12/92

DATE DUE

			PRINTED IN U.S.A.

12/92

DRAMA
CRITICISM

Guide to Gale Literary Criticism Series

When you need to review criticism of literary works, these are the Gale series to use:

If the author's death date is:	You should turn to:
After Dec. 31, 1959 (or author is still living)	**CONTEMPORARY LITERARY CRITICISM** for example: Jorge Luis Borges, Anthony Burgess, William Faulkner, Mary Gordon, Ernest Hemingway, Iris Murdoch
1900 through 1959	**TWENTIETH-CENTURY LITERARY CRITICISM** for example: Willa Cather, F. Scott Fitzgerald, Henry James, Mark Twain, Virginia Woolf
1800 through 1899	**NINETEENTH-CENTURY LITERATURE CRITICISM** for example: Fyodor Dostoevsky, Nathaniel Hawthorne, George Sand, William Wordsworth
1400 through 1799	**LITERATURE CRITICISM FROM 1400 TO 1800** *(excluding Shakespeare)* for example: Anne Bradstreet, Daniel Defoe, Alexander Pope, François Rabelais, Jonathan Swift, Phillis Wheatley
	SHAKESPEAREAN CRITICISM Shakespeare's plays and poetry
Antiquity through 1399	**CLASSICAL AND MEDIEVAL LITERATURE CRITICISM** for example: Dante, Homer, Plato, Sophocles, Vergil, the Beowulf Poet

---

Gale also publishes related criticism series:

CHILDREN'S LITERATURE REVIEW

This series covers authors of all eras who have written for the preschool through high school audience.

SHORT STORY CRITICISM

This series covers the major short fiction writers of all nationalities and periods of literary history.

POETRY CRITICISM

This series covers poets of all nationalities and periods of literary history.

DRAMA CRITICISM

This series covers dramatists of all nationalities and periods of literary history.

ISSN 1056-4349

R

DRAMA CRITICISM

Criticism of the Most Significant and Widely Studied
Dramatic Works from All the World's Literatures

VOLUME 2

Lawrence J. Trudeau, Editor

Jelena Krstović, Zoran Minderović, Joann Prosyniuk,
and Mark Swartz, Associate Editors

 **Gale Research Inc.** · DETROIT · LONDON

REC '92

Since this page cannot legibly accommodate all copyright notices, the acknowledgments constitute an extension of the copyright notice.

While every effort has been made to ensure the reliability of the information presented in this publication, Gale Research Inc. neither guarantees the accuracy of the data contained herein nor assumes any responsibility for errors, omissions, or discrepancies. Gale accepts no payment for listing; and inclusion in the publication of any organization, agency, institution, publication, service, or individual does not imply endorsement of the editors or publisher. Errors brought to the attention of the publisher and verified to the satisfaction of the publisher will be corrected in future editions.

The paper used in this publication meets the minimum requirements of American National Standard for Information Sciences—Permanence Paper for Printed Library Materials, ANSI Z39.48-1984.

Contents

Preface   vii
Acknowledgments   ix

Preface

Drama Criticism (*DC*) is principally intended for beginning students of literature and theater as well as the average playgoer. The series is therefore designed to introduce readers to the most frequently studied playwrights of all time periods and nationalities and to present discerning commentary on dramatic works of enduring popular appeal. Furthermore, *DC* seeks to acquaint students with the uses and functions of criticism itself. Selected from a diverse and often bewildering body of commentary, the essays in *DC* offer insights into the authors and their works but do not require that the reader possess a wide background in literary studies. Where appropriate, reviews of important productions of the plays discussed are also included to give students a heightened awareness of drama as a dynamic art form, one that many claim is fully realized only in performance.

DC was created in response to suggestions by the staffs of high school, college, and public libraries. These librarians observed a need for a series that assembles critical commentary on the world's most renowned dramatists in the same manner as Gale's *Short Story Criticism* (*SSC*) and *Poetry Criticism* (*PC*), which present material on writers of short fiction and poetry. Although playwrights are covered in such Gale literary criticism series as *Contemporary Literary Criticism* (*CLC*), *Twentieth-Century Literary Criticism* (*TCLC*), *Nineteenth-Century Literature Criticism* (*NCLC*), *Literature Criticism from 1400 to 1800* (*LC*), and *Classical and Medieval Literature Criticism* (*CMLC*), *Drama Criticism* directs more concentrated attention on individual dramatists than is possible in the broader, survey-oriented entries in these Gale series. Commentary on the works of William Shakespeare may be found in *Shakespearean Criticism* (*SC*).

Scope of the Series

By collecting and organizing commentary on dramatists, *DC* assists students in their efforts to gain insight into literature, achieve better understanding of the texts, and formulate ideas for papers and assignments. A variety of interpretations and assessments is offered, allowing students to pursue their own interests and promoting awareness that literature is dynamic and responsive to many different opinions.

Each volume of *DC* presents:

- 10-12 author entries

- authors and works representing a wide range of nationalities and time periods

- a diversity of viewpoints and critical opinions.

Organization of an Author Entry

Each author entry consists of some or all of the following elements, depending on the scope and complexity of the criticism:

- The **author heading** consists of the playwright's most commonly used name, followed by birth and death dates. If an author consistently wrote under a pseudonym, the pseudonym is listed in the author heading and the real name given on the first line of the introduction. Also located at the beginning of the introduction are any name variations under which the dramatist wrote, including transliterated forms of the names of authors whose languages use nonroman alphabets.

- A **portrait** of the author is included when available. Most entries also feature illustrations of people, places, and events pertinent to a study of the playwright and his or her works. When appropriate, photographs of the plays in performance are also presented.

- The **biographical and critical introduction** contains background information that familiarizes the reader with the author and the critical debates surrounding his or her works.

- The list of **principal works** is divided into two sections, each of which is organized chronologically by date of first performance. If this has not been conclusively determined, the composition or publication date is used. The first section of the principal works list contains the author's dramatic pieces. The second section provides information on the author's major works in other genres.

- Whenever available, **author commentary** is provided. This section consists of essays or interviews in which the dramatist discusses his or her own work or the art of playwriting in general.

- Essays offering **overviews and general studies of the dramatist's entire literary career** give the student broad perspectives on the writer's artistic development, themes and concerns that recur in several of his or her works, the author's place in literary history, and other wide-ranging topics.

- **Criticism of individual plays** offers the reader in-depth discussions of a select number of the author's most important works. In some cases, the criticism is divided into two sections, each arranged chronologically. When a significant performance of a play can be identified (typically, the premiere of a twentieth-century work), the first section of criticism will feature **production reviews** of this staging. Most entries include sections devoted to **critical commentary** that assesses the literary merit of the selected plays. When necessary, essays are carefully excerpted to focus on the work under consideration; often, however, essays and reviews are reprinted in their entirety.

- As an additional aid to students, the critical essays and excerpts are prefaced by **explanatory annotations.** These notes provide several types of useful information, including the critic's reputation and approach to literary studies as well as the scope and significance of the criticism that follows.

- A complete **bibliographic citation,** designed to help the interested reader locate the original essay or book, follows each piece of criticism.

- The **further reading** list at the end of each entry comprises additional studies of the dramatist. It is divided into sections that will help students quickly locate the specific information they need.

Other Features

- A **cumulative author index** lists all the authors who have appeared in *DC, CLC, TCLC, NCLC, LC, CMLC, SSC,* and *PC,* as well as cross-references to related titles published by Gale, including *Contemporary Authors* and *Dictionary of Literary Biography.* A complete listing of the series included appears at the beginning of the index.

- A **cumulative nationality index** includes each author featured in *DC* by nationality, followed by the number of the *DC* volume in which the author appears.

- A **cumulative title index** lists in alphabetical order the individual plays discussed in the criticism contained in *DC.* Each title is followed by the author's name and the corresponding volume and page number(s) where commentary on the work may be located. Translations and variant titles are cross-referenced to the title of the play in its original language so that all references to the work are combined in one listing.

A Note to the Reader

When writing papers, students who quote directly from any volume in the Literary Criticism Series may use the following general formats to footnote reprinted criticism. The first example pertains to material drawn from periodicals, the second to materials reprinted from books.

[1]Susan Sontag, "Going to the Theater, Etc.," *Partisan Review* XXXI, No. 3 (Summer 1964), 389-94; excerpted and reprinted in *Drama Criticism,* Vol. 1, ed. Lawrence J. Trudeau (Detroit: Gale Research, 1991), pp. 17-20.

[2]Eugene M. Waith, *The Herculean Hero in Marlowe, Chapman, Shakespeare and Dryden* (Chatto & Windus, 1962); excerpted and reprinted in *Drama Criticism,* Vol. 1, ed. Lawrence J. Trudeau (Detroit: Gale Research, 1991), pp. 237-247.

Suggestions are Welcome

Readers who wish to suggest authors to appear in future volumes of *DC,* or who have other suggestions, are cordially invited to contact the editor.

Acknowledgments

The editors wish to thank the copyright holders of the excerpted criticism included in this volume, the permissions managers of many book and magazine publishing companies for assisting us in securing reprint rights, and Anthony Bogucki for assistance with copyright research. We are also grateful to the staffs of the Detroit Public Library, Wayne State University Purdy/Kresge Library Complex, and the University of Michigan Libraries for making their resources available to us. Following is a list of the copyright holders who have granted us permission to reprint material in this volume of *DC*. Every effort has been made to trace copyright, but if omissions have been made, please let us know.

COPYRIGHTED EXCERPTS IN *DC*, VOLUME 2, WERE REPRINTED FROM THE FOLLOWING PERIODICALS:

American Theatre, v. 3, January, 1987. Copyright © 1987, Theatre Communications Group. All rights reserved. Reprinted by permission of the publisher.—*The Antigonish Review,* n. 9, Spring, 1972 for "An Aran Requiem: Setting in 'Riders to the Sea' " by Daniel J. Casey. Copyright 1972 by the author. Reprinted by permission of the publisher and the author.—*The Antioch Review,* v. XXV, Spring, 1965. Copyright © 1965 by the Antioch Review Inc. Reprinted by permission of the Editors.—*Black American Literature Forum,* v. 22, Winter, 1988 for an interview with Wole Soyinka and Anthony Appiah. Copyright © 1988 Indiana State University. Reprinted by permission of Indiana State University, Brandt & Brandt Literary Agents, Inc. and Anthony Appiah./ v. 19, Winter, 1985 for "Images of Men in Lorraine Hansberry's Writing" by Steven R. Carter. Copyright © 1985 Indiana State University. Reprinted by permission of Indiana State University and the author.—*The Christian Science Monitor,* March 4, 1987 for "Nigerian Drama Blends Plot, Pageantry" by John Beaufort; March 30, 1988 for "New Chapter in Wilson Saga of Black Life" by John Beaufort. © 1987, 1988 by the author. All rights reserved. Both reprinted by permission of the author.—*CLA Journal,* v. XXV, September, 1981. Copyright, 1981 by The College Language Association. Used by permission of The College Language Association.—*Commentary,* v. XXVII, June, 1959 for "Thoughts on 'A Raisin in the Sun' " by Gerald Weales. Copyright © 1959, renewed 1987 by the American Jewish Committee. All rights reserved. Reprinted by permission of the publisher and the author.—*Comparative Drama,* v. 20, Summer, 1986. © copyright 1986, by the Editors of *Comparative Drama*. Reprinted by permission of the publisher.—*Daily News,* New York, December 9, 1966. © 1966 New York Daily News. Used with permission.—*Drama Survey,* v. 4, Summer, 1965. Copyright 1965 by The Bolingbroke Society, Inc./ v. 5, Summer, 1966 for "Theme and Image in Lorca's 'Yerma' " by Robert Skloot. Copyright 1966 by The Bolingbroke Society, Inc. Reprinted by permission of the author.—*Éire-Ireland: A Journal of Irish Studies,* v. IV, 1969 for "The Structural Craftsmanship of J. M. Synge's 'Riders to the Sea' " by Paul M. Levitt. Copyright 1969 © Irish American Cultural Institute, 2115 Summit Ave., No. 5026, St. Paul, MN 55105. Reprinted by permission of the publisher and the author.—*Financial Times,* January 30, 1978. © Financial Times Limited 1978. Reprinted by permission of the publisher.—*Forum,* v. 17, Winter, 1979 for "The Treatment of Madness in 'Love for Love' " by Retta M. Taney. Copyright, 1979, by Events Publishing Company, Inc. Reprinted by permission of Current History, Inc. and the author.—*Freedomways,* v. 19, fourth quarter, 1979. Copyright © 1979 by Freedomways Associates, Inc. Reprinted by permission of *Freedomways*.—*The Listener,* v. 99, February 2, 1978 for "The Funny Side" by John Elsom. © British Broadcasting Corp. 1978. Reprinted by permission of the author.—*Massachusetts Studies in English,* v. VIII, 1982 for "In Defense of Hedda" by Lisa Elaine Low. Copyright © 1982 by *Massachusetts Studies in English*. Reprinted by permission of the author.—*Modern Drama,* v. XII, February, 1970; v. XIII, September, 1970; v. XX, September, 1977. Copyright 1970, 1977 *Modern Drama*, University of Toronto. All reprinted by permission of the publisher.—*Neophilologus,* v. LXXII, April, 1988 for "Yerma: 'Una Tragedia Pura y Simplemente' " by Guadalupe Martinez LaCalle. © 1988 by H. D. Tjeenk Willink. Reprinted by permission of the publisher and the author./ v. LVI, July, 1972. © 1972 by H. D. Tjeenk Willink. Reprinted by permission of the publisher.—*The New Republic,* v. 142, February 29, 1960. © 1960 The New Republic, Inc. Reprinted by permission of *The New Republic.*—*New York Post,* October 12, 1984; March 2, 1987; March 27, 1987, March 28, 1988. © 1984, 1987, 1988, *New York Post*. All reprinted by permission of the publisher.—*The New York Times,* May 27, 1947; February 17, 1960; December 9, 1966; October 12, 1984; March 2, 1987; March 28, 1988. Copyright 1947, 1960, 1966, 1984, 1987, 1988 by The New York Times Company. All reprinted by permission of the publisher.—*Newsday,* March 2, 1987; March 27, 1987. © Newsday, Inc. 1987. Both reprinted by permission.—*The Personalist,* v. XLIV, July 1963. Reprinted by permission of the publisher.—*Plays and Players,* v. 25, March, 1978. © 1978 Plusloop. Reprinted with permission of the publisher.—*Research in African Literatures,* v. 14, Spring, 1983; v. 19, Winter, 1988. Copyright © 1983, 1988 by the University of Texas Press. Both reprinted by permission of Indiana University Press.—*Saturday Review,*

Aristophanes

c. 450 B.C.-c. 385 B.C.

INTRODUCTION

The comedies of Aristophanes are numbered among the greatest creations of the ancient Greek theater; they are hailed as a triumph of the creative imagination over the constraints of reality, a flight into the realm of absolute freedom. Aristophanes is admired in particular for his ability to imagine fantastic worlds in which human nobility and love triumph over stupidity, egotism, politics, violence, and malice. Although he severely criticized Athenian society in his comedies, Aristophanes's devastating satirical wit, as critics have observed, seems overshadowed by his profound humanism: the purpose of his ridicule is to expose, and thereby to combat, evil. Aristophanes's fictional world, though hardly realistic, is not totally incredible; it offers, in the words of Cedric H. Whitman, "another reality, a truth beyond truth . . . which is, in fact, the spirit's formulation of the way things are."

Little is known of Aristophanes's life. He was born an Athenian citizen during Pericles's rule (c.460-c.430 B.C.), when Athens, heading a maritime empire, stood at the zenith of its political might. The Peloponnesian war (431-403 B.C.), a power struggle between Athens and Sparta, provided a tragic backdrop in many Aristophanes's comedies, and the eventual defeat of Athens deeply offended the poet's patriotism. Consequently, he detested Pericles's successor Cleon, a ruler representing the will of a mercantile plutocracy who viewed war as a lucrative venture. As a traditionalist to whom the land-owning aristocracy and the peasantry represented the soul of the Greek nation, Aristophanes harshly condemned the new leaders of Athens for waging a politically opportunistic war which led to the gradual destruction of Athenian agriculture. Despite his political sympathies, however, the poet never succumbed to political partisanship, affirming in his works the ideals of Greek unity and humanism.

Aristophanes is considered the chief representative of fifth-century B.C. Athenian comedy, usually termed "Old Comedy." The works of his principal rivals Cratinus and Eupolis exist only in fragments, while eleven of Aristophanes's comedies survive out of an output of about forty-four, constituting an oeuvre which scholars believe to be the apex of the Old Comedy. Critics have commented on Aristophanes's artistic originality and individuality, while noting that his comedies are nevertheless rooted in the mythic and religious origins of the Greek theatre. As a literary form, comedy emerged from the ritual celebrations of Dionysus, a Thracian divinity adopted by the Greeks as the central figure of a fertility cult. More specifically, as Aristotle stated in his *Poetics,* comedy evolved from the cult's traditional bawdy procession, whose participants hurled obscene insults—a familiar feature of Aristophanic comedy—at the onlookers. As both laughter and obscenity were, from time immemorial, credited with the power

to ward off evil, Aristophanes's salaciousness, often found excessive in modern times, reflects ancient cultic practices. The formal structure of the Old Comedy was also influenced by the Dionysian cult. For instance, the *parabasis*—the section of the play where the chorus, interrupting the plot, approaches the spectators and directly addresses them on behalf of the poet—originated in Dionysian ritual. Other essentially cultic features include the *agon,* or dispute, and the *komos,* the orgiastic ending of the play. Indeed, the term *komos,* from which the word *komoidia,* or comedy, developed, refers to the orgiastic aspect of the Dionysian procession. The actors' masks, body padding (*somation*), the giant phallus worn by the male characters (all the actors were male), and the animal chorus appearing in *Sphēkes* (*Wasps*) and *Batrakhoi* (*Frogs*) also stem from Dionysian rituals. The Dionysian celebrations were eventually formalized as the Dionysia, official religious festivals first recorded in the sixth century B.C. The ceremonies included a dramatic contest, participation in which was vital for a playwright's career. Tragedies and comedies were performed, the jury awarding prizes to the three best works in each genre. The most important festivals for drama were two Athenian events: the Lenaean Dionysia, held in the month of Gamelion (January-

February), and the Great (or Urban) Dionysia, celebrated in the month of Elaphobelion (March-April).

The principal themes of Aristophanes's comedies mirror the poet's profound dissatisfaction with the political reality of Athens. In *Akharnēs* (*Acharnians*), his earliest preserved play, which received the first prize at the Lenaean festival in 425 B.C., an Athenian peasant excludes himself from the Peloponnesian war by cleverly obtaining a separate truce with Sparta. An often-cited example of Aristophanic individualism, the main character of *Eirēnē* (*Peace*), produced in 421 B.C., flies to Mt. Olympus on a dung beetle—in a parody of Euripides's *Bellerophon*—to see what the gods have in store for his war-torn city. In *Hippeis* (*Knights*), performed in 424 B.C., the decrepit Demos, symbolizing the Athenian people, is paradoxically rejuvenated after his favorite, a repugnant tanner (a transparent allusion to Cleon, who owned a tannery), is outwitted and replaced by an even more repulsive sausage-seller. The obsessive litigiousness of Athenian citizens is lampooned in the *Wasps,* staged in 424 B.C., in which Bdelycleon ("Cleon-hater"), driven to despair by his father Philocleon's ("Cleon-lover") compulsive attachment to jury duty, tries to keep the old man from the law courts by detaining him at home. Philocleon is eventually permitted to conduct a trial involving two dogs, one of which is named Cleon. *Ornithes* (*Birds*), produced in 414 B.C., considered the playwright's masterpiece by many critics, depicts a bird community which, perhaps due to its location between heaven and earth, manages to avoid both divine excess and human folly.

In his portrayals of human foibles, Aristophanes effectively contrasted the stereotypically Athenian *polypragmosyne,* a blend of extreme zeal, short-lived enthusiasm, and meddlesome ingenuity, with two characteristically Spartan traits: *apragmosyne,* conservative caution, and *hesychia,* a yearning for the quiet country life. In *Nephelai* (*Clouds*), produced in 423 B. C. at the Great Dionysia, the poet tackles a type of warped intellectual *polypragmosyne.* The play, with its chorus of clouds symbolizing the nebulousness of self-serving intellectual endeavors, lambastes the Sophists, or professional intellectuals, for introducing a spirit of moral and logical relativism into Athenian society. The chief Sophist, according to Aristophanes, is Socrates, who, from his *phrontistērion,* or "thinkery," directs a preposterous school fostering useless research and logically sound dishonesty. Many commentators have asserted that, given the philosopher's unequivocal condemnation of the Sophists, Aristophanes's portrayal of Socrates seems unfair. The comedy was not well received, obtaining the third prize—a crushing defeat, according to the poet. In the *Frogs,* produced in 405 B.C., Aristophanes, turning to the issue of innovation for its own sake, depicted a poetry contest between the playwrights Aeschylus and Euripides. Aristophanes's description of the contest includes blasphemy in the form of ridiculing the gods, as well as brilliant parodies of Euripides, the dramatist he considered the voice of innovative superficiality in Athenian culture. Aristophanes's case against the older playwright is so erudite and impeccably argued in the *Frogs* that scholars have extolled him as one of the great critics of Greek literature.

Three comedies, *Lȳsistratē* (*Lysistrata*) and *Thesmophoriazoūsai* (*Thesmophoriazusae*), both staged in 411 B.C., and *Ekklesiazoūsai* (*Ecclesiazusae*), performed in 392 B.C., identify women as the moving force in society. While the *Thesmophoriazusae,* replete with burlesque situations and parodic episodes, describes a terrified Euripides fleeing the female celebrants of the Thesmophoria (a festival in honor of Demeter the Legislatrix) who seek revenge for his unflattering portrayal of women, and the *Ecclesiazusae* imagines a city ruled by female politicians, *Lysistrata* pictures women as saviors of society. During the Peloponnesian war, Lysistrata, an Athenian woman, organizes a strike with the help of a Spartan ally; with their followers, the women proclaim that there will be no sex until the men stop fighting. This theme provides Aristophanes ample opportunity to regale his audience with much comical obscenity, but there is a tone of profound sorrow underlying the erotic hilarity, particularly in the scenes where the poet voices his sympathy with the war widows and other bereaved women. A comedy about the tragic human condition, *Lysistrata* is also, according to critics, the poetic expression of Aristophanes's humanism and his desire for Greek unity. *Ploutos* (*Plutus*), Aristophanes's last extant comedy, likewise addresses a universal topic. Produced in 388 B.C., the play deals with humankind's yearning for a world in which fortune favors only the deserving. In the comedy, Plutus, the god of wealth, who is traditionally depicted as blind, has his sight restored, but when he effects an equitable distribution of wealth the result is nothing but chaos.

Critics have often praised Aristophanes's ability to create imaginary scenarios and to reach astounding levels of absurdity. Although his characters are based on real Athenian incompetents, strident demagogues, and greedy vulgarians, the crucial element of Aristophanes's art is fantasy. As Carroll Moulton observed in response to commentators who characterize Aristophanes's plays as generally episodic and loosely structured, "the coherent unities in comic poetry are to be sought in the unique reality of fantasy itself." The comic poet was an unsurpassed master of the Greek language. Abounding with labyrinthine allusions, complicated puns, hyperbolical verbal constructs, and startling analogies, Aristophanes's language is the essential ingredient of his stage magic. He employs the full range of Greek discourse, adding neologisms, dialectal variations, a wealth of vulgarities, even gibberish, and he often rises from popular speech to sublime poetry. Some of Aristophanes' lyric segments, such as the beautiful parabasis of the *Birds,* are considered among the greatest accomplishments in Greek literature. As Albin Lesky emphasized, it is his language, more than the comedy of situation, that carries Aristophanes's humor; thus, "the variety of his language mirrors the variety of content, which mingles the real and the fanciful in a number that has never since been equalled."

Aristophanes's fame waned after his death and he was eventually eclipsed by Menander, the chief representative of the New Comedy. Urbane, refined, inoffensive, and replacing the raucous hilarity of the Old Comedy with polite irony, the New Comedy appealed to the cosmopolitan urban elite of the Greek-speaking world in the fourth and third centuries B.C. Thus it was Menander, not Aristophanes, who provided a blueprint for the Roman comedy that followed, which in turn exerted a decisive influence on the European stage. In Western Europe, Aristophanes's fame was rekindled during the Renaissance revival of Greek learning: his greatness was recognized by the Dutch humanist Desiderius Erasmus, and by François Rabelais, in whose satirical prose commentators have discerned the euphoric spirit of Aristophanic comedy. Playwrights whose work bears some influence of Aristophanes include Ben Jonson and Jean Racine, the French tragedian whose only comedy, *Les Plaideurs,* is an adaptation of the *Wasps.* The French critic and poet Nicolas Boileau-Despreaux, author of the influential *Art Poetique* (1674), decried the "fury" of the Old Comedy, condemning Aristophanes' treatment of Socrates, which François Marie Arouet Voltaire also found execrable. But the comic poet was emulated by Henry Fielding, who excoriated politicians on the stage with Aristophanic gusto. Aristophanes was also praised by such Romantic writers as Heinrich Heine, Samuel Taylor Coleridge, Percy Bysshe Shelley, and Robert Browning. The German philosopher Georg Friedrich Wilhelm Hegel ranked him among the giants of European literature, a judgment with which twentieth-century commentators generally concur.

As the author of a challenging and inspiring oeuvre, Aristophanes remains an intriguing subject for scholars. The comic poet is among those writers who ultimately elude definitions and explanations; despite a multitude of commentaries and elucidations, critics still encounter unexpected meanings in his plays. As John Addington Symonds wrote, Aristophanes defies the critic who attempts "to interpret the secret of his strength and charm. The epithets which continually rise to our lips in speaking of him—radiant, resplendent, swift, keen, changeful, flashing, magical—carry no real notion of the marvellous and subtle spirit that animates his comedy with life peculiar to itself."

PRINCIPAL WORKS

PLAYS

Akharnēs   425 B.C.
Hippeis   424 B.C.
Nephelai   423 B.C.
Sphēkes   422 B.C.
Eirēnē   421 B.C.
Ornithes   414 B.C.
Lȳsistratē   411 B.C.
Thesmophoriazoūsai   411 B.C.
Batrakhoi   405 B.C.
Ekklesiazoūsai   392 B.C.
Ploutos   388 B.C.

PRINCIPAL ENGLISH TRANSLATIONS

The Comedies of Aristophanes   (translated by Benjamin Binkley Rogers)   1924
Complete Plays of Aristophanes   (edited by Moses Hadas) 1962
Four Comedies   (translated by Dudley Fitts)   1962
The Frogs, and Other Plays   (translated by David Barrett)   1964
Four Comedies   (translated by Richard Lattimore and Douglass Parker)   1969
Lysystrata, The Acharnians, The Clouds   (translated by Alan H. Sommerstein)   1973
Complete Plays of Aristophanes   (edited by Moses Hadas) 1984
Clouds   (edited by Kenneth J. Dover)   1989
Lysistrata   (edited by Jeffrey Henderson)   1991

OVERVIEWS AND GENERAL STUDIES

Moses Hadas   (essay date 1950)

[*Hadas was a distinguished American scholar whose many works, including* A History of Greek Literature *(1950) and* Hellenistic Culture: Fusion and Diffusion *(1959), range over the entire field of classical literature. In the following excerpt, he discusses Aristophanes's political conservatism as it is reflected in his comedies and surveys the plays in terms of Aristophanes's contributions to Old Comedy.*]

It is important to realize that comedy too was part of a religious ritual [in ancient Greece], though there was little of the solemnity which we associate with religion. Comedies were presented in the same theater as tragedy and at the same festivals, though on special days and hours. Both forms told a story by acting it out in verse dialogue, with an obviously traditional chorus for song and dance, but comedy's explosive fantasy and boisterous bawdiness seemed calculated to put it at the farthest remove from the somber dignity of tragedy. It is difficult to know whether, as many scholars hold, the heroically obscene elements in comedy are direct vestiges of a fertility rite in which comedy originated, or whether they are there because incongruity is a capital element in the ridiculous, and indecency is incongruous in Greek literature. All the kinds of things that have ever moved men to laugh are to be found in Old Comedy: slapstick and subtle word play, invective and burlesque, dialect and mumming, and ever and again the physiological jokes, excretory and reproductive. The mask and costume of the comic actor set the tone. He was ridiculously padded on belly and behind, and his short jacket just fell short of the crotch, which was decorated with a colossal phallus. Exculpations of Aristophanic humor on the ground that it is clean dirt and not prurient miss the mark. Every type of sex joke from the infantile to the most sophisticated is represented; no female human or divine appears on the stage without the suggestion being made that she be put to sexual use forthwith. Aristophanes is not prurient because his comedy is a comedy of pure wit, which attacks the head and not the entrails. None of the characters engages the audience's sympathy as human beings; with none can the audience identify itself. They are like characters in Rabelais, not Cervantes; like the Marx Brothers, not Charlie Chaplin.

For us Old Comedy means Aristophanes. The Alexandrians joined Cratinus and Eupolis with him to make a Comic Three as a pendant to the tragedians, but it appears that Aristophanes towered above his rivals by a much greater interval than any of the three tragedians was separated from his. On the other hand, the titles and scrappy fragments of Aristophanes' rivals suggest that they differed from him in quality and degree but not essentially in kind. (pp. 99-100)

Before considering Aristophanes' individual plays it will be convenient to notice certain peculiarities common to all of them. The structure of comedy, while not nearly so regular as tragedy, still maintains a pattern of its own. A prologue, either a monologue or dialogue, puts the audience in possession of the plot. Always it is based upon some wildly fantastic idea, contrary to all human experience, such as ascending to heaven to obtain peace or establish-

Characters of Old Comedy.

ing a utopia in the clouds or descending to Hades to fetch a poet or calling a sex strike. Once the premises of this world-destroying idea are accepted, the consequences are natural. The first part of the play has to do with achieving the idea. Usually there is an *agon,* or conflict, vigorously enacted by two parts of the chorus, advocating or opposing the innovation in question. A special and wide variety of meters is employed in the *agon,* usually culminating in a kind of patter song. Somewhere about the center of the play there is a *parabasis,* where the chorus steps forward and speaks directly in the name of the poet, with little reference to the subject matter of the play. Toward the end the idea which was to be realized is shown in action. Usually the plays end with the "hero" going off for a revel and feast with some young woman, with whom there is to be a sort of marriage. Scholars have labored to show the ritual genesis of these various parts, and especially of the "marriage" at the end. Whatever validity their arguments may have, it may be remarked that the only psychologically suitable "solution" for comedy is the relaxation and renewal implicit in such a revel. Considering the nature of comedy its regularity and refinement are more remarkable than its looseness. Whatever the expectations of other Greek writers may have been, it is clear that Aristophanes was writing for a single performance and had no thought of becoming a classic. Language is used with exuberance, new formations are freely coined, liberties are taken with meter. Yet the lyrics in Aristophanes are among the most exquisite in the language.

Aristophanes' primary aim, obviously, was to give expression to his ebullient wit, to entertain, to win the prize; but he was an Athenian, and had convictions on many subjects, and it is inevitable that these convictions should appear in his writing. These convictions, in music and education as well as in politics, are consistently and pronouncedly conservative. So outspoken is he in his attacks on democratic leaders and favorite democratic policies that competent critics have gone to the absurd length of declaring that he was in the pay of the oligarchical, pro-Sparta party. On the other hand, it cannot be maintained that his ridicule of democratic leaders is a natural comedian's device, anything new or strange being an easy mark for ridicule. In fact, his audience was substantially identical with the ecclesia which voted for the leaders and policies he attacked. Time and again he claims that the poet's function is to instruct and guide, notably in several passages in *Acharnians* and *Frogs,* as for example (*Frogs* 1054 f.): "Boys at school have a teacher to instruct them, but poets are the teachers of men."

Aristophanes disliked anything that disturbed the old-fashioned disciplines. He did not like the Sophists with their trains of eternally arguing young men. He did not like the new fashions in music, the new self-consciousness of the suppressed classes. Particularly he attacked Cleon, Pericles' successor as leader of the democracy. Ancient authorities are at one in condemning Cleon, but in this respect the impartiality of none is above question. The fact is that Cleon continued the policies of Pericles, but whereas Pericles was himself a "gentleman," Cleon was not. As against the jostling merchant and sailor class, the conservative and land-holding class had real admiration for

Spartan conservatism and discipline, and little to gain and much to lose by the war. In the passions of war years there is little room for moderates. In foreign policy Aristophanes' moderation was surely on sound grounds. What he desired, as *Lysistrata* shows, was in fact the only thing that could have saved Greece: peace between Athens and Sparta and a pan-Hellenic union to present a united front against the powers of the east. The crying need for such union to avert inevitable doom is in the background of Thucydides' history, and was urgently advocated by Isocrates. But however farseeing Aristophanes' policy may have been, the fact remains that he was tender-minded to the Spartans and their friends and their friends' ideas, and opposed the representatives of those who were associated with new ideas.

Because of his concern with immediate problems and personages and their human backgrounds rather than with eternal verities, Aristophanes' teeming plays are incomparably our most important help for real knowledge of the people of Greece. He breezes through the museum hall where the majestic figures stand fixed, and they drop their poses and move about and talk, about everything that men talk about. When Dionysius, tyrant of Syracuse, asked Plato to describe the constitution of Athens, Plato sent him the works of Aristophanes. But however useful such knowledge may be, and whatever instruction the political issues in which Aristophanes took part may provide, his prime claim is as a genius of exuberant wit, a true creator who fashioned worlds in fantasy, as he fashioned man himself in Plato's charming and lifelike picture in the *Symposium*.

The first extant play is **Acharnians,** presented in 425 B.C. when the author was twenty, which won the prize over Cratinus and Eupolis [at the drama competition]. Dicaeopolis makes an individual peace with Sparta, but as he is about to celebrate the long intermitted vintage festival he is attacked by a chorus of Acharnian charcoal burners who represent the war party and wins a hearing by a parody of Euripides' *Telephus*. In a seriocomic speech he shows that the causes of the war were trifling, and wins over half the chorus, who are engaged in a violent agon by the other half. These call in the general Lamachus to assist them, but the general too is beaten in argument, and the chorus, uniting on Dicaeopolis' side, deliver the poet's parabasis. Then Megarians and Boeotians bring in for sale the good things Athens has lacked. A herald summons Lamachus to a hard campaign, and another Dicaeopolis to a wine party. Lamachus returns wounded, and Dicaeopolis reels in, having won the prize for drinking, on the arms of pretty flute girls, whom he leads out in procession. If we are astonished at the temerity of a poet who could say a word for the enemy and many words for pacifism amid the passions of war, we must be amazed at a democracy which permitted and sponsored such a play in time of war, and gave it first prize. *Acharnians* shows a keen freshness, but it is in every way equal to Aristophanes' most mature work. It has the characteristic topsy-turvy fantasy of a one-man peace, beautiful lyrics, the rollicking burlesque of Euripides, vigorous exposition of an idea, tireless energy, and a reveling finale. If we admire the political tolerance of the audience, or, alternatively, their

greater devotion to art, we must also admire their cultivation, for constantly Aristophanes' parodies of tragedy assume a close and wide familiarity with the poets. We have no better evidence for the general culture of the community which produced the intellectual giants of fifth-century Greece.

The fresh and mercurial inventiveness which makes *Acharnians* delightful is gone from *Knights* (424 B.C.), which is a virulent and unrelieved attack, not upon war, but upon the man Cleon. The play starts with a transparent allegory as two slaves of crotchety old Demos ("the people"), got up to resemble the generals Nicias and Demosthenes (the older editions so name the characters), complain of the bullying of Demos' new favorite, a Paphlagonian leather-seller, who represents Cleon. Among the oracles they steal from Cleon is one which foretells that Cleon shall be supplanted by a sausage-seller. The sausage-seller appears, and is persuaded that his rascality and impudence qualify him; Cleon accuses his slaves of treason, and the chorus of knights, possibly riding pick-a-back, rush to their assistance. Cleon dashes out to complain to the senate; but Sausage-seller has outdone Cleon in brazenness, and when both seek to win over Demos, Sausage-seller (now named Agoracritus) succeeds. During a second parabasis Sausage-seller (who had apparently assumed his earlier character only to out-Cleon Cleon) has rejuvenated Demos by stewing him in a pot, and he comes forth determined to abolish innovations and restore the old-fashioned ways. A few months before *Knights* was presented Cleon had brought to a successful conclusion at Sphacteria the most brilliant exploit of the war (what part he had in originating it is questionable), which caused the Spartans to propose peace. In the play Demosthenes says (54 ff.): "The other day I kneaded a Laconian cake at Pylos, but the Paphlagonian with rascally effrontery dodged in and snatched it up and himself served up the cake I had kneaded." On the other hand, a minor exploit of the knights at Corinth is glorified (595 ff.). This and the unrelieved vituperation of Cleon throughout the play are the principal evidence of Aristophanes' attachment to the oligarchical party. It is said that the mask-makers refused to provide a mask of Cleon for this play, and that Aristophanes played the part himself. Cleon doubtless sat in the front row during the performance, the right of proedria having been conferred upon him for the exploit at Pylos. The part of this play which Eupolis helped write was the second parabasis; possibly Eupolis' use of the same passage in his own *Maricas* is the basis for Aristophanes' charge in *Clouds* (553 ff.) that Eupolis' *Maricas* was a distortion of his own **Knights.**

Compared to the treatment accorded Cleon in **Knights,** Socrates is handled almost with affection in *Clouds* (423 B.C.), but readers are most offended with *Clouds* because of the reverence which has come to be paid Socrates. The play is damaging indeed (in his *Apology*, twenty-five years later, Socrates was to blame it for creating prejudice against him) and on false grounds, for he did not study natural science, did not charge fees, was not a Sophist. But a caricaturist who wished to attack the Sophists could scarcely avoid making Socrates his butt; not only was he the best known teacher (but without the aura of sanctity which generations have given him), but his physical idiosyncrasies invited caricature. It is said that when the mask-maker's art was applauded on his double's first appearance, Socrates stood up in the theater to show the likeness. It is not Socrates but science (which questioned all traditions) and the glib seekers for new knowledge which would permit them to evade responsibility that are pilloried. The contest between Just and Unjust Reason or between traditional and modern education exhibits Aristophanes' nostalgia for the old, but as in his preference of Aeschylus over Euripides the praise of the old is not unqualified. Our text of the play is a revision, which was never officially presented, and there are, consequently, serious inconsistencies in plot. The original play ran third, being defeated by Cratinus' *Pytine* and Amipsias' *Connus.*

Wasps (422 B.C.) is directed against the institution of large paid juries and their subservience to such leaders as Cleon, and incidentally against ill-founded pretenses to grand manners. The question of pay for public service was an important one in the Greek democracy, for without pay decisions would be left in the hands of those who could afford leisure. It is Aristophanes' point that with only a fraction of the state income supposedly used for such purposes (656 ff.) the demagogues purchase loyalty to themselves. The scene of Philocleon's attempted escapes when his son has shut him in is delightfully funny, as is the trial scene of the dog.

In *Peace* (421 B.C.) a farmer called Trygaeus ascends to heaven on a beetle to procure an end to the war. The gods have washed their hands of the Greeks and left War to work his will. He has buried Peace, and the chorus eventually succeed in drawing her up, to the consternation of those who profit by war and the hearty satisfaction of all others. The text as we have it is probably a conflation of two editions, but it is full of charm and high spirits. *Peace* contains what has been called the earliest idyllic poetry of the Greeks. The second parabasis (1140 ff.) which begins, in the Rogers translation,

> Ah, there's nothing half so sweet as when the
> seed is in the ground,
> God a gracious rain is sending, and a neighbor
> saunters round—

has been aptly described by Gilbert Norwood as "a blend of Hesiod, Theocritus, and Christmas as portrayed by Dickens."

There is an interval of seven years until *Birds* (414 B.C.), which attacks no specific abuse but is literally escapist, in that its heroes, wearied of the Athenian atmosphere, decide to build a utopia, which they call Nephelococcygia ("Cloudcuckoosbury"), in the sky. In fantasy, poetry, construction, good humor, *Birds* shows Aristophanes at his best, and the play is usually regarded as his masterpiece. The delegation of the gods who have come to conclude terms with the new city, which has made itself a bottleneck for sacrifices ascending from earth, is one among many delightful touches; another is the reception accorded malefactors and public nuisances who plague life on earth when they come up to exploit a virgin field. The bird lyrics are delightful, especially such a piece as the hoopoe's serenade to its mate (209 ff.):

> Awake, my mate!
> Shake off thy slumbers, and clear and strong
> Let loose the floods of thy glorious song,
> The sacred dirge of thy mouth divine
> For sore-wept Itys, thy child and mine;
> Thy tender trillings his name prolong
> With the liquid note of thy tawny throat;
> Through the leafy curls of the woodbine sweet
> The pure sound mounts to the heavenly seat.
> —B. B. Rogers

In the other plays indecency is incidental; in *Lysistrata* (411 B.C.) it is central, and yet the play is in a sense the most serious of the eleven. The debacle at Syracuse in 413 had left its mark. Now, the poet implies, no rational solution of the political problem seems possible, and only so fantastic a scheme as a sex strike on the part of the women can offer hope. The operation of the strike is excruciatingly funny, especially where the young wife teases her panting husband so unmercifully, but the play as a whole is sad. Talk of state policy in the interstices of the sexual theme is quite grave, and the political message of the whole is on a high level, being an advocacy of a panHellenic union to save Greece from destruction.

The sparkle that is wanting in *Lysistrata* is to be found in fullest measure in *Thesmophoriazusae,* presented a few months later, at the Great Dionysia of the same year. At their private festival the women are to try Euripides for traducing their sex, and after applying in vain to Agathon, Euripides persuades his kinsman Mnesilochus to attend disguised as a woman and to protect his interests. The scene where Mnesilochus is singed and scraped and dressed for his role is riotous. At the women's assembly Mnesilochus is suspected when he suggests that Euripides has not revealed a fraction of women's iniquities. When he is put under guard, Euripides in disguise tries to save him by brilliant parodies of rescue scenes from his own *Telephus, Palamedes, Helen,* and *Andromeda.* If *Birds* stands first for fantasy and charm, *Thesmophoriazusae* is irresistible for its energetic and highly literate fooling.

Thesmophoriazusae is rather flattering to Euripides than otherwise. There is no ridicule in the parodies, the charges of the women are proven unjust, and Euripides is spared the broad insinuations made about Agathon. But in *Frogs* (405 B.C.) we have aspersions on Euripides (but almost as serious ones on Aeschylus) based on well-considered and legitimate critical criteria. Dionysus goes to Hades to fetch Euripides, for there are no more good tragic poets. There an elaborate contest takes place to determine whether Aeschylus or Euripides is the better poet. After tests of various elements of their art Dionysus is still at a loss and propounds a political question: What should be done with Alcibiades? Eventually, Aeschylus is chosen. It is clear that Aristophanes learned much from Euripides and knew and liked his poetry; what he objects to is the encouragement Euripides gave to the bright young men who were endlessly chattering of their new social and philosophical ideas. The adventures of Dionysus and his slave Xanthias on their way to Pluto's court are sidesplitting; the songs of the chorus of initiates in Hades are enchanting.

Ecclesiazusae ("Women Assemblymen," 392 B.C.) seems

the work of an ebullient spirit grown weary. On the basis of the play alone one might surmise that something had happened to the author; what had happened was that his city had fallen and the spirit was gone out of its people. The project of women sitting in the ecclesia was almost as wildly improbable as going to Hades to fetch a poet; but the fact that it is not absolutely impossible is significant. All reasonable means had failed, and nothing could be worse than conditions as they were. The parody of the communist ideas later to be set forth in the fifth book of Plato's *Republic* shows that these ideas, including a better position for women, were being discussed. Most readers feel that Aristophanes is for the first time disgusting in the picture of the three hags who, following the new law that the least favored must come first, quarrel over and pull about a young man who is trying to make his way to his sweetheart in a balcony, with whom he sings pretty duets.

If *Ecclesiazusae* shows the old spirit crushed, *Plutus* (388 B.C.) is altogether on a humbler level. It has so far departed from Old Comedy that it is counted with Middle Comedy, of which it is, indeed, our only specimen. No individual or institution could take exception to its doctrine: good men are afflicted with poverty because Plutus (Wealth) is blind; his blindness is healed, and everything is made right. The play is entertaining enough, and there are amusing scenes when adjustments are made after the god has recovered his vision; it is respectable in moral and decent in language; and its Greek is easy to read. From antiquity it has been a favorite schoolbook, and there are at present 146 manuscripts of it. But the glory is gone. Instead of choral lyrics there is now merely the mark *chorou* indicating where a choral interlude was to be provided, as there is also in places in *Ecclesiazusae* and as there was to be in New Comedy. (pp. 102-09)

> *Moses Hadas, "Drama," in his* A History of Greek Literature, *Columbia University Press, 1950, pp. 74-110.*

Albin Lesky (essay date 1957-58)

[*An Austrian classicist and educator, Lesky is the author of numerous publications on topics related to ancient Greece. Critics have praised his* Die griechische Tragodie (1958; Greek Tragedy, 1965) *as a scholarly, lively, and insightful study. In the following excerpt from his* Geschichte der griechischen Literatur (1957-58; A History of Greek Literature, 1966), *he reviews Aristophanes's oeuvre, with particular emphasis on the common themes and motifs of the Old Comedy. Commenting on the form and content of Aristophanes's comedies, he asserts that "the variety of his language mirrors the variety of content, which mingles the real and the fanciful in a manner that has never since been equalled."*]

If we were asked whether the Attic genius was most fully and characteristically shown in Sophocles or in Aristophanes, we should have to reply 'In both'. Either by himself is only half the picture: to see it whole we must view together the sublime poetry of human suffering and the colourful extravagance of a comic invention which has never known a rival.

[Various popular usages, the Attic carnival, and several other nuclei of primitive comedy] are taken up into the supreme creations of Old Comedy; but how much else there is to make up the fascinating motley of these delightful plays! The manifold richness of life in Athens' proudest days, the heights and depths of her ambitious politics, her well-stocked markets, the foibles of her eccentrics (not all of them harmless), the inrush of new ideas and the revolution in art—all this is caught in a magical mirror in the hand of a genius who never allows us to lose sight, behind these thousand flickering lights, of the realities of life and the seriousness of his own convictions.

The Alexandrians were the first to divide the history of comedy into three stages: the Old Comedy, culminating in Aristophanes, the New, best represented by Menander, and a Middle Comedy in between. If we try to give figures and to date the change between 400 and 320, we must remember that the boundaries are in fact very fluid. (pp. 417-18)

[We define Aristophanic comedy as political, but not] as comedy dealing with current politics, although Old Comedy does take much of its material from that source: the epithet rather refers to the intimate association of the genre with the common life of the *polis,* an association which in its closeness is unequalled anywhere else in Greek literature.

Aristophanes himself gives us an interesting light on the history of comedy in the parabasis of the *Knights* (517), where he proves how fickle the taste of the Athenian public is by citing examples of the rise and fall of earlier writers. (p. 418)

Aristophanes, from the urban deme of Cydathenaeum, was born in the happy days of the Periclean peace, in those years when the building of the Parthenon was begun. We know that he presented his first play in 427 when he was very young: thus we will not go far wrong if we suppose that he was born about 445. There is little known about his life. In the *Acharnians* (653) he says jokingly that the Spartans coveted Aegina because they wanted to rob him; so presumably he had possessions on the island. This may be connected with the expulsion of the Aeginetans in 431 and their replacement by Attic cleruchs. Every one of his plays attests his lively concern for the political and literary life of his day and his close familiarity with the great national poets. We have no ground for assigning him to any given political party. Political satire thrives in opposition to the régime of the day, whose weaknesses it always seeks to expose. In the service of the establishment it degenerates into pure propaganda. The comedies of Aristophanes were mostly written in a period when the structure of Athenian democracy was being undermined by the war and by its own internal deficiencies. It was on these that Aristophanes discharged the vessels of his satire. We shall not discuss the question whether he was basically an opponent of the democracy. What we have said must not be interpreted as if the poet's expressions on the questions of the day were dictated by a kind of mechanical opposition. He was only able to throw such a lurid light on all that seemed questionable or dangerous because amid all the headlong changes around him he retained a lively sense of

Ancient vase painting of a komos, an early form of comic performance which gave rise to Greek comedy.

the power of tradition and conservatism, which are as necessary for the life of men and countries as those forces which beckon forwards.

Aristophanes took part in public life, as we see from an inscription from the early fourth century, which speaks of Aristophanes of Cydathenaeum as a prytanis.

The last dateable play is the **Plutus** of 388. He wrote later the **Cocalus** and **Aeolosicon,** which were staged by his son Ararus, himself a writer of comedies like two other sons of Aristophanes. We may therefore say that the poet died in the 'eighties; but we cannot establish a more precise date. (p. 425)

The first of Aristophanes' plays to be produced was the **Banqueters** (Δαιταλησ) which won the second prize in 427. A father has had his two sons brought up very differently: one in the good old school, the other under the modern rhetoricians. He now compares the results in the form of an agon [dispute] between the two sons in his presence, in which it is seen how the fashionable methods lead to the collapse of all true education and decent feeling. The view has been put forward that this play, unlike the **Clouds,** tilted at practical and forensic education rather than the contemporary philosophical and sophistic teachings. The

later pieces show, however, that the boundaries are very hard to draw. At all events, the debate on education owed its sharpness and actuality to the impact of the sophists, and thus in his very first play we find Aristophanes called to grapple with them. The theme remained a living one down to the time of Terence's *Adelphi.* (p. 426)

The oldest of the extant plays [by Aristophanes] is the **Acharnians,** which won against Cratinus and Eupolis at the Lenaea of 425. Scholars are divided here in a way which is symptomatic of our whole approach to Aristophanes. The question is put: Is the **Acharnians** a free play of fancy, without any serious taking of sides, or is it a creation of the poet's deep convictions, part of his struggle against the war and the Athenian war-party? To us such a question seems to sunder a unity which is the secret of the great master of Old Comedy.

When Aristophanes wrote this play, Athens was sorely beset by epidemics and by the destruction of her crops and fields at the enemy's hands; the rural population above all, wretchedly housed between the Long Walls, had every reason to sigh for peace. Thus it is the peasant Dicaeopolis, his very name expressive of justice, who features here as the hero of peace. It is sheer comic fantasy when he procures a private truce of thirty years from Sparta—the truce is given bodily form as a skin of wine!—and leads a happy life in a little island of peace among all the hardships of war. But he has a hard task to defend his treasure against the chorus of brutal charcoal-burners from Acharnae, who will not give up the war until the ravaging of their homeland is avenged. But he is able to win them over and to enjoy the pleasures of the situation he has contrived, which stand in sharp contrast to the sufferings of the swaggering war-hero Lamachus.

Despite all their freedom and fantasy, the comedies of Aristophanes are made up of formally differing and separate scenes, which in earlier times had had a life of their own. . . . The fairly clear articulation of the *Acharnians* will enable us to illustrate and characterize some of the more important of these constructional elements.

The piece begins with a prologue-speech in which Dicaeopolis vents his ill-humour over the hard times. This form of introduction may have been influenced by the type of prologue which Euripides had developed for tragedy, but underneath it lay the old and essentially popular form of the speech to the public. In comedy at that time the audience could be directly addressed and the dramatic illusion temporarily shelved: this contact with the spectators continued down to the time of New Comedy. The vigorous development of the aside comes largely from this root. It seldom occurs in Euripides; where it does, one must reckon on comic influence. A good example of this direct address to the public comes in the prologue-scene of the *Knights* (36 ff.), which has another interesting feature in its opening: the explanatory and introductory speech does not come until after a scene of dialogue. This feature recurs in others of Aristophanes' plays, and in Menander's hands became typical of New Comedy. In this close contact between comedy and its public we see again how intimately in this art-form the classical literature of Athens was associated with the whole population, and how it drew strength and life from this quarter.

In the *Acharnians* the prologue that gives us our bearings is followed by a sequence of scenes satirizing proceedings in the ecclesia [assembly] and leading rapidly to the point where Dicaeopolis receives the wonderful drink that is his separate peace. Next comes the entry of the chorus—the parodos—here taking the form of a ferocious hunt for the bringer of peace. In discussing the origins of comedy, we saw that the original part played by the chorus was the parabasis, which in this play does not come till later. The parabasis [during which the chorus addresses the audience] derives its name from the procession or parade of the chorus, which was once the first appearance that it made in the action. We now find it embedded in the play, as the result of a process of growth. . . . In the fully developed form the chorus entered long before the parabasis, in a parodos like that of tragedy, and naturally we can suppose tragic influence. The same influence was no doubt at work in the development of scene-division in comedy.

After its parodos the chorus lies in ambush, and Dicaeopolis comes out of the house at the head of a little procession, which we may consider as the descendant of one of those phallic processions which Aristotle mentions as

the beginning of comedy. The chorus jumps out upon Dicaeopolis, and after various preliminaries . . . , we come to the decisive battle of words, in which the advocate of peace has to plead his case with his head already on the block. He succeeds in dividing the chorus—the ease with which it splits into two opposing halves is a traditional feature of the comic chorus. Those who still hanker for war call on Lamachus to help them and take the opposite part to Dicaeopolis. But he does no good, is laughed to scorn, and the chorus finally comes over completely to Dicaeopolis. (pp. 427-29)

After the parabasis the *Acharnians* very well illustrates that sequence of scenes which we reckoned among the basic elements and which is also well preserved in the *Peace* and *Birds*. Dicaeopolis, making ready for the delights of festival, has proclaimed an open market. The first to come to it is a poor wretch from Megara, which had suffered severely from the war: he has his two daughters in a sack and seeks to sell them as piglets. Next comes the inevitable sycophant, and is smartly sent about his business. The third is a Boeotian with all manner of good things, including the prized Copaic eels. The Canephoria is then proclaimed, and Dicaeopolis prepares himself to celebrate it fittingly. But he has to keep off some unbidden guests, who try to cadge some of his peace-drink. In the last scene before the rudimentary second parabasis there is a scene of stichomythia which most amusingly contrasts Dicaeopolis, revelling in the feast, and Lamachus, who has just received his orders, arming himself for the battle and the camp.

The closing section again exemplifies a standard feature, although we must emphasize once for all that all the standard features in Old Comedy are merely the framework which the poet's genius fills with a unique life and gaiety. Dicaeopolis returns from a drinking contest victorious and in the highest spirits, while Lamachus, who has been most unheroically wounded while jumping over a ditch, is carried onto the stage groaning and howling. The contrast is further heightened. The tipsy Dicaeopolis is not alone: he has a girl on each arm, and he minces no words in describing the joys that await him. The play ends with an uninhibited komos, in which the erotic element is very pronounced. There is of course no lack of the erotic in Aristophanes, but it undoubtedly plays a specially prominent part in the end of the plays. We have only to consider how frankly the union of Trygaeus and Opora is spoken of at the end of the *Peace*: in the *Birds* greater decency is preserved, but again a marriage forms the end. . . . (pp. 430-31)

Cleon was not able to frighten Aristophanes by his action over the *Babylonians.* In the *Acharnians* (300), with an allusion to Cleon's work as a tanner, he promised to cut up Cleon into boot-soles for the knights. Thus he already had in his mind the plan for the comedy which brought him victory at the Lenaea in 424—one of the greatest successes of his life. From the passage quoted we can infer that at the time of writing Aristophanes was already confident of the collaboration of the knights—members of a conservative *corps d'élite*—in the chorus of the play which bears their name. At a time when scholars did not pay overmuch attention to the monuments, it was fashionable to think of cavalry manœuvres executed by proud Athenian knights. Nowadays we prefer to follow the black-figure vases which portray men with masks of horses, carrying others on their backs. This is another example in Aristophanes of the old and enduring tradition of the animal chorus.

As the play opens, two slaves, whom we recognize as the generals Nicias and Demosthenes, are deploring their lot in the service of their master Demos of the Pnyx. Life has been intolerable since a new slave, a Paphlagonian, has been practising his rascality in the house, getting round Demos by flattery and having his own way in everything. But they are able to lay hands on the Paphlagonian's collection of oracles, and they find the comforting assurance that he will meet his match in a sausage-seller who is an even baser wretch than he. The sausage-seller soon arrives and does full honour to the promise. From this point on the play consists for long stretches, both before and after the parabasis, in a series of agon-scenes, in which the two worthy contestants strive each to surpass the other in vulgarity and vilification, in speeches which they deliver before an ecclesia summoned for this purpose, in producing ludicrous oracles, and finally in entertaining their master Demos. The Paphlagonian's prospects grow steadily dimmer, until finally, on the strength of an oracle, he has to acknowledge in the sausage-seller his fated successor, and he yields to him.

While the two competitors are off the stage, preparing the entertainment for Demos, there is a snug scene between the latter and the chorus (IIII) which is very important for the understanding of the whole. The old lord Demos shows himself in a new light, and makes it clear to the knights that he is not so stupid after all. He does in fact see through these rascals who are battening on him: he is deliberately letting them wax fat, but at the right moment he will take back all that they have stolen. We can see that Aristophanes is giving a charitable interpretation of Demos so as to avoid being reproached with a defamation that amounted to *lèse-majesté* [gross insult]. But this section, which gives us a rest from the noisy altercation that has gone before, has another purpose also: it is to prepare us for the surprising *coup de théâtre* at the end. After the [repetition of part of the parabasis which is not uncommon in the older plays] the sausage-seller and Demos come on again. But what a sausage-seller, and what a Demos! The glib swindler of the early scenes comes on garlanded and in festal garments to give the glad tidings that he has boiled Demos young again. This is an old myth-motif, well known from the story of Pelias and its dramatization by Euripides. Then Demos himself enters—no longer the feeble old man, but in the prime of life, dressed in the style of the great days of Marathon and Salamis, the true embodiment of 'holy, violet-crowned Athens', and wildly acclaimed by the chorus as king of the Hellenes. Now everything will be different, everything will prosper. The new adviser takes Demos to task for his previous faults, but consoles him by saying that the blame really rests on the traitors around him. But from now on Demos will behave better in every way.

This startling reversal at the end has always puzzled schol-

ars, and some have declared that it defies all logic and psychology. This is true by our own standards, but the thing looks different if we accept the 'logic' of Old Comedy, which was at liberty whenever it chose to flit from the thousand problems of reality to the bright world of dreams. We see the right of it only when we bear in mind that the poet had to consider the feelings of his own public, who could only accept a play like this if it gave a cheerful prospect of a better time to come—the ultimate consolation in times of adversity. If we choose to interpret the end as bitter irony, we may reach a conclusion that satisfies our own notions, but we go a long way from the free and fanciful world of Aristophanes. (pp. 431-32)

Aristophanes went off in a different direction when he brought out the *Clouds* at the Dionysia [drama competition] of 423. What we have now is a fairly drastic revision of the play as then performed. It was a failure, which the author took greatly to heart. Cratinus came first with the *Pytine,* Amipsias second with the *Konnos,* which also concerned itself with Socrates. Aristophanes rewrote it later, but did not put the new version on the stage.

The play seems to begin as a bourgeois comedy of manners, but the fantasy of Old Comedy soon shows through. The peasant Strepsiades has defied the advice of Pittacus and taken himself a wife of higher social rank. His son Phidippides lives up to these origins and to his distinguished name, devotes himself to horses and brings the old man to the verge of ruin. After a sleepless night Strepsiades can see only one way out: the boy must go to the thinking-shop (phrontisterion) to learn the art of winning cases, just or unjust. But the youngster will not hear of these people, Socrates or Chaerephon, and so Strepsiades himself in his old age must try to learn the new art of perverting the truth. But the scenes where the length of a flea's hop is being measured, where the origin of a gnat's hum is discussed, and where Socrates observes the sun from a hanging basket, all these only enable Strepsiades to make himself a laughing-stock by his boundless stupidity. Now it is Phidippides' turn. For his instruction the dispute is staged between the dikaios logos and the adikos logos, the just and the unjust cause—the most brilliant of all the agon-scenes in Aristophanes, in which the representative of a new age, which knew how to take its pleasures unhindered by morality and justice, triumphs over the advocate of ancient piety and morals. Here is a school that suits Phidippides, and he makes such good progress that his father is delighted with his skill and is enabled to rid himself of two pressing creditors (the traditional sequence of encounters and dismissals). But over dinner inside the house he falls out with his son over the latter's infatuation with Euripides, and Phidippides commits the ultimate and inexpiable crime of beating his own father. Thanks to his schooling he is clever enough to justify his action as a requital of what he suffered from his father as a child. In a sudden revulsion of feeling, which gives no difficulty in comedy, Strepsiades regrets having associated with knaves to learn their knavery, and goes with his slaves to burn down the thinking-shop.

The play is named after the chorus of Clouds, a very complex poetical creation. At first these Clouds provide a vehicle for splendid poetry: their first song is one of the most beautiful in Greek literature; next, as the divinities worshipped by the dwellers in the phrontisterion, they serve as an example of 'enlightenment' and are associated with all sorts of metaphysical theorems. At the end, however, they underline the moral tone of the action and dress themselves in a kind of Aeschylean piety. When Strepsiades reproaches them with having led him into his perverse behaviour, they give a deeply meaningful reply: thus do they always when they see a man inclined towards evil, so that he may fall and learn through suffering to reverence the gods.

The central problem raised by the *Clouds* is the representation of Socrates. . . . (p. 433)

Aristophanes knew enough of Socrates to represent many of his characteristics to the life. But at the same time he hastily brought him in to his general attack on the new ways of thought, of speech and of education which were destroying the good old ways, in short, into his attack on the sophists. This was possible because to the Athenians of that day Socrates inevitably appeared—without the distinctions obvious to us today—simply as a representative of suspect innovation, of a way of thought which called everything into question. How far Aristophanes shared the views of the many, how far he used them for his own purposes—these are questions which we cannot now answer. But the suggestion that his play had a double meaning, and that through all the ridicule one can perceive a serious representation of Socrates clearly set apart from the sophists, is one which ignores the nature of Old Comedy. (p. 434)

In the *Wasps* we have the same conflict between father and son as before in the *Daitales* and the *Clouds,* but here the situation is reversed, and a son is plagued by the folly of his father. Here again they are at opposite poles politically. Their names, Philocleon and Bdelycleon, indicate that the father is as warm in his support of that controversial statesman as the son is in detesting him. Philocleon is the embodiment of a passion that was epidemic at the time. The Greeks of all ages loved litigation—a reflection perhaps of what has been called their competitive nature. It was a very fine thing for a man to enjoy the pleasure of feeling important as a juror and to be paid for it as well. Pericles had introduced payment of jurors: in 425 Cleon raised it from two to three obols. It was necessary to secure a large number, since the Heliaea consisted of six thousand lay judges chosen by lot, who had to divide into committees of several hundreds to deal with individual cases.

The struggles of Bdelycleon against his father's inordinate love of jury-service provide the stuff of the drama until the parabasis, which at v. 1009 is strikingly delayed. The form of the exposition is familiar: a dialogue between two slaves leads up to a continuous account given by one of them. They are guarding the father on the son's orders—Bdelycleon has shut him up in the house—to keep him away from the law-courts. Philocleon's amusing attempts to break out (one of them borrowed from the ruse of Odysseus in the cave of the Cyclops) provide scenes of rich comedy. The chorus now comes to find Philocleon—a chorus of jurors, dressed as wasps with long stings. They are gnarled old men, good old-fashioned Athenians, but possessed by the same passion. An agon follows in which Bdelycleon has a theoretical discussion of the question with his father and defends his own point of view. The chorus is convinced, but the young man then arranges a private court in which the old man decides a lawsuit between two dogs. The dog Labes of Aexonae has been accused of cheese-stealing by a dog from Cydathenaeum. In the latter we recognize Cleon, who brought an action for embezzlement in 425 against the general Laches of Aexonae (we know him from Plato's dialogue). It is a pretty point that the verdict of 'not guilty', which was given in the historical trial, is here arrived at only through an oversight on the part of the infatuated Philocleon.

It is nothing new to us to find Aristophanes ending his play along different lines from those which he has followed in the first part. Here again there is a change of theme in the parabasis, where Bdelycleon tries to bring his boorish old father into a better frame of mind and into more refined company. But once again Aristophanes is sceptical of experiments in education, and this one also brings unexpected fruits. The old man behaves abominably at the dinner-table, starts all sorts of quarrels, and steals a pretty flute-girl from his companions. Thus Aristophanes brings in that coarse erotic element which is typical of his closing scenes. The final komos here is particularly disorderly. The old man dances like one possessed, and challenges the bystanders to compete with him. This brings in the three dwarfish sons of Carcinus, and they all finally go dancing off the stage.

The part following the parabasis is effective enough in its slapstick comedy, but it is not very carefully constructed. Twice the rejuvenated Philocleon gets up to his mischief off-stage, and twice the slave Xanthias comes on to the stage to make an appropriate report (1292, 1474). On the first occasion the events coincide in time with the typical fragment of parabasis, on the second with a song from the chorus praising the conversion of Philocleon. After the old man's behaviour at the table this is rather hard to take, and everything would go more smoothly if we transposed the two strophes and the piece of parabasis. The latter would then be at a greater and more normal distance from the main parabasis. But in a piece composed like this one such conclusions cannot claim any certainty.

When Aristophanes wrote the *Peace* for the Dionysia of 421, he could be confident that the play was topical. After the death of Cleon and Brasidas, the peace parties on both sides gained ground, and in April 421, very nearly at the time of the Dionysia, the peace was concluded which was expected to last for fifty years. Despite the extreme topicality of the play, Aristophanes had to concede first place in the contest to Eupolis with the *Colaces.*

Again it is two slaves who begin the play, and one of them, directly addressing the audience as so often, expounds the situation. They are having a thin time, these slaves, in giving the necessary care and provender to a gigantic dung-beetle kept by their master, the vinegrower Trygaeus. This creature is to serve its enterprising owner as transport to heaven, where he will ask Zeus what he has in mind for the war-weary Hellenes. Again the fanciful invention has a specific target: the ride on the dung-beetle is a parody of the *Bellerophon* of Euripides, in which the hero tried to reach heaven on his winged steed. For this purpose some stage machinery was used which readily lent itself to ridicule. But in Aristophanes the enterprise has a happier issue than in the tragedy. Trygaeus reaches his goal and enters into discussions with Hermes. He notes with disapproval that the gods have withdrawn into the highest aether to be away from the endless horrors of war, and that Polemos reigns unchecked. He has shut up the goddess of peace, Eirene, in a pit, and he is now about to take the cities of Greece and bray them in a gigantic mortar. Polemos is shown in person making his arrangements, while Trygaeus listens unnoticed. The scenes of eavesdropping that are common in later comedy are foreshadowed here. Luckily Polemos' servant Kydoimos (the fear of battle personified) is unable to provide a pestle—Cleon and Brasidas are dead—and so Polemos has to go back into the house to make another. Trygaeus seizes the opportunity, calls on the Greeks, who appear as the chorus, gains the support of the anxious Hermes for his plan, and leads the rescue of Eirene, who is pulled up from her pit by ropes. At the same moment two goddesses appear—Opora, goddess of fruitfulness, and Theoria, who stands for joy at festivals. After a conversation with Hermes, in which the causes of the war are recalled in ludicrous travesty, they all return to earth, not by the dung-beetle on a stage flying-machine (Trygaeus and his three goddesses would have overloaded it), but by simply climbing down a route which is pointed out by Hermes with a light-hearted breaking of the dramatic illusion. (pp. 435-37)

At the Lenaea of 414 Philonides produced for the author his *Amphiaraus.* Again it was a story of rejuvenation, taking place in the shrine of that hero in Thebes. If we are right in supposing that miraculous cures had their share of attention in the play, there was a thematic parallel to the later *Plutus.*

At the Dionysia of the same year Aristophanes brought out the most highly wrought of all his extant plays, the *Birds.* It features the flight of two human beings from the miseries of the world into a fairyland, and it combines the boldest flights of fantasy with the most delicate poetry in a way that gives perennial delight and constantly invites imitation. The scenes are more numerous and varied and at the same time more closely knit than in any other of his plays.

When Aristophanes was writing this play, the Sicilian expedition was already in hand—that venture which aroused such hopes and such forebodings. The most determined attempts have been made to find allusions in Aristophanes to this great event, but we must admit that Aristophanes does nothing to reward such determination. The two friends Pisthetaerus and Euelpides, whom we find when the play opens walking through a wood led by crows and jackdaws, give as the reason for their flight the passion for litigation at Athens—nothing more. In this piece the free play of fantasy is overwhelmingly more important than any concrete political purpose.

Of these two friends Pisthetaerus (True Friend) shows

himself as a man of action and sense, while Euelpides (Good Hopes) takes the part of a bomolochos or buffoon. They ask the hoopoe if it knows of a city where one can live quietly and enjoy oneself. This is a happy touch, since the hoopoe was once king Tereus, the son-in-law of Pandion, king of Athens. The outcome of their exploration is quite different, namely the founding of the bird-city, but we should not immediately declare that there are two different strands in the plot. In fact one theme leads naturally to the other. The hoopoe's suggestions are none of them satisfactory, and Pisthetaerus consequently comes to think that the birds themselves ought to found a city in mid-air from which they could starve out the gods and make them more obliging. The chorus of birds—a colourful troupe—is summoned up by a monody from the hoopoe, in which, as in other lyrical parts of the play, the sounds of nature and the artistry of words are so combined that the woods in springtime seem to be echoing with a hundred strains of birdsong. (p. 438)

Now comes another period of a few years in which we do not know what Aristophanes wrote, until in 411 he brought out two plays—the *Thesmophoriazusae* and the *Lysistrata*—both dealing with women, but with very different basic themes. We do not know which play came out at which festival, but the *Lysistrata,* with its panhellenic terms of reference, was most likely brought out at the Great Dionysia.

The Thesmophoria was a festival common to all Greece, celebrated by women at the time of sowing: men were rigidly excluded. In Athens it took place in the Pnyx, where the women spent the day of the festival in leafy bowers. Aristophanes' play is built upon the invention that the women of Athens at this feast are plotting serious measures against their incorrigible adversary Euripides. The writer of so many plays of intrigue has devised a stratagem for his defence against this threat: he proposes to smuggle a friend in woman's clothing into the secret festival. So he has arranged with Mnesilochus, a kinsman by marriage, to depute this part to Agathon, whose effeminate manners mark him out for it. Agathon is rolled out upon the stage from the very ecstasy of composition (like Euripides in the *Acharnians*), but he refuses to undertake so hazardous an enterprise. Mnesilochus steps into the breach, but he has to be shaven and singed before he puts on the women's clothes from Agathon's wardrobe. The poet then makes us witnesses of the solemn assembly, in which eloquent complainants demand the death of Euripides for bringing their faults onto the stage and making men suspicious. The speech of Mnesilochus in defence is not exactly acclaimed, since he makes it a point in Euripides' favour that he has not revealed the worst of woman's character. The whole section is remarkable for its bringing in themes and stories in the manner of the Milesian tales or the Decameron. We must suppose that such stories were current and popular even then.

At last Mnesilochus is unmasked. He tries to save himself by Telephus' stratagem (previously parodied in the *Acharnians*). He snatches the child of the principal speaker and flees to an altar. But what the swaddling clothes contain is in fact a wineskin. That Athenian women greatly appreciated the gifts of Bacchus is a frequent theme in comedy, and is unlikely to have been a malicious invention.

Guarded by one of the women, Mnesilochus stays sitting on the altar while the chorus in its parabasis sings the praises of women and depreciates men. Thus the context of the play gives new life to the immemorial battle of words between the sexes which had been probably part of the amusement of the spring festival since the earliest times.

In his mortal danger Mnesilochus scribbles appeals for help on votive tablets and throws them outside, just as Palamedes in Euripides' play wrote of his sufferings on oar-blades and threw them into the sea. Euripides finds the appeal, and the sequence of episodes after the parabasis here takes the form of a series of attempts at rescue—brilliant and fantastic parodies of scenes in Euripides—separated by songs from the chorus. In the first Mnesilochus is Helen, and Euripides Menelaus, trying to free his wife as in the play of 412. But the only upshot is that Euripides is taken into custody by one of the Scythians who served as police in Athens at that time. Next comes the *Andromeda,* but Perseus-Euripides is no more successful. Mnesilochus is not freed until the third attempt, when the poet comes to terms with the women, promising a truce in future, and with their co-operation and that of a pretty street-walker gets the better of the stupid Scythian.

It can be seen from what we have said that this play battens on contemporary tragedy, but we cannot give any impression of the completeness with which tragic parody permeates it even in individual lines and words.

Aristophanes wrote another comedy under the title **Thesmophoriazusae,** which differed considerably from the extant play.

In the *Lysistrata*—again produced by Callistratus—the women have a quite different end in view. They aim at stopping the war, and thus this play takes its place beside the **Acharnians** and **Peace.** But its tone is very different: in the earlier plays we heard much about the miseries of war, and there were many home thrusts against those who profited from the common calamity; but the **Lysistrata** breathes a spirit of forgiveness and conciliation. It is significant that in the middle of his city's struggle for existence Aristophanes could express so openly the conviction that there was a good deal to be said for Sparta, and that Athens could do no better than extend the hand of friendship to her. Here Aristophanes looks far beyond the Athenian horizon and shows a true panhellenic feeling. In consequence the allusions to domestic politics are infrequent in this play, despite all the tension that must have preceded the oligarchical putsch. It is characteristic of Aristophanes that his obscenity is not abated one whit by his seriousness of purpose.

Like others of Aristophanes' plays (**Clouds, Wasps, Ecclesiazusae**), the comedy opens at the break of dawn. The heroine of the piece and inventor of the stratagem is Lysistrata, whose seriousness of character keeps her above the general obscenity, which here is very great indeed: she is waiting for her helpers whom she has summoned from

Boeotia and the Peloponnese. One by one the conspirators arrive, but as soon as Lysistrata unfolds her plan—a sex-strike to compel the men to make peace—we see how hard such a sacrifice seems to them. The general tone of the play is well reflected in the fact that Lysistrata's best helper is the Spartan woman Lampito. The agreement is solemnized by a sacrifice (of a wineskin!), and the other measure prudently proposed by Lysistrata is carried out: the older women occupy the city to secure the state treasury, from which the men pay the expenses of the war.

From the very beginning of the *Lysistrata* there are two opposing choruses; but we cannot be sure whether they were two whole choruses or the halves of one. Certainly this was not an innovation: the use of two choruses disputing one with the other was an old feature. First the chorus of old men comes on to storm the city and drive out the women. The chorus of women with ready tongues and buckets of water keeps the men in check. The dispute between the choruses is now followed in this beautifully constructed play by an agon of individuals. A high official arrives—a member of the college of probouloi which was set up with extensive powers in 413. A proboulos appears also in the *Demes* of Eupolis. In our play his authority avails him little; he has to hear a vigorous denunciation by Lysistrata of the faults of the men who aspire to rule, and he has to withdraw covered in confusion. There now follows, in obvious ring-composition, a further scene of conflict between the two choruses, singing one against the other. (pp. 439-41)

The great peace-treaty is preceded by a treaty between the two choruses, who now come together and form one. The Spartan ambassadors come to discuss terms, and Lysistrata appears accompanied by Forgiveness—another of those allegorical figures that come at the end of Aristophanes' comedies. She addresses both parties, and reminds the conflicting Greek nations of their common destiny in a speech which is one of the most noble and serious in Aristophanes. It is only natural that the spirit of the komos should now assert itself in feasting and dancing. The end is damaged, but not much appears to be missing.

We can well understand why this splendid play has been so often imitated, especially in times which have known the horrors of war. But we can also understand why all such attempts on stage or screen are doomed to failure. The incredible frankness with which sex is handled—yet without any prurience—is unacceptable to modern taste, while to Aristophanic comedy, its nature and origins being what they were, such frankness was quite indispensable. Here if anywhere we can see how necessary an historical sense is for full enjoyment of ancient literature. (p. 442)

[**The Frogs**] begins with a kind of prelude at the house of Heracles, to which Dionysus comes with his slave Xanthias to enquire the way to the underworld. Heracles has been there before to fetch up Cerberus, and Dionysus thinks it advantageous to go down in the costume of Heracles, with club and lion-skin, to make a good impression. The purpose of the venture is to bring back Euripides, who had died a little before: the god of the stage cannot endure his absence. He justifies his expedition in a conversation with Heracles on the pitiful state of the tragic stage in Athens.

With a lightning change of scene, as allowed by comedy, we find ourselves beside a lake in the underworld: Dionysus enters Charon's boat, where he has to row manfully himself. Here he is greatly troubled by the croaking of a subsidiary chorus of frogs, which gives the play its name. Xanthias is not allowed on board, and so he runs round the lake (i.e. round the orchestra) over which his master is rowing. In rather a similar way, although more ceremoniously, the god was borne through the city in his boat on wheels at the spring festival.

After going some little way on their journey, during which Dionysus gives several proofs of the most striking cowardice, the two meet a chorus of Eleusinian initiates, who are allowed to celebrate their festivals even in the underworld. (This is the first appearance of the chorus.) Their hymn of invocation to Iacchus is a pearl of Aristophanic poetry.

The value of the Heracles-costume becomes rather doubtful at this stage. At the sight of the supposed dog-stealer, Aeacus, the porter of hellgate, becomes furiously incensed and rushes off to fetch a policeman. Alehouse-women, whom Heracles has eaten out of house and home, fall upon the new arrival like maenads. But there is some consolation: a serving-maid of Persephone's comes with a charming invitation. In the course of these rapid episodes Dionysus makes Xanthias repeatedly change clothes with him so that he can pass off the slave as Heracles when it suits his book. In consequence, when Aeacus comes with the constables, it is impossible to establish which is the god. The matter is comically tested by flogging them both, but this leads to no certain result. In the end Aeacus sends the two heroes into the palace so that the gods of the underworld can decide.

The parabasis, the last that we have from Aristophanes, is shorn of its nonresponsional parts, so that it shows the same form of epirrhematic syzygy that we have met in the second parts of the older plays. Its theme—an earnest and persuasive appeal to Athenians to heal the wounds within their city and to reach out the hand of forgiveness to political offenders—occasioned a second presentation of the play, according to Dicaerchus in the hypothesis. A pupil of Aristotle's deserves belief on such a point: but the date of the second presentation is uncertain. Most probably it was in the same year: perhaps even at the same festival.

After the parabasis Aeacus and Xanthias come on, having now struck up a friendship as between servants. From their conversation we hear of a dispute that has broken out in the underworld: Euripides is laying claim to the throne of tragedy, but the holder, Aeschylus, is defending it. It is now time for the two men's art to be examined and compared, and Dionysus is to be the umpire. It is obvious that the plot has here been changed. Dionysus originally went on this expedition in order to recover Euripides, but now there is to be a contest between the representatives of venerable tradition and of modern tragedy. But it would be wrong to talk of two plots side by side in the play, and to invent theories to account for the facts mentioned above. One such theory suggests that the contest was thought of

while Sophocles was still alive, while the fetching back of Euripides was suggested by the parlous state of the stage after the former's death. We should be better employed in appreciating the art by which the poet twists the two themes together into an organic whole and gains the opportunity for an animated agon. It is true, however, that Sophocles died while the play was in Aristophanes' mind, and this fact called for notice. The poet does this with a few light touches: we see this most clearly in those charming passages which express respect and admiration for the great tragedian. (pp. 443-44)

Of the late plays only two survive. If we can judge from them, common features were the reduction within narrow limits of topical references to men and affairs of the day, and the increased scope allowed to pure invention.

So we find it in the *Ecclesiazusae* (*Women in Parliament*), which was produced two years after the treaty of alliance between Athens and Sparta, that is, in 392. Comparison with the *Lysistrata* is inevitable. In both plays women conspire in a revolution, in both it is one woman who holds the leading strings of the enterprise, and in both the play opens with a conspiratorial meeting at an early hour—here actually in darkness. But while the *Lysistrata* was concerned with the most burning of topical questions, namely the ending of the war, it is a comic Utopia that is depicted here. In the *Lysistrata,* behind all the fantasy, we felt an earnest hope and exhortation that reason might be suffered to prevail, but in the *Ecclesiazusae* the free play of fantasy leads light-heartedly to a *reductio ad absurdum.*

The women of Athens have had enough of the unsatisfactory government of men, and they propose to take over themselves. They sneak into the ecclesia in disguise to force through the necessary legislation: but first they listen enthralled to a speech from their leader Praxagora expounding her policy. They form themselves into a chorus, sing a song about what they are doing to do, and go into the ecclesia. Thus after the parodos the stage is empty, permitting a scene in which Blepyrus, the husband of Praxagora, is informed of the total revolution by Chremes, who has just come from the assembly. The chorus also comes back, and with it Praxagora, who outlines the programme of the new régime to her husband in a protracted agon in long verses. Basically it is simple: poverty is to be abolished, since all is to belong to all. We have seen before that Aristophanes often keeps his plots moving by entwining one sequence of themes with another. So here the original theme of the regiment of women drops out of sight, and the rest of the play turns on the enforcement of a primitive communism. While the play has no parabasis, in all other ways it keeps the old form of composition. The agon is followed by a series of episodic scenes throwing an ironical light on the new régime. A loyal citizen, all ready to give up his goods, is confronted with a sceptical smart-alec who is waiting to see how things turn out. There is a wholly mad and wholly Aristophanic scene—if that is not a tautology—concerned with the execution of an important point in the programme: women are to be assured of an equal share in the delights of love by making the old women mate before the young ones have their chance. Thus a young man who would fain fly to his love becomes the sorry victim of some Megarian hags like the daughters of Phorcys, who have all the allurements of a coven of witches.

Praxagora's revolution turns out differently in reality from what she intended. Here again she is unlike Lysistrata, and in the second half of the play she is seen no more on the stage. The end is negligently sketched. A serving-girl calls Blepyrus to the communal feast which the other citizens have already enjoyed. This gives an excuse for the comastic ending that custom demanded, and Blepyrus comes on contentedly enough with some women of the town. How far the ironical tone of the previous scenes is maintained is difficult to say. At all events the invitation of the audience to go and have a good dinner—at their own houses (1148)—and the contrast between the description of the wonderful fare that is waiting (ending with a word of 168 letters!) and the pease-pudding that is served both point in this direction. The appeal to the judges is relegated to the closing section, since there is no parabasis in which to place it. (pp. 446-47)

The last piece that we have from Aristophanes is the **Plutus,** which he produced in 388. He had brought out a play of the same name in 408. The little that we know about it suggests that the first **Plutus** was on the same theme as the extant play.

The age-old complaint of the unjust distribution of blessings is treated here in a kind of fairy-story which leaves out much of the personal invective and obscenity which were the stock-in-trade of Old Comedy.

Once again in late Aristophanes we find the theme of the **Daitales** and **Clouds,** The aged Chremylus has gone to Delphi to ask the god whether he would not do better for his son's career by training him to be a rascal. The god has answered with his favourite irrelevance that Chremylus is to take into his home the first man that he meets outside the temple. This turns out to be Plutus, whose blindness is responsible for the bad state of the world. He is to recover his sight by a miraculous cure in the temple of Aesculapius. This project is opposed by Penia, poverty personified, who stands up for herself in an agon of the old style with Chremylus. When Poverty praises her blessings, it is not the poverty of the beggar that is meant in this sociologically important section, but the poverty which makes a man work for his daily bread, not for luxuries. Much that Poverty says is close in spirit to the closing chapter of Herodotus.

This play also shows a twining of different themes, leading in fact to considerable uncertainty. Plutus is to have his sight when he distributes wealth to the good and just, but the notion is now slipped in that all men are to be both rich and good, which is contradicted by the scene with the sycophant in the later sequence of episodes.

The healing of the blind god is related in detail by the slave Carion, who with Aristophanic lack of inhibition tells in the same breath of the trickery of the priests and the wonders wrought by the god. (pp. 447-48)

One observes with regret that amid all the critical work on the surviving plays there has been little attempt to bring out the elements of Aristophanes' humour. Despite his frequent use of comedy of situation, it is his language above all that carries his humour. In verbal point and wit, sometimes brilliant, sometimes overdone, he is inexhaustible. . . . He twists the meanings of words and makes use of similarities in sound—devices, in fact, which are common in popular speech in every age. From this quarter too comes his trick of exploiting every possibility of playing on form and meaning of proper names. He is very fond of compounds of three or more elements, which reach a monstrous complexity sometimes. . . . A constant feature of his language is the appearance of heterogeneous elements side by side. Basically he uses the Attic of his own time; but just as he often sinks below it with coarse vulgarisms, so he frequently rises above it to the spacious realm of poetic language. His purpose in this case is usually to achieve a comic effect by parodying the stilted language of tragedy: sometimes, however, especially in lyrical passages, he uses poetical expressions with no such end in view. Thus the variety of his language mirrors the variety of content, which mingles the real and the fanciful in a manner that has never since been equalled. (p. 449)

> *Albin Lesky, "The Flowering of the Greek City State," in his* A History of Greek Literature, *translated by James Willis and Cornelis de Heer, Thomas Y. Crowell Company, 1966, pp. 241-641.*

Alan H. Sommerstein (essay date 1972)

[*In the following excerpt, from an essay written in 1972 but not published until the following year, Sommerstein discusses Aristophanes's* The Acharnians, The Clouds, *and* Lysistrata, *commenting on their technical, historical, and cultural background. He places these works in the context of Greek dramatic competitions and explains some of the customs that influenced them. Sommerstein also points to the dramatist's verbal virtuosity, providing examples of Aristophanes's prodigious linguistic imagination.*]

[Aristophanes'] lifetime was a time of extreme political turbulence. At the beginning of his career Athens was at the height of her power and fame. For a generation the city had been governed by a radical form of democracy, under which all citizens had both an equal share in policy decisions (which were taken by an Assembly of the whole citizen body) and an equal chance of appointment to executive office or to the Council which dealt with routine public business and prepared the agenda for the Assembly (since appointment was by lot—military and diplomatic posts necessarily excepted). Such a system might not appear conducive to either rational or consistent policymaking, and the triumphs of Athens between 462 and 431 would scarcely have been possible if one man, Pericles, had not been able to control the Assembly by his personality, his popular policies, and the power that comes from success. Under his leadership Athens transformed what had been a military alliance directed against the Persian empire into a league of subject states paying tribute to herself. Athens was greatly enriched, and spent much of the money on a programme of public building then unparalleled anywhere in Greece; but the subject states, and others who feared they might become so, were naturally resentful. Eventually Sparta, the greatest military power in mainland Greece (for Athens' empire was an essentially maritime one), was persuaded that Athenian power was a menace to the independence of other states, and forced Athens into war. This was in 431.

Two years later Pericles died. His successors, Cleon and his like, self-made men for the most part, tended to follow rather than lead public opinion, a failing memorably depicted in *The Knights* where Cleon is presented as a grasping and toadying slave of the personified People of Athens. (These new politicians were also more sensitive to satire: Pericles never prosecuted a comic poet.) The war dragged on indecisively until 421, when, it having become clear that neither side could defeat the other, peace was concluded. Before long, however, Athens was back on her imperial trail, attempting to subdue Sicily, and Sparta again felt compelled to stop her. The Sicilians defeated and destroyed the Athenian expedition; Sparta, on the advice of the brilliant former Athenian general Alcibiades, seized and fortified a base in Athenian home territory; and the crisis resulted which forms the background to *Lysistrata.* For a few months in 411–410 Athens even abandoned her democratic system, but soon restored it, and continued the war. Most of her subject states, however, had by now revolted, and the Spartan alliance, with backing from Persia, was far the stronger side. In 405 Athens suffered a final and catastrophic naval defeat, and the following spring she surrendered unconditionally.

The victors deprived Athens of all her overseas possessions, and even for a time of part of her own territory. A small group of oligarchs seized power and inaugurated a reign of terror, but within a year the democratic system was again re-established, never again to be challenged until Athens fell under Macedonian domination. From now on, however, Athens could never be quite what she had been. She no longer had the resources of the whole Aegean behind her, and while she did again very soon become one of the leading powers of Greece, she never again became *the* leading power. The transformation of Athens from the political to the intellectual centre of Greece was under way.

Aristophanes' work reflects, towards the end of his career, the early stages of this transformation. His last two surviving plays are concerned, not (like *The Acharnians* or *Lysistrata*) with immediate political issues, nor (like *The Clouds* or *The Frogs*) with the moral dangers inherent in contemporary thought and literature, but with the theoretical Utopias that philosophy had begun to construct, and their ludicrous possibilities if put into practice. In these plays he becomes a keen-eyed but detached observer of society. During the war, on the other hand, he is very much part of society; he has his diagnoses for its ills, and his prescriptions as well, and he means them to be taken seriously.

Of this last point I am sure. It has often been said, especially in recent years, that in Aristophanes political and social thought is purely incidental and always subordinated to the desire to amuse his audience and win the prize. I do not see how this view can be reconciled with the fact that when *The Clouds,* which is in fact, if not in name, a tragedy, failed at its first performance, Aristophanes' reaction was to include in his revision of the play an address to the audience in which, in effect, he rebukes them for not appreciating a comedy whose merits lay 'in her words and in her action'. The Aristophanes of the *Symposium* also seems to expect to be taken seriously, though very much afraid that he may not be. If, then, we ask what were Aristophanes' social, political and intellectual attitudes, we are not talking about something that does not exist.

We certainly cannot detect in Aristophanes any burning attachment to the established democratic system. Again and again he emphasizes the fickleness and gullibility of the sovereign people; and it is noticeable that the politicians about whom he is most venomous are all strongly democratic—Cleon, Hyperbolus, Cleophon, and others. There is no such campaign against more 'right-wing' leaders such as Nicias, and even Alcibiades is attacked on the score of his sexual rather than his political activity. In *The Frogs* Aristophanes explicitly recommends that civic rights should be restored to those who had taken part in the oligarchic coup of 411, and that the direction of affairs should be entrusted to 'men of good birth and breeding'— two classes which would certainly overlap at a number of points. He never goes so far as to express himself in favour of oligarchy, and it would be an exaggeration to describe him as anti-democratic; but he was certainly distrustful of the way the system was currently working.

One of the reasons for this distrust was undoubtedly the eagerness of the Assembly to plunge into war and their reluctance to make peace even when . . . the opportunity stared them in the face. Aristophanes detests war, at any rate the current war against Sparta, for many reasons, of which the most prominent, in *The Acharnians* and in *Peace,* is the forcible separation of the country people from their land, a separation especially bitter in the 420s when that land was constantly being ravaged by the enemy. (The return to the land is also mentioned in *Lysistrata,* line 1173, as the blessing of peace *par excellence.*) As *Lysistrata* makes quite clear, though, Aristophanes was no simple-minded pacifist, and he had a deep love for his own city.

In the literary and intellectual sphere, as we see from *The Clouds* and *The Frogs,* Aristophanes saw a marked contrast between old and new, Aeschylus and Euripides, traditional and sophistic education. He did not regard the old as perfect; Right in *The Clouds,* for all his high moral tone, is a dirty old man, and Aeschylus is treated as in many ways antiquated and crude. Nor are old men in Aristophanes as a rule morally superior to young men. But he was very suspicious of the new styles. In poetry his treatment of Euripides is on the whole good-natured; serious criticism is reserved for *The Frogs,* when Euripides is dead and his work can be reviewed as a whole. There can be no question, though, what Aristophanes thought of the new kinds of education that were coming into fashion. Not that the attitude he expresses in *The Clouds* was unique to him. One of the plays that defeated *The Clouds* in 423— *Connus,* by Ameipsias—also included a portrayal of Socrates which, to say the least, did not contradict that in *The Clouds;* and the same is true of all other references in comedy to Socrates, and indeed to philosophers in general, well into the fourth century. The inference can hardly be resisted that this was also the attitude of the ordinary Athenian to such people. It is understandable. The 'enlightenment' of the last third of the fifth century, as is the way of enlightenments, together with a great deal of truth introduced a great deal of nonsense, and dangerous nonsense at that. The ordinary Athenian saw the nonsense, lumped the truth together with it, and rejected the whole package. The intellectual, like Thucydides, distinguished between the two. Aristophanes did not make the distinction.

The old-versus-new attitude extends even to religion. Although in fifth-century Athens 'impiety' was a serious crime, impiety did not include laughing at the many absurdities in the traditional ideas of the gods and their activities. Aristophanes can happily, in *The Birds,* entertain the idea of the gods being deprived of food and sex by an aerial blockade and then deposed from the sovereignty of the universe; and the theme of Zeus starving from a shortage of sacrifices turns up again in *Plutus* and in Aristophanes' speech in the *Symposium.* Denying the existence of the gods was another thing: this was part of the indictment later preferred against Socrates. That indictment also referred to Socrates allegedly believing in 'other new deities'; and it is new deities and new cults that Aristophanes is particularly scathing about—witness the remarks of the Magistrate in *Lysistrata* (lines 387-9), about the worship of Asiatic gods such as Sabazius and Adonis. Otherwise, though he may parody religious observances, Aristophanes never jeers at them; which is not surprising, for the very performance of one of his comedies was itself part of a religious observance.

Comedy at Athens, like tragedy, was always produced in connection with one of the festivals of the god Dionysus—the Lenaea in the lunar month of Gamelion (corresponding roughly to January) and the City Dionysia in Elaphebolion (corresponding roughly to March). The Lenaea, at which *The Acharnians* and probably *Lysistrata* were produced, was essentially a local Athenian affair, since foreigners were unable to attend in any numbers owing to the extreme difficulty of sea travel in winter. (Aristophanes in *The Acharnians* draws attention to this fact to protect himself from being again accused of 'slandering the City in the presence of foreigners'.) The City Dionysia was the occasion when the wealth of Athens, political, literary and musical, was displayed to the world. Victory at the City Dionysia was thus more highly coveted than at the Lenaea, and defeat more keenly felt.

The City Dionysia lasted for five days in normal times, but during the war with Sparta it was reduced to four. (Comedy was the main sufferer from the curtailment of the programme, the number of competitors being cut from five to three.) Before the festival began, the statue of its patron god, Dionysus Eleuthereus, was brought in procession from a temple just outside the city, near 'Academe's Park' (see *The Clouds*), to the theatre, where the god remained throughout the festival, watching the performances and

sometimes (as in *The Frogs*) seeing himself take part in them. On the day after this procession there was another, when numerous sacrifices were offered; the sponsors (*choregi*: see below) of the various performances took a leading part in the procession and dressed themselves magnificently. The rest of this day appears to have been devoted to contests of boys' and men's choruses singing and dancing the lyric performances in honour of Dionysus known as dithyrambs.

On the next day (the second of the festival proper) the dramatic performances began. First, however, various important public ceremonies were performed: announcements were made of the award of golden crowns to citizens who had rendered important services to the state; the gold and silver brought by the subject states as tribute (see *The Acharnians*) was displayed to the audience in the theatre; and those young men, just reaching their majority, whose fathers had been killed in battle, paraded in the theatre and were presented with a set of armour at the public expense. Thus the audience which then settled down to watch three tragedies and a satyr play by one poet, and a comedy by another, had been forcibly reminded that it was also the People of Athens, that courage and public spirit had made their city great, and that it was up to them to keep it so.

This audience was enormous by modern theatrical standards. The capacity of the Theatre of Dionysus was about 14,000, and there can be little doubt that it was always full during the Dionysia. There seem to have been no restrictions of age, sex or citizen status governing attendance: Plato in his *Gorgias* makes Socrates say that 'poets in the theatres' direct their eloquence at a public 'consisting of children, women and men, slave and free, all at once'. This is not contradicted by the fact that Stratyllis in *Lysistrata* can address the audience as though it consisted entirely of adult male citizens; for she is speaking to the audience in its political capacity as 'the People', and only adult male citizens had political rights. In any case, the men will have been in a majority and will have had the exclusive right to the best seats. (A passage in *Peace* implies that the women sat apart from the men, in the back rows.) Many foreigners were present, most notably the official delegates from the three hundred or so Greek states subject to Athens, who had come bringing their tribute; these delegates, as well as Athenian officials and priests, had reserved seats in the best parts of the theatre. The most privileged seat of all, the centre place in the front row, was that of the priest of Dionysus.

Preparations for the festival had begun several months before. Soon after taking office in the summer, the Chief Archon took in hand the arrangements for the City Dionysia, and his colleague the King-Archon (who involuntarily became a performer in *The Acharnians*) those for the Lenaea. These magistrates had two main duties in connection with tragedy and comedy. On the one hand, they had to select the poets who were to be allowed to compete. It is not known how they did this or what advice, if any, they took; for, being chosen by lot, they did not normally have any literary qualifications themselves. There are hints that it was the practice for poets to read their work to the mag istrate. This task of his, at any rate, was very delicate and often gave poets occasion for complaint, justified or not.

The other main responsibility of the archon in charge of the festival was to nominate sponsors (*choregi*) to equip the choruses and organize the performances generally. He chose men of considerable means, who were then required to undertake the task as a compulsory civic duty. Sometimes he received applications from people volunteering to be *choregi*, for despite the expense involved a *choregia* was regarded by many as an honour: defendants in lawsuits often pointed to the number and magnificence of their *choregiae* as proof of their public spirit.

Each comic *choregus* was responsible for one play. Acting on the advice of the poet, he had to train and costume the Chorus, hire any additional singers, dancers or musicians needed (such as appear, for example, at the end of *Lysistrata*), and provide a dinner afterwards for all concerned in the production. He also probably had to pay and costume any actors over and above the three provided by the state (which may explain why, although in some plays Aristophanes certainly needs four actors, in others such as *The Birds* he goes out of his way to ensure that no more than three are required).

It is not altogether clear how actors were selected. It is known that poets sometimes acted in their own plays, or employed professional actors of their own choice; and it is very tempting to believe that Aristophanes himself took the part of Dikaiopolis in *The Acharnians.* On the other hand, we know that in the early fourth century five principal actors ('protagonists') were chosen by the state and allocated by lot, one to each poet; what we do not know is when this system was introduced. At the Lenaea a prize was awarded to the best comic actor; surprisingly, it was not till a century after Aristophanes' time that a similar prize was introduced at the City Dionysia.

It was normal for poets to produce their own plays, and it was as producers (*Didaskaloi*) that their names appeared in the official records of the festivals. Thus Aristophanes himself produced *The Clouds.* For his first play, *The Banqueters,* however, he had asked a friend, Callistratus, to act as producer (probably because he had not attained the age of majority), and this arrangement was so successful that he frequently repeated it. *The Acharnians* and *Lysistrata* were both produced by Callistratus. There can be little doubt that the audience were well aware of the real identity of the author; indeed in *The Knights,* the first play he produced himself, Aristophanes, through the mouth of the chorus-leader, says to the audience that many of them had been asking him 'why he had not long ago asked for a Chorus in his own name'. (He says that the reason is that he considers comic production to be the most difficult job that exists, and goes on to exemplify this statement in considerable detail; he does not deign to mention that had he asked for a Chorus in his own name for the Dionysia of 427, he would not have got one.)

When *choregus,* poet and producer (if any) had completed their preparations, two days before the festival, a preview (*proagon*) was held in the Odeon, not far from the theatre. The poet (or the producer—it is not clear which) presented his actors and chorus, without their masks and costumes, and announced the title of the play. In some cases this will have given the public a fairly good idea what the play was about: after the hints given in *The Acharnians,* they will not have been very surprised when a play announced as *The Knights* turned out to be an attack on Cleon. In other cases the audience would have been put in a mood of mystified expectation: a play called *The Clouds* might have been about anything (since it does not seem that it was announced what roles the actors would play), and certainly no one would expect the Chorus of *The Wasps* to consist, as it did, of elderly jurymen.

Productions at the dramatic festivals were always competitive. The prizes were allotted by a panel of judges selected by a complicated procedure designed to ensure that the judging should be both competent and fair. Competence was secured by the initial selection, which was made by the Council; the *choregi* were entitled to make nominations at this stage. Corruption was as far as possible eliminated by leaving the final appointment of the judges until just before the contest, and then choosing ten by lot. At the end of the contest the ten voted, but only five of the votes, drawn out of an urn by the presiding archon, were counted. The judges appear to have written their names on their voting tablets, so that, at least in the case of those whose votes were counted, it was known how each judge had voted. Thus there was some possibility of influence being brought to bear on them, either by the general feeling of the audience or by powerful individuals. Nevertheless, the judges' decisions usually seem to have been reasonable from the critic's point of view; and the limits of influence are shown by the fact that Cleon was unable to prevent the victory either of *The Babylonians* or of *The Knights.*

Technically the competition was not between plays or between poets but between choruses; thus when all was ready for a play to begin, the crier proclaimed *Eisage ton choron* ('Bring on your chorus'; this is the proclamation translated in *The Acharnians* as 'Let your play commence'). This practice continued even though it had long been regular for a play to begin with dialogue and for the Chorus only to come on later. The comic chorus consisted of twenty-four; there could also, as in *Lysistrata,* be additional dancers, and any of the actors could be given a song. The Chorus normally has a distinctive character, and some at least of its songs are written to reflect this character; others, however, need not do so. Thus in *The Acharnians* the Chorus consists of old men of Acharnae when it enters, and so it remains for much of the play. But towards the end it becomes (in Dover's phrase) 'the hero's claque'; and at one point it seems to speak as the mouthpiece of the author. Even in *The Clouds,* where the plot requires that the Chorus should retain its character throughout, it can speak as a Chorus taking part in a competition and demand, with menaces, to be given the first prize.

Lysistrata is exceptional in having two choruses, presumably of twelve each. The motive is dramatic, not musical, since all female parts whatever were played by men.

It was not quite a rule of the competition, but the overwhelmingly regular practice, that once the Chorus had appeared on the scene it had to remain until the end of the play, and then leave. Some flexibility was allowed: in *The Women's Assembly* the Chorus of women goes off to the Assembly and returns one scene later, and in *Lysistrata,* after the final departure of the Chorus, the actors and additional dancers remain for a concluding song. But in general the Chorus had to be present, and this imposed some restrictions on the plot. In particular, nothing can be done with the knowledge of the Chorus of which it disapproves and which it is willing and able to stop. In tragedy this could be a handicap, and Choruses are sometimes made to take oaths whose implications they do not fully realize, so that when they understand the situation and wish to intervene they cannot do so without perjuring themselves. Aristophanes is able to turn this power in the hands of the Chorus to advantage. In *The Acharnians* the Chorus tries to stop the hero's 'personal peace' by violence. In *Lysistrata* the two Choruses fight each other. Only in *The Clouds,* of our three plays, does the Chorus not intervene in the action; and it turns out in the end that its non-intervention was deliberate, and has far graver consequences than any intervention would have done.

The Chorus normally danced as it sang, and the dance-movements were regarded as an important part of the total effect of a choral ode, but unfortunately we know very little about them.

In addition to normally having to keep his Chorus on the scene of action, the dramatist was also under a restriction on the number of actors who could have speaking parts. The maximum permitted was four, and these had between them to play all the characters; indeed, as has already been mentioned, some of Aristophanes' plays, such as *The Birds,* seem to have been deliberately constructed so that they could be performed with only three actors. This restriction meant that the author could not, like a modern dramatist, carry a large number of characters through the play, since it would be confusing for the same part to be played by different actors in different scenes; in comedy, indeed, it is regular for only one or at most two to have parts which bring them on stage in all or most of the scenes, and characters whom one might have expected to be of some importance in the play, like Lampito in *Lysistrata,* can simply disappear. *The Clouds,* with three characters carried through the play, is exceptional in this respect, and presented Aristophanes with a problem for which he found no satisfactory solution. It was impossible for him, with only four actors at his disposal, to have a debate between Right and Wrong with Strepsiades, Pheidippides and Socrates all present; so before the debate begins, Socrates, without giving a reason, has to excuse himself.

It may be interesting to see how Aristophanes arranged *Lysistrata* in such a way that four actors could play some twenty parts. The first actor takes the part of Lysistrata, who appears in almost every scene. The other three actors seem to have fairly equal loads. The second actor to appear comes on first as Calonice, then in quick succession as First Woman and Fourth Woman, then as Calonice again; after this he would probably not be needed until near the end, when he would again have to make a couple of quick changes, appearing as First Layabout, then First

Diner, then First Layabout again. The third actor begins as Myrrhine, then takes Second Woman and Fifth Woman, then becomes Myrrhine again for the famous scene in which Cinesias is tantalized; after this he probably takes the parts of the Magistrate, the Negotiator, the Doorkeeper (who probably remained unseen behind the door) and, in the final scene, the Athenian.

The fourth actor in *Lysistrata* appears to have been a specialist in dialect roles. He appears first as Lampito, then as the Magistrate, then as Third Woman, then as Cinesias (who probably staggered off after singing his last line), then in successive scenes as the Spartan Herald and the Spartan Ambassador, and in the final scene as Second Layabout, Second Diner and the Spartan.

The rule about number of actors was rigid, the rule about the continuous presence of the Chorus nearly so. More elastic were certain conventions about the structure of the play. The basic form was something like this:

(1) A prologue (so-called), in which the opening situation was expounded and the movement of the plot begun.

(2) The *parodos* or entry of the Chorus, often marked by a long and varied song-and-dance movement.

(3) A series of scenes interspersed with songs by the Chorus; the central scene was usually a formal debate (*agon*) on the crucial issue of the play, with speech balanced against speech and song against song.

(4) The *parabasis,* in which the Chorus partially or completely abandoned its dramatic role and addressed the audience directly in the absence of the actors. It normally consists of three songs (S) and three speeches (s), in the order S_1-s_1, S_2-s_2, S_3-s_3; S_2 corresponds metrically to S_3 and s_2 to s_3, and the first speech (s_1) often ends with a passage to be rattled off very rapidly (theoretically in one breath), called a *pnigos*.

(5) Another series of scenes interspersed with choral songs. The songs in this section generally contained jibes directed at prominent individuals (the Chorus of *Lysistrata* explains why it is departing from this custom); one of them was often expanded into a brief second *parabasis* (as in *The Acharnians*).

(6) A concluding scene of general rejoicing, often associated with a banquet or a wedding.

None of the plays [discussed here] conforms exactly to this pattern, and it is clear that there was no obligation on the poet to follow the conventions at all closely if they did not suit him. The *parodos* of *The Clouds,* for example, consists of only a single song, though a very beautiful one. *The Acharnians* has no *agon;* this is certainly because, if it had had one, somebody would have had to argue in favour of war, and Aristophanes is careful, in all his plays on the theme of peace, not to allow the case for war to be presented. For the same reason, although *Lysistrata* contains a scene in the form of an *agon,* it is completely one-sided: the Magistrate is never given a chance to argue. Again, *Lysistrata,* with its divided Chorus, can have no *parabasis;* in place of this we find a scene between the two Choruses, with alternating song, dance, speeches and violence. The speeches are directed partly at the opposing Choruses, but mainly at the audience; there is even (lines 698-9) a direct address to an individual member of the audience. Even the final scene of rejoicing is dispensable; we might have thought that when in *The Clouds* the triumphant Strepsiades took his son home and put his creditors to flight, an ending of that kind was coming, but the Chorus has already given us a hint that it is not to be so, and instead of rejoicing the play ends in destruction. The leader of the Chorus says that it is time to go, and they go—in total silence. The judges evidently did not approve of the original ending of *The Clouds,* and there is evidence that the ending was one of the parts altered when Aristophanes revised the play; the new ending, had the revised version been performed, would have been scarcely more to the judges' liking.

At both the City Dionysia and the Lenaea, comedy and tragedy were performed in the Theatre of Dionysus, which can still be seen just to the south-east of the Acropolis. The plan of the theatre was circular. Over half the circumference was occupied by the spectators' seating, around the circular *orchestra* or dance-floor where the Chorus usually performed. Behind the *orchestra* stood a building called the *skene,* originally no more than a dressing-room, but in Aristophanes' time decorated with an architectural façade and (probably) three doors. Part of the *skene* was on two floors; the upper floor was used a good deal in comedy, as in *The Acharnians,* where Euripides is upstairs writing a play. The rest of the *skene* was lower and had a flat roof: it is on this that Dikaiopolis' wife stands in *The Acharnians* to watch the Dionysiac procession, and in *Lysistrata* the roof does duty as the battlements of the Acropolis. It is likely that the same background was used for every play; when, as in *The Acharnians* and *The Clouds,* the single *skene* building had to represent two or more houses, curtains were hung between the doors.

Whether there was a raised platform in front of the *skene* has long been a matter of controversy, but a painted vase found in Attica, and dating from about 420 B.C., appears to settle the question. The painting shows a comic actor posturing as the hero Perseus, while two spectators look on. The actor stands on a wooden platform approached by four steps. It is thus now generally agreed that there was such a platform in the Theatre of Dionysus; the steps may well have extended the full length of the platform, since in some tragedies a full Chorus of fifteen apparently sits on these steps. There were also probably steps at the ends of the raised platform, which would be used by actors coming in from the wings. Near the top of the central steps stood a small altar, much used in tragedy for prayer and the burning of incense.

The platform was a convenient device for marking off the actors visually from the Chorus, but there was no objection to the actors coming down to the *orchestra* or even to the Chorus mounting the platform, as the Men's Chorus must do ('I doubt if I have any hope / Of hauling these logs up the slope') when attempting to burn the women out of the Acropolis in *Lysistrata.*

Between the ends of the *skene* and the auditorium there were broad side passages (*eisodoi* or *parodoi*) for the entrance and exit of the Chorus and of those actors who did not emerge from the 'house' or 'houses' in the *skene.*

Two pieces of machinery were available for use in tragedy and comedy. One, known as the *eccyclema,* was a device of some kind for bringing tableaux and immobile characters (such as dead bodies in tragedy) out of the *skene* into view; its exact nature is disputed, but it seems most likely, from the language used to describe it in *The Acharnians,* that it was a pivoting arrangement rather like the modern revolving stage, such that the whole front of the 'house' opened up. (This is why, later on in *The Acharnians,* Dikaiopolis tells his slave to 'lock up the house'). The other device was a crane from which a car could be suspended, so that gods and heroes in tragedy could be shown flying through the air. It is on this crane that Socrates first appears in *The Clouds.*

The comic actor's costume was traditionally characterized by grotesque padding, and it seems that this was still normal for most characters in Aristophanes' time. Over this actors wore tights and (if playing a male part) a very short tunic which left uncovered a large leather phallus. (Female characters wore long gowns, often dyed yellow.) Much play, of course, is made with the phallus in *Lysistrata;* and in *The Clouds,* when Aristophanes says that he does not bring on 'a great thick floppy red-tipped leather tool', it is likely that the operative word is 'red-tipped', i.e. circumcised; for at least two jokes in the play are more easily managed by an actor wearing a phallus than by an actor without one.

Certain characters would wear special costumes, or carry marks of their identity or profession. Lamachus in *The Acharnians* probably wore a military cloak (*phoinikis*: the 'scarlet uniform' referred to elsewhere by Lysistrata). In *Lysistrata,* Lampito and her Peloponnesian companions no doubt wore the sheepskin gowns referred to in the song which closes the play; the Scythian policemen (and policewoman) would be recognized by their bows and quivers, the Spartan herald by his wand of office.

The costumes of the Chorus, if they represented human beings, were similar to those of the actors; it is not certain whether Choruses of men would wear phalluses, but it is most likely that they did (the supernumeraries who represent the Odomantian soldiers in *The Acharnians* would certainly have to). Choruses of animals or birds, on the other hand, gave the costume designer plenty of opportunity to exercise his imagination; it seems he did not give his imagination much rein in the case of *The Clouds,* where the Chorus appears simply as women, and this may have been partly responsible for the play's failure.

Actors and chorus all wore masks, which were typically made with grotesque exaggeration of features. The use of masks may have been religious in origin, or it may have been merely a device employed by early actors to emphasize the fact that the actor was, for the purposes of the performance, not himself but someone else; masks were retained mainly for two quite practical reasons—firstly, they made it easier for one actor to play many different roles; secondly, in such a large theatre and with only natural lighting, a bold and exaggerated mask would be far more easily visible to the audience than the features and expressions of the actor's own face.

There appears to have been a repertoire of stock masks available for any play; several of them are represented in contemporary art. Some masks, however, must have been unique or nearly so; that of Pseudartabas in *The Acharnians,* for example, must have raised an instant laugh with its single gigantic eye. When a living individual was caricatured on the stage, it was normal to commission a mask recognizably like him. We know that this was so because in *The Knights* Aristophanes apologizes for not using such a portrait-mask for the character who represents Cleon; the mask-makers, he says, were too frightened to take the responsibility of producing one. One reason for the choice of Socrates as the 'professor' in *The Clouds* may well have been that, as we know from other sources, Socrates had an unusually ugly face which lent itself easily to caricature in a mask.

The comic mask normally included a beard, apparently of real hair. The chief character of *The Poet and the Women* is given a shave on stage. Beardlessness at this time was a sign of effeminacy, and so the notoriously effeminate Cleisthenes and Strato (Pseudartabas' 'eunuchs' in *The Acharnians*) are given beardless masks, and Dikaiopolis twits Cleisthenes as 'he of the long black beard'.

The masks and the unchanging back-scene are not the only features of Athenian theatre production that would have been offensive to an audience brought up on early-twentieth-century naturalism. Since the performances took place in the daytime and in the open air, it was not possible to indicate visually whether the action was supposed to be taking place in daylight or darkness. *The Clouds* begins at night; but the Athenian audience will only have known this because the characters are asleep and one of them, on waking, complains how long the nights are.

Again, it was impossible, except by the use of the *eccyclema,* to show action taking place indoors. In general this would not be too disturbing, because much more of the business of Greek life than of ours was in any case done in the open air; but sometimes it created difficulties. The first scene of *The Clouds* may again serve as an example. Strepsiades and his son must have been lying *in front of* the *skene*. In real life they would of course have been indoors, since the weather is supposed to be quite cold, cold enough for Pheidippides to want five blankets; in the play they must needs be outdoors. It would probably be nearer the truth to say that it does not occur to the audience to ask whether they are inside or outside; they are too interested in Strepsiades' problems and what he is going to do about them. When Strepsiades points out to his son the door of the Thinkery, then, indeed, they must be outside their house; until that point the question of their exact location just does not arise.

This indeterminacy of place makes it easy to have changes of imaginary setting without change of scenery, or gaps in imaginary time without intervals. (The 'dramatic unities' are not only not classical, they are not even Aristotelian:

they are Renaissance misinterpretations of Aristotle.) *The Acharnians* begins on the Pnyx, but when Dikaiopolis walks 'home' (i.e., probably, up the steps towards the *skene*) we find we are in front of his house. In *Lysistrata,* the action is continuous up to the ignominious retreat of the Magistrate; when the women next appear, we find five days have elapsed. So long as the audience knows those facts about the imaginary situation which matter for the purpose of the play, there is no incongruity felt.

Aristophanes' merits as a comedian can for the most part be left to speak for themselves; but I should like to say a few words on two aspects of his technique.

On the one hand, Aristophanes is a master of dramatic structure. It may be of interest to illustrate this from a part of his work that has sometimes been thought rather naive in this respect, the second half of *The Acharnians.*

It has many times been said that in early comedy we tend to find after the *parabasis* a succession of disconnected scenes, and *The Acharnians* and *The Birds* are treated as typical examples. I will not speak here of *The Birds;* but in *The Acharnians,* though we certainly have a succession of scenes, they are not disconnected. Their unifying theme is stated by the Chorus in the centre of this section of the play, at the very beginning of the exquisite ode that sums up the message of the whole play:

> Look you, citizens of Athens,
> See the gain that wisdom brings!

—'wisdom' being here synonymous with willingness to make peace. Before and after this ode, the scenes rise to a climax. First, Dikaiopolis sets up his market, and makes an exchange with the Megarian, giving him goods of little value and getting in return goods of perhaps slightly greater value in the two girls; an Informer is driven out with contumely. Then he buys a vast load of good things from the Boeotian, including the much-coveted eels of which Boeotia had a monopoly and which (as Aristophanes again complains in *Lysistrata*) were totally unobtainable in wartime; and for these he pays less than nothing—for that is certainly the price at which we are meant to rate Nicarchus. After this Dikaiopolis chooses his own customers, turning away Lamachus' servant and the Farmer, but condescending, like an amused god, to show favour to an anxious bride. Next he is invited to the usual concluding dinner-party (while the 'unwise' Lamachus is forced to go off and get chilblains) and returns with two ravishing conquests; but even now he is not finished: the climax is still to come. Dikaiopolis has won the Pitcher Day drinking contest, and he has come to claim a prize from the King-Archon—the very magistrate who is shortly (so the author hopes, and his hopes were justified) going to award another prize to the play itself. And so *The Acharnians* ends.

Another aspect of Aristophanes' genius, which has to be mentioned here because in a translation it cannot be reproduced but only imitated, is his dexterity at all forms of juggling with words. I shall give some examples of this from the beginning of **The Acharnians.** This passage provides a favourable field for word play, because nothing whatever is happening. Dikaiopolis is merely whiling his time away, waiting to see if the Assembly will begin less than five hours late. While he is waiting, he fires off a few jokes.

One of the first of these occurs almost at once. 'The number of things that have pained me,' says Dikaiopolis, 'is *psammakosiogargara,*' literally 'sand-hundred-heaps'. Aristophanes invents these improbable compounds with zest; in **Lysistrata,** 'lettuce-seed-pancake-vendors of the Market Square' and 'innkeepers, bakers and garlic-makers' are just one word each (each word filling a whole line of verse). The idea is carried to its logical conclusion at the end of **The Women's Assembly,** where the main item on the menu for the concluding feast is described in one 170-letter word.

Another trick is the so-called *para prosdokian,* 'contrary-to-expectation': the speaker makes us quite sure what we are going to hear next—and then says something quite different. After completing his list of theatrical joys and sorrows, Dikaiopolis goes on, 'Seriously, though—in all the years I've—' and we expect to hear something like, 'In all the years I've lived, I have never been so distressed as I am now.' What Dikaiopolis actually says is, 'In all the years I've washed, I've never had so much soap in my eyes as—yow!—as I have now.'

Then there is the pun, as dear to Aristophanes as to Shakespeare, or more so. In this speech we have the pun which I have translated into one on 'sale' and 'sail'. In the original it is neater: 'My deme, which never said "Buy charcoal" (*anthrakas priō*), nor vinegar or oil; it knew not "buy" (*priō*), but provided everything for itself without needing a saw (*priōn*).'

On another pun, of rather a different kind, the whole plot of **The Acharnians** depends. Two lines early in the play—one spoken by the demigod Amphitheus to the Assembly, the other later on by Dikaiopolis to Amphitheus—are identical: *spondas poiēsai pros Lakedaimonious monōi,* 'alone to make peace with the Spartans'. But from one use of the line to the other the construction of *monōi,* 'alone', has changed. When Amphitheus uses it, *monōi* agrees with the subject, and the meaning is that Amphitheus is the only person authorized to make peace. In Dikaiopolis' mouth *monōi* is a 'dative of advantage', 'to make peace *for* me alone'. This is the 'personal peace' of which Dikaiopolis afterwards reaps the benefits. It need only be added that when the peace-treaty (*spondai*) is finally brought by Amphitheus, it takes the very agreeable form of three wine-skins suitable for pouring libations (also called *spondai*). (pp. 12-35)

> *Alan H. Sommerstein, in an introduction to* The Acharnians, The Clouds, Lysistrata *by Aristophanes, translated by Alan H. Sommerstein, Penguin Books, 1973, pp. 9-38.*

THE ANARCHIST PLAYS

CRITICAL COMMENTARY

Douglas J. Stewart (essay date 1965)

[*In the following excerpt, Stewart characterizes Aristophanes as a writer who took great pleasure in anarchy; he examines* The Acharnians, Peace, Knights, *and* Lysistrata *as comedies in which Aristophanes turns various kinds of order upside down, and creates a new, imaginative order. The dramatist's chief delight, Stewart contends, "is in shaming and upsetting the established order, political, customary or intellectual."*]

In the *Symposium* Alcibiades remarks, with Plato's evident approval, that Aristophanes has been "bitten by the madness of philosophy"—a lead few have cared to pursue. And despite the anecdotal gossip in later antiquity connecting Plato and Aristophanes, scholars have spent little time seeking the possible affinities which may have given rise to the reports, for instance, that Plato wrote the poet's epitaph, kept an edition of his plays as bedside reading, and even got many of his ideas from them or from friendly conversation while the older man still lived. We do not treat such "information" as solidly factual, but we usually seek the plausibility behind the circumstantial imagination of early biographers. Though not much in this case, for, we tell ourselves, "comedy" is one thing, and "philosophy" quite another. Not only is comedy "literature" but Old Comedy is a fantastic, starkly vulgar form of it, while philosophy is all logic and high seriousness. [Ulrich von] Wilamowitz, the generalissimo of twentieth century classicists, rejected the genuineness of the "Platonic" epitaph, denying that Plato could possibly have valued Aristophanes as highly as does the epitaph. This judgment does justice neither to Plato nor to Aristophanes. There is more than a little Aristophanes in Plato: the impish temper, the free-wheeling imagination, the moral insights, the juxtaposition of clowning and sublimity (and, some would add, the same high-handed treatment of adversaries).

But Plato needs less attention on this point than Aristophanes. Philosophy has not set up such severe formal canons that one is debarred from seeking aids to understanding wherever they may be found. If the author of *Protagoras* and *Euthydemus* is suspected of learning some tricks from a comic poet, the student may go to work and try the case with whatever tools he has at hand. But if the comic poet claims to be teaching *philosophia* even in the innocent fifth century acceptance of the term, the student is met by an assortment of injunctions, derived from a theory of literature anachronistically defined, which artificially hamper his movements. Too much so in the case of Aristophanes.

Aristophanic criticism has a spare and confused record. In a [1964 anthology, *Theories of Comedy,* edited by Paul Lauter], over 500 pages are filled with observations on the subject, comedy. But among all the collected opinions from Plato to the present there is only one extensive or important treatment of the first extant comic writer in Western literature—by Hegel! This is symbolic and typical:

symbolic in that only a philosopher could be found to dwell upon Aristophanes; and typical in that so little of what is said about the genus Comedy—however valid with respect to later work—has anything to do with Aristophanes. Study of Aristophanes is mostly an argument carried on in mutually incomprehensible languages between those who take Plato's hint and see Aristophanes as a kind of philosopher, teaching men to think, as he claims over and over again, and those who would study him as they study other "literature," but never quite get him in their sights.

Naturally enough, literary critics as a rule of procedure refuse to admit that philosophy and literature are the same thing. And seeing something which outwardly resembles what we call "drama," they are perhaps too quick to invoke their generally useful rules as metaphysical certainties, and forbid critical access to those who wield tools appropriate, they say, to another "field." Yet it is hard to avoid seeking "intention," even if this is *usually* a fallacious procedure, when your author is forever telling you what he means and what good he is doing your life, your morals, and your mental habits. On matters of characterization Aristotle's offhand judgment that comedy shows us characters a little worse than real life is as wide of the mark as are the modern attempts to assimilate Aristophanes' heroes to common types, the picaro, the braggart, and the "rose-pink ladies and mad grammarians" of later comedy, for his characters are walking mental states, and their only dimensions are stupidity and intelligence; they are neither interesting nor important for personal foibles. Again, literature which sets out to convert and correct *normally* comes under the head of what [Northrop] Frye calls "naive allegory," but does one call *Lysistrata, Acharnians,* or *Peace* "naive"?

I would suggest that criticism gets nowhere unless we take Aristophanes at his word, at least provisionally, granting as a working hypothesis that here, even if nowhere else in literature, someone managed to write stuff that could be examined validly both in its literary modalities and in its intellectual "content," and indeed which must be examined in both at once. Our own reactions tell, I think, the true story: he has the power, unlike almost anything in literature, to fascinate and unnerve his audience; he provokes not coolly synthesized responses, but awed prostration of the faculties. We take his effrontery personally. We are *involved:* he hectors and editorializes, and we cheer or boo. We quite rightly feel that he is making demands upon us, that his proposals are real and not hypothetical shapes. Heine called his work, "the jubilee of death and the fireworks of destruction," and said that the appearance of a live Aristophanes would swiftly be attended by a chorus of furious policemen. No less today, I fear. We could not remain aloof. We would have to *do something* with him, as with a live Socrates. From the D.A.R. to the French Academy our society would feel compelled to take a stand on his uncomfortable presence. This is more than amusement, more than a parade of types, more than satire. We laugh at comedy of later vintage which twits our weaknesses without distressing us with demands for instant and heroic reform; we do not feel personally challenged. But Aristophanes makes the challenge and we respond, with

love or fear, and usually with both at once, to our own critical puzzlement.

Here the view will be advanced that this engagement he produces is due directly to his freedom—a freedom which invades every "genre" and tortures every idea to test its worth, a freedom which acknowledges no laws of society or art save those which meet his stringent intellectual standards. And further it is proposed that this freedom—which is so complete as perhaps to deserve the gloss, *anarchy*—is that aspect of his performance most worth attention, for it is or ought to be the meeting ground whereon students of Aristophanes the Philosopher and students of the literary Aristophanes can compose their differences.

Aristophanes' chief delight is in shaming and upsetting the established order, political, customary or intellectual. *Acharnians* heartily endorses the pleasures of an anarchy consisting in treasonous dealings with the enemy, while *Ecclesiazusai,* near the other end of his career, goes the whole way with subversion of both the regime and the constitution of the state. *Wasps* seemingly attacks the courts and the majesty of law, while *Lysistrata* approvingly portrays the subversion of family discipline. In *Birds* the very constitution of the universe is snubbed and Peithetaerus extorts the sceptre from Zeus himself. In *Knights* Athenian politics is equated with buffoonery, while Demos, personifying the sovereign people, is a deaf and childish old fool. In each of these plays the character who plots the subversion of the status quo is crushingly successful and crowns his victory in orgies of socially unprofitable indulgence, untouched by the threat of retribution or thoughts of any consequence whatever. This seems the work of a devoted anarchist. But we must examine the content of this anarchism, for anarchy is not usually enjoyable, and mere destructiveness rarely inspires pleased admiration for the charm and elegant good taste of the destroyer.

Is this the "jubilee of death and the fireworks of destruction"? Gilbert Norwood modifies Heine thus: (Aristophanes proceeds) " . . . not indeed reducing the universe to nothing, but blowing it to pieces and building with the shards a new fantastic universe that lasts a rainbow moment like the soapbubble blown by a child." Aristophanes destroys order only to create a more gorgeous if not a more orderly world. Whether from mere wish-fulfillment or from deep antisocial tensions, we all respond to the destruction of the established order and its replacement by the madly inverted world of the poet's imagination. In this procedure Aristophanes begins with nothing refined or subtle; he first engages us by finding that human itch which every picaresque character endeavors to scratch. We sympathize with successful rascals, from Gil Blas (one might say, from Odysseus) to the Gentle Grafter. But the artful rogue is always found leading an episodic life, traveling forever in a cycle from desperation, to scheme, to scrape, to success, to desperation again. The appeal is definitely to our taste for stratagem and suspense, with no higher aim or hope in the author's mind or ours. The stratagems have no deeper import than the rescue of the schemer that he may scheme the more. Aristophanes uses this mechanism, but to do much more than fascinate: he employs it to lower our guard, to render us helplessly receptive to the power of his paradoxes. His schemers, moreover, are no common schemers, and they are driven to scheming by something far different from any rashness or misdeeds of their own. Here we see the poverty of assimilating, "type" criticism. Aristophanes' heroes are in no sense rascals or buffoons. Frye says that "The comic hero will get his triumph whether what he has done is sensible or silly, honest or rascally." Were this true everywhere else in comic literature, it still would not be so for Aristophanes: Trygaeus, Dicaeopolis, Peisthetaerus and Lysistrata get their triumphs because they are ineffably wise, and perfectly honest—especially with themselves. It makes *all* the difference in the world that they *know* what they are about and why it is wise and good. Their schemes may be desperate, but heroically so—perfect instruments in the hands of master reformers. The glory of the plots is the subtlety of these schemes, perfectly tailored to the problem attacked and admirable, even millennial, in their results. And it is particularly in the treatment of results that we must look for our philosopher. It is easy to overthrow convention; it is more than a little difficult to supply an alternative which does not simply reapportion the old stupidities.

In **Acharnians** Dicaeopolis is sick of war; and more, he is bored with it. It is soon made clear that tender-hearted pacifism is not the mainspring of the action. War is wrong because it is preposterous and contemptible; it revolts the intelligence of anyone who, like Dicaeopolis, is immune to its specious claims. He defeats all representatives of the "war mentality" not because he is simpler and kindlier but because he is smarter. He is too clever to be defeated in either debate or ambuscade, and he is too intelligent to fall into any of the faults of his opponents or inferiors. He arrives at the assembly earliest of all, dutiful but bored:

> —and then, since I'm alone
> I moan, yawn, stretch, fart,
> Ponder, scribble, pull my hair, and cast accounts.
>
> (29-31)

He comes solely to push for peace, ready to hoot if any other subject finds a speaker. The first to rise is one Amphitheus, who is crazy. Claiming irrelevantly to be divine, he is hustled from the meeting with no chance to make the case for peace. This Dicaeopolis deplores. There follows the report of the special embassy to Persia, who have wined and dined and wasted their appropriation. They lead on the Persian emissary who gives them the lie in bad Greek: they have accomplished nothing and Persia is in no mood to help Athens. Dicaeopolis in disgust seeks out Amphitheus and dispatches the harmless fool to conclude a private treaty with Sparta for himself and his family. In the space of 130 lines, two important contrasts have been effected: between Dicaeopolis' clear-eyed common sense and the pompous folly of Amphitheus, whose nonsensical introduction spoiled his good and proper purpose, as Dicaeopolis had observed and between Amphitheus, for all his folly, and the calculating, incompetent ambassadors. Dicaeopolis stands at least two removes from credentialed authority in the direction of brains and honor.

Amphitheus returns in an economical forty-five lines, bringing a treaty and a raging pell-mell Chorus. The Acharnian charcoal burners were quick to learn of the treason and they ache to punish anyone who would treat with their mortal enemies, the Spartan ravagers of their vineyards. Dicaeopolis, unimpressed, will first celebrate the festival of Dionysus, for the first time in years on his own land, protected by his new-found immunity from war. The charcoal burners approach, making heavy weather of their woes, confusedly cursing both the Spartans and the man who can now escape their depredations, and leaving us in doubt whether they want relief or revenge. Dicaeopolis appears bearing the furbishments of the sacrifice and feast, ignores the Chorus, and sings the hymn to Phales, the godlet of copulation and fertility, greeting this long-neglected presence, who can now be accorded his natural and proper devotion by one

> . . . freed of troubles, battles (*machai*),
>   and *Lamachuses.*
>
> (269-70)

War is not simply and solely the direct source of anguish and disruption for the few; as well for the many it brings a whole string of woes, great and small, and creates a class of oppressive annoyances like Lamachus, the general who with his punning name stands for the professional military mind, so called. All this is contrasted with the joys of country life, clearly specified and represented (in the hymn at least) by the opportunities for casual fornication. The charcoal burners began their threats, and now cannot be ignored. Replying, Dicaeopolis first defines the question—his right to make the treaty, not Spartan guilt—then demonstrates that provocation came from both sides, and finally proposes to make a formal defense, with his head on a chopping block against his failure to convince. As the Chorus is unmoved, he suddenly takes direct action, threatening, unless he gain a chance to plead his case, to stab the Chorus' dearest progeny—a basket of charcoal. This marvelous foolery is a parody of Euripides, to be sure, but it also calls the charcoal burners back to cases. They may rant about the abstractions, treason, justice and revenge, but charcoal is their living. The choice of charcoal cancels out their unrealistic illusions and recalls their minds to practical matters. But this gains Dicaeopolis merely time; he is not yet assured of success. It is not enough to convince the practical man that charcoal is more useful than dialectic. One must then challenge the makers of opinion and bring a reformed opinion back to the people. Our hero gains an adjournment and rushes off to interview Euripides, the profound questioner, to borrow suitable armament. The ensuing consultation is a great favorite and needs no paraphrase here. I am content to observe that the scene is a masterful assertion of the natural right of comedy to pronounce upon things of importance. As it turns out, Euripides supplies no arguments at all, no fine speeches, no convincing sentiments—only filthy rags and tawdry props. The irony of the scene invites the conclusion that these trappings alone separate comedy from tragedy as a source of wise comment upon man's state, as Dicaeopolis makes plain, beginning his great speech:

I shall discourse on the city's affairs, though in
    a comedy;
For comedy, too, knows what justice is.

(499-500)

This "justice" (*to dikaïon*) was the constant preoccupation
of Athenian civic and intellectual life. Here now is an uncompromising challenge from an unexpected quarter: Aristophanes too lays claim to a portion of the debate, and
even demands to lead it.

The substance of this justice is to dismiss the causes of war
as trivial—a minor commercial rivalry here, the kidnap-
ping of a few whores there (we are reminded of Herodotus), the rages and heavy bluster of Pericles over this silly
insult. Suppose, he asks, the Spartans had kidnapped a
"Seriphian dog"—surely the most worthless commodity
available—wouldn't Athens have collected a billion-dollar
emergency fund and sailed off in all directions to punish
Sparta? Small wonder then that our serious mistreatment
of Megara finally drove the Spartans to war on behalf of
her ally. But "we have no sense", either to avoid war, or
to grasp its salient issues. Is it not obvious that the war has
no real cause, that its operative effects are absurdly dispro-
portional to either the ostensible causes or the likely political results? Why do we stand for laws with no more sense
in them than the most casual drinking songs? Half the
Chorus is convinced, and the other half turns upon its colleagues. The obstinate half of the Chorus now invokes its
savior, Lamachus, with the lightning glance and the terrible armor. It is a poor choice. This champion, the brave
stormer of cities, is a veritable Achilles of confusion. He
appears at the charge not knowing who or where the
enemy is. Dicaeopolis pretends to fear his armor and
plumes, and asks that they be removed from sight, only
to suggest sundry crude uses for them. Lamachus is appalled that a beggar (D. still wears the rags of Euripides'
Telephus) should so mock his dignity. Mockery turns to
allegations of self-serving ambition. Lamachus has no real
answer and goes off, vowing in highest patriotic style to
war forever with the enemy, while Dicaeopolis vows instead to trade forever with the enemy, or anybody else, but
not with Lamachus. This contrast between war and trade,
between sterile and productive activities, is a constant
motif in Aristophanes, and here balances the two representatives of peace and war. Although there may sometimes be good reasons for war, Lamachus does not know
them. Although there might be good reasons to embargo
trade, Dicaeopolis knows that they are not presently operative and he will act accordingly. Lamachus is the man
who subsists on generalities, with no mind and no taste for
examination of the particular facts. Dicaeopolis spears
every generality with a sharp, though coarse, intelligence.

Opening his free-trade market, he attracts first an impoverished Megarian, who sells his two daughters, disguised
as pigs, to prevent their starving. The Megarian and his
daughters, in the midst of the elaborate notice given the
girls' sexual promise, contrast starkly with the folly of
war. They illustrate not so much the desperation of the
small combatant in wartime, for the scene is not pathetic,
but the complete and intellectually repugnant reversal of
values which war entails, whereby it is a *mercy* to sell one's
children, even as animals. Next appears a Boeotian, selling

every kind of produce. But only his eels attract Dicaeopolis. The exchange proves a problem: the Boeotian
wants only what he cannot get at home. Nothing Dicaeopolis offers appeals to him until one Nicarchus appears to denounce the trade in "contraband" and attempts
to confiscate the eels. With comic "justice" he proves to
be the proper "currency"—for Athens has a surfeit, but
Boeotia none, of this product—and he is set upon, trussed
up like a wineskin and carried off slung on a shoulder-pole.
So much for one cause of war: the busybodies who enforce
the absurd embargo would be sold off for their true
worth—a pot of eels. With him goes the suspicious folly
that motivates him and other partisans of war.

Now a troupe of new characters appears—Athenians this
time. They stand for two basic needs, agriculture (food)
and marriage (sex). A farmer begs some "peace-balm" (for
peace has suddenly become a healing urgent in D.'s possession) for his ravaged eyes. He has wept so much for his
stolen cattle that he cannot see to hunt for them. But Dicaeopolis refuses to help and returns to his *menu*. A
groomsman appears, begging some of the balm for a newly
married couple who fear the groom's imminent call to service. He gets nowhere, but the bridesmaid does; war is no
fair burden for a wife—and some of the balm is sent along
to the bride with earthy instructions for its nightly application. It is doubtful whether Dicaeopolis' first refusals are
simply callous: the farmer wasted his eyesight in futile
weeping when what was wanted was clear-sighted action;
the institution of marriage is the first victim of war, but
the safe-keeping for "peace-balm" is with the wives who
can convince their husbands in the most elemental way of
the advantages of peace.

Lamachus now reappears, summoned to active duty. Dicaeopolis is simultaneously summoned to a banquet. The
two now call for the appurtenances of their "professions":

> L. Now bring me here my helmet's double
>   plume.
> D. And bring me here my thrushes and ring-
>   doves.
> L. How nice and white this ostrich-plume to
>   view.
> D. How nice and brown this pigeon's flesh to eat.
> L. Man, don't keep jeering at my armor so.
> D. Man, don't keep peering at my thrushes so!
>
> . . . . .
>
> L. Boy, bring the framework to support my
>   shield.
> D. Boy, bring the bakemeats to support my
>   frame.
> L. Bring here the grim-backed circle of the
>   shield.
> D. And here the cheese-backed circle of the
>   cake.
> L. Is not this—mockery, plain for men to see?
> D. Is not this—cheese-cake, sweet for men to
>   eat?

(1103-08; 1123-28)

Dicaeopolis' glutton's catalogue nicely turns each of Lamachus' preparations into a hollow mockery. There is perhaps nothing grand or noble about cheese-cake or roast pigeon, but they are at least useful. The contrast is not be-

tween the ideal and the real, but between the humble and the useless. Peace needs no justification in dithyrambic terms: it need only be contrasted with the costly and sterile tools of war. War and the belligerent mentality need no horrific indictments: they need merely be compared with the simplest needs and desires of the most ordinary man on the street.

When Lamachus returns, badly injured (through his own clumsiness), he and Dicaeopolis comment *alternis versibus* on their recent experiences: Lamachus is sore, unhappy, and embarrassed should Dicaeopolis see his humiliation; Dicaeopolis gloats over the bawdy good times he has had at the feast. Relaxed and generous, he kisses Lamachus— who can only bite back! The proud, self-conscious general is full of folly and inhumanity to the end, and as he apostrophizes the air about his hurts, Dicaeopolis sings a witty *obbligato,* contrasting his own riotous indulgence in a close and obscene parody. Lamachus, the beaten "victor," is carried to his cot in a faint; his peace-mongering "conqueror" goes to his couch with two girls at once. Thus has the anarchist won the day, but by subverting the accepted order he has recast things in a better and more intelligent order. Common sense—a realistic appraisal of the real goods of this life—not only makes war unnecessary, but exposes with devastating point what is wrong with war. It is fomented by vain fools, fought by braggart fools, and borne by simple fools. Surely *Acharnians* offers no remedy for the Peloponnesian War in particular, nor is it really an indictment of political leadership. It rather points out that when all the claims of policy and all the abstract reasoning have had an airing, most of men's troubles come from their infatuation with pride and humbug. As it turns out, the anarchy of the poet is a system far more reasonable than the status quo ruled by King Precedent, Queen Vanity, and the brainless minister Sloth. For Aristophanes, anarchic overthrow of the status quo is necessary to show how preposterous are the "rules" by which we are constrained to do useless things for stupid reasons simply because it is expected. The "rules" of the new "anarchy" are right and intelligent, because they have been carefully considered. The "rules" of the status quo are too often never considered at all because we are too lazy to think and too satisfied with the world's symbolic guarantees of our own unfounded self-esteem. Aristophanes' anarchy is less an attack on "the system" than upon the unthinking way we progressively exchange more and more of our real goods for the flattering unrealities of which all systems are so appallingly productive. Aristophanes teaches us to compare the artificial world of self-conscious vanity with the wholesome effects of shedding all poses and accepting the freedom to see things as they really are. Only the cold-eyed realist, who sees his own figure for what it is, fearlessly can strive toward genuine goals, unencumbered by delusions of his own dignity. Only the realist—whose realism begins with a good laugh at himself—can reshape reality from top to bottom, subvert the accepted and bring fantasy to a practical success.

In *Peace* Trygaeus has no fears of the accepted order, nor of the weight of thoughtless "opinion." Zeus alone, he theorizes, can establish peace among the Greeks. From high speculation he descends to the shrewdest space-

engineering, determining that a dung beetle would be the optimum mode of transport—only one food supply will do for both steed and passenger. This combination of daring and craft, of vulgarity and immensity, is really a revelation of Aristophanes himself, who could say with Trygaeus:

> I fly on behalf of all the Greeks,
> A contriver of unheard-of daring.
>
> (93-4)

He who flies to heaven on a dung beetle has laid hold of every province of thought, and acknowledges no limits in custom or art to his powers of speculation and comment. The whole universe, from barn floor to Olympus, is his claimed domain. Aristophanes, too, "flies" beyond the normal limits of the human imagination, doing unheard-of things, on behalf of the Greeks. His intellectual command of every aspect of life emulates Trygaeus' panoramic view of Greece as he sails heavenward, both in scope—and in methodology. The play rehearses many of the themes of *Acharnians:* the bravado of warmongers; the trifling causes of war; the preposterous suspicions attendant upon conflict; and more delightful contrasts between the implements of war and peace. What is new and suggestive is the appearance of a lively kind of low-life symbolism. The great statue of Peace is one case, as is the "salad" into which War would grind the cities of Greece. But more vigorously applied is the symbolism of the female figures, Opora and Theoria ("Harvesthome" and "Mayfair" in Rogers' rendition) who accompany Peace to earth. Opora is to be married to Trygaeus, who is rejuvenated for the occasion, while Theoria is turned over to the whole Council, with explicit instructions for the completest sexual use to be made of her. The bawdiness of the marriage preparations while holding the symbolism down to earth enhances its meaning. These female figures, symbols of abundance and prosperity, not only suggest the obvious joys which return with peace, but imply that they are superior to the competence of either Trygaeus or the Council, unless and until both the State and Trygaeus are renewed. Without such renewal, the State cannot enjoy Theoria adequately or for long. And the details of this reform and rebirth are found in Trygaeus' prayer to Peace:

> . . . O put an end to the whispers of doubt
>   These wonderful clever
> Ingenious suspicions we bandy about;
> And solder and glue the Hellenes anew
>   With the old-fashioned true
> Elixir of love, and attemper our mind,
> With thoughts of each other more genial and kind.
>
> (993-98)

The Greek for "thoughts . . . genial and kind" is rather more intellectual in tone than the English: they are *syngnômê* and *nous,* really, forgiveness and intelligence. Without good sense, without unrelenting exercise of intelligence that implies forgiveness, the Greeks will never reap the advantages prepared for them by the unprecedented journey of Trygaeus. Bold, because brilliant, Trygaeus has rescued Peace where others had failed, or never tried. He has violated the "rules" of heaven's "air space" to rescue the Greeks as well (from the salad), of whom the very gods have despaired. But only if they share Trygaeus' uncluttered vision and wisdom will they keep their prize, Peace, and their safety. They must aim as high as heaven in their thoughts, but happily forsake all foolish sense of dignity if a dung beetle proves necessary for the trip. We should all be heroes had we Pegasus to ride. But only a healthy self-contempt frees our brains for the realization that here and now a dung beetle is not only the realistic choice, but probably the more suitable one, given both the problems we face and the natures we possess. Unless men see clearly their comic posture, forgiving and forgetting harmless slights to empty pride, they will do nothing but serve as salad greens for the god of War.

The details of **Knights** are well known, and a discussion of its political allusions and topical bearing is beyond the scope of this essay. But one may address the problem often raised in the reader's mind by the rude and cynical attitude toward the institutions and function of government which seems to inform the play. It is not anarchistic in the crude sense of, say, a Cynic's attack upon the sinful nature of government as such. The concern of the slave Demosthenes is not fear that democracy will devolve into tyranny, but that the refusal of Demos to rule himself, to act *democratically,* will plunge Demos (and himself) over the edge into chaos; in other words, that the present anarchy of mind which affects Demos will extend and objectify itself until the household is consumed. The play is hardly a dismissal of all government as corrupt or useless, and it demands, through Demosthenes, not less government, but more real exercise of authority. The introduction of the sausage-seller, Agoracritus, achieves what Jaeger calls "the wildly impossible task of squaring the circle in politics"—the State's reform through the agency of a worse rascal than now afflicts it. But there is surely a distinction to be made: Agoracritus is a slob, but a realistic one. He lays no claim to any surer knowledge than that of his own condition, origins, and mental state. Paphlagon-Cleon puts on airs, claims a higher wisdom. When defeated by facts, he resorts to oracles, *which he really believes.* Paphlagon takes himself seriously; but Agoracritus, although an oracle declares a wondrous destiny for the "seller of guts," has serious reservations. He feels no pride when saluted as "savior of the city," and self-mockery laughs at his sudden renown when he recalls that his youthful adventures in pilferage were the real presage of his call to greatness. In bidding for the support of Demos, the butcher is wittier, more imaginative, and more outrageous, but through the persiflage we can see that he cares nothing for his own dignity and position. He enjoys the game of baiting the Paphlagonian and he wins because he keeps his humor and his self-contempt. Having gained the day he swiftly makes himself unnecessary by renewing Demos' health and vigor so that he can see his best interests for himself. Restored in hearing and temper, Demos can regret his mistakes in good earnest and set about managing his own affairs. It would be wrong, then, to look for specific political advice in the play, since such would doubtless detract from the major point, that a vigorous people, awake to its political responsibilities, needs no managers, even if, as Demos irrelevantly adds, it is somehow so blest as to survive them all. And the corollary: one's choice in politicians should first of all discriminate between realists, whatever their vulgarity, and self-

infatuated "indispensable" men, whose virtues, however great, are debased by a belief that their policy is good because it is theirs. Even a sausage-seller is better than a Cleon if he remembers what he is and refuses the temptations of power with a hearty laugh at himself. The merits and accomplishments of a Cleon, or of anyone else, are hindered and nullified by lust for domination and pride of place.

Perhaps the best play for illustrating this constructive anarchy at work is the *Lysistrata.* The play gathers together motifs which occur in separate earlier plays and of course places sex, a casual accompaniment in the other comedies, at the center of the construction. It suits my purpose as a keystone of this study, however, for a different reason. In the plays already discussed Aristophanes attacked and sought to reintegrate human nature as it operates in various social roles. The *Lysistrata* is essential Aristophanes because it tackles essential man—essential man and woman.

A sex strike is declared by the women of Greece for the purpose of forcing men to end the Peloponnesian War. But to see in the denial of conjugal rights a political theme or a desperation born of the generalized agony of war is to blur and spread the colors too far. Sex is not the earthy means to a higher good. Sex is the whole thing. Its denial is the means to its triumphant return. And the conditions under which it returns carry the real meaning of the play. It would be incorrect to see the plot as a subversion of the family and the state. For in fact the anarchic engineering of *Lysistrata* is a perfect paradox. Anarchy casts out anarchy. The cause of female discontent is emphatically that the men have forsaken their women in their preoccupation with war and its essentially childish politics. It is men who have overthrown the most fundamental law of civilization—the requirement of secure and peaceful cohabitation of the sexes in the family. War is an unreal substitute for sex, as are the women's weird religious practices of which both Lysistrata and the *proboulos* [commissioners] complain. But he, like all men, fails to comprehend the cause. Strange religions attract the women only in compensation for the loss of their men, who pursue the wholly perverse worship of war and ambition. The most unnatural effect of war is the disruption of the family. For the women this hardship is not so diffuse in its effects that they do not see the real cause of the war, which is the very inability of the men to see it. Men fail to see it because they do not know themselves; and they do not know themselves for the same reason that their knowledge of women and sex is deficient. And it is this one-way comprehensibility of the sexes that dictates the whole development of the play.

The treatment of sex must sound strange to modern ears. It is at once blatantly moral and enthusiastically vulgar, and seems to mock by anticipation a modern sophistication which desires to be very little of either. Moreover, while our generation seems to think sex (as portrayed) is funny because sex (in practice) is a low form of fun, Aristophanes maintains that sex is fun because it is funny, and sex is funny because man is funny. The thesis is not that war is Hell and therefore even sex should be foregone to stop it. Rather, it is that sex is ridiculous and this is the

Scene from a National Theatre of Greece presentation of The Knights.

best thing about it. Aristophanes seems to say, first, that sex is *the* driving necessity in life (which we might be prepared to accept), but then he adds (what we don't care to believe) that sex is also perfectly ridiculous, and so are we. A denial of sexual access stops the war, but only because the denial focuses men's attentions upon sex, and in its ridiculousness they see their own. And a man who sees what a comic sight he is (the actors wore *erect* phalluses, Wilamowitz reminds us) is in no condition to fight wars, oppress captives, or make inflammatory speeches. We take sex very seriously, but Aristophanes believes that some things are too important to be taken seriously. Like sex. Like the human race. Where better address his attack on all that bedevils mankind than upon this instinct which means so much to man and yet can teach him how comical he is? And in the case of the men—how one-sided and false is their understanding of sex, of women, and of their own posture! Men have usually treated women as mere sexual objects; when they are so treated in return, it baffles and embarrasses them.

For men, sex is conquest and pride, as is everything else they do. For women, sex is security, productivity, and the forum of common sense. Men are generalizers and plunderers. Women are creatures of frugality and detail.

Throughout the play the contrasting traits of the sexes, the keys to all the action, are rendered in faithful and idiomatic consistency with the main fact, sex, and what it teaches, or ought to, about the whole individual. The smoky torches of the old men's half-chorus represent their waning or imaginary sexual capacities, and at the same time, the confused ardors and ill-advised counsels of military ambition. The crones' water-pots are not only their way of bringing sexually over-ambitious old men back to their senses, but are also general female common sense, dousing truculent folly. The coquettish Myrrhine and the enfevered Cinesias in the seduction scene not only portray in frankest tones the effects of the sex strike, but also the natural impetuosity of men and the natural fussy carefulness of women. Men are as hasty and impetuous in making war as they are in the boudoir—for the same reasons. Women are as careful and detail-ridden in their desires for peace as they are in bedroom protocol, again for the same reasons. In one of the most effective analogies in the play, Lysistrata speaks of Greece as a bundle of wool:

Just as a woman with humble dexterity, thus with her hands
        disentangles a skein,

Hither and thither her spindles unravel it, drawing it out and
                     pulling it plain,
So would this weary Hellenic entanglement soon
   be resolved
                     by our womanly care,
So would our embassies neatly unravel it, drawing it here and
                     pulling it there.

                                            (566-70)

The ills of Greece are to be set right with consummate patience and care: by washing and carding and generally understanding the materials in hand. Everyone knows what
masculine impatience does to a tangled thread. In contrast, men view Greece as mere geography, and at the end
of the play, when they contrive to see geographical features in the body of Lysistrata, they reveal what is too true
of their sex. Their double-meaning jokes about geography
and physique, for which they lust equally, describe perfectly a nature whose mainspring is an undifferentiated response to thoughts of heedless plunder, whether of women
or territories. It is a case of "humble dexterity" over
against boastful clumsiness. Women know what wool, and
peace, really are: men definitely do not know that countries are more than territories, or that women are more
than gratification-machines.

These are the realities of sex—the *given* in the natural relations of the sexes. But the play is sex in both its reality and
its unreality. Sex in its absence directs attention to its
claims as something real over flattering delusions like
glory. But as war is the product of unrealities at work
upon the unreflective mind, so its products are yet more
absurd. The absence of sex is not an isolated phenomenon.
If war drives out sex, if men prefer its unreality, let them
have their fill, the poet says, and introduces a whole train
of absurdities. Since the men refuse the modest proposal
that women take over the management of public finance,
there is, until the resolution of the basic issue, a far more
complete reversal of sexual roles. We see women chanting
war songs and men in full armor shopping for soup and
onions. Men, who breathe fire against the enemy, confess
defeat by "an unbeatable women, fiercer than leopard or
fire." Men are unaccountably reticent about sex, until the
grand reconciliation (cf. 980 ff: having been treated by
women as mere sexual instruments, they all too soon appear as little more—to their acute discomfort), while
women are curiously brazen. Women make speeches and
conduct diplomacy, while men are as strangely impotent
in statecraft and political argument as they are frustrated
in sex.

Each of the sexes, left to itself, is a disordered abstraction.
Together they may engage in a superficial battle; but this
is unimportant. There is no *curing* the fact that men will
always be hasty, vulgar, and rapacious; women will never
be purged of their caution, fussiness, frivolity, and coquetry: but these differences can never be allowed to overrule
life. They are contained and made productive when the
sexes live together; they are merely aggravated and driven
into fruitless erraticism when they are apart. Religious fanaticism and war are simply the inevitable outlets for the
peculiarities of the sexes in default of the proper recourse.

The respective tensions created by the radical differences
of the sexes can rather be allayed by dissolving them in
gaiety and insobriety, as the celebration at the end of the
play makes clear. And the big problem is the male sense
of dignity. War, it becomes clear, feeds men's lust for
noise, bravado, and trumpery. Only the greater indignity
of enforced celibacy teaches them that dignity itself must
be thrown overboard if one is to resolve any but the most
superficial problems of life. When they see how foolish
they are in women's eyes—scaring old marketwomen with
their armor, posturing in the assembly, and fighting over
nothing—then only do they realize that their present embarrassment is only what they deserve. The poet shows
that both sexes must forget, not understand, one another's
incomprehensible notions of dignity and gaily become undignified together in that undignified posture they both
understand.

The *Lysistrata* encapsulates Aristophanes' "philosophy."
His destruction of the accepted order and his reconstruction of a better world are the two sides of his "anarchy."
The sex strike is anarchy, but it brings about a better sexual climate than preceded it; for while it is in effect, the
dominant differences between the sexes are played out at
every level, only to show more clearly that these differences are just more proof of their necessarily complementary nature. When sex becomes the crisis, human nature
sees itself more accurately. War is not only a poor substitute for sex; it is the inevitable substitute men choose when
they forget what sex teaches them about themselves. Sex
has no match for concentrating one's thoughts. Aristophanes' "blue" wit helps one properly discount pale generalities and muddy enthusiasms. Life is more than sexual intercourse; but the mentality and traits of the sexes, which
make life largely what it is, can be studied no better than
against the background of that relationship wherein they
must come to terms with nature. And they must come to
terms: otherwise, nature, with a permissive curse, will
allow them to plunge into the separate abysses which
await them. Nature with its lively vulgarity will not permit
us to nail down a cozy corner of the world in which to
nurse our pride and forbid entrance to the Aristophanic
spirit: it will either cajole us or destroy us. But we cannot
help thinking that the mere experience of reading Aristophanes has presented us the opportunity of the happier
choice.

Aristophanes is of course no professional philosopher.
Like many people (in [Gilbert] Ryle's language), he is
good at thinking with concepts, but not much for thinking
about concepts. For him, ideas in themselves are not objects of interest. They become fascinating when they move
men, especially when they are misunderstood and move
men to foolishness. In a sense he is the philosopher of misunderstanding. His immersion in the particular may deny
him a place in the formal history of Greek philosophy, but
he practices that informal philosophy, that "free play of
consciousness" for which Arnold congratulated the Greek
spirit. His mind is astonishingly free of the "petrification,"
the unthinking allegiance to misunderstood "talismans"
which typify the mind untouched by "Hellenism." (Although he found a good deal more stubborn confusion and
unbalanced "Hebraism" among his fellow Hellenes than

Arnold must have imagined.) And thus the paradox of his creative anarchy. Probably no one has better understood the pernicious tendency of ideas half-understood and turned into fetishes to lead men into quackery and corruption. Anarchic overthrow of the accepted order is his way of calling men to attend to the thoughts they do not understand and to examine the humbug on which they feed. He finds that the only way of teaching men the truth about themselves is to invent impossibilities about the world they think they know. The philosophers, as professional men of ideas, must learn much from him about the efficacy of the ideas they study. Plato must have learned. For the affinity between them is no new conjecture. Surely, for instance, it was surmised by a Lucian who tried so hard to be both at once. They were both, in the language of Euelpides, *zetounte topon apragmona,* "seeking a land of un-business," the place free of those accumulated superstitions and "decorative inutilities" which forbid reflection. The Platonic "myth" and the Aristophanic "anarchy" are not very far apart, for the fantasy-worlds they picture put us on the track of thoughts which have at least a chance to better our much too thoughtless existence. And they both show that in the "unreal" world one can at least think clearly and see one's own true stature, or lack of it, while the "real" world is populated by the pompous and the fanatical, the frauds and the self-deluded, the people in *Lysistrata* who put five cents' worth of soup in fifty-dollar helmets and fail to see the irony of the occasion. (pp. 189-208)

> *Douglas J. Stewart, "Aristophanes and the Pleasures of Anarchy," in* The Antioch Review, *Vol. XXV, No. 1, Spring, 1965, pp. 189-208.*

BIRDS

CRITICAL COMMENTARY

August Wilhelm Schlegel   (lecture date 1808)

[*Schlegel was a German critic, translator, and poet. With his younger brother, Freidrich, he founded the periodical* Das Athenäum *(1789-1800), which served as a manifesto for the Romantic movement. He is perhaps best known for his translation of Shakespeare's works into German and for his* Über die dramatische Kunst und Literatur *(1809-11;* A Course of Lectures on Dramatic Art and Literature, *1846). In the following excerpt from that work, Schlegel briefly discusses the significance of Aristophanes for Old Comedy and discusses his style in* Birds, *praising the dramatist's craft and handling of philosophical ideas in that piece. Schlegel's comments were originally delivered as a lecture in 1808.*]

Of the Old Comedy but one writer has come down to us, and we cannot, therefore, in forming an estimate of his merits, enforce it by a comparison with other masters. Aristophanes had many predecessors; *Magnes, Cratinus,*

Crates, and others; he was indeed one of the latest of this school, for he outlived the Old Comedy. We have no reason, however, to believe that we witness in him its decline, as we do that of Tragedy in the case of the last tragedian; in all probability the Old Comedy was still rising in perfection, and he himself one of its most finished authors. It was very different with the Old Comedy and with Tragedy; the latter died a natural, and the former a violent death. Tragedy ceased to exist, because that species of poetry seemed to be exhausted, because it was abandoned, and because no one was now able to rise to the pitch of its elevation. Comedy was deprived by the hand of power of that unrestrained freedom which was necessary to its existence. . . . The Old Comedy flourished together with Athenian liberty; and both were oppressed under the same circumstances, and by the same persons. So far were the calumnies of Aristophanes from having been the occasion of the death of Socrates, as, without a knowledge of history, many persons have thought proper to assert (for the **Clouds** were composed a great number of years before), that it was the very same revolutionary despotism that reduced to silence alike the sportive censure of Aristophanes, and also punished with death the graver animadversions of the incorruptible Socrates. Neither do we see that the persecuting jokes of Aristophanes were in any way detrimental to Euripides: the free people of Athens beheld alike with admiration the tragedies of the one, and their parody by the other, represented on the same stage; they allowed every variety of talent to flourish undisturbed in the enjoyment of equal rights. Never did a sovereign, for such was the Athenian people, listen more good-humouredly to the most unwelcome truths, and even allow itself to be openly laughed at. And even if the abuses in the public administration were not by these means corrected, still it was a grand point that this unsparing exposure of them was tolerated. Besides, Aristophanes always shows himself a zealous patriot; the powerful demagogues whom he attacks are the same persons that the grave Thucydides describes as so pernicious. In the midst of civil war, which destroyed for ever the prosperity of Greece, he was ever counselling peace, and everywhere recommended the simplicity and austerity of the ancient manners. So much for the political import of the Old Comedy.

But Aristophanes, I hear it said, was an immoral buffoon. Yes, among other things, he was that also; and we are by no means disposed to justify the man who, with such great talents, could yet sink so very low, whether it was to gratify his own coarse propensities, or from a supposed necessity of winning the favour of the populace, that he might be able to tell them bold and unpleasant truths. We know at least that he boasts of having been much more sparing than his rivals in the use of obscene jests, to gain the laughter of the mob, and of having, in this respect, carried his art to perfection. Not to be unjust towards him, we must judge of all that appears so repulsive to us, not by modern ideas, but by the opinions of his own age and nation. (pp. 153-55)

[The] **Birds** transports us by one of the boldest and richest inventions into the kingdom of the fantastically wonderful, and delights us with a display of the gayest hilarity: it is a joyous-winged and gay-plumed creation. I cannot concur with the old critic in thinking that we have in this work a universal and undisguised satire on the corruptions of the Athenian state, and of all human society. It seems rather a harmless display of merry pranks, which hit alike at gods and men without any particular object in view. Whatever was remarkable about birds in natural history, in mythology, in the doctrine of divination, in the fables of Æsop, or even in proverbial expressions, has been ingeniously drawn to his purpose by the poet; who even goes back to cosmogony, and shows that at first the raven-winged Night laid a wind-egg, out of which the lovely Eros, with golden pinions (without doubt a bird), soared aloft, and thereupon gave birth to all things. Two fugitives of the human race fall into the domain of the birds, who resolve to revenge themselves on them for the numerous cruelties which they have suffered: the two men contrive to save themselves by proving the pre-eminency of the birds over all other creatures, and they advise them to collect all their scattered powers into one immense state; the wondrous city, Cloud-cuckootown, is then built above the earth; all sorts of unbidden guests, priests, poets, soothsayers, geometers, lawyers, sycophants, wish to nestle in the new state, but are driven out; new gods are appointed, naturally enough, after the image of the birds, as those of men bore a resemblance to man. Olympus is walled up against the old gods, so that no odour of sacrifices can reach them; in their emergency they send an embassy, consisting of the voracious Hercules, Neptune, who swears according to the common formula, by Neptune, and a Thracian god, who is not very familiar with Greek, but speaks a sort of mixed jargon; they are, however, under the necessity of submitting to any conditions they can get, and the sovereignty of the world is left to the birds. However much all this resembles a mere farcical fairy tale, it may be said, however, to have a philosophical signification, in thus taking a sort of bird's-eye view of all things, seeing that most of our ideas are only true in a human point of view. (pp. 166-67)

> *August Wilhelm Schlegel, "Lecture XII," in his* A Course of Lectures on Dramatic Art and Literature, *edited by Rev. A. J. W. Morrison, translated by John Black, revised edition, 1846. Reprint by AMS Press, Inc., 1973, pp. 153-73.*

Gilbert Murray   (essay date 1933)

[*A British educator, humanitarian, translator, author, and classical scholar, Murray has written extensively on Greek literature and history and is considered one of the most influential twentieth-century interpreters of Greek drama. In the following excerpt from his full-length study of Aristophanes, he discusses the social and political climate that influenced the writing of Aristophanes's* Birds. *Murray points to a kind of resignation on the part of the dramatist, noting that in this play he seems less hopeful of any improvement in Greek politics, and correspondingly more interested in the escape that art can provide from everyday reality.*]

Most of the plays of Aristophanes are so strongly political, or at least so much inspired by public movements in con-

temporary Athenian life, that scholars when they treat of a play like the *Birds,* which on the face of it is as fanciful and as far removed from politics as *A Midsummer Night's Dream,* can hardly help asking themselves what it means, or—more prudently—what state of affairs in Athens formed the soil from which it sprang. It was produced at the Great Dionysia in the spring of 414 B.C. The great fleet which was to undertake the conquest of Sicily had set sail the previous summer, and had met so far with no great success or defeat. What was the feeling in Athens, or rather in those circles of the Athenian 'intelligentsia' to which Aristophanes belonged?

Some scholars have spoken of the 'dark shade of the fatal Sicilian expedition'; but that is to read into the spring of 414 B.C. the feelings of the winter of 413. The expedition had not yet failed. Others, like Mr. Rogers, consider that 'Athens was at the height of her power and prosperity' and that 'no shadow of the coming catastrophe dimmed the brightness of the outlook'. The first view would take the *Birds* as a reaction against despair, the second represents it as an overflow of sanguine hopes and high spirits. I doubt if either is quite satisfactory, though I find more approach to truth in the first. (pp. 135-36)

To touch for a moment on the actual situation in Athens, it was a time both of trouble and of *Hubris.* Mêlos had fallen in the winter of 416-415. At the same time the vast project was formed and debated of sending an overwhelming armada, such as no Greek city could withstand, against Syracuse. If Syracuse were conquered all Sicily would become subject to Athens; and if Sicily fell, how could Carthage resist? What a vista then revealed itself! This scheme was enthusiastically urged by Alcibiades and vainly opposed by Nicias. Thucydides regarded it as an act of madness due to the folly of an excited populace and corrupt demagogues. Just before the fleet sailed, however, there occurred an extraordinary outrage, the history of which throws much light on the psychology of the Athenian mob. It was usual to have in front of the more important buildings a 'herm' or boundary pillar with two human characteristics: a bearded head, making the herm into the god Hermes, and a *phallus erectus* as an emblem of generation and fertility. On a single night, just before the fleet was to sail, all these images, except one that accidentally escaped, had their noses and phalli knocked off and were left mutilated. It is at first sight difficult for us to understand either the motives that led to the outrage, or the extraordinary state of public fury that it caused.

To the ordinary man in ordinary times such figures would, of course, be taken for granted and cause neither scandal nor enthusiasm. But the mutilation of them at a moment of extreme crisis, when it was of the first importance to have all the omens favourable, might well make a terrible impression. It would not merely be a crime against the gods which cried for punishment; it would actually have the effect of depriving a powerful god of his power to help. Such monstrous malignity, the people would feel, must have some abnormal motive behind it, some wish to paralyse and ruin Athens. It must be the work of oligarchs, of would-be tyrants, or traitors, or else of some deliberate enemies of the gods.

In reality, perhaps, the motives were not so abnormal after all. There must have been among the more intellectual circles of Athens many who had sat at the feet of Protagoras and Anaxagoras and Socrates and whose ideas of God were utterly unlike such foolish idols. Then, outside philosophical circles, there were men who had travelled and knew how these phallic figures made the Greeks ridiculous in the eyes of foreigners. More important still, every serious critic of Greek civilization must have seen what a paralysing effect was produced on public action by the innumerable superstitions and scruples of the populace. A wrong tinge in the victim's liver had more than once wrecked a Spartan campaign: soon after this a whole Athenian army was to be lost because of an eclipse of the moon. We can appreciate the strength of such terrors, and the repulsion which they inspired among the intelligent, from Theophrastus's picture of the 'Superstitious Man' and from the enthusiastic reception of Epicurus's doctrine of deliverance. At this particular moment Lysias tells the Athenians of a society called the Κακολαιμονισται, like the 'Hellfire Clubs' of the eighteenth century, which deliberately met and dined on forbidden days (αποφραδεσ ημεραι) and in other ways 'showed their contempt for our gods and customs'. There were men who occasionally parodied the Eleusinian Mysteries, which in many ways must have been tempting to parody. A generation later the pious Euthyphro in Plato's dialogue mentions that when he speaks in the Assembly about oracles foretelling the future, people laugh and think him cracked. A reasonable free-thought was no doubt spreading steadily during the fifth century throughout the educated classes, and writers like Thucydides and Aristophanes had risen well above the level of that ευηθεια ηλιθιοσ or *Ur-Dummheit* which still lurked in the traditional religion.

At this particular moment, however, public feeling took fright. Unscrupulous or ignorant demagogues lashed it to fury. A number of people believed to be guilty of the mutilation were put to death, others fled the country. The enemies of Alcibiades accused him but would not consent to hold an immediate trial. They let him start for Sicily but afterwards had him pursued and arrested, not for mutilating the Hermae—which was the last thing he was likely to do on the eve of his own great adventure—but for some alleged profanation of the Mysteries. And the armada set sail, in spite of all previous oracles and omens, under the shadow of an awful apprehension.

In this situation Aristophanes produced the *Birds.* His hero, Peithetairos, or 'Winfriend' and his companion, Euelpides, 'Hopefulson', are utterly sick of Athens, sick of the high prices, the burden of debt, the everlasting informers, the ferocious law-courts, and the whole cloud of anxiety. It was in this year that Euripides represented his hero Ion as refusing to accept a princely fortune in Athens because he will not live in a city 'filled with fear' (φοβου πλεα, *Ion* 601). The two friends want advice about some place where one can live in peace, and can think of no better adviser than King Têreus, who was once married to an Athenian princess, and then was turned into a bird, the Hoopoe, and must by now have flown all over the world. Guided by a crow and a jackdaw they find Têreus, looking

odd, but not odder than he was described in Sophocles' tragedy, and Euelpides explains what he and his friend want. 'There is', says the Hoopoe, 'a place that might suit you on the shores of the Red Sea'. . . . 'No. Not by the sea. An official ship from Athens might come and arrest us.' (Like Alcibiades.) 'There is Lepreon in Elis' . . . where the Spartans had just founded a colony of Helots who had fought under Brasidas! 'There is the region of Opûs in Locris' . . . where the population was particularly hostile to Athens and the Athenians had deposited a military post to control them! None of these is attractive. 'But what is it like here among the birds?' 'Not bad. You don't need a purse; and you find plenty to eat in the gardens.' At this point Peithetairos, hitherto silent, interrupts with a great shout. He sees a magnificent possibility. Let the birds unite and found one great city; let them put a wall round the air! Then they can rule mankind as if they were locusts, and master the gods by controlling their food-supply—which consists of course in the steam of sacrifices from the earth. The Hoopoe explodes in delight and admiration. He calls his wife, the Nightingale, from the thicket (their domestic differences seem to be forgotten, and her song is represented by a flute), and the two summon a grand gathering of the birds. The chirruping song of the Hoopoe is lovely, and presently the air is thick with 'long-throated birds', οιωνων ταναοδειρων, and loud with their musical cries. The number of birds known is remarkable. A flamingo comes first; then a cormorant and other individual birds which give a chance for jests at the fat Cleônymus and others of Aristophanes' special butts; then comes the whole army: halcyon, widgeon, francolin,

> Jay and turtle, lark and sedge-bird, thyme-finch,
>   ring-dove first, and then
> Rock-dove, stock-dove, cuckoo, falcon, fiery-
>   crest and willow-wren,
> Lammergeyer, porphyrion, kestrel, waxwing,
>   nuthatch, waterhen.
>
> (Rogers.)

'Why are they summoned?' they ask the Hoopoe. 'To speak to two men here. . . . ' 'Men?' they scream in horror. 'Men, our bitterest and wickedest enemies! Are you mad? Where are they that we may peck their eyes out?' There follows a sort of battle dance, in which the two men arm themselves with pots, saucers, and spits, rather like Tweedledum and Tweedledee, until at last the Hoopoe succeeds in inducing the Birds to listen to reason.

Peithetairos expounds the ancient rights of the Birds. They were once kings, a claim which he illustrates by many examples; and now he can show them how to recover their kingdom. The Birds listen spell-bound. They are melted to tears by his description of the way in which they are now treated, pelted like madmen, driven out of the temples where others have sanctuary, snared, limed, caged, eaten and, as if that was not enough, drowned in thick sauces! He shows in detail how they can make or mar mankind; how they can rule much better than the gods who have usurped their throne. The Birds are wild with enthusiasm and accept the plan. The two men are taken into the Hoopoe's dwelling in the rock to be provided with wings.

The Birds left alone break suddenly into a lyrical summons to the Nightingale: . . . 'Dear one, tawny-throat, best-beloved of birds . . . you have come, you have come, we have seen you.'

Her fluting is to lead their song, which then begins in long anapaests. It is a great cosmogony in the style of Orpheus or Musaeus, addressed by 'the Birds of the Sky, who live for ever, ageless and deathless, and filled with immortal thoughts, to the dimly existing tribes of men, little-doing, moulded of clay, strengthless multitudes that fade as the leaf.' . . . These birds, like Keats's nightingale, were 'not born for death'; no hungry generations trod them down, such as were now harassing Athens. They explain how in the beginning of things the Birds were born of Erôs and Chaos, how they are older than the Olympian gods, how in spite of their dethronement they still guide and direct human life, and how all signs and omens are 'birds'. Later in the parabasis they explain how their City will be an asylum for the misfits of the world; for father-beaters—since birds freely fight their fathers—for fugitives, for slaves and outcasts and barbarians, and for all, one might say, who are ashamed or unhappy among men. Then they expatiate on the usefulness of wings, chiefly for getting out of the theatre if you are bored or have other business, but also for climbing in the world, like Dieitrephes, the basket-seller, on his wings of wicker.

As often in Aristophanes, there is here a rush of real feeling and beauty, quickly apologized for and turned off with a laugh. And curiously enough, the feeling turns out to be based on something more than mere fancy; for the birds, as objects of worship in the Aegean area, were really older than the Olympian gods. Their sanctity goes back to pre-Hellenic times. Birds were in Greece, bringing thunder and rain, or giving signs to prophets, long before the anthropomorphic band of warlike Olympians descended from the northern forests: the eagle and the swan before Zeus, the owl before Athena, the dove before Aphrodite. There must have been more relics of pre-Hellenic cults extant in Aristophanes' time than we generally realize; but none the less it was a remarkable feat of imaginative guesswork, aided perhaps by some special love of birds in themselves, that enabled Aristophanes to catch this glimpse of a truth so long hidden from the generations after him.

Re-enter Peithetairos and Euelpides in their new wings, and in high spirits. What shall the city's name be? 'Nephelokokkûgia', suggests Peithetairos, a name which seems at first sight to be simply 'Cloud-cuckoo-land', but, since there seems to have been a wind called $\kappa o\kappa\kappa\upsilon\gamma\iota\alpha\sigma$, may carry a connotation embracing winds as well as clouds and cuckoos. Euelpides is sent off to help in the building and is not seen again. Peithetairos begins a solemn inaugural sacrifice, but the priest, who appears with a long prayer to the birds, parodied from Athenian ritual, at last calls so many birds that Peithetairos sees there will not be nearly enough for them to eat. He drives the Priest off, and is starting the sacrifice himself, when he is interrupted by an anonymous poet bringing a hymn in honour of the city and its founder ready-made, together with a lyrical request for baksheesh. This does not seem promising, but the man's verses are of the old severe school like Pindar or Simonides, so he has to be treated

well. He is provided with the Priest's jerkin, but is still cold, and not contented till he has his tunic as well. Peithetairos begins afresh when in there bursts a $X\rho\eta\sigma\mu o\lambda o\gamma o\sigma$, or collector of oracles, with some momentous revelations, among them a divine command that the first holy man to arrive shall receive a cloak and new shoes. Peithetairos, however, happens to have another oracle strictly enjoining that the first religious imposter shall receive a stick between the ribs, and the oracle-monger vanishes. He is followed—rather to our surprise—by Metôn, the great astronomer and reformer of the calendar, who is treated with similar disrespect; then by a supercilious and well-dressed Commissioner, sent by the Ecclesia to supervise the ceremonies. 'Will he take his fees and go?' asks Peithetairos. 'Of course he will. His time is precious and he has a motion to propose at the Assembly.' The 'fees' descend upon him and the Commissioner flies, but before he is well away there comes a man provided with books full of laws and decrees which may be useful in the new City. As Peithetairos drives off one of these nuisances on one side the second returns on the other side, and both threaten him with legal proceedings for assault, for *lèse-majesté,* for impiety, and for sacrilege, till he proceeds to extremities, and gives up for the time being the attempt to sacrifice in the open air. He goes indoors.

After another chorus about the help which the Birds can give to man, a curse on Philocrates the bird-seller, and a description of the happy life of birds in the summer, when the grasshopper, 'maddened with the sunshine and the rapture of the noon', sings below them, a Messenger announces to Peithetairos that the City wall is now built; but the description of it is barely finished when there comes news of a trespasser—some profane mocker who leaps over new walls, like Remus. Out goes a regiment of ten thousand falcons to arrest him. The guards presently return with a surprising prisoner—Iris, the rainbow messenger of Zeus, who is on her way to mankind to inquire why the sacrifices have stopped. Peithetairos affects extreme indignation. By what gates did she enter? Has she a passport? Have the ornitharchs given her a permit? Iris is bewildered. 'What is all this about permits and passports and ornitharchs? She is bearing a message from the Olympian Gods. . . . ' 'Olympian Gods indeed! We are the Gods now, we Birds, and so you can tell your Olympians.' His bullying increases to such a point that the poor young goddess bursts into tears, and flies away to complain to her father.

Then comes the Herald back from the earth, where the revolution has been accepted with enthusiasm. Mankind, who used to be Sparta-mad, are now Bird-mad. Instead of going 'long-haired, unwashed and half-starved, like Socrates', they rise at dawn and fly to the $\nu o\mu o\delta$—law, or, with a change of accent, meadow—they settle on $\tau\alpha$ $\beta\iota\beta\lambda\iota\alpha$—books or papyrus beds—and fill their crops with $\psi\eta\phi\iota\sigma\mu\alpha\tau\alpha$—decrees or pebbles. Above all, they are clamouring for wings and are coming in crowds to get them. Instantly baskets and baskets of wings are brought, and there is some farcical business which cannot now be followed about the mistakes of the slaves in bringing them. They are only just in time, when in comes a

Πατραλοιασ, or Father-beater, clamouring to be made an eagle 'and fly over the unharvested sea'.

A father-beater is not, of course, a parricide, though he might become one: he is a 'bright young thing' who shows what he thinks of that iron parental discipline which was almost a religion in antiquity, by thrashing those who try to exercise it. We have had a case already in the *Clouds* (1320-1443). This *Patraloias* is treated with far more consideration than the prophets and the statute-mongers. He has come to the Birds because all young cocks fight their fathers. 'Yes,' says Peithetairos, 'but our law is also that of the storks. The young storks always feed their father.' This is a blow to the *Patraloias;* he has had his journey for nothing! The Birds are a fraud! 'Not quite,' says Peithetairos. 'Let your father be. We will fit you out as a soldier's orphan, with wing, crest and spur: now, off to Thrace with you, if you want fighting, and defend it against the barbarians!' The orphans of men slain in war were provided by the Athenian State with shield, helmet, and spear; and Aristophanes feels that the average rowdy half-criminal youth who during the long war had become a pest in Athens, had at least some stuff in him and might be a good man on the frontiers; which the other visitors in this scene could never be.

The next is a rather important historical character, Kinêsias, the most famous of Athenian lyric poets. One of his victories is recorded in an extant inscription. He is condemned by Plato (*Gorg.* 502a) as one whose art aims only at producing pleasure, not good; in this he followed his father, Melês, 'who, however, while aiming at pleasure produced only boredom.' The lyrics with which he enters now, delightful as they are, show what Plato meant. They are all ethereal gleams and clouds and wings and snowflakes, rather like some of the prettiest songs in Euripides' *Helena*. We shall have more to say about this interesting person later on; here it is only his verses that come into question. The air, he explains, is his true home:

> Our dithyrambs' best beauties are but schemes
> Of mist and light and dark and cloudy gleams
> And fast wing-beating.

And Peithetairos proceeds to 'fast-wing-beat' him off the stage, rebuffed but still determined to be a winged thing and 'peragrate the air'.

In his place comes another singer, threadbare and sinister and badly in need of wings. He is an informer who makes a special business of serving writs on rich people in the islands. 'A charming trade! I congratulate you', says Peithetairos. 'Can't you dig?' 'No, never learnt.' 'Can't you do anything honest?' 'Come, no preaching. I want wings; wings, for business purposes. It is beautifully simple. I will fly to the island, serve the writ, fly back to Athens, bring on the case, get the islander condemned *in absentia* and there you are! I will spin there and back like a top.' 'Just so,' says Peithetairos, 'I'll make you spin', and whips him off yelling.

Returning he discovers a new arrival, of different type; a mysterious person so swathed in cloaks and veils that he can neither see nor be seen, nor even hear properly. 'Who are you?' 'Is any god following me?' 'No, but who are

you?' 'What time is it?' 'Early afternoon. Who are you?' 'Closing time or later?' 'Oh, you make me sick!' 'Thank you. Is it cloudy or clear?' 'Confound you, stupid!' 'Thanks, in that case, I'll unroll.' He unrolls. 'My dear Prometheus!' cries Peithetairos, for it is indeed that friend of man and enemy of Zeus. 'Don't speak my name,' he exclaims; 'and please hold this umbrella over me, lest Zeus should see!' Prometheus has come to betray the secrets of Olympus. There is famine among the Gods; the barbarian gods up north are already starving and threatening to invade. Ambassadors will soon come, but Peithetairos will be wise to make no terms unless, first, the sceptre is given back to the Birds, and secondly, he has the beautiful Basileia (Sovereignty) to wife. The umbrella duly returned to him, Prometheus departs.

Peithetairos promptly sets to work on the preparation of a tempting feast, and after a short Chorus the Embassy arrives. It consists of Poseidon, the old aristocratic god, patron of the Athenian Knights; Heracles, the strong beefy youth with more appetites than brains; and an absurd figure who proves to be a representative of the barbarian gods, a Triballian. He cannot understand or make himself understood, but he responds more or less to threats and blows from Heracles. 'Oh, Democracy!' sighs Poseidon, regarding him. Poseidon proposes terms of peace, but Heracles has his eyes glued on the cookery. (It consists, by the way, of some oligarchic birds who were condemned to death for conspiring against the State.) Peithetairos demands the restoration of the sceptre. The Birds will watch over men and see that they perform their oaths both to Birds and to Gods. Heracles eagerly agrees; the Triballian jabbers unintelligibly, but when Heracles asks him if he wants a hiding he apparently says yes. Poseidon is reluctantly giving way, when Peithetairos mentions as a slight extra that he also wants Basileia for his own. This Poseidon definitely refuses. Heracles hesitates. Poseidon appeals to him not to give up his whole inheritance, but Peithetairos whispers in his ear that he is not the heir of Zeus at all, being illegitimate, so that Heracles, left angry and confused about the point of law, but indubitably anxious for his dinner, consents. Everything now depends on the Triballian. He jabbers at some length, and the majority decide that he has consented; so Poseidon is outvoted and Peithetairos has his desire. After another short chorus we have his triumphal Kômos. The royal bride, Basileia, is brought to him; surrounded by his faithful Birds he dances with her his wedding dance, he discharges the lightning and the thunder, and is hailed as Kallinîkos, the Victorious, the Highest of the Gods!

Δαιμονων υπερτατε: actually 'Highest of the Gods'. One would have thought such words impossible. Greek doctrine is full of the punishments of those who make themselves equal to even the lowest orders of the gods, yet Peithetairos dances off in triumph. We cannot tell how the audience felt about it. The fact that the *Birds,* which we moderns mostly consider the poet's masterpiece, only obtained a second prize does not take us far, for there are many ways in which the play may have failed to catch the taste of the public.

But it does seem strange that the poet should have had this

successful pursuit of a great kingdom in the clouds staged just at the time when, as Thucydides and Plutarch tell us, Athens was going mad after a kingdom in the west almost as cloudy, and yet should have intended no particular political reference. Nevertheless it is impossible to discover any direct allusion, or even any clear attitude towards the schemes for the conquest of Sicily and Carthage. It cannot be an intentional encouragement of them, yet on the other hand it does not read like satire. It seems to be just an 'escape' from worry and the sordidness of life, away into the land of sky and clouds and poetry. If people want a cloud empire, here is a better one!

It was, we are told, in the previous year that Syracosios had brought forward his proposal for the prohibition of personal attacks in comedy. If so, the decree was either never passed or never really operative, for the personal references in the **Birds** are, if anything, more numerous, though on the whole lighter and less severe, than in the earlier plays. Most of them are concerned with literature; at least eleven poets or musicians come in for some chaff. With them may go the prophets Lampon and Diopeithes; the boasters, like Theogenes and Aeschines, and the many obscure persons who are likened in passing to some bird or other. There is mostly a careful avoidance of controversial politics: two cautious references to Nicias, one to Alcibiades, none to the warlike Lamachus—whom Aristophanes had attacked in the **Acharnians** and was to praise so handsomely after his death. Cleon dead and Hyperbolus ostracized are both now outside the picture; Euripides is not mentioned. But with all this reticence the old champion cannot keep his hands off some people. They are mostly of the same type, cruel war-mongers, informers, and traders on the superstition of the public.

There is Cleônymus, usually compared to Falstaff, but really a much more sinister figure; one of Cleon's jackals (κολακεσ), an informer, an oppressor of the Allies. It was he who moved in 425-424 B.C. the doubling and in some cases the trebling of the tribute; it was he who proposed a reward of a thousand drachmae for information about the mutilation of the Hermae and joined his ally Peisandros in inflaming the fury of the frightened mob. For these things Aristophanes must have hated him, but they hardly afford matter for good jokes. In the two earliest plays, the **Acharnians** and the **Knights,** Cleônymus was just a low hanger-on of Cleon's, very poor, very dirty, and with an enormous appetite (**Ach.** 844; **Kn.** 958, 1292 ff.). But from the satirist's point of view he improved. He became excessively fat; in war his belly betrayed him; and gods and men had laughed to see him running from the battle of Delium (424 B.C.) with his shield flung away. From the **Clouds** (423 B.C.) onward there is little mercy for the 'big Jackalonymus shedder-of-shields', the professional 'Never-betray-you' of the mob. A slave in the **Peace** dreams of an eagle seizing an Aspis—the word means both asp and shield—which it bore high into the air and then . . . then Cleônymus threw it away! In the **Birds** the Chorus tell of a strange tree in the land where there are no hearts; it is not exactly useful for anything, but still it is large and greasy and timid; in the spring it bursts into a bloom of figs and falsehoods, and in the winter sheds its—shields! (1473 ff.)

A similar figure is Peisandros, also a great Jingo and a great fat man, like a stout Acharnian ass. In the **Babylonians** we hear of him stirring up war; Lysias the orator says he found the confusion of war convenient for stealing in. In the **Peace** Peisandros' 'crests and eyebrows' make all decent people sick. Like Cleônymus, however, he suffered from nerves at the sight of real fighting. Not only a comic writer, like Eupolis, mentions that he went all the way to Pactôlus and was still the worst coward in the army; but the sober Xenophon (*Symp.* ii. 14) wonders what would happen to him if he did a sword-dance, since he cannot look at a spear! He seems to have had some dealings with the Socratics, for the Chorus (1553 ff.) describe how in some shadowy land where Socrates the unwashed brings souls to light (ψυχαγωγει) Peisandros had come looking for his ψυχη—the word means both 'soul' and 'courage'—which had absconded in his lifetime; how he sacrificed a camel to recover it and how there appeared something that looked like a ψυχη (ghost) but it was only—a starved philosopher. In the storm against the Hermocopidae he outdid Cleônymus. Cleônymus had a reward of 1,000 drachmae offered, but Peisandros had it raised to 10,000 and actually carried a resolution for the torturing of citizens to obtain evidence. First a violent demagogue, he joined the oligarchs and took part in the reign of terror of the Four Hundred, and fled with them to Deceleia (410 B.C.). A sinister and repulsive figure, a type of what Aristophanes loathed.

'There is nothing like wings. Why, Dieitrephes, whose wings were only made of wicker, got chosen first a tribe-commander, then a General commanding cavalry, and now does great things and is a . . . tawny Hippalector' (ξουθοσ ιππαλεκτρυων). So we are told at v. 798. A hippalector is a mythical monster compounded of a horse and a fighting cock, used as a figure-head for ships. We hear again that the words of Dieitrephes can 'give people wings'; in v. 1442 he 'sets young men flying' with desire to join the cavalry. One gets a fairly clear impression of this strange man: 'the lunatic, the Cretan, barely of Attic race', as Plato Comicus calls him; one of 'three shameless wild beasts', as he is to Cratînus (Plato, *Heortai,* 31; Cratinus, *Chirônes,* fr. 233). Fierce and half-mad, he excited the young men to martial ardour. In that shocking affair in 413, when the savage Thracian mercenaries made the massacre at Mycalessus, killing all the children in the school, and were so suitably cut to pieces by the pursuing Boeotians, Dieitrephes was in command. Doubtless the Thracians had got out of hand: Dieitrephes can hardly have ordered such doings. We do not hear of any charges of dishonesty or blackmail against him. He was not a squalid criminal. And curiously enough, though we do not know how he died, Pausanias mentions a statue of him, pierced with many arrows, set up by public decree on the Acropolis.

Then there is that Kinêsias who was flapped out of Nephelokokkugia and left flying in the air. There was much more against him than his newfangled verse and music. He had not yet committed his great crime of 400 B.C. when he proposed and carried a decree abolishing the chorus in Comedy; nor had Aristophanes yet perpetrated against him—or at least against his name—the unforgettable yet scarcely malignant insult of the *Lysistrata.* But there were other things. He was accused of impiety. He had notoriously defiled a shrine of Hecatê, one of those humble domestic objects of superstition which provoked the scorn of the intellectuals. He was actually a member of the 'Hellfire Club', the Kakodaimonistae. He seems to have been antidemocratic. He was twice in the courts against Lysias, who says that he 'deserted his art of poetry and made money by turning informer'. An extant inscription contains the decree proposed by him in honour of Dionysius I of Syracuse. It is interesting to notice in Aristophanes the difference of tone between the mocking of the rival artist Kinêsias, whose style he dislikes, and his grim onslaughts on war-mongers and informers. Aristophanes genuinely hates corrupt politicians and demagogues; but there is always a twinkle of good-nature in his most mischievous onslaughts upon artists. A passing accusation of unnatural vice, based on a poet's treatment of anapaests or his absence of beard, would no doubt be taken by Agathon and others in the spirit in which it was meant.

Cleisthenes had no art to excuse him, but it is difficult at first blush to see why he should be pursued with such relentless ridicule. True, he wore no hair on his face, a Macedonian fashion which did not prevail in Athens till about the time of Aristotle, but that in itself was hardly a sufficient crime. Of course, it makes him 'like a woman'. When the Clouds see Cleônymus they become timid deer, when they see Cleisthenes they look like women. In the *Thesmophoriazusae* it is Cleisthenes who comes among the women, as one of themselves, to warn them of Euripides' plot. When Mnesilochus, after shaving, looks in the mirror he seems 'just like Cleisthenes'. In the *Birds* we are asked how things can be expected to go well with a city where Athena the Maiden stands in full armour and Cleisthenes holds a shuttle. In the *Acharnians* he is called o Σι βυρτιον, the son (or pupil) of a famous trainer of athletes, and we cannot say whether this means that the beardless man was really a great athlete—which would make most of the jokes rather better—or just the reverse. But the clue to Aristophanes' hostility is not far to seek. We hear in the *Knights* that Cleisthenes was one of the 'beardless' orators in the Assembly (1373 f.). And Lysias definitely calls him an informer.

> He is one of a gang of men who have made profit out of the city's misfortunes and caused the gravest public wrong. They have persuaded you to condemn men to death without trial. They have brought about many unjust confiscations, banishments and degradations from civic rights. For money they would always try to get the guilty acquitted in the courts and the innocent destroyed. (*Lys.* xxv. 25.)

No doubt there is exaggeration in the pleader's statement, but it gives us just the light that we needed on Cleisthenes' real activities. It was not the absence of beard that enraged Aristophanes. A sŷcophantês without a beard would be hated for his smooth cheeks, but a bearded one would be just as much hated for his shagginess.

Aristophanes is still the same man that he was in the *Babylonians,* except that some of his illusions have gone. He no longer hopes with the old confidence to achieve real

peace, to restore good feeling between Athens and her subject Allies, to get politics once more into the hands of decent people or see King Demos clothed and in his right mind. He talks but little politics. He lives in literature, in μουσικη. Even in μουσικη, of course, all is not well; the young people nowadays do not know and love the great old poetry as they ought, and as for some of these new musicians, the less said of them the better! But in the realm of the Muses he can forget the world, its fears and its poverty and its intrigues; he can find wings for men or at least for the souls of men; he can laugh again, and laugh not bitterly but happily, laugh with an intoxication of fun and wild fancy and beautiful words, with no more bitterness in his heart . . . except of course for war-mongers and informers and persecutors, plague take the lot of them! (pp. 139-63)

> *Gilbert Murray, in his* Aristophanes: A Study, *Oxford at the Clarendon Press, 1933, 268 p.*

Cedric H. Whitman (essay date 1964)

[*Whitman was an American classicist whose books include* Sophocles: A Study in Heroic Humanism *(1951),* Homer and the Heroic Tradition *(1958), and* Euripides and the Full Circle of Myth *(1974). In the following excerpt from his* Aristophanes and the Comic Hero *(1964), he explores some of the themes of Aristophanes's* Birds *and the playwright's treatment of them. Whitman posits that one of the main concerns of the play is nothingness, and that the characters' actions center around the idea of recreating order in their world through the use of language.*]

The *Birds* is, as a rule, regarded as the most mysterious of the comedies. Interpreters who seek the essence of the plays in current political or social situations have found in the *Birds* some cause for embarrassment. It is not a "peace" play exactly, and it is not a play against Cleon, who was now dead; Euripides, for an exception, is not even mentioned in it; Socrates has a brief stanza, but no more. One commentator has seen in it a political allegory having to do with Alcibiades and the Sicilian expedition, but his theory turns the *Birds* into a cryptographic political treatise so intricate that no one could possibly have detected the meaning even in its own time. Who would suspect from watching a performance that the birds were the Athenians, the gods the Spartans, and the hero a cross between Alcibiades and Gorgias of Leontini? Other interpreters, more realistic, but inclined, perhaps, to settle for too little, have regarded it as a flight of purest fancy having little to do with anything. But poetry cannot be quite so lacking in relevance to experience, though the *Birds* is indeed a flight of fancy. A third group, favoring an Aristophanes who is more a moral reformer than a political one, sees the play as a condemnation of the Athenian vices of gullibility, fickleness, waywardness, and superstition. Perhaps; but then it must be asked why the hero Peithetaerus, whose operations can scarcely be called supremely moral, is so marvelously successful, even to ascending the throne of the whole world; and the answer has to be that after the end of the play the gods struck him down, and of course everybody knew that that was going to happen. This is to pull a rabbit, and not a very pleasing rabbit, out of a very old hat. One tries in vain to imagine, after the triumphant riotings of the last scene, the thoughtful Athenians turning homeward, spiritually admonished, and murmuring, "Ah, that Peithetaerus is headed for a bad fall! Good old Aristophanes has straightened us out again."

Yet for all these differences of interpretation, the **Birds** is also regarded as the poet's masterpiece, and a glance at the scenario may suggest the reason, or one of the reasons. Two aging Athenians, Peithetaerus and Euelpides, disgusted with the life in Athens, its tumult of business, war, debts, and litigation, have decided to consult the birds about a better place to live. Guided by a crow and a jackdaw which they have bought, they seek the Hoopoe, who was once Tereus, King of Daulis, and husband of the Athenian princess Procne. This first stage of the search introduces the theme of a pristine world, far away and long ago, under the rule of Tereus and Procne, who here, their crimes forgotten, represent not only the carefree world of pastoral bliss but also a further range of knowledge, "all that men know, and all that birds know." The next theme is more hardheaded, however, and concerns the world of empire. The two Athenians make a compact with the birds, and convince them that they, the birds, are the original gods, who have been cheated of their rights by the Olympians. They proceed to build a new city in the air, Cloud-cuckoo-land, and intercept the smoke of sacrifices rising to heaven, thus bringing the gods into parley. Zeus capitulates and yields to the now winged Peithetaerus his scepter and the Princess Basileia, and therewith complete supremacy. Thus outlined, the play appears like an escapist manifesto, the utopian dream of a new and perfect city where men can live as freely and happily as birds. The utopian theme is certainly there, but so too is the theme of power, and close scrutiny of the way the two work together, and of the motifs through which they develop, reveals beneath the broad laughter a striking poetic intuition, laced with deep and wistful irony.

The **Birds** is strangely free of political concerns; there are the usual topical allusions, indeed, but they are passing ones, and there is no consistent reference to any specific issue or issues of the city, as there is in the five preceding plays. In the **Birds** comedy seems to detach itself, to a degree, in search of a broader and more symbolic scheme; and though the old form persists, it becomes more free of the immediate topicalities on which it once relied so heavily. In this freedom from parochial concern lies one of the play's chief claims to supremacy: its scene is the world, not merely Athens. Moreover, it has a greater dramatic unity than any of the comedies so far, a unity unbroken even by the parabasis. Normally the parabasis of the chorus marks an interruption in the progress of the play, as the chorus comes forward, and, speaking as much in the poet's person as in character, addresses the audience about matters quite outside the drama. There is no such breaking of the illusion in the **Birds;** rather the parabasis abets the illusion, with its famous parody on cosmogonic poetry explaining how the world was created by birds, the original gods. The demands of dramaturgy have triumphed in the **Birds** over

the need for certain traditional components, and the result is a play of singularly sustained dramatic force.

But what is dramatized? The earlier plays of Aristophanes regularly mingle their fantasy and satire in such a way that the satiric element provides a clue to the meaning of the fantasy. Out of the satire on the war party rises the great individualist Dicaeopolis with his fantastic peace; out of the satire on interminable litigation rises the fantasy of the **Wasps,** the dream of personal power blending into the inescapable vortex of nature. With the element of a satiric nucleus apparently lacking in the **Birds,** one is left with the fantasy itself, to discover its relevance as best one may from an analysis of its structure and motifs.

The hero himself is clear. He is not Alcibiades or Gorgias, or anyone else, though Gorgias . . . may have some relevance to the meaning of the play. The hero is simply the man of heroic *poneria* par excellence; more properly, he becomes that in much the same way Dicaeopolis did. Like Dicaeopolis, he represents the individual fugitive from an increasingly impossible society, and he also reaches the point where he is suddenly inundated by a vision of supremacy, which he immediately implements with all his resources. He is the grandest and most successful of all Aristophanes' heroes. Even before he becomes inspired, the germ of his *poneria* is implicit in his name: Peithetaerus, "Companion-persuader" (if that is the right form), certainly implies the suspicious powers of rhetoric and guile. His companion's name, Euelpides, "McHopeful," suggests naïveté, if not exactly innocence. One might justifiably regard these two, perhaps, as two familiar aspects of Athenian character, cleverness and gullibility, but in fact these possibilities are not dramatically exploited, for Euelpides is not duped. Rather he acts as the principal foil to Peithetaerus' boundless vision until he is no longer necessary, partaking of the fantasy and eventually disappearing into it.

Up to the point where Peithetaerus gets his great idea, Euelpides does more of the talking; he has his eye more firmly on the object than does the visionary Peithetaerus. It is Euelpides who discusses with the Hoopoe the possible whereabouts of a city which will be free of the faults of Athens; Peithetaerus during this scene is the aloof, brooding mastermind whose thoughts have not yet come to fullness. But from the point where the mastermind suddenly springs into action and begins erecting its gigantic fantasy of a bird city in the air, the objectivity and realism of Euelpides take the form of earthy comments characteristic of the role of buffoon, and swing into a poised and familiar dramatic relation to Peithetaerus' inspired leadership. Euelpides contributes little or nothing to the structure of the fantasy, but his practical remarks throughout the agon fall with sudden dull thuds in the interstices of Peithetaerus' airy verbiage. This is familiar comic technique—to blow up a large balloon and then burst it—and Aristophanes makes use of it often, but it is a major principle in the **Birds.** Not only in the scenes with Euelpides, but roughly everywhere, lyrical fancy and vaporous superstructures of wit and sophistry alternate with a trudging realism which, for all it may bring us back to earth in a sense, never really wins the day; the fantasy goes on with tireless rhythm, unperturbed by the dragging weights of what is usually called reality. If the process were reversed, if soaring fancy foundered on ineluctable fact, one might discover a common-sense view, and the **Birds** might be taken as similar to Brueghel's "Fall of Icarus," where a winged man has just fallen out of the sky into the sea, his legs still visible, but nobody takes notice; the ship sails on, and the peasant goes on driving his furrow. Here is just the opposite: the balloon never quite bursts; it just loses a little air and then shoots higher. References to everyday familiarities only feed the fantasy, through Peithetaerus' genius for turning everything to advantage. Here *poneria* achieves its most developed sense, in that the self-advantage which it pursues is identified with nothing less than the restructuring of the world itself, and challenges the authority of Zeus, the god of things as they are. Euelpides' part is to embody the solid facts which dissolve before the skilled language of the demiurgic man of words.

All this is nonsense, of course, but in the sense of nonsense poetry, which, at its best, regularly juxtaposes real and imaginary things or words in such a way as to exloit the real in favor of the imaginary. In reading Edward Lear's "Pobble Who Has No Toes" we may doubt the existence of Pobbles, but not of toes; yet, in the long poem which tells how this Pobble lost his toes despite his mother's warning to take care of them, toes make the Pobble as clothes make the man. Their solid factuality does not detract at all from the imaginary Pobble's reality. And in the lovely Pogo lyric

> How pierceful grows the hazy yon!
> How myrtle petal thou!
> For spring hath sprung the cyclotron—
> How high browse thou, brown cow?

the sudden appearance of the cyclotron is a bit of a shock; yet, the cyclotron is carried along somehow in the pastoral air, and the song pursues its serene and gentle way.

The observation that the **Birds** is nonsense may not seem to be either very helpful, or very different from the interpretation previously rejected, that it is a flight of purest fancy, signifying nothing. But the answer may be that a work may signify nothing in one of two senses, for "nothing" is a metaphysical term. The word may mean "absence of anything," and thus be quite negative; but it may also have the more positive meaning of the articulable conception "nothing," or "nothingness," and in this second meaning it is as useful to thought and criticism as zero is to a mathematician. By the hypostasis of language "nothing" becomes something to which we give a name, and about which we may invent a whole series of predicates which signify, no doubt, nothing, but which may be the rightful language of absurdity. In any case, when we speak this language, we play with words and give them a primacy over their meanings which inverts our usual sense of reality. The **Birds** plays with language in a way far beyond any of the other comedies, and the sense of reality undergoes considerable change by consequence. If the word play "Katagela" in the **Acharnians** creates a city with metaphoric existence in Sicily, the **Birds,** which is one vast, finely woven texture of word plays, creates the absurd and wonderful metaphor of Utopia, Nowhere, the ideal city of

Nephelococcygia. One of the ways to say in Greek "You are talking nonsense," is ουδεν λεγεισ, "you talk nothing." If we take that "nothing" in the second sense, it becomes clear what Aristophanes is about; for the nothing that people talk is the reality which they possess. The word is all, it creates consciousness, and its enormous vitality stubbornly resists fact. A word becomes image or metaphor, and the image or metaphor lives in the mind, independent of reason and far more compelling. Philocleon suffered from an ineradicable image of himself, but Peithetaerus' imagery includes also a world appropriate to himself, and he manufactures it. Images and metaphors are dream substance and make dream worlds, and every world is an absurdity, a verbal nothing. All this is beyond satire, as handled in the **Birds;** it is a poetic weft comically adumbrating the world in which we live, the world where there can be no tragic reversal or recognition, the world of *poneria* and the self, where the persuasive and manipulable word is king.

To interpret so may seem to do historical violence, by introducing modern ideas of relativism, subjectivism, and the question of the relation between reality and language. But such ideas are by no means exclusively modern. Probably around the third quarter of the fifth century B.C. Gorgias composed a book called "On Non-being," or "Concerning Nature," in which, according to Sextus Empiricus, he maintained three propositions: first, that nothing exists; second, that if anything exists it is not intellectively graspable; and third, that even if it is intellectively graspable, it is incommunicable. The last of these is the most relevant to the **Birds,** and is really the source of the other two; for Gorgias believed that speech, and speech alone, is what is communicated, and that speech does not correspond to reality. His mode of reasoning may not be wholly flawless, but there can be no doubt that he is facing the epistemological problem of communication:

> For if the real things, which have external existence, are visible and audible, and commonly perceptible by the senses, and of these things the visible ones are grasped by vision, the audible ones by hearing, and there is no interchange, how then can these be communicated to another person? For the instrument by which we communicate is speech, and speech is not "existent real things"; therefore it is not real things which we communicate to our neighbors, but speech, which is different from existent objects. And so, just as the visible cannot become the audible and the reverse, so too, since reality exists externally, it could not become our speech.

It has been said by a number of scholars that Gorgias is here doing no more than displaying his ingenuity with words, in a playful refutation of Eleatic metaphysics. Even if this view were correct, the treatise "On Non-being" would be not merely an argument, but also an object lesson on the power of speech. But it has been recently demonstrated that this theory of communication and reality is wholly consistent with the rest of the work of Gorgias, and in particular with his theory of *peitho* (persuasion), and *apaté* (deception, illusion) as the psychic and aesthetic basis of the rhetorical art. Certainly relativism and subjectivism were nothing new in the late fifth century, after Protagoras and even Democritus. Gorgias simply pressed matters further, in denying all knowable connection between being, or reality, and the communicative medium of language, and in asserting that language is the controlling factor in the life of the psyche. As it has been well stated [by C. P. Segal in "Gorgias and the Psychology of the Logos," *HSCP* 66, 1962]: " 'Reality' for him [Gorgias] lies in the human psyche and its malleability and susceptibility to the effects of verbal coruscation. Thus his rhetoric, though concerned primarily with a technique of verbal elaboration, rests ultimately upon a psychology of literary experience. These two, psyche and *logos,* lie both within the realm of tangible experience and become for Gorgias the new reality."

If such views were indeed characteristic of Gorgias, whose influence was great, one must assume an intellectual climate in which subjectivism, relativism, and the priority of speech to reality were familiar if not always approved theories; theories which, in fact, one finds Plato later retrospectively combating. But in the fifth century, in at least some intellectual quarters, the persuasive "deception" of speech created the *doxa,* or private opinion, upon which people acted, in a world where ultimate or final truth was undiscoverable. Speech assists and directs the "subjective restructuring of the world," and thus occupies a position of power analogous to, if not identifiable with, divinity itself. And it is precisely such a psychology which underlies the *Birds* of Aristophanes. The airy empire of the birds is created out of words by that demiurge of persuasion, Peithetaerus, in a vast "subjective restructuring of the world" which is both lyrical and ironic. Peithetaerus knows his Gorgias, and though Gorgias undoubtedly felt that the rightful ends of rhetorical persuasion were good, for the comic hero no such scruple need exist: *peitho* and *apaté* are the most serviceable modes of *poneria,* in that they build their own reality and lead on to the boundless.

One cannot begin to analyze in full the way this underlying idea is worked out in the *Birds,* but a few examples will serve to illustrate, for essentially everything contributes toward it, even the parabasis, as pointed out earlier. The play begins with a dramatized metaphor. The two Athenians, turning their backs on troubled Athens, are going to visit the birds. Euelpides makes sure we get the joke, because going to the birds is like going to the crows, which is Greek for going to the dogs:

> Isn't it dreadful, here we are, we two,
> Ready and willing to go to the crows,
> And cannot find the road?

Or, as it has been translated with succinct felicity: "Two of us for the birds, and we can't even find the road!" The metaphor in hand may be no more than simple slang, but to stage two characters who pace out the actual steps of "going to the birds" has the unmistakable effect of putting language itself in the controlling position. Once evoked, the phrase plots the poetic course of the play through a preposterous series of verbal pyrotechnics whose iridescent web of innuendoes gradually reveals the poet's gay but profound reflection upon his world.

The image goes deeper than the slang phrase. Peithetaerus and Euelpides leave their world to go to the birds, which

is going to the crows on the one hand; but it is also a return to nature. At first they seek another city, better than Athens, but when none can be found, Euelpides asks what life is like among the birds:

> HOOPOE: Not a bad way to spend your time.
> First of all, here we live without a purse.
>
> EUELP.: Then you get rid of a great deal of life's hugger-mugger.
>
> HOOPOE: We feed in gardens on white sesame,
> On poppy seed and mint and myrtle berries.
>
> EUELP.: You live the life of newlyweds!

This passage is double-edged, for it points to two aspects of the life of nature, *physis.* The remark about the purse reminds us that one of the reasons why the two men left Athens was their desire not to have to pay debts. Further, one is reminded of Strepsiades in the *Clouds,* where nonpayment of debt is regarded as natural enough if you can get away with it; and one can get away with it with the help of Unjust Discourse, whose basic principle is the φυσεωσ αναγκαι, the necessities of nature. Nature is here again invoked, after the late sophistic fashion, as an antimoral force, and one which in the human creature does not naturally acquiesce to law, let alone create it. To escape *nomos* and to arrive at the fulfillment of *physis* becomes therefore a natural desideratum. On the other hand, the Hoopoe's description of the life of birds is the first of a series of marvelous pastorales exalting the innocence of nature and the sweetness of birdsong, which reaches up toward the harmony of the gods themselves. And yet, both views go somehow together, for the gods are indeed above morality, in that state of divine supremacy toward which, as said often before, the comic hero also strives, yet without renouncing his humanity, his "necessities of nature." . . . [In] the *Wasps* Aristophanes studied nature as a trap, a vicious circle coming always round upon itself. But in the *Birds* nature's innate antinomies are drawn with a clearer sense of the unity of all natural phenomena. And if the outcome involves, as it does in the *Wasps,* some unexpected turns, yet the presence of a true comic hero, Peithetaerus, who can include multitudes of inconsistencies, keeps the fantasy triumphantly afloat to the last, so that the vicious circle itself becomes a victory.

Nowhere has Aristophanes given fuller expression to the comic dream, and in no way could he have reached more subtly into the psychology of his contemporary audience. To return to nature is to evade, or better, to transcend law, and most of the advantages of Nephelococcygia amount . . . to a happy lawlessness. Yet such is scarcely the moral. Half the charm of the *Birds* lies in its paradox, in its exploitation of the ambiguities of the *nomos-physis* debate. Not only is nature a term of ambiguous value; there are further equivocations and puns on *nomos,* which with one accentuation, can mean either "law" or "song," and then with a different one, "pasture," or the haunts of birds. Peithetaerus and Euelpides cannot live in Athens, with its laws, bailiffs, and bother; they will seek songs and pastures, the lawless *nomos* which is *physis,* the life of nature, fit for birds and gods. And this, incidentally, is the reason why the *Birds* does not arise from any specific issue in the city, as the other plays do; the city itself is the issue, or pretext, for the fantasy, and there is no need to satirize a part when the whole is dismissed and transformed. (pp. 167-77)

The equations of the *Birds* cancel out. In order to evade the imperial metropolis, the imperial metropolis must be rebuilt; in order to achieve reality, reality must be denied existence; in order to find meaning, language must be handed over to its most limitless ambiguities; the return to nature, with its songs and pastures, becomes a return to the city, with its laws and conventions. But what does it all mean? Is it that the *Birds* is meaningless and without relevance apart from its fine artistry? Hardly so; but it is about meaninglessness, the circle of inscrutable nature again, the absurdity which calls for the heroic act of individual freedom and self-transformation. Meaning is a word, and it requires a hero to give the word meaning. In the *Clouds* and in the *Wasps* Aristophanes dealt in various ways with the problems of nature, law, and education, but in both plays he abandoned temporarily the heroic figure of transcendent fantasy, save insofar as Philocleon may be said to approach it. The result was drama bifurcated by dialectic, and ending in ironic unresolved images of nature as insurmountable. In the *Birds* the hero returns, grotesque and grand, a bird-man-god who commands all and unites all in himself, and so resolves the ambiguities of nature and the world. But the tool is language, and the underlying secret is the acquiescence to the view that meaning is a created structure, a heroic achievement. The hero gives what meaning he will to the words of which he builds his empire, and by such masterful transvaluations, the world from which he fled becomes the world which he commands. The terms may be nonsense, but they effect the self-authentication which is indispensable to heroic experience. The *Birds* is the crown of Aristophanes' works in that it unites the unilinear heroic fantasy of the "polis" plays with the intellectual dilemmas of the "education" plays, in a mysterious and shimmering comedy whose range and import are unequaled, save, perhaps, by the somber and wholly different *Frogs.*

The *Frogs* . . . is in some way the opposite of the *Birds;* it is a quest for meaning beyond mere words, a deeply concerned effort to penetrate to the heart of a world on the verge of disappearance. Profound and beautiful as it is, however, it has not quite the visionary breadth and encompassing totality of the *Birds,* nor has it the detachment and creative freedom which arise from the full heroic acceptance of nothingness. When the world begins to appear meaningless, as well it might have to the mature Aristophanes in 414, one may be free, if one is Aristophanes, to dramatize its nonsense with an irony so detached and yet so imaginative that the product is something like a myth; a myth gives a view of the whole world, and so does the *Birds.* Its detachment and involvement are mingled in an equal suspension which Aristophanes never repeated; and hence it is at once the gayest and the saddest of the plays. Neither a reform play, a political play, nor an escape play, the *Birds* is about nothingness—and therefore everything. (pp. 198-99)

Cedric H. Whitman, in his Aristophanes and the Comic Hero, *Cambridge, Mass.: Harvard University Press, 1964, 333 p.*

CLOUDS

CRITICAL COMMENTARY

Alan H. Sommerstein   (essay date 1973)

[*In the excerpt below, Sommerstein discusses the intellectual background of* Clouds *and the sources of Aristophanes's dislike of the Sophists.*]

In the 420s Greece, and in particular Athens, was in an intellectual ferment. The eternal verities were being questioned. New forms of education were coming into existence, and new kinds of morality too. The young, men like Alcibiades, took all this up with enthusiasm. The old were suspicious: would not these new-fangled ideas destroy the cohesiveness of society and lead to anarchy or despotism? And how about the new teachers, the sophists as they were called? Why couldn't they work for a living like everybody else? Aristophanes, though in years a contemporary of Alcibiades, believed (at least for the purposes of his comedy) that the old were right; and *The Clouds* is his exposure of what the 'new learning' stands for and what it leads to.

It had all started, as far as Athens was concerned, with Protagoras, who had spread the gospel that it did not matter whether the gods existed and that all values were relative. Then there had been Anaxagoras, who had meddled in geology, astronomy, and heaven knows what else, had declared the sun to be a stone and not a god, and finally had been sent into exile by an Athenian court. More recently the Sicilian Gorgias and others had arrived in town and begun to teach the new art of rhetoric, training their disciples to concentrate not on being right, but on getting people to believe that they were right. And already there were many who proclaimed that all previous codes of morality had been superseded, and that from now on might was right. These four elements—atheism, scientific inquiry and speculation, rhetoric, and the new morality—all appear in *The Clouds,* and all are ascribed to Socrates.

Socrates himself was forty-five when *The Clouds* was originally written. A few months before he had behaved with notable courage during the Athenian retreat from Delium in Boeotia—which perhaps did not endear him to his comrades, who thought of him as swaggering and conceited. In Athens he had gathered round him a circle of rich young men, who listened eagerly as he questioned those who thought themselves clever, and proved that they had never worked out the grounds on which their opinions were based. But he had nothing to do with atheism, physical science or rhetoric, and his moral inquiries were directed not at setting up a new morality, but at providing foundations for the old one to stand on. Why then did Aristophanes attribute to him all the (in his view) least desirable characteristics of rival teachers?

It is quite likely that Aristophanes did not know the difference. Socrates gave young men an unconventional education, and that was enough. Besides, Socrates was easily the best known of the various 'sophists'. The others were mostly foreigners who came to Athens from time to time. Socrates was an Athenian citizen and, except for military service and other public duties, never left the city. So, if one wished to caricature an individual 'sophist', Socrates was the obvious choice.

Mud, however, once thrown, has a tendency to stick; and, if we are to believe Plato (and it seems unlikely that his account is false in essentials), the mud thrown at Socrates by Aristophanes and other comic poets stuck so well that when Socrates was charged in 399 with 'corrupting the young' and with 'not believing in the City's gods but in other strange deities', his accuser said in court that Socrates believed the sun to be a stone and the moon to be earth (which were Anaxagoras' views, not his). It was not just *The Clouds,* of course. Quotations preserved from other comedies show clearly that Socrates was always being got at in them, and being presented very much as he is presented in *The Clouds.* The Athenians who sat on the jury in 399 would have been superhuman if twenty-five years of this had not prejudiced them, quite apart from other considerations Aristophanes must bear his share of the responsibility.

Although Aristophanes unreservedly condemns the new learning, that does not mean that he uncritically approves of the older generation. Strepsiades (whose name means 'Twister') is quite ready to get out of paying his debts by dishonest means, and Right, the champion of the old education, has an interest in young boys which is overdone even for fifth-century Athens. Strepsiades takes his revenge on Socrates, but not before he has been suitably punished himself. The play, indeed, could almost be described as a tragedy showing how wickedness recoils on itself; and the Clouds behave very much as gods do in tragedy: they lead Strepsiades down the primrose path of evil, which is also the way he wants to go himself, and let him fall over the cliff at the end of it.

The Clouds, in fact, is an unusually serious comedy, and it was too serious for its original audience. When it was originally produced, in the spring of 423, the judges placed it third and last. As we can see from *The Wasps,* Aristophanes was very bitter about this. Some time between 420 and 417 he set to work revising *The Clouds,* but the revision was never completed and the play was never produced again. Despite this, it is the revised version that we possess, and it bears marks of its incomplete state. These, however, are not such as would be noticed in a modern production. (pp. 107-09)

> *Alan H. Sommerstein, in an introduction to "The Clouds," in* The Acharnians [and] The Clouds [and] Lysistrata *by Aristophanes, translated by Alan H. Sommerstein, 1973. Reprint by Penguin Books, 1988, pp. 107-09.*

Alexis Solomos   (essay date 1974)

[*Solomos is a noted Greek theater director and author.*

In the following excerpt, he recreates the circumstances surrounding the first staging of Clouds *in order to explore some of the reasons for Aristophanes's attack on Socrates and the Sophists.*]

In the spring of 424 B.C., there lived in Athens an unhappy old poet and a happy young one. The old poet was at the end of his life; he felt tired and looked back with bitterness at his whole life's work which had now fallen into ruins. A number of years ago he was the king of laughter in Athens, but now he inspires nothing but pity from those he encounters in the streets or from those who attend his comedies in the theatre. For two consecutive years he has been defeated at the Lenaea and the second prize he did receive was perhaps given to him as a mere consolation. The once audacious old poet who made even Pericles tremble has now no other company than his wine jug, which has been his great love as well as the cause of his decline. Late at night he returns home from the tavern and there, "on a filthy sheepskin," Cratinus goes on snoring.

The young poet is not yet twenty-six and already all Greece has cheered him. He is the man who, more than anybody else, makes the soldiers relax from the miseries of war with his god-sent laughter. He is, moreover, the idealist who fights for peace, often endangering his personal freedom. In the small towns where the Greeks build walls, demolish walls, moan and groan, one of his quips comes every now and then by word of mouth to bring the balm of gaiety. Cleon, of course, is always after him, trying to trap him; on the other hand, Eupolis, Ameipsias, and Phrynichus, even the old Cratinus, are dangerous rivals. But the glory of dramatic creation and the love of his fellow Athenians have made our young poet spiritually immune. Therefore, he is no longer afraid to declare publicly his name—Aristophanes, son of Philip, of the Cydathenaeon deme and the Pandionis tribe—an immense ego.

With his next play, Aristophanes is resolved to compete in the Great Dionysia. And to avoid being disqualified in advance, he will submit a harmless literary satire, which will by no means damage Cleon's authority. His anti-Cleonic attacks will be heard again, as in the two previous years, in the Lenaea. He will thus expand his theatrical campaign on both Dionysiac fronts. He plans the *Merchant Ships* for January and the *Clouds* for March.

From the *Merchant Ships* (*Holcades*) we possess about fifty lines, but we are ignorant of its fate in the competition. According to the grammarians, peace was the main subject of this comedy, in which Aristophanes assaulted "the bellicose Lamachus and the reactionary Cleon." In other words, the politician and the military man, who had begun their stage careers in the *Babylonians* and the *Acharnians,* reappeared in new adventures. They had become by now stock characters, and the public looked forward to laughing at them. Scholars even go so far as to surmise the plot: the Athenians and the Spartans, wishing to exchange their complaints, ship them to each other. The cargoes of complaints, however, are so enormous that by looking at them the two rivals decide to make peace.

The *Clouds,* on the other hand, is one of the best known plays of Aristophanes and, without doubt, the one that has given us more trouble than any of the others. It contains the most puzzling riddle in the poet's entire production and one of the major question marks in the history of literature. Why did Aristophanes attack Socrates? Why did the young and intelligent playwright present the wisest and most virtuous man of his time as a ridiculous and improbable buffoon—an exaggerated combination of the Homeric Thersites and the Sileni offered in abundance by the satyr drama? This question, especially in connection with the condemnation of Socrates twenty-four years later, transcends the narrow limits of literary criticism to become a historical enigma.

Numberless pages have been written to explain the Aristophanic Socrates, as well as Plato's subsequent attitude toward the man who ridiculed his beloved teacher. In our opinion, the position taken by Aristophanes in the *Clouds* is in full accord with the policy he has so far maintained. His target here is the prevailing educational system which he considers the cause of the overall degeneration of Athenian thought. Under its influence, the citizens vote for Cleon and carry on a disastrous civil war. The subject is not unsimilar to that of the *Banqueters,* though more passionately treated. In the former play, the problem of youth was simpler: their shortcomings were laziness, illiteracy, and sophisticated blabber. The *Clouds* aims at a more dangerous evil: the inclination of youth to the new philosophic theories which shake the foundation of religion, family, democracy, and morality.

In those days, many schools of higher education had been opened in Athens, most of them directed by foreign sophists. From the picture that Plato will give us in his *Protagoras*—where three famous sophists meet in the house of the rich Athenian Callias—we get an idea of how important and how eccentric these teachers were. Aristophanes could very well have chosen one of these three sophists as his hero. Why didn't he do so? Someone has said that Attic comedy tactfully limited itself to attacking none but Athenian monsters. On the other hand, our playwright may have been unwilling to slander any actual school; he didn't hold responsible this system or that, but modern education in general. This is, perhaps, one of the reasons why he chose Socrates, who was a native Athenian, did not have a school of his own, and in the public eye was not so very different from the teachers of revolutionary and preposterous ideas.

We must not forget that the Socrates we know today is mostly the Socrates that Plato has created. The ideal personality, immortalized by the faithful pupil, will first appear nearly thirty or forty years after the *Clouds,* when the early dialogues will be published. Only then will the enormous difference between Socrates and the sophists become obvious, as well as the deeper significance of the former's teachings. For the average Athenian of Aristophanes' time Socrates is nothing more than a peculiar type of the agora, a barefooted and impecunious tramp who frequents the gymnasium, lectures on new and never-heard-of-before ideas and is always amusing because he makes fun first of all of himself. Although he never has enough money to pay for a meal, he is invited to dinners as a special attraction, because he is able to deliberate until dawn and drink without getting tipsy. It is not very likely that he has, as

yet, created his famous method or fathomed the mystery of the human mind. His present theories may be identical to a certain extent with all the strange things that the sophists are telling their students about astronomy, geology, geometry, or even, as Aristophanes mocks, about whether gnats hum from their mouths or their behinds (*Clouds,* 157-58). In the classic Greek century the sophists were generally regarded like the surrealists or the existentialists in our own era; and very probably every person of daring ideas, unshaven and unkempt, would be deemed a sophist. So the pre-Platonic Socrates may have been a victim of such a misunderstanding; because even in his days of posthumous glory the orator Aeschines will refer in one of his speeches to "Socrates the sophist."

The Platonic Socrates that we are more familiar with, therefore, is not the original Socrates. Aristophanes, responsible for the oldest portraits of Cleon and Euripides, was also the first to give a picture of the forty-seven-year-old philosopher. This practice was eagerly exploited by some of his fellow playwrights and, henceforward, Socrates became a fashionable attraction on the comic stage. We discover many invectives referring to the philosopher, about his dirty and shabby cloak, his absurd chatter, his poverty, and so on. "I too hate Socrates, the impecunious," Eupolis says, "who thinks about everything and only forgets to think how to eat." Aristophanes was the first to accuse Socrates—arousing Voltaire's wrath many centuries later—of stealing the athletes' clothes in the palaestra for the sake of his students (*Clouds,* 179). Similar thefts were exploited by Ameipsias and Eupolis. After all, Attic Comedy had license for even worse charges. An unwritten theatrical privilege made comedy the executioner of all the great figures, from Aeschylus to Pericles and from Homer even to its own god Dionysus.

At any rate, the Socrates of the comic poets was the first Socrates to appear in history. It was, furthermore, the only depiction of himself that Socrates lived to know. On the contrary, the Platonic dialogues are posthumous appraisals, in which one might discern more of Plato's own way of thinking than of his quasi-legendary master's. It may not, therefore, be too daring or sacrilegious to surmise that, between the caricature made by Aristophanes and the hagiography made by Plato, the first bears more likeness to the human original. In fact, the Aristophanic view finds its advocates to a considerable degree in Xenophon, not to mention Plutarch, Diogenes Laertius, and ancient anecdotology. No matter how biased our playwright was in his social sermon, it is unlikely that he distorted the real Socrates more than he had done the real Cleon or the real Euripides; and we know well (from Thucydides' descriptions of the former as well as from the tragedies of the latter) that whatever Aristophanes wrote about them remains within the bounds of probability. Notwithstanding the laughable exaggeration that ancient comedy could make use of, the Athenian spectators would never accept a false theatrical semblance. Thus, we may blame Aristophanes for his lack of understanding of the Socratic mind, but we can by no means reject altogether the plausibility of his Socrates.

Many things have been written both by ancients and moderns, with the purpose of justifying or of analyzing the comic poet's attitude toward the philosopher. Some, for instance, said that Anytus and Meletus instigated the Aristophanic attack; yet the two accusers of Socrates could not have been more than children when the *Clouds* was produced. Others have maintained that Aristophanes was jealous of Socrates, because Archelaus, the art-patron king of Macedonia, had invited the philosopher to his court and not him. And the old *Life* vaguely states that the comic poets had "some controversy" with the philosophers.

Perhaps the following speculations may cast some light on Aristophanes' choice of his comic hero:

1. He chose this free-lance philosopher who never had a school of his own, in order to avoid libeling any of the particular sophistic academies.

2. It is a well-known truth that our comic poet, although he hits *en passant* many petty nuisances, never condescends to fight seriously except with those standing high. "Having the temper of Heracles, I fight with the greatest," he himself will comment on his audacity (*Wasps,* 1030). His heroes, when they are real characters, will always be the most prominent Athenian statesmen, generals, or tragic poets. So the fact alone that he dedicates a whole play to Socrates signifies that he picks him out as the most important, and for that reason the most dangerous, teacher of the young.

3. Attic Comedy was supposed to present familiar faces; the likeness of the mask would guarantee half of the success. Quite naturally, the wandering Socrates was, for the man-in-the-street, a more familiar face than the various sophists known to academic circles alone. Therefore, just by his appearance on the stage, he could create mirth, for even such a favorite disciple as Alcibiades admitted that to meet Socrates was, at first, a funny experience. With his Silenean features, his bald head, his belly, his bare feet, and shabby clothes, Socrates offered the comic poet a ready-made figure of Megarian farce. So the mere external appearance of the philosopher must have been a great temptation to Aristophanes.

4. Socrates was himself a man with an acute sense of humor, always ready to laugh when people teased him. Aristophanes, therefore, feared no reprisals. He knew that the starving sage responded good humoredly to every joke made at his expense. There is a story, mentioned by Diogenes Laertius, that once a man kicked Socrates, and when the latter's friends asked him why he did not sue the offender, Socrates replied "What for? If a donkey kicked me, would I sue him?"

The deeper reason, however, which compelled Aristophanes to write the *Clouds* was not a matter of joking. He wanted to attack collectively all the imposters of education, all the philosophic quacks by whose influence, he thought, young Athenians were being led astray and old ideals were being forsaken. If he became the moral instigator of Socrates' later condemnation, it was beyond his intention. Socrates was destined to serve as the scapegoat for the sins of the sophists; no one among them drank the hemlock and none even became so famous a comedy character as he. What argues for Aristophanes' innocence of

purpose is Plato's complaisance toward him. If the playwright had been seriously responsible for the philosopher's condemnation, Plato would not have included him, as friend among friends, in the famous *Symposium,* written fifteen years or so after Socrates' death. About Plato's attitude toward Aristophanes we shall speak in due time. Now the future author of the *Dialogues* is not more than four or five years old and not, as yet, acquainted either with the Socrates wandering in the agora or the Socrates wandering among the Aristophanic clouds.

A chronological detail, however, seems to be anything but flattering to the playwright. During the summer of 424 B.C., while Aristophanes was sitting comfortably in his home worrying about peace, Socrates, as a plain soldier, was fighting for his country at Delion. The noncombatant Aristophanes, in the *Clouds,* shoots the recruited philosopher for leading young people away from the patriotic ideals of Aeschylus and the Marathon warriors. He attacks at a moment when the poor defendant is much more Aeschylean and much more Marathonian than his heartless prosecutor.

The two comedies of Aristophanes are approved by the respective archons in charge of the two festivals and are performed in the same year. The *Clouds,* attended by the Athenians in the City Dionysia of 423 B.C. is not, at least in its entirety, the *Clouds* that we know. Ancient grammarians inform us that "two *Clouds* are mentioned"; moreover, taking their information from Eratosthenes, they distinguish between what the playwright wrote in "the performed *Clouds*" and what he writes in "the modified" version. The modified version is the one which has come down to us, and philologists date it three or four years after the original one. In the next chapter we shall try to discover the reasons which compelled Aristophanes to rewrite this play, as well as the reasons which made posterity retain the second version of the comedy, leaving the first to oblivion.

According to the valuable Argument VI of the *Clouds,* the second play "is similar to the first and has been revised in various parts . . . generally it has been reworked throughout; some elements have been taken out and new ones have been added and many changes have been made in the structure and the characters. The parts transformed altogether are the *parabasis* of the chorus, the scene where Just Reason speaks to Unjust, and finally the burning of the house of Socrates." The elements given by this Argument help us to reconstruct, *mutatis mutandis,* the performance of 423 B.C.

The comedy opens in the house of Strepsiades, where the old father and his son are sleeping. Actually, the son is snoring profoundly, whereas the father cannot find peace. Strepsiades is a typical Aristophanic elder, whose *moira* [fate] had him born in the country but married in the city. Contrary to Sheridan's Sir Peter Teazle who had to suffer a country wife, Aristophanes' hero has had a hell of a time with his city wife. "When at night we went to bed together, I smelled of wine, figs and sheep and she of perfumes" (49-51).

The fruit of that incongruous coupling was a single son

Pheidippides, named so because the aristocratic mother insisted that in the boy's name the word *hippos* (horse) be incorporated as a sign of knighthood. When the son grew up, he was caught in the cross-fire between his parents, who had conflicting ideas about his education. The maternal influence being more drastic, the son took the road to laziness, snobbishness, and flattery, a perfect example of the depraved younger generation. The result was that he learned nothing and is currently caught up in debts.

Utterly nonchalant, the young Pheidippides sleeps and "farts," wrapped in five blankets, while the poor sire keeps ruminating about his son's expenses, debts, and horses. The last cock has already crowed when Strepsiades makes his decision. He wakes up the young man and implores him to follow him. (They will not go far: if their house was indicated by the left door of the proskenion, they only walk to the right door, where we must imagine the sophists' school.) Along the way the old man tells the sleepy youngster that he must enroll as a student of those wise teachers. Thus, he says, "if you study the Unjust Reason, taught by them, we will not have to pay a penny of your debts" (117-19).

The urgings of the old man are all in vain, for the son is adamant in his refusal to obey. "How shall I be able to face my fellow knights, if I become one of those pale and miserable students?" he exclaims (119-20). Furious, Strepsiades sends him to hell and decides, as the last resort, to enroll himself. So he knocks at the door, while the son returns to his bed.

The scene that follows (126-275) is the second part of the prologue, for the chorus entrance has not yet taken place. Still it has the character of an episode, because two new characters, the student and Socrates, make their appearance. This student who opens the door, scowling because the knocking has made him miscarry a philosophic idea, agrees to let Strepsiades have a glimpse of the school's interior; and this is technically realized by the *ekkyklema* [a theatrical machine], which presently reveals the sanctum with all the unshaven and pale-faced scholars, who, like nuns in ecstasy, are prostrated. The old man asks, quite astonished, what they are doing in that position. "They are doing research on the Underworld," the student replies. "And why do their behinds point at the sky?" "Because they study astronomy" (192-94).

The student, however, orders his fellows to disappear because they must not "stay too long in the open air." And then, all of a sudden, Strepsiades sees, high above their heads, an incongruous spectacle: over the central door of the proskenion [proscenium arch] there hangs a basket in which a man is sitting. "Who is that fellow hanging in the air?" he asks. And the student replies with monosyllabic veneration: "He!" (219).

With the help of the *mechane* [deus ex machina], the teacher descends to earth like a Euripidean god. In fact, the first words he utters, when Strepsiades interrupts his lofty brooding, bears a divine grandeur:

SOCR.: Why do you call me, O mortal?

STREP.: Tell me first, what are you doing up there?

SOCR.: Air-borne, I examine the sun.

(223-25)

And when the ignorant visitor inquires why it is necessary to get into a basket to study the sun, the sage explains that "If from below I should look up I would not discover anything: the earth attracts and absorbs the fluids of thought, like the sap of the cress." And the poor retarded old man whispers: "No kidding, so the cress also thinks! . . ." displaying the same astonished admiration as, centuries later, Molière's would-be-gentleman before the new horizons of philosophy.

In the meantime, the space-surveying Socrates has landed, though he will remain "in the clouds" throughout the play. He is the antipode of common sense: an eccentric and highbrow mastermind; an intellectual snob. As such, he belongs to the comic tradition of all the pedantic professors of the universal stage. As Lamachus is the ancestor of all braggart soldiers (**Acharnians**) and the Aristophanic elders the originals of all pantaloons and gerontions, so this Socrates is the first pedant or doctor of the theatre. Nevertheless, although lizards excrete on his skull while he is contemplating the stars, he is a person of enormous authority. He impresses with his eloquence and profundity. The explanations he offers about natural phenomena are even scientifically convincing. In creating his sage's theories, Aristophanes borrowed indiscriminately from the sophists and the natural philosophers, maybe also from genuine Socratic pronouncements of the early period. It is quite illuminating for the history of Greek thought that the first instruction that Socrates gives to the amazed Strepsiades concerns the substitution of new gods for the old ones. Thus, after praying to Air, to Ether, and to the Clouds, he invokes those last-mentioned powers to appear before the elderly novice.

The *parodos* [first appearance of the chorus] of the chorus does not take place at once, as in the previous comedies. The Clouds' song is heard from afar (275 ff.) answering Socrates' call. Thunder is heard at the same time, frightening Strepsiades, who is trying to discern the strange goddesses arriving over the top of Mt. Parnes.

The teacher tells him why these Clouds are the most precious of all the new divinities and why they protect the philosophers; in so doing he also explains to us why Aristophanes chose them for the chorus of this play: "These Clouds, great and heavenly, are the goddesses of the idle: they offer knowledge and shrewdness, discussion and excessive talk, skill in lying and the art to attack and to get away with it" (316-18). In other words, the dialectic expertise of the sophists is no more than cloudy masses, dull and empty, thundering and made of thin air.

The Clouds appear (probably at line 358) still singing; it is a strange and rare chorus, not only in its symbolism but also in its physical appearance. Comedy choruses usually were human beings, men or women, having in common either a geographical origin, a profession, or a vice. In other cases, they belonged to the kingdom of animals or semihuman beings. We can easily visualize most of them in their costumes, masks, plumes, horns, or tails. Even Cratinus' *Androgynes* can, with a little effort, be imagined. Yet, what could possibly have been the aspect of other choruses, personifying abstract ideas, such as the *Laws* or the *Riches,* the *Islands* or the *Cities?* We possess no description of them and the vase-paintings do not help us in any way. One such case is the misty and mystic chorus of this comedy. The only thing that we are told is that they look like "mortal women" and that they have "noses" (341, 344). As for the way they move and for their general comportment, we cannot help recalling Brecht's admiring description of Mei Lan-fang's art: "He could imitate a passing cloud."

Now, with the Clouds sitting around, like priestesses of the New Thought, the systematic conversion of the old man begins (364). The first thing that he learns is that what causes rain and thunder is the Clouds and not Zeus, whom he had always imagined "pissing through a sieve." Socrates explains those facts with a popularizing method that could be envied by all our school texts; as, for instance, the simile of the thunder: "In the Panathenaean festival, when your belly is full of soup, you suddenly begin to thunder" (386-87).

Strepsiades, however, has no time to waste; he only wants to learn what is necessary for him to do in order to slip "like an eel" out of his creditors' hands. He is ready even to masquerade as a sophist. In a passionate song, he swears allegiance to the Clouds and follows Socrates inside the mystic halls, after having stripped naked, in accordance with the rules of the school (509).

At this point, we have the *parabasis,* only 152 lines after the *parodos,* something quite unusual in Aristophanic comedy. The *parabasis* is one of the three parts of the play which, according to our information mentioned above, were revised some years later in the second version. So, the extant *parabasis* is inspired primarily by the failure of the 423 B.C. performance of the play. It is a vigorous apology by the poet and a bitter retrospection of his career. It is the only instance of an Attic comedy narrating the chronicle of its own performance and also the unique case of a play writing its own autobiography. Aristophanes' chief point is that the 423 B.C. *Clouds* was the best play the Athenians had ever seen and that they—public and judges—were unable to appreciate it (518-25). Aside from being an interesting literary document, however, this *parabasis* [in which the chorus addresses the audience] does not tell us anything about the topic discussed in the original one. Perhaps only the *epirrhemas* (575-94 and 607-26), which mention persons and events of 423 B.C., belong to it.

In the subsequent episode (627 ff.) Socrates comes out of his school swearing. He never before has had such a helplessly idiotic student. Nonetheless, he makes a final effort to educate the naked Strepsiades. Of this course, which is extended on grammatical, etymological, and rhetorical subjects, we should like to emphasize one particular episode not only because it brings to our minds the well-known introspective method of Plato's *Dialogues,* but also because it foreshadows in a funny way the psychoanalytic methods of our own century. The sage orders his student to lie down on a couch and try to concentrate: "Now think as deeply as you can and get together your thoughts" (700-701). He adds that if he is unable to continue one thought, he must jump quickly to another. Accordingly, Strepsiades remains for a while alone with his subconscious, and yet he is unable to concentrate. "What have you been thinking?" Socrates asks. "Whether the bed-bugs will spare any part of me," the old man answers. A second concentration follows, with no better results. This time Socrates has had enough, and therefore sends away the helpless sophist-to-be. The Clouds, pitying the old man, suggest to him a compromise—to send his son in his place (812).

Up to this point, we have had a parody of the sophist's teaching. The following episode is a parody of the parody. Proudly imitating the airs of the great teacher, Strepsiades instructs his son. He swears by the Goddess Fog and laughs at the young man's obsolete ideas, to believe "at his age" in Zeus and other such things. The young man shakes his head in despair and wonders what is the best thing to do, to appeal to the court for guardianship of his father or order him a coffin. He has no time to decide, however, because the old man has already called for Socrates.

Here the *agon* [dispute] of the comedy takes place (889-1104). It is the second of the parts modified by Aristophanes, and so we must again make the distinction clear. The surviving *agon* is a duel between two opposed mentalities, two different ways of life, personified as the Just and the Unjust Reason. The Just, who advocates the old manner of living, is senile and ugly; he has endowed the past with good morals and has brought up the victors of Marathon, but he stinks of mold and outdatedness. The Unjust is young and handsome, bisexual, verbose, impertinent, and rich, because he earns a lot from his sophistries. Their dialogue is not only a battle for supremacy but also a combat to gain the young Pheidippides. It resembles, in its wild fanaticism, the battles to be fought one day between angels and demons for the souls of the dead.

Just Reason enumerates in a lyrical sermon the virtues of ancient education, when youthful beauty was admired and sons respected their fathers. He advises Pheidippides to choose a simple and natural life which is better for health, physical appearance, and character, as well as a pleasure in itself. In spite of this nostalgia for the past, Aristophanes, as [Werner] Jaeger has noted, does not preach a return to bygone days. "He was not a rigidly dogmatic reactionary. But he was living in an age of transition when thoughtful men shrank from being whirled along in a constant stream of innovations, seeing good old things destroyed before they were replaced by something equally good."

Unjust Reason has nothing else to boast about except his ability to make the crooked straight and the unjust just. Yet this ability is all he needs in order to demolish with sophistries the honest arguments of his antagonist. Unlike the sausage-seller (**Knights**) or Aeschylus (**Frogs**), who won their *agons* because they deserved to win, the Unjust Reason wins because he ought *not* to. With this ironic conclusion, Aristophanes makes his satire more piercing.

The outcome of the duel is unexpected and droll; not only does Pheidippides join at once with the Unjust Reason, but also the Just Reason himself, throwing away his investments, declares: "I come with you to become a fairy!" Such is the magic attraction of philosophic deception and moral depravity that, Aristophanes postulates, whatever wise and honest was left in our country was swept away by deceit.

A conventional lapse of time allows Pheidippides to enroll in the school and attend the courses. Meanwhile (1114-30) the chorus tells the audience about the services offered by the Clouds, not so much to sophists, as to vegetation. Then (1145 ff.) Strepsiades and Socrates meet in the street and kiss each other fondly. Our old buffoon is still in agony about how to pay his creditors. The professor calms him down by telling him that his son has graduated from the school with honors and is now a master in deceit. The proud father calls his son, and as soon as he sees him he notices with joy the results of sophistic education in his physiognomy, namely, that "Attic look," the familiar facial expression of the Athenian wise-guy who knows how to find his right by wronging others. Saying good-bye to Socrates, the old man takes the graduate home to celebrate (1212).

The comedy, however, has a tragic conclusion. No sooner have we witnessed how happy Strepsiades is in dispelling his creditors with his sophistic counterattacks, than we see him running out of his house screaming, while his son pursues him with a whip (1321 ff.). The new education has surpassed the old man's expectations. The whole trouble started, he tells us, when he asked his son to sing with the lyre some patriotic melodies of Simonides, whereupon the young man answered, quite cynically, that those were old stuff and, instead, began to sing from Euripides about how a brother and a sister had committed incest. Strepsiades could not prevent himself from swearing at Euripides, and at once Pheidippides started to beat him. The old man now tries to move his son with reminiscences of his childhood—in a parody, we might say, of Clytaemnestra begging Orestes for her life. Yet the well-educated son remains unmoved. Bringing forth solid sophistic arguments, he proves to his father that he has *justly* punished him:

> PH.: When I was a child, didn't you beat me?
>
> ST.: Yes, for your own good, because I loved you.
>
> PH.: Isn't it right then for me to love you and beat you, since beating means loving?
>
> (1409-12)

Exhausted from the *stichomythia,* and from the beating too, the poor Strepsiades raises his arms to heaven and curses his offspring: "May you fall into abysmal Hell along with Socrates and Unjust Reason!" And, like the repenting King David, he asks the true gods to help him punish the school-master.

Here, in the final episode of the play and in the *exodos* [exit] of the chorus, we encounter the third modified passage (1493-1510). The surviving version presents the old man ordering his servants to set fire to the school. Socrates and the students appear amid the flames and smoke coughing. "What are you doing up there on the roof?" the philosopher shouts to the demented old man. And he with savage satisfaction answers, "Airborne, I examine the sun!" The 423 B.C. version, undoubtedly, displayed a more extended final episode. There was a dialogue between Strepsiades and the god Hermes, who came to advise him about the burning. One can also suspect that Socrates' humiliation and downfall were not restricted to a single suffocated cue, and that the exodus of the chorus did not consist of a single line: "Let us go now, we have danced enough for today." The burning of the Socratic precincts must have been one of the basic ingenious ideas of the comic poet. He might even have borrowed it from a real happening: the fire which, according to a legend, destroyed the school of Pythagoras.

Around this performance many anecdotes have grown up. Aelian tells us that Socrates himself was sitting in the theatre and when his "double" appeared in the orchestra, he stood up so that everybody could see at whom the satire was aimed. Plutarch, on the other hand, records a conversation which supposedly took place when the play was over: "Aren't you angry, Socrates?" somebody asked him. To which the philosopher answered: "No, by Zeus; as they tease me at banquets, so they tease me at the theatre."

At that City Dionysia—the first in which Aristophanes appeared after a two-year expulsion—the Clouds met with disaster. It was the most terrible defeat that our playwright had so far experienced, a trauma that he will not easily overcome. Not only had he been spoiled with three victories in four consecutive years, but he also thought of the Clouds as his wisest play to date and the best comedy that the Athenians had ever watched.

All the same, the judgment was not favorable. We gather from the *parabasis* of the Wasps and of the second Clouds that the judges and the public were not yet ready for that kind of intellectual message and so they misunderstood it. Theatre art is like a chariot race; the man who runs faster than all the others has the greatest chance to break his neck (cf. Wasps, 1050). What the true cause of the unfavorable verdict was we shall never know; it will remain a question open to conjectures of all kinds, just as the other two unanswerable questions related to the Clouds: why did the poet attack Socrates and why did he re-write and then apparently not finish the comedy?

Winner of the competition was old Cratinus' Wine Jug (Pytine). This play did not oblige the spectators to worry about the dangers of unorthodox philosophy or meditate on the sophists' good or bad faith. It was an innocent comic allegory on drunkards, easy as wine to swallow. It had the additional interest that the comic hero was the playwright himself in a ruthless self-derisive confession. A few fragments which have survived enable us to restore the plot, supplying plaster where the marble is missing. A middle-aged Athenian, married to Dame Poetry, falls in love with a glamorous prostitute Intoxication; and for her sake he abandons his home. His legal wife goes to court. Her complaint is that "in days gone by he cared only for me and didn't have an eye for tarts; but now in his old age Intoxication has made him a different man." Up to this point the comedy refers to well-known events: it is the old

Cratinus, pub-crawler and derelict, twice beaten by Aristophanes, and, as his young rival has said, "wandering around with his laurel crown withered, a prey to his thirst for wine" (*Knights,* 533-34). The comedy, however, proceeds to future miracles. The friends of the comic hero break all his jugs and pitchers and oblige him to return to a dry and virtuous life. The poor man protests: "When you drink water, you think of nothing wise." Nevertheless, much against his will, he returns to his lawful wife Poetry.

The dramatic denouement is repeated in real life. The comedy's victory revived the ancient Cratinus and his withered laurels blossomed again. We might note that, contrary to Euripides, who, in his last tragedy, will return to the worship of Bacchus, Cratinus, in his last comedy, becomes a renegade to the wine-god. The paradoxical conclusion of this play is that only water brings real inspiration.

The *Wine Jug* must have been Cratinus' last comedy, for there is some vague information that the old playwright left this world soon after his artistic restoration. Let us add that one of the fragments contains the well-known invective on Aristophanes:

> "Who are you?" a smart spectator might have asked. "A subtle word-mincer, epigram-chaser, Euripidaristophanizer!"

It seems that the judges, acclaiming the old poet at the expense of a younger one, did no more than put into practice Aristophanes' own preaching. Had he not always, in fact, stressed the Just Reason of the old and the Unjust Reason of the young? Now his own whip was turned against him and slashed him. We might also say that, in the event of the *Clouds'* failure, there was mutual benefit to both Cratinus and Socrates. Unknown to them, each one brought about the rightful rehabilitation of the other.

Thus, among the crowds leaving the Dionysus theatre on that spring evening, there walked a happy old man and an unhappy young one. And, somewhere in the distance, a barefoot philosopher strode blithely toward the river Ilissus. (pp. 105-25)

> *Alexis Solomos, "The 'Clouds' and Socrates,"*
> *in his* The Living Aristophanes, *translated by*
> *Alexis Solomos and Marvin Felheim, The University of Michigan Press, 1974, pp. 105-25.*

FROGS

CRITICAL COMMENTARY

John Vaio   (essay date 1985)

[*In the following excerpt, Vaio describes the themes and structure of the two plots of* Frogs—*long considered unrelated and discordant—and demonstrates their interrelatedness. Through the interplay of the plots, he notes,*

"Aristophanes suggests the close relation between dramatic art and the moral and political concerns of the city-state."]

A kaleidoscopic whirl of time, place, and action is endemic to Aristophanic comedy. From Athens to Heaven or Hell is the matter of a few words and gestures. No illusionistic scenery constrained the playwright's invention. No French schoolmaster of the seventeenth century was stationed in the Theater of Dionysus to impose the allegedly Aristotelian unities on the recalcitrant comic poet. Nor was Monsieur [Eugène] Scribe there to urge the canons of the "well-made play." Consistent and logical development of dramatic action was not the artistic goal of that untrammeled spirit. In his plays the plot may change suddenly and unexpectedly at any moment. The surprising and the inconsequent were the stock in trade of Aristophanes and his fellow craftsmen, who reveled in illogicality, as did their audience, a keen-witted band capable of following and enjoying the most intrepid zigging and zagging of the comic fantasts.

So protean a drama has often perplexed classical scholars, not least of all in the case of *Frogs,* a play seemingly concocted out of two distinct dramatic ideas—two separate plots, in effect. This bipartite dramatic structure is the great literary problem of the play and raises important questions of Aristophanic technique, which are the main subject of this paper. But first a brief resumé of the action is in order.

The divine patron of ancient drama, Dionysus, is going straight to Hell to fetch back Euripides. The god is a fanatical devotee and must retrieve his favorite playwright. The collection of hacks left in Athens is just too much to bear. So off to Herakles' house to ask half-brother, a notorious Underworld traveler, how to get there. The action of the first part of the play (lines 1-673) follows consistently from this premise. The divine voyager meets a few surprises on his way, but nothing that varies from the dramatic idea of the prologue, Dionysus' journey to Hades to bring back Euripides.

The action, interrupted at line 674 by the parabasis, begins again at 738, but with a completely new premise. Aeschylus, of whom not a word in part I, has previously occupied the throne of honor as the greatest tragic poet but is now being challenged by Euripides. Pluto will hold a contest to decide between the two, and Dionysus, as god of the dramatic festivals, is chosen as judge. From line 738 to line 1413 there is no reference to the dramatic premise of part 1.

Such reference occurs, however, at lines 1414 ff., but with a surprising and significant change. Dionysus refuses to pass judgment and is reminded by Pluto of his purpose in going to Hades. The former then restates that purpose as follows: "I made my descent here after a poet . . . in order that Athens might be saved and continue to hold her dramatic festivals."

This revised statement of intent motivates the quiz on foreign policy that follows. But some fifty lines later Euripides reminds Dionysus of an oath he swore to bring *Euripides,* not merely "a poet," back home. Dionysus does not deny this, but chooses Aeschylus anyway. God and victor then depart to save Athens amidst general rejoicing.

How might one account for the discontinuity of dramatic plan and the illogicalities of the penultimate scene? One theory (still maintained in influential circles) holds that *Frogs* is a hastily and haphazardly concocted farrago of two independently conceived plots, intended for two separate plays. This view, however, presupposes canons of dramatic consistency and logical development of action that disappear before the evidence of the other extant plays. *Frogs* is a single comedy built on two distinct, but not incompatible, dramatic ideas, combined in a manner that can be paralleled in other Aristophanic works. Moreover, the presence on stage of the protagonist in both parts of the play is itself an important unifying factor. Here one may compare Philocleon in *Wasps.*

But for the critic of philosophical spirit there had to be a deeper unity. Matters religious and mythological implicit in the play were explored to produce an interpretation of stupendous metaphysical solemnity. In place of Aristophanes' protagonist, a genial but cowardly aesthete, there emerges a Dionysoparsifal, virtually an antique clone of Wagner's hero. Gone is the jovial jokesmith who uses Aeschylus' exposition of the true nature of dramatic art as the foil for his clownish wit. He is wholly submerged into a character of deep seriousness that develops inwardly from the shallow aestheticism of the opening scenes to the perfect wisdom and understanding of the final exaltation.

What develops in *Frogs* is not a character (symbolic or otherwise), but a theme. And that theme may be briefly stated: tragic drama cannot be judged on aesthetic criteria alone. Of greater importance is the social, moral, and political "message" of these plays and its probable effect on the lives of the citizens of Athens.

My purpose here is to suggest that the ethical and civic value of tragedy, the central theme of the second part of *Frogs,* is introduced and partly developed in the opening scenes of the play. It would be useful then to begin our inquiry by examining this theme as it is presented in the later scenes, where it informs and determines the action on stage at the beginning and at the end of the Great Contest.

The first full statement of the theme in question occurs in the second half of the *agôn,* which begins the Great Contest—the first round (as it were) of the battle of poetic champions. Euripides has just completed his indictment of Aeschylean tragedy: the charges included bombastic trickery, unintelligibility, and detachment from reality (lines 907-79).

Aeschylus replies by cross-examining his rival (lines 1006 ff.). "What," he asks, "is the proper reason for admiring a poet?" Euripides answers that a poet ought to be admired for his cleverness and the moral instruction he gives the people in the cities. Aristophanes has thus obviously and ruthlessly set up the hapless Euripides to be hoist with his own petard.

For Aeschylus proceeds to show how the true poet encourages and improves civic morality and how the false poet corrupts it (lines 1013-17). The former makes men worthy citizens, noble, patriotic—full of martial spirit. Compare these to the products of the counterfeit playwright: morally worthless rascals who loaf about the marketplace and desert their city in time of crisis.

And who are the models for the true poet's heros? The great warriors of Homer's epics, lion-hearted men like Patroclus and Teucer, represented on stage to inspire every citizen to emulate their example of martial courage (lines 1042-44). The false poet, on the other hand, litters his plays with whorish adultresses, harbingers of suicidal trauma for noble Athenian matrons (1049-51). He dresses kings in rags and so teaches wealthy citizens how to avoid income tax by crying poor (1063-66). He turns the youth from the good old education of the wrestling schools by inspiring them with a desire for the new rhetoric. And what is the result? Sailors talk back to their commanders instead of obeying them unquestioningly (1069-74).

Aeschylus ends his condemnation with grotesque but amusing exaggeration (1078-88). By representing pimps on stage, women giving birth in temples, and sisters sleeping with their brothers, by uttering such paradoxes as "to live is not to live," Euripides has filled the city with a gang of bureaucrats and clownish politicians who act like monkeys, all bent on deceiving the people. And the last, heinous crime? Why, since the people don't exercise, there's no one able to run in the ritual torch races anymore! In short, political and private morality in all its forms is the province of the poet-teacher. And his dramas are to be judged by determining their effect on this morality.

Apart from a brief passage (1301-8) in which Aeschylus accuses his rival of swiping melodies from the songs of whores—we see Euripides' muse, a tart so ugly that even irrumation is out of the question—the rest of the contest (some three hundred lines) does not directly take up questions of morality, but is concerned with matters of style, melody, rhythm, and finally the sheer weight of words.

Aeschylus has had the final word in the *agôn* and in the parts of the contest that followed. But Dionysus hesitates to pass judgment and has to be reminded by Plato that unless he does so, he will not achieve his purpose in going to Hades (1411 ff.). Here two points deserve notice. First, the motivation for Dionysus' reluctance—he doesn't want to make an enemy of either poet—is employed by Aristophanes primarily to restate the central theme of lines 1006-98. Dionysus' judgment will now be based ostensibly on the poets' direct political advice to Athens.

Second, Dionysus' reason for going to Hades has changed significantly since the prologue. "Come, learn this from me," says the wine-god to the rival poets. "I came down for a poet. What was my purpose? In order that the city might be saved and go on holding dramatic festivals. So the poet I intend to take back with me shall be the one who is likely to give the city some good advice" (1415-21). Dionysus then proceeds to solicit their opinions on a major political question: what to do about Alcibiades—a far cry from the god's purely aesthetic and Euripidean longings in the prologue.

What has happened? Has Dionysus' association with Aeschylus reawakened an old fondness, which prompts the god to accept the view that the poet teaches his city political and moral wisdom? . . . Or may we say that the god's growing awareness of his own identity has given him a deeper understanding of the genre over which he presides? Careful examination of Dionysus' remarks made during the contest (895-1410) commends neither view. For example, during the long recitative in which Aeschylus criticizes Euripides' plays for their immorality (1006-98) the god only twice comments seriously on the discussion (1012, 1023 f.), and in the second of these instances he *criticizes* Aeschylus sharply for the effect of his militaristic drama; otherwise Dionysus amuses himself (and presumably the audience) with peripheral jokes and side remarks (esp. 1036-38, 1089-98).

What Aristophanes has done is to combine two elements of his play—the initial dramatic idea (the descent into Hades to bring back a specific dramatic poet) with the central theme of the *agôn* (the importance of the moral and political content of tragedy). Dionysus thus suddenly becomes the principal exponent of this theme. The resulting change in the god's purpose is not in itself inexplicable, but no attempt to explain it is made by Aristophanes, who neither raises the question nor explicitly resolves it. Dramatic logic and consistent characterization are not primary concerns of Old Comedy. And here they take second place to the poet's desire to restate the theme of lines 1008-89 in the person of the protagonist.

The final test concerns the poet's political sagacity and rounds out the picture of tragedy presented in the half-serious, half-ridiculous contest that is the second part of **Frogs.** Aesthetic criteria based on formal considerations of style, melody, rhythm, and dramaturgy are not sufficient for sound judgment of the art of tragedy: the content as well as the form of poetic drama must be examined to determine the poet's influence on the moral and political life of his fellow citizens.

Aeschylus is the poet chosen by Dionysus to return to the world of the living and bring renewed life to Athens: within terms of **Frogs** he emerges as the true poet and potential saviour of his city, the embodiment of the social and political importance of drama (esp. 1482-1515).

We shall now examine the first part of **Frogs** to determine whether the text supports the thesis of this paper, namely, that the central theme of part 2 (the importance of the moral and political content of tragedy) is introduced and developed in part 1, thus establishing a thematic link between the two dramatically separate sections of the play.

We begin with the meeting of Dionysus and Herakles in the prologue (35-165). Here we learn that Dionysus is going to Hell to bring back Euripides, so great is his desire for that cleverest of poets. The tragedians left on earth are all mere hacks, according to their divine patron. There's not a creative artist left capable of truly noble utterance. "What do you mean by 'creative'?" asks the dull-witted lion tamer. "This is what I mean," explains his patient half-brother. "I mean the kind of poet who can write a bold and audacious phrase, something like this." He then goes on to cite three examples. First, "O Ether, bungalow of Zeus"—a comic distortion of a phrase taken from Eu-

ripides' *Melanippe the Wise.* Second, "Time's foot" (taken from *Alexander*). The third example is a prosaic rendering of a notorious phrase from *Hippolytus:* "My tongue has sworn; my mind remains unsworn." Fairly or not, the phrase was criticized as a glaring example of Euripides' immorality, in this case the justification of perjury. Dionysus' notion of a clever and creative poet appears based mainly on considerations of style and manner. At least he makes no comment here on moral content.

The moral question, is, however, raised implicitly first by Dionysus himself some thirty lines earlier and then by Herakles at 103 ff. At 78 ff., when asked why he does not bring Sophocles back rather than Euripides, Dionysus answers as follows. (1) He wants to see if Sophocles' son can write without his father's help. And (2) since Euripides is a versatile rogue (πανουργοσ), he would be ready to join the god in escaping from Hades. Compare 1520 f. at the end of the play, where Euripides, defeated and discredited, is called "rogue" (πανουργοσ), as well as "liar" (ψευδολογοσ) and "buffoon" (βωμολοχοσ). Thus already at 80-81 we have a hint at Euripides' immorality.

At 102, in reply to Dionysus' citations from Euripides mentioned above, Herakles asks, "Do you like this stuff?" and is rudely dismissed as a boor incapable of aesthetic judgment. But Herakles' objections to Euripides are of interest to us, if not to his half-brother. (1) The kind of poetic conceit that Dionysus is so fond of is "down-right humbug" (104). The Greek word, κοβαλα ("knavish tricks"), implies that such ideas do actual harm. Compare lines 1014 f., where the products of the false poet are κοβαλοι, "impudent and mischievous imps," as well as διαδρασιπολιται, αγοραιοι, and πανουργοι.

Herakles' second objection serves further to suggest that Dionysus' taste is morally questionable: the *bons mots* selected from Euripides are "utterly and completely rotten" (106). The key word, παμπονηροσ, is ambiguous and may refer to the manner as well as the morals of Euripides' verse. It is on both counts that Euripides loses the contest in part 2.

Thus the aesthetician of tragedy, who enjoys Euripides' contrived and immoral verse, is contrasted with the crude but morally straight embodiment of the sterner virtues of an earlier heroic age. The central theme of the Great Contest is set in motion early in the play and is further developed some forty lines later in Herakles' description of Hades' mud and ever-flowing crap, wherein miserable sinners lie in perpetual punishment (145 ff.).

And who are these malefactors? Men who violated the law of hospitality. Men who enjoyed the services of a young hustler, then absconded with the money owed the unlucky youth. Other sinners are mother-beaters, sons who struck their fathers, or men who swore false oaths. . . .

With the exception of the outhustled hustler, all these represent infractions of serious moral taboos of Greek society. But Herakles' list does not end here. Completing the roll call of sinners against common morality and emphasized by his position at the conclusion of the list is the man who sinned not against the moral code, but against the aesthetic canons of poetic taste, the man who so loved the wretch-

Antique vase illustration of a scene from Frogs.

ed verse of the incompetent tragic poet Morsimus as to have an entire speech copied out for his own delectation (151).

The line is an example of two standard comic devices: incongruity and the unexpected. But in view of the questions of literary judgment raised only forty lines earlier, we should not dismiss this as mere comic mannerism. The aesthetic sinner shares the same fecal bath as his moral counterparts. No distinction is made between them regarding their punishment. They are judged alike, and their juxtaposition points the way to the later criticism of drama on ethical as well as stylistic grounds.

This interpretation is strengthened by another important passage occurring two hundred lines later. But let us first consider Dionysus' remark capping Herakles' allusion to Morsimus. "By the gods!" exclaims their kinsman, "you ought to add one more to your list of sinners. The man who has learned a war-dance by Kinesias" (152 f.). The allusion is to avant-garde innovations in choreography, rhythm, and melody that threaten to corrupt the stately refinement of earlier lyric poetry.

Another artistic sinner is thus added by the divine aesthete to join Morsimus and the moral peccants in the foul and fecal mire of Hell. More grist for our thematic mill—but not out of character for Dionysus either, since he is hypercritically opposed to ultramodern tendencies in tragedy (92 ff.).

Herakles continues his description of the Underworld by depicting the blessed band of Initiates who will direct Dio-

nysus on his way to Pluto's door: saints instead of sinners, the divine breath of flutes instead of the foul stench of feces and mud. The Initiates are the main chorus of the play, and it is their leader's address to the audience at lines 354 ff. that concerns us.

Whatever the precise religious nature of their cult (or cults, for that matter), it is clear from the text of the parodos that the chorus introduces several ideas connected with ancient mystery religions, ideas of great importance to this play. These include the hope of a blissful existence after death, which awaits initiates who have led a moral and pious life on earth (454 ff.). These ideas are explicitly and emphatically stated (or rather sung) in the parados, and their relevance to the contest of part 2 (with its moral concerns) and to Aeschylus' return to life requires no further discussion here. We merely note that the symbolic value of the religious beliefs represented and enunciated by the chorus renders any of their pronouncements of particular importance.

Let us now turn to 354 ff., a "half-serious, half-jesting imitation of the proclamation made before the beginning of mystic ceremonies to warn all who were uninitiated or impure to keep out of the way."

A common feature of Old Comedy is that its characters (including the chorus) frequently acknowledge the fact that they are performing a comic drama in the Theater of Dionysus, as distinct from their roles within the play itself. Thus the chorus functions explicitly on two levels: as a chorus of religious initiates within the drama and as a comic chorus outside it. Both aspects are exploited in the passage we shall now examine.

Who are the profane who must keep far off from the chorus, that is, the band of initiates and at the same time the chorus in our comedy? The list begins as follows: whoever has no experience of such words (as the chorus will utter) or is not pure in judgment, or has neither seen the rites of the noble muses nor danced in them; whoever has not been initiated into the Bacchic rites of the tongue of bull-eating Cratinus or enjoys vulgar, clownish jokes which occur out of their proper place (354-58).

Aristophanes' technique here is to vary certain religious formulae and apply them to the just appreciation of comedy. The lines refer directly to the experience and discernment of a true judge of comic drama, while never losing their distinct religious overtones. Thus purity of judgment refers primarily to the unbiased and clear intellect needed to judge comedy. But at the same time the ethical connotations in this context are unmistakable and not irrelevant to the task of literary criticism.

Again, Cratinus is a grand old poet of a bygone era as opposed to the hacks of today, pilloried by Dionysus at the beginning of the prologue. To have seen his comedies was to be *initiated* ($\epsilon\tau\epsilon\lambda\epsilon\sigma\theta\eta$, 357) into "the Bacchic rites of his tongue," that is, plays produced at Bacchus' festival. And lest we forget, Cratinus used that noble tongue to soak up a lot of wine in his day. And Bacchus is none other than the god who calls himself "Dionysus, son of wine-jar" (22). Finally, the great comedian is called "bull-devourer," a cultic epithet of Dionysus, here used probably to refer to the vigor and crudeness of Cratinus' old-fashioned verse.

The cunning verbal shifts employed by Aristophanes to clothe the product of his art in the mystic robes of high religion is partly comic hocus-pocus. But the implication that drama itself may represent the most profound beliefs of that religion, beliefs enunciated by the chorus soon after this passage—namely, salvation for the city and its citizens guided by and striving for the highest moral standards—is made explicit near the beginning of the contest in part 2 and again at the end of the play.

The list of the profane, forbidden to join the choral dance, does not end with those who have not the pure understanding of the mysteries of true comedy. The coryphaeus proceeds to add a long list of political offenders: the man who does not try to end factional strife, or is not good-natured toward his fellow citizens, or promotes and encourages party strife for personal gain, or solicits bribes in office during a national crisis, or exports contraband to the enemy or persuades a foreign power to aid that enemy (359-65).

The technique is like that of the earlier passage in which aesthetic malefactors were plunged into the same hellish mire as their moral counterparts. Here the crimes are political, added to the list of unfortunates who cannot behold the mystic revelations of drama. Thus ethical, artistic, and political motifs are combined through juxtaposition and

interconnection, and look ahead to the criticism of drama in the second part of the play.

The association of crimes against the state with faults of artistic appreciation continues at 366 with another blast against the malefactor of 152 f., the lyric poet Kinesias. The latter is not named, but is probably to be identified with the wretch excluded from the comic mysteries for pouring diarrhoetic offerings over the shrines of Hecate, while leading the music of dithyrambic choruses. Given the corrupt musical tendencies of this miserable victim of gastric distress, we have here a glaring example of gross impiety and simultaneously of bad art—a lapse (may we say?) of taste and waste.

The final victim of choral exclusion combines both political and dramatic motifs. He is the politician lampooned by the comic poet, who actually dares assault the high person of comedy's self by reducing the amount of the prizes awarded the poets (367 f.). Note that the dramatic festivals are here called "the mystic rites of Dionysus celebrated by our fathers." Again the language and religious connotations of the mysteries are grafted onto drama.

To sum up: The implications of Herakles' brief criticism of Euripidean conceits—that they are morally suspect and dangerous—are further developed in the description of the Stygian sea of mire and *merde* [excrement], where the immoral and the inartistic meet the same malodorous fecal fate. The next stage in this developing combination of motifs is the proclamation of the leader of the mystic chorus. Here the inartistic are placed on the same profane level as political criminals who threaten the stability of the state. Motifs of false dramatic art, immorality, and political perversion have been brought together by the dextrous manipulation of various comic devices. In this way Aristophanes suggests the close relation between dramatic art and the moral and political concerns of the city-state. The nature and significance of this relation is the sum and substance of the later scenes: the great contest for the throne of dramatic poetry leading to the victory of Aeschylus.

Frogs is admittedly a play that falls into two parts, each based on a different dramatic idea, in effect, a play with two plots, which though not contradictory are never clearly combined in the action. But if in such a play important motifs are introduced and developed in the early scenes and later explicitly and fully related to one another in such a way as to determine the action of the end, then a significant link between both parts has been established. And coherence of theme may be seen as one constructive element in the poetic technique of a dramatist who consciously and openly disavows logical coherence of action. (pp. 91-101)

John Vaio, "On the Thematic Structure of Aristophanes' 'Frogs'," in Hypatia: Essays in Classics, Comparative Literature, and Philosophy, *William M. Calder III, Ulrich K. Goldsmith, and Phyllis B. Kenevan, eds., Colorado Associated University Press, 1985, pp. 91-102.*

LYSISTRATA

CRITICAL COMMENTARY

Gilbert Murray   (essay date 1933)

[*In the following excerpt, Murray comments on Lysistrata, focusing on its themes, the characterization of
Lysistrata herself, and on the play's reliance on tradition. Murray concludes that Aristophanes's comedy is a
great play, as it makes "its appeal not to laughter alone
but also to deeper things than laughter."*]

The *Lysistrata* was acted in the early spring of 411 B.C.
(February?) and was therefore composed in the atmosphere of the previous year. The Sicilian catastrophe of
413 B.C. had filled the city with consternation, so Thucydides tells us. Athens had lost her army, her ships, and the
flower of her youth; her treasure was nearly exhausted,
and she looked in vain for new sources of strength. The
allies one by one began to revolt and to join the Spartans:
Euboea, Lesbos, Chios, Erythrae went over to the enemy,
and afterwards Miletus and Rhodes. The Persian satrap
Tissaphernes also had just made a military alliance with
Sparta. Faced with this desperate situation, the Athenians
were cool and resolute. They built up painfully a fleet of
100 ships and a fair army, and one by one began recapturing the revolted cities. Athens was not yet conquered; by
410 B.C. indeed she had regained the command of the sea;
but the strain must have been terrible. The oligarchical
government of the Four Hundred began proposing rather
futile terms to Agis for a permanent peace, which of
course was much harder to obtain in present conditions
than it had been in 421 B.C. It was now that Aristophanes
made one last half-farcical half-tragic appeal.

A strange idea came to him. The times were not normal.
The strain of war and the heavy mortality seem to have
produced that spirit of feverish licence and pleasure-
seeking which often accompanies the shedding of much
blood. London, Paris, Vienna and Berlin knew it in the
late war. Historians have described its excesses in the
French Revolution and in the plague of Naples, to take
only two instances out of many. 'What sensible thing are
we women capable of doing?' asks Cleonîkê in this play;
'we do nothing but sit about with our paint and lipsticks
and transparent gowns and all the rest of it' (42 ff.). 'If this
were a festival of Bacchus or Aphrodite, instead of a serious peace meeting', says Lysistrata, 'it would be impossible to squeeze through the crowd; but now there is nobody
here!' Later on, when continence is required of them, they
break down: when they do take the resolve, they soon
begin to fall away from it. 'Our whole sex is a mass of lust'
(ωσ παγκαταπυγον ημετερον απαν γενοσ), says
Lysistrata in her wrath, though there is never any suggestion that men are better. It is taken for granted that they
are not. It was the same, doubtless, with all Athens: the
reaction from the strain and disappointment of the great
war left a deep and lasting mark.

Aristophanes, heavy-hearted for once and almost bitter,
has the thought that these very lusts might be made an instrument to save Athens. Let the women use the cosmetics
and scents and transparent gowns and the like as means
to get mastery over the men and compel them to stop the
war! 'If they do not stop it', says Lysistrata (33 ff.), 'the
alternative is clear—there will be no Peloponnesians left'
('I should not mind that', says her hearer), 'no Boeotians,
and as for Athenians . . . but I say no more.'

Gradually the women gather. It has been difficult for them
to come: one was attending to her husband, who was starting for the war; another to the servants; others doing various things to the children, washing, feeding, putting to
sleep and the like (16-19). Lysistrata and her friend Cleonîkê are there first; then Myrrhinê, a little frivolous; then
others; then at last Lampito from Sparta, brown with the
sun and 'strong enough to choke an ox'. With her come
women from the other enemy states, Corinth and Thebes.
They have come together to hear Lysistrata's great secret
plan for stopping the war, and are prepared to accept it
whatever it is. They will do anything. They will gladly die
or cut themselves in pieces if only the war can be stopped.
At last Lysistrata—the name is a real Greek name and
means 'Dismisser-of-armies'—explains her plan. Men
cannot live without women; let the women refuse to have
any intercourse with men until the war stops. There is a
painful silence. Then a voice: 'I can't do it. Let the war go
on.' 'Nor I; let the war go on.' 'Anything else you like,
dear Lysistrata, but not that. There is nothing else like it.'
The Spartan woman has not spoken. Lysistrata turns to
her and beseeches her help. If they two stand together. . . . 'Difficult, by the Twin Gods,' says the Spartan in
her strong Doric; 'but . . . all right! We must have peace.'
The two strong wills are enough. The others follow and
a great oath is taken. The women swear, not over a shield,
like the heroes in the *Seven Against Thebes,* but over a
great basin of wine—that beverage, one part wine, and
three parts water, which was the Athenian woman's substitute for tea. Just as the ceremony ends, a loud *Ololûgê,*
or Woman's cry of Joy, in the distance tells them that their
colleagues, the Old Women, have seized the Acropolis.

There is a tension of feeling in the writing, and a closeness
to tragedy in the circumstances, which would have been
fatal to a Comedy if they had been consistently carried
through. That would never do. The play must be a farce,
and since the feast is a phallic festival, it follows that the
style of joke is determined. The play is, of necessity, indecent and more than indecent. The *phallus erectus* is treated
as a kind of symbol, standing for all the thwarted desires
and expectations that would arise in men alienated from
their womankind.

To resume the story: on hearing of the seizure of the
Acropolis a Chorus of Old Men—tough Marathonian vct-
erans of the sort that Aristophanes loves—arrive on the
scene with wooden logs and fire to burn the women out,
but are confronted by a Chorus of Old Women with pails
of water, ready to defend their friends. After a quarrel in
which the Old Men are drenched with water, there enters
a Proboulos, or Commissioner, with four Scythian policemen, whom he orders to force the gates and arrest Lysistrata. She comes out to parley, and the Commissioner
calls on a policeman to seize her forthwith. At this there

appears another woman, and another and another and another, till the police are outnumbered. The Commissioner none the less insists on making an attack—the attack and defence forming a mimetic dance for the Chorus. Repulsed with loss, he consents to parley, and demands an explanation. 'Why have they seized the Acropolis?' Lysistrata explains. They want to get possession of the Treasure in the Parthenon, so that the war cannot be carried on, and the Women may save Athens . . . and you yourself. 'But I don't want to be saved!' cries the Commissioner. 'You will be, all the same.' 'But what have you women to do with war or peace?' 'I will tell you,' says Lysistrata, and proceeds to describe the previous state of things.

> You never allowed us to utter a sound,
> But you needn't imagine, for that,
> That our thoughts were content. We watched
>   what you did
> From the quiet rooms where we sat,
> And perhaps we would hear of mistakes you had
>   made
> In some first-class public affair.
> Then, pain in my heart and a smile on my lips,
> I would ask with an innocent air,
> 'Did the peace-offer come to the Council to-day?
> And what was it settled to do?
> And will the decree be inscribed on the stone?'
> 'Be off! That's nothing to you,'
> Said my husband. 'You just hold your tongue.'
>   So I held it.
>
> A WOMAN: I wouldn't have held mine!
>
> COMMISSIONER: You would!
> Or else you'd have used it for screaming, my lass!
>
> LYSIS: I held it! I quite understood.
> Then later, perhaps, when a rumour arrived
> Of some still stupider act,
> I might ask: 'What made them, my love, do a
>   thing
> Which seems so perfectly cracked?'
> At once he looked up at me under his brows:
> 'Attend to your spindle', he said,
> 'And remember that War is the business of men,
> Or you'll soon have a pain in your head.'
>
> COMM: A thoroughly sensible husband you had!
>
> LYSIS: Is it sensible, never to take
> The advice of a friend, and never confess
> When you know you have made a mistake? . . .
> Well, years went by, and we heard in the street,
> One day, two gossiping men;
> 'Not a fighting-man left in the place', said the
>   first;
> 'Not one', said the other. So then,
> We saw it was up to the women, at last,
> To muster their forces and cope
> With the plague that was ruining Hellas. Why
>   wait?
> If we waited, what was there to hope? . . .

Up to this point there is no mistaking the underlying seriousness of Lysistrata's tone: then comes the inevitable turn towards farce and even 'Knock-about'.

> So now, if you're ready to listen in turn,
> And accept the good counsel we give,
> And stay perfectly silent, we'll save you perhaps,

> And, with all your faults, help you to live.
>
> COMM: Our faults! *You'll* save us, you? Nonsense, I say,
> And unbearable nonsense!
>
> LYSIS: Keep still!
>
> COMM: Keep still and let you do the talking, you
>   jade?
> Not I. Strike me dead if I will!
> And you in a veil!
>
> LYSIS: Would a veil of your own
> At all help you? You've only to ask it.
> If that's the objection, that's making you frown,
> There; wrap it well over, and pull it well down,
> And then you'll be silent! . . . And take as a
>   crown
> On top, this elegant basket.

Veiled and 'with his head in a bag', the Commissioner is reduced to silence, while Lysistrata announces her programme. If Erôs and Aphrodite give aid, her women will stop the war. First, they will put an end to the men's foolish habit of going to the market in armour, buying fish or cabbage or figs with a spear and a Gorgon shield, and terrifying the old women who keep the stalls. Then the women will take up the whole tangle of public affairs and treat it as they treat their balls of wool: wash out the mere dirt, pick off the burrs, smooth out the bits that get together in lumps, and then unite all together—citizens, resident aliens, foreigners who are friendly, and those Athenians who have been disfranchised—in one general skein of Good Will.

> COMMISSIONER: It is really too much! With
>   their balls
>   and their skeins
> These creatures think themselves clever.
> You have nothing whatever to do with the War;
> Just remember that!
>
> LYSIS: Nothing whatever?
> Why, it falls upon us twice as hard. What about
> The sons whom we bear in our pain
> And send to the armies?
>
> COMM: Ah, no more of that;
> Don't stir old sorrows again.
>
> LYSIS: And then, at the time when youth is at
>   brim,
> In the crown and flower of our lives,
> We lie all alone, with our men at the wars.
> And it's not so bad for the wives,
> But it's hard on the girls, sitting there in their
>   rooms,
> Growing older, day after day.
>
> COMM: But, bless us, men also grow old!
>
> LYSIS: Yes, of course,
> But quite in a different way.
> The man who returns, though his hair may be
>   grey,
> Can at once get a maiden for mate.
> But a woman's hour is short; it is gone
> As she grasps at it, just too late.
> No one will come for her. There she must sit
> Taking omens, while twilight is falling!

COMM: (*complacently*). Come, a stout old man
with a leg and an eye. . . .

LYSIS: (*exploding*). Oh, why don't you die? I can
never think why!
There is not too much time with your coffin to
buy,
And the honey-cake—I'll come and knead it.

ANOTHER: I'll tie
The funeral ribbons all round you!

ANOTHER: And I
Bring the gifts for the grave, some wet and some
dry!

LYSIS: What more do you want? The boat waits
for you; fly!
Bestir yourself! Charon is calling!

It is not easy to make out exactly all the elaborate 'business' that is intended here. Evidently Lysistrata loses all patience, and the poor Commissioner, who had felt so young and bridegroom-like the moment before, goes off, with funeral bands tied round his body and funeral libations poured over his head, to show his outraged person to the authorities. There is a short choral Agôn, or Strife, between the Old Men and the Old Women, when Lysistrata returns in anxious thought. Her troops, it seems, are of poor material. The women have, apparently, been about five days in the Acropolis, and some are beginning to desert. She has caught three or four already, and now there are others. One of them remembers that she has left a lot of wool out where the moths will get it, another is anxious about a silk robe, another expects her confinement and cannot stay on the Acropolis because she has been frightened by the sacred Snake! Lysistrata firmly turns them back, comforts them with an oracle, and locks them in. The two Choruses then tell stories at each other. 'There was once', say the men, 'a hero called Melanion, who hated women, and went to the wilderness to avoid them.' 'There was once', answer the women, 'a certain Timon in Athens, who hated men, because he saw what they were like', and so on. At last comes the first sign that the enemy is weakening! A man is seen drawing near. It is Kinêsias, the husband of Myrrhinê, and it is obvious from his appearance why he has come. Lysistrata gives directions to Myrrhinê to lead him on, play with him, madden him and cheat him, and so leaves her. Myrrhinê in a scene of a hundred lines carries out her instructions more than adequately. Kinêsias is easily induced to promise that he will vote for peace, and to repeat his promise. Myrrhinê slips back into the Acropolis and he is left planted. He has scarcely left the scene in lamentation when there appears a Herald from Sparta eager for a Peace Conference. Preliminaries are arranged. Meantime the two hostile Choruses look at each other. The Old Men still strongly disapprove of the Women's conduct, but the Old Women flatter them a little, and rearrange their cloaks, which have fallen off; one man has got an insect in his eye and a woman gets it out for him and wipes his eye, and then—in spite of his protest—kisses him! After this they form one Chorus. We should expect a mocking song, attacking certain individuals, but Aristophanes makes his Chorus say simply that at a time like this they will not speak ill of any one. Recon-

ciliation is what is needed, between parties in Athens itself, as well as between Athens and Sparta.

In the next scene we have the entrance of the Spartan Envoys; the Athenians meet them, but they cannot make terms without Lysistrata. She enters with an allegorical figure, Diallagê, or Reconciliation, who takes Athenian and Spartan by the hand and joins them together. Then Lysistrata speaks. She is a woman, but after all she can think, and she has learnt history and politics in the only way that was open to ordinary people at the time, by listening to the words of her father and her elders. She accuses both Spartans and Athenians of great sin, in forgetting their common religion, gods and altars, and tearing one another like enemies. Do the Spartans not remember how Athens sent Kimôn to help them when they were nearly overthrown by the Messenian Revolt and the earthquake which came at the same time? Do the Athenians not remember how the Spartans sent Cleomenes and delivered Athens from the tyrants? Now let them be reconciled.

'We agree,' say the Spartans; 'though of course we must have Pylos again.' 'Never!' begin the Athenians, when Lysistrata checks them. They ask then for other places in payment for Pylos; the Spartans say 'Not all those!' Lysistrata again intervenes and both agree that the details do not really matter. The Reconciliation is made. The Athenians join their wives, and the Spartans theirs, who seem in some unexplained way to be present—the Old Comedy did not stick at small points of that sort—and the whole concourse goes in to a great banquet . . . materials for which have been secretly saved up by the women out of their allowances. A public banquet was a difficult undertaking in 411 B.C. After a short Chorus the feasters come forth again. The Spartans have been charming; and as for us, says an Athenian, we are so much better all round when we are a little drunk! When sober, we are too clever. We pay no attention to what other people really say but concentrate on discovering their motives for not saying something which they have not said, so that we never can give a straightforward account of any negotiations! A Spartan sings in broad Doric and dances what seems to be a Spartan war-dance in honour of the great deeds done by Athens and Sparta alike against the Persian. There is a procession of Spartans and Athenians, each man with his wife, an Attic hymn, and finally a Spartan hymn ending in an appeal to Athena of the Bronzen House, $\tau\alpha\nu$ $\pi\alpha\mu\mu\alpha\chi\text{o}\nu$, 'the All-warrior' or 'All-daring'.

A curious ending to a Peace Play, if indeed it is the end; though the final note here is not so much a eulogy of the comfort and ease of Peace, such as we had in the *Peace* and the *Acharnians,* as an appeal to the two great Greek Cities, Athens and Sparta, to stand together against all enemies of Hellas instead of working for their own mutual destruction. But probably the last few lines of the comedy are lost.

The message of the play, in any case, is considerably different from that of the *Acharnians* or even the *Peace.* In the *Acharnians* the cry was 'I hate the Spartans as much as you, but this war is senseless and makes every one miserable. Get rid of the war-mongers and fire-brands, and let us return to our farms and enjoy ourselves.' In the *Peace* the chief fire-brands were dead: every city in Greece was sick of war—except some neutrals, who made money by it. One pull, all together, and they can cheat the Gods who wish to destroy them and the politicians and informers who thrive on their sufferings. In the *Lysistrata* things are so dark that it is no good blaming anybody. There is no word against the democrats or the oligarchs, the mob or the conspirators, or even against any individual. They have all done badly; let them say no more about it but hold together. Above all, let them be reconciled with the great and noble enemy, Sparta. The old alliance, the deeds of mutual help, the old songs and choric dances of Sparta, the old steadfast habit and the tradition of heroism are called to mind, and the Spartan ideal set up beside the Athenian. One almost wonders, considering how near Athens was to her final collapse, that Aristophanes should dare to take this tone of free equality towards the enemy. But after all no one knew yet how the war would end. Athens was showing marvellous energy, and had still some big victories to come. She was not yet forced to approach Sparta as a suppliant.

The Old Comedy never takes much trouble with its characters. That was left for Menander and the New Comedy. Aristophanes generally has one central figure, the *scurra senex,* the shrewd and witty Old Man, who mocks at the various shams and impostures that rule the day, while the minor figures are only types. In this play there is no *scurra senex:* Lysistrata herself takes his place. There are women with names, Cleonîkê, Myrrhinê, the Laconian Lampito, who shines out in one scene, and perhaps others: but, except for differences of dialect, it is often not possible for an editor to decide which one is speaking, or even to keep their characters consistent throughout. It seems to be Myrrhinê, for example, who says that her husband has been away in Pylos for seven months (104); yet it is her husband who turns up at 1. 845 with no mention of having been away at all. The one consistent and well-characterized human being in the play is Lysistrata. She has a touch of the heroic. She dominates every group, male or female, in which she finds herself. She is fully in earnest, and ready for all emergencies. When the plenipotentiaries from Athens and Sparta are met, the Leader of the Chorus calls to her:

> Bravest of women, now for you!
> To-day be terrible and weak,
> Daring and timid, proud and meek,
> And ever with resources new!

She reminds one of Peithetairos in the *Birds,* that convincing leader of desperate enterprises. It is noteworthy, also, that her dignity is never compromised, the regular mark of respect which Aristophanes pays to his best heroes. She is never caught flinching or lying or wanting to drink; she has no husband or lover of her own, or, if the 'wife of Lycon' is really she (270), that is all we ever hear of Lycon. Her language is in dignity well above the standard of the other characters. The others, for example, often say innocent things which have indecent double meanings, but not Lysistrata. When she does use a coarse phrase it is a brutal truth rather than a joke. Indeed, Lysistrata herself, like the whole play, illustrates well that curious divided allegiance in the comedian's mind which we have noticed be-

fore. He cannot help admiring the thing he mocks at, or perhaps rather he selects for the object of his laughter the thing that secretly fascinates him: Socrates, who makes the conventional world seem hollow; Euripides, whose verse and ideas haunt his imagination; the women who genuinely and whole-heartedly want peace and who have at least not shown themselves so desperately deluded as the men.

The *Lysistrata* is from time to time produced on the modern stage. There have been performances in London, in Paris, in Boston, and in New York, and recently in Cambridge. People are perhaps fascinated by the idea of doing something which, in the foolish modern euphemism, is called 'daring'. But, apart from their various degrees of 'daringness', such performances achieve little. They lack the two things which make the *Lysistrata* not merely a tolerable but an inspiring work of art. They lack utterly the background of traditional ritual; a ritual to which fertility was the main object of desire, and the phallus the recognized symbol of fertility. Without that background the play becomes consciously obscene instead of simply taking the indecency in its stride. It is hard to think of a modern parallel. But I once knew an English family which had a house full of reproductions of Italian religious pictures, showing the martyrdoms of numerous saints, and brought to it a Chinese nurse. The nurse besought them to take away these pictures: no doubt it was highly desirable that wicked men should be punished, but these punishments were dreadful and the pictures kept her awake at night with fear. To Western Christians the martyrdoms were merely part of a familiar tradition and consequently in no way shocking; to the Chinese woman, unused to the tradition, they came as fresh suggestions and caused a violent shock. She would not hang such pictures on her walls unless she wished to gloat on tortures, nor would a modern author write such a play as the *Lysistrata* unless he wished to revel in τα φαλλικα.

The modern performances suffer also from a greater lack. The *Lysistrata* has behind it much suffering and a burning pity. Aristophanes had more than once risked his civic rights and even his life in his battle for peace, and is now making his last appeal. It is owing to this background of intense feeling that the *Lysistrata* becomes not exactly a great comedy, but a great play, making its appeal not to laughter alone but also to deeper things than laughter. (pp. 164-80)

> *Gilbert Murray, in his* Aristophanes: A Study,
> *Oxford University Press, Inc., 1933, 268 p.*

Jay M. Semel   (essay date 1981)

[*In the following excerpt, Semel discusses Aristophanes's treatment of gender conflict in* Lysistrata, *stating that to the playwright, "sex differentiation is simply a metaphor for human incompletion."*]

Aristophanes' *Lysistrata,* as does most Greek drama, focuses on persons moving in the face of adversity toward a definition of self and social role. Invariably this entails the testing of one's capacity to reconcile individual human desires, passions, and instincts with that combination of abstract principles and pragmatic political expediencies demanded by society for the maintenance and well-being of the State. In *Lysistrata,* the reconciliation is extraordinarily successful: the Peloponnesian War is stopped and Panhellenic unity achieved solely because of the need to satisfy sexual desires. In fact, this self-fulfillment generates a far-reaching harmony leading to the restoration of the family, the polis, the entire Greek world, and finally the gods themselves.

The first lines of the play, which call for "a debauch in honor of Bacchos," immediately underline the constant emphasis on sexuality, and the specific reference to Bacchos—or Dionysus, as he is often known—recalls the context for the performance: the play is given at the Theatre of Dionysus during the Athenian Festival of Dionysus. The festival was a holiday, a time to escape normal routine and responsibility, to revel and drink and dance, and to indulge one's humanity; but here, as in the dramatic process described earlier, individual pleasure led to more noble ends: the festival honored a god, it demonstrated the patriotism of the Athens community, and it ushered in a new season of the year. And the comedies performed as part of the festival incorporated a similar process. On stage, men mocked themselves and the State. They were raunchy and ribald. They played female roles or exaggerated their own maleness by sporting yard-long leather phalluses. However, by the conclusion, the jokes, the mocking, and the grotesqueries would evolve into a reassertion of human value and classical order.

A brief recounting of the myth of Dionysus's origins sheds considerable light, albeit a rather ironic light, on the thematic concerns of *Lysistrata.* Dionysus was a child of the great god Zeus and of the mortal woman Semele. After the baby had been conceived, Semele, encouraged by jealous Hera, demanded that Zeus, who hitherto had remained invisible, expose himself to her. He did reveal his full glory, but the sight of the overwhelming godhead was too much for Semele: legend has it that she was annihilated by the thunderbolt emitted from his presence. Zeus then reached into her remains to retrieve the fetus, and, assuming a maternal role, implanted it in his thigh, finally giving birth to Dionysus when he was full term. Needless to say, the notion of male supremacy, potency, and responsibility embodied in the myth is sharply ridiculed in the drama.

More important than providing cultural or mythic connections, the first lines of the play serve to characterize the nature of women and to define Aristophanes' comic method:

> Women!
> Announce a debauch in honor of Bacchos,
> a spree for Pan, some footing fertility Fieldday,
> and traffic stops—the streets are absolutely clogged
> with frantic females banging on tambourines.
> No
> urging for an orgy!

But *today*—there's not one woman here. Here, Lysistrata, the title figure of the play and the leader of the women's revolt, is complaining about and making fun of her colleagues' concern for the trivial and the physical when more important matters are at hand. Women, who need no urging for an orgy but who are late for a meeting called of all wives of soldiers fighting the war, obviously lack any sense of political responsibility. Of course, under Lysistrata's direction, the women do come and get organized, initiate and emerge victorious from the war of the sexes, and end the Peloponnesian War. But in spite of their triumphs, the women never abandon their original "trivial" interest in sex. All of the incredible diplomatic achievements come only because the women want to make love with their husbands all of the time, and not just when the men are home on furlough.

Much of the drama's humor is founded on the women actually affirming the female stereotype. They never really change into soldiers or politicians; they simply assert their femininity. Lysistrata even goes so far as to tell Kleonike that she would be happy if only they could live up to the slanderous male view of women as sly, deceitful monsters of intrigue. And, significantly, the intrigues she has in mind are necessary to gain human pleasure. The issue at hand is not some vague principle, but something "immense," "pressing," "unthinkably tense," so important that Lysistrata has spent sleepless nights "kneading it, mulling it, filing it down". Similarly, Kleonike advises against the annihilation of the enemy city-state of Boeotia, not out of a sense of diplomacy or even of compassion, but because she enjoys eating the eels that come from there, eels which nicely suggest her sexual interests as well.

To insure a permanent access to eels and to their men, Lysistrata proposes that the women from all over Greece form an alliance to work for peace. Kleonike, doubtful about the enterprise, observes that women lack practicality and wisdom: "There's nothing cosmic about cosmetics—and Glamour is our only talent". But Lysistrata realizes that feminine accoutrements are not a weakness, but a strength: "slippers and slips, rouge and perfumes, negligees and decolletage" can be used in a wise, practical way and can even achieve cosmic results. She then announces her plan to have the women accentuate their womanliness, entice their husbands, and then deny their husbands. And in denying their husbands, the women are rejecting the fragmented lives the war has forced on them. If they cannot have the whole, neither can their men. Lysistrata knows that a married man "wants harmony—cooperation".

The link between womanliness, sexuality, wholeness is the point of that scene which occurs when the women arriving at the meeting inspect each newcomer's body. Lampito's complexion, figure, and bosom are praised; and as she is flatteringly fondled, she is accused of and admits to being healthy and strong enough to strangle a bull. Ismenia arrives and her body becomes representative of her cultivated family and her country. She is the image of picturesque Boeotia; "her verdant meadows, her fruited plain," and "her sunken garden where no grass grows. A cultivated country". In similar fashion, when Lampito says of a Lorinthian girl that "her kinfolk's quality—mighty big back there," Kleonike, inspecting the girl's behind, observes, "She's mighty big back *here*". In short, the women's bodies reflect their strength, their ancestry, and their country. Similarly, the peace ultimately attained in the play will be embodied by a beautiful young woman.

The women, who miss their husbands and realize that lovers are now impossible to come by and that even leather do-it-yourself kits are no longer available, are a little reluctant to give up the little sex they do have when the husbands manage a furlough; but they soon assent whole-heartedly to Lysistrata's scheme. They take an oath swearing to "withhold all rights of access or entrance/from every husband, lover, casual acquaintance"; but unlike the men, who usually slaughter an animal to take a blood oath on their shields, the women use domestic ceramic pots filled with wine. Blood, sacrifices, and shields lead to blood, sacrifice, and war, whereas wine gives human pleasure. And should the women fail, they have no intention of falling on their swords: they'll just settle for drinking water. The scene may poke fun at women who do not lend the proper dignity to serious matters, but its sharpest barb is aimed squarely at the values of men and of a society which considers serious only that which is destructive or painful.

To put it in the proper perspective, the scene is switched to the Temple of Athene at the Akropolis, where a chorus of old women is bravely defending the gates against an on-slaught of old men. The difficulty the men have keeping their torches lit and their logs up comments on their impotency, but the men's assault on the Temple also clarifies the nature of the war they have been fighting over the last several years. Above all, the Peloponnesian War is an attack on Athene and everything she represents. The men have exhausted the treasury there, having used the money for their futile military endeavors. It is a war on Greece, because the combatants are Greek city-states. It is a war against women, for ultimately it is they and their children who have suffered. And, of course, it is a war against the deity Athene, goddess of Wisdom, which is to say the men are fighting a sacrilegious and stupid war.

The men lack the wisdom and the ability to win because in both the battle between the sexes and in the all-encompassing Peloponnesian War (throughout the drama, the little war mirrors and trivializes the big one) they are fighting for the wrong things. The men call out for "victory, male supremacy . . . and a testimonial plaque", while the women pray for salvation "from battles, insanity, Man's inhumanity". This contrast is also reflected in their choice of weapons: whereas the men possess torches and battering rams, the women employ the defensive agent of water contained in household pitchers. The water and pitchers carry obvious sexual overtones, especially as they put out the male torches, but they bear other associations as well. When the old men's leader scoffs at the idea that his fire can be doused, he is answered by his woman counterpart, "You'll see when the facts soak in". A few lines later, she says that she will give him a bath "pure enough for a blushing bridegroom." And when the men are thoroughly inundated, and indignantly inquire what the women think they're doing, the response is: "If you must know, I'm gardening. Perhaps you'll bloom". So the women's weapon—the water—is equated with the truth, the purification of a marriage ceremony, the growth

and fertility of the garden. Certainly these elements are not associated with traditional military spirit, and that's exactly the point. The women's alternative to traditional warfare is not just something silly or pleasant; it is quite effective. The old women win.

In spite of all, the claim is made that the women have no say in civil matters and have no stake in the war. To this, the leader of the women's chorus offers a strong rebuttal: "I hold stock in Athens—stock I paid for in sons". In fact, the women insist that it is they who have borne the greatest burden of the war: their sons have died; the married women have wasted the best years of their lives, and young virgins have had "nothing to do but grow old"; and feasts in honor of Hekate, the goddess of childbirth, have been spoiled.

Demanding an end to the manhandling of government, Lysistrata advises on the best way to set straight the city's affairs, using an elaborate domestic metaphor. Like wool, the city should first be cleansed of the sheep-dip of corruption, its leeches cudgeled, the snarls combed out, and the citizens carded together "in a single basket of common weal and general welfare". Out of this is spun a bobbin of yarn which is woven "without bias or seam, a cloak to clothe the city of Athens". Lysistrata's reducing the operation of government to a household chore deflates the men's immense sense of self-importance; it also makes the crucial point that the best government is an extension of homely virtues and skills, not a denial.

Yet having raised the wool to the high level of state policy, Aristophanes makes certain to bring it down again to a more personal level. And so the symbolic value of the wool is changed from public to pubic. Their political headway suddenly becomes quite unimportant to the women. Mad for men, they try to tunnel under or hoist themselves over the walls. When they are caught, they insist that they are deeply concerned for their wool left at home. Lysistrata understands the suffering involved when one's wool is unspread or one's flax is unpeeled, but she demands the women remain for the duration. Perceiving that the old wool alibi hasn't been particularly successful, another woman pleads that she must get home because she's having a baby. Somewhat skeptical, Lysistrata taps the woman's bulging belly and hears a metallic ring. Undaunted, the woman explains that it is a boy baby; but when her dress is lifted, a bronze helmet is discovered. The interest in wool and babies is a transparent masking of obvious sexual needs; but unless the men begin to recognize the primacy of this need and stop the war, there will remain the terrible frustration, the ruined wool of homelife, the lack of real babies. Boys must stop being bronze-helmeted soldiers and begin to be boys again.

And indeed the men do begin to discover—painfully and obviously—their maleness. Kinesias, bearing an immense erection, calls out desperately to his wife: "I can't hold out much more. / I'd rather be dismembered. / *How long, ye gods, how long?*" Interestingly enough, he uses the same appeals as the women did when they were trying to escape to their men; he brings his son to inspire his wife's maternal instincts; he mentions the wool at home being ruined through disuse; he now sees, as she has seen, how empty life is when a loved one is absent:

> —Life is a husk. She left our home and happiness went with her. Now pain is the tenant. Oh, to enter that wifeless house, to sense that awful emptiness, to eat that tasteless, joyless food—it makes it hard, I tell you.
> Harder all the time.

His wife, Myrrhine, resists his urgings and her urges, tantalizes and teases him, but does not give in. She knows that joy can only be restored to the home when they are all at home all of the time.

But that time is not far off, for a veritable phalanx of men in erectus converge to lament their plight:

> —I've been up for hours. I was up before I was up.
> —And what are you—a man? a signpost? a joint stock company?
> —Hit ain't the heat, hit's the tumidity.
> —The words are different, but the malady seems the same.

Clearly the men are ready to submit; and to satisfy their desires and end their frustrations, they will settle for "peace from any person, at any price". The willingness to stop the Peloponnesian War on such grounds trivializes the men's reasons for starting and continuing the war, but once more there is the strong suggestion that trivial human pleasures are better than bad politics, and that good politics are founded on trivial human pleasures, and that human pleasures are never really trivial.

Therefore when peace comes, it is no mere abstraction, but a strikingly beautiful, stark naked woman who is the literal embodiment of Greece: she serves as a map of the region during the subsequent peace talks. Following a general agreement about the deposition of the land, the Athenian representative has "an urgent desire to plow a few furrows," and the Spartan also feels the need "to work a few loads of fertilizer in". These remarks show that in turning their swords into plowshares, the men will not abandon their sexuality, but simply change its direction. It has become, at least metaphorically, a force associated with the stable and life-giving pursuits of making a home and renewing the earth.

Similarly, the participants agree that the most effective unifying force during the peace talks was the wine consumed. The commissioner has discovered that sobriety and "cold-water diplomacy" caused much mistrust and suspicion, while wine leads to "total pleasure, the free-and-easy / give-and-take of friendship".

If the drama has demonstrated the strength and validity of the women's credo of personal and domestic fulfillment, it has also helped to redefine the traditional concept of masculinity. The phallic weapons—spears, torches, and battering rams—have proved to be at best impossible encumbrances, at worst terrible destructive agents. But if this was the case with phallic symbols, the phallus itself fared no better. Characters with erections did not appear strong or potent or heroic, but frustrated and downright silly. Phallic strength and dignity are contingent upon

consummation; and so in terms of this drama, a man's integrity is achieved when he is at home making love to his woman.

While it is apparent that the couples formed are greater than the sum of their parts, it is equally apparent that the only fully realized individual in the drama is Lysistrata. She is principled, knowledgeable, political. She is articulate and forceful enough to make the women restrain their passions; farsighted enough to realize that the men will not be able to restrain theirs. That she lacks the coarse lust of her colleagues is not a sign of her sterility, but an indication of her self-control and self-contained confidence. Aristophanes leaves her uncoupled in the drama to emphasize this wholeness; and given her single condition, it is significant that the reader cannot, is not even tempted to, categorize her as mannish, maternal, non-feminine. In the drama, the men hail Lysistrata as one who is a totality of qualities:

> Hail, most virile of women! Summon up all your experience:
> Be terrible and tender,
> lofty and lowbrow,
> severe and demure.

As has been stated, sex differentiation is simply a metaphor for human incompletion.

Appropriately, at the play's conclusion all differentiation is abolished. Lysistrata, symbol of individual integrity, oversees action leading to a more comprehensive kind of unity. Imbued with Dionysian spirit and spirits, men embrace their women and their former foes in a ring of Panhellenism and dance and sing in honor of the deities watching over the scene. And the play which began with an urging for an orgy has come full circle to complete harmony. (pp. 28-36)

> *Jay M. Semel, "Sexual Humor and Harmony in 'Lysistrata'," in* CLA Journal, *Vol. XXV, No. 1, September, 1981, pp. 28-36.*

WASPS

CRITICAL COMMENTARY

K. J. Dover   (essay date 1972)

[*Dover is an eminent English classical scholar whose books include* Greek Popular Morality *(1975),* Greek Homosexuality *(1978), and* The Greeks *(1980). In the following excerpt, he examines Philocleon's negative character traits and discusses the role of the law courts in* Wasps.]

THE CHARACTER OF PHILOKLEON

[The] principal character of an Aristophanic comedy sometimes behaves, with apparent impunity, in an uninhibited way which in real life would incur strong social disapproval or even severe legal penalties. The average member of the audience, identifying himself with such a character, may achieve a vicarious revenge on the social and political order within which he is compelled to live. Philokleon [in *Wasps*] is noteworthy for the readiness with which he inflicts on others drunken violence and insults to a degree which incurs threats of prosecution for *hýbris*. Recent commentators have remarked on the sympathy and affection which he evokes in the spectator and in the reader. I admit that he evokes mine; and yet I remain astonished at the hidden strength of antinomian sentiment which that sympathy and affection imply. Aristophanes has invested Philokleon with such defects of character that beside him Dikaiopolis, Trygaios and Peisetairos are almost prigs. Let us list the charges.

1. What Philokleon likes about jury-service is not merely the opportunity to exercise arbitrary and irresponsible power but the opportunity to do *harm*. He expresses his spite in his declaration to the chorus (320-323) that he longs to escape and go with them to the court (literally) 'to do something bad', and (340) that his son

> won't let me judge cases or do any wrong (*literally,* 'anything bad').

To some extent, what he says can be regarded as exmplifying [a] kind of dramatic inconsistency . . . , but the emphasis conveyed by repetition is notable.

2. When the chorus suggests to him (354f.) that he should climb down from the window on a rope, it alludes specifically to an occasion when, as a soldier at the capture of Naxos, he stole some spits. Philokleon agrees wistfully (357),

> Yes, I was young then, and able to steal.

The chorus-leader has earlier recalled to his fellows, as they lament their vanished youth (236-239):

> . . . when you and I were on garrison duty at Byzantion, and as we made the rounds at night we pinched the baker's bowl and got away with it, and chopped it up and boiled some pimpernel.

Later in the play (1200f.) Philokleon boasts of 'stealing Ergasion's vineprops' as 'the most valiant deed' of his life.

3. In the context of his exploit at Naxos he also says (358f.):

> And no one kept watch on me, but I could run away with impunity. But now soldiers arrayed in arms stand guard on the passes . . .

Whereas in his present circumstances he wants to 'run away' *through* the 'enemy' (i.e. Bdelykleon and the slaves) in order to do his public duty, the language he uses and the contrast he draws with his own soldiering days suggest that in those days he took whatever chance he had to run away out of danger; and cowardice is not to be found elsewhere among the characteristics of the 'comic hero'.

4. When boasting of the jurors' power, Philokleon tells us (583-586) that if a father dies and leaves his daughter (and a share of his property with her) to a husband whom he has named in his will, the jurymen do not worry in the least about the will and the seal which proves its validity, but award the daughter and the property to whoever petitions them persuasively enough. One cannot easily imagine Dikaiopolis behaving in this way, which is not only fundamentally contemptuous of law but has some affinity with a cowardly delinquency which earned very strong disapproval, injury (*kákēsis*) to widows, orphans and heiresses.

5. In 607-609 Philokleon relates with gusto how when he comes home from court, carrying his fee (in the usual Greek manner) in his mouth, his daughter makes a fuss of him and fishes it out of his mouth with her tongue. This kind of kiss was (naturally enough) known to the Greeks as highly erotic . . . , and the passage is the only one in comedy which dares to hint at the enjoyment of incestuous contacts.

In short, Philokleon is not merely a comic character who does what the man in the street would really like to do; he seems to be the kind of man (fortunately, there are not many of them) who as a soldier loots from unarmed civilians but keeps clear of an armed enemy, and in old age spends his days in the infliction of pain on others and his evenings in running his hand up his daughter's skirt. If we still like him, why do we? Is it that Aristophanes, by some dramaturgical skill which resists analysis, has compelled us to like him? Or is it that we, through a deficiency of imagination which prevents us from reacting to fictitious creations as we do to the people and situations encountered in our own lives, have misunderstood Philokleon and his creator's intentions? Trygaios in *Peace* (54, 65) is regarded by his slave as 'insane' when he purposes to fly up to Olympos, but no one calls him that when he has brought back peace. Philokleon, on the other hand, is 'sick' (71, 87, cf. 119-124) so long as he is gripped by his obsessive desire for jury-service, and 'insane' (1486) at the end of the play when his insatiable aggressiveness turns in a different direction. Bdelykleon describes his 'sickness' as one 'inborn, from the beginning, in our city' (651); and this points to an interesting relationship between the personality of Philokleon as an individual and those aspects of the jury system which are also satirized in the play.

THE LAW COURTS

If Philokleon wishes to spend all day and every day serving on juries, why should anyone mind? In particular, why should his son wish to prevent him from performing with conscientious enthusiasm a public duty which gave him such pleasure and interest in life during his declining years? If it is *wrong* for Philokleon to serve on a jury, is it wrong because (*a*) it is a job for younger men, or (*b*) Philokleon brings the wrong attitude to the job, or (*c*) it is beneath the dignity of well-to-do citizens, or (*d*) trial by jury is itself wrong? If (*c*) is the case, the implication is that only the poor, glad of the three obols a day maintenance, should decide issues at law; if (*d*) is the case, the implication is that justice should be left to what Hesiod, moralizing indignantly three centuries earlier, called 'bribe-hungry nobles'. There is no hint of (*c*) or (*d*) in *Wasps,* any more than *Knights* hints that the sovereignty of the people should be restricted. It is interesting to see that Aristophanes does not suggest a conflict between town-dwelling idlers who sit on juries and virtuous farmers who become the jurors' victims. Indeed, in *Peace* 349 the chorus which articulates the hopes of Attic farmers and identifies itself a few lines later (358) as belonging to the hoplite military class says that if only peace will come,

> You won't find me a fierce, bad-tempered juror
> any more.

The idea that jury-service is better performed by younger men is not, taken by itself, an idea which Aristophanes is likely to have entertained, nor is it very practical; it is only reasonable that men who are past military service and have time on their hands because they have retired from day-to-day preoccupation with estate or craft or trade should spend some of that time on public service, and a mass of old men sitting as a jury is the democratic equivalent of an immemorial feature of human society, the elders of the community sitting as judges.

Why Philokleon's obsession is bad for the community is indicated to us at the end of the prologue, when his name and Bdelykleon's are revealed to us (133f.). It is by no means normal practice to tell us the names of the chief characters before they have appeared; Dikaiopolis's name is first revealed at *Ach.* 406, the Sausage-seller's ('Agorakritos') almost at the end of *Knights* (1257), Strepsiades' at *Clouds* 134 (after he has knocked on the door of the school), Trygaios's at *Peace* 190 (not in the expository prologue, but after his arrival on Olympos), and Peisetairos's not until *Birds* 644. When we hear that the old man is 'Philokleon' and his son 'Bdelykleon', immediately after we have been told that the old man is mentally sick with an obsession for jury-service and the younger man has done everything in his power to get him cured (just as he would have tried to cure him of severe arthritis or cancer), we cannot help relating the names to an aspect of political life which has been satirized in *Knights* and is in any case familiar to us; we are thus half prepared for the terms in which Bdelykleon will argue—and persuade the chorus, which, like the chorus of *Acharnians,* is ultimately amenable to reason—that his old father should stay at home.

Athenian juries were in a sense committees of the sovereign assembly, but committees of a rather special kind; they could not be called to account, nor was there any appeal against their verdicts, and to this extent they were themselves sovereign. Since prosecutions for administrative corruption, procedural irregularity, military failure and bad political advice were common, the juries had it in their power to make and break political careers, and the death penalty was inflicted quite readily. It is this irresponsible exercise of power which Philokleon and his aged friends find so congenial: to have distinguished men weeping, flattering them, begging them for mercy; to settle an inheritance lawsuit without regard for what the testator's will actually says; to be courted by Kleon and other politicians; to be welcomed home and made a fuss of, because of the extra three obols they bring. I, says Philokleon, enjoy the power of Zeus himself, and (626f.):

> When my lightning flashes,
> the rich and the proudest of men
> gasp and shit themselves.

Bdelykleon's argument is designed to prove that this power is illusory, and that the jurors are slaves (682, cf. 515-521); the real power lies with the politicians. This he 'proves' by arithmetic: the total income of the Athenian state is two thousand talents a year (twelve million drachmai), and how much of that is paid out at half a drachma a day to six thousand jurors? Where does the rest go? Not a difficult question, if we are permitted to do a little more arithmetic on the cost of fighting a major war and administering a large city, but we are not permitted; Bdelykleon successfully conveys the impression that somehow or other the money all goes to *them,* the politicians who manipulate in their own interests those very juries which they seem so to flatter and cherish. It is hinted that the ferocity of the old men and their unwillingness to forego the pleasure of convicting a defendant are a nasty kind of compensation for the inferior status which necessarily follows physical enfeeblement, an inferiority for which the outward forms of respect could not compensate enough. Their character is therefore well suited to exploitation by politicians, and to this extent *Wasps* satirizes an aspect of the same political style already satirized in *Knights;* the 'disease' of Philokleon is only an individual case of what Bdelykleon calls (651) 'a disease long endemic in our city'. Kleon appeals to the worst in people, and the loyalest of all his supporters will be a man devoid of shame, honesty, manliness, magnanimity and human kindness.

The Greeks did not rate the virtues of compassion and forgiveness as high as we do, but they did recognize them as virtues; this is clear not only from drama but also from fourth-century oratory, where juries are rarely criticized for harshness but often chided or complimented (according as the speaker is prosecutor or defendant) for habitual mildness. There is no room for doubt that the portrayal of Philokleon as flattered, but not moved, by appeals for pity is intended to be a portrayal of a disagreeable, un-Greek, un-Athenian way of behaving. Moreover, although Athenian law required indictments for offences against the community to be initiated by individuals, it is observable that the orators who initiate such indictments take some trouble to justify themselves—sometimes as personally wronged by the defendant, more often as moved to patriotic duty by the community's great peril—in a way which suggests that they are very anxious not to be thought busybodies. In the same way, too, too great an enthusiasm for spending one's time in jury-service might have incurred criticism as evidence of an insufficient inclination to mind one's own business. Aristophanes' 'heroes' do not refer to cases on which they have sat in judgment, and without *Wasps*—even making allowance for *Peace* 349 . . . we should not get the impression from comedy that the Athenian judicial system differed significantly from ours.

Philokleon's austere life as a juryman has something in common with the intellectuals' disregard of ordinary comfort in *Clouds;* both are deviations from a normal valuation of comfort and enjoyment and relaxation. But whereas Aristophanes would have answered the question, 'How is scientific research to be carried on? by saying 'Not at all', we can hardly imagine that he would have advocated the abolition of all prosecutions and lawsuits. If we assume that he is in no way suggesting that there should be any constitutional change in the recruitment, size and powers of juries, the general implication of *Wasps* is very close to that of *Knights:* it is moralizing, not politics, and it belongs—like most Greek comedy and much of the satirical literature of our own culture—within the tradition of didacticism directed not towards structural change but upon human attitudes and patterns of behaviour. (pp. 125-31)

K. J. Dover, "Wasps," in his Aristophanic Comedy, *University of California Press, 1972, pp. 121-31.*

Kenneth J. Reckford   (essay date 1977)

[*Reckford is an American classicist whose writings include* Horace *(1969). In the following excerpt, he explores the connections between dreams and comic catharsis in* Wasps, *emphasizing Aristophanes's use of symbolism, word play, and unusual associations.*]

[I take as a] point of departure two peculiarities of Aristophanes' *Wasps* which critics have largely ignored. One is the prominence given to dreaming and dream-interpreting in the prologue; the other is a significant play on the words καθαιρειν [being clean] and καθαροσ [clean] in the parabasis [in which the chorus addresses the audience] and elsewhere. I want to show that both of these features are important and that they illustrate the nature and meaning of Aristophanes' comedy.

Of the two, the *catharsis* motif is more immediately connected with the plot of *The Wasps.* It first occurs in Xanthias' report of how Bdelycleon tried to cure his father's jury-mania (115-24). . . . After (a) persuasion failed, Bdelycleon tried three other forms of psychotherapy. (b) He "cleansed" his father. The term is highly ambiguous. It refers most likely to a traditional rite of purification by which defilements were cast out; the healing ceremony presumably included a ritual bath. But this catharsis-and-washing treatment failed. Later on, and more pertinently than he realizes, Bdelycleon will refer to his father as the proverbial "ass-hole you can't get clean."

After that wash-out came (c) the Corybantic treatment. Although this attempt is not explicitly labeled as a catharsis, mention of the "drum" reminds us of how, in the Corybantic rite, repressed emotions were liberated through exciting musical rhythms. Since, by this means, a person's special psychological ailment revealed itself for diagnosis, and an appropriate remedy could be discovered, including religious sacrifice and prayer to the appropriate divinity, Plato classifies this rite as cathartic: it belongs, that is, to the type of "healing madness" which, under Dionysus' general patronage, drives out actual insanity. That is why Aristophanes has Xanthias combine (c) with (b) under the common heading of τελεται, "ceremonies" or "rites" of purification. Both provide religious and psychological healing, as also does (d), the forced incubation of Philocleon in the temple of Asclepius at Aegina: dream therapy this time under the auspices of Apolline religion.

We shall not succeed in differentiating Bdelycleon's efforts more precisely. They shade off into each other; they share various elements of purification, purgation, and emotional release; and they belong together as "therapy" and "catharsis" much as today, for all their differences, we might lump together an encounter group experience, psychiatry on the couch, the sacrament of Confession, and participation in a large rock music festival. In *The Wasps,* these attempts at psychotherapy also share a common result. They all fail. From emotional treatments, as from the more rational "therapy of the word," Philocleon rebounds into the jury court; indeed, the more effort is made to restrain or change him, the more extraordinarily he springs back. The prologue thus introduces the central theme of *The Wasps,* which is, depending on our perspective, either "the failure of therapy" or "Philocleon's escape."

Yet this same failure, or triumph, is related significantly to Aristophanes' own comic purposes by his use of the words καθαιρειν and καθαροσ. The wasp leader, speaking for Aristophanes, begins the parabasis by asking the audience to pay attention "if you love something καθαρον." He means a good clean comedy unpolluted by wornout vulgarities. The term then submerges for almost thirty lines in which Aristophanes criticizes his audience for having done him wrong. Despite his multiple benefactions, some surreptitious (much as a ventriloquist speaks through other people's bellies) and some open (φανερωσ), on his own responsibility; despite the fact that he was not puffed up by his enormous successes, but demonstrated high moral conduct and never prostituted his Muse for private (sexual) ends; and despite, finally, his consistent bravery in attacking in various plays no ordinary people but a certain appalling and hideous and ferocious monster, not to mention lesser "shivers and fevers" that preyed on ordinary folk: still Aristophanes' audience betrayed him, they let him down (1043-45). . . . And yet [*The Clouds,* which the audience failed to appreciate in 423,] was an excellent play. By Dionysus, it was! Those who failed to "get it" then should be ashamed of themselves—not the playwright, whom the "clever people" commend for his unusually daring effort. What remains is for the audience to make amends by cherishing (θεραπευετε) original poets in the future; that way, if they store up their clever ideas, the clothing of the Athenians will smell sweetly of—*cleverness* all the year long. (pp. 283-85)

[Aristophanes] compares his services as αλεξικακοσ [warding off evil] and καθαρτησ [purifying] to those of Heracles "cleansing" Greece of monsters. With "Heraclean temper," Aristophanes faced up to a monster that combined the worst features of many horrible creatures, including the Hydra and the dog Cerberus (more about dogs elsewhere); he did not cower, did not stoop to—taking bribes, but fought, and still fights, for his ungrateful public. All this self-praise was traditional and expected. Aristophanes must have enjoyed posing as a champion, a hero, and a National Asset, much as Picasso in his later years liked to portray himself in such various and splendid roles as hero, warrior, Olympic victor, lover, and bullfighter. What is new and subtle is the way Aristophanes combines the political claim, to be a public benefactor, with the literary one, to be writing a new, improved, clever, and daring sort of comedy whose success depends on the audience "getting it clearly" (γνωναι καθαρωσ). Combine the two ideas, and Aristophanes is offering his comedy to the public both as "good clean fun" and as healing therapy—claims, to be sure, which must be evaluated in terms of *The Wasps* taken as a whole (for the parabasis occupies an ironic position *within* the play's development). But this raises the next question. What relation, if any, exists between Bdelycleon's attempts to cure his father and Aristophanes' attempts to improve Athens and the Athenian theatre?

Let me defer this question for now in order to introduce a second theme, of dreaming and dream-interpreting, which is closely related to the themes of comic meaning and comic catharsis. The dream section (lines 1-53) is usually treated as *captatio benevolentiae* [a plea for benevolence] and passed over quickly. In [M. D.] MacDowell's words, "The chief function of this passage is to provide a string of jokes to get the audience warmed up." True enough: the prologue scenes seduce the audience, as usual, into a relaxed and attentive frame of mind: this is familiar fun, and the more relaxing because it *is* familiar. We notice that this year Aristophanes takes special pains to keep the audience on his side. At the same time, however, his joking points to a series of important affinities between dreaming and dream-interpreting on the one hand and jokes and comedy on the other. Both involve psychic relaxation; both introduce us to a nonsense world of absurd and fantastic combinations and transformations; and both, when rightly understood, produce in us *a healing catharsis, a clarification through release, and a series of ultimately joyful recognitions*. But this is to anticipate much. Let us begin with the obvious preliminary: with relaxation.

The two weary slaves guarding Philocleon nod off and dream. Through relaxation not just the slaves, but the audience with them, pass over a bridge from everyday anxieties to the world of transforming fantasy. (pp. 286-87)

In the first discussion, of Xanthias' eagle-and-snake dream, the idea of *relieving anxiety* is prominent. In this dream, an eagle flies into the agora carrying an *aspis* (asp); but right away, before we can ask whether this portent heralds good or ill, it clarifies its own meaning. The *aspis* turns punningly into a brazen shield which is thrown away by—Cleonymus. In short: our attention was engaged, only to be discharged in laughter at a familiar Aristophanic joke. "Oh, he's making fun of Cleonymus again!" Sosias makes the point differently, comparing Cleonymus to a riddle such as people pose at drinking-parties, a riddle that required a punning short-cut answer. . . .

Xanthias is alarmed, as people are by strange dreams. Does it portend some dreadful consequence? Not so, says Sosias as dream-interpreter and therapist: don't be anxious! But Xanthias has the last word, explaining his anxiety with a joke that in fact interprets the dream finally and solves the riddle. Since the phrase αποβαλων οπλα is equivocal, meaning to "throw away arms" or to "lose one's testicles," the dream turns out to be a comic dramatization of a very basic sexual anxiety. What seemed a simple joke builds to stronger laughter, greater relief of pent-up feelings and anxieties: in small, yet programatically, to a healing catharsis.

Yet Xanthias' model dream is only a preliminary: the "big" dream of Sosias that follows is more complex and more significant, for it concerns the "hull" ship of state. Sosias has dreamed of an assembly of sheep on the Pnyx, each with its mantle and staff; they were being harangued by a monstrous whale. The audience will be ready for political satire; they are accustomed to the use of comic "likenings" as a basic form of insult; a series of hints . . . leads unmistakably—especially if one knows Aristophanes and remembers *The Knights*—to the identification of the whale as the corrupt, bellowing demagogue Cleon; and to drive the point home, Xanthias anticipates the audience's happy recognition ("He's talking about *Cleon!*") by an indirection or disguise so transparent that it can *only* point to Cleon: "Ugh. Don't say it! Your dream stinks horribly of rotten leather." The allusion is a comic trademark. Leather goes with the tanner Cleon just as chervil goes with Euripides' greengrocer mother. It is a symbol that the audience cannot fail to grasp. By now, without being told explicitly, they have "gotten" the joke and interpreted the dream. (pp. 287-89)

[Aristophanes thus uses] the dream-machinery as a device for entertaining his audience with a string of witty jokes against the usual people (Cleonymus, Cleon, Theorus). This is true: Aristophanes is warming to larger political themes, and he is entertaining the audience and putting them in a happy and receptive mood; yet the connections which he implies . . . between jokes and dreams and comedy are significant for our understanding of *The Wasps* as a whole and of Aristophanic comedy generally. We see, first, that jokes and dreams share a common mechanism of disguise and discovery, build-up and resolution, absurd surface appearance and revelation of some latent idea or meaning. Freud has given us psychological insight into the connections here intimated by Aristophanes; he has illuminated the role of the unconscious in jokes, as in dreams, though without by any means exhausting the nature and meaning of these relations. Secondly, Aristophanes connects the interpreting of dreams and "getting" of jokes with the raising and alleviation of anxiety. When Sosias concludes that he should pay his two obols and retain the services of that fine dream-interpreter, Xanthias, Aristophanes may be laughing at a well known type of fraud. The two-bit dream-interpreter belongs with the oracle-monger and other itinerant fortune-tellers. Yet there seem to have been a few serious psychiatrists in Aristophanes' time who attempted to relieve people's anxieties and to help them lead happier lives through counseling them and interpreting their dreams; and at the least, Aristophanes' jokes show that he was interested in the idea, and probably in some specific methods, of *psychiatric healing*.

What is more certain is that the dreaming and dream-interpreting of the prologue is closely connected with the later plot of *The Wasps* and with the poet's intention in writing it; for Xanthias, our dream-interpreter, also guides the expectations of the audience. What will this play be? . . . [Aristophanes' answer contains the phrase λογιδιον γνωμην εχον.] The phrase suggests something like a fable with a point or moral: and since this "little story" will not (like *The Clouds*?) be "more clever" than the audience, they are evidently expected to get the point, or γνωμη; contrast their previous failure, depicted in the parabasis, to "get the point" of *The Clouds* and hence to receive the appropriate comic catharsis (1043-45, quoted above). As though to forestall a repetition of that disaster, Aristophanes has Xanthias take the audience with him step by careful step: he tells them that the father of his *sleeping* master has a *peculiar* disease which they can only *get* and *interpret* correctly with his guidance (71-73). . . . Although the guessing-game which follows provides more *captatio benevolentiae* as well as a pretext for a new string of personal jokes, it also connects dream-interpreting with watching and grasping comic action. The implication, I think, is that the main action of *The Wasps* will resemble a dream, in its peculiar and absurd formations and transformations, but that if it is rightly received, like a dream that is rightly interpreted, it will give great pleasure and great healing.

After [the] transitional section, Xanthias introduces us to the comic plot: first, to Philocleon's manic obsession with the jury court; then, to the various forms of therapy attempted, but without success, by Bdelycleon. The last of these, incubation in Asclepius' temple, nicely connects our scenes: for had it worked, it would probably have done so by means of a healing dream. In a dream or dreamlike vision Asclepius himself might have come, his ministers or health-giving snakes might have appeared, or in some way or other, a health-giving prescription might have been revealed to the sick man's relaxed and open mind. Yet it seems that this effort at psychotherapy failed with Philocleon, as the others had previously, and as (to anticipate) Bdelycleon's subsequent, most imaginative efforts must also fail. But what of Aristophanes' own similar attempt? Will he succeed where Bdelycleon fails? Will his audience get the point this time and receive the healing catharsis? The answer, I want to suggest, is ambiguous. Insofar as Aristophanes, like Bdelycleon, tries to manipulate and control his audience, or simply to reform them, he is bound to fail. Yet this very failure provides a still better catharsis, a deeper, more comic recognition, and—to pursue our analogy—something like the best, most hopeful interpretation of a very significant dream.

The play's chief pattern is of constraint and escape. It appears twice in the prologue: in Xanthias' report of Bdelycleon's therapeutic efforts and their resounding failure, and in the wild scene of Jack-in-the-box farce, in which Philocleon keeps popping out of his house by door or window or roof, while Bdelycleon and the slaves shove him back inside. We should remember this basic struggle during the three major scenes that follow, namely:

> (i) a paramilitary contest between Philocleon's guards and the wasp-chorus of old jurors who came to his rescue but are repulsed; this leads to
> (ii) the Agon, a formal debate or contest in persuasion between Philocleon and Bdelycleon, ending in the son's victory; this leads in turn to his presentation of the jurycourt-at-home, including
> (iii) the trial of the dog. This is at once a satirical

skit, an exercise in play therapy, and an indirect struggle between father and son which ends, once again, in Philocleon's discomfiture and defeat.

In reviewing these scenes, we should maintain a multiple perspective. First, we should ask: what does Bdelycleon teach his father? How true is it, and how effective? Second: we should observe Bdelycleon's own character and methods, and ask, does he fight (reeducate) fairly? The answer, to anticipate, is clearly no; and this is related to key issues of freedom vs. control and even democracy vs. tyranny (or oligarchy). And third: we should pay special attention to Philocleon's emotional reactions, his identity crisis. I shall assume in the following discussion that our sympathies are divided, as Aristophanes intended them to be, between the sensible but spoilsport son who is basically parental and the demented but terribly vital father who is often childish. Comic heroes frequently evoke such divided response: Falstaff, for example; or perhaps Mr. Toad, in *The Wind in the Willows,* when he tricks Ratty, escapes from house-confinement, and runs off to steal a motor car. We find ourselves necessarily on both sides of the recurrent game.

(i) Most of the key issues of *The Wasps* are first spelled out between the siege-relieving operation and the formal debate. Bdelycleon wants, he says, to induce Philocleon to change his "earlyrisinginformerlawsuitlaborious" habits for a better, more comfortable lifestyle. This his father rejects. Bdelycleon also says that his father has been deceived and wrongly "habituated" by people who use him for their purposes; with "new instruction," he will recognize his mistakes and embark on a new, better life. The question here raised, whether Philocleon is a king or a slave, managing or duped, comes so close to the issues of *The Knights* that we may anticipate a definite answer: Philocleon is deluded and used by the demagogues. So the Agon will show. But the earlier scene also raises the question whether Bdelycleon is an anti-democratic conspirator. The chorus are paranoid, of course: we are meant to laugh at those people who see a conspiracy behind every vegetable stall or brothel; yet there is a grain of truth in their suspicions. Even more important is the issue raised by the wasp-jurors at 540-45: are old men worth anything? Or are they just hollow shells? Aristophanes has portrayed his chorus as weak, weary, ordinary old men living mainly on memories. They look to Philocleon as their hero because he is the roughest, toughest of them all—or rather has been, because at present he is pining away like a lovesick girl in a Euripidean tragedy. The parody is marvellous fun—Philocleon as Danae in her tower, or as Stheneboia. It looks forward to the great paratragic scenes of *The Thesmophoriazusae.* But it also shows how much Philocleon's jurymania *is* an erotic passion and the very heart of his vitality and feeling of identity. Without it, he must grow sick, must look toward death—although of course comic heroes never die like lovesick heroines, nor do they fade away. They always bounce back. The attempts of the chorus to revive Philocleon's spirits through song, dance, and encouragement, point to the larger healing power of comedy itself, which goes well beyond anything Bdelycleon can offer. But this is anticipating. Let us consider the Agon.

(ii) The *argument* works out so clearly in Bdelycleon's favor that people tend to ignore his trickiness and the psychological crisis of his father. From the first, Philocleon makes himself vulnerable as he reveals his childish infatuation and megalomania. He lives and thrives in court; enjoys himself there, as at a musical or dramatic performance; relishes his power over rich defendants who fear and flatter him; gains erotic thrills; finds increased respect, comfort, and independence at home: in sum, he feels like Zeus as he lightens and thunders! The statement is wildly exaggerated. It also shows, as the portrayal of Demos in *The Knights* did earlier, the importance of private feelings behind the facade of public behavior and policy.

Rebuttal comes easily enough. Bdelycleon uses a few simple statistics, as politicians will, to show how his father is deceived and manipulated by the politicians: how they enjoy the real power and the big bribes, while Philocleon is kept poor and dependent like a slave *or savage-tempered watchdog.* The point is well taken—and it is Cleon who is mainly pointed at. Yet Aristophanes equally means us to observe the rhetorical skills and sophistries that Bdelycleon uses. He makes notes carefully. He knows how to project the right *ethos* of good will, how to mitigate anger in his audience, how to increase their pity. Thus he begins by asking "Daddy dear" to relax his frowning brow. He uses a tricky first person plural, asking his father to consider "what *we* get now." Cleverly, too, he diverts Philocleon's anger into indignation at the politicians who have tricked him, at the officials who order him around, and—ultimately—at Cleon. He also bribes Philocleon with a fantasy picture of the riches he ought to enjoy, and with the promise of the real comforts and pleasures he will enjoy under his son's management once he agrees to give up the jury courts and stay at home.

At the same time, we watch Philocleon's violent reactions to the argument. He is "stirred to his depths" by the revelations; his mind is "drawn over;" he doesn't know "what is happening" to him. As the argument proceeds, a strange numbness is "poured over" his hand; he can no longer hold up his sword; he is $\mu\alpha\lambda\theta\alpha\kappa\sigma\sigma$: soft, weak, sick. The joke rests on the identification of voting tablet and sword; it also raises the issue of sexual potency, to which I shall return. Once more Philocleon plays the tragic lover, frustrated and despondent. "Where is my soul?" he asks. This is tragic parody with a point, for Philocleon's identity is in question. But his deep anxiety is diverted, as Bdelycleon wished, into anger at Cleon. The angry outburst, "I wish I could catch Cleon red-handed," $\kappa\lambda\epsilon\pi\tau\sigma\nu\tau\alpha$ $K\lambda\epsilon\omega\nu\alpha$ $\lambda\alpha\beta\sigma\iota\mu\iota$, introduces (and punningly summarizes) the subsequent scene, of the dog's trial.

(iii) [This scene] combines a wish-fulfilment fantasy, of the jury-court at home, with some acute satire directed at the conduct of political trials in general and the repulsive tactics of Cleon in particular. Like Philocleon, the audience are made to see that "Labes" (Laches), who stole some "Sicilian cheese," is a great deal less guilty than the greedy Dog (Cleon) who prosecutes him—for not having produced the customary bribe. This does not mean that the indictment is false. On the contrary: our attention is drawn to all the tricks of judicial pleading which unscrupulous lawyers use to get their clients off. We are also made aware of how much Bdelycleon stage-manages the entire trial. Not only does he act as presiding judge and even "lawmaker" (*thesmothetês*); when things look bad, he intervenes as counsel for the defense; he uses every trick in the book to play on the jury's pity; he even introduces Labes' little whining puppies; and then, when all else fails, he simply tricks Philocleon into casting his decisive vote into the Urn of Acquittal instead of Condemnation. This final deception sums up the whole pattern of manipulation and control used by Bdelycleon—in the interest, naturally, of his father's return to sanity and good judgment.

Indeed, before the trial scene began, Bdelycleon's prayer to Apollo made his intentions clear enough (875-84). He wants to remove toughness, anger, bitterness; in their place he hopes to induce tenderness, kindness, pity. Although these are ordinary rhetorical aims, Bdelycleon's language and movements suggest that he is acting as a doctor or wizard or a *magic cook* ready to perform a saving transformation. There are significant parallels between his prayer and Socrates' invocation of his cloud divinities in the fraudulent *phrontisterion* ["Thinkery"] in *The Clouds;* still more, between Bdelycleon's terms of surgery and cooking and the key dramatic metaphor of rhetoric as cooking in *The Knights,* culminating in the magical re-cooking of Demos into his former self. Just so, Bdelycleon hopes to transform his father's character through the magical cooking of play therapy and psychodrama—a hope which, as we shall see, is intimately connected with Aristophanes' own aims and methods as a comic poet.

But again: if we watch Philocleon's reactions, we observe that this particular therapy kills more than cures. Once again, the old man is overcome, weakened, "made soft." This is largely a joke—what a disaster for Philocleon to pity a defendant, let alone acquit one!—but there is real pathos in his words just before he faints: "So then, I am nothing." Earlier he pretended like Odysseus to be *Outis,* "Nobody;" now he has lost his identity. It is a kind of death. His last words too are pathetic, as he gives in to Bdelycleon's renewed offer of a comfortable retirement: "All right, if that's what you think best." He has given up. His resignation comes very close to tragedy, like Falstaff's famous lines after his great hopes are disappointed: "Master Shallow, I owe you a thousand pounds." Although the chorus proceed into their usual "Go ye rejoicing" song, we are left with the impression more of failure than of success—of a therapy that has led to a loss of self, a psychological death.

FAILURE OF CATHARSIS: ARISTOPHANES AND BDELYCLEON

Precisely at this point the actors withdraw and the chorusleader voices Aristophanes' claims to be a heroic $\kappa\alpha\theta\alpha\rho\tau\eta\sigma$. The timing of these remarks makes some connection between Bdelycleon's use of therapy and Aristophanes' comic catharsis inevitable. Have there been earlier hints of such a connection?

In the Agon, Philocleon described the various ways in which defendants bribed and humored him and worked upon his pity. Some flattered him; some bewailed their "poverty;" while others used funny stories (566-67). . . . Whether they tell stories or a funny fable of Aesop, or just make jokes, their aim is consistent. They want to make Philocleon feel pleasure and laugh so that he will "lay down his temper." And if that form of *anapeithein* (a word combining the ideas of persuasion and bribery) doesn't work, they can always resort to sheer pathos, bringing in their bleating kids. The parallelism is striking. Make Philocleon laugh or cry, and you will have banished his angry mood. Later on, Philocleon tells of his pleasure when gifted defendants recite a tragic speech or play on the pipes for his entertainment. The point is satirical. It seems, the courtroom rivals the theatre as a place of entertainment; we shall see more of this in the dog's trial. But isn't Aristophanes doing what those guilty defendants do: isn't he making them laugh in order to teach them the desired lesson and perform the desired catharsis of their feelings? Certainly, many passages from Aristophanes' plays, and especially from *The Peace,* suggest that he means to bring the audience to a cheerful frame of mind in which they will recover the natural perspective, of country, peace, and celebration, in which right attitudes can be maintained, right decisions worked out. If this were all, then our "good humor man" would be a supermanipulator and persuader. But is it all? Let us reserve judgment; and let us also remember that Aristophanes himself has provided the evidence linking him with Bdelycleon. And he continues to provide it.

Most strikingly of all, Bdelycleon steps out of character just before his rebuttal, merging momentarily with the comic poet (650-51). . . .

We might recall the way in which Dicaeopolis' speech in *The Acharnians* moved back and forth between different levels of meaning: between parody of Euripides' *Telephus,* the requirements of the comic plot, and the pleading of Aristophanes to his audience for peace and fair play. Thus Aristophanes speaks through Dicaeopolis who is "transparently" disguised as Telephus pretending to be a beggar. Very similarly, we have just heard, behind Bdelycleon, the voice of Aristophanes the would-be public therapist. The longtime, deeply ingrained disease of Philocleon merges with that of Athens. On the surface, Bdelycleon is uttering a rhetorical platitude: "I'm just not up to the demands of this extraordinary subject and occasion." But he also says more than he intends. He and the τρυγωδοι, the comic playwright and his troupe, are *not* up to performing the desired catharsis. Their γνωμη, their most intelligent planning, will not suffice. (pp. 290-98)

A number of parallels may be drawn . . . between Bdelycleon's tactics in his rebuttal and the comic tactics, whether of Aristophanes or the Sausage-seller, which worked so effectively in *The Knights.* In that play, the Paphlagonian (Cleon) was beaten at his own game; he was outshouted, outdone in disgustingness, and outbribed: hence the sausage-seller wins the chance (now reversing himself into an aristocratic saviour) to take Demos in hand and to transform him, through magical cooking, into the vigorous Demos of old. This splendid accomplishment implies total victory for the comic poet working behind the scenes and

for all his true and right values. Now it seems that in *The Wasps* Bdelycleon is pushing for a similar victory and reformation, and by similar means. Again, an infatuated old man (= the gullible Athenian public) must be disabused of his illusions; he must be shown how the politicians (notably Cleon) have manipulated and controlled and deceived him for their own purposes; and to do this, the enemy must be outbribed, beaten at their own game. In *The Knights,* this is done with sweaters and pillows and cakes; in *The Wasps,* by a fantastic evocation of imperial riches that should rightly be Philocleon's but in fact go mainly to the politicians and demagogues who manage him. Of course, Bdelycleon's promises of a comfortable retirement constitute a further bribe; so too does his wonderful jurycourt at home with its play therapy, its entertainment.

Enough was said earlier to suggest how Bdelycleon uses the dog trial as an entertainment- and substitution-bribe to give Philocleon satisfaction while actually keeping him indoors and out of trouble, and also as a psychodrama that will teach him to be kinder and more compassionate. There is much emphasis on the way he is made to weep with pity for the defendant and his helpless little whining puppies. He undergoes an emotional catharsis—although he blames it on the hot soup, and it is only temporary. On another level, the trial of the dog resembles the kind of fable which defendants used to tell in court to put the jury in a good humor. And on still another level, it resembles the plot of *The Wasps,* which was described earlier as a λογιδιον γνωμην εχον, a little story or fable with a point (or moral). The irony is complex but no more so than in *The Acharnians:* for here, as there, the poet includes in his play an exposure of his comic intentions and methods—there, educational; here, therapeutic ones— that were hidden behind the masks, the costumes, and the comic plot.

Let us assume Aristophanes' honesty, defer the question of his final intentions, and move with the plot itself towards the wild reversal which utterly destroys any attempt (whether by Bdelycleon or by Aristophanes) at moral reformation and reeducation. Certainly, Bdelycleon tries: he dresses his father in new clothes, much as he would like to dress him in new, civilized, polite habits to consort with "gentlemen" at a party. It is an uproarious scene of trying to improve human nature. There are many borrowings from *The Clouds,* from scenes of Socrates trying to teach Strepsiades (who resisted with a kind of saving stupidity); and there are many ironies pointing to Bdelycleon's managerial tendencies, his resemblance to Cleon himself (do you become like the enemy whose weapons you adopt?), and the essential bankruptcy of his bourgeois aims—to get his father into the country club. The metaphor of cooking recurs: Philocleon almost melts away in the furnace of his new clothes; he begs Bdelycleon to get a meathook ready to pull him out. So too, the idea of sleeping and dreaming: Philocleon is led to the "couch" and, as he says, given not a real feast but a "dream-dinner." But once again, it is the spring mechanism at work. The more Philocleon's nature is restrained, the more violently it will break forth. When Philocleon goes to the party, gets roaring drunk, makes an ass of himself, insults everybody, steals a flute girl, and comes reveling home with her, knocking things over on the way, stealing food, and beating up tradespeople—this is the break-out that we have somehow been expecting all along. For the son, it is utter disaster; for the father, a final escape from manipulation and control, yet with a fully appropriate excuse: "You *told* me I shouldn't think about lawsuits any more!"

Still another strong irony is the way the fable or funny story backfires. Bdelycleon had instructed his father in polite conversation (λογουσ σεμνουσ) befitting clever people (δεξιοι). His idea of civilized conversation includes edifying stories and anecdotes (provided, we might say, they get past the censor): and later on, when Philocleon worries rather prophetically that he might get drunk and offend people, his son reassures him: in polite society, you can always soothe ruffled feelings by means of a funny story or a fable (1256-61). Presumably, if he took this advice, Philocleon would succeed like one of the defendants he described earlier, who brought the jury to a serviceable good humor. What actually happens is that Philocleon reverts when drunk to the most primitive types of humor. At the dinner party, he was splendidly vulgar; onstage, his "Aesopic" meanderings add insult to injury. As he raves on about Aesop and the Delphians and something about a beetle, his longsuffering son carries him bodily into the house—at which disastrous point the chorus sing a mocking little song praising Bdelycleon for his *cleverness* and his success—so far as it goes—in reforming his father's character and bringing him to a new and very civilized style of life.

The joke is on Bdelycleon, whose instruction and therapy have backfired. But it is equally on Aristophanes; hence, I think, the special emphasis on funny stories and fables that don't work out the way they should. We should remember that Aristophanes claimed to be a καθαρτηδ in both the social and the literary realm. We could say, he claimed to cleanse Athens of its faults and demons, and comedy of its tired vulgarities and ploys. And yet: just as the reformation of Philocleon explodes into ruins, failing very much like an experiment *in a fable,* where some creature reverts suddenly to its former nature, or some disguise is stripped off, or someone's attempt at a new way of life fails, prompting the moral, "Stick to your own trade" (or nature)—at the same instant, Aristophanes' *Wasps* relapses into the old vulgarities which constitute the old self of Old Comedy. What Xanthias announced would be a "little story with a point," cleverer than most, but not too clever for the audience, turns into beating and screaming and running and knockabout farce and some wonderfully obscene by-play about a torch which is really a naked flute girl. Bdelycleon is knocked down, in a true life boxing story; Aristophanes' chariot of reform crashes again. And we are glad. Shut up again in the house, the irresponsible Philocleon re-emerges finally to perform a joyful, drunken, and triumphant dance. "An impossible business, by Dionysus!" cries Xanthias the would-be warder. Precisely: it *is* an impossible business to reform human or Athenian nature; and (by Dionysus!) comedy in the end must be about human freedom, which now includes the freedom not to be re-educated or reformed or brainwashed or made the involuntary object of a cathar-

sis—even a comic catharsis. The greater the constraint of attempted reform, the wilder the escape, the more manic the final dance. The old man is mad, and Athens is mad, and nothing can be done about it ("Drink hellebore!" cries the helpless Xanthias); and if there is a victor in the end, it is the god of madness, Dionysus himself.

DREAM-INTERPRETATION AND COMIC CATHARSIS

I want now to borrow the Aristophanic freedom to reverse myself and ask whether *The Wasps* does not offer a healing catharsis after all, albeit a different one from the kind we have been discussing. It is, after all, the nature of Dionysian religion to provide that temporary abandonment of self-possession that enables people to escape the greater insanity to which the self-willed rationalist like Pentheus may or must succumb. And although the wild ending of *The Wasps* is a tribute to Dionysus and a reaffirmation of the primitive and irrational, whether in human nature or in comedy, yet even Philocleon's clownish dancing and joking are planned by Aristophanes as part of the total play. A larger catharsis is intended and achieved, under the auspices of Apollo and Dionysus, than either Bdelycleon within the plot, or Aristophanes-as-Bdelycleon, might have desired or even imagined.

That is why it is time to return to the idea of dreaming and dream-interpretation which preceded the Bdelycleon-Philocleon plot, suggestively framing the comic action. In the prologue, Aristophanes set up important analogies between dreams and jokes or riddles, dream-interpretation and comedy. He also invited the audience to join his troupe in interpreting the play's action as if it were a strange yet favorable dream. They will get the point and the benefit of it, though not without his guidance. This does *not* mean (for Aristophanes is often ironic about the audience's power of comprehension) that every symbol in the play will be allegorical and self-revealing and unequivocal. . . . ; it *does* mean that this peculiar comedy will present its meanings in symbolic form, like a dream; that the audience are invited to try to understand these meanings; and that such understanding (again, as of a significant and favorable dream) will be accompanied by some kind of healing. Since this catharsis is different from that discussed earlier, I want to treat it as a series of *recognitions,* each one corresponding to a different kind of symbolic form or action. We shall move at once from simpler to more complex symbols—the dogs, the wasps, and "escape"—and from correspondingly simple to complex forms of recognition provided for the audience, though not necessarily fully grasped by them.

The trial of the dog combines absurdity with obvious allegorical meaning, much as Sosias' dream in the prologue did. There, a whale harangued an assembly of sheep, and close by sat the crow-headed man; here, one dog prosecutes another in domestic court, kitchen utensils and puppies appear, a cheesegrater takes the stand to give testimony, and a rooster (briefly mentioned in the text, but prominent on stage) crows from time to time to keep the jury awake. The scene has the peculiarity of a dream and much of the charm of fable or fairy-tale, but like Sosias' dream earlier, it serves the purposes of an easily recognizable satire on the jury system and especially on Cleon. The audience will take pleasure in "getting" the joke, seeing through the disguise (it is conceivable that "Dog" appeared with features of a Cleon portrait-mask combined with features of a dog), and appreciating the points thus scored against Cleon. The satire here remains transparent, the "symbolism" obvious, from beginning to end. Like Orwell's *Animal Farm,* it is a "little fable with a point."

Probably, too, the dog comparison was familiar and expected, however beautifully Aristophanes develops it here. Already in *The Knights* he had portrayed Cleon as a villainous dog. Perhaps Cleon had claimed in actuality to be the "watchdog" of the people, and this claim had struck Aristophanes' funny bone; certainly it is demolished in the counter-oracle produced by the sausage-seller (*Knights* 1030-34) about a Cerberus which flatters the Athenian people—and licks up all the food when they aren't looking. It is possible that the word-play which Aristophanes exploits, between $\kappa \upsilon \omega \nu$ ("dog") and $K \lambda \epsilon \omega \nu$ [Cleon], had become a satirical commonplace in Athenian political life, rather like a cartoon. In *The Wasps,* Aristophanes goes further, making $K \lambda \epsilon \omega \nu$ a riddling amalgam of $\kappa \upsilon \omega \nu$ and $\kappa \lambda \epsilon \pi \tau \omega$, "to steal:" thus his name is interpreted as "stealing dog," and Philocleon's angry wish,

$$\kappa \lambda \epsilon \pi \tau \text{o} \nu \tau \alpha \ K \lambda \epsilon \omega \nu \alpha \ \lambda \alpha \beta \text{o} \iota \mu \iota,$$

contains in itself the essential elements of the dog trial: the stealing, Cleon, and also *Labes*—the latter being an amalgam of the general Laches and the root $\lambda \alpha B$-, "to get" or "grab."

Aristophanes clearly meant his audience to enjoy themselves following the clues which point to the poet's attack on Cleon. He pretends, through Xanthias, to put them off the track, saying that he won't resort to the old ploy of chopping Cleon into mincemeat; but much of the fun of the play comes from the way Cleon keeps coming in, one way or another, like an unforgettable obsession. The dreams point to Cleon; the protagonists' names involve relations to Cleon; people keep mentioning Cleon; and sooner or later—sooner, if they are quick to pick up hints, but later in any event—the audience are provided with the happy recognition of Cleon and Laches behind the dog trial—the familiar beneath the absurd. Nobody in the audience will miss the point that Aristophanes is getting at Cleon, that in his view Cleon is much guiltier than Laches or anyone else who might be put on trial. (They probably *will* miss the further suggestion that most everybody steals at some point or other, that the jurymen and Philocleon have stolen, and that the whole courtroom is pervaded by the atmosphere of deception and fraud symbolized in the name of the clock, the $\kappa \lambda \epsilon \psi \upsilon \delta \rho \alpha$ or "water-stealer.") Again, the audience will appreciate Aristophanes' picture of himself in the parabasis, as Heracles struggling with a Cerberus-monster. It makes a nice political cartoon. They will also catch the idea conveyed later on, that Aristophanes, though he pretended to submit, has taken a surprise vengeance on his enemy Cleon, as "the vinepole fooled the vine"—although as it turns out, the joke is also on Bdelycleon and on Aristophanes himself.

At first sight, the symbolism of the wasps seems as easy to interpret as that of the dogs. Indeed, Aristophanes talks about it explicitly, through the chorus-leader. He had just finished explaining how *The Clouds* was a fine play despite the audience's failure to appreciate it, to "get" its point; thus he compared himself to an ambitious chariot-driver who, in the effort to outreach his opponents (i.e., to write a comedy of ideas, not just tired slapstick) crashed and broke his—*idea.* ($\epsilon \pi \iota \nu \text{o} \iota \alpha \nu$). This time—and the contrast is pointed—the chorus say they will explain the "idea of the sting" ($\eta \ \pi \iota \nu \text{o} \iota \alpha \ \tau \eta \sigma \ \epsilon \gamma \kappa \epsilon \nu \tau \rho \iota \delta \text{o} \sigma$) so that even an ignorant person will understand it. So the wasp-chorus comically explain their own symbolism, point by analogical point. They are (they explain) very courageous beings; when the barbarian came with fire and smoke to loot their hives, they flew out angrily, fought, stung, and conquered him. And still today, as jurors, they exhibit the same temper; they "swarm" into various courts; they provide a livelihood for themselves by "stinging" (= voting to condemn); and they resent those stingless drones who have no [good] (i.e., never served in the army) yet share their privileges and their fee.

So far, the point is clear enough, despite Aristophanes' casual way of confusing wasp-traits with those of bees or hornets. The wasps are jurymen and veterans. Earlier, they pursued invaders with anger and spears; now they pursue defendants (and Aristophanes is playing, as often, on the literal and figurative meanings of $\delta \iota \omega \kappa \omega$ [pursue] and $\phi \epsilon \upsilon \gamma \omega$ [flee]) with the same anger, the stylus, and the voting tablet. Would the audience "get" the further implication that for these old men, jury duty is a kind of surrogate warfare? Probably not, or not very consciously: yet it is clearly important to Aristophanes that the aggressiveness which Bdelycleon has been trying to mitigate or exorcize is the very quality of temper that saved Athens in her time of peril. Even Aristophanes takes pride in his own Heraclean $\text{o} \rho \gamma \eta$ [wrath]. Wasps need their sting; we all need passion and power; and once more, when Bdelycleon introduces his father to a new life-style, he begins by removing his everyday jury coat which is *also* the coat that used to serve him so well in military campaigns. Take it away, like a hero's armor, and the old man's identity goes with it.

So far, the sting connotes aggressiveness and the jurymen's power. But that is not all. It seems clear that the sting is also a sexual symbol and that Aristophanes is teasing his audience by making this point obvious on stage without saying anything about it in his explanation. Sex is to be expected in Old Comedy, and sexual symbolism is appropriate in this dreamlike comedy; but how is it represented here, and what does it mean? Through most of *The Wasps,* the "sting" is prominent and the phallus is not. The chorus of old jurymen are weak and tired; their sexual exploits lie back in the same remote past, now nostalgically viewed, as their military ones: yet when they are roused, they can still attack the enemy in military formation and with extended stings at the ready. "Erect stings!" they cry in their battle scene; "Attack the enemy in the rear!" However this scene was acted out—and it must have been hilariously funny—the stings in it evidently stand not just for anger, but for anger as a sexual surrogate. The phalluses of the wasp chorus remain coiled up innocuously, but their stings retain a vitality, a life of their own.

The same symbolism applies, though less obviously, to Philocleon. From the beginning, his jurymania was described in terms of erotic obsession, partly for the fun of parodying Euripides' lovesick heroines, but even more to indicate that for Philocleon, power is an aphrodisiac. His jury life provides him with that repeated thrill of potency that makes him feel most alive. Hence all those jokes about "mussel shells" or "unsealing the wills" of pretty heiresses. If we go further, as I think we should, and interpret Philocleon's stonelike hardness as an expression of this inner feeling of sexual potency which his jury service provides, then we may also understand why Bdelycleon's attempts to "soften" his father make him feel impotent, sick, and old. Take away his sting and you take away his life. Of course, since this is comedy and not tragedy, Philocleon rebounds into sexual hybris, animal vitality. His "rope" may be old and rotten, as Bdelycleon insists it is; yet his revival and rejuvenation are sufficient, somehow, to cheer our hearts.

Did Aristophanes' audience "get" this fuller meaning of the sting? Probably not, any more than modern critics have: the wasp symbolism is hardly as transparent or as allegorical as that of the dogs. Yet Aristophanes, despite all his teasing, must have expected the *recognition* corresponding to the symbolism of the wasps and their stings to be available to the audience, as it is still available to us today. The point this time is more than satirical. It is a general truth about human nature. People, not least old people, require a sense of power and value; take that away, and they will not be happy, no matter how many substitute-comforts you may shower them with. In a way, therefore, Philocleon comes close to the great tragic heroes like Achilles and Ajax (and Medea) in the way he cares, passionately cares about his $\tau\iota\mu\eta$ [honor]. And his rebellion is ultimately right. It is hard to say what the practical implications of such a recognition might be. It is even harder to deal with Philocleon the wasp than with Cleon the dog. The complex wasp symbolism points to a dilemma: what *can* we do, after all, about these terrible old men? Understand them better, perhaps; but the negative moral remains, that this is not an illness that comedy (or any other treatment) can easily cure.

Our third idea, of *escape,* is more metaphor than symbol; it is conveyed more in feeling and action than in words; yet it is crucial to the final and very positive interpretation which this dreamlike play requires. For although we have stressed Bdelycleon's failure, the play can more justly be entitled, "Philocleon's Escape." The basic pattern was played out in the slapstick scenes before and after the entrance of the chorus. Philocleon is shut up within the house and tries to escape, is pushed in, pops out again, and so forth. Similarly, Bdelycleon's efforts to re-educate and reform his father are attempts to confine him, to keep him in. Bdelycleon is a spoilsport and a jailer, though with the best intentions. Will the old man elude the "watch?" Will he make his escape somehow, like Odysseus from the Cyclops' cave? Again and again he is foiled; he seems to be "Outis" more than Odysseus; yet in the end he escapes, by the implied help of Dionysus the looser of bonds, into unregenerate animal nature and drunken revelry. It is a final dramatization of the idea $\alpha\pi o\phi\epsilon\upsilon\gamma\omega$ [escape], used

throughout the play of defendants trying to "get off free," now transferred at the end to the runaway Philocleon himself. His final dance signifies happiness and victory, not unlike Alexander the Great's famous dream of a dancing satyr.

What kind of recognition goes with this dominant escape theme? This time, I think, it is a recognition less of the mind than of the heart: not satirical like the dog-allegory, nor thought-provoking like the wasps symbolism, but recognition as the *recovery* of an energy and hope which we once possessed, which (under various pressures) we had forgotten, and which, now rediscovered, promises a more confident and vital way of life. This rejuvenation movement is anticipated in the first ode of the parabasis (1060-70). Of old, say the chorus, they were valiant in dancing, in warfare, and in sex; now these things pass and heads grow grey: *and yet* (key words in comedy) they *must* reattain youthful vigor; for looking at today's effeminate youth, they feel surprisingly vigorous after all. This plea and affirmation is answered by the recovery of their champion, Philocleon. An ironic recovery, to be sure, as he plays the ardent lover wishing to escape the constraints of paternal domination—but the paradoxical truth is that Philocleon *is* more youthful, passionate, and energetic than his anxious son, who is old and crusty before his time. His recovery is the playwright's final healing gift to the chorus, who go out dancing, and behind them, to the Athenian people: for if Philocleon's defeat and disillusionment point to the need of accepting reality, as intelligent and sane people must accept it, yet Philocleon's successful rebellion and escape demonstrate the energy and erotic passion and hopefulness—those very Athenian traits—which make living in the real world not just tolerable, but deeply worthwhile.

If I am right, then Aristophanes has presented Athens after all with a healing catharsis. It has many features in common with the forms of psychotherapy attempted by Bdelycleon: the therapy of the word, the purification rites, the Corybantic music and dance, the Asclepian incubation. As *The Frogs* later attests, Aristophanes regarded the experience of producing or watching comedies as participation in a Dionysian rite; and it is above all Dionysus who presides over and guarantees the catharsis shaped by comedy: through the relaxation of tension, through the dream-like experience of a fluid world in which things turn into each other and the normal laws of scientific and critical thought are relaxed, and through the various recognitions, emotional as well as intellectual, which arise out of the experience of that transformed and transforming dream-world. Such a comic catharsis is a magnificent gift. What Aristophanes says in the parabasis is true. Yet his truthfulness is guaranteed by the way he exposes every single trace of fraud or deception or coercion, *even by himself,* that might accompany the desired catharsis. Bdelycleon is a shadow of Aristophanes: he is what Aristophanes either was, or might have been; for just as Bdelycleon, the would-be reformer, adopts his enemies' tricks and becomes like them in the end, so comedy itself could become manipulative, could use its devices of joke and fable and play for uncomic purposes of behavior modificaton and propaganda. The path to demagoguery is paved with good intentions. Yet in the end Aristophanes' play is non-coercive and it is honest: non-coercive like a dream which, on being rightly interpreted, brings out its own true story from our unconscious feelings and thoughts; and honest, because it includes the exposure of its own shadow side, its inherent dishonesty.

At the same time, *The Wasps* is a deeply democratic play: not only because it casts a vote against oligarchy, against turning over the management of affairs to clever people like Bdelycleon, or Aristophanes himself, but also because it reaffirms the fundamental unity of Old Comedy and of its audience. To be sure, the prologue and parabasis of this play seem to show a widening gap between Aristophanes' new comedy of ideas and the old vulgar farce, and also between the "clever people" in the audience who can "get" the poet's clever ideas and those others who do not—as with *The Clouds* the previous year. Such a division threatens unity, much as the Cleon-whale "divides the people" in Sosias' dream. But does Aristophanes accept this division? At first, he seems to; when he suggests that the audience are "clever" ($\delta\epsilon\xi\iota\sigma\iota$) and so will be able, at least with his guidance, to follow the new comedy, he seems insultingly condescending; yet he gives enormous weight to the ridiculing of cleverness and clever people in the last part of *The Wasps*. The chorus make fun of Bdelycleon, who turns out to be rather silly after all. They also lampoon various "clever people" who turn out to be idiots and perverts—ingenious perverts, to be sure. Yet it would be wrong to read the end of *The Wasps* as an unequivocal rejection of intellect. The last scenes, vulgarity and all, belong to an integrated comedy which can appeal to its varied audience on several levels of thought and feeling at one and the same time. It brings many kinds of wholeness, many kinds of healing.

Let me suggest, finally, that the positive themes of escape and recovery for which I have been arguing in *The Wasps* can be found, spelled out in much more explicit terms, in the next year's play. In *The Peace,* Athens returns to health, together with the rest of Hellas. The Athenian people have been sick with a war neurosis whose symptoms are suspiciousness, litigiousness, and bad temper generally; but now, restored to the blessings of peace, leisure, and the countryside, they recover their earlier good humor, their enjoyment of life, and the same perspective that accompanies such enjoyment. Rejuvenation and reform thus go together in *The Peace* as they could not in *The Wasps*. The roughness of bad-tempered jurors will be sloughed off, to everybody's gain including their own; they will turn youthful again, sleek, and tender—but clearly with no loss of sexual potency! On careful study, *The Peace* is filled with motifs taken from *The Wasps* but inverted, much as *The Wasps* inverted so many motifs from *The Clouds.* Thus the magic cooking works this time: Peace will "compound better humors" in the Greek peoples and will "mix them together" in friendship as in a good sauce (996-99). (This is much nicer than the crazy salad which War makes of cities, using such ingredients as Sicilian cheese and Attic honey.) A "demon hard to purge" (1250: ω δυσκαθαρτε δαιμον) is transferred from the hero to a nuisance type, a scapegoat; for Trygaeus himself is not insane as people think but rather a master of that creative

madness which by-passes the limits of feasibility and accomplishes what we all want done. This time, too, the fable works for progress. Trygaeus borrows something like Aesop's beetle (which we remember from Philocleon's drunken scene) and rides it in comic and fabulous fashion to Olympus. Conversely, the negative warnings that you can't change human nature so often found in fable and proverb are used this time by Trygaeus, with comic inversion, against the religious imposter who cited them as a necessary obstacle to peace. "You won't make the crab walk straight," proclaimed Hierocles; "you can't make the rough hedgehog smooth" (1083, 1086). And so Trygaeus, excluding Hierocles from the sacrificial feast, answers his protests with a firm reminder: "You won't make the rough hedgehog smooth" (1114).

It seems strange in retrospect that, although the crab proverb was never quoted in *The Wasps,* still that play ended with a dance of the "crabs," tiny spinning children of Carcinus the old king crab himself. It is a wonderful nonsense dance, delightful in its own right like the lobster quadrille in *Alice* or Edward Lear's owl and pussycat dancing to the light of the moon. Could it also be a riddling dramatic embodiment of that same unmentioned proverb, "You won't make the crab walk straight?" That was the point: nobody, not even a comic poet, can straighten out Philocleon or the Athenian jury system or human nature itself. And yet: even if crabs won't walk straight, these crabs at least can evidently dance—and what could be more fun, or a better symbol of energy, excitement, and very hope, than their spinning dance? (pp. 298-312)

Kenneth J. Reckford, "Catharsis and Dream-Interpretation in Aristophanes' 'Wasps'," in Transactions of the American Philological Association, *Vol. 107, 1977, pp. 283-312.*

FURTHER READING

OVERVIEWS AND GENERAL STUDIES

Croiset, Alfred and Maurice Croiset. "Aristophanes and His Contemporaries." In their *Abridged History of Greek Literature,* pp. 248-64. 1904. Reprint. New York: AMS Press, 1970.
    Includes an overview of Aristophanes's life and works.

Harriott, Rosemary. *Aristophanes: Poet and Dramatist.* London: Croom Helm, 1986, 194 p.
    Explores the dramatic, poetic, and narrative techniques used by Aristophanes.

Harsh, Philip Whaley. "Aristophanes." In his *A Handbook of Classical Drama,* pp. 265-312. Stanford, Calif.: Stanford University Press, 1944.
    A survey of Aristophanes's comedies; includes a discussion of structure, principal themes, and historical context.

Heath, Malcolm. *Political Comedy in Aristophanes.* Gottingen: Vandenhoeck und Ruprecht, 1987, 61 p.
    Maintains that any discussion of Aristophanes's come-

dies must include an analysis of the author's political intent.

Henderson, Jeffrey. *The Maculate Muse.* New Haven, Conn.: Yale University Press, 1975, 251 p.

Examines the function of obscene language in Aristophanic comedy.

Lord, Louis E. *Aristophanes: His Plays and His Influence.* New York: Longmans, 1927, 183 p.

A study of Aristophanes's influence on Greek, Roman, Italian, French, English, and German literatures.

Moulton, Carroll. *Aristophanic Poetry.* Gottingen: Vandenhoeck und Ruprecht, 1981, 152 p.

An analysis of Aristophanes's principal poetic procedures. Moulton asserts that, contrary "to the generally accepted notions of Aristophanic comedy as episodic and loosely structured, . . . the coherent unities in comic poetry are to be sought in the unique reality of fantasy itself."

Murray, Gilbert. "Comedy." In his *A History of Ancient Greek Literature,* pp. 275-93. New York: D. Appleton, 1937.

Traces Aristophanes's dramatic career and offers a general evaluation of his oeuvre.

Nussbaum, Martha. "Aristophanes and Socrates on Learning Practical Wisdom." In *Aristophanes: Essays in Interpretation,* edited by Jeffrey Henderson, pp. 43-97. Cambridge: Cambridge University Press.

Examines the philosophical questions raised by Aristophanes in his *Clouds.* According to Nussbaum, the *Clouds,* "by showing the potential violence of the democratic man, and monumental indifference to the rights, the dignity, even the lives of his fellow citizens," seems to bolster Plato's ideal of an enlightened aristocratic state.

Platt, Arthur. "Aristophanes." In his *Nine Essays,* pp. 45-64. Cambridge: Cambridge University Press, 1927.

Defines Aristophanes's comedic art as a "revolt against convention," asserting that "he has carried this revolt further than any other writer."

Spatz, Lois. *Aristophanes.* Boston: Twayne, 1978, 164 p.

A general overview of Aristophanes's life and works, including analyses of the principal comedies.

Stuart, Donald Clive. "The Origin of Greek Comedy. Aristophanes. Menander." In his *Development of Dramatic Art,* pp. 101-36. New York: D. Appleton, 1928.

A study of the structure, basic characteristics, and distinctive features of Aristophanes's comedies.

Sutton, Dana. *Self and Society in Aristophanes.* Lanham, Md.: University Press of America, 117 p.

Discusses the tension between society and the individual in Aristophanes's comedies. Sutton observes that "every Aristophanic hero is in his own way striving to create a personal utopia."

Ussher, R. G. *Aristophanes.* Oxford: Oxford University Press, 1979, 44 p.

Comments on Aristophanes's extraordinary "range and command of lyric language." In addition, Ussher focuses on staging and performance issues.

FROGS

Allison, Richard H. "Amphibian Ambiguities: Aristophanes and His *Frogs.*" *Greece & Rome* XXX, No. 1 (April 1983): 8-20.

Discusses the function and stage presentation of the frog chorus in Aristophanes's play.

Arnott, Peter. "Aristophanes and Popular Comedy: An Analysis of the *The Frogs.*" In *Western Popular Theatre,* edited by David Myer and Kenneth Richards, pp. 169-85. London: Methuen, 1977.

Compares the comic techniques of Aristophanes and Molière.

Hooker, J. T. "The Composition of the *Frogs.*" *Hermes* 108, No. 2 (1980): 169-82.

Identifies and explains certain compositional deviations from Old Comedy conventions.

LYSISTRATA

Marsh, David R. "The Double Chorus in the 'Lysistrata' of Aristophanes." *Proceedings of the Pacific Northwest Conference on Foreign Languages* 22 (16-17 April 1971): 193-96.

Discusses the relation of the double chorus, a unique feature of the play, to the story of gender conflict in *Lysistrata.*

Vaio, John. "The Manipulation of Theme and Action in Aristophanes' *Lysistrata.*" *Greek, Roman, and Byzantine Studies* 17, No. 4 (Winter 1973): 369-80.

Argues that certain compositional inconsistencies in *Lysistrata* were not lapses but rather characteristic features of Aristophanes's dramatic technique.

For further information on Aristophanes's life and career, see *Classical and Medieval Literature Criticism,* Vol. 4.

Albert Camus

1913-1960

INTRODUCTION

Camus is considered one of the most important literary figures of the twentieth century, having received the Nobel Prize in literature in 1957. An Algerian-born French writer, Camus produced works in many genres, including dramas, novels, essays, and short stories. Throughout his highly varied career he consistently, often passionately, explored the various ways people attempt to come to terms with, and sometimes overcome, the fact that they live in a universe without meaning. Although he is better known for his fiction and essays, Camus himself regarded drama as his favorite medium, calling it "one of the great joys of my life." His early days as an actor, director, and playwright in Algiers grew into a love for the theater which he maintained throughout his career. However, compared to his influential novels *L'Etranger* (*The Stranger*), *La Peste* (*The Plague*), and *La Chute* (*The Fall*), and his philosophical essays *Le Mythe de Sisyphe* (*The Myth of Sisyphus*) and *L'Homme révolté* (*The Rebel*), Camus's plays are the least respected of his literary output. Of his four original dramas, only *Caligula* was enthusiastically received when first presented; the response to *Le Malentendu* (*The Misunderstanding*) and *Les Justes* (*The Just Assassins*) was lukewarm, and *L'Etat de siège* (*State of Siege*) was judged a failure. His stage adaptations of such works as William Faulkner's novel *Requiem for a Nun* (*Requiem pour une nonne*) and Fyodor Dostoyevsky's novel *The Possessed* (*Les Possédés*) were more successful. In fact, Camus considered adapting dramas as creative and challenging a task as writing original pieces.

Camus spent the first twenty-seven years of his life in Algiers, the capital of what was then the French colony of Algeria. Born into a poor family, he was raised in a second floor apartment in a working-class section of the city. When Camus was just a year old, his father, Lucien Auguste Camus, was killed during World War I at the first battle of the Marne. Upon her husband's death, Camus's mother, Catherine Sintès Camus, took her sons Lucien and Albert to live with her mother and brother. Because she was partially deaf and much affected by her husband's death, Catherine left the rearing of her sons to her own strong-willed mother. Despite the lack of an intellectual atmosphere at home, Camus was nonetheless a superior student at school. An instructor, Louis Germain, recognized potential in the boy and encouraged him to excel. Germain lent him books to read, spent extra time tutoring him, and persuaded his autocratic grandmother to permit Camus to remain in school rather than go to work. He also urged his young student to vie for the scholarship that allowed him to attend the prestigious Lycée Bugeaud high school. Camus later dedicated his Nobel Prize acceptance speech to this first mentor.

While in his early teens, Camus was an active sports en-

thusiast. He swam often and was an avid soccer player, serving as goalie for the Racing Universitaire Algérois (RUA). As an adult, he wrote, "After many years during which I saw many things, what I know most surely about morality and the duty of man I owe to sport and learned in the RUA." Camus's sports activities came to a halt when, at seventeen, he contracted tuberculosis, a disease with which he was to be afflicted for the remainder of his life. Undaunted by his illness, Camus entered the University of Algiers in 1932. There, with professor Jean Grenier as his new mentor, he studied Greek literature, poetry, and philosophy, and discovered the works of Pascal, St. Augustine, Kierkegaard, and Plato. Grenier, an unorthodox thinker whose views tended to the ironic and skeptical, exerted a lasting influence on Camus's intellectual development. In forming his own philosophy, Camus increasingly analyzed the nature of the "absurd." The absurd refers to the perception that human beings, who constantly strive to make sense of the world, live in a godless universe where their lives have no meaning outside their own existence. Camus believed, however, that one can overcome the apparent meaninglessness of life through purposeful action. He felt that to accomplish this each person must first recognize that life is absurd and then rise above that absurdity. The refusal to either surrender to meaninglessness, or to avoid the struggle altogether, forms the basis of Camus's theory of "revolt": the deliberate and ceaseless confrontation with the absurd.

In 1936, Camus earned his *diplome d'études supérieures* in philosophy but his physical condition prevented him from undergoing the *agrégation,* a gruelling academic competition for teaching positions. Camus instead turned to journalism, writing for the *Alger-Républican.* During this period, he became involved in politics, joining the Algerian Communist Party in 1935. Germaine Brée has pointed out that, like other leftist students, Camus was "anti-Mussolini, anti-Hitler, anti-Franco, rather vague on facts and enthusiastically in favor of social reform in France." Also in 1935 he and a group of amateur actors in Algiers formed the Communist *Théâtre du Travail* (Worker's Theater), a troupe devoted to bringing outstanding plays to working class audiences. This experience allowed Camus to develop talents as an actor, director, and adaptor. In 1936 he collaborated with three student friends on a controversial play, *Révolte dans les Asturies,* a propagandistic work about a 1934 Spanish miners' strike. When it was written, Spain was on the brink of civil war, and the political mood was strained in Algeria as well. As a result, the mayor of Algiers banned the play, and it was never performed. Camus eventually became disillusioned with the Communist party and broke all ties with it in 1937. He continued, however, to work with the theater group until 1939, though he changed the name to the *Théâtre de l'Equipe* (Team Theater).

By 1942, the year in which both *The Stranger* and *The Myth of Sisyphus* were published, Camus had moved to Paris where he became a part of the French resistance movement against German occupation. He was also writing *The Plague,* while simultaneously working as a reader at the Gallimard publishing company during the day and writing for the underground newspaper *Combat* at night. Despite taking great precautions, Camus barely escaped being caught by the Nazi gestapo on at least one occasion. When Paris was liberated in 1944, *Combat* became a fullfledged daily newspaper, and Camus remained its editor until 1947.

Except for *Révolte dans les Asturies,* all of Camus's original dramas were first performed between 1944 and 1949. *The Misunderstanding* was Camus's first produced play, opening in 1944 to mixed reviews. Camus's attempt at a "modern tragedy" tells the story of a man's murder by his mother and sister. In the play, Martha and her mother run an inn in a bleak town in Europe. Longing to escape to a sunny land near the sea, they decide to murder rich customers to gather the money needed. The long-absent son Jan reappears with his wife Maria, intending to help his mother and sister. Hoping to surprise them, he decides to conceal his identity. He leaves Maria at another hotel and presents himself as a stranger at his mother's inn. Ironically, he is murdered by his family and thrown into the river. When Jan's passport is found, revealing his true identity, the mother kills herself. The next day, coming in search of her husband, Maria meets Martha, who tells her of

Jan's death. Martha insists that life is meaningless and advises Maria to become insensitive "like a stone," indicating that she herself will commit suicide. Maria cannot accept such a view of the world and calls out to God for help. An old servant appears in response, and she repeats her prayer. He, however, replies with the single word "No." Camus continued to revise this somber play from 1944 to 1958. Critics have noted the work's dramatic unity (the events in the play take place in less than twenty-four hours), its fatalism, and its characters who represent such reactions to the senselessness of the human condition as rebellion, despair, and acceptance.

Caligula, often considered Camus's most significant dramatic work, was first staged in early 1945, though it was begun as early as 1938. The character Caligula is based on the historical figure Gaius Caesar, called Caligula, who became emperor of Rome at the age of twenty-five. A gentle man at the onset of his reign, Caligula evolved into a cruel and heartless ruler who was eventually assassinated. In Camus's portrayal of the emperor, Caligula is transformed into a tyrant after the death of his sister-lover Drusilla. Her death makes clear to the emperor that "men die and they are unhappy." Since life is absurd or meaningless, Caligula reasons, every act is equally senseless. He then proceeds to prove his point by destroying accepted conventions. He seduces a man's wife, with the man himself as witness; causes a famine; and tortures his subjects indiscriminately. His aim is to educate the self-deluding patricians—members of Rome's aristocracy—on the meaning of the absurd. A segment of the oppressed people, led by the patrician Cherea, stage a revolt that culminates in the assassination of the emperor. Although Caligula laments, "I didn't take the right road, I came out nowhere. My freedom is not the right kind," his final words are defiant: "I am still alive." *Caligula* has been interpreted as a political allegory about the German occupation of France during World War II and as Camus's attempt to write a tragedy according to classical Greek models. Most scholars agree, however, that *Caligula* is a penetrating analysis of the nature of the absurd and a warning that individual liberty must affirm, not destroy, the bonds of humanity. Critics note that Caligula revolts against the absurdity of the universe—a response that Camus advocates—but does so in a way that the author rejects.

Following a lecture tour to the United States and Canada in 1946 and the publication of the critically acclaimed novel *The Plague* in 1947, Camus's next dramatic venture was *State of Siege,* produced in 1948. The play is an allegorical work condemning totalitarianism. It concerns the people of Cadiz, Spain, and their attempts to overcome the death and destruction of the plague, personified in the form of the town's new leader Plague and his secretary Death. Plague imposes a repressive administration of killing in which his secretary systematically checks off a list the names of those people who will become infected with the disease. Diego, a physician, rebels and rouses his fellow citizens to similar revolt. Diego himself contracts the disease, and the secretary Death attempts to seduce him. Refusing to give in to death, he strikes her, and all of his symptoms of the disease immediately disappear. In retaliation, Plague and his assistant check off names even more rapidly. Diego's fiancée Victoria becomes infected. Diego offers his life in exchange, but Plague proposes to spare them both if they leave Cadiz. Diego refuses and continues the struggle. Plague is ultimately driven from the city, but Diego dies of the disease. *State of Siege* was one of Camus's favorite works, but at its Paris opening the play was roundly condemned. French author René Barjavel remarked: "Since I have been going to the theatre, I believe that I have never suffered as much." Camus wrote in the introduction to the English translation of the play that *State of Siege* "had without effort achieved critical unanimity" and "a complete cutting up." Some audiences assumed that *State of Siege* was an adaptation of *The Plague,* but Camus averred that the play is not based on his novel. In fact, when compared to Camus's own works, *State of Siege* is most similar to *Caligula,* also a "play with death," Brée has observed. "This time, however, death alone does not hold sway, for *State of Siege* also concerns love and life."

Camus's next play, *The Just Assassins,* opened in 1949, a year after *State of Siege.* Treating the subject of terrorism in the early 1900s, the plot is derived from *Souvenirs d'un terroriste* (1931), the memoirs of Russian revolutionary Boris Savinkov. Camus's play involves a Socialist group that plans to assassinate the Tsar's uncle Grand Duke Sergei. The young poet Ivan Kaliayev, who is motivated by noble ideals, is chosen to throw a bomb at the Grand Duke's carriage as it takes him to the theater. Regarding his mission as a "crusade which is also a martyrdom," as John Cruickshank has noted, Kaliayev is willing to die for his actions without regret. Kaliayev does not throw the bomb, however, when he discovers that there are children in the carriage. One of his comrades, Stepan, insists that the presence of children should not have stopped him. Kaliayev protests that the murder of children is dishonorable, and his lover Dora—also a member of the group— agrees. He succeeds in his second attempt, but is captured and sentenced to die. In prison Kaliayev resists several temptations to repent and is ultimately executed. Dora, however, begins to have doubts, perceiving the contradictions between her noble ideals and terroristic murder. Nevertheless, she asks for the assignment to throw the next bomb, stating, "It's so much easier to die from one's inner conflicts than to live with them." *The Just Assassins* was greeted with opposing reactions. The Communist newspaper *L'Humanité* found the characters unrealistic and the play itself "worse than cold—icy." But *Le Populaire,* a Socialist party publication, reviewed it as "powerful and moving." Critic Alba Amoia has praised the "controlled tone and realistic dialogue" of the play, calling it "an effective stage vehicle and a compelling objectification of some of Camus's deepest thoughts on justice. . . ."

Over the next ten years Camus published the essay *The Rebel,* the novel *The Fall,* and the collection of short stories *L'Exil et le royaume* (*Exile and the Kingdom*), but did not write another original play, opting instead to concentrate on adaptations. Among the most highly regarded of these are *Les Esprits,* adapted from Pierre de Larivey's comedy of the same name; *Un Cas intéressant* from Dino Buzzati's comedy *Un Caso clinico; Requiem pour une*

nonne; and *Les Possédés.* In this same period Camus gradually fell from popular favor. His break with his longtime compatriot the existential writer Jean Paul Sartre due to a political quarrel in 1950 left him disheartened, and his refusal to comment on the Algerian war for independence in the mid-1950s brought criticism from both the French and the Algerian sides. Camus had just emerged from a long-lived writer's block, full of ideas for future writings, when he died suddenly in a car accident outside Paris on 4 January 1960.

Critical reception of Camus's dramatic output is mixed. Although he is admired as a director and innovator, and his plays are generally well regarded as written texts, the consensus among scholars is that his emphasis on philosophical issues leads Camus to create characters that are often merely representatives of specific ideologies. As a result, his plays are commonly judged stiff, formal, and lifeless. In spite of marked fluctuations in Camus's popularity—his rise to literary fame in the 1940s occurred as rapidly as his fall from popular favor in the years preceding his death—his literary significance remains undisputed. Although his plays have not elicited as much scholarly attention as his novels, essays, and short stories, they have been the focus of considerable study. "Camus's dramatic output is sometimes considered slim," Brée has remarked, "and his incursion into the theater merely a brief episode in his literary career. . . . Yet his plays continue to live in Little Theaters throughout the world, are frequently discussed in scholarly essays, and seem more alive in many minds than other more resoundingly successful dramas."

PRINCIPAL WORKS

PLAYS

Révolte dans les Asturies   1936 [collaborator, with Anne Sicard, Alfred Poignant, and Yves Bourgeois]
*†*Caligula*   1938-39
   [*Caligula,* 1947]
Le Malentendu   1944
   [*Cross Purpose,* 1947; also published as *The Misunder-standing,* 1958]
**L'Etat de siège*   1948
   [*State of Siege,* 1958]
**Les Justes*   1950
   [*The Just Assassins,* 1958]
Les Esprits   1953 [adaptor; from the play of the same name by Pierre de Larivey]
Un Cas intéressant   1955 [adaptor; from the play *Un Caso clinico* by Dino Buzzati]
Requiem pour une nonne   1956 [adaptor; from the novel *Requiem for a Nun* by William Faulkner]
Les Possédés   1959 [adaptor; from the novel *Besy* by Fyodor Dostoyevsky]
   [*The Possessed,* 1960]

OTHER MAJOR WORKS

L'Envers et l'endroit (essays) 1937
  ["Betwixt and Between" published in *Lyrical and Critical,* 1967]
Noces (essays) 1938
  ["Nuptials" published in *Lyrical and Critical,* 1967]
L'Etranger (novel) 1942
  [*The Stranger,* 1946]
Le Mythe de Sisyphe (essay) 1942
  [*The Myth of Sisyphus,* 1955]
Lettres à un ami allemand (essays) 1945
  ["Letters to a German Friend" published in *Resistance Rebellion and Death,* 1961]
La Peste (novel) 1947
  [*The Plague,* 1948]
L'Homme révolté (essay) 1951
  [*The Rebel,* 1954]
La Chute (novel) 1956
  [*The Fall,* 1957]
L'Exil et le royaume (short stories) 1957
  [*Exile and the Kingdom,* 1958]
Oeuvres complètes (collected works) 1962
‡*La Mort heureuse* (novel) 1971
  [*A Happy Death,* 1972]

*These works were translated and published as *Caligula and Three Other Plays* in 1958.

†This work was written in 1938-39, published in 1944, and first performed in 1945.

‡This work was written in 1937 but was not published until 1971.

AUTHOR COMMENTARY

Why I Work in the Theatre (1959)

[*In the following essay, Camus discusses his love for theatrical work, the benefits of which he believes are twofold. Staging a play allows him to concentrate his creative talents in a sort of religious "rite," free from the vanity that comes with fame; it also pulls him out of the artistic vacuum in which writers work, letting him form instead a collaborative fellowship with directors and actors during the creative process. This piece originally appeared in French as "Camus vous parle" in Le Figaro littéraire, 16 May 1959 and was later reprinted in his Théâtre, Recits, Nouvelles.*]

Why do I work in the theatre? I've often asked myself why. And up to the present, the only answer I've been able to make will strike you as discouragingly banal: simply because the theatre is one of the places in the world in which I am happy.

Look out, though; that reflection is less banal than it seems. Nowadays, happiness is a touchy subject. People have rather a tendency to hide their pursuit of it even from themselves, to regard it as a kind of rosy-hued ballet for which they ought to make excuses. Sometimes I read that

men of action who have given their all to public activity find refuge or shelter in their private lives. There's a little contempt, isn't there, in such a notion? Contempt and—the one doesn't exist without the other—nonsense. I, for one, have observed many cases of the reverse situation: people who have found refuge in public life in order to escape their private lives. The powerful are often flops at happiness, which explains why they cannot be gentle.

Being happy today is like living in sin: You must never admit it. Don't say innocently, without considering evil, "I'm happy." Immediately you will read your condemnation on curled lips all around you: "Oh! You're happy, my boy! And tell me, what are you doing about the orphans in Kashmir, and the lepers in the New Hebrides? *They* aren't exactly happy!" Well, what is to be done? So immediately we become as sad as toothpicks.

Yet I am sorely tempted to believe that in order to be really useful to people who are in misery, we must be strong and happy. The person who regards his life as a burden and who sinks under his own weight, can't help anyone. But the person who controls his feelings and his life can give effectively. I knew a man once who didn't love his wife, and was in despair over it. One day he decided to devote his life to her (in overcompensation, in other words). From that moment, the life of the poor woman, which until then had been bearable, became absolute hell. You see, her husband was ostentatious in his self-sacrifice, and quite shatteringly devoted. That's how it is these days: People devote themselves most to those human beings they like least. Such morose lovers marry, in fact, for the worst, never for the best.

Is it any wonder, under the circumstances, that the world looks ill, and that it becomes difficult to paste a picture of happiness over it—especially when one is a writer? Nevertheless, I cling to my respect for happiness and for happy people; for the sake of hygiene, I try to be in one of the settings of my happiness as often as possible—namely, the theatre. Unlike certain other more transitory joys, mine in the theatre has persisted for over twenty years, and much as I might want to, I don't think I could do without it. In 1936, I reorganized a defunct troupe in a dance hall in Algiers, and put on plays ranging from Malraux to Dostoevski to Aeschylus. Twenty-three years later, on the stage of the Théâtre Antoine, I was able to put on an adaptation of Dostoevski's *The Possessed.* Even I was astonished at such rare faithfulness—or such long intoxication. I wondered what the reasons could be for my obstinate virtue, or vice. And I found that there were two kinds: one that concerned my own nature, the other that concerned the nature of the theatre.

My first and less dazzling reason, I recall, was that through the theatre I escape from what irks me in my career as a writer. I escape first of all from what I call the frivolous traffic jam. Suppose your name is Fernandel, Brigitte Bardot, Aly Khan, or, more modestly, Paul Valéry. In any case, you have your name in the newspapers. And as soon as you have your name in the newspapers, the traffic jam begins. Mail rushes at you; invitations pour in; presumably they must be answered. A large portion of your time is taken up in refusing to waste it. Half your human energy is used thus in saying no, in all sorts of ways. Isn't that silly? Of course it's silly. But that's how we are punished for our vanity by vanity itself. I had noted meanwhile that everybody regards work in the theatre with awe, even if it too is a vain profession, and that all you need do is to announce that you are in rehearsal. Immediately a desert forms around you. And when you have the cunning, as I do, to rehearse all day and part of the night, well, frankly, it's paradise. In that respect the theatre is my monastery. The tumult of the world dies at the base of its walls; inside its sacred enclosure, for two months, sworn to a single meditation, turned toward a single goal, a community of working monks, isolated from the century, prepares the rite that will be celebrated one evening for the first time.

Does the word "monks" surprise you? A sophisticated press, or a sophomoric one (I don't know which), may lead you to picture theatre people as animals, sleeping late and divorcing often! I would be deceiving you, no doubt, if I were to tell you that the theatre is more banal than that, or even that people in it get divorced far less frequently than in textiles, in sugar, or in journalism. It's simply that when there is a divorce case involving people in the theatre, other people naturally talk about it more. Let's say that the heart of our Sarah Bernhardt engages the public interest more than that of M. Boussac. That's quite understandable. Yet an acting career calls for some of the stamina and control of an athlete. Acting is a profession in which the body counts, not because it is used profligately, but because one is constrained to keep it in shape. Being virtuous is a matter of necessity, which is perhaps the only way to be virtuous.

In any case I prefer the company of people in the theatre, virtuous or not, to that of the intellectuals, my brothers. As everyone knows, intellectuals are seldom amiable; they don't get along well together. There is another reason that I can't explain fully. In the company of intellectuals I always feel as if there's something about me that takes forgiving; I invariably have the impression that I've broken one of the rules of the clan. Such a feeling dispels my spontaneity, and without spontaneity I bore even myself. On the stage I am spontaneous. I don't think about whether to be or not to be, and the only things I share with my collaborators are the trials and joys of a common enterprise. Such a state, I believe, is called fellowship, and has been one of the great joys of my life. I lost it in the days when I left a newspaper we were doing as a team, and found it again as soon as I returned to the theatre.

A writer works in solitude, is judged in solitude, and, above all, judges himself in solitude. That is not right, and it is not healthy. If he is constituted normally, the hour comes when he needs to see other faces, to feel the warmth of human contact, which even explains most of the involvements of a writer: marriage, academe, politics. Anyway, these expedients settle nothing. No sooner has he lost his solitude than he begins to miss it. He would like to have, at one and the same time, both his slippers and a great love; he would like to be an academician without ceasing to be a nonconformist; and if he is engaged in politics, he would like to have others negotiate and kill in his stead, but only on the condition that he reserve the right to denounce them for it. Believe me, the career of an artist today is not a sinecure.

The theatre offers the fellowship I need, together with the heavy servitude and the limitations that all men and all minds need. In solitude, the artist reigns—but over a vacuum. In the theatre he cannot reign. What he wants to do depends upon others. The director needs the actor, who needs him. This mutual dependence, when it is recognized with the humility and the good humor that are appropriate to it, forms the solidarity of the profession, and gives a body to its daily fellowship. In it we are all linked together without the loss of anyone's freedom (or almost so). Isn't that a good prescription for the society of the future?

But let's get this much straight: Actors are just as deluded as any other human species, including their director, and sometimes even more so when you have permitted yourself to love them. But the delusions (if delusions they are) happen most often after the period of work is over, when each returns to his solitary nature. In this profession, whose people are not strong in logic, it is said with equal conviction that failure breaks up the company, and so does success. There's nothing to that. What breaks up the company is the end of the hope that held them together during rehearsals. It is the proximity of the goal (opening night) that has held them together in such intimate fellowship. A party, a movement, a church are also fellowships; but the goals they seek become lost in the night of the future. In the theatre the fruit of the work will be harvested, for better or for worse, on an evening known long in advance, an evening that each day's work brings closer. Individual men and women become a team through sharing a common adventure, and pursuing a single goal, which will never be better or more beautiful than on the long-awaited evening when the dice are cast.

The builders' trade guilds, the collective studios of painting during the Renaissance must have experienced the kind of exaltation known by those who work on a big show. Their achievements have endured long beyond the moment of execution; contrariwise, a show is transitory—and its participants love it all the more because one day it must die. Only in my youth have I known such fellowship: the same strong sense of hope and unity that accompany the long days of training leading up to the day of the match. What little I know of morale, I learned on football fields and on the stage. They have been my true universities.

The theatre also helps me to flee the abstractness that threatens all writers. Just as in my days as a newspaperman I preferred setting up pages in type to wording those quasi sermons that are called editorials, so too in the theatre I like the way the work takes root in a jumble of spotlights, platforms, canvas and props. I don't know who said that to be a good director you have "to know the weight of the scenery with your arms," but it's a great rule in art. And I love this profession which obliges me to consider simultaneously the psychology of personalities, the placing of a lamp or a pot of geraniums, the texture of a cloth, the weight and counterweight of a heavy piece that must be flown above the stage. When my friend Mayo designed the sets for *The Possessed,* we agreed that we had to begin by thinking in terms of solid settings (an ugly room, furniture—reality, in short), in order to raise the production, little by little, to a more elevated plane, less rooted in matter; finally, we would stylize the *décor.* The play wound up in a kind of unreal madness, but it started out from a precise place, burdened with matter. Isn't that the very definition of art? Not reality alone, nor imagination alone, but imagination taking flight from reality.

Enough of personal reasons for my presence in the theatre. They are the reasons of a man, but I have the reasons of an artist too—and the latter are more mysterious. First of all, I find the theatre a place of truth. To be sure, people generally call it a place of illusion. Don't you believe it! It is society, above all, that lives among illusions, and you will certainly find fewer hams on the stage than around town. Take, for example, one of those nonprofessional actors who cuts a figure in fashionable circles, or in the administration, or simply at opening nights. Put him on the stage, in this exact spot; throw four thousand watts of light on him, and the play will become unbearable. You will see him, in a sense, absolutely naked in the light of truth. Yes, the spotlight's blaze is merciless, and all the faking in the world will never conceal the true identity of the man or woman on stage, in spite of disguises and costumes. And I am absolutely sure that even those people I have known long and well in life would be truly and fundamentally revealed to me only if they were willing to rehearse and perform with me in a work involving characters of another century and another nature. Those who love the mystery of the heart, and the truth concealed in human beings, must come to the theatre; it is there that their insatiable curiosity receives at least partial gratification. Yes, believe me, to make the truth come alive, put it on a stage.

Sometimes I am asked, "How can you reconcile the theatre and literature in your life?" To be sure, I have had many professions, out of necessity or taste, and since I have continued to be a writer, it must be assumed that I have managed to reconcile them somehow. I even feel that the moment I consent to be a writer only, I shall stop writing. And where the theatre is concerned, the reconciliation is automatic; to me the theatre is the highest of literary forms, and certainly the most universal. I once knew and loved a director who was always saying to his authors and his actors, "Write, or act, for the one nitwit in the audience." He was not advising them to be stupid or common, but only to speak to everyone present. Actually, nitwits didn't exist for him; everyone deserved having an interest taken in him. But speaking to everyone is not easy. You always run the risk of aiming too low or too high. There are authors who want to address themselves to what is most stupid in the public; believe me, they succeed very well. There are others who want to address themselves only to those who are supposedly intelligent; they almost always fail. The former prolong that very French dramatic tradition which might be called The Epic of the Bed; the latter throw a few vegetables in the philosophic stew. On the other hand, when an author does succeed in speaking to everybody with simplicity while remaining ambitious about his subject, he serves the true tradition of art; he brings together all classes and all spirits in the audience

in a single emotion or a single laugh. Only the very great achieve that.

I've also been asked (with a solicitude that overwhelms me, you may be sure), "Why do you adapt scripts when you could be writing plays of your own?" I *have* written plays of my own, and I shall go on writing others; and I shall resign myself in advance to the fact that in so doing, I may be providing those same persons who ask the question with grounds for wishing I had stuck to my adaptations. When I write *my* plays, it is the writer who is functioning, but in accordance with a broad, over-all scheme. When I *adapt,* it is a case of the director working according to the terms of his concept of the theatre. I believe, in fact, in the total show, conceived, inspired and produced by the same soul; written and directed by the same man. Such an approach makes possible the attainment of a unity of tone, style and rhythm that comprise the absolute essentials of a show, and which I may pursue perhaps more freely than others who have not been, as I have, author, playwright and director. In short, I am the servant of the texts (translations, adaptations, or what have you)—but when they are put in production on a stage, I reserve the right to fashion them in accordance with the needs of the direction. I collaborate with myself, in other words, a fact that eliminates the friction between author and director. And I feel so little degraded by this work that I shall continue to pursue it whenever I have the opportunity. I should feel that I had deserted my duties as a writer only if I agreed to put on shows that might please the public through degraded means—the kind of highly successful production you used to see (and still can) on our Paris stage, which turns my stomach. I certainly don't feel that I deserted my career as a writer when I staged *The Possessed;* the production is the embodiment of what I actually know and believe about the theatre.

Perhaps it won't be possible to serve what I love in the theatre much longer. The very nobility of this demanding profession is being threatened today. The incessant rise in costs and the bureaucratization of professional companies are pushing the theatre, little by little, toward further commercialism. Too many such commercial managements acquire glitter more through their incompetence than by any other means, and they have no right to imprison that franchise which a mysterious fairy godmother once gave them. And so this place of grandeur may turn into a place of squalor.

Is that any reason to give up the fight? I don't think so. A spirit of art and madness lurks incessantly beneath the balconies and behind the drapes. It cannot die, and it prevents all from being lost. It awaits each one of us. It's up to us to see that it finds expression. We must prevent it from being banished by the shopkeepers and the mass-producers. In return, it will keep us on our toes, and save our good and solid humor. To receive and to give—isn't that the happiness and the ultimately innocent life about which I was speaking at the beginning? And we need life itself, strong and free.

Let's get to work on the next show. (pp. 58-9, 70-1)

Albert Camus, "Why I Work in the Theatre,"

translated by Sue Davidson, in Theatre Arts,
*Vol. XLIV, No. 12, December, 1960, pp. 58-9,
70-1.*

OVERVIEWS AND GENERAL STUDIES

Allan Lewis   (essay date 1962)

[*Lewis is an American critic and educator who has written extensively on modern theater. In the following excerpt, he provides a general introduction to Camus and
his dramatic works.*]

The sudden death of Albert Camus in an automobile accident at the age of forty-six, three years after he had won
the Nobel Prize for literature, was a major loss to France
and to the contemporary theatre. He had written but five
plays, in addition to his novels, collections of essays, and
adaptations for the stage, but under the reorganization of
André Malraux, he was given his own theatre where as director and producer he would have had full freedom to experiment. He had long hoped for such an opportunity, and
once wrote that the theatre was "one of the places in the
world where [he was] happiest."

Camus belongs to the theatre of ideas, but unlike [Jean
Paul] Sartre, he was never convinced of certainty, and his
doubt made him all the more human. His ideas were few,
but in coming to them he had eliminated many others in
order to explore those few more exhaustively. In *Noces,*
he said:

> It takes ten years to have an idea all one's own—
> about which one can speak. Naturally, it's a little
> discouraging.

Though he was not an existentialist, he was close to Sartre
in affirming a universe without God, but he did not erect
a philosophical system of ethical values. He was content
to say that "man's responsibility is to do nothing to increase suffering." His own anguish, which is the central
theme of his plays, is the fear that we may have failed to
do that which would spare another human being. Men
must act, and Camus, like Sartre, believed in the "committed" writer, but only because inaction may fail to prevent
or lessen the misery of others. We cannot rely on chance.

> The time of irresponsible artists is over. We shall
> regret it for our little moments of bliss. But we
> shall be able to admit that this ordeal contributes
> meanwhile to our chances of authenticity . . .
> The freedom of art is not worth much when its
> only purpose is to assure the artist's comfort.

He sought a positive affirmation of life even if it lay only
in the freedom to search for that affirmation. In his essays
on rebellion, he wrote:

> . . . I am tired of criticism, of disparagement,
> of spitefulness—in short, of nihilism. It is essen-
> tial to condemn what must be condemned, but
> swiftly and firmly. On the other hand, one
> should praise at length what still deserves to be

praised. After all, that is why I am an artist, because even the work that negates still affirms
something and does homage to the wretched and
magnificent life that is ours.

It is the most succinct reply to [Eugéne] Ionesco and
[Jean] Genêt.

Camus was born in Algeria, the son of an agricultural
worker, and knew poverty and the struggle to gain a university education. Never completely at home in Europe,
he always longed for the sun and the sea of the African
coast. He formed his own theatre group in Algiers, mostly
with students and workers, and wrote his first play, *Caligula,* for them, but it was not produced until years later in
Paris. His fame was the result of his novels, *The Stranger*
and *The Plague,* and a book of essays, *The Myth of Sisyphus,* in which occurs the oft-quoted phrase, "There is
only one really serious philosophical problem—suicide."
His essays contain more serenity, hopefulness and resolution than the plays, which, with their moments of doubt,
the thinking out of human problems, the action prior to
resolution, are pessimistic. They deal with loneliness, with
crime that is accidental and fatal, with "groping in the
dark . . . dreaming of justice," yet contributing to injustice. Above all, to Camus—as to many—the source of anxiety is the absence of any real reason for living, a problem
covered over by habit and sentiment. The symbol of dislocation and futility is Sisyphus rolling his rock up the
mountain and having it roll down just as he reaches the
top, but Camus respected man and found "help in hope,"
and in preserving those few values "without which a
world, even transformed, is not worth living in."

Le Malentendu (*The Misunderstanding*), written while
Camus was living in the mountains of central France as
a member of the Resistance, was his first produced play.
The scene is an inn in Bohemia, run by Martha and her
mother. To save money to escape from their barren, dismal surroundings, they kill the occasional guest who arrives, dispose of his body, and rob him of his funds. The
son, Jan, returns after a long absence and expects to be recognized without giving his name. Instead, he is murdered.
This is the misunderstanding. Aware of what they have
done, mother and sister commit suicide. It is a gloomy
play in which the inner conflicts are insufficiently visualized. Camus, like others of the theatre of ideas, is less concerned with psychological motivation than with philosophical implications. He called his play "a work of easy
access," but the access is choked by the emphasis on the
verbal; yet, paradoxically, the theme is the absurdity of relationships that depend on words. The failure of Jan to say
the right word leads to his death. Camus tells in one of his
essays of a visit to Prague. A stranger dies alone in his
hotel room, while the narrator next door, aware that
something wrong is taking place, studies a shaving cream
advertisement. Leaving things to chance, through inaction
permitting the accidental to happen, may lead to another's
death and our own failure to lessen human misery. When
Jan is alone in his room at the inn, he says:

> The evenings are depressing for a lonely
> man . . . and I know what it is. It's fear, fear of
> the eternal loneliness, fear that there is no an-
> swer.

The play is also the story of the son's return—"He came unto his own and his own received him not." All the characters are lost in their private solitude, and though they may be of the same blood, there is no recognition. Their lives touch but do not communicate.

The Old Man, who is the servant and accomplice of Martha and her mother, moves silently throughout the action. When, in the final scene, Jan's widow calls upon God for help, the Old Man enters and says, "No"—his only word in the play. Camus wrote that the Old Man could not have helped if he had wanted to, for pain is solitary. But there is an implication of the distance between man and God, of the lack of any explanation for ugliness and brutality.

Les Justes (*The Assassins*), which deals with the murder of the Russian Archduke by a band of terrorists, is a discussion of ends and means, of the relationship between ethics and politics. Camus said that he admired the assassins because "they understood the limits of action," and that there is no good or just action that does not recognize those limits. Our world today is run by men "who go beyond those limits and kill others without dying themselves . . . Justice serves as an alibi throughout the world for the assassins of justice." In the most dramatic scene, the Grand Duchess comes to the prison cell to interview her husband's murderer, the one who threw the bomb. She offers him the grace of God and the forgiveness of man. He angrily rejects both. He must accept death, for otherwise he would not have had the right to take a life, and would not have recognized the limits of his action. Is murder ever justified, even if done to restore justice and better all humanity? It is the question raised by the Resistance fighters and by [Bertolt] Brecht in *Die Massnahme* (*The Expedient*) and by Sartre in *Les Mains Sales* (*Dirty Hands*).

L'Etat de Siège (*State of Siege*) is the weakest of the plays. It is a treatise about the effects on men of being closed within a sick society. Despite the production by [Jean-Louis] Barrault, it won little acclaim. The plague is more skillfully treated in the novel. The best of Camus' dramatic work is *Caligula,* the first play he wrote, and one of the finest examples of the theatre of ideas.

Caligula, Emperor of Rome, is overwhelmed by the death of Drusilla, his sister and mistress. He goes off to the wilderness to be alone with his grief, and when he returns he has discovered a new truth: that "men die; and they are not happy." He will no longer be content with the usual and the commonplace. He will find happiness even if he has to destroy the world to do so, for he alone has the power to be free. He begins with truth as he sees it, tearing away the outward appearance of lies and deception that have become rooted in all government and seeped through to all of life. He kills and murders and destroys, reveling in the sensuous release that he believes is happiness. For he, the Emperor, is "the unpunished murderer" in a world of scorn and hatred, but his happiness is illusory and his freedom brings loneliness and the anguish of being a man. He has shed tears of love, but now he weeps because "the world's all wrong." He says:

> I knew that men felt anguish, but I didn't know what that word anguish meant. Like everyone

else, I fancied it was a sickness of the mind—no more. But no, it's my body that's in pain . . . but worst of all this queer taste in my mouth. Not blood, or death, or fever, but a mixture of all three. I've only to move my tongue and the world goes black, and everyone looks . . . horrible. How hard, how cruel it is, this process of becoming a man!

His loneliness is deceptive. One is never alone. There is always the future and the past, and

> those we have killed are always with us. But they are no great trouble. It's those we have loved, those who loved us and whom we did not love; regrets, desires, bitterness, and sweetness, whores and gods, the celestial gang! Always, always with us! . . . If only in this loneliness . . . I could know, but for a moment, real solitude, real silence, the throbbing stillness of a tree.

He casts out love to go beyond love. He will love the moon and attain the impossible. In mounting fury, he plays before the mirror the image of himself, and in the final scene, strangles his faithful mistress Caesonia, so that he may achieve beyond love "the glorious isolation of man." He has searched for the impossible "at the confines of the world, in the secret places of his heart" and knows that his freedom has led to nothing. He smashes the mirror and exclaims, "Soon, I shall attain the emptiness beyond all understanding." The young poet Scipio and the old cynic Cherea, the disinterested minds who love him for his madness, are the ones who destroy him. As the conspirators plunge their daggers into his body, Caligula cries, "I'm still alive."

Camus condemns the Emperor's absolute nihilism. No man can save himself alone. Caligula refuses to escape the absurdities of life by accepting the accessible refuge of God's unknowable justice, and rejects faith in another life that may transcend this one. He would make the impossible attainable here on earth, change the order of the universe, cause laughter from pain, beauty from ugliness, and he observes his power in a mirror for he alone is witness of his deeds. He fails because he chose a way without humanity. The result is isolation and hate, and he smashes the mirror that reflects his failure. But he lives on after death, since his was the supreme effort of the passion for the impossible, which Camus stated is as "valid a subject for drama as adultery or avarice."

Sartre had Goetz in *The Devil and the Good Lord* turn to evil as the only creative act left to man. Caligula turns to evil to imitate the gods. His error lies in negating man. In his preface to the play, Camus wrote that "one cannot destroy everything without destroying oneself . . . Caligula is a superior suicide . . . Unfaithful to mankind through fidelity to himself, Caligula accepts death because he has understood that no one can save himself all alone and that one cannot be free at the expense of others." In this sense, *Caligula* is a modern morality play, a debate on the nature of man. Though the conclusion seemingly is nothingness and a return to what had existed before, the Emperor's rebellion exposes the emptiness of an ill-considered nihilism, a rebuke to the facile writing of despair. Camus could offer little in the way of positive answers, and he rejected the glib assumptions of indifference to life. During the Resistance he had said that, though this world has no superior meaning, "I know that something in it has meaning. It is man, because man is the sole being to insist on having a meaning." He accepted no systematic concepts either of totalitarianism or existentialism—the end may not justify the means. However, his outlook was not one of fear but of devotion to the task of serving human dignity by "means which are honorable in the midst of history which is not honorable." And he added, "I should not want to change eras, for I know and respect the greatness of this one. Moreover, I have always thought the maximum danger implied the maximum hope." (pp. 211-17)

> Allan Lewis "The French Theatre-Giraudoux, Sartre, Camus," in his The Contemporary Theatre: The Significant Playwrights of Our Time, *Crown Publishers, Inc., 1962, pp. 191-217.*

Germaine Brée   (essay date 1964)

[*Brée is a French-born American critic and translator. Her critical works are devoted to modern French literature and include studies of Marcel Proust and André Gide and* The French Novel from Gide to Camus *(1926). Here, Brée examines Camus's four original plays,* Caligula, L'Etat de siège, Le Malentendu, *and* Les Justes, *considering in turn the conflict each work presents between human desire for happiness and a meaningless universe. Each play shows people struggling to impose order on the world by means of a "totalitarian logic," an effort that results in destruction and failure. According to Brée, "the greatest tragedy in Camus's theatrical world . . . is to make of this earth 'a desert,' that is, to destroy that part of life which is joy and love."*]

The Emperor, Caligula, is the first of the forces of perversion Camus unleashed on the stage. *Rien* (nothing) is the leitmotiv of the play, and Caligula is the man who carries this theme to its ultimate limits, a privilege that only an all-powerful emperor enjoys, as he himself recognizes. In *Caligula,* Camus chose to project upon the stage the extreme consequences of the nihilism with which he grappled in his first works. His emperor is a victim, not a hero, of *l'absurde,* suffering from a form of *hubris* which in Camus's eyes is peculiarly modern and at the heart of much evil in our time.

The Emperor's fall really takes place before the curtain rises. Until the death of his beloved sister Drusilla, Caligula was a perfect emperor, a man who spoke of love, justice, and friendship, a man who aspired to be a just man. When he returns after Drusilla's death and his three-day disappearance—a symbolic descent into hell—he returns a man possessed. He has struggled with the meaning of death and comes back transformed. He sees that death negates life, love, friendship, justice, human beings, human values; that death delivers up the human being to an arbitrary, impersonal, mechanical fate. From this powerfully simple, negative, intellectual vision, Caligula draws extreme consequences: everyday living, individual habits and social institutions, are shams, contemptible forms of mockery with which human beings delude themselves. From his de-

tached vantage point he looks down on life and sees around him only hypocrisy, dissembling, cowardice, a worthless and miserable "play."

Since he is emperor and since he is in possession of an incontrovertible truth he is doubly free; he is free to impose the truth upon his subjects, he is free to tear away the mask of their false security as he pleases. In the name of truth he undertakes a peculiar form of ruthless and disinterested mental warfare upon his subjects. Caligula is now a man with a purpose—an educator, not a tyrant—the would-be savior of humanity.

This is the easiest level of action for the spectator to follow, and the richest in theatrical effects. Camus gives full play to a macabre, inventive form of "black" humor, using for its maximum effect the strange mad acts Suetonius records [in his *Lives of the Caesars,* Camus's source for *Caligula*]. The dramatic situation is simple and its dynamism authentic. On the one hand are the Patricians, types rather than characters, straw men who incarnate the complacent, righteous attitudes of good citizens; on the other is the all-powerful Emperor, who sets out to challenge the authenticity of their attitudes and to introduce them to the truth. At the beginning the spectator is likely to be on the side of the Emperor, on the side of his truth against their shams. But as the perspective changes the spectator reluctantly abandons Caligula, though not to join the Patricians.

Caligula's educational method is direct. Like Hamlet, he deliberately stages a play within a play; he reserves the main part for himself, impersonating his own truth, taking upon himself "the stupid and incomprehensible" aspect of "the gods." To his subjects he leaves only one role, that of victim, and in their anguished faces he eagerly searches for the horror he himself wishes to escape. In one scene after another he acts out a wild and murderous double parody: the parody of the absurd working of social institutions, the parody of the no less absurd workings of fate. He violates all the rules of both games as he applies his system arbitrarily in all realms of life from table manners to religious ritual. All men, in terms of the natural order of things, are condemned to death: therefore all men, according to the legal language of society, are guilty. This is the first axiom on which Caligula works. Caligula, the Emperor, represents the natural order of things, therefore all Caligula's subjects are guilty, therefore Caligula can treat them as he wishes. The "Treatise on Execution" he claims he is writing develops this amiable theme.

In the capricious scheme of humiliation, cruelty, and murder that Caligula then works out for the practical application of his theory, he sets the stage, calls the tune, changes the rules at will; he takes the wife of a Patrician under the man's eyes as he might take a glass of wine; he confiscates possessions, imposes humiliating duties upon the Patricians, creates an artificial famine in his empire, impersonates Venus in a burlesque religious ceremony, and ever and always tortures and condemns to death.

On the stage, act by act, we watch Caligula unconcernedly destroy the Patrician's unconscious assumption: if life is conducted according to certain rules, life will be righteous and secure. But whereas before the Emperor's revelation the Patricians lived in a perhaps harmless enough state of complacent blindness with regard to their ultimate fate, they are now plunged into a world so deadly in its arbitrary mechanisms that they cannot tolerate its existence. From the beginning of Act II in *Caligula* a wave of revolt arises; refusing the role of victim allotted to them, not by nature but by a fellow man, their emperor, the Patricians at last become rebels. Their complacency is destroyed; Caligula's rule is intolerable and Caligula's pedagogical career is at an end.

This is, however, only an outer line of action and it is, perhaps, a weakness in an otherwise powerful and original play that there is a disproportion between the theatrical force of the outer spectacle—the somewhat too facile *reductio ad absurdum* and re-education of the Patricians—and the tragic inner drama of which it is only a counterpart. One tends to lose sight of the real conflict and the real tragedy, which is personal and not essentially social in kind. The real center of the play must be sought in Caligula's relationship with himself and with the people of his own race: his friends, Helicon, Scipio, and Cherea; his mistress, Caesonia. They alone participate in his inner drama and each at some point will leave Caligula, who moves beyond them until he faces only his own immeasurable solitude. Caligula's inner tragedy is marked by two symbolic gestures: at the end of Act I he wipes from the mirror the past image of himself; at the end of the play he breaks the mirror and the intolerable image it reflects. Thus before his assassination at the hands of both his subjects and his former friends he admits his self-destruction.

"You have not recognized your real enemy," says Cherea at the beginning of Act II, as the Patricians begin to plot Caligula's death. It is to Caligula's friends that we must turn for the real action and intent of the play. Drusilla's death revealed to Caligula that men die and are not happy. In a world ruled by death human happiness is an illusion, since human life has lost its value. In order to live at all Caligula must, therefore, have something beyond life—the moon, the impossible—and to Helicon he entrusts the mission of getting the moon. The Patrician's real enemy is in the very logic of this conclusion; Caligula, Cherea warns, is a man moved by the highest and most mortal passion, a "philosophy without objections," negating man and the world. And Caligula is "the only artist who has brought his thought and his action into harmony." Therein lies his power, the attraction which emanates from him, and his significance. He is the mad Emperor who, in Camus's eyes, holds sway over a time—our time—which tends to consider an individual life as nothing compared to the moon, that symbol of any ideal state lying beyond the limits of our present lives.

Caligula's problem—how to live without hope—is solved in different ways by Helicon, Caesonia, Scipio, and Cherea, those alter egos with whom he can, to a certain limit, converse. Helicon is the "spectator" of Caligula, he who fails to get the moon for the Emperor and who with Caesonia is the Emperor's henchman. In the 1958 version of the play Camus etched his figure more clearly than before. A former slave, freed by Caligula, he despises the fu-

tility, selfishness, and cowardice of the "free men" who run the state. For Helicon the Emperor's experiment is perfectly legitimate; anything is better than insignificance and the *status quo*.

Caesonia knows no truth other than that of her body and to this truth she is faithful unto death—as she is faithful to Caligula. Her body tells her quite early in the game what Caligula discovers only in the end: that the Emperor's enterprise is useless. "If evil is on this earth, why wish to add to it?" she asks. And to the Emperor's contention that he must "give the impossible a chance," she opposes the suggestion that "what is possible also deserves to have its chance." Inevitably Caligula's revolt against death leads him to destroy this voice too purely of the flesh, that flesh which he hates because it is marked for death. His last act will be to strangle Caesonia deliberately.

Scipio, the seventeen-year-old poet, is carried forward in life on a great tide of love—love for the beauty of the earth, love for others, love for Caligula. Caligula, who coldbloodedly murders Scipio's father, will teach him the value of hatred. "Pure in good" as Caligula is "pure in evil," Scipio draws from his initiation into the dark injustices of life a powerful commitment on the side of all that lives against all that kills. It obliges him to take sides against the Emperor.

Like Caligula, Cherea "lives within the truth" without delusion and without hope, and it is he alone who can confront the Emperor and come out unharmed. For he lives in an intermediate zone between Caligula and Caesonia; he has accepted not only the "meaning of death" but also the certainty of life. He has no need for the moon, and it is he who challenges the wisdom of Caligula's attempt to bring one's thought and actions into harmony. For he recognizes a realm superior to the realm of thought, the relative human order in which reign those "truths of the flesh" that are lived and not demonstrated. These Caligula bypasses or destroys in his longing for the absolute. Since without these Cherea cannot live, the Emperor becomes his enemy.

Step by step in the play Caligula's being is dislocated, emptied of humanity. For one brief instant at the end Caligula faces what he has become, not a superman but a solitary, desperate, frightened, empty shell: Caligula or the state of inhuman nothingness; "I am nothing . . . Nothing, Caligula, nothing."

All three levels of the drama—the awakening of the Patricians, the rejection of Caligula by his friends, Caligula's own self-destruction—reach their climax in Act IV when Caligula calls upon the poets to compete: "Topic: Death—time limit, one minute." After a hilarious parody of various poetic approaches, in which Camus as author takes great delight, Scipio presents his poem on death:

> Pursuit of happiness which makes men pure,
> Sky streaming with sunlight,
> Unique and wild celebrations, my rapture without hope.

And indeed, in its entirety the play is a dramatic interpretation of this theme. Caligula himself, in a subterranean way, is an ally of these expansive forces of life which he negates, releasing them in the Patricians, sparing them when he meets them in Scipio and Cherea. The play itself is a cry of alarm and a call to awareness, as Camus discerns in our apathy a sickness of the heart and mind which may lead us to sell our human birthright for a mental delusion we call certainty. Through Caligula, therefore, Camus challenges us to think. But perhaps it is too much to ask of the average spectator that he move, unprepared, into this fairly complex mental universe. Nonetheless, one cannot easily forget Caligula and his bitter experiment nor the price he pays: "I did not take the right path, I have accomplished nothing. My liberty was not of the right kind." The play, in all its aspects, stands high among contemporary productions. In the years after 1938 the road of history so closely followed the pattern of action of Camus's Caligula that the last words of the Emperor have a prophetic ring: "I am still alive."

L'Etat de siège merely projects upon the stage, in broader perspectives and more massive effects, the outer impact of a Caligula-like social experiment. The themes in the two plays are essentially the same, but whereas in *Caligula* it is only the action of the individual that matters, the action in *L'Etat de siège* involves a city as an entity, as Camus moves from a metaphysical to a social plane. The inhabitants of Cadiz live as a matter of course in the natural fullness of a life accepted unquestioningly; a vague traditional social order subsists, inefficient and without content, represented by the governor, the judge, the church. The Plague imposes upon Cadiz a rigid bureaucratic collective organization, a theoretical abstract order, a mechanical social order similar to the mechanical laws that govern the universe. From this, Camus draws a number of more or less facile burlesque effects. But, like Caligula's arbitrary government, the rule of the Plague is life-destroying: it eliminates love, freedom, and adventure, the very substance of human life. Justice becomes vengeance; love turns into hatred; honor becomes cowardice; the flow of human words carrying questions, comments, answers, fears, doubts, and delights is stopped, as all mouths are gagged. This until Diego, the young student and lover, out of the excess of his despair shouts the words of revolt which loosen the gags, free the citizens, save his love, and cost him his life.

For in Cadiz—as elsewhere perhaps—justice does not lie primarily in the judge, nor in the law; power is not in the government nor in force; and love is not contained in a word. This Nada sees—Nada, the nihilist, the destructive principle *par excellence*—and he aligns himself wholeheartedly with the Plague in his immeasurable Caligula-like contempt for such irrational imaginary entities. And the devilish parody of social order takes over as the source of order is perverted.

The force of revolt in this play is embodied in the hero, Diego, who becomes a central and unambiguous figure as he escapes from the deadly grip of the Plague. He stirs up the latent forces of energy and freedom among the inhabitants of Cadiz, awakening the citizens from their lethargy, calling them back to life.

The pattern is simple and clear: like the Patricians, the people of Cadiz have fallen prey to a negative, rationaliz-

ing power, a power destructive at its very source, a false god, a false pope, wrought out of their failure to trust the great generous forces of the life they feel within them. Their salvation lies in an attack upon the usurper and depends upon their faith in the expansive energies of love and imagination which assure their victory over the negative, subversive power of the mind divorced from the heart.

More even than in *Caligula,* the spectator must accept the characters not as personalities but as abstract forces incarnate, those very forces whose existence Nada would deny. They are there in their positive form: courage in Diego, pure love in Victoria, for example; and in their negative form they are perverted incarnations: law without justice in the judge, government without power in the governor, power without humanity in the Plague. The movement of the play itself is contained in the images projected on the stage: the imprisonment behind the closed doors of Cadiz, for example; the movement toward sunlight and air; the bursting open of the bonds of slavery which accompanies Diego's rebellion and victory. Two atmospheres struggle, rather than two ideas, rather than two clear-cut conceptions of good and evil.

In *L'Etat de siège,* as in *Caligula,* it is the atmosphere that counts; this is a difficult medium to handle, yet one that Camus had to attempt to master if he was to project upon the stage what he wished to convey. The two dangers he attacks are indifference and abstraction, those two facets of a latent nihilism which, he seems to indicate, are already in control of our institutions. Indifference and abstraction make of our human values empty concepts and shameless parodies, delivering us up as captives to the absurd. The stage in Camus's hands, therefore, becomes the *décor* of a mental universe, and the characters that live their short lives upon it are reasons, emotions, forces, inner and outer attitudes, which try to impose their own form upon the play, creating the situation and the inner dynamism of the action. Allegorical in nature, these two plays have very little connection with the current "well-made" psychological or realistic play, and yet by their very realistic technique they remain outside the realm of the so-called poetic drama.

Both plays deal with a form of alienation, and in each case the alienation is simultaneously individual and social. *Caligula* goes from the individual to the social; *L'Etat de siège* from the social to the individual. In both plays the dramatic difficulty lies in the presence on the stage of two kinds of beings both embodied by actors. Caligula and Cherea embody beings of different caliber: as Caligula becomes stronger Cherea fails to reach the stature he needs to play his part as opponent to Caligula. The Plague and his secretary are distinguished from the rest of the cast by the type of costumes they wear, but their relations with such human beings as Diego are disconcerting, for it is hard to project death on the stage in the form of a secretary with a notebook and keep a coherent dramatic atmosphere. But it is harder still to project a sort of double allegory, to project the plague, for example, simultaneously in the form of a mediocre bureaucrat and as a social disaster incarnating a totalitarian tyranny. Diego himself is essentially the incarnation of an attitude—the force opposed to Nada's nihilism and yet a human being in love with Victoria.

In both these plays through essentially nonhuman characters Camus sets up forms of "logical delirium" to which he gives full rein; he allows them to act at first as though they were autonomous, uninvolved in any reality beyond their own, and then proceeds to show how they mutilate that part of humanity which they ignore and how eventually they are destroyed by it. Beyond the willing suspension of disbelief necessary for the enjoyment of any theater, the two plays consequently require that the spectator be aware that the play, the make-believe on the stage, contains a meaning beyond itself. And here Camus leaves much to the spectator, refusing to state his themes in rational terms—as does, for example, [Jean-Paul] Sartre—within the dialogue of the play. The dialogue consequently has a hieroglyphic quality which is at first puzzling, as this dialogue between Helicon and Caligula on Caligula's return clearly illustrates:

> HELICON: You look tired.
>
> CALIGULA: I walked a great deal.
>
> HELICON: Yes, you were away a long time (*silence*).
>
> CALIGULA: It was difficult to find.
>
> HELICON: To find what?
>
> CALIGULA: What I wanted.
>
> HELICON: And what did you want?
>
> CALIGULA: (*still in a matter-of-fact tone*) The moon.
>
> HELICON: What?
>
> CALIGULA: Yes, I wanted the moon.
>
> HELICON: Ah!

In its matter-of-fact nonchalance this exchange of remarks is an excellent bit of dialogue, but in terms of its meaning it moves too fast for the unprepared spectator, and for the moment at least both its meaning and its relation to the action on the stage may well be lost to him. To Camus, dialogue is not an explanation of action; it cannot be divorced from action and yet it is not a comment on it. To understand the dialogue the spectator must first grasp the play in its totality and then follow an intellectual path as Camus designates it. This path leads not only toward a discussion of ideas—that is relatively habitual and easy—but it leads also toward the delineation of issues that touch upon an experience of life and cannot be stated in simple terms of right and wrong. In *Caligula* and *L'Etat de siège,* the spectacle itself, disconcerting though it be in terms of our theatrical habits, may be sufficiently rich to hold the attention of the spectators during the performance, but this is not so true of either *Le Malentendu* or *Les Justes.*

Le Malentendu is entirely symbolical. The land-locked inn in the center of Europe where mother and daughter so reluctantly carry out their self-imposed duty of murder; the silent servant; the son Jan, who brings with him a wealth of love and life in his wife, his fortune, and his experience of happiness—all these are symbolic rather than human. But Maria, the son's wife, seems to be an ordinary human being, and Jan himself moves between the two levels or two dimensions of the play, halfway between the human and the symbolic. And yet it is Jan's adventure which furnishes the meaning behind the spectacle—a meaning not easily or quickly grasped.

From the strictly realistic point of view of the psychological play with a well-constructed plot, *Le Malentendu* fails to answer one question: For what reason did the son Jan first abandon the inn, his mother and sister? No psychological play would have left the question unanswered. Camus does not give us any reason for Jan's long absence nor does he explain, very satisfactorily, the reason for Jan's return. Though Jan says that he realized, at his father's death, that he was needed, this hardly tallies with the weary round of murder with which his mother and sister had been so long engaged. And the dead father is artificially introduced, one feels, only to "make sense" in terms of the "well-made" play where all is rationally explained; in the symbolic structure of the play it is no more than an irrelevant detail. Nothing in *Le Malentendu* can or need be rationally explained: it is not a psychological play.

The first act of *Le Malentendu* introduces the two forces that will precipitate all four participants into disaster. First the mechanism of murder set off automatically by the stranger's arrival:

> MARTHA: Mother, we must kill him.
>
> MOTHER: No doubt we must kill him.
>
> MARTHA: You speak strangely.
>
> MOTHER: I am tired, it is true. And I wish that he at least could be the last. It is terribly tiring to kill. And though it matters little to me whether I die facing the sea or in the center of our plains, I should like it if, afterwards, we could leave together.
>
> MARTHA: We shall leave and it will be a great moment! Make an effort, mother, there is little to do. You know that it's not even a question of murder. He'll drink his tea, he'll sleep, and while he is still alive we'll carry him to the river.

In the meantime Jan is carrying out a plan of his own. "I came here to bring my fortune and, if I can, happiness." But to the question his wife, Maria, raises, Jan gives no answer. "There is only one way," Maria replies. "It's to do what the first-comer would do, to say, 'Here I am,' to let one's heart speak."

> JAN: The heart is not so simple.
>
> MARIA: But it uses only simple words. And it wouldn't be very difficult to say: "I am your son, this is my wife. I've lived with her in a country we loved, facing the sea and the sun. But I was not happy enough and today I need you."
>
> JAN: Don't be unfair, Maria. I don't need them, but I realize that they must need me and that a man is never alone.

Like Martha, his sister, Jan thinks in terms of duty. He has come "to find his mother and country" on the one condition that his family recognize him. Recognition is the key denouement of innumerable plays: recognition of the hero's real situation in tragedy, recognition of identity in drama and comedy. Jan, drugged by the tea his sister serves him, will never know what his real situation is nor his destiny. And Martha and the mother will recognize Jan's identity only after he is dead when, too late, they grasp the tragic irony of their situation. But here again the recognition by means of an outer sign as in drama—in this case a passport—seems extraneous to the spirit of the play, which hesitates, poised halfway between a suspense based on an inner hazardous progression toward the discovery of the truth and a chance recognition by outer material signs.

It is easy enough to follow literally the action of the play. Martha, without knowing it, sacrifices her brother to her dream of happiness and loses all: her dream, her brother, her mother's love, her desire to live. The mother, in a moment of desperate revelation, discovers love as she follows into death the son she helped to kill. Jan fails to make the gift of love and happiness he bore, and destroys the happiness and love he shared with Maria. It is Martha who, in the end, draws from that literal level of the play a first and partial "metaphysical" conclusion, as before her suicide she faces a distraught Maria:

> I tell you, we are robbed. What is the use of the great appeal of our being, the great vigilance in our souls? Why this aspiration toward the sea or toward love? It's all derision. Your husband now knows the answer, that frightful home where in the end we'll all be huddled together. . . . Understand that your suffering will never equal the injustice done man. And finally, listen to my advice. For I owe you some advice at least, since I killed your husband.
>
> Pray to your god that he make you comparable to stone. That's the happiness he reserves for himself, that's the only true happiness. Do as he does, make yourself deaf to all cries, and be as stone while it is still possible. But if you are too cowardly to enter into that blind peace, then come and join us in our common home. Goodbye my sister! Everything is easy, as you see. You can choose between the stupid felicity of pebbles and the slimy bed where we await you.

And as Maria cries to God for help in her distress she gets her only answer from the old servant who at last finds a voice to say No!

But this is not the final meaning implicit in the play. The meaning is contained in the development of the action; it is obscure and hard to find and it does not entirely support Martha's interpretation. The end, of course, remains unchanged: Maria's appeal to a miraculous revelation from beyond the human realm is still rejected. The cold and haunting distress is the same: Martha, Jan, and their mother are dead, they have been "robbed" of the meaning of their acts. But at each turn in the play one word could have been said or left unsaid, one move made or not made,

or a decision taken, and perhaps the course of the action would have changed—in so far as it could be changed. "Your method is not the right one," cried Maria to Jan; and neither as a matter of fact is Martha's. Someone could have looked at the passport; the mother could have arrived in time to take away the drugged cup of tea; Martha might have wavered had Jan not mentioned the sunny lands from which he came; and Jan might have declared his identity.

The very structure of the play is ironical and its real implications are carried in its strange blind movement, the "illogical blind accident" of which Spengler wrote. "I shall count on the force of things," said Jan at the beginning, strong in his knowledge that he is the son and brother, that his intentions are generous, and that "with time" the stranger will be recognized as the son. But the force of things is not to be counted upon and Jan, who "is in no hurry," is already too late. The path of murder is a path that can be followed in but one direction, it allows for no return. Jan ignores the reality confronting him. The tragedy is obviously conceived as a tragedy of situation, tragic because a third path perhaps could have been found not implicit in "the force of things," the nightmarish force of inertia, nor in the force of Martha's will.

All through the play the "illogical blind accident" is opposed by a "truth of the heart," a muffled truth, half heeded and never quite understood, from which comes an impression of slowness and a sense of frustration. Possibly, it implies, there is another solution besides the two Martha proposes when her enterprise fails, another choice besides the indifference of the stones or a despair which leads to suicide, a choice made from the heart.

Behind the play one senses great personal anguish and the dark years of the 1940's, when Europe had, like Camus's inhospitable inn, become a charnel house, a mother wearily slaughtering her sons, hallucinated by dreams of a future felicity. And to the generous *élan* of her favorite children who brought to her rescue their ideal of love and happiness she could answer only in death. The initial fiction of the inn is left far behind as we fumble toward a meaning veiled in the silence which the dialogue delineates but never breaks—a feat in itself.

The conception of the play is powerful and its atmosphere hallucinating, but the characters and plot never quite give form to the questions it poses. The situation and dialogue do not completely complement each other, though the words spoken—particularly by Martha—often have a resonance and an intensity worthy of tragedy. Jan and, even more, Maria are never completely convincing, and the sense of their conversation at the beginning of the play, referring as it does to a plot behind the plot, seems somewhat artificial. The mother and Martha dominate the play like two great masked figures, reducing Jan and Maria to a stature that is never quite adequate.

Les Justes might almost be called a second *Malentendu* presented in terms of a concrete political action; Yanek in a sense is a second Jan, and Dora another Martha who kills the Maria she might have been. To a normal theater-going audience the most evident crux of the action may seem highly abstract and academic: Can a man deliberately kill another in view of the future good of all humanity? To this question Savinkov's terrorists gave an answer, an answer which **Les Justes** questions. [Boris Savinkov was a Russian terrorist whose *Souvenirs d'un terroriste* provided the basis for **Les Justes.**] As in Savinkov's Memoirs, the play follows the destiny of Yanek, his successive choices in successive situations, and each choice is openly debated on the stage: the choice of terrorism itself between Yanek and Stepan and between Dora and Yanek in the opening scenes of the play; the limits of terrorism between the group of terrorists after Yanek's first failure to throw the bomb; the relations of the terrorist to society, law, and religion in the prison scene; and, finally, the rebound, the effect of the terrorist's execution upon his comrades. A problem play without doubt, and a play not of one but of several situations—and therein lies its weakness. Yet there is an underlying theme, which, had it been strong, might possibly have bound the successive situations together and given the play an inner dynamism: Dora's tragic evolution.

Undoubtedly Camus's scrupulous respect for Savinkov's Memoirs hampered his treatment of Dora, yet it is Dora who carries in depth the tragic theme which is not Savinkov's but Camus's. Only at the end of the play, when the fact of Yanek's death really penetrates Dora's being, does this theme break through. Is Yanek's death, accepted and foreseen, really justified by the abstract hope in a better future for Russia? The immediate impact of his death is to empty Dora of hope, to draw her away from Yanek's universe of love and fraternity into Stepan's deadly world of vengeance and hatred. Dora has entered the grim inn of **Le Malentendu** and will follow in Martha's footsteps.

But along the way the play, situation by situation, explicitly raises a number of questions implicit in its title **Les Justes.** Until the end of the third act and the throwing of the bomb, the question is debated from the point of view of the terrorists: Russia and her people suffer from injustice and the suffering is intolerable. All agree that the Grand Duke, the incarnation of injustice, must die, for to kill the Grand Duke is a step toward establishing justice. The "just," therefore, have judged and condemned: the Grand Duke is guilty and the sentence of death is justified.

But the problem then shifts from the logical to the ethical: for Yanek [Kaliaev], injustice must be fought in the name of life, love, and happiness for all. For Stepan, who has just come out of prison, who has already been a victim of the law, injustice must be fought in the name of hatred and vengeance. For Yanek and Dora, though the death of the Grand Duke is necessary, to kill is evil, thus he who kills enters into a pact with injustice. The killer is guilty, so he must die, but he is his own judge and executioner; the double human sacrifice saves his act from the stigma of human irresponsibility. For Stepan, the Grand Duke is justly condemned and his death is a matter not of guilt but of rejoicing. Yanek and Dora respect the human being beneath the abstraction; Stepan has nothing but contempt for him.

The second debate, centering upon Yanek's refusal to kill two children, is merely a prolongation of the first: it fur-

ther delineates the problem of the individual responsibility of the "just judges" and the nature of their verdict. To kill children is, to Yanek, an act of both social and human injustice, which turns into murder his difficult act of justice. For Stepan, a couple of children are of no account when they stand in the path of justice; in his eyes Yanek's sense of responsibility should not be first for human beings but for results.

After the throwing of the bomb the spotlight shifts, as it did in *L'Etranger,* to the existing social forms of justice; the debate continues as various codes of justice clash. First Foka comes face to face with Yanek. Foka, a prisoner and criminal who killed three people in a fit of drunkenness, is now the executioner, and every execution cancels one year of his sentence. The irony is obvious and perhaps a little artificial. Yanek admits that Foka—even in murder—is his brother, but he refuses to admit Foka's contention that they are brother executioners. And his conduct supports his point, for he refuses all alibis and goes voluntarily to his death.

Skouratov, the chief of police, is a Stepan further along in his career. "One begins by wanting justice and one ends by organizing a system of police," he states as he interviews Yanek. The debate with him prepares the audience for the entrance of the Christian Grand Duchess, when Skouratov, setting aside the theoretical aspect of the problem, puts it in terms of the flesh-and-blood destruction of a man:

> KALIAYEV: I threw a bomb against tyranny.
>
> SKOURATOV: No doubt. But it's the man who got it. . . .
>
> KALIAYEV: I carried out a verdict.
>
> SKOURATOV: No doubt. No doubt. We've nothing against the verdict. What is a verdict? It's a word around which one can argue through night after night. What we don't like . . . no, you wouldn't care for the word . . . Shall we say that it is the amateurishness of the thing, its slight untidiness. The results are unquestionable. Everybody saw them. Ask the Grand Duchess. There was blood, you understand, a lot of blood.

For Skouratov, justice is a matter of appearances: blood is an "untidy thing" and ideas live in a harmless world all their own. What is essential for Skouratov is that Kaliayev play according to the rules of the game: he must admit he is guilty, and if he repents and atones by giving information to the police concerning his organization, he will obtain his grace. In his system of values the Christian approach to the problem comes merely as a help to the police. His matter-of-fact proposal is violently rejected by Kaliayev, but before he leaves he fires a parting shot: "If your idea is not strong enough to kill children, does it warrant you to kill a Grand Duke for its sake?" Like Stepan, he cannot see the value of a limit.

It is with the Grand Duchess that Yanek Kaliayev first really faces the human consequences of his crime and its essential absurdity, for, as the Duchess tells him, the man he killed was a man who dozed after lunch and who spoke of justice as does Kaliayev, whereas the children he spared are not innocent but already hardhearted and afraid of the poor. The theme of justice is now replaced by the theme of injustice: "Certainly you, too, are unjust. The earth is a desert," says the Grand Duchess. And from this universal guilt of man she appeals to God's forgiveness and justice; but in this universal guilt she drowns Kaliayev's one strength: his sense of personal responsibility. It is the sense of personal responsibility, not of guilt, that carries Kaliayev to a death worthy of a man; his self-respect is the force that gives him faith in his oneness with his group. Kaliayev has escaped from the senseless social machinery of murder and reprisal which Stepan and Skouratov embody; he lives, kills, and dies without contempt. Therein lies the "exemplary" value of the play. As Camus pointed out in an article, there is a world between a Kaliayev and the "complacent" bureaucratic organizers of mass murder in our time.

Les Justes, like *Le Malentendu,* may not seem at first fully to come to life on the stage, but that it lives in its full force in the universe of Albert Camus is unquestionable. In a sense *Les Justes* delineates more clearly than any of the three other plays the issues which Camus raises and which concern him deeply. The greatest tragedy for any man in Camus's theatrical world, whether Caligula, Martha, or even Kaliayev, is to make of this earth "a desert," that is, to destroy that part of life which is joy and love or, in the case of a social tyranny like that of the plague, to make their enjoyment nearly impossible. A second tragic error is to abandon that which gives man his dignity: his sense of responsibility. In each play just such a destruction lies at the source of the action; when the sense of responsibility is perverted it becomes a sense of guilt which in its wake brings the judge and with him collective humiliation and collective irresponsibility. Tragically dangerous also are the forms which revolt can take, in this state of separateness and irresponsibility, as the result of the aspiration of a human being for happiness and coherence, for example such perverted forms as the "logical delirium" of Caligula or Martha's murderous dream of a future Eden. Such revolt ends in the destruction of others and the annihilation of self.

The society attacked by the Plague or challenged by Caligula or Kaliayev seems unaware of the mortal dangers inherent in its own structure. Through these plays Camus obviously attacks a society he sees as using three main forms of persuasion, all conducive to irresponsibility: mystification, miracle, and abstract authority. Of these Caligula makes short shrift.

Camus's characters on the stage move between two limits: the irresponsibility of a Foka and the monstrous perversions of a Caligula or a Martha. The fluctuations of the play project the anguished experience of these individuals as they measure the distance between their aspirations and the realities offered by both society and the cosmos.

Essentially the combat is an inner one, as heart and mind struggle in their attempt to come to terms. And it is the mind in each play that forces the issue that starts the ac-

tion: the mind with its totalitarian logic that sets up its own tribunal and tries to impose upon reality the coherent world of certainties in which it feels at ease and justified. Caligula or the Plague attempts to operate this transmutation; and, because all men escape in part from irrefutable logic, all men, in their eyes, are guilty.

This intellectual perversion is what Camus fought as he also fought the social solution offered by certain proponents of Christianity, the solution proposed by Fyodor Dostoevsky's Grand Inquisitor [in *The Brothers Karamazov*]. "You have elevated men and taught them pride," accuses the Grand Inquisitor, judging Christ. The perversion of Christ's message he proposes is to keep men humble and satisfied with simple "permitted joys," to make them deaf to that "great inner aspiration" of which Martha speaks. In contrast, Camus proposes in each of his plays that man "be proud of his revolt," but that the revolt be, like Diego's, one of the heart and not merely of the head. Beyond the order of the universe with its mechanism indifferent to humans, beyond the constructs of logic, and beyond the empty forms of social irresponsibility lies the possibility of reaching a human order conciliating heart and head, truth and aspiration. It cannot be argued, it can be lived, and each play shows that it cannot be denied. That is why, no doubt, Dostoevsky's world furnished Camus with those elements he most needed as playwright and why *Les Possédés* is perhaps, with *Caligula,* his best play.

It may well be that Camus's plays will never be popular as theater; the vision they seek to express is confined too narrowly perhaps to Camus's intimate experience and may not be immediately evident to his spectators. And in his effort to give the theater a language cut down to the essential, Camus may not have always succeeded in creating the perspectives a spectator needs in order to catch the mood of the play and its general orientation, if not its meaning. It may well be, too, that a great tragic theater needs to rely on semi-legendary, semihistorical figures which cannot be created and for which the allegorical figure of "any" man cannot be substituted. Dora cannot become the equivalent of an Electra, nor Jan of an Orestes, nor can the spectator accept their situation with the same abandon.

But the nature of the problem raised in Camus's plays, the quality of the language, and the originality of the dramatic situations lift them out of the immediate and the topical. It is quite clear that they are not dictated by a theoretical approach, such as permits the deft handling of the current problem play. They move from the concrete to the abstract and not in the reverse direction. Whether the concrete situation is strong enough to carry the full weight of the thought is debatable. (pp. 168-90)

Germaine Brée, in her Camus, *revised edition, Rutgers University Press, 1964, 280 p.*

CALIGULA

PRODUCTION REVIEWS

Brooks Atkinson   (review date 17 February 1960)

[*As drama critic for the* New York Times *from 1925 to 1960, Atkinson was one of the most influential reviewers in America. Upon his retirement from the* Times, *the Mansfield Theatre in New York was renamed the Brooks Atkinson in honor of his contributions to the theater. His publications include* Skyline Promenades *(1925),* Henry Thoreau: The Cosmic Yankee *(1927), and* East of the Hudson *(1931), as well as many collections of his criticism. The following is a review of an English-language production of* Caligula, *adapted by Justin O'Brien and directed by Sidney Lumet. It premiered in New York on 16 February 1960 and featured Kenneth Haigh in the title role. Atkinson here calls* Caligula *a modern* Tamburlaine, *concluding that, like Christopher Marlowe's sixteenth-century tragedy, the play's presentation of "gratuitous horror piled on horror," ultimately becomes repetitive and hollow.*]

What [Christopher] Marlowe's *Tamburlaine* was to the sixteenth century, Camus's *Caligula* is to ours.

Without the poetry, of course. For Camus's portrait of self-consuming power, which opened at the Fifty-fourth Street Theatre last evening, is leaner in style. Under Sidney Lumet's direction, it has been produced with a kind of ruthless grandeur—a bold setting by Will Steven Armstrong that thrusts Caligula's horrors in the faces of the audience and a spectacular performance by able actors.

But Marlowe's *Tamburlaine* has a monolithic insistence that becomes repetitious as it progresses. Camus's *Caligula* has a similar rhythm, gratuitous horror piled on horror. Out of respect for Camus's purity as a writer of inner dialogues, Mr. Lumet has given the play all the color and sound of a big theatre style. And Kenneth Haigh, as Caligula, drawn between youthful petulance and demoniac fury, is superb.

But the sound and fury become a little hollow before the last scene is played. In view of the modest content of the drama, it seems at the end to have been overproduced.

It is the story of a Roman emperor who uses his power to achieve the impossible. He tries to achieve personal freedom by liberating himself from everything that is human. "Men die, and they are not happy," says Caligula early in the play. In the preface to the printed text (translated by Justin O'Brien) Camus quoted that line as symptomatic of what he was trying to say.

In 1938, when he wrote the play, both Hitler and Stalin were drunk with power. In 1945, when it was produced in Paris, the power of Hitler was broken, although Stalin's

Gerard Philipe as the tyrant in the 1945 Paris production of Caligula *at the Théâtre Hébertot.*

was more massive than before. Since Camus's political convictions changed with his ripening experience, it would be erroneous to try to draw exact parallels between his play and political conditions. But it is a fact that he wrote *Caligula* when excesses of power were shaking the world.

Caligula portrays the evil progress of a megalomaniac who is destroying life around him, not for political or materialistic aggrandizement, but to free himself of the encumbrances of friendship, society and love. He plunges himself into oblivion. *Caligula* is a bare play, without rhetoric, almost with passion. It is almost as though Camus were drawing a blueprint of self-destruction and evil.

Possibly Mr. Lumet has intended to compensate for the bareness by his imposing production. The costumes are splendid. The soldiers' costumes have a warrior-like ferocity. Entrances are solemn and ominous. In the carnival scene at the opening of the second act, the roll of drums and the clashing of cymbals are explosive bits of ingenious and disciplined showmanship.

In addition to Mr. Haigh's impressive performance, the cast includes a number of other excellent actors—Colleen Dewhurst as a tragic queen in the part of Caesonia, Phillip Bourneuf as the patrician who dares defy the tyrant, Edward Binns as Caligula's henchman, Clifford David as a young poet who cannot be frightened. The cast is long and uniformly able.

Only six weeks after Camus's absurd and cruel death deprived the Western world of one of its noblest spirits, it is a sobering experience to hear his thoughts spoken on the stage. The thoughts come from twenty-two years ago. Unfortunately, they are not so pertinent now as thoughts he may have had later and thoughts he took to his grave.

There will be more enduring monuments to his memory than this withdrawn and repetitive drama of horrors.

> *Brooks Atkinson, " 'Caligula' Bows," in* The New York Times, *February 17, 1960, p. 31.*

Walter Kerr   (review date 17 February 1960)

[*Kerr is a Pulitzer Prize-winning American drama critic, essayist, and playwright. Throughout his career, he has written theater reviews for such publications as* Commonweal, *the* New York Herald Tribune, *and the* New York Times. *Below, he offers guarded praise for the Broadway production of* Caligula, *admiring the stage settings and Kenneth Haigh's performance as the emperor, but finding the shocking events of the play so excessive that they lose their impact. Consequently, in his judgment, the play lacks suspense and a sense of progression.*]

Kenneth Haigh, as the emperor Caligula, announces in the first few moments of the play at the 54th Street, that he is going to be the first ruler ever to "use unlimited power in an unlimited way." He is going to kill whom he likes, ravish what wives he chooses, declare famines on the instant, turn himself into a golden-wigged Venus, try absolutely everything on his unfettered march toward the impossible. He learns, shortly before he plunges from a tower

to the knives that finally await him, that when everything is possible, nothing is.

Has Albert Camus' play fallen into precisely the same trap, or is it the current performance that makes the evening seem like the four whirring wheels of a high-powered automobile racing immobile on ice?

Of promised power there is plenty. Designer Will Steven Armstrong's disembodied stairways scoop massively upward with the swirl of a humming dynamo. Kenneth Haigh, stumbling first onto the stage in dirty black tatters and ascending later to a pinnacle on which he can show contempt for the gods themselves, holds nothing back. There is no thrust of his arms, no shower of speech, no motion of retching disgust that he is not willing to make with all of the urgency, openness, and passionate belief at his headlong command.

In the staging, director Sidney Lumet has had the courage of his author's tryst with the absurd. Caligula wants the moon in his arms; short of the moon, he wants to ram poison down the throat of an unoffending courtier, to crack the neck of the mistress who has grown old serving him, and to dance in the great court at midnight in a petaled white skirt with two dark panels that suggest the wings of a graceful, and fatal, insect. Mr. Lumet has hurled Romans to the right, doubleheaded axes to the left, and spitting challenges at the audience as though his conscience were on fire.

Yet there is a treadmill under foot. One crime is really not more shocking than the last. When the first bloodied body has been carted away, or the first deliberately insane law handed down to the empire, we have grasped—to the full, apparently—the uttermost limits of one man's absolute freedom. The murder of Scipio's father does not distress us more than the slaughter of Cassius' sons: when they follow one another, scene by scene, the footfall is familiar, the measured tread monotonous.

In short, drama itself seems to observe the law that our moon-maddened hero must discover for himself. If there are no limits to what a character in a play may do, then the play itself is without intelligible boundaries—without a pattern that forms, without a forward movement that we can either desire or yearn for. The sky is open to us, but the sky has no shape.

The fact that the late Mr. Camus' play has been enormously successful in France, however, leads to other questions. Is there somewhere in the performance a secret, insistent, almost imperceptible reduction in size? How much does it matter that Mr. Haigh's voice clearly escapes control now and then, that his silences sometimes seem to offer so much more than the restless soliloquies that follow? It is always possible that a play about absolutism has not been done absolutely enough—with the anvil stroke and the untroubled resonance of a monster utterly sure of himself.

There are certainly sound performances from Philip Bourneuf as a clear-headed intellectual who cannot be swerved from his course, from Colleen Dewhurst as a mother-wife who has worshiped no god other than her own body, from Clifford David as a poet who cannot help the love he bears even to Caligula.

But in precisely what way should we laugh when Caligula appears on a half-shell in corkscrew curls, when he paints a suppliant's fingernails and then his bald head, when a prissy old patrician purses his lips in a deadpan moue out front? The play means to touch the outrageous, the unspeakable, the ultimate defiance of all human value in these passages. But the light titters that spring up in the auditorium suggest that only a casual, rather flighty, cynicism has been arrived at, not the soul-destroying and mirthless laughter that might accompany sheer negation.

Between the impossibility of moving forward when there is no forward to move to, and a certain readiness of tone and style that thin out a satanically majestic experiment in living, *Caligula* continually stirs interest and then finds its temperature falling.

> *Walter Kerr, in a review of "Caligula," in* New York Herald Tribune, *February 17, 1960, p. 19.*

John McClain   (review date 17 February 1960)

[*Although he ranks the acting and writing superior, McClain concludes that* Caligula's *demonstration that "the entire negation of moral principles" can lead only to destruction seems simple and obvious.*]

Caius Caligula ruled the Romans from A.D. 37 to 41; and as a philosophic profligate established records which still stand unchallenged in history. Although only 29 when he was assassinated by popular demand, he had endeavored on a basis of pure logic to defy all the conventions of his time: loyalty, decency, and even the common conceptions of right and wrong.

These are the elements from which Albert Camus fashioned the play, *Caligula,* which opened at the 54th Street Theatre last night.

It has been given a towering production by Chandler Cowles, Charles Bowden and Ridgely Bullock; the cast, headed by Kenneth Haigh is spectacular in procedure and costume; Sidney Lumet's direction is suitably flamboyant, but I couldn't divorce myself from the fact that I was spending too much time with an idiot boy.

Endless essays can be written on the theory of a selfish existence—the entire negation of moral principles—but the world is old enough now, as it was then, to convince us that this is only a detour to destruction.

It took the boy Emperor a long and bitter time to arrive at this conclusion, and while his experiment is presented with some superior acting and impressive writing, the final verdict seems simple and inevitable.

Along the way there are many arresting scenes in which Caligula callously rejects those close to him, in which he exhibits his obsession to defy the hatred and stupidity of the Gods, as he puts it, and to prove, by logic, that the impossible can be true.

This leads him to multiple executions, climaxed by the strangling of his mistress. When he is aware that there is a plot to take his life he makes no effort to prevent it, accepting the logic by which he lived.

Mr. Haigh, in the extremely strenuous title role, gives a brilliant account of himself. His speech is brittle and sure (if occasionally reminiscent of the British outlander's accent from [John Osborne's] *Look Back in Anger*), and his final moments in the face of death are played in energetic good taste.

He is given sympathetic support by Philip Bourneuf, an unfailing professional, in the role of Cherea; Edward Binns, as Helicon, and Colleen Dewhurst, as Caesonia. Then there are such others as, Clifford David, Frederick Tozere, Sorrell Booke and Frederic Warriner in the large supporting cast.

Will Steven Armstrong has evolved the decorative costumes and an austere set, mostly stairs and platforms, which still lend majesty to the proceedings.

But, however disguised in the skillful double-talk of the late author, and with all its elaborate mountings, *Caligula* impressed me as an over-extension of a quite small idea.

> *John McClain, "Over-Extension of a Small Idea," in* New York Journal-American, *February 17, 1960.*

Richard Watts, Jr.   (review date 17 February 1960)

[*Watts was an American journalist and critic whose career spanned forty years at the* New York Herald Tribune *and the* New York Post. *Here, he admires the philosophical questions of good and evil that* Caligula *raises but claims that Camus ineffectively dramatized his ideas. As a result, Watts asserts, Camus's "portrait of the rigorous idealist . . . becomes a picture of a sadistic monster who is part clown."*]

Caligula seems to me at the same time a fascinating play and a failure. The English adaptation by Justin O'Brien of Albert Camus' philosophical drama about the notorious young Roman Emperor, which opened last night at the 54th St. Theater, combines a lurid theatrical excitement with some of the distinguished French author's most provocative speculations on the perversities of the human condition, and yet my final impression is that its subtlety of ideas gets lost somewhere within the melodramatic confusion of its portrait of a sadistic madman.

It is true that Camus refuses to admit that Caligula was a madman. What passes for his madness, the drama appears to be telling us, was the despairing effort of a too rigorously logical idealist, who believed in the absolutes of human behavior and dreamed of achieving the impossibility of perfection. Baffled by his failure to bring about the absolute of goodness, and stricken by the death of the sister who was also his mistress, he turned to the absolute of evil and tried to destroy mankind in the secret wish that it would destroy him.

"It would tax your understanding," Caligula tells his later mistress, Caesonia, at one point, and I am afraid that this is pretty much what happens. But it is not because the ideas are incomprehensible so much as that they are often approached with such obliqueness, and are so frequently present by hints and inference, that they are dimmed rather than illuminated by the narrative. Camus was clearly capable of capturing dramatic effectiveness, but I can't feel that he has here dramatized sufficiently the ideas he was proposing.

What happens is that his portrait of the rigorous idealist turned in on himself becomes a picture of a sadistic monster who is part clown. When Caligula dons women's clothes and impersonates Venus, he is more a buffoon than a terrifying figure, and, when he is indulging in his cruelty, the spectacle is more a detailed record of his crimes than a dramatization of them. In depicting a philosophical dreamer transformed into a creature of inhumanity, Camus is often vivid but most of the humanity has been drained from his drama, also.

Yet, because Camus had a wonderfully stimulating mind, it is stimulating to watch it probing into philosophical problems of good and evil and the desperation of tormented mankind, even when he is so oblique about it. Although this is the first professional production of *Caligula* I have seen, I heard it at a reading and once attended a performance at Yale, it has never failed to provide additional food for contemplation. That is one of its great virtues. Its weakness is that it always seems dissatisfying in dramatizing its many ideas.

It is vastly helped by Kenneth Haigh's sensitive but dynamic portrayal of the lengthy title role. The other parts are much less important, but there are excellent performances by Colleen Dewhurst as Caesonia, Philip Bourneuf as Caligula's most intelligent foe, Edward Binns as an ex-slave loyal to the Emperor, and Clifford David as a troubled young poet. Save for an unfortunate final scene, where Caligula falls to his death in the manner of Peter Pan flying on a wire, the staging is admirable. The Camus drama is a most stimulating failure.

> *Richard Watts, Jr., "M. Camus Studies a Roman Emperor," in* New York Post, *February 17, 1960.*

Robert Brustein   (review date 29 February 1960)

[*Brustein is an American essayist, educator, and critic. He has directed drama programs at both Yale and Harvard universities and has been a panel member of the National Endowment for the Arts. His writings include* The Theatre of Revolt: An Approach to the Modern Drama *(1964),* The Culture Watch: Essays on Theatre and Society, 1969-1974 *(1975), and* Critical Moments: Reflections on Theater and Society: 1973-1979 *(1980). In the review below, Brustein deplores the "stupefying opulence" of the Broadway production of* Caligula. *In the critic's opinion, director Sidney Lumet attempted to make this drama about "the individual's relationship to his universe" acceptable to American audiences, which rarely like or understand such philosophical pieces.*]

In a world of surprises, Broadway still remains predictable. Once you are able to swallow the jawbreaking news that Albert Camus' *Caligula* will be performed on the main street, everything that follows—from the half-respectful, half-hostile bafflement of the daily press to the stupefying opulence of the production—becomes as inevitable as the digestive process. Unable to soften down this dangerous play of ideas, Sidney Lumet, the director, has chosen to drown it out, imposing over the pop-pop of explosive thought a recurrent din of more familiar Broadway sounds: resounding gongs, breaking mirrors, mournful string arpeggios, clashing cymbals, stamping feet, and vibrating drums. And just in case some meaning should still find its way through the thunder, he has introduced visual distractions as well: langorous, mute courtesans lolling diaphanously on the floor; armies of half-clad, powdered male torsos marching militarily through the action; running Olympic leaps performed up, down, and over a precarious group of stairs; and murky battles fought in the gloom with sword and fire. As for the acting, while it is mixed (patricians from the classical theater, plebeians from the Studio), it is rarely blessed. Colleen Dewhurst contributes some sturdy, matronly moments as Caligula's mistress and Sorrell Booke is amusing and loathsome as the emperor's comic foil; but, as Caligula, Kenneth Haigh alternates too abruptly between grim irony, which he controls, and temper tantrums, which he doesn't, while stumbling floppily around the stage like an Eton schoolboy dizzy on his first cigarette. Meanwhile, the entire spectacle—periodically bathed in a frenzy of colored lights exceeding even Stanley Kowalski's orgiastic imagination [in Tennessee Williams's *A Streetcar Named Desire*]—is spread over a grey raked apron which is thrust into the orchestra like the launching platform of an aircraft carrier. Designed to be performed in cool, classical quiet, the current *Caligula* production is a credit to the memory of Cecil B. DeMille, and might even bring a gleam of envy to the imperturbable features of Tyrone Guthrie.

But let us (reversing the usual Broadway procedure) dispense with the production and examine the play. For, while, hardly a model of dramatic art, it contains, in Justin O'Brien's lucid translation, some of Camus' most provocative ideas. Written when the author was only twenty-five, *Caligula* is a study in total refusal. Camus characterizes the Roman emperor as an early nihilist with an artist's craving for form, clarity, and order in a world without meaning. Brought, through the death of his sister, to the realization that life is absurd and imperfect ("Men die, and they are not happy"), Caligula determines to work out the inexorable consequences of this conclusion. Rebelling against the very conditions of life, he exercises complete freedom without obedience to moral, spiritual, or canon law. "If God is dead," observed [Fyodor] Dostoevsky [in *The Brothers Karamazov*], "then everything is permitted." Caligula's absolutism is an attempt to achieve the impossible (symbolized by the "gentle, weightless, and naked" moon), to impose on life a form and purity which it does not possess.

Elsewhere, Camus once predicted that "the rebel, who at first denies God, finally aspires to replace him," and Caligula's crimes soon become his aspiration towards divinity. Observing that "there is only one way of equalling the gods—all that's needed is to become as cruel as they," Caligula conducts his reign according to the same heartless justice he sees operative in the universe. What results is a reign of dispassionate terror. Patricians are ordered to disinherit their sons and leave all the state ("Governing amounts to robbery. . . . As for me, I shall rob openly"); wives are ravished, sons tortured, and fathers murdered out of sheer whim. Everyone is guilty—not of any particular crime, but because they are subjects of Caligula, because they are alive under a merciless god. After making his divinity physically manifest as Caligula-Venus rising from a seashell (homosexuality is merely another expression of his license and revolt), his personal suffering begins to overwhelm him. He has achieved that solitariness necessary to the Promethean rebel, his contempt for mankind has reached its zenith, and he is ready to die. But he soon realizes, just before he is assassinated, that he too is guilty. Though liberated from memory, illusion, happiness, and the desire for security, he has recognized no limits, and his own fear of death signifies that his freedom has not been pure. Camus' final position goes beyond nihilism: man must refuse the divinity he has inherited from a dead God in order to share in the "struggles and destiny" of suffering humanity.

Caligula, obviously, is not a work which Americans will understand readily or accept with any enthusiasm when they have understood it. Camus eventually works his way through to a liberal-humanist platform, but he arrives there the hard way, without sentiment, moralizing, or didacticism, having come through the tenebrous forest of nihilism. While we in America have left unexplored even the borders of this forest, Camus recognized that nihilism was the central position against which he had to define his own, since it was the inevitable culminating point of 19th Century thought. It is still a powerful force in Europe, partly accounting for the excesses of Hitler and Stalin (in its most monstrous shape), and (in more harmless form) for the vacillating anarchy and authoritarianism of French government.

But the impact of nihilism on France has also resulted in some of the most original drama written in the last decade, a drama which—in the direction of its thought—would be almost inconceivable in America. For while we are trying to come to terms with human conditioning, the French are trying to explore the boundaries of human limitation; while we are seeking security, ease, and happiness within the social unit, the French are seeking metaphysical freedom outside of human institutions; while our key words are *adjustment* and *affirmation,* the key words in France are *alienation* and *negation.* In consequence, our plays— with their official tone, their pious pronouncements, and their social-psychological orientation—seem to be the work of a collective, embodying the collective's distrust of freedom, heroism, and individual salvation. In this early play of Camus, on the other hand, as in so much current French drama, the individual's relationship to his universe is once again being fully explored. (pp. 21-2)

> *Robert Brustein, "Nihilism on Broadway," in* The New Republic, *Vol. 142, No. 9, February 29, 1960, pp. 21-2.*

CRITICAL COMMENTARY

John Cruickshank   (essay date 1959)

[*In the excerpt below from his* Albert Camus and the Literature of Revolt *(1959), Cruickshank examines* Caligula *in terms of Camus's theory of the absurd—the tension between a chaotic universe and the human need for order and reason—and his concept of revolt—the refusal to give up the struggle against meaninglessness. Arguing that Caligula's actions are a form of rebellion against the absurd, Cruickshank observes that the reign of terror "has the threefold purpose of accepting the fact of the absurd, making a personal protest against it by bringing it out into the open, [and] forcing others to recognize the truth Caligula has discovered."]

Although *Caligula* reached the Parisian stage fifteen months after *Le Malentendu* its composition preceded that of the latter by five years. It was completed in 1938, published in 1944 and performed in September 1945. Paul Œttly produced it at the Hébertot with Gérard Philipe in the title part.

Caligula has a straightforward historical basis. Its subject is the third of the twelve Caesars described by Suetonius [in his *Lives of the Caesars*]. Caius Caesar Caligula came to power in A.D. 37 at the age of 25, and reigned for four years until his assassination in A.D. 41. For the first eight months of his reign he proved a relatively enlightened and generous ruler. He largely reversed the policy of Tiberius and made a series of concessions by freeing state prisoners, bringing about progressive changes in the judicial system, etc. During this same period, however, he conceived an incestuous love for his sister Drusilla and announced his intention of marrying her. Then Drusilla suddenly died and almost overnight Caligula's character seemed to change completely. He abruptly became a monster of vice and cruelty. Suetonius speaks of him as being 'rather a monster than a man'. He killed, tortured or condemned his subjects until some members of his court rebelled openly and assassinated him. In his play Camus draws directly from Suetonius. *Le Figaro* of 25 September 1945 quotes him as saying that he invented nothing, added nothing, but accepted the account of Caligula given by Suetonius—'un journaliste qui savait voir'. Thus one finds, both in Suetonius and in Camus' play, references to Caligula's restlessness and insomnia, his apparent madness, his grimacing in front of the mirror, his wooing of the moon. The same is true of many other details including his murder of his mistress, Caesonia, his orders to arrange a famine in the land, his scheme to open brothels as a source of income for himself. Two of the most dramatically effective scenes in the play are also derived from Suetonius: the worship of Caligula dressed up as Venus in Act III, sc. i, and his 'poetic contest' on the subject of death in Act IV, sc. xi. Although he took so many facts from Suetonius Camus naturally interpreted them in a way that suited his own ideas at the time the play was written. *Caligula* belongs to the period in which he was most acutely aware of the absurd. In an article [in *Opéra*, 12 September 1945] Marc Blanquet reports him as saying:

> I have been all the way with the character I

chose as my subject and could not do otherwise despite the moral lesson which, I think, emerges from the play. This is that one cannot be free by being against other people.

The case history of Caligula is associated by Camus with the absurd. The play opens a day or two after the death of Drusilla and this event makes Caligula really conscious of the absurd for the first time. It appears, however, that Drusilla's death in itself has upset him less than the features of the human condition which it indicates. It has revealed to him, he tells Helicon, that 'men die and are not happy' (*Caligula*, I, v). The death and despair of human beings constitute his discovery of the absurd. Having become aware of the absurd in this way Caligula both accepts its inevitability and rebels against it. Although he really regards it as an inescapable reality he also tries to evade its consequences for himself by intensifying those consequences for other people. He wants to enter what he himself describes as the realm of the impossible. This is why he desires the moon:

> This world as it is is not to be endured. Therefore I need the moon, or happiness, or immortality, something which is mad perhaps, but which does not belong to this world.

Caligula thus exemplifies one form of revolt against the absurd, a form which Camus soon rejected. Caligula adds after the remark just quoted that the seemingly impossible may perhaps be obtained if one is logical to the utmost limits. In the context of the absurd this all-embracing logic means reducing everything to the same level of unimportance and turning upside down most conventions and sanctions. The logic of the absurd makes the greatness of Rome and Caesonia's arthritis equally unimportant. This logic also brings complete freedom to the individual who wields power and authority. Furthermore it tells him that all human beings are condemned to death so that whether they die sooner or later matters little. It is this kind of logic that Caligula has bitterly decided to follow to its conclusion and this decision sets the main action of the play in motion. Caligula institutes a cruel and capricious reign of terror among his subjects. It has the threefold purpose of accepting the fact of the absurd, making a personal protest against it by bringing it out into the open, forcing others to recognize the truth Caligula has discovered. As Act I comes to an end he beats furiously on a gong and shouts to Caesonia:

> Life, Caesonia, life is the opposite of love. It is I who tell you so and it is I who invite you to an unsurpassed celebration, to a public trial, to the finest of all spectacles. And I need people, spectators, victims, the guilty. Bring in the guilty. I need the guilty. All of them are guilty. I want the condemned to be brought in. . . . Judges, witnesses, the accused, all of them condemned in advance!

The remaining three acts of the play show the effects of Caligula's decision. He imposes arbitrary suffering. At a whim he kills individuals or has them killed. His cruelty is appalling in its consequences, though one can at least admire the way in which he exposes the shallowness, the mediocrity, the hypocrisy of many of his subjects. At one point, in the course of some comments on his own cruelty, he says to Scipio:

> The rivalry of the gods has its irritating side for a man who loves power. I have suppressed it. I have proved to these illusory gods that, provided a man has the will, he can carry on their ridiculous trade without prior training.
>
> SCIPIO: That is blasphemy, Caius.
>
> CALIGULA: No Scipio, it is lucidity. I have simply realized that there is only one way of being equal with the gods. It is enough to be as cruel as they are.

Statements like these make it clear that Caligula is a certain kind of *révolté* [rebel], but by his rebellion against the absurd he only intensifies it. The motives of his revolt—a desire for lucidity and a readiness to act in accordance with the truth he finds—would have Camus' approval, but the methods of his revolt are utterly wrong. Caligula himself begins to realize this towards the end of the play. Having strangled Caesonia, he mutters in Act IV, sc. xii: 'yet murder is no solution'. In the next scene, which is also the last, he condemns his actions as a whole. Not only does he decide that murder is no solution; he adds: 'I have not taken the right road, I have achieved nothing. Mine is not the right kind of freedom.' Camus' own comment on Caligula's mistake is contained in a note included in the programme for the Hébertot production:

> . . . if his integrity consists in his denial of the gods, his fault is to be found in his denial of men. One cannot destroy everything without destroying oneself. This is why Caligula depopulates the world around him and then, in keeping with his own logic, does what is necessary to arm against himself those who will ultimately kill him. Caligula's story is that of a high-minded type of suicide. It is an account of the most human and most tragic of mistakes. Caligula is faithless towards humanity in order to keep faith with himself. He consents to die, having learnt that no man can save himself alone and that one cannot be free by working against mankind. But at least he will have rescued some souls, including his own and that of his friend Scipio, from the dreamless sleep of mediocrity.

One of the other main characters in the play, Cherea, makes this last point. He says that Caligula forces people to think by making them insecure, by jolting them out of the rut, and this is really why he arouses their hatred. He shatters their easy assumptions and makes them face unpalatable truths. This is the aspect of Caligula's behaviour which Camus admires, and Cherea understands it. It is also understood by Scipio. Caligula says that Scipio is pure in the realm of good as he himself is pure in the realm of evil. This enables Scipio to understand the ideals pursued—and also perverted—by Caligula. One can say, in fact, that four different attitudes to Caligula's behaviour are indicated in the play. The patricians generally are too sunk in mediocrity to understand him. The outraged attitude they display centres round their own unimportant lives and their private wealth. Caesonia does not understand him either, though she uneasily accepts his actions.

By accepting his logic she seals her own fate since this very logic finally requires her to become one of Caligula's victims. An attitude of comprehension is found in Cherea and Scipio. Camus thus uses them in part at least, to explain more fully to the audience the apparently outrageous and demented activities of Caligula. To some extent they act as a chorus, as in ancient tragedy, since they reveal the real nature of Caligula's revolt and indicate two different attitudes to it based on a proper understanding of its metaphysical nature. Cherea understands it and rejects it utterly. He is convinced that Caligula must be removed and he works for this end. Scipio also understands Caligula's reaction to the absurd but in his case understanding prevents him from joining the assassins. He says to Cherea: ' . . . I cannot be against him. If I killed him my heart, at least, would still be on his side.' When pressed further by Cherea he adds: 'The same flame consumes our hearts. . . . My misfortune is that I can see reason in every attitude.' Cherea now considers that Scipio has been completely corrupted by Caligula's logic. He has accepted abstract logic rather than practical reasonableness because of the depths of his own despair. Cherea regards it as the worst of all Caligula's crimes to have wrought this transformation in the purity of Scipio. He leaves Scipio in order to make final preparations for the assassination of Caligula.

Readers of *L'Homme révolté* will find *Caligula* particularly interesting because it contains an imaginative projection of various ideas more fully explained and discussed in the later essay. For the audiences of 1945, however, especially those unacquainted with Camus' other writings on the absurd, the play was perhaps chiefly interesting as a kind of political morality. Several of the first critical notices made this point by speaking of similarities between the megalomania of Caligula and of Hitler, between Caligula's attitude of mind and that revealed by some Nazi theorists, between Caligula's actions and those of Hitler, between Caligula's suicidal death and Hitler's self-immolation in the Berlin bunker. These are genuine aspects of the play of course, and they contributed to its first success. *Caligula* contains various ideas also discussed in *Lettres à un ami allemand.* But a more important aspect of the play remains. How good a play is *Caligula* in itself, independent of its apparent topicality in 1945 or its special interest now for those who know Camus' other writings well? I think the answer should be that it is a good play, for several reasons. For instance, the subject-matter itself clearly provides Camus with a wealth of material. This material is dramatic, spectacular, and it moves steadily and inevitably towards a climax. Camus, by having such material at his disposal, was therefore able to adopt the natural order of his subject while retaining tenseness and dramatic density. In the case of *Le Malentendu* one may feel that a rather limited amount of dramatic material is being artificially, if cleverly, expanded for the purposes of a full-length play. This is not so in *Caligula* which is free from wordy *longueurs*. At the same time it has been suggested that the play is unsatisfactory after the first act. From then on we have a series of situations logically derived from Caligula's earlier decision to try to achieve the impossible. The result, it is argued, is a sequence of tableaux which are striking enough in themselves but lack real dramatic connection with one another. In a sense this is undoubtedly true,

and it may appear to be a serious criticism of *Caligula* as a drama for the stage. My own feeling is, however, that the cumulative effect of these tableaux and their rise towards a climax ensures their effect in the theatre. In addition, the fact that they all have a direct logical link with Caligula's first decision gives them a collective necessity and preserves their dramatic unity.

This unity is also strengthened by the domineering and neurotic figure of Caligula himself. The play is organized around him. He gives it a dramatic centre and dramatic impact. His personality holds the attention of the audience. He is repellent and yet fascinating, a tyrant and also a victim, a madman whose logic nevertheless cuts cleanly through the muddle-headedness and hypocrisy of many of his subjects. Camus also makes dramatically effective use of his tempestuous beating on the gong and his repeated self-scrutiny in the mirror. This latter device has obvious symbolical as well as direct meaning, and this indicates another source of strength in the play. The character of Caligula allows the play to appeal to the audience on two distinct levels. For those who do not grasp the philosophical ideas fully, or who find them too abstract to hold their attention, the play can still appeal as an unusual and powerful psychological study. Caligula himself is no mere abstraction; his very inhumanity is humanized. This also means that for those who accept more readily the metaphysical nature of Caligula's revolt it has a double interest. The success the play enjoyed on its first performance is partly due, I think, to this unified duality which allowed Camus to give psychological body to his admittedly didactic intentions. Some critics, it must be added, found the play too abstract on its first performance in spite of everything. One said it was philosophy, not theatre, and another described it as being literature but not drama. Most of the leading critics were enthusiastic, however, and several claimed *Caligula* to be the most impressive new play to have reached the Parisian stage since before the war. (pp. 194-200)

John Cruickshank, in his Albert Camus and the Literature of Revolt, *1959. Reprint by Oxford University Press, London, 1960, 249 p.*

R. W. B. Lewis   (essay date 1960)

[*In the following essay, Lewis contends that in each of* Caligula's *four acts, the Roman emperor methodically breaks his ties to humanity: with Caesonia, with Scipio, with Cherea, and, finally, with himself.*]

Within days of Camus' death, it was being said (with an air of surprise) that, for all he seemed so characteristically a man of the theater, his dramatic achievement was not, as it turned out, very large or impressive. Four plays of uncertain merit, and nothing original since *Les Justes* in 1949; adaptations of Calderón, Lope de Vega, Faulkner and Dostoievsky; towards the end, administrative activities. The enumeration is not inaccurate; and in appraising the apostle of *mesure,* one does not want to make immoderate claims for his work in the theater, nor for *Caligula* in particular. But such reckoning can be as misleading as it would be for Camus' fiction (only one novel, really, along with a couple of novellas and a handful of short stories), or for his essays and articles. The fact is, of course, that Camus—as he always insisted—was one of those writers "whose works form a whole in which each one is illuminated by the others." Each one, it might be added, is a necessary aspect of the others, and often contains those others, including writings yet to come, in nearly visible essence. Camus' dramatic work, in short, is not a fragment to be isolated, for inspection, from his performance in other genres. It is a constant dimension, constantly expanding, of his total artistic accomplishment. It was, for him, one more vocabulary, one more set of resources, with which to take hold of the shifting chaos reflected everywhere in his pages; just as the actor was one more prototype (along with Don Juan and Napoleon) of what Camus used to call "the absurd man." Camus' theatrical dimension was large and pervasive; and no work, in my opinion, more rousingly illustrates the scope and intent of it—and its dependence, for full understanding, upon his other writings—than the first of his plays, *Caligula.*

Written in 1938, *Caligula,* like *Noces,* is distinctly a pre-war creation; and though it was composed in Algeria for local production, it is hard not to see a part of the spiritual condition of late pre-war continental France in the sagging morality and jumpy opportunism of the Roman patricians, as they whine and cower before the lethal derision of Camus' protagonist. But the date of composition is more important as an aid to identification. Albert Camus, in 1938, was exactly as young as the 25-year-old Roman lad who began his own career, his blood-curdling four-year rule as Emperor of Rome and successor to Tiberius, in 37 A.D. *Caligula* is, first of all, an emphatically youthful play about an emphatically youthful hero ("All young people behave like that," says one of the patricians, hopefully); and through all its persistent horrors there rings an irrepressible exuberance that—in Camus' case—the swift maturing process of the war years would soon dispel.

This communicated zest is, among other things, the sheer joy of artistic creation. *Caligula* expresses the same self-conscious literary excitement that we sense (to take one of countless examples) in young Christopher Marlowe's apprentice drama about an imperial superman, *Tamburlaine.* It is the excitement of the discovery of vocation: an emotion so powerful that, with *Caligula* as with *Tamburlaine,* the insatiable aspirations of the hero appear as vital analogues to the creative aspirations of the author. The life-begetting impulse apparent in the writing vies and mingles with the death and destruction enacted on the stage; story and tonality engage in a strained but artistically happy marriage; and poets and poetry, actors and dramatic presentations become literal and significant elements in the action of the piece, investing it with a quality of being that no summary of the plot could hope to suggest. The result, as Camus describes the dark congested reign of one of history's most repulsive tyrants, is (not a tragedy but) an extravaganza which takes as its inner and actual subject the very idea of extravagance: that is, strictly, of "wandering outside." The great attraction of supreme power, Caligula remarks thoughtfully, is that it gives the impossible a chance; and this play is the only work of Camus which really does so.

In *The Myth of Sisyphus,* Camus would commit himself "to exhaust[ing] the field of the possible," and to hanging doggedly inside it. The urge to transcend, to wander outside the limits of human possibility, would then be denounced as one of the characteristic modern modes of suicide. To be sure, Caligula's transcendent urge was also, in a manner of speaking, suicidal: as Camus underlined in his 1958 preface to the American edition of the play. *"Caligula,"* Camus declared—but this is the older and more austere Camus talking—"is the story of the superior suicide," who "does what is necessary to arm against him those who will eventually kill him." That is a neat capsule of the play's plot; though, as Camus went on to say, it is not the fact but the terms of the Emperor's rebellion that must be seen as unacceptable. At the outset, indeed, Caligula plainly bespeaks Camus' own refusal to accept the condition of things: that condition which the shock of his sister Drusilla's death leads Caligula to recognise and reject: a universe in which "men die and they are not happy." In that extraordinarily bare and eloquent phrase of the pre-Christian Caligula, we hear the unmuffled voice of the post-Christian Camus, uttering his absolute statement about the source of the tragic nature of contemporary experience. Camus' personal response was to dedicate both his art and his moral energy to what, following [André] Malraux here as elsewhere, he called the "refabrication" or "rectification" of the universe. But to rectify the universe, according to Camus, was, precisely, to *humanise* it. The way of Camus' Caligula, on the contrary, was to dehumanise it, literally to attempt to depopulate it: and this, or so it would seem in retrospect, was the young man's grandiose error. And yet, as dramatized, Caligula's deadly ambition—set, as it is, amidst a good deal of erotic highjinks and set against the whimpering bewilderment of most of the other persons in the play—takes on a curiously exhilarating character; even as Caligula, the man, becomes a curiously, contradictorily engaging personality. For by giving its head, for once, to an extravagance he would thereafter resist with all his force, Camus composed what, within the framework of all his later writings, comes to us as the major showpiece for his compelling anti-themes.

These are the great themes that animate the realm of the impossible. Among them is the familiar awareness of nothingness, of *rien.* But nothingness is not grimly confronted here, acknowledged and deplored, as it would be in *Cross-Purposes* and *The Myth of Sisyphus.* It is, rather, reached out for, it is leaped towards and celebrated: from its multiple iteration in the play's opening scenes (when it is sounded with the booming regularity of the gong the Emperor strikes, rhythmically, to accompany the nihilistic oath he forces on his terrified mistress, Caesonia) onward to Caligula's wild admission, a second before his assassination, that his entire quest has concluded in *"Rien! rien encore!"* The cry is a shout of triumph as well as an ultimate confession; for "nothing" has become an end to be accomplished, a reality to which Caligula nearly reduces the world he rules over. And throughout the quest, Caligula proceeds with a kind of fierce and knowing joy directly against the notion that Camus would erect into a central theme, and a principle of right conduct: the theme of *mesure,* of balance, of control and limitation. Dr. Rieux, in *The Plague,* stands for Camus' ideal of well-balanced rebellion; but about Caligula everything is excessive, out of control—beginning with his extravagant grief over the loss of Drusilla ("*Cela dépasse les bornes,*" grumbles one of the patricians.). "I invite you," Caligula says magniloquently to Caesonia, "to a feast without limit . . . to the most beautiful of spectacles." *Caligula* itself, needless to say, is that feast and that spectacle.

And the limit Caligula seeks mainly to surpass, equally obviously, is the limit of humanity. In *The Rebel,* the determining theme and the note of its unswervable humanism was Camus' contention—echoing the reply of Homer's Odysseus [in the *Odyssey*] to the goddess's offer of divinity and a permanent home on her magic island—that "We shall choose Ithaca . . . This world remains our first and last love." The anti-theme of *Caligula* is the defiant rejection of Ithaca and the ultimate strangulation of the aging, faithful Penelope of the piece; while Caligula himself assumes the role of the goddess, and appears before the gaping nobles in the guise of Venus. That second-act scene is as antic and histrionic as anything in the play; but Caligula is impersonating the only divinity that he (or Camus) could manage to discern: something deceitful, perverse, malicious and utterly unpredictable; the dispenser of a loathsome or, betimes, maddeningly prankish grace.

Such is the image of divinity implicit in *The Plague,* and represented by the incalculable epidemic which mysteriously destroyed one person and spared another; and such is the image made quite explicit in *The Rebel.* In *Caligula,* it is the tribune Cherea who makes Camus' more customary thematic point:

> I have the taste and the need for security. Most men are like me. They are not capable of living in a universe where, at any moment, the most bizarre thought can enter into reality; where, most of the time, it does enter, like a knife in the heart.

Cherea's words define not only a whimsical tyrant and an insupportable Rome; they define an unsolvable godhead and an appalling kingdom of grace—as seen from the side of human reason. But where, in *The Rebel* and *The Plague,* the perspective was largely on the tough-hearted and clear-minded effort to resist so intolerable a deity, in *Caligula* the focus is on the deity itself. The figure of Cherea (unless the part is performed with uncommon skill) tends to fade before that of the Emperor; and as it does so and as Caligula looms and expands, the anti-theme gets its full chance of expression, gets itself articulated with something like genuine high spirits and genuine high comedy. Both elements are grounded in the creative excitement I have alluded to; but within the play, the playwright's excitement is merged with the hero's excited aspirations towards, and notions of, divinity. "I have taken on the stupid and incomprehensible visage of the gods," he tells Scipio. "And that is blasphemy, Caius." "No, Scipio, it is the dramatic art! The error of these men is that they do not believe enough in the theater."

Camus, in 1938, believed so much in the theater that his histrionic enjoyment illuminated not only the imaging of a hateful theology, but also the exposure of what is perhaps the most significant of *Caligula's* anti-themes: the theme of total isolation. This, again, is not something asserted and feared; it is something lusted after and, at the end, accomplished, after the departure of Scipio, the revolt of Cherea, the killing of Caesonia and the (presumed) assassination of Helicon. Isolation is the chief anti-theme in the sense that its opposite—human fellowship as the key resource for those who stick to the possible in a senseless cosmos—would become the bedrock of Camus' compassionate humanism. And in the construction of *Caligula* it is a periodic tension between the lust for isolation and the longing for an authentic human encounter that moves the action forward.

Such an "agon" emerges consistently in the climax of each act. For the play is composed of a series of analogous movements, beginning in each case with a relatively crowded stage and thickening into a public spectacle of some kind; and then shifting and concentrating into the effort and the revealed failure of some personal and private relationship. Those parallel rhythms are analogies to each other; but they are also synecdoches, enactments in small, of the entire and over-all action—which is, exactly, a deliberate movement from the crowded center of a populous Empire to a position of complete solitude. The pattern I am suggesting warrants, perhaps, a brief elaboration.

After introductory moments wherein various patricians prowl and conspire, muttering their hopes or resentments or fears, we are treated—in Act I [of the French four-act version]—to a display of startling political and financial imperial decisions; in II, to a banquet modelled, one guesses, on those techniques of sexual humiliation discoverable in the Marquis de Sade's *Juliette;* in III, to an obscene religious rite, a histrionic Black Mass, with the Lord's prayer meticulously inverted to serve the worship of an androgyne Venus ("Spread across our faces thy impartial cruelty, thy objective hatred; open before our eyes thy hands full of flowers and murders . . . "); and, in IV, to a poets' contest, at which the assembled court listens to hurried improvisations on the theme of death. Few modern plays have even attempted so rich and various a presentation of the public contours of experience, in the classical and Elizabethan manner; far more characteristic of this dramatic era is Camus' *Cross-Purposes,* with its tight and inward little domestic parable and its cast of five persons. But it is to be noted that the public spectables that occupy the middle of each act in *Caligula* do not merely dramatize, they rambunctiously *subvert* the governmental, the social and familial, the religious and the artistic dimensions of the "Roman" life being depicted. And it is to be noted that these recurring ceremonies lead regularly to a moment when some purely private encounter is investigated and then, similarly, invaded and subverted.

Four successive times, after the pageantry has been dissipated and the patricians dismissed, Caligula confronts one or another of the very few persons with whom a relationship is imaginable. In Act I, it is his mistress whom the Emperor submits to the exquisite torture of a dreadful oath of allegiance ("You will be cruel." "Cruel." "Cold and implacable." "Implacable." "You too will suffer." "Yes, Caligula, but I am going mad!") The second act concludes with a surprising intimacy springing up between

Caligula and the young poet Scipio, whose father the Emperor has had executed—and with Caligula's abrupt denial of the incipient relationship, or of any other ("Is there nothing in your life that resembles some silent refuge, like the approach of tears?" "Yes, Scipio, there is." "What is it?" "Contempt!"). It is the turn, in Act III, of the rational tribune Cherea, who is persuaded despite himself that it is after all possible for two individuals "whose pride and spirit are equals, to speak to each other, once in their lives, from the bottom of their hearts"—only to have that experience, too, torn to pieces as an illusion, even as Caligula tears in pieces the conspiratorial document Cherea had written. And finally, in the play's denouement, Caligula (having dispatched his one remaining companion, Caesonia) confronts Caligula, his own staring image in the mirror; haranguing himself in a long last effort at relationship—only to demolish that possibility as well, in the conclusive gesture of smashing the mirror and turning to throw himself on the swords of the inrushing assassins.

The absolute solitude arrived at in the closing instant is then, dramatically speaking, altogether appropriate: the end towards which the play and its hero have been determinedly moving from the outset. In pursuit of his negative ideal, Caligula must explore the varieties of possible personal relationship, if only to demonstrate the fragility or fraudulence of all of them: the heterosexual relation (with its portion of mother-son involvement, and a hint of further incest); the relation of masculine love (with its portion of father-son involvement, for Caligula curiously but understandably replaces for Scipio the father he has murdered); the intellectual companionship of equals; and the relation of the psyche to itself. All are experimented with, undermined and rejected; and the action fulfills itself—with a burst of horrified enthusiasm—in the established fact of utter and permanent alienation.

The movement, or action, I have been describing is plain enough in the printed text, and it was made glowingly evident in the Paris production of 1958, directed by Camus. But it was largely smothered in the American presentation of 1960, and in a way worth mentioning for the inverse light it sheds on the play. The performance, for one thing, was heavily over-produced; characteristically, the reviewers praised the production and dismissed the play that lay buried beneath it. The set was mammoth and overwhelming; hordes of extras, many of them naked to the groin, pounded up and down huge flights of steps in total disorder; one had the impression of klieg-lights and Cecil B. De Mille. But such lavish expenditure merely concealed the exuberance *within* the play by imposing a spurious and distracting boisterousness from without. The production did not trust the play; and the play in action no longer trusted itself. It no longer, for example, trusted the obscenity in the Venus scene to become apparent through language and grouping, but required the unfortunate actress playing the part of Caesonia to contribute a series of pantomime obscenities ("bump-and-grinds") to punctuate—and in fact completely to divert the American audience from—the superbly blasphemous words of the prayer.

But the graver defect of all this was to blur fatally the characteristic rhythm of the action—its progression in act after act, and throughout the play as a whole, from the collapsing public spectacle to the failing private encounter. The latter element was made impossible from the beginning, and for another reason. It is not possible to enact the subtle motion towards and the painful failure of the human relationship, if the personages of the stage have—as actors—no visible relation, have nothing to do with one another, to start with. Cherea and Caesonia, Helicon and Scipio, the assorted patricians and their wives: all, in the American production, appeared to have wandered on to the same set by accident. There was no surprise and little impact in Caligula's inability to arrive at some common basis for understanding or for love. This scattered quality is not, it should be added, peculiar to the American presentation of *Caligula:* it is something inherent in the contemporary American theater, and under present circumstances it is probably incorrigible.

The American production has closed (for the wrong reasons), but the play remains—complex and extravagant, nihilistic and exhilarating, perverse and blasphemous and profoundly moral. (pp. 52-8)

> R. W. B. Lewis, " 'Caligula': Or the Realm of the Impossible," in Yale French Studies, Vol. 25, Spring, 1960, pp. 52-8.

Louis Z. Hammer   (essay date 1963)

[*Hammer is an American educator, poet, and playwright. In the following essay, he explores Caligula's attempt to control death. According to the critic, Caligula mistakenly believes that by taking the lives of others he exerts power over death. Camus shows, however, that the only power a person can wield against death lies in resisting it, in "holding onto life until he is absolutely forced to give it up."*]

Caius Caligula became the ruler of Rome in 37 A.D., at the age of 25, and remained as Emperor until his assassination in 41 A.D. He is the fourth of the Caesars described by Suetonius in his *Lives of the Twelve Caesars.* The observations of Suetonius, a sharp-eyed journalist, furnished Albert Camus with most of the incidents for his play, *Caligula.* In the present essay I shall offer an interpretation of this work which is, I think, consistent with its action and dialogue as well as with the thought Camus has expressed in other works.

Camus wrote the play in 1938. Because of the war, it was not produced until 1945, when it was given an enthusiastic reception in Paris. Many saw in its portrayal of a self-destructive absolute monarch an image that could quickly be applied to recent political events. France had just emerged from the Nazi occupation, and the parallel between Caligula's Rome and Hitler's Germany seemed particularly close.

While this parallel cannot be denied, I think it would be quite a mistake to view the play as centered on the theme of absolute political power. Camus was concerned with a more fundamental problem, one that is found at the roots of the human condition. To state the matter baldly, the play has to do with the question whether life does or does not have a meaning. Some may wonder whether this is really a question that anyone would take the time to bother about. But they should be reminded that Caligula was only 25 years old when he became the Caesar, and that it sometimes happens that at this age young men do raise such questions, perhaps before they know better. But not only was Caligula 25 years old; this was also Camus's age when he wrote the play.

This is, then, a young man's play about a young man. But it is about a young man who, at the age of 29, was able to say, "my life seems so long." These are the words of a man ready for death. And in the case of Caligula, they are the words of a man who prepared his own death and his own executioners. As Camus remarked [in the introduction to *Caligula and Three Other Plays*] "*Caligula* is the story of a superior suicide."

For approximately eight months after becoming the Caesar, Caligula, who had been a stormy, impetuous, often cruel young man, was the model of an enlightened ruler. He reformed the judicial system, freed state prisoners, allowed tax concessions. During this early period of his reign Caligula developed a deep passion for his sister Drusilla. (Suetonius accuses him of committing incest with all of his sisters, but Drusilla he seems really to have loved.) However, Drusilla died suddenly. Her death so affected Caligula that he abruptly left the city at night and traveled as far as Syracuse, returning after three days. Overnight he had turned into the embodiment of cruelty and vice. Having given a brief account of Caligula's early reign, Suetonius says very abruptly: "So much for Caligula as emperor. We must now tell of his career as a monster." It is this career of Caligula as a monster, but a strangely attractive monster, with which Camus is concerned in the play.

It is reasonable to suppose that Camus was attracted to the figure of Caligula because he saw in the young emperor an aspect of himself. It is Caligula's rebellion rather than his cruelty that attracted Camus; it is his own suffering rather than the suffering he caused others which makes Caligula strangely appealing. Camus at 25 was just young enough to appreciate Caligula's peculiar kind of lucidity that expressed itself in absolute rebellion, and old enough, decent and experienced enough, to recognize where Caligula went wrong. He remarks. "I have been all the way with the character I chose as my subject and could not do otherwise despite the moral lesson which, I think, emerges from the play "[*Opéra*, 12 September 1945]. The Caligula of this play is definitely Camus's own creation, though most of the details of the action are suggested by Suetonius.

Caligula, as Suetonius described him, seemed to Camus to represent perfectly a phenomenon in which he was acutely interested, namely, the experience of the "absurd." The death of Drusilla has revealed to Caligula, as he tells his henchman Helicon, that "Men die; and they are not happy." A common discovery, one would think. As a philosophical statement, it is to be classed among the most elementary. Camus says, "I look in vain for philosophy in these four acts. Or, if it exists, it stands on the level of this assertion by the hero: 'Men die; and they are not happy.'

A very modest ideology, as you see, which I have the impression of sharing with Everyman."

One has to agree with Camus that the philosophical statements are on the most elementary level—"Men die; and they are not happy"—and then say that a profound question of action may occur when the level of philosophical statement is even the most elementary. For one of the central problems of this play is the relation between thought and action, or, more broadly, between the reasoning mind and the material world. The propositions which thought furnishes may be extremely simple, but what to do about them, how to act in the light of them, may be a highly complex problem.

Camus begins the discussion of absurdity and suicide in *The Myth of Sisyphus* with this assertion: "There is but one truly serious philosophical problem, and that is suicide. Judging whether life is or is not worth living amounts to answering the fundamental question of philosophy. All the rest—whether or not the world has three dimensions, whether the mind has nine or twelve categories—comes afterwards." Should a man who observes that "Men die; and they are not happy" do away with himself on that account? In the discussion just mentioned, Camus says further, "The principle can be established that for a man who does not cheat, what he believes to be true must determine his action. Belief in the absurdity of existence must then dictate his conduct." Or, to use Caligula's words, one must "be logical." But to "be logical" in Caligula's sense is not simply to think rigorously; it is to maintain a rigorous consistency between thought and action.

The "absurd" is one of the central notions of Camus. *The Myth of Sisyphus* is devoted to an examination of it; *The Stranger* is the story of a man who lives the "absurd"; and *The Rebel* begins with a discussion of "absurdist" reasoning. Briefly, the "absurd" is a relationship between the mind seeking to use reason and the material world about which it attempts to reason. The relationship is one of disparity, for the world will not offer itself to the categories of the mind. To experience the "absurd" is to face "the silence of the universe," to attempt to find ultimate meaning and to be denied it. Life presents itself as though it had a meaning, but when we seek to probe that meaning we come up against a silent rock. The mind finds itself unable to cope with a residual surd factor in the nature of things, a factor that, try as we will, remains resistant to thought.

Caligula experiences the absurd upon the death of Drusilla. His transformation seems to be the result, not of his grief over her loss, but of the awareness that comes upon him of the contingency of human life and the complete indifference of the universe to man's presence in it. One moment this beautiful, joyful creature is alive, and the next moment she is gone, and it is as if she had never been. Beauty and joy, life and love are not sustained. Rather, the universe shows a huge lack of concern with them. In the wake of life and joy come death and despair; silence encompasses the best and the worst. What then is the value of human life and what difference does it make whether one dies sooner or later, since one will die eventually? One is alive now, and that it the sole reality.

Caligula reacts to the "truth" he has discovered—that human life has no ultimate meaning—by absolute revolt. Instead of acting within the limits of this knowledge, instead of living within the bounds of possibility, he gives way to a passion for the impossible, for the moon. In this he aspires to rival the gods. In Act III he asserts: "Well, I've proved to these imaginary gods that any man, without previous training, if he applies his mind to it, can play their absurd parts to perfection." Since all men die, all men must be guilty; this is the natural order, and Caligula represents that order. Therefore, all the subjects of Caligula are guilty and can be punished. This is the new bill of rights.

"[L]iving . . . ," Caligula says, "is the opposite of loving." Love requires the lovers to believe that they will be joined to each other throughout eternity. But Caligula has discovered that death comes to all and that we can know nothing of a life beyond death. One must be lucid: life is the opposite of eternity and therefore the opposite of love. What men call love is simply an animal act. Caligula's passion for the impossible, for being absolutely free to act consistently with any truth he has discovered, is so intense that he sets about pitilessly to act according to his truth. In Caligula's new Rome life suddenly drops in value. The Treasury becomes of first importance. In fact, human life, the Treasury, his mistress's arthritis, all become of equal importance and of equal unimportance. Caligula attempts to stand up to this indifferent universe, not to meet it on its terms, but to reject these terms. If the universe cares nothing for human valuations, then he, the Emperor, will care nothing. He will not accept the supposed condition under which man must adopt meaning while the universe disowns any meaning. Caligula wants the moon, that cold, lucid, aloof light that looks at men brightly but does not warm them or care for them. He wants the moon in the name of an honesty which sets itself against chimeras and, in its strange way, wants to be faithful to life.

In the three years that elapse during the play, Caligula has subverted all the values of civilized society. Even the sophisticated Romans have had enough. Cherea is a leader of the nobles, the voice of enlightened reason, and ultimately Caligula's nemesis, since he understands Caligula's passion for the impossible. He observes:

> True, it's not the first time Rome has seen a man wielding unlimited power; but it's the first time he sets no limit to his use of it, and counts mankind, and the world we know, for nothing. That's what appalls me in Caligula; that's what I want to fight. To lose one's life is no great matter; when the time comes I'll have the courage to lose mine. But what's intolerable is to see one's life being drained of meaning, to be told there's no reason for existing. A man can't live without some reason for living.

Caligula has had any number of patricians put to death, he has taken some of their wives for his brothel, he has made the patricians trot along beside his litter when he goes out into the country. At any moment he is likely to visit upon them some unheard-of indignity. Naturally, they are incensed and want to take revenge. Only Cherea, however, opposes Caligula because he has destroyed the foundations of society, and not simply because the Emperor has wronged him. He is against Caligula, but this does not mean he is for the weak and self-centered patricians. Cherea understands that Caligula has sowed the seeds of his own destruction and he prevails on his fellow patricians to give Caligula more time, to wait, as he says, until Caligula's "disinterested malice" has become genuine madness, and then to strike. When Caligula asks Cherea why he opposes him, Cherea, speaking, it seems, for Camus, replies: "Because what I want is to live, and to be happy. Neither, to my mind, is possible if one pushes the absurd to its logical conclusions."

Perhaps no relationship in the play reveals better the extent to which Caligula's illness has proceeded than that between Caligula and Scipio, a young poet who has adored him and whose father the Emperor has murdered. In an affecting scene at the end of Act II, Caesonia has just urged Scipio, who has real cause to hate Caligula, to try instead to understand him. Caligula asks Scipio about the poems he has written and speaks knowingly and sensitively of Scipio's innermost feelings for the beauties of Nature, even guessing the content of his poems. He has completely won over the sensitive youth, telling him that "the same eternal truths appeal to us both," when, abruptly changing this tone he snarls, "Your poem sounds very good indeed, but, if you really want my opinion. . . . All that's a bit . . . anemic." Scipio is horrified, calls Caligula a "loathsome brute" and tells him how horribly lonely he must be. Caligula replies that he is never alone, "Those we have killed are always with us. But *they* are no great trouble. It's those we have loved, those who loved us and whom we did not love; regrets, desires, bitterness and sweetness, whores and gods, the celestial gang!" Scipio is again moved and asks Caligula if there is no "secret solace" in his life, to which Caligula replies: "Yes, I have something of the kind . . . Scorn." With this decisive utterance the act ends.

We see Scipio again in Act IV being asked by Cherea to join in the overthrow of Caligula. Scipio refuses, saying that while he is not *with* Caligula he cannot be *against* him: "The same fire burns in both our hearts." Scipio now despairs of ever taking sides, and Cherea comments: to have instilled despair into a young heart is fouler than the foulest of the crimes he has committed up to now."

After this scene, the play whirls through its denouement. Caligula has summoned all the patricians who tremble with fear that their plot has been discovered and that Caligula will put them to death. Cherea alone is steadfast, perhaps because he knows that Caligula wishes to die.

Caligula has ordered an amusement, a contest among the poets on the subject: death. Time limit: one minute. Scipio is requested to compete. After one minute each poet is to step forward and read what he has written, that is until Caligula blows a whistle ordering him to stop. The winner is the poet who can read through his poem without being stopped. The other poets barely begin before they are interrupted. Scipio is allowed to read three lines before he is stopped:

> Pursuit of happiness that purifies the heart,
> Skies rippling with light,
> O wild, sweet, festal joys, frenzy without hope!

"You're very young to understand so well the lessons we can learn from death," Caligula says. The poets are marched out. Scipio tells Caligula that "I shall go away, far away, and try to discover the meaning of it all."

Caligula is left alone with Caesonia. Led on by his ruthless "logic" he strangles her too, and just before the conspirators rush in to assassinate him, he weeps: "I have chosen a wrong path, a path that leads to nothing. My freedom isn't the right one."

Though its action parallels rather closely actual historical events, *Caligula* is not an historical play. The Rome of the drama is not historical Rome, but a poetic Rome. It is not accident that Scipio the poet comes closest to probing Caligula's heart, or that Caligula stages a spectacle play within the play—a public rite in which the Emperor appears dressed as a grotesque Venus—, or that he holds a contest among the poets on the topic of death. Caligula, as he himself says, is a kind of poetic dramatist creating his own version of man's relationship to the nature of things. The setting is Rome, an aesthetic city, a sealed-off city, the scene of an inner struggle, the struggle within Caligula's soul.

Caligula creates a new kind of space in which a recognizable human environment disappears. Rome becomes the space in which to express the Emperor's frenzy. In it women are raped openly, men are murdered, the role of the gods is taken over by a man. Every sort of dislocation is permitted in this space; it is a dream-space, the space of the impossible, a chaotic inner world externalized. No wonder Cherea reacts so strongly as he sees the meaning of men's lives undermined. For him Rome is an institution in which men associate to achieve a common good. The city of Rome is for him the locus of this association. When he walks through Caligula's Rome he is in an altogether different city. It is the creation of a madman, not the environment of sane and responsible human beings.

In his novel *The Plague,* Camus gave us another sealed-off city which is both an actual and mythical place, the city of Oran in Algeria. For ten months the inhabitants of Oran are cut off from the outside world while the plague ravages the city bringing with it physical suffering, death and the terror of solitude. The plague-ridden city of this fable is akin to Caligula's Rome. The plague is a spiritual as well as a physical disease. Like Caligula's madness, it brings about dislocations which awaken a sense of reality among a people who had taken the order of their lives too much for granted.

There is also a disordering of time; the conflict between youth and age is very much a part of the play. Caligula constantly taunts the old patricians and causes them to suffer countless indignities. Maturity, in the form of Cherea, in the end destroys Caligula. But youth and age almost become fused one with the other. Caligula feels like an old man at 29. At 30, Caesonia sees herself as an aging woman. Scipio, a boy of only 17, is forced to leave youthful innocence behind him, to leave Rome in order to go in quest of himself. At the same time, old men become like prattling children again, denied any of the reverence due their age.

All of this is consistent with Caligula's denial of any meaningful, progressive sequence to life. If there is no ultimate meaning to human existence, he reasons, it does not matter whether a man dies sooner or later. Time has lost all of its usual divisions; a genuine future ceases to exist. Time is only a prolonged and empty present which must be filled up, a kind of immense hole, the emptiness of which continually cries out to be relieved by violent acts. Caligula, like Macbeth, has murdered sleep; it is no longer in his power to escape the prolonged present which can end only with death, the obliteration of time.

Caligula is constantly aware of time. In the contest he holds among the poets, the subject is death, time limit: one minute. He attempts to impose his control on time, but what he cannot do is to make time move for him in a meaningful sequence. In *The Plague* Camus has Tarrou record in his journal this entry: "*Query:* How contrive not to waste one's time? *Answer:* By being fully aware of it all the while. *Ways in which this can be done:* By spending one's days on an uneasy chair in a dentist's waiting room . . . by listening to lectures in a language one doesn't know: by traveling by the longest and least convenient train routes, and of course standing all the way." This droll entry points up Caligula's dilemma: When one is most aware of time, i.e. the context in which meaningful acts occur, one cannot act in a meaningful way. To possess an overdeveloped sense of time is to lose the dynamic and structure of time. Time for Caligula is no longer the medium of events; it has become a substance that weighs on him. And the horror of his condition is that his own death will serve only to prove the extent to which his own life has been a negation of life. Death terminates, but also underscores, the sweetness of a life that has been lived fully as a series of human events. But it cannot function in this way for Caligula because he has cut the living nerve of time.

Disruption of the order of space and time is part of the syndrome that Camus is examining in this play, namely, the passion for the impossible. Caligula wants to achieve what even the gods cannot achieve. Caesonia, who pleads the case for the possible, tells him: "You can't prevent the sky from being the sky, or a fresh young face from aging, or a man's heart from growing cold. . . . There's good and bad, high and low, justice and injustice. And I swear to you these will never change." Caligula, however, will not accept the necessity in the order of things that ordains what is possible. His acute sensitivity to the suffering implicit in the human condition drives his passion for justice. He cannot stand the inequities of human life. If the order of the universe is such that it condones these inequities, then he will reject the universe. He will supersede God with the man-god. If God's order is denied, then the way is open for man to become God. And to the man who has become God, everything is allowed; crime is permitted.

Caligula very much resembles [Fyodor] Dostoevski's hero, Ivan Karamazov [in *The Brothers Karamazov*], who also rebels against injustice, only to condone murder. The truth of things as they are is not acceptable to Ivan because the suffering of children must be taken in the bargain. But to reject the truth of things as they are is to assert that there are no limits to what might be. And if there are no limits, what then is to prohibit murder? Although the servant Smerdyakov is the one who actually kills old Fyodor Karamazov, Ivan in the end holds himself guilty of this father's murder because he has fostered the principle that everything is allowed.

Like Ivan, Caligula rebels against the injustice of the world, and carries his rebellion to its "logical" end. His thoughts and actions show a coherence that is the expression of a kind of lucidity. He has attained a certain form of freedom, freedom from an exterior order. He has detached himself from the system of nature and of the human species. In fact, he has denied that there is a nature, and he has assumed for himself the terrible burden of Creation, the bringing into being of a system of "possibles." But this is the task of God, and Caligula discovers that he is not God, a fact which he really must have known all along. Caligula has set himself against man as he is, against the human species as it has been constituted, in the name of a freedom that would allow him to rise above that species and its limitations.

The tragedy of his position is that he is trapped by his own membership in the human species. Man is a social and political animal, and cannot become himself except with other men. The kind of freedom Caligula has chosen cannot work because it is a denial of this fundamental condition. To express the freedom he has assumed, Caligula must give himself the power of life and death. Moved by the death of Drusilla, he wants to destroy death. But the absolute, the impossible power needed to destroy death is also the power to destroy life. Following his passion to acquire this impossible power, he achieves only a limited power: he destroys other life. Death remains as the nucleus of the possible, and death remains in control of Caligula. He tells Scipio that he is never lonely because those he has killed are always with him. He might have said that death too is his constant companion, a companion waiting to strike at the proper moment. Death has taken charge in Caligula's Rome, and the deaths he has caused cause his destruction, an outcome for which Caligula is prepared from the beginning. In seeking his freedom in being against other men and against the conditions under which men have to live with each other, against the possible, he has affirmed the supreme power possessed by the possible. That is why his last words are: "I'm still alive!" In recognizing that he has chosen the wrong kind of freedom, he acknowledges that the only freedom which a man can acquire is freely to accept those moments that are given to him in which to be alive within the limits of possibility. And this possibility is defined by that nature which men have in common. In crying that he is still alive in the moment before his death, Caligula for the first time honors life and defies death in the only way open to a man. A man cannot rebel against death by trying to abolish death, but only by holding onto life until he is absolutely forced to give it up. There is perhaps another more sinister meaning in his cry that he is still alive: that the passion for the impossible, which he represents, is still alive in the world.

Camus holds that for the man who has experienced the absurd and is moved to rebel against the universe, there is only one legitimate course to follow. He must remain alive to face "the silence of the universe." If he is honestly playing the game that life forces him to play in the face of the absurd, he must persevere without consolation. He must not hope for salvation in a future life, nor should he allow himself to be beguiled by the myth of the ultimate perfectability of man on this earth—a revolutionary goal which only brings new forms of tyranny. Like Meursault, the hero of *The Stranger,* he must say that any vision he may have of a Heaven after death must be of "A life in which I can remember this life on earth."

The man who lives the absurd, who plays the game fairly, must reject suicide because to end his own life is to destroy that human power of awareness by which the absurd originally came into view, and which constitutes him a man. To commit suicide is to call it quits, to end the contest with the impenetrable universe. The only nobility man can achieve is to refuse to end the contest, his only power the power to go on living. Absolute rebellion will result only in handing to the universe a victory over man all the sooner. Murder and destruction also are not allowed because they deprive other men of the opportunity to continue to put their humanity in the face of the universe. The true rebels rebels not against life but against death. "And if I find killing easy, it's because dying isn't hard for me," Caligula observes in a revealing moment.

Camus has put into this play, as he says, a "moral lesson." But it is a lesson to be found on the far side of the play, after Caligula's violence has run its course. After going all the way with Caligula, we see the hero of the absurd as he should be; and what he should be is not what Caligula was.

This is reflected in the imagery of the play. Caligula wants the moon, and he identifies the moon with the impossible. The light of the moon furnishes a kind of lucidity out of which is developed the "logic" of absolute rebellion, a "logic" of the impossible. The other source of light, the true source of light, which illumines both the possible and impossible, is the sun. After all, the moon shines only with a light reflected from the sun. The impossible appears only because the possible shows it up. The proof of the association of the sun with the possible is that the sun warms and sustains life, while the moon simply looks on with a hard brilliance. The sun was the dominant image of Camus's life. He was born and spent his youth in Algeria, and it is in the sensation of tanned bodies luxuriating under the African sun that he found a continuing source for the recognition of human reality. In the final analysis Camus does not appeal to logical argument to sustain his claim that the rebel must operate within the limits of the possible. He bases the claim on the direct contact with other persons. He finds in the relationship with another person what Hazel Barnes [in *The Personalist* 41, No. 4, (Autumn 1960): 443-47] calls "emotional absolutes." My seeing, hearing, touching other human beings helps to define the limits of my action because this experience furnishes me with a reality which I cannot deny except by denying myself. The tenderness one feels when one observes the helplessness of a child, the revulsion one feels when one sees an old man degraded, convince one of his solidarity with the human race.

It is the image of human beings under the sun—too brilliant to look at directly, thus the image on the far side of the play—that sustains the race through all of its possibilities. To realize these possibilities, men will have to rebel against the conditions in which they find themselves. It will not however be the moon that they seek, but rather to stand in the full light of the sun, for, as Camus has said [in his *The Rebel, An Essay on Man in Revolt*]: "rebellion cannot exist without a strange form of love." Camus calls for a rebellion that keeps to its love. The moral lesson of *Caligula* is contained in these words from *The Rebel:* "Whatever we may do, excess will always keep its place in the heart of man, in the place where solitude is found. We all carry within us our places of exile, our crimes and our ravages. But our task is not to unleash them on the world; it is to fight them in ourselves and in others." (pp. 322-35)

> Louis Z. Hammer, "Impossible Freedom in Camus's 'Caligula'," in The Personalist, Vol. XLIV, No. 3, July, 1963, pp. 322-36.

Francine and Albert Camus in Stockholm, at the time he was awarded the Nobel Prize.

David R. Ellison   (essay date 1990)

[*In the following excerpt, Ellison provides a concise description of the general content and structure of* Caligula, *describing the play's central themes of guilt and art. Perceiving a total absence of innocence in the world and concluding that all humans are guilty, Caligula assumes the role of judge and arbitrarily defines innocence and guilt. Furthermore, Caligula considers his actions creative:* "his monstrous acts, in his view, amount to artistic creation."]

The first Paris performance of *Caligula* took place on September 26, 1945, with Gérard Philipe in the title role. Camus had worked on this his best play for a number of years (notes on the principal themes of *Caligula* can be found in the author's *Carnets (Notebooks)* very shortly after the completion of *Nuptials* and at the earliest stages of the composition of *The Stranger*), and was to revise it on a continual basis until 1958, when it achieved its definitive form. As we shall see, *Caligula* is a play based on ideas that are central to Camus's general philosophy or worldview; its dialogues echo both the problem of the absurd as developed in *The Stranger* and *The Myth of Sisyphus* and also the theme of revolt as found in *The Plague* and *The Rebel.*

Although the Parisian audiences of 1945 were unanimous in their praise of the acting talent of Gérard Philipe (who was to become one of France's greatest luminaries in the theater and in the cinema), the first reviewers of *Caligula* expressed reservations about the play's sometimes verbose and extravagant scenes, in which the expression of intellectually complex views seemed to take precedence over dramatic action and the continuity of the plot line. Like [Jean-Paul] Sartre, Camus had created a "theater of ideas": he placed characters on the stage with whom, for the most part, the spectator would have difficulty identifying and empathizing, but whose profound moral and spiritual dilemmas would constitute an enigma worthy of one's concentrated attention. The principal purpose of the theater according to Camus was to make the audience think, to shock it into reflection by upsetting its mental habits and routines. In choosing one of the most puzzling and outrageous figures from ancient history as the central character of his drama, Camus could guarantee his spectator both an intellectual challenge and an aesthetically enhanced questioning of the values on which cultivated human beings have traditionally based their laws, their arts, their civilization as such.

Caius Caesar Germanicus (12-41 A.D.), surnamed Caligula because, as a young man living in a military camp in the Roman province of Germania, he wore soldiers' sandals (called *caliga* in Latin), began his reign as Emperor in an enlightened, liberal style, but soon underwent a complete change in his personality. Historians traditionally have assumed that an illness of some sort was responsible for the transformation of Caligula into one of Rome's worst tyrants, into a man who forced his subjects to adore him as king and as a god. Influenced by his Egyptian slaves, he worshipped the goddess Isis, and himself demanded to be recognized as "The New Sun." His four-year reign was characterized by arbitrary arrests and murders; he himself was assassinated in 41 A.D.

1. GENERAL CONTENT AND STRUCTURE OF THE PLAY

At its most basic level, *Caligula* is a study of excess—excess of desire, of power, and even, as we shall see, of idealism. As was the case in *The Myth of Sisyphus,* there is no place in the universe of this play for moderation or tranquility of spirit. Like Don Juan, the metamorphosing *comédien,* and the military conqueror, who led exemplary "absurd lives" in *The Myth,* Caligula pushes his own existence to the limit of its possibilities. At the same time, however—and it is herein that the imaginary worlds of *The Myth* and of *Caligula* do not coincide—in his play Camus is not content to present the problem of the absurd from the perspective of the individual consciousness: as spectators, we are not merely aware of the Emperor's aspirations, volition, despair, and crimes, but also of the way in which his actions impinge upon the lives of his subjects and advisors. Nowhere in *The Myth* does Camus consider the consequences of Don Juan's seductions or Alexander's triumphs; the people who fall victim to the grand designs of the "absurd heroes" remain invisible to the philosopher-essayist. This is not the case in *Caligula,* where Camus was careful to surround his Emperor with secondary characters who must choose between passive fear of the tyrant and open resistance to his schemes.

The entirety of the play is constructed on a balancing of the Emperor's actions against the reactions of the characters with whom he comes into daily contact. Camus has his audience penetrate the claustrophobic world of a ruler's inner sanctum, in which court intrigue (what, in today's jargon, we would call "political in-fighting") is rampant and transparent. As spectators, our gaze is always directed at Caligula, but occasionally we must view his thoughts and actions through the interposed consciousness of the courtiers.

The play begins with the clear and direct exposition of the problem: why and in what way has Caligula changed? During the first two scenes of Act I we do not see the protagonist, but hear about him from his concerned courtiers, who worry at his inexplicable absence. The general assumption is that the Emperor has left the palace out of grief for his sister Drusilla, who has died just recently. It had been rumored for some time that brother and sister had an incestuous relationship, but this possible "fact" does not seem to account for Caligula's recent behavior and for the brusqueness of his departure. When we encounter Caligula for the first time, we see a man who is distraught and disheveled, who is suffering from an inner crisis at first difficult to define. In the first important prolonged scene of the play (I,4) he tells us of his desire to possess the moon, and states, in a bland tone: "Les hommes meurent et ils ne sont pas heureux" ("Men die and are not happy"). It is the coupling of the Emperor's strange, apparently mad aspirations (expressed initially as his desire to "have" the moon) with his discovery of the absurdity of human existence (our unhappiness *and* our mortality) that sets in motion the various dramatic conflicts of the play.

In Act I, after an expository section on Caligula's past and on his current unstable frame of mind (scenes 1-7), we witness the changed ruler's first decree, which foreshadows all the atrocities to come. Caligula orders all citizens of the Empire to disinherit their children and to will their fortunes to the State (I,8). In so doing, the ruler wishes to "change the order of things" and to "confound the categories" on which civilized society is based. He now sees his function not as lawgiver and guarantor of civil peace, but rather as all-powerful judge in need of guilty persons for the exercise of his arbitrary power. The first act ends with Caligula contemplating himself in a mirror.

There is an interval of three years between Act I and the three remaining Acts of the play. Camus has chosen to show us the very beginning of Caligula's transformation and the bloody conclusion of his reign, and has kept close to historical chronology. At the beginning of Act II, we learn, once again through the eyes of the courtiers, not only what the Emperor has done in concrete terms, but also the rumors circulating about him: we learn that the populace at large lives in fear of his every act, all the more so since there seems to be no reasonable explanation for his choices and decisions. In Act II we meet the two most important secondary characters in the play, both of whom serve as foils to Caligula: the first, Cherea, a man of common sense who desires nothing more than an undisturbed existence; the second, Scipio, a poet whom the Emperor simultaneously admires and mocks. At this point in the play, we observe what might be called Caligula's "distorted logic." He liberates the slaves in his palace so that senators might serve him (II,5), and he declares that everyone in his realm must ultimately die *because* he is absolute master (II,9). In other words, everyone is by definition a slave and everyone is by definition guilty in an Empire that knows only arbitrary whim and decree.

Act III begins with a grotesque scene: we witness Caligula disguised as "Venus" emerging from behind a backdrop of his own making. In this short instance of "play within a play," we discover how important theatricality has become to the Emperor. He desires to be the protagonist in a drama of his own creation; his spectators, of course, are not allowed *not* to applaud. Adding to the outrageousness of the scene itself (the actor who plays Caligula wears a woman's tunic, makes effeminate gestures, and at one point paints his toenails) is the blasphemous arrogance of the ruler: he informs his subjects that it is through his power that the gods are able to descend to earth (III,1). Caligula is not merely portraying Venus in an outlandish way: he is suggesting that he participates as much, or perhaps more, in godliness, than she. When Scipio observes that Caligula's actions are indeed blasphemous, the latter responds: "No, Scipio, it's dramatic art. The error of most men is not to believe sufficiently in the theater. Otherwise they would know that it is permissible for anyone to stage celestial comedies and to become god. One need only harden one's heart." As Act III progresses, Caligula demonstrates the extremes to which he is willing to carry his arbitrariness. When he discovers incontrovertible proof that Cherea is among a group of conspirators seeking to depose him, the Emperor decides, on a whim, to destroy the proof and thus to declare Cherea "innocent." In so doing, Caligula acts not out of uncharacteristic altruism, but rather in defiance of all logic (and even his own self-preservation) so that he might surpass even the gods in his power. In his dialogue with Cherea, Caligula puts it this way: "with the disappearance of this proof I see the dawn of innocence on your face. What an admirably pure forehead you have, Cherea. Innocence is so beautiful! Admire my power. The gods themselves cannot restore innocence without prior punishment."

As could be imagined, Act IV is, in the strict Greek sense, the *catastrophe* of the play—that is, the final action in the drama that negates or overturns all that has preceded. The conspiracy that Caligula chose to ignore for his own reasons of power and of narcissistic self-absorption succeeds in the end. The Emperor cannot stand in the way of an inevitable death that he himself has caused: the suffering that he has inflicted on the people surrounding him returns in his direction in a final moment of retribution. Caligula, by the conclusion of the play, has refused the tranquil happiness sought after by Cherea, the love offered him by his mistress Caesonia, and the promise of fulfillment in art as achieved by the poet Scipio. He has affirmed that the only real happiness consists of "universal disdain, blood, hate all around me, the unequaled isolation of the man who holds his entire life in his vision, the measureless joy [*joie démesurée*] of the unpunished assassin." In the end, of course, it is precisely this thirst for the limitless, the *démesuré,* that causes the protagonist's downfall, that brings on his ultimate and tragic punishment.

2. INTERPRETIVE ISSUES

a. Excess (Démesure)

At the end of the first section of **The Myth of Sisyphus** Camus had asked the question: "Is there a logic unto death?" The purpose of the remainder of the essay was to prove that such a logic did indeed exist, but that its endpoint, rather than being suicide, was the lucid acceptance of the absurdity of the world coupled with an obstinate, constantly renewed revolt of the consciousness. The hero of **The Myth** is the individual human who knows himself to be condemned to a universe characterized by the irrational but whose desire for clarity is never assuaged. Although at first there might seem to be very few points of contact between the noble mythical figure of Sisyphus and the ostensibly "unhinged" Caligula, nevertheless it is notable that the point of departure of Camus's play is exactly the same as that of the philosophical essay. At two crucial points of **Caligula,** the protagonist asserts his will to "remain logical until the end." The first instance of this phrase is near the beginning of the play (I,4), when Caligula notes, on the one hand, that all people are unhappy and destined to die, and, on the other, that he wants to possess the moon. In this context, to be logical until the end means to deny one's own mortality (to become a god) and to pursue an object that is properly inaccessible. The second occurrence of the phrase is in a monologue that Caligula pronounces in the scene preceding his important confrontation with Cherea (III,5). At this stage of the play, the protagonist is surrounded by the death and destruction that he himself has caused, and realizes that even if he could possess the moon now, this "transfiguration" of the world

would not reverse the course of events nor would it restore life to those who had disappeared through the arbitrariness of his decrees.

The dialogue between Caligula and Cherea in III,6 is one of the pivotal moments in the play, in that for the first time Camus clearly opposes to the protagonist's philosophy of excess another philosophy, another way of being in the world. This is one of the brief and rare moments in the dramatic progression in which the spectator manages to look beyond the bloody realm of the Emperor, to glimpse a far calmer horizon. In response to Caligula's exposition of his thirst for absolutes, Cherea says:

> I want to live and to be happy. I think that neither is possible when one pushes the absurd to its limit. I am like everyone. To free myself from my condition, sometimes I wish for the death of those I love, I desire women whom the laws of family and of friendship prohibit me from desiring. To be logical, I should then kill or possess. But I judge that these vague ideas are not important. If everyone tried to realize them, we could neither live nor be happy.

The principal difference between Caligula and Cherea is that the latter, in accepting the limitations of his human condition, refuses to follow the logic of his desires to their conclusion. Cherea's notion of happiness is one of moderation and simplicty; according to him, the realization of one's wishes is not equivalent to a life well-lived. Within the universe of **Caligula,** Cherea's statements are noteworthy for their extreme brevity and for their disappearance under the sheer weight of the protagonist's will-to-power. Yet we should remember what Cherea says and the simplicity with which he speaks, because his mode of reasoning and his conception of life foreshadow the stubborn modesty of Dr. Rieux, the hero of **The Plague.**

b. Power, Evil, Resistance

In reading **Caligula,** we must not forget that the play was written during World War II and performed not long after the Liberation. The 1930s and first part of the 1940s in Europe had been a period in which political democracy had been under siege, both from the Nazi far-right and from the Marxist far-left. Following a world-wide economic depression came a total war that submerged the Continent in death and in despair and that caused dislocation to all political systems that advocated the freedom of the individual. The first audiences of Camus's play were not insensitive to the fact that the Roman Emperor, in his abuse of power and in the arbitrariness of his decisions, could be likened to much more recent despots—Franco, Hitler, Mussolini, and Stalin come to mind—all of whom had followed a certain "logic" to its most extreme political and social consequences. Camus's play did not deal in mere abstractions, therefore; the problems of power and of evil had emerged as being historically real, incorporated as they were in the concrete manifestations of bombs, torture chambers, and death camps. In **Caligula** the spectator experiences the inevitability with which the pursuit of an absolute degenerates into the exploitation and enslavement of human beings, who have become mere means to the end of the dictator's narcissistic enjoyment of his short-lived capacity to alter the face and facts of the world.

In his representation of the Emperor's entourage, Camus has given us an interesting portrait of fear and courage as well. Most of the secondary figures in the play live in awe of Caligula's power and fawn on him at every opportunity, much to his distaste (abject flattery is boring to an intelligent if devious monarch). But two of the characters—Cherea and Scipio—stand up to him, and both gain the respect of their adversary. In these courageous individuals who are unwilling to succumb to the will and vision of their ruler, post-war French audiences could see fictional/theatrical equivalents of those of their countrymen who had joined the Resistance. What I am suggesting here is not that *Caligula* be reduced to a mere political allegory (this was certainly not the author's intention), but that we recognize in its form of representation the potential for direct political and historical relevance. Put differently, one might say that the era in which *Caligula* no longer resonates with such relevance will be a happy one indeed: a time when dictators no longer exist and have become incomprehensible because they are unimaginable.

c. Judgment and Art

Throughout the play, when Caligula exercises his formidable power over his subjects, he most often assumes the role of judge. The Emperor, precisely because he has absolute political authority, presumes to be both judge and jury; no voice of opposition can be heard in his realm, which is also his universal court. Toward the middle of Act IV, when his actions have reached the epitome of arbitrariness, Caligula orders the organization of a poetic contest, in which he will evaluate all entries (IV,12). The contestants are given one minute to write a poem on the subject of death. We learn in this scene that Caligula himself has penned a treatise on the same theme, and that the lyrical but excessively subtle literary efforts of the court poets apparently fall short of the insights the ruler thinks he has gained on death during his three years of tyranny. At the conclusion of IV,12 Caligula sends away the poets (perhaps an allusion to Plato's famous banishing of the poets from his Republic [in *The Republic*]) and chooses to keep only Scipio, whose verses seem to have moved him. In a very important short assertion, Caligula reveals to us why he considers himself to be an artist and why he feels justified in condemning the writers of mere ornamental verse: "I have written only one composition. But in it I prove that I am the only artist Rome has ever known, the only one, you know, Cherea, who has made his thoughts and actions coincide." What Caligula implies here is that his reign can be "read" as one enormous "poem": his monstrous acts, in his view, amount to artistic creation. The only reason he spares Scipio from his generalized condemnation of the court art-functionaries is that he finds in Scipio a temperament or sensibility somehow attuned to his own. He cannot judge an individual who has, in his own way, understood death.

At the end of the play, the two characters who remain untouched by the increasing folly of the Emperor are Cherea and Scipio—those two individuals in whom Caligula sees strong resistance to his power and whom he is, therefore,

incapable of judging. In a crucial sense, the entirety of *Caligula* turns on the question of judgment. In his final monologue, as he contemplates himself one last time in the mirror before succumbing to the conspirators, the protagonist raises the question of his guilt, and cries out: "But who would dare condemn me in this world without a judge, in which no one is innocent?" If we move back to the beginning of the play, we can see that Caligula's initial discovery of the absurdity of the world (the unhappiness and mortality of the human being) caused him to assume that the very notion of innocence was an impossibility. We are all condemned to death and to subsisting for a while on a planet characterized by the irrational. Given the absence of innocence, there can be no judges, *unless* one presumes to become the unique judge and redefine the parameters of innocence and guilt. Caligula's reign of terror begins and ends when he decides, in an act of egocentric will, to *create* (by constantly disrupting and redefining them) the lines of demarcation between guilt and innocence.

Caligula the arbitrary judge is thus at the same time Caligula the artist of evil. The unusual combination of the themes of judgment and of art is at the center of the play; the way in which we interpret the subtle interplay of the two apparently disparate elements will determine our overall reading of *Caligula.* Further, although the overwhelming atmosphere of evil and of excess is perhaps unique to this one play, nevertheless we can see echoes of its thematic network in other works of Camus. (pp. 81-93)

David R. Ellison, in his Understanding Albert Camus, *University of South Carolina Press, 1990, 232 p.*

FURTHER READING

BIOGRAPHIES

Brée, Germaine. *Camus.* New Brunswick: Rutgers University Press, 1959, 275 p.
> A major study of Camus's personality and writings. Brée's discussion of Camus's drama is excerpted above.

Lottman, Herbert R. *Albert Camus: A Biography.* Garden City, N. Y.: Doubleday and Company, Inc., 1979, 753 p.
> Traces Camus's life and intellectual development and includes a critical examination of his works.

Thody, Philip. *Albert Camus: 1913-1960.* New York: The Macmillan Company, 1961, 242 p.
> Study of the body of Camus's work. Thody suggests that it was in Camus's "later theatrical work that he was most exclusively an artist, working with no ambition other than the purely aesthetic one of producing a good play."

OVERVIEWS AND GENERAL STUDIES

Amoia, Alba. *Albert Camus.* New York: Continuum, 1989, 156 p.

Includes a summary of the themes and the dramatic issues of each of Camus's four original plays. Amoia discusses Camus's exploration of the absurd in *Caligula,*
the "stark and sordid picture of an inhuman condition"
in *The Misunderstanding,* the contrast between the depiction of death and the "lyrical invocation" of nature
in *State of Siege,* and the ethics of political murder in
The Just Assassins.

Brée, Germaine. *Albert Camus.* New York: Columbia University Press, 1964, 48 p.

Concise overview of Camus's career including a discussion of his dramas as well as his fiction and expository
writings.

———, ed. *Camus: A Collection of Critical Essays.* Englewood Cliffs, N. J.: Prentice-Hall, Inc., 1962, 182 p.

Includes essays on Camus's plays; discussions of his social, political, and philosophical views; and assessments
of specific literary works.

Couch, John Philip. "Camus' Dramatic Adaptations and
Translations." *The French Review* XXXIII (October 1959):
27-36.

Discusses Camus's work as a theatrical adaptor and
translator. In several instances Couch finds Camus's versions brilliant interpretations of the original works and
important contributions to Camus's own body of work.

Freeman, E. *The Theatre of Albert Camus: A Critical Study.*
London: Methuen & Co., 1971, 178 p.

Only available book-length study devoted exclusively to
Camus's drama, from the writer's early efforts with the
Worker's Theater to the original plays and the adapta-
tions of his final period.

Garnham, B. G. "Camus." In *Forces in Modern French
Drama: Studies in Variations on the Permitted Lie,* edited by
John Fletcher, pp. 129-46. New York: Frederick Ungar Pub-
lishing Co., 1972.

Discusses Camus's entire dramatic output, from *Révolte
dans les Asturies* to his late adaptations and translations.
Garnham finds that "the human condition, the place
and purpose of man in the world" forms a consistent
theme throughout all of Camus's theatrical works.

Reck, Rima Drell. "The Theater of Albert Camus." *Modern
Drama* IV, No. 1 (May 1961): 42-53.

Examines how Camus's dramas reveal his philosophical
beliefs. Reck also contends that all of Camus's characters who "seek self-identity fail to recognize the futility
of such a task in an absurd universe."

Reed, Peter J. "Judges in the Plays of Albert Camus." *Modern Drama* V, No. 1 (May 1962): 47-57.

Examines the figures of justice in Camus's four major
plays. Reed defines two types of judges in the dramas:
the "just judge" who remembers "he is judging human
beings, not simply administering legalities," and the "arbitrary judge" who does not meet this requirement.

Sonnenfeld, Albert. "Albert Camus as Dramatist: The
Sources of His Failure." *The Tulane Drama Review* 5, No.
4 (June 1961): 106-23.

Observes several defects in Camus's dramatic techniques. Sonnenfeld contends that "Camus ultimately
failed as playwright because he consistently tried to
force into the dramatic form themes and situations per-

fect for his prose narratives but totally alien to the
stage."

CALIGULA

Abraham, Claude K. "*Caligula:* Drama of Revolt or Drama
of Deception?" *Modern Drama* 5, No. 4 (February 1963):
451-53.

Argues that considered as a play rather than a philosophical study, *Caligula* is disappointing. Abraham
charges that because he struggles against the absurd,
"Caligula seem[s] heroic for a while," but when the emperor finally admits that he accomplished nothing, the
audience, "like Caligula and his empire, has the right to
feel somewhat frustrated."

Aston, Frank. "*Caligula* Scores at 54th." *New York World-
Telegram and The Sun* (17 February 1960).

A review of the New York debut of *Caligula* that deems
the work a "fascinating drama" containing not only
"brilliantly challenging dialogue" but "noisy and fierce"
action. Aston especially appreciates the lead performance of Kenneth Haigh, who, the critic claims, mastered a physically and technically demanding role.

Braun, Lev. "The Challenge of Caligula." In his *Witness of
Decline—Albert Camus: Moralist of the Absurd,* pp. 43-52.
Rutherford, N. J.: Fairleigh Dickinson University Press,
1974.

Interprets *Caligula* in terms of Camus's own philosophical development. Braun places the composition of the
play during a period in which the successful rise of fascism was leading Camus to question his own liberal beliefs.

Clurman, Harold. Review of *Caligula. The Nation* (5 March
1960): 213-14.

A review of the 1960 Broadway staging of *Caligula* that
judges Sidney Lumet's direction "intelligent, faithful
and sometimes ingenious." Clurman finds the lavish scenery and costumes "irrelevant" to the play's meaning,
however.

Gassner, John. "Fables on Broadway." In *Dramatic Soundings: Evaluations and Retractions Culled from Thirty Years
of Dramatic Criticism,* edited by John Gassner, pp. 485-86.
New York: Crown Publishers, Inc., 1968.

Reprints a review of the 1960 staging of *Caligula* that
condemns the opulence of the production. "A more inappropriate approach to Camus' philosophical play
could hardly be imagined," Gassner charges.

Harrow, Kenneth. "*Caligula:* A Study in Aesthetic Despair."
Contemporary Literature 14, No. 1 (Winter 1973): 31-48.

Compares the Roman emperor to characters in other
Camus works written in the same period as *Caligula,* in
an attempt to discover why "Caligula alone is moved to
despair over the confrontation with the absurd." According to Harrow, Caligula, unlike the other heroes, refuses to accept his destiny and avoids confronting death.

Sprintzen, David. "*Caligula.*" In his *Camus: A Critical Examination,* pp. 65-77. Philadelphia: Temple University Press,
1988.

Analyzes *Caligula* as Camus's exploration of various
ways of coming to terms with an absurd universe. Al-

though Caligula's attempt is shown to be a failure, Sprintzen observes, the play offers no better alternative.

Stoltzfus, B. F. "*Caligula*'s Mirrors: Camus's Reflexive Dramatization of Play." *French Forum* 8, No. 1, (January 1983): 75-86.

> Offers an interpretation of *Caligula* as a play about a play: "Caligula is simultaneously actor, director, choreographer and script writer for a dramatic poem whose subject is death," Stoltzfus states.

THE JUST ASSASSINS

Freeman, E. "Camus's *Les Justes:* Modern Tragedy or Old-Fashioned Melodrama?" *Modern Language Quarterly* 31, No. 1 (March 1970): 78-91.

> Asserts that for the first three acts of *Les Justes,* "Camus points his play in the right direction for a genuinely dramatic and tragic consummation," but then steers it in the direction of sentimentality and melodrama when he has Kaliayev refuse to kill the Grand Duke's children.

THE MISUNDERSTANDING

Barnes, Hazel E. "Recognition and Engagement: To Leap or Not to Leap." In her *The Literature of Possibility: A Study in Humanistic Existentialism,* pp. 155-75. Lincoln: University of Nebraska Press, 1959.

> Discussion of the failure of the characters in *The Misunderstanding* to either transcend or to comprehend the absurdity of existence. Barnes claims that Camus's intent in this drama was to show "the absurdity of things as exemplified in gratuitous human suffering and in the misunderstanding and hatred existing where there might 'more naturally' have been love and mutual help."

Behrens, Ralph. "Existential 'Character-Ideas' in Camus'

The Misunderstanding." *Modern Drama* 7, No. 2 (September 1964): 210-12.

> Proposes that each character in *The Misunderstanding* is "the embodiment of some aspect of Camus's thought": Maria represents a "normal" outlook on life, the old man "complete detachment from life," Jan and his mother failed existentialist rebels, and Martha the "incarnation" of rebellion.

Church, D. M. "*Le Malentendu:* Search for Modern Tragedy." *French Studies* XX, No. 1 (January 1966): 33-46.

> Comprehensive study of *The Misunderstanding* as Camus's attempt to form a modern tragedy. Church observes several successful aspects of Camus's experiment—including the conversational dialogue, masterful images, and lyrical passages—as well as several failures, including ambiguous language and simplistic characters.

Merton, Thomas. "Three Saviors in Camus." *Thought* XLIII, No. 168 (Spring 1968): 5-23.

> Reveals how *The Misunderstanding* symbolically considers the problem of modern communication. By refusing to show his love for his mother and sister "in plain and obvious terms," acting instead on the "unrealistic reasoning" that they will welcome him as a stranger, Jan contributes to his own demise.

Parsell, David B. "Aspects of Comedy in Camus's *Le Malentendu.*" *Symposium* XXXVII, No. 4 (Winter 1983-84): 302-17.

> Examines *The Misunderstanding* for its comic elements, arguing that in this play "Camus sought to arrive at tragedy through an inversion or parody of comic structure." Parsell detects several "staples of the comic repertory" in *The Misunderstanding* and points out that Jan envisioned the surprising of his mother and sister as a little comedy.

For further information on Camus's life and career, see *Contemporary Authors,* Vols. 89-92; *Contemporary Literary Criticism,* Vols. 1, 2, 4, 9, 11, 14, 32, 63, 69; *Dictionary of Literary Biography,* Vol. 72; and *Short Story Criticism,* Vol. 9.

William Congreve

1670-1729

INTRODUCTION

Also wrote under the pseudonym Cleophil.

Universally acknowledged as the greatest comic dramatist of the Restoration, Congreve is best known for the unflagging wit with which he infused a repertoire of plays still widely performed and read today. His skillful representations of human behavior in society—effected primarily through the brilliant banter of his characters in such celebrated plays as *Love for Love* and *The Way of the World*—have established his preeminence within an age renowned for its exhibitions of intelligent and imaginative wit.

Born at Bardsey in Yorkshire, Congreve was the son of a country gentleman of modest means. After his father joined the army and received a lieutenant's commission, the family moved to Ireland, where Congreve received his earliest schooling. At age twelve, Congreve entered Kilkenny College, one of the great educational institutions of the British Isles; there he became friends with Jonathan Swift, a fellow student. Congreve's curriculum—which included reading, writing, Classical languages, and theology—was rigorous, but did not prevent his enjoying school holidays with Swift and other friends or regularly attending dramatic performances by his fellow students and by visiting Dublin players. In 1686 Congreve was accepted into Trinity College, Dublin, where he intensified his studies in theology and, particularly, Classical literature. Like many restive students, Congreve, gregarious and fond of amusement, availed himself of Dublin's many diversions, such as the renowned Smock Alley Theatre, though this was officially forbidden to Trinity residents. Congreve thus became well-grounded in the dramatic presentations popular during this time—among them works by Thomas Shadwell, Thomas Southerne, John Dryden, and other Restoration playwrights. He avidly read works on dramatic theory as well. It is conjectured that Congreve was probably more familiar with the theater than most young gentlemen of his era by the time he came to London in early manhood.

In 1691 Congreve enrolled in the Middle Temple, London, to study law. He found this pursuit uninspiring, though London afforded him opportunities to meet many men with literary inclinations similar to his own. He soon established himself as a wit and promising writer with the novel *Incognita; or, Love and Duty Reconcil'd,* and before long joined the literary circle that met regularly with Dryden in Will's Coffee House. Congreve soon became Dryden's friend, legal adviser, and literary protégé; his legal acumen enabled him to negotiate arrangements between Dryden and his publisher, while years of rigorous training allowed him to make numerous important contributions as translator to Dryden's editions of Classical authors. Dryden recognized the younger man's sensitivity not only to good translation but to the nuances of his own tongue,

and predicted Congreve's literary success. This came with the production of *The Old Batchelour* in 1693, for which its author received enthusiastic acclaim. Dryden and Southerne, impressed by a draft of the play, had helped Congreve refine and polish it. Some critics complained that Congreve was merely a creation of his mentor Dryden, but most commentators acknowledged the unique brilliance of his witty dialogue.

Like the majority of plays produced during this period, *The Old Batchelour* was written with specific players in mind; it was performed with a cast of the most popular and accomplished actors available. Many biographers surmise that Congreve created the role of the virtuous and witty ingenue Araminta specifically for actress Anne Bracegirdle, the object of his lifelong, though unrequited, love. The theatrical debuts of each of Congreve's subsequent plays featured Bracegirdle in the heroine's role.

Despite ringing endorsements from such notable figures as Dryden and Swift, *The Double-Dealer* inspired much less enthusiasm than had its predecessor. In a letter to a friend, Dryden accounted for the drama's lukewarm reception this way: "The Women think [Congreve] has exposed their Bitchery too much; and the Gentlemen are offended with him; for the discovery of their Follyes: and the way of their Intrigues, under the notion of Friendship to their Ladyes Husbands." However, the overwhelming success of his subsequent drama, *Love for Love,* both redeemed Congreve's popularity and considerably increased his income, as he was given a full share in a new acting company under William III's protection. In 1696, traveling with Southerne, Congreve visited Ireland, where he received a master of arts degree from Trinity College and was briefly reunited with his parents. It is believed that contact with Southerne, the author of several successful tragedies, may have prompted Congreve to test his ability in what most critics of the age considered a higher dramatic form, tragedy. Ignoring gibes and unsolicited warnings from fellow coffeehouse wits who were convinced his endeavor would fail, he wrote *The Mourning Bride,* which many critics praised liberally for its morality as well as its literary merit.

Given the generally positive response he had received thus far, Congreve was unprepared for Jeremy Collier's fervent attack on his work in *A Short View of the Immorality and Profaneness of the English Stage,* published in 1698. Collier, a clergyman, launched indictment after indictment against the profligacy he deemed evident in Congreve's work. Congreve replied with *Amendments to Mr. Collier's False and Imperfect Citations,* which professes the essential morality of all well-crafted art. This lucid rebuttal displays Congreve's characteristic wit but is colored by his own badly disguised contempt for Collier's fervent moralism and social standing—an emotionally charged tack which gave Collier the upper hand in the argument and spawned subsequent skirmishes as well. Weary of being drawn into further confrontations, Congreve concentrated on writing his last comedy, *The Way of the World.* Performed in 1700, it enjoyed only moderate success, a reception Congreve interpreted as indicating his work's opposition to the "general Taste."

After several months on the Continent at health spas for treatment of gout and advancing blindness, Congreve turned to the composition of a libretto, *The Judgment of Paris,* which was well received by the public despite the low esteem then accorded opera. Early in the eighteenth century, Congreve collaborated with fellow dramatist John Vanbrugh in the establishment of a new theater, the Haymarket. This project was financed by members of the Kit-Kat Club, a literary-political society which included members of nobility as well as such renowned contemporaries of Congreve as Joseph Addison and Richard Steele. While the Haymarket Theatre soon failed, Congreve's association with influential members of the Kit-Kat Club proved profitable, enabling him to secure two government posts and a lifelong appointment as Secretary of Jamaica. By 1706 ill health compelled Congreve to curtail much of his writing. No longer the prolific artist of his youth, he resided quietly in London until his death in 1729.

The late seventeenth-century "comedy of manners" reached its zenith with the staging of Congreve's comedies, particularly *The Way of the World.* Plays of this type commonly feature contrived, often bewilderingly complex plots depicting illicit love affairs and intrigues; satire is directed at the morals and attitudes of a highly sophisticated aristocratic society, and emphasis is placed on verbal wit and brilliant dialogue rather than character and plot development. The persons in these works are often presented as simple "types" or "humors" figures—characters possessing a single predominating trait, such as jealousy or gullibility. *The Old Batchelour,* Congreve's first comedy, is esteemed for its skillful handling of these conventions. The play's theater premiere was applauded by audiences and reviewers for the dazzling wit with which Congreve had vitalized the stock situations. However, the author's subsequent comedies go beyond the narrow confines of the genre, introducing innovations that sometimes dismayed early audiences. *The Double-Dealer,* for example, probes beneath the folly that is central to Restoration comedy, presenting a distinctly threatening undercurrent of vicious malevolence in the character of the scheming Maskwell. Congreve also experimented with the Neoclassical "unities" of time and setting in this comedy, the action of which unfolds entirely within the confines of Lord Touchwood's house in a three-hour period, the same length of time it takes to perform the play. Despite Dryden's enthusiastic approval, theater patrons were largely unreceptive to *The Double-Dealer,* and Congreve determined to refocus on more conventional aspects of comedy in his next production.

Love for Love was both a critical and popular success. Treating the related pursuits of love and money, the comedy depicts numerous characters anxiously seeking through marriage to satisfy both of these desires. The plot focuses on Valentine's struggle to avoid financial ruin and his simultaneous pursuit of Angelica, whom he hopes to win with lavish displays. She, however, steadfastly refuses his advances until he despairs of gaining her love with money. Finally, in a desperate attempt to convince Angelica of the depth of his love, Valentine renounces financial concerns, insisting: "I have been disappointed of my only Hope; and he that loses hope may part with any thing. I never valu'd Fortune, but as it was subservient to my Pleasure; and my only Pleasure was to please this Lady: I have made many vain Attempts, and find at last, that nothing but my Ruine can effect it. . . . " Thus assured of Valentine's genuine love, Angelica assents to marriage. As Albert Wertheim has observed, "clearly Angelica and Valentine rise above the other characters as they affirm a relationship based upon love for love instead of love for money." Significantly, Angelica's role as Valentine's teacher reasserts the prominence of the virtuous woman in Restoration drama, and her refusal to submit to Valentine's designs highlights Congreve's astute commentary on male-female relationships in the society of his day.

The Way of the World, presently considered Congreve's masterpiece despite its modest reception by the dramatist's contemporaries, manipulates conventional devices of deception and misunderstanding to communicate the author's wry evaluation of love, human relationships, and the institution of marriage—a favorite target of Restoration humor. The intricate plot and myriad interrelations among characters in the play are so complex as to be nearly impenetrable to the audience. The society thus depicted defies most of the characters' attempts to control it; only the central figures Mirabell and Millamant can succeed in such a world, for their dazzlingly fluid wit allows them to adapt to rapidly changing conditions. William Van Voris and others have argued that the perplexing intricacy of *The Way of the World* is intentional; Congreve, Van Voris claims, "placed scenes of brightly witty scheming beside scenes of increasingly violent extravagance, so the gilded world of the first act seems about to shatter into fragments by the last." The critic concludes that the union of Mirabell and Millamant—founded on a hard-won trust—represents the necessary corrective to this chaotic society, affirming the existence, amid corruption and marriages of convenience, of genuine values and real love.

From the time of Collier's attack on Congreve's works to the twentieth century, the dramatist's critical reputation has fluctuated according to changes in prevailing moral standards. Nineteenth-century critics routinely condemned his plays as scandalous and immoral, though Congreve did have supporters during these years who urged that his plays be judged not according to present taste and morality but as the products of a more licentious age. Modern critics have discovered penetrating examinations of Restoration society and morals beneath the ornate surfaces of Congreve's comedies. As Van Voris has observed: "If we watch the figures [in Congreve's plays] closely and are not preoccupied with the machinery of the intrigues, we can gain a real insight into the World and into the values by which it should be judged."

PRINCIPAL WORKS

PLAYS

The Old Batchelour   1693
The Double Dealer   1693
Love for Love   1695
The Mourning Bride   1697
The Way of the World   1700
The Judgment of Paris   (opera libretto)   1701

OTHER MAJOR WORKS

Incognita; or, Love and Duty Reconcil'd [as Cleophil] (novel)   1692
Amendments of Mr. Collier's False and Imperfect Citations from the "Old Batchelour," "Double Dealer," "Love for Love," "Mourning Bride" (criticism)   1698
The Works of Mr. William Congreve. 3 vols.   (drama and poetry)   1710
A Letter from Mr. Congreve to the Right Honourable The Lord Viscount Cobham (poetry)   1729
William Congreve: Letters & Documents (prose)   1964

OVERVIEWS AND GENERAL STUDIES

George Henry Nettleton   (essay date 1914)

[*In the following excerpt, Nettleton presents an overview of Congreve's dramas, noting their relations to the works of his precursors and successors in this genre. While acknowledging weaknesses in plot and characterization in many of the author's plays, Nettleton asserts that Congreve's verbal brilliance renders him a pre-eminent English playwright.*]

In an age that prided itself on wit and elegance of style, William Congreve (1670-1729) was the wittiest and perhaps most graceful writer of English comedy. Born near Leeds, schooled at Trinity College, Dublin, Congreve came to London as a law student, published a minor novel, contributed to a poetical translation of Juvenal, and at twenty-three had won [John] Dryden's favour and general applause with his first comedy, *The Old Bachelor* (1693). Dryden declared that 'he never saw such a first play in his life, and that the author not being acquainted with the stage or the town, it would be a pity to have it miscarry for want of a little assistance; the stuff was rich indeed, only the fashionable cut was wanting.' This assistance Dryden himself helped to give, and [Thomas] Southerne, an early sponsor for Congreve, generously hailed him as Dryden's successor. In comparison with Congreve's later work, *The Old Bachelor* won disproportionate success. Its characters were largely conventional, yet even Captain Bluffe, a cowardly blusterer anticipated in the first English comedy, *Ralph Roister Doister,* has a certain vividness and individuality. Fondlewife recalls [William] Wycherley's Pinchwife [in *The Country Wife*], and Heartwell, the 'surly old Bachelor, pretending to slight Women, secretly in love with Silvia,' has some touches of Manly [in *The Plain Dealer*], while some of the characters of the underplot suggest [Ben] Jonsonian humours. Yet if *The Old Bachelor* somewhat lacks originality in characterization, Bellmour's words in the opening act might well have been Congreve's own invocation, 'Wit, be my faculty!' It was more than a decade and a half since [George] Etherege had produced *The Man of Mode* and Wycherley had taken a cynical farewell of comedy in *The Plain Dealer*. With a style more graceful than Etherege's and wit more sparkling than Wycherley's, Congreve showed that there had appeared a new master of comedy.

Though far less gross and brutal than Wycherley, Congreve has a tone of subtle but pervasive immorality which he later strove vainly to disprove. In answer to Jeremy Collier he urged that the end of a play pointed the moral. Unfortunately Collier [in his *Defence of the Short View of the Profaneness and Immorality of the English Stage, &c.*] found the real moral of *The Old Bachelor* in its closing lines:

> What rugged ways attend the noon of life!
> Our sun declines, and with what anxious strife,
> What pain we tug that galling load, a wife!

In the Epistle Dedicatory prefixed to his next play, *The Double-Dealer* (1693), Congreve makes an unconvincing reply to the charge that 'some of the ladies are offended' by its immorality. It is fair to note, however, that, in the dénouement, Cynthia's virtue escapes even Maskwell's plots and is rewarded by union with Mellefont, Lady Touchwood is driven off by her husband with an orthodox 'Go, and thy own infamy pursue thee,' and Maskwell is seized and held for punishment. Though all is not well that ends well, the curtain no longer falls on the dishonoured husband amid derisive laughter.

In the Epistle Dedicatory, Congreve claims originality of plot and deliberate intention 'to preserve the three unities of the drama.' Yet the admirable scandal scene (III, 3) recalls Olivia's scene with Novel and Plausible [in *The Plain Dealer*], and Molière's still earlier passages in *Le Misanthrope*, while the obscure turns in the labyrinth of plot are even further complicated by a network of bypaths and meanders. Congreve has perplexity, not unity, of action. The characters of **The Double-Dealer** are familiar types— Mellefont, the lover, Careless, the confidant, Maskwell and Lady Touchwood, villains, Lord Froth and Brisk, coxcombs, Lady Froth, 'a great Coquette,' Lady Plyant, 'insolent to her Husband, and easy to any pretender.' Lady Plyant's sesquipedalian words possibly suggest Mrs. Malaprop [in Richard Brinsley Sheridan's *The Rivals*], but there is little 'mathemacular demonstration,' to borrow one of her phrases, of Mrs. Malaprop's 'nice derangement of epitaphs.' Even with the aid of the soliloquy, a device comparatively infrequent in Restoration comedy, though defended by Congreve in the Epistle Dedicatory, the devious ways of Maskwell are followed with difficulty. Plot is subordinated to brilliancy of dialogue. The numerous technical defects in dramatic construction perhaps account for the somewhat indifferent reception at first accorded **The Double-Dealer,** but its vividness of characterization and vitality of phrase eventually established it in a popularity which lasted through the eighteenth century.

Love for Love (1695) was the first play produced at the new Lincoln's Inn Fields Theatre, by [Thomas] Betterton and the actors who had revolted from the Patent Theatres. Its success was well merited, for in it wit is married to grace of diction. Valentine, a young spendthrift who is lucky in love, has had many successors in English comedy, among them, Young Honeywood in [Oliver] Goldsmith's *Good Natur'd Man* and Charles Surface [in Sheridan's *The School for Scandal*]. His wit does not stop with his assumption of madness. In a way that curiously recalls Hamlet, he 'uses his folly like a stalking-horse and under the presentation of that he shoots his wit.' Jeremy, his witty servant, takes after his master, as do Sheridan's Fag and David. Jeremy, who 'waited upon a gentleman at Cambridge,' cites Epictetus, Seneca, Plato, and Diogenes in a single speech, as readily as Fag alludes to Jupiter's masquerades in love. The ceaseless showers of wit fall alike on master and man. Sir Sampson Legend, Valentine's father, is a vigorous portrait of the crusty father. Scandal is the familiar confidant of Restoration comedy, not too busy to neglect his own intrigue. Foresight, 'pretending to understand Astrology, Palmistry, Physiognomy, Omens, Dreams, &c,' though in point of fact not an anachronism, seems dramatically a Jonsonian character, out of place amid Congreve's beaux and belles. Miss Prue, an admirable example of the Restoration perversion of the

ingénue, is essentially of the same type as Wycherley's Mrs. Pinchwife and Miss Hoyden in [John] Vanbrugh's *Relapse.* Miss Prue has some admirable scenes—one where Tattle initiates her into the mystery of saying one thing while meaning the opposite—another with her sailor suitor Ben, whose awkward advances lead to a mutual disagreement which anticipates the scene of Tony Lumpkin and Miss Neville [in Goldsmith's *She Stoops to Conquer*]. Comedy borders dangerously upon farce when Tattle, thinking he is wedding Angelica in nun's disguise, is tricked into marriage with Mrs. Frail—a situation possibly saved by the fact that the marriage takes place off the stage. Congreve's Dedication of the play shows that he was not unconscious of the danger in its length, but unflagging zest of dialogue, skill in characterization, and more effectiveness in plot construction than he usually attained made **Love for Love** an acting comedy success.

Congreve's sole tragedy, **The Mourning Bride** (1697), has often been viewed as a solitary excursion into an alien dramatic field, and unrelated to his comic work. Yet in the villainy and passion of Maskwell and Lady Touchwood may be found strains of tragic suggestion, just as Wycherley's *Plain Dealer* does not depart too far from *Le Misanthrope* to forget entirely the grim aspect of misanthropy. Doubtless it would be fantastic to exaggerate in Wycherley and Congreve the sombre threads in the weave of comedy, yet the latter's venture into the realm of tragedy is perhaps not an extraordinary and unheralded phenomenon. From the modern standpoint it seems the irony of fate that **The Mourning Bride** achieved in its own day greater success than Congreve's comedies. It held the boards through most of the eighteenth century, and the passage at the end of the first scene of the second act elicited Doctor [Samuel] Johnson's famous eulogy of it as 'the finest poetical passage he had ever read'—a dictum whose extravagance has reacted too severely against even a reasonable appraisal of a fine passage. The customary modern verdict, that Congreve's departure from comedy proved his incapacity for tragedy, is perhaps testimony to the change of popular taste quite as much as to the author's lack of judgment in essaying an uncongenial task. Plot and characters are, indeed, artificial, and the probabilities are stretched almost beyond the limits of the possibilities. That its writing took three years suggests that it was a tragedy not born, but made. Yet Congreve's shortcomings are those of all but a few of the Restoration tragic dramatists. **The Mourning Bride,** in fact, though written in blank verse, resumes in many respects the habits of heroic drama. It develops themes of love and honour in the foreign setting of Granada, and adopts a happy issue for the heroic loves of the Princess Almeria and the noble Osmyn. The modern reader might prefer either a full tragic solution or an anticipation of the dénouement by a somewhat lighter handling of the earlier tragic elements. The final surprise seems rather a let-down than a wind-up. There has been no comic relief, and the advent of Osmyn at the end comes as a fortuitous trick, not as a logical dramatic climax. The plot, complicated by the motives of 'cross purposes' and 'mistaken identity,' has, apart from its artificiality, more coherence and vigour in development than is characteristic of Congreve's comedies.

Gosse believes that the blank verse 'is the parent of Thomson's,' and that Congreve's real model is Milton [Edmund Gosse, *Life of William Congreve,* 1924]. Apart from such possible bearings on the history of poetry, Congreve's verse is of interest chiefly in some good, if rather conventional, lines, some of which are familiar in quotation. The Prologue sets a higher standard than Congreve attained either in comedy or in tragedy:

> To please and move has been our poet's theme,
> Art may direct, but nature is his aim;
> And nature missed, in vain he boasts his art,
> For only nature can affect the heart.

Congreve is a great literary artist, but without the gift that blends art with nature.

The Dedication of *The Mourning Bride* had termed it a 'poem constituted on a moral whose end is to recommend and to encourage virtue.' This high purpose did not shield Congreve from Collier's determined attack in the following year, nor did that attack deter the dramatist from one further venture in comedy. Notwithstanding the fact that *The Way of the World* (1700) contained Congreve's most brilliant character creation, it met with a reception so lukewarm that the author was somewhat piqued. 'But little of it,' he writes in his Dedication, 'was prepared for that general taste which seems now to be predominant in the palates of our audiences.' Even [Richard] Steele, in his Commendatory Verses, admits that it was caviare to the general by asking:

> How could, great author, your aspiring mind
> Dare to write only to the few refined?

Congreve's Dedication voices a deliberate intention to depict not the gross fools 'which are meant to be ridiculed in most of our comedies' but 'some characters which should appear ridiculous, not so much through a natural folly (which is incorrigible, and therefore not proper for the stage) as through an affected wit; a wit, which at the same time that it is affected, is also false.' With evident pique at critics who failed to note such subtleties, Congreve added that 'this play had been acted two or three days, before some of these hasty judges could find the leisure to distinguish betwixt the character of a Witwoud and a Truewit.' In a letter to [John] Dennis, Congreve had defined 'humour' as 'A singular and unavoidable Manner of doing or saying any thing, peculiar and natural to one Man only; by which his Speech and Actions are distinguish'd from those of other Men,' and had declared that '*Humour* is from Nature, *Habit* from Custom, and *Affectation* from Industry.' He had further asserted: 'The saying of humorous things does not distinguish Characters; for every Person in a Comedy may be allow'd to speak them. From a witty Man they are expected; and even a *Fool* may be permitted to stumble on 'em by chance. Tho I make a difference betwixt *Wit* and *Humour;* yet I do not think that humorous characters exclude Wit: No, but the Manner of *Wit,* should be adapted to the *Humour.*' Yet Congreve's own weakness lay in his inability to adapt his own wit to the various characters he should have differentiated. His 'fools' are permitted to stumble on too many brilliants. His diamond beds are without sand. Even in *The Way of the World,* Foible, the maid, like Congreve's

earlier servants, has the wit of her betters. The unconscious humour of Goldsmith's Diggory is closer to life than the brilliant quips of Congreve's servants. It is small wonder that critics overlooked a theoretical distinction that seemed without a difference in practice.

Yet if, in Dryden's words, *The Way of the World* 'had but moderate success, though it deserves much better,' the judgment of posterity has gone far to correct the error. Millamant, Congreve's most brilliant character creation, has commanded [William] Hazlitt's eulogy [*Lectures on the English Comic Writers,* Lecture IV] and George Meredith's tribute to the 'perfect portrait of a coquette' [*An Essay on Comedy,* 1897]. They had been anticipated, however, by an earlier critic, her lover Mirabel: 'I like her with all her faults; nay, like her for her faults. Her follies are so natural, or so artful, that they become her; and those affectations which in another woman would be odious, serve but to make her more agreeable' (I, 2). She enters with a flash, and goes off in a blaze of wit. Even amid the ceaseless pyrotechnics of Congreve her departure seems like the extinction of a brilliant rocket. Yet Millamant is an artificial creation—beautiful and fragile as Dresden china. She has the wit, but not the humanity, of Shakespeare's Beatrice [in *Much Ado about Nothing*].

Congreve's wit is his supreme strength and perhaps his greatest weakness. It led him to sacrifice not merely naturalness in character and dialogue, but effectiveness of plot. In his comedies the action usually halts while the train of wit passes gaily by. Sheridan, with greater dramatic art, showed that brilliant wit need not clog the movement of plot, for even the scandal scenes which have at times been instanced to the contrary have some justification, apart from their brilliancy, as a necessary background for Lady Teazle [in *School for Scandal*]. Yet it would be unfair to judge Congreve chiefly by his defects. To supreme wit he added grace of diction. He has the ease of [Joseph] Addison. He is a sort of *avant-courier* of eighteenth-century felicity of phrase and delicacy of diction. Hazlitt's eulogy, if somewhat superlative in expression, is sound in essence: 'His style is inimitable, nay perfect. It is the highest model of comic dialogue. Every sentence is replete with sense and satire, conveyed in the most polished and pointed terms. Every page presents a shower of brilliant conceits, is a tissue of epigrams in prose, is a new triumph of wit, a new conquest over dulness.' In the record of English comedy Congreve holds a foremost place. His early work, especially *The Old Bachelor,* shows the influence, without the malignant bitterness, of Wycherley. In comic spirit he seems rather the descendant of Etherege and the ancestor of Sheridan. With Etherege's weakness in plot, he has greater ease of dialogue; in brilliancy and ceaseless wit, he vies with Sheridan. In his hands the comedy of society is touched with rare literary skill. It is artificial comedy, but the art is masterly. (pp. 122-32)

George Henry Nettleton, "Congreve, Vanbrugh, and Farquhar," in his English Drama of the Restoration and Eighteenth Century (1642-1780), *1914. Reprint by Cooper Square Publishers, Inc., 1968, pp. 120-40.*

Virginia Woolf   (essay date 1937)

[*Woolf is considered one of the most prominent literary figures of twentieth-century English literature. Like her contemporary James Joyce, with whom she is often compared, Woolf is regarded as one of the most innovative of the stream of consciousness novelists. Concerned primarily with depicting the life of the mind, she revolted against traditional narrative techniques and developed her own highly individualized style. Her works, noted for their subjective explorations of characters' inner lives and their delicate poetic quality, have had a lasting effect on the art of the novel. A discerning and influential critic and essayist as well as a novelist, Woolf began writing reviews for the* Times Literary Supplement *at an early age. Her critical essays, which cover almost the entire range of English literature, contain some of her finest prose and are praised for their insight. In the following essay, originally published in 1937 in the* Times Literary Supplement, *Woolf offers a general appreciation of Congreve's works, attesting to the playwright's wealth of memorable characters and his "genius for phrasemaking."*]

The four great plays through which Congreve is immortal take up very little space, and can be bought very cheaply; but they can be seen very seldom, and to read them, silently and in solitude, is to do them an injustice. The best way to repair that injustice is to consider them with the author's help more critically, if more coldly, than we are able when the words are embodied on the stage. Congreve, the man of mystery, the man of superb genius who ceased to use his genius at his height, was also, as any reader may guess from almost any page, of the class of writers who are not so entirely submerged in their gift but that they can watch it curiously and to some extent guide it even when they are possessed by it. Whatever he has to say in a letter, in a dedication, in a prologue about his art is worth listening to with all our ears. Let us then put to him some of the questions that the remembrance of his plays has left over in the mind before we allow the Tattles and the Foresights, the Wishforts and the Millamants to sweep us off our feet.

First there is the old grievance which, though it sounds elementary, must always have its say: the grievance that is summed up in the absurd names he gives his characters—Vainlove, Fondlewife, and the rest—as if we were back again in the age of mummer and cart, when one humour to one character was all the audience could grasp or the actor express. To that he replies, ". . . the distance of the stage requires the figures represented to be something larger than the life," a warning to the reader to suppress the desire for certain subtleties which the playwright cannot satisfy, a reminder that the imponderable suggestions which come together on silent feet in fiction are denied the playwright. He must speak; the speaking voice is the only instrument allowed him. That introduces a second question: they must speak, but why so artificially? Men and women were never so witty as he makes them; they never speak so aptly, so instantly, and with such a wealth of figure and imagery as he would have us believe. And to that he replies, "I believe if a poet should steal a dialogue of any length, from the extempore discourse of the two witti-

est men upon earth, he would find the scene but coldly receiv'd by the town." People on the stage must be larger than life because they are further from us than in the book; and cleverer than life because if he set down their actual words we should be bored to distraction. Every writer has his selection to make; his artifice to enforce; these are the playwright's. These are the methods by which he puts us in the frame of mind needed for his purpose.

Still there remains another grievance which is not so elementary nor so easily laid to rest; and that is, of course, the plot. Who can remember the plot when the book is shut? Who has not been teased by its intricacies while the book is open? As everybody is agreed something must happen, and it matters very little what happens if it serves to make the characters more real, or more profound, than they would otherwise have been; a plot should put the characters on the rack and show them thus extended. But what are we to say when the plot merely teases and distorts the character, and distracts us from any more profound enjoyment than that of asking who is behind that door, who is behind that mask? To this Congreve the critic gives us no satisfactory answer. Sometimes, as in the preface to **The Double Dealer,** he prides himself that he has maintained "the unities of the drama." But a certain doubt declares itself elsewhere. In the dedication to **The Way of the World** he envies Terence. Terence, he points out, had "great advantages to encourage his undertaking for he built most on the foundations of Menander; his plots were generally modelled and his characters ready drawn to his hand." Either then, one must conclude, the old weatherworn plots which slip into the mind so smoothly that we scarcely notice them—the legendary, the prehistoric—are the only tolerable ones, or we are forced to suppose that the plot-making genius is so seldom combined with the genius for creating character that we must allow even Shakespeare to fail here—even Shakespeare sometimes lets the plot dictate to the character; suffers the story to drag the character out of its natural orbit. And Congreve, who had not Shakespeare's miraculous fecundity, who could not cover up the farfetched and the mechanical with the abundance of his imagination and the splendour of his poetry, fails here. The character is squeezed to fit the situation; the machine has set its iron stamp upon live flesh and blood.

But, now that we have dismissed the questions that hang about an unopened book, let us submit ourselves to the dramatist in action. The dramatist is in action from the very first word on the very first page. There are no preliminaries, no introductions; the curtain rises and they are in the thick of it. Never was any prose so quick. Miraculously pat, on the spot, each speaker caps the last, without fumbling or hesitation; their minds are full charged; it seems as if they had to rein themselves in, bursting with energy as they are, alive and alert to their finger-tips. It is we who fumble, make irrelevant observations, notice the chocolate or the cinnamon, the sword or the muslin, until the illusion takes hold of us, and what with the rhythm of the speech and the indescribable air of tension, of high breeding that pervades it, the world of the stage becomes the real world and the other, outside the play, but the husk and cast-off clothing. To attempt to reduce this first impression to words is as futile as to explain a physical sensa-

Portrait of Congreve in his early twenties, by Henry Tilson.

tion—the slap of a wave, the rush of wind, the scent of a bean field. It is conveyed by the curl of a phrase on the ear; by speed; by stillness. It is as impossible to analyse Congreve's prose as to distinguish the elements—the bark of a dog, the song of a bird, the drone of the branches—which make the summer air. But then, since words have meaning, we notice here a sudden depth beneath the surface, a meaning not grasped but felt, and then come to realize something not merely dazzling in this world, but natural, for all its wit; even familiar, and traditional. It has a coarseness, a humour something like Shakespeare's; a toppling imagination that heaps image upon image; a lightning swiftness of apprehension that snatches a dozen meanings and compacts them into one.

And yet it is not Shakespeare's world; for just as we think, tossed up on the crest of some wonderful extravagance of humour, to be swept into poetry we come slap against hard common sense, and realize that here is a different combination of elements from the poet's. There is tragedy—Lady Touchwood and Maskwell in *The Double Dealer* are not comic figures—but when tragedy and comedy collide it is comedy that wins. Lady Touchwood seizes her dagger; but she drops it. A moment more and it would have been too late. Already she has passed from prose to rant. Already we feel not that the scene is ridiculous, for there is passion there; but that it is unsafe. Congreve has lost his control, his fine balance is upset; he feels the ground tremble beneath him. Mr. Brisk's comment, "This

is all very surprising, let me perish," is the appropriate one. With that he finds his feet and withdraws.

The world that we have entered, then, in Congreve's comedies is not the world of the elemental passions. It is an enclosure surrounded with the four walls of a living-room. Ladies and gentlemen go through their figures with their tongues to the measure dictated by common sense as precisely as they dance the minuet with their feet; but the image has only a superficial rightness. We have only to compare Congreve's comedy with [Oliver] Goldsmith's or with [Richard Brinsley] Sheridan's, let alone with [Oscar] Wilde's, to be aware that if, to distinguish him from the Elizabethans, we confine him to a room, not a world, that room is not the drawing-room of the eighteenth century, still less is it the drawing-room of the nineteenth century. Drays roar on the cobbles beneath; the brawling of street hucksters and tavern rioters comes in at the open windows. There is a coarseness of language, an extravagance of humour, and a freedom of manners which cast us back to the Elizabethans. Yet it is in a drawing-room, surrounded by all the fopperies and refinements of the most sophisticated society in the world, that these ladies and gentlemen speak so freely, drink so deeply, and smell so strong. It is the contrast, perhaps, that makes us more aware of the coarseness of the Restoration dramatists than of the Elizabethan. A great lady who spits on the floor offends where a fishwife merely amuses. And perhaps it was for this reason that Congreve incurred first the majestic censure of Dr. Johnson [in his *Lives of the English Poets,* 1779] and then the more supercilious contempt of the Victorians who neglected, Sir Edmund Gosse informs us, either to read him or to act him [in his *Life of William Congreve,* 1924]. More conscious than we are of the drawing-room, they were quicker repelled perhaps by any violation of its decencies.

But however we may account for the change, to reach *The Way of the World* through *The Old Bachelor, The Double Dealer,* and *Love for Love* is to become more and more at loggerheads with Dr. Johnson's dictum:

> It is acknowledged, with universal conviction, that the perusal of his works will make no man better; and that their ultimate effect is to represent pleasure in alliance with vice, and to relax those obligations by which life ought to be regulated.

On the contrary, to read Congreve's plays is to be convinced that we may learn from them many lessons much to our advantage both as writers of books and—if the division is possible—as livers of life. We might learn there, to begin with, the discipline of plain speech; to leave nothing lurking in the insidious shades of obscurity that can be said in words. The phrase is always finished; nothing is left to dwindle into darkness, to sound after the words are over. Then, when we have learnt to express ourselves, we may go on to observe the indefatigable hard work of a great writer: how he keeps us entertained because something is always happening, and on the alert because that something is always changing, and by contrasting laughter and seriousness, action and thought, keeps the edge of the emotions always sharp. To ring so many changes and keep up so rapid a speed of movement might well be enough, but in addition each of these characters has its own being, and each differs—the sea-dog from the fop, the old eccentric from the man of the world, the maid from the mistress. He has to enter into each; to leave his private pigeonhole and invest himself with the emotions of another human being, so that speech meets speech at full tilt, each from its own angle.

A genius for phrase-making helps him. Now he strikes off a picture in a flash: " . . . there he lies with a great beard, like a Russian bear upon a drift of snow." Now in a marvellous rush of rapid invention he conveys a whole chapter of guttersnipe life.

> That I took from the washing of old gauze and weaving of dead hair, with a bleak blue nose, over a chafing dish of starv'd embers, and dining behind a traverse rag, in a shop no bigger than a bird cage.

Then, again, like some miraculous magpie he repeats the naïve words, follows the crude emotions, of a great gawky girl like Miss Prue. However it is done, to enter into such diverse characters is, the moralists may note, at any rate to forget your own. Undoubtedly it is true that his language is often coarse; but then it is also true that his characters are more alive, quicker to strip off veils, more intolerant of circumlocutions than the ordinary run of people. They are reduced to phrase-making oftener than we could wish, and fine phrases often sound cynical; but then the situations are often so improbable that only fine phrases will cover them, and words, we must remember, were still to Congreve's generation as delightful as beads to a savage. Without that rapture the audacity of his splendid phrases would have been impossible.

But if we have to admit that some of the characters are immoral, and some of the opinions cynical, still we must ask how far we can call a character immoral or an opinion cynical if we feel that the author himself was aware of its immorality and intended its cynicism? And, though it is a delicate matter to separate an author from his characters and detach him from their opinions, no one can read Congreve's comedies without detecting a common atmosphere, a general attitude that holds them together for all their diversity. The stress laid on certain features creates a common likeness as unmistakable as the eyes and nose of a family face. The plays are veined through and through with satire. "Therefore I would rail in my writings and be revenged," says Valentine in *Love for Love.* Congreve's satire seems sometimes, as Scandal says, to have the whole world for its butt. Yet there is underneath a thinking mind, a mind that doubts and questions. Some hint thrown out in passing calls us back to make us ponder it: for instance, [in *The Double Dealer*] Mellefont's "Ay, My Lord, I shall have the same reason for happiness that your Lordship has, I shall think myself happy." Or, again, a sudden phrase like "There's comfort in a hand stretched out to one that's sinking" suggests, by its contrast, a sensibility that trembles on the edge of tears. Nothing is stressed; sentiment never broadens into sentimentality; everything passes as quickly as a ray of light and blends as indistinguishably. But if we needs must prove that the cre-

ator of Sir Sampson Legend and old Foresight [in *Love for Love*] had not only a prodigious sense of human absurdity and a bitter conviction of its insincerity but as quick a regard for its honesty and decency as any Victorian or Dr. Johnson himself, we need only point to his simplicity. After we have run up the scale of absurdity to its sublime heights a single word again and again recalls us to common sense. "That my poor father should be so very silly" is one such comment, immensely effective in its place. Again and again we are brought back to sanity and daylight by the sound of a voice speaking in its natural tones.

But it is the Valentines, the Mirabells [in *The Way of the World*], the Angelicas [in *Love for Love*], and the Millamants [in *The Way of the World*] who keep us in touch with truth and, by striking a sudden serious note, bring the rest to scale. They have sharpened their emotions upon their wits. They have flouted each other; bargained; taken love and examined it by the light of reason; teased and tested each other almost beyond endurance. But when it comes to the point and she must be serious, the swiftest of all heroines, whose mind and body seem equally winged, so that there is a rush in the air as she passes and we exclaim with Scandal, "Gone; why, she was never here, nor anywhere else," has a centre of stillness in her heart and enough emotion in her words to furbish out a dozen pages of eloquent disquisition. "Why does not the man take me? Would you have me give myself to you over again?" The words are simple, and yet, after what has already been said, so brimming with meaning that Mirabell's reply, "Ay, over and over again," seems to receive into itself more than words can say. And this depth of emotion, we have to reflect, the change and complexity that are implied in it, have been reached in the direct way; that is by making each character speak in his or her own person, without addition from the author or any soliloquy save such as can be spoken on the stage in the presence of an audience. No, whether we read him from the moralist's angle or from the artist's, to agree with Dr. Johnson is an impossibility. To read the comedies is not to "relax those obligations by which life ought to be regulated." On the contrary, the more slowly we read him and the more carefully, the more meaning we find, the more beauty we discover.

Here perhaps, in the reflections that linger when the book is shut and *The Way of the World* is finished, lies the answer to the old puzzle why at the height of his powers he stopped writing. It is that he had done all that was possible in that kind. The last play held more than any audience could grasp at a single sitting. The bodily presence of actors and actresses must, it would seem, often overpower the words that they had to speak. He had forgotten, or disregarded, his own axiom that "the distance of the stage requires the figures represented to be something larger than the life." He had written, as he says in the dedication, for "the *Few,*" and "but little of it was prepar'd for that general taste which seems now to be predominant in the palates of our audience." He had come to despise his public, and it was time therefore either to write differently or to leave off. But the novel, which offered another outlet, was uncongenial; he was incorrigibly dramatic, as his one attempt at fiction shows. And poetry, too, was denied him, for though again and again he brings us to the edge of poetry in a phrase like "You're a woman, One to whom Heav'n gave beauty, when it grafted roses on a briar," and suggests, as [George] Meredith does in his novels, the mood of poetry, he was unable to pass beyond human idiosyncrasy to the more general statement of poetry. He must move and laugh and bring us into touch with action instantly.

Since these two paths then were blocked, what other way was there for a writer of Congreve's temperament but to make an end? Dangerous as it is to distinguish a writer from his work, we cannot help but recognize a man behind the plays—a man as sensitive to criticism as he was skilled in inflicting it on others; for what is his defiance of the critics but deference to them? A scholar too with all the scholar's fastidiousness; a man of birth and breeding for whom the vulgar side of fame held little gratification; a man, in short, who might well have said with Valentine, "Nay, I am not violently bent upon the trade," and sit, handsome and portly and sedate as his portrait shows him, "very gravely with his hat over his eyes," as the gossips observed him, content to strive no more.

But indeed he left very little for the gossips to feed upon; no writer of his time and standing passed through the world more privately. Voltaire left a dubious anecdote; the Duchess of Marlborough, it is said, had an effigy of him set at her table after his death; his few discreet letters provide an occasional hint: "Ease and quiet is what I hunt after"; "I feel very sensibly and silently for those whom I love"—that is all. But there is a fitness in this very absence of relics as though he had consumed whatever was irrelevant to his work and left us to find him there. And there, indeed, we find something beyond himself; beyond the many figures of his fertile and brilliant imagination; beyond Tattle and Ben, Foresight and Angelica, Maskwell and Lady Wishfort, Mirabell and Mellefont and Millamant. Between them they have created what is not to be confined within the limits of a single character or expressed in any one play—a world where each part depends upon the other, the serene, impersonal, and indestructible world of art. (pp. 76-84)

> *Virginia Woolf, "Congreve's Comedies," in her* Collected Essays, Vol. I, *edited by Leonard Woolf, Harcourt Brace Jovanovich, 1967, pp. 76-84.*

Albert Wertheim   (essay date 1986)

[*In the following essay, Wertheim examines themes of love and money in Congreve's comedies, comparing his treatment of these motifs to that of his contemporaries.*]

It is often the case that in the works of second- and third-rate writers we come closest to seeing the preoccupations of an age. For in their works, unalloyed by authorial talent or invention, we find baldly stated the attitudes and ideas artfully and inventively presented in the works of their more gifted contemporaries. Such is the case of *A Wife to be Lett* (1724) by Mrs. Eliza Haywood, whom Pope took to task in *The Dunciad* and whom Swift described as "A stupid, infamous, scribbling woman." The conflict in Mrs.

Haywood's play centers around the idea of the union of the sexes as a strictly monetary arrangement rather than as a consummation of romantic love. In the closing couplet of the second act, Toywell, a mercenary fop, asserts:

> When her Fortune's gone, the loveliest of Woman
> In this wise Age is fit Wife for no man.

The contrasting view is given at the close of the fourth act by a reformed rake:

> Ye false-nam'd Pleasures of my Youth farewel,
> They charm'd my Sense, but you subdue my Soul.
> Tho fix'd to you alone, I've pow'r to change,
> While o'er each Beauty of your Form I range.
> Nor to those only need I be confin'd,
> But changing still, enjoy thy beauteous Mind.

With little subtlety, Mrs. Haywood pits extremes of thoroughly crass behavior against extremes of thoroughly romance attitudes. In the plot that gives the play its title, a thoroughly exploitative husband is prepared to rent out his wife for a fee of £2000. In another plot, Celemena has no second thoughts at all about losing her £10,000 portion in order to follow the dictates of her heart:

> Well, let me consider—Here's a Coach and Six with my Father's Commands and 10,000*l.* to back it—On the other hand, 16 *s.* a Day, and the Title of a Captain's Lady, with a reasonable Suspicion of being turn'd out of doors with never a Groat—But then, on this side, I've a Fool—on that, a Man not disagreeable, and of allow'd sense—One marries me upon Compact, the other generously runs the risque of a Fortune— Well, *Gaylove,* I think you carry the day.

Mrs. Haywood paints her portraits without life, color, or shading.

The conflict of marriage based on romantic feeling versus marriage based on a cash nexus, so flatly and unsubtly presented in *A Wife to be Lett,* is also the one that informs most of the best getting-married plays from the 1690s to [Richard Brinsley] Sheridan's *The Rivals* (1775). It is the conflict central to plays like [George] Farquhar's *The Constant Couple* (1700), *The Recruiting Officer* (1706), and *The Beaux' Stratagem* (1707); [Richard] Steele's *The Tender Husband* (1705) and *The Conscious Lovers* (1722); [John] Gay's *The Beggar's Opera* (1728) and *Polly* (1729); [Henry] Fielding's *A Modern Husband* (1732); and [George] Colman and [David] Garrick's *Clandestine Marriage* (1766). Viewing Congreve as a transition figure between the love-game comedies of [George] Etherege and [William] Wycherley, which appeared a quarter of a century before **The Way of the World,** and the marriage comedies of the eighteenth century, which so often dwell on questions of portions and jointures, one can see how economic matters make their presence felt in comic drama after 1688, the date usually cited as the onset of England's Commercial Revolution.

The "Glorious Revolution"—the ascension of William and Mary to the throne of England in 1688—is a major landmark in English political, constitutional, and social history. As historians are becoming increasingly aware, however, 1688 is an even more important landmark in English economic history, largely because of the consequences of British commercial interests in the New World and the growing wealth derived from trade as opposed to land. By 1688, as W. W. Rostow [in *The Stages of Economic Growth,* 1964] and others have shown, England was ready for economic "take-off" and ready to become the first industrial nation. Although in drama before 1688 the opposing claims of romance versus finance had already made their mark in Elizabethan plays—for example, Shakespeare's *The Taming of the Shrew* (1594) and *The Merchant of Venice* (1596), [Thomas] Middleton's *A Trick to Catch the Old One* (1605), [John] Fletcher's *Wit without Money* (1614), and [James] Shirley's *The Brothers* (1641)—in the period following 1688, the new economic circumstances in England and the new wealth created through entrepôt trade make the economic questions in courtship and marriage comedies particularly acute ones. As the major comic playwright writing in the decade following 1688, Congreve provides us in his four comedies with a useful measure for gauging the growing importance of financial concerns in marriage comedies.

As it is found in the four comedies of Congreve, the question of the conflation of love and money is recognizable but muted. Though financial marriage arrangements are central to the plots of *The Double Dealer* (1693), *Love for Love* (1695), and *The Way of the World* (1700), and though Sir Joseph Wittol's desire to marry Araminta's £12,000 fortune forms one plot interest in *The Old Bachelor* (1693), Congreve's main characters are at once wise enough to know that marriage for money alone is foolish and urbane enough to recognize that London courtship and romance courtship are incongruent. It is only the most excessive of all Congreve's characters, Lady Wishfort, who seems to read romances with any seriousness. Her comparison of her maid to "*Maritornes* the *Asturian* in *Don Quixote*" (3.1.37-8), probably in Durfey's version, is only less excessive than her idea that she and Mrs. Marwood head for the nearest pastoral landscape:

> Well Friend, you are enough to reconcile me to the bad World, or else I wou'd retire to Desarts and Solitudes; and feed harmless Sheep by *Groves* and *Purling Streams.* Dear *Marwood,* let us leave the World, and retire by our selves and be *Shepherdesses.*
>
> (5.1.131-35)

The very thought of Lady Wishfort, the foppish, "superannuated" would-be coquette and Mrs. Marwood, the most jaded of all Congreve's town ladies, as shepherdesses is as ludicrous as it is inconceivable. It is, at the same time, only Congreve's two out and out villains, Fainall in *The Way of the World* and Maskwell in *The Double Dealer,* who consider marriage strictly in its nonromantic context, as a means to pecuniary ends.

Though Congreve sees the possibilities of romantic and mercenary excess, he nonetheless maintains an urbane distance from the fundamentally antithetical demands of marriage as the fruition of courtship on the one hand and marriage as the culmination of economic negotiation on the other. This is evident in his first comedy, *The Old*

Bachelor, which separates the courtship plots involving Bellmour and Vainlove from the money plot concerning the bilking of the foolish Wittol by the confidence man Sharper. In *The Old Bachelor,* two young men about town, Vainlove and Bellmour, are united by their complementary amoristic tastes. Vainlove relishes only pursuit and courtship; his friend, Bellmour, enjoys the consummation of an affair. They work happily in tandem: the one tracks down agreeable young women and woos them; the other beds them down. It is striking, however, that although Vainlove and Bellmour's activities are not shaped by a profit motive, their association is like a business partnership, as their friend Sharper aptly underlines when he describes their union of Neoplatonic friendship and physical consummation with a monetary image: "He does the drudgery in the Mine, and you stamp your image on the Gold" (1.1.220-21). Throughout *The Old Bachelor,* moreover, the love games of Vainlove and Bellmour are juxtaposed to the confidence game of Sharper, who hopes to fleece Sir Joseph Wittol. Picking up Sharper's monetary imagery, Bellmour says of the Sharper-Wittol relationship, "a little of thy Chymistry *Tom,* may extract Gold from that Dirt" (1.1.345-46). Here as elsewhere, the plots of *The Old Bachelor* are related metaphorically, but metaphorically only. The love plots exist separately from the money plot.

In the main plot or plots, the fortunes of the two women are hardly spoken of. Vainlove pursues the airy Araminta who is described as "a kind of floating Island; sometimes seems in reach, then vanishes and keeps him busied in the search." Bellmour pursues the witty and disdainful Belinda. Although it is known that Araminta is a "great fortune," Vainlove seems unconcerned about Araminta's financial assets. The less idealistic Bellmour is aware of his Belinda's wealth but surely does not treat it with great seriousness:

> SHARPER: Faith e'en give her over for good-and-all; you can have no hopes of getting her for a Mistress, and she is too Proud, too Inconstant, too Affected and too Witty, and too handsome for a Wife.
>
> BELLMOUR: But she can't have too much Money—There's twelve thousand Pound *Tom*—'Tis true she is excessively foppish and affected, but in my Conscience I believe the Baggage loves me, for she never speaks well of me her self, nor suffers any Body else to rail at me. Then as I told you there's twelve thousand Pound—Hum—Why faith upon second Thoughts, she does not appear to be so very affected neither—Give her her due, I think the Woman's a Woman, and that's all. As such I'm sure I shall like her; for the Devil take me if I don't love all the Sex.
>
> (1.1.161-75)

These speeches sensitize the audience to Belinda's considerable fortune and make them aware, too, that Bellmour is not entirely ignorant of her £12,000. Still, the pursuit of Belinda is almost entirely an amorous one, and John Harrington Smith [in *The Gay Couple in Restoration Comedy,* 1948] rightly asserts that Congreve's audience must have delighted in "a love game as had not been seen since the time of Etherege."

The minor plot of **The Old Bachelor** is quite another matter. In it, the foppish Sir Joseph Wittol and his *miles gloriosus* [braggart soldier] companion, Captain Bluffe, lose their gold in hopes of gaining the rich Araminta. Setter, Bellmour's pimp, ruminating aloud so that Wittol and Bluffe can be sure to hear him, inspires their fortune hunting:

> Were I a Rogue now, what a noble Prize could
> I dispose of! A goodly Pinnace, richly laden,
> and to launch forth under my Auspicious Con-
> voy. Twelve Thousand Pounds, and all her Rig-
> ging; besides what lies conceal'd under Hatches.
> (5.1.221-25)

Both Wittol and Bluffe take the gilded bait, each bribing Setter to match him with Araminta. And in their pursuit of Araminta's £12,000, both Wittol and Bluffe are deprived of courtship and even of the sight of their betrothed. Their comic punishment is that they are married off respectively to Bellmour and Vainlove's shared former mistress, Silvia, and her maid Lucy. Although the love games of Bellmour and Vainlove may be linked metaphorically to the monetary duping of Wittol and Bluffe, Congreve keeps the two plots largely separate, and there seems a distinct reluctance on Congreve's part to recognize the con game and the love game not merely as analogous but as conflated social realities.

In the later comedies, some of that reluctance is overcome, but Congreve's world is, for the most part, homogeneously aristocratic; and neither Mellefont in **The Double Dealer,** nor Valentine in **Love for Love,** nor Mirabell in **The Way of the World** is *forced* to consider a wealthy match either outside or within his class. True, Mellefont and Valentine face the possibility of disinheritance and financial ruin, but Congreve does not have either think of recouping his losses through marriage. Quite the contrary: Mellefont is prepared to marry Cynthia without money, and Valentine hopes to outwit his father so that his own fortune may be commensurate with Angelica's. Mellefont's and Valentine's views are not, however, those of the playwright, and it is the women who must teach them what appears to be Congreve's concept of happiness in marriage.

The Double Dealer is unique among Congreve's comedies, for Mellefont, its hero, is neither rake nor wit. Those traits belong instead to the mercenary villain, Maskwell. Mellefont's innate virtue, his ingenuous and blind trust in the unscrupulous Maskwell, and his near loss of Cynthia bring him dangerously close to sentimentality and to the heroes of sentimental comedy. He is, however, like Valentine in **Love for Love,** both rescued and educated by his more discerning female counterpart. The central difficulty in **The Double Dealer** turns on a financial issue: through the scheming of various characters and of Maskwell in particular, Mellefont stands to lose his own inheritance as well as the hand and fortune of Cynthia. But Mellefont's boyish romantic attitude is such that he is prepared to surrender his monetary interests if he can marry Cynthia. And he is prepared to have her with or without her money. Mellefont's idealistic enthusiasm is, however, significantly

adjusted and redirected by a wiser, more pragmatic Cynthia:

> MELLEFONT: I don't know why we should not steal out of the House this moment and Marry one another, without Consideration or the fear of Repentance. Pox o'Fortune, Portion, Settlements and Joyntures.
>
> CYNTHIA: Ay, ay, what have we to do with 'em; you know we Marry for Love.
>
> MELLEFONT: Love, Love, down right very Villanous Love.
>
> CYNTHIA: And he that can't live upon Love, deserves to die in a Ditch—Here, then, I give you my promise, in spight of Duty, any temptation of Wealth, your inconstancy, or my own inclination to change—
>
> MELLEFONT: To run most wilfully and unreasonably away with me this moment and be Married.
>
> CYNTHIA: Hold—Never to Marry any Body else.
>
> MELLEFONT: That's but a kind of Negative Consent.—Why, you wont baulk the Frollick?
>
> CYNTHIA: If you had not been so assured of your own Conduct I would not—But 'tis but reasonable that since I consent to like a Man without the vile Consideration of Money, He should give me a very evident demonstration of his Wit: Therefore let me see you undermine my Lady *Touchwood,* as you boasted, and force her to give her Consent, and then—
>
> MELLEFONT: I'll do't.
>
> CYNTHIA: And I'll do't.
>
> (4.1.27-51)

Mellefont's stress upon marriage based on love is applauded, but his easy surrender of both money and wit are not. Of course, Mellefont's proper demonstration of wit, the successful undermining of Lady Touchwood, will, in effect, secure the "Fortune, Portion, Settlements and Joyntures" against which he has just so vocally protested.

Mellefont's education about wit, money, and love is done in the context of Lord and Lady Froth on the one hand and of Machiavellian Maskwell on the other. The Froths are poetasters and false wits, who celebrate their affection by writing "Songs, Elegies, Satires, Encomiums, Panegyricks, Lampoons, Plays, or Heroick Poems" (2.1.1-26), but whose supposed wit has as its end only self-adulation, self-admiration, and self-congratulation. The use of wit—or in this case false wit—merely for egocentric and nonutilitarian purposes is presented and rejected by Congreve as well as by Cynthia (3.1.626-34). Maskwell is a character not as easily rejected, for he has both true wit and utilitarian purpose. For these reasons he is not rendered foolish like the Froths and almost defeats Mellefont. He is a forerunner of Fainall, who is very nearly a match for Mirabell in **The Way of the World,** and like Fainall, he is rendered a Machiavel by the primacy of his utilitarian ends, his acquisitiveness. He tells Mellefont that he has tricked Lady

Touchwood and "if I accomplish her designs (as I told you before) she has ingaged to put *Cynthia* with all her Fortune into my Power" (2.1.427-29); and when Mellefont exits, Maskwell, in a long Machiavellian soliloquy, exclaims:

> Success will attend me; for when I meet you [Mellefont], I meet the only Obstacle to my Fortune. *Cynthia*, let thy Beauty gild my Crimes; and whatsoever I commit of Treachery or Deceit, shall be imputed to me as a Merit.
>
> (2.1.439-43)

Later, when he seems nearly successful in obtaining Cynthia and the inheritance Lord Touchwood had planned to settle on Mellefont, Maskwell soliloquizes, "This is prosperous indeed—Why let him find me out a Villain, settled in possession of a fair Estate, and full fruition of my Love, I'll bear the railings of a losing Gamester" (5.1.85-8). What makes Maskwell reprehensible and villainous from Congreve's point of view is not that his wit is used to betray others, for certainly this could be said of Bellmour, Valentine, and Mirabell. It is, rather, his concentration upon the acquisition of money. Whether Maskwell has any affection for Cynthia beyond his affection for her fortune is never clear. Even Cynthia's beauty is transmuted into precious metal by Maskwell, for it will "gild" his crimes. He sees, moreover, that Cynthia's money is something to be held and controlled, for he speaks of having Cynthia's fortune put "into my Power" and of being "settled in possession of a fair Estate." Maskwell's possessiveness is such that he wishes to use his wit primarily to bring him a bundle of money and only secondarily the young lady who accompanies it.

To a ruthless business mentality like Maskwell's, a friend like Mellefont is expendable when he becomes a competitor in the economic marketplace. If he can possess Cynthia's estate, says Maskwell, "I'll bear the railings of a losing Gamester." The object of Maskwell's game playing is the possession of money, and here Congreve has Mellefont differ radically and importantly from him. Early in the play, Cynthia and Mellefont describe marriage through the imagery of games. Cynthia quips, "Still it is a Game, and Consequently one of us must be a Loser," to which Mellefont replies, "Not at all; only a Friendly Tryal of Skill, and the Winnings to be Shared between us" (2.1.168-71). For Maskwell, marriage is a game of winners and losers with the former in control of the marriage settlement. For Mellefont, by contrast, marriage and getting married are a game, but the "Tryal of Skill," the play, is more important than any monetary prize; and, furthermore, "the Winnings" are to be *shared* or, as some editions read, "laid out in an Entertainment." What Mellefont and the audience are taught through Cynthia and through Congreve is that the reasons for getting married should be based upon love and should transcend fortune, which is not to say that a loving couple should marry without money if it is in the power of their wit to secure it. In *The Double Dealer* wit must be used to secure the love of a young lady and then to secure the settlement she should bring with her, but step one must greatly outweigh and precede step two.

By making Maskwell such an outright villain and Mellefont so amiable and trusting a fellow, Congreve allows the question of romance versus finance in marriage to be one that need not engage much of the audience's attention. Mellefont's values are after all largely in the right place. He prefers love to settlements and jointures; and he sees any money brought into the marriage by either partner as funds that the married couple may jointly enjoy. Cynthia's task is simply to encourage Mellefont not to lose what, by virtue of the marriage arrangements already drawn up, is nearly his. The questions of money and love are furthermore pushed into the background by Congreve's satiric portraits of three other couples, the Froths, the Plyants, and the Touchwoods. These comic characters and the plots in which they move serve to draw the audience's attention away from the issues besetting the Mellefont-Cynthia-Maskwell triangle. It is in *Love for Love* that Congreve places the questions concerning the relationship between money and love in the foreground and at the center of his comedy. This play abounds in talk of fortunes, inheritances, settlements, deeds of conveyance, and estates. A loan broker and an estate lawyer receive extended comic treatment. And a sometimes nasty, frequently comic, world driven nearly mad by the precedence of material values is the potent image that Congreve has pass before the eyes of his audience.

Love for Love has no fewer than eleven characters of major importance, all of whom are, with the exception of Mrs. Foresight and Scandal, directly affected by the financial state of affairs in the play. Mrs. Foresight, who is financially secure in her marriage to Foresight and who has no children to marry off, has nothing to lose or gain by the monetary transactions of the play. Since, however, she has in the past made a presumably financially advantageous marriage to Foresight, she can use her experience to counsel and abet her sister in Mrs. Frail's attempts to attain financial security through marriage. Likewise, Scandal, whom the play pairs with Mrs. Foresight and who is her worldly-wise male counterpart, has no personal loss or gain at stake in the money that will pass hands in the play; but he serves, nonetheless, to advise and abet his friend Valentine in affairs of the pocketbook as well as of the heart. At the center of Congreve's witty but acquisitive world stand Valentine and Angelica, whose positions toward courtship, marriage, and money create the central interest of the comedy. Those positions not only are treated directly but also are examined indirectly through each of the several other actions of the comedy. In part, the point of *Love for Love* can be located in its title, for although there is much courtship for purely sexual ends and much courtship for purely acquisitive ends, there is no true love for love except that displayed between Angelica and Valentine during the final moments of the play.

The two most patent fortune hunters in *Love for Love* are Mrs. Frail and Mr. Tattle, who, through Congreve's poetic justice, emerge married to each other. Yet Congreve is no harsh judge, for he knows that Mrs. Frail is no mean-spirited, avaricious Maskwell but rather is a victim of the way of the world who must do what she can to mend or make her fortune. Sight unseen, therefore, she is prepared to set her cap for the rough tar, Ben, whose promise of inheritance obliterates his unpromising personality. To her successful sister, she dispassionately explains:

> You have a Rich Husband, and are provided for, I am at a loss, and have no great Stock either of Fortune or Reputation; and therefore must look sharply about me. Sir *Sampson* has a Son that is expected to Night; and by the Account I have heard of his Education can be no Conjurer: The Estate You know is to be made over to him:— Now if I cou'd wheedle him, Sister, ha! You understand me?
>
> (2.2.489-96)

And when the estate is taken from Ben and seems to revert to Valentine, she can just as dispassionately have no qualms about marrying Valentine despite his seemingly demented state. That Ben is crude or that Valentine is mad makes little difference, for it is the estate that matters. As Mrs. Foresight shrewdly comments, "after Consummation, Girl, there's no revoking. And if he should recover his Senses, he'll be glad at least to make you a good Settlement" (4.1.473-75).

As in most love comedies, there are winners and losers in *Love for Love,* but—in a way that sets them apart from Etherege's and Wycherley's characters—the wins and losses are realistically reckoned in pounds sterling rather than in mistresses. This sense of gain and loss informs Tattle's as well as Mrs. Frail's *Weltanschauung* [world view]. Valentine's servant Jeremy convinces Tattle that, in return for some tangible rewards, Angelica can be tricked into marrying Tattle. Jeremy's lure is Angelica's fortune, to which Tattle has already shown himself not indifferent. " 'Tis an Act of Charity, Sir," observes Jeremy, "to save a fine Woman with Thirty Thousand Pound, from throwing her self away" (5.1.209-11). Tattle's assurance of success is expressed with images, like Mrs. Frail's, stressing marriage as a game of chance played for monetary stakes:

> I have some taking Features, not obvious to Vulgar Eyes; that are Indications of a sudden turn of good Fortune, in the Lottery of Wives; and promise a great Beauty and great Fortune reserved alone for me, by a private Intriegue of Destiny.
>
> (5.2.267-71)

When Mrs. Frail marries Tattle believing him to be Valentine, and when Tattle married Mrs. Frail believing her to be Angelica, Congreve momentarily allows Tattle and Frail to be comic proxies for Valentine and Angelica in order to project what it would be like for the main couple to marry for fortune and estate only. Despite their dislike for one another, however, the two fortune hunters, Mrs. Frail and Tattle, do not make a bad match; and they will likely survive even more swimmingly than Silvia and Sir Joseph, their forerunners in *The Old Bachelor.*

The economics of getting married are delineated in another key through the marriage preparations for Ben and Miss Prue. Here Congreve presents a radically mismatched couple, he "a Sea-Beast" and she "a Land-Monster," who are brought together by Sir Sampson and Foresight, their parents, to unite jointure and settlement. Sir Sampson is perhaps the character most corrupted by

the material values that color the way of *Love for Love*'s world, but even the otherworldly astrologer Foresight, comically lost in the stars, seems not completely oblivious to the prime mover, prosperity, that guides the realities of the beau monde:

> SCANDAL: But I fear this Marriage and making over this Estate, this transferring of a rightful Inheritance, will bring Judgments upon us. I prophesie it, and I wou'd not have the Fate of *Cassandra,* not to be believ'd. . . .
>
> FORESIGHT: But as to this marriage I have consulted the Stars; and all Appearances are prosperous—
>
> SCANDAL: Come, come, Mr. *Foresight,* let not the Prospect of Worldly Lucre carry you beyond your Judgment, nor against your Conscience— You are not satisfy'd that you act justly.
>
> (3.1.543-57)

Congreve does not take pains to let us see exactly how much worldly wisdom resides beneath Foresight's otherworldly humour, but he is pellucid in his portrayal of Sir Sampson Legend.

If there is a villain in *Love for Love,* Sir Sampson is it; and he is, appropriately, the one character publicly exposed, disgraced, and punished at the close of the comedy. Sir Sampson not only plans to dispose of Ben as he would a piece of property, but in his treatment of Valentine he replaces the obligations of parental love with loveless legal and monetary obligations. When Valentine sues for his father's blessing, Sir Sampson tellingly replies, "You've had it already, Sir, I think I sent it you to day in a Bill of Four Thousand Pound" (2.1.274-75). Valentine continues to urge the obligations of parental love; Sir Sampson counters with an argument for paternal despotism and the divine right of the father, unashamedly setting forth the purely capitalistic paradigm of the family as an arrangement of economic exploitation and dependence:

> why Sirrah, mayn't I do what I please? Are not you my Slave? Did not I beget you? And might not I have chosen whether I would have begot you or no? Ouns who are you? Whence came you? What brought you into the World? How can you here, Sir? . . . Did you come a Voluntier into the World? Or did I beat up for you with the lawful Authority of a Parent, and press you to the service?
>
> (2.1.323-32)

Valentine rightly terms his father's behavior "Barbarity and Unnatural Usage," an unnaturalness and barbarity bred by a monstrous materialism that allows children to become inanimate goods or property to be disposed of according to the whims of their fathers, the despotic property holders. The monstosity of Sir Sampson's attitude is brought out to its fullest by Angelica, who wins his favor by feigning to share his materialism, "If I marry, Sir *Sampson,* I'm for a good Estate with any Man, and for any Man with a good Estate" (3.1.253-54). She aphoristically echoes his depersonalization of human relationship in favor of economic egotism. Her trick works so well that

Sir Sampson proposes marriage and reveals himself prepared unfeelingly to disinherit both his sons:

> SIR SAMPSON: Odd, Madam, I'll love you as
> long as I live; and leave you a good Jointure
> when I die.
>
> ANGELICA: Aye; But that is not in your Power,
> Sir *Sampson;* for when *Valentine* confesses him-
> self in his Senses; he must make over his Inheri-
> tance to his younger Brother.
>
> SIR SAMPSON: Odd, you're cunning, a wary Bag-
> gage! Faith and Troth I like you the better—But,
> I warrant you, I have a Proviso in the Obligation
> in favour of my self—Body o'me, I have a Trick
> to turn the Settlement upon the Issue Male of
> our Two Bodies begotten. Odsbud, let us find
> Children, and I'll find an Estate.
>
> (5.1.119-29)

The voice of intelligence, judgment, and wit in **Love for
Love** belongs to Angelica, and it is she, therefore, who
teases both Valentine and his father to show their best and
worst selves respectively. She tests both father and son,
and rewards them accordingly:

> I was resolv'd to try him [Valentine] to the ut-
> most; I have try'd you [Sir Sampson] too, and
> know you both. You have not more Faults than
> he has Virtues; and 'tis hardly more Pleasure to
> me, that I can make him and my self happy, than
> that I can punish you.
>
> (5.1.574-78)

For his generous love, Valentine receives a public declaration of Angelica's love for him. For his unnatural and materialistic barbarity, Sir Sampson is publicly exposed; and
for his plan to disinherit his sons and marry Angelica, he
is rendered a fool open to both the ridicule and scorn of
all.

The events involving the Foresights, Mrs. Frail, Ben and
Prue, and Sir Sampson and Angelica merely form a dramatic context for the education of the comedy's central
character, Valentine. That education is, furthermore, the
product of Valentine's two principal teachers, Scandal and
Angelica. When at the close of **Love for Love,** Angelica
gives heart and hand to Valentine, she says she "was re-
solv'd to try him to the utmost"; but in the course of that
trial, Valentine learns what no character other than Angelica knows: the importance of love for love.

In the first act of the play, Congreve introduces a Valentine impoverished by courtship. At heart a romantic, Valentine takes pleasure in the prospect of becoming a misog-
ynist poet or philosopher, roles his reduced finances will
support. He hopes as well to gain Angelica's love, the love
he had not gained through prodigality, through the charm
of his current romantic poverty. At the same time that he
maintains a romantic pose, Valentine also possesses a
sharp wit, has fathered a bastard, and has not been untouched by the way of the world. His worldly education
has taught him what it has taught the other characters: in
this world money triumphs over love. That knowledge,
combined with his innate romanticism, has led Valentine
first upon a mad course of proving his affection for Angelica by spending vast sums in her behalf and then to a belief

that his current resultant poverty is the ultimate demonstration of his love:

> Well; and now I am poor, I have an opportunity
> to be reveng'd on 'em all; I'll pursue *Angelica*
> with more Love than ever, and appear more no-
> toriously her Admirer in this Restraint, than
> when I openly rival'd the rich Fops, that made
> Court to her; so shall my Poverty be a Mortifica-
> tion to her Pride, and perhaps, make her com-
> passionate that Love, which has principally
> reduc'd me to this Lowness of Fortune.
>
> (1.1.49-56)

This romantic view would justify Valentine's further im-
poverishing himself by signing away his inheritance to his
brother Ben.

Signing a deed of conveyance would be, as Scandal chides,
"A very desperate demonstration of your love to Angelica," and he argues astutely, "you have little reason to believe that a Woman of this Age, who has had an indifference for you in your Prosperity, will fall in love with your
ill Fortune; besides, *Angelica* has a great Fortune of her
own; and great Fortunes either expect another great Fortune, or a Fool" (1.1.343-44, 350-54). The correctness of
Scandal's comment on the monetary basis of love relationships specifically and on social behavior generally is
brought home to Valentine by various characters who are
heard from in act 1. They include the pragmatic, philoso-
phizing Jeremy, who speaks of the need to leave a master
bereft of credit; the past mistress who now writes for child
support; the loan broker Trapland, whose friendliness in
flush times has been replaced by an uncharitable readiness
to clap insolvent debtors into irons; Mrs. Frail, who carries the news of the proposed, economically motivated arranged match between Ben and Prue; and Sir Sampson's
steward, sent to act on his master's barbarous demand for
Valentine's deed of conveyance.

By the end of the first act, Valentine, in the context of the
other characters, does indeed seem to have acted naively,
and Scandal's observation and couplet, which close the
act, are well taken:

> I'll give an account of you, and your Proceed-
> ings. If Indiscretion be a sign of Love, you are
> the most a Lover of any Body that I know: you
> fancy that parting with your Estate, will help
> you to your Mistress.—In my mind he is a
> thoughtless Adventurer,
>
> Who hopes to purchase Wealth, by selling Land;
> Or win a Mistress, with a losing hand.
>
> (1.1.675-81)

Apparently, it is Scandal's wordly teaching upon which
Valentine then proceeds to act. His feigned madness is
principled by a pragmatic, materialistic outlook that will
enable him to keep his estate, and provide him with the
land and the winning hand that Scandal asserts are necessary for marriage to Angelica. Valentine's feigned madness is, furthermore, simply his satiric exaggeration of the
mad, unprincipled proceedings of the rest of society. "All
mad, I think—Flesh, I believe all the *Calentures* of the Sea
are come ashore for my part" (4.1.356-57), is, after all,

what the plain-dealing Ben so aptly says of the entire cast of *Love for Love.*

As the play shows it, Scandal's teaching may have the ring of truth, but it is, nonetheless, flawed; and as Valentine's teacher, his *magister ludi,* Congreve replaces Scandal with Angelica. In act 4, Valentine recites to Angelica the lessons he has mastered under Scandal and receives reproof instead of expected reward. He admits that he "has worn this Mask of Madness, only as the Slave of Love, and Menial Creature of your Beauty" (4.1.702-04), and that, furthermore, his efforts to retain his estate and inheritance, to match fortune for fortune (which Scandal has said is necessary for winning "Women of this Age"), are proof of his affection. Instead of falling into his arms and ending the comedy, as Valentine anticipates, Angelica gives him a telling and heuristic rebuff:

> VALENTINE: The Comedy draws toward an end, and let us think of leaving acting, and be our selves . . . my seeming Madness has deceiv'd my Father, and procur'd me time to think of means to reconcile me to him; and preserve the right of my Inheritance to his Estate . . .
>
> ANGELICA: How! I thought your love of me had caus'd this Transport in your Soul; which, it seems, you only counterfeited, for mercenary Ends and sordid Interest.
>
> VALENTINE: Nay, now you do me Wrong; for if any Interest was considered, it was yours; since I thought I wanted more than Love, to make me worthy of you.
>
> ANGELICA: Then you thought me mercenary— But how am I deluded by this Interval of Sense, to reason with a Madman.
>
> (4.1.707-08, 715-30)

Angelica here affirms that Valentine has acted as madly and as badly as the rest of the world. Placing mercenary interests above love, Valentine has adulterated and transmogrified the love between the sexes in precisely the same way that Sir Sampson has adulterated and transmogrified the love between parent and child. In this short exchange, Angelica successfully reveals that neither prodigality nor avarice need mix with love and that to posit mercenary ends as a necessary prelude to marital love, as most of the characters in *Love for Love* do, is for her nothing short of madness.

Congreve's title, of course, is the core of Angelica's educational philosophy; and Valentine must come to understand the concept of generosity that avoids and transcends both prodigality and avarice which is implicit in the title. It is only when, through Angelica's guidance, he masters the idea of generosity that Valentine can have both his woman and his money:

> VALENTINE: I never valu'd Fortune, but as it was subservient to my Pleasure; and my only Pleasure was to please this Lady: I have made many vain Attempts, and find at last, that nothing but my Ruine can effect it: Which, for that Reason, I will sign to—Give me the Paper.
>
> ANGELICA: Generous *Valentine!* . . . Had I the

> World to give you it cou'd not make me worthy of so generous and faithful a Passion: Here's my Hand, my Heart was always yours, and struggl'd very hard to make the utmost Tryal of your Virtue.
>
> (5.1.544-64)

Of all his comedies, Congreve's *Love for Love* is the one that turns most centrally on the conflation of money and the affairs of the heart. *The Old Bachelor* separates the two concerns by dividing them into two plots, and *The Double Dealer* overwhelms the concern for Mellefont's and Cynthia's fortunes with a strong Machiavel and a constellation of manners comedy stock figures. In *Love for Love,* however, no character is unaffected by the impact of money, yet Congreve seems to shy away from the implications of his own satire. Perhaps this is Congreve's own form of generosity. Clearly Angelica and Valentine rise above the other characters as they affirm a relationship based upon love for love instead of love for money or money for money; but at the same time, the other characters are not, except Sir Sampson, really condemned or punished. Scandal and Mrs. Foresight consummate their affair, Mr. Foresight remains unchanged, Ben happily returns to the sea, and Miss Prue will, as she herself predicts, probably fulfill her destiny and run off with one of the servants. Tattle and Mrs. Frail are married but even they realize that they will likely manage quite well; and though Tattle's fortune is not what Valentine's is or what Ben's would have been, it will nevertheless serve the purpose of rescuing Mrs. Frail from her economic dilemma. Even Sir Sampson, who is condemned and punished, is not in a class with Congreve's out and out villains, Maskwell and Fainall, and his punishment is merely the exposure of his failures as a parent and suitor; there is no concomitant economic punishment as there is for Maskwell and Fainall. Even with Angelica, the central intelligence of the play, Congreve seems to skirt some of the realities of economics by placing Angelica's fortune entirely in her own hands. This rare situation, in short, frees Angelica from any economic control including that of her guardian Foresight. As a totally free agent, absolute mistress of her vast £30,000 fortune, she can enjoy the luxury of teaching Valentine to be generous.

In *The Way of the World,* which is less centrally about money than *Love for Love,* Congreve nonetheless comes closest to treating the question of money convincingly. In *The Double Dealer,* Cynthia's settlement is not in question, it is only a matter of whether it will go to Maskwell or Mellefont; in *Love for Love,* Angelica's considerable fortune is entirely at her own disposal; but in *The Way of the World,* Millamant's £12,000 is only partially in her own hands, for Lady Wishfort controls £6,000, exactly half of it. Millamant, therefore, can only in part be her own mistress and affirm the primacy of love, for she is also in part liable to the loss of half her monies if she marries without her aunt's consent. How Mirabell and Millamant deport themselves, consequently, seems a more true test and more convincing example of Congreve's attitudes toward marriage than those found in his earlier comedies.

Dividing the control of Millamant's £12,000 fortune equally between the heroine and her aunt, Congreve places Millamant at the theoretical center of *The Way of the World.* She could conceivably marry for love thereby forfeiting £6,000; or she could marry the unsuitable Sir Wilfull Witwoud, her aunt's choice, thereby losing Mirabell but keeping her fortune intact. Neither choice is a happy one, but, the conventions of comedy being what they are, an audience has every right to expect that Millamant either alone or together with Mirabell will use her wit to trick Lady Wishfort and the other blocking characters in such a way that Millamant can have Mirabell as well as her full £12,000 intact. The desired result is achieved, but how it is achieved has not been given enough consideration. It is remarkable indeed that in a society where jockeying for financial position seems so much the way of the world, and in a plot where the disposal of Millamant's fortune is so central an issue, Millamant herself never once discusses her money nor does Mirabell ever once discuss with Millamant his elaborate plotting to secure the £6,000 pounds under Lady Wishfort's control. Millamant is, nonetheless, certainly aware of what is happening around her, as she reveals the one time Mirabell unsuccessfully attempts to broach the subject:

> MIRABELL: Can you not find in the variety of your Disposition one Moment—
>
> MILLAMANT: To hear you tell me that *Foible's* married, and your Plot like to speed—No.
>
> MIRABELL: But how came you to know it—
>
> MILLAMANT: Unless by the help of the Devil you can't imagine; unless she shou'd tell me her self. Which of the two it may have been, I will leave you to consider; and when you have done thinking of that; think of me. *Exit.*
>
> (2.2.480-89)

Millamant parries before Mirabell can thrust, at once acknowledging her awareness of Mirabell's doings and forbidding him to speak to her of them. Before the astonished Mirabell can react, she turns with physical and linguistic flourish to exit, but leaves him with the injunction, "think of me." Like so much that happens in *The Way of the World* between Mirabell and Millamant, much of the communication is effected precisely by what is *not* said. Unlike Angelica, Millamant need not stop to reprove the hero's acquisitiveness or remind him to concentrate more on love than on fortune. She merely deflects the topic of conversation, yet wittily and pointedly reminds Mirabell not to lose sight of his real object: "think of me."

The singular and superior relationship between Mirabell and Millamant is made by Congreve to look all the more singular and superior by the characters around them. As everyone who has ever seen or read *The Way of the World* immediately senses, consciously or unconsciously, the foppish Petulant and Witwoud, the plain-spoken but boorish Sir Wilfull, and the passionate Lady Wishfort set off by their various flaws the patently superior wit and style of the lead couple. More discrimination is necessary to measure Mirabell and Millamant against Marwood, Fainall, and Mrs. Fainall, for these three are no fools and fall only slightly short of Mirabell and Millamant's level of intelligence and poise. Yet Mirabell and Millamant do emerge superior and not merely because they are less passionate

and less malicious, though that has something to do with placing them above Marwood and the Fainalls. What distinguishes Mirabell and Millamant is, finally, what also distinguishes Valentine and Angelica from the rest of the characters in *Love for Love,* namely their generosity and their attitude toward the relative importance of money as a basis for marriage or love relationships.

If Mirabell and Millamant fail to talk of money, the two characters who are most closely compared to them, Fainall and Marwood, can think of little else. Their relationship to the other characters and even to each other is repeatedly marked, often dominated, by their prodigality and acquisitiveness. Reminiscent of the union of [Ben] Jonson's Subtle and Face [in *The Alchemist*] the relationship between Fainall and Marwood is an explosive one and one that is a business partnership held together by money:

> MRS. MARWOOD: It shall be all discover'd. You too shall be discover'd; be sure you shall. I can but be expos'd—If I do it my self I shall prevent your Baseness.
>
> FAINALL: Why, what will you do?
>
> MRS. MARWOOD: Disclose it to your Wife; own what has past between us.
>
> FAINALL: Frenzy!
>
> MRS. MARWOOD: By all my Wrongs I'll do't— I'll publish to the World the Injuries you have done me, both in my Fame and Fortune: With both I trusted you, you Bankrupt in Honour, as indigent in Wealth.
>
> FAINALL: Your Fame I have preserv'd. Your Fortune has been bestow'd as the prodigality of your Love would have it, in Pleasures which we both have shar'd. Yet had not you been false, I had e'er repaid it—'Tis true—Had you permitted *Mirabell* with *Millamant* to have stoll'n their Marriage, my Lady had been incens'd beyond all means of reconcilement: *Millamant* had forfeited the Moiety of her Fortune; which then wou'd have descended to my Wife;—And wherefore did I marry, but to make lawful Prize of a rich Widow's Wealth, and squander it on Love and you?
>
> MRS. MARWOOD: Deceit and frivolous Pretence.
>
> (2.1.187-208)

Marwood's passion is conflated with prodigality. Fainall's circuitous plotting to obtain everyone's money is as complex and extravagant as Mirabell's scheme to gain Lady Wishfort's blessing and loosen her grip on Millamant's £6,000 by extricating the aunt from a marriage with a valet. What distinguishes the two schemes, however, is that for Fainall all things and all women are sacrificed to his egotistical desire for money. Any feeling for Marwood is at best an afterthought, as is clear in the priorities revealed in Fainall's declaration that he desires money to "squander it on Love and you." He loves for money, he marries for money, and he plots for money. Mirabell, by contrast, acts with greatest honor toward Mrs. Fainall, his former mistress, and toward the money she has placed in his trust, and he omits all question of money in his discourses with Millamant. His plotting is meant to place at her disposal the money that is rightly Millamant's and not to secure it for himself. Mirabell's elaborate plot is, after all, well under way long before Millamant has given any consent, verbal or written, to marry him.

At the heart of Mirabell and Millamant's relationship is the famous "Contract" or "proviso" scene of act 4. For every critic this scene takes on signal importance as the representation of what the relationship between the hero and heroine actually is and what it will be after marriage. Norman Holland [in *The First Modern Comedies,* 1959] and Virginia Birdsail [in *Wild Civility,* 1970] stress the harmony of temperament and the maturation of Millamant; Kathleen Lynch [in *The Social Mode of Restoration Comedy,* 1926] places the proviso scene in the context of the dramatic sources and analogues Congreve likely knew, and Maximillian Novak [in *William Congreve,* 1971] goes on to show that against the literary background Lynch documents, Mirabell and Millamant play wittily with the proviso convention because their understanding is already such that provisos are superfluous. Ian Donaldson [in *The World Upside Down,* 1970] notes in passing that the proviso scene does not touch "upon the cold mercantile facts" raised in Wycherley's *The Gentleman Dancing-Master,* an analogue Lynch overlooked. Donaldson here indicates precisely what is remarkable about the verbal contract Mirabell and Millamant agree to. In the mock formality of its legal language, its *imprimis* and *item,* it calls to mind the usual marriage contracts in which the clauses concerned settlements and jointures, the financial arrangements that were to provide the legal setting for a union officially recognized in a church ceremony. Mirabell and Millamant "convenant" a great many things, most of them trifles that are nonetheless indicative of the social and love relationship they already have and wish to foster in the future. As is often the case, however, in the discourses between Mirabell and Millamant, what is unspoken is as important as what is stated. That the issue of money is never once part of their legalistic convenant, though in the world outside the theater it was always the heart of the legal marriage convenant, shows at once Mirabell and Millamant's awareness of the monetary ways of the world as well as their determination not to define their love verbally by the economic strictures of the traditional marriage contract. The content of the proviso scene italicizes the primacy of love and personal relationships that Mirabell and Millamant affirm as the proper basis for marriage. Money, in not being mentioned, is given a distinctly peripheral place. The actual monetary agreements that would have to have been reached in the written contract, seemingly drawn up off stage somewhere between the fourth and fifth acts, are never either specified or discussed by the principals. Congreve's emphasis upon the importance of love over concerns about money is further italicized by providing Mirabell and Millamant with a real financial issue, namely, Lady Wishfort's control over half of her niece's fortune. For Angelica, whose fortune is entirely in her own hands, her attitudes, however laudable,

can be judged a luxury. Millamant's is an attitude that must necessarily be more hard won and, therefore, more credible.

In the concluding scene of *The Way of the World* the avarice of Fainall and the generosity of Mirabell collide. In a proviso scene of his own, Fainall proposes a contract that would enable him to control Lady Wishfort and, consequently, her estate; he demands that Mrs. Fainall "settle on me the remainder of her Fortune, not made over already" (5.1.268-69), and insists upon immediate possession of the half of Millamant's fortune held by Lady Wishfort. Since all things seem to be going Fainall's way, he gives vent to what is for him obviously the optimum social relationship, malevolent economic despotism. Lady Wishfort may enjoy her "own proper Estate during Life; on the condition you oblige your self never to Marry, under such penalty as I think convenient" (5.1.252-54). Mrs. Fainall not only is to make over her fortune to her husband but must, says Fainall, "for her Maintenance depend entirely on my Discretion" (5.1.269-70). As Fainall senses his strength, he revises his demands to insist upon his sole control of Lady Wishfort's estate as well as his wife's (5.1.433-36). His machinations are, however, foiled by Mirabell and the contents of the black box:

> MIRABELL: Mr. *Fainall,* it is now time that you shou'd know, that your Lady while she was at her own disposal, and before you had by your Insinuations wheedl'd her out of a pretended Settlement of the greatest part of her fortune—
>
> FAINALL: Sir! pretended!
>
> MIRABELL: Yes Sir. I say that this Lady while a Widow, having it seems receiv'd some Cautions respecting your Inconstancy and Tyranny of temper . . . she did I say by the wholesome advice of Friends and of Sages learned in the Laws of this Land, deliver this same as her Act and Deed to me in trust, and to the uses within mention'd. You may read if you please—tho perhaps what is inscrib'd on the back may serve your occasions.
>
> FAINALL: Very likely, Sir, What's here? Damnation! *A deed of Conveyance of the whole Estate real of* Arabella Languish *Widow in trust to* Edward Mirabell. Confusion!
>
> MIRABELL: Even so Sir, 'tis *the way of the World,* Sir: of the Widows of the World.
>   (5.1.535-54)

Why, one is led to ask, should Congreve allow his comic plot to hinge on a providential black box and its hitherto obscure contents? Why, too, is Mirabell's elaborate hoax necessary when he might so easily compel Lady Wishfort to permit his marriage to Millamant by flourishing Mrs. Fainall's deed of conveyance? The obvious answer is that Congreve forces his audience to dwell upon Mirabell's generosity, especially in contrast to the exposition of Fainall's character. There is, however, a still more important answer, namely, that the audience in asking the second question comes to realize that Mirabell could not have won Millamant through blackmail that threatened the financial ruin of her cousin or aunt. In the 162 lines (432-594) comprising Fainall's seeming triumph and his consequent defeat, Millamant remains silent, but consistent with her presentation throughout *The Way of the World,* she is not only present on the stage but eloquent in her silence. Her presence amid the revelations whereby Mirabell saves Mrs. Fainall and Lady Wishfort makes the audience realize that had Mirabell used the black box to obtain Lady Wishfort's consent he would have shown that he sought Millamant's money more than the lady herself, and, more important, would have revealed a culpable, mercenary character, not unlike Fainall's, by the very nature of blackmail based upon economic mastery. In the last speech of the play, Mirabell relinquishes the deed of conveyance to its owner and projects a new, enlightened view of money in marriage:

> For my part I will Contribute all that in me lies to a Reunion, (*To Mrs.* Fainall) in the mean time, *Madam,* let me before these Witnesses, restore to you this deed of trust. It may be a means well manag'd to make you live Easily together.
> (5.1.615-19)

Mirabell conveys the sense that in those marriages like the Fainalls' where love does not overshadow economics there is a second best choice, namely, to use economics so that the couple may "live Easily together."

Although in the courtships that take place in his comedies Congreve acknowledges the importance of money in a way that Wycherley and Etherege do not, he finally avoids having his characters make their choices in the context of real monetary pressures. In *The Old Bachelor* marriage for love and marriage for money are separate issues relegated to separate plots; and characters like Mellefont, Valentine, and Mirabell, who acknowledge the need for both love and money, never have to make a serious choice *between* them. Congreve's world is a game board that includes a desired young lady and a bundle of money. To win the game, the male player must bring these two objects to the same square on the board, and the game is not over until there is a winner. Like the witty couples found in the comedies of Elizabethan dramatists such as John Fletcher or in the comedies of Congreve's more immediate forebears, Etherege and Wycherley, Congreve's main couples are primarily expert players of the mating game. Their game has, however, been made more complex and difficult by adding financial obstacles to the sexual ones. And it is precisely those financial obstacles that will increasingly come to occupy the descendents of Valentine and Angelica and of Mirabell and Millamant as they are found in the comedies of Steele, Gay, Fielding, Garrick, and Sheridan. (pp. 255-72)

> *Albert Wertheim, "Romance and Finance: The Comedies of William Congreve," in* Comedy from Shakespeare to Sheridan: Change and Continuity in the English and European Dramatic Tradition, *edited by A. R. Braunmuller and J. C. Bulman, University of Delaware Press, 1986, pp. 255-73.*

LOVE FOR LOVE

PRODUCTION REVIEWS

Brooks Atkinson   (review date 27 May 1947)

[*Atkinson was the drama critic for the* New York Times *from 1926 to 1960. Upon his retirement from that post, the Mansfield Theatre in New York was renamed the Brooks Atkinson in honor of his contributions to the theater. His publications include* Skyline Promenades *(1925),* Henry Thoreau: The Cosmic Yankee *(1927), and* East of the Hudson *(1931), as well as many collections of his drama criticism. In the following review, Atkinson describes John Gielgud's 1947 production of* Love for Love *at New York's Royale Theater, in which Gielgud himself played Valentine. He finds the staging "uneven," expressing disappointment in Gielgud's Valentine while commending the performances of the remainder of the cast. He especially praises Jessie Evans's Prue, asserting that "since long interludes in this* Love for Love *are tedious, the sheer gusto and vulgarity of her acting are gratefully entertaining."*]

Since Congreve's *Love for Love* is a notorious classic, one must naturally speak of it with respect. But Mr. Gielgud and his company, who revived it at the Royale last evening, make it seem inferior to [Oscar] Wilde's *The Importance of Being Earnest,* which no one is required to treat with respect. Generally it is polite to pretend that a very old play, which has somehow survived, seems younger than plays of today. But Congreve's artificial comedy, first produced in 1695, seems at least 100 years old now, although Wilde's decorous Victorian prank seems eminently modern.

Nor is the performance of *Love for Love* as perfect a jest. Many of Mr. Gielgud's recent actors have back-tracked with him from Victorian to Restoration. But the performance as a whole lacks the brittle, lacquered uniformity of the previous work. Mr. Gielgud's lack of humor turns Valentine into an ascetic, colorless young man who is burlesquing Shakespeare when he is not acting a prig. Technically, Mr. Gielgud is a brilliant actor. But since he is not playing Congreve artificially, his Valentine emerges as a pleasant, well-mannered young man without much strength of personality—more at home in a library than at Will's coffee house.

As the director Mr. Gielgud has done better by the other actors than by himself. Adrianne Allen and Marian Spencer, as Mrs. Frail and Mrs. Foresight, respectively, are playing with wit and coquetry; and Pamela Brown, as Angelica, is acting with high style that skilfully separates Congreve from nature. George Hayes' Scandal is nicely mellowed by sin. As the choleric Sir Sampson Legend, the irate, vainglorious parent, Malcolm Keen is playing with good spirit.

In so mincing a comedy, a little hearty playing is always refreshing. Cyril Ritchard's dissembling, fatuous Tattle is capital fooling with its skipping embroidery. Richard Wordsworth's Irish serving rascal is affably humorous. As

John Gielgud, Cyril Ritchard, and George Hayes in the 1947 production of Love for Love *at the Royale Theatre, New York.*

[*In the following review, Barnes praises John Gielgud's staging of* Love for Love, *asserting that the actor-director "deserves full credit for a gay and stylish production." While lamenting that the plot of this comedy is so complex that at times it "virtually requires a diagram," Barnes maintains that the staging is successful because of a number of memorable scenes and good acting.*]

William Congreve's **Love for Love** has been given a brilliantly ribald revival by John Gielgud and his excellent company at the Royale. As in his earlier production of *The Importance of Being Earnest,* the English actor-manager has struck a happy balance between wit and artifice. The lines of the celebrated Restoration comedy crackle across the stage with a rich bawdy and satirical eloquence. What is more to the point, they are backed up by captivating characterizations and elegant bits of horse-play, two centuries and a half have not withered a lusty show in the current offering.

Gielgud deserves full credit for a gay and stylish production. In addition to playing the central role of Valentine, who becomes impoverished and counterfeits madness for love of his fair Angelica, he is responsible for a remarkably fluent staging of the classic. There are intervals, to be sure, when Congreve forgot about stage action, or swung to the opposite extreme by complicating his farce until it virtually requires a diagram. They occasion infrequent lulls or periods of confusion at the Royale. The high points of the play, when the half-witted coxcomb, Tattle, is making love to the dumb yokel, Miss Prue, or Valentine is becoming entangled in his pretended lunacy, are rare good fun.

The star is assisted at every hand by full-bodied and riggish portrayals. Cyril Ritchard is particularly good as a mincing London Lothario of 1695, while George Hayes contributes a sardonic and restrained interpretation of the free-speaker, Scandal. Adrianne Allen is delightful as Mrs. Frail, whose matrimonial schemes land her the least desirable of the beaux at hand; Marian Spencer is decorously wanton as old Foresight's young wife and Pamela Brown is altogether coquettish as the hard-to-get heroine.

Then there is Malcolm Keen, boisterous and paternally remiss as Valentine's hard-hearted father, caricaturing Sir Sampson to the queen's taste. Robert Flemyng is fine as his seafaring younger son. John Kidd is properly ancient as the illiterate and superstitious Foresight, and Jessie Evans is an apple-cheeked and silly Prue. Congreve has been well served by players in the latest revival of his sturdy comedy of manners. The trappings of the piece are in perfect keeping with the material, with handsome settings by the late Rex Whistler and fancy costumes by Jeanetta Cochrane. There are laggard scenes in **Love for Love,** but on the whole it is an artful and highly amusing addition to late-season theater going.

the blunt and graceless sailor, Robert Flemyng is giving an entertaining performance. As the country-bred daughter, Jessie Evans has a part that can be played broadly. And since long interludes in this **Love for Love** are tedious, the sheer gusto and vulgarity of her acting are gratefully entertaining.

As an example of dramatic literature, **Love for Love** is sententiously written with an elaborate plot that seems hardly worth so many convolutions. Mr. Gielgud has chastened some of the earthier words, mercifully omitted the sailors' hornpipe and culled out some of the verbosity. Rex Whistler's settings of Restoration London are done with taste, but with less distinction than Jeannette Cochrane's costumes. Restoration costumes are a designer's holiday.

Despite the licentiousness of Restoration manners, Congreve wrote **Love for Love** with wit and elegance. Mr. Gielgud has taken it too much at face value. He plays Valentine as though he believed in the essential high-mindedness of the character. Perhaps this is the reason why the performance as a whole is so uneven—rueful romance dampening the hard raillery of the Congreve text. The Wilde was better because it was unalloyed make-believe without a single honest word all evening.

Brooks Atkinson, in a review of Love for Love, in The New York Times, *May 27, 1947.*

Howard Barnes, "Gielgud Scores Again," in New York Herald Tribune, *May 27, 1947.*

William Hawkins   (review date 27 May 1947)

[*In the following review of John Gielgud's production of* Love for Love, *Hawkins describes various weaknesses in the play that detract from its appreciation by modern-day audiences, but comments favorably on the performances of many of the players.*]

The proposition of seeing *Love for Love,* by William Congreve, as of seeing any Restoration play, suggests an evening of good-natured bawdy conversation and a whirl of intrigue moving with brittle intricacy.

John Gielgud's production of the play, which opened last night to a most distinguished audience, proved that it needs a wealth of comic invention to keep it more than intermittently amusing in this day and age.

The play seems to be done with an awesome fidelity to tradition that would undoubtedly appeal more to a British audience than an American one. Here and now it seems bloodless, and only here and there funny.

There is a maze of plot about various love affairs that has no particular point beyond excusing a series of epigrammatic remarks couched in the free language of courtship in the 17th Century.

Some of these speeches are crystal-clear and brilliantly amusing. Others have the humor of bald frankness. The artificial romances, appropriate as they may be to the period, have a way of going home the long way round and distending the space between the bright peaks.

In all honesty it should be said that *The Importance of Being Earnest,* which Mr. Gielgud's company treated so brilliantly, is mighty tough to follow.

The star is a courtly hero, sly with the comment that needs a leer, and sure of the bravura of his mad scenes. A bitterness that makes his character real burns in his love scene with Angelica.

Cyril Ritchard as the foppish satyr Tattle, brings an energetic style to all his scenes. His vigor and sustained manner make many of the other players colorless. Not so however, the Prue of Jessie Evans, whom he teaches about romance far too successfully for his own comfort.

Miss Evans plays a bumptious maid with a whole hearted broadness that picks the play up and whirls it in the air. Her approach is athletic and punchy, but her eagerness is real whether mad, glad or sad.

Robert Flemyng contributes another full-blooded portrait as the sailor Ben who almost gets a fortune and a wife. He brings a lusty sea-going freedom into the drawing room, and with a clear-cut, effective idea of what he is up to, makes his presence felt every moment he is on the stage.

Pamela Brown shows again a dewey gracefulness and a rare sense of elegance. As Angelica she has style, warmth and strength.

Adrianne Allen is a handsome Mrs. Frail, opportunist with her affections, who aims at many men and gets one she would least like to have. As her sister, Mrs. Foresight, Marian Spencer has a particularly lovely moment at the end of the first act as she hints an invitation to an extra-marital romance.

As Jeremy, the servant of Valentine, Richard Wordsworth gives a dexterous picture of a cunning, though good humored rogue.

Since *Love for Love* is a talky play it could do with more physical vibrancy than it gets here. Proof of this lies in the fact that so many of the really memorable moments are those that are pictorial for their agility.

One remembers with delight and some relief Miss Evans' headlong dive at Mr. Ritchard and her flight from him, Mr. Ritchard's mincing off stage with his ridiculous muff, and Mr. Gielgud's desperate antics with a blanket during his mad orations.

> William Hawkins, " 'Love for Love' Bawdy
> But Brittle in Revival," in New York World-
> Telegram, *May 27, 1947.*

Louis Kronenberger   (review date 28 May 1947)

[*A drama critic for* Time *from 1938 to 1961, Kronenberger was a distinguished historian, literary critic, and author highly regarded for his expertise in eighteenth-century English history and literature. In the following review, he comments generally on reasons for the failure of theater presentations of Congreve's masterpiece,* The Way of the World, *and the comparative stage success of* Love for Love. *He remarks favorably on John Gielgud's staging of the latter play, commending especially the performance of the cast.*]

Once more John Gielgud has put us in his debt. His *Love For Love* is stylish and spirited, and infinitely more of a stage piece than a waxwork. If it isn't so brilliant an achievement as was Mr. Gielgud's *Importance of Being Earnest,* it plainly didn't offer him so brilliant an opportunity. This is not to damn it out of hand as the inferior play. But being 200 years older than *Earnest,* it is a little more garrulous, a little stiffer in the joints. Thanks to having been written in 1695, it includes, for example, an old codger interested (as his original audience was) in astrology: for a present-day audience, he is merely an unutterable bore. But it is not age alone that makes Congreve's play less rewarding, production-wise, than Wilde's. There is also the fact that Congreve's cannot quite be acted all in one style, and so cannot seem so great an achievement in sheer style.

Artistically, *Love for Love* cannot hold a candle to Congreve's *Way of the World* which is, without any doubt whatever, the finest stage comedy in the English language. Yet it is not hard to understand why *The Way of the World* has generally failed in the theater, and *Love For Love* has so many times succeeded. *The Way of the World* is marvelously high-bred, but a little low-pitched. The very thing that makes *Love For Love* a lesser play—its streak of very broad comedy—makes it infinitely more playable. Without boorish Ben and hoydenish Miss Prue—without, for that matter, the more farcical moments of Valentine's feigned madness and the less corseted moments of virtually everybody's sex life—*Love For Love* would have a far grander air; but it would prove, I fear, much duller company.

Yet, if no patrician comedy of manners like *The Way of the World, Love For Love* is not mere Restoration bawdry, either. It too is concerned with manners, and even with manner. However often its bedroom doors may open and shut, all its worldlier characters speak to perfection the language of the drawing-room. It is, indeed, their speech that matters most. In the artificial style, there has never been a greater master of polished and witty dialogue than Congreve. Often, no doubt, his lines are too literary to have naturalness; but they never lack consummate ease.

Obviously, how to speak such lines is something of a problem; as is how to play such roles. Americans generally can't: when they're not being too prosaic, they're being too elegantly mincing and mannered; they're choking all the life out of the play through attempting a way of life. The English usually know better. They can achieve a very real elegance on occasion, but they don't confuse it with enervation; and what they most go after is a certain aplomb. That distinguished Mr. Gielgud's *Importance of Being Earnest;* it distinguishes his *Love For Love.* Moreover, the frightfully foppish Tattle has it quite as much as the mettlesome Angelica or the insolent Valentine; it is what, more than any other single thing, keeps the play going.

Love For Love is not the perfectly inlaid production that *Earnest* was able to be, but Mr. Gielgud has staged it skilfully and there are some very good performances. One of these is Mr. Gielgud's own as Valentine; another is the Angelica of Pamela Brown, a pretty fascinating actress; a third the Ben of Robert Flemyng. Other good marks go to Cyril Ritchard, Adrianne Allen, Jessie Evans and George Hayes, among others; and to Rex Whistler for his settings.

> Louis Kronenberger, "Gielgud Gives New Life to a 252-Year-Old Play," in PM Exclusive, May 28, 1947.

CRITICAL COMMENTARY

Maximillian E. Novak   (essay date 1971)

[*Novak is an American educator and critic who has written extensively on Restoration and eighteenth-century literature. In the following excerpt, he discusses "the romantic foundation" for Congreve's social satire in* Love for Love, *asserting that the irrationality of love is a central theme in the play. Novak also describes Congreve's use of dialogue to effect distinctive characterizations in this work.*]

> Valentine in Love for Love is (if I may so call him) the Hero of the Play; this Spark the Poet would pass for a Person of Virtue, but he speaks too late. 'Tis true, he was hearty in his Affection to Angelica. Now without Question, to be in Love with a fine Lady of Thirty Thousand Pounds is a great Virtue! But then abating this single Commendation, Valentine is altogether compounded of Vice. He is a prodigal Debauch-

ee, Unnatural and Profane, Obscene, Sawcy, and Undutiful; and yet this Libertine is crown'd for the Man of Merit, has his Wishes thrown in his Lap, and makes the Happy *Exit.* I perceive we should have a rare Set of Virtues if these Poets had the making of them! . . . To sum up the Evidence. A fine Gentleman, is a fine Whoring, Swearing, Smutty, Atheistical Man.
> Jeremy Collier, *A Short View of the Immorality and Profaneness of the English Stage.*

A typical opening for a Restoration comedy reveals the rake-hero reading a volume of Lucretius or Epicurus and expounding on Libertine themes. "Thou great Lucretius! Thou profound Oracle of Wit and Sence!" exclaims Bruce at the start of [Thomas] Shadwell's *Virtuoso.* Shadwell eventually reforms his libertine, and, except for this apostrophe to Lucretius, it would be difficult on the basis of his actions in the play to detect that he was either a wit or a debauchee. Congreve's opening to *Love for Love* is a notable reversal of the convention; Valentine, who has been reading the stoic philosopher Epictetus, preaches a mocking anti-Epicurean sermon to his servant, Jeremy: "Read, read, Sirrah, and refine your Appetite; learn to live upon Instruction; feast your Mind, and mortifie your Flesh." Jeremy's reply is pragmatic and practical: none of the stoics or cynics, or even Plato, will help Valentine pay his debts. Valentine, however, insists that his poverty will not prevent his loving Angelica even more than when he was wealthy enough to compete with the rich fops surrounding her. "So shall my Poverty be a Mortification to her Pride," he continues," and perhaps, make her compassionate the Love, which has principally reduc'd me to this Lowness of Fortune." The combination is curious—philosophy, wit, and passion. But to Congreve these were the qualities of an ideal comic hero, however immoral and unchristian Jeremy Collier may have thought him.

ROMANTIC AND SATIRIC THEMES

The outlines of Congreve's play *Love for Love* bear some resemblance to the famous story from [Giovanni] Boccaccio's *Decameron* in which the hero impoverishes himself for love of a wealthy lady; has to withdraw to a farm without even the slightest acknowledgment that she is aware of his existence; sacrifices his last possession, a falcon, to feed her when she comes to ask a favor; and finally is rewarded by her love. So Valentine ruins himself for love of Angelica, gives up all as a final gesture of despair over losing her, and gains her in the end. The details are very different, but the substance, with its emphasis on true gentility, is the same; the resemblance suggests the romance foundation on which Congreve is constructing his satire. We are most aware of it at the end, when Angelica matches Valentine's moving confession of love with her own praise of Valentine's generosity, but we are always aware that Valentine is capable of intense passion and of acting upon it. He was a libertine, remains a wit, and is capable of true love. Like Mellefont [in *The Double Dealer*], he is also capable of being victimized and deceived, but in Congreve's scheme of things, this vulnerability is a minor drawback.

That Congreve should have stressed the satiric elements

in his most romantic play may appear curious, but in the prologue he begins by speaking of *Love for Love* in terms of a varied comic feast with "Humour" and "Plot," but of the chief ingredient as satire:

> We've something too, to gratifie ill Nature,
> (If there be any here) and that is Satire.
> Tho' Satire scarce dares grin, 'tis grown so mild
> Or shews its Teeth, as if it smil'd
> As Asses Thistles, Poets mumble Wit,
> And dare not bite, for fear of being bit.

Congreve proceeds to lament the demise of satire since [William] Wycherley's Manly in *The Plain Dealer* lashed the age, and he clearly conceives of satire in terms of direct invective, such as that delivered by a constantly satiric spokesman—a misanthrope like Manly or personified figures like Folly or Truth. Congreve's very imagery refers to the hieroglyph of satire with its smiling face, ass's ears, and lash. Although it seems fair enough to allow Congreve some knowledge of his intention, the question of what the satire is all about remains.

When *Love for Love* was revived in 1965 by the National Theatre of England, many critics felt that heavy sociological overtones had been added to the play and regretted the passing of the stylized production in the 1940's with John Gielgud, which had taken [Charles] Lamb's concept of the artificiality of Restoration comedy as a starting point for a vision of a world which had existed only in the elaborate imagination of those playwrights. Confronted with a realistic interpretation and with sets determinedly placing the play in the late seventeenth century, the critics of the 1960's discovered that it was far more materialistic than they had supposed. Penelope Gilliat [*The Observer Weekend Review* (24 October 1965)], who thought it should be renamed "Love for Loot," probably was unaware that, seven years before Congreve's play was produced at Lincoln's Inn Fields Theatre, [Thomas] Durfey had already written a play called *Love for Money* (1689) and that Congreve may have been echoing Durfey's title.

A comparison of the two plays is enlightening. Whereas Durfey presents a situation involving a general chase after an heiress of fifty thousand pounds—a girl who is still in a boarding school among her fellow "Romps," girls just entering puberty—Congreve reduces the fortune of his heiress, gives her maturity and intelligence, and reserves the adolescent role for Miss Prue. Moreover, Durfey's play has a burlesque quality and a wryness not found in Congreve. As absurd as Congreve's Miss Prue is, she is not so off-color as Durfey's Molly and Jenny, who at thirteen and a half have just discovered sex and cannot tell whether or not it is as interesting as cheesecakes and custard. At one point in Durfey's play there is a dialogue of sensibility between the hero, Young Meriton, and the heiress, Mirtilla, over the question of love without money. She is ignorant of her fortune, though he is not; and, when he mendaciously urges her to marry him and live in poverty, she exclaims:

> 'Tis not for my own sake that I deny, but Sir for yours; if we were married, perhaps I should love ye, nay love ye dearly; perhaps have children too, some half a dozen pretty smiling Blessings

to cling around and help Life's tedious Journey with the dear nonsense of their prating Stories. But should the freezing hand of Want afflict us, what should we do, but sit by our small fire, Tears in our Eyes and throbbing Griefs at Heart, to see our little Flock of unfledg'd *Cupids,* shivering with Cold as wanting necessaries, who looking wishly on us seem to say, why would you marry thus to make us miserable.

Though he may have agreed with the idea behind it, Congreve wisely chose to avoid such appeals to sentimentality. Yet Durfey's play is actually far more bitter: the two schoolgirls, Molly and Jenny, are dragged away by their seducers (one of the girls symbolically drops her doll), while Young Meriton deceives Mirtilla to get her fortune. For all its farcical comedy, Durfey's play is about the rape of innocence, but Congreve's is about what the title suggests: love for the sake of love. That some men might marry strictly for money was the immediate context of his play; that Valentine should act unwisely and still find his reward is the beautiful, satisfying fairy tale which Congreve serves as a delightful feast.

The satire, then, is not concerned with the problem of love for money, but with the entire context of social action; and, for this purpose, Congreve creates a cast of satiric figures. Valentine's friend, Scandal, is actually a "plain dealer," who is cynical about all human motivation, particularly that of women. Valentine's servant, Jeremy Fetch, regards the social world of his master with much the same skepticism and pragmatism with which Henry Straker considers the actions of Jack Tanner in G. B. Shaw's *Man and Superman.* Even the "fools" are capable of satiric invective. Ben is brought in from the sea to present an unworldly but not unperceptive insight into London life, while Prue comes from the country to learn the art of lying and deceit—the art of being a woman in society. Even Tattle has moments of vision, if not of himself, at least of the world around him; and the absurd old men, Sir Sampson and old Foresight, occasionally offer a corrective to the lives of those around them. More than any of Congreve's plays, then *Love for Love* involves debate and points of view. It would be doing violence to Congreve's art to suggest that it was a play of ideas, but it is one of contrasts and paradoxes.

Some of the ambiguity of *Love for Love* may be due to Congreve's borrowings from Molière's *Don Juan* (1665). In addition to adapting the entire scene involving the attempted gulling of the scrivener, Trapland, Congreve seems to have taken some major hints from that play. What if Don Juan were to reform through true love? What if he were to be seen as a victim rather than as a vicious seducer of everyone in sight? Molière has his hero assume the garb of a hypocrite to fool his enemies and win over his father; Congreve has his hero assume the role of a madman who believes he is Truth. Molière's hero, like Valentine, has almost ruined his father through his debts; but suppose the father were cruel and lacking in understanding? And what if Don Juan had to face a woman like Angelica, witty, sophisticated, and intelligent? Could this experience not save him and reform his life? Need he be led by the Commandant down to hell? Though Don Juan usually acts more like a villain than a hero, more a Maskwell than a Mellefont, Don Juan, like Valentine, serves a satiric function in his attacks on the hypocrisy of the world.

WITS AND FOOLS

But it would be a mistake to regard *Love for Love* in the light of any single influence. The relation between Valentine and Angelica is very much like that between Captain Darewell and Berenice in Durfey's *The Marriage Hater Match'd* (1692); the mad scenes as well as the character of Tattle owe something to Durfey's *The Richmond Heiress* (1693); and the general sophistication of the discussions of sex and seduction are indebted to [Thomas] Southerne's *The Wive's Excuse* (1692). *Love for Love* is almost as derivative as **The Old Batchelor,** but never was a play more Congreve's own. The unique combination of character, language, and plot—all are his. Most of all the wit is pure Congreve, for, while [John] Vanbrugh was often more insightful and Southerne more subtle, no other writer of the time had so much fancy.

Valentine's opening dialogue with Jeremy allows Congreve to display his own and his characters' powers of fancy as his hero suggests that he resolves to rail at the world and to take revenge upon the wits by writing a play, a suggestion which brings forth Jeremy's offer to resign and his brilliant attack on the authors at Will's Coffee House:

> I never see it, but the Spirit of Famine appears to me, sometimes like a decay'd Porter, worn out with Pimping, and carrying *Billet doux* and Songs; not like other Porters for Hire, but for the Jests sake. Now like a thin Chairman, melted down to half his Proportion with carrying a Poet upon Tick, to visit some great Fortune; and his Fare to be paid like the Wages of Sin, either at the Day of Marriage, or the Day of Death. . . . Sometimes like a bilk'd Bookseller, with a meagre terrify'd Countenance, that looks as if he had written for himself. . . . And lastly, in the Form of a worn-out Punk, with Verses in her Hand, which her Vanity had preferr'd to Settlements . . . as if she were carrying her Linnen to the Paper-Mill, to be converted into Folio Books of Warning to all young Maids, not to prefer Poetry to good sense; or lying in the Arms of a needy Wit, before the Embraces of a wealthy Fool.
>
> (I. i. 108-32)

When Scandal enters a few minutes later to be informed of Valentine's desire to rail like a satirist in his writings, his response is in a different style:

> Rail? At whom? the whole World? Impotent and vain. Who would die a Martyr to Sense in a Country where the Religion is Folly? You may stand at Bay for a while; but when the full Cry is against you, you shan't have fair play for your Life. If you can't be fairly run down by the Hounds, you will be treacherously shot by the Huntsmen.—No, turn Pimp, Flatterer, Quack, Lawyer, Parson, be Chaplain to an Atheist, or Stallion to an old Woman, any thing but Poet; a Modern Poet is worse, more servile, timorous, and fawning, than any I have nam'd: Without

> you could retrieve the Ancient Honours of the Name, recall the Stage of Athens, and be allow'd the Force of open honest Satire.
>
> (I. ii. 25-39)

In these passages we have a good example of . . . Congreve's ability to render each character distinct with the individual's own words. Jeremy, Rabelaisian and expansive in his satire, begins with a personification of the spirit of famine, which haunts the world of poetry and wit around Will's; and he then builds a pattern of related similes, though the porter and the old prostitute are connected to poetry only through a fanciful process of association. But this seemingly illogical process (John Locke called it in his *Essay concerning Human Understanding* a kind of "madness") allows Jeremy to deliver his wry warning to Valentine all the more effectively. Jeremy's wit is both less sharp and more expansive than that of his betters. Scandal is almost a satirist by profession; in his diatribes he joins together pimps, quacks, lawyers, parsons, and poets, implying, by a device that [Alexander] Pope was to use so brilliantly a few years later, that they are all the same. Scandal's longing to "recall the Stage of Athens" and with it the strong, personal satire of Aristophanes is significant; he is all for direct attack and abuse.

Valentine's responses to his servant and friend are pithy and tend toward understatement. When the crowd of duns is announced below, he merely remarks on the resemblance between the debtor and the great man who is courted by those seeking favors. It is left to Scandal to take up the suggestion and to moralize and apply it to the ways of the world. When in his pretended madness, he assumes the paradoxical role of Truth, Valentine also becomes a railer and a satirist; but, as Congreve remarked, by assuming another persona Valentine functions almost as a new character.

Though Jeremy, Valentine, and Scandal are clearly the satirists within the play, the norm from which they satirize the world is not always too clear. Since Valentine has been indiscreet; Jeremy, foolish in remaining with an impoverished master; and Scandal, unwise in railing against the evils of the world, their standard can hardly be good sense. Some of the basis for their satirical stance appears in their treatment of Trapland. He is a fool, or at least he is made to seem one; yet he has come, like the other creditors, to collect what is his due. When he finally demands payment, Scandal threatens to make him regurgitate the wine he has drunk at their invitation. To Trapland's protest that he never asked for the wine, Scandal retorts, "And how do you expect to have your Mony again, when a Gentleman has spent it." If the analogy bears little logical connection to the situation, it does convey the contempt of a gentleman for a merchant, a wit for a fool, and a young man for an old one. The standpoint is that of the libertine ethic which regards age as ridiculous and which places a high premium on freedom of spirit and the play of passions. Valentine may be in the process of changing his philosophical position from Epicurus to Epictetus, but there is little sign of it in the play; and he has certainly lost none of his wit in the process. He has few of the conventional virtues of Mellefont. His disgust with Margery, the nurse of his illegitimate boy, for failing to smother him in bed may be part of his witty pose, but it is hardly endearing. If he is rewarded at the end, it is for his generosity and *noblesse*. In short, **Love for Love** uses an aristocratic standard of behavior to belabor its gallery of fools.

But Congreve's gift is to make the world of the fools a very human world. When Tattle enters and is informed that Scandal will never speak well of him, he exclaims with some justification, "How Inhuman!" For, if Tattle is silly with his elaborate pretense at secrecy about his affairs with women, while revealing all, at least his gallery of paintings is composed of portraits of the women he has seduced. Scandal's gallery, on the other hand, has mainly caricatures and what he calls "Hieroglyphics," symbolic representations of the vices, passions, and professions. Scandal and the satirists deal in a non-human world of grotesques; Tattle is a fool, but his folly is human.

The same may be said of Foresight, who is so foolish and indeed so helpless in his folly as to be a character at whom we laugh without the slightest disapproval, for he transcends moral judgment. He is Congreve's finest "humours" character, for his superstition dominates his entire life, whether as an astrologer or a cuckold. His old nurse treats him like a child as does his wife, whose sleep he has never disturbed in all their years of marriage. Angelica teases him about his cuckolded state, but his anger flares only when he thinks she is insulting the "Celestial Science." Her remarks to her uncle are a good example of the way so much of the play involves a series of extended images on the subject of astrology and (after Ben's entrance) the sea. "I have a mind to go abroad," says Angelica, "and if you won't lend me your Coach, I'll take a Hackney, or a Chair, and leave you to erect a Scheme, and find who's in Conjunction with your Wife. Why don't you keep her at home, if you're jealous of her when she's abroad? You know my Aunt is a little Retrograde (as you call it) in her Nature. Uncle, I'm afraid you are not Lord of the Ascendant, ha, ha, ha." When Foresight becomes angry enough to attempt a witticism on the lack of virgins among the signs of the zodiac, he is so ineffectual that he merely provokes Angelica to genuine laughter.

They are interrupted by the threatening but equally foolish figure of Sir Sampson Legend who, in the extravagant language of a traveler, addresses old Foresight as Nostradamus, Fircu, Albumazar, Haly, and any other astrologer of contemporary books of fortune that pops into his mind. Like old Foresight, Sir Sampson is a "humours" character, reminiscent of Sir Epicure Mammon in [Ben] Jonson's *Alchemist* in the way ideas seem to grow in his mind and in the way he convinces himself of mad ideas through his own language. He enters with a Hobbesian theory that a child owes his parents a debt for having been conceived by them, rather than owing them obedience because of gratitude—the more customary attitude of the times. Sir Sampson is an egoist; and, as George Meredith suggested, egoism inevitably brings down the imps of laughter. He boasts of his travels, tries to force his sons to actions they find odious, convinces himself that Angelica can find him an attractive man, and boasts of his sexual powers. He is capable of the most servile flattery of Foresight to get him to marry his daughter Prue to Ben, and of deceiving his

son with false affection when he thinks him mad. In other words, he is the ideal comic villain—threatening enough to endanger the future of the lovers but foolish enough to make us doubt the possibility of his succeeding.

Suspended somewhere between the wits and the fools is Ben, that "veriest Wag in Nature; an absolute Sea-Wit," as Angelica calls him mockingly. Certainly Ben is not a thorough fool. Though he may be innocent enough to be tricked by Mrs. Frail, even she knows that he will not be overly surprised if he is rejected by her. The fact is that life at sea has completely separated Ben from the other characters socially, morally, and linguistically. His values are relatively simple: "We're merry Folks, we Sailors, we han't much to care for. Thus we live at Sea; eat Bisket, and drink Flip; put on a clean Shirt once a Quarter—Come home, and lye with our Landladies once a Year, get rid of a little Mony; and then put off with the next fair Wind" (III. xv. 89-94). When he attempts to be witty, he speaks entirely in nautical similes and metaphors; and most of our laughter is directed at the absurdity of these remarks, not at their cleverness. But Ben wins our respect because he is entirely his own man. He is willing to obey his father only to the extent of proposing to Miss Prue; and, when Scandal suggests that Ben might be lying, he tells him, "Look you, Friend, it's nothing to me, whether you believe it or no. What I say is true; d'ye see. . . ." Angelica may mock him, but she cannot destroy the integrity of his world any more than he can impinge upon hers.

Ben has something of the quality of Voltaire's Huron in *L'Ingénu*. Both are noble savages let loose on society, and both make social manners seem a bit stiff and hypocritical. Instead of a delicate or subtle song of love, Ben and his shipmates bawl out a bawdy ballad. With little knowledge of gallantry in love, Ben can still give good advice about women to both his father and Tattle. Ben is not the first sailor to appear on the Restoration stage. Wycherley's Manly in *The Plain Dealer* (1677) was a ship captain, and Captains Porpus and Wilding in Durfey's *Sir Barnaby Whigg* (1681) are both sea wits. There is even a captain named Sea Wit in William Davenant's *News from Plymouth* (1635). And even the nautical language was fairly commonplace, for something like Ben's accent appears in Porpus's remarks to his wife on finding two men in her room: he sees her "in danger to prove a Fire ship—forc'd to a surrender by a thorough-shot betwixt Wind and Water, and then to be Mann'd by the Enemy in the Fore-Castle and Poop—with a Pox t'ee." But Ben, a far cry from Durfey's licentious cuckold, remains at the end unchanged and uncontaminated by society. He has been rejected by two women and disinherited by his father, but he still has the sea and other lands to sail to, and, for him, that is the important thing.

His feminine counterpart, Miss Prue, is another matter. Where Ben's world, in which "it's but a Folly to lie," has its own very real values, hers is merely the reverse of that of the adult and the city: she has yet to grow up and lose her country ways. For Congreve, the country can only mean ignorance and barbarity; and childhood, the lack of that maturity which constitutes a complete human being. The Restoration understood very literally those laws that

Anne Bracegirdle, the actress who originated the roles of many of Congreve's heroines, including Angelica in Love for Love *and Millamant in* the Way of the World.

exempted children, along with the insane, from a role in society. Even in the next century, biographers and novelists avoided lengthy discussions of their subjects' childhood, because they regarded such material as trivial or "low." Miss Prue is only at the threshold of life—adult life. Old enough to be seduced, she is ready to run off with Robin, the butler, when Foresight refuses to let her have Tattle. She represents that paradox that so much delighted the libertines—animal sensuality slightly veiled by an innocent education. What she must learn before she can be considered socially acceptable is to control her sex drive or, better yet, to disguise it; and Mr. Tattle willingly begins her education in deceit.

It should be pointed out that the art of lying and of disguise is as much a part of Angelica's life as it is of Mrs. Foresight's and Mrs. Frail's, for it is little more than the art of being a woman in society. Angelica hides her feelings toward Valentine until the very end; but we know just how strong her feelings are from her concern at his madness, from her asides when she feels she is being tricked, and from her final confession that she may seem as fond in the future as she appeared indifferent before. When Valentine, dropping his mask of insanity, asks for some answer to his proposal of love, she pretends to think him

mad: "Wou'd any thing, but a Madman, complain of Uncertainty? Uncertainty and Expectation are the Joys of Life. Security is an insipid thing, and the overtaking and possessing of a Wish, discovers the folly of the Chase. Never let us know one another better; for the Pleasure of a Masquerade is done, when we come to show our Faces; but I'll tell you two things before I leave you; I am not the Fool you take me for; and you are mad, and don't know it." The speech bears some resemblances to those of Belinda and Cynthia in the earlier plays [in *The Old Batchelor* and *The Double Dealer,* respectively], but Angelica's defense of disguise is itself defensive. She is sure of her affection for Valentine, but she is not at all certain how disinterested he is. She is, after all, an heiress; and, if she is not surrounded by a train of fops like Millamant [in *The Way of the World*], she is pursued by Tattle and Sir Sampson. We also know that Valentine wasted his four thousand pounds in vying with the crowd of suitors about her. Thus, she lies and affects an uncharacteristic coldness and self-interest to protect her tender emotions as well as her fortune.

What gives Angelica the self-control that all the other women in the play lack? When Mr. Tattle gives Prue her lesson in lying at the instigation of Prue's step-mother and her sister, his central lesson is that women must give a clue to their real feelings while giving a surface impression that is exactly opposite. "O Lord," exclaims Prue, "I swear this is pure,—I like it better than our old-fashion'd Country way of speaking one's Mind" (II. xi. 49-51). To test his pupil, Tattle asks Prue to kiss him. She refuses and quickly kisses him; Tattle leads his "apt Scholar" to the bedroom a few minutes later. Only the entrance of the Nurse prevents the final act of seduction. Prue learns nearly everything but discretion, a quality rarely found in a young girl; but in this instance she is not very different from Mrs. Foresight and her sister. Mrs. Foresight sleeps with Scandal after sending her husband off to bed and then denies everything the next morning. As for Mrs. Frail, in the words of Scandal, "we all know her." Only an education in the ways of the world separates Prue from the other women, but their actions may vary according to their condition. Mrs. Foresight has to look elsewhere than to her husband for sexual satisfaction, and her sister has not had the good fortune to find a husband until Tattle is tricked into matrimony. Now Angelica has two substitutes for sexual relations denied to the other ladies. She is genuinely in love with Valentine with a love that looks forward to marriage, and she spends a large part of her time torturing him by pretending complete indifference. The sexual aggression that goes into such behavior can sustain women on the coldest nights.

In creating the character of Angelica, Congreve drew on a common contemporary stage type which found its archetype in [Francis] Beaumont and [John] Fletcher's *The Scornful Lady* (1616), a play which Congreve obviously knew thoroughly. The Scornful Lady punishes Loveless, her admirer, with commands and indifference. She confesses in an excellent soliloquy that she does not understand her motivation for humiliating her admirer but admits, "I had rather die sometimes than not disgrace in public him whom people think I love, and do't with oaths, and am in earnest then." Only when Loveless provokes her jealously does she yield. A similar type is Berenice in Durfey's *The Marriage Hater Match'd* (1692), who rants against "that hellish vice called Love," and says, after she surrenders to it, that her lover will find her actually as soft and kind as "a plain dull silly House-dove."

MADNESS AND TRUE LOVE

The pleasure these women find is partly in revenge, the obverse passion of love, and partly in the power which their sex gives them over men. As Congreve observed throughout his writings and particularly in his love poems and songs, the lover craves favors of his mistress; and every favor she gives is a gain for the man. The woman's sovereignty ends with marriage; until that time, the man is the suitor, obeying his mistress's whims unquestioningly. For the woman, marriage involves obedience to the will of the man, and Congreve's women are reluctant to surrender what power they have. Marriage is a goal received, and the achievement is always less satisfying than the pursuit. As Congreve's Semele sings:

> I love and am lov'd, yet more I desire;
> Ah, how foolish a Thing is Fruition!
> As one Passion cools, some other takes Fire,
> And I'm still in a longing Condition.
>
> (III. ii. 1-4)

Thus, while she still has power over her lover, Angelica makes him suffer by her scorn, by her indifference, and, finally, by the greatest affront she can offer him—a prospective marriage to his cruel father, Sir Sampson.

But, instead of using Valentine's forfeiture of his right to his inheritance to increase her personal estate, Angelica tears up the deed and addresses her "Generous Valentine" in words of deep affection: "Had I the World to give you, it cou'd not make me worthy of so generous and faithful a Passion: Here's my Hand, my Heart was always yours, and struggl'd very hard to make this utmost Trial of your Vertue" (V. xii. 71-5). Her confession shows no reversal of character comparable to Durfey's transformation of Berenice into a "silly House-dove." Angelica has revealed her feelings clearly enough to the audience when she tells Tattle, who has found in Valentine's feigned madness an excuse to angle for Angelica, "O fie for shame, hold your Tongue, A passionate Lover, and five Senses in perfection! when you are as mad as Valentine, I'll believe you love me, and the maddest shall take me" (IV. xvi. 24-7). This statement is a key one, for the madness, or at least the irrationality, of love is the central theme of the play.

With Valentine, the madness of love has caused the ruin of his estate, but it eventually results in his gaining Angelica; for, if the alternative to true love is a life spent in the pursuit of self-interest or in the folly of self-love, what choice have Valentine and Angelica but to plunge into madness? And, if Valentine is mad to ruin himself for love and Angelica for marrying him in his poverty, what are we to think of the other characters—Foresight, for example, who, coming to hear Valentine prophesy, finds in the ravings of Truth things "Mysterious and Hieroglyphical"? Actually, Valentine's statements after he assumes the dis-

guise of Truth are merely realistic, satirical descriptions of everyday life, perhaps the least mad parts of the play:

> Oh, Prayers will be said in empty Churches, at the usual Hours. Yet you will see such zealous Faces behind Counters, as if Religion were to be sold in every Shop. Oh things will go methodically in the City, the Clocks will strike twelve at Noon, and the horn'd Herd Buz in the Exchange at Two. Wives and Husbands will drive distinct Trades, and Care and Pleasure separately occupy the Family. Coffee-Houses will be full of Smoak and Strategem. And the cropt Prentice, that sweeps his Master's Shop in the Morning, may ten to one dirty his Sheets before Night. But there are two things that you will see very strange; which are wanton Wives, with their Legs at Liberty, and tame Cuckolds, with Chains about their Necks. But hold, I must examine you before I go further; you look suspiciously. Are you a Husband?
>
> (IV. xv. 22-39)

Had Foresight even the perception of a Polonius [in Shakespeare's *Hamlet*], he might have found a method in Valentine's ravings. And is not Ben right in thinking that his father has gone mad in planning to marry Angelica at his age?

The maddest joke of all comes near the end as Tattle and Mrs. Frail sneak off disguised as friar and nun, respectively; the one thinks to marry Angelica; the other, Valentine. Their costumes represent a direct reversal of roles for "Turk Tattle" and the promiscuous Mrs. Frail, and their marriage provides the properly absurd contrast with the union of the hero and heroine. Congreve has frequently been accused of bad taste in resorting to the hackneyed, improbable device of a marriage in disguise. Gellert Alleman, in his *Matrimonial Law and the Materials of Restoration Comedy,* has shown that in Restoration England marriages in masks did occur on rare occasions, but that a marriage involving some mistake in the parties participating in the ceremony could be renounced. To search for a justification for Congreve's device on historical grounds, however, would be a mistake. It belongs to the absurd dramatic world of *Love for Love,* and that world has only the most tangential relation to reality; it is a final mad trick in which the two most self-seeking characters find their match in a marriage which will be as bad as that of Valentine and Angelica will be ideal.

Valentine points out the moral to Tattle: "Tattle, I thank you, you would have interposed between me and Heav'n; but Providence laid Purgatory in your way—You have but Justice." "I never lik'd any Body less in my Life," says Tattle of his new wife; and Mrs. Frail tells her sister, "Nothing but his being my Husband could have made me like him less" (V. xi. 37-8). Valentine, on the other hand, has attained what is the only "Heav'n" on earth: a good marriage. There is another moral—this one delivered by Angelica to Scandal—a feminist moral. Angelica argues that the fault in courtship usually lies with the men, not with the women. If there were more lovers like Valentine to persevere in their love "even to Martyrdom," there would be more women to reward them. The language in this section is obviously religious, and its significance did not escape Collier's notice. The fact is that Congreve is placing his "Heav'n" in the present life rather than in the one to come. *Love for Love* is a moving play, but not if we are oriented to thinking of life as a vale of tears and as a stopping place on the way to a better life. Congreve distributes his rewards and punishments on earth.

In actuality, only Sir Sampson and Tattle are severely punished; and this fact says something about the nature of the play. Congreve has presented a plot; but, with the exception of the marriage in disguise, there is little mechanical plotting. Our interest is sustained mainly by the characters; and, in this sense, *Love for Love* is as original as *The Double Dealer.* The characters are drawn so clearly, so individually, that they seem to exist outside the action of the play and, like [Luigi] Pirandello's family in *Six Characters,* to continue their lives after the curtain falls: Old Foresight will continue being cuckolded by his wife; Ben, go back to the sea and his dreamy life; Scandal, continue his materialistic, satirical approach to the world; and Prue, grow up. As her ignorance is replaced by sophistication, lies will come more naturally to her.

Love for Love is the height of Congreve's mimetic art. Because it is so artful, it seems entirely self-contained; because it is so real, it seems to burst its borders in time and space. Congreve encloses his action in twenty-four hours, but he has taken it out of the suggested confinement of time and space which we find in *The Double Dealer.* Ben is pulled in from the sea, Prue from the country; Foresight is a wanderer among the stars; Sir Sampson has "made a Cuckold of a King, and the present Majesty of *Bantam*" is his illegitimate child; and the place of assignation for both Mrs. Foresight and Mrs. Frail is that house of ill fame, The World's-End. This expansiveness is also represented by a wider spectrum of characters from different social strata.

Congreve also makes a distinct technical advance in *Love for Love.* There is his usual deliberate building up of characters before they appear on the stage, but Congreve now handles this method in a way that appears perfectly natural. The dialogue is as witty as that in *The Old Batchelor,* but the association of ideas—the process which Congreve imitated in his witty dialogue—operates without strain and with the quality of ordinary conversation. The first exchange between Foresight and Sir Sampson, in which each becomes progressively more irritated, is something Congreve would have been incapable of a few years before. And most of all, Congreve has found his mode—lyricism, romanticism, and optimism superimposed upon that world of cynical libertines and imbecile cuckolds which was the tableaux of Restoration comedy. This play was his gayest and in many ways his best comedy. It is hardly surprising that, after this triumph, he should have turned to *The Mourning Bride* and tragedy as a new field to conquer. (pp. 107-21)

> *Maximillian E. Novak, in his* William Congreve, *Twayne Publishers, Inc., 1971, 197 p.*

Retta M. Taney (essay date 1979)

[*In the following excerpt, Taney examines the madness theme in* Love for Love, *focusing particularly on Valentine's demonstration of two definitions of insanity—"divine creative madness" and "a treatable mental disorder"—in the "mad" scenes of Act IV. Valentine's ultimate success in the play, the critic argues, represents a "triumph of healthy chaos" over the "corrupt sanity" of society.*]

From the title page of Tonson's 1695 edition of *Love for Love* through the final scene, the theme of madness and the treatment of the disease are of paramount importance to the plot, tone, and balance of the play. The title page epigraph is from Horace *II Satire* iii, ll. 184 and 271: "Stripped of lands and paternal wealth, he goes mad by regular system and method." This phrase indicates the psychological bent of the play and suggests classical overtones. In the course of the play, madness itself is dramatically defined both in the classical creative sense and in the contemporary destructive sense. The juxtaposition of these two antithetical approaches ensures a conscious tension in dramatic treatment of Valentine's situation.

Despite multiple critical readings of the play, there is a basic agreement about the ultimate triumph of positive creativity which shapes the principal characters. In *The Development of English Drama in the Late Seventeenth Century,* Robert D. Hume acknowledges that the "fairytale quality is marked at the end"; Rose Zimbardo, in *Wycherley's Drama,* credits Congreve with showing "through action and through character disclosure . . . the good nature, the sentimental goodness of heart, that lies beneath the brilliant witty manners of hero and heroine"; Bonamy Dobrée, in *Restoration Comedy,* affirms that "a passionate ardour for the finer side of life breathes constantly from his [Congreve's] pages"; and in *A Preface to Restoration Drama,* John Harold Wilson sees that finer side in a hero and heroine who are "good natured, and . . . cling to a few principles of decency and honor." This suggestion of positive results is not necessarily achieved through the most direct method, and the idealized end is only effected through the indirection of the "play" of the mad scene.

In the first three acts, Congreve prepares the audience for the central scenes of mock lunacy in Act IV. Shortly after the opening of Act I, Valentine confides to his servant Jeremy and his friend, Scandal, that he will write a play in order to "rail in my writings and be revenged." Scandal—described in the Dramatis Personae as "a free speaker"—argues against impotent raving:

> Turn pimp, flatterer, quack, lawyer, parson . . .
> anything but poet; a modern poet is worse, more
> servile, timorous, and fawning, than any I have
> named; without you could retrieve the ancient
> honours of the name, recall the stage of Athens,
> and be allowed the force of open honest satire.
>
> (I. ii)

Scandal's advice may be cynical, but it is realistic. Both young men are aware that, as Virginia Ogden Birdsall says in *Wild Civility: The English Comic Spirit on the Restoration Stage,* "in a case like Valentine's, where his prosperity depends on social acceptance and where there has been a clear commitment to the adult world, free speaking is only possible by indirection." The only escape from this adult world is into the world of childhood. Valentine can only achieve the spontaneity of the child by performing the play he has been threatening to write. Although Valentine never executes his design on paper, his alter ego in the mad scene fulfills the wildest hopes of his misanthropic attitude. He speaks out with force and brilliance before the astonished characters who are both his audience and his cast.

This desire to write, this suggestion of inspiration—in the classical sense—suggests the divine creative madness revered by the ancients. On the opposite side of the coin, the audience is assured that "love and pleasurable expense" have been Valentine's greatest faults. Although these youthful follies make him sympathetic, this love, which could be interpreted as the disease known as "love melancholy" and pleasurable expense, an indication of dissipation, are both factors which lead not to divine madness but to a treatable mental disorder. In this precarious condition, which combines divine madness and treatable lunacy, only a catalyst is necessary to trigger Valentine's behavior.

As the domestic difficulties between father and son stalemate, Sir Sampson seeks a solution in Ben, his most malleable child. Ben and Valentine never appear together on stage: for Ben has found, naturally, the world that his elder brother must create artificially. For Ben there is no lasting adult world. His commitment to civilization lasts as long as he is "port-bound," but his heart remains "as sound as a biscuit." Although he never achieves Valentine's depth of discovery, his happiness is assured by his willingness "to retreat to the world of innocence whence he has come" [according to Birdsall]. Although Johnson may complain, "The Sailor is not accounted very natural" [Samuel Johnson, "The Life of William Congreve," in *The Comedies of William Congreve,* edited by Norman Marshall, 1948], Ben can make justifiable accusations of madness against the sophisticates who would ensnare him in their treachery. The threat posed by the deed of conveyance which transfers Valentine's right to his inheritance to his brother Ben pushes Valentine over the edge of dramatic sanity and into the virtuoso mad scenes of Act IV.

The juxtaposition of Valentine's threatened madness with the activities of old Foresight, that student of ancient astrologers crammed with spurious knowledge of the future, plays into the classical theme which functions in the comedy. The establishment of this frame early in the play leaves Valentine free to go as mad as he likes as long as he includes classical allusions and contemporary references in his ravings. But Congreve sets limits on his performance by balancing him and Angelica.

If Valentine and Ben avoid meeting because Valentine protests, "when he rises I must set," there are precious few confrontations between Valentine and his love. When they are together, Angelica is at the height of her power over Valentine. Her control lies as much in her refusal to admit her love for Valentine as in her barbed view of their situation. In *William Congreve,* Maximillian E. Novak argues that "For the woman, marriage involves obedience to the will of the man, and Congreve's women are reluctant to

surrender what power they have." This situation is apparent from the couple's first meeting in III. iii. Angelica is protesting that she has never acknowledged love for Valentine; he accuses her of uncertainty—of saying neither "yes" nor "no." Angelica immediately parries: "You mistake indifference for uncertainty; I never had concern enough to ask myself the question." She makes free with her denials.

In Act III, she denies to Tattle her "passion" for Valentine. The denial is not only consistent with her tantalizing inconsistency but it also serves to mark her as a character free of an overpowering humor, a defect which would imbalance her function in the order of the play. Her wholesome chiding of her Uncle Foresight for his obsession with portents and her warning to him about his wife—"There are a great many horned beasts among the twelve signs, uncle. But cuckolds go to heaven"—is the warning of a playful but clear-sighted woman. The establishment of Angelica's solidity is necessary to the moment when she, as physician, will refuse to support Valentine's carefully created mock delusionary system.

In Act III. x, just past the middle of the play, Scandal appears with the news of Valentine's breakdown:

> Something has appeared to your son Valentine. . . . He speaks little, yet says he has a world to say; asks for his father and the wise Foresight. . . . He has secrets to impart, I suppose to you two.

Significantly, Valentine appeals to the quack astrologer and the cynic—the hopelessly outdated man and the man of the times. As a believer, Foresight has no real function in the mad scene and is prudently excluded from anything more than a choric participation. But Sir Sampson, the unnatural father, the conniver and contriver, who has proudly asserted, "there's no time but the time present, there's no more to be said of what's past, and all that is to come will happen," is ripe to be the physician of his ailing son.

The central "mad" scenes of Act IV deal with the treatment of the disease in three stages by three different types of physicians. First, there is an attempt to deceive the patient by figures who should represent order and protection and whose dealings with the madman result in failure. Second, the patient is given therapy by the one physician whose very presence, though desired by the madman, is a threat to his stability. Third, the patient begins to cure himself in a seemingly whimsical yet psychologically sound solution which resolves itself in Act V.

In *The First Modern Comedies: the Significance of Etherege, Wycherley, and Congreve,* Norman Holland contends that *Love for Love* "is based on the idea of an education or therapy." This concept is illustrated as the "mad" scenes are played out, and Valentine, who is trying to buy time by playing at being *non compos* while showing a taste for the "open honest satire" called for by Scandal, is both educating his antagonists and being educated by his wholehearted commitment to his "madness." This double activity puts him in the ranks of the late-century rake who is moving "to a new ethic of communion founded in knowledge of self " [John Traugatt, "The Rake's Progress from Court to Comedy: A Study in Comic Form," *Studies in English Literature* 6 (Summer 1966)].

If the madness of Valentine is essential in a consideration of the play, performances of his mad scenes should not be ignored. Kenneth Muir ["The Comedies of William Congreve," in *Restoration Theatre,* ed. John Russell Brown and Bernard Harris, 1967] insists that the play "acts even better than it reads" and that "Valentine's pretended madness [is] inevitably successful on stage."

In the twentieth century, Valentine has received two significant interpretations before audiences who represent a society particularly attuned to the systematic treatment of mental disorders. When Sir John Gielgud played the role in London in 1943, he was given points for "a witty grace, a perfect command of the Congrevean prose rhythms and the nicest sense of Shakespearian parody in the mad scene [*Times* (9 April 1943)]. Gielgud had burlesqued his own popular interpretation of Hamlet, still fresh in audience memory, and, consequently, insured the success of the scenes. Muir seems to be recalling Gielgud when he notes that "the actor who keeps Congreve's rhythms automatically registers his points." The Hamlet allusion was not simply a clever theatrical point of reference for a well-informed audience. Arthur W. Hoffman has found clear parallels between Valentine's lines and those of the Prince who also chooses the antic disposition ["Allusions and the Definition of Themes in *Love for Love,*" in *The Author in His Work,* ed. Louis L. Martz and Aubrey Williams, 1978].

In 1965, the National Theatre Company of Great Britain mounted the play with a young actor, John Stride, who seemed to concern himself more with broad, superficial antics and less with the complexity of Valentine's situation. By 1965 the mad scenes of the play were considered the necessary accoutrements of a classic. The heavy sociological overtones of the 1965 production caused a regretful backward glance at Sir John's 1943 stylization, and the critical suggestion that "updating" a classic in a thesis production which stressed an overwhelmingly mercenary bent was not necessarily an improvement of the piece or a service to the theater.

In Act IV, Valentine does not appear until the sixth scene. He immediately begins a process of self-identification. To Sir Sampson's introduction of himself and Buckram, Valentine responds with an identification of himself—"I am Truth"—and an invective against those who abuse this identity:

> I am Truth. . . . I have been sworn out of Westminster Hall the first day of every term. . . . But I'll tell you one thing; it's a question that would puzzle an arithmetician . . . whether the Bible saves more souls in Westminster Abbey, or damns more in Westminster Hall.
>
> (IV. vi)

The presence of the lawyer Buckram provokes the Truth personality; for Buckram, far from being a valid representative of lawful authority, is the archetypal legal trickster whose perversion of the law makes him the target for the attack by the mistreated Truth. Buckram, who has come

to aid in the duping of Valentine, is himself duped and unwittingly supports Valentine's first major sham delusion. This support is essential for the confrontation with Sir Sampson. Significantly, Valentine asks for and receives his father's blessing. Sir Sampson's seeming solicitude provokes Scandal's aside: "Miracle! The monster grows loving." Within that brief encounter, a Christian union is ironically fulfilled. Valentine's identification with Truth is one step from an identification with Christ, a natural psychotic progression. He looks upon his father who "loves" him and thus the Trinity of Father, Son, and Holy Spirit—theologically the eternal love of the Father for the Son—is established. This unity operates only for the purpose of ultimate disruption; for Sir Sampson is an unnatural father and the love is a semantic trick to make Valentine sign the deed of conveyance. Ultimately, Valentine completely perplexes his father, who admits: "I know not what to do, or say, nor which way to go." Thus the first physicians, Buckram and Sir Sampson, are completely routed by the madman's vision of himself as avenger, and the libertine has become the spokesman for the social order. For Novak, Valentine's views are peculiarly modern: "The libertinism of Restoration comedy . . . permitted a truly moral concern with . . . relationships between man and his society" [Maximillian E. Novak, "Congreve as the Eighteenth-Century's Archetypal Libertine," *Restoration and 18th Century Theatre Research* 15 (November 1976)].

In these scenes, Congreve emphasizes the correct inversion of order, for Valentine's apparently psychotic behavior is really a proper reaction to the unnatural environment provided by his corrupt doctors. Only the addled Foresight stumbles upon a clue when he admits to Scandal that he is inclined to "reverence a man whom the vulgar think mad."

Subsequently, Valentine, deliberately mistaking the loose Mrs. Frail for the virtuous Angelica, spins a classical tale of their forthcoming marriage:

> I have a secret to tell you—Endymion and the moon shall meet us upon Mount Latmos, and we'll be married in the dead of night—but say not a word. Hymen shall put his torch into a dark lanthorn, that it may be secret; and Juno shall give her peacock poppy-water, that he may fold his ogling tail, and Argos's hundred eyes be shut. . . . Nobody shall know but Jeremy.
>
> (IV. xvi)

Then he offers the paradox: "Angelica is turned nun, and I am turning friar, and yet we'll marry one another in spite of the Pope." This seeming nonsense more than furthers the intrigue of the plot. It joins the classical and Christian themes to show Valentine, in his comic manipulation of Mrs. Frail's marriage to Tattle, at the height of his madly creative powers. Into this situation, Angelica enters as his "therapy."

The true Angelica is the object of his love and the dramatic point Congreve makes is that love, because it is irrational, triumphs over Valentine's carefully constructed false irrationality. The tension within Valentine, as the appearance of the true love threatens the false lunacy, is resolved as he reveals himself to her:

> You see what disguises love makes us put on. Gods have been in counterfeited shapes for the same reason, and the divine part of me, my mind, has worn this mask of madness, and this motley livery, only as the slave of love, and menial creature of your beauty.
>
> (IV. xviii)

Refusing to support the classical mode, Angelica mocks— "Mercy on me, how he talks! Poor Valentine!" Her mockery extends beyond his pose of madness to strike at the man himself and that part of his personality which has yet to be revealed. In a play where all other romantic relationships fail because they are based on duplicity or the culpable lack of self-knowledge, the obstinacy of Angelica is beneficial to both. It reveals [according to Norman Holland] that the reality "which is higher and larger than 'continued Affectation' " can be attained only through an examination of self. Angelica's seeming obtuseness draws from Valentine the plea, "let us think of leaving acting and be ourselves." At this point, the only course he can see is to betray—and, therefore, demolish—the entire fantasy structure. This act, Valentine imagines, will reveal his true self, but Angelica only admits a man who has shammed his way to his fortune by "mercenary ends and sordid interest." Because of Angelica, Valentine is forced back into the pose he has rejected. Her parting remarks are significant:

> Never let us know one another better; for the pleasure of a masquerade is done when we come to show our faces. But I'll tell you two things before I leave you: I am not the fool you take me for; and you are mad and don't know it.
>
> (IV. xx)

In *The Cultivated Stance: The Designs of Congreve's Plays,* W. H. Van Voris calls these "the saddest lines in the play." And, if they were the closing lines, they would be. They are, rather, lines of very real concern; for Angelica must shift Valentine from the temporary center of his pose, and, at this point, she cannot offer him the means for a successful transition.

By the end of Act IV, both masks are intact. Through the workings of Angelica, the pose of Valentine's lunacy has been altered, but the concept of madness remains dominant. Valentine's madness must be repositioned in another context, one which will dispel the transitory pleasures of the masquerade for more certain knowledge. Alternatively, he must remain forever mad: that is, unconscious of his true self.

In Act V, Angelica continues the masquerade and Sir Sampson is again thoroughly manipulated, this time by the lady. Once she has that most important stage property, the deed of conveyance, she issues one of her warnings: "If you remember, the strongest Sampson of your name pulled an old house over his head at last."

In this final act there is much talk of madness. Foresight calls Tattle mad and fears the malady will infect his daughter Prue. It does. Ben calls his father mad, and Tat-

tle and Mrs. Frail, disguised as friar and nun, make a mad marriage. When everyone is thoroughly confused, Valentine reveals himself to himself. First, he admits the deception to his father: "I thought, sir, when the father endeavored to undo the son, it was a reasonable return of nature." Valentine's admission of his deception, a revelation which is economically destructive, is the first of two moves. His second move is to freely offer the long-awaited signature to the deed, and his explanation is based on the irrational—his love for Angelica: "I never valued fortune, but as it was subservient to my pleasure; and my only pleasure was to please this lady. I have made many vain attempts, and find at last that nothing but my ruin can effect it: which, for that reason, I will sign to—give me the paper." It is this total renunciation that evokes Angelica's response, "Generous Valentine!" and causes her to tear the bond which would ruin him.

The act which Scandal sees as disaster has, in fact, been his salvation. Valentine is straightforward; Angelica responds accordingly. Novak agrees that "genuine love, however irrational that may be, is not part of . . . folly." Thus, both manifest their love publicly before the unloved and loveless who have fruitlessly attempted to understand their mystery. Van Voris' view of Valentine is that "He has at last realized his identity. He has not discovered it; he has built it so that in effect it is the last of all his many masks . . . that he is ready to wear in the face of time and ruin. Angelica is . . . too lonely in her own desires to refuse him any longer." It is as difficult to see Valentine peeled, like Peer Gynt's onion, having to mask his nothingness forever, as it is to see an independently wealthy woman with a flock of suitors being forced to accept, out of loneliness, a marriage with a man whose affectation will lead to perpetual isolation for them both.

By the standards of Valentine's society, his act is neither sane nor logical, nor even canny, and yet in his offer to sign the bond is a victory—the victory of his just, loving madness over corrupt sanity. The madman has become his own physician and reclaims his sanity, his true self, through total renunciation. This behavior establishes a new order in which he achieves economic, social, and romantic victories.

The final words of the play are given to the crown of his victory, Angelica, who replies to Scandal's compliment to her "exemplary justice":

> The miracle today is that we find
> A lover true: not that a woman's kind.
>
> (V. xii)

The character Scandal sees Angelica as miraculous; the critic Birdsall sees the same in Valentine: "He is . . . as much a 'Miracle' as Angelica herself—and also, by implication, that ideal balance of 'Love for Love' that they at last achieve." The earlier use of "Miracle"—a reference to Sir Sampson's seeming affection for Valentine—now shows that the monstrosity is in those who are incapable of the extremes of social behavior in order to achieve ultimate harmony beyond the compass of the other characters.

Though the motivation for Congreve's Valentine stems

from an accepted classical background, Valentine goes mad according to the system and method set down by his creator. Congreve combines the ancient vision of the lunatic as the inspired creator with the contemporary vision, which sees Valentine as a creature unable to function and dangerous to ordered society. Congreve's victory lies in the triumph of this classical-contemporary madness over the pitfalls of the seeming social order, a triumph of healthy chaos over corrupt sanity. (pp. 15-19)

Retta M. Taney, "The Treatment of Madness in 'Love for Love'," in Forum, *Vol. 17, No. 2, Winter, 1979, pp. 15-20.*

THE WAY OF THE WORLD

PRODUCTION REVIEWS

B. A. Young   (review date 30 January 1978)

[*In the following review, Young offers a favorable assessment of John Barton's 1978 Royal Shakespeare Company production of* The Way of the World *at London's Aldwych Theatre. The critic admires particularly the clarity with which the play's complicated relationships are presented.*]

No one denies that the plot of Congreve's great comedy [*The Way of the World*] is hard to follow. John Barton, in his splendid production for the RSC, has done much to make it easier. The opening conversation between Mirabell and Fainall is spoken by Michael Pennington and John Woodvine almost as if it were directed at the audience to explain what is to come—though at no cost to the elegant language in which it is couched. I doubt if a newcomer to the play could really absorb much of the complicated relationships revealed, even with the aid of the family tree thoughtfully included in the programme, but it is a good start.

From this crystalline beginning the action builds up in a kind of dramatic crescendo where the comedy becomes more and more free as the tale becomes more and more elaborate. The great classic scenes—Lady Wishfort at her toilet, Mirabell's proposal to Millamant, and so on—are beautifully played, yet they do not seem like "turns" in the smooth continuum where the detailed excellence of even the smallest points holds the attention fast.

The décor and the admirable costumes are by Maria Bjornson. Furniture, screen and a balustrade around that tiresome balcony left over from the Aldwych's attempt to be the Globe make up all the scenery—quite enough save in Act One, where the chocolate-house looks as forbiddingly bare as if the Aldwych had now decided to become the Warehouse. The songs are most naturally integrated into the action: even Sir Wilfull Witwoud's outbursts are heard with patience by the company, for that rustic knight

is allowed enough decency by Bob Peck under his country gaucherie to emerge as a kind of gentleman.

One of the joys of the play, indeed of most Restoration plays, is that hero and heroine are mature, adult, experienced people rather than the *ingenus* of either sex that came in with the matinee idol cult. Judi Dench, looking unusually tall and even slim, gives Millamant a knowing face and a knowing voice, superbly interpreting her silliness, her instant self-contradictions, even her giggles, as part of a deliberately put-on personality.

Mirabell, in Michael Pennington's hands, is as serious and reserved a character as John Woodvine's Fainall, cool and thoughtful, a mile away from the silly wits, whether he is organising the cruel deceit of Lady Wishfort or resolving the matter of Mrs. Fainall's estate. The scene in which he and Millamant exchange terms for their betrothal is played quietly and intimately, and although Millamant seems to be making all the conditions, Mirabell is in charge.

The out-and-out comic figures are all given their measure of dignity—all, that is, but Nickolas Grace's nimbly asinine Witwoud, where Congreve has firmly left that quality out. Beryl Reid's Wishfort is the relic of a handsome lady. She excels in the scene at her dressing-table, where she is given uncommonly good support from Bobbie Brown as her maid; but elsewhere when she is coping with drunken Sir Wilfull for instance, she is still mistress in her own house and human enough to earn some sympathy for the universal mockery she attracts.

Mrs. Fainall is very coolly played by Carmen du Sautoy, a quality emphasised by the plainness of her costumes. In contrast, Marjorie Bland's Mrs. Marwood, dark hair curling around her face like gorgon-serpents, has something of the witch blended with her social charm. The servants Foible, Mincing and Waitwell are sharply individualised; I only quarrel with Waitwell's standing with his hands in his pockets as he talks to Mirabell. Perhaps he is practising impertinence for his pretended gentility later.

B. A. Young, "The Way of the World," in Financial Times, *January 30, 1978, p. 11.*

John Elsom   (review date 2 February 1978)

[*An English dramatist and critic, Elsom has written extensively on British theater. His numerous publications include* Post-War British Theatre *(1976),* Is Shakespeare Still Our Contemporary? *(1989), and* Cold War Theatre *(1992). In the following review of Barton's staging of* The Way of the World, *Elsom objects to the verbal additions made by Barton to clarify the play's plot, maintaining that "the insertion of explanatory names just ruins the rhythm of the lines." He adds that, despite good performances by Judi Dench as Millamant and Beryl Reid as Lady Wishfort, the production is lethargic, making Congreve appear to be a "second-rate satirist and not a first-rate comic stylist."*]

The Way of the World is sometimes said to reflect a singularly heartless and amoral society; but after [Peter Barnes's] *Laughter* and [Charles Wood's] *Dingo*, Congreve's cynicism seems innocent, a matter of false lovers and fortune-hunting. John Barton's RSC production aims for narrative clarity; and, of course, *The Way of the World* has a notoriously complicated plot. Barton tries to unravel it for us. The opening scene in the chocolate house between John Woodvine's Fainall and Michael Pennington's Mirabell is taken at a very deliberate, cocoa-stirring pace; and throughout, Barton adds words, usually names, to clarify the script.

Thus, in the scene between Mirabell and Mrs Fainall, Congreve wrote the line (spoken by Mirabell) that she may consent to my marriage with her niece', and Barton has added 'to Millamant'. 'Have I,' says Mrs Marwood (Marjorie Bland), ' . . . sacrificed my friendship to keep my love inviolate?' And Barton inserts 'to her' after 'friendship'. These may seem tiny points; but there are a lot of them, and it is not just in a 'hands off the classics' spirit which makes me wonder whether Barton has not aimed for the wrong kind of clarity.

Congreve's story is a muddle because it is conventional and not very important, just as you do not have to follow the stories in pantomimes too closely. It does not matter. All you have to recognise are the cipher characters—the dashing lover, the artful mistress, the lustful dowager, the cousin from the country—and sit back and enjoy the speeches and scenes which Congreve has given them. The insertion of explanatory names just ruins the rhythm of the lines. See how those two words 'to her', in the line quoted above, spoils the neat balance between friendship and love, which in turn sets up the last word of the sentence, 'inviolate'.

This production works best when Judi Dench (as Millamant) and Beryl Reid (as Lady Wishfort) get to work on their speeches so that the lines seem as elegant or as funny as they were when Congreve wrote them. Elsewhere, a ploddingness descends, which makes even the scene between Mirabell and Millamant about the provisos of marriage seem pedantic. The root problem is that we still accept the Jeremy Collier line that Congreve was describing a corrupt and licentious society. All societies are corrupt and licentious. What is different about Restoration dramatists and, later, Congreve is that they were caught between a feeling of relief that the hard days of puritanism were over and a foreboding that direr punishments could be nigh. They loved the town elegance of which they pretended to disapprove. Barton makes the foppish fashions look tatty, the lovers inelegant and the fools just unfortunate. He approaches Congreve in the spirit of Brecht and Weill, making him look like a second-rate satirist and not a first-rate comic stylist. Nobody wants a return to the old boisterous playing of Restoration comedy, nor to powder-puffery; but we have yet to find a modern way of capturing urban eloquence.

John Elsom, "The Funny Side," in The Listener, *Vol. 99, No. 2545, February 2, 1978, p. 153.*

Ned Chaillet   (review date March 1978)

[*In the following review of John Barton's production of*

The Way of the World, *Chaillet praises the performances of the cast, focusing especially on those of Beryl Reid as Lady Wishfort and Judi Dench as Millamant. However, Chaillet maintains that poor stagecraft detracted from Barton's production.*]

The confusions of *The Way of the World* have become an easy joke. Determining who is related to whom, by whose half-brother or former wife, proves ample diversion to those who prefer counting blades of grass to noticing the forest. But, without book in hand, and without perusing the family tree provided in the Aldwych programme, any attentive theatre-goer will understand the comedy of Congreve's play. The rattle of funny exposition is as clear in the Royal Shakespeare Company's production as it ever gets, and the fine points can be left to literary genealogists since much of the laughter is provided by the unfolding of duplicity and chaotic emotional connections.

Every separation of characters in the opening scenes brings them together with others who reveal hidden alliances and sexual intrigues, as husbands, wives and lovers betray each other for love and money. What matters most is that Lady Wishfort controls the money that is due to her niece, Millamant, and has powers over her daughter, Mrs Fainall. The matriarchal fortunes of the family are threatened by two men, Mirabell, who has loved or pretended love to nearly every woman in the play, and Fainall, Mrs Fainall's husband, who is involved in an affair with Mrs Marwood and is determined to cut loose his wife and keep her money.

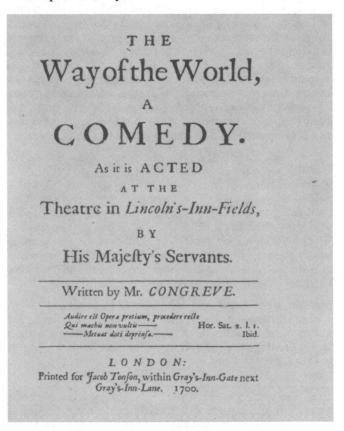

Title Page of the first edition of The Way of the World.

The legalistic means by which Mirabell emerges victorious, protecting his one-time lover Mrs Fainall, from her husband's plot and winning Millamant in marriage—and a stake in the family fortune—against the opposition of Lady Wishfort, are clear in performance, and the scholarly intricacies of Restoration law and marriage practice hardly matter. So greatly do several of the parts open up to inventive performance, and so eagerly are those characters seized on by some of the actors, that some chunks of the performance would be enjoyable to people without more than a smattering of English, let alone knowledge of the plot.

Yet for all the glory of Beryl Reid's creation of Lady Wishfort and for all the charm of Judi Dench's Millamant, it cannot be counted a successful production. Before counting its several blessings, it would be useful to suggest some of its faults.

Since matters of budget led the RSC to install a permanent set at the Aldwych, the encircling balcony that curves round the stage has served to encompass everything from Shakespeare to Brecht. It has been effectively masked for Ibsen and Ben Jonson, but is left in full view for Congreve. It does not make the ideal setting for a Restoration comedy of manners and only once, as background for a garden, does it not actually distract attention from supposed scenes.

Granted that Restoration stagecraft may have relied on doors and the stage apron more than on inhabitable sets, there were still appropriate backdrops. Nor is it enough to suggest that isolated furniture in the RSC's production of [Bernard Shaw's] *Man and Superman* conveyed everything that was necessary for Shaw's comedy of manners, for there the sets faded into blackness, focusing the attention on the actors in the play. In *The Way of the World* attention is completely fragmented with a screen here, a couch elsewhere, making up a single incoherent room. The balcony is not ignored, since it is always visible, but the hanging of chandeliers around it does not bring it into the play, it merely accentuates its obtrusiveness.

The miscalculation of design extends to the appearance of the play's romantic hero. Michael Pennington's Mirabell is draped in a costume the colour of sand and faded blue velvet. With his sandy hair he blurs into the softness of his clothes and when he speaks he declines to emphasise his dialogue, choosing a potentially effective, languorous approach to character amid the extravagance surrounding him. Instead of becoming noticeable, he all but disappears. A not inconsiderable piece of acting, considering Mr Pennington's usually unmistakable presence.

His soft-spokenness may come from a position of strength within the text, but he is not the only figure to fade on the stage. Mrs Fainall and Mrs Marwood contribute their lines prettily, but are never very different from one another. It is left for Congreve's greater caricatures to fill the stage.

Even the smaller caricatures have success, from Nickolas Grace's foppish Witwoud, merrily exclaiming, 'I confess I do *blaze* today', to Bob Peck's Sir Wilfull Witwoud, glorious in drunkenness, though deprived by obvious whispering of a useful credibility when he proclaims his willingness to marry Millamant. Eliza Ward's Foible steals some moments of merriment, but it is hard to steal anything but honour from her mistress, Lady Wishfort.

Miss Reid is brassy, wicked and vain, conscious that it is bad for one's reputation to have servants answer the door with bottles of cherry brandy in their hands but easy prey for any supposed knight seeking a well-off widow. She rasps out her lines with authority and irony and brings an unexpected quality of slapstick to her character, displaying ludicrously alluring positions on a bed and gazing with rapt admiration at the bare barrel of a pistol.

The other full achievement of John Barton's production is Miss Dench's Millamant. Artificially endowed with a resounding giggle, she can be convincing about the advantages of pinning up her hair with poetry and still fight the worthy battle against dwindling, by degrees, into a wife.

Mr Barton makes final use of the play's confusions in a delightfully tangled version of the dance of celebration. The triumph of laws and masculine wiles is not capped by a perfect, orderly bringing together of all parties in a handsome movement, but is undermined by further confusion as inappropriate partners first take, then disregard, each other. It suggests an interpretation that might have proved interesting elsewhere in the production. (pp. 28-9)

> *Ned Chaillet, in a review of "The Way of the World," in* Plays and Players, *Vol. 25, No. 6, March, 1978, pp. 28-9.*

CRITICAL COMMENTARY

William Van Voris   (essay date 1958)

[*In the following essay, Van Voris counters criticism that finds* The Way of the World *excessively convoluted in plot and superficial in characterization. He contends that the complex machinery of the author's plot allows him to present his characters from a multiplicity of viewpoints and thus facilitate a "real insight into [their] world and into the values by which it should be judged." Van Voris concludes that the play is an apt expression of the thought and temper of the Restoration aristocracy.*]

"Oh, those insufferable Congreve plots!"

Everyone has heard this complaint: "For all the busyness of language and intrigue in *The Way of the World,*" so the criticism goes, "the play is but a Restoration carousel, spinning and bobbing to the old tunes—fornication, marriage, and some bright witty jokes. We are perfectly willing to accept the play as a stylistic masterpiece, to snigger at complaints about its immorality or its lack of verisimilitude; we properly admire the handsomely carved mains and withers of the figures, even suppose that they represent certain Restoration mores; but in the end nothing really happens to them, and so they remain but twirling manikins. The greatest geniuses show us characters alive, bending or growing under the stress of events, not the mere dizzy motion of an intrigue which is at best a trivial symbol for an idle, aristocratic world."

But this is wrong. Although Congreve cast his final play as a carousel, my point is that his form is a dramatic device which enables us to see his posturing characters from several points of view as they circle before us. If we watch the figures closely and are not preoccupied with the machinery of the intrigues, we can gain a real insight into the World and into the values by which it should be judged. Congreve's theatre is the theatre of witty insight and when we share his insight, his gilded carousel is no more trivial than a Picasso clown.

In more conventional terms, the exposition of the characters and their situations in *The Way of the World* is not complete until the epilogue. Because of this Congreve's play is more difficult to understand than a comedy using an archtypical structure, such as *L'Ecôle des Femmes*. In Molière's comedy we are first introduced to the characters and their situation and then we watch them develop through a series of episodes. It is all very funny and very clear. On the other hand, the kind of exposition that occupies the first act of Molière's play occupies the whole of Congreve's. Congreve was a late baroque playwright, classical in his elaboration of Ciceronian rhetoric and Terence-like intricacy. His aristocrats are so complex and so circumspect that we must see them many times in many different situations before they are properly defined. When at last we fully understand what is happening, when we see the unity beneath the violence and the beauty in the conventions, the play is over.

Take Mirabell, the man of many loves, the plum of the aristocratic World who knows it perfectly. To Fainall he is both the bright contriver of farce and male gossip: ". . . I got a Friend to put her [Lady Wishfort] into a Lampoon, and compliment her with the Imputation of an Affair with a young Fellow, which I carry'd so far, that I told her the malicious Town took notice that she was grown fat of a sudden; and when she lay in of a Dropsie, persuaded her she was reported to be in Labour. The Devil's in't, if an old woman is to be flatter'd further . . . " (I. i). Schooled by Rochester, Mirabell is also to Fainall the ironically analytical and passionate lover of Millamant, "I like her with all her Faults; nay, like her for her Faults. Her Follies are so natural, or so artful, that they become her" (I. iii). To his servants Mirabell shows the amused arrogance of the Restoration aristocrat, "Sirrah, *Waitwell*, why sure you think you were marry'd for your own Recreation, and not for my Conveniency" (II. vii). To a fool who courts Millamant he shows a streak of Cavalier violence, "Have you not left off your impudent Pretensions there yet? I shall cut your Throat, sometime or other, Petulant about that Business" (I. ix). To Mrs. Fainall, his former mistress, he candidly reveals his chilly expedient hypocrisy when explaining why he made her marry, "Why do we daily commit disagreeable and dangerous Actions? To save that Idol Reputation. If the Familiarities of our Loves had produc'd that Consequence, of which you were apprehensive, where cou'd you have fix'd a Father's Name with Credit, but on a Husband?" (II. iii). To old Lady Wishfort he plays the facetious Restoration precieux, a creature stepping from

[Edmund] Waller's verses with his tongue in his cheek, "Ah Madam, there was a time—But let it be forgotten—I confess I have deservedly forfeited the high Place I once held, of sighing at your Feet; nay kill me not, by turning from me in Disdain" (V. ix). To Millamant, in public, he plays the fashionable relativist, "Beauty is the Lover's Gift; 'tis he bestows your Charms—your Glass is all a Cheat" (II. iv). In private, attempting to explain his absurd intrigue of blackmailing Lady Wishfort into allowing his marriage with her niece, he is driven by Millamant's flippancy into playing the sententious and stuffy male, "You are merry, Madam, but I would persuade you for a Moment to be serious. . . . Can you not find in the variety of your Disposition one Moment . . . " (II. v). Only in the famous bargaining scene, when he approaches the serious with calculated and outrageous banter, does he succeed with her, and then he reveals a natural domestication greater than her own and a sensitive aspiration for beauty quite as fine. Mirabell is, in short, the truest of wits; he is a character of great diversity of mood and incisive, speculating intelligence, given stability and unity by a studied grace and brought to life without touzling so much as a curl of his peruke.

Something of the same complexity and circumspection is apparent in the other characters. Millamant is a coquette so witty that she can toy with wit as if it were a fan, "Sententious *Mirabell*! Prithee don't look with that violent and inflexible wise Face, like *Solomon* at the dividing of the Child in an old Tapestry Hanging" (II. v). The affectation guards and embellishes the young girl very much in love and a little afraid, "Well, If *Mirabell* should not make a good Husband, I am a lost thing;—for I find I love him violently" (IV. vii). Fainall acts the jaded sophisticate because he is a desperate husband, "Death, am I not married? . . . Am I not imprison'd, fetter'd? Have I not a Wife?" (II. ii). And, near the level of farce, the same complexity holds true for Lady Wishfort, Sir Wilfull and the fops. Congreve's purpose for all his characters was roughly the same—to allow us to see around the masks which they affect. His concern for masks, for the illusions with which characters clothe themselves is similar to [Luigi] Pirandello's. Unlike the Italian, however, Congreve avoided melodramatic events which rip the masks away; rather, he contrived to spin a character before us in such a way that we can catch him negligently laying the mask aside or expediently adjusting another to his face.

As each view gives us a new insight into the complexity and passions of character, each view of the society which the characters represent brings its clearer insight into the violence which lies beneath the formal surface.

The first act shows a chocolate house, the public world of the men. As all the talk goes on between the audience and Betty the waitress, an outsider, appropriately, reputation is the theme of the act. Here the comedy is truly of manners; everything is in terms of deportment before the public view. The gallants are accordingly merciless with the reputations of others—Mirabell's description of Lady Wishfort is a case in point—but jealous of their own. The society is burnished to a high gloss of Restoration elegance and unless we watch and listen very closely, we can hardly tell the difference between Mirabell, Fainall and Witwoud. "Impudence and Malice pass for Wit." The theme which unifies the act is amplififed by variations that are not essential but certainly delightful. The farcical gossip of Mirabell is paralleled by the gossip of Witwoud. Petulant, he says, in order to affect popularity would "call for himself, wait for himself, any and what's more, not finding himself, sometimes leave a Letter for himself" (I. viii). Similarly, the mistrust, the arrogance, the forced aphorisms of Mirabell and Fainall are echoed and mimicked by the fops.

Whatever conflicts there are in the act come from reiterated hints that passion, malice, and confusion lie behind the balanced phrases and controlled gestures. The farcical gossip serves this function; so do the ambiguous allusions of the wits. Even the exposition of Mirabell's intrigue is used as a kind of dramatic rhetoric. In the first act we know nothing but that he has secretly contrived a marriage of his servants, that he has ordered them to meet him soon in the park, and that what he has done amuses him.

When Waitwell and Foible meet him in the park at the end of the second act ready to deceive Lady Wishfort and to be paid, they come as a final variation on the theme that has been woven through the immediately preceding scenes. The latent passion of the first act becomes apparent as the theme of the second; the desire for love and money, a handsome number of pounds in or out of Hoare's Bank. In the long public walks of the park we hear nothing of this; all is fashionably witty. But when the characters separate and pair in the shadowed arbors, we see them scramble and plot. There Fainall rants at his mistress—they are poor. There Mirabell icily reveals his plots to Mrs. Fainall—he wants Millamant and her estate.

The third act shows us why. We approach Lady Wishfort's drawing room somewhat circuitously through the chocolate house and the park. When we arrive we are in the lively center of the aristocratic world and all is violence and pretense. Ironically she is the titular head of this aristocracy, but she is more outrageous than any of the others. Told by Marwood that her maid has been talking to Mirabell, she tipples, bellows, and flounders among the gilded bric-a-brac until her decorums are as cracked and peeled as her face. It is all very funny—and somewhat frightening. Unwittingly she and Foible chart their world, as she plans revenge on Mirabell:

> LADY WISHFORT: I hope to see him hung with Tatters, like a *Long-Lane* Penthouse, or a Gibbet-Thief. A slander-mouth'd Railer: I warrant the Spendthrift Prodigal's in Debt as much as the Million Lottery, or the whole Court upon a Birth-Day. I'll spoil his Credit with his Tailor. Yes, he shall have my Niece with her Fortune, he shall.
>
> FOIBLE: He! I hope to see him lodge in *Ludgate* first, and angle into *Black-Fryars* for Brass Farthings, with an old Mitten.
>
> (III. v)

The school of [architect Christopher] Wren built clear windows in these baroque townhouses and now we are able to look through them straight into the stews and pris-

ons of London that lie outside. When Sir Wilfull enters at the end of the act bellowing at the fops, yanking off his boots, and stinking like all the manure heaps of the home counties, the picture is complete. The World is tiny, bounded by the park, the chocolate-house and by a social precipice. There is no escape from it, only a fall and death. It is little wonder that the characters scramble and scheme for the money that secures them.

But most of them are unable to control their world, and their muddle-headedness turns into a wild hysteria in the fourth act. As in all of Congreve's plays, the realistic yields to a fantastic serio-comic nightmare: the fourth act opens with the deluded Lady Wishfort archly preparing to meet Mirabell's disguised clown and valet, and closes while she fumbles with her preciosité and slobbers to be seduced, "All Chastity and Odour." In the meantime Fainall, who has discovered his wife's past relations with Mirabell, prepares his own blackmail of the old lady and to confuse her gets Sir Wilfull and the fops drunk. The squire bellows songs; Witwoud belches sour-breath and similes; Petulant snarls. Only the lovers are safe from this. Locked above the chaos, Mirabell and Millamant meet and bargain for a marriage that will allow each his identity and that will save them from dwindling too quickly to pale nonentities or from scampering like violent fools. "Let us be as strange as if we had been marry'd a great while; and as well bred as if we were not marry'd at all" (IV. v).

Such contrasts between scenes of controlled formal elegance and incontinent and often farcical emotions are characteristic of all Congreve's comedies, but in *The Way of the World* he used what amounts to a kind of "montage" technique, alternating increasingly raucous scenes with those of increasingly stylized urbane dialogue with greater frequency as the play continues. To do this he used the intrigues of Mirabell and Fainall not for themselves, but as devices to exaggerate the contrasts by which he controlled the fluctuating tone and pace of the play and increased its conflicts. It is Mirabell's intrigue that causes Lady Wishfort desperately to invoke her absurd decorums for a disguised valet and just as desperately to break them before the arched eyebrows of her family. The same intrigue starts Foible lying, Mrs. Fainall palely simpering, the wits jabbering, Mirabell posing. It is his suspicion of an intrigue between Mirabell and Mrs. Marwood that drives the hysterical Fainall to wrench his mistress's arm in the park; it is his and Marwood's acrid contrivance that causes the drunken vulgarity of the squire and the fops and brings about Lady Wishfort's disillusionment. The intrigues are the machines that spin the characters for the wits' convenience and our amusement and understanding. The plotting, the arrangement of the sequences produced by the intrigue, is more important. Congreve built his elaborate ironic parallels to allow the thematic development of his acts; and to intensify the conflicts of the World he also placed scenes of brightly witty scheming beside scenes of increasingly violent extravagance, so the gilded World of the first act seems about to shatter into fragments by the last. Significantly, when Lady Wishfort is told by Marwood and Fainall that she is attempting to seduce a valet under the nose of his wife, she runs screaming after Foible, "Begone, begone, begone, go, go,—That I took from washing of old Gause and weaving of dead Hair, with a bleak blue Nose, over a Chafing-dish of starv'd Embers, and Dining behind a Traverse Rag, in a shop no bigger than a Bird-Cage.—go, go, starve again, do, do" (V. i).

We have now seen about all we need to know of this World. It is upon the basis of what is shown that the two sober and sharp-eyed men and their mistresses proceed to try to manage it. This is the problem that occupies the final act.

Fainall and Marwood look upon Lady Wishfort's romance. Foible's perfidiousness and Mrs. Fainall's adultery with Mirabell as so many symbols of a world in which everyone is a kind of fraud. They believe that all forms are merely matters of convenience used to shield stupidity and lust, hence all social formulas are nonsense. They therefore ask the old question of persons shrewd enough to see social imbecilities but too unimaginative to conceive of social unity—Why not? Why not blackmail Lady Wishfort? Why not desert Mrs. Fainall? Why not force Millamant's money into their own hands and gratify their own passions? Lady Wishfort herself asks, "What's Integrity to an Opportunity?" so, they think, does everyone. It is "all in the Way of the *World*."

They are, in short, characters straight from [Thomas] Hobbes's jungle of Eden [in *The Leviathan*]:

> I put for a general inclination of all mankind, a perpetual and restless desire for power after power, that ceaseth only in death. And the cause of this is not always that a man hopes for a more intensive delight than he has already attained to, or that he cannot be content with a moderate power; but because he cannot assure the power and means to live well which he hath at present, without the acquisition of more.

Restless to be rid of a pallid wife, restless to escape, restless to satisfy their passions, Fainall and Mrs. Marwood threaten divorce, invoking the mechanics of the law itself as a weapon for their illegality.

> What, and have your Name prostituted in a publick Court; yours and your Daughter's Reputation worry'd at the Bar by a Pack of bawling Lawyers? To be usher'd in with an *O Yes* of Scandal; and have your Case open'd by an old fumbler Leacher in a Quoif like a Man Midwife, to bring your Daughter's Infamy to Light; to be a Theme for legal Punsters, and Quiblers by the Statute; and become a Jest, against a Rule of Court, where there is no Precedent for a Jest in any Record; not even in *Dooms-day Book;* To discompose the Gravity of the Bench, and provoke naughty Interrogatories in more naughty Law *Latin;* while the good judge, tickl'd with the Proceeding, simpers under a Grey Beard, and figes off and on his Cushion as if he had swallow'd *Cantharides,* or sate upon *Cow-Itch.*
>
> (V. v)

Even the code of honor is meaningless to them; when the indignant and sober Sir Wilfull challenges him, Fainall waves the "*Bear-garden* Flourish" aside. Why not?

Mirabell has the superior insight to answer. He gains admittance to Lady Wishfort by his graceful formality, reveals Fainall's and Marwood's motives to the family, has Millamant pretend to accept Sir Wilful so Lady Wishfort cannot under any circumstances seize her property, and, finally, produces a "Deed of Trust" from Mrs. Fainall. He, it seems, is in complete control of the Fainall fortunes. This, he says, is truly "*the Way of the World,* Sir; of the Widows of the World" (V. xiii), that is, the knowledgeable. Mirabell has shown that Fainall is many times a fool, a man who does not even know his wife, let alone his world. Nor does he know his Gassendi nor his Locke. Mirabell has produced what is in effect a kind of social contract to preserve the unity of the passionate, bewildered, and cacophonic family. It comes as a surprise, but it is inevitable; the very existence of rapacious persons in a confused world necessitates some such agreement of trust to protect the weak and the wise from those who would prey upon them. England itself had rediscovered this old truth at this time under William of Orange and the ruling Whigs. The play is resolved by this final exposition of a unity in the diversity of the family.

For all his affectations, then, Mirabell has the insight to be honest. And he is honest in all the senses of the term as it was used in the 17th century; he has integrity and he has aristocratic grace. Therefore he can reassert the value of the gilded world even when it seems cracked and tarnished. From Montaigne and the true Precieuses the Restoration learned that the astute person could turn manners into an art. And it is this ability that allows Mirabell to triumph in the world he has helped to preserve. Granted the social forms can be absurd when taken at their face value: the fops see nothing but the facade of fashion and are therefore merely witnesses of the World; Lady Wishfort is more foolish than the servants in her trust of "decorums" and we find that she has almost ruined her daughter by a formalistic education designed to turn her into "another me." Mirabell, however, can turn an intrigue or an entrance into high comedy. Where Fainall's intrigues are merely brutal, Mirabell's are ingenious *divertissements* [diversions]. Significantly, he alone of all the characters truly loves Millamant because he can see that she is triumphant in weaving the rare and the beautiful from commonplace conventions. It is no coincidence that most of her images are drawn from art and poetry; as she sails by the brambles of the park "with her Fan spread and her Streamers out," she is more attractive than the others in the play as surely as the play itself is more felicitous than other Restoration comedies using similar conventions.

If *The Way of the World* has never been a very popular commodity, it was not meant to be; it was written, much to [Richard] Steele's astonishment, for "the Few Refin'd" after Congreve, the Whig aristocrat, had lost confidence in the general public during the Collier controversy. The refined would not expect merely another story of Restoration sex; the refined could discover in the curious carousel an image of themselves, an image which gathers together some of the best ethical and political thought of a violent and fascinating class which developed an enduring constitution and fine critical art to resolve a century of violence, extravagance, and deceit. (pp. 211-17)

William Van Voris, "Congreve's Gilded Carousel," in Educational Theatre Journal, *Vol. X, No. 3, October, 1958, pp. 211-17.*

Louis Kronenberger (essay date 1969)

[*In the following excerpt, Kronenberger asserts that, more than any other play,* The Way of the World *distinctly embodies the worldly attitude that characterizes Restoration comedy.*]

There has never been a body of literature more notable—indeed, more notorious—for its worldly tone than Restoration comedy. Nor is this simply because its plots abound in sexual license, that over it there hovers a sense of dissoluteness; it is equally because its plots pivot on trickery and that over it there hangs a sense of deceit. Its recurrent butt, its endless dupe, is the cuckold, who far from being sympathized with is to be made sport of. Nor, as in earlier, as in Elizabethan literature, is sexual license a matter of lustiness, of warm-hearted gallants and wanton ladies: when we move on to the Restoration, though we advance to a higher social world, we descend to a baser moral one. There is much less a sense of lustiness than of laxness; of animal spirits than of animal cunning; of love as an end in itself than of love as a rung on a ladder. Infidelity springs much less from a warm or foolish heart than from a kind of heartlessness. Into all the era's brittle assignations, its loveless lovemaking, go those companion motives of worldliness—personal ambition, fortune hunting, money. It is no wonder that, in the form of Jeremy Collier's celebrated *Short View of the Immorality and Profaneness of the English Stage,* Restoration comedy should in its own day have been strongly condemned, or that in ages more moral thereafter it should have been roundly denounced.

All the same, it has in many ways been rather unfairly denounced, not just because those who have done so most loudly have often been mere lip-service moralists, and not just because they have quite lacked appreciation of its literary merits; but because to a marked degree it is an honest picture of the life it portrays; because, again, it possesses the particular virtues, as well as faults, that go with its subject matter; and finally, because it is a special body of work, created less by the usual sort of professional than by what we may call the gentleman author, who might well have participated by night in the activities and intrigues that he recorded next morning.

Now in every age there have been what can be called gentlemen authors: in English literature we have, among others, Sir Philip Sidney, [John] Dryden, [Henry] Fielding, [George Gordon, Lord] Byron, [Percy Bysshe] Shelley, [Algernon Charles] Swinburne, all of them wellborn and some of them clearly possessed of genius. But in every age the wellborn more often tend to write like Queen Victoria, who underlined hundreds of words that she had far better have left out. Nor has there been much incentive among the wellborn to write well; authorship was until recently looked askance at; and though society might not mind if its members wrote skillfully, it minded even less if they didn't. It was more pleased when its members talked wittily, but it seldom assumed that they would. Most of the greatest society wits—Chamfort and [Richard Brinsley] Sheridan, Sydney Smith and Oscar Wilde—have been outsiders.

But just here the Restoration was rather different. Any number of its wellborn people were witty; a large number, indeed, were truly talented. Society for once not only repeated all kinds of good remarks; it coined them. Society not only went, night after night, to the playhouse; it often wrote the plays. This means, moreover, the most dissipated sections of society—the very people who stayed up late breaking all the commandments, who gambled and drank when they might have been reading and writing. They led scandalous lives and sometimes wrote scandalous plays, but they equally led stylish lives and wrote stylish plays, and could be as witty when alone with their pens as in company over the wine. There is something remarkable about a group of wastrels who should have been almost as concerned with the portrayal of pleasure as with the pursuit of it. And as a result, if these gentlemen authors produced an indecorous literature, it was yet a real literature of a kind. Lord Rochester, Lord Dorset, Sir Charles Sedley, Sir George Etherege, the Duke of Buckingham—and Dryden, though so much more than a gentleman; and Congreve, though he came well after the others—never, certainly, have we been so forcibly reminded that the Poets' Corner is only a stone's throw from the House of Lords.

Now what these men produced is rightly called artificial comedy; artifice is what shapes it, starches it, forms its very essence. But though artificial in itself, it mirrors a good deal that is real. These men wrote, more than we may imagine, about the wantons they knew and the rakes they were and the childish brutal pranks they played; about their own frivolities and lack of feeling, about their desire to dazzle, their need to ridicule. Autobiographical in any strict sense their plays are not, but at times they perhaps come as close to autobiography as to fiction. Rochester and Etherege, for example, took part in a notorious prank that began with tossing some fiddlers in a blanket and ended with one of their victims dying of his wounds. The wonder is that in coming so close to autobiography, they yet managed on occasion to come equally close to art. But they did, and all the more remarkably for refusing to work hard, for insisting that they only worked at all when they had nothing better to do. Obviously, they posed in all this; but then they never plodded. The result, as we might suppose, is often careless, often capricious, tenuous, sometimes plagiarized; but often elegant, often witty and perceptive, and sometimes full of truth.

It is not my purpose to provide a conspectus of Restoration comedy, though in many ways a worldlier *body* of work would be hard to find. *The Way of the World,* as the crowning play of that literature, is a sufficiently key play as well. But this is in some sense true because only Congreve could have made it both. Others who were equally suited by temperament were endowed with less talent; others with equal, and indeed one with superior, talent were less fitted for stage writing. On Dryden, we feel, stage comedy never sat easily: despite a keen sense of the absurd and a mastery of satire, he lacked the ability to frisk and romp; besides, the Restoration stage has a striking indoors quality, at odds with Dryden's outdoor vigor. No one would make words march as he did; but words that should skip, and splash one another with water, and mock while they seem to caress, and elude while they seem to consent—these were not his forte. And where Dryden found his true worldly calling in a vigorous, striding, deep-chested satirical poetry, something at which he remains unmatched, so a [William] Wycherley failed, as I venture to think, to find his proper role at all. He too had a vigorous talent, and had often violent emotions, so that *he* often cannot keep life inside a drawing room. His age and his place in society led him to write for the theater, and with too little restraint and often a wrong kind of coarseness; in a later age he would almost certainly have turned novelist, and been as comfortable a figure in the world of Fielding and [Tobias] Smollett as he can be a marginal one in that of [George] Etherege and Congreve. His name and Dryden's alone stand as high as Congreve's in the Restoration theater; but Congreve's alone fully graces, fully fits the Restoration on its comic and worldly side.

Strictly speaking, Congreve is not of the true generation of Restoration playwrights; when he began writing plays, not Charles II or even James II occupied the English throne, but rather William and Mary. The Revolution of 1688 had intervened, and brought with it something of a social as well as political revolution. William of Orange was a brilliant but cold, sickly, boorish figure with no love for the theater and none for London. There was no considerable court life, no stir of frivolity and fashion. The world of fashion may itself not have changed its morals for the better, but at least it pretended to. It was this touch of gray in the moral landscape, this hint of chill in the moral air, that led to Jeremy Collier's attack on the theater. In that attack Congreve was not spared, and it would be idle to suggest that he worked on a morally higher plane than had most of his predecessors. He was as little shocked as they by what he saw, and on occasion could be almost as shocking. But because he was so much more delicate an artist, with the theater itself much less gross a bear garden, there emerges a greater refinement of tone. [Edmund] Burke said of the court of Marie Antoinette that "vice itself lost half its evil by losing all its grossness." There, it seems to me, Burke was rather dangerously suggesting that aesthetics can do the work of morality, was rather implying that it is only half as ill-behaved to poison your uncle artistically as to slice him up with a meat ax. Actually, in real life, the premeditation involved in well-wrought immorality makes not for lesser guilt but for greater; but in literature, an elegant depiction of vice does tend to have, for a time at least, a genuine lure.

Congreve, in any case, stands apart from the earlier generation of Restoration playwrights as much for tone as for talent. Etherege, notably in *The Man of Mode,* has admirable ease and airiness and a sort of fashionable rattle, a constant fizz; but he is not endowed with such style and breeding as we encounter in the best of Congreve, who is at once in the literary sense a patrician and in the temperamental sense an almost too urbane worldling. And just so, he much less represents a period than a tradition: he does not simply mirror Restoration manners, he embodies the civilized point of view. If anything, I think, we shall find that it is the Restoration that makes Congreve a little less than completely civilized, that it is the Restoration that tarnishes him with a certain period cynicism, a certain modish sophistication. Of the completely civilized man we require something that, in the final reckoning, Congreve never quite gives us. We do not expect him, from the seriousness of an occasion, to raise his voice; but we ask that he do more than raise his eyebrows. He need not be warm-hearted, but it must not be mere indifference or imperturbability that he conveys, it must be a kind of serenity. On the other hand, in an ability to appraise life in the very act of savoring it, in a fine appreciation of tangible civilized virtues Congreve is beautifully a master. As that, he is a type it is not easy to do exact justice to—one that can be about equally overpraised and undervalued.

Congreve's claims to embody, in spirit no less than style, the civilized point of view derive chiefly from the last and by all odds most distinguished of his plays, *The Way of the World,* which is, indeed, the finest of Restoration comedies. In his three previous plays, Congreve had either done something inferior or something different. In his first play, *The Old Bachelor,* he had made plain that a witty new playwright had arrived on the scene, but also that nothing new in playwriting had arrived at all. He borrowed the plots, the characters, the situations, the general atmosphere, the interminable amorousness, exactly as he found them, offering not creation but brilliant rewrite. *The Old Bachelor* is like something in a child's drawing book, where the picture is printed beforehand and the child colors it as he sees fit; Congreve's coloring is brilliantly precocious, but the design is not his own. In his second play, *The Double Dealer,* he has stopped copying and begun to write, and at his best not just the wit and style are delightfully Congrevian, but the attitude is as well: the trouble here was that the main action is melodrama and only the subordinate part stylish and witty. Congreve's third play, *Love for Love,* is a genuine success, indeed by far his most successful theater piece, full of liveliness and sprinkled with true worldly wit: in it Congreve has plainly mastered his medium, has written creditably in terms of pleasing others. But it was only with *The Way of the World* that he came to write entirely to please himself; into *The Way of the World* he poured everything, we feel, that earlier—whether from craving commercial success or worrying over artistic failure—he had consciously or unconsciously withheld or watered down.

As a result, the difference between *The Way of the World* and Congreve's earlier work is less a matter of degree than of kind. This becomes evident, I think, if we consider the quality which Congreve is best known for and which best conveys his worldliness—I mean his wit. Now, witty though *Love for Love* often is, it nowhere equals *The Way of the World,* whether in amount, or degree, or effect. But that there is much more wit, or even much better wit, in *The Way of the World* is not the final point. The final point is that wit, in *The Way of the World,* is not a mere ingredient but a kind of essence. The play is not, so to speak, witty; it is wit. We can speak of it as wit as we can speak of an ode of Keats' as poetry, or an oration of

Burke's as eloquence. The wit of *The Way of the World* is a way of writing, so that a speech in the play is almost as hard to paraphrase as a stanza in the *Ode to a Nightingale.* The idea is completely married to the words, and if you kill them off, the idea will fling itself into the same grave.

I shall not try to define wit, in part because no definition can be altogether adequate, in part because none can be sufficiently alive. But wit, like poetry, demands (as it provides) a peculiar climate, a particular atmosphere. Like poetry, wit lives in a house without stairs, moving upward in a rush, in sudden dizzying leaps; though where poetry is a kind of bright creature with wings, wit is more like a witch on a broomstick. But a kind of lightning suddenness is part of the thing itself. And as important as there being something bright about them both, there must be something concentrated. We may think of them as brilliantly clothed, but must also see them as essentially naked. Such concentratedness, such speed, makes both true wit and true poetry, however else they differ, into something barer and more direct than other forms of expression. That is why they can prove fatiguing: we have so much to absorb in so little space. One reason why *The Way of the World* finds it hard to succeed in the theater is that, theatrically, it moves too slow, with talk where there might better be action. But a perhaps deeper reason is that verbally it moves too fast: the wit has us panting to keep up with it. Such writing is too concise for the stage.

Moreover, the pervasive and carpeting wit of *The Way of the World* depends on context, and even on character. Detached from the play, deprived of its atmosphere and attitudes, the wit loses immeasurably. For it is wit and only seldom witticism, purring so smoothly that we are not always aware of how sharply it bites. It would rather be well-bred than emphatic, it would rather chime like a clock than go off like a gun. With, say, an Oscar Wilde, wit is the lights and bells on a Christmas tree, where with Congreve it is the sap in a living tree trunk. Moreover, at its most characteristic and impressive, Congreve's wit is inseparable from his worldliness, is the very lens through which he surveys the world. Listen to Witwould telling what trouble Petulant took in order to make himself seem sought after:

> Why he would slip out of this chocolate-house, just when you had been talking to him. As soon as your back was turned—whip he was gone; then trip to his lodging, clap on a hood and a scarf and a mask, slap into a hackney-coach, and drive hither to the door again in a trice; where he would send in for himself—I mean, call for himself; wait for himself; nay, and what's more, not finding himself, sometimes leave a letter for himself.

The whole tone of the play is as worldly and urbane as one could ask for. Indeed, Congreve has so perfectly captured what might be called drawing-room elegance that we may not realize that he has exhibited its limitations as well as its luster. So brilliant at times is his brushwork and his coloring, so unified his tone, that we are in the midst of a fairyland of fine manners: this is how we might expect people to talk in Heaven. But these, at the same time, are peo-

ple we must expect to find in Hell. Inwardly they can be as tarnished as they are polished without. The play is well named, for its concern is not with this person's follies or that one's vices, but with leisure-class society in general, its incentives of pleasure, its temptations to betray or misbehave. Indeed, it is the social scene as a whole that is of thematic importance in the play; the actual plot, the individual intrigues, are often tediously complicated, and are perhaps more of a drawback to the play's success than the talkiness of the dialogue and the fatiguing brightness of the wit. *The Way of the World* is the most distinguished product of the Restoration theater, but there is no use going into it at length as a play in the technical sense, because even if it is rather better than it is usually thought to be, as playwriting it is still not impressive; and to try to work up enthusiasm for *The Way of the World* on the basis of its stagecraft would be like trying to work up enthusiasm for Chartres Cathedral on the basis of its acoustics. We must judge it for what its characters represent as symbolic figures, and not as puppets of the plot. Nonetheless, the plot does often serve to point up not only how self-indulgent and inconstant these people are, but how frustrated and foiled. They cannot, many of them, have what they want in the way of a husband or a lover; they cannot dare believe in friendship or hope for love. They are trapped by the baseness of their own view of life and by the very selfishness of their own desires. Even in suffering they can find no salvation, for they do not know how to suffer; they can only, when they feel pain, try to inflict it elsewhere.

This is something apprehended amid the spin and sparkle of language and wit, something that is a matter of tone; the teaching of the play, so far as it does teach, is in the tone. Congreve is, on the one hand, too sensitive an artist to try to teach more overtly; but on the other hand, I would think, too baffled and skeptical and perhaps superficial a philosopher to know how. He has far too much taste and sensibility to acquiesce cynically in what he sees of life, yet too ingrained and pessimistic a sense of the way of the world—and doubtless too great an affinity for it—ever to protest very much. We must look elsewhere for writers with more severe and positive values, for writers who aspire beyond tone to something like vision. But *The Way of the World* furnishes, in its own aesthetic fashion, a sense of the melancholy in life, of the awful hell of life. There is here a kind of paradox: no tone could be more civilized than Congreve's, yet no story better suggests how little being civilized avails.

But how much it avails in art. No naturalistic approach could bring off a Millamant or contrive, beyond even the verbal merits of *The Way of the World,* its decisive sense of style. When at length, well into the second act, Millamant appears and Mirabel salutes her with his celebrated words—"Here she comes, i' faith, full sail, with her fan spread and streamers out, and a shoal of fools for tender"—with what a splash, with what an air of the great world, she enters. Mirabel so glorifies Millamant in those words, we are scarcely aware that he is also making fun of her. She enters, there is some give-and-take, and then comes the business of the letters:

MILLAMANT: Mincing, what had I? Why was I so long?

MINCING: O mem, your laship stayed to peruse a packet of letters.

MILLAMANT: Oh, ay, letters—I had letters—I am persecuted with letters—I hate letters. Nobody knows how to write letters; and yet one has 'em, one does not know why. They serve one to pin up one's hair.

WITWOUD: Is that the way? Pray, madam, do you pin up your hair with all your letters? I find I must keep copies.

MILLAMANT: Only with those in verse, Mr. Witwoud. I never pin up my hair with prose. I think I tried once, Mincing.

MINCING: O mem, I shall never forget it.

MILLAMANT: Ay, poor Mincing tift and tift all the morning.

MINCING: Till I had the cramp in my fingers, I'll vow, mem. And all to no purpose. But when your laship pins it up with poetry, it fits so pleasant the next day as anything, and is so pure and so crips.

WITWOUD: Indeed, so crips?

MINCING: You're such a critic, Mr. Witwoud.

Here again it is not just the language or the fancifulness, but a certain turn and heightening, an effect of style, that gives this trivial little scene distinction; the same style that gives the play the exact pitch, the sure mark of high comedy; that adds a kind of breeding to the brilliance. It is the decisive element in a prose of the best sort—a prose that for word choice, rhythm, movement, can equal fine poetry but is not, in any usual sense, the least poetic. Indeed, it never loses a certain low-pitched dryness and coolness, a certain colloquial ease. It remains domesticated. Sterne, in his own way, can be the same kind of prose writer, can keep the same kind of colloquial ease.

Such dry, cool, yet invincibly stylish prose perfectly fits Congreve's conveying to us that the way of the world is no passing fashion but an eternal fact. Rather than the struggle against defeat that we find in drama, we find in such high comedy as this a skepticism which is very nearly defeatism. One knows here, or suspects, or fears, what the world can be like, or life can be like, or love can be like. Millamant holds Mirabel off throughout most of the play, but this cannot be regarded simply as a conventional plot device or as the coy tactics of a "romantic" heroine. The point is that Millamant is not just choosing a man, or even choosing one man from many: she is deciding whether to marry. Now it is assumed in novels and plays that everyone wishes to marry; indeed, marriage is the only way an ordinary writer has for indicating that certain characters lived happily ever after. But the issue is not so simple; the idea of marriage, which is not the same thing as the idea of mating, could be very disquieting, very much of a dilemma, to a clever, high-mettled, attractive, much-sought-after girl who is as much her own mistress as Millamant.

The marriage-contract scene between Millamant and Mirabel is so witty and delightful as mere banter that we almost fail to notice the altogether realistic basis of the bargaining. We are so pleased with Millamant's remark about how she "may dwindle into a wife" that we may miss the point of her conditions, which are that the marriage may not dwindle into a farce or deteriorate into a failure. Congreve, like other masters of comedy, employs a kind of paradox: he suggests the tarnish of life through the glitter, the lees through the froth, the clouds and shadows through the all-too-passing moment of sunlight. The marriage-contract scene is in its way Mozartian: here are the shimmer and gaiety of those who apprehend how fugitive is pleasure, how fraudulent are so many well-intended vows, how touched with melancholy is life. Reading the scene, we may of course ignore everything but its charm, and will have been notably rewarded; but there is more to it than charm. All earnest souls, all people who judge things by mere size and weight, distrust and dismiss gaiety as minor and even frivolous. But we ought not to be deceived; there is not only more health in the moment of joyousness, but very likely more resonance and depth. What could be gayer than Natasha at the ball in *War and Peace*—or more beautifully memorable? What has more brilliance than the court scenes in *The Charterhouse of Parma* and yet, at bottom, more of the hard truth of life? And who, in a way, for all his celebrated dispiritedness is gayer, brisker, more playful, more full of spring and wit than Hamlet?

Millamant seems to me an extremely successful creation as much for what Congreve did not make her as for what he did. Thus, he did not make her lovable: there is nothing warm-hearted or self-effacing or innocently girlish about her; you cannot imagine her being terribly kind to people she has no interest in, or staying home from a ball to sit at a sick aunt's bedside. She is not in the least noble-minded, she is not even, by modern standards, very humane. She is spoiled, she is pert, she is given to airs and affectations, she is invincibly feminine, she is an incorrigible coquette. She makes light of most things, she makes fun of many. She is a very superior girl who knows her own worth; and like anybody who is honest about it, she loves being sought after and complimented and courted.

The point is that she is the very best product of a certain world; the point is, equally, that she does not rise above it. She is captivating rather than lovable, and easier to find fault with than to resist. She has taste and sensibility and perceptiveness, and at moments that incomparable hoity-toityness wherewith women always have, if not the last word, then something like the last laugh. Nowhere has she it more superbly than in commenting on the vanity and fatuousness of "lovers" (we should say "suitors"):

> Lord, what is a lover that it can give? Why one
> makes lovers as fast as one pleases, and they live
> as long as one pleases, and they die as soon as
> one pleases; and then, if one pleases, one makes
> more.

One particular virtue about Millamant is that, though a perfect character of artificial comedy—endowed with an air too perfect for real life—her actual behavior and motivations are convincingly realistic. She is incomparable for her graces, not for her good qualities. And it is a tribute to Congreve's honesty that he made Millamant a radiant figure without making her a romantic or entirely girlish one.

Set against Millamant, most of the other characters, including Mirabel, rather tend to pale. But as worldlings, and worldling types, a number of them are effective, and something in particular might be said for Witwoud, the sort of fellow who must be always in the know and never caught napping, who never lacks a smart or clever answer or an up-to-date bit of gossip or slang: a very good kind of second-rater, really, whom we almost admire till we see him come up against somebody better. I don't share the usual opinion about how tragic Lady Wishfort is—pathetic, yes, and a truly wretched figure, burning with sexual desire while grown old and ugly. But she is too much a fool, too shallow, too gullible, for us to care about *her;* what we feel for is her situation, is that of anyone unloved and wanting love. She is also, and I think wisely, made quite farcical: were she not, she might, without becoming tragic, be too uncomfortably realistic for artificial comedy. (pp. 55-69)

> Louis Kronenberger, "The Way of the World,"
> in his The Polished Surface: Essays in the Literature of Worldliness, *Alfred A. Knopf, 1969,*
> *pp. 55-72.*

Susan McCloskey   (essay date 1981)

[*In the following excerpt, McCloskey examines the depiction of familial relationships in* The Way of the World, *contending that the play attests to Congreve's preoccupation with the changing structure of the family during the Restoration period. "The play is about the Wishfort family's gradual transformation," she states; "bound by wealth and status, the sprawling kinship structure presented in the first three acts collapses, to be replaced in the final acts by a conjugal family intimately bound by ties of love."*]

With the exception of *The Old Bachelor* (1693), a highly conventional first play, Congreve's comedies focus on relations within families. Each play in turn deals with characters bound by increasingly complex genealogical and emotional ties. As a playwright interested in manners, Congreve found in such compact (and unruly) communities a microcosm of society, and in the relations between siblings, spouses, and parent and child a network of associations perfectly suited to dramatic representation. For instance, *The Double Dealer* (1694) assembles Touchwoods and Plyants, related already by marriage, to witness a second match between the two families. Interests more at odds are hard to conceive. In love with her step-nephew Mellefont, Lady Touchwood connives to block his marriage to her brother's child. While she works with Maskwell, Mellefont's avowed friend, to carry out her scheme, her brother, Sir Paul Plyant, struggles to prevent his wife's infidelity with Careless, the step-nephew's true friend. No more straightforwardly, the Legends and the Foresights begin *Love for Love* (1695) linked only by friendship; after a series of comic close calls, they end the play as prospec-

tive in-laws. Before this happy unravelling occurs, Valentine Legend, Sir Sampson's son, feigns madness to circumvent his father's plans to cut off his inheritance, and fears he will lose Angelica Foresight to his father's brisk courtship. His brother Ben returns from sea to pay halfhearted court to Prue Foresight and to teach Sir Sampson the limits of parental power. While lust, greed, and Ben's bluff practicality tax the Legend family ties, lust alone rends those of the Foresights. Mr. Foresight vainly studies the movement of heavenly bodies in order not to observe the exorbitant tendencies of his wife's, sister-in-law's, and daughter's undeniably earthly ones. Finally, *The Way of the World* (1700) exaggerates the dynastic convolutions of its predecessors. Lady Wishfort presides over a collection of orphans tenuously related to her by blood and law. Much of the play's comedy—and the audience's confusion—stems from the characters' bafflingly precise definitions of their connections to one another. To Fainall, for instance, Mirabell describes Lady Wishfort as Millamant's "aunt, your wife's mother, my evil genius" (I. 1. 20-1). Finall replies in kind, identifying Sir Wilfull as "half brother to this Witwoud by a former wife, who was sister to my Lady Wishfort, my wife's mother" (I. 1. 174-75).

In the number and variety of the relationships detailed, all three plays attest to Congreve's preoccupation with the family. In *The Way of the World,* however, Lady Wishfort's fractured family commands his attention not only as a synecdoche for society, but on its own terms. The play

Jessica Tandy as Lady Wishfort and Nancy Wickwire as Mistress Marwood in a 1965 production of The Way of the World *at the Guthrie Theater, Minneapolis.*

is about the Wishfort family's gradual transformation: bound by wealth and status, the sprawling kinship structure presented in the first three acts collapses, to be replaced in the final acts by a conjugal family intimately bound by ties of love. Congreve's focus on the family in the process of change, forced by circumstance to redefine its sense of itself, can be sharpened in performance, making delightfully clear the ways in which his last play summarizes the social and moral emphasis of his dramatic career.

Recent scholarship on the family in England indicates that Congreve chose the family as his focus at a crucial stage in its historical development. Despite the criticism leveled at the unwieldy scope of his work and its method, Lawrence Stone's study, *The Family, Sex, and Marriage in England, 1500-1800* (New York: Harper and Row, 1977) presents a model for the family's transformation over time with which few scholars quarrel. Stone argues that the family of the sixteenth and seventeenth centuries was a hybrid, retaining on the one hand traits of the kin-dominated family of the Middle Ages, and anticipating on the other the conjugal family of the eighteenth century to the present time. By 1700, this transitional phase had nearly ended. Sharper lines were being drawn between the immediate and the extended family. Affection between husband and wife came increasingly to be regarded as the basis for marriage; less frequently, except among the aristocracy, was wedlock an alliance to improve the wealth or social position of the kin. Love between spouses extended to love for the children of the union, who began to acquire the special status unknown even to their Elizabethan predecessors. In short, as a congeries of economic, political, religious, and social forces worked to erode the kinship system as the dominant family pattern, the unit at the heart of that system—the conjugal group of mother, father, and children—emerged in its place.

This shift in emphasis, from the extended to the immediate family, and the changes in marriage and parenting such a shift implies, was perceptible even, or perhaps especially, to the men and women of Congreve's own day. The coexistence of old and new forms of the family and motives for marriage rendered flexible a formerly more rigid system of mating and multiplying. Stone presents John Verney's experience in courtship as an index to extremes among the options. In 1674, Verney sought a wife with the shrewd calculation of the merchant he was, discussing settlements with the father, discussing nothing with his intended bride (who remained ignorant of his existence), and worrying that the young woman might fail to please him. The match never took place—for reasons of finance, not sexual appeal. In 1680, though, the same seemingly heartless merchant fell so passionately in love that financial considerations shrank to lilliputian proportions. This match did transpire, to the apparent and continuing delight of both partners—and their offspring. Writing to his wife during her third pregnancy, Verney sends "love to the little ones and"—a charming phrase—to "the kicker in the dark." In the space of a mere six years, the merchant who regarded marriage as a financial arrangement came to adopt the thoroughly modern notion of marriage as the

union of lovers. His transformation, at the very least, is a startling one.

Perhaps no more than Verney himself did Congreve comprehend the myriad causes of this reorientation of attitude toward marriage and family. But as his last play, *The Way of the World,* demonstrates, he closely observed the process in which Verney participated. What the family in history took two centuries to accomplish, Congreve compresses into five carefully structured acts. Through the first three acts, he describes Lady Wishfort's chaotic family, an extended kin group with all the stability of a house of cards. Their tangled relationships would baffle even an audience of professional genealogists. All the children (save Arabella Fainall) are orphans, and feel bound to one another less by blood and affection than by varieties of self-interest. In their disarray, they appear an easy mark for Fainall, who wishes to seize the family's fortune and blight its fame. The last two acts involve Mirabell's attempts to defend the family against Fainall's assault. He assumes the central role abdicated under pressure of circumstance and incapacity by Lady Wishfort, the grudgingly acknowledged matriarch. He then moves to revitalize the decaying family, first by guaranteeing its future, then by directing its present. In the fourth act, he gains Millamant's consent to a love match and—rare in Restoration comedy—to maternity. Then in the fifth act, he forges the divided kin into a community sufficiently strong to resist Fainall's designs. Through his efforts, a new kind of family emerges from the old. The men and women onstage in the play's closing moments enact this reorganization, letting us see how the ramshackle kin group unites around the stable center that Mirabell, Millamant, and their promised offspring will provide. As this process takes place, the play's often-cited complexities resolve into simplicity. Our earlier difficulty in deciding who is what to whom suddenly seems remote. Such a transformation—nearly as dazzling as John Verney's—invites retrospective attention to the sleight of hand by which a family in its death throes becomes one eager for its perpetuation on new terms.

Congreve's magic begins with his portrait of Lady Wishfort's family and her world through the first three acts. To define the conditions within a decaying society, he chooses an inherently dramatic index: the kinds of relations the family's members maintain. We are meant to find these relationships indecipherably complex. But Congreve thrusts us into his labyrinth with a guide, focusing our attention on one kind of relationship at a time. Acts I through III successively deal with friendship, with love, and with kinship—or this family's distorted equivalents. Each act supplies evidence that the traditional bonds have been severely frayed. For instance, four supposed friends meet at the chocolate house in Act I as if to demonstrate that men prefer the company of those they detest. Mirabell and Fainall, Witwoud and Petulant profess friendship to observe each other's movements at close range: a rival under surveillance can less readily gain the upper hand. In the second act, lovers turn out to be equally suspicious, as four couples transform the byways of St. James's Park into an emotional maze. The Fainalls meet to exchange insults. Fainall and Mrs. Marwood wander down a private path, not to rendezvous, but to hurl recriminations at one another's heads. As Mrs. Fainall chides her former gallant, Mirabell, who then encounters Millamant in one of her flightier moods, they supply further proof that the men and women associated with this family mean by "love" a variety of things. Detestation, surfeited passion, mutual wariness, and the stern notion that "one's cruelty is one's power" (II. 1. 348) have more to do with the tender passion than the audience might have supposed. Like the men in the chocolate house, these unhappy couples testify to old bonds about to snap under new strains.

The first two acts show us *what* is wrong with this society; the third tells us *why*. To emphasize its central role in the confusion of his characters' affairs, Congreve makes kinship the focal relationship of the play's central act. His spiteful lovers and mistrustful friends converge on Lady Wishfort's apartments, demonstrating that when charity does not begin at home, its failure often ends there. True to the precedent of the opening acts, in which friendship and love come nearly to mean their opposites, kinship too undergoes radical redefinition. Sir Wilfull's arrival in London might have occasioned a happy reunion, but in Lady Wishfort's family, his visit proves that kinship is a euphemism for unfortunate accidents of birth. Millamant leaves the room when her cousin arrives; Witwoud prefers not to acknowledge his half-brother after their twelve-year separation. Not until Lady Wishfort makes her tardy entrance does anyone present work himself up to a brief and singularly tepid show of family feeling:

> LADY WISHFORT: Nephew, you are welcome.
>
> SIR WILFULL: Aunt, your servant.
>
> FAINALL: Sir Wilfull, your most faithful servant.
>
> SIR WILFULL: Cousin Fainall, give me your hand.
>
> LADY WISHFORT: Cousin Witwoud, your servant; Mr. Petulant, your servant. Nephew, you are welcome again . . .
>
> SIR WILFULL: . . . I thank you, aunt.
>
> [III. 1. 524-32]

Each successive "nephew" or "aunt" or "cousin" sounds more hollow than the last. The very perfunctoriness of the exchange suggests that the ties first joining these men and women are those least happily acknowledged. Had Fate not played them dirty tricks at birth or marriage, Lady Wishfort's wards—with the single exception of Sir Wilfull—would have no part of this joyless gathering. As Witwoud observes and as the third act confirms, "Tis not modish to know relations in town" (III. 1. 470-71)—or anywhere else, for that matter.

Unrelated to Lady Wishfort's family by birth or marriage, Mirabell seems to have spent his adult life remedying that fortunate oversight. Former lover and legal advisor to Mrs. Fainall, pretended gallant to Lady Wishfort, determined suitor to Millamant, benefactor to Waitwell and Foible, and companion to Fainall, Witwoud, Petulant, and Sir Wilfull, this Mirabell cultivates the ties to the family its own members prefer to deny. He is in fact the cyno-

sure Lady Wishfort should be. But the nature of this outsider's involvement in the family's affairs goes beyond these ties: he acts as well as a moral arbiter in Lady Wishfort's stead. While she pines for sex, he plots for marriage. While she murders reputations on cabal nights, he preserves Mrs. Fainall's name, counsels Petulant against ill manners, and reproves Millamant for her unseemly toleration of fools. As he contemplates a lifetime association with the Wishfort family, he finds himself thoroughly displeased with the status quo. "How can you find delight in such society?" (II. 1. 393) is the question he asks Millamant, having himself considered the answer with great care. As the play's last two acts demonstrate, he never comes to share her belief in the tonic effect of foolish companions. For him, the delight of such society lies in its complete revamping.

Prior to the fourth act, Mirabell can do little but remonstrate against his companions' poor behavior. But in the fourth act, he starts acquiring the power needed to reform his intended family. Significantly, he directs his energies toward matrimony, the institution on which the perpetuation of families depends. His earlier schemes to gain Millamant without loss of her fortune confirm his marriage-mindedness: he has paid court to Lady Wishfort, sent Waitwell and Foible to be married at Duke's Place, and brought Waitwell back as her ladyship's suitor, Sir Rowland. Not wishing to trick Millamant into the union that requires for success her free consent, Mirabell abandons plots for persuasion. In their justly famous proviso scene, he enlists Millamant's aid—and, more importantly, her love—to define the marriage that will avoid the Fainalls' poor precedent. In the course of the scene, the young lovers establish the terms of a relationship that will provide the stable center around which Lady Wishfort's family of orphans can regroup.

In keeping with his portrait in Acts I through III of Lady Wishfort's world, in which the odds favor failed relationships, Congreve places the proviso scene in an important modifying context. Mirabell must woo and win Millamant while Lady Wishfort schemes for her own nuptials with Sir Rowland, and while Sir Wilfull and Petulant look to bumpers of wine for the courage to court Millamant themselves. These comically flawed attempts at courtship define the attitudes toward marriage that have deprived the family of stability, making likely its present muddled affairs. Lady Wishfort regards marriage as a means to satisfy her sexual longings without murdering her reputation. Petulant sees marriage as the easiest way to gain the social position his peculiar talents have denied him. Sir Wilfull prefers bachelorhood, but struggles against personal inclination when his aunt orders him to pay court to his cousin. So partial is this triumph of familial obedience over good sense that Sir Wilfull forgets his cousin's name when he proposes their dictated match. By contrast, the exquisite reasonableness of Mirabell's courtship shares nothing with these radically compromised views of matrimony. Together, he and Millamant define an achievable ideal in wedlock and establish the precedent for successful relationships so clearly required by Lady Wishfort's alienated kin.

The proviso scene is a model of mutual understanding, reciprocity, and respect, all informed by a sophisticated sense of play. A couple with serious reservations does not, after all, draw up a marriage contract dealing with arrangements at dinner and the proper beverages at afternoon tea. Motivated neither by lust, social ambition, nor the command of an imperious aunt, this young couple announces a new, single motive for matrimony: love. Conscious of Millamant's skittish resistance to possible imprudence (half her fortune depends on her aunt's unlikely consent to this union), Mirabell slowly leads her beyond the desire for personal independence within marriage to a calm acceptance of the risks and rewards of a shared life. Millamant in turn tempers Mirabell's habitually singleminded pursuit of his goals by exercising her cherished maiden privilege: the freedom teasingly to oppose his wishes even when they happen to be her own.

At no point in the scene is this artful inconsistency more apparent than in this exchange—a peculiarly domestic one in any romantic comedy, let alone one written during the Restoration:

> MIRABELL: . . . When you shall be breeding—
>
> MILLAMANT: Ah! name it not!
>
> MIRABELL: Which may be presumed, with a blessing on our endeavors—
>
> MILLAMANT: Odious endeavors!
>
> MIRABELL: I denounce against all strait-lacing, squeezing for a shape, till you mold my boy's head like a sugar loaf, and instead of a man-child, make me the father to a crooked billet.
> [IV. 1. 230-37]

Mirabell takes no more seriously than Millamant her avowed distaste for "breeding." Her feigned horror—like so many other expressions in this delicately indirect scene—in fact attests to the contrary feeling: readiness to become the unlaced mother to Mirabell's shapely offspring. In a play about family, the lovers' accord on this point is significant. Already the best of friends and the truest of lovers, Mirabell and Millamant agree to become the closest of kin—father and mother, as well as husband and wife. When they do, they recapitulate the sequence of the first three acts, substituting success for their companions' failures. In defiance of the world's precedents, they formulate their own. And in defiance of the slightly altered proverb, they teach the old world a new trick.

But old habits die hard. Once Mirabell has won his lady in the fourth act, he faces in the fifth a threat to her present family—and, in future, his own. He parts from his fiancée only to discover that Fainall and Mrs. Marwood have busily advanced their scheme to push Lady Wishfort's tottering family over the brink into ruin. Planning to deprive Lady Wishfort of remarriage, and Mrs. Fainall and Millamant of their estates, the villains put to a severe test the notion that "one's cruelty is one's power." From their cynical observation of the world and its ways, they know that the threats of scandal and poverty will rend the already tattered fabric of kinship, friendship, and love. Success requires only that they isolate their victims and argue the easy case of self-interest's priority over all other claims.

Their principal victim, appropriately, is the head of the family whose ruin they intend. Early in Act V, we watch a beleaguered Lady Wishfort crumble as Mrs. Marwood imagines Mrs. Fainall's trial for adultery with Mirabell. Unnerved by the prospect of such a scandal, she weakly resists Fainall's harsh terms for its avoidance. Because she is isolated from those who might restore her scattered wits to sense, she uses her scant time for reflection to no good end. What sees her through this crisis is her uncanny instinct for doing what is worst for her family: she simply decides to dissociate herself from her kinsmen's fates. Expecting a negative reply, she has already asked Mrs. Fainall, "Is it possible thou shouldst be my child, bone of my bone, and flesh of my flesh?" (V. 1. 129-30). But now she abandons such speculation for certainty. Millamant and Sir Wilfull enter her presence not as niece and nephew, but as "Egyptian plagues" (V. 1. 289). Sir Wilfull needs only to remind her of their relationship to provoke her flat denial of the ties of blood: "Out, caterpillar, call me not aunt! I know thee not!" (V. 1. 291). Her disclaimers of kinship signal the utter dissolution of the old family structure; its center nervously repudiates all responsibility to hold. By the middle of Act V, then, Fainall and Mrs. Marwood seem to have achieved their ends with an almost unbecoming ease.

But unknown to the villainous pair, Mirabell has anticipated her ladyship's abandonment of power and responsibility, and devised a dazzlingly simple counter-offensive to Fainall's attack. His scheme depends in part on a bit of shrewd foresight predating the play's commencement. Having long possessed Mrs. Fainall's deed of trust, he knows that her estate is secure against Fainall's claims. (Millamant need only agree to marry Sir Wilfull to protect her fortune.) But Mirabell deliberately conceals knowledge of this deed from Lady Wishfort's wards. His purpose is not merely to prevent penury, but to redefine the family's sense of itself. By encouraging them to think their crisis more severe than it is, he hopes to translate apparent danger into the occasion for concerted action. The opportunity to act as a family may finally instruct them in what one is. So, while we watch Fainall and Mrs. Marwood badger Lady Wishfort into accepting their demands, Mirabell works offstage toward his benevolent double ends. He obtains Waitwell's release from prison, rejoins Millamant, and sends Mincing to summon Sir Wilfull and Foible. As he beckons character after character to this offstage parley, he apparently presents to each a simple alternative. They may subscribe to Fainall's version of self-interest, act independently to save their own necks, and risk almost certain failure. Or they may acknowledge their interdependent interests, cooperate in Mirabell's plot, and guarantee success. Only fools would puzzle long over such a choice—which perhaps explains why Mirabell fails to include Witwoud and Petulant in the confederates' assembly.

Just at the moment in Act V when Fainall and Mrs. Marwood feel confident of victory, Mirabell begins to pay out the dividends of his offstage negotiations. In the middle of

Act V, the drawing room in which Lady Wishfort has endured her lonely and entirely comic victimization slowly starts to fill. Armed with the dictates of the same law Fainall has invoked, Mirabell's allies confront their opponents, behaving at once like seasoned troops and accomplished actors. Millamant and Sir Wilfull enter to announce with straight faces their wedding plans. Mirabell then appears to beg her ladyship's pardon—and, not at all incidentally, to isolate Fainall and Mrs. Marwood by winning Lady Wishfort to his side. Mrs. Fainall, Foible, and Mincing come forward to testify to Fainall's adultery. Then Waitwell appears with the deed of trust, followed by Witwoud and Petulant, who dimly recall having witnessed its signing. Each entrance loosens Fainall's grasp on another endangered estate, until he holds in his hand nothing but the sword he turns on his wife. But his violence is easily contained. United for the first time by a common cause, the ten confederates simply banish the villainous couple from the stage.

A mere second elapses between Fainall's and then Mrs. Marwood's departure and the beginning of a celebration. The five men and five women remaining onstage rejoice not only in their deliverance, but in the second triumph their unprecedented cooperation has achieved. Mirabell's strategem has succeeded. Having *acted* as a family, these poor friends, worse lovers, and still more reluctant kin now *become* one, and rush to proclaim the ties they have learned, through crisis, to value. Lady Wishfort promptly embraces her daughter, pleased that Mrs. Fainall has miraculously "inherited" the "prudence" her mother so notably lacks (V. 1. 522-23). Mrs. Fainall hails Mirabell as her "cautious friend," Sir Wilfull reclaims his half-brother, and Mirabell and Millamant declare their love so openly that Sir Wilfull scrambles to conceal a blush (V. 1. 524). As they name one another properly—"daughter," "mother," "nephew," "friend," "lover," "aunt," "cousin"—their clarity makes our earlier confusion seem causeless. Unlike poor Witwoud, we are no longer "in a maze yet" (V. 1. 542-43). This outburst of reconciliation unravels the tangled relationships, as the ties first joining these characters to their displeasure now bind them to their evident delight. Kinship, which so recently seemed to blight the possibilities of friendship and love, now complements both.

Confirming this new unity, Mirabell and Millamant, Sir Wilfull and Mrs. Fainall, Waitwell and Foible, Lady Wishfort and Witwoud, Mincing and Petulant join hands in the expected dance. But this aspect of their celebration complies in no simple way with comic convention. Indeed, if this essay's argument is correct, the final dance provides an occasion to render the play's theme through its blocking, to translate the dance into an emblem of the old kinship structure Congreve and Mirabell have set out to rearrange. Its choreography should be emphatically linear: parallel lines of men and women bowing and curtseying, coming together and breaking apart, passing in pairs under the other dancers' raised arms. They trace in their movement a pattern like a family tree, with its sets of horizontal lines indicating relationship through marriage and vertical lines expressing relationship through birth. The dancers should repeat the pattern again and again, sus-

pending the dramatic action to emphasize the crucial moment when it resumes. For once this dance ends, its precise angles should immediately be played against the characters' final configuration onstage, illustrating through this changing geometry how the new family's structure evolves from the old.

The lovely, stylized dance ends in circumstances that reinforce its potentially emblematic nature. Finding the exercise too taxing, Lady Wishfort suddenly breaks from her partner and disrupts the graceful image of her family's accord. She is apparently no more able now than before to keep her family together. If they wish to preserve their unity, her kindred require a structure more permanent than the dance—or even the kinship system whose network it traced. By retreating from the festivities, Lady Wishfort tacitly permits that structure to emerge; she can in fact "hold out no longer" (V. 1. 558). At this critical moment in the play details of blocking might again assume thematic importance. The final phase of the family's reorganization should begin as Mirabell escorts her exhausted ladyship to a chair, calming her fears about Fainall's reprisals. He then returns to center stage to present Mrs. Fainall with the deed of trust. As the interrupted dancers gather around him, their action acknowledges his leadership and declares an allegiance his predecessor could never command.

But now the family's leader comes in a matched set, and two more replacements of the old by the new mark the play's final moments. As Millamant moves to Mirabell's side, the young lovers succeed the loveless, childless Fainalls as the family's married partners, and hold out to it the promise of a new generation. With the other "players at the end of the last act" assembled around them, they give to the old family a new center and shape (V. 1. 479-80). Degrees of care and affection, rather than the sequence of births, determine proximity to this center—and the players' arrangement on stage should again emphasize this point. Mrs. Fainall, Sir Wilfull, Waitwell, and Foible form a circle around Mirabell and Millamant, earning their places through early and continued loyalty. Mincing attends Lady Wishfort in her nearby chair, at the circumference of an imagined second ring. Doomed by invincible self-love to a peripheral role in the family's affairs, Petulant and Witwoud linger downstage, detached from the rest of the company. The play should end with this picture of men and women at ease in an informal grouping quite unlike the tightly controlled pattern of the dance. In their movement from the first to the second pattern of blocking, the characters enact the kindred's reorganization as a conjugal group: rigid lines relax into the roughly concentric circles emanating from the center Mirabell and Millamant define.

The most important achievement of the play's final moments, however, involves neither the kin's lost dominance, the conjugal family's imminent triumph, nor the success of a marriage based on love and awaiting little kickers in the dark. Congreve's fascination with his society's forms and customs, the changing values that turn a merchant like Verney into a romantic, dictates only what happens to Lady Wishfort's relations. His skill as a comic dramatist controls what happens to his play. As his characters find themselves plucked from ruin, snatched from disgrace, and delighted to have friends, be lovers, and embrace kin, they leave Congreve's audience with an impression far different than they had initially encouraged. The muddle synonymous with Lady Wishfort's world has disappeared; Mirabell's world is altogether a tidier place. The perplexed era of the cabal, feigned courtship, secret marriage, eavesdropping, blackmail, and brandished swords has ended—at least for the time. A more hopeful age appears to have begun. Mirabell and Millamant can marry, Sir Wilfull can travel, and Witwoud and Petulant can continue to rail and gamble, confident that the family's new sense of itself makes possible a happier progress through the corridors of the chocolate house, through the avenues of St. James's Park, through confusion, uncertainty, and distress—in short, through all the ways of the world. (pp. 69-79)

Susan McCloskey, "Knowing One's Relations in Congreve's 'The Way of the World'," in Theatre Journal, *Vol. 33, No. 1, March, 1981, pp. 69-79.*

FURTHER READING

BIOGRAPHIES

Gosse, Edmund. *The Life of William Congreve.* New York: Charles Scribner's Sons, 1924, 181 p.

> Expanded version of Gosse's 1888 biography. Gosse examines Congreve's life and literary career, offering critical commentary while reviewing the reception of his works.

Hodges, John C. *William Congreve The Man: A Biography from New Sources.* New York: Modern Language Association of America, 1941, 151 p.

> Uses newly discovered material to "make possible a more discerning and more sympathetic reading of Congreve."

Lynch, Kathleen M. *A Congreve Gallery.* Cambridge, Mass.: Harvard University Press, 1951, 196 p.

> Illuminates Congreve's life and works through the exploration of his friendships.

Taylor, D. Crane. *William Congreve.* New York: Russell & Russell, 1963, 252 p.

> Critical biography. Taylor devotes individual chapters to each of Congreve's plays, and appends a chronological bibliography outlining the publication of various tracts prompted by the Jeremy Collier controversy.

OVERVIEWS AND GENERAL STUDIES

Archer, William. Introduction to *William Congreve,* edited by Felix E. Schelling, pp. 1-40. New York: American Book Company, 1912.

> Denigrates the "inextricable tangle" of most of Congreve's plots but lauds his characterization and dialogue.

Archer asserts that Congreve's indifference to moral precepts renders him the "last of the ancients" rather than the "first of the moderns."

Avery, Emmett L. *Congreve's Plays on the Eighteenth-Century Stage.* New York: The Modern Language Association of America, 1951, 226 p.

> Discusses the production and reception of Congreve's plays in the eighteenth century relative to other Restoration dramas revived during that period.

Child, Harold. "William Congreve." In his *Essays and Reflections,* edited by S. C. Roberts, pp. 105-14. Cambridge: At the University Press, 1948.

> Refutes critics who have dismissed Congreve's work as shallow, maintaining that his plays reveal "sustained and varied emotion," "moral notions," and "extraordinary psychological perception."

Davies, Thomas. "Congreve." In his *Dramatic Miscellanies,* pp. 185-227. 1784. Reprint. New York: Benjamin Blom, 1971.

> Reviews Congreve's dramas, discussing their sources, characters, and early productions.

Dobrée, Bonamy. "Congreve." In his *Restoration Comedy 1660-1720,* pp. 121-50. 1924. Reprint. Westport, Conn.: Greenwood Press, 1981.

> Influential reassessment of Congreve's comedies. Dobrée examines the relationship between style and thought in Congreve's works, concluding that the author was "too much of a poet to accept the surface of life, [and] too little a poet to find beauty in the bare facts of existence."

——. "William Congreve: I. His Life" and "William Congreve: II. His Work." In his *Variety of Ways: Discussions on Six Authors,* pp. 46-65, 66-85. 1932. Reprint. Freeport, N.Y.: Books for Libraries Press, 1967.

> Concludes that Congreve distinguished himself by the brilliance of his prose and not by any noteworthy expressions of philosophical or moral questions.

Edgar, Irving I. "Restoration Comedy and William Congreve." In his *Essays in English Literature and History,* pp. 52-70. New York: Philosophical Library, 1972.

> Asserts that Congreve's superior wit and "marked refinement of language" enhance his employment of plots and conventions established by earlier Restoration dramatists.

Fujimara, Thomas H. "William Congreve." In his *Restoration Comedy of Wit,* pp. 156-96. Princeton, N.J.: Princeton University Press, 1952.

> Explains Congreve as a transitional figure whose comedies demonstrate the libertine wit of the Restoration giving way to the moral seriousness of the eighteenth century.

Hazlitt, William. "On Wycherley, Congreve, Vanbrugh, and Farquhar." In his *Lectures on the English Comic Writers,* pp. 133-76. London: Taylor and Hessey, 1819.

> Contends that Congreve's style and dialogue are elegant but his characterization limited. According to this influential critic, "the springs of nature, passion, [and] imagination are but feebly touched" in Congreve's works.

Holland, Norman N. *The First Modern Comedies: The Signif-*

icance of Etherege, Wycherley and Congreve. Cambridge, Mass.: Harvard University Press, 1959.

> Highly regarded study of the conflict between social conventions and natural desires in Restoration drama.

Hunt, Leigh. Introduction to *The Dramatic Works of Wycherley, Congreve, Vanbrugh, and Farquhar,* edited by Leigh Hunt, pp. ix-lxxxiv. London: George Routledge and Sons, 1875.

> Charges that Congreve's "love is spare and sorry; his belief in nothing, abundant"; his characters "heartless"; and his plots convoluted. "Wit for wit's sake," Hunt concludes, "becomes a task and a trial."

Jantz, Ursula. *Targets of Satire in the Comedies of Etherege, Wycherley, and Congreve.* Salzburg Studies in English Literature No. 42: Poetic Drama and Poetic Theory, edited by James Hogg. Salzburg: Institut für Englische Sprache und Literatur, Universität Salzburg, 1978, 242 p.

> Studies the three writers' contrasting approaches to such conventions and subjects as fops, dupes, women, and marriage.

Kronenberger, Louis. "Congreve." In his *Thread of Laughter: Chapters on English Stage Comedy from Jonson to Maugham,* pp. 117-45. New York: Alfred A. Knopf, 1952.

> Discusses the distinguishing features of Congreve's art and thought, assessing biographical influences on his comedies.

Leech, Clifford. "Congreve and the Century's End." *Philological Quarterly* XLI, No. 1 (January 1962): 275-93.

> Contends that Congreve's comedies reconcile not only the "diverse and often conflicting elements of Restoration comedy" but also the ascendant moral seriousness of the eighteenth century.

Love, Harold. *Congreve.* Oxford: Basil Blackwell, 1974, 131 p.

> Maintains that Congreve created natural characters whose relationships are realistic.

Lynch, Kathleen M. "Congreve." In her *Social Mode of Restoration Comedy,* pp. 182-213. New York: The MacMillan Co., 1926.

> Surveys the *précieuse* tradition in England, examining its influence on Congreve's thought.

Morris, Brian, ed. *William Congreve.* London: Ernest Benn, 1972, 176 p.

> Collection of nine diverse critical essays, including "Congreve on the Modern Stage" by Kenneth Muir and "Congreve's Sense of Theatre" by Gareth Lloyd Evans.

Muir, Kenneth. "William Congreve." In his *Comedy of Manners,* pp. 96-125. London: Hutchinson and Co., 1970.

> Favorable overview of Congreve's comedies. Muir lauds the author's ability to individuate characters through dialogue.

Perry, Henry Ten Eyck. "William Congreve." In his *Comic Spirit in Restoration Drama,* pp. 56-81. 1925. Reprint. New York: Russell & Russell, 1962.

> Traces the development of Congreve's artistry. Perry examines themes common to Congreve's works, and discusses the influence of George Etherege and William Wycherley on his comedies.

Roussel, Roy. "William Congreve and the Conversation of Opposites." In his *Conversation of the Sexes: Seduction and Equality in Selected Seventeenth- and Eighteenth-Century Texts,* pp. 124-59. New York: Oxford University Press, 1986.

> Detailed examination of male-female relationships in Congreve's comedies.

Snider, Rose. "William Congreve." In her *Satire in the Comedies of Congreve, Sheridan, Wilde, and Coward,* pp. 1-40. 1937. Reprint. New York: Phaeton Press, 1972.

> Addresses Congreve's satiric treatment of conventional male and female roles and of traditional social institutions.

Stephen, Sir Leslie. "Congreve, William." In *The Dictionary of National Biography,* Vol. IV, edited by Sir Leslie Stephen and Sir Sidney Lee, pp. 931-34. London: Oxford University Press, 1921.

> Assesses Congreve's work as both flawed and essentially base.

Strachey, Lytton. "Congreve, Collier, Macaulay, and Mr. Summers." In his *Portraits in Miniature and Other Essays,* pp. 41-9. New York: Harcourt, Brace and Co., 1931.

> Investigates the essence of Congreve's comedy and its attendant moral issues.

Thackeray, William Makepeace. "Congreve and Addison." In his *English Humorists of the Eighteenth Century,* pp. 48-92. Boston: Estes & Lauriat, 1891.

> Discusses Congreve's literary career, highlighting prominent features in his works. Thackeray concludes that "we have had in Congreve a humorous observer . . . to whom the world seems to have no moral at all, and whose ghastly doctrine seems to be that we should eat, drink, and be merry when we can, and go to the deuce (if there be a deuce) when the time comes."

Turner, Darwin T. "The Servant in the Comedies of William Congreve." *CLA Journal* I, No. 2 (March 1958): 68-74.

> Illustrates the diverse roles of confidant, arch-deceiver, and wit played by servants in Congreve's comedies.

Van Voris, W. H. *The Cultivated Stance: The Designs of Congreve's Plays.* Dublin: The Dolmen Press, 1965, 186 p.

> Elucidates Congreve's "main assumptions," describing how these "are revealed in the designs of his four comedies and his tragedy." Van Voris also examines Time as a recurrent theme in Congreve's works.

Williams, Aubrey L. "Poetical Justice, the Contrivances of Providence, and the Works of William Congreve." *ELH* 35, No. 4 (December 1968): 540-65.

> Argues that "the major works of Congreve are brilliant demonstrations of a providential order in human events."

―――. *An Approach to Congreve.* New Haven, Conn.: Yale University Press, 1979, 234 p.

> Examines each of Congreve's major works in "an attempt to provide the reader with an opportunity to decide for himself whether the playwright's imaginative vision is consistent with a Christian normative order—or with some putative Epicurean or Hobbesian or 'despiritualized' order—or with no order whatever." The opening chapters of Williams's study discuss the "still commonly shared, and fundamentally Christian, vision of human existence" that characterized Congreve's milieu.

LOVE FOR LOVE

Eaton, Walter Prichard. "Congreve's *Love for Love*." In his *Drama in English,* pp. 165-70. New York: Charles Scribner's Sons, 1930.

> Studies various aspects of *Love for Love* as they pertain to theatrical productions of the play.

Lyons, Charles R. "Congreve's Miracle of Love." *Criticism: A Quarterly for Literature and the Arts* VI, No. 4 (Fall 1964): 331-48.

> Contrasts the immature and corrupt liaisons of the minor characters in *Love for Love* with Valentine and Angelica's relationship, which represents sane, fulfilling love.

Milhous, Judith, and Hume, Robert D. *"Love for Love."* In their *Producible Interpretation: Eight English Plays, 1675-1707,* pp. 260-88. Carbondale: Southern Illinois University Press, 1985.

> Analyzes significant critical readings of *Love for Love,* outlining several "stageable interpretations" of the play.

THE WAY OF THE WORLD

Hinnant, Charles H. "Wit, Propriety, and Style in *The Way of the World.*" *Studies in English Literature, 1500-1900* XVII, No. 3 (Summer 1977): 373-86.

> Examines Congreve's conception of wit as elucidated in *The Way of the World.*

Kaufman, Anthony. "Language and Character in Congreve's *The Way of the World.*" *Texas Studies in Literature and Language* XV, No. 3 (Fall 1973): 411-27.

> Contends that distinctive dialogue effectively characterizes the players in *The Way of the World.*

Kimball, Sue L. "Games People Play in Congreve's *The Way of the World.*" In *A Provision of Human Nature: Essays on Fielding and Others in Honor of Miriam Austin Locke,* edited by Donald Kay, pp. 191-207. University, Ala.: University of Alabama Press, 1977.

> Proposes that the gaming imagery in *The Way of the World* is Congreve's "metaphor for life and love."

Lyons, Charles R. "Disguise, Identity, and Personal Value in *The Way of the World.*" *Educational Theater Journal* XXIII, No. 3 (October 1971): 258-68.

> Maintains that *The Way of the World* "explores the problem of value in a world dedicated to appearance, focusing upon the relationship of power and vulnerability in the sexual relationship."

Mueschke, Miriam, and Mueschke, Paul. *A New View of Congreve's "Way of the World."* Ann Arbor: University of Michigan Press, 1958, 85 p.

> Detailed study of Congreve's artistry in *The Way of the World.*

Snider, Alvin. "Professing a Libertine in *The Way of the World.*" *Papers on Language and Literature* 25, No. 4 (Fall 1989): 376-97.

> Asserts that *The Way of the World* represents Congreve's attempt to "assimilate the Epicurean tradition even while rendering it absurd and exposing its inadequacies in respect to 'real' experience."

For further information on Congreve's life and career, see *Dictionary of Literary Biography,* Vols. 39, 84; and *Literature Criticism 1400-1800,* Vol. 5

Everyman

c. 1495

INTRODUCTION

"*Everyman* is the most immediately impressive of the medieval moral plays, the one most often performed in modern times, and the one with which the whole idea of the moral play is synonymous," wrote W. A. Davenport, and most modern commentators agree with this assessment. *Everyman* achieves a simple beauty and dignity in its dramatic treatment of the medieval Catholic church doctrine concerning "Holy Dying," whereby a person forsakes earthly attachments and prepares his or her soul for salvation. Furthermore, this profound moral message is conveyed with gentle humor through vividly depicted characters. Long judged to be of historical interest only, a literary curiosity from a distant time, *Everyman* was revived on stage at the beginning of the twentieth century to great acclaim. The renewed interest in the play stimulated by William Poel's 1901 production has lasted to the present day, with audiences and critics discovering contemporary relevance in its poignant blending of spiritual and worldly concerns.

The play centers on the figure of Everyman, a wealthy man in his prime. Suddenly called by Death to make his reckoning before God and unprepared for such a trial, Everyman unsuccessfully tries various means to postpone the summons. As he embarks on his journey to meet God, he seeks assistance from his life-long companions Fellowship (friends), Kindred and Cousin (family), and Goods (material wealth), but all abandon him. Good-Deeds, with whom he has a passing acquaintance, responds, but since Everyman has neglected her in life, she is too weak to go along. She advises him, however, to call on Knowledge (awareness of sin). Knowledge escorts Everyman to the holy man Confession, who directs him to do penance. As he does so, Good-Deeds is strengthened and finally able to accompany him to his final reckoning. Everyman now wears the garment of Contrition, and his journey, until now a quest for spiritual health, increasingly takes on the quality of a pilgrimage to his salvation. Everyman, Knowledge, and Good-Deeds are joined by Beauty, Strength, Discretion (reason), and Five Wits (the senses). After donating his wealth to charity, Everyman follows the advice of Knowledge and Five Wits and receives the sacraments of Communion and Extreme Unction from a priest offstage. Meanwhile, Knowledge and Five Wits converse on the subject of corrupt priests in the Church. Coming to his grave, Everyman is again deserted by all his companions except Knowledge and Good-Deeds. Knowledge, however, remains behind as Everyman and Good-Deeds together descend into the grave.

Everyman was composed by an unknown author in the late fifteenth or early sixteenth century. As a morality play, it rose out of the rich medieval history of dramatic works based on Scripture. The morality play genre developed from the tradition of mystery and miracle plays,

Title page to an early edition of Everyman.

which enact such biblical stories as Noah's flood or Christ's crucifixion. In the course of time mystery plays were influenced by other medieval genres, including sermons, instructive discourses on moral themes, and scholarly commentary on the Bible. As a result of these influences, the characters and situations depicted in dramas became less realistic and more abstract. Thus, morality plays such as *Everyman* are allegorical dramas which present religious or ethical lessons by means of characters representing abstract virtues like "Mercy" and vices like "Greed." Specific influences on *Everyman* include the literature describing the *Danse Macabre* (Dance of Death), in which each dancer in turn is accosted by Death and confronted with his or her sins; the *Ars Moriendi* (Art of Dying) treatises describing a dying man's repentance and regaining of spiritual health; and *psychomachia,* allegorical depictions of battles between virtues and vices for a human soul. However, the primary source of *Everyman* may be the Dutch play *Elckerlijc* (c. 1490), attributed to Peter of Diest. Scholars generally believe that *Everyman* is a translation of *Elckerlijc,* though the question is still open to debate. The close similarity of the text and tone of the plays has led critics to agree that one must be a translation of the other. Regardless of which work is the earlier, critics add, *Everyman* remains a complex work that suggestively interweaves a variety of traditional themes and motifs.

The text of *Everyman* survives in four early sixteenth-century editions: two complete printings by John Skot (or Scott) entitled *Here begynneth a treatyse how the hye fader of heuen sendeth dethe to somon euery creature to come and gyue a counte of theyr lyues in this Worlde, and is in maner of a morall playe (The sumonȳg of eueryman)* (c. 1522-29 and c. 1530-35) and two redactions by Richard Pynson (c. 1510-25 and c. 1525-30), which are extant only in fragments. In subsequent centuries, *Everyman* was considered little more than an artifact and appeared only in collections of pre-Elizabethan drama that sought to catalogue England's literary heritage. Such anthologies include Thomas Hawkins's *The Origin of the English Drama* (1773) and W. Carew Hazlitt's edition of Robert Dodsley's *A Select Collection of Old English Plays* (1874). No separate editions appeared until after the play's twentieth-century revival. Since then, it has been reprinted numerous times, including A. C. Cawley's 1961 edition, which is both highly regarded and widely available. In addition, the play has been adapted and translated into various languages; Hugo von Hofmannsthal's German adaptation *Jedermann* is particularly noteworthy, having achieved great popular success in performance at the 1911 Salzburg Festival.

William Poel's 1901 production of *Everyman* overthrew the longstanding perception that allegorical morality plays were dull, didactic, and had little to offer contemporary audiences, thus sparking critical and popular interest in the play. The primary concern for early twentieth-century critics was the question of *Everyman*'s relationship to *Elckerlijc.* In 1939 E. R. Tigg argued that the Dutch drama was the earlier work; and although in 1947 Henry de Vocht presented a vigorous case to the contrary, most scholars now concur with Tigg and consider *Everyman* a translation of *Elckerlijc.* Subsequent critics have noted plays similar to *Everyman* and *Elckerlijc* in various European languages. These researchers have identified the story of a man who is abandoned by his friends when confronted by death as a tale of great antiquity and have traced it back to a Buddhist parable transmitted to the West through *Barlaam and Josaphat,* a work that has been attributed to St. John Damascene.

Critics have investigated numerous other aspects of the play, including the religious doctrine it portrays, its interrelated themes and structure, its style, and its characterization and use of allegory. They disagree as to the religious views expressed in *Everyman,* some arguing that it reflects the teachings of the medieval Catholic church exclusively, and others detecting the spirit of the Protestant Reformation and the teachings of Martin Luther. The fact that Everyman is saved through his actions (good deeds) as well as through his faith places the play within the Catholic rather than the Protestant tradition, which stresses that faith alone is essential for salvation. However, episodes such as the discussion between Knowledge and Five Wits on corrupt priests suggest the influence of the Protestant reform movement. Critics who hold this view argue that *Everyman* was composed sometime after 1517, when Luther wrote his *Ninety-Five Theses* and broke with the Catholic Church. Scholars have also commented on the close interrelatedness between the play's structure, themes, and imagery. *Everyman* possesses a two-part construction. The first movement traces the central figure's descent into despair as his friends desert him and is described in terms of a quest, a series of adventures undertaken by a hero in search of truth or spiritual awareness. The second movement, depicting his spiritual rebirth and ascent to salvation, is similarly presented in terms of a pilgrimage, a devotional journey to a holy place. Not only does Everyman undergo several trials, but his friends do as well. This testing of Everyman's companions—all of whom fail except Good-Deeds—reflects the medieval belief that friends must prove themselves before they can be accepted as true. Good-Deeds's loyalty additionally points to the Christian notion of friendship as a gift from God. Thus, this figure not only signifies Everyman's own positive acts but represents God's blessing as well.

Critics also praise the poetry of *Everyman,* which is written in a clear, direct style with little of the artificiality and ornateness typical of much of the literature of the time. Another aspect of the play that has received much attention is its characterization. Such figures as Fellowship and Knowledge function both as allegorical representations of abstract concepts and as highly individualized, human characters. Cousin, for example, pleads "the cramp in my toe" as an excuse not to accompany Everyman. These sensitive and often humorous portraits make *Everyman* unique among morality plays. Besides studying stylistic issues, scholars have tried to determine the manner in which *Everyman* was first staged. No stage directions or costuming instructions appear in the text and there are no records of performances before the twentieth century. Indeed, even the title of Skot's printing (*a treatyse . . . in the maner of a morall playe*) raises doubts whether *Everyman*'s author intended it to be performed. Researchers have therefore turned to other morality plays, such as *The Castle of Perseverance* (c. 1400-25), for which early staging information survives, for clues as to how *Everyman* may have been first presented.

Everyman is considered the finest of the medieval morality plays. Its vivid characterization, unadorned poetic style, and closely interwoven themes, images, and plot, critics agree, combine to create a peerless artistic achievement. The message of redemption and salvation the drama conveys continues to move audiences, and Everyman's poignant cry, "O Death, thou comest when I had thee least in mind!" retains its universality.

PRINCIPAL EDITIONS

Here begynneth a treatyse how the hye fader of heuen sendeth dethe to somon euery creature to come and gyue a counte of theyr lyues in this Worlde, and is in maner of a morall playe (The sumonȳg of eueryman) c. 1522-29

Here begynneth a treatyse how the hye fader of heuen sendeth dethe to somon euery creature to come and gyue a counte of theyr lyues in this Worlde, and is in maner of a morall playe (the somonȳg of eueryman) c. 1530-35

Everyman. A Morality (in *The Origin of the English Drama*) 1773

Everyman: A Moral Play (in *A Select Collection of Old English Plays*) 1874

Everyman 1902

Everyman (in *Materialien zur Kunde des älteren Englischen Dramas*) 1904

Everyman (in *Everyman and Medieval Miracle Plays*) 1956

Everyman 1961

Everyman (in *Medieval Drama*) 1975

The Summoning of Everyman 1980

Everyman (in *Three Late Medieval Morality Plays: Mankind, Everyman, Mundus et infans*) 1981

OVERVIEWS AND GENERAL STUDIES

A. C. Cawley (essay date 1961)

[*In this excerpt from the Introduction to his 1961 edition of* Everyman, *Cawley examines numerous aspects of the play, including its meaning, style, versification, and staging.*]

MEANING OF EVERYMAN

Everyman is completely a product of the medieval world. Printed in the same decade as Machiavelli's *Il Principe* (1513), Erasmus's *Novum Instrumentum* (1516), and Luther's *Theses* at Wittenberg (1517), *Everyman* is untouched by either Renaissance or Reformation.

Everyman is a dramatic and allegorical presentation of the medieval Catholic doctrine concerning Holy Dying. This doctrine, reduced to its simplest terms, is that a dying man makes a good Christian ending by giving up his trust in worldly things, by clinging to his good deeds, and by preparing himself through penance to receive the last sacraments worthily. In consequence of his penitential acts he returns to a state of grace, revives the merit of his good deeds, and by God's mercy ensures his salvation.

This is the essential doctrine which the playwright enlivens with his fable and characters. The fable of the Faithful Friend is an allegorical representation of Everyman's rapid spiritual growth and development in the presence of death: he learns that he must part with all outward things (goods, friends, and kinsmen) before he can be illumined

within and come to realize that his soul's salvation depends on Christ and His sacraments. Like Sir Thomas More meditating on 'the deep conceived fantasy of death', Everyman experiences a severance of 'the soul from the love and affections of the body' even before his body and soul are separated by death.

Although several of the characters in *Everyman* are vividly personified and have a very real existence on the literal plane, they also have a theological meaning underlying their surface liveliness. Everyman himself is a representative Catholic Christian rather than a 'representative of the whole human race' [W. R. Mackenzie, *The English Moralities from the Point of View of Allegory*]. He is also typical of the average Christian of any denomination in the sense that he is neither very good nor very bad. But, unlike many of his fellow Christians, he has had lavished on him the gifts of fortune, grace, and nature. His gifts of fortune are his goods and friends, his gifts of grace are knowledge and good deeds, and his gifts of nature include strength and beauty.

The gifts of fortune are not bad in themselves, but Everyman has wasted them and put his love of them before his love of God. Thus abused, Everyman's gifts of fortune undergo a transformation: his worldly wealth becomes a peril to his soul; his friends and kinsmen are reduced to the level of fair-weather companions, who encourage him in sinful living and then abandon him to the consequences of his sin. On the surface, then, characters like Fellowship, Kindred, Cousin, and Goods are lively representatives of the world and the flesh, and bear a strong resemblance to the Vice of the later moral plays. But, allegorically, they signify the gifts of fortune, abused and deformed by the sinful Everyman.

Good Deeds is Everyman's principal gift of grace. . . . [Her] theological meaning is made plain by a passage in Chaucer's *Parson's Tale*: 'Now been ther thre manere of almesse: contricion of herte, where a man offreth hymself to God; another is to han pitee of defaute of his neighebores; and the thridde is in yevynge of good conseil and comfort, goostly and bodily, where men han nede, and namely in sustenaunce of mannes foode.' To the poet of *Everyman* there can be no faith without good works, any more than good works alone can have merit towards salvation.

Hardly less important than Good Deeds is her sister, Knowledge, who ultimately represents knowledge of God. John Gaytryge's *Sermon on Shrift* emphasizes that no man can come to everlasting bliss 'with-owttene knaweynge of Godde'. But while this is the supreme end of all knowledge, it cannot be reached without self-knowledge: 'As sayth saynt bernarde / ther is none saued / wythoute to haue knowleche of hym selfe. for of this knowleche groweth humylyte. which is moder of helthe.' Everyman's memory of his good works goes together with an increasing awareness of his sin and spiritual sickness to induce in him humble feelings of contrition, and this prepares him to receive worthily the sacrament of penance.

There is evidently a close connexion between Everyman's

knowledge and his five wits (i.e. senses). It is Knowledge who introduces Five Wits to Everyman (662-63); it is Five Wits who preaches on the seven sacraments and the spiritual power of the priesthood (712 ff., 730 ff.), and Knowledge who ventures in reply to criticize the behaviour of sinful priests (750 ff.). The explanation of this connexion between Knowledge and Five Wits is that the five senses, both outer and inner, are the means by which a man attains to knowledge of himself and knowledge of God. A parallel is provided by the moral play *Wisdom,* where the five wits (controlled by reason) are said to bring a man to 'knowynge of yowrsylff' and to knowledge of the 'Godhede incomprehensyble'.

Everyman's gifts of nature—strength and beauty—need little comment. Long before *Elckerlijc* was translated into English, Strength had been included among the *dramatis personae* of *The Pride of Life* (c. 1400-25), in which the King of Life summons his knights Strength and Health to his aid. It is noteworthy that although Everyman's gifts of fortune are the first to desert him, his gifts of nature are the next, closely followed by Discretion and Five Wits.

Everyman may be called a lenten penitential play or an allegorical drama concerned with the Four Last Things (Death, Judgment, Heaven, and Hell). Within these limits it is a strongly dramatic presentation of the theme of death. But it would be quite wrong to give the play the status of a tragedy. Moral plays in general conform to the medieval idea of comedy in that they begin harshly and end harmoniously. *Everyman* is no exception to this rule: God's strict justice is, in the end, tempered by His great mercy, and the soul of Everyman is saved. When a Christian playwright has the dramatic gifts of the author of *Elckerlijc–Everyman,* his theme of repentance and holy dying will provide the material for an impressive play; but the tragic elements of disaster and overwhelming evil are bound to be absent.

The Castle of Perseverance gets nearer than *Everyman* to being a tragedy since its protagonist (Humanum Genus) dies 'unhousel'd . . . unanel'd', and after death his soul is narrowly saved by his cry for mercy, which Peace and Mercy successfully interpret as a sign of contrition. This is the sort of near-tragic moral play which, under Calvinist influence, produced the tragedy of *Faustus.* But the poet of *Everyman* will have nothing to do with posthumous salvation. By means of the sacrament of penance Everyman prepares for the salvation of his soul in advance of its separation from his body. Like Humanum Genus he cries for mercy; but he has made sure of receiving it by virtue of his good works and penitential acts, and his soul is at once welcomed into the 'heavenly sphere'. His reckoning is crystal-clear: there is no wrangling over his soul by the Four Daughters of God. The concluding words of Doctor in *Everyman* (912-13) read rather like a stern reproach to Humanum Genus for sailing so close to damnation:

> after dethe amendes may no man make,
> For than mercy and pyte doth hym forsake.

Behind the different attitudes expressed in *The Castle of Perseverance* and *Everyman* towards contrition in relation to the other parts of the sacrament of penance there lies an old theological controversy concerning the function of

contrition. William of Ockham maintained that contrition alone is enough to ensure salvation, while Duns Scotus held that the grace of contrition is given in and through the sacrament of penance. It is certain that the author of *Elckerlijc–Everyman,* like Scotus, could accept nothing less than the full sacrament of penance as necessary for the soul's salvation.

STYLE

Every commentator on *Everyman* remembers to praise its natural and appropriate language. But it is also worth remembering that the plain, clear diction of *Everyman* was a triumph of compromise achieved at a time when most writers of verse and prose vacillated between the extremes of aureate diction and colloquial language. These extremes are found, for example, in *Mankind* (c. 1450-1500), in which the artificial 'Englysch Laten' of Mercy and the gutter-bred colloquialisms of New-Guise, Nowadays, and Nought are equally extravagant and obscure. The poet of *Everyman* occasionally uses aureate diction at moments of great solemnity, as he does just before Everyman scourges himself for his sins (581 ff.). But for the most part he can be dignified or colloquial, according to the speaker and occasion, without resorting to either artificiality or meanness. In fact, he does for poetic style what [the first English printer William] Caxton deliberately tried to do for prose style. Caxton, faced with the same undesirable extremes of aureate splendour and colloquial meanness, [in his prologue to *Eneydos,* 1990] rejected both in favour of a style 'not ouer rude ne curyous, but in suche termes as shall be vnderstanden'. The search for a serviceable 'middle style' in verse and prose went on long after the time of Caxton and the author of *Everyman,* and busily engaged the attention of such scholars as Ascham, Wilson, and Cheke. Even to-day a poetic dramatist like T. S. Eliot is still looking for a twentieth-century equivalent of the neutral style used so successfully in *Everyman.*

One historian of the drama [A. W. Ward in *A History of English Dramatic Literature to the Death of Queen Anne,* 1899], while praising the 'sustained force' and 'simple solemnity' of the action of *Everyman,* considers that it is impaired by its repetitions. But an examination of the verbal repetitions in the play does not support this view. Most of the phrases which are used two or more times are convenient rhyming tags; but they also draw our attention to some of the cardinal points of the action, and for this reason the repetition of them is didactically effective. On one occasion the reiteration of the phrase *moost nede* is sharpened by contrast, when Cousin's use of this phrase in conversation with Everyman (357-58):

> Trust not to me; for, so God me spede,
> I wyll deceyue you in your moost nede

is echoed by Good Deeds in a context of exactly opposite meaning (522-23):

> Eueryman, I wyll go with the and be thy gyde,
> In thy moost nede to go by thy syde.

Sometimes a verbal repetition extends over several lines, and in one instance—where Death and Goods use the same form of words in addressing Everyman—the repetition serves to bring together the transitoriness of man's life and the impermanence of his earthly possessions. Several times a repetition is deliberately contrived in order to emphasize the hollowness of promises made by persons like Fellowship, Kindred, and Strength. Finally, we may notice the repetition by Death of his command to Everyman to hurry up and lose no time in beginning his journey, followed throughout the play by repeated references to the passing of time. This repetition intensifies the urgency of the action, and it is not long before the reader feels almost as concerned as Everyman himself that he should finish his preparations before the end comes.

It will thus be seen that the verbal repetitions in *Everyman* have a purpose and help to create a certain effect. They are not attributable to the translator's laziness or impoverished vocabulary; nor can they be said to impair the action of the play.

One other aspect of the language of *Everyman* may be commented on: the translator's use of proverbial sayings. Many of these sayings are put into the mouth of Everyman, who tricks out both his folly and his wisdom in proverbial dress. His foolish presumption finds words ready-made for it before the experience which is to chasten him (316):

> For kynde wyll crepe where it may not go;

and, after that experience, his hard-won wisdom is also cast in a proverbial mould (379):

> Lo, fayre wordes maketh fooles fayne.

Everyman has a proverb for every occasion: his optimism and pessimism are equally well expressed in the traditional saws of every man.

VERSIFICATION

Everyman, unlike *Elckerlijc,* is very irregular in the matter of verse-length, verse-forms, and rhymes. The number of syllables in a line ranges from four to fourteen. The verse-forms are a welter of couplets and quatrains, together with occasional tail-rhymes, five-, six-, and seven-line stanzas, rhyme-royal stanzas, and octaves. There are more than a hundred imperfect rhymes: some are examples of assonance and some are due to corruption of the original text, but this still leaves several pairs of words which fail to rhyme, as well as end-words without companion rhyme-words.

At a first glance, then, the versification of *Everyman* looks a slipshod affair, no better than that of *Hickscorner (c.* 1515-16), which it closely resembles, and decidedly inferior to that of *Wisdom* and *Mankind,* in which different stanza-forms are regularly used to distinguish between the morally good and bad elements in the play.

And yet there is something to be said in favour of the versification of *Everyman,* unsatisfactory though it may be. To begin with, it is wrong to regard the individual verses in *Everyman* as lame pentameters. Occasionally an iambic-decasyllabic or iambic-octosyllabic line occurs, but many of the longer lines can only be read as freely rhythmical verses, which perhaps are a development of the native accentual line. In these verses the number of unaccented syllables between the stresses is variable, and sometimes

there is a division into two half-lines by means of a medial pause, with each half-line hovering 'between two and three stresses in a manner analogous to the Anglo-Saxon types D and E' [C. S. Lewis, in *Essays and Studies* XXIV (1938)]. For example, a line like the following (394):

> I lye here in corners, trussed and pyled so hye

reads well enough if the above stressing is observed, but Procrustean violence is needed to force it into an iambic pattern.

It should also be said on behalf of the versification of *Everyman* that its verse-forms are not entirely haphazard. Some of the very short verses seem meant to mark a quick exchange of dialogue, while rhyme-royal and octave are used in passages of exceptional gravity. These may be signs that the author-translator of *Everyman* is feeling his way towards a dramatic use of different verse-forms. Again, the rhyme-words are often skilfully distributed between two or more speakers, with the result that the dialogue is more rapid and flowing.

In general, the moral plays of the fifteenth and sixteenth centuries show an enterprising use of dignified and popular rhythms and stanzas. *Everyman* is no exception. Even Saintsbury, who [in *A History of English Prosody,* 1906] disapproved so strongly of 'the apparently skimble-skamble long doggerel of the earlier plays', is willing to admit that in these plays can be detected a striving towards freer, more dramatic rhythms and stanzas. We may agree with Saintsbury that the attempt was often unsuccessful. But the fact remains that the freely rhythmical verses of *Everyman* harmonize inconspicuously with its neutral style, so that we find ourselves [like T. S. Eliot in his essay "Poetry and Drama"] 'consciously attending, not to the poetry, but to the meaning of the poetry'.

STAGING

It is not known whether *Everyman* was originally acted out of doors, as were *The Castle of Perseverance* and *Mankind,* or whether it was an indoor entertainment like the majority of the interludes. But it is clear that *Everyman,* in common with all other Tudor plays, depended for its staging on two things: an unlocalized acting area (*platea*) and a structure (*sedes*) representing a definite locality within this area.

Most of the action of *Everyman* is unlocalized; the only *sedes* mentioned in the play is the 'hous of saluacyon' (540), to which Everyman goes to receive the sacrament of penance from Confession. Something can be learnt about the nature of this *sedes* by comparing it with the castle in *The Castle of Perseverance,* to which Humanum Genus resorts after Penance and Confession have persuaded him to abandon the World, the Flesh, and the Devil. The central importance of the castle, in both a literal and a figurative sense, is emphasized by the contemporary plan of the staging of the play. In this plan the castle occupies the centre of the acting area, while its battlements above and its dungeon below—furnished with the death-bed of Humanum Genus and with the cupboard of Covetousness—are prominently displayed. From the play itself we learn that the battlements of the castle represent the state 'of vertu & of grace' (1559) to which Humanum Genus returns after receiving the sacrament of penance; and that the dungeon represents death in sin from which there is no escape, except by God's grace. In *Everyman* the 'house of saluacyon' is no less central in importance, since the salvation of Everyman is the end of all the action. It therefore seems reasonable to assume that the house of salvation, which is the dwelling-place of Confession, also had its battlemented heights, where God stood and spoke to sinful mankind at the beginning of the play and where Everyman's soul was received with angelic song at the ending. Further, the grave of Everyman (794) is related to the house of salvation much in the same way as the dungeon and death-bed of Humanum Genus are to the heights of the castle in *The Castle of Perseverance*. It is probable, then, that Everyman's grave stood at the foot of the house of salvation and was connected with it, so that Everyman could enact his own salvation by entering his grave and ascending from it to the heights of the 'heuenly spere' (899).

In the absence of stage directions in the early prints of *Everyman* we are driven back on the play itself for information about properties, costumes, and the number of actors. The properties to which reference is made are Death's dart (76), Everyman's account-book (104, 502 ff.), the bags and chests belonging to Goods (395 ff.), the penitential scourge (561, 605), and the crucifix (778). There is no reason to doubt that all these properties had a physical existence.

The only allusions to costume are to the gay clothing worn by the unregenerate Everyman (85-6, 614) and to the penitential robe which he puts on after he has scourged himself (638 ff.). This change of costume to symbolize a change of heart is frequently found in the moral plays.

Although *Everyman* has seventeen speaking parts, seven of the *dramatis personae* (Messenger, God, Death, Fellowship, Kindred, Cousin, and Goods) have finished speaking and left the stage by line 462—almost exactly half-way through the play. This means that their parts could have been doubled by the actors who played seven of the remaining ten parts. On this reckoning not more than ten actors were needed in all.

Collier has observed [in *The History of English Dramatic Poetry to the Time of Shakespeare,* 1831] that 'In the performance *Every-man* must have wanted much of the character and variety, which were found in some other contemporary productions'. It is no doubt true that plays like *Mankind, Wisdom,* and *The Castle of Perseverance,* enlivened as they are with dances, processions, and secular music, were more popular productions in their day than *Everyman* could have been. Yet the stark simplicity of the theme of *Everyman* is perfectly matched by its stage setting, with the house of salvation rising up and dominating the action of the play. Such simplicity and harmony of theme and presentation are extremely effective. (pp. xix-xxxi)

> *A. C. Cawley, in an introduction to* Everyman, *edited by A. C. Cawley, Manchester University Press, 1961, pp. xix-xxxi.*

Geoffrey Cooper and Christopher Wortham (essay date 1980)

[*In the following excerpt from the Introduction to their edition of* Everyman, *the critics survey the play's relation to medieval drama, the religious spirit it conveys, and its language and poetic style. Cooper and Wortham also discuss possible methods of staging* Everyman *and offer an overview of several ways of interpreting the drama.*]

EVERYMAN AND MEDIEVAL DRAMA

Although medieval religious drama and the great secular plays of the Elizabethan period may seem to be worlds apart, they embody a continuous development. Shakespeare's works do not spring miraculously from the spirit of the Renaissance alone, as did Athene fully grown and fully clothed in her regalia from the head of her father Zeus. Behind Shakespeare, contributing to his craftsmanship in many ways, there is a vigorous native tradition. This tradition was several hundred years old and still very much alive well into Shakespeare's lifetime.

The first medieval plays seem to have been prompted by the liturgy, i.e. set forms of prayer and worship in the Church. Central to the liturgy is the Mass, itself a dramatic re-enactment of the Last Supper albeit stylized and with many accretions. The liturgical year, then and now, incorporated a wide and varied range of readings from the Bible; these readings were interspersed at various points in the Mass. It followed quite naturally that some of the readings became dramatized eventually, partly because they recount many inherently dramatic situations and events, partly because human beings are drawn to dramatization as a means of communication, and partly because a more vivid means of re-enactment than mere reading could bring home the vitality of the Bible to an audience that was largely illiterate and without its own recourse to the text.

From the twelfth century to about 1450 the genre of the mystery play, with several related forms, grew and predominated. From about 1400 to the mid-sixteenth century the morality play ran its relatively brief but highly influential life cycle. Written towards the end of the fifteenth century, *Everyman* is one of the later morality plays.

The seed of medieval religious drama was probably sown when priests celebrating the Mass began to interpose dramatized scenes into the order of service. These playlets became excessively long in relation to their place within the liturgy. In addition, bishops grew uneasy at the thought of clerics taking on a second (and dubious) profession—that of acting. Yet some form of compromise seemed advisable. The compromise, after a number of interim measures failed, was achieved when the plays passed into the hands of lay performers and were attached to the public feast of Corpus Christi. The feast of Corpus Christi became formally recognized in 1311. Municipal corporations in the larger centres now took overall responsibility for the performance of religious drama. The mystery plays were grouped in cycles, the order of performance following biblical chronology. Many a town in England and Europe had its own cycle to be performed at Corpus Christi at various points or "stations" in the town. One common mode of performance was to transport the players from one station to another on wagons, which would also serve as raised platforms for staging plays. Individual guilds of craftsmen and labourers took responsibility for plays that bore some relation, sometimes an ironic one, to their calling: the water drawers of Chester acted in that town's version of *Noah's Flood.*

Only four of the Corpus Christi cycles performed in many English towns have survived in complete or substantially complete form. Of these four, two show the guiding hand of a single author through a significant portion of the cycle. These shadowy figures are known as the York Realist and the Wakefield Master. The surviving manuscript for the Wakefield cycle, sometimes called the Towneley cycle because it was long in the possession of a family of that name, dates from the second half of the fifteenth century, some time after the cycle would have taken its final form. Unfortunately a great number of the mystery plays have been lost, the manuscripts having been destroyed by sincere but misguided religious reformers who found the plays obscene and blasphemous.

The genre of the moral play or the morality play, as it has become popularly known, seems to have emerged at about the end of the fourteenth century. It is known that a great many morality plays were written, their numbers probably running into hundreds, but very few have survived in more than fragments. The earliest substantial fragment of a morality play in English, *Pride of Life,* dates from between 1400 and 1425. Probably slightly later is *The Castle of Perseverance,* which is almost complete and next to *Everyman* is one of the best plays to survive. *Everyman* is one of the last of the genuine morality plays. It was, as we have noted, written at the very end of the fifteenth century, at a time when the structure of the essentially religious morality play was being taken over and adapted for the first secular drama of the Tudor period, some seventy years before the birth of Shakespeare.

Speculation on the origin of the morality play has brought forth some interesting but inconclusive theories. One is that this kind of drama grew out of a particular form of sermon. Another is that medieval commentaries on the moral doctrine of the Bible provided the basis. A third looks to stock themes in formal debates or disputations. All of these have something to do with the development of the morality play, but none can fully account for it. The simple truth is that allegory, which governs the structure of the morality play and invites certain themes, is so common in other medieval literature that its appearance in the drama occasions no surprise.

A working definition of the morality play might run as follows: the morality play is an allegorical drama which expounds religious or ethical lessons. Such a definition really says very little, but it is impossible to define the genre more precisely because its surviving representatives are so various.

The distinction between the allegorical morality play and the more "realistic" mystery play has far-reaching consequences. It must be recorded that many of the mystery plays have an allegorical meaning, but in these plays the allegory is generally covert, whereas in the morality play it is overt. The mystery play, re-enacting biblical events through the portrayal on stage of the people involved in the events, is concrete where the morality play is abstract. The presentation of historical material in the mystery play inevitably lays stress on incident and any thematic or moral point is conveyed through the means of the incident, whereas in the morality play theme and moral are paramount so that the plot is subservient. The practical consequence of the central difference between the mystery play and the morality play is that in the latter, e.g. *Everyman,* the author is not bound by historicity: his plot is his own entirely, constrained only by thematic and doctrinal considerations. Freedom is always a challenge; one of the most engaging aspects of *Everyman* is the way in which the playwright meets this challenge.

Everyman represents in dramatic form what so many Gothic cathedrals represent architecturally, that is a taste for intricate and carefully patterned, though not necessarily symmetrical, structure. Majesty of conception combines with earthy humanity, nobility is tempered with warmth and humour. In art, including literary arts, and architecture the medieval mind had a delightful capacity for what may best be called "wonder". This capacity slowly eroded in later centuries and was finally eliminated by the neo-classical canons of good taste and decorum at the end of the seventeenth century. The capacity for wonder allowed men to see that God was not only just and merciful but also witty. As one literary historian has put it [Kitty Scoular, in *Natural Magic,* 1965], wonder was "compounded of religious awe and the capacity for being surprised, an acceptance of the world both as the Creator's joke and His riddle, veiling and yet revealing divine truth."

From an aesthetic point of view, *Everyman* marks a high point in the medieval art of patterned structure. If our modern sensibilities prevent us from seeing the humour in its high purpose, or make us feel that there are elements within it which are out of keeping with its grand design, we should be prepared to attribute such responses to our own limitations rather than to uncouthness in the playwright.

THE PLOT OF EVERYMAN

The plot of *Everyman* is simple enough in its broad outline. The play begins with a prologue spoken by a Messenger; God then speaks from his celestial throne, stating his policy towards man and justifying the apparent cruelty of death, through which Everyman is shortly to be summoned to appear before his Creator; God calls Death and orders him to fulfil the divine command. Although by way of introduction to the main action of the play, the action thus far is central to the theme as stated in the full title to the play. Everyman, confronted with the imminence of his end by the sudden appearance of Death, turns successively to his friends (Fellowship), to his family (Kindred and Cousin), and to his material possessions (Goods) for solace and company on his hard journey. In each appeal he is rejected and, because his scale of values is perverted, each disappointment is worse than the last, so that by the mid-point in the play Everyman is close to despair. At this crucial moment Everyman begins to re-assess himself and in the second half of the play climbs slowly and painfully towards true values. The upward journey involves a second set of desertions, not by the external props of people and possessions this time, but by his own inner attributes of Beauty, Strength, Discretion and Five Wits. Everyman has to learn that, although these attributes can and should be helpful in the quest for salvation, they too have to be shorn away as soul leaves body at the moment of death. His Good Deeds and Knowledge, on whose guidance he has depended through the second half of the play, go with him to the graveside. Here, at the terminal point in human experience, Knowledge must leave him because she is part of Everyman's corporeal nature, but Good Deeds, having been reunited with Everyman's incorporeal soul through the sacrament of confession and strengthened by other sacraments (the eucharist and extreme unction), goes with Everyman into the grave. Thus Everyman is spared from his dread of isolation at the last. An Angel welcomes Everyman before God at the other side of the grave and a Doctor (of Divinity) speaks the epilogue.

One may discern a fall-and-rise pattern in the sequence of Everyman's fortunes through the play, a pattern which may be represented visually thus: V. Although not exactly symmetrical, the overall impression given by the play is one of symmetry. As in the more purely visual arts, departures from absolute symmetry give life to a work and serve to point up significant features. Beside the central fall-and-rise pattern, from which Good Deeds stands out as an exception and Knowledge as a partial exception, there are other items of symmetry: the Messenger's prologue and the Doctor's epilogue encapsulate the story, the latter fulfilling what the former had promised; and the figure of Death, seen by Everyman in his unregenerate state as malignant, gives way to the welcoming Angel. From the pattern of the outer portion of the play, God's speech stands out in isolation, as does the role of Good Deeds from the action of the inner portion of the play. These two asymmetrical features, which linger in one's memory after one has received the whole experience of the play, emphasize the twofold doctrine that man is to be saved by faith and good works. (pp. ix-xii)

. . . . .

RELIGION IN EVERYMAN

Literary critics are hesitant, and rightly so, about stepping outside their normal sphere of competence. But *Everyman* is a religious play and calls for comment on its theology and its exposition of devotional practice. Professor Cawley [in his 1961 edition of *Everyman*] finds that "*Everyman* is completely a product of the medieval world" and that it is "untouched by either Renaissance or Reformation." Sir Edmund Chambers, sensing an undercurrent, albeit on the basis of a gross misapprehension, suspects [in *English Literature at the Close of the Middle Ages*] that the play has "a Protestant temper rather than a Catholic one." Lawrence Ryan, in his article on "Doctrine and Dramatic Structure in *Everyman*" [*Speculum* XXXII (1957)], states that the play dramatizes "the scheme of salvation according to an orthodox view."

These views are inadequate. By the end of the fifteenth century, when *Elckerlijc* was written, and by the early sixteenth century, when it was translated into English as *Everyman*, orthodoxy was no longer a simple matter to determine. Many of the seemingly straightforward and even innocent statements in *Everyman* should be reexamined in the light of the times. The times were turbulent: controversy, feud, schism, and even open war on the issues of religious orthodoxy broke out on a scale never known hitherto in the history of Christianity. When the first known printed copy of *Elckerlijc* appeared, c. 1495, Martin Luther was a schoolboy not far from the place where the play was printed. When John Scott brought out his edition of *Everyman* in 1525, Luther had already broken with Rome, taking thousands of followers with him; his bitter argument with Erasmus, his former admirer, was now at its height. In England Henry VIII was accorded the title of *Fidei Defensor* [Defender of the Faith] by the Pope in recognition of his work in refutation of Luther but would himself be excommunicated a few years later.

More than a century before the Reformation, the first signs of fatal discord had appeared in western Europe. In the latter part of the fourteenth century a great reformer, whose aims were to promote a return to spirituality and to purge the corrupt Church in the Low Countries where he lived and worked, gave birth to a new movement. This man was Gerard Groote (1341-84) and his movement became known in the fifteenth century as the *Devotio Moderna*. The name itself tells a good deal. Within the *Devotio Moderna*, and as a result of Groote's efforts, a new kind of religious community emerged. It all began in 1374 when Groote turned his own house over to women who wished to live together in religious fellowship, but without taking vows or supplying the dowry required by convents of the established orders. In time the group became known as the Sisters of the Common Life. During Groote's lifetime his male disciples banded together similarly; after his death many more community centres were founded and these men called themselves the Brethren of the Common Life. Groote himself was a priest, but many of his followers were laymen. They submitted themselves to live in piety according to the rules of the house, but were free to withdraw at any time. Recent scholarship has questioned the extent of the role played by the Brethren and the Sisters in the gathering surge of the *Devotio Moderna,* but their influence was profound.

The Brethren of the Common Life quickly became established as educators and found themselves in charge of schools of two thousand and more pupils, vast in any age and the more so then. Many men destined for fame and high office were associated in their early years with the Brethren: among them were Desiderius Erasmus and Martin Luther. Luther maintained a high regard for the Brethren, even though he was under their care for only a year and probably did not attend their local school. Members of an earlier generation of pupils of the Brethren of the Common Life include Thomas à Kempis, author of the *Imitation of Christ,* and Nicholas of Cusa, a prominent theologian.

Within the *Devotio Moderna* and among the Brethren all

was far from settled. Once a reforming movement starts, there is no knowing where it will stop; some will always want to go farther than others and new divisions emerge. Erasmus and Luther are both entirely comprehensible in terms of their common background. Both were highly critical of the same deficiencies and malpractices, but with one great difference: Erasmus insisted to the last that reform must come from within the established Church; with symbolic aptness, Luther posted his ninety-five theses *outside* the church door.

Elckerlijc and *Everyman* bear the marks—and the scars—of their time. Controversial issues are subtly subdued and do not disrupt the calm and dignified flow of the play's action. But *Everyman* asserts a view of man's spiritual needs which is unmistakably related to the reforming movement, and which is remarkably similar to the position adopted by Erasmus. In short, the play affirms the authority of the Catholic Church piously yet without complacency.

Although we are going to compare the play with a number of ideas expressed by Erasmus, there is no veiled hint that Erasmus may have written it: the play has nothing of Erasmus' witty, trenchant style and if he had written it we should have known about it, for Erasmus kept a carefully tabulated list of all his own prolific writings. We have picked out three points for specific comparison. In the first place, the play enjoins simple piety. Everyman's forgotten faith, which he recovers in the second half, makes no appeal to the dazzling arguments of medieval scholastic theology. His faith rests upon a few straightforward biblical texts and upon the simple piety built on them. Erasmus' life was devoted to learning, but he rejected the intricacies of scholastic theology in accordance with a dominant mood which was making itself felt within the *Devotio Moderna*. Secondly, in both the play and the thought of Erasmus there is a revulsion against fanatical extremism. As a Christian Humanist, Erasmus is for moderation in all things; the play retains some of the "contempt for the world" tradition from earlier centuries, but the strongest voice is for moderation. Even Goods, which have become evil in *Everyman* only because of man's excesses, could have worked for Everyman's salvation "yf thou had me loued moderately" (431). Thirdly, in the discussion on priesthood (713-68) corruption within the Church is condemned with feeling, but the final statement is an unequivocal affirmation of authority: the office of priesthood must be honoured with obedience and reverence, however scandalous the abuses perpetrated by individual members of the clergy.

We have noticed affinities with Erasmus; before going on to some of the more problematical teachings of the play it will be as well for us to note points of radical difference between the play and Luther. There are two which seem most obvious. To begin with, there is in the play the central theme of salvation through both faith and works (Good Deeds). Some time after the composition of *Elckerlijc* and shortly before its translation into English, Luther promulgated his doctrine of justification by faith alone in *The Freedom of a Christian* (November 1520). In *Everyman* faith is taken for granted as being necessary for salva-

tion—it is in faith that Everyman takes the advice of Knowledge—but faith alone is not enough and the final reckoning will be made in terms of Good Deeds, the only true friend to accompany Everyman into the grave and beyond. The other difference between the play and Luther which calls for immediate comment lies in Luther's concept of the priesthood of all believers. He did not suggest that the Christian Church could do without an ordained ministry, but he envisaged a more dominant role for the laity in the way of active ministry. Lines 767-68 in *Everyman:*

> We be theyr shepe and they shepeherdes be,
> By whome we all be kepte in suerte

indicate that however receptive the author may have been to reform within the Church, it did not occur to him to suggest the kind of change which Luther would make. In this respect *Elckerlijc* is ante-Reformation and *Everyman* is anti-Reformation.

In other respects *Elckerlijc* and *Everyman* may not be so clearly categorized. For example, lines 737-39 could easily be taken as absolute vindication for the Catholicism of the play:

> With v. wordes he may consecrate,
> Godde's body in flesshe and blode to make,
> And handeleth his Maker bytwene his [handes].

The doctrine of transubstantiation is affirmed, but these lines are not at variance with Luther's new doctrine of consubstantiation either. By consubstantiation Luther maintained the teaching of the real presence of Christ in the eucharist while differing from Aquinas and other orthodox theologians in holding that the bread and wine were not reduced to mere "accidents" but remained essentially what they formerly had been.

Luther reduced the number of sacraments from seven to three, and later to two. He acknowledged baptism, the eucharist and confession, but ultimately rejected the last. The vindication of the seven sacraments in *Everyman* is certainly pre-Reformation, but two factors in the play's teaching on the sacraments indicate that the play moves on the shadowy middle ground between Catholicism and proto-Protestantism. Both factors centre on the sacrament of confession.

All the early prints of *Elckerlijc* omit confession, or penance, from their list of the sacraments, but in the early prints of *Everyman* penance is tagged on at the end. In medieval listing, penance usually comes third. And Luther, we recall, removed penance from his sacraments after some deliberation. The uncertainties over confession seem to be more than a coincidence; they seem to be related to a common source. It is probable that the omission from the Dutch text was deliberate and that it was the consequence of a controversy within the *Devotio Moderna:* from Groote onwards there had been some doubt about the value of sacramental absolution given by a priest in confession, on the ground that God alone converts the sinner and turns him from his sinful ways. At the heart of the controversy was the question of the priest's jurisdiction—were his powers as unlimited as biblical authority (Matthew 16.19) seemed to declare? The penitential rite remained highly regarded, nevertheless, as a devotional means towards the sinner's restoration to God. The roll-call in *Everyman* of seven sacraments compared to six in *Elckerlijc* may be interpreted as a sign of embarrassment resulting from a conflict between orthodoxy and the reforming movement. The specific inclusion of the sacrament of penance in *Everyman* suggests the hand of a translator who was more conservative than his original author.

The other factor concerning the sacrament of penance is too basic to the whole construction of the play for the translator to have amended by discreet modification. Let us remember that Everyman goes to the allegorical figure of Confession to confess his sins, but that he goes to Priesthood to receive the other two sacraments befitting his last moments. For sheer doctrinal and allegorical consistency Everyman should have gone to Priesthood for all three sacraments. Not unreasonably, Cawley thinks that Priesthood "is indistinguishable from *that holy man Confessyon* (539), who hears his confession and gives him absolution" and that the same actor would have taken both parts. Up to a point, the text supports this view: Confession is a "holy man" who lives "In the hous of saluacyon" (430) and who imposes penance on Everyman in the way that a priest would in dispensing the sacrament (561-63). However, the allegorical mode, which always keeps a little distance from everyday reality, does not encourage a highly specific reading in this instance: the allegory keeps the idea of confession a little aloof from human administration. If Cawley is right in his suggestion, based upon comparison with *The Castle of Perseverance,* that the house of salvation where Confession dwells is the same edifice where God stands and speaks to sinful mankind at the beginning of the play, then one has even more reason to doubt the identification of Confession with Priesthood: visually, as well as conceptually, Confession resides with God and not with man.

There is a textual crux in *Everyman* when the penitent addresses Confession as "moder of saluacyon" (552). Cawley explains this unusual mode of address to a masculine figure as "a figurative description of sacramental confession." This explanation supports the view that the dramatist wishes to maintain a clear distinction between the sacramental value of confession and human agency. The reader may be interested to note that the phrase "that holy man" is the translator's addition: the Dutch text of *Elckerlijc* simply has "Waer woent biechte", or "where dwells confession." The Dutch text does, however, include the phrase "moder of saluacyon." Whatever licence the translator may have taken with the Dutch text, there is ample evidence in both that the nature and role of Confession is controversial.

The dramatic realization of God in the play is of importance for what it reveals of contemporary formulations about God. The long-standing controversy as to whether God was to be visually represented by a man or whether God would have been a disembodied voice is a separate issue not relevant to this one. The point is that throughout God's speech the Holy Trinity speaks with one voice. . . . [We can observe] the conjoint attributes of God the Fa-

ther, God the Son (or Christ) and the Holy Spirit in God's first long speech.

The doctrine of the Holy Trinity, teaching that God is distinct in persons but one in being, is one of the central mysteries and paradoxes of Catholicism, going back to the early Church. A startlingly new approach to the Trinity had been put forward some fifty years before *Elckerlijc* by Nicholas of Cusa. Nicholas of Cusa, as we noted earlier, received his education from the Brethren of the Common Life. In *De Docta Ignorantia* (1440) Nicholas adopted a quasi-mystical approach in which he stressed the unknowability of God: the best we can do, he said, is to progress from the ignorance of the child to the learned ignorance of the wise man who knows that he knows nothing. This attitude led Nicholas to reject the idea of persons in God as an unhelpful human fabrication. He did not reject the concept of the Trinity, however, but only the attempt to describe God in human terms. The Trinity, he said by way of simile, is like a circular piece of water with no apparent inlet or outlet: the mystery is explained when one discovers that within the lake is a spring, which feeds a stream, which in turn swells out to become a lake. In explanation of his simile, Nicholas says that God the Father is the spring, Christ the stream, and the lake of the Holy Spirit proceeds from the two and links them.

In *Everyman* God speaks in the first person singular both as the Father and the Son (cf. 22 and 31) and laments that the people, blind to the Holy Spirit, "know me not for theyr God" (26). The concept of God here is not one of separate persons but essentially the same being in different manifestations and seems to be more like the God of Nicholas of Cusa than the God of Aquinas. Here again one may discern the influence of the *Devotio Moderna.* The emphasis on a triune God rather than a Trinity is characteristic of fifteenth-century devotionalism.

Later in the play, and on a different theme entirely, there is the much-discussed episode or digression, as it is sometimes called, on priesthood. Satire and allegory had always kept company together and, besides, a number of sources and analogues for *Everyman* have been adduced in justification of the satirical element in the play. The existence of satire in the play is unremarkable in itself, but certain aspects of the satire indicate that the concerns of the fifteenth-century reforming movement are present. In the speech in which Knowledge contributes criticisms of the contemporary Church, two principal areas of corruption among the clergy are given prominence: they are simony [selling church positions] and breaches of the vow of chastity. Such abuses had been condemned for centuries, but with renewed vigour by followers of the *Devotio Moderna.* Gerard Groote wrote a book entitled *De Simonia ad Beguttas* in which he defined simony and all the kinds of spiritual buying and selling which went with it. Furthermore, he saw the refusal of convents to accept postulants *sine symonia et sine pactu,* i.e. without a financial premium, as an extension of the same abuse; his anger against monastic corruption led to his founding of the first community of the Sisters of the Common Life. As to failures in chastity, Groote attacked the clergy of the Low Countries in his *Sermo contra focaristas.* Priests were keeping concubines, or *focariae,* quite blatantly and in this practice Groote saw an especially grave cause of scandal. In Knowledge's speech (750-63) Groote's concerns are summarized.

Followers of the *Devotio Moderna* would probably be most surprised and dismayed, were they to return to this earth, to find themselves remembered chiefly as reformers in anticipation of the Reformation. The greater intention of the movement, as its name implies, was to renew spirituality and to this end the movement was prolific in devotional works far more concerned with positive aids to spirituality than with the largely negative criticisms of failure. *Elckerlijc* itself may be seen as one response to the devotional impulse; it certainly shares a number of characteristics with such writings of the time.

Devotional writing is by nature a record of personal, sometimes idiosyncratic, experience and it is difficult therefore to generalize about the works which came out of the milieu of the *Devotio Moderna.* There are common characteristics, however, which *Elckerlijc* shares with these works and which the translator of *Everyman* preserves. One is the kind of language used by the Brethren of the Common Life—their art of simple, lucid expression. In *Everyman* the translator renders accurately the limpid simplicity of his Dutch text. If the play lacks the verbal riches of Elizabethan drama, and it does, it has rare directness and clarity. The paring down of language is the verbal correlative of the desire to strip life of its inessentials, a devotional exercise in itself and one which underlies the action of the play. To the author of such a work, personal glory as the reward of literary endeavour is anathema and hence it is not surprising to find that the authorship of *Elckerlijc* is uncertain and its translator unknown.

Much of the devotional writing of the fifteenth century reveals the same lack of concern for scholastic theology which we have already commented upon in Erasmus. One of the resultant dangers was a decline in intellectual quality. R.R. Post goes so far as to maintain [in *The Modern Devotion,* 1968, quoting M. T. P. Van Woerkum] that "this lack of intellectual penetration in the long run caused Groote's Devotionalist movement to shrivel and peter out." However, if the play is without that heady intellectual excitement which Dr Faustus experienced at the University of Wittenburg, its spiritual programme is as safe as Faustus' was dangerous.

We continue this part of our discussion of *Everyman* with a comparison between the play and *The Imitation of Christ* written by Thomas à Kempis, a brother of the Common Life. In the *Imitation* and in the play, which followed a generation later, spirituality is serenely reposed upon faith in received doctrine. As one editor of the *Imitation* [L. Sherely-Price, 1952] has commented: "In the *Imitation,* as in the lives of the Saints, will be found sincere and reasoned loyalty to the teachings of Christ and the Holy Catholic Church, and Thomas lays emphasis on right belief as the prerequisite of right life." While there is a vein of contention in *Everyman,* as we have already seen, the overall mood is one of acceptance and endorsement of established doctrine: difficulties over the status of confession and criticisms of clerical abuses should be kept within the wider context of submission to authority, as enjoined by Five Wits at the end of the debate on priesthood at lines 765-68.

One obvious difference between the *Imitation* and the play is that the former is concerned with holy living, the latter with holy dying. The difference is only one of emphasis, however, since the *Imitation* encourages the reader to meditate on death and the audience at the play is offered precepts for life as well as death. In its degree of emphasis on death, the play is closer to much fifteenth-century devotional writing than is the *Imitation* itself. In this writing there is a tradition of meditation upon the four last things: death, judgment, hell and heaven. *De spiritualibus ascensionibus* by Gerard Zerbolt, one of the most prolific writers in the Brethren of the Common Life, is an example. *Elckerlijc* and *Everyman* have inherited this tradition. The connexion between the Brethren and the play becomes firmer still when one takes into account that the meditation on the four last things in Zerbolt, à Kempis, and others occurs in conjunction with the theme of the imitation of Christ.

In the latter stages of *Everyman* there is a drawing-in of parallels between the penitent protagonist and the Passion of Christ. We should note that it was the Passion, used in the broader sense to include the events from the Last Supper onwards, rather than the whole life of Christ which was the focus for meditation among the Devotionalists, including à Kempis. In the play the first reference to the Passion as Christ's redemptive act of love for man occurs in God's speech, lines 29-33. Thereafter it is not until lines 561-64 that we are specifically reminded of the Passion. The great difference between the second reference and the first is that Everyman is no longer alienated from God but is undergoing a process of identification with the Passion:

> Here shall you receyue that scourge of me,
> Whiche is penaunce stronge that ye must endure,
> To remember thy Sauyour was scourged for the
> With sharpe scourges, and suffred it pacyently.
> (561-64)

The particular form of penance allotted to Everyman, i.e. flagellation, was common but by no means predominant in the Church at the time. That a dying man should literally be required to scourge himself seems most unlikely, so we may assume that the allegory is looking to a metaphorical basis of connexion between the scourging of Christ and the satisfaction to be made by Everyman in completion of the penitential rite. From this moment in the play the pilgrimage itself begins to carry increasingly explicit comparisons with the part of the Passion known as the Way of the Cross. The whole question of pilgrimage will concern us later in this Introduction, but it will be as well to note here that well before the play was written pilgrimage as practised by Christians had become identified with the Passion. In Chaucer's *Canterbury Tales* the pilgrimage becomes symbolic

> Of thilke parfit glorious pilgrymage
> That highte Jerusalem celestial.

The pilgrimage through death to the New Jerusalem heralds the beginning of Everyman's imitation of Christ's last agony in the play, lines 493-94. Just before Everyman receives the scourge of penance and uses it in satisfaction for his past sins, he appeals to the Virgin Mary, who witnessed her Son's crucifixion, for help in the form of prayers of intercession on His behalf:

> And, Lady, that I may, by meane of thy prayer,
> Of your Sone's glory to be partynere;
> By the meanes of His Passyon I it craue.
>
> (601-03)

The reference to the saving power of Christ's Passion, followed by renewed reference to scourging completes the process of making explicit what had formerly been implicit, i.e. that the penitent Everyman has identified himself with the Passion.

Once Everyman has received the sacraments he is in fit state to die and to die in the manner of Christ. As the moment of death approaches, Everyman alludes several times to the Passion, his own words echoing Christ's. Calling on Beauty, Strength, Five Wits, Discretion and Knowledge to go with him, Everyman tests their loyalty, saying:

> Now set eche of you on this rodde your honde,
> And shortely folowe me.
>
> (778-79)

"Rodde" refers to the crucifix which the penitent would be wearing. Some time before Christ was arrested He prophesied his end and tested his disciples in these words:

> Whosoever will come after me let him deny himself,
> and take up his cross, and follow me.

The simple, yet powerful, accompanying symbolism of action at this moment in the play is enough to suggest to the audience that Everyman's own Way of the Cross has begun.

The last words of Christ upon the cross in Matthew's gospel are: "My God, my God, why hast thou forsaken me?" (Matthew 27.46) This sounds like despair, but in fact Christ is quoting the prophetic twenty-second psalm, which predicts the circumstances of the crucifixion. This ambiguity demonstrates the paradoxical nature of Christ as true God, foreknowing all with confidence, and as true man, experiencing the terror of being abandoned in the dying flesh. Similarly, in faith and fear Everyman cries out; "O, Iesu, helpe! All hath forsaken me" (851).

According to Luke's gospel Christ's last words are: "Father, into thy hands I commend my spirit" (Luke 23.46). Christ is again quoting a psalm, this time psalm 31.5. These are Everyman's own last words, said first in English at line 880 and then in Latin at lines 886-87:

> In to thy handes, Lorde, my soule I
> commende; . . .
>
> *In manus tuas . . .*
> *. . . commendo spiritum meum.*

The identification of Everyman with Christ is now complete.

INTERPRETATIVE APPROACHES

The sheer diversity of sources and analogues which have been argued for in *Everyman* is testimony enough to the play's richness. *Everyman* is open to many interpretative approaches, a few of which we shall now consider in outline. There will be some overlap with what we have said under preceding headings.

1. *The quest*

From fairy tale to epic, literature reveals and proclaims the inquisitive, restless spirit of man. In many countries at many times this spirit has found expression in tales of exploit and adventure: a hero, a warrior, or a prophet undertakes a journey through mortal dangers in a search or quest for a dragon to be slain, a beautiful maiden to be rescued, or a truth to be found. Sometimes the tale of a quest is no more than an exciting narrative, fit to keep drowsy children awake at bedtime. But often the quest is more profound, necessitating a journey by a protagonist towards self-realization, towards deeper insights into the truth of his own being and the world about him. The journey may be presented in literal or "realistic" terms, as in Ernest Hemingway's novel *A Farewell to Arms,* or in the elaborate extended metaphor of allegory, as in Edmund Spenser's *The Faerie Queene.*

The medieval romance, which lies somewhere between fairy tale and epic and which partakes of the qualities of both, is the genre most integrally related to the theme of the quest. In fact, although "quest" is simply derived from the Latin for the verb "to seek", by long association the word has become identified with the medieval romance. In the quest literature of the romances the concerns are aristocratic and, in the English tradition of the romance, tales of King Arthur and the Knights of the Round Table are the most frequent subject matter. Perhaps the finest example is *Sir Gawain and the Green Knight.* Behind the courtly exterior of this and other romances, there lie universal significances. Even in Shakespeare's generation Edmund Spenser could still seek to recapture the mood of the bygone chivalric romance in order to promote the new Protestant religion, which drew largely upon the common people for support.

Everyman, as the play's title indicates, is more proletarian than the aristocratic literature of the romance, yet it has attributes in common with the romance. In the play, as in the romance, there is a process of spiritual growth through a hazardous journey in which values are tried and proven, or rejected if false, through ordeal. The V-shaped structure of *Everyman* has its parallels in the romance, with the shearing-off of falsehood represented through the pitfalls and dangers encountered on the way. The process is necessary as a prelude to spiritual rebirth. Of particular interest to the student of *Everyman* is the imagery of the play, which echoes that of the quest in romance literature.

In the imagery of *Everyman,* God is continually referred to in a way that is completely familiar to the medieval mind: He is represented as the most powerful being in the universe on the supernatural plane, which is unknown to man's earthly experience, in terms of the most powerful being known to man on the natural plane. This most powerful of beings is, of course, the king. Everyman's quest will take him to judgement before the King of Heaven (see lines 19, 494) in a manner not unlike that of the medieval knight on return from his perilous adventures. As Sir Gawain, after his long and frightening journey to meet the Green Knight in fulfilment of a commitment that seems certain to bring about his death, returns to King Arthur for judgement on his deportment—so Everyman endures trials, including that of death itself, as he returns to stand before his Creator. The figure of Death affirms the reality and puissance of God when he tells Everyman that he has been sent to summon Everyman by "the chefe Lorde of Paradyse" (110) who dwells in "mageste" (91) and "magnyfycence" (159).

Once Everyman has accepted that he must shortly die, and he takes some convincing, he has to explain his plight to those whom he would take for company and in doing so speaks as the knight who has been given a special mission to accomplish. To Fellowship he says:

> Commaunded I am to go a journaye,
> A longe waye, hard and daungerous,
> And gyue a strayte counte, without delaye,
> Before the hye Iuge Adonay.
>
>   (242-45)

To Kindred and Cousin he explains, rather deviously evading the blunt truth:

> I was commaunded by a messenger,
> That is a hye kynge's chefe offycer.
>
>   (329-30)

The evasion is functional in the play, not only for what it reveals of Everyman's own short-coming, but also for the insight offered into Everyman's imaginative transformation of the task before him.

Everyman has to explain—and partly veil—what lies before him when he introduces the subject of his impending death to his false friends. When he comes to his Good Deeds he discovers that his plight is known and needs no explanation. Nevertheless, the chivalric metaphor continues as a channel of communication between Good Deeds and Everyman now that the metaphor is no longer needed as a means of partial self-deception or for the deception of others. Good Deeds declares:

> Euery Man, I haue vnderstandynge
> That ye be somoned a counte to make
> Before Myssyas, of Iherusalem Kynge.
> And you do by me, that iournay with you wyll
>   I take.
>
>   (492-95)

When Good Deeds speaks of Everyman having to appear before the Messiah, King of Jerusalem, he is of course referring to the risen Christ of the New Jerusalem. In this statement strands in the imagery of the play converge and become interwoven. Everyman's journey is both a quest and a pilgrimage, for Christ is both King and God.

Pilgrimage is a practice common to many religions, usually taking the form of a visit to a shrine or holy place. Within a religion there may be different kinds of pilgrimages, addressed to different purposes. In modern Catholicism, for example, pilgrims go to Lourdes for healing. In the Middle Ages pilgrimages to the Holy Land (as opposed to more local pilgrimages like that of Chaucer's pilgrims to Canterbury) had a special significance: such pilgrimages were commonly undertaken from all over Europe as acts of devotion and atonement. Shakespeare's Henry IV is obsessed with his guilt for overthrowing and murdering Richard II; he yearns, ever more as his life draws to its end, to make the pilgrimage to Jerusalem in expiation, but the nearest he approaches his goal is to die in the Jerusalem Chamber of his own palace. So, for fifteenth- and sixteenth-century audiences at the play, the metaphor of the pilgrimage to Jerusalem to describe sinful Everyman's death would have seemed especially apt.

A final point to note is that the imagery of the journey as quest gives way progressively to that of the journey as pilgrimage. This development is commensurate with the spiritual growth of Everyman.

2. *Mysticism in Everyman*

Mysticism has a long history both in the East and the West. It is a term which has acquired opprobrious connotations, unfortunately, through being loosely associated with the occult and some rather outlandish religious cults and sects. More properly applied, the term "mysticism" involves two principal aspects: one is a vision of cosmic order that absorbs and transcends the fragmentary, contradictory and severely limited perceptions we have of the world about us; the other is the process by which the unifying and transcendent vision is achieved.

To the extent that *Everyman* is a mystical play, the mystical element is manifested more through process than through vision. A mystical reading reinforces the meaning of the journey and helps to explain the events of the journey. One of the puzzling things about the play is the apparent betrayal of Everyman's inner attributes and the concomitant misguidedness, or apparent misguidedness, of Good Deeds and Knowledge in having urged Everyman to call them together. An examination of the play's mysticism helps to resolve the problem.

At the most obvious level we accept the departure of Beauty, Strength, Five Wits and Discretion as part of the natural order of things. . . . St Thomas Aquinas enumerates five proofs for the existence of God by application of sense data to the evaluative faculty of reason. In *Everyman* Five Wits represents the senses and Discretion the faculty of reason. Quite rightly, Everyman is encouraged to use his five senses and his discretion because they are, in the terms employed by Aquinas and other theologians, God-given means through which man may come to a fuller understanding of his life on earth and his future in heaven. However, at the moment of death, man is stripped of these temporal aids. We all know this, but our wordly preoccupations blunt such perceptions. For good reason, it seems, the translator of *Everyman* (in a passage which has no parallel in *Elckerlijc*) makes his Doctor insist at the conclusion to the drama that such divine gifts as sensory perception and reason will forsake us, as will the more patently ephemeral Strength and Beauty. There is nothing mystical so far. But a purely common-sense approach does not account fully for our aesthetic response to this part of the play.

Let us look at the second set of desertions in another way. The playwright invites his audience to share imaginatively his protagonist's moment of death, to experience death while still alive. To experience the unexperienceable, for we cannot die and yet continue to live, requires a leap of the imagination. The playwright invites us to make the leap by following for the brief duration of the play a way that was well known to medieval mystics and practised by many as a way of life: this is the *via negativa*, the way of negation of self. The principle on which the *via negativa* operates is that we are separated from God by our individuality and that we may reach towards reunion with Him by eliminating individuality. The discipline of asceticism, which is common to many religions and which is rooted in the earliest Christian practices, was conceived as a practical means towards the purpose of reunification with God. Asceticism was a way of conditioning body, mind and soul for the contemplation of the divine being and achieving a sense of oneness with Him.

The writings of many medieval mystics have preserved for posterity a record of contemplation achieved through the *via negativa*. Among them, St John of the Cross expresses ideas which seem to offer particularly fruitful comparison with *Everyman*. Although St John of the Cross wrote his works some time after *Elckerlijc* and *Everyman*, the comparison is valid because all these works bear the mark of a common tradition. As we read the following extract from St John's treatise, *The Ascent of Mount Carmel*, let us have in mind the bipartite structure of *Everyman* with its two sets of desertions:

> For a soul to attain to the state of perfection, it has ordinarily to pass through two principal kinds of night, which spiritual persons call purgations or purifications of the soul; and here we call them nights, for in both of them the soul journeys, as it were, by night, in darkness.
>
> The first night or purgation is of the sensual part of the soul; and the second is of the spiritual part.
>
> And this first night pertains to beginners, occurring at the time when God begins to bring them into the state of contemplation; in this night the spirit likewise has a part. . . . And the second night, or purification, pertains to those who are already proficient, occurring at the time when God desires to bring them to the state of union with God.
>
> We may say that there are three reasons for which this journey made by the soul to union with God is called night. The first has to do with the point from which the soul goes forth, for it has gradually to deprive itself of desire for all the worldly things which it possessed, by denying them to itself; the which denial and deprivation are, as it were, night to all the senses of man. The second reason has to do with the mean, or the road along which the soul must travel to this union—that is, faith, which is likewise as night to the understanding. The third has to do with

> the point to which it travels—namely, God, Who, equally, is dark night to the soul in this life. These three nights must pass through the soul, or, rather, the soul must pass through them—in order that it may come to Divine union with God.

Much of what may be said by way of comparison is self-evident, but it may be as well to summarize. The persistent metaphor of the journey in St John awakens one to a further dimension of meaning to the journey in *Everyman*. In the second paragraph of the extract just quoted we discern a close parallel with what happens in *Everyman*. The way of purgation is first of the outer adjuncts to and extensions of personality, i.e. all the status-giving relationships and possessions that we shore up to conserve our sense of identity and self-importance. Then follows the second task, the elimination of all the more intimate and inwardly-identifying features of selfhood. St John's formulation is a little different in detail from what happens in *Everyman*, but the pattern, the process, is virtually identical. The symbolism of the dark nights suggests fear, apprehension and pain in renunciation as being necessary and inevitable. As Everyman prepares to go through the knot of death he must undergo such human anguish. Finally, in both St John's treatise and in the play, the soul which has divested itself of all mortal attachments is ready for union with God.

In this scheme of things, Good Deeds and Knowledge are quite right to direct Everyman to Five Wits and Discretion, both aids to faith in a Thomist formulation, because faith is vitally important to the development of the soul towards union with God. But because the development of the soul takes it past the point where the senses are beneficial, to where they become a hindrance, in fact, the second set of desertions is in no way incompatible with the counsel given by Everyman's well-intentioned advisers. On a mystical level of interpretation, what the playwright is doing is to offer the death of Everyman as an analogue for the audience to take home with them and to apply it to their lives. Those who have seen the play may thus relate the art of holy dying, which Everyman has discovered late, to the mystical art of holy living and so be prepared in good time for that which has taken Everyman by surprise.

The speculative mysticism of St John of the Cross ascends to rarified heights of contemplation. For more earth-bound mortals the practical day-to-day path offered by Thomas à Kempis may be of greater value. The *Devotio Moderna* was deeply concerned with the spirituality of everyday life, and it was in response to this need that à Kempis wrote the *Imitation of Christ*. It is hard to know whether to describe the *Imitation* as a mystical work. Contemplation of the life and death of Christ in the *Imitation*, especially in the passage on "The Royal Road of the Holy Cross", has affinities with the more speculative writings. Certainly the shearing off of non-essentials in *The Ascent of Mount Carmel* and the contemplation of Christ's Passion in the *Imitation* are both glimpsed in *Everyman*, where both elements are combined harmoniously in the expression of a single spiritual impulse.

3. *An existentialist interpretation*

From whatever direction one approaches *Everyman,* at the centre there is always the same crisis—the onset of death. Dying brings about a sudden and radical change in Everyman's circumstances, necessitating a complete reappraisal of self and values. Existentialism, as a philosophical approach to the nature and meaning of existence, draws upon crises such as that which faces Everyman.

Existentialism is a rather forbidding name for a straightforward way of looking at the world. The name itself is little more than a hundred years old; what the name describes is an attitude of mind as old as the Bible, to which many existentialist writers have recourse for endorsement of their views. Because existentialism is a way of looking at the world and not a system of ideas, it is not necessarily Christian or the property of any one Christian denomination. It takes widely differing forms, as in the Protestantism of Kierkegaard, the Catholicism of Gabriel Marcel, the Judaism of Martin Buber, and even the atheism of Sartre.

Existentialism takes for granted the existence of man and the universe. It also asserts his capacity to understand and interpret his existence. It further asserts the wholeness of man as a being comprised of intellect, emotions, intuitions, and instincts; and it insists that man's interpretation of himself and the world about him must be the product of the totality of all his modes of perception working together. Existentialism approves of reason, but it is part of a movement in reaction against the rationalism of much eighteenth-century philosophy.

All existentialists, whether religious or agnostic or atheistic, share a common pursuit. They seek authentic existence. The existentialist maintains that many people drift or are blown across the surface of life, never thinking deeply, never caring greatly, never prepared to commit themselves to values that really matter. Such people the existentialist will declare to be inauthentic. Everyman, as he is when we meet him at the beginning of the play, is one of those people whose superficiality condemns them. He has lived complacently in a world of received ideas, without ever questioning the validity of what he has received and, by sheer default of mind and will, accepted. Furthermore, Everyman's inauthenticity is evil because the society in which he insouciantly lives is evil.

In his first moment of distress, Everyman turns to Fellowship. But Fellowship has been a good friend only "in sporte and playe" (201). Superficiality breeds not only evil but also mere frivolity. Kindred, to whom Everyman appeals next, is incorrigibly frivolous and incapable of taking anything seriously. All he can offer Everyman is a wench for wassailing:

> Ye shall haue my mayde with all my herte;
> She loueth to go to feestes, there to be nyse,
> And to daunce and a brode to sterte.
> I wyll gyue her leue to helpe you in that iourney,
> If that you and she may a gree.
>
> (360-64)

Goods, who complains that he is too brittle and may not endure (425), is equally frivolous and much more malicious:

> Mary, thou brought thy selfe in care,
> Wherof I am gladde.
> I must nedes laugh; I can not be sadde.
>
> (454-56)

Sometimes something happens which makes it impossible for a man to continue in his inauthentic way. It may be that he has a blinding flash of insight or it may be that insight is thrust upon him through a sudden change of circumstance. Men with spontaneous insights are rare, however; the record of life and literature is of the latter situation. Shakespeare's King Lear is a fine example of a man who leads a dangerously inauthentic existence until authenticity is forced upon him. Through foolish notions he loses all that he has taken for granted—his status as monarch and father, food, clothing, shelter. At the middle of the play, and in this respect *King Lear* closely resembles *Everyman,* desolation and isolation bring Lear to ask himself what it really means to be a man; from this point he begins to reshape his values and he is on the way to authentic existence.

In literature which presents a protagonist as a man on the way to an existential reexamination of himself, isolation is a recurrent motif. The novels of Joseph Conrad almost invariably tell the story of men who have become in some way isolated, who have become alienated or exiled in some terrible situation; the experience is turned to spiritual advantage, even if it is too late for recovery in any other sense, and insight is achieved. This is true even of Mr Kurtz in *The Heart of Darkness* who at the end of his life, and with his last breath, can only whisper: "The horror, the horror." Some existentialists would describe the crisis which confronts King Lear and Mr Kurtz as a "boundary situation", that is one where the protagonist arrives at the boundary of his received ideas and must travel beyond them without familiar and comforting landmarks.

Religious existentialists often look to death—a unique and isolated event within the life of every man—as the boundary situation *par excellence*. A favourite text is the parable recounted in Chapter 12 of Luke's gospel. In this parable a rich man decides to pull down his barns and build bigger ones for storing his food and goods; having exercised his worldly providence to immense material satisfaction, he resolves to eat, drink and be merry. God interrupts his complacency, however, and says to him: "Thou fool, this night thy soul shall be required of thee: then whose shall those things be, which thou hast provided?" (Luke 12.19). *This* night: there is no escape from death, which comes as a moment of truth to the man who has lived the lie of temporal security. Everyman, carefree, rich and in the full flush of worldly enjoyment, is served with the same summons.

To summarize, three related aspects of existentialism are: (1) the need for a total human response to life, engaging all the human faculties, (2) the application of these faculties towards achieving authenticity, and (3) the boundary situation as the providing ground for the first two. To what extent are these existential concerns the concerns of *Everyman*?

In the play, Everyman, for so long as he lives, is a combination of body and soul. His relationship with his body is paradoxical: his human faculties respond to his call for help on the way to salvation, the reward promised for spiritual authenticity, and yet he must be parted from them. We have noted how this paradox operates on the mystical level; it operates existentially as well. In approaching the severance of body and soul in death, his human understanding is enhanced by the assistance of the very faculties which he must soon lose. His Knowledge is joined during a vital part of his journey by his Five Wits (the organs of sight, hearing, touch, taste and smell), his Discretion, and even his Beauty and Strength. Thus it is seen that the *Everyman* dramatist insists on the importance of the whole man that corresponds closely with modern existentialist contentions.

On the application of all faculties towards achieving authenticity, not much more need be said. Good Deeds and Knowledge emphasize their presence as a purposeful presence. Good Deeds describes Discretion, Strength and Beauty as "persones of grete myght" (658), and Knowledge adds immediately afterwards:

> Also ye must call to mynde
> Your Fyue Wyttes as for your counseylours.
> (662-63)

To which Good Deeds rejoins:

> You must haue them redy at all houres.
> (664)

Good Deeds and Knowledge are not misguided fools. Their advice is sound in existential as well as in mystical terms. It is only Everyman's limited understanding, for he is still on the way to enlightenment, which makes these counsellors seem like deserters. What is important is that he has now gained sufficient understanding to heed the advice of his true friends.

The boundary situation, the realization of the incapacity of false values to sustain the dying man, is the focal point of the play. It is to this that the action of the first half leads. So momentous is the coming of death that Everyman takes some time to grasp what it means for him. His attempt to bribe the personified messenger (120-23) is one of the humorous moments in the play, and it is humour to a purpose. Everyman is so steeped in his life of inauthentic materialism that he can respond only in terms of his familiarity with the ways of this world. He argues and pleads with Death, accepting the overwhelming fact only when Death concludes the conversation with words reminiscent of the parable from Luke's gospel:

> For thou mayst saye this is the daye
> That no man lyuynge may scape a waye.
> (182-83)

Acceptance of the fact marks Everyman's first step towards salvation, but as yet he remains bound to his false values. So he has to go through the disillusionments of the first half of the play to reach his boundary situation.

Once Everyman has learnt that his material values will be of no further use to him, he experiences the full terror of isolation. Alone, bereft of all that he had held dear to him, he begins his central soliloquy. He has nothing left and, as yet, nothing to take its place. At the nadir of his fortunes, close to despair, he acknowledges the truth of his spiritual state:

> And so I am worthy to be blamed;
> Thus may I well my selfe hate.
> (477-78)

Fortunately for him, unlike Conrad's Mr Kurtz, there is just enough time for constructive reappraisal. His isolation, not experienced simply as an intellectual idea but as a shattering blow to his whole being, leads him to discover who his true friends are.

It would be perverse, even foolish, to see in the fifteenth-century play of *Everyman* an exact replication of twentieth-century existentialist attitudes. There are elements in the play which undoubtedly separate it from us in outlook. But the modern existentialist maintains that he is only giving a name to what has long persisted in human thought, rather than creating a new perspective, and to this extent *Everyman* lends itself to such an interpretation.

4. *The theme of friendship*

An enquiry into the nature of friendship is a subsidiary theme which runs through the play. For those modern readers who do not find much interest in the theological and doctrinal issues of *Everyman,* the ethical enquiry into the nature of friendship will still seem relevant. Some students have declared that, apart from the undisputed dramatic strength of the play and its purely aesthetic appeal as a finely-constructed artefact, this enquiry into the ethics of friendship is what gives *Everyman* a lasting appeal.

In the ancient world of Greece and Rome and in medieval Europe, friendship had a more carefully formulated role in society than it has today. We tend to think of friendship much more casually. Many treatises from the ancient and medieval periods testify to the importance of friendship in imparting and sustaining moral values. Of the classical works on the subject, Cicero's *De Amicitia* is a fine example. Here, following Aristotle, Cicero defines the qualities to be found in friends and friendship. His concept of friendship proceeds from the proposition that friendship is worthy of the name only when it is morally and spiritually improving. For Cicero, its foundation and continuance depend upon the virtue of the participants: friendship lasts so long as the friends are good, in a moral sense, and decays when there is corruption in the persons. Hence the desertion of Everyman by Fellowship, Kindred, Cousin, and Goods is only to be expected.

Medieval concepts of friendship owe much to classical ideals, with the addition of other characteristics attributable to the cultural developments of the intervening centuries. In medieval literature the ethical values of friendship are often seen in application to a rare and special relationship between two people; classical authors see friendship in terms of selective but wider groups of relationship. In some of the medieval models of friendship, two men swear undying loyalty to one another and will undergo any hardship in the cause of that bond, even to the point of death. Chaucer's *Knight's Tale* is an example of such friendship put to the test, for the two men have the misfortune to fall in love with the same woman; in this case love destroys friendship. In *Everyman* there is no such conflict or complication, but throughout the play the protagonist finds himself rejected when he attempts to find the values of true friendship in those who are unworthy and therefore incapable of it. Everyman needs only one true friend to go all the way with him, even to death, and Good Deeds ultimately fills the role.

The test which Everyman imposes on his would-be friends in turn, i.e. their willingness to die with him, conforms with the medieval paradigm of friendship: friendship is not true unless it has been tried and tested through ordeal. Everyman applies the test, with disastrous but inevitable consequences, until he looks to Good Deeds. In his acceptance of the trial of friendship by ordeal, Good Deeds acts like a sworn true friend. And so the acting out of motifs associated with the ethical ideal of friendship serves the purpose of reinforcing the main doctrinal theme of the play, which is that good works are necessary for salvation.

The classical and medieval secular traditions of friendship acquired added strength of meaning when reinforced by Christianity. Friendship was seen as a special gift of God. St Ambrose expounds the Christian dimension to friendship in *De Officiis Ministrorum,* as does Peter of Blois in *De Amicitia Christiana.* In *Everyman* the gift which the protagonist receives in friendship of Good Deeds symbolizes the operation of another gift of God, known as actual grace, within his soul.

Actual grace, in Catholic theology, is manifested in the supernatural help which the Holy Spirit gives to sinners in order to recognize their sinfulness and to repent. Through actual grace Everyman begins to realize what is necessary for his salvation. Good Deeds cannot be efficacious while one is in a state of mortal sin (see lines 514-15) and mortal sin can only be removed through sanctifying grace, which is normally conveyed through the sacraments. The first whisperings of the sin-stricken, immobilized Good Deeds are the promptings of actual grace in Everyman's soul. Everyman's forgotten friend tells him to call upon Knowledge; Knowledge bids Everyman to go to the sacraments; through the sacraments Everyman's Good Deeds are freed of the bonds of sin and are able to accompany him. Friendship with Good Deeds is vital: only through the guidance of this faithful friend is Everyman able to set his feet in the right direction upon the spiritual journey to redemption.

LANGUAGE, STYLE AND VERSIFICATION

By the end of the fifteenth century modern standard English had almost fully developed. Modern English is based upon the Middle English spoken in the East Midland district, strongly modified by London dialect and usage. *Everyman* is an early example of modern standard English. Superficially the text has a "medieval" look about it, but that is largely because of the spelling, which had not been standardized by this time and was still largely phonetic. Apart from spelling, there are some items of vocabulary and usage which would not be familiar to a modern reader. . . . By and large, the text of *Everyman* presents no greater problems to the twentieth-century reader than the Elizabethan drama of some seventy years later does. Although *Everyman* is generally grouped with medieval

drama by virtue of its link with medieval dramatic traditions, in language as well as in religious thought it has closer affinities with the Renaissance.

Plays of the late fifteenth and early sixteenth centuries clearly show that dramatists of the time were faced with a problem of style. Most of the plays lack stylistic consistency to some extent and range from the excessively aureate to the excessively colloquial within themselves. Erasmus, in his treatise for students of rhetoric entitled *Of The Two Kinds of Style,* says that there are two kinds of style possible—one highly ornamented, the other very plain; both, he says, have their dangers and limitations. Classical rhetoricians had identified three styles, but for our purposes Erasmus' distinction will suffice. What the *Everyman* dramatist managed to achieve was a happy blend of the two, though the emphasis is more on an austere and dignified plainness stripped of colloquial banality than on incorporation of consciously elevating rhetorical devices. It is the style as much as the doctrinal and devotional matter which identifies the play and its original, *Elckerlijc,* with the reforming movement of the Low countries. What the translator of *Everyman* has done is to achieve dramatic strength through variations in style, without losing the consistency which characterizes the work. At some moments, for example in the speeches of Kindred and Cousin, the language approximates to the ordinary domestic level of common people; at others, as in Everyman's prayer of penitence (lines 581-607), the poetry is as exultant as the spirit.

The versification of *Everyman* has received little critical attention in its own right. Most often rhyme and rhythm have been compared with *Elckerlijc* for the purpose of detecting priority. Cawley notes that the verse-forms are "a welter of couplets and quatrains, together with occasional tail-rhymes, five-, six-, and seven-line stanzas, rhyme-royal stanzas, and octaves." Cawley also notes that there are more than a hundred imperfect rhymes, some of which are examples of assonance and others due to corruption of the original text. Undoubtedly there are oddities in the rhyme sequence and it would require considerable ingenuity to justify all of them, but the description of the verse-forms as a "welter" is excessively harsh. To be fair to Cawley, he goes on to say that the verse-forms are not entirely haphazard and that "Some of the very short verses seem meant to mark a quick exchange of dialogue, while rhyme-royal and octave are used in passages of exceptional gravity." *Everyman* resembles *Elckerlijc* in that the principal verse-form is the rhyming couplet; in both the Anglo-Saxon pattern of the heavily accented line containing four or five stresses with a median pause is the dominant characteristic of the versification, however, so that rhyme schemes with their variants are subservient to the powerful rhythmic thrust of the line. Because of the Anglo-Saxon rhythm the actual number of syllables to the line varies greatly. Exceptionally short lines in *Everyman* are mostly derived from half-lines in *Elckerlijc* and are used for emphatically brief interchanges. For example, compare lines 92-3 from *Everyman:*

EUERY MAN: What, sente to me?

DETHE: Ye, certaynly.

with the split line 75 of *Elckerlijc:*

> ELCKERLIJC: Aen mi ghesonden?
>
> DIE DOOT: Jae ick, certeyn!

Commentators have pointed out, in the process of establishing the priority of *Elckerlijc,* that the translator was faced with a number of problems in maintaining rhyme. Commonly, the **Everyman** dramatist employs rhyming tags; sometimes these affect the strength of a line, giving it a rather lame conclusion. To illustrate this point we compare lines 690-91 of *Elckerlijc* with the corresponding lines 721-22 of **Everyman.** In the Dutch, "leven" (= life) rhymes with "seven":

> Hier in desen aertschen leven
> Die heylighe sacramenten seven

In English "life" and "seven" simply cannot be persuaded to rhyme; accordingly, in **Everyman** the words are placed within the line and rhyme-tags are added:

> Here in this transytory lyfe for the and me
> The blessyd sacramentes vii. there be.

Here is an example of weak writing in the face of the problem of translation, intensified by translating verse into verse. Nevertheless, the translator of **Everyman** deserves commendation for the overall quality of style and versification.

EVERYMAN ON THE STAGE

The surviving English morality plays were written to be performed. All manner of clues in the texts of the plays leave us in no doubt about that. Taking performance for granted, we are confronted with more difficult questions—what kind of staging? were the performers professionals or amateurs? what sorts of people would have been in the audience? To some extent these questions are interrelated and an answer to one will help to answer another.

To show the range of possibilities within the genre of the morality play, we shall comment briefly on two diverse exemplars, *The Castle of Perseverance* and *Mankind. The Castle of Perseverance* is an early play (*c.* 1400-25): it requires an immensely complicated set, as a plan of the acting area incorporated into the original manuscript shows; it calls upon a large cast; and it is a very long play of over 3000 lines. All these factors point towards amateur performance. Professional troupes of strolling players, such as Shakespeare recalls and lampoons in *Hamlet,* did not become established until later in the century. They relied upon plays which could be adapted to a variety of settings and which required a minimum of props to be carried about from town to town—*The Castle* is far too elaborate for that. The troupes were small, often consisting of no more than four actors—in *The Castle's* large cast of thirty-three there is little scope for doubling parts. And finally, the length of the play suggests a festival atmosphere rather than an entertainment relying upon the limited span of attention that can be expected from a casual audience. *Mankind,* on the other hand, is considerably later (*c.* 1475-1500) and is into the period of the first professional play-

ers. Unlike *The Castle,* the stage setting is undefined—it is anywhere and nowhere; the cast is much smaller and the script also allows for doubling, thereby requiring no more than six players. Furthermore, the play is much shorter than *The Castle,* being only 907 lines in length and capable of being acted in little over an hour. These are indications enough, but we may add that an appeal to the audience for money early in the play leaves us in no further uncertainty!

Partly because **Everyman** is a translation and therefore has no specifically English roots, the circumstances surrounding its first performance in the sixteenth century—if indeed it was actually performed—are not easily determined. Although it shares much with *Mankind* in date, flexibility of setting, relative smallness of cast—with the maximum of doubling it can be performed by a company of seven—and brevity, nevertheless it lacks two characteristics generally found in the shorter English morality play designed for professional performance: there is no bawdiness to speak of in **Everyman,** although there is much dry humour, and there is no knockabout farce to eke out and palliate the overriding didacticism. It is most probable that *Elckerlijc* was first performed as a school play in one of the educational institutions fostered by the Brethren of the Common Life, but the Brethren had no exact equivalent in England. No record of performance survives. It is even possible that Pynson's first edition (the **C** text) was printed for purely polemical reasons since, in his official capacity as King's printer, he issued a number of political and controversial books concerned with the Reformation. The headnote to both Dutch and English versions of the play may be interpreted to mean that the play is intended as a closet drama, i.e. to be read rather than performed: the Dutch headnote describes the play as a "schoon boecxken", a beautiful book, and the English one calls it "a treatyse"; furthermore, both speak of it as being "in den maniere van" or "in the manner of " a play, as though the form needs some explanation. With these reservations and unresolved issues in mind, we may now proceed to consider the ways in which **Everyman** may have been performed when it was first rendered into English.

The most crucial editorial problem concerning the actual staging of **Everyman** is that of stage directions. Apart from the directions "God speketh" between lines 21 and 22, "Dethe" between lines 63 and 64, "Euery Man" between lines 86 and 87, and "Felawshyp speketh" between lines 205 and 206, there are none. *Elckerlijc* is even less helpful, directing only that God speaks first. From what we know of early sixteenth-century stagecraft and stage conventions, it would seem that there are three broad possibilities as to the manner in which **Everyman** would have been presented.

First of all, there is the kind of setting familiar to us from *Mankind* and its kindred plays. This is unlocalized, but, by a convention so widespread throughout all forms of medieval drama as to be universal, there is at least one portion of the acting area given some form of concrete being: it may be as humble as a chair or as imposing as a church, and it is symbolized by some form of stage property. The action takes place in the area within and adjacent to the identified place. Given such a setting, the action proceeds in a sequence of scenes, such as we experience in the conventional theatre of today, with actors making entrances and exits. The text of *Everyman* supports this manner of presentation. Everyman is directed by Knowledge to seek Confession and, on enquiring where to find the holy man, is told: "In the hous of saluacyon" (540). Within three lines Knowledge can say: "Lo, this is Confessyon" (543). Characters who are about to be seen by the audience and who have already been seen by an actor on stage are, it is reasonable to assume, separated from the acting area by a curtain or wings or some device. So it may be argued that the play is intended for a defined, though unlocalized, acting area having "on stage" and "off stage" facilities and with a localized area symbolically represented within the acting area. A large cross and, perhaps, a chair for Confession to sit on would be enough. So far, so good. Cawley, however, sees the house of salvation as a more complex structure: "It would be reasonable to assume," he says, "that the house of salvation, which is the dwelling-place of Confession, also had its battlemented heights, where God stood and spoke to sinful mankind at the beginning of the play and where Everyman's soul was received with angelic song at the ending." He bases this assumption on the dubious analogy of the castle in *The Castle of Perseverance*. It may well be that God is present, overseeing the action throughout the play, but the spare stage directions, unlike those of *The Castle*, leave us unconvinced that the dramatist intended so complex a structure as Cawley envisages. It is equally possible that God is present only for his speech and that He then withdraws or, as in the case of some mystery cycles, He is present for part of the time. It is also possible that only his voice is heard, that He is not seen at all. All this should be enough to show that within the conventions of presentation here suggested a great deal must remain a matter of speculation.

Another possible, though less likely, mode of presentation was that of *The Castle of Perseverance* where performances ranged over a large acting area and were given in the round. A number of plays and play cycles were produced in this way. There was, for example, a two-day performance of a cycle of mystery plays in Lucerne in 1583 for which the acting area was an entire square in the town centre, within which a number of localized acting areas were designated by structures of various kinds. It seems that the scenes were changed not by shifting scenery but by shifting the actors around the square. An advantage of presenting *Everyman* in this way would be that in his peregrinations the constant metaphor of the pilgrimage would be visually reinforced in the action. In such a mode of presentation there would be no exits and entrances: Everyman would make his way from one area or station to another and converse there with the figures who would already be waiting in readiness.

The third (and least likely) way, which comprises elements of the first two and some additional features, is that which was used for performance of festival plays at Mons and Valenciennes early in the sixteenth century; this system may also have been used for the York and Chester cy-

cles of mystery plays in England as well as in various parts of Europe. Instead of performing a sequence of plays on individual pageant wagons, a long stage is created by placing platforms side by side in a straight line; the action then moves from platform to platform along the single long stage. (pp. xxii-xliv)

No less important than stage arrangements to a sixteenth-century audience would have been the question of costuming. A simple setting was often complemented with elaborate costuming. To a public accustomed to iconological interpretation in the visual arts, the details of costuming were highly significant. Many medieval and Renaissance plays, including those of Shakespeare, have left many clues concerning costuming; *Everyman,* unfortunately, offers very few hints, but those which exist should not go unnoticed. God begins: "I perceyue, here in my maieste", which confirms that He would have been presented in the manner which had become conventional through the mystery plays—as a king or emperor. Everyman is first described as being dressed "gayly", indicative of a worldly man, vain and wealthy, and he later changes this raiment for the "garment of sorowe", called "Contrycyon": change in costume, in drama of this period, symbolized a change of heart.

THE STAGE HISTORY OF EVERYMAN

Whether *Everyman* was performed or not, the play must have achieved immediate popularity, for it was published no less than four times, and by two different printers, within about ten years. The subject matter was not only popular in England: between 1536 and 1549 five versions of the basic *Elckerlijc* drama appeared on the Continent, three in German and two in Latin. After the morality and mystery plays were overshadowed by the rise of the great drama of the Elizabethan period—during this early Protestant period the old Catholic religious plays were also deliberately suppressed—plays like *Everyman* were long forgotten. Not until 1773 was *Everyman* reprinted in England, and then only as a curiosity. Medieval drama began to attract serious attention only in the nineteenth century and it was not until 1901 that there was a major revival of *Everyman,* in the production by William Poel for the Elizabethan Stage Society in London. Other major revivals include a production by Professor Nevill Coghill at Oxford in 1934, as an outdoor production, and restaged in the following year for performance in Tewkesbury Abbey. In recent years *Everyman* has been put on by Universities and Colleges throughout the English-speaking world and the play has become recognized on literature and drama syllabuses as a great and historically significant work. (pp. xliv-xlv)

Geoffrey Cooper and Christopher Wortham, in an introduction to The Summoning of Everyman, *edited by Geoffrey Cooper and Christopher Wortham, University of Western Australia Press, 1980, pp. ix-li.*

PRODUCTION REVIEWS

The *Athenæum* (review date 20 July 1901)

[*The twentieth century revival of interest in* Everyman *began with William Poel's July 1901 production in the Master's Court of the Charterhouse in Canterbury. Poel, an English actor and manager, founded the Elizabethan Stage Society, an organization devoted to producing Shakespeare's plays in accordance with theatrical conventions of the poet's age. Although financially unsuccessful, surviving only from 1894-1905, the Society had an enormous impact on subsequent stagings of medieval and Renaissance drama. The critic finds that this presentation of the play demonstrates that "the primitive drama, which seems so dull and didactic, may well have passioned our forefathers—is, indeed, capable of passioning us."*]

To Mr. William Poel, the secretary and originator of the Elizabethan Stage Society, we are indebted for some quaint and edifying illustrations of our early stage. None of the previous experiments has had quite the value and interest of the performance given last Saturday afternoon under the shade of the venerable walls of the Charterhouse. The place was admirably suited to the entertainment, which consisted of the anonymous morality of *Everyman* and the scene of the interrupted 'Sacrifice of Isaac' from the *Histories of Lot and Abraham,* which is the fourth of the Chester miracle plays. That the scene was better suited than the court of Fulham Palace, which witnessed Ben Jonson's *Sad Shepherd,* or than the halls of the various Inns of Court which have been placed at the Society's disposal, may not perhaps be said. The environment was, however, in keeping with the action, and the two were so harmonious that it became easy to conceive the mimic performance real, and to believe that we were spectators of, and almost participants in, a great historical tragedy. Tragedy indeed, in its naïve simplicity and uncompromising sincerity, *Everyman* is—that "tragedy to those who feel" which is our general lot, the great unending problem of life, responsibility, and death. There are many points from which the entertainment may be regarded, and from all it is significant. The first thing that strikes one is that the primitive drama, which seems so dull and didactic, may well have passioned our forefathers—is, indeed, capable of passioning us; the second that this particular piece, played no better and no worse than on the occasion it was, is capable, when its merits are known, of attracting all London and becoming the "sensation" of a season. Temptations to ridicule presented themselves, and the smile rose occasionally to the lips. It died there, and sank before the absolute sincerity of the whole. Amusement never degenerated into mockery.

What are the obligations of the English dramatist to the *Elckerlijk* assigned to Peter Dorland of Diest, the Belgian mystic, the author of the *Viola Animæ,* or to the *Barlaam and Josaphat* of John of Damascus, we are unable to say. After the delivery of a species of prologue by a messenger, the scene, like that of *Festus* or of one of Goethe's prologues to *Faust,* opens in heaven with a speech from God,

Everyman and friends in the 1901 production. From left to right: Knowledge, Discretion, Beauty, Five Wits, Strength, Everyman, Good Deeds.

described in the programme by the Hebrew name Adonai, complaining of the lewdness of life of men and their neglect of His worship. Death then approaches, and is told to bid Everyman to his final pilgrimage. Everyman comes capering to his lute in festive garb and singing to his mistress. Having received from Death his instruction to prepare for immediate departure, he seeks by bribery to obtain a respite. When this effort is vain he summons Fellowship, Kindred, and Goods or Wealth; but though ready enough to accompany him to scenes of debauch or even aid him in a murder, they refuse to accompany him on so grievous a journey. Good Deeds is so weak she can neither stand nor crawl. She is none the less helpful, and brings to him her sister Knowledge, by whom he is led to Confession. By means of penance he is then prepared for death; and after he has received the sacraments he dies penitent and pardoned, deserted by his former associates Strength, Beauty, Discretion, and Five Wits, but supported by Good Deeds, whose strength and stature are augmented, and by Knowledge.

The presentation was naturally naïve. Adonai was shown as an elderly man with a curling grey beard. Death had no scythe, but had, as in some illustrations we recall, a drum and a trumpet. He had also, it may incidentally be mentioned, a strong Scotch accent. Everyman, who was admirably played by a woman, was a bright and dapper youth in the opening scenes, and in the later presented a tragic figure. Designs for the dresses are supplied on the title-page of an edition of the morality printed by Skot, and are given in facsimile in the first volume of Hazlitt's [edition of Robert Dodsley's *A Select Collection of Old English Plays,* 1874]. In preference to these, Mr. Poel has taken others from Flemish tapestries of the early fifteenth century. Whencesoever obtained, they were admirable, and the entertainment was lifelike and impressive.

A review of "Everyman," in The Athenaeum, *Vol. 2, No. 3847, July 20, 1901, p. 103.*

C. E. Montague (review date 1 November 1902)

[*In the following excerpt, originally published in the* Manchester Guardian, *Montague praises William Poel's 1902 Manchester production. Montague maintains that although the set designs were in a sense inappropriate—based on late fifteenth century Italian art works rather than early fifteenth century English—they were effective in conveying the medieval spirit to a modern audience. He also admires the simple and understated method of acting, which, he claims, created the "right tragic effect" in the play.*]

[*Everyman*] was presented with what seemed to us amazing ingenuity, judgment and care. We are not prepared to define the medieval spirit, but the performance had not lasted five minutes before one felt that the mind was being adroitly filled with reminiscences of everything that before had brought it nearest to late mediaeval ways of looking at life and death. Mainly, it must be confessed, they were Italian reminiscences, not English. The "Messenger" who spoke the prologue was a study in the ascetic's wax-like anticipation, in living flesh, of that fine austerity of death which is fully expressed in art nowhere but on the sculp-

tured tombs on the floor of the Florentine church of Santa Croce; the decoration of the canopied recess from which God spoke the opening lines was a typical landscape background of Bellini, with topped trees and a distance of mountains; the angel sitting on the steps was in every detail, if we remember rightly, the angel of Botticelli's "Tobit"; Everyman in his grave clothes came straight from the "Last Judgment" of Orcagna, where the grave is giving up its dead; the figure of Confession was, to the life, one of the blithe angelic monks who look so like happy, serious, pretty and good children, with tonsures, on the tombs sculptured by Mino da Fiesole. All very much out of place, a captious spectator might say, in a reproduction of an English play ascribed by some to the early fifteenth century, and placed later than the end of the fifteenth century by no good authority. In a narrow sense that may be true, but not in a sense that is more important. Most Englishmen whose imaginations have conceived in the slightest the frame of mind most characteristic of the Middle Ages have got at it through Italy—at Florence, Assisi, and Venice—and an anachronism or a dozen anachronisms are nothing so long as you are helped to make the nearest approach which your ignorance renders possible to the right mood for listening to the play.

Another thing that was beyond praise in the performance was the severe seriousness and simplicity of method which the whole company achieved. We have never seen actors grimace less, or stand so still. This simplicity and reticence never lapsed into insipidity or lifelessness. It nearly always gave the right tragic effect of outward expression purged and refined down to its pure essentials by the stress of intense feeling. The set and immobile face, level delivery, and almost unchanged position of Death were curiously effective in enhancing the solemnity of his first message to Everyman; they affected you like so many symbols of an inexorable fixity in the sentence. There was the same excellent discretion in the gait of Death when he did walk or run. A little more would have made it ridiculous. As it was, it was unexpected and disquieting. About the wisdom of the extent to which the dialogue was intoned we are not quite sure. Much of it undoubtedly was extremely effective; but in one case, that of Good Deeds, there was a rather overdone plaintiveness, and the words of a few of the speeches were not clearly audible. There can be no such doubts about the stage management, which was masterly; nothing could have been better arranged to give the effect intended than the half-heard Mass behind the scenes, and the ingenious *naïveté*—no mere affectation or infanticism—of the burial of Everyman and of the ensconcing of Goods behind a curtain was admirably conceived, as was everything in the scenery, the dresses, and all the accessories. (pp. 162-63)

C. E. Montague, in an excerpt in William Poel and the Elizabethan Revival *by Robert Speaight, William Heinemann Ltd., 1954, pp. 162-63.*

Elisabeth Luther Cary (review date January 1903)

[*In the following review, Cary examines the background of* Everyman *and lauds nearly every aspect of Philip Ben*

Greet's 1903 New York production. She singles out Edith Wynne Matthieson's portrayal of the title character for particular praise, observing that "subtle feeling for the psychological situation rasies her performance to a very high level of modern dramatic art."]

The morality play of *Everyman* seems to have aroused among its audiences a feeling in which admiration, interest, curiosity, and bewilderment are more or less evenly blended. It is a departure from the routine drama not quite easy to accept without explanation. A performance so consistent, so simple, so genuine, so moving, and so entirely outside the bounds of modern convention is disturbing unless the tradition to which it conforms is clearly in mind. And if we examine the tradition of this play we have the clue to all the important work of the interesting company who are responsible for it, and who are attempting to revive the substance, form, and spirit of mediæval and of early Elizabethan drama.

The outline of the literary history of *Everyman* shows it to belong somewhere in the latter part of the fifteenth century, and probably to have been derived from a Dutch play whose author seems to have been "an historian and theologian of a speculative and mystic turn of mind."

It is a very perfect example of the English morality as it existed before theological controversy, intellectual progress, or realism broke in upon the purely orthodox religious drama designed primarily to inculcate reverence for the Church.

Briefly the allegory runs as follows: The High Father of Heaven, observing His creatures, finds them without due fear of His law and "rightwiseness," and sends to Everyman Death, the mighty messenger, to show him the pilgrimage he must take, and to warn him to bring a sure reckoning of his life, good deeds and bad. Everyman, in the person of a careless youth, astounded, begs to know if he may have company on his pilgrimage. Death responds "if any be so hardy" as to wish to go with him there is no embargo. Everyman then takes account of his friends and turns to Fellowship, with whom so many a day he has been "good friends in sport and play," and prays him to bear him company, but Fellowship, who will gladly follow him to feast or to murder, declares:

> For no man that is living to-day
> I will not go that loath journey.

Everyman, cast down by this reverse, next bethinks himself of his kindred, since, according to the old proverb, "Kind will creep where it may not go." He again suffers disappointment, and, reflecting that "fair words maketh fools fain," repairs to Riches, whom all his life he has loved, beseeching him piteously:

> All my life I have had my pleasure in thee,
> Therefore I pray thee now go with me:
> For, peradventure, thou mayest before God Al-
>   mighty
> My reckoning help to clean and purify,
> For it is said ever among
> That money maketh all right that is wrong.

Riches, however, "sings another song," and informs his friend that should he go with him his fortunes would not

be bettered, since his love is "contrary to the love everlasting."

Everyman, despairing now, and hurt to the heart by the unreadiness of his comrades, remembers his Good Deeds, and to her he hastens. Good Deeds reminds him of her frailty and bondage to his sins:

> Here I lie, cold in the ground:
> Thy sins have me so sore bound,
> That I cannot stir.

But she directs him to her sister Knowledge, who will help him to "make that dreadful reckoning."

Up to this point the play has kept along the line of purely human interest. Everyman, in the lusty health of his youth and poignancy of natural feeling, is a figure of flesh and blood, claiming kinship with all the inhabitants of the world. The moral scene now shifts. Everyman is brought under the dominion of the Church (represented by Knowledge). She leads him to Confession, puts into his hands the scourge of Penance (thus freeing Good Deeds from his sins), wraps him in the robe of contrition, and brings him to Death with his reckoning crystal clear. Shortly before the consummation he has summoned to his aid his abstract qualities, Beauty, Discretion, Strength, and Five Wits (the five senses), but these also forsake him as he nears the grave, into which he sinks, supported by Knowledge and Good Deeds.

To render this mediæval symbolism harmoniously a mediæval setting is obligatory, and the English company, under the direction of Mr. Greet, give the mediæval impression with skill and with much beauty of general effect. The stage is modelled on the ancient plan. The actors come and go almost from among the audience. There is no curtain; there are no changes of scene: the stage is never empty. Two monks sit throughout the piece on the steps before the proscenium to indicate the character of the audience when a Father Ambrose or a Father Chrysostom might have taken the title rôle. Above the stage is aloft, partially screened from view, from which is heard the arraignment of Everyman by the Deity and the singing of the angels who welcome the ransomed soul. Death is a grim figure, built upon suggestions gained chiefly from old woodcuts, but singularly without the effect of travesty to even an audience accustomed to veil realities. The part of the "Messenger" or "Doctor" who delivers the impressive prologue and epilogue is taken by Charles Rann Kennedy, whose work is known in England for its delicate scholarship, and the important rôle of Everyman is filled by Mrs. Kennedy (Edith Wynne Matthieson). Her interpretation is the fire of life to the *naïve* little play which, with all its qualities, could very easily be made an affair of external and merely archæological interest. Subtle feeling for the psychological situation raises her performance to a very high level of modern dramatic art, while the simplicity and frankness of the allegory are not sacrificed in the least degree. Everyman's hold upon the audience is gained and kept by the truly inspiring and noble art with which his representative character—that of a soul belonging to humanity at large rather than to man or woman in particular—is maintained, and his decline from the animation of abundant life to utter physical frailty is portrayed. The rise of his spirit from the rebellion of worldly desires to the obedience of religious faith and the gradual subduing and graying of his bright temper into conformity with the counsels of his ghostly advisers are accomplished with the most satisfying regard for proportion and feeling for what a painter might call the aërial perspective. The part demands a singular combination of intellectual comprehension and emotional force, and fortunately has been undertaken by one in whom these qualities are adequate to the very difficult task of expressing the soul through a text of almost childlike simplicity. All the quaint and solemn mysticism of the piece seems to circle about the central figure in something of the fashion of Death's labyrinthine course across the stage, adding to the effect of strangeness and mystery, but completely dominated and kept in place by the compelling beauty of the conception and the power and charm of the acting. (pp. 43-45)

> Elisabeth Luther Cary, " 'Everyman' a Morality Play," in The Critic, New York, Vol. XLII, No. 1, January, 1903, pp. 43-5.

CRITICAL COMMENTARY

Lawrence V. Ryan   (essay date 1957)

[Ryan is an American medievalist whose works include Roger Ascham (1963) and a 1967 edition of Ascham's posthumously published The Scholemaster (1570). In the excerpt below, Ryan examines the intertwined nature of theology and dramatic structure in Everyman and defends the theology as indispensable for understanding the work. Quotations are taken from W. W. Greg's edition of Everyman in W. Bang's Materialien zur Kunde des älteren englischen Dramas IV (1904).]

As the title pages of the two early editions printed by John Skot make clear, **Everyman,** like other examples of its kind, is conceived as a didactic work under a dramatic form: "Here begynneth a treatyse how ye hye fader of heuen sendeth dethe to somon euery creature to come and gyue a counte of theyr lyues in this worlde / and is in maner of a morall playe." Thus, in any judgment of its effectiveness, one must bear this conception in mind. Yet no extended or adequate analysis of the play, from the point of view of the relationship between form and purpose, has so far appeared in print. Most of the commentary written over the past half century has concentrated on attempting to establish the priority of composition of **Everyman** or the Flemish morality *Elckerlijc* and on determining the meanings of such pairs of words in the two versions as *kennisse-knowledge, roeken-rood,* and *duecht-good deeds.* As a result, scholars have largely neglected the question of the dramatic structure of **Everyman.** On the other hand, the impression made by this morality on modern audiences as pure drama has served to obscure its original doctrinal purpose. William Poel, who revived it successfully soon after the beginning of the twentieth century, once ex-

F.W.G. Gilly as Death in William Poel's 1901 production of Everyman in the Quadrangle of the Charterhouse, London.

pressed an opinion which is characteristic of, and possibly helped to shape, the modern reaction:

> I did not myself produce **Everyman** as a religious play. Its theology is indefensible. One can very easily tear it to pieces in that respect. But the whole story, Eastern and not Catholic, in its origin, is beautiful as a piece of art; it offers a hundred opportunities from the point of view of beauty, and it leaves an impression that is fine and chaste.

The approaches of both Poel and the controversialists over the priority of the English-Flemish versions have provided valuable insights to the play, but they fail to get at the essential point about **Everyman**—that is, the relationship between the doctrine that the author wishes to present and the dramatic means he employs to convey that doctrine to his audience.

It is not necessary in studying this relationship to deal with the question whether **Everyman** is a translation or an original work; although it differs from *Elckerlijc* in certain important details, the general structure of the two moralities is very similar. Nor would it be wise to try to convince the modern audience that it ought to react with full sympathy and comprehension to the lesson presented in the play. But Poel's objection, that its "theology is indefensible" and "can very easily" be torn to pieces, along with his finding more valuable than the clearly presented ideas of the work only a vague sort of fineness and chasteness, is not a valid one and ignores the fact that the doctrinal content is the reason for being of *Everyman.* This article will be an attempt to demonstrate that the theology involved is indispensable, not indefensible, and furthermore, that it gives the play its characters, structure, significance, and even its dramatic impressiveness. Without the theology the artistic merit may not be fully appreciated. The story does not by itself carry the burden; in other words, the real meaning and thus the true and legitimate effect of the work depend not on the action alone, but on a proper comprehension of what the action signifies.

The preacher-playwright of *Everyman* is interested in answering the important question: What must a man do to be saved? His chief problem is to reduce the complex answer to terms of simple dramatic representation without falsifying or obscuring the doctrine. In both respects he achieves success, conveying his teaching through fitting details of "characterization," through simultaneously occurring emotional and doctrinal climaxes, and, most important of all, through the representation of an action which brings into harmony the natural, dramatic, and theological elements of Everyman's experience.

Inherent in the theme are excellent possibilities for subtle irony and surprising turns of fate. For in dramatizing the scheme of salvation according to the orthodox view, the author was faced with two apparent paradoxes. According to Catholic theology, man, having fallen by Adam's original sin, is incapable of saving himself through his own efforts. Only through the graces earned in the redemption by Christ—in which one must believe—is the free gift of salvation made available. After professing his faith, however, one must also continue to coöperate with grace; that is, he must live well in the life of grace in order to achieve heaven. In addition, the benefits of the redemption are passed on to all men through the ministration of Christ's church, of which one must be a member to gain eternal life. Here the paradoxes arise. First, though man is incapable of doing anything by himself to merit salvation and is saved by the Sacrifice on the Cross, yet he is finally judged on the basis of his own good works. The believing Christian must perform good deeds because the precept of charity so commands him and because failure to do so is a grave sin of omission, particularly in a man whose will is supposed to be in harmony with that of God. . . .

That is one difficulty. The second is that while Christ died for all men, only through membership in his church may anyone be saved. This belief in turn poses two problems. It rules out the strictly Calvinistic doctrine of special election. Everyone does receive sufficient grace to save his soul. Nevertheless, even St Thomas Aquinas admits that why some men are saved and some reprobated is one of the unfathomable mysteries of the divine will. Thus, the author of *Everyman* is careful to show that while some may not share in its benefits, the redemption was intended for all. Early in the play, God says:

> I hoped well that euery man
> In my glory shulde make his mansyon
> And therto I had them all electe.
>
> (ll. 52-4)

But the author also points out that God's graces in their fulness flow to men only through the church and through the sacraments, which are administered by the clergy. In one speech, Five Wits informs us:

> No remedy we fynde vnder god
> Bute all onely preesthode.
>
> (ll.745-46)

The problem of presenting these ideas efficiently and without confusion has determined the structure of the morality. *Everyman* goes far beyond the overly simple moral lesson that is likely at first glance to be taken as its theme: "Do good deeds and you will be saved." It offers, in effect, a concise presentation of the orthodox teaching on the matter of man's salvation. For the play to be a success, the audience at the end not only must be exposed to but must comprehend the rather involved message revealed step by step through the experience of Everyman.

Structurally, the play turns on two climaxes, growing out of the abandonment of the hero by two theologically and dramatically distinct groups of "friends" in whom he has placed his confidence. Introduced between these two series of desertions are, first, the appearance of Knowledge and Good Deeds, the former character remaining with him until "all is made sure," the latter being the only one to accompany him into the grave; and, second, an episode in which Everyman prepares for death by receiving the last sacraments. An examination of the characters introduced and of the structure shows how both the most effective drama and the clearest revelation of doctrine have been achieved. The action begins with God's sending Death to summon Everyman before the judgment seat. Though one may not make too much of the fact, since there is no reason for another character to be on stage at the time, it is perhaps significant that Death finds his victim walking alone. Dramatically, the aloneness of Everyman in this episode makes him a more pathetic figure. And his isolation is certainly meaningful from the theological standpoint: he is really alone and destitute of help or true friends, because at the moment he has no one to plead for him before God's throne. Having been told by Death, "Se thou make the redy shortely" (l. 181), Everyman calls in turn on Fellowship, Kindred, Cousin, and Goods for help, but each one refuses to accompany him on his final pilgrimage.

The names and characterizations of this set of false friends make it plain that Everyman takes the natural course in first seeking help outside himself when faced with his greatest crisis. The pathos of his being abandoned by the creatures he has loved most arouses sympathy, but the author wishes also to teach and remind the audience, even as he solicits their pity, that foolish and sinful men inordinately love transitory things which can avail them nothing in the end. The first painful step in Everyman's spiritual education and regeneration is his discovery that excessive love of passing things has placed him in danger of hell-fire. The characterizations here are done with touches of individuality and ironic humor, for Fellowship, Kindred, and

Cousin make rash promises to stand beside Everyman through all manner of hardship; earthly attachments seem to be man's truest friends when one has them fully at his command. Fellowship is rashest of all in his boastful pledge:

> For in fayth and thou go to hell
> I wyll not forsake the by the waye.
>
> (ll. 232-33)

Then, upon learning the cause of Everyman's sorrow, he shows his true colors and explains that he will be a constant companion in every kind of sinful doing, but as for making the final pilgrimage with his friend,

> I wyll not go that lothe iournaye
> Not for the fader that bygate me.
>
> (ll. 268-69)

Kindred and Cousin in their turn raise the hero's hopes with promises to hold with him in "welth and wo" and with him "to liue and dye," but when he explains what he wants of them, they too depart with lame excuses. Here he learns that it is not true that "ouer his kynne a man may be holde [*sic* for *bolde*]" (l. 326). Finally, Goods, whom he has loved best of all, tells him unsympathetically that his inordinate attachment to her has ensnared his soul.

The author, in an improvement over other versions of the story, is careful to make these false friends appear in a climactic order according to the increasing danger of each as a distraction from one's Maker. In *Barlaam and Josaphat,* when the hero is called to give his reckoning before the king, two of his three friends desert him while the third remains faithful. These three friends represent, successively, abundance of wealth, wife and child and kindred, and the man's virtues and good deeds. In *The thrie Tailes of the thrie Priests of Peblis,* the appeal is made to riches, kindred and friends, and alms deeds and charity—in that order. The expansion of the number of false friends and the rearrangement of their appearances by the author of **Everyman** constitute a great improvement. First, there is the advantage of dramatic climax gained by substituting a triple for a double refusal. Besides, the writer clearly distinguishes Fellowship from Cousin and Kindred, since he represents a different kind of danger to the soul. Fellowship is willing to help Everyman to "ete & drynke & make good chere Or haunt to women the lusty company" (ll. 272-73). He is likely to lead the hero into sins of the flesh. Cousin and Kindred, however, are dangerous in another way. The hero is likely to misplace his trust in the love and loyalty of his family at a time when he should look to God alone for love and support. Such a mistake would be natural enough because of the close ties that bind members of a family together: "For kynde wyll crepe where it may not go" (l. 316). Yet none of these false friends is so serious a threat as Goods. The love of human creatures, while it may lead one astray, as too much of it has misled Everyman, is not incompatible with love of God. But no man can "Deo servire, et mammonae" [serve God and mammon] (Matthew vi, 24). Excessive love of worldly goods closes the soul to love of any higher object. These unfaithful friends, personifications of external and ephemeral relationships and possessions, promise much, but have finally no solace to offer Everyman. In fact, because of the manner in which the author presents them, it is obvious that they are not only unavailing, but may even be actual hindrances to salvation provided one gives too much attention to them.

The reversal of the pattern of desertion, along with the separation of Fellowship, Kindred, and Cousin into recognizably individualized "characters," not only provides a more realistic and convincing order of climax than that of other versions of the story, but is also dramatically necessary since the episode with Goods is the natural preparation for and transition to the calling forth of Good Deeds.

Left alone after the departure of all these characters, the hero is close to despair. The soliloquy summarizing his discovery of the vanity of his hopes is the first of the two climaxes of the play. Although no remedy seems to be at hand as the speech begins, the time is appropriate for the reversal of fortune, which coincides with the correct theological moment for Everyman to turn at last to something that can save him. The man who loves any creature more than the Creator himself is still a graceless sinner. But now, having been abandoned by all his false loves, Everyman at last remembers his Good Deeds. His turn in this direction is the right one, and it is not mere chance that he makes it. The author has prepared for it through one of the speeches of Goods:

> But yf thou had me loued moderately durynge
> As to the poore gyue parte of me
> Than sholdest thou not in this dolour be
> Nor in this grete sorowe and care.
>
> (ll. 431-34)

The hint that almsgiving, a form of good deeds, would have been to his true advantage, turns the thoughts of Everyman, after he has finished summarizing his disappointments up to this stage, to the one friend who can be of assistance to him.

At this point, however, the author has had to present his doctrine with extreme care. First of all, the church teaches that good works, though they are naturally good and are never to be taken as anything but good, are availing to salvation only to the Christian in the state of grace. Secondly, it is also dogma that man is unable even to begin repentance for his misdeeds unless God supply the first motion in him. God is a wrathful judge, as the opening of the morality indicates, but at the same time he is the merciful Saviour who provides Everyman with the grace to repent. Consequently, Good Deeds is represented as willing to help the hero, but so "sore bounde" by his sins that she "can not stere." There is a moment of dramatic suspense here in order that the audience may grasp the full import of the situation: good deeds in themselves are as nothing if a man be in the state of sin. What hope, then, since Everyman, since all men, are sinners? Good Deeds provides the answer shortly. She has a sister,

> Called knowledge whiche shall with you abyde
> To helpe you to make that dredefull rekenynge.
>
> (ll. 520-21)

A true understanding of the significance of the character Knowledge is crucial to a proper interpretation of the play. Actually, the dialogue shows what she stands for, and the *Elckerlijc-Everyman* controversy has demonstrated that Knowledge here means "contrition" or, better, "acknowledgment of one's sin." Nevertheless, erroneous interpretations of the word persist. Popularly, Knowledge is usually taken as representing comprehension of intellectual truth or (possibly through the influence of the motto of Everyman's Library) learning or merely understanding. But it is evident that the protagonist is not in need of knowledge in the first two senses, and for knowledge in the third sense the author uses the word *cognition* or *intellection,* as when Everyman asks Knowledge to

> gyue me cognycyon
> Where dwelleth that holy man confessyon.
> (ll. 538-39)

Another error has been to take the character as standing for "faith" or "the grasp of the divine law and the divine plan of the universe" [L. A. Cormican, "Morality Tradition and the Interludes," in *The Age of Chaucer,* edited by Boris Ford, 1954]. The events of the play, however, show quite certainly that none of these interpretations is correct.

Doctrinally, the character represents the only kind of knowledge that can profit Everyman in his condition—awareness of and acknowledgement of his sin—for she offers to lead him out of his misery by taking him "To confessyon that clensyng ryuere" (l. 536). At this point, such an offer is proper, for Everyman had already made the first tentative acknowledgment of his fault when he said to Goods: "I gaue the that whiche sholde be the lordes aboue" (l. 458). He is now prepared to repent, but the author takes care to make clear that the motion to repentance has not originated in the sinner himself. Joy begins to fill Everyman's spirit, but with it comes a sense of humility at his own powerlessness. Having just previously recognized, by looking into the book of his own good deeds, that he has nothing to his credit, he says, "Our lorde Iesus helpe me" (l. 506). This is not a mere ejaculation. As his account now stands, only the mercy and merit of the Saviour can help him. And the motion to repent does come from above, as Everyman now tells us twice. First he says that he is in

> good condycyon . . . in euery thynge
> And am hole content with this good thynge
> Thanked by [be] god my creature.
> (ll. 524-26)

A short while later, having confessed his sins, he declares that he will begin his penance, "yf god gyue me grace" (l. 607).

As he carries out his penance, Good Deeds rises from the floor. Up to this moment she has been unable to move, but now that Everyman has fulfilled the requirements of the sacrament—contrition, confession, and satisfaction—he is in the state of grace, and his good works have value for his salvation. Furthermore, carrying out the penance is itself a good work because penance is an act of love (*caritas*) as well as of reparation. Even the flagellation of Everyman helps to strengthen his Good Deeds. Immediately after the penance is completed and the sinner puts on the "garmente of sorowe" (l. 643), Good Deeds and Knowledge introduce to him four "persones of grete myght"—

Beauty, Strength, Discretion, and Five Wits. Again the author's dramatic and pedagogical timing coincide perfectly. Everyman, already made joyous by his confession and the strengthening of his Good Deeds, becomes actually jubilant at the sight of so many friends to assist him on his journey: "lacke I nought," he says, naming all of them in turn, "I desyre no more to my besynes" (ll. 680, 683).

The addition of this second set of friends to the traditional story is an innovation of the author and contributes to both the dramatic effectiveness and the clarification of the doctrine toward the exposition of which the entire play is unerringly directed. A second and more surprising climax is prepared by the introduction of these personifications. The hero's exultation is ironic, for upon seeing the grave, all of these counsellors will desert him, even as his false friends had done. Here the intent of the author in creating the new set of characters becomes clear. He brings them in at the moment when Everyman is certainly renewed in sanctifying grace. The new friends, as their names indicate, are properties of Everyman himself, not external things like the first group of companions. They are the natural endowments, good in themselves, that make man the flower of creation and help him to fulfill his natural destiny. But according to Christian teaching man has been called by a free gift of God to a supernatural destiny to which these qualities are unavailing in any way unless, as St Paul says, men prepare themselves, "induentes novum eum [hominem]" [put on the new man] (Colossians iii, 10; Ephesians iv, 24). Only after the protagonist, by penitence and forgiveness, has been restored to the life of grace, are the natural powers and qualities sanctified and made effectual for his new life. Once again, the technique of the author is to reveal points of doctrine to the audience in their natural order and as Everyman discovers them through his experience. This incident is also a skilful preparation for the final revelation of the play. The fact that man's unassisted natural powers can not help him toward salvation implies that nothing performed by him without divine aid, even his good works, can bring him to the end for which he was created. But elevated by grace and the supernatural virtues that accompany it, the natural powers and virtues can be exercised to help toward, in fact, must necessarily be exercised properly for one to achieve perfection and salvation.

Still, even in the state of grace the Christian may come to rely too much on these natural powers. The author, having presented the more obvious message in the first climax, proceeds to a more subtle lesson here. There is a danger of Pelagianism [a doctrine asserting the importance of individual will] in the man who lives well; he may attribute his sanctity to his own efforts rather than to the free gift of God's grace. Dramatically and doctrinally, the author begins now to bring his play to a resolution with the two episodes that finally drive home his point and leave Everyman assured of salvation as he descends into his grave. The first of these is the so-called "digression on priesthood," which is not really a digression at all but a theologically essential and (if properly understood) dramatically appropriate situation. The second is the final desertion of Everyman by all save his Good Deeds.

As the four counsellors "of grete myght" enter, they too pledge themselves to remain with Everyman in his need, but the promises, while perhaps equivocal, are not rash nor intentionally deceitful as were those of the earlier set of friends. For these characters can not really be false friends, or else Good Deeds and Knowledge would not have presented them to Everyman. Each gives a pledge that is in keeping with his nature (ll. 684-93). Strength appropriately will stand by Everyman "in dystres Though thou wolde I batayle fyght on the groũde." Five Wits assures him that "though it were thrugh the worlde rounde We wyll not departe for swete ne soure." Beauty promises to remain "vnto dethes houre," and Discretion informs him that "We all gyue you vertuous monyeyon That all shall be well." None boasts rashly that he will stay with the hero "and thou go to hell," for these qualities do not lie to him; being good in themselves, they give him no ill counsel or misinformation. Nevertheless, irony in the situation is provided by the fact that the somewhat obtuse Everyman does not listen to their speeches attentively, for he evidently supposes that they mean to accompany him into the grave. Thus, at the second climax, their departure, in the natural order in which they would leave a dying man, Beauty first, then Strength, Discretion, and finally Five Wits, dismays Everyman. Again he has been abandoned by the things that have meant most to him: "I loued them better than my good dedes alone," he laments (l. 857). The audience, too, is likely to be surprised and moved; for it comes as a blow that these qualities, which help man to realize the perfection of human nature, are in themselves of no consequence before the judgment seat. Most amazing of all is the fact that Knowledge does not accompany one beyond the grave. "O all thynge fayleth saue God alone," says Everyman (l. 841), and hears from his one remaining friend that "All fleeth saue good dedes and that am I" (l. 873). At last, through the vicissitudes of experience, the hero has learned his lesson: even the redeemed Christian in the state of grace is capable of forgetting that his natural properties and accidents are in themselves not the instruments of salvation. In themselves, they are merely temporal aids, and they help on the supernatural level only if a man has received the gift of grace. That he is in a state of grace, one demonstrates by his good works, which are acts of love showing that his will is in harmony with the will of God.

The reason for adding this second climax involving a set of characters not found in other versions of the story has been made apparent by the action. The original tale of the man and his three friends is simple and moving, but it is so simple that what the author of **Everyman** understood to be the complete truth about man's salvation could not be represented within its narrow terms. Even in preparing for the first climax of the play with its more obvious lesson, he saw fit to expand the number of episodes and to rearrange them so that the natural order in which Everyman would turn to sources outside himself for help, the theological order in which these externals represent increasing danger to his spiritual welfare, and the order of dramatic logic are made perfectly to coincide. It is disheartening to see the rejection by friends and kindred, but it is the greatest disillusionment of all to learn that wealth, which on earth can buy nearly everything and seems to be man's greatest good, is useless and may be fatal to the soul. This ordering, of course, provides for a smooth and natural transition from the chiding of Everyman by Goods for his neglect of almsgiving to the hero's appeal to his Good Deeds.

But the doctrine is more complex than what the action up to this stage presents to the audience, and the writer was required to find an effective means to dramatize the rest of his message. The action might have been finished off quickly with the confession episode followed by the descent of Everyman and Good Deeds into the grave. Such an ending would have been simple enough to bring about and would have satisfied the formal requirements of dramatic art. It would not, however, have been quite so moving, nor would it have given the audience a fully accurate revelation of what a man must do to be saved. To watch someone receive no help from any external source as he goes to judgment is pathetic enough; to discover the hard truth that one may not even depend on his own powers is a bitter thing. Yet the four counsellors are truly "of grete myght" and are not to be despised or reprehended; they do help Everyman on his earthly journey even if they are unable to enter the grave with him. The author has introduced them to remind the audience of man's utter dependence upon God, for love of whom one must direct all one's powers toward performing the good works that win him mercy on the day of doom.

Nor is Knowledge to be blamed for remaining behind. At the last, Everyman sees why this is so and expresses gratitude for her constant guidance. Acknowledgment of sin is necessary only to the moment of death; after death it is not necessary, since the redeemed sinner, having performed his good works in keeping with the will of God, rejoices in the divine forgiveness and has no need of sorrow for past transgression when judgment is passed upon him. As Dante symbolizes it in the *Purgatorio,* the soul is first washed in Lethe, the river of forgetfulness of sorrow for past sin, and then in Eunoë, the river of remembrance of good deeds (Cantos xxxi and xxxiii). Knowledge is Everyman's chief guide up to the end. Until death Good Deeds remains in the background, since good works are not given their reward until after death, when the soul has arrived in heaven and the will is certainly and eternally conformed to that of God. Acknowledgment of sin, leading to the sacrament of penance, is thus the first and most important step to salvation, and one must go on acknowledging sin until "all is made sure." Knowledge remains with the hero until she sees "where he is become." She is the only character left on stage at the end, when the angels announce the reception of Everyman into heaven, thus symbolically driving home her significance in the play.

But what may be said about the dramatic value of the "digression on priesthood?" To a modern audience, this may seem like a flaw in an otherwise perfectly realized work of art. But if it does seem so, that is because a modern audience, absorbed in the action for its own sake and preferring to believe that man should depend exclusively on his own powers to work out his salvation, is likely to overlook the sacramental emphasis of the play. The author is very careful (ll. 717-18) to state the doctrine that the seven sacraments are "the cure For mannes redempcyon," and he deals specifically with the three that are received upon the approach of death—penance, holy eucharist, and extreme unction. Furthermore, the church teaches that the sacrament of penance is necessary for the restoration of grace to the mortal sinner, unless he make an act of perfect contrition for his offenses against God. But Everyman does not have perfect sorrow, since his concern is not that he has offended an all-good and all-loving creator. It is at first motivated only by a desire of avoiding punishment for his sin, and is rather to be called attrition than contrition. Besides, according to church doctrine, even perfect contrition implies an intention of confessing one's sins sacramentally when the opportunity occurs. Hence the need for Knowledge to lead Everyman to *sacramental* confession in order that his Good Deeds may be able to rise. Next the hero, having become truly contrite through the instruction of Knowledge and the grace of the sacrament, is advised to

> Go to presthode . . .
> And receyue of hym in ony wyse
> The holy sacrament and oyntement togyder.
>   (ll. 707-09)

that is, holy eucharist and extreme unction. At this point comes the "digression" of Five Wits and Knowledge, during part of which the main character is offstage for the only time in the play. It is the absence of Everyman and the introduction of these speeches immediately before the final climax that trouble persons who criticize the passage as a structural weakness. Yet, if one bears in mind that this is "a treatyse . . . in maner of a morall playe" intended to dramatize Everyman's discovery of the way to eternal bliss, the suitability and even the stage effectiveness of these speeches become clear. The eulogy of priesthood is important at this moment because of the incalculable value to Everyman of penance and the eucharist. Echoing various passages in Scripture, Five Wits tells Everyman of priests that

> God hath to them more power gyuen
> Than to ony aungell that is in heuen
> With .v. wordes he may consecrate
> Goddes body in flesshe and blode to make
> And handeleth his maker bytwene his hande
> The preest byndeth and vnbyndeth all bandes
> Both in erthe and in heuen.
>   (ll. 735-41)

Since normally only the sacrament of penance can restore grace to the mortal sinner, the power of the priest to bind and unbind is obviously crucial in the scheme of salvation. Everyman is also urged to receive the eucharist, for although the church does not hold that the reception of Christ's body and blood is absolutely necessary, there are weighty authorities to emphasize its importance. Christ himself had said, "nisi manducaveritis carnem Filii hominis, et biberitis ejus sanguinem, non habebitis vitam in vobis" (John vi, 54). And Aquinas, while he does not say that actual reception of the eucharist is essential, argues that at least the implicit desire to receive it is fundamental to the consummation of the spiritual life. Now the author sends Everyman offstage for twenty-two lines to partake of the last sacraments while Knowledge and Five

Wits deliver to the audience a sermon designed to stress the validity of the sacraments regardless of the moral condition of the minister. The very fact that it contains an admonition to the clergy to lead upstanding lives is the clue to the significance of the sermon in the action. If priests give scandal by their conduct, the faithful may stay away from the sacraments and, by so denying themselves access to the means of grace, perhaps lose the opportunity to be saved.

The communion of Everyman is not dramatized, possibly out of a sense of decorum, and the supposedly digressive sermon serves here to express a truth that the hero has learned through his experience. The "digression" is skilfully wrought, even to the point of presenting the lesson chiefly through the speeches of Five Wits, rather than one of the other characters, because "A sacrament is a visible [that is, sensibly evident] sign which imparts grace to our soul" [Wilhelm Faerber, *Cathechism for the Catholic Parochial Schools of the United States,* 1942]. Moreover, the episode is dramatically timely, for it occurs just before the natural powers will be weakened and must depart from Everyman, leaving only the grace received through the sacraments to sustain him and to make his Good Deeds effectual. Thus, when for a moment he again feels abandoned, "O Iesu helpe all hath forsaken me" (l. 851), he and the audience become ready for the final lesson. Again Good Deeds is ready to come to his aid, but at this final climax she is really able to assist him, having been made efficacious by the infusion of grace which Everyman has received from the sacraments administered by the priest. This, then, is the message of the play which dramatization of Everyman's escape from his original predicament has made clear. In order to be saved not only must a man perform good deeds; he must perform them as a faithful Christian with the aid of the graces that are channeled to him through the church. Though death is the conclusion, the moment is one of release and exaltation, as in Sophocles' *Oedipus at Colonus,* for the meaning of the pattern has been fully revealed to the protagonist as he reaches the end of the tragic experience. Like Oedipus, Everyman discovers that it is better for a man to face reality and to learn what he really is and has, no matter what suffering the discovery may cost him, than to spend his life in pursuing illusions.

A successful play reveals what it has to say through the experience of its characters; all other message is dramatically gratuitous and were better put into some sort of Shavian preface [characteristic of playwright Bernard Shaw]. *Everyman,* conceived primarily to expound doctrine and to inspire to the good life, is powerful in both teaching and moving because in its construction the doctrinal and dramatic orders have been made perfectly to coincide and because what one learns from the play grows naturally out of the action itself. Instead of being "indefensible" and inessential to an appreciation of the work, the theology presented actually determines the structure of the morality and helps to give it the place it admittedly deserves as the most successful thing of its kind in English literature. (pp. 722-35)

Lawrence V. Ryan, "Doctrine and Dramatic

Structure in 'Everyman'," in Speculum, *Vol. XXXII, No. 4, October, 1957, pp. 722-35.*

Dennis V. Moran   (essay date 1972)

[*Below, Moran maintains that* Everyman's *action mirrors the medieval notion of the ages of man and that the play represents Everyman's entire lifetime rather than just his "eleventh hour conversion." Quotations are taken from A. C. Cawley's 1961 edition of* Everyman.]

The morality *Everyman* clearly stands in some debt to the theme of the Dance of Death that permeated late medieval sermons and homiletic literature. More a popular obsession than a theme, the Dance largely developed in historical consequence of the Black Death and the frequent outbreaks of plague that persisted through the late fourteenth and fifteenth centuries in both England and France. The sudden, often hideous, death threatened by the plagues, which the homilist and preacher glossed in graphic physical detail as divine retribution for sin, bore heavily on the medieval conscience and imagination. It is not surprising, therefore, that the terrifying figure of personified death inevitably found its place in the traditional psychomachia [battle of virtues and vices] of Catholic allegory.

Despite this debt, *Everyman*'s elaboration of death does not reflect the physical grotesqueries and unrelieved morbidity that characterize the Dance of Death. Indeed the play is less an elaboration than a profound celebration of the art of Christian dying, the *ars moriendi* of the Latin church. Through the combined and complementary mediums of dramatic action and language, the play makes visually clear to its audience the utter certainty of death, and instructs it with uncluttered simplicity in the means, both human and spiritual, which God has put at man's earthly disposal that he might avoid hell and merit eternal salvation. As such, the developing stress in the play falls on the infinite mercy of God as opposed to His justice. "Christ cannot save thy soul, for he is just," Lucifer informs Faustus [in Act II, scene i of Christopher Marlowe's *Tragical History of Doctor Faustus*], suppressing one critical factor in the divine equation. "This mater is wonders precyous," announces the Messenger who heralds *Everyman* and its theme, "but the entent of it is more gracyous, / And swete to bere awaye".

Death's entrance in *Everyman* comes with appalling suddenness. The allegorical alter-ego of the biblical thief in the night, he strikes terror in the heart of complacent Everyman, calling him abruptly from earthly concerns to an awful consideration of last things. "Everyman," he commands, "stande styll! Whyder arte thou goynge / Thus gayly?" The effect of his menacing physical presence and the stark question he poses is made dramatically clear in the anguished tone of Everyman's reply to his summons. "O Deth, thou comest when I had the leest in mynde!"

This sudden appearance of Death sets powerfully into motion the thematic issues of *Everyman* and invests them with a suspense that largely explains the obvious dramatic appeal of the play. Yet though his presence, seen or unseen, dominates the action throughout and initially sets Everyman off on his disillusioning search for comfort in false friends, Death physically quits the stage with four-fifths of the play remaining and the terror aroused by his summons almost wholly subsides with Everyman's return to sanctifying grace. Indeed, however gracious his manner might have been in consequence of that return, Death the character does not claim Everyman; rather at the appointed hour, comforted by the hope Knowledge and Good Deeds insure, Everyman yields himself to God with the resigned "commendo" of Christ on the cross. The vivid contrast between the character Death, whose spectral prefigurement of eternal suffering for sin sets the anxious tone of the first half of the play, and the peaceful form of Everyman's dying makes its didactic point lucidly clear to the audience: death can hold no terror for the sinner who cooperates with God's grace.

Despite *Everyman*'s exemplary emphasis on death—the terror it holds for sin and the hope it offers repentance—the play has deceptively much to say about the life of Everyman. Students of the play, however, tend to overstress the *dramatic* entrance and presence of Death to the exclusion of larger considerations that disclose more about the nature of life than the nature of death. I suggest it is absurd to hold visually in mind the idea that Everyman is dying when death confronts him or to interpret too literally the day Death allots him, however much such a reprieve illustrates the mercy of God. The time allowed Everyman projects the fullness of life's experience, defined and circumscribed, as Everyman is made to recognize, by the natural fact of death. Stressing too literally the dramatic presence of Death and the eleventh-hour reprieve he offers reduces the content and quality of Everyman's experience to a *deus ex exemplo*. Everyman's achievement is not cheaply or superficially won; it is the result of a progressive experience through life and disillusionment, culminating with a satisfying intellectual and psychological exactness in knowledge. This progression is implied in surprising detail throughout the play.

Following his confession and return to the state of grace, Everyman, along with Good Deeds and Knowledge, is joined by Beauty, Strength, Discretion, and Five Wits, in that precise order. These four characters personify attributes natural to human life, and though they are sanctified and given proper direction by the grace Everyman enjoys, they are *not* gifts that come directly in consequence of Everyman's state of grace. Gifts of nature, they are part of Everyman's essential humanity, albeit perverted and debased by his sins. That this is so is made clear in Death's admonition to Everyman early in the play, well before he achieves the knowledge that leads to repentance. Instructing him that his life is but lent him and that others will possess it when he is gone, Death says, "Everyman, thou arte made! Thou hast thy wyttes fyve, / And here on erthe wyll not amende thy lyve" (168-69). The irresistible implication is that man sins by perverting the natural gifts God has given him.

The introduction of these four attributes toward the end of the play is clearly intended to define their natural function in human life and to mark allegorically the physical devolution of all men into death, for precisely implied in the sequence that these attributes depart Everyman is the pattern of man's life from youth to old age. Beauty and strength characterize youth, while strength continues on into middle age, to the senility of old age, signified in Everyman's loss of discretion or his capacity to make discriminating, practical judgments. The extremity of old age puts Everyman on the immediate threshold of death with the loss of his five wits or bodily senses. The loss of these five, comprehended in the unity of the *sensus communis* of scholastic epistemology [theory of the nature of knowledge] and psychology, implies Everyman's inability to experience physical life.

Dramatically the departure of these naturally good attributes illustrates the transitoriness of physical life; doctrinally their departure emphasizes the solitary, indispensable role of Good Deeds, who along with Knowledge is visually isolated on the stage with Everyman. This visual isolation makes all the more effective Good Deeds's otherwise commonplace observation "all erthly thynges is but vanyte", as Everyman prepares himself for immediate death.

That Knowledge remains with Everyman is consistent with her allegorical function and the human faculty she personifies, though her presence is somewhat ambiguous. Among other things, Knowledge represents Everyman's experience of the world, his awareness of sin, and his understanding of God's mercy and grace. Telling Everyman that she will remain with him "tyll I se where ye shall become" (863), she obviously serves, along with Good Deeds, to comfort Everyman in his natural fear of physical death and, given Everyman's history of sin, to guard him from despair. It must be stressed that Everyman does not despair with the defection of his human attributes; though frightened, he is continually instructed and strengthened by Good Deeds and Knowledge, both allegorical projections of his own moral awareness and achievement. To interpret Everyman's fear as despair is to miss altogether the significance of Knowledge and the efficacious force of Good Deeds.

A human attribute, knowledge nonetheless derives from the cognitive faculty of the soul, and it is scholastically sound that the character Knowledge survives the defection of purely physical attributes. She does not, however, accompany Everyman on his journey and actually steps out of allegorical character, implying a wider comprehension, to point the moral to the audience.

> Now hath he suffred that we all shall endure;
> The Good Dedes shall make all sure.
> Now hath he made endynge;
> Me thynketh that I here aungelles synge
> And make grete ioy and melody
> Where Everymannes soule receyued be.
>   (888-93)

This ambiguity, I suggest, is due to the author's own uncertainty about the ultimate nature of supernatural life and the disposition of human knowledge within it, an uncertainty shared by other medieval theologians, whose conception of the afterlife and the soul's form of knowledge there was largely speculative.

The fixed progression of man's life into death, defined here in the sequential departure of Beauty, Strength, Discretion, and Five Wits, is a theme common to the English morality play as well as the sermon and countless other homiletic works. The character Mankind in *The Castle of Perseverance,* for instance, is dramatically represented as passing from youth to old age, and the nature of the temptations posed him and the sins he commits correspond to the set stages of his life. *Ratis Raving,* a didactic poem of the fifteenth century, enumerates at deadly length seven ages of man, anticipating Jaques' catalogue in the second act of *As You Like It,* while *The Parlement of the Thre Ages,* a fourteenth-century alliterative poem, elaborates three ages in a pictorial tableau that embraces the beauty and strength of youth and the senility of old age. As in *Everyman,* the progress implied in these successive stages illustrates the ceaseless movement of life into death and the consequent vanity of earthly aspirations and concerns.

If the full passage of life into death is implied by Everyman's loss of his human attributes, a complementary progression is also suggested in the first half of the play where Everyman in turn seeks out Fellowship, Kindred, and Goods to accompany him on his pilgrimage, itself a conventional medieval figure for the course of life. These temptations, either to sin or to a misplaced confidence in earthly things, are presented in an order that reflects the growth of youth into age, of the sensual pleasures of early manhood passing on into the avarice of autumnal years.

In his conversation with Everyman, Fellowship consistently speaks with the self-satisfied flippancy of irresponsible youth. Shrinking evasively from the uncomfortable reality of death, he poses to Everyman the enticements of sensual pleasures commonly associated with youth. Everyman's perception of his falseness, tellingly indicated in the sarcasm of his reply, at once marks the rejection of temptation and the beginning of his growth into knowledge.

> FELLOWSHIP: . . . yf thou wylte ete & drynke
>   & make good chere,
>   Or haunt to women the lusty company,
>   I wolde not forsake you whyle the daye is
>   clere,
>   Trust me veryly.
>
> EVERYMAN: Ye, therto ye wolde be redy!
>   (272-76)

Since the natural instinct to family can apply to any and all stages of man's life, the character Kindred admittedly does not fit a precise stage in the sequent progression of man's life from youth to death. Nor does Kindred, along with Cousin, so much personify a temptation to sin as a temptation to a false confidence in earthly relationships, which in the ultimate face of death justify no confidence whatsoever. Nonetheless, set between Fellowship and Goods, Kindred can be interpreted to personify the natural preoccupations of man passing out of the reckless pleasures of youth to the more conservative concerns of wife, children, and family.

Played false by Kindred, Everyman next seeks comfort and assistance from Goods. That Goods brings to three the number of "friends" who betray Everyman and that he enters the stage when he does is significant in point of the sources generally assigned the play. In *Barlaam and Josaphat,* for instance, the protagonist is betrayed successively by wealth and kindred, while good deeds remains faithful. In the third tale of *The Thrie Tailes of the Thrie Priests of Peblis* the appeal is made unsuccessfully to riches and kindred and later, successfully, to alms and charity. In noting *Everyman*'s addition of a third refusal, Professor Lawrence V. Ryan argues [in *Speculum* XXXII (1957)] that the combination of three refusals gives the theme of betrayal a greater intensity and that the distinction of fellowship and kindred allows for a different set of temptations to be dealt with.

The positioning of Goods in *Everyman,* however, is not merely random. By placing the attraction of material wealth last, the author gives it the force of climax, while at the same time implying that avarice represents the last significant temptation in man's pilgrimage to death. It is surely no coincidence that during the late fourteenth and fifteenth centuries the sin of avarice was given increasingly heavier stress in sermons and homiletic literature, to the point where it rivalled pride and in some cases outdistanced it as the deadliest of the Deadly Sins. Furthermore medieval writers of the time consistently stressed avarice as a sin peculiar to advancing years and age. Just as sensuality characteristically afflicted youth, covetousness afflicted middle age. (pp. 324-28)

The association of avarice with middle age is consistently made in *The Castle of Perseverance.* Past forty and anxious about his increasing years, Mankind seeks comfort in Covetyse, who claims that a full purse offers the best protection against the variable winds of age. As with Everyman, avarice constitutes the last temptation posed Mankind, and the explanation given him on the temporal nature of riches by the Boy (VII, 2969ff.), himself the messenger of Death, corresponds in every detail with the self-revelation of Goods to Everyman. The emphasis on advanced age and its susceptibility to avarice is clearly stated in the prologue that sets the themes of *The Castle.*

> Hard a man is in age, & Covetouse be kynde;
> Whanne all oþer synnys man hath for-sake,
> Eure þe more þat he hath, þe more is in his
>   mynde
> To gader & to gete good with woo & with
>   wrake . . .
>
>   (92-5)

Gauged then by conventional medieval descriptions of the ages of man and the sins and temptations peculiar to them, the sequence of alternate hope and betrayal that leads to Everyman's isolation and subsequent understanding is hardly a random one. The author has clearly structured his material to offer the allegorical projection of a life passing from youth into age, though a life whose awareness is intensified by the certain realization of ultimate death and the fragility of existence. A complementary pattern, conceived in terms of the gifts of nature rather than the gifts of fortune, can be seen in Everyman's possession and subsequent loss of Beauty, Strength, Discretion, and Five Wits. And while the gifts of fortune prove false and the gifts of nature prove unstable, the gifts of grace, whose

fruits are knowledge and good works, remain steadfast through the pilgrimage of life into eternity.

The fullness of life implied in these progressions makes Everyman's ultimate achievement of knowledge psychologically and intellectually valid, a validity that other English moralities lack. Everyman's awareness of himself and the world grows steadily through time and nourishes itself on the bitter bread of disillusion. The reflective effect of this on the audience, I suggest, is not the *deus-ex-exemplo* effect of an eleventh-hour conversion, however dramatic Death's appearance is at the outset of the play. Everyman's struggle is honestly joined and won, and that this struggle has more to do with the nature of life than with the nature of doctrine very possibly explains the play's continued appeal to different audiences. (p. 329)

> *Dennis V. Moran, "The Life of 'Everyman',"*
> in Neophilologus, *Vol. LVI, No. 3, July, 1972,*
> *pp. 324-30.*

Carolynn Van Dyke   (essay date 1982)

[*Van Dyke is an American academic whose works include* The Fiction of Truth: Structures of Meaning in Narrative and Dramatic Allegory. *In the following excerpt, she discusses the allegorical nature of the characters in* Everyman. *She asserts that the various figures are not merely "types" or "categories" but individualized characters as well. At the outset of the drama Everyman responds to these figures only as individuals, and he undergoes a process of learning to view them in their larger, allegorical, context. Quotations are taken from David M. Bevington's* Medieval Drama *(1975).*]

Beginning actors must find the script of *Everyman* perplexing. They are likely to have been taught that the "imaginative ability to put [oneself] truly in the place of a fictitious character in a meaningful way . . . provides the vitality of all good acting" [Robert L. Benedetti, *The Actor at Work,* 1976]. They may have been encouraged to cultivate that ability through "a program of self-questioning: Who is this character? How old is he? Where was he born? What were his parents like?" [John Dolman, Jr., *The Art of Acting,* 1949]. It is sobering to contemplate the heroic, if not blasphemous, labors of imagination by which students might apply that advice to such roles as Death, God, Fellowship, and Knowledge. And if they sensibly abandon the attempt at empathetic projection, they face the equally difficult task of enlarging the definition of a dramatic role. Similar, if less pressing, difficulties confront all readers and spectators who wish to understand the "characters" of allegorical drama, personifications which are also dramatis personae.

One apparently simple solution is provided by traditional definitions of allegory. If "an allegory is but a translation of abstract notions into a picture-language" [according to the nineteenth-century critic Samuel Taylor Coleridge], then the allegorical dramatist employs his actors only as porters for pieces of dogma. That definition is also, of course, a negative judgment. In *English Religious Drama* [1893], Katherine Lee Bates opens her chapter "Moralities" with a charmingly devastating concession: "The very word is like a yawn." In a more analytic vein she explains that "these old plays manage it to be so dry and tuneless . . . because in these is committed the cardinal sin of literature,—the forsaking of the concrete for the abstract." That is, the "characters" of morality plays are bogus people, abstractions in human disguise. Given the prevalence of that idea, it is not surprising that morality plays were not staged between the Middle Ages and the twentieth century.

In 1901, however, when William Poel defied the grim anticipation of "those who knew their dramatic history" by producing *Everyman,* Bates's judgment was challenged. "In Poel's performance," according to a recent study [Robert Potter, *The English Morality Play: Origins, History, and Influence of a Dramatic Tradition* 1975], "the 'lifeless abstractions' of the medieval text turned out to be what they must always, invisibly, have been—not walking categories, but realized figures, parts in a play." There followed a theatrical reclamation of *Everyman,* based on a new vision of the play's cast. As Glynne Wickham writes [in *Shakespeare's Dramatic Heritage,* 1969], nearly seventy years after Poel,

> Fellowship, Kindred and Cousin, Strength and Discretion may all be abstract personification and, as such, contemptuously dismissed as shadows rather than characters by some literary critics of mediaeval Morality Plays; but each is characterized broadly and firmly enough for the imaginative actor to fill in just enough detail to endow the character with a personality. The spectator can then easily take the last step and equate this personality with a real-life character of his own acquaintance.

For Wickham the actors are not carriers of abstract ideas; on the contrary, each abstract name is a portmanteau for any number of personalities, one of which the actor must display. Thus we can witness, for instance, Fellowship with a North Country accent, Everyman in jeans and a reefer jacket, and Death as a "Marine Commando."

Wickham's approach has helped make *Everyman* playable, but it has not been universally welcomed. As he anticipated, certain "literary critics of mediaeval Morality plays" have denounced the tendency toward deallegorization. Lawrence V. Ryan [in *Speculum* 32 (1957)] argues that "the impression made by this morality on modern audiences as pure drama has served to obscure its original doctrinal purpose." Following Ryan, Joanne Spencer Kantrowitz [in *Comparative Drama* 7 (1973)] defines the moral play as "a didactic, allegorical drama" whose personae are "simply a convenient means of representation."

A predictable compromise between pure doctrine and pure drama has been articulated by Michael J. Warren [in the *Dalhousie Review* 54 (1974)]. *Everyman* presents two kinds of meaning simultaneously, according to Warren: the "simple fiction" concerns an individual who must go to Jerusalem, while the "allegory of that plot" is about a representative human being preparing for death. The actors particularize their roles, but the audience is led "to construct a series of conceptual syntactic formulations for what is presented in spatial terms." Unfortunately, however, the two-meanings theory leaves the director and critic with certain problems. The play contains many overtly doctrinal speeches which intrude on the "simple plot" about the journey to Jerusalem and baffle any attempt to conceptualize that plot, since they clearly do not need conceptualization. Warren tries to preserve two levels by conceptualizing the doctrinal discussions as the thoughts of a "representative soul." For instance, Everyman hears a lecture from Good Deeds and then one from Knowledge because his "unremitting concentration on the current worthlessness of his Good Deeds forces him to the recognition that they can be restored to value only by his use of his knowledge." As Warren concedes, however, certain speeches are somewhat too long to be thoughts, some of them are addressed directly to the audience, and several are delivered while the representative soul is offstage, otherwise occupied. Should the diligent allegorizer decide that only actions, not speeches, are to be conceptualized, he must account for other anomalies: Death leaves Everyman alive and then fails to return as promised, even though Everyman does in fact die; Discretion, Strength, Beauty, and Five Wits are introduced to Everyman late in his life—long after, in fact, he has been said to possess one of them. In short, if the playwright of *Everyman* was trying to parallel dialogue or action with allegorical meaning, he was a very poor geometrician.

Thus none of the obvious descriptions of the cast of *Everyman* seems adequate. The characters are not simply abstractions; they are not simply human beings; they are not human beings on one level and ideas on another. All those formulations are based on theories about the nature of drama or allegory or both. Discussions of allegory are usually theoretical, of course, for critics commonly assume that the real meanings of allegory are by definition not literal ones and thus cannot be discerned empirically. But if theoretical description has indeed failed, it may be best to approach the dramatis personae of *Everyman* through the text of the play.

A natural starting point is the protagonist. Everyman is on the one hand the most easily individualizable of the play's roles, for he easily becomes anyman—or, by an ironically surprising extension, any woman. Thus he confirms Wickham's sense of the cast as individuals with general names. On the other hand, Everyman does not begin as an individual. God's opening speech employs "everyman" as a collective pronoun (lines 40-41, 60-62):

> Euery man lyueth so after his owne pleasure,
> And yet of theyr lyfe they be nothynge sure.
>
> They be so combred with worldly ryches
> That nedes on them I must do iustyce,
> On euery man lyuynge without fere.

God shifts from "he" to "they" in referring to "euery man," as V. A. Kolve [in "*Everyman* and the Parable of Talents" in *The Medieval Drama,* edited by Sandro Sticca] has noted, providing divine confirmation for the suspicions of innumerable freshmen that the term may be technically singular but is ineluctably plural in spirit. Only after God's collective decree do we see the individual who bears the name Everyman. The entrance of that individual, blithely ignorant that he represents Death's generic victim, produces a powerful effect which might well be called dramatic, even though it has little to do with conflict among characters. The drama is the enactment of a metamorphosis. John C. Webster [in "The Allegory of Contradiction in *Everyman* and *The Faerie Queene*," in *Spenser and the Middle Ages,* edited by David A. Richardson (1976)] writes that, in referring both to all men and to a single character, **Everyman** "forces us to entertain *both* meanings, even though they are logically contradictory, and to do so simultaneously." I would modify Webster's statement: we do indeed entertain both meanings simultaneously, but "contradictory" is an inaccurate description of the relationship between a category and its members. The collective "euery man" becomes the singular Everyman by a shift in perspective, an act of re-cognition. We cannot account for such effects if we see Everyman as an individual on one "level" and all mankind on another, for the drama of his appearance depends on the mutual convertibility of category and individual. The medium of exchange for that conversion is, of course, language. It appears, then, that the center of Everyman's composite identity is his name.

The audience's re-cognition of the categorical "euery man" as the individual Everyman is repeated, in reverse, by Everyman himself in his encounter with Death. Asked where he is going and whether he has forgotten his Maker, Everyman offers, as Webster puts it, the "extraordinarily non-plussed and (from our informed point of view) obtuse reply: "Why askest thou? / Woldest thou wete?' " Even when informed about Death's identity, he still responds as if to "a random encounter with an obnoxious stranger" who can perhaps be bribed. The resulting humorous irony is not incidental. Webster explains that "we are . . . previewing a major theme of the play, that the logic of literal things is not the only logic in the universe, that being saved depends on one's ability to keep seeing double, to keep both the literal and figurative possibilities of language in mind at once." "Literal" and "figurative" are unfortunate terms here, since Everyman's "literal-mindedness" is his myopic focus on the figurative representative of death. But if we substitute "concrete" and "abstract" for those terms, Webster's point becomes clear. Everyman responds to the individual agent and the particular encounter, not to the concept which they embody. He thus demonstrates for the first time what Thomas Van Laan calls a blindness to "any values higher than those of world and time."

The kind of naïveté which Everyman displays toward Death is usually regarded as a chronic condition of allegorical personae. C. S. Lewis writes, [in *Spenser's Images of Life,* ed. Alastair Fowler (Cambridge: 1967)] " . . . to the characters participating in an allegory, nothing is allegorical," and Robert E. Wood [*South Atlantic Bulletin* 43 (May 1978)] cites "the essential condition" of allegory, that the characters react to circumstances in their realistic rather than their allegorical significance." That "essential condition" is violated with astonishing regularity in the major allegories, as it is here. If allegorical meanings were inaccessible to Everyman, we would have to find an allegorical correlative for his encounter with Death. The obvious allegorization is "Everyman has died," but of course he has not. Short of accusing the playwright of violating

"allegorical logic," as does Webster, we may as well accept the allegory literally—that is, according to the text. Everyman's meeting with Death is not his expiration but his encounter with death. In a particular sensual experience, a frightening conversation with a stranger, he confronts God's message about his own mortality. The play constitutes, in part, Everyman's education in allegorical vision, which is the recognition of the particular and timebound as the universal.

His education continues in the well-known scenes with Fellowship, Cousin, and Kindred. Warren points out that those characters "have a dual quality; at times they appear as Everyman's friends in their particularity, and at others in their abstract roles as representative figures and aspects of Everyman's thought. The first attendant problem, however, is that the separation is never exact." That "problem" is not the playwright's lapse, but his point. Fellowship is a particular human friend, but, being that, he must obey the laws of friendship (lines 213-14):

> I wyll not forsake the to my lyues ende,
> In the waye of good company.

Kindred generalizes about his loyalty (lines 325-26), but his unthinking reliance on clichés reveals him as only too typical. Cousin's pitiable claim to a particular exemption from Everyman's journey—"I haue the crampe in my to" (line 356)—confirms, ironically, his categorical frailty. The point is not that the characters are particularly weak friends and kinsmen; neither, however, is it simply that earthly friends and kindred cannot figure in anyone's final reckoning. What amuses and moves us is Everyman's enlargement of perspective, from the promises and evasions of his friends and kin to what he has always known about friendship and kinship.

After his human friends desert him, Everyman turn to Goods, who, like Death, is not a category but an abstraction. Goods is also like Death in being an actor, of course, and it is in the latter form that Everyman first responds to him. "Vp, let vs go thyder to-gyder," he urges (line 424), as if Goods were really a man. What he must learn is to take Goods's name literally (lines 394-97):

> I lye here in corners, trussed and pyled so hye,
> And in chestes I am locked so fast,
> Also sacked in bagges. Thou mayst se with thyn
>   eye
> I can not styre; in packes, lowe I lye.

Goods is lying not just under bags, though the actor is sometimes represented that way, but *in* bags; being Goods, he can "folowe no man one fote" (line 426). He resembles a human being only in his ability to expound his nature to anyone who will listen. His representation by an actor is not meaningless, however, for the illusion that Goods can accompany Everyman is exactly the illusion of potency and loyalty often produced by material goods. Thus Goods, like Death, Fellowship, Kindred, and Cousin, teaches Everyman to understand particularities through the categories whose names they bear and whose laws they must obey.

Goods's amusing self-exposition evinces particularly

clearly the function of the actors in *Everyman:* they enact their roles, which are their names. The names designate individuals whom the text invites the actors to personalize, but they simultaneously designate categorical laws which define the individuals. Thus far, the play's peculiar power has arisen from the revelation of those laws to Everyman, to the audience, and to some of the characters themselves. After Goods the dramatis personae alter, for "good deeds," "knowledge," and "confession" do not denominate classes of people or even of material objects. The actors who play these more abstract roles will enact their names in a new way: instead of showing that particular phenomena manifest universal principles, they reveal the force and meaning of universals in the phenomenal world. The change begins with Good Deeds, and it constitutes Everyman's conversion.

Unlike his appeals to Fellowship, Kindred, Cousin, and Goods, Everyman's meeting with Good Deeds is not an experiment but an acceptance of instructions given him some time ago (lines 106-108):

> And loke thou be sure of thy rekenynge,
> For before God thou shalte answere, and shewe
> Thy many badde dedes, and good but a
> fewe. . . .

Everyman admits somewhat ruefully after his disappointment with Goods that he will "neuer spede / Tyll that I go to my Good Dede" (lines 480-81). In that context the appearance of an actor named Good Deeds is a sign of Everyman's spiritual progress. The actor is usually dismissed as a conventional equivalent for Everyman's good deeds, on the assumption that "the medieval imagination" could personify anything at all without considering "moral or metaphorical logic." As such she is another instance of sloppy allegorical geometry, for Everyman's good deeds have already been represented—in the account book to which Death referred and which now lies "vnder the fete" (lines 503-505). Good Deeds will in fact emphasize her own redundance by saying to Everyman, "Than go you with your rekenynge & your Good Dedes togyder" (line 529). Taken as a code for "good deeds," Good Deeds also has produced an apparent doctrinal problem: Everyman's good deeds seem to play the decisive role in his salvation, implying a theology of "works" which Arnold Williams [in *The Drama of Medieval England,* 1961] finds essentially unChristian and attributes to the plot's Buddhist origin. But if we abandon the assumption that the actors are merely ciphers for ideas, we can see in Good Deeds's redundance a solution to the theological problem. Because Everyman's good deeds are recorded in his account book, their appearance also as a personification—an agent capable, after he has repented, of going with him to God and pleading on his behalf—is literally gratuitous. The actor is not simply good deeds but good deeds made manifest and potent by God's grace and Everyman's repentance.

Good Deeds's gratuitous personification is reinforced by the materialization of Knowledge. Knowledge is probably the most controversial personification in the play, having been identified with many and diverse kinds of knowledge. As Warren says, "there is no sound reason why Knowledge should not be accepted simply as knowledge since that is the name of the character." Such acceptance will be easier, however, if we take seriously Knowledge's appearance as a character, in a particular context. Throughout the play Everyman has behaved as though ignorant of anything but empirical reality. Unlike the protagonists of other morality plays, however, he appears as an adult; Death asks him, "Hast thou thy Makere *forgete?*" (line 86; emphasis added), and God's opening speech makes clear that he has had ample opportunity to learn "my lawe that I shewed, whan I for them dyed" (line 29). His apparent ignorance of intangible truth is illusion, sinful blindness "of ghostly syght" (line 25). The first half of the play disillusions Everyman, forcing him to acknowledge what he knows. The appearance of Knowledge, following that of Good Deeds, confirms Everyman's disillusionment. Anyone who translates the encounter with Death as "Everyman is dead" will probably assume that the encounter with Knowledge means "Everyman has learned," but both readings are inaccurate. Everyman is in fact encountering knowledge, accepting knowledge as his guide and companion. Something with no obvious empirical manifestation is thereby externalized and personified as a more vocal and potent agent than Fellowship and Goods.

Knowledge convinces Everyman to seek confession, which accordingly materializes before him (lines 535-43). At this point Everyman accepts not only the reality of the intangible fact called confession but also the provisional nature of its tangible form; that is, he recognizes the man called Confession as only one manifestation of his name. Knowledge first calls Confession "that clensynge ryuere" (line 536); Everyman then speaks of "that holy man, Confessyon" (line 539) and is directed to the "hous of saluacyon" (line 540). When Confession materializes, presumably as a male actor, Everyman addresses him as "O gloryous fountayne" and then, oddly enough, as "moder of saluacyon" (lines 545, 552). The incompatible appositives are not careless aureation but a sign that Everyman has escaped the tyranny of particular material forms. Even as he responds appropriately to the priestlike agent who manifests confession to him, he also perceives the aspects of confession designated by "river" and "mother." The alternative metaphors bring him as close as earthly man can come to apprehending confession itself.

Everyman has at last achieved spiritual sight, the recognition of the spiritual as real and of the material as radically metaphorical. That vision lets him understand Confession's shifting references to penance—first as a "precyous iewell" and then, four lines later, as "that scourge" (lines 557, 561). Everyman himself brings the metaphoric epiphany to a climax in his reverent, rhapsodic *pronominatio* (lines 581-91):

> O eternall God / O heuenly fygure,
> O way of ryghtwysnes / O goodly vysyon,
> Whiche dyscended downe in a vyrgyn pure
> Bycause he wolde euery man redeme,
> Whiche Adam forfayted by his dysobedyence:
> O blessyd God-heed, electe and hye deuyne,
> Forgyue me my greuous offence!
> Here I crye the mercy in this presence.
> O ghostly treasure, O raunsomer and redemer,
> Of all the worlde hope and conduyter,

Myrrour of ioye, foundatour of mercy. . . .

After his prayer Everyman "wade[s] the water" of penance on a dry stage (line 617) and is given Contrition to wear (lines 638-50). Objects appear here in response to their names, and visible actions depend on invisible conditions. Everyman will shortly be directed to the prototype for such miraculous materialization: the sacrament in which a man may "with v. wordes . . . [handle] his Maker bytwene his handes" (lines 737-39). The play itself is now virtually transubstantiated, its actors and dialogue translucent to spiritual reality.

Understandably, some directors and critics feel that the play should end at this point. Like the allegories of Langland, Spenser, and Bunyan, however, *Everyman* continues past the moment of supreme vision into anticlimax. Indeed, the reference to transubstantiation just quoted opens a discussion of the intransigence of the material: Knowledge explains that Priesthood, which holds the power to manifest God, is itself subject to fleshly corruption (lines 750-63). Everyman has been directed to Priesthood as he was to Confession, but the encounter apparently occurs offstage while Knowledge and Five Wits converse. That Priesthood does not appear as an actor might be taken as a development of the allegorical vision achieved with Confession, an indication that actors are not needed now to manifest spiritual realities. On the contrary, however, the dialogue concerning Priesthood draws our attention to the problem of the inevitable embodiment of the spiritual reality. Spoken of as "they," "he," and "thou," Priesthood clearly has multiple forms, some of them perhaps present in the audience, and Knowledge raises the possibility that its spiritual power may depend on the purity of a particular materialization. The play's intangible realities have not transcended their material basis, after all; Everyman is still alive.

That is why he must encounter a new and ambivalent set of agents. Discretion, Strength, Beauty, and Five Wits imitate both the reliable guides who have recently materialized and the would-be companions who deserted Everyman earlier. Everyman deliberately evokes them in obedience to Good Deeds's and Knowledge's instructions; the actors constitute another metamorphosis of truth. That is, Everyman is not receiving discretion, strength, beauty, and physical sensation but recognizing those qualities and capacities as companions and counselors "of grete myght" for his journey to death (lines 658, 663). That they will abandon him at the grave does not invalidate them. As Lawrence Ryan points out, their promises to Everyman are entirely honest: Strength "wyll by you stande in dystres, / Though thou wolde in batayle fyght on the grounde" (lines 684-85); Five Wits will remain "though it were thrugh the worlde rounde" (line 686); Beauty will not depart "vnto dethes houre" (line 688). If beauty and the five senses often mislead the Christian, this Beauty and this Five Wits, responding to the control of Good Deeds and Knowledge, faithfully superintend Everyman's charitable testament and his visit to Priesthood. Their materialization is part of his proper disposition of his life in preparation for death. Nonetheless, it is his life which Everyman is disposing, and the disposition can lead him up to the grave but not beyond it. At the grave Discretion,

Strength, Beauty, and Five Wits drop their formerly ritualistic diction and turn as colloquial as villagers (lines 800-801, 816-25):

I crosse out all this. / Adewe, by Saynt Iohan!
I take my tappe in my lappe and am gone.

Ye, I haue you ferre ynoughe conueyde.
Ye be olde ynoughe, I vnderstande,
Your pylgrymage to take on hande.

Go thryst the in to the grounde.

Their earthiness completes their enactment of their names: capable of attaining spiritual status, they are of course fundamentally sensual. Beauty cannot "smoder" in the grave and "[i]n this worlde lyue no more," as Everyman would have her do (lines 796-98), for she is inseparable from life in the world. The "persones of grete myght" thus materialize twice—as effectual aids in Everyman's salvation and then as homely creatures, aids only for that part of his salvation which can be enacted in the world.

The colloquial curtain lines of Strength, Beauty, and the rest complete a pattern in the play's style of acting which is also the pattern of its meaning. Initially Everyman and his friends are as realistic as the most traditional director could wish. They are doubly realistic, in fact: they behave like familiar individuals, and they sustain the conviction that the world of individuality is the primary locus of reality. Thus when they later display categorical limitations, they demonstrate the subjection of all individual phenomena to the laws of a different reality. From that other reality come Everyman's new friends, beginning with Good Deeds. The actors who embody Good Deeds, Knowledge, Confession, Discretion, and so forth are clearly not autonomous creatures; their materialization is sacramental, and they accordingly speak and act ritualistically. Even at their most impersonal, however, the actors inevitably suggest personality: we imagine Good Deeds as sweet and gracious, Knowledge as more direct, and Confession as paternal and eloquent. If, as I have argued, those characters' material forms not only represent but also redefine their names, the suggestions of personality are doctrinally meaningful. At the same time, hints of personality are necessary consequences of the concepts' embodiment—concessions, in fact, to our sensual apprehension. Even in experiencing conversion, even in sensing God's presence, Everyman can approach the intangible only through images. As he nears death, the human images that have strengthened his spiritual vision reveal afresh their personalities, their inseparability from the material world. They have come full circle, back to the realism of Fellowship, Kindred, and Cousin. But Everyman does not complete the circle, and neither do we: as the play reverts to realism, we pass beyond the play.

Everyman ends with the actors' unmasking. First Everyman and Good Deeds violate the theatrical illusion called the "fourth wall" by addressing the audience directly. "Take example, all ye that this do here or se," Everyman begins (line 867). Then Knowledge, continuing the direct address, appears to drop her identity as a personification: "Now hath [Everyman] suffred that *we* all shall endure" (line 888; emphasis added). Finally a "Doctour" summarizes the action as if it had yet to occur, transforming Everyman back into every man and the other characters' names back into common nouns (lines 905-11):

> And remember Beaute, V. Wyttes, Strength, &
>   Discrecyon,
> They all at the last do Eueryman forsake,
> Saue his Good Dedes there dothe he take.
> But be-ware, for and they be small,
> Before God he hath no helpe at all:
> None excuse may be there for Eueryman.
> Alas, how shall he do than?

In those breaches of illusion the actors transfer their roles from the play's microcosm back to the wider reality of doctrine and universal experience. They thus reenact for us the lessons that Everyman has learned: that there is no permanent separation between individual action and universal reality, that all embodiments are vehicles of general truth, and that Everyman himself—that is, we ourselves—must dissolve as autonomous creatures to achieve our fullest identity.

The student of acting who fears that he cannot imaginatively realize the roles of *Everyman* is halfway toward understanding those roles. As categories and abstractions, they cannot be fully realized by any creature. By the same token, however, their embodiment in individual actors is not fictional representation, as in post-Renaissance theater; still less is it the arbitrary convention of a bogus dramatization. It is a function of the relationship between object and word, a relationship which *Everyman* dramatizes with unparalleled power. *Everyman*'s allegorical cast is in fact literal: its dramatis personae are words, realizable in many dimensions. In presenting those roles, the skillful actor must call upon the techniques of realistic characterization, upon the more impersonal tones and gestures of ritual, and, above all, upon his own allegorical vision of the metamorphoses of reality, the points at which, in Robert Potter's fine phrase [in *The English Morality Play*], "the Truth comes true." (pp. 311-24)

> *Carolynn Van Dyke, "The Intangible and Its Image: Allegorical Discourse and The Cast of 'Everyman',"* in Acts of Interpretation, the Text in Its Contexts 700-1600: Essays on Medieval and Renaissance Literature in Honor of E. Talbot Donaldson, *edited by Mary J. Carruthers and Elizabeth D. Kirk, Pilgrim Books, 1982, pp. 311-24.*

Stanton B. Garner, Jr.   (essay date 1987)

[*In the excerpt below, Garner examines the tension in* Everyman *between its "theatricality"—the physical presence of actors and props in performance—and the abstract, spiritual concepts it attempts to convey. Unlike the morality play* Mankind, *which, with its lively action and variety of stage effects, invites the audience's involvement with the performance itself,* Everyman *progressively strips away all theatrical effects, leaving only the play's moral message. Garner observes that this paring away of the physical aspects of a performance mirrors Everyman's own abandoning of earthly attach-*

ments. Quotations are taken from David M. Bevington's Medieval Drama *(1975).*]

Over the past twenty years, the English morality play has undergone radical literary revaluation at the hands of David Bevington, Robert Weimann, Robert Potter, and others who have probed its structural and thematic elements, its antecedents in the "popular tradition of the theater," and its developments and influences. This work has done much to uncover the literary and artistic power of these plays which, for so much of their intervening history, have been approached as simple moral fables, primitive in their dramatic technique as well as their didactic impulse, less interesting (for the most part) than the cycle plays that preceded them and the Elizabethan drama that eventually followed. But if it is true that a work of art must be understood in its medium to be fully appreciated—if Michelangelo's statues, for instance, must be studied in terms of the compositional tension between the roughness of stone and patterns of sculpted form—then the morality play remains in a kind of no man's land, for these plays have yet to be adequately valued as theater pieces, written for the stage and intricately dependent upon performance for their realization. There have been exceptions, but for the most part the study of morality drama has abstracted it from its medium and relegated it to the printed text where it has been confined for centuries.

The reasons for this tendency are numerous and complex, involving biases and assumptions that infuse the study of drama at all levels and in all fields. Most fundamentally, the general disregard for performance derives from the Aristotelianism [based on the views of art defined by Aristotle in his *Poetics*] that still characterizes most dramatic criticism, with its strict divisions of the elements of a play and its tacit dismissal of performance under labels such as "spectacle." This critical approach has narrowed the analysis of drama to matters of plot, character, and theme, all considered in a kind of literary abstraction without recourse to the theatrical medium that determines and shapes dramatic elements. In the case of morality drama, the neglect of performance has been influenced by two more particular factors: the paucity of evidence concerning how these plays actually *were* performed, and our classroom view of *Everyman* as the paradigmatic morality—a misleading choice, since of all the moralities *Everyman* seems (at first glance) to be the least dependent on performance, its streamlined simplicity fully available on the page.

But whatever the specific conditions of its staging—whether indoors or outdoors, for instance—the evidence marshalled by scholars of the medieval theater indicates that morality drama was indeed designed to be performed, and that this was accompanied by what we might today call "theatrical" success. This success is not surprising, since these plays are aware of their own existence in performance, draw upon performance in various ways, and in fact constitute some of the most sophisticated artistic and moral explorations of theatricality in English drama. In suggesting some of the ways by which these plays manipulate their own theatricality, I will focus on the two moralities which have received the most critical attention in recent years: the lively, topsy-turvy *Mankind* and the starker *Everyman,* a play whose striking bareness becomes an even more remarkable manipulation of performance in light of the earlier play. I hope to demonstrate that, in each of these plays, the stage constitutes not simply an added effect, but a fundamental condition of meaning.

"Theatricality," as it will be used here, refers to a play's existence in the moment of performance, in all its physicality and immediacy, and the many ways by which a play calls attention to this moment. It is conventional to speak of the moralities in the context of sermons, moral tracts, and other medieval works of literature and art—to compare their mischief figures, for instance, to the devils grinning from the borders of illuminated manuscripts. But such comparisons neglect the crucial difference between these plays and their more strictly literary and visual counterparts: in performance, a stage devil is physically *there,* in real proximity to the audience, and with every gesture and movement he draws attention to his immediacy. This kind of histrionic self-display is what is usually meant by "theatricality," but I am using the term more fundamentally, to include all the ways in which a play exists in the moment, as well as all the aspects of performance which a play draws upon: objects, movements, light, sound, even the physical stage space itself. A play, of course, is more than this: like a printed literary work, the materials of the stage point beyond themselves, and suggest a fictional world which they both embody and signify. Drama, to some extent, always seeks to transcend theater's bare physicality, and this is particularly true of the moralities, whose effects hinge on abstract levels of narrative and allegorical significance. At the same time, beneath fiction and allegory, these plays never lose contact with their theatricality, that dimension of all plays that is irreducibly here and now.

Theatricality, in other words, is an essential component of that tension, inherent in all drama, between the material reality of performance and the fictional realm which it is made to represent—that tension implicit in Hamlet's skull, which is both stage prop on the performance level and the remains of "poor Yorick" in the play's story. What is significant in the present context is how pertinent this dualism is to the central moral and dramatic oppositions of morality drama itself. Both *Mankind* and *Everyman* contrast an abstract salvation scheme with the distracting presence of the here-and-now, and both present a protagonist torn by this conflict: Mankinde abandons Mercy's teaching for the temptations around him, whereas Everyman must confront the consequences of such an abandonment. In keeping with morality drama's didactic function, and its dual conception of "Mankind" as character and as spectator, each play extends this conflict to its interaction with its audience, exploiting that dualism of dramatic performance between the immediate and the abstract, between what we directly experience and what it means. Both plays present the entertaining immediacy of performance as a form of diversion, which "dis-tracts" attention from the invisible realities of the eternal to the sensory realities of the moment, though (as I shall argue) they do so with different dramatic results. *Mankind,* through a barrage of stage diversions, involves its audience in its character's "fall" from Mercy's admonishments, while

Everyman engages its audience in the triumph over temptation through a stark anti-theatricalism, in which the things of the stage (like the things of the world) are steadily stripped away.

Mankind, as F. J. Furnivall recognized [in his edition of *The Macro Plays,* 1904], is cast in a tripartite structure, and its beginning and end are ruled by Mercy, who serves as spokesman for the play's morality of vigilance and its theology of forgiveness. (pp. 272-75)

The middle third of *Mankind* is ruled by the mischief figures: Mischeff, the "three N's" (Nowadays, New-Guise, and Nought), and Titivillus. They represent in concert, as Mercy outlines at the play's close, the Flesh, the World, and the Devil. The dramatic fact, though, is that this clear allegorical identification comes long after they have left the stage for good, when their dramatic *effect* in the play is at an end. While they hold the stage, these figures constitute the heart of the play's diverting theatricality, establishing a stage presence so disrupting that it actually works against the conceptual calm on which allegory and other more abstract levels of comprehension depend. Indeed, so pronounced is this theatricality that some have seen this middle third as a corruption of an originally more streamlined dramatic text. These suspicions are understandable when we consider the havoc these figures wreak on Mercy and what he represents—interrupting his initial sermonizing with nonsense parodies and (if we take Nought's boast at 113 to indicate a stage direction) physically tripping him up.

But whether or not their scenes represent graftings upon a more purely homiletic play, the theatricality of these mischief figures corresponds strikingly to the world of temptation and danger within the play's moral scheme. The essence of their threat to Mankinde, after all, lies in their ability to draw him away from his spiritual certainties, and it is significant that they accomplish this through distraction: a board implanted in the ground, a whisper in the ear as he sleeps, a confusing tangle of activity. As Mercy warns Mankinde, Titivillus sets out to "ronde in yowr ere, and cast a nett befor yowr ey" (303), and this is effected through a wearying barrage of tricks and antics. Through their frenetic, assaultive theatricality, the mischief figures exert a similar distracting power over that other Mankinde, the audience. In contrast to Mercy, whose physical presence on stage is no doubt as stolid as his latinate verse, the mischief figures dance, prance, and tumble; they holler and sing. In short, they engage in the business of circus clowns, drawing attention through ostentatious self-display. They enter and move onstage with a bewildering randomness, filling the stage less with clearly delineated moral abstractions than with a chaos of individual bodies. Significant in this regard is the frequency with which they call attention to particular body parts: face, neck, feet, anus, genitals. Titivillus, himself adorned with an oversized head, announces himself with this focus: "I com, with my leggys under me!" (454). Such references, and the gestures that accompany them (New-Guise clutching his "jewllys," for instance, and later putting his head in a noose) suggest the extent to which their antics draw attention toward the particular—toward those components of performance that are most specific and inert. It is in keeping with this "objectifying" of the stage that much of the activity of the play's middle sequence centers around stage props, and that attention is repeatedly focused on the *materiality* of these props: a fake head's size, a shovel's weight, a board's thickness. (pp. 276-77)

It is useful to set *Mankind* within the broader development in oratory and the arts evident by the late middle ages, when "the calm, reflective statements of the romanesque era came steadily to be replaced by more forceful, demonstrative and individualistic forms of expression, emotional, theatrical, and often deliberately shocking" [Glynn Wickham "Medieval Comic Traditions and the Beginnings of English Comedy" in *Comic Drama: The European Heritage,* edited by W. D. Howarth, 1978]—the development suggested, for instance, by the proliferation of intricately realistic detail in Flemish painting, and of popular, even comic, elements in the medieval sermon. What *Mankind* demonstrates is that this intrusion of the "demonstrative" bore particular fruit within the morality tradition, where the very medium of performance could be made an element of its didactic impulse and its typical narrative and moral patterns. Moreover, the success with which the theatricality of the stage, its props, and its actors were incorporated within *Mankind*'s broader oppositions suggests a dramaturgical source, not only for the secular moralities that followed, but also for the great plays of the age of Elizabeth and James. Short of its didactic frameworks, theatricality makes itself felt in the broader thematic frameworks of these plays, and it retains some of the structural features of the earlier moralities: a tendency toward distraction and confusion; a pronounced awareness of the theatrical event itself; and a focus on the momentary and the particular, which often stand in direct contrast to broader, more abstract patterns of value. The influence of the Vice on English Renaissance drama has been well established, but the more general legacy of theatricality itself has not been adequately explored. Though participating in differing moral spheres, we can find versions of *Mankind*'s theatricality in [William Shakespeare's] *1 Henry IV,* [Thomas Dekker's] *The Shoemaker's Holiday,* and [Ben Jonson's] *Volpone,* as well as in the darker dramatic worlds of [Shakespeare's] *Richard III,* [Cyril Tourneur's (?)] *The Revenger's Tragedy,* and [John Webster's] *The Duchess of Malfi.*

Against this background—of *Mankind* and what we might call a tradition of "English theatricality"— *Everyman* appears all the more striking. For *Everyman* is radically different in its theatrical technique from the earlier *Mankind,* a consequence of its different dramatic emphasis. A play about endings, its dominant mode is retrospect: the distractions of life flourish in the past, and are represented in the present only so that the play can dramatize their falling away. The things of the world are banished, in other words, as part of a gradual triumph of the things of the spirit. Dramaturgically, this *contemptus mundi* [scorning the world] tenor is reflected in a profound anti-theatricalism, unrivalled among the moralities (and among virtually all of English drama)—a steady suppression of the immediacy of performance toward the invisible spiritual pattern that stands as its referent.

The play's stage action, as it is suggested by the text, contrasts noticeably with the frenetic movement that the text of *Mankind* calls for so insistently. *Everyman* features seventeen characters (compared to *Mankind*'s seven) but these characters are carefully grouped within the action and on stage, and they make no attempt to disrupt these groupings; when they move, they do so with an almost processional simplicity. Felawship evokes revelry and boisterousness (272-75), but his imaginative projection is counterpointed by the sparseness of the present, and its relative stillness. Speeches give few cues for gesture, save those appropriate to explanation and illustration; in much the same way as Mercy's speeches, those of *Everyman* consistently draw attention toward spiritual action and its consequences, toward allegorical—not material— identity. Goodes, for instance, displays himself to Everyman and to us, but—unlike the mischief figures of *Mankind*—we are concerned less with the actor displaying his body than we are with his abstract significance. Indeed, insofar as the actor playing Goodes represents the temptation of material wealth, it is precisely his physicality that is discredited as delusory. In keeping with this ascetic suspicion of the physical, there are few props in *Everyman,* and those props that *are* dictated by the text—book of reckoning, scourge, garment of sorrow, rood—point beyond themselves; the emphasis is on their *sacramental* quality, that divine reality which suffuses, and thereby transforms, the prop's mere *objectness.* Attention, in *Everyman,* is continually deflected from presence to meaning, and this process occurs against a subdued stage.

One of the most remarkable dramaturgical features of the play is the frequency with which characters anticipate, or summarize, its action. It is not generally noted that the main action of *Everyman* is introduced three times: by the Messenger, by God, and by Dethe. Each discusses Everyman's condition, his impending journey, and what it all signifies on the level of allegory. The Messenger, for instance, presents the following outline:

> Here shall you se how Falawship and Jolité,
> Bothe Strengthe, Pleasure, and Beauté,
> Will fade from the[e] as floure in Maye;
> For ye shall here how our heven Kinge
> Calleth Everyman to a generall rekeninge.
>
> (16-20)

At least one critic has considered this Prologue "somewhat superfluous," [Thomas F. Van Laan in *PMLA* 78 (December 1963)], but the effects of such introductions on the audience's experience of the dramatic action are significant to the play as a whole. For one thing, by highlighting the journey motif, they underscore the plot's streamlined linearity, as well as its simplicity, thereby providing the play with a clearly arranged beginning, middle, and end. Not all of the play's events are specifically anticipated, but the outline within which they occur is set in place with a rigor absent even from Mercy's stern warnings. In so doing, these anticipations significantly adjust the audience's conceptual relationship to the unfolding action. As Bertolt Brecht understood so well, devices like this serve to distance the audience from the moment, its suspense, and its immediacy; they shift the audience from participants to observers, focusing their attention on the stage and what it is being made to signify. This distancing strategy continues throughout the play, as characters recapitulate the action that has taken place and speculate as to future outcomes. Abandoned by his kinsmen, for instance, Everyman sums up both the rejection and its lesson:

> A, Jesus, is all come hereto?
> Lo, faire wordes maketh folles faine;
> They promise, and nothinge will do, certaine.
> My kinnesmen promised me faithfully
> For to abide with me stedfastly,
> And now fast awaye do they flee;
> Even so Felawship promised me.
>
> (378-84)

Using language in a radically different manner from that of *Mankind*'s mischief figures, Everyman reflects upon what has happened, abstracting from his experience those meanings which constitute its lasting significance, pressing the stage moment ever further into the background.

Unlike *Mankind,* which has as its moral beacon a vision of a spiritual life lived in the here-and-now, *Everyman*'s *terminus* is the world beyond man's world, the spiritual realm that encloses the material. This movement toward the unseen is reflected in the play's steady movement beyond performance, off stage. Characters in *Mankind* enter and exit randomly, but (with the possible exception of Everyman after his confession, if this indeed occurs offstage) no character who exits the stage world of *Everyman* ever returns. The focus remains on Everyman as a character alone, who traverses the stage only to lose most of what he finds, and the play's dramatic progression is a steady deepening of what V. A. Kolve calls [in "*Everyman* and the Parable of the Talents," in *The Medieval Drama,* edited by Sandro Sticca, 1972] "that movement-into-aloneness generic to tragedy." It is a culmination of this play's steady anti-theatricalism, its refusal to rest in the objects of the stage, that the play's climax—Everyman's death—is a stage exit, and that the triumph of his salvation is not shown, but described, by the Angel that welcomes Everyman's invisible spirit: "Here-above thou shalte go, / Bicause of thy singuler vertue" (895-96). The play ends as the Doctor provides a final recapitulation of Everyman's story, now freed from its embodiment on stage. And as the stage recedes, the thesis which it has demonstrated moves into the foreground. "This morall men may have in minde" (902): *Everyman* completes itself on the audience's inner stage of memory and judgment as action becomes lesson, pure in its conceptual autonomy.

Everyman presents us, in many ways, with a theatrical paradox. On the one hand, its demonstrative force depends on its embodiment in performance—its "bodying forth" in props and actors, words and actions. Good Dedes owes her homiletic power, in large part, to the actress' material presence onstage, and to the physical arts of declamation and presentation upon which she draws. At the same time, the play resists the distraction threatened by this embodiment—the tendency of all performance to intrude itself on its own, non-conceptual terms. Like a tightly patterned dance, the play's power lies in the insistency with which it keeps its energies under control, subordinating display to design, rendering inconceivable *Mankind*'s theatrical extravagance. This tension gives *Everyman* its distinctive stage vitality: simple, even severe, its activity charged with the power of abstraction.

The contrast between these two plays, so near to each other historically, could not be more pronounced. *Mankind* dramatizes the conflict between world and spirit by drawing the audience into the entertainments of performance—pulling them into a medium which is not simply a vehicle for allegory but an actual, material presence. The tautness and power of *Everyman,* on the other hand, results from the ways in which it works against its condition in performance, paring away its theatrical inessentials, finally abandoning the things of the stage as it does those of the world in which the stage has its existence. In each case, we can appreciate that performance and theatricality are not mere incidentals to morality drama; rather, they are essential components of dramatic meaning and dramatic effect. We do these plays a disservice by consigning their performance features to the less serious realm of "popular entertainment," or by seeing their frequent bareness as "literary" in the same terms as the printed text. The morality play may indeed be "the archetype of the theater of ideas in our western tradition of drama" [as Potter says in *The English Morality Play,* 1975], but it is an archetype aware of its status as a performance from. As such, its achievements and its influences are of a different kind and magnitude than we have traditionally allowed, meriting critical approaches more sensitive to these differences. Like all vital artistic forms, morality drama is deeply rooted in the medium for which it was created: in the theatrical moment where it finds its life. (pp. 280-85)

> *Stanton B. Garner, Jr., "Theatricality in 'Mankind' and 'Everyman',"* in Studies in Philology, *Vol. LXXXIV, No. 3, Summer, 1987, pp. 272-85.*

FURTHER READING

Conley, John. "The Doctrine of Friendship in *Everyman*." *Speculum* XLIV, No. 3 (July 1969): 374-82.

  Analyzes *Everyman* in terms of medieval traditions surrounding friendship.

Davenport, W.A. "Pride, Death and Tragedy." In his *Fifteenth-Century English Drama: The Early Moral Plays and Their Literary Relations,* pp. 15-35. Cambridge: D.S. Brewer, 1982.

  Analysis of the tragic elements of *Everyman.* Davenport claims that the central figure's "painful acquisition of knowledge of self and the world is a tragic theme."

Fifield, Merle. *The Castle in the Circle.* Muncie, Ind.: Ball State University, 1967, 48 p.

  Studies the staging of morality plays and argues that *Everyman* is best presented on a round platform. Fifield then constructs a performance of the play utilizing surviving set designs and blocking instructions from a medieval production of *The Castle of Perseverance.*

Goldhammer, Allen D. "*Everyman:* A Dramatization of

Death." *Quarterly Journal of Speech* 59 (February 1973): 87-98.

> Compares the stages of death presented in Elisabeth Kübler-Ross's *On Death and Dying* (1969) with those through which Everyman passes to argue that the play shows death as "a learning process."

Kolve, V. A. "*Everyman* and the Parable of the Talents." In *The Medieval Drama,* edited by Sandro Sticca, pp. 69-98. Albany: State University of New York Press, 1972.

> Uses the New Testament parable to demonstrate that *Everyman*'s medieval audience would have considered the play to be as much about life as death.

McRae, Murdo William. "Everyman's Last Rites and the Digression on the Priesthood." *College Literature* XIII, No. 3 (Fall 1986): 305-09.

> Argues that the discussion between Knowledge and Five Wits reinforces the play's reformist teachings and its overall concern with the "tension between the lofty goal to purify the Church and the worldly recognition that the Church is inhabited by the sinful."

Munson, William. "Knowing and Doing in *Everyman*." *The Chaucer Review* 19, No. 3 (1985): 252-71.

> Maintains that the theology underlying *Everyman* stresses the importance of human striving as well as knowledge, and encourages the play's audience "to see that to affirm Christian truth is to affirm the process of venturing . . . and of learning."

Potter, Robert. "The Idea of a Morality Play." In his *The English Morality Play: Origins, History and Influence of a Dramatic Tradition,* pp. 6-29. London: Routledge & Kegan Paul, 1975.

> Provides the religious background of medieval morality plays.

Schreiber, Earl G. "*Everyman* in America." *Comparative Drama* 9, No. 2 (Summer 1975): 99-115.

> Provides information on successful *Everyman* productions and adaptations, concentrating on Hugo von Hofmannsthal's *Jedermann* (1911), Walter Sorell's *Everyman Today* (1948), and Geraldine Fitzgerald and Jonathan Ringkamp's *Everyman and Roach* (1968).

Speaight, Robert. "*Everyman* and Euripides." In his *William Poel and the Elizabethan Revival,* pp. 161-78. London: William Heinemann, 1954.

> Describes the circumstances behind Poel's production of *Everyman,* the first modern staging of the play, and details Poel's disagreements with the play's theology.

Stevens, Martin. "The Reshaping of *Everyman:* Hofmannsthal at Salzburg." *The Germanic Review* XLVII, No. 2 (March 1973): 117-31.

> Traces the sources and stage history of Hugo von Hofmannsthal's successful *Jedermann,* an adaptation of *Everyman.*

Thomas, Helen S. "The Meaning of the Character Knowledge in *Everyman.*" *Mississippi Quarterly* XIV, No. 1 (Winter 1960-61): 3-13.

> Observes that Knowledge represents a "wisdom figure whose function it was to counsel Everyman wisely . . . and to send him to the Sacrament of Penance."

Tigg, E. R. "Is *Elckerlijc* Prior to *Everyman*?" *Journal of English and German Philology* 38 (October 1939): 568-96.

> An important study of the relationship between *Everyman* and the Dutch play *Elckerlijc.* On the basis of stylistic and other analyses, Tigg concludes that *Elckerlijc* is the elder work and *Everyman* an English adaptation.

Van Laan, Thomas F. "*Everyman:* A Structural Analysis." *PMLA* LXXVIII, No. 5 (December 1963): 465-75.

> Detects a two-part structure in *Everyman* that melds the religious and dramatic elements of the drama, giving it universal appeal. According to Van Laan, the first part traces Everyman's descent into despair and the second part follows his rise to salvation.

Vocht, Henry de. *Everyman: A Comparative Study of Texts and Sources.* Louvain: Ch. Uystpruyst, 1947, 228 pp.

> Textual comparison of *Everyman* and *Elckerlijc* that judges *Everyman* the earlier play. De Vocht argues that the sound Christian doctrine in the English play and the unclear phrasing in the Dutch prove *Elckerlijc* is an unsuccessful translation from the English.

Federico García Lorca

1898-1936

INTRODUCTION

García Lorca is considered one of Spain's foremost twentieth-century dramatists. Critics have noted that all the main streams of Spanish culture converge in his plays; he combined elements of Spanish and Classical literature with folk and gypsy ballads to create an idiom at once traditional, modern, and personal. Lorca's often startling imagery—harshly realistic yet lyrical, sometimes violent and primitive—attests to his ambition to revivify Spanish literature by depicting the beauty, excitement, and danger of life lived close to nature. His drama takes many forms, ranging from experimental puppet plays and farces to tragedies patterned after Greek classics. Lorca is best known for his rural trilogy, comprising *Bodas de sangre* (*Blood Wedding*), *Yerma,* and *La casa de Bernarda Alba* (*The House of Bernarda Alba*). Evocative and powerful, his dramas transcend their particular milieu, creating what Gwynne Edwards has described as "mirrors in which we see ourselves."

Born in rural Andalusia near the city of Granada, García Lorca grew up in a culture rich in myth, storytelling, and folk music, the influence of which is manifested throughout his works. After attending school in Almería, he studied literature and law in Granada. There he published his first work, *Impresiones y paisajes,* a prose depiction of the austere, melancholy countryside surrounding Castile. In 1919 he moved to Madrid and lived for several years at the Residencia de Estudiantes, a flourishing center for writers, critics, and scholars of cultural liberalism. Here Lorca met the surrealist artist Salvador Dalí, who later recalled that "the personality of Federico García Lorca produced an immense impression on me"; to Dalí, Lorca was "the poetic phenomenon in its entirety and 'in the raw,' viscous and sublime, quivering with a thousand fires of darkness and of subterranean biology, like all matter endowed with the originality of its own form." Shortly after he began his studies at the Residencia, García Lorca wrote his first play, *El Maleficio de la mariposa* (*The Butterfly's Evil Spell*). Incorporating poetry, music, and dance, and with a butterfly and a cockroach as the protagonists, this poetic drama, staged in Madrid in 1920, failed as a theatrical production.

Biographers have speculated that his initial lack of success as a playwright was bitterly disappointing to Lorca; for the next several years, he devoted himself almost entirely to writing poetry. His first volume of verse, *Libro de poemas,* is a compilation of ballads based on gypsy folklore Lorca encountered during his youth. He continued to depict the culture of rural Andalusia in *Canciones* and *Poema del cante jondo,* both of which reflect his interest in the traditional Andalusian ballad form known as *cante jondo,* or "deep song." Lorca's best-known collection of poetry, *Primer romancero gitano* (*The Gypsy Ballads*), is

widely regarded as a masterpiece of Spanish verse. In this volume, comprising eighteen poems written between 1924 and 1927, García Lorca presented images of gypsy village life in the traditional ballad form, creating poetry that is both thematically accessible and lyrically complex. In 1929 he visited New York, studying English at Columbia University and writing poetry—including much of the acclaimed volume *Poeta en Nueva York* (*Poet in New York*)—and dramas which reflected his horror at mechanized urban civilization. His return to Spain in 1930 marked the beginning of his most productive and successful period as a dramatist. In addition to directing La Barraca, a federally sponsored traveling theater troupe, at this time Lorca wrote several plays, including the rural trilogy. He also completed *Doña Rosita la soltera* (*Dona Rosita the Spinster*), a drama in which a woman waits in vain through three decades for her fiancé to return to Spain and marry her. Shortly after the outbreak of the Spanish civil war in 1936, García Lorca was abducted from a friend's home and murdered. Although Lorca was not overtly political, it is generally accepted that he was killed by Nationalist followers of Francisco Franco. The details surrounding his death remain a mystery.

García Lorca's first mature dramatic effort, the verse play *Mariana Pineda* (1927), revolves around a more conventional hero than those of *The Butterfly's Evil Spell;* Mariana Pineda was a folkloric figure who was executed in the early 1800s because she would not reveal the whereabouts of her lover Pedro, an anti-government rebel. The play as a whole dramatizes such concepts as unrequited love, powerful passion, and tragic death. Considered one of Lorca's minor plays—faulted for its ambiguous allusions and melodramatic elements—*Mariana Pineda* is nevertheless regarded as significant for its indication of the direction Lorca's later drama would take. Edwards describes Mariana as "a forerunner of many of Lorca's great female characters who love and hope and wait in vain." Lorca went on to explore love and romance in *La Zapatera prodigiosa* (*The Shoemaker's Prodigious Wife*) and *El Amor de Don Perlimplín con Belisa en su jardin* (*The Love of Don Perlimplín and Belisa in the Garden*). Both plays are farces in which young and sensual women marry older men; the women express and demand unrestrained passion that is beyond the capabilities of their husbands, resulting in impotence and frustration for the men. Critics have pointed out that the conflicts engendered by repressed passion, presented with humor in Lorca's farces, emerge later in much darker tones in *Blood Wedding, Yerma,* and *The House of Bernarda Alba.*

During his time at Columbia University, García Lorca began work on two dramas that reflect the influence of Surrealism, particularly as defined in André Breton's *Manifeste du surrealisme* (1924). In both *El Público* (*The Public*) and *Asi que pasen cinco años* (*If Five Years Pass*), Lorca attempted to write freely and without inhibition in order to reveal the workings of the subconscious mind. As Lorca's brother Francisco noted, "the part [Lorca] turned over to a process of unconscious cerebration was enormous." Lorca himself deemed the two works unplayable, describing *The Public* as "a poem to be booed at"; nevertheless he declared that "these impossible plays contain my true intention."

Epitomizing many of Lorca's artistic preoccupations, *Blood Wedding,* the first work in the trilogy of rural tragedies, depicts the inevitability of death, the price of personal honor, and the powerlessness of human reason in the face of passion. A young woman, referred to simply as The Bride, must choose between The Bridegroom—her fiancé, and the socially sanctioned choice—and her lover Leonardo. She resigns herself to the marriage, but immediately after the wedding runs away with Leonardo. The Bridegroom's Mother, knowing that a confrontation between the two men will result in her son's death, nonetheless sends her son after the lovers to vindicate the family's honor. The Bridegroom catches up with The Bride and Leonardo in the forest, and the two men kill each other in a duel. *Blood Wedding* is essentially poetic in style, incorporating lullabies and wedding songs, as well as abstract characters like the Moon and Death who speak their lines in verse. This drama afforded Lorca a vehicle to express the view that repression of the elemental passions results in violence and even death. *Blood Wedding* received enthusiastic reviews in Madrid and in Latin America, but English-speaking audiences reacted adverse-

ly to the play, perhaps because, as some critics pointed out, the society depicted was too foreign. Stark Young wrote of the New York premiere that *Blood Wedding* is "an importation that is against the beat of this country," but he also praised Lorca for eloquently capturing the Spanish character.

Yerma, the second play of the trilogy, centers on a young woman who is obsessed with the idea of bearing a child. Although they have been married for two years, Yerma and her husband Juan have been unable to conceive; the cause of their infertility is left unspecified, but Lorca suggests that Juan's indifference to the idea of starting a family contributes to the problem. Yerma feels neglected by her husband and mocked by the villagers for her inability to fulfill her role as mother; with everything around her fertile and life-giving, nature itself seems to taunt her. Yerma's thwarted longing for motherhood leads her to consult the local sorceress and to participate in a surreal fertility rite which proves unsuccessful. The sorceress also counsels Yerma to take a lover, suggesting that she could conceive a child with a different man, but Yerma's code of honor prevents her from doing so. Having exhausted all options available to her, Yerma finally confronts her husband, who admits that he is happier without children. At the height of her frustrated longing, Yerma strangles Juan. Referring to the child she will never conceive, she proclaims "Now I'll sleep without startling myself awake, anxious to see if I feel in my blood another new blood. My body dry forever!. . . I myself have killed my son!" In this play Lorca conveys his themes not only through the words and actions of the characters, but also through the songs, dances, and poems incorporated into the piece. Although the drama garnered mixed reviews, *Yerma* received much critical attention and secured García Lorca's international reputation as a significant playwright.

In the last play of the trilogy, Lorca deliberately downplayed the poetic and surreal elements that had become his trademark. He labelled *The House of Bernarda Alba* a "photographic documentary," having written the play in severe, simple language, starkly realistic and devoid of lyricism. At the beginning of the drama, Bernarda Alba announces, upon returning from her husband's funeral, that she and her five daughters will maintain an eight-year period of mourning. Despite what Carl W. Cobb has described as "an undercurrent of fury and rebellion," Bernarda's tyrannical hold over her family is unchallenged by all except Adela, the youngest daughter. Seeking to escape the atmosphere of severe sexual repression in her home, she sneaks out of the house to meet her lover Pepe el Romano. When Bernarda realizes what has transpired, she reaches for her gun and shoots at Pepe; although she misses, she allows Adela to believe that Pepe is dead. In a final act of desperate rebellion, Adela hangs herself in her room. The play closes with Bernarda still attempting to assert her authority and to maintain family honor by insisting that Adela died a virgin. Despite Lorca's claim that the language of *Bernarda Alba* contains "not a drop of poetry," many critics have pointed out the play's poetic essence. In a manner reminiscent of both Greek tragedy and the folk customs of García Lorca's native Andalusia, Bernarda's perverse allegiance to honor, pride, and tradition results in suffering, hatred, and ultimately, death.

García Lorca's work has won the admiration of audiences worldwide as well as the respect of numerous critics. In general, García Lorca is considered most successful when dealing with such universal themes as death, honor, and passion. Though scholars regard his experimental dramas as significant to the development of his career, they feel that the rural tragedies best represent Lorca's style. A few critics have faulted him for occasionally sacrificing dramatic intensity to poetic effect, but the majority agree that he achieved an admirable balance between the two in his later plays.

PRINCIPAL WORKS

PLAYS

El Maleficio de la mariposa   1920
 [*The Butterfly's Evil Spell,* 1954; also translated as *The Spell of the Butterfly,* 1957]
**Los Títeres de Cachiporra*   1923-31
 [*The Billy-Club Puppets,* 1963]
Mariana Pineda   1927
 [*Mariana Pineda,* 1950]
El Publico   1929-30
 [exists only in an incomplete version; translated in Lorca's "The Public": A Study of This Unfinished Play and of Love and Death in the Work of Federico García Lorca, 1974]
La Zapatera prodigiosa   1930
 [*The Shoemaker's Prodigious Wife,* 1941]
†*Asi que pasen cinco años*   1931
 [*If Five Years Pass,* 1941]
El Amor de Don Perlimplín con Belisa en su jardin   1933
 [*The Love of Don Perlimplín and Belisa in the Garden,* 1941]
‡*Bodas de sangre*   1933
 [*Blood Wedding,* 1939]
Yerma   1934
 [*Yerma,* 1941]
Doña Rosita la soltera   1935
 [*Doña Rosita the Spinster,* 1941]
§*La Casa de Bernarda Alba*   1936
 [*The House of Bernarda Alba,* 1947]
From Lorca's Theater: Five Plays of Federico García Lorca   1941
Three Tragedies of Federico García Lorca   1947
Comedies   1954
Five Plays: Comedies and Tragicomedies   1963

OTHER MAJOR WORKS

Impresiones y paisajes   (sketches)   1918
Libro de poemas   (poetry)   1921
Canciones   (poetry)   1927
Primer romancero gitano   (poetry)   1928

[*Gypsy Ballads,* 1951]
ǀ*Poeta en Nueva York*   (poetry)   1929-30
 [*Poet in New York,* 1940]
Poema del cante jondo   (poetry)   1931
Llanto por Ignacio Sánchez Mejías   (poetry)   1935
 [*Lament for the Death of a Bullfighter;* published in *Lament for the Death of a Bullfighter, and Other Poems,* 1937]
Obras completas   (drama and poetry)   1938-46
Deep Song and Other Prose   (lectures, poetry, and essays)   1980

*This trilogy was published posthumously in 1948.

†This work was published posthumously in 1937.

‡This work was translated (1934) and produced in New York (1935) with the title *Bitter Oleander;* script is unpublished.

§This work was published posthumously in 1944.

ǀThis work was published posthumously in 1940.

AUTHOR COMMENTARY

The Authority of the Theatre   (1934)

[*In the following excerpt taken from a speech given on the opening night of* Yerma *in 1934, Lorca expounds on the nature and importance of theater. He asserts the need for the playwright to constantly challenge and, in turn, be challenged by society. He also stresses that the role of the dramatist is to teach his audience and to maintain the dignity of the dramatic arts.*]

Necessity and struggle, grounded on a critical love, temper the artist's soul, which easy flattery makes effeminate and destroys. The theatres are full of deceiving sirens, garlanded with hothouse roses, and the public is content, and applauds dummy hearts and superficial dialogue; but the dramatic poet who wishes to save himself from oblivion must not forget the open fields with their wild roses, fields moistened by the dawn where peasants toil, and the pigeon, wounded by a mysterious hunter, which is dying amongst the rushes with no one to hear its grief.

Shunning sirens, flattery, and congratulations, I have accepted nothing in my honor, on the occasion of the first night of **Yerma:** but it has been the greatest pleasure of my short life as a writer to learn that the theatre world of Madrid was asking the great Margarita Xirgu, an actress with an impeccable artistic career, luminary of the Spanish theatre, and admirable interpreter of the part of Yerma, together with the company which so brilliantly supports her, for a special production.

For the interest and attention in a notable theatrical endeavor which this implies, I wish, now that we are all together, to give to you my deepest and sincerest thanks. I am not speaking tonight as an author, nor as a poet, nor as a simple student of the rich panorama of man's life, but as an ardent lover of the theatre of social action. The theatre is one of the most useful and expressive instruments for a country's edification, the barometer which registers its greatness or its decline. A theatre which in every branch, from tragedy to vaudeville, is sensitive and well oriented, can in a few years change the sensibility of a people, and a broken-down theatre, where wings have given way to cloven hoofs, can coarsen and benumb a whole nation.

The theatre is a school of weeping and of laughter, a rostrum where men are free to expose old and equivocal standards of conduct, and explain with living examples the eternal norms of the heart and feelings of man.

A nation which does not help and does not encourage its theatre is, if not dead, dying; just as the theatre which does not feel the social pulse, the historical pulse, the drama of its people, and catch the genuine color of its landscape and of its spirit, with laughter or with tears, has no right to call itself a theatre, but an amusement hall, or a place for doing that dreadful thing known as "killing time." I am referring to no one, and I want to offend no one; I am not speaking of actual fact, but of a problem that has yet to be solved.

Every day, my friends, I hear about the crisis in the theatre, and I feel always that the defect is not one before our eyes, but deep down in its very nature; it is not a defect of the flower we have before us, of a play, that is, but deeply rooted; in short, a defect of organization. Whilst actors and authors are in the hands of managements that are completely commercial, free, without either literary or state control of any kind, managements devoid of all judgment and offering no kind of safeguard, actors, authors, and the whole theatre will sink lower every day, beyond all hope of salvation.

The delightful light theatre of revue, vaudeville, and farce, forms of which I am a keen spectator, could maintain and even save itself; but plays in verse, the historical play, and the so-called Spanish *zarzuela,* will suffer more and more setbacks, because they are forms which make great demands and which admit of real innovations, and there is neither the authority nor the spirit of sacrifice to impose them on a public which has to be overruled from above, and often contradicted and attacked. The theatre must impose itself on the public, not the public on the theatre. To do this, authors and actors must, whatever the cost, again assume great authority, because the theatre-going public is like a school child; it reveres the stern, severe teacher who demands justice and sees justice done; and puts pins on the chairs of the timid and flattering ones who neither teach themselves nor allow anyone else to teach.

The public can be taught—I say public, of course, not people—it can be taught; for, some years ago, I saw Debussy and Ravel howled down, and I have been present since at loud ovations given by a public of ordinary people to the very works which were earlier rejected. These authors were imposed by the high judgment of authority, superior to that of the ordinary public, just as were Wedekind in Germany and Pirandello in Italy, and so many others.

This has to be done for the good of the theatre and for the glory and status of its interpreters. Dignity must be maintained, in the conviction that such dignity will be amply repaid. To do otherwise is to tremble behind the flies, and kill the fantasies, imagination, and charm of the theatre, which is always, always an art, and will always be a lofty art, even though there may have been a time when everything which pleased was labeled art, so that the tone was lowered, poetry destroyed, and the stage itself a refuge for thieves.

Art above all else. A most noble art, and you, my actor friends, artists above all else. Artists from head to foot, since through love and vocation you have risen to the make-believe and pitiful world of the boards. Artists by occupation and by preoccupation. From the smallest theatre to the most eminent, the word "Art" should be written in auditoriums and dressing rooms, for if not we shall have to write the word "Commerce" or some other that I dare not say. And distinction, discipline, and sacrifice and love.

I don't want to lecture you, because I should be the one receiving a lecture. My words are dictated by enthusiasm and conviction. I labor under no delusion. As a good Andalusian I can think coolly, because I come of an ancient stock. I know that truth does not lie with him who says, "Today, today, today," eating his bread close to the hearth, but with him who watches calmly at a distance the first light of dawn in the country.

I know that those people who say, "Now, now, now," with their eyes fixed on the small jaws of the box office are not right, but those who say, "Tomorrow, tomorrow, tomorrow," and feel the approach of the new life which is hovering over the world. (pp. 58-61)

> *Federico García Lorca, "The Authority of the Theatre," in* Playwrights on Playwriting: The Meaning and Making of Modern Drama From Ibsen to Ionesco, *edited by Toby Cole, Hill and Wang, 1960, pp. 58-61.*

OVERVIEWS AND GENERAL STUDIES

Angel del Rio   (essay date 1941)

[*In the essay below, originally published in Spanish in 1941, del Rio describes the development of Lorca's "fresh creative genius" from his earliest plays, through his experiments with surrealism, to his mature works, and ending with his rural trilogy. Del Rio traces the influences on Lorca's dramas, discussing elements of myth, pagan and Christian rites, folklore, and Classical tragedy. According to del Rio, Lorca's career culminates in* The House of Bernarda Alba, *"a complete and inspired masterpiece."*]

As is so often the case in Spanish literature, Lorca's dramatic work is inseparable from his poetry and is a natural emanation from it. We have many examples of this: Gil Vicente, Lope de Vega, the Duke of Rivas, Zorrilla; in modern times, Villaespesa, Marquina, Valle-Inclán, Unamuno, and the Machado brothers. In European Romanticism we frequently find the phenomenon of lyrical poetry being turned into dramatic poetry. In this respect, as in so many others, Lorca can be placed within the framework of the Romantic attitude. But let us understand Romanticism not as a school of a certain period, but as a manner of feeling and artistic expression.

Lyricism and Romanticism seem to be fused from the start of his career. His first play, *El maleficio de la mariposa* (*The Spell of the Butterfly*) was written at the same time as his Symbolistic early verse and was animated by the same inspiration as his poems about insects and animals.

Leaving aside the dramatic intensity of his poetry, especially that of the *Gypsy Ballads,* his dramatic work developed side by side with his poetic work, both oscillating between the two magnetic poles of his inspiration and his style, the poles of the select and the popular, the capricious and the tragic, the stylized grace whose art was close to the art of the miniature painter, and the anguished passion within a whirlwind of sensuality.

MARIANA PINEDA

In 1927, several years after the premature *Spell of the Butterfly,* Lorca really began his dramatic career with *Mariana Pineda.* Conceived in the popular vein, the work suggests a childhood ballad: "Oh, what a sad day in Granada." It follows a technique similar to that of many of his first poems and songs. We see here the attempt, probably intuitive, to fuse elements of the classical and Romantic theater and to do so with a modern flair. From the classical tradition he takes the essential spirit, the dramatization of a popular ballad in whose verses the drama is suggested. On the other hand, from the Romantic era he takes the historic theme, the feeling of background, and above all the character of the heroine, an angel sacrificed on the altar of love. Judged on its own merit, the work lacks true dramatic dimensions. It is a static picture. Only in one or two dialogues between Pedrosa or Fernando and Mariana can we catch a glimpse of the clash of wills without which there can be no drama. As for the intimate conflict of the heroine, Marianita, it is barely sketched. From the very beginning she seems predestined to her end; she is the embodiment of sacrifice: neither the hope of saving herself, nor the certainty of Don Pedro's love for her can change her tone of resignation:

> Through this love true
> that devours my simple soul
> I am turning marigold
> through suffering for you

She is revealed to us not through action nor in intimate dramatic soliloquies but in lyrical fugues, as in the beautiful ballad that begins with the lines, "With what an effort / the light leaves Granada!" In the rest of the play the same thing happens. The best moments are due to the presence of lyrical elements, either directly, separated from the action, as in the ballads describing the bullfight in Ronda and the arrest of Torrijos, or as a lyrical motif in contrast to the dramatic action. The latter we find in the ballad of Clavela and the children or the song in the garden, "Beside the water." In many scenes there is a pathetic, almost musical atmosphere. On the whole we detect

throughout the play the lack of maturity of an author who is experimenting with a new technique. Even his verse has a naïve and occasionally clumsy cadence. Though doubtless inferior to the poetry of these years, in which Lorca had already written many of his *Gypsy Ballads, Mariana Pineda* is not without interest. In more than one way we can catch a glimpse in it of the great merit which the best dramatic work of Lorca was to exhibit. There is a clear feeling for the tragic and a faultless good taste: aesthetic dignity saves the most dangerously poor passages, those on the border of immature and trite melodrama, like the scene of the conspirators, the seduction attempt on the part of Pedrosa, and the chorus of novices. Above all, there is a conscious effort of innovation in his intention to synthesize in the theater the plastic, lyrical, dramatic, and musical arts into a superior unity. For this reason Lorca took great pains to "tune up" each scene within a stylized atmosphere of colors, lights, allusions, and constant musical interludes and backgrounds, until at the end of the play a sort of operatic and symbolic apotheosis is achieved.

At its premiere during the period of Primo de Rivera's dictatorship many people saw in the main theme a political intention which was completely alien to its spirit. Such eminent critics as Enrique Díez Canedo, however, pointed out the mistake of interpreting the principal character as a revolutionary symbol. Mariana Pineda as Lorca conceived her was, he wrote, "a ghost who embroiders her flag, not as a symbol of liberty, but as a lover's gift. And only when she understands that in the soul of her beloved the love for freedom is stronger than the love for herself, does she become transfigured and convert herself into a symbol of that very liberty" (*El Sol,* Madrid, Oct. 13, 1927). This meaning is clear throughout the play and is explicitly stated in the final words of the heroine:

> I am Liberty because love willed it so.
> Pedro: the Liberty for which you left me.
> I am the Liberty wounded by mankind.
> Love, love, love, and eternal solitude.

Only in a few words by Don Pedro, in scene 2, can we possibly see a direct allusion to politics:

> It is not the time to think of fancies, it is time
> to open the breast to beautiful realities at hand,
> of a Spain covered with wheat and flocks of
>   sheep,
> where people eat their bread with joy,
> in these wide eternities of ours
> and this keen passion for breadth and silence.
> Spain buries and treads on her old heart,
> her wounded heart of an errant peninsula
> and we must save her soon with our hands and
>   our teeth.

Outside of these lines, the play develops through exclusively artistic channels, within a typically Lorcan world in which social preoccupations seldom exist, except as a projection of deeper human problems.

SHORT PLAYS, FARCES

Far better constructed, although of less emotional intensity, are the works which followed *Mariana Pineda.* We find in them again the same qualities—expertness, self-confidence, stylization—as in his *Book of Songs,* but here enriched by a well-defined and conscious ironic grace.

Three farces in prose, written between 1929 and 1931, make up this phase of his work and constitute at the same time a group by themselves within his theatrical writings. The first is *Amor de Don Perlimplín con Belisa en su jardin (The Love of Don Perlimplín for Belisa, in His Garden)*, not produced until 1933 but written long before then. Then came *La zapatera prodigiosa (The Shoemaker's Prodigious Wife)*, first presented in the *Teatro Español* of Madrid in 1930 and later in an enlarged version in the Coliseum Theater in 1935; and finally the delightful *Retablillo de Don Cristóbal (In the Frame of Don Cristóbal)*, a farce for puppets dated 1931 in the Losada edition of Lorca's complete works.

They have in common the same stylized popular background and a similar theatrical technique which results from the combination of elements taken from the courtly comedies at the end of the seventeenth and the beginning of the eighteenth centuries, from the Italian stage, from the puppet theater, and from the modern ballet. Each one, depending on which element predominates, has its particular character.

The Love of Don Perlimplín is the most cultivated of the group in technique and the most lyrical in spirit. Although not distinguished by the careful technique or the lively movement of *The Shoemaker's Prodigious Wife,* it is nevertheless superior in its poetic qualities. Always within the framework of irony, we can detect passages of beautiful lyricism, as in Perlimplín's lament: "Love, love, wounded love," and in Belisa's song: "Along the banks of the river." In the third scene—Perlimplín's suicide—buffoonery is raised to an atmosphere of delicate melancholy. The playfulness of the farce becomes impregnated by a pathetic aura, diffused in soft tones like the sonatas of Scarlatti, which were used by Lorca as melodic interludes, or like the poetic theater of Musset, which Lorca had read with great interest. We find ourselves at the limit of pantomime where an intentional dehumanization of characters takes place, and nevertheless we perceive in the comic profile of Don Perlimplín his sentimental anguish, caused by a love which is at the same time pure and grotesque.

The Shoemaker's Prodigious Wife is a stylization of pure folk charm, the most complete and successful work of this group. Directly inspired by folklore, the shoemaker and his wife, the chorus of neighbors, the dialogue and the action are conceived with a picaresque, old Spanish flavor, which reminds us of certain short plays of the Golden Age. The popular ballad of the shoemaker preserves the common and clumsy flavor of the ballads commonly recited by blind men, refined through touches of the best poetic quality. The play is an exercise in wit: the few dramatic scenes are expressed in a knowing gradation through the contradictory feelings of the shoemaker's wife toward her husband. Throughout she is bad-tempered and tender, piquant and impudent. The farce is resolved in the triumph of love, when the shoemaker and the shoemaker's wife are reunited. Even within the framework of comedy Lorca places a trace of bittersweetness, when after the reconciliation of the couple the work closes with the half serious, half ironic lamentations and insults of the shoemaker's wife: "How unfortunate I am with this man that God has given me!" We should take notice of this ending, basically a happy one, because it is the only time that it occurs in Lorca's dramatic works, which are primarily concerned with frustrated love. As in his other plays, the music—song, rhythm, background—has an essential role, producing an effect of unreality and giving the play the subtlety, grace, and movement of a ballet.

In the Frame of Don Cristóbal, like *Los títeres de Cachiporra (Cachiporra's Puppets)*, comes from the period of the first youthful experiments and was inspired directly by the puppet theater. It is not much more than a game, a folk Andalusian *divertissement;* it is important only as an example of Lorca's versatility, that constant search for a better integration of the arts which characterizes his theatrical writings as much as his poetry. It also reveals the piquant background of malicious country wit which was part of his mental makeup and added spice to his conversation. *In the Frame of Don Cristóbal,* full of naïve fantasy, is a magnificent example of "naughtiness" and spontaneity.

These short unpretentious plays illustrate typical aspects of Lorca's artistic personality; his more profound self we find in his treatment of anguish and tragedy, but even here we shall continue to find a counterweight of light and joyfulness, of pleasure generated by wit and innocent irony.

EXPERIMENTS IN SURREALISTIC THEATER

Asi que pasen cinco años (If Five Years Pass) and some scenes from the drama *El público (The Public)*, written between 1929 and 1930, belong to the period in which he was interested in Surrealism. This work comes a little after or at the same time as his poems about New York City. They coincide with the climax of Surrealism in France and its reflection in Spain, with Alberti in poetry and Gómez de la Serna and Azorín on the stage. Lorca never made up his mind to stage them, and it is possible that once the vogue for this kind of art had passed, he did not pay much attention to them.

The fragments that we know from *El público* do not give us an accurate idea of the total work. It seems to have been inspired by the problem of reality and poetic "superreality" on the stage and in real life. Besides, we can detect in several episodes a vein of perverse and abnormal sensuality corresponding to the preoccupations which must have tormented him during those years. The characters are beings of fantasy and beings taken from real life, without any distinction between them. All act and speak with the same incoherent automatism. The play is full of bloody and violent images mixed with humor. In the first extant scene he formulates the poetic idea of the metamorphosis of forms, which constitutes the basis of all Surrealistic aesthetics:

> *Figure covered with little bells:*
>   If I should change into a cloud . . .
> *Figure covered with tendrils:*
>   Then I would change myself into an eye.

This is an idea which inspired some of the poems of *Poet in New York.* It reminds us especially of **"Death"**: "What an effort, / what an effort of the horse / to become a dog," etc.

If Five Years Pass ("a legend about time in three acts and five scenes") is of greater interest than *El público*. Here the theme is a combination of two typically Lorcan preoccupations: the passing of time and the frustrations of love. The central characters, the young man and the fiancée, are new versions of Marfisa and Don Perlimplín and the waiting for a wedding which never takes place is almost a foretaste of *DOÑA ROSITA LA SOLTERA* (*Doña Rosita the Spinster*). The technique and the atmosphere are, however, completely Surrealistic. It is an atmosphere of dreams, with masks, mannequins, clowns, or real people like the rugby player or the card players dehumanized in the manner of the characters of Gómez de la Serna, to whose influence this work is largely indebted. Lorca manages to sustain an unreal atmosphere suspended somewhere between humor and drama and with an undercurrent of mysterious sensuality. As in the best of his plays, the lyric elements are ever present. The scene of the dead child and the cat in the first act has all the characteristics of his poems about children, including the use of images, the "white handkerchief," "the roses that wounded my throat," the "voice of silver," the "fish through the water," and so forth. Many other poetic fragments of this play bear the imprint of the best of Lorca, as this delightful song of the rain:

> I return for my wings,
> let me return.
> I want to die being dawn,
> I want to die being
> yesterday.
> I return for my wings,
> let me return.
> I want to die being a spring.
> I want to die away from the sea . . .

The dialogue, whether in prose or in verse, almost always shows a growing mastery of the theatrical technique which the poet was slowly acquiring through his various experiments. Lorca never confined himself to a definite type of poetry or of drama nor to the inflexible formula of any fixed school. Thus, having learned all he could from it, he soon abandoned Surrealism and returned for inspiration to the feelings and themes of Spanish reality where his art finally found its focal point.

DONA ROSITA THE SPINSTER

Leaving aside till later the analysis of *Blood Wedding* and *Yerma,* which in our opinion occupy a unique place in the dramatic works of Lorca, we now come to examine the last play staged during the poet's life, in which the sentimental attitude of his first years reappears, but enriched by all the experiences of his artistic development.

Doña Rosita the Spinster, or The Language of Flowers, was produced in Barcelona by Margarita Xirgu the thirteenth of December, 1955. It had enormous success and the critics saw in the play a new trend of Lorca's already many-sided dramatic art. If his tragedies represent a balance between lyricism and drama, *Doña Rosita* is the fusion of poetry and comedy, with subtle historical overtones.

The author describes the work as "a poem of Granada in 1900 divided into various 'gardens' with scenes of singing and dancing." Like *Mariana Pineda,* to which it bears a strong resemblance in technique and mood, it deals with the evocation of a period. But the shading of the poetic, plastic and emotional elements of the play is better achieved. The direct romanticism of the earlier work now becomes soft irony. The intense drama of love becomes diluted and is dissolved into lyrical fragrances. The somewhat artificial pathos of *Mariana Pineda* is replaced by a sweet melancholy, a pure and intense emotion. Doña Rosita, a woman (the most important characters in Lorca's plays are always women), is not a heroine but rather a symbol of womanhood in the Spanish provinces at the end of the century. Thus we have a lack of real dramatic intensity. In order to become a deep psychological play it would have had to delve into the individual soul of the characters. This is precisely one of the main shortcomings in all of Lorca's plays, including his tragedies, where passion never quite acquires full psychological embodiment and always remains skin deep, with no motivation other than a kind of tragic destiny before which the characters submit with hardly a struggle. What happens in *Doña Rosita* is that the poet turns this limitation into his main creative force. The drama of resigned love incarnated in Doña Rosita, the endless waiting for the sweetheart who will not return, is consciously subordinated to a more impersonal anguish: what moves the spectator is neither the passion nor the suffering of the protagonist but the bodiless presence of time itself hovering over the stage and the life of every character. Lorca is a master of creating a lyrical atmosphere, and in this play he succeeds completely. The evocation of those quiet years from 1890 to 1910 in which Spanish life seemed to be at a standstill as if it had lost all its vital springs gives us a perfect picture of both reality and trite pathos, touching in its irony. All the sentimental mood of the play, all its lyrical quality find their maximum expression in the "language of flowers," a symbol of existence without desires and without ambitions, and a symbol at the same time of the slow withering of Doña Rosita:

> The rose? It was still open
> but night was coming fast
> and the thud of sad snow
> was weighing on its branch;
> when the shadows returned
> the nightingale still sang,
> but she, with deathly pallor
> into the darkness shrank,
> and when a metal horn
> sent shivers through the night
> and the wind embraced the mountain
> falling asleep on its lap
> she lost her petals and died
> while dawn gathered her last sigh.

Some critics have mentioned the influence of Chekhov. There seems to be a definite similarity between both writers. The end of the play, when the mother, the governess, and Rosita leave the house, taking with them all their memories, while the wind softly moves the curtains and the stage is engulfed by the weight of loneliness, cannot but remind us of the almost identical end of *The Cherry Orchard.* Other points of coincidence with Chekhov, whose works Lorca doubtlessly knew, could be found. There is the fact that both turn to nature when looking for a symbol of action and a lyrical background. The atmosphere in *Doña Rosita* reminds us in many ways of the melancholic atmosphere in *Three Sisters.* But the parallels seem to end there. There can be no similarity between Lorca's characters, as simple as shadows, and the characters created by the Russian playwright, who are at the brink of desperation, and struggle tragically while looking for a justification of their existence. Chekhov's lyricism is the result of a delving into the deepest layers of human feelings and human anguish; in Lorca lyricism is a poetic fact alien to every intellectual and psychological motivation.

Neither in *Doña Rosita* nor in his dramas can Lorca's art be characterized by its intellectual strength. Its essence is rather an instinctive intuitive penetration and an extraordinary gift for poetical expression.

MATURE WORKS

Born during a period of permanent crisis in art and in society, Lorca was bound to reflect in every facet of his work the varied experiments of the new aesthetics, struggling to find a firm basis and solid ground. This variety of styles can be explained by the influx of new literary movements, the new "isms" that have dominated the arts since the First World War. It differs nevertheless from the variety and the changes in style to be found in the works of many poets or artists of our time, inasmuch as throughout Lorca's works a personal accent and the expression of a personality basically impervious to outside influences can be detected. The development of his different facets was carried through a long process of growing simplicity and integration. The abundant and sometimes confusing themes and feelings of his youthful poetry became increasingly pure and simple; the experiences and artistic forms suggested by the changes in modern sensitivity and the restlessness of his own moods became increasingly better integrated. This phenomenon need not be ascribed only to Lorca; it can be observed in every true artist, in almost any period. What seems to be characteristic of Lorca is its pervasive importance and at the same time its fruitfulness. Without sacrificing any essential element in his inspiration, he managed to create a synthesis which finally became stabilized around certain folk themes. These folk themes were "popular" in the best sense of the word, because of the essentially traditional nature of style and form and because of the spiritual and poetic contents. In *Blood Wedding, Yerma, Lament for the Death of a Bullfighter,* we find the same human, elementary, passionate mood of the *Poem of the Cante Jondo* and the *Gypsy Ballads.* The poet comes back to the Andalusian world, but now, in a splendid artistic plenitude, all that was marginal or merely picturesque disappears, only essences remain.

POETIC TRAGEDIES

In *Blood Wedding* (another English title for the same work is *Bitter Oleander*), which had its premiere in the Beatriz Theater in Madrid in 1933, Lorca for the first time finds the right expression for the passionate intensity vibrating in the inner recesses of his best poetry: a peasant tragedy. At times the dehumanized, stylized art of his songs and stage artifices make us forget the frantic trembling of life and nature which the voice of this dark and passionate poet brought to us from the time of his earliest creations. This constantly present trembling of life can be found in the dramatic quality of his lyrical poetry as well as in his tragedies, where it comes to be felt with all its violence, subordinating the lyrical content to the dramatic tone in a perfect fusion which Lorca had to achieve if he wished to express fully his most complete self.

"I was," the Fiancée says, "a burnt woman, full of sores outside and within. And your son was a drop of water from whom I expected children, earth, health." Here is the essential element of tragedy: beings who are scorched by a deep passion against which it is futile to struggle. The situation is a simple one and an old one: the rivalry within a family, and the rivalry of two men for a woman who struggles between the attraction of a fiancé, who offers her peace of mind, and the more powerful attraction of her lover. However, having been abandoned by her lover, Leonardo, who, in the meantime, has killed off many relatives of her prospective bridegroom's family, the Fiancée finally decides to get married. The preparations for the wedding are clouded by premonitions. The wedding takes place in an atmosphere full of bad omens; there is the presence of Leonardo, now married to another woman, the flight of the lovers, and the death of the rivals after a pursuit and a frantic struggle in the forest. At the end we find the three women, the Fiancée, the Mother, and Leonardo's Widow, expressing their hatred, their sorrow, and their loneliness when confronted by death, among the lamenting chorus of the neighbors.

Using this basic and timeless plot, Lorca creates a drama in which the dark and somber passion of tragedy becomes stylized within a lyrical and musical framework, but without losing any of its intensity. Straightforward to the point of being schematic in the exposition and development of dramatic conflict, he makes use with admirable economy of all the known devices of his art. Music has a role, together with folk poetry, in the lullabies and wedding songs, and in the rhythm which envelops the action (especially noticeable in the psalmodic tone of the concluding lamentations). Lyricism has its role in the characteristic themes of Lorca's Andalusian vision: the horse, the knife, the rider, the flowers, or in the nocturnal symbolism of the scene with the woodcutters and the moon. The tiniest slip in the handling of any of these elements of the play would have reduced it to a melodrama of local color and have destroyed the nobility of its inspiration by scenes of facile and mannered lyricism.

Blood Wedding is saved from these dangers through its balance and precision. Although some of its musical interludes or lyrical fugues might better have been eliminated, they nevertheless do not break the classical structure of the plot, nor do they destroy the cold and objective pathos of the forces which move the characters and even give them a universal meaning.

Sensuality, hatred, love, and tragic destiny bringing with

it a bloody and violent death are the central themes of this play. Underneath them as the source of all these human and elemental events, raising tragedy to the level of inescapable fatality, is the earth, the land, which possesses and inspires all the characters. Leonardo will say as his only justification for his criminal love:

> For the guilt cannot be mine,
> for the guilt is in the land
> and this fragrance that arises
> from your breasts and from your hands.

The woodcutters in their symbolic commentary during the scene of the crime will explain the earth's power as a fate, an end, a goal which gives birth to human desires, the desires of the two lovers, and also provides an end to them:

> FIRST WOODCUTTER: They were deceiving each other and finally blood was more powerful than either one of them.
>
> THIRD WOODCUTTER: Blood.
>
> FIRST WOODCUTTER: We must follow the blood's path.
>
> SECOND WOODCUTTER: But blood that sees light the earth drinks up again.

The earth is above all the wet clay which nourishes the roots of grief and the hatred of the Mother, the true incarnation of the moving pathos of tragedy. In the final scene she says to the Neighbors,

> Your tears are tears only of the eyes. And my tears will come when I am alone; they will come up from the soles of my feet, from my roots, and they will burn more than blood.

The earth is the only companion of her solitude, because in it there lie the beings born from her womb:

> I will make out of my dream a cold dove of ivory which will carry camellias of frost to the churchyard. But no, not a churchyard: a bed of earth . . . I do not wish to see anyone. The earth and I . . .

The earth is the only consolation, because it changes the blood of the dead into a new fountain of life, and so when the Fiancée appears before the Mother asking to be sacrificed in atonement for her guilt, she controls her impulse toward vengeance and hardly looks at her:

> But, what do I care for your honor? Why do I care for your death? What do I care for anything? Blessed be the wheat, because my sons are beneath it; blessed be the rain, because it moistens the face of the dead; blessed be God, who lays us out to rest.

The play should have ended here. Lorca fell into the temptation of closing upon a lyrical-musical-symbolic scene and added a chorus where there are allusions to sunflowers, bitter oleanders, sweet nails, and small knives and which spoils to some degree the tragic tone of the final scene.

Blood Wedding is a work of the highest artistic rank. In it we can detect the breath of classical influence, a touch of Mediterranean tragedy and even a certain Shakespear-

ian quality. The sources are many. From the Spanish traditional comedy it has borrowed the peasant touches and the technique of fusing music and action. The whole atmosphere of the wedding scene is reminiscent of Lope de Vega. Modern touches can be found in the symbolism of death, which seems inspired by Maeterlinck, and in the Andalusian folk background accompanied by realistic details that suggest the Machado brothers. The poet's use of naked tragedy also brings to mind D'Annunzio or Valle-Inclán, but it is without the literary affectation of D'Annunzio or the purely verbal charm and the archaic atmosphere of Valle-Inclán. When we mention these influences, we are not speaking about direct and literal influences but rather of vague subconscious memories (with a possible exception to be made in the case of Lope). Essentially Lorca does not abandon for even one second his own peculiar poetic world and his usual method of composition, with all its limitations and all its genius. A typically Lorcan play with its mixture of different elements, *Blood Wedding* does not have a clear precedent or source. It may very well miss becoming a world classic because of its local color and the fact that its action seems limited and appears to lack real spiritual content. The lukewarm reception by the public of its English and French versions shows that many of its values are lost in translation and that a great deal of its atmosphere can be communicated only to a Spanish-speaking public steeped in Spanish artistic traditions. But even with all these reservations, it is impossible to doubt the exceptional value of this play. The unity of its poetic elements, the moving clarity of its drama, and the breath of folk life that animates it make it the most complete and beautiful masterpiece of Lorca's theater and place it well above the mediocre productions of today's Spanish dramatic literature.

Yerma, written two years later, is similar in its main idea and its technique to *Blood Wedding.* In many ways it is a more finished product. The subject is a more ambitious one. Lorca had been elaborating it for many years. It deals with a love frustrated because of man's powerlessness to respond to woman's passion. The subject appears in some of Lorca's earliest poems and reappears later as an obsession in *Mariana Pineda,* in some of the *Gypsy Ballads,* in *Don Perlimplín,* in *If Five Years Pass,* in *Doña Rosita.* Sometimes he deals with spiritual love, sometimes with sensuous lubricity. In *Yerma* the situation develops within the framework of frustrated motherhood, and the passion becomes intimate and spiritualized. The play's structure follows an order in which dramatic elements predominate. The lyrical elements—songs, washerwomen's chorus—are less important. The tragic conflict acquires greater density because within a primary climate of passion surrounding the characters there is a more complex hierarchy of forces. As in *Blood Wedding,* there is a suggestion of pagan forces struggling in Yerma's soul against her moral sense of duty, until she is incapable of giving in to either of the two forces and decides to kill her husband.

In spite of all this and perhaps because of its ambitious scope, *Yerma* does not quite reach the artistic level of *Blood Wedding.* It does not have the same artistic unity; the dramatic motivation is less clear. In *Blood Wedding* everything is concrete and basic, earthy, within a folk poetic atmosphere. In *Yerma* at bottom every element strains toward abstraction. We could well suspect that Unamuno's presence hovered around Lorca's subconscious while he was writing *Yerma.* The very character of the heroine reminds us of Unamuno's literary creations. Her last words, after killing her husband, seem inspired by the author of *The Tragic Sense of Life:*

> Do not come near me for I have killed my son.
> I myself have killed my son!

Doubtlessly Lorca wanted to go beyond Unamuno's disembodied approach to tragedy; he wanted to add to it life, blood, individuality. He managed to do so up to a point, but in order to give to Yerma's intimate anguish all its pathos and its universal meaning he needed instruments for abstract reasoning and at the same time for subtle psychological penetration. These Unamuno possessed abundantly but Lorca lacked, being an intuitive spontaneous artist. Lorca's domain extended from direct speech to symbols, from folk elements to stylization. That is why the reading of *Yerma* is somewhat disappointing. We do not find in it the lyrical pathos or the burning dialogue of *Blood Wedding.* Perhaps on stage the effect would be more positive. Lorca's theater is in great measure a spectacular theater and words lose a great part of their meaning when read outside a total atmosphere that was posited at the very moment the work was written. Lorca was a past master in the rendering of dramatic elements in terms of visual details, rhythm, and lyrical symbols.

Yerma is one more step toward the intensification of tragedy. This purpose seems also to inspire Lorca's last tragedy, *The House of Bernarda Alba,* which according to his friends he finished a short time before his death. This last play was, with *Yerma,* part of a trilogy on the theme of sexual obsession and unfulfilled love, a theme, as we have pointed out previously, that is one of Lorca's most characteristic and permanent, since it is at bottom a projection of the conflict between pagan and Christian attitudes which is ever present in the Andalusian soul and basic for the psychology and the artistic temperament of Lorca.

Adolfo Salazar, one of the poet's friends who had heard Lorca's reading of the play, has published the following synopsis of it:

> Seven women, without a man, in a country house, closed down by a recent mourning, within the calcinated atmosphere of an Andalusian August. Bernarda Alba is a character that seems to come out of the classical Greek stage, as does Yerma, as does the Mother in *Blood Wedding;* a crazy old woman, long time a widow; an old servant; and the four daughters of Bernarda Alba. Seven women without a man who try to catch a glimpse of Pepe el Romano's warm shadow. Three anguished, dry, laconic acts. Words of ice beneath which beats rancor; the hatred of one woman toward another in whom she suspects a possible rival. Because Pepe el Romano, who is never seen on the stage, is constantly present and his corduroy trousers dance before the eyes of the seven women tortured by sex. A brutal episode: the distant beating, of which only the rumor is heard, of the woman who commit-

ted adultery . . . Pepe el Romano succeeds in evading the hundred eyes of Bernarda—Argus and Medusa under the guise of a vestal virgin watching over the chastity of her daughters. The adulteress . . . Pepe el Romano's portrait under the pillow . . . The youngest daughter, the one who was not yet bitter. A noise in the barn. A woman hung from a rope . . . Bernarda's form grows larger. She ascends a mythological peak. Silence! Not a word of this outside of this house! Silence! Let no one suspect anything. The hatred of the rejected ones is the only responsory for the dead girl.

Salazar adds that every time Lorca finished reading a scene he exclaimed with enthusiasm: "Not a drop of poetry! Reality! Realism!" This seemed to be his goal and aspiration: to reach cold, objective, essential tragedy, tragedy without any lyrical addition. He was reaching a serene maturity without having lost any of his fresh creative genius. It is therefore not surprising that in the *House of Bernarda Alba* he may have achieved a complete and inspired masterpiece, anticipated by *Blood Wedding* and prepared by *Yerma,* which, although less accomplished as works of art, had already given him a first classical pattern. (pp. 140-54)

Angel del Rio, "Lorca's Theater," translated by Gloria Bradley, in Lorca: A Collection of Critical Essays, *edited by Manuel Duran, Prentice-Hall, Inc., 1962, pp. 140-54.*

Garcia Lorca in 1927 at his family home in Granada.

Francisco García Lorca   (essay date 1947)

[*In the following excerpt from his prologue to Lorca's* Three Tragedies, *originally published in 1947, the dramatist's brother examines the themes and style of several of Lorca's plays, focusing on his procedure in writing for the theater. Francisco Lorca here emphasizes his brother's constant experimentation with poetry in drama and his intuitive approach to composing, noting that "the part he turned over to a process of unconscious cerebration was enormous."*]

Doña Rosita, perhaps the most lyric in tone of all [of Federico García Lorca's] plays, contains more elements of reality in it than all the plays which preceded it. Naturally, there are different planes of reality in this work, as in almost all of them. Here, there is a reality made poetic: the atmosphere of Granada. It is what one might call the play's spirit, and it would still be in it even without a single direct reference—just as it exists, in another way, in *Don Perlimplín.* In *Doña Rosita* the evocation of the atmosphere, and of the period, are created without sparing a single detail. Proper names of Granada families, real happenings, real persons, and literary ones, appear. Some of the incidents which would seem most improbable spring straight from reality. Many of the phrases of the Economics Instructor—"I do not possess a sufficient volume of experience . . . ," and others—are out of the speech of persons known in the Spanish faculty. Never till then had the poet so resorted to actual happenings as in this play, the only one for which he 'did research.'

I remember seeing 1900 almanacs and magazines on his work table in our Granada garden. The ballad about the language of the flowers was made from a little book that contained, besides the language of the flowers, that of stamps, the fan, dreams, etc. The allusions to automobile races and such other details are taken from books. What is more, the description of the *mutabile* rose, which constitutes the play's essence, and the descriptions of the *hispid* and *inermis* roses are data out of an old botany book which the poet, Moreno Villa, showed Federico, and which finally crystallized the idea of *Doña Rosita.*

This play haunted the poet's imagination for many years and was the longest in maturing among all that he wrote. Its conception was such a task to him that I know that when he saw it finished it was a load off his shoulders. To understand this statement better, one must know how Federico 'worked': abandoning projects, forgetting themes, and then letting them be reborn in his memory to the spark of some new reality. More than by thinking things out, by allowing things—to say it with an Unamunesque phrase—to think him out: until those two worlds met and welded—which was the time to write. And then, what ease, what simplicity and at bottom, what joy in the task of creating.

But he would not spare his errors or his weaknesses until he overcame them. I believe that with *Doña Rosita,* written with great care, he overcame the private failure of *Mariana Pineda.* One can almost imagine something like a rivalry with the city of Granada itself—a desire to possess it artistically and to express it. From Mariana Pineda's lyric Granada he moved to a more complex Granada

which he loved and disdained, over which he laughed and wept. I do not want to speak of the outcome of this relationship, which seems an awful vengeance of the city against the soul that best expressed it.

Likewise, to me, *The Love of Don Perlimplín* is the victory over that other frustrated exercise of his, *The Butterfly's Evil Spell,* with which this play has a number of thematic relationships. This is the Butterfly which, freed now, still flutters among the plays in *The Shoemaker's Prodigious Wife.*

This innate tenacity of his character surprises me, as I consider it today. It is a tenacity unperceived by those who saw him pass through life, voluble, vagabond, a troubadour.

Into the three plays that make up this book, reality enters in diverse fashions. Reality and dramatic (that is to say, poetic) values are balanced in different ways. (pp. 18-19)

Blood Wedding was inspired by a newspaper account of an incident almost identical with the plot of the play, which took place in Almería. However, many years passed before he decided to write the play; it had a gestation period almost as long as *Doña Rosita* did.

After grasping reality, it was as though he needed to draw away from it, to dream on it anew, then to incorporate the live persons into his own poetic mythology. It is perfectly apparent that the characters in *Blood Wedding* went through this evolutionary process.

I do not know how many times he told me about the play. Then he would forget it; later it would reappear, but transformed (he never wrote down a play's outline) until, fully conceived at last in his fantasy, he wrote it. If I remember correctly, *Blood Wedding* only took a week to write; but in maturing it took years.

Most times he did not himself know what was going to happen in a play—yet it would later surprise me how he would have foreseen, in a first act, what would have its justification in a third. The part he turned over to a process of unconscious cerebration was enormous. And it is not only for such works as *If Five Years Pass* that this statement holds true, but in great measure for all of them.

His procedure in writing for the theatre did not vary greatly from the one he adopted for poetry. What was perhaps a play's essential part he entrusted to instinct. If he had not been a born playwright he could never have brought a dramatic work to realization.

In *Blood Wedding* there is a palpable (and I do not know if I should add, but involuntary) intention of taking the play's atmosphere away from any nature of a newspaper story. From the field of the very human passions of concrete beings he removes to an unreal world, one in which the appearances of mysterious and fantastic players (as in the personification of the Moon and Death) are possible. Then he makes the flesh-and-blood characters rise to a plane less real, one which converts them into forces whose incentives are outside themselves. At the play's climax, one of the characters says this:

"For the fault is not mine;
the fault is the earth's."

And a lesser one:

"Blood that sees the light
is drunk up by the earth."

In this fusion with nature—for more than nature it is Earth herself they tread on—the characters have lost individuality. They have moved away from the newspaper account from which they came but they have gained in human and poetic significance. They have been converted into anonymous beings who possess a country's generic character, who are opposed by a tragic personage, their fate, and who are led by this fate among songs and premonitions toward death. As the great poet, Pedro Salinas, says, "*Blood Wedding* gives body, dramatic realization, and the category of great art to a concept of human life borne along time's length in a people's innermost being and traditionally remembered and kept alive in it: the concept of human fatality" [*Literatura Española del Siglo XX,* 1941].

Thus there is a greater abundance of poetic themes in this work; the turning to verse in climactic situations is frequent. Even more: the moments of the play's greatest dramatic intensity are in verse. But Federico never turns to this technical device without a careful preparation. The final episode of the next to last scene, an episode unequaled in dramatic sensuality, is preceded by a series of fantastic appearances which makes the use of verse and of the characters' poetic expressions seem natural. This to such a degree that the episode is imbued with a tone that surpasses in realism the scenes of greater realistic intention.

To some critics this is the play which best achieves an integration of poetry and drama. It is the most spontaneous and simple because the poet does not struggle against his poetic instinct; he gives himself over to it, but without forgetfulness of his previous experiences.

In spite of this, Federico considered that his theatre would benefit by a more austere technique, progressing toward drama by the roads furthest removed from lyric forms. It is curious that in *Yerma,* while seeking a design simpler in elements and further purged of the ingredients of fantasy, instead of staying closer to reality he moved away from it. Of the trilogy contained in this book, *Yerma* is the play which has the smallest number of elements directly inspired by reality. Federico turned to a theme present in all his lyric and dramatic work—that of a frustrated instinct for motherhood; this theme he embodied in the character that is the most symbolic in all his theatre, perhaps the most dramatic and, I was about to say, the most poetic.

The drama centers about the violence with which the main character lives her personal conflict. It has been argued—a little childishly, to my notion—that Yerma's dramatic obsession is not entirely justified psychologically, since it could have a solution. And in effect, it could have one, and there would be no drama, by making Yerma cease to be Yerma—that is to say, by making her cease to feel her maternal instinct tragically. Or, with the easy solution (entirely problematical in another sense) of changing men. It would not be worth the effort to falsify Yerma's character

by making her violate her sense of duty—another defining trait of her character—so that afterward she might continue being Yerma as before. This solution is proposed in the play and rejected.

In spite of the fact that in *Yerma* reality appears as the well of direct inspiration in lesser measure than in the other two plays, the secondary characters, to my judgment, have a greater individuality than those in *Blood Wedding.* In spite of Yerma's poetic atmosphere, in spite of the fact that in it poetic speech—which continues to have that characteristic poetic realism—is not abandoned but simply made purer, the characters no longer live submissive to forces extraneous and superior to themselves, but with themselves as centres. As a case in point, I cite that the Moon does not, as in *Blood Wedding,* prepare the blood's pathway. The Pagan Crone (in all his theatre, one of the characters most alive) chooses her own road as, fundamentally, Yerma herself does.

The drama is not determined by external accidents or, finally, by such chance as the meeting of two persons. In *Blood Wedding,* a knife can be drama's final reason. The poet is shaken that an insignificant hazard, an inert and tiny object, should be able to put an end to the blood's live torrent. But in *Yerma* the conflict is determined by a force that struggles against itself within the soul. A violent anxiety of fertility and sterility, or on another plane, of life and death—as in all of Federico's plays. Man's essential drama.

The instrument which brings death to that child who never existed except in the form of a desperate hope is Yerma herself. The solution, if the term may be so used, she gives out of her own flesh. It is the right thing for the play that Yerma should kill with her own hands and not with a knife, as in *Blood Wedding;* those hands held the power of death, embodied by now in the central character herself. In the final scene, prepared by a frenzied dance to life, what is mourned is nothing other than the symbolic death of Yerma, now without direction or justification. It is Yerma who dies, just as it was she who was in final agony before. In the play's dramatic conception everything is a reference to the single character. . . . At the play's dress rehearsal in Madrid Don Miguel [de Unamuno] was present. With great generosity, he said to the author: "This is the play I wish I had written."

A confluence of traditional Spanish theatre tendencies, plastic and musical, is brought about in this play. This is achieved in a purer classic conception, toward which the poet turned his eyes in search for simplicity and sobriety. It is already expressed in the very title, *Yerma*—"Barren." An invented name, symbolic, univocal, which answers the play's conception in a perfect fashion.

Apropos of this, let me be forgiven if I recall the sureness and exactness with which Federico named his plays. Common, everyday objects he liked to call by fantastic and capricious names—many times by invented ones; and he carried this game, like others, to his life's end. But poetic things he liked to call by their own names. He is perhaps the only poet of his generation who did not endow his books of poems with literary names. His first book is called, simply, **Book of Poems.** He called **Songs** a book of songs and **Gypsy Balladeer** a book of ballads. Other titles stand as examples of the tendency: **Poems of the Cante Jondo, Lament for Ignacio Sánchez Mejías, Poet in New York.**

The only exception, and this but a relative one, is the book written in homage to the Arabic Andalusian poets, the **Divan of the Tamarit.** Here the literary lies in the use of the word 'divan' to mean collection; it is otherwise justified, however, since Tamarit is the Arabic name for the district in which the Granadine garden where this book was written is situated.

The same thing could be said of his plays. Wherever a literary name is used, an ironic allusion that goes beyond the term's aptness is implied, as in the subtitle of **Doña Rosita, the Spinster,** which is, **The Language of the Flowers.** Take too, **The Love of Don Perlimplín and Belisa in the Garden**—a play which the poet has called an 'allelujah.' Particularly meaningful is the title **If Five Years Pass** for, beyond its poetic implication, the phrase might be the exact wording in simple prose of what happens in the play. Everywhere in Federico we find a double affirmation of poetry and truth.

Of the titles which made up this trilogy we have already cited **Yerma. Blood Wedding** is the only one which makes no reference to a proper name: the most directly poetic of the three titles, and the least personalized.

In **Blood Wedding** the theme—as the poet promises and fulfills—is more the noun, *wedding,* than the characters themselves. Thus in the cast appear the Mother, the Bridegroom, the Betrothed, etc. But there is only one character with a name of his own—Leonardo: the most realistic character in the play, and the most 'biographical.' Though he also is destroyed by his destiny, he, more than the others, moves toward events of his own will. It is not that his will is stronger than that of the Mother or the Betrothed, but that things happen to them, while basically he, Leonardo, goes looking for them to happen. The most dramatic character is the Mother; to her the greatest number of things outside the radius of her will happen. She is the chosen character of the blind forces. That is why Leonardo, the most individualized character, is the one who least stands out, the one who is furthest from the conception expressed in the title, **Blood Wedding.** And this in spite of the fact that that blood is his.

Yerma is the transition point toward **The House of Bernarda Alba.** And in this latter, just the opposite of **Blood Wedding,** all the characters have names. The title, which alludes to a family atmosphere dominated by one figure, applies to the context with the same exactness and expresses the dramatic conception which guided the poet. Bernarda Alba is no longer only a given name, but a family name. Even the oppressive monotony of a dominant and tyrannical character is expressed in the magnificent alliteration of the a's: **La Casa de Bernarda Alba.**

This play . . . boasts such economy of lyric elements as to make almost a display of virtuosity out of it. The poet intensified his own tendencies to such an extreme that he achieved a work that lies at the farthest point of his drama's roads. Even though his own express statement would not be needed for an interpretation such as this, he did tell me that with this play he closed the cycle, gathered in this trilogy, of rural dramas—a cycle so alike in its character and themes, so diverse in conception and technical resources.

The House of Bernarda Alba, of these plays, is the one which has the most direct inspiration in reality. In this it is the exact opposite of **Blood Wedding,** in which everything is invented except the plot. In **Bernarda,** everything except the story is inspired by reality. The story was potentially possible in the given setting; the characters are modified, as is natural, to make the plot possible.

But not a single one of the characters, even those who do not take part but are merely alluded to, and not a single act of those who serve as background proceed directly from the poet's imagination. And in spite of this basic reality, I would say that this is his most artful play and the one which is most disciplined in technique. In a certain way, it is the most *artistic* in its strangeness. His tendency of making female characters the most important ones in his theatre is accentuated until he produces a drama of women only. (pp. 19-26)

Bernarda as a drama is characterized not only by the part played by reality, but by the interpretation of this reality, since the real basis only provides the artistic matter. In the play I think we may perceive a certain type of realism—and this is an approach already anticipated in others of his plays—nearer to the interpretive forms which have been considered as typically representative of what is Spanish.

In no other work of the author's do we find with such power the affirmation of the character of the personages, the defense of their individuality. Others of his poetic creatures, since they are conceived on another plane, struggle against their destinies, but at bottom convinced that it is impossible to overcome the unappeasable forces which play with man's fate.

"You have to follow the blood's road . . . " "When things reach their centres . . . "—there is no one who can stand against them. Certainly this conformity with destiny—to say it with a religious word, this resignation—is human and Spanish. But it also is, and more representatively so, in a certain way, the will's steadfastness before destiny and before death. In this sense, the psychological attitude of the characters has changed in **The House of Bernarda Alba.**

And the play's dramatic tension is born precisely out of the clash of these wills. Of the domineering will of the mother, upheld by the forces of tradition, of custom, of social values—and of the deaf and invincible wills of the daughters, dragged by their thirst for living and by impulses and instincts which clash with each other in their turn. And over all of them, a tragic sense of life against which nothing avails. That is why it is curious and why it underscores the attitude of the central character that, when she is faced with the death of the daughter who has hanged herself with the cord with which the mother symbolically would have bound all of them, Bernarda finishes the drama with a shout of triumph, an illusory triumph, like Doña Perfectá's.

Here it would be opportune to cite the different road down which the playwright turned to achieve an artistic interpretation of reality. Before, the poet's world abounded in signs and objects which were either already poetic in themselves or else in everyday objects which had been put through the tollhouse of his poetry. Now he put himself to the test not only of permitting ugly or vulgar realities to enter into his world, but of selecting them with this very criterion in mind. On the other hand, however, I believe I can perceive that his literary tone has not much changed. In the other works there is a point of poetic violence, reiterated evidence of life's dramatic poetry. Here there is rather the somewhat anguished reiteration of the dark shadows that fall across a daily life. One could say that it is not so much that his eyes have changed, but that they are looking on reality's other aspect—and that out of this he achieved a stylization as literary as that of his other works. Perhaps more. I dare to hazard that *The House of Bernarda Alba* could be a fecund way, to deepen what has been called Spanish reality. It surprises me how the same poet who has struck the greatest note of tenderness in the Spanish theatre could strip himself of it to the point which he has been able to do in this play. Everything has been foreset to avoid the temptations of turning to lyricism or tenderness. Here is a dark, closed recess into which the atmosphere's flooding light, the flesh's dolorous passion, and the tragic fate of persons filter through the bars. It is a symbol of the poet's own esthetic position. The world with all its harshness, against which Bernarda and her daughters vainly defend themselves, passes before their windows in visions full of fury or drunk with dirty eroticism. These are the visions which burned the poet's imagination as a child, and which he now recasts in a defined scheme, sure and palpitant with truth. Scenes of lights and violence, hard, Goyesque—somewhat, and infinitely Spanish. And there, among these woman-figures, contained, self-burning, dark-souled—the serving women, trailing a low and picaresque undertone. This outlook arrives at something like a new, different vision by the force of surpassing previous stages. But as it happens, his work's enormous coherence makes it apparent that this aspect of reality had already been announced and expressed in previous moments of his poetry and drama. As at other times, what he has done is to isolate and construct upon materials contained in his previous work.

The fact of his being gifted with that very Spanish acumen of discovering the negative side of things confirms—and constitutes one of the reasons for his power—his sensitivity to all aspects of poetry. He has the facings of the three traditional poetic fronts: epic, lyric and dramatic. I do not here concern myself, as may be seen, with anything save a recapitulation of values—and for this purpose it is enough for me not to falsify them. It could be said that all the important poets of his time and his tongue surpassed him in something, but he surpassed them all in the poetic integration of his work—a complete work.

It is the privilege of the lyric poet to cultivate his own medium, to clarify and deepen it until it has become perfect and unimprovable. It is the privilege of men like my brother to be open to all the calls of poetry, to its innumerable voices, and to be able to follow it to all its redoubts. Consequently there are poets who, in different intensities, are always doing over the same things. Federico was always doing different things, following poetry along different paths—even at those times when he seemed to continue along one path, as may be seen in [his] trilogy.

And within his work's variety which, for the reasons before expressed, has to be very high, unity is assured because of the unflagging poetic ability of the man who interwove his life and death with his work, and who already during his life was, among those who knew him, something of a legendary poet. (pp. 26-29)

> *Francisco García Lorca in an introduction to* Three Tragedies of Federico García Lorca, *translated by James Graham-Luján and Richard L. O'Connell, New Directions, 1956, pp. 1-33.*

Morris Freedman   (essay date 1967)

[*Freedman is an American educator and critic whose works include several studies of modern drama and American literature. In the following essay, he examines* Blood Wedding, Yerma, *and* The House of Bernarda Alba, *particularly discussing the conflict in each between individual passion and societal morality.*]

With Lorca we enter an altogether different landscape in the modern drama, the landscape of passion. His three great tragedies—*Blood Wedding, Yerma, The House of Bernarda Alba*—are stripped nearly bare of the details of setting and time, that sense of locale we need for Ibsen, Wilde, Shaw, or O'Casey. Yet we do not leave the area of reality, as we do with some of Strindberg and of Pirandello. Lorca empties his drama of nearly all forces but passion. Even his settings always seem nearly barren, simply all whites or all blacks, so that only the colors emerge that are evoked by the action and the characters. The motivation and energy for plot are in passion; the definition of character is through passion. There is no "thought," no "idea" of any significance.

Lorca is preeminently the playwright of passion in the modern theater although we can find elements of Lorca in Williams, Osborne, O'Neill, and Genet; but in each of these there is a significant admixture of other thematic material. Lorca's passion is not related to a program, as in D. H. Lawrence, or in Williams, or in Genet. Lorca's "blood consciousness" is a consciousness of what is, already; of what must be observed, acknowledged, assimilated, lived with, understood, and, finally, even forgiven. Lorca's passion is rooted in an established social context. The tragedy in his plays comes from the tension between passion, which is necessarily always entirely individual and personal and whimsical, and the society in which the individuals move, which defines them and also gives a particular value and shading to passion and its manifestations. In Lorca, the conflict is between passion and honor, where passion is the mark of the personal (willful and private and powerful in its needs) and honor that of the social (rigid and public and equally powerful in its rules and taboos, the denial of needs).

Blood Wedding offers a bare plot, as spare as a scenario for a ballet, nearly melodramatic in its familiarity and excesses, but only as a skeletal structure to enclose the several domains of passion which combine to give the play its enormous intensity and energy.

The passion of the Mother is both personal and general, her own particular agony enlarged to the dimensions of universal maternal passion. The play opens immediately with a clear indication of the boundaries of maternal passion: her sense of loss of her husband and son is separate and different from her surviving son's sense of loss of father and brother. Throughout the play she continues to define herself as a widow and bereaved mother. At one point, she asks "Can you really see me? Don't I seem mad to you?" That is, does she have an existence outside her loss of husband and son. When she speaks to her son, the Bridegroom, about how to treat his wife, she evokes again the memory of her lost husband, having learned about such matters, she says, from him.

But it is not passion alone which defines the Mother, either as an individual or as a force. It is also honor. Mothers live not only in family but also in society. Honor and passion mingle in the mother to nourish her growing lust for vengeance. And at the end of the play it is her fulfilled but terribly thwarted passion that comes to match and balance the terribly unfulfilled *potential* passion of the bride, who will never be wife or mother and has not even been a beloved, except in hope.

Maternal passion has its domain in the heart of proper society. The other pole of passion in ***Blood Wedding*** is that of the lovers, outside that society. The lovers are awed by the passion they rouse in themselves. Leonardo says: "To burn with desire and keep quiet about it is the greatest punishment we can bring on ourselves." And the Bride replies a little later: "And I know I'm crazy and I know my breast rots with longing; but here I am. . . . " And in her final self-justification, to the mother of the Bridegroom she betrayed:

> You would have gone, too. I was a woman burning with desire, full of sores inside and out, and your son was a little bit of water from which I hoped for children, land, health; but the other one was a dark river, choked with brush, that brought near me the undertone of its rushes and its whispered song. And I went along with your son who was like a little boy of cold water—and the other sent against me hundreds of birds who got in my way and left white frost on my wounds, my wounds of a poor withered woman, of a girl caressed by fire. I didn't want to; remember that! I didn't want to. Your son was my destiny and I have not betrayed him, but the other one's arm dragged me along like the pull of the sea, like the head toss of a mule, and he would have dragged me always, always, always—even if I were an old woman and all your son's sons held me by the hair!

The Bride insists to the Mother: "You would have gone, too." That is, "You who know what it is to act on passion would have gone, too."

When they are alone in the woods, an area set off from the everyday world, the lovers are very conscious of how their passion appears to that world. The bride refers to herself as a bitch. "I, too," says Leonardo to her, "would want to leave you if I thought as men should." But the passion that provides the energy to break through the barriers of honor, to get outside the walls of society, must be as great as it is illicit. It must in its intensity equal the passion of the mother; the passion of vice must balance the passion of virtue.

Passion, then, in Lorca has strength to form its own moral universe. Tragedy comes when this new universe of passion must be opposed by the larger and older universe of logic, of order, of society. The opposition is stated now prosaically, now lyrically, from the center of the passionate universe (the lovers), from outside it (the Woodcutters, who remind one of the detached gravediggers in *Hamlet*): "You have to follow your passion," one says, "They did right to run away." But what must necessarily happen, as it happens in *Romeo and Juliet,* is that passion unrooted in an ordered universe cannot survive beyond the initial momentum. It can only frustrate ironically. Everyone in ***Blood Wedding*** is left bereft, although the Bride seems most punished. The Mother has been a wife and mother and she has had a measure of vengeance. The Bride must go on living as a woman who has destroyed both husband and lover through passion.

Yerma's life shadows the life of the Bride: if the Bride had not fled with Leonardo, she might have found herself a Yerma. Yerma does not love her husband. She has no pleasure in her emotional life; there is only a flicker of response, empty as a conventional flirtatious gesture or intonation, in her contact with another man than her husband. She has so turned inward she has no capacity to feel normally. She is admonished at one point by an old woman: "Men have got to give us pleasure, girl." But her only impulse toward pleasure is maternal. Her wish to be a mother is hysterical in its excess, and perhaps, thus, self-defeating because it does not accommodate calmly and compromisingly to the possibilities. (One has to think only of how Mita solved her problem in Pirandello's *Liolà,* also a folk drama, to recognize the potential immediacy of Yerma's salvation.)

It is properly not clear from the text whether Yerma or her husband is infertile. It is clear that Yerma has lost the capacity to make union, to give herself in passion to a man, specifically to her husband, but also, as the old women who hover about the action of the play suggest, to any man. Yerma is limited by the demands of honor, the established social ritual, in working out her maternal drive. One old woman says flatly that only men can help Yerma, although she is willing to try black magic: witches, the supernatural, come more within the proper social limits than adultery. Unable to break out of her armor of honor, fashioned by the passion of her own regard for society, she turns her passion inward. She speaks of becoming her own son; she addresses her body; she describes herself as being on the edge of sanity.

Yerma's passion in a sense has less to do with maternity than with sheer fertility. Becoming a mother, that act alone, isolated from the biological and emotional realities, seems to be enough to fulfill her passion. "For I'm hurt, hurt and humiliated beyond endurance," she says, "seeing the wheat ripening, the fountains never ceasing to give water, the sheep bearing hundreds of lambs, the she-dogs; until it seems the whole countryside rises to show me its tender sleeping young, while I feel two hammer-blows here, instead of the mouth of my child." Juan, her husband is himself not interested in passion, merely the sensual; he is phlegmatic and resigned: wearing himself out physically seems to be equal for him to fulfilling himself physically. He has not the vitality in any case to rouse himself to the pitch of passion that Yerma requires, and it is poetically just, if ironic, for Yerma to murder him at last, to take out her frustrated passion, so to speak, against the frustrator, thus once and for all eliminating any possibility to have her need for maternity "honorably" satisfied.

Murder is scarcely more honorable than adultery, of course: if Yerma is finally to find power to pierce her armor of honor, she might have found a lover to father her child. But Yerma has gone far out of the territory of the reasonable or plausible, driven by her inner and constrained by her outer passion. She has entered a mad, surrealistic landscape, where murder and motherhood, destruction and creation, sterility and fertility, become equated because exactly opposite, exactly self-cancelling.

In *The House of Bernarda Alba,* we have what amounts to a nunnery and all that implies of the suppression of passion: nunneries are refuges from the usual passion of the world. Bernarda Alba is sadistically compulsive about order, pathological about cleanliness. As in *Yerma,* in which the two old maids spend all their time keeping their house spotless, so the barrenness, immaculateness of Bernarda Alba's establishment are related to sterility; her house is not merely a denial of passion but a denigration of it. Bernarda, loudly: "Magdalena, don't cry. If you want to cry, get under your bed."

We remember that in *Blood Wedding,* Leonardo lives a "disordered" life: he cannot hold down a job, he is hot-tempered and impatient, he comes from a line of murderers. He is thematically equated with a wild stallion. But none of this is pejorative, merely descriptive; Leonardo is of that world where violence alone is heroic. The Bridegroom represents order, cleanliness, and wealth. Bernarda Alba is rich and viciously opposed to irregular emotions: "Hot coals in the place where she sinned," she screams horribly about the local girl who has given herself to a number of men. As we hear the threat of the galloping stallion in *Blood Wedding,* threatening the orderly arrangement of events, so one hears the hoofbeats of the caged animal in *Bernarda Alba,* a tattoo of threatening disaster again.

Bernarda Alba is an extreme distillation of social honor; she exemplifies a passion that has gone too far in excluding the mortally impulsive, irrational, emotional, self-indulgent. It has become in its extremity antipassion. When one daughter says, "I should be happy, but I'm not," Bernarda Alba replies, "It's all the same." (Of course, it's not all the same, not even for Bernarda, as her frenzy to undo things at the end of the play testifies.) In effect, Bernarda is a Satanic spirit, living in an atmosphere of death, perversion, and denial. The play starts with a funeral and ends with a suicide; between we have sadism, insanity, onanism. There are black curtains on the windows. Sexual passions are outside this territory: the stallion drumming in his stall; the village escapades. No men appear on stage. The setting is on the edge of action. The only action that occasionally can burst out in Bernarda Alba's house is the poultrylike squabbling of the sisters, a parody of life.

In *The House of Bernarda Alba,* then, we get an extended examination of the pathology of social passion, of an honor that is contemptuous of the individually human, that is, finally, self-defeating. Bernarda Alba did bear five children, but we are to gather that this was in the cause of social honor, that whatever private passion she might have begun with has attenuated into nothingness, been distorted into self-hatred. She hates her daughters. Bernarda Alba's passion is exercised in the extinguishing of passion: the sadist can only have definition through the masochist, his diametrical opposite. As the play opens, we see Bernarda Alba finally retiring into the "ideal" existence, waiting primly for death, her social duties done, indifferent to the suppressed but smoldering vitality of the unattached daughters. Bernarda Alba fears and hates sex in any form, for sex means only life.

The conclusion of *Bernarda Alba* crystallizes earlier thematic hints and motifs. Adela hangs herself on learning, mistakenly, that her lover has been killed. In a veritable hysteria, Bernarda Alba shrieks that Adela died a virgin, forbids tears except in private, and calls for silence, silence, silence, as the curtain descends. Cleanliness, purity, silence, defining marks of death itself, envelope Bernarda Alba's house. "Death must be looked at face to face," she pronounces as Adela's body is cut down.

In *Blood Wedding,* the tragedy develops from the opposed passions of the lovers and those of the world they move in; the forces are embodied in Leonardo on one side, in the mother on the other. But there is a continuum in passion; it comes full circle, wherever it may start. The text opens with a chilling litany by the Mother about knives ("Cursed be all knives. . . . everything that can slice a man's body") and closes with the Mother and Bride chanting alternately about "a tiny knife / that barely fits the hand, / but that slides in clean / through the astonished flesh / and stops at the place / where trembles, enmeshed, / the dark root of a scream." Initially impelled by opposing passions, the Mother and the Bride are joined together in the common passion of bereavement: passion becomes a moral force for making the human experience, wherever it may start, a final common and vital one, enclosing all possibilities, including conflicting ones.

In *Yerma,* we do not have external oppositions; Yerma herself encloses the opposites that destroy her: passion and honor themselves unwind the tragedy in her, her own passion, her own honor, both too great to yield or accommodate to the other. Her individual, nearly maniacal impulse toward motherhood, so private, so violent, is not less than her obsessed sense of her place in society, even when the evidence is offered to her of the death implicit in proper sterility. Like Lady Macbeth, she rises steadily to a height of mania, oppressed by the too great burden of reconciling private need with public prohibition. She breaks, and in breaking is finally freed of the restraints of taboo; self-abandoned, she murders, fulfilling at last, while utterly cancelling, her private passion. Honor finally asserts its own passionate power.

Bernarda Alba climaxes this trilogy of the tragedy of passion by seeming to assert that it is "honor," passion perverted by a sense of the social that excludes the human, which somehow survives and even triumphs, however abominably, over the personal passion. We may thus read these tragedies as concluding on a pessimistic note: the world of Bernarda Alba is one in which human impulses may not range freely, must be constrained, even expunged, even at the risk of the ugliest consequences, of perversions of passion and of life, including madness, self-stimulation, torture, suicide. But the very extremity of this view suggests its own rebuttal; Bernarda Alba's mode cannot sustain itself except by a restlessly conscious, eternally remorseless exercise of death-dealing. The professional murderer himself dies a measure with each death he arranges. The Nazis, the hired hands of Murder, Inc., Bernarda Alba act out a slow suicide. But the victims, whatever the intimidation, unless they conspire in their own long day's dying, hold on to life, one way or another. Even as Bernarda Alba is hysterically improvising her sterile stagecraft for the future, managing the appearance of Adela's suicide ("Take her to another room and dress her as though she were a virgin"), arranging to face death daily, another daughter, Martirio, mutters: "A thousand times happy she, who had him." (For every Eichman there is a Bruno Bettelheim, more than one, to man's glory.) The personal, physical passion continues to assert its independent power. Honor may finally turn to antipassion, as in Bernarda Alba, certainly with its own power, but the primal force is personal passion.

Lorca's tragedy, then, resides in the domain of passion: passion destroys itself and its possessors, the personal can ultimately only come in conflict with the social, the social enlarges itself into vengeance or into death-serving sterility. Life and fulfillment may reside in passion alone, but precariously, never without risk, not casually. Humans cannot truly be alive without passion, but with passion they must wage a running, alert, and subtle battle with those guerilla forces intent on its destruction. It is the classic opposition between life and death itself; and death, of course, as Freud not least has sadly indicated, is an expression, a wish, of life itself. But to celebrate passion is to celebrate life, living, feeling, reaching, erring: vitality, vivacity, whimsicality, impulsiveness, energy of every sort. There is a final rightness about Lorca's characters who strive toward goals that define them as they live, as there is about Oedipus, and to fail is simply—and greatly—to be human. (pp. 89-98)

> *Morris Freedman, "The Morality of Passion:*
> *Lorca's Three Tragedies," in his* The Moral
> Impulse: Modern Drama From Ibsen to the

Present, *Southern Illinois University Press,*
1967, pp. 89-98.

Frederick Lumley   (essay date 1967)

[*In the following essay, Lumley surveys Lorca's career as a dramatist, examining his progression toward the "pure folk tragedies" for which he is best known. Linking Lorca's works with the Spanish concept of* duende *("incantatory force"), Lumley also stresses the importance of locale and national spirit in Lorca's dramas.*]

There is a word in Spanish which defies translation: *duende* (literally it means 'elf' or 'hobgoblin'). It signifies that incantatory force which distinguishes the artist from all others; it is a quality of greatness which cannot be acquired. But it is more than that. It requires a living interpreter at an 'exact present'. All the arts are capable of it, but in Spain they are inspired by it. We witness it when a dancer, for example Antonio, holds an audience by his *zapateado,* so that they feel and shake to the very tempo of his movements; unless a bull-fight is alive with it the ceremony becomes meaningless. For *duende* is something which can make even a modern sophisticated audience aware of primitive emotion. "One only knows that it burns in the blood" is how Federico García Lorca once described it in a lecture on **"The Theory and Art of the Duende"**.

Lorca's own plays depend absolutely on the creation of this strange power. Since his drama is merely a natural extension of his ballads in terms of the theatre, the most important element is always the audience and their ability to identify themselves with his leading characters. From his very first theatre piece, **The Witchery of the Butterfly,** written with the delicate fantasy of a boy poet, to the grim realism of his last completed work, **The House of Bernarda Alba,** everything depends on their ability to come across to the audience, who will be not so much entertained as animated and haunted by an apprehension unrelated to reason. An audience on Broadway or Shaftesbury Avenue which does not know that it is already in Granada, which does not fear the wild mountain-sides of the Sierra Nevada, which remains indifferent to the strange lyricism, unaware of the mystifying bond between romance and death, unafraid of the tyranny of Bernarda Alba, can never hope to enter the spirit of his plays by any intellectual process. They will only see in such a performance what Wolcott Gibbs described in an American production of **Bernarda Alba** as "apt to seem more comic than really dramatic".

In an interesting article on "Lorca's Audience" by Mary Otis (*Theatre Arts,* May, 1951), this failure of Lorca to establish himself with American audiences is discussed, and Miss Otis suggests that his inability to do so is not because the productions have been too Spanish for American understanding, but "not Spanish enough". "In Spanish dancing", as Miss Otis emphasises, "the genuine thing is always unconsciously recognised". On the other hand, we have the comment of Rafael Nadal, who, writing on the New York failure of **Blood Wedding** (produced under the ridiculous title, **Bitter Oleander**), believes that "whether we like it or not, Spain is from many points of view a world apart, and an attempt to transfer, in Lorca's most Spanish poetry, Spanish values of men and things met with an almost unsurmountable barrier." This barrier is not only confined to the English-speaking public, for **Blood Wedding** also failed in its Paris production in 1938, in spite of an excellent translation, praise from Left-wing critics and the politically favourable atmosphere of the time. Arturo Barea, writing of this production, explains that it had to fail "because foreign spectators only understood it through a laboured intellectual process, not through the swift, piercing associations and sensations it produced in a Spanish public. Indeed, in any Spanish public—for in Hispano America it was as great and lasting a success as in Spain itself ". It would seem that there is danger of Lorca's plays losing their *duende* more or less completely without an audience which, if not Spanish-speaking, has a knowledge of, and sympathy for things Spanish.

To understand Lorca, then, we have to understand Spain, the hopes and sufferings of Spain, the rules of conduct and honour in Spain, the pride of the people, life and death in Spain. "I am a Spaniard and it would be impossible for me to live outside my geographical boundaries", Lorca once told a journalist. Throughout his entire work, Lorca is excessively a Spaniard, both in thought and action. Spain has always presented life in a sharper perspective than that of other European countries; it is at once exaggerated in its simplicity and passion. The strident colours are brighter and darker; a merciless sun hides nothing. In this nation with such a tremendous zest for living the elongated shadow of death is everywhere present. If in other nations death is kept in the subconscious mind, in Spain it is for ever in the conscious. The capacity for living is made one with a capacity for dying; death should be triumphant, not an euphemism which is to be politely whispered. With this vision of death, it is understandable that religion in Spain should be so vastly important, rigid and extreme. In religion, as in politics, as in honour, the Spaniard imposes the severest discipline.

It is not without consequence that Spain has remained throughout history isolated, outside the European sphere of influence and culture. Spanish writers have written directly for the Spanish people, and an attempt during the eighteenth century to impose a pseudo-classicism on the Spanish stage as in France was to kill the Spanish drama until a return to its own tradition was made in the nineteenth century. Spanish art and music are equally distinguished in their perception of national temperament. Indeed, the arts in Spain have not and never have had the civilising pattern of European arts, for as Lope de Vega wrote in *The New Art of Writing Plays in This Age* (1609): "But since we are so far away from art and in Spain do it a thousand wrongs, let the learned this once close their lips." Spanish individualism can swim against the spirit of an age and bring its own rewards.

Lorca was less successful when he tried to expand his horizon; he was never the poet of burning intensity away from his Andalusia. His visit to America did not result in any broad understanding of the American scene or interest in their way of life. His **Poet in New York** is a testament of

his failure there. His voyage, however, terminated a vitally important stage in his career, for he was able to realise that he was not to be the poetical opposite number of his artist friend Salvador Dali, who seemed in his painting to possess a universality that made him as much at home in America as elsewhere. It was a very different Lorca that was to return to Spain, for he had decided to abandon his gipsy romances and devote himself more and more to playwriting. But it was still Andalusia that attracted him for his themes.

Not only was he regional in writing about Andalusia, but he chose his own Granada, with its ancient towers nestling beside the bleak mountain-sides, or Cordoba, "remote and lonely", rather than Seville with its softer colours and more inviting calm. Lorca was an Andalusian minstrel who selected his themes from the diversity of life around him, from the people he met, to be recited preferably to the people he knew.

Lorca immediately reminds us of Burns in our own literature. Both are poets of international renown, yet both are essentially regional poets who, writing about their own locality, become the national poets of their respective countries. Lorca in New York was no more at home than Burns would have been in Oxford; the very thought of an Anglicised Burns, a Burns with a 'B.B.C. accent', is beyond the wildest probabilities of farce. But in spite of the distance between Scotland and Spain, the poet of Tam O'Shanter might well have chosen the subject matter of **Preciosa and the Wind,** though their interpretation of ideas would reveal the fundamental differences between Ayrshire and Andalusia. These differences are, of course, national differences, not a different vision of poetry and its uses. Both Burns and Lorca were masters of the ballad, and the *duende* that comes from good storytelling.

Because Lorca was never so happy as in his Andalusia, he disregarded the advice of his friends not to go south to Granada in July, 1936. His tragic murder, which has been dramatically investigated by Mr. Gerald Brenan in his book *The Face of Spain,* was to turn Lorca for a time into a Republican martyr, thus unfortunately identifying him with a political cause. His politics had never been more pronounced than wishing to be friends with everyone in all countries, and not sacrificing the latter for narrow nationalism. If anything, at any rate on the surface, Lorca was more conservative than progressive, and plays such as **Mariana Pineda** (1929), as Arturo Barea has pointed out, might well at another time have been taken up by the Right, instead of being championed as an attack on the decaying dictatorship and monarchy of the era.

The truth is that Lorca could not help becoming identified as a poet of the democratic movement, for it was the progressives who were the intellectuals and who had supported and encouraged him. Moreover, the emotional onslaught against the conventional rigidity of the middle class such as his folk tragedies ventilated, ensured powerful enemies. His plays portrayed much that was wrong in the state of Spain, and while some believed his satires an occasion for a political demonstration (much to Lorca's disgust), others took exception to the 'realism' they saw in the mirror. These were the years when Spain seemed on the road to freedom of thought and social justice; a new renaissance had arrived for Spanish literature. It was the Republican government who appointed Lorca director of La Barraca, a national theatre company which toured Spain with a repertory of classical plays by such authors as Lope de Vega, Cervantes and Calderón. This work stimulated Lorca and encouraged him also to write and produce his own plays for his company.

For the last six years of his life Lorca was a professional playwright working within his company; his earlier failures were a closed chapter, for now he had made contact with his public and gathered confidence in each play he wrote. His poetical evolution led him, ironically enough in his last play *The House of Bernarda Alba,* to reducing the lyrical element so drastically that he could go no further in this direction; he had written a play which had been pruned bare, consisting only of bones and the impact of Spanish realism. But even though Lorca rejoiced that there was not 'one jot' of poetry in this play, its whole conception is that of a poetic vision, a drama, with the economy and precision of a well-made ballad.

Those who only know Lorca through this severely disciplined work can have little idea of the gradual evolution of Lorca's arrival there; those, on the other hand, who know him only by his other plays would find it difficult to believe that a mind so unusually sensitive to the qualities of lyricism should have deprived itself so completely of its opportunities.

It is true that the struggle between poetry and prose in his plays does not always lead to satisfaction, but it is a conflict which all poets have to solve for themselves in the theatre. Their fusion can only be arrived at by experiment. In these experiments Lorca was tempted by other methods, such as surrealism, which he finally discarded, and rightly so, in order to concentrate on his pure folk tragedies. For it is by these that Lorca is remembered. In them he endeavoured to introduce into the Spanish theatre the folk speech, lyricism and poetic imagination while at the same time to reduce life to an outline or skeleton of bare essentials. He wished to replace the bourgeois realism of the commercial theatre of his day, which was not specifically Spanish, with a return to the beauty of the Spanish language as spoken by peasants who retained its purity. Lorca wished to ally this with a return to the traditional Spanish theatre, the models set by Lope de Vega and Calderón, which had been discarded. For though Jacinto Benevente had for so many years been acknowledged as Spain's leading dramatist (he was a Nobel Prize winner in 1922) he had surprisingly neglected much of the tradition of the Golden Age (in fact he shares with Lope de Vega only the distinction of having had a long life in which to write a superabundance of plays). Lorca delighted in the lyrical and emotional elements in Lope de Vega's plays, specially in his own productions of them. But possibly he revered more the austerity and spiritual exploration found in the plays of Pedro Calderón de la Barca, and especially his concept of honour which figures in many of his works. We must, however, remember that Lorca was only in the tradition of these Spanish classical writers, they were only the forefathers of a common heritage.

. . . . .

The world of Federico García Lorca (1898-1936) was from his early childhood an imaginary world of the theatre, and the whole of life was to him a mysterious drama in which he was an actor. In a preface to *Three Tragedies* his brother Francisco tells us how the first toy that Federico ever bought was a model theatre. Since there were no plays provided he had to make them up for himself. We are also told that one of his favourite games was to play as priest and deliver a sermon to his sisters, the servants, and any others who would willingly participate; the only condition was that everyone had to weep. Life was to Lorca an occasion for tears and laughter, and that was what he wanted of his audience.

It is not perhaps surprising that Lorca failed to establish a *duende* with his Madrid audience in his early career. Its urbanity was far removed from the childhood simplicity needed to give way to a flood of tears. *El Maleficio de la Mariposa (The Witchery of the Butterfly),* presented during the 1919-1920 theatrical season by Martinez Sierra, ran for one performance and was vigorously booed. Written before he was twenty, the subject matter of this piece was related closely to Lorca's verse written about the same time. He tells us of the longing of a sordid cockroach to know the world of a wounded butterfly. Eventually the butterfly is able to use its wings again and flies away to the world the cockroach will never know. For the cockroach life becomes unbearable because of the witchery of the butterfly.

In 1927 Lorca, with the aid of Salvador Dali, who designed the sets, had his first full-length play, *Mariana Pineda,* produced. The play, an historical romance, takes for its heroine a woman from Granada who embroiders a Republican flag in preparation for a revolution in the 1830's. When the police discover the plot the cowardly revolutionaries flee abroad and she is arrested; unwilling to betray the names of the conspirators, although they have deserted her, she dies on the scaffold. Mariana, however, is not made to die for a political cause; like Lorca himself, she is not interested in politics, but is an innocent victim caught in their web. It must be remembered that the place of a Spanish woman is at home; she would evoke little sympathy in dying for a political cause. It is, on the other hand, very much in the Spanish tradition for a woman to sacrifice herself for love. Mariana Pineda is in love with a liberal conspirator. How can she show this more fittingly than to embroider a flag for him with his party's emblems on it? It is through her love that she must die, and die alone, for all the revolutionaries are shown up as pitiable funks.

Lorca calls this play a 'popular ballad'. To the obvious dramatic opportunities in the theme he has introduced many lyrical passages of distinction, but it is not altogether a satisfying play. His greatest difficulty is to make his characters appear to live instead of remaining merely figures in a plot. Perhaps this is an inevitable danger for a writer of ballads, where so much less importance is attached to characterisation than in a play.

After *Mariana Pineda* Lorca started writing a series of

plays which experimented with the folk idiom on the stage, and which were to clear the ground for his more important folk tragedies. *Amor de Don Perlimplín con Belisa en su Jardín (The Love of Don Perlimplin for Belisa in his Garden)*; *La Zapatera Prodigiosa (The Marvellous Shoemaker's Wife)*; and *Retabillo de Don Cristobal (In the Frame of Don Cristobal)* form the three plays of this group. Perlimplin is a dear old rich bachelor who, urged on by his housekeeper Marcolfa, rashly asks for the hand in marriage of Belisa, a voluptuous beauty who lives next door. She accepts readily, but it is not long after their wedding night that Perlimplin learns that she has a lover. He tells her he will be content to love her as a father does a daughter. In the last scene Perlimplin approaches Belisa while she is waiting for her lover. He tells her that if she really loves her lover, he does not want him ever to abandon her, and "so that he may be yours completely, it has occurred to me that the best thing is to stick this dagger into his gallant heart". Perlimplin runs after a figure and after a while returns, wrapped in a red cape. He is wounded, and before falling dead in Belisa's arms rejoices that Belisa is now able to have a soul as well as a body. Through his own suicide he has given Belisa a soul. It is indeed a play for tears and laughter.

The Marvellous Shoemaker's Wife, the most successful of this series, may be described as a poetic farce, with song and dance interwoven in its theatrical structure. The young sensual shoemaker's wife is, like Belisa, married to a nonentity of a husband, far older than herself, and no match for her insatiable desires. In fact, for the poor shoemaker life is made a hell, and he is eventually forced to flee from his home. The marvellous wife turns his workshop into an inn which all her lovers frequent. The shoemaker returns in disguise and finds that with all the temptations available to his wife, she has nevertheless remained faithful to him. Everything would seem ready for a happy ending, but no . . . when the disguise is discarded we are back where we were, and the merry-go-round begins again.

In the Frame of Don Cristobal is a puppet farce, a highly spirited piece which opens with the poet addressing the audience about the meaning of his play, and having an argument with the producer about what he is allowed to say (the producer of course wins). Again it is a story of a faithless wife, Rosita, who having been bought in marriage by Cristobal, offers herself to any man, and when she gives birth to quadruplets pleads that they are Cristobal's children. He beats her to death for it.

There are two plays belonging to Lorca's surrealist period *Así que Pasen Cinco Años (If Five Years Pass)* and *El Público (The Audience)*. *If Five Years Pass* is a highly complex play, which has as many incidents, characters appearing and disappearing, as one might expect to pass through the mind when contemplating a span of five years. It is certainly too meandering for any adequate synopsis of contents, and the title itself tells us all we need to know about the plot. On the stage its violently surrealist approach must either conquer the audience or dumbfound them. A list of the characters: Young Man, Old Man, Stenographer, Manikin, Valet, the Friends, the Betrothed,

the Rugby Football Player, Cat and Boy, three Gamblers, a Harlequin, a Clown . . . requires a fertile imagination to envisage them all as complementary characters in the framework of a play. There is no doubt that Lorca was attempting to rid himself of all the restrictions of dramatic conventions and achieve in the theatre the complete freedom of a poet. His other surrealist experiment, *The Audience,* may be considered as an attack on the commercial theatre, in which the audience itself is on trial.

After these *ballons d'essai* Lorca finally turned to his folk tragedies, where his genius was best fitted to assert itself. *Bodas de Sangre (Blood Wedding)*; *Yerma; Doña Rosita la Soltera (Doña Rosita the Spinster)* and finally *La Casa de Bernarda Alba (The House of Bernarda Alba)* complete Lorca's drama. The heroines of these plays compel our admiration, for their portraiture of Spanish womenfolk is Lorca's superb achievement. In his plays the women accept the stern code of honour which is more important to them and their families than life, and should they fail, should they be driven by sexual passion to forfeit their virginity or honour they are aware of their punishment. An honest woman commits suicide to protect her purity.

In *Blood Wedding* (1933) the emphasis is on the word blood; blood is associated with the blood of old family feuds which have never healed. The characters in this play are nameless, except the one who causes the bloodshed, for this is a study not of characters so much as of attitudes and ethics. The only living son of a mother who has seen her husband and other sons killed in a feud murder, is planning to marry a girl who was previously engaged to Leonardo, a member of the family who took part in the murder. Leonardo has since married the girl's cousin, but it is not a happy marriage and Leonardo still loves the girl he was to marry. The wedding takes place between the son and the girl, but after the ceremony the bride suddenly elopes with her old lover.

When her father hears the news, he pleads: "It can't be she. Perhaps she's thrown herself into the cistern."

To which the mother curtly replies: "The pure and honourable throw themselves into the water. Not that one, no! But now, she's the wife of my son! Two clans. Here there are two clans."

They all join in the hunt to avenge the crime, and the mother knows that in doing so her only son is going to his death. "The hour of blood has come again."

So the young lovers are pursued through the woods, and in the beginning of the third act, set in the dark, supernatural atmosphere of the weeping forest, Lorca brings a sombre lyrical imagination to bear on the mounting tension of the human hunt. Symbolism is also present; three woodcutters represent a mournful Greek chorus; then the moon, the messenger of death, rises, lighting the stage with "an intense blue radiance". The moon gives way to the beggar woman, who personifies Death. In the final scene the bride returns leaving behind the bodies of both husband and lover, and submits herself to her mother-in-law's fury; the mother strikes her and she falls to the ground:

BRIDE: Leave her: I came to let her kill me so that I would be taken away with them. (*To the Mother*) But not with your hands: with hooks of wire, with a sickle, and with a force that will break my bones. Leave her. I want her to know that I am clean, that I shall go mad, but that they will bury me without a single man's ever having seen the whiteness of my breasts.

MOTHER: Be quiet: be quiet: What does that matter to me?

BRIDE: But I went away with the other, I went. (*In anguish*) You would have gone. I was a burnt-up woman, full of wounds within and without, and your son was a spring of water from which I expected sons, land and health: but the other was a dark river full of branches which rushed towards me with the song of its reeds and its stifled song. I ran with your son who was like a little boy made of cold water, but the other sent me hundreds of birds which impeded my course, and left frost in my wounds of a poor pining woman, a girl caressed by the fire. Your son was my aim and I never deceived him, but the arm of the other swept me away like a great sea-wave, like the butting of a mule, and he would have swept me away even had I been old and all the children of your son had been clutching my hair . . . Revenge yourself on me. Here I am. See how soft my throat is. It would be less trouble to cut a dahlia in your garden. But not that! I am chaste, chaste as a newly born child. And strong enough to prove it. Light the fire. We'll put our hands in it—you for your son, I for my body. You'll pull yours out first.

MOTHER: But what does your honour matter to me? What does your death matter to me? What does anything matter to me? Blessed be the corn because my sons lie under it, and it wets the faces of the dead. Blessed be God who lays us out together to rest. [Translation by Mr. Roy Campbell.]

Blood Wedding was the first play of major importance which Lorca wrote, the first play where his maturity had developed to a point where he was as much a dramatist as a poet.

The following year Lorca was determined to move along the road towards dramatic realism, while still retaining important lyrical scenes. **Yerma** is still described as a 'tragic poem'. Like **Blood Wedding** it is a tragedy which underlines the Spanish acceptance of sex as borne by women and the torment suffered by the soul of a woman who adheres to the conventions and must reject all compromise. The word 'Yerma' means 'unsown' or 'uncultivated' and in this particular play it refers to a woman who is sterile, through no fault of her own. She only married to have children, but she fears her husband is impotent. She becomes obsessed with the desire for a child, and she is attracted by Victor, a strong shepherd whom she knows would be able to consummate her love. Clearly they were made for each other. But Yerma is a Spanish woman first. Although she is driven to hate her husband for his frigidity she has her code of honour. Although her body feels the

need for children, her soul thirsts for children, better to remain barren than give herself to a man who is not her husband. In vain she consults other women, but they cannot comfort her. The behaviour of her husband drives her near frustration. He tells her that "life is sweeter without children. I am happy not having them". Yerma must resign herself to this fact, but this she will not do. Instead, in an embrace, she seizes her husband by the throat and in a mad frenzy of passion strangles him. Her tortured being could no longer accept, there was no other outlet for her emotions; what she did was instinctive. Now she can find peace, knowing for certain she will be barren for the rest of her life.

> Withered! Withered, now I know it for certain, and alone. I am going to sleep without ever waking in a start to see if my blood feels another new blood. Barren forever . . . what are you all looking at? What do you want to know? Don't come near, for I've killed my son. I myself have killed my son!

Doña Rosita the Spinster (1935) restrains the passions and there is little action or drama in its study of spinsterhood and old age in nineteenth-century Granada. But whether intentionally or not, the play makes a more open attack on the narrowness of middle-class life which was to be interpreted politically. Rosita waits in vain for the return of her fiancé, who many years before went abroad and who has actually married somebody else. The deception, however, is kept up by Rosita, who remains always faithful to him.

The House of Bernarda Alba completes the journey to dramatic—or should one rather say Spanish—realism. Everything is subjected to realism, right down to the names of the characters. In an article by Claude Couffon in *Le Figaro Littéraire* (26 December, 1953) Lorca's cousin Doña María told M. Couffon that "Bernarda Alba and her daughters really existed. They lived in a little village in the open country, where the parents of Federico owned property: Valderrubio. The two houses were adjoining. The actual well was mid-way. It was one summer, when he was staying at Valderrubio, that Federico discovered this strange family of girls over whom their mother, widowed for many years, exercised a tyrannical guard. Intrigued by this, he decided to overhear the intimate life of the Albas. Using the well as an observation-post, he spied, studied, took notes. Two months later the play had taken shape." And we learn from Doña María that even the mysterious character of Pepe el Romano, who is behind the action in the play but never actually appears, played the same rôle in real life and had the name Pepe el Romilla.

There are no male characters in **Bernarda Alba**. The female studies of his previous plays had been so important—whereas one soon forgets his male characters—that it seems as if Lorca was determined to consecrate a play entirely to them. So we have Bernarda Alba, the domineering head of five daughters (aged thirty-nine to twenty), only the youngest of them attractive and not yet resigned to being a spinster. The daughters know nothing about what goes on outside their windows; they are barred, and the stifling atmosphere of repression, suppressed desires, results in a clash of wills. A marriage has been arranged between Pepe el Romano and the eldest daughter Angustia, but Pepe has already seen the attractive youngest daughter Adela and meets her in the stables. Their meetings are betrayed one night by another jealous sister who is also in love with Pepe, and Bernarda rushes out of the room with intent to shoot Pepe. Adela is given the false news that he has been killed, whereas in fact Bernarda missed. Believing him dead, Adela goes and hangs herself in her room. Bernarda orders them to:

> Cut her down! My daughter died a virgin. Take her to another room and dress her as though she were a virgin. No one will say anything about this! She died a virgin. Tell them, so that at dawn, the bells will ring twice.

For the others the house remains a prison, of jealousy, bigotry, unhappiness, ruled by the rod of iron of Bernarda.

In **The House of Bernarda Alba** Lorca reached the end of an experiment in playwriting, and it resulted in his most successful play. Throughout his life Lorca had never been content with doing things the same way twice, and whether he had at last found where he really wanted to go, or would, had he lived, have started new experiments, we shall never know.

That Lorca died in his prime of life is one of the greatest tragedies that could have happened, not only for Spanish literature, but for world theatre. Of all the dramatists of his era, he was the one who was capable of achieving the calibre of greatness. Many atrocities were committed on both sides in the Civil War; what is done is done. Lorca was a victim of the forces of violent death he himself described so vividly, for it was by always living in face of death that he lived so fully, with every moment precious to him. Death continually lurked by his side, haunted his imagination, and he lived forever under the presentiment of its shadow. Lorca found no consolation in the Catholic conception of death, and nowhere in his writing does he show any reference to a belief in any life beyond. For him, death was an eternal sleep which deprived one of the senses. So be it. Lorca has survived death, and lives every time his work creates that *duende* of which he was master. His name lives on as do his plays. As an epitaph we can quote his **Cásida de la Huída:**

> I want to sleep for a while,
> For a while, a minute, a century,
> But all shall know that I have not died,
> That there is a stable of gold on my lips,
> That I am the little friend of the West wind,
> That I am the giant shadow of my tears . . .
>
> (pp. 92-104)

Frederick Lumley, "A Spanish Tragedy: Federico Garcia Lorca," in his New Trends in 20th Century Drama: A Survey Since Ibsen and Shaw, *Barrie and Rockliff, 1967, pp. 92-104.*

BLOOD WEDDING

PRODUCTION REVIEWS

Stark Young   (review date 27 February 1935)

[*An American playwright, poet, novelist, and translator, Young served for twenty years as drama critic for such journals as* the New Republic, Theatre Arts Monthly, *and the* New York Times, *and the best of this criticism is collected in* Immortal Shadows *(1948). He is especially acclaimed for his translations of Anton Chekhov's dramas. In the following excerpt from his review of* Blood Wedding *(here called* Bitter Oleander*), he discusses the difficulty of making Lorca's Spanish drama accessible to an English-speaking audience. Young asserts that the wedding customs portrayed by Lorca as well as the whole atmosphere of the play are foreign to American playgoers; consequently,* Blood Wedding *"racially . . . is hopelessly far from us." Nevertheless, he praises the simplicity, poetry, and gravity of Lorca's drama.*]

Bitter Oleander is by a genuine poet, and the piece itself is said to have made some dramatic history in Spain. In the story of Señor Lorca's play the bride runs away with a former lover, now married; there is a stabbing and the mother of the bridegroom is left without any of her men. There are dances and songs, a wedding and so on.

Many passages in the performance that the Neighborhood Playhouse gives are clear and moving. The drawing in various scenes is clean and final. The whole approach is, to a considerable degree, stylized and simplified. The direction indicated is noble, Giottesque and right. The fact remains, nevertheless, that such a direction can achieve fruition only through the traditional and racial.

Racially the play is hopelessly far from us. A country like ours, where the chief part of a wedding is the conference between mothers-in-law, the trousseau, the presents and the going-away gown, can scarcely be expected to feel naturally in terms of wedding songs, grave and passionate motivations, rich in improvisations and earthborn devotions. No amount of dance lessons, chantings and drill can remove this portion of **Bitter Oleander** into what is convincing. The whole of it is at best is an importation that is against the beat of this country.

Bitter Oleander, in its poetry and in its method, suggests now and again D'Annunzio's *Daughter of Jorio,* one of the most hopelessly inexportable fine dramas of our time. For the seventh century B.C., for Sappho's era, in the Grecian isles, there are many motifs and movements and lyricisms in **Bitter Oleander** that would have been easy. Mr. Lorca's bold and poetic mind expects a flowering toward the splendor and rigor and gravity of the heart. Fundamentally the difficulty of this play for our theatre is that we cannot sufficiently take it for granted, with all its full choric passion, its glowing simplicity and its basis in a Latin tongue, whose deceiving simplicity mocks translation.

Another way of praising Mr. Lorca is to say that the

Leonardo and the Bride in the Madrid production of Blood Wedding, *1962.*

Neighborhood Playhouse does not desert its high tradition in attempting the production of his play.

The performances were in general sincere and painstaking, though the tempo of the whole was too slow. Of them all Miss Nance O'Neill's seemed to me by far the best. She has a genuine comprehension of the simplification, the meaning expressed by combination of details, the innate discipline that characterize such a role as that of the Spanish mother. As words, all this may sound plausible enough; but for such roles Miss O'Neill is unique on our stage.

> *Stark Young, in a review of "Bitter Oleander,"*
> *in* The New Republic, *Vol. LXXXII, No.*
> *1056, February 27, 1935, p. 78.*

CRITICAL COMMENTARY

Allan Lewis   (essay date 1962)

[*Lewis is an American critic and educator who has written extensively on modern theater. In the following discussion of* Blood Wedding, *Lewis examines the strict moral code of early twentieth-century Spain, which, he suggests, is presented in Lorca's drama as being "in violent opposition to the natural flow of the emotions."*]

All three [of Lorca's major tragedies], **Blood Wedding, Yerma,** and **The House of Bernarda Alba,** are aspects of a central theme: the conflict between the law of honor and the law of the passions. They are intense lyrical dramas of sex in which woman, who should be fruitful, remains unfulfilled. The worship of virginity to preserve the right of inheritance, the code of moral conduct to insure the continuity of life, is in violent opposition to the natural flow of the emotions, but the code is preserved. The rotting past weighs down the living, and the women are left alone among the dead, or go mad with frustration, "dried up forever." Out of the tragedy of women is implicit the story of Spain herself.

In **Blood Wedding,** the first three scenes are components of one situation—the contractual marriage arrangements, suppressed love, and the blood feud of two families. The second act is the serenade to the bride and the wedding feast. The last act is the pursuit in the forest and the mourning of the dead. The form is a musical orchestration of changing rhythms, folk songs, and lamentations, a verse drama in which there is no concern with psychological motivation but with pagan forces in a primitive pageant of revolt, vengeance, and death.

Of all the characters, only Leonardo has a specific individualized name, for his is the passion that is the propulsive force. The others are abstractions: the Mother, the Bride, and—in the expressionistic fantasy of the forest scene—the Moon and Death. Lorca thus employs as did the creator of the dream play, Strindberg, before him, a touch of reality to make the fantasy more real. Leonardo's intensely personal self holds the abstract quality of the others close to the earth.

The Mother is convention, the code of honor, the strength of the land, the embodiment of the preservation of the family blood. Hers is the tragedy, for she senses the doom in the initial scene as she sends her remaining son to the fields to cut the grapes.

> Cursed be all knives and the scoundrel who invented them.

The metaphors of the poems are now incorporated into the dramas, where they become integrated with the lives of the characters and essential elements in the theme. The knife to cut the grapes will also cut down the young men, and the Mother's premonition of death rises to the living image of the moon. Throughout the play, concrete objects are used as symbols of death, which as Lorca once said are known to all, for in "Spain the dead are more alive, dead, than in any other place in the world; their profile cuts like the edge of a barber's knife." He even enumerated the everyday objects that, to others, sound like obscure images but to the Spaniard carry associations of "the frozen air of departure from this life": the beards of shepherds, the full face of the moon, the fly, "the cutting outline of eaves and bay windows," and water which the horse will not drink but which is the giver of life.

The play opens with a staccato exchange between mother and son, simple one-word rhythms, as he leaves for work in the vineyard—here land is in need of water—dry lands which the father "would have covered with trees," as he would have covered her with sons had he lived longer. From the land that needs to be made fertile, they turn to talk of the girl he would like to marry. The themes are interrelated, for marriage means children and sons to work the fields. Women, like the earth, must give life, and sex in the traditional code of the Church is for procreation, not pleasure or passion. The Mother is the earth—violent, lusty, tender, strong, but no longer fertile, for a knife has taken her husband. She is the preserver of life from whom life has been taken.

> I looked at your father and when they killed him, I looked at the wall in front of me. One woman with one man, and that's all.

The son must carry on, and she will be content with "six grandchildren." She agrees to arrange the marriage, even though the girl had once been in love with Leonardo Félix, whose family is responsible for the death of her men. Leonardo has been married for two years and has a child "and another one coming." Like Shakespeare in *Romeo and Juliet,* Lorca contrasts the power of love which springs from passion and brooks no obstacle, and the contractual marriage, which is planned to unite two families. Paris is worthy and honorable, but he seeks the hand of Juliet by discussion with old Capulet. The Bridegroom likewise pursues the established pattern of order. But Leonardo, like Romeo, is unrestrained—individual love that knows no barriers—and acts impulsively and takes the consequences. Juliet knows that "it is too rash, too unadvised, too sudden, too like the lightning." This is the common theme of all great tragedy, Greek as well as Shakespearean—the rash act that brings down the world of reason and crushes the transgressor. With Lorca, the form is a folk ballad of symbolic beauty and surging emotion.

The rest of the play is the working out of what has been announced in the opening scene. In Leonardo's home, his Wife and Mother-in-Law sing a lullaby to the child. Like so many cradle songs, it is filled with cruelty and premonition of disaster, but it is one of Lorca's finest lyrics with its repeated images of the stream, the flies, the horse with the bleeding hooves and frozen mane, "and deep in his eyes a silvery dagger." Relations between Leonardo and the women in his home are strained, for they know he rides at night to see his former love. The Wife is the symbol of patient suffering that must be endured for the sake of her son. The code makes the man the master; woman's role is to obey and be faithful. Leonardo tries to hold back his anger when he learns of the marriage, but it is too powerful and he races out of the house in a violent outburst as the lullaby resumes.

The nuptial contract is discussed by the Mother and the Bride's Father. The sex theme is carried over into the joining together of two farms. The Father says, "How beautiful it is to bring things together." The Bride is quiet, subdued, and gives her consent with full awareness of her duties—"a man, some children, and a wall two yards thick for everything else." When she is alone with the Servant, she hears Leonardo's horse on the plains and her repressed love rises to torment her. The cold marriage is played against the unmanageable fire of man for woman. The Bridegroom has been proper and respectful, the parents have followed the ancient customs, the Bride has attempted obedience—but the sound of the horse's hoofs beats like an ill omen against this wall of conformity.

The second act opens with the Bride dressing for the wedding. She is determined to love her betrothed. Then Leonardo arrives in advance of the other guests, and tells her:

> To burn with desire and keep quiet about it is the greatest punishment we can bring on ourselves . . . When things get that deep inside you there isn't anybody can change them.

The dry rivers now run swollen and fast, and the Bride trembles with excitement as she replies:

> I can't listen to your voice . . . It pulls me along and I know I am drowning—but I go on down.

The villagers interrupt with a serenade, and with dance and music and flowers escort the couple to the church. Leonardo is left alone with his Wife. She recalls her own wedding day when she left her home "shining with a star's glow." She can endure no more humiliation. She orders Leonardo to accompany her to the ceremony.

The banquet after the wedding is another opportunity for song and dance and gaiety. The Mother and Father look forward with hope for future "hands to chastise and dominate the soil." Her father boasts that his daughter "is wide-hipped" and well able to bear children. Leonardo stalks in the background. Unable to bear the thought that another man will possess the Bride that night, he runs off with her. The Bridegroom's Mother, who had thoughts only of preserving her son, knows now that there will be no children, that her only son will die, but she rallies all to kill "quickly and well," for though it is the end of the family line, its honor must be maintained. "The hour of blood has struck again!"

The scene in the forest is a feast of death. The action moves beyond the home into nature itself, in an expressionistic fantasy of specters, symbols come alive, and the reality of the young lovers pursued by the Bridegroom. The Woodcutters who chop down life, shadows in the dark, gloat over the impending meeting of the young men and the desecration of the bridal bed. The Moon appears, a young Woodcutter with a white face, and calls for red blood to "spurt over the mountains" of her chest, and offers to aid Death, the Beggar Woman, with her fullness "to light up the waistcoat and open the buttons; the knives will know the path after that." Leonardo and the Bride, exhausted from the pursuit, halt in the darkness of the woods. The Bride is filled with regret and shame:

> What lamenting, what fire
> Sweeps upward through my head!
> What glass splinters are stuck in my tongue!

Their mutual recriminations serve to arouse their love, and in a sensuous embrace they transform their violence into a recognition that they are joined forever. The Bride says:

> Nails of moonlight have fused
> my waist and your chains.

They run off. The Moon appears to light up the forest. Two violins are heard in the distance, then two shrieks, but the sounds are cut short, and the Beggar Woman "opens her cape and stands in the center of the stage like a great bird with immense wings," as she welcomes the bodies of two young men.

The final scene is the funeral dirge. Only women are left, for that is all that remains of life. In black against the white walls, they mourn the dead. The Bridegroom's Mother is resolute and strong, facing death with pride, without wailing, now that her son "is a fading voice beyond the mountains." All that is left for woman is to water the graves, "the bed that shelters them and rocks them in the sky." The Bride returns to weep alongside the Mother. In wild fury, the Mother leaps upon her and shouts, "Where is my son's good name, now?" Herein lies the peculiarly Spanish flavor of Lorca's play. The Mother's husband and sons have been wiped out. Vengeance and hatred have spilled her family's blood, and she is all alone. Yet her main concern is with the honor of her family. The Bride is conscious of her guilt. She had meant to respect

her vow, but the Bridegroom was "a little boy of cold water," whereas Leonardo was "a dark river, choked with brush." She tells the Mother, "Your son was my destiny . . . but the other one's arm dragged me along like the pull of the sea." And she adds that she is still a virgin, that not "a single man has ever seen the whiteness of my breasts." Leonardo's wife joins the mourners, and as the bodies are carried to the village, the Mother and the Bride lead the chorus with a lament to death.

The Bride:

> . . . fish without scales, without river,
> so that on their appointed day, between two
> and three, with this knife,
> two men are left stiff,
> with their lips turning yellow.

The Mother closes the play with:

> And it barely fits the hand
> but it slides in clean
> through the astonished flesh
> and stops there, at the place
> where trembles enmeshed
> the dark root of a scream.

The emphasis on virginity and the Bride's willingness to undergo an ordeal by fire as a test of her purity are remnants of the feudal code and the law of the Church, deeply imbedded in the people of Spain. The Bride has been swept away by an uncontrollable desire. She has denied her wedded husband the right to make her fertile, but she has not been violated by another man. Her purity remains with her body, destined to wither unfulfilled. Adultery is beyond law and destroys all continuity of land possession by casting doubt on rightful heirs. Lorca is not treating of social reform nor recommended change, but of emotions choked by a persistent morality, and he held his theme within those limits.

The play, like folk ballads, is a pageant of life stripped to its bare essentials. The real and the symbolic merge in concrete images, then blur into vague and imperceptible shadows. Analysis injures its vitality, for as a whole the play leaves the impression of the cry of the earth for ripeness and fecundity. Tradition and honor and the imposed morality crush the outpouring of life that is secretly admired but outwardly condemned. All that is left of the struggle between passion and reserve is a chorus of wailing women. The stark ballet of the forest scene is a dance of death, but whereas Strindberg employed expressionist techniques to emulate the flow of dreams, and O'Casey as well as Ernst Toller and Georg Kaiser to visualize social forces, Lorca uses them to portray a primitive battle for survival. (pp. 248-55)

> *Allan Lewis, "The Folklore Theatre—García Lorca," in his* The Contemporary Theatre: The Significant Playwrights of Our Time, *Crown Publishers, Inc., 1962, pp. 242-58.*

Gwynne Edwards (essay date 1980)

[*In the following excerpt, Edwards explores the character and function of Lorca's stage settings in* Blood Wed-

ding, emphasizing the dramatist's use of mood, imagery, and rhythm.]

It has been said of Chekhov that 'it is very much his method of building a play to keep violent acts and emotional climaxes away from the center of things . . . ' Of Lorca's rural tragedies we can justifiably say the opposite, for they reveal the most powerful human passions and the most violent confrontations. Indeed, the trivia of human lives, the ordinary events and the desultory conversations that are the stuff of many dramatists, are almost entirely absent. Instead, Lorca goes to the heart of the matter, stripping away the commonplaces of experience in favour of all that is heightened, intense and concentrated. This is, of course, the material of melodrama, and for many theatregoers, particularly the more phlegmatic North European, it remains the difficulty of appreciating fully Lorca's plays. He is, indeed, very Spanish and very Andalusian, rarely given to understatement. But if his plays are a series of hammer blows, we should not assume that, in terms of stagecraft, they are in any way crude.

Let us consider, firstly, the character and function of the stage settings [in **Blood Wedding**]. There are seven in all, each of them different, and some of Lorca's stage directions are much more detailed than others. They do, however, have one important thing in common, for the play, though dealing with the stuff of real life in a Spanish village, is far from naturalistic, and the sets, far from being cluttered, are spare and simple, as stark and as stripped of detail as the heightened emotional situations to which they form a background. The stage pictures are an integral part of the scene.

Act I, Scene One, conveys, above all else, the obsessive nature of the Mother's grief for her dead husband and her elder son, and her fear for her one remaining son. The stage picture that sets the scene and forms the frame for the expression of its powerful emotions is very simple. Lorca has, in the published text, just one short instruction: [*A room painted yellow.*] He does not specify its tone, but we may imagine the harsh yellow of the bare kitchen walls forming a background to the black of the Mother's dress. Within this frame she will be seated as the curtain rises, downstage in all probability. The combination of colours and the static posture of the silent figure create a mood of dark, brooding melancholy before a word is spoken. The words and actions that follow are anticipated by the setting and harmonize with it at every stage.

The second scene initially suggests the domestic bliss that exists in the house of Leonardo and his wife but gradually presents the ominous and disruptive nature of Leonardo's passion for his former sweetheart. The stage picture is suggested here in detail:

> *A room painted rose with copperware and wreaths of common flowers. In the centre of the room is a table with a tablecloth. It is morning.*
> [*Leonardo's* MOTHER-IN-LAW *sits in one corner holding a child in her arms and rocking it. His* WIFE *is in the other corner mending stockings.*]

Every element is important—the predominant rose colour of the walls, the glow of the copperware, the brightness of the flowers, of the light of morning, and the tablecloth. We have not a clash but a harmony of colour very different from Scene One. The seated figures of the women have a different effect too, for they blend into the background, creating a sense of balance and tranquillity. The spectators are lulled by its soothing impact, but, in contrast to Scene One, the ensuing actions, involving Leonardo's violent conflict with the Wife and Mother-in-Law, offset the stage picture and are themselves thrown into greater relief by it.

The stage settings for Act III are interesting in a different sense. The events of the first two Acts, leading to Leonardo's abduction of the Bride, are, though heightened, on a human plane. The sets, portraying the rooms of the various houses or the landscape outside those houses, are, reduced to the bare, necessary elements, accompaniments to human affairs and emotions. By the final Act the action is transposed to the level of the supernatural, for the awesome figures of Moon and Death control and manipulate the lives of human beings. The sets should be seen now not as stage pictures which accompany and underline the conflicts within and between human beings but as frames which emphasize their smallness and insignificance.

Act III, Scene One, for instance, presents Leonardo and the Bride concealed in the wood, pursued by the Bridegroom and his companions, and then Leonardo and the Bridegroom hounded by the Moon and Death. The stage picture is briefly described, but it suggests the elements necessary to convey to us the vastness and the mystery of the forces that circumscribe human lives:

> *A forest. It is night-time. Great moist tree trunks.*
> *A dark atmosphere. Two violins are heard.*
> [THREE WOODCUTTERS *enter.*]

While the earlier sets are precise, even though their starkness gives them a certain symbolic quality, the setting of the great wood is, in accordance with the movement of the play, much more symbolic.

The dialogue, for all its seeming naturalness, is highly stylized. In Act I, Scene One, the exchanges, firstly between the Mother and the son, then between the Mother and the Neighbour, are carefully constructed, full of repetitions of words and phrases that convey to us the obsessive nature of the Mother's grief and fear. The son asks for a knife with which to cut the grapes, the word unleashes her emotions, and in the outburst that follows, 'knife' or 'knives' occurs six times, 'pistols' twice, and 'guns' once. In addition, there are throughout the passage the same repeated patterns of speech:

> If I lived to be a hundred I'd talk of nothing else . . .
> . . . No, I'll never be quiet.
>
> No. No. Let's not quit this talk.
> No . . . If I talk about it it's because . . . Oh, how can I help talking about it . . .

Through the language and its insistent rhythms Lorca reveals to us with power and immediacy the emotions that haunt the Mother throughout the play. The son's lines are few in comparison but they are important in terms of contrast. His adoption of different emotional positions—resignation, aggression, coaxing, cajoling—both fail to stem the tide and throw into greater relief his mother's obsessive concerns.

In the middle section of the scene the Mother's obsessions remain a constant undercurrent. There are two important pauses that accompany her allusions to her son's future wife, for they reveal the thinking processes that underlie her words. Firstly:

> Forgive me.
> [*Pause.*]
> How long have you known her?

And secondly:

> Go on. You're too big now for kisses. Give them
> to your wife.
> [*Pause. To herself.*]
> When she is your wife.

At other points the idea of her being left alone is repeated twice: 'I'll be left alone. Now only you are left me . . .' 'I have no one but you now!' She refers to her dead husband three times. The tempo is slower but the dialogue still reflects the Mother's nagging and insidious worries. Finally, in the scene's concluding moments her questions, repeatedly punctuating the conversation and becoming more insistent, acquire an obsessive character, building to the climactic revelation of the name of the Bride's former sweetheart and the confirmation of the Mother's fears:

> You know my son's sweetheart?
> And her mother?
> How do you remember it?
> Who was the boy?
> Félix, a slimy mouthful.
> [*She spits.*]
> It makes me spit—spit so I won't kill!

The Mother appears again on three occasions and the patterns already noted in the dialogue occur again, suggesting the narrow areas of emotional experience in which she moves, the repeat performances which she is always giving. In Act II, Scene Two, in the conversation with the Bride's father after the wedding, the mention of Leonardo's name has the same effect on her as the previous reference to the knife. The Mother uses the word 'blood' six times and, to a lesser extent, 'killing', 'killed', 'knife-wielding'. We note, too, precise echoes of Act I, Scene One:

> When the talk turns on it, I have to speak. And
> more so today. Because today I'm left alone in
> my house.

The repetitions and rhythmic patterns of the dialogue given to the Mother must be seized upon by the actress who wishes to convey to the audience the intensity and permanence of the Mother's obsessive thoughts and feelings.

Lorca's use of poetry can be considered in relation to many scenes. In Act I, Scene Two, for instance, Lorca uses verse to heighten mood and atmosphere in what is a fairly static situation rather than one which, presenting characters in conflict with each other, demands the cut and thrust of prose dialogue. Secondly, the use of poetry here is in no way jarring, for, taking the form of a lullaby, it fits perfectly into the context of the scene. But its effect is magical and beautifully managed. The delicate colour tones of the stage setting and the gentle rocking of the baby are enhanced by the words and rhythms of poetry, especially in the lullaby's refrain:

> WIFE [*softly*]: Carnation, sleep and dream, the
> horse won't drink from the stream.

But slowly, in its central section, the lullaby becomes, more than an accompaniment to the sleeping child, a lament for the thirsty, bleeding horse, and, in a marvellously evocative way, the earlier associations with the room and the baby are transformed into the sinister splash of blood and the icy light in the horse's eyes that glints like a knife:

> MOTHER-IN-LAW: . . . His poor hooves were
> bleeding, his long mane was frozen, and deep in
> his eyes stuck a silvery dagger.
>
> And his blood was running, Oh, more than the
> water.

The poetry in performance, with due attention to its powerful pictorial and rhythmic qualities, should construct a verbal picture which takes the spectators' attention from the visual picture of the room and only slowly allows them to return to it, but with the verbal picture and all its ominous implications firmly imprinted on their minds. No producer should ignore the different levels on which the lullaby works.

The middle section of the scene, in prose, presents Leonardo in relation to his wife and mother-in-law and the emotional tensions that exist between them. In contrast to the slow tempo of the lullaby and the static postures of the women who intone it, there are now three dramatic climaxes, each more powerful than the previous one, the carefully graded interplay of word, action and movement about the stage to the point where Leonardo storms out. The conclusion of the scene returns to the lullaby in a way which links its implications firmly to the characters themselves. Its impact should be much harsher, coloured by the weeping of the Wife and the Mother-in-Law in such a way as to make the lamentation for the horse a simultaneous lamentation for themselves:

> MOTHER-IN-LAW: Carnation, sleep and dream,
> the horse won't drink from the stream.
>
> WIFE: [*weeping, and leaning on the table*]: My
> rose, asleep now lie, the horse is starting to cry.

By this stage the figures of the women, initially part of the tranquil setting of the room, are a discordant element within it.

In Act II, Scenes One and Two, poetry is used in the form of song in association with the wedding. In the first scene the Servant begins to intone the song that, taken up by others as the scene unfolds, builds slowly into a moving and lyrical celebration of marriage and of the Bride and Bridegroom:

> Awake, O Bride, awaken,
> On your wedding morning waken!

> The world's rivers may all
> Bear along your bridal Crown!

Its effectiveness in the scene lies at first in the fact that its optimism, caught in the imagery and the gently insistent rhythms, is bounded on either side by the conflict of the Bride and Leonardo within themselves and in relation to each other. It is, indeed, swamped by the savagery of their clash. But then the song is taken up again, sung by the guests, the distant chorus coming slowly nearer, growing and assuming a sustained momentum that banishes the earlier tensions of the scene. In addition, the performance of the song, essentially stylized in the distribution of its lines and refrains and through the movements of the singers, raises the action to a more symbolic plane, substituting individual passions with and absorbing them into generic and universal patterns. Here, as in Act I, Scene Two, poetry both heightens the atmosphere of the scene itself and, through its allusive nature, extends its meaning. The song acquires the character of age-old ritual, the Bride and Bridegroom the mythical proportions of archetypal lovers, and the joy of the guests the impulse towards all that is creative and harmonious that is deeply rooted in human nature. As the scene ends, the incantation begins to fade with the departure of the guests for the wedding, and snatches of song are interwoven with a return to the tension between Leonardo and his wife. A magical and harmonious climax has been built only to descend again into the final and more ominous discord of personal relationships. It is a scene in which the performance of the poetry in terms of changing tempo and emphasis and the suggestion of its different levels of meaning is both demanding and vitally important.

In the first two Acts poetry takes the form of songs, but in Act III it is part of the dialogue itself, both between the supernatural figures of the Moon and Death and between Leonardo and the Bride. Indeed, even in the prose dialogue of the Woodcutters that begins Scene One the rhythms of poetry are very prominent and, in performance, must acquire that insistent, inescapable beat that will create the sense of inevitability that pervades the scene:

> FIRST WOODCUTTER: By now he must be loving her.
>
> SECOND WOODCUTTER: Her body for him; his body for her.
>
> THIRD WOODCUTTER: They'll find them and they'll kill them.
>
> FIRST WOODCUTTER: But by then they'll have mingled their bloods. They'll be like two empty jars, like two dry arroyos.

This poetic prose leads into the poetry itself, into the Moon's anguished, menacing soliloquy:

> I want no shadows. My rays
> must get in everywhere,
> even among the dark trunks I want
> the whisper of gleaming lights,
> so that this night there will be
> sweet blood for my cheeks . . .

In contrast, Death, in the form of an old woman, delivers her lines in an urgent yet sinister whisper:

> They won't get past here. The river's whisper
> and the whispering tree trunks will muffle the
> torn flight of their shrieks.

If the potential of the scene, whose atmosphere lies as much in its poetry as in anything else, is to be realized on the stage, every attention must be given to the delivery of the lines in terms of pitch, rhythm and changing tempo.

The poetry of the concluding section, revealing to us the passion, the guilt and the fear of the Bride and Leonardo, conveys those emotions to us in a form more stark and more immediate than any prose could do. Lorca's stage direction suggests the intended effect: [*This whole scene is violent, full of great sensuality.*] It is a mood which must be caught in the delivery of lines as simple yet as evocative as these:

> LEONARDO: The birds of early morning are calling among the trees. The night is dying on the stone's ridge. Let's go to a hidden corner where I may love you for ever, for to me the people don't matter, nor the venom they throw on us.

As a last example there is the final elegy for Leonardo and the Bridegroom. This is a static scene, the mourners in set positions. The movement of the scene lies solely in the movement of the lines they speak. Through repeated lines and rhythms there is created a sustained momentum. Moreover, there will be an interplay not merely of lines but of voices, of the Wife, the Bride, the Mother, the Neighbours, which will vary the tone of the passage and maintain its sense of forward movement, giving to the whole a ritualistic, chorus-like effect:

> MOTHER: Neighbours: with a knife, with a little knife, on their appointed day, between two and three, these two men killed each other for love. With a knife, with a tiny knife, that barely fits the hand but that slides in clean through the astonished flesh and stops at the place where trembles, enmeshed, the dark root of a scream.
>
> BRIDE: And this is a knife, a tiny knife that barely fits the hand: fish without scales, without river, so that on their appointed day, between two and three, with this knife, two men are left stiff, with their lips turning yellow.
>
> MOTHER: And it barely fits the hand but it slides in clean through the astonished flesh and stops there, at the place where trembles enmeshed the dark root of a scream.

There should be no restraint, no holding back in the speaking of these lines. Their intense emotion must be transmitted to us by the whole range of vocal resources that the actors can command.

The first of these two scenes is the real climax of the play, and in its effectiveness lighting plays a significant part. Elsewhere lighting is used to enhance atmosphere, as in Act I, Scene Two, or to suggest a change of mood, as in Act II, Scene One, where darkness gives way to dawn, conflict to the greater optimism of the wedding. In Act III, Scene One, it does these things to a much greater degree, in accordance with the greater dramatic nature of the scene, and it also pinpoints the climactic moments of the scene. It begins in darkness—*A dark atmosphere*—which, allowing us to see only the shapes of the trees and the dim forms of the woodcutters, cloaks the stage in mystery and foreboding. When the Moon appears there is at first *a shining brightness at the left* and then—*The stage takes on an intense blue radiance.* The blue light, illuminating the whole stage, creates a very eerie effect and a setting in which the figure of the Moon, with a white face and in the centre of the stage, is literally spotlighted. Within this cold light the Moon's soliloquy becomes more chilling. With the Moon's exit and the appearance of Death the stage reverts to darkness, an appropriate setting and accompaniment to her furtive movements and then to the searching of the Bridegroom. Within the darkness the movements of individuals, the slow movements of the Woodcutters, the passionate words of the Bride and Leonardo, the music of the two distant violins, demand our attention even more, are emphasized more because of the darkness. Finally, as the Bride and Leonardo try to escape, the blue light fills the stage again, dramatically spotlighting their death, giving to the ending of the play that sense of something cold, inhuman, merciless, from which there is no escape. It is an impression enhanced further by the way in which the black shape of Death enters and dominates the downstage area, silhouetted against the light in a wonderfully evocative and dramatic stance: [. . . *She opens her cape and stands in the centre of the stage like a great bird with immense wings . . .*] (pp. 156-66)

> Gwynne Edwards, in Lorca: The Theatre Beneath the Sand, *Marion Boyars, 1980, 310 p.*

THE HOUSE OF BERNARDA ALBA

PRODUCTION REVIEWS

Richard Watts Jr.   (review date 8 January 1951)

[*Watts was an American journalist and drama critic. In the following review of a 1951 American National Theater and Academy (ANTA) production, he concedes that* The House of Bernarda Alba *was "worth doing," but posits that "the theatre of Spain does not fit any too snugly into the American stage." For Watts, the stylized elements of the play, "hauntingly lyric" in the original Spanish, seem "a little flat and unpersuasive" in translation.*]

Federico Garcia Lorca, the Spanish playwright who was murdered by his country's Fascists in 1936, is a figure of international literary importance, and the American National Theatre and Academy was fulfilling one of its proper functions when it offered his most famous drama, *The House of Bernarda Alba,* as the fourth item in its subscription season at the ANTA Playhouse last night. It must be added, however, that the production provided additional

evidence that the theatre of Spain does not fit any too snugly into the American stage and presents barriers that it is not easy to cross.

The House of Bernarda Alba is a somber and brooding tragedy about a family of girls ruled over by a grim and tyrannical matriarch who seeks to suppress their natural instincts in the interest of her own stern social code. With the father dead, the mother drives the young women into a lengthy period of mourning in which they are to be cut off completely from association with men, with the not altogether surprising result that they are filled with bitterness, hatred and general unrest and the youngest of them commits suicide after it had been discovered that she was having a secret love affair with the eldest daughter's fiance.

The conflict between natural instincts and the forces that try to suppress them seems to be one of the dramatist's favorite themes, and there is no denying that, in *The House of Bernarda Alba,* he goes about his story with a single-minded intensity that is capable of engendering considerable dramatic power. Although on the English-speaking stage there appears to be a certain artificiality in the theatrical style of Garcia Lorca, it is still evident that he is a playwright of authentic tragic force. There are moments in the play that are highly impressive in their concentrated emotion.

The mood of ominous impending doom that hangs over the unhappy household of savage old Bernarda is captured in both the writing and the production with effective skill and presents the most successfull feature of the drama. But the tragedy itself, it seems to me, is made less moving and believable than its materials should make it through a kind of artificial stylization that may be eloquent and hauntingly lyric in the original Spanish but is a little flat and unpersuasive in its English translation. The final effect, which might have been devastating, is somehow far from overwhelming.

For me, one of the troubles with the play's effectiveness is the acting of Katina Paxinou as the matriarch. I have now seen Miss Paxinou on the stage in *Hedda Gabler* and on the screen in *For Whom the Bell Tolls* and *Mourning Becomes Electra,* and I must confess that her art continues to escape me. There is something about her highly mannered style that seems to me grotesque and extravagant, rather than powerful and moving, and this struck me as being all the more noticeable last night because that style happened to be contrasted with the less ornate playing of the other members of the cast.

Such interesting young actresses as Ruth Ford, Helen Craig, Mary Welch and Kim Stanley are prominent in the all-woman cast, and they all play skillfully, but I couldn't escape the feeling that they were in a different play from the one in which Miss Paxinou was appearing. The set and the costumes by Stewart Chaney and the direction by Boris Tumarin are of help in creating the mood that is the most successful feature of *The House of Bernarda Alba,* and I certainly agree that the tragedy was worth doing. But I am also sure that Garcia Lorca must have been a finer playwright than he seems in the American theatre.

A production of The House of Bernarda Alba *at Columbia University, New York.*

Richard Watts Jr., "The Grim Home of Bernarda Alba," in New York Post, *January 8, 1951.*

William Hawkins   (review date 8 January 1951)

[*Hawkins served as drama critic for* the New York World-Telegram *from 1946 to 1956. In the review below, he addresses the American National Theater and Academy production of* The House of Bernarda Alba, *praising the play's "fantastic emotional power" but noting that it fails "to use silence and stillness."*]

The House of Bernarda Alba is the best known and probably the finest play of Federico Garcia Lorca, surely one of the most powerful of modern playwrights.

This is a story of Spain half a century ago. Its fantastic emotional power springs from the desperate suppression of five young girls by their proud mother.

The tension of the drama is created by negating natural impulses, until the situation bursts open in a panic of crazy events.

The already suppressed children of Bernarda are faced with eight years of strict mourning for their father. Here in a small, dull town, they have position and are considered wealthy. Almost none of the village men are considered by Bernarda to be good enough for her daughters.

One Pepe finally woos the 39-year-old Augustias, a half-sister of the others, who has money in her own right. The youngest girl is so desperately in love with him that she would sacrifice her reputation, her honor and her standing in the town for the rest of her life. She even threatens to become his mistress after he has married the older girl.

A third sister, crippled and hopeless of love, also yearns for Pepe. She is determined to destroy the youngster's romance. When the mother finds out what is going on, there is complete and irremediable tragedy.

The most remarkable element of this production is the performance of the star, Katina Paxinou, as Bernarda. She is a haughty disciplinarian to her fingertips, ramrodlike and immovable.

She dispels such force of character that the strange, remote play becomes entirely believable.

Where this production weakens is in its inability to supply the play's inherent demands for smooth ensemble playing.

Despite this, in its own way each performance has interesting color. Helen Craig is the dark, plain older girl, and Kim Stanley is the fiery young rebel. Ruth Ford is the bitter meddler, in whom I missed some explicit manifestation of the physical disability the others discuss.

Tamara Daykarhanova has some brief but quite lovely moments the maddened old grandmother. Ruth Saville seemed to me howlingly miscast as the old retainer.

The play moves gracefully. There is a particularly effective scene as all the daughters silently eavesdrop on their mother from a row of dim archways. If the direction has a major fault, it is the failure to use silence and stillness. Only Miss Paxinou makes pauses effective, and this is a play where unspoken hatreds are the bloodstream of the drama.

William Hawkins, "Lorca Play Pivots on Love and Hate," in New York World-Telegram & The Sun, *January 8, 1951.*

CRITICAL COMMENTARY

Sam Bluefarb   (essay date 1965)

[*Bluefarb is a British-born educator and critic. In the excerpt below, he explores various oppositions and tensions in* The House of Bernarda Alba, *including death versus life, sterility versus fertility, and maleness versus femaleness.*]

Something of the background [of *The House of Bernarda Alba*]: The opening scene of the play is one of mourning, mourning for the death of Bernarda's husband, Antonio María Benavides. (In spite of the circumstances, it is somehow difficult to imagine someone like Bernarda ever having a husband, yet the daughters are there, some sort of testimony—no matter how dubious—to the fact of the conjugal relationship! There is also that certain attitude, almost a culture syndrome of many Latin women, towards the conjugal state itself, where marriage is often looked upon by the women as a fate to be endured rather than an experience to be enjoyed, and where the woman's status is often referred to as *obligada,* with all the moral, physiological, and legal duties which the word suggests.) This first scene sets the tone of the entire play, and everything that follows that scene. All his life Antonio has been a profligate, and in the words of La Poncia, the maid, who also, among other things, expresses this stoic endurance of the Latin woman, "two weeks after the wedding a man gives up the bed for the table, then the table for the tavern, and the woman who doesn't like it can just rot, weeping in a corner." The remark is specifically applied to Evaristo, her own dead husband; but it may be applied to all men, including—as La Poncia implies—Pepe el Romano, Angustias' fiancé, and Antonio himself. But now another servant passes a kind of posthumous judgment of loss upon Antonio, who true to form has been carrying on with the servant herself:

> Let them put you in a coffin with gold inlay and brocade to carry it on—you're no less dead than I'll be, so take what's coming to you, Antonio María Benavides—stiff in your broadcloth suit and your high boots—take what's coming to you! You'll never again lift my skirts behind the corral door!

The scene of course suggests another character in another play, a character whose philanderings are also the harbingers of other people's dooms: Captain Alving in Ibsen's *Ghosts.* In both plays—*Ghosts* and *Bernarda Alba*—these heads of households (about whom we can only know through other people) find themselves married to women in whom the milk of the life force has dried up or curdled. In both plays, the men, perhaps symbolic of a thwarted virility (though the reference may be somewhat ambiguous in Antonio's case) cause that virility to expend itself on the crude, but sensually provocative women of the lower classes (both Antonio and Alving make up to servant women). And in another instance, though the sexual and class relationships are reversed, another Scandinavian, Strindberg, has presented his own example of lower class virility in the person of Jean, the valet in *Miss Julie.* What these women lack in education, decorum, finesse, they

more than make up for by their earthy sensuality—in the minds of their paramours at least. Thus, like Alving and his relationships (or lack of them) with Mrs. Alving, Antonio, no longer satisfied with Bernarda, seeks elsewhere for the satisfaction which only a woman who lacks Bernarda's moral (or immoral?) scruples, can give him. But with Antonio's death—and it seems to be a "timely" death, since the daughters are now full grown and more than ready for marriage—the house falls to the women.

Symbolically, as has often been pointed out, this conflict between a virility now dead (Antonio) and a virility which is still potential (Adela, the youngest of the daughters) is represented by the cleavage between the inside of the house and the outside, and by the clash between them. Inside, there is mourning and restraint; outside, singing and freedom. Appropriately enough, the singing here comes from a band of reapers who are passing the house on their way to those fertile fields which "beg to be taken," to use a pathetic fallacy. The fertility of the outside world is of course represented by the hot sunlight, the swarming colors of the village streets and the bright fields which lie beyond them; the farms, the lusty singing, which itself can only be thought of as a kind of spontaneous hymn to fertility, a melodious celebration—all of these form the backdrop of a ritual from another age of tragedy. The song itself transcends mere suggestion:

> The reapers have set out
> Looking for ripe wheat;
> They'll carry off the hearts
> Of any girls they meet.

Ripeness, fertility, joy in the biological urge through song—the significance of the melodious chorus of reapers lies in these. But, as if in a kind of non-melodic counterchorus to the melodious chorus, a monotoned anti-strophe to the tuneful strophe of the reapers, three of the sisters, Amelia, Martirio, and Adela, comment on the passing reapers:

AMELIA: They don't mind the sun.

MARTIRIO: They reap through flames.

ADELA: How I'd like to be a reaper so I could come and go as I pleased. Then we could forget what's eating us all.

MARTIRIO: What do you have to forget?

ADELA: Each one of us has something.

The strophe of the reapers obtrudes again, but this time more distantly, from farther away, as though all the joy and life contained in their words were already passing out of existence for the girls:

> Throw wide your doors and windows,
> You girls who live in town
> The reaper asks you for roses
> With which to deck his crown.

There is a kind of sadness too about the stallion penned in the corral, who, in his eagerness to break out and find the potential of his own fertility with the mares, kicks at the walls of the corral, and in a sense repeats the action of his late master. But it is in the tension between the sisters who find *la casa* "adequate" (though scarcely more than that!) and Adela, who does not, that these meanings come alive even more strongly.

Life inside the house, such as it is, is sterile. And this sterility is perhaps most effectively symbolized by a virility grown old and moribund, the eighty-year-old grandmother, Maria Josefa, who, having no baby of her own to nurse, is now forced—in her senility—to make believe that the lamb she carries in her arms is her baby. Even here, Josefa's senility itself not only expresses the sterility within the house, but the larger spiritual senility which has in its turn been brought on, or at least aggravated by, that sterility. Beyond this, even the house itself—where no men except mourners may now tread, and that only beyond the patio—seems to appear as one enormous and sterile womb; it is not entirely accident that the title of the play itself should contain within it the word "house." Without too much wrenching of analogical, though *not* poetic, logic—Freudian or otherwise—the play might well have been called *The* Womb *of Bernarda Alba!*

What builds up to this feeling of sterility (as opposed to virility), life (as opposed to death), are the constant references to these and related matters. Martirio, one of the daughters who seems to be a kind of major domo of repression, a paler second self of Bernarda, says:

> It's better never to look at a man. I've been afraid of them since I was a little girl. I'd see them in the yard, yoking the oxen and lifting grain sacks, shouting and stamping, and I was always afraid to grow up for fear one of them would suddenly take me in his arms. God has made me weak and ugly and has definitely put such things away from me.

While the mother rejects the male world through a kind of bitter, perverted strength and courage, Martirio—even the name bears ironic connotations—does so through weakness and fear. For she has accepted her own fate, not so much by conviction as by fear that she herself, in her knowledge of Adela's affair with Pepe, can never have the satisfaction of having the kind of hope that Adela can have. Rather than join Adela in what could be her own unsuccessful breakaway (as Adela's finally turns out to be), she rejects the world outside, to chant her own hymn of sterility and death inside the house—all of those things which her mother ("admirably") represents for her. And while she too hates her mother, her jealousy, and her hatred of her sister Adela is composed of an even more incandescent stuff.

Bernarda's statement early in the play—apart from the context and the contingency of ritualistic mourning (and in spite of Antonio's siring of her daughters!)—sets the tone for the greater need of mourning for the loveless life itself, for the meaninglessness of an existence with, or without, men:

> For the eight years of mourning, not a breath of air will get in this house from the street. [read *life* for "air"] We'll act as if we'd sealed up the doors and windows with bricks. [The house now becomes a tomb.] That's what happened in my father's house—and in my grandfather's house.

Meantime, you can all start embroidering your hope-chest linens.

As Professor Morris Freedman puts it, Bernarda has set herself up as a housekeeper, a "Mother Superior," of a "do-it-yourself nunnery." The epithet, wry as it is, is apt, in the context of the play. There is something of a Menckenesque iconoclasm about it, without its necessarily carrying pejorative connotations about the real thing. Yet, surely, the image is not inapposite. For as the true nunnery represents the quest for a *life* beyond life (or even a spiritual life in the present life)—and here the contrast is crucial—so does Bernarda's "do-it-yourself" institution represent a flight from life, both physical *and* spiritual—a flight towards physical and spiritual death. It is, in short, as Professor Freedman has put it, "a denial of *all* human passion,"—even spiritual passion; accordingly, like so many other "do-it-yourself" counterparts at less dramatic levels, Bernarda's effort, lacking professional know-how, and the success that comes of that know-how, must come to rest in an amateur, but expensive, failure—the failure of life to assert itself over death. For even in Bernarda's perfectionism ["For a hundred miles around there's no one good enough to come near them."], we are already permitted to see the kind of "purity of aims" and the "nobility of purpose," which, in the words of Henry Miller, makes for a "universe of death." And the irony is made even more bitter in the scene where the girls are prevailed upon by Bernarda to get to work on their *hope*-chests [my emphasis].

Yet, for all her insistence on malelessness, Bernarda, and through her, her daughters, become—as if it were in the very nature of the default, or because of it—obsessed with maleness. Poncia is relating the details of a prurient incident to Bernarda; it concerns the men of the village and their Sabine abduction of one of the village women, Paca la Roseta.

> PONCIA: They were talking about Paca la Roseta. Last night they tied her husband up in the stall, stuck her on a horse behind the saddle, and carried her away to the depths of the olive grove.
>
> BERNARDA: And what did she do?
>
> PONCIA: She? She was just as happy—they say her breasts were exposed and Maximiliano held her as if he were playing a guitar. Terrible!
>
> BERNARDA: And what happened?
>
> PONCIA: What had to happen. They came back almost at daybreak. Paca la Roseta with her hair loose and a wreath of flowers on her head.
>
> BERNARDA: She's the only bad woman we have in the village [Bernarda's ideas of badness seem to be peculiarly singleminded.].
>
> PONCIA: Because she's not from here. She's from far away. And those who went with her are the sons of outsiders too. The men from here aren't up to a thing like that.
>
> BERNARDA: No, but they like to see it, and suck their fingers over it.

These last words of Bernarda, ironically, are nothing more

than an unwitting commentary on her own and Poncia's preoccupation with the verbal motion picture of pruriency—the preoccupation, if not obsession, of women without men—with the details of unashamed sex. If there is any "finger-sucking" here it is of course Bernarda's. Poncia's word-pictures, and Bernarda's questions, are the reverse side of the coin of the rougher, no-holds-barred tavern pruriency of the men. But where the men eventually translate their words into action, and thus find release—as in the episode of Paca la Roseta—the women can only find a dubious "release" in the non-release of verbal masturbation. This is both their fate as women trying to live up to a code of social values and as symbols of that declining—if still iron-gripped—code. And it is their curse too. For it is their fate to go on *talking* about the life outside the house, with its arousing escapades of "shame" and "shock," the better to insulate themselves from their unacknowledged fear of that life. But where D. H. Lawrence often makes this the explicit statement of his themes (talk and cerebration as a kind of death), Lorca, even more powerfully, because so implicitly, shows it in the actions (or lack of actions) of his characters.

The other characters, apart from Bernarda herself, draw in, or away from, her as the necessity of the drama determines. There seems to be in them both a quality of repulsion from, and fascination for, the indomitable energy—death-inspired though it is—of Bernarda. And to this extent, the others are both dominated and fascinated by her. Bernarda, like her "sister" Mrs. Alving in Ibsen's *Ghosts* and her "cousin" Madam Ranevsky in Chekhov's *Cherry Orchard*—both of whom, like Bernarda, also represent a certain kind of death—is an "arranger," to use Professor Freedman's word for the type. At the beginning of the play, she is there to arrange the mourning for her husband, and to arrange his funeral; throughout the play, she arranges—with some impressive success—the lives of her daughters; at the end of the play, with Adela's suicide by self-strangulation, she sends out instructions:

> Cut her down! My daughter died a virgin. Take her to another room and dress her *as though* [my emphasis] she were a virgin. No one will say anything about this! She died a virgin. Tell them, so that at dawn, the bells will ring twice.

But Martirio, as if to undo the effect of Bernarda's words, has her short moment of rebellion, which soon returns to submission after she has had her say. Of Adela and Pepe, she can at last say: "A thousand times happy she, who had him."

Bernarda not only arranges matters within the house, but her arrangements even affect those who are outside. The twenty-six-year-old Pepe el Romano is to marry the forty-year-old Angustias—for her dowry. But even of this cynically uneven match it is Bernarda who supervises the details. Of course she is aware of the incongruity, the "unnaturalness" of such a match—or, at its mildest, its unsuitability. Of *course* she is aware that Pepe's match with any of her other daughters—even the soured Martirio—would be an even more natural arrangement than the sort of paradoxical extreme which Pepe's and Angustias' represents. Yet it is decorum, her concern for the social con-

ventions of her milieu, that prompt her into pushing the Pepe-Angustias match. It is as if she were able to anticipate the impossible position she will be placed in by having Angustias remain, before the world, a spinster one day longer. And while it is true that Bernarda is strong-willed, she is not so strong-willed that appearances do not have their effect on her. Indeed, it is primarily her concern for appearances that motivates her into the kind of tyranny she must wield over her daughters. Thus, in spite of the disparate ages between the two, Bernarda pushes Angustias into the marriage with Pepe el Romano. But of course, even here—*especially* here—the marriage points up with brilliant clarity the nature of the larger problem within the house itself: for both Pepe and Angustias the marriage will itself be a kind of death. And each will repeat, like the "Ghosts" before them, the monstrous motions of Antonio and Bernarda. Pepe, true to Poncia's prognostications, will, if he hasn't done so already, tire of Angustias, and Angustias herself will live out her deathlike life much like Bernarda before her.

If there is the least bit of life in this tragedy of thwarted life, and the abrasively familial relations growing out of that life, it is best represented by Adela in her natural and strong desire for Pepe, and of course in Pepe's illicit return of that desire for her. It is not the "morality" or the "rightness" of that desire that is important, for judged by those standards, it is probably as outrageous as is its opposite in the play—the crushing or repression of desire. And we cannot even assume that it is Pepe himself that Adela desires. But under her limited circumstances he is "available" and he is willing. Perhaps under freer, less restrained circumstances, Adela would have chosen someone else. But there can only be the one choice—and the one *chance*—in this instance.

Adela is not only the most vital of the five sisters, she is also the youngest: she is twenty, old enough to understand with the deep instinctive knowledge of her newly-awakened womanhood that the life about her in the house is a form of death, bent on claiming her to its fold too; yet she is young enough to have thus far escaped the blandishments of that death as represented by Bernarda's complete dominance, her obsessive concern for decorum, the social pressures, and for the Latin woman's greatest dilemma: the cross of *obligacíon*. But because she resists these—and Lorca's tragedies generally arise because of the individual's resistance to what society regards as "right"—Adela must inevitably die. If she makes her peace with the living death inside the house, then she may be permitted to "live" on in a scarcely less dubious "life." But if she resists, then she will, as she must, face the only other alternative: she must pay for her "sin" by dying. And Adela, like Shaw's Joan before her—even perhaps for similar though not identical reasons—chooses the latter. Thus death, which opens the play and sets its tone, also closes it. Yet, after Adela's death, we somehow feel a certain release which we do not feel at the sight of the mourning for Antonio's, a sense that Adela must have felt herself at the moment when she has taken her own extreme action to break out of the living death. Even so, while life goes on much as it has done before, appearances, at whatever cost, must be kept up. Thus Bernarda's "Tell them . . . she died a virgin." But the audience offstage—and perhaps even on—knows otherwise!

I should like to say a word or two about the significance of color in this play. The dominant colors are of course the spectrumless "colors" of black and white—the black as seen in the dresses and skirts and shawls of the mourning women—a hue which almost seems to be a national color for the women in Latin countries—and white. The walls of Bernarda's house are of course all painted white. And this goes beyond the contrivance and the esthetic demands of the dramatist's or scene designer's art, either expressionistic or realistic. In point of fact it is immensely realistic, for the walls of countless farmhouses scattered over the continent of Europe are often whitewashed or calcimined in that chalky hue. Yet the realism here, such as it is—and in spite of Lorca's symbolic and poetic powers—is immensely successful, both as symbol and as poetry. For the realism, as in all effective realism grounded in a greater truth, has symbolic force. The white walls are white at one level because of the exigencies of climate, humidity, insulation, cheapness, etc. Yet, since white is universally—at least in the Western world—the hue of sterility, of "purity," if one wishes, the walls obviously suggest the sterility within them. In effect, the colors in the play present a chiaroscuro, or better, a checkerboard, where white and black represent the two kinds of death: white—sterility, the incapability of life to bring itself forth, reproduce itself; and black—where life *has* managed to reproduce itself, yet, where the iron-clad law of that reproduction demands payment by way of its dissolution. In each instance the implication is one of the *absence* of life, the presence of death. Perhaps this is what Melville saw in the whiteness of the White Whale, or in the almost copper blackness of Ahab's sea garb. Adela's green dress relieves the stark contrasts between the whites and the blacks, sterility and death, by pathetically suggesting Adela's own wish fulfillment for fertility, the color of green in her dress, itself so symbolic of fertility.

Thus, even through these stark contrasts of color, the play symbolizes those other greater contrasts and tensions: the house as opposed to the streets; the world inside the house as opposed to the world outside. In the house, the blacks and whites—death and sterility—which dominate; in the streets, the bright swarm of sunlit colors which beat down with the strong life-giving light of the sun itself, while the greenness of the fields—that fertile greenness—glitters beneath the sun. In the house, there is the coolness of the blacks and the whites, which even suggests the dank and musty chill of tombs and decaying shrines, where no sunlight may enter, and where even the thermal appeals to cold and warmth, as distinct from the visual appeals to the colors, become fitting figures. In the streets and in the fields beyond the streets, lies the hazy fecundating heat of the sun—with its encouragement to song and fertility. But finally, beyond the colors, which graphically evoke those contrasts we have already spoken of, there are other contrasts. And they present themselves almost as a kind of contrapuntal fugue which runs through the play: Librada's living child, born out of wedlock (again, the revolt against the mores of the social order) and the murder of that child to hide the "enormity" of the first crime. There is the contrast between Bernarda herself, who symbolizes, and energetically maintains, the social decorum, and Antonio María Benavides, Bernarda's husband, who, if anything, represents the virile side of the family, where death dominates, and who early in the play dies, himself, as a kind of immolation to, and anticipatory warning of, the fact that such a life of profligacy must lead to death; finally, we also have in the play the contrasts [as Professor Freedman sees them] of "the ordered, clean life as opposed to the disordered, dirty life." The terms here should not be taken at their literal or even first level connotations, but should rather be given certain poetic latitudes, where the "ordered, clean life" is, in reality, nothing more than the order and cleanliness of death, of the washed corpse dressed up neatly for the last viewing; and where the "disordered, dirty life" becomes in its fullest measure the throbbing, pulsating life of the streets outside the house, in the village, and beyond the village to the "dirt," the *earth* if one wishes, of the fertile fields from which life-giving sustenance is gotten. All of these contrasts—the house and the village; the stark blacks and the sterile whites as opposed to the fertile greens; the iron-clad law of Bernarda and the breaking of that law by Antonio, and by Adela after him—all of these point to the central tensions of the play itself, those tensions that arise from the greatest conflict of them all, the life instinct in its struggle with the forces of death. (pp. 111-20)

Sam Bluefarb, "Life and Death in García Lorca's 'House of Bernarda Alba'," in Drama Survey, *Vol. 4, No. 2, Summer, 1965, pp. 109-20.*

YERMA

PRODUCTION REVIEWS

John Chapman   (review date 9 December 1966)

[*Chapman was an American editor and drama critic. In the following review, he addresses a Lincoln Center Repertory Theater production of* Yerma, *commenting on its performances and staging and describing it as "a spectacle, a dance, a musical and a haunting picture of life."*]

In Federico Garcia Lorca's dramatic poem, **Yerma,** simple in outline, Yerma is a young married woman of Andalusia who wants a child. But her husband does not. She yearns for this child, begs, goes to female witch doctors and prays at a shrine of fertility. She refuses an offer of extramarital help. She strangles her husband and mourns, "I have killed my son."

But, as it was produced last evening by the Repertory Theatre of Lincoln Center at the Vivian Beaumont Theatre, this outline has been brilliantly, impressively filled out, and it becomes a spectacle, a dance, a musical and a haunting picture of life in some unnamed Spanish town at an unspecified time.

The original production of Yerma *in Madrid, 1934, starring Margarita Xirgu (right) as Yerma.*

Everything contributes to the simple beauty of this production, from the stark yet graceful translation of Garcia Lorca's poem by the poet W. S. Merwin to the speaking of it by Gloria Foster, as the child-hungry Yerma, and the speaking of it by Frank Langella, Tom Rosqui, Aline MacMahon, Maria Tucci and many others.

The setting, devised by David Hays, is merely a flat, round, thrust stage, covered by a reddish, threadbare carpet and backed by some white adobe movable walls. With simple props unobtrusively brought on and off by the players themselves, this stage becomes many scenes, including Yerma's home, a river where the peasant women do their washing and a shrine. These scenes and more are vividly imagined, rather than pictured.

Often there is a background of music by Stanley Silverman, a concert guitarist and a faculty member of the Berkshire Music Center. Sometimes this music becomes song, and it is movingly sung by Miss Foster. The choreography of the wild rite before the shrine has been admirably staged by Jean Erdman.

There is a fine, repressed performance by Langella as Yerma's husband, and a sweet one by Rosqui as a young shepherd who might have had Yerma had events been different. Miss MacMahon, who always displays subtle authority, holds the stage in the role of a wise old woman who has had nine children and tells Yerma it is easy.

The production has been staged by John Hirsch, a guest director who comes from Hungary by way of Canada. His work in bringing a tragic poem to the stage is splendid,

and it adds greatly to the stature of the Lincoln Center company.

John Chapman, " 'Yerma' Splendid at Beaumont," in Daily News, *New York, December 9, 1966.*

Walter Kerr   (review date 9 December 1966)

[*Kerr is an American dramatist, director, and critic who won a Pulitzer Prize for drama criticism in 1978. A long-time drama critic for* the New York Times, *as well as the author of several book-length studies of modern drama, he has been one of the most important and influential figures in the American theater since the 1950s. In the following review, Kerr praises the actors and stage set in the Lincoln Center staging of* Yerma *but asserts that the translation of the drama by W. S. Merwin has failed to give the production "any evocative or integrated stage life."*]

The program notes for the Lincoln Center Repertory Theater production of Garcia Lorca's **Yerma** extend us the courtesy of including one of the author's non-dramatic poems. In a ballad called **"The Faithless Bride"** a young man is slipping down to the riverbank, now that all the lanterns are "smothered" for the night, with a woman he means to seduce:

> The starch of her petticoat
> rang in my ears
> like the noise of ten knives
> ripping a piece of silk.
> Without silver light in their leaves
> the trees had grown bigger
> and a horizon of dogs
> barked from far off on the river.

I have quoted W. S. Merwin's translation at this length because both the imagery and its translation seem to me quite striking. Curiously—at least as **Yerma** is now being performed—the same able translator has not been able to give the same sort of metaphor any evocative or integrated stage life.

Yerma is a "tragic poem" in six scenes, without intermission, relating the mounting despair of a Spanish mountain woman who cannot conceive a child. For six scenes she speaks of little but her barrenness, so that the play comes to seem as obsessed with fertility as she does. No one can enter her house, or so much as pass her door, without at once touching on the subject of the babies that aren't there.

But now the imagery obtrudes, as though the playwright had been sending his actors and actresses separate telegrams to be inserted into the narrative, and coming as deliberately as it does it takes on a highly self-conscious coloration. "When I see you and the other women filled with flowers inside . . . " the distraught heroine begins, but the moment she begins we find ourselves recoiling from the obviousness, if not the stickiness, of the formally intrusive words.

Gloria Foster, the sleek black-haired Yerma with heavy-lidded eyes and a face straight out of Gauguin, asks neighbor Maria Tucci what is it like to be expecting a first-born. "Did you ever hold a wild bird in your hand? That's how it is, but in your blood," is the reply. As the years pass, and as hostility deepens between the deprived bride and her pale, evasive husband, the language goes right on seeking synonyms for her by now thoroughly described plight. Striking her breasts the woman cries, "I feel two blows of a hammer here instead of my baby's mouth," and, falling to the ground, "When I went out to pick my carnations, I ran into a wall—this is the wall I have to beat my head against."

Gradually, at the Vivian Beaumont, the business of listening to constructions that really do seem like artificial carnations brought in to relieve a moody monotone turns into something of a game. When Miss Foster refuses to give up her yearning "even if you tell me to stick needles into the softest part of my eyes," we feel an urge to analyze, to talk back, to get into the game. What is the softest part of the eyes? And has this phrase really done anything other than decorate a solemn song that is standing still?

Certainly a part of the difficulty lies in the playwright's urgent wish to sustain for nearly an evening's length a single, compulsively reiterated state of mind. Though the years slip by, nothing alters. A shepherd who has once stirred the heroine's blood visits her, blandly, politely. A village crone, played with no-nonsense authority by Aline MacMahon, scolds Yerma once, scolds her twice. The tension with husband Frank Langella continues, a matter of strained conversations, implied mutual injury, hurt glances and curt words. But not until the sixth scene—which is a good one—does a direct challenge, or any real candor, erupt between them. Because we are so long circling the subject, words must work overtime.

But there is an additional burden imposed upon the poetic "atmosphere," I think, by the portentiousness, the studied pausing, the statuesque earnestness of the playing. Under John Hirsch's direction, line after line, thought after thought, comes in regular, almost uninterested sequence—rather as though the effect of verse were simply a matter of eternally equal stresses. A visitor whips in at the door. "Come," she says to Yerma. Yerma whips past her. "Come," she says to the visitor. Surely, a ballad, even in its metrical strictness, can change its emotional pace, race its heartbeat?

In fact, we do arrive at a moment of shock and of revelation, though not until the chanted lament is virtually done with. In the very last sequence, Mr. Langella steels himself to speak what has always been *his* truth. He hasn't wanted children. "It doesn't matter to me," he says directly, taut with challenge. Whereupon Miss Foster puts her claws to his neck and most believably drains the life from him, killing her husband and killing her promise of a son in one ultimate gesture. We sit up. There has been a hard, cruel core to the play, after all. Why haven't we felt a whisper of such mettlesomeness, or seen a tendon go truly taut, before?

Visually, Mr. Hirsch has arranged some attractive set pieces: two black-clad sisters of the husband searching an empty room silently, by lamplight; Nancy Marchand,

ready to add prayer and magic to Yerma's cause as she stomps about a farmhouse as though she had learned to walk on the steeper mountainsides. And composer Stanley Silverman has added echoes of mandolins slipping in at the windows to blend with sung soliloquies on stage. More than that, he has given a chorus of washing women, thrashing away at their clothes on a rocky river bank, what is probably the evening's one genuinely exhilarating lyric lift.

David Hays's settings—a pattern of leaves sprayed on a moldering wall, a tall rectangular opening of frayed burlap through which cold light can invade a childless room—are just fine.

> *Walter Kerr, " 'Yerma' at Lincoln Center," in* The New York Times, *December 9, 1966, p. 60.*

CRITICAL COMMENTARY

Robert Skloot   (essay date 1966)

[*Skloot discusses the major themes in* Yerma: *desire, sterility, repression, and honor. He also explores the play's "richness of language and imagery," commenting on Lorca's use of several image groups and noting that many images are presented as simultaneously positive and negative. The author of this essay wishes to note here that, in the twenty-six years since this piece was written, the understanding of Lorca's work and of gender issues has been revised significantly. An updated analysis would, he stresses, acknowledge more recent investigations of the subject and newer methodologies used in contemporary dramatic criticism.*]

The second part of Lorca's trilogy, **Yerma,** was written and produced in 1934. The tragedy concentrates on and revolves around one woman. Unlike the mother in **Blood Wedding,** she has nobody to share her tragic destiny; she shoulders her entire burden and suffers her final downfall painfully alone. **Yerma,** however, is not less rich in imagery or artistry, nor less powerful than the play which preceded it. I disagree with [Angel] del Rio when he writes:

> . . . perhaps because he tried to achieve a purpose of greater scope, we believe that **Yerma** does not reach the artistic level of the other tragedy. It does not have the artistic unity of **Bodas de sangre,** nor does the dramatic motivation appear as clear. In the latter everything is concrete and elemental within a popular and poetic environment. In **Yerma,** in fact, everything seeks abstraction.
> [*Vida y Obras de Federico García Lorca,* 1952]

There is, I think, a greater intensity in **Yerma** because the dramatic elements of the play are so directly aimed at the central figure, so that we are witness to a greater personal tragedy. What del Rio overlooks in his comment on the play is the richness of language and imagery of **Yerma.** He has failed to see that Lorca has intentionally used his language to support and extend the basic image-metaphor of the play—the word "yerma." The word, meaning barren or uncultivated, perfectly and completely describes the theme of the tragedy.

The dramatic motivation becomes clear once we understand how the Spanish code of honor operates, and what its place is at the center of the drama. Further, it is not only the play but Yerma herself who seeks abstraction, as she slowly abandons what is concrete in her life (reason and religion can be thus described) and seeks solace and a solution to her problem in non-rational ways. It is curious, however, that although we can easily accept a surrealistic intrusion in *Blood Wedding* in the forest scene, we find it more difficult to do the same in the scene at the hermitage in *Yerma.* This is because in the earlier play the departure from realism stood by itself, separate from the drama, although linked by a common body of imagery. An identical situation occurs in the Laundresses's scene in *Yerma.* But the ballet and chorus in act three of *Yerma* exist within a scene which begins and ends realistically. This makes us uncomfortable, although it does not negate the theory (and Lorca's own claim) that the trilogy shows the playwright's attempt at an ever increasing realism in his mature work.

The story of Yerma is tragically human in the most universal sense of the word. She is a woman frustrated, a woman obsessed, a woman trapped by her desire to bear children, a privilege that has been denied her by her husband Juan who may or may not be impotent. [Arturo] Barea writes [in *Lorca: The Poet and His People,* 1949] that Juan "refuses the spiritual cooperation [needed] in creating a child." "Her [Yerma's] fatal error," writes [Anthony] Aratari, "lies in having unknowingly separated the womb's fruitfulness from love for man, in having separated good from good" [*Commonweal,* 12 August 1955]. Both critics are correct in their analysis of Yerma's lack of children.

Juan's life is centered on his land and his flocks, which he cares for from sunrise to sundown, and even into the night. Yerma despises the sensual pleasure he takes from her body, a substitute for his lack of desire for children. This Yerma believes to be the cause of her sterility. "What matters to me is what I can hold in my hands," Juan finally declares to his wife (III, iii) and this precipitates the most violent action of Yerma's life, and the most violent of the play. But there is truth in the statement, as we shall later see, that: "In reality, it is Yerma, not her drudge of a husband, who has no purpose and no time for love" [Walter Maria Guggenheimer, *Frankfurter Hefte* XIV, No. 11, October 1959].

Juan covets the earth greedily, blindly, unable to see that Yerma is the earth itself, the potential source of life, and, equally important, the violent force of death.

> That which for Yerma constitutes the axis of her life, the core of her soul, the burning and imperative problem of her existence, is, for him [Juan], something meaningless, indifferent, impractical, alien, remotely existent and ethereal. One cannot imagine a declaration more expressive of the ultimate disparity of their lives.
>
> [Ofelia Machado Bonet, in *Federico García Lorca,* 1951]

We must understand, however, that Juan does not think this way about children—he asks Yerma to bring her brother's child to live in their house—but about Yerma's obsessive dream for children. The difference between the two is the difference between the story and the imagery of the play. Although Juan does refuse "spiritual cooperation," it is also Yerma's imprisoned passion, and her fidelity to her code of honor in the face of enormous temptation, which compel her to destroy her life and leave her forever "tierra yerma," barren earth that not even a successful farmer like Juan could have made productive. Both husband and wife must share the blame for their childless household.

Lorca is primarily interested in the code of honor of his central character, and it is upon the code that emphasis should be placed, not on frustrated motherhood. Critics who have concentrated on Yerma's frustration have failed to see that the central image "yerma" applies to her sterile code as well. It is the same code which we saw in *Blood Wedding;* the code which, because it is taken to an extreme, makes life more painful and dry rather than fruitful and rich.

Act One begins with Yerma sleeping on stage "in the strange light of a dream." A shepherd appears leading by the hand a child dressed in white. The light and mood change, and we are back to reality again, having seen in Yerma's mind in the first seconds of the drama, the essence of the story. The dream-shepherd is, like the real one who will appear later, Juan's opposite: the man who loves both land and women tenderly and naturally, a man who is both a protector and guider of children.

The foil for Yerma is Maria, a simple peasant who is pregnant after five months of marriage while Yerma remains childless. Yerma, who has built her life around an imaginary flock of children, just as Juan has built his real life around a flock of sheep, is made to appear more knowledgeable about matters concerning children than others in the play. But knowledge only causes Yerma pain. To hide the pain she turns her thoughts to a dream world which, as the play progresses, becomes less and less a source of comfort.

Indeed, Yerma lives two lives, one of hard actuality where the plot prevails, and one of hopeful fantasy where the images become the chief concern. When the realities of life overpower her, Yerma retreats to the dream world. This is what most angers her husband, for he cannot prevent her mind from escaping while his is entrenched in a real world below.

The shepherd Victor presents to Yerma one of the many temptations she will face in the play. They are strongly attracted to each other, both physically and spiritually, as we hear in Yerma's conversation with the old woman in act one and later when Yerma leaves her place to stand where Victor stood and breathe in his spiritual essence.

Victor's character, although sympathetic, is not entirely favorable. He is a wanderer, and possesses a dull shyness in direct variance to the "typical" Spaniard. He has nothing of the active passion of Leonardo in *Blood Wedding.* But importantly, Victor is shown as the man who could have made Yerma productive had conditions been different. When Victor finds Yerma making diapers for Maria's child, he advises her to "try harder," one of the several ironic remarks in which he proves his lack of understanding of Yerma's situation.

Other characters appear who will alternately tempt and taunt Yerma. An old pagan woman who has borne many sons can only say when pressed for advice that "these are matters of honor," (I,ii) which is perfectly true in Yerma's case. Even God cannot help Yerma she says, only man.

Juan angrily denounces Yerma when he finds her alone with Victor, suspecting that something physical will take place between them. His mistaken impression will grow, commensurate with Yerma's desire, to great proportions. Juan's fear of public scorn and social criticism, of some concern here, will play a vital role in **The House of Bernarda Alba.** Of greater importance is that Juan's fear is linked to the code of honor, and occasions his remark: " . . . families have honor. And that honor is a burden which rests on us all" (II,ii). Juan, for all his agricultural success, is spiritually and emotionally barren. He bases his life on the sterile code and acts as he does, wrongly, because he is as bound by the code as his wife is. His thoughts are barren even if his land is productive; just the opposite of Yerma whose dreams are lofty as her life is empty.

The second act of *Yerma* begins with a chorus of singing washer-women. They represent the world outside Yerma's personal tragedy yet are fully aware of her problem. They are the first to tell us that Juan has brought his two aged sisters-in-law to his house to spy on Yerma. Never, however, do they mention Yerma by name, nor is it ever mentioned in the play until the sisters, silent throughout their whole scene, dramatically shriek both the name and the curse. The sisters are "beatas," old, shrivelled, perverted spinsters who haunt Spanish homes and churches as self-appointed overseers of religious and moral standards. Later, with Victor gone and the sisters' spying and Juan's presence intolerable, Yerma escapes the house to consult a conjurer. She is left no alternative but to turn aside from the sterile Christian morality, and to seek the aid of pagan sorcery.

In the last act, everything becomes clear, even to Yerma. Even if violence will not solve her problem, she must commit it as an affirmation of the life that is in her and the death that is in and around her. In the final scene at the mountain hermitage, Yerma has come to join in the ancient fertility ritual. The highly symbolic play-within-a-play is enacted, surrealistic and sensual. A chorus appears to comment on the dance of the Male and Female, as they perform a ballet interpretation of Yerma's pilgrimage to the mountains. The commentary is rich in all the natural imagery which Lorca loved; the dance is erotic and sensuous in the extreme. Its story is sexual, but beautiful and not ugly, as Lorca specified in his stage directions.

This is Yerma's last dream. It is an echo of her first dream which began the play, but whereas the earlier dream was plain and simple, this is wild, passionate and complicated. Yerma's imagination is on the rampage. Her hallucina-

tion, with all its fantastic images, is the last time she will escape into the fertile area of her mind. When the dream ends, Yerma is snapped back to her barren reality, where the old pagan woman offers one final but dishonorable way for Yerma to have children. Of course, she refuses.

When Juan arrives he finally admits that he never cared for his wife's dream. He asks from life only land, honor, and periodic satisfaction of his sexual desires. He has not suffered with her, and will not. [Miguel de] Unamuno explains this [in his *The Tragic Sense of Life,* 1921]:

> Lovers never attain to a love of self-abandonment, of true fusion of soul and not merely of body, until the heavy pestle of sorrow has bruised their hearts and crushed them in the same mortar of suffering. Sensual love joined their bodies but disjointed their souls; it kept their souls strangers to one another; but of this love is begotten a fruit of their flesh—a child. . . . For men love one another with a spiritual love only when they have suffered the same sorrow together, when through long days they have ploughed the stony ground bowed beneath the common yoke of a common grief. It is then that they know one another and feel one another, and feel with one another in their common anguish, they pity one another and love one another. For to love is to pity; and if bodies are united by pleasure, souls are united by pain.

The stage directions read:

> *Yerma gives a shriek and seizes her husband by the throat. He falls backwards. She chokes him until he dies. . . .*

Bursting with passion, imprisoned by her honor, Yerma has sacrificed one to the other. With an ironic touch, Lorca ends the play with the chorus of the pilgrimage heard in the background.

The motivations for Yerma's actions are clear and consistent. She is a woman trapped in a bitter conflict.

> For Lorca, also, the myth would be the expression of that fundamental conflict which we call life, a vision of the world as a demand for man to affirm his individuality in the face of forces so brutal as to appear indomitable. We perceive easily the noble and heroic naturalness with which the human being accepts the uneven struggle, and his simultaneous refusal to accept the final defeat.
> [Juan Lopez-Morillas, in his *Intelectuales y Espirituales,* 1961]

Her passion forbids her to accept her barrenness or to accept humility or martyrdom as a solution to her problem. Her code of honor forbids her running off with Victor or the pagan woman's son, and flouting moral and social convention like the bride in **Blood Wedding.** Witchcraft, of course, is no answer. The whole tragedy is meaningless unless we see that Yerma had no choice but to commit violence.

And when Yerma simultaneously commits murder and suicide, she kills with her hands, strengthened with a superhuman passion, the hands which would have held and caressed a child if she had had one. She strangles Juan as he comes to kiss her and take pleasure in her body. She takes his life, and the life of her unborn child, in an embrace from which they will never escape. Juan is at last committed to the earth where he will exist as he existed in life—cold, greedy and blind. For Yerma, pathetic, instinctual, lonely, barren and tragic, there could have been no compromise.

Thus far, we have dealt with the story of Yerma and with its philosophical implications. In discussing the imagery and symbolism of **Yerma,** we must note that Lorca used both in a different way than in the other two plays of the trilogy. In **Blood Wedding** and **The House of Bernarda Alba,** Lorca's imagistic and symbolic skill was employed in an antithetical or dialectical technique, by which is meant that each symbol had a definite and logical opposite in the play. The sun is opposed to the moon, opening is opposed to closing, water is opposed to thirst and drought, freedom is opposed to imprisonment, until ultimately, good is opposed to evil.

This is not Lorca's method in **Yerma;** here he uses a synthetical means of expression. Images in **Yerma** do not have opposites so much as they oppose themselves in a complicated pattern, so that one image, instead of being pitted against another, contains within it its own inherent conflict. The clue to what Lorca is doing here is found in his subtitle to the play: "a tragic poem." **Yerma,** far more than either the play which preceded it or that which came after it, is a poem. Looked at in this light, **Yerma** takes on an added dimension.

In our discussion of the play, we have implied that no matter where the impotence lies, either in Yerma, in Juan, or in both, our sympathies lie with Yerma. But we must see that Lorca intentionally created a character more complicated than she first appears. Since we cannot put aside the central question of the source of the sterility, we must conclude that Lorca would not place the impotence at a specific source, and as a direct result of this, produced a play-poem filled with synthetical imagery, with a deliberate ambiguity at its center.

As indicated earlier, the sterility may be of two sorts, biological or spiritual. Because either or both are possible, **Yerma** is divided into two distinct but intertwined parts: the plot-story which is basically realistic (the biological), and the imagery-symbolism (the spiritual).

It is difficult to believe entirely in Juan's impotence in spite of the old woman's protestations in Act Three, especially since her own son has come to the mountain to find a woman, his house also being barren. Further, the sisters Juan has brought to spy on Yerma are noticeably ineffectual since Yerma is always escaping from them. Nor should we overlook the fact that Juan is one of the most successful and, importantly, hard working farmers in the district to the extent that he even buys Victor's flock. The irony that he should be productive in the fields and unproductive at home seems to be too heavy-handed to be entirely convincing. Victor's remark to "try harder," really applies neither to Yerma, who couldn't "try any harder," nor to Juan who at home hardly "tries at all." Maria's success in bearing children is based on the fact that she doesn't nor shouldn't have "to try," but merely waits—as Lorca would seem to desire in these matters if the world were a better place—confident that nature will take its course.

The case against Yerma is more convincing. Her obsession allows love to play no part in her life. Material and spiritual considerations are obscured by her desire. If Juan is cold, greedy and blind at his death, the same could be said of Yerma in life. She is a strangely fascinating but unappealing creature, given to extremes and wild flights of fancy. Her singlemindedness, including her absolute denial of sexual pleasure conditioned in part by the strictness of her code, makes her a tremendously powerful but repellent figure. Most important, we must see that Yerma *was born to be barren,* as her name indicates. We remember that she comes from a family where children abound, and yet she is singled out to be childless. She is thus marked from birth, and her fate is announced every time her name is mentioned. Yerma never refers to herself as "yerma," but "seca" (dry—she describes Juan in these terms also), and finally as "marchita" (withered). She fears to address herself in her own terms for fear of the truth of her destiny. She herself even says meaningfully that "some things never change." Ironically and unwittingly, Victor shows his helplessness when he curses Yerma with a desire to see her fate extended to another generation, which is an impossibility. "If it's a girl," he says, "you give her your name."

The story of the play is really Yerma's growing realization of her barrenness, and her ultimate acceptance on her own terms, of her fate. But if we look at the play with Yerma barren from the beginning, which Lorca wanted us to see as entirely possible, we see the problem that he must have faced in his use of symbols and images. Whereas in the other two plays of the trilogy he could ally certain images with the "good," and oppose them to the images allied with the "bad," here the protagonists were both "good" and "bad," or better, not "good" or "bad." Images, then, had to serve dual causes, and this is a key to understanding the play.

Water imagery is most important. Dryness, barrenness, thirst, rivers and streams appear everywhere. All around Yerma is fecundity. Crops and sheep thrive, and nature makes a constant mockery of Yerma's life. Not that the land is naturally productive, it isn't. But hard work makes it so, and it is a bitter symbolic pill for Yerma to know that Juan forsakes her bed to be busy all night with the irrigating.

Lorca writes of rural Spain where "children come like water." Yerma goes to the well for water, offers Juan a drink (which he refuses), and embittered, grows "to hate the water from these wells" The laundresses's scene is set by "a fast flowing mountain stream." It is water which must slake the thirst of passion's heat and extinguish the flame of desire.

But water is not entirely "good." It is not only a life-giving force, but stands for death as well. Children may die from a careless "swallow of water," as indeed Yerma's dream child does at the end of Act One when "he cried as though drowning." The old woman who asked God to "send His lightning against those men of rotted seed who make puddles out of the happiness of the fields" is echoed later by Yerma whose curse is "a puddle of poison on the wheat heads." Also, Yerma's passion is a flood (II,ii) sweeping everything in its path. And not only are water's functions perverted, water itself is. The stream has a "torn voice," the river "carries red mud," "gives salt," and above all, the current is icy, too cold to be endured.

Children, we would assume, would be "good." But infants are careless and tiresome. They wail and wet. "We must suffer to see them grow," Yerma says, even if she is "torn and broken" by them. Worse still, children kill, for they are killing Yerma in Victor's song which he is really singing about her. Ironically, Yerma compliments Victor on his voice but she misses the meaning in the words. And children also steal. When Juan leaves for the fields at the end of Act One, it is to guard them against thieves which only a moment before Victor indicated were children. Children are also "doves of fire," and it is a fire that has burned Victor (I,ii).

Needles are important because Yerma is always sewing, for herself and for others. They are used to make the clothes of Yerma's imaginary children. But the little needles can also kill babies, (I,i) just as they caused the "wounds of our Lord." Juan looks at Yerma with "two needles," even as she earlier wished for "needles in the weakest part of my eyes." Juan admits that what matters to him is "what my eyes can see," and we recall that Yerma said "I could see myself in his eyes," even though as a child.

Mountains are important in **Yerma.** Yerma would like to be a "mountain of fire" in bed with Juan, and the mountains issue forth "a river of single men." The mountains are icy and yet still send down children as if frigidity were necessary for fecundity. Yerma wants "to go up the mountain, but [she has] no feet," and yet does climb to the hermitage where she is told that she has feet to leave her house (III,ii), something she will not do. Mountains are called breasts (I,i), and breasts are called doves (II,ii) and give milk, and both doves and milk are white, as is the dream child in act one, the dawn (II,ii; III,ii) and the Female in the ballet. White is also the color of lace which Yerma sews with her needles, the color of ice and snow on the mountains, and the color of the jasmine, the flower which is everywhere in the play because it is the matrimonial flower. Jasmines and roses are flowers and Yerma is called an open flower (I,ii), calls her womb a flower (II,ii), calls old age upon herself as a "withered flower," and yearns for the rose to join with the rose to make one rose in her (III,ii), and end her torment from the "thorns upon her cheek" which are, of course, needles.

Thus in **Yerma,** Lorca has made his images with inherent contradictions and woven them through his play like threads in a fabric, each joined to another and reminding us of others in turn. He does this in his prose, but especially in his poem-songs. If there is one "good" activity in **Yerma,** it is singing, even in bed, for its mention is always associated with childbirth and happiness. And yet the words of the songs are both bitter and sad.

Prolonged barren existence has caused great changes in Yerma. It has, above all, undermined her femininity. (In his last play, Lorca takes this technique to the extreme and makes Bernarda a totally masculine creature.) While early in the play she is spoken of as a beautiful woman, and even has seen herself "as if I were my own daughter," halfway through the play, seized by one of her usual premonitions, she exclaims: "I'll end up believing I'm my own son." Her final tragic outcry is the epilogue to her very masculine act: "I myself have killed my own son!" Her barrenness, the denial of reproduction, has truly destroyed Yerma's femininity.

Yerma also undergoes a religious mutation. She first mentions God when she remarks to the old woman, at least half seriously, that He will help her with her problem. The old woman blasphemes, and advises Yerma to seek man, not God. By the next act Yerma's religious disillusion is complete as she refers to herself as "a part of this wasteland abandoned by the hand of God." Maria's advice to "remember the wounds of our Lord," and Victor's farewell wish "may God hear you," are obviously useless.

Full of bitterness, Yerma sarcastically remarks that "God is God," and recognizes that according to her code of honor, Juan is her "only salvation." The old woman is ironic when she gives Yerma the typical Spanish farewell "God go with you," none the less so because Yerma is leaving to turn her blasphemy from word to deed at the hermitage. When religion, one of the main supports of Spanish life, is removed, Yerma is that much closer to the murderous abyss. Because Christ is often seen as a shepherd leading His flock, because Christ appeared unrecognized to Mary Magdalene as a gardener, and because in literature Christ is often referred to as the lamb of God, any mention of God in this play becomes a highly ironic commentary on Yerma's loss of faith, especially since both Juan and Victor religiously tend their flocks. Along with his imagery, Lorca has undercut religion as well.

We have seen that **Yerma** is a play about barrenness and sterility. This extends to and is derived from Yerma's code. Yerma is bound by it and kills by it. Juan too lives by the code. His chief worry is believing, mistakenly, that Yerma has violated the code, the ultimate manifestation of his sterile mind and lack of understanding. "My life's in the fields, but my honor's here. And my honor is yours too," he tells her. Juan's erroneous belief that Yerma is unfaithful to him denies her any peaceful refuge at home.

In his use of symbols and images, Lorca altered his artistic technique from anthetical to synthetical. [Guillermo] Diaz-Plaja's remark about Lorca's work applies just as well to the imagery in **Yerma:** "All Lorca's work is a simultaneous exaltation in which life and death contrast and mutually illuminate each other" [*Federico García Lorca,* 1954]. Realism, we note, lapses often, not only in the scene at the hermitage, but at many places along the way, most notably in the songs. As a rule, the songs can only be partially understood for their narrative value, but are connected to all parts of the play by their imagery and symbols.

With consummate skill, Lorca the poet put the entire drama into its title, and named at the same time his central character and one of the abundant multiple symbols. Lorca the playwright then sewed them all, like Yerma herself, into the whole tragedy and every part of it. (pp. 151-61)

> *Robert Skloot, "Theme and Image in Lorca's 'Yerma'," in* Drama Survey, *Vol. 5, No. 2, Summer, 1966, pp. 151-61.*

Guadalupe Martinez Lacalle   (essay date 1988)

[*In the following excerpt Martinez Lacalle demonstrates that* Yerma *follows the typical structure of Classical drama. She also focuses on Yerma's gradual realization and eventual acceptance of her fate.*]

The numerous interpretations to which Lorca's **Yerma** has given rise bear witness to the enormous interest generated by this "poema trágico en tres actos y seis cuadros". While numerous critics have sung the praises of the work's overwhelming lyrical and dramatic power, and the richness of its rural imagery and symbolism, others, on the

Garcia Lorca, pictured here in front of a poster for the theater troupe La Barraca.

other hand, have even gone so far as to cast doubt on its aesthetic and dramatic worth, suggesting that the dénouement is a failure because it does not ring true to human life. My purpose in the present article is to analyse the play in the light of the author's expressed intention in writing it and to suggest that it is in fact a classical tragedy and, poetically and dramatically, a work of considerable range and power. (p. 227)

We are dealing [in **Yerma**] then with a universal theme—that of the sterile woman. And yet the personal experiences of this woman have as their setting a modern rural society—that of the Spain of the 1930's—where monogamy is the rule and procreation is held to be a primary purpose of marriage, beliefs which in both cases have deep religious and social roots. Socially speaking, therefore, Yerma can hardly be said to belong to the lofty world of Greek tragedy. . . . [What] Lorca is seeking to do is to express this universal theme in contemporary terms, giving it a more specifically human dimension.

Let us examine how closely Lorca follows the classical model. The four characters referred to by the author are Yerma herself, Juan, Víctor and the Old Woman. But in **Yerma** we have not a plot but a *fabula*, i.e. a series of stages in the character development of the protagonist which constitute the action and which are underlined by the choruses. These choruses are fundamentally that of the washerwomen at the beginning of Act II and that of the romeros in the cuadro containing the dénouement. Both of them add significantly to the dramatic, poetic, metaphorical and visual dimension of the play, the music and dance contributing to the spectacular element of this tragedy. In this complex tragedy, the protagonist's only "action"—the expression of her thoughts in prose, verse and song—is her evolution from a woman who still hopes to become a mother to one in whom all hope of motherhood has died—the trajectory, in other words, of a character who falls from her initial state, moving from ignorance of her destiny to awareness of her tragic reality. It is a process of struggle and suffering (pathos) through which Yerma comes to realise her initial error, her catastrophic hamartia, and which leads her to recognition (anagnorisis) and acceptance of her tragic fate and to final isolation. Her suffering is that of the archetypal fertile woman, the potential mother, whose vital impulse consists in imitating (mimesis) the process of Creation itself but whose fate prevents the fulfilment of her raison d'être. This tragic suffering—that of a morally good woman, constant and true to herself, of a believable character—evokes in the spectator feelings of terror and pity: the aristotelian catharsis.

The inescapable fate which has made the protagonist the victim of sterility is expressed in the metaphorical title of the play (there are of course also allusions to her fatal destiny scattered throughout the work). The name Yerma is derived from the adjective *yermo*, which, according to the second definition provided by María Moliner, "se aplica al terreno sin árboles y no cultivable o no cultivado" [*Diccionario del uso español*, 1981]. The title foreshadows the dénouement of the play, the ennobling catastrophe; my primary concern at the moment, however, is with the implications of the word *yermo*, since nobody will ever know why Yerma—this "campo seco donde caben arando mil pares de bueyes"—is barren: whether because she herself is sterile ground in which no seed can germinate, or because she has not received a seed capable of fertilising her. Does the fault lie with Juan, whose seed, according to the insinuations of the Old Woman in Act I, is "podrida"? Or with Yerma, for receiving good seed in barren ground?

And yet if it is her destiny to remain barren, how can we speak of fault at all? There is therefore both tragic irony and a tragic ambiguity in the play's title. As Calvin Cannon has pointed out [*Symposium* 16 (1962)], if either of them were indeed at fault, Yerma would stir our compassion, but she would not be tragic. But in her underlying internal conflict, Yerma oscillates between a belief that she is innocent and Juan guilty and vice versa. This oscillation furnishes the tragedy with its dramatic and poetic tension and any account which dispensed with it, for example by treating Yerma's behaviour as merely the product of a disturbed mind, would destroy much of the grandeur and tragedy of the play.

The idea of guilt appears early on in the play, but the chorus of the washerwomen in Act II brings it unambiguously to the fore. In this chorus there is only one character who defends Yerma in the face of the accusing tone adopted by the other women, saying: "Ella no tiene hijos, pero no es por culpa suya". One washerwoman blames Juan, another Yerma: both accusation and defence are emotional in character and have their origins in deeply rooted popular beliefs. It is their poetic and lyrical potential which appeals to Lorca. We are moving here in the realm of the mysterious and intuitive, which reveals a state of mind which is destined to destroy what on the surface was "un canasto de rosas". One of the washerwomen declares sententiously: "Tiene hijos la que quiere tenerlos". With a hostility not entirely free of envy, she accuses Yerma on the one hand of not accepting her destiny and on the other of lacking the will to have children, which, at least according to the lyrical dimension of the play (in what is clearly another reflection of rural beliefs), is, along with sexual passion, an indispensable requirement for conception. The scene, which has considerable poetic and dramatic power, ends with an erotic hymn to conception, full of sexual and life-giving symbols—water, current, seed, sex seen as a flower—contrasted with those associated with "la casada seca".

The character, the moral grandeur, of Yerma make her stand out from the rest of the community and isolate her within it. She is also an anomaly in terms of the prevailing code, which identifies womanhood with motherhood. In her thirst for motherhood (she does not want to raise the children of another, such as the nephew which Juan suggests), Yerma affirms her will against social norms and distances herself from them. She is thus different from the other women in the play. As Lorca himself has indicated, he is contrasting in this work—tragically and metaphorically—death, represented by Yerma's infertility, and the living poem of natural fertility which surrounds her. The Old Woman with her fourteen children, the washerwomen, etc., live according to the rhythm of the seasons: they are born, they grow, they reproduce and they die, putting up with the vagaries of fortune and accepting whatever may fall to their lot, allowing themselves simply to be borne along by time and life. Hence their advice to Yerma that "Lo importante de este mundo es dejarse llevar por los años", and their accusation that she is unwilling to accept her fate: "Todo esto son cuestiones de gente que no tiene conformidad con su sino". They are impervious to any human value which might raise them beyond the realm of the purely physical; bound as they are to the earth, they are happy without being conscious of their happiness. One might, indeed, go so far as to say that all the characters in the play, with the exception of Yerma herself, are spiritually barren. Yerma is the ideal mother. She has a far deeper understanding of child-rearing than the mothers around her and, unlike them, wants to experience all the physical, emotional and spiritual sensations involved in the conception and development of a child. She understands the suffering involved in this process and is willing to confront it. (pp. 227-29)

This tragically suffering Yerma, the noble woman who stands out from her community, is, at the start of the play, still calm, affectionate to her husband and hopeful of fulfilling her existential role. By Act III she is saying that she no longer loves her husband. Her initial error was to marry Juan, a man with whom she can never fulfil herself as a human being. At the same time, she realises that with Victor she would have found complete fulfilment. Her hamartia stems from a choice which was neither fully free nor totally determined, as befits a classical tragic hero. Yerma, as she points out to her husband, was happy to get married. She makes the same point to the old woman: "Me lo dio mi padre y yo lo acepté. Con alegría. Esta es la pura verdad". In other words, Yerma did not object to an arranged marriage, it was not imposed on her by her father and she married, as she herself goes on to state, primarily with the thought of children in mind: "Yo me entregué a mi marido por él [the child], . . . pero nunca por divertirme".

It is important to bear in mind the moral principles which govern the society of Lorca's rural trilogy, on obedience to which depends the stability and order of his world. These principles are the reflection of a mentality, a way of thinking. Among the better-off sections of the community marriages were a matter of convenience: sexual attraction between the partners did not necessarily come into it, either developing after the marriage or never developing at all. We should also bear in mind that according to the version of canon law then in force (*Código de Derecho Canónico*) the primary purpose of marriage was procreation, the relief of lust being only a secondary consideration. . . . As Yerma realises that Juan lacks the two things which she and her community consider indispensable for conception (sexual passion and the will to create), she says (Act III): "Cuando me cubre cumple con su deber, pero yo le noto la cintura fría, como si tuviera el cuerpo muerto, y yo, que siempre he tenido asco de las mujeres calientes, quisiera ser en aquel instante como una montaña de fuego". In other words, and despite her initial scruples, her desire to have children makes her want to compensate for her husband's coldness and erotic deficiency.

But let us examine Yerma's process of self-discovery. At the beginning of the action, on a morning radiant with spring sunshine, the protagonist dreams. Her subconscious desire takes concrete shape upon the stage as a shepherd enters leading a child dressed in white by the hand. This dream, as well as establishing the theme of the tragedy, also prefigures her destiny, for the colour of the child's dress is a metaphor for death and lack of fulfilment. In the dialogue with Juan which follows, it is made clear that he has no interest in children: "No tenemos hijos que gasten". All he is interested in is his money and his reputation. Shortly afterwards, the words of Victor show the contrast between the two men: "En esta casa hace falta un niño". In the presence of Victor Yerma has a kind of subconscious intuition of what might have been and now never will be: she asks Victor whether he can hear a child crying "como ahogado". In the first stage direction after Victor's exit, Yerma is lost in thought and *"acude al sitio donde ha estado Victor y respira fuertemente, como si aspirara aire de montaña"*—in other words, the vivifying air, the breath of life that she cannot find in her husband. In all her subsequent encounters with Victor, both the stage directions and the dialogue make it clear that their attraction is mutual.

After three years of childless married life, an anguished Yerma begins to confront, courageously yet tragically, a whole world of suspicion, taboo and social observance. She seeks advice from strangers, to the detriment of that external honour which Juan so jealously seeks to guard, in the hope that they will help her to relieve her anguish and solve her problem. The insinuations of the Old Woman—"¿A ti te gusta tu marido?" and "¿No tiemblas cuando se acerca a ti?"—give her food for thought, for she has only experienced such feelings with Victor, and that some time ago. Yerma thus becomes aware of the erotic attraction she feels for the shepherd. When he takes leave of her after selling his sheep to Juan, *"Yerma queda angustiada, mirando la mano que ha dado a Victor"*. The identification of Victor with the shepherd of the first act is made clear. With him Yerma would have experienced a complete and natural bond and her life would have been fruitful. The presence in the play of Victor, therefore, enables Yerma to discover her error. Yet neither he nor the Old Woman's son nor the young studs at the romería are considered as a solution to the sterility of the protagonist. Her destiny ties her inescapably to Juan. (pp. 230-32)

Yerma is of good stock, in other words of prolific ancestry. Juan, on the other hand—or so we are told by the Old Woman—comes of a rather infertile family: "Ni su padre, ni su abuelo, ni su bisabuelo se portaron como hombres de casta". Hence Yerma's fury when her honour is put in doubt. Honour is this tragedy serves to underline the noble character of the protagonist and the gulf which separates her from the rest of the characters. (p. 232)

In the gradual isolation to which the protagonist is condemned her husband's lack of understanding plays no small part. A dogged worker who counts his money at night, there is not a single suggestion in the text that his ambitions go beyond the realm of the purely material, and although he is concerned about Yerma's material wellbe-ing, he cannot understand her spiritual and psychological needs. He is clearly not a very interesting character, but it can be said of him that he is morally good. They are two characters whose fundamental urges are mutually exclusive. Yerma gradually comes to the conclusion that her husband is blameworthy, as for example when she tells Dolores (after the latter says that Juan is good and that he is also suffering): "No sufre. Lo que pasa es que él no ansía hijos". (p. 233)

Yerma's solitude, and the lack of understanding of the other characters, reach their peak in the dénouement at the romería. . . . This is the moment when the tragic heroine arrives at her anagnorisis, the recognition that she is a woman who will never be fertile:

> ¡Marchita, sí, ya lo sé! ¡Marchita! . . . Desde que me casé estoy dándole vueltas a esta palabra, pero es la primera vez que la oigo, la primera vez que me la dicen en la cara. La primera vez que veo que es verdad.

This is followed by the final confrontation with her husband, who has been lying in wait. He also suffers, but his bitter complaints denote once again his lack of understanding. Yerma's vital impulses are dismissed as "cosas oscuras, fuera de la vida . . . cosas que están en el aire". When he says shortly afterwards "No tenemos culpa ninguna", he is quite right, for the fault is no one's: it is to be found in fate, in Yerma's passionate longing for motherhood. The dramatic tension increases when he states openly that he does not care and never has cared about a child, that he never wanted one. Juan, in rejecting the desire for renewal, does not behave as an "hombre de casta": he therefore declares himself guilty. Then, in a display of passion without precedent in the play and possibly due to the effects of wine, he tries to seduce his wife, but it is too late. Echoing her words in the previous scene, but with a different meaning (yet another example of the incompatibility of these two characters), he says: "A ti te busco. Con la luna estás hermosa". When he tries to kiss her, it is now she who rejects her husband, crying: "Eso nunca. Nunca". Yerma will not now accept erotic passion devoid of procreative purpose. The stage directions reads: *"Le aprieta la garganta hasta matarle"*. And in her recognition she repeats: "Marchita, marchita, pero segura. Ahora sí que lo sé de cierto. Y sola . . . Con el cuerpo seco para siempre." Yerma's is not a violent character, and yet her passion, the blood of her fertile stock, urge her towards destruction with gigantic force. Yerma has found her identity as a barren woman and triumphantly accepts her destiny when she strangles Juan. Finally, before the chorus of pilgrims which has gathered around, she accepts full responsibility for her act: "¡No os acerquéis, porque he matado a mi hijo, yo misma he matado a mi hijo!". These words bring the tragedy to a close. In killing Juan, she is symbolically killing the child that might have been, for Juan, as I have repeatedly stated, is her only chance of conceiving. Juan may be considered a scapegoat, a propitiatory sacrifice, the *pharmakos* of the Greeks—the victim of an adverse destiny.

The tragedy ends with the triumphant and liberating cry of an ennobled woman, who, with her integrity intact and definitively alone, takes charge of her own destiny. It is an irrevocable ending, which closes the door on any chance of beginning over again. The tragic chant of the pilgrims' chorus is heard in the background as the curtain falls.

The aristotelian catharsis is felt to the full. The audience's emotions are purged by the horror provoked by the tragic and irreversible ending, the development of which it has followed step by step, and the pity provoked by the sight of the heroine valiantly struggling against her destiny and finally accepting it—a destiny which she does not deserve, since she has no moral blame or conscious responsibility for it.

Yerma's passionate longing for motherhood—the tragedy of the woman who, as I hope to have shown, is **Yerma**—achieves in Lorca's hands the heights of classical tragedy, the theme, action and characters being expressed through the magic of words—the metaphors and symbols drawn from the rural environment so beloved of Lorca, the poet and dramatist. (pp. 234-35)

> *Guadalupe Martinez Lacalle, "Yerma: 'Una Tragedia Pura y Simplemente'," in Neophilologus, Vol. LXXII, No. 2, April, 1988, pp. 227-37.*

FURTHER READING

AUTHOR COMMENTARY

García Lorca, Federico. "Lorca Discusses His Plays," edited by Barnard Hewitt; translated by Rupert C. Allen, Jr. *Tulane Drama Review* 7, No. 2 (Winter 1962): 111-19.

> Translated interviews and excerpts of Lorca's writings on the theater taken from the "Entrevistas" section of his *Obras completas.*

OVERVIEWS AND GENERAL STUDIES

Adams, Mildred. *García Lorca: Playwright and Poet.* New York: George Braziller, 1977, 204 p.

> A critical biography. Adams concludes that Lorca can be understood only through an objective study of his life and work, with a particular emphasis on the effect his visits to North and South America had on his work and philosophy.

Allen, Rupert C. *Psyche and Symbol in the Theater of Federico García Lorca: Perlimplín, Yerma, Blood Wedding.* Austin: University of Texas Press, 1974, 224 p.

> Surveys three of Lorca's dramas in terms of their characters, who "unfold, grow, and meet their fate in a dense realm of shifting symbols."

Cobb, Carl W. *Federico García Lorca.* New York: Twayne Publishers, Inc., 1967, 160 p.

> A biographical and critical study. Cobb illustrates "a basic duality" in Lorca's body of work between traditional Spanish elements and Surrealist aspects.

Colecchia, Francesca, ed. *García Lorca: A Selectively Anno-*

tated Bibliography of Criticism. New York: Garland Publishing, 1979, 313 p.

> Divided into sections on the author's life, general criticism of his work, and criticism of individual dramas and poetry collections.

———, ed. *García Lorca: An Annotated Primary Bibliography.* New York: Garland Publishing, Inc., 1982, 281 p.

> A comprehensive bibliography including sections on Spanish editions of Lorca's plays and poetry; on translations of his works into twenty-five languages, including English; and on Lorca's interviews and correspondence.

Crow, John A. *Federico García Lorca.* Los Angeles: University of California, 1945, 116 p.

> A comprehensive examination of Lorca's poetry and theater. Crow, a fellow-student and friend of Lorca while both were attending Columbia University in New York, praises Lorca for his "complete identity with the soul of his nation."

Duran, Manuel, ed. *Lorca: A Collection of Critical Essays.* Englewood Cliffs, N.J.: Prentice-Hall, 1962, 181 p.

> Includes essays by such critics as William Carlos Williams, J. B. Trend, Roy Campbell, Edwin Honig, and Angel del Rio.

Higginbotham, Virginia. *The Comic Spirit of Federico García Lorca.* Austin: University of Texas Press, 1976, 181 p.

> Asserts that "the comic passages in Lorca's plays were important and related to the playwright's outpouring of fear and frustration."

Honig, Edwin. *García Lorca.* Norfolk, Conn.: New Directions Books, 1944, 242 p.

> Examines the works of Lorca, whose "genius grew . . . out of a richly functioning Spanish tradition."

———. "Lorca to Date." *Tulane Drama Review* 7, No. 2 (Winter 1962): 120-26.

> Examines the unpublished works of García Lorca and assesses his critical reputation.

Lima, Robert. *The Theatre of García Lorca.* New York: Las Americas Publishing Co., 1963, 338 p.

> Surveys Lorca's plays, "analyzing each under several critical, historical and biographical microscopes."

Otis, Mary. "Lorca's Audience." *Theatre Arts* XXXVI, No. 5 (May 1951): 37-9.

> Examines typical responses to Lorca's theater, concluding that, if an American audience fails to be moved by one of Lorca's plays, "it is not because the production is too Spanish, but because it is not Spanish enough."

Wells, C. Michael. "The Natural Norm in the Plays of F. García Lorca." *Hispanic Review* XXXVIII, No. 3 (July 1970): 299-313.

> Depicts the contrast between natural and unnatural elements in Lorca's works. Wells asserts that in the early plays, the conflict is "represented as the contrast between individuals," while in the later plays it is manifested as the "clash of forces within single characters."

BLOOD WEDDING

Gaskell, Ronald. "Theme and Form: Lorca's *Blood Wedding.*" *Modern Drama* V, No. 4 (February 1963): 431-39.

Asserts that of Lorca's three rural tragedies, *Blood Wedding* "is at once the most original and the most impressive."

Palley, Julian. "Archetypal Symbols in *Bodas de Sangre.*" *Hispania* L, No. 1 (March 1967): 74-9.

Examines the prevailing metaphors and symbols of *Blood Wedding,* concluding that they "confirm the play's structure and weave together the various parts of its acts and scenes."

Touster, Eva K. "Thematic Patterns in Lorca's *Blood Wedding.*" *Modern Drama* VII, No. 1 (May 1964): 16-27.

Explores some of the difficulties that arise from the fusion of poetry, music, and drama in *Blood Wedding.*

Zimbardo, R. A. "The Mythic Pattern in Lorca's *Blood Wedding.*" *Modern Drama* X, No. 4 (February 1968): 364-71.

Refutes the notion that Lorca's drama is narrow and parochial. Using *Blood Wedding* as an example, Zimbardo asserts that Lorca's work is "elemental in the way ancient drama is elemental."

THE HOUSE OF BERNARDA ALBA

Bentley, Eric. "The Poet in Dublin." In his *In Search of Theater,* pp. 215-32. New York: Alfred A. Knopf, 1953.

An analysis of *Bernarda Alba* "as discovered in production."

Cueto, Ronald. "On the Queerness Rampant in the House of Bernarda Alba." In *Leeds Papers on Lorca and on Civil War Verse,* edited by Margaret A. Rees, pp. 9-42. Leeds: Trinity and All Saints' College, 1988.

An in-depth study of the world of Bernarda Alba. Cueto concludes that "Lorca's foreignness [is] more apparent than real."

Sharp, Thomas F. "The Mechanics of Lorca's Drama in *La casa de Bernarda Alba.*" *Hispania* XLIV, No. 2 (May 1961): 230-33.

Examines the setting and symbols in *The House of Bernarda Alba* as effective vehicles for Lorca's significant themes.

Torrente Ballester, Gonzalo. "Bernarda Alba and Her Daughters, or a World without Pardon." In *The Theatre Annual,* edited by John V. Falconieri and Blanche A. Corin, pp. 7-18. Cleveland, Ohio: Western Reserve University Press, 1963.

Presents an analysis of the characters in *Bernarda Alba.*

YERMA

Cannon, Calvin. "The Imagery of Lorca's *Yerma.*" *Modern Language Quarterly* XXI, No. 2 (June 1960): 122-30.

Maintains that *Yerma* relies not on plot but on imagery to confirm the "tragic conflict . . . between fruitfulness and barrenness."

Correa, Gustavo. "Honor, Blood, and Poetry in *Yerma.*" *Tulane Drama Review* 7, No. 2 (Winter 1962): 96-110.

Describes *Yerma* as "an essentially Spanish tragedy," containing elements of "power and vitality, tenderness and delicacy, together with luminosity."

Lott, Robert E. "*Yerma:* The Tragedy of Unjust Barrenness." *Modern Drama* VIII, No. 1 (May 1965): 20-7.

Traces the character and theme development of *Yerma,* concluding that Yerma's desperate action at the end of the play could be interpreted "as a self-deliverance from her terrible impasse."

Parker, Fiona and McMullan, Terence. "Federico García Lorca's *Yerma* and the World of Work." *Neophilologus* LXXIV, No. 1 (January 1990): 58-69.

Argues that Lorca broadens the scope of *Yerma* through an examination of the characters' roles in the working world and that "the daily grind is a central theme and a vital issue" in the play.

Sullivan, Patricia L. "The Mythic Tragedy of *Yerma.*" *Bulletin of Hispanic Studies* XLIX, No. 3 (July 1972): 265-78.

Asserts that, "because of the interpenetrating nature of man and the cosmos in *Yerma,* not only the dramatic characters but also the entire dramatic action, culminating in tragedy, achieve the level of myth."

MEDIA ADAPTATIONS

Blood Wedding (Bodas de Sangre). Carlos Saura, 1981.

Dance film, choreographed by Antonio Gades, based on Lorca's play. In Spanish with English subtitles.

For further information on García Lorca's life and works, see *Contemporary Authors,* Vols. 85-88; and *Contemporary Literary Criticism,* Vols. 5, 9, 14, 25, 40.

Lorraine Hansberry

1930-1965

INTRODUCTION

Full name Lorraine Vivian Hansberry.

The first African American and the youngest person to win the New York Drama Critics' Circle Award, Hansberry is best known for her play *A Raisin in the Sun*. The story of a black working-class family and their decision to move into a white neighborhood, *A Raisin in the Sun* paved the way for the acceptance of African-American drama by Broadway producers and audiences. Although dismissed by some militant blacks as assimilationist, *A Raisin in the Sun* nevertheless garnered praise as a sensitive and revealing portrait of a black family in America. In her study *Lorraine Hansberry,* Anne Cheney observed: "A moving testament to the strength and endurance of the human spirit, *A Raisin in the Sun* is a quiet celebration of the black family, the importance of African roots, the equality of women, the vulnerability of marriage, the true value of money, the survival of the individual, and the nature of man's dreams. A well-made play, *Raisin* at first seems a plea for racial tolerance or a fable of man's overcoming an insensitive society, but the simple eloquence of the characters elevates the play into a universal representation of all people's hopes, fears, and dreams."

Hansberry was born into a middle-class family on Chicago's South Side in 1930. In 1938, Hansberry and her family moved into a segregated white neighborhood, deliberately violating the city's "covenant laws," which legally sanctioned housing discrimination. When ordered to abide by the law, Hansberry's family, with the help of the NAACP, took their case to the Illinois Supreme Court, which declared the laws unconstitutional. During the trial, white neighbors continually harassed the Hansberry family; in one incident, a brick thrown through their living room window barely missed Hansberry's head. As a result of her parents' dedication to the struggle for civil rights, she became acquainted with sacrifice and injustice at an early age.

Hansberry became interested in the theater while still in high school; later, upon enrolling in the University of Wisconsin in 1948, she studied the works of August Strindberg and Henrik Ibsen and was inspired by a production of Sean O'Casey's *Juno and the Paycock.* She left the university in her second year, briefly studying painting in Chicago at the Art Institute and at Roosevelt College, then continuing her studies in Gaudalajara, Mexico. She moved to New York City in 1950 to begin her career as a writer, working on short stories and plays and engaging in various political activities. She reported for Paul Robeson's radical *Freedom* magazine, writing reviews of books and dramas by African Americans and composing articles censuring various forms of social injustice. In addition, she participated in crusades against poverty, the military arms race, and U.S. involvement in South America. Dur-

ing a protest against racial discrimination at New York University, she met Robert Nemiroff, a white writer who, like herself, was an advocate of liberal politics. A romance developed and in 1953 they married. Nemiroff encouraged Hansberry in her writing efforts, going so far as to salvage her discarded pages from the wastebasket. One night in 1957, while the couple was entertaining a group of friends, they read a scene from Hansberry's play in progress, "A Raisin in the Sun." The impact made by the reading prompted Hansberry, Nemiroff, and friends to push for the completion, financing, and production of the drama within the next several months.

After enjoying solid success at tryout performances on the road, *A Raisin in the Sun* made its New York debut on 11 March 1959 at the Ethel Barrymore Theatre. It was the first play written by a black woman to be produced on Broadway and the first to be directed by an African American (Lloyd Richards) in more than fifty years. When *A*

Raisin in the Sun won the New York Drama Critics' Circle Award, Hansberry became the youngest American and the first black artist ever to receive the honor, competing that year with such theater luminaries as Tennessee Williams, Eugene O'Neill, and Archibald MacLeish. In June 1959 Hansberry was named the "most promising playwright" of the season by *Variety*'s poll of New York drama critics.

Hansberry originally named her play *The Crystal Stair* after a line in the Langston Hughes poem "Mother to Son," but she later changed its title to *A Raisin in the Sun,* an image taken from another Hughes piece, "Montage of a Dream Deferred." Set in a run-down apartment in Southside Chicago after World War II, the play focuses on the Younger family: Lena, the matriarch; her son Walter Lee, a chauffeur; her daughter Beneatha, a college student; Walter Lee's wife Ruth; and their son Travis. In the opening scene, Ruth rouses her family early on Friday morning. She is described by Hansberry as a woman whose disappointment in life clearly shows in her demeanor. Walter, in contrast, is a lean, intense man whose voice contains a quality of indictment. His question—"Check come today?"—immediately alludes to the central conflict of the play. Walter's father has died, leaving a ten thousand dollar insurance policy to Lena. Lena, Walter, and Beneatha long to partake in the American Dream, which for them entails escape from their ghetto surroundings into middle-class respectability. They regard the insurance money as the key to the realization of their hopes, and they all envision different and, due to the relatively small size of the policy, mutually exclusive paths to this goal. Beneatha, who is slim and intense like her brother but distinguished from her family by having had more formal education, intends to use the money for her tuition to medical school. Walter plans to persuade his mother to give him the money so that he, along with two other men, can invest it in a liquor store. However, Lena, a woman whose noble yet unaffected bearing attests to an inner strength, uses part of the money as a down payment on a house in a predominantly white neighborhood, a decision that she feels benefits the family members equally. She entrusts the rest of the money to Walter, who gives it to an acquaintance so that they can start the business. Walter is humiliated when the man runs off with the money, and the family is left with the newly purchased home as its only asset. A representative from the white neighborhood, intent on preventing the black family from moving into the neighborhood, offers to buy back the home. Walter refuses, even though the white man's money would more than make up for the sum recently lost. Walter submerges his individualistic, materialistic aspirations—for a time, at least—and rallies to support Lena's family dream. The play ends as the Youngers close the door to their apartment and head for their new home. For Walter and his family, whose desires are frustrated, this ending leaves unsettled the question posed by Hughes in "Montage of a Dream Deferred":

> What happens to a dream deferred?
> Does it dry up
>   like a raisin in the sun?
> Or fester like a sore

> and then run?
> Does it stink like rotten meat?
> Or crust and sugar over—
>   like a syrupy sweet?
> Maybe it just sags
>   like a heavy load.
> *Or does it explode?*

Because the play explores a universal theme—the search for freedom and a better life—the majority of its first-run audience greatly admired the work. According to Gerald Weales in *Commentary, A Raisin in the Sun* spurns the features of both the traditional Negro show—folksy and exotic—and the protest play, which is typified by black characters denouncing the injustices of white oppression. "If the play were only the Negro-white conflict that crops up when the family's proposed move is about to take place" Weales observed, "it would be editorial, momentarily effective, and nothing more. Walter Lee's difficulty, however, is that he has accepted the American myth of success at its face value, that he is trapped, as Willy Loman [in Arthur Miller's *Death of a Salesman*] was trapped, by a false dream. In planting so indigenous an American image at the center of her play, Miss Hansberry has come as close as possible to what she intended—a play about Negroes which is not simply a Negro play." Subsequent critics have admired Hansberry's ability to capture in *Raisin* the turbulence of the time in which it was written. "The spirit and struggles of the Younger family," Margaret B. Wilkerson has noted, "symbolized the social progress and setbacks characteristic of the 1950s." Similarly, Amiri Baraka, initially one of the harshest critics of the play, later admitted that *A Raisin in the Sun* is "the quintessential civil rights drama," and he admired Hansberry's anticipation of the Civil Rights Movement of the 1960s. *Raisin,* he stated, "dealt with the very same issues of democratic rights and quality that were being aired in the streets. It dealt with them with an unabating dramatic force, vision, political concreteness and clarity that, in retrospect, are awesome." Critics agree that, by blending pressing political issues with a sensitive and realistic depiction of an African-American family, Hansberry produced a work that transcends the limits of both sentimental drama and the protest play, creating instead a work of lasting and universal significance.

A Raisin in the Sun's original run on Broadway lasted nineteen months, totalling 530 performances. In 1961, a film version of the drama was released, starring the actors from the original Broadway cast Sidney Poitier and Claudia McNeil as Walter Lee and Mama. Hansberry won a special award at the Cannes Film Festival and was nominated for a Screen Writers Guild award for her screenplay. She then began work on *The Sign in Sidney Brustein's Window,* a play about a Jewish intellectual who vacillates between social activism and paralyzing disillusionment. The play was produced on Broadway but had mixed reviews and poor sales. Hoping to keep the play alive, a group of Hansberry's friends and admirers organized a campaign to improve ticket sales and raise donations. The play eventually received 101 performances and closed on 12 January 1965, the day Hansberry died of cancer at the age of thirty-four.

Although Hansberry and Nemiroff divorced in 1964, he remained dedicated to the playwright and her work. Appointed Hansberry's literary executor after her death, he collected and published her writings in the autobiographical *To Be Young, Gifted and Black: Lorraine Hansberry in Her Own Words.* Nemiroff also edited and published her last three plays: *Les Blancs,* a psychological and social drama about a European-educated African who returns home to protest colonialism; *The Drinking Gourd,* a black woman's story of slavery and emancipation; and *What Use Are Flowers?* a fable about an aging hermit who, in a ravaged world, tries to impart to children his remembrances of a past civilization.

A Raisin in the Sun is ranked with Arthur Miller's *Death of a Salesman,* Tennessee Williams's *Glass Menagerie,* and Eugene O'Neill's *Long Day's Journey into Night* as a classic in American theater. Recently the play has attracted a new generation of admirers. To mark the twenty-fifth anniversary of *A Raisin in the Sun* in 1984, Nemiroff published an expanded edition of the play, which restored material removed from the first production. *A Raisin in the Sun* was also adapted for television in 1989, staring Danny Glover, Esther Rolle, and Kim Yancey.

Although Hansberry wrote other plays, her name remains associated first and foremost with *A Raisin in the Sun.* Full of power, compassion, and emotional appeal, *Raisin* is considered, without question, Hansberry's best work.

PRINCIPAL WORKS

PLAYS

A Raisin in the Sun   1959
The Sign in Sidney Brustein's Window   1964
To Be Young, Gifted and Black: The World of Lorraine Hansberry [adapted by Robert Nemiroff]   1969
Les Blancs [adapted by Robert Nemiroff]   1970
*Les Blancs: The Collected Last Plays of Lorraine Hansberry [adapted by Robert Nemiroff]   1972

OTHER MAJOR WORKS

The Movement: Documentary of a Struggle for Equality (essays)   1964; also published as *A Matter of Colour: Documentary of the Struggles for Racial Equality in the USA,* 1965

*This work includes *The Drinking Gourd* and *What Use Are Flowers?*

AUTHOR COMMENTARY

Willy Loman, Walter Younger, and He Who Must Live (1959)

[*In the following essay, Hansberry examines critical reaction to* A Raisin in the Sun *and discusses Walter Lee Younger's role, which she feels has been commonly misunderstood as that of a failure. She goes on to compare Walter with Willy Loman, the protagonist in Arthur Miller's* Death of a Salesman, *noting that Walter's struggle is a more positive one and that he manages to hold on to a greater share of his personal dignity than Miller's character.*]

Some of the acute partisanship revolving around *A Raisin in the Sun* is amusing. Those who announce that they find the piece less than fine are regarded in some quarters with dramatic hostility, as though such admission automatically implies the meanest of racist reservations. On the other hand, the ultra-sophisticates have hardly acquitted themselves less ludicrously, gazing cooly down their noses at those who are moved by the play, and going on at length about "melodrama" and/or "soap opera" as if these are not completely definable terms which cannot simply be tacked onto any play and all plays we do not like.

Personally, I find no pain whatever—at least of the traditional ego type—in saying that *Raisin* is a play which contains dramaturgical incompletions. Fine plays tend to utilize one big fat character who runs right through the middle of the structure, by action or implication, with whom we rise or fall. A central character as such is certainly lacking from *Raisin.* I should be delighted to pretend that it was *inventiveness,* as some suggest for me, but it is, also, craft inadequacy and creative indecision. The result is that neither Walter Lee nor Mama Younger loom large enough to monumentally command the play. I consider it an enormous dramatic fault if no one else does. (Nor am I less critical of the production which, by and large, performance and direction alike, is splendid. Yet I should have preferred that the second-act curtain, for instance, had been performed with quiet assertion rather than the apparently popular declamatory opulence which prevails.)

All in all, however, I believe that, for the most part, the play has been magnificently understood. In some cases it was not only thematically absorbed but attention was actually paid to the tender treacherousness of its craft-imposed "simplicity." Some, it is true, quite missed that part of the overt intent and went on to harangue the bones of the play with rather useless observations of the terribly clear fact that they are old bones indeed. More meaningful discussions tended to delve into the flesh which hangs from those bones and its implications in mid-century American drama and life.

In that connection it is interesting to note that while the names of Chekhov, O'Casey, and the early Odets were introduced for comparative purposes in some of the reviews, almost no one—with the exception of Gerald Weales in *Commentary* [June 1959]—discovered a simple line of descent between Walter Lee Younger and the last great hero in American drama to also *accept* the values of his culture,

Willy Loman. I am sure that the already mentioned primary fault of the play must account in part for this. The family so overwhelms the play that Walter Lee necessarily fails as the true symbol he should be, even though *his* ambitions, *his* frustrations, and *his* decisions are those which decisively drive the play on. But however recognizable he proves to be, he fails to dominate our imagination and finally emerges as a reasonably interesting study, but not, like Arthur Miller's great character—and like Hamlet, of course—a summation of an immense (though not crucial) portion of his culture.

Then too, in fairness to the author and to Sidney Poitier's basically brilliant portrayal of Walter Lee, we must not completely omit reference to some of the prior attitudes which were brought into the theatre from the world outside. For in the minds of many, Walter remains, despite the play, despite performance, what American radical traditions *wish* him to be: an exotic. Some writers have been astonishingly incapable of discussing his purely *class* aspirations and have persistently confounded them with what they consider to be an exotic being's longing to "wheel and deal" in what they further consider to be (and what Walter never can) "the white man's world." Very few people today must consider the ownership of a liquor store as an expression of extraordinary affluence, and yet, as joined to a dream of Walter Younger, it takes on, for some, aspects of the fantastic. We have grown accustomed to the dynamics of "Negro" personality as expressed by white authors. Thus, de Emperor, de Lawd, and, of course, Porgy, still haunt our frame of reference when a new character emerges. We have become romantically jealous of the great image of a prototype whom we believe is summarized by the wishfulness of a self-assumed opposite. Presumably there is a quality in human beings that makes us *wish* that we *were* capable of primitive contentments; the *universality* of ambition and its anguish can escape us only if we construct elaborate legends about the rudimentary simplicity of *other* men.

America, for this reason, long ago fell in love with the image of the simple, lovable, and glandular "Negro." We all know that Catfish Row was never intended to slander anyone; it was intended as a mental haven for readers and audiences who could bask in the unleashed passions of those "lucky ones" for whom abandonment was apparently permissible. In an almost paradoxical fashion, it disturbs the soul of man to truly understand what he invariably senses: that *nobody* really finds oppression and/or poverty tolerable. If we ever destroy the image of the black people who supposedly do find those things tolerable in America, then that much-touted "guilt" which allegedly haunts most middle-class white Americans with regard to the Negro question would really become unendurable. It would also mean the death of a dubious literary tradition, but it would undoubtedly and more significantly help toward the more rapid transformation of the status of a people who have never found their imposed misery very charming.

My colleagues and I were reduced to mirth and tears by that gentleman writing his review of our play in a Connecticut paper who remarked of his pleasure at seeing how "our dusky brethren" could "come up with a song and hum their troubles away." It did not disturb the writer in the least that there is no such implication in the entire three acts. He did not need it in the play; he had it in his head.

For all these reasons then, I imagine that the ordinary impulse to compare Willy Loman and Walter Younger was remote. Walter Lee Younger jumped out at us from a play about a largely unknown world. We knew who Willy Loman was instantaneously, we recognized his milieu. We also knew at once that he represented that curious paradox in what the *English* character in that *English* play could call, though dismally, "The American Age." Willy Loman was a product of a nation of great military strength, indescribable material wealth, and incredible mastery of the physical realm, which nonetheless was unable, in 1946, to produce a *typical* hero who was capable of an affirmative view of life.

I believe it is a testament to Miller's brilliance that it is hardly a misstatement of the case, as some preferred to believe. Something has indeed gone wrong with at least part of the American dream, and Willy Loman is the victim of the detour. Willy had to be overwhelmed on the stage as, in fact, his prototypes are in everyday life. Coming out of his section of our great sprawling middle class, preoccupied with its own restlessness and displaying its obsession for the possession of trivia, Willy was indeed trapped. His predicament in a New World where there just aren't any more forests to clear or virgin railroads to lay or native American empires to first steal and build upon, left him with nothing but some left-over values which had forgotten how to prize industriousness over cunning; usefulness over mere acquisition, and, above all, humanism over "success." The potency of the great tale of a salesman's death was in our familiar recognition of his entrapment which, suicide or no, is *deathly*.

What then of this new figure who appears in American drama in 1958; from what source is he drawn so that, upon inspection, and despite class differences, so much of his encirclement must still remind us of that of Willy Loman? Why, finally, is it possible that when his third-act will is brought to bear, *his* typicality is capable of a choice which *affirms* life? After all, Walter Younger is an American more than he is anything else. His ordeal, give or take his personal expression of it, is not extraordinary but intensely familiar like Willy's. The two of them have virtually no values which have not come out of their culture, and to a significant point, no view of the possible solutions to their problems which do not also come out of the self-same culture. Walter can find no peace with that part of society which seems to permit him and no entry into that which has willfully excluded him. He shares with Willy Loman the acute awareness that *something* is obstructing some abstract progress that he feels he *should* be making; that *something* is in the way of his ascendancy. It does not occur to either of them to question the nature of this desired "ascendancy." Walter accepts, he believes in the "world" as it has been presented to him. When we first meet him, he does not wish to alter *it;* merely to change *his* position in it. His mentors and his associates all take the view that the institutions which frustrate him are somehow impeccable, or, at best, "unfortunate." "Things being as they are," he must look to *himself* as the only source of any rewards he may expect. Within himself, he is encouraged to believe, are the only seeds of defeat or victory within the universe. And Walter believes this and when opportunity, haphazard and rooted in death, prevails, he acts.

But the obstacles which are introduced are gigantic; the weight of the loss of the money is in fact, the weight of death. In Walter Lee Younger's life, somebody *has* to die for ten thousand bucks to pile up—if then. Elsewhere in the world, in the face of catastrophe, he might be tempted to don the saffron robes of acceptance and sit on a mountain top all day contemplating the divine justice of his misery. Or, history being what it is turning out to be, he might wander down to his first Communist Party meeting. But here in the dynamic and confusing post-war years on the Southside of Chicago, his choices of action are equal to those gestures only in symbolic terms. The American ghetto hero may give up and contemplate his misery in rose-colored bars to the melodies of hypnotic saxophones, but revolution seems alien to him in his circumstances (America), and it is easier to dream of personal wealth than of a communal state wherein universal dignity is supposed to be a corollary. Yet his position in time and space does allow for one other alternative: he may take his place on any one of a number of frontiers of challenge. Challenges (such as helping to break down restricted neighborhoods) which are admittedly limited because they most certainly do not threaten the basic social order.

But why is even this final choice possible, considering the ever-present (and ever so popular) vogue of despair? Well, that is where Walter departs from Willy Loman; there is a second pulse in his still dual culture. His people have had "somewhere" they have been trying to get for so long that more sophisticated confusions do not yet bind them. *Thus the weight and power of their current social temperament intrudes and affects him, and it is, at the moment, at least, gloriously and rigidly affirmative.* In the course of *their* brutally difficult ascent, they have dismissed the ostrich and still sing, *"Went to the rock, to hide my face, but the rock cried out: 'No hidin' place down here!'"* Walter is, despite his lack of consciousness of it, inextricably as much wedded to his special mass as Willy was to his, and the moods of each are able to decisively determine the dramatic typicality. Furthermore, the very nature of the situation of American Negroes can force their representative hero to recognize that for his *true* ascendancy he must ultimately be at cross-purposes with at least certain of his culture's values. It is to the pathos of Willy Loman that his section of American life seems to have momentarily lost that urgency; that he cannot, like Walter, draw on the strength of an incredible people who, historically, have simply refused to give up.

In other words, the symbolism of moving into the new house is quite as small as it seems and quite as significant. For if there are no waving flags and marching songs at the barricades as Walter marches out with his little battalion, it is not because the battle lacks nobility. On the contrary,

he has picked up in his way, still imperfect and wobbly in his small view of human destiny, what I believe Arthur Miller once called "the golden thread of history." He becomes, in spite of those who are too intrigued with despair and hatred of man to see it, King Oedipus refusing to tear out his eyes, but attacking the Oracle instead. He is that last Jewish patriot manning his rifle in the burning ghetto at Warsaw; he is that young girl who swam into sharks to save a friend a few weeks ago; he is Anne Frank, still believing in people; he is the nine small heroes of Little Rock; he is Michelangelo creating David and Beethoven bursting forth with the Ninth Symphony. He is all those things because he has finally reached out in his tiny moment and caught that sweet essence which is human dignity and it shines like the old star-touched dream that it is in his eyes. We see, in the moment, I think, what becomes, and not for Negroes alone, but for Willy and all of us, entirely an American responsibility.

Out in the darkness where we watch, most of us are not afraid to cry. (pp. 7-8)

> *Lorraine Hansberry, "Willy Loman, Walter Younger, and He Who Must Live," in* The Village Voice, *Vol. IV, No. 42, August 12, 1959, pp. 7-8.*

Me Tink Me Hear Sounds in de Night   (1960)

[In the following essay, Hansberry laments the limited role of African Americans in American theater and ex-

Lorraine Hansberry.

amines some of the factors that contribute to their exclusion from fuller participation in all aspects of producing a drama. She cites stereotypical roles, categorization of plays as "Negro" or not, and a false sense of realism (which dictates that "white" roles be played only by whites) among the main reasons for the persistence of this trend in theater.]

I was visited some weeks ago by a young actress, a member of the cast of a quite successful Broadway show, who had herself won considerable praise from critics and audiences. I also knew her to be among the truly serious students of her profession: one of those devoted actors who spend so many self-imposed extra hours per week in dance, acting and voice studios. She was twenty-four, deeply talented, profoundly dedicated to her work, possessed of a vigorous Broadway credit and—a Negro.

So we spoke at length of her career. Had she, for instance, had offers of other work when the current show closed? "Well," she told me between two sighs, "there is a fall-coming show that I was called in to read for. It turned out to be an opportunity to play Young Negro Problem again." She explained discerningly that an American author, on the incomplete, if desperately welcome, rebound from stereotypes, had written a part for someone who was to make an entrance as a Social Question and exit as a Social Question. And that swiftly.

"How," she asked, "can anybody study for *that?* How can you find shading and character in the absence of shading and character?" As an actress she wanted to know how it was possible to interpret humanly that which was simply devoid of human definition. When would contemporary dramatists not be afraid to invest Negro characters with ordinary human complication, now that, to some degree, more overtly obnoxious traditions had started to fade?

Thinking of her excellent notices in the current show, I asked if what she had described had *really* been the only sign of future work. She laughed and replied, "Oh, no. I had a television call to read for a *traditional.* Not a maid; the *other* category, the 'native girl' bit. And, thought I, a job is a job. So I got the script, studied the lines, and went to the reading. And I read: *'Me sit on me hummock and me tink me hear sounds in de night and den . . .* 'I finally just choked up on it, and closed the book and thanked the people for hearing me, and left. I just can't make that scene any more, my dear. Dis here native is tired of sittin' on de hummock!"

When she departed I was left to reflect on the general situation of Negroes in the American theatre. The authors of the two plays we had discussed were not singularly stupid or untalented people; the question was larger and deeper than their mere inadequacy in dealing with certain kinds of characterization. They had been trapped creatively by an old, monumentally encompassing and deeply entrenched legacy from history.

The sixteenth-century spirit of mercantile expansionism that swept Europe, and gave rise to colonial conquest and the European slave trade, was also father of a modern concept of racism. The concept made it possible to render the African a "commodity" in the minds of white men, and to alienate the conscience of the rising European humanism from identification with the victims of that conquest and slave trade. In order to accommodate programs of commerce and empire on a scale never before known in history, the Negro had to be placed arbitrarily outside the pale of recognizable humanity in the psychology of Europeans and, eventually, of white America. Neither his soul nor his body was to be allowed to evoke empathy. He was to be—and, indeed, *became,* in a created mentality of white men—some grotesque expression of the mirth of nature; a fancied, static vestige of the primeval past; an eternal exotic who, unlike *men,* would not bleed when pricked nor revenge when wronged. Thus for three centuries in Europe and America alike, buffoonery or villainy was his only permissable role in the halls of entertainment or drama. And notwithstanding the few later exceptions in Europe (the most distinguished of course, being the career of Ira Aldridge, an American-born Negro actor of the nineteenth century who toured Europe in Shakespearean companies and achieved considerable recognition), in America the sight or even the notion of a Negro gripped in the complex agonies of a Hamlet outraged a cultural legend as today it yet embarrasses it.

That is why, 140 years ago, local hoodlums descended on the African Repertory Theatre Company at Bleecker and Mercer Streets in New York City, and harassed its actors and audiences out of existence. And that is why Negroes are not integrated in our theatre today.

It is this old historical situation that confronts a theatre, some of whose dramatists are currently baffled by Negro character, and whose producers and their receptionists are reduced to rudeness or apologetic embarrassment as they face the miraculously stubborn and increasing battalion of dark, hopeful faces among the multitude of other hopeful faces in their famous outer offices.

Presumably talent, all talent, is as good for the theatre as democracy is for a democratic nation. But to say so is to ignore that breathlessness and perplexed expression in the countenance of our theatre as it asks, over and over again, "What can *realistically* be done about integrating the Negro in the theatre, given the present racial climate in the United States?"

The question implies that to integrate Negro actors in most dramatic situations is to perpetuate a social lie and invalidate the responsibility of art. It also has a way of starting at the point where artistic questions *are* relevant. It rather sneakily ignores a stupendous area where "art" has nothing to do with discrimination in the theatre. For instance, I have never had the experience of purchasing a ticket from a Negro in a Broadway box office; I cannot imagine it to be a matter of either art or qualification, since, I can testify from personal experience, short-temperedness is not limited to white people, and it is that trait, we have all come to assume, that is the prime qualification for those legendary posts. Nor have I ever purchased a box of mints, or received my program, from a Negro lobby vendor or usher. And, to proceed to more important areas, I have not, in my wanderings backstage, found my 10 per cent represented in the handling of flats, lights or properties, or calling time to the actors. Only on the rarest of occasions have I spotted Negroes in the orchestra pits (I believe only at New York's City Center does that phenomenon occur with even minimal regularity); and never, of course, wielding the baton, despite the lingering legend of a certain people's acute "musicalbility." Similar observations may be made of the chorus lines in our musical comedies.

As for the situation among other echelons of the theatre—the actors, writers and directors—I think only the first two deserve more concentrated thought than the categories already covered. Directors should be men or women who are sufficiently talented to have works of art put under their direction. I cannot believe that their height, diet, place of birth, or race will affect those talents. Naturally it is to be desired that a director have adequate cultural reference to his script, but intelligence dictates that we do not hesitate to appoint plays with Japanese settings to Americans, or American settings to decidedly English directors, and so on. When they are good directors they direct well; when they are poor ones they direct poorly. I have never been able to tell by the quality of a mounting what kind of accent a director has; only whether or not he has done a professional and imaginative piece of work. It would, indeed, take an imaginative piece or argument to show how or why it should be different for Negro directors.

The question of the employment of Negro actors, however, does raise interesting questions, which, it may be argued, in a different sociological atmosphere would be only minor questions of production techniques. But at the moment a fascinating and revealing dichotomy exists within the theatre's most literate circles with regard to the use of Negro actors. People who are most bored and outraged by what they call Ibsenesque or Shavian "boxes" on the imagination of the contemporary theatre, who long for fancy and illusion to take utter command, who can deliver whole sermons on the Philistinism of breaking "real eggs" on stage, very often are, astonishingly enough, among the first to shout betrayal of "realistic" attitudes if one speaks of putting a Negro actor into a non-Negro role. It is most curious. Whoever said, for instance, that Queen Titania was white—or anything else? Or the incidental postman, policeman, clerk or schoolmate in that contemporary play? Or *all* the people in that New York City crowd scene that is allegedly in Times Square. It takes rather more of a trick to imagine a good many urban American scenes without Negroes than with them.

But, above all, to defend a color barrier in the theatre is to ignore or argue against its essence, which has always been illusion. We do not get the blind to play the blind, or infants to play infants. Nor do we move Southern mansions or oceans on stage. It is not necessary. Our theatre must attain a sufficient degree of maturity and sophistication to put aside artificial barriers, to acknowledge that any truly qualified actor, Negro or white, who is made up properly, can do the job. I am speaking, of course, of roles that specify particular skin and hair coloring. When such matters are irrelevant rather than intrinsic, they should be viewed for what they are, and not be made the imagined basis for such barriers.

With regard to Negro writers, the theatre is yet saddled with the notion that their materials are necessarily parochial, and consequently without interest to the general theatregoing public. It is a difficult attitude to prove by looking back over the last six or seven years, when a fast total of *three* scripts by Negro writers was allowed to reach the Broadway stage for judgment by *the public*. It is interesting to note that of the three, two were quite first-rate efforts. The first found a steady and appreciative audience off Broadway when its Broadway run came to a close, and a subsequent motion-picture sale made a rather tidy sum for its investors. The second not only copped a prize, and earned over a million and a half at last count; it ran more than a year (an excellent record, in view of the disturbingly poor showings made by dramas these days), and got itself scheduled for national tour this season; it received production and translation throughout the world, and only its motion-picture production schedule prevented the American company from being sent abroad, as requested by our government, *to represent our national drama*. That is a peculiar kind of parochialism. And even the third show, a dreadful little piece, lasted several weeks too long, in my opinion, before it was buried. Viewed from any point of view, it is hardly a ratio that the rest of Broadway could duplicate.

The above should not be confused, as it often is, with the production of "Negro shows" by non-Negro writers, a somewhat different field. Such shows can be produced more easily, and they are in an area that requires the most revolutionary transition. In the theatre it is our dramatists and musical-comedy book writers who have the largest responsibility for presenting our world to us with ever-increasing penetration and illumination. Sad to say, they have, with only a few fine and notable exceptions, an exceedingly poor tradition to draw on with regard to Negroes because of the scale of the old alienation.

The Negro, as primarily presented in the past, has never existed on land or sea. It has seldom been a portrait of men, only a portrait of a concept, and that concept has been a romance and no other thing. By its very nature white supremacy longed for the contentment of the Negro with "his place"; one is always eager to believe that *somebody else* is exhilarated by "plenty of nuttin'." Since real-life Negroes—with their history of insurrection, "underground railways," mass enlistments in the Union army, petitions, delegations, organizations, press and literature and even music of protest—have failed to oblige, the white writer, in the main, has not failed to people *his* "Negro world" with Negroes who did not seem to know that slavery was intolerable, or that the subsequent and lingering oppression was a form of hell on earth. Thus in the make-believe domains of Porgy and Brutus Jones, only the foibles of *other Negroes* are assaulted; otherwise the heady passions of this particular happy breed are committed only to sex, liquor and mysteriously motivated ultra violence, usually over "dis or dat womans." A larger scale of dreams and anguish eluded their creators, and showed some otherwise great creative imaginations to be incapable of the recognition of the universal complexity of humankind.

This does not imply that malice has always been the intent. It would be as foolish to think that Mark Twain or Mrs. Stowe tried to defeat their own humanist protests as to suppose that Marc Connelly, in a different vein, ever dreamed that he was writing a racist document in "The Green Pastures." Rather, it is a matter of a partially innocent cultural heritage that, out of its own needs, was eager to believe in the colossal charm, among other things, of "childlike" peoples. From that notion, presumably, came the tendency to find non-Negro dramatic and musical materials rendered "quaint" when performed by "all-colored casts." From such an astonishing idea we have been treasured with the likes of "Carmen Jones" in the past, and will undoubtedly be treated to something like "Honeychile Tosca" in the future before it is exhausted. It is also interesting to note, in view of the hoped-for transition, that these translations "to the Negro" have generally meant (aside from adding saxophones and red dresses) haphazardly assaulting the English language beyond recognition, as if the Negro people had not produced an idiom that has a real and specific character, which is not merely the random exclusion of verb endings.

That does not suggest a counterdesire to see Negroes talking (or behaving) just like "everybody else" because, by and large, Negroes do no such thing, as conscientious playwrights will swiftly discover. And neither does "everybody else." American speech is as varied as the wind, and few of our sophisticated writers would dream of putting the speech of Texans into the mouths of New Yorkers for any purpose save that of the broadest comedy. So there is nothing extraordinary in the expectation that Negro speech must eventually be presented with artistic respect for its true color, nuances and variations as they exist for each class and generation.

Finally, I think that American writers have already begun to believe what I suspect has always been one of the secrets of fine art: that there are no simple men. Chinese peasants and Congolese soldiers make drastic revolutions in the world while the obtuse and myth-accepting go on reflecting on the "inscrutability and eternal placidity" of those people. I believe that when the blinders are dropped, it will be discovered that while an excessively poignant Porgy was being instilled in generations of Americans, his truer-life counterpart was ravaged by longings that were, and are, in no way alien to those of the rest of mankind, and that bear within them the stuff of truly great art. He is waiting yet for those of us who will but look more carefully into his eyes, and listen more intently to his soliloquies. We must not be intimidated by the residue of the past; the world is paying too large a price for the deception of those centuries; each hour that flies teaches that Porgy is as much inclined to hymns of sedition as to lullabies and love songs; he is profoundly complicated and interesting; everywhere he is making his own sounds in the night. I believe that it is within the cultural descendants of Twain and Whitman and Melville and O'Neill to listen and absorb them, along with the totality of the American landscape, and give back their findings in new art to the great and vigorous institution that is the American theatre. (pp. 9-11, 69-70)

Lorraine Hansberry, "Me Tink Me Hear Sounds in de Night," in Theatre Arts, Vol. XLIV, No. 10, October, 1960, pp. 9-11, 69-73.

OVERVIEWS AND GENERAL STUDIES

Alex Haley   (essay date 1979)

[*Haley gained fame for writing Malcolm X's "as told to" autobiography and established his reputation with the highly acclaimed historical novel* Roots: The Saga of an American Family *(1976), which traces the author's African-American ancestry back to a tiny village in Gambia, West Africa and which inspired one of the most ambitious television productions ever undertaken. In the following essay, Haley discusses characterization in Hansberry's* A Raisin in the Sun, Les Blancs, *and* The Sign in Sidney Brustein's Window, *asserting that her plays reflect her commitment to the improvement of society.*]

. . . For me, this is one of the most affirmative periods in history. I'm very pleased that those peoples in the world whom I feel closest to: the colonial peoples, the African peoples, the Asian peoples are in an insurgent mood, and are in the process of transforming the world, and I think for the better. I can't quite understand pessimism at this moment; unless, of course, one is wedded to things that are dying out, which should die out, like colonialism, like racism. . . .

[***Lorraine Hansberry Speaks Out: Art and the Black Revolution*** (record album)]

These words of our late sister, Lorraine Hansberry, were not spoken during the late 1960's explosions within such American urban ghettos as Watts, Detroit and Harlem. Nor was she protesting the Cambodian bombings of 1972. Instead, the year was 1959 and Sister Lorraine was expressing herself in an interview on "60 Minutes." Matching tone for tone the acerbic quality of host Mike Wallace's voice, she was responding to his comment that her play *A Raisin in the Sun* ended on an affirmative note.

Especially when one reflects upon the 1959 date, one is aware that Hansberry's entire corpus of work was characterized by her singular penchant for sensing signs of change in the air, and by her ability to make accurate forecasts that were years in advance of a mass acceptance. We have but to recall that during the decade following the statement quoted above, the Civil Rights Movement, first surfacing in Southern isolation, crescendoed into national and even international significance along with other diverse causes which, collectively, saw an unprecedented number and social range of Americans taking up the banners of protest.

Now, on the threshold of 1980, the historical adage again

rings clarion true that "every revolution devours [many of] its own." The toll has been heavy on many drained by exposure to Watergate, inflation and recession. Indeed, not a few have fallen by the wayside, disheartened and lacking faith. The ennui that characterized the Eisenhower years parallels in many ways the apathy of today, which certainly would have sorely frustrated and displeased Hansberry. For she envisioned a world in which good men and women face injustice boldly, and lift their voices to combat it. Throughout her creative lifetime, she served as a model for us all, using as her weapons her verbal articulateness and her powerful pen.

For instance, in a most gripping dramatic example of the triumph of man over his circumstances, in *A Raisin in the Sun,* Walter Lee Younger stretches to the full height of his manhood. A black man who has been systematically disenfranchised, Walter develops a burning need to surmount the poverty of his life. When his dream to own a liquor store vanishes with the money remaining from an insurance policy, Walter will surely crawl back into the hole of his ghetto apartment—we *think.* But not only are we surprised, we are enlightened by the new dimensions that are revealed in Walter, when he musters the internal strength to inform the white Mr. Lindner that he and his family *will* resist all obstacles, that they *will* move into the white middle-class neighborhood.

With a similarly characteristic Hansberry stroke, in *The Sign in Sidney Brustein's Window,* one of her best plays, she helps us to examine the question of faith. A product of the post-war intellectual malaise that found expression in Sartre and Camus, Sidney Brustein has adopted the philosophy of apathy. He no longer thinks he has the energy to devote to politics. But in the end, he—and we—find his commitment to be so strong that despite his wife's desertion and the suicide of a young sister-in-law, he stands firmly against injustice in an affirmation of life. He becomes "a . . . fool who believes that death is waste and love is sweet and that the earth turns and men change every day and that men wanna be better than they are . . . and that hurt is desperation and desperation is energy and energy can *move* things. . . ."

In *Les Blancs,* Hansberry assigns to Tshembe Matoseh the conflict of racial identity versus personal identity. An African intellectual, English-educated, he returns to his homeland only to find it divided by the struggle for independence. Having left behind his English wife and London's creature comforts, and both attracted and repulsed by what he sees in his native Africa, he wishes he could forget the homeland ties but finds that he simply cannot. Ultimately, he discovers that his "two identities" are as one—inextricably intertwined; that it is equally impossible to divorce himself either from the moral rectitude of independence or from his conscience as an intellectual, and he joins the band of rebels as their leader.

The list of Hansberry's contributions is lengthy, but one thing in particular has always struck me as unique, perhaps due to my own special interest in this subject. She wasn't the *first* black writer to illuminate the relationship between the American Black and Africa (that credit belongs to the Harlem Renaissance writers), but she was the first to *popularize* the notion. Merely by the force of *A Raisin in the Sun*'s success, she helped to dispel the myth of the "cannibal" African with a bone in his hair. Her educated African character, Asagai, was certainly the first time a large audience had seen and heard an African portrayed as carrying himself with dignity and as being, moreover, a primary spokesman for sanity and progress. It must also have been the first time a mass audience had ever seen a black woman gracefully don African robes or wear an "afro" hairstyle.

In *Les Blancs,* Hansberry forthrightly states her position on the question of colonialism. At a time when Algeria had exploded and Kenya was in turmoil, she dramatized the African quest for independence. And despite the then unpopularity of her thinking, she supported the concept of self-rule.

Although her works were attended by protest, Lorraine Hansberry was no utopian sentimentalist. She didn't blindly worship one group to indict another. Rather, in her passionate understanding, she treated all of her characters equally. Mr. Lindner, in *A Raisin in the Sun,* is not a cardboard reactionary but a human being whom years of socialization have made racist. His sweat and his voice betray his nervousness over his mission to bar the Youngers' entry into his community. He tries, albeit comically, to justify his presence, explaining that his "welcome committee" deplores the violence that has occurred in some areas over integration. When he makes his pathetic offer to purchase the Youngers' new home at a profit to them, we almost pity his ignorance.

Conversely, just as she avoided creating stereotyped villains, Hansberry fleshed out her heroes with sometimes unflattering humanity. Sidney Brustein's drunken debauch when his wife leaves him; Walter Lee's cruelty to his wife, stemming from his frustration at being deprived of his manhood; Tshembe Matoseh's ambivalent desire to bury his head in the sand and avoid involvement in the independence movement signal Hansberry's understanding of the struggles that engulf and frustrate individuals—and which drive humanity.

And yet, Hansberry never gave up hope that eventually, however clumsily, people could solve their social conflicts. "I think that the race of man is obviously worth saving, ridiculous as it can be."

Lorraine Hansberry's death in 1965 came within a month of the assassination of Malcolm X, when I was just completing *The Autobiography of Malcolm X.* I had personally been in her company but once, briefly, among others at her home. Some months before, I had heard that she was ill, next that she was very ill, and then one morning I read in the paper that she was in a hospital, failing. I went there; none but her family was being admitted, and so I put my name on the list with the names of others who had also just felt we should come there where she was.

I feel now that, were she still among us, in her gentle and yet firm way she would still beckon us to persist, to have faith, and to continue to work for a better world. The final words of Sidney Brustein, trying to make sense out of the loss of his sister, are the most fitting testament for *our* sister:

> . . . That is the first thing: to let ourselves feel again. . . . Then tomorrow we shall make something strong of this sorrow. . . .
>
> (pp. 277-80)

Alex Haley, "The Once and Future Vision of Lorraine Hansberry," in Freedomways, *Vol. 19, No. 4, fourth quarter, 1979, pp. 277-80.*

Steven R. Carter (essay date 1985)

[*An educator who specializes in African-American, African, and Caribbean literature, Carter has published numerous essays in those areas, including studies on Ishmael Reed, Ngugi wa Thiong'o, and Michael Anthony. In the following essay, he explores Hansberry's ideas on women's rights by focusing on her treatment of male characters' attitudes towards women in* A Raisin in the Sun, The Sign in Sidney Brustein's Window, *and* Les Blancs.]

Until recently, Lorraine Hansberry's commitment to women's rights was little noted; it was, however, pro-found. In a radio interview with Studs Terkel in 1959, Hansberry observed "that obviously the most oppressed group of any oppressed group will be its women" and that when they are "twice oppressed" they often become "twice militant." She expressed her respect for such militancy unequivocally in her ironically titled, unpublished essay **"In Defense of the Equality of Men":** "In deed and oratory, in their recognition of direct political action as the true key to social transformation, American Feminist leaders, in particular, set a path that a grateful society will undoubtedly, in time, celebrate." Noting the efforts that women's groups have made toward enlarging "the Constitutional promises of the American Republic to include the largest numbers of its people of both sexes," she further contended that "we might well long for the day when the knowledge of the debt all society owes to organized womanhood in bringing the human race closer together, not pushing it farther apart, will still the laughter in the throat of the uninformed." Although Hansberry once established her devotion to the cause of women's equality by resigning from a job as a production secretary for a theatrical producer because her primary duty was to serve coffee, the best demonstration of her militancy lies in her many yet-unpublished feminist essays and the feminist implications of her published works.

A scene from The Sign in Sidney Brustein's Window. *Sidney (Gabriel Dell) is flanked by his wife (Rita Moreno) and banjo-playing Alton Scales (Ben Aliza).*

Actually, of course, her whole way of life was a repudiation of the limitations that society has tried to place on women. Instead of seeking fulfillment in the traditional, limiting roles of homemaker, mother, pillar of the church, and sexual toy, she sought it in areas in which men did—in artistic creation, in intellectual speculation, in political struggle, in public speaking, in deserved acclaim, and in the pursuit of knowledge about all aspects of life. She peopled her dramas with many powerful female characters whose strength was like that of their creator and with some whose lives were made lame by their efforts to accept socially dictated roles.

Hansberry's bitterness over the subject status of women was tempered, however, by her belief that some remarkable men (and women) would always spring to defend the rights of others. In an unpublished essay written in 1957 and titled **"Simone de Beauvoir and *The Second Sex:* An American Commentary,"** Hansberry observed that "in times past, woman, ignorant, inarticulate has often found her most effective and telling champion among great men" and argued "that if by some miracle women should not ever utter a single protest against their condition there would still exist among men those who could not endure in peace until her liberation had been achieved." Moreover, she believed that "to the extent that the Feminist leaders pronounced *man* rather than ideology as enemy they deserved correction"; she was similarly opposed to white racism rather than to whites.

Partially as a result of her belief that ideologies and systems were the true enemies, she was able to create many convincing and sympathetic male characters with whom a man could easily identify. At the same time, she carefully emphasized the ways in which these sympathetic creations are caught in the web of sympathetic conditioning in male supremacy and the resulting harm that they do to women and themselves. Thus, among her most important male characters are multidimensional figures who are admirable in many respects, who struggle valiantly against a variety of personal and social pressures, who frequently arouse the audience to cheer on their efforts, and who, nevertheless, sometimes callously and sometimes subtly, oppress the women entangled in their lives.

Consider Walter Lee Younger, Jr., in *A Raisin in the Sun.* Walter Lee is a black chauffeur who wants to tear down the economic and social wall built around him and his family by a white racist society, provide greater freedom for his son than he himself has had, and give his family a chance to experience a fresher, more tolerable, more human environment. All of these are admirable aims and gain our sympathy. However, Walter Lee's resentment of the economic pressures placed upon him by the white supremacist structure of his society leads him to display hostility toward his wife for increasing his financial burden by becoming pregnant, toward his mother for not giving him the insurance money she receives from the death of his father, and toward his sister for wanting some of the insurance money to help her continue to study to become a doctor. His bitterness toward his sister is exacerbated, moreover, because he reflects the conventional view that she

should "go be a nurse like other women—or just get married and be quiet." However, once his mother gives him what remains of the money after she has made a downpayment on a house in a white neighborhood and he sees the chance of changing his life, he behaves more gently and responsively to all three of the women, taking his wife to the movies for the first time in ages and holding hands with her afterwards, warmly presenting a gift to his mother, and affectionately teasing his sister about the ambition and idealism he had previously scorned in her.

Walter Lee's ability to alter his behavior after gaining the money clearly shows the extent to which he has been influenced by financial pressures. His new sweetness and concern last only until he loses the money, whereupon he retreats into an agonized and resentful isolation. By the play's end, however, when whites offer to buy the house Walter Lee's mother had bought as a means of keeping the Younger family from "blackening" their neighborhood, Walter Lee realizes that he can accept this money only at the expense of his respect for himself, his family, and his race, and he finally concedes his family's importance to him. He learns that his pride in himself and his pride in his family are inseparable, that anything harming one also harms the other, and he further sees that the three women in his life have always helped him bear the burdens of living in a racist system and are now prepared to be powerful allies in the struggle against this new racist insult, in spite of the implicit threat of harm which comes from not accepting it. Significantly, at the moment Walter Lee announces his decision to place dignity before money, he discusses his pride in his wife and his mother—and in the fact that his sister is "going to be a doctor." His maturing into manhood thus includes not only a gathering of his own strength to fight the racist system but also a recognition of the strength and talents of women. Apparently, the web of male supremacist conditioning can at least be torn, if not destroyed. In our last view of him, Walter Lee is trying to convince his sister that she should marry a rich suitor, but he is not serious; this is an argument between one strong-willed individual and another, and Walter Lee knows he has no chance of winning it. He is just having fun—and so is she.

In the same play, there are two other examples of male chauvinism. Both of the men interested in Walter Lee's sister, Beneatha, display traditional attitudes toward women, though in varying degrees. The middle-class American black George Murchison regards Beneatha's desire to be a doctor as laughable, and when she tries to talk to him seriously, he advises her "to cut it out, see— The moody stuff, I mean. I don't like it. You're a nice-looking girl . . . all over. That's all you need, honey, forget the atmosphere. Guys aren't going to go for the atmosphere—they're going to go for what they see. Be glad for that." Not surprisingly, she dismisses him as a fool. Her other suitor, the African student Joseph Asagai, cannot be so easily dismissed, however, since he is somewhat complex and highly appealing. His beguiling mixture of idealism and sophistication, his seeming role as spokesman for many of Hansberry's political and philosophical views, and his willingness to die either to free his country from colonialism or simply to aid its progress—all lend him the aura of a romantic hero. Nevertheless, he is capable of such insensitive comments as "between a man and a woman there need be only one kind of feeling" and "for a woman it should be enough." In spite of all his revolutionary attitudes, Asagai is, in this one area, a traditional—and fallible—male. Unlike George Murchison, however, he is willing to listen to Beneatha and to take her career goals seriously, thus enabling their relationship to grow and leaving open the possibility that he may eventually free himself of his remaining chauvinism.

Along the same lines, consider Sidney Brustein in **The Sign in Sidney Brustein's Window.** An extraordinarily sensitive Jewish liberal who cares deeply about the sufferings of others, who strongly opposes all forms of social and political oppression, and who displays concern to the point of meddling daily in the lives of those around him, Sidney compels his wife to distort her character by living up to his fantasy image of her. To cope with the strain of residing in New York City, with its filth, its widespread social and economic injustice, and its inordinate amount of crime (the play opens with a discussion of the death of a seventeen-year-old junkie who had worked for Sidney), he has evolved a fantasy of living Thoreau-like in the pure air of the mountains with only a spritely, barefooted mountain girl beside him, and he has pressured his wife Iris to be that girl. This fantasy is not a full-time refuge for him but a retreat for those moments when social and personal strife became too painful. Because of her attraction to Sidney, Iris had originally been content to play this role for him. However, having come from such an environment and considering it boring, she has become increasingly dissatisfied with his fantasy about her and strives to make him aware of her true, urban-loving personality. The strain between his fantasy and her reality finally drives her to leave him, and only when a succession of painful experiences, including the sellout of a political candidate Sidney supported and the suicide of his sister-in-law Gloria, teaches him the necessity of facing life head-on, without any refuge, is she able to return to him and have him respond to her real self.

Gloria's tragedy is crucial to Sidney's development, since it leads him to see how his male-supremacist fantasizing has harmed his wife. As a call girl recruited for her innocent, all-American-girl appearance, Gloria has been paid to let men make her part of their warped sexual fantasies, and she has suffered such mental and physical abuse that she begins taking drugs to escape. After being severely beaten by one of her clients, she decides to break free from the life by marrying Sidney's friend Alton Scales, only to find that Alton has been told about her profession and is so appalled by the destruction of his idealized conception of her that he is unwilling even to talk to her. Still reeling with shock from this, she is approached by another of Sidney's friends, who wants her to aid him in a perverted sexual fantasy. She deliberately takes an overdose of drugs, saying, "Papa—I *am* better than this! Now will you forgive me—?" The motivation for Gloria's suicide is similar to Hansberry's interpretation of Marilyn Monroe's suicide. In an unpublished letter about *After the Fall,* Arthur

Miller's slightly fictionalized drama concerning Monroe, Hansberry argued that "the concept of 'woman' which fashioned, warped and destroyed a human being such as Marilyn Monroe (or 'Audrey Smith' . . . or 'Lucy Jones'—daily) IS HIDEOUSLY WRONG—and she, *in her repudiation of it,* in trying tragically to RISE ABOVE it by killing herself is (in the Shakespearean sense) right."

Sidney is reflective enough to understand what has been done to Gloria and the reason that she killed herself, and he realizes that he, like Alton and Gloria's clients, has caused immeasurable damage by upholding a false concept of woman. He also realizes that he must free himself from all such concepts and see his wife as the individual she is if their marriage is to be preserved. At the same time, he decides that he must take a stand against the drug pushing that helped to destroy the seventeen-year-old boy and Gloria, and he finds that his wife wishes to be an ally in this struggle.

The full complexity of Hansberry's view of men is revealed in her portrayal of Alton Scales. Like Walter Lee, Asagai, and Sidney, Alton is a character with many admirable and sympathetic traits. A black so light he could pass for white but chooses to remain true to his heritage no matter what the cost, Alton is also a compassionate person who becomes deeply moved by the death of a junkie, a former Communist who left the Party because he considered the Russian suppression of the Hungarian freedom fighters an outrage. Where Alton differs from Walter Lee, Asagai, and Sidney is in the degree to which right and wrong, the sympathetic and the unsympathetic, are entangled in his most important act, his rejection of Gloria for having been a prostitute. We cannot avoid being moved by his story of how his father's pride was hurt by having to accept the "white man's leavings" to survive; neither can we fail to respect the racial pride that makes him want to identify fully with his fellow blacks and their struggles. However, his view of Gloria as another piece of the "white man's leavings" which must be rejected for the sake of racial pride not only displays a racist attitude (as Sidney points out, Alton *might*—eventually—have been able to accept a black prostitute) but is also a callous and chauvinistic act. He loses sight of Gloria as the individual he loves and regards her only, in almost Victorian terms, as a "fallen" woman. We have witnessed the narrowness of his sexual attitudes earlier, when he calls a homosexual acquaintance "Fag Face," and we realize that he is being no less insensitive toward Gloria. Thus, our feelings toward Alton are necessarily mixed: We must see him variously as hero, victim, and oppressor; must both respect and feel sorry for him; and must condemn the ideas and system that make him act blindly and cruelly toward women, and other men.

Finally, consider the Reverend Torvald Neilsen and Tshembe Matoseh in **Les Blancs.** Although he never appears on stage, Rev. Neilsen is talked about enough to make it clear that he is modeled on Albert Schweitzer. He possesses all of Schweitzer's wonderful accomplishments and qualities, such as his talent for music (Schweitzer the organ, Neilsen the cello), his encyclopedic knowledge, his medical ability, his far-ranging philosophy, and his well-publicized capacity for self-sacrifice; he also possesses Schweitzer's outstanding flaw, his desire to be Big Daddy to everyone, females and blacks definitely included. When a delegation of blacks approaches Neilsen with a petition for the Governor General requesting proportional representation in the legislature, Neilsen responds, " 'Children, children . . . my dear children . . . go home to your huts! Go home to your huts before you make me angry. *Independence indeed!*" His most cruel decision, however, is his refusal to assist in the delivery of a child from a black woman who has been raped by a white man because Neilsen believes that the child is "the product of an evil act, a sin against God's order, the natural separation of the races." This decision is sexist as well as racist since, even granting his assumptions, it fails to acknowledge that the woman had no share in the "sin," that she was manifestly sinned against and needed help. As his wife observes after his slaughter by rebelling blacks, Neilsen "was a good man . . . in many ways" who "did some amazing things," but he let the self-imposed responsibility that came from his role as "White Man in Darkest Africa" warp his judgment—and his compassion.

Perhaps the definitive choice concerning women is made by Tshembe Matoseh. Tshembe is a black Hamlet torn between staying with the Ophelia-like European wife who offers him security, love, children, comfortable nights in front of the "telly," and a way of living within society as it is presently constituted, or heeding the spirit of a black woman warrior who reminds him of the injustices inflicted on his father and his people and who challenges him to be his "father's son" and pick up the spear of purifying change. The woman warrior is linked to others of the past, including Joan of Arc, Queen Esther, Columbia, and La Passionara, and she calls Tshembe to a combat demanding leadership and strength from both men and women. In accepting her challenge, Tshembe accepts a world in which women do not cater to his comfort but stand as forceful, independent allies in the continuing fight for human development and equality.

Through these and through other equally complex and credible male characters, Hansberry makes a more moving and more disturbing case against man's oppression of woman than if she had created male villains with no redeeming traits. She shows all too clearly and painfully the manifold ways in which the doctrine of male supremacy can damage the characters of even the most sensitive, intelligent, and heroic females—and males—in our society. Conversely, she argues that, in Sidney Brustein's words, "people wanna be better than they are"; that men and women can change, become partners in struggle, and develop a society that nurtures equality. (pp. 160-62)

> *Steven R. Carter, "Images of Men in Lorraine Hansberry's Writing," in* Black American Literature Forum, *Vol. 19, No. 4, Winter, 1985, pp. 160-62.*

A RAISIN IN THE SUN

PRODUCTION REVIEWS

Gerald Weales   (review date June 1959)

[*The following review was written just after* A Raisin in the Sun *won the New York Drama Critics' award for best play. Weales observes numerous shortcomings in the work but nevertheless judges it a good play. "Its basic strength lies in the character and the problem of Walter Lee, which transcends his being a Negro," Weales states. "The character's difficulty, however, is that he has accepted the American myth of success at face value, that he is trapped . . . by a false dream."*]

The playwright who is a Negro is faced with a special problem. Broadway has a tradition of Negro shows, inevitably folksy or exotic, almost always musical, of which the only virtue is that Negro performers get a chance to appear as something more than filler. The obvious reaction to such shows is the protest play, the Negro agitprop, which can be as false to American Negro life as the musicals. A playwright with serious intentions, like Miss Hansberry, has to avoid both pitfalls, has to try to write not a Negro play, but a play in which the characters are Negroes. In an interview (New York *Times,* March 8, 1959), Miss Hansberry is reported as having said to her husband before she began *Raisin,* "I'm going to write a social drama about Negroes that will be good art." However

---

ETHEL BARRYMORE THEATRE

PHILIP ROSE and DAVID J. COGAN

present

SIDNEY POITIER

in

a raisin in the sun

A New Play by
LORRAINE HANSBERRY

with

CLAUDIA McNEIL	**RUBY DEE**
LOUIS GOSSETT	DIANA SANDS
IVAN DIXON	JOHN FIEDLER

Directed by
LLOYD RICHARDS

Designed and Lighted by
RALPH ALSWANG

Costumes by
VIRGINIA VOLLAND

Playbill of the Broadway opening.

good the art, unfortunately, the play will remain, in one sense, a Negro play. The *Times* interview made quite clear that Miss Hansberry was aware that she was writing as much for the American Negro as for the American theatre. Similarly, an article on Sidney Poitier, the play's star, in the *New York Times Magazine* (January 25, 1959), made the point that Poitier avoided roles that might "diminish the Negro's stature as a human being." Whatever his ambitions as an artist, the Negro playwright, like the Negro actor, is still forced into a propaganda role. The publicity for *A Raisin in the Sun,* the news stories about it, the excitement it stirred up among Negroes (never until *Raisin* had I seen a Philadelphia theatre in which at least half the audience was Negro) all emphasize that it is a play written by a Negro woman about Negroes, a fact which could hardly have been forgotten when the Critics' Award was passed out.

Having suggested that objectivity is impossible with respect to *A Raisin in the Sun,* I should like to make a few objective remarks about it. The play, first of all, is old-fashioned. Practically no serious playwright, in or out of America, works in such a determinedly naturalistic form as Miss Hansberry in her first play. The semidocumentary movies that cropped up at the end of World War II, and then television, particularly in the [Paddy] Chayefsky school of drama, took over naturalism so completely that it is doubtful whether the form will ever again be comfortable in the theater. It is now possible to accept on stage the wildest fantasy or the simplest suggestion; but the set that pretends to be a real room with real doors and real furniture has become more difficult to accept than a stylized tree. Ralph Alswang's set for *Raisin,* as murky and crowded and gadgety as the slum apartment it represents, is ingenious in its detail; but the realistic set, like the real eggs the young wife cracks for an imaginary breakfast, reaches for a verisimilitude that has become impossible. *Raisin* is the kind of play which demands the naturalism that Miss Hansberry has used, but in choosing to write such a play, she entered Broadway's great sack race with only a paper bag as equipment. Her distinction is that she has won the race this year, which proves, I suppose, that narrow naturalism is still a possible—if anachronistic—form.

If the set suggests 1910 and Eugene Walter, the play itself—in its concentration on the family in society—recalls the 30's and Clifford Odets. It tells the story of the Younger family and their escape from a too-small apartment on Chicago's South Side to a house in which they have space and air and, unfortunately but not insurmountably, the enmity of their white neighbors. The conflict within the play is between the dreams of the son, Walter Lee, who wants to make a killing in the big world, and the hopes of his mother and his wife, who want to save their small world by transplanting it to an environment in which it might conceivably flourish. The mechanical means by which this conflict is illuminated—the insurance money, its loss, the representative of the white neighborhood association—are completely artificial, plot devices at their most devised. Take the loss of the money, for example. From the first moment that Walter Lee mentions his plans for a profitable liquor store, his connections, the need for

spreading money around in Springfield, the audience knows that the money will be stolen, supposedly, in good naturalistic tradition, the audience should sit, collective fingers crossed, hoping that he might be spared, that the dream might not be deferred and shrivel, like a raisin in the sun, as the Langston Hughes poem has it. I found myself, fingers crossed, hoping that the inevitable would not come, not for the sake of Walter Lee Younger, but for the sake of the play, of which the solid center was already too hedged with contrivances. No one's crossed fingers did any good.

Of the four chief characters in the play, Walter Lee is the most complicated and the most impressive. He is often unlikable, occasionally cruel. His sense of being trapped by his situation—class, race, job, prospects, education—transfers to his family, who become to him not fellow prisoners but complacent jailers. Their ways of coping with their condition are his defeats, for to him the open-sesame that will release him (change his status? change his color?) is money. The play is concerned primarily with his recognition that, as a man, he must begin from, not discard, himself, that dignity is a quality of men, not bank accounts. Walter Lee's penchant for taking center stage has forced his wife to become an observer in his life, but at the same time she is an accusation. For most of the play she wears a mask of wryness or the real cover of fatigue, but Miss Hansberry gives her two scenes in which the near-hysteria that lies beneath the surface is allowed to break through. The mother is a more conventional figure—the force, compounded of old virtues and the strength of suffering, that holds the family together. She is a sentimentalized mother figure, reminiscent of Bessie Burgess in [Clifford Odets's] *Awake and Sing,* but without Bessie's destructive power. The daughter, who wants to be a doctor, is out of place in this working-class family. Not that her ambition does not belong with the Youngers, but her surface characteristics—the flitting from one expensive fad to another—could not have been possible, on economic grounds alone, in such a household. Although Miss Hansberry, the daughter of a wealthy real estate man, may have enjoyed poking fun at a youthful version of herself, as reported in the *Times* interview, the result of putting the child of a rich man into a working-class home is incongruous.

Despite an incredible number of imperfections, *Raisin* is a good play. Its basic strength lies in the character and the problem of Walter Lee, which transcends his being a Negro. If the play were only the Negro-white conflict that crops up when the family's proposed move is about to take place, it would be an editorial, momentarily effective, and nothing more. Walter Lee's difficulty, however, is that he has accepted the American myth of success at its face value, that he is trapped, as Willy Loman [in Arthur Miller's *Death of a Salesman*] was trapped, by a false dream. In planting so indigenous an American image at the center of her play, Miss Hansberry has come as close as possible to what she intended—a play about Negroes which is not simply a Negro play.

The play has other virtues. There are genuinely funny and touching scenes throughout. Many of these catch believably the chatter of a family—the resentments and the shared jokes—and the words have the ring of truth that one found in Odets or Chayefsky before they began to sound like parodies of themselves. In print, I suspect, the defects of **Raisin** will show up more sharply, but on stage—where, after all, a play is supposed to be—the impressive performances of the three leads (Poitier, Ruby Dee, and Claudia McNeil) draw attention to the play's virtues. (pp. 528-29)

> *Gerald Weales, "Thoughts on 'A Raisin in the Sun'," in* Commentary, *Vol. XXVII, No. 6, June, 1959, pp. 527-30.*

A. Alvarez   (review date 15 August 1959)

[*An English poet and noted critic, Alvarez is best known for his controversial anthology* The New Poetry *(1962) and the polemical introduction to that work in which he argued that British poetry since World War II had suffered from excessive meekness and civility. Alvarez called for poetry that expresses the immediacy and vitality of human experience. In the following review of a later performance in the play's original run, he writes that* A Raisin in the Sun *is occasionally trite and sentimental but that it succeeds in showing its themes to be universal. Alvarez adds that "as a vehicle for the actors it is superb."*]

It is a sound rule in the theatre that excellence is inversely proportional to tears shed; that is, the bigger the catch in your throat as the curtain comes down the more suspect the play will seem half-an-hour later. On this account *A Raisin in the Sun* (Adelphi) is highly questionable. At the end of it the handkerchiefs were out in force and the audience, though they elbowed each other as savagely as usual through the doors, were speechless. True enough, Miss Lorraine Hansberry's play has most of the ingredients of the classic tear-jerker: a poor but honest family on the wrong side of the tracks; a benevolent despot of an Old Mum; her ageing son who is eating his and his wife's heart out for lack of an opportunity in life; his pert kid sister who goes to medical school and has a couple of admirers in tow, one intellectual, one rich. There is also a large insurance cheque, most of which the son is promptly conned out of. More than that, the dialogue is occasionally as predictable as the situations: the mother hands the cash over to her son with the words, 'It isn't very much, but it's all I got in the world'. He, presumably, passed it on to the con man murmuring, 'Take it, it was my mother's'.

Yet, although **Raisin in the Sun** occasionally slips over into triteness, it makes an extraordinarily compelling evening's theatre—which shows once again, I suppose, the degree to which drama is an extra-literary activity. As a play it may be patchy, but as a vehicle for the actors it is superb. One reason is that a powerful rhetoric comes naturally to Miss Hansberry. This puts her in a rather small club of writers, most of the other members of which are Celts. But with a difference: the rhetoric of a talented Negro writer always gives you the impression that it is about something, which is certainly not true of the Irish or the Welsh. Miss Hansberry has more than a gift of the gab; she also has a great deal to say on questions that deep-

ly concern her. So her rhetoric is not just colourful; it has a natural dignity, which presumably has something to do with the fact that the rhythms and diction of passionate Negro speech come straight from the Bible. The language is felt and meant to a degree where it can afford to be simple. Finally, Miss Hansberry's characters continually talk about the subjects which concern all Negroes: the jobs they can get, the areas they can live in, the strategies by which their pride is preserved or undermined, the problem of assimilation and racial independence. This means that the otherwise nice, rather sentimental family life, with its humdrum quarrels, ambitions and pieties, is continually strengthened by outside loyalties and outside hatreds.

It also means that the coloured actors have a chance to act out their feelings on these subjects. 'What's Hecuba to him, or he to Hecuba, That he should weep for her?' The answer, on this occasion, was clear. And the actors made one feel this, often to the point of discomfort. When Earle Hyman delivered his tirade against the hypocrisy of the whites in their trafficking with Negroes, he did so across the footlights, directly *at* the audience. He needed no Method to make this speech ring true.

But resentments and credos apart, Mr Hyman gave an excellent performance. However much he sympathised with the son, he managed to endow him with the necessary unpleasantness; he made no attempt to soften the nerves, self-pity and edgy dissatisfaction. And when in the end he did retrieve his pride, he made it seem just as knife-edged an affair as his earlier tantrums. His rather brittle vigour was a perfect foil to Juanita Moore's Mama. Miss Moore had to cope with most of the play's clichés. But she is an actress of so beautifully dignified a simplicity that she carried the bad lines as effortlessly as the good. The best moment in the play was, it seems, entirely her creation when, after the financial tragedy breaks, she sits down very slowly, shaking her head and murmuring 'Mm-mm, mm-mm'. I had always thought this ability to create a whole world of experience out of a mere gesture was the exclusive prerogative of Anna Magnani. Kim Hamilton, as the wife, was as tired and depressed as was needed, though her performance was slightly hampered by a fixed smile which glowed through everything, like the dial of Big Ben on a stormy night. Olga James, as the kid sister, gave a vigorous show of teenage temperament, and John Adan was peculiarly unselfconscious as the child of the family. Lloyd Richards, the director, was so strict in maintaining the pace and so imaginative in using every dramatic opportunity that it's a pity he was not a little tougher with the platitudes in the text. (p. 190)

> *A. Alvarez, "That Evening Sun," in* New Statesman, *Vol. LVIII, No. 1483, August 15, 1959, pp. 190-91.*

CRITICAL COMMENTARY

Margaret B. Wilkerson   (essay date 1986)

[*Wilkerson is an educator in the field of African-American Studies. In the following essay, she discusses*

Original cast members Sidney Poitier, Claudia McNeil, Ruby Dee, Glynn Turman, and Diana Sands in a scene from A Raisin in the
Sun.

*social, historical, and artistic factors that have contribut-
ed to the continuing success of* A Raisin in the Sun. *Arguing that Hansberry anticipated such important movements as the rise of black militancy in the United States,
the beginning of independence for African nations, and
the women's rights movement, Wilkerson focuses on the
play's characters and themes that attest to Hansberry's
development of her ideas.*]

Rarely, if ever, has a play by a Black-American been accorded the status of a classic. Parochialism and polemics,
critics have claimed, render works based on Black experience unattractive and of limited or temporary appeal. Yet
Lorraine Hansberry's **A Raisin in the Sun,** the first play
by a Black woman to be produced on Broadway and to
win the New York Drama Critics' Circle Award in 1959,
has become an American classic within a quarter of a century. According to Samuel French, Inc., an estimated two
hundred productions were mounted during the 1983-84
theatre season alone, including critical successes at the
Goodman Theatre in Chicago, Yale Repertory Theatre,
and the St. Louis Repertory Theatre. In a [November 9]
1983 review in the *New York Times,* Mel Gussow called
this play about a 1950s Black family in Chicago "an en-

during work of contemporary theatre." [In "Yale Marking 25th Anniversary of **Raisin in Sun,**" *New York Times,*
1 November 1983] Lloyd Richards, director of the Yale
Repertory and director of the original 1959 production,
labeled **A Raisin in the Sun,** "An historic . . . and . . .
a timeless piece." Frank Rich, in his 1983 review of the
Goodman Theatre revival ["Theater: **Raisin in Sun,** Anniversary in Chicago," *New York Times,* 5 October],
claimed that the play was dated only by "its dependence
on plot mechanics." The St. Louis Repertory Company's
production attracted unprecedented sell-out crowds in
1984, while a 1986 production at the Roundabout Theatre
drew the admiration of off-Broadway audiences. What accounts for the extraordinary appeal of **A Raisin in the
Sun**? How has it transcended the racial parochialisms of
American audiences?

A variety of factors have contributed to its enduring success: the finely crafted text; a brilliant cast in the original
production and subsequent casts with talented performers; its historic reception on Broadway in the 1958-59 season and subsequent impact on a new generation of artists;
and the events of the past quarter century that confirmed
Hansberry's prescience. However, textual additions and

revisions since the original production, some as recent as 1984, have sharpened the major issues of the play, revitalizing the work for contemporary audiences. This essay will discuss the various social, historical, and artistic factors that have contributed to the play's contemporary relevance and popularity, with particular focus on recent script revisions published by Samuel French, Inc., in the 1984 Anniversary Edition of the play.

The history of that first production is the stuff of which theatre legend is made. "Housewife's Play Is a Hit," read one local headline [in the *New York Daily Mirror,* 16 March 1959], indicating the sheer luck and nerve that allowed *A Raisin in the Sun*—a play written by an unknown Black woman, produced by inexperienced newcomers, and directed by an untried young Black man—to reach the professional New York stage. Although Sidney Poitier brought "star quality" to the show, the other performers (with the exception of Claudia McNeil) had yet to make their mark on the American theatre. Yet the talent of this first cast proved extraordinary and the chemistry perfect for a memorable show. Today the names of playwright Lorraine Hansberry, director Lloyd Richards, producers Phil Rose and David Cogan, actors Sidney Poitier, Claudia McNeil, Lou Gossett, Glynn Turman, Diana Sands, Ivan Dixon, Ruby Dee, Ossie Davis, understudies Douglas Turner Ward, Lonne Elder, Beah Richards, and others are widely known for their contributions to theatre.

Starting from a half empty house in New Haven, *A Raisin in the Sun* attracted larger audiences on its out-of-town trials through Chicago and other cities until a last minute rush for tickets in Philadelphia earned it a Broadway house. It had taken a year to raise the $100,000 needed for the show—the "smart money" would not take a risk on a serious play about a Black family. The tenuousness of its production life ended, however, with its New York opening. The show ran on Broadway for nineteen months and won the New York Drama Critics' Circle Award against such plays as Tennessee Williams' *Sweet Bird of Youth,* Archibald MacLeish's *J.B.,* and Eugene O'Neill's *A Touch of the Poet.*

The play's phenomenal reception can be attributed, in part, to its timeliness, for this drama reflects that moment in U.S. history when the country was poised on the brink of cataclysmic social and legal upheavals that would forever change its character. In his 1959 review of the show ["No Clear Path and No Retreat," *New York Herald Tribune,* 22 March], Walter Kerr observed that Hansberry "reads the precise temperature of a race at that time in its history when it cannot retreat and cannot quite find the way to move forward. The mood is forty-nine parts anger and forty-nine parts control, with a very narrow escape hatch for the steam these abrasive contraries build up. Three generations stand poised, and crowded, on a detonating-cap."

The tensions of the times that Kerr sensed in the play had been captured earlier in a short, provocative poem ["Harlem"] by Langston Hughes, a work that had given Hansberry the title and theme of her drama. "What happens to a dream deferred," asked the poet in his historical collection of poems on Harlem. "Does it dry up like a raisin

in the sun . . . or does it explode?" Lorraine Hansberry answered by fashioning a play about the struggles and frustrations of a working-class Black family living in Chicago's South Side ghetto during the 1950s. Crowded into a cramped, roach-infested kitchenette, this family of laborers wages a constant battle to survive and to maintain hope for a better future. When Lena Younger (Mama), the elder of the household, receives a $10,000 widow's benefit, each family member sees the money as fulfillment of a private dream. The conflict is sharpest between the dual protagonists of the play, Mama and her thirty-five-year-old son, Walter Lee, who lives with his sister (Beneatha), his wife (Ruth), and son (Travis) in his mother's home. Walter, frustrated by his dead-end chauffeur's job, wants to invest in a liquor store as a way out of their economic and psychological trap. But Mama, seeking more physical space for the family and the psychological freedom it would bring, puts a down payment on a house that happens to be in Clybourne Park, a white neighborhood. Her decision decimates Walter who views the money as his last chance to gain some economic control over his life. When Mama realizes how deeply her decision has hurt her son, she entrusts him with the remaining money with a portion to be placed in a savings account for his sister's college education and the rest for Walter to do with as he wishes. His good fortune is short-lived, however, because he loses the money in a dubious business deal. A disillusioned man, Walter faces his mother and family in a highly emotional scene; when presented with the opportunity to recover his losses by selling out to the Clybourne Park Association (which is determined to keep the neighborhood white), he decides to take their offer despite its demeaning implications. However, Walter comes to realize that he cannot live with this denigration of his family's pride and consequently rejects the proposal. The play ends as the family begins to move to the new house.

The spirit and struggles of the Younger family symbolized the social progress and setbacks characteristic of the 1950s, and the Broadway audience of that time could not help but notice. In 1955, three years before the opening of *A Raisin in the Sun,* the Supreme Court had declared racial segregation in public schools illegal, marking a climax to decades of advocacy and legal challenges, but initiating a new level of resistance. The Montgomery bus boycott was staged the same year, marking the beginning of Martin Luther King's visible leadership in the Civil Rights Movement. Boycotts and sit-ins intensified as federal troops were called in to prevent interference with school integration in Little Rock, Arkansas. As the struggle continued in the United States, it was also raging in Africa as Ghana became an independent nation, signaling the imminent demise of European colonialism.

During the play's run and shortly thereafter, Black and white Freedom Riders headed South and were greeted by a wave of terrorism as Southern segregationists retaliated; lunch counters in over 100 Southern cities were integrated; sit-ins and protests accelerated; Martin Luther King was arrested and jailed repeatedly; Black children were murdered, and churches were burned by racists, while the President of the United States shattered precedent by declaring that segregation was morally wrong. The bloody years continued as public figures like Medgar Evers and President John F. Kennedy were assassinated.

"[Hansberry] saw history, whole," wrote Frank Rich in his 1983 review of the play, " . . . the present and the future in the light of the past." The time was ripe for a play that could somehow bridge the gap between Blacks and whites in the U.S. while communicating the urgency and necessity of the civil rights struggle. Black militancy born of anger, frustration, and deferred dreams was captured in the explosive and desperate Walter Lee. Rosa Parks's sudden refusal to move to the back of the bus, which became the catalyst for the historic Montgomery Bus Boycott, was mirrored in Lena Younger's apolitical decision to live in Clybourne Park, and her unintentional challenge of the restrictive covenants of the day. The rise of independent African nations was reflected in the presence of Asagai, the African student, who brings home the reality of his people's struggle for liberation, while Beneatha's adulation of things Africaine anticipated a new wave of hair and dress styles that Black Americans would soon adopt. In an uncanny way, Hansberry sensed what was to come. Her prescience extended even a decade beyond to the assertion of women's rights and women's equality through the assertive Beneatha who aspires to be a doctor, and the loyal, loving Ruth who seriously contemplates an abortion. The play touched the vibrating nerve of a country on the verge of change and a people on the move.

The timeliness of the play was equalled only by the captivating characters with whom white audiences were willing to identify and of whom Black audiences could be proud. Lena Younger was a strong point of identification. She was everybody's Mama—strong, caring, determined—the glue that held the family together. The self-sacrificing love of wife and mother were recognizable in Ruth's quiet strength and giving nature. Although Walter Lee was a new kind of character for white audiences, intended as a "ghetto hero" by Hansberry, the generational conflict with his mother was very familiar. For Blacks, Walter was a welcome affirmation of the urgency and potency of the Black struggle, while his sister, the ebullient Beneatha, represented its intellectual potential. Each character was molded with skill, humor, and the best tools of realistic theatre. The human qualities of Hansberry's characters came through without negating their racial integrity, and the play was loudly acclaimed on that account.

Critics praised the play as much for what it did not do as for its achievements. It presented characters who were neither sentimentalized nor stereotyped. There was no special pleading. The play was honest and had integrity. It did not preach political dogma, reviewers claimed. Even the F.B.I. file on Hansberry confirmed that the play was not propagandistic, according to the agents' report. Apparently, it did not pose a danger to the Republic. Because the humanity of this family was so brilliantly exposed, white audiences could see themselves reflected in those Black faces. Because the racial experience was so authentically portrayed, Blacks found a new voice and created a vital, provocative theatre movement in the next decade. However, during the 1960s, Black critic Harold Cruse [in his *The Crisis of the Negro Intellectual,* 1967] labeled the play a "glorified soap opera," reflecting a few reviewers' growing impatience with realistic plot structures and disagreement with what they perceived to be the play's political views. Nevertheless, the vitality and sharp definition of characters, the wit and humor of its sparkling dialogue, and the continued affirmation of the play's "message" by Black and white audiences alike, have far outweighed that criticism, causing audiences to return year after year to relive the now well-known rituals of the Younger family. However, *A Raisin in the Sun* is also a play of ideas and functions on a deeper, philosophical level, which until recently has been obscured to some extent by the racial prism through which it was originally viewed.

Writing in her scrapbook of reviews, Hansberry agreed with a 1959 passage ["*A Raisin in the Sun* Premieres at Schubert," January 24] by Daniel Gottlieb of the *Hartford Times:* the playwright "manages to weave the threads of the Negro-white conflict, materialism vs. spiritualism, and the individual vs. his conscience into the play." The seductiveness of material values is at issue in the play and the Youngers' struggle for a spiritual and economic future poses fundamental questions about the American dream of success. As Gregory Mosher, Director of the Goodman Theatre [quoted in Tom Valeo's "Issues Raised by *Raisin* Haven't Begun to Dry Up," *Chicago Sunday Herald,* 2 October 1983, sec. 5], asks, "Is Walter Lee right when he says money is all that matters? How important is economic success in securing rights for a minority group? Such goals give you power, but do they also corrupt you?" In order to advance materially, must the Youngers also become materialistic? The contradiction between the profitable, economic values of acquisition, power, and status and the "unprofitable" values of integrity, justice, and freedom runs deep in the American psyche. Walter's desire to "make it" is as American as Mama's determination to retain the family's pride and honor.

Although the original production script contained ample confirmation of this theme, events of the last twenty-five years both offstage and on have helped audiences to perceive these fundamental issues more clearly. The reinsertion of some omitted lines has sharpened and clarified the philosophical content without altering the basic structure of the play. Some scenes were cut in the original production in order to minimize risk; the producers and director chose to keep the playing time as tight as possible without sacrificing the playwright's values. Among the scenes and lines that were eliminated were three portions of dialogue which have since been restored to more recent publications and were included in 1983-84 productions. These sections offer important insights to the character of Walter Lee and Mama, the play's dual protagonists, and greatly strengthen the articulation of the fundamental theme.

The debate over materialism and integrity is framed by Walter Lee and Mama whose conflict drives the play. However, the full implications of Walter's desires must be grasped in order to perceive the deeper levels of the debate. The New American Library edition (1966) and the 25th Anniversary edition published in 1984 restored a scene which is key to this understanding. Inserted at the end of Act II, Scene 2, the scene shows a brief moment between Walter and his young son, Travis. Walter, who has just been entrusted with the remaining $6500 by his mother and who sees his dream of economic success within his grasp, speaks in a tender tone not heard before from him:

> You wouldn't understand yet, son, but your daddy's gonna make a transaction . . . a business transaction that's going to change our lives . . . That's how come one day when you 'bout seventeen years old I'll come home and I'll be pretty tired, you know what I mean, after a day of conferences and secretaries getting things wrong the way they do . . . 'cause an executive's life is hell, man— . . . And I'll pull the car up on the driveway . . . just a plain black Chrysler, I think, with white walls—no—black tires. More elegant. Rich people don't have to be flashy . . . though I'll have to get something a little sportier for Ruth—maybe a Cadillac convertible to do her shopping in . . . And I'll come up the steps to the house and the gardener will be clipping away at the hedges and he'll say "Good evening, Mr. Younger." And I'll say, "Hello, Jefferson, how are you this evening?" And I'll go inside and Ruth will come downstairs and meet me at the door and we'll kiss each other and she'll take my arm and we'll go up to your room to see you sitting on the floor with the catalogues of all the great schools in America around you . . . All the great schools in the World! And—and I'll say, all right son— it's your seventeenth birthday, what is it you've decided? Just tell me where you want to go to school and you'll *go*. Just tell me, what it is you want to be—and you'll *be* it . . . Whatever you want to be—Yessir! You just name it, son . . . and I hand you the world!

The placement of this speech is critical to its import for it catches Walter in a rare, reflective moment. Throughout the play, the audience has seen the restless side of Walter, constantly at odds with his family, desperately trying to convince his strong-willed mother of the importance of his plans. This speech is Walter's only chance in the play to explain his ideas fully, without interruption and criticism. While the speech verifies Walter's desire to shape a better future for his son, it also signals a shift in his value system—one which will make the outrageous offer from the white homeowners' association both attractive and logical. Walter is willing to buy into a system of roles and class stratification in order to realize his dream. His image is typical Americana—the independent male who controls the world and around whom the universe revolves. Wife, secretary, gardener, Cadillac, sports car—all are complements to his material universe. His manhood is at stake, he believes, and the women around him with their traditional values are holding him back.

Walter's speech was also deleted from the 1961 film version of the play. In its place was a brief exchange between Mama and Walter in which Walter equates his investment opportunity with his parents' move North out of the economic and spiritual traps of the Deep South. The money represents his chance to board his generation's train to the North. Without the Walter/Travis scene, however, the text lacks the subtle class and sexist implications of the American dream that Walter seeks.

To sharpen this fundamental debate, Lena Younger/Mama must be rescued from the persistent image of passivity, accommodation, and self-satisfaction associated with the Black Mammy stereotype. She must be revealed for what, in fact, she is, according to Hansberry [in her October 5, 1963 address to the American Academy of Psychotherapists, **"The Origins of Character"**]: "The Black matriarch incarnate: The bulwark of the Negro family since slavery; the embodiment of the Negro will to transcendence. It is she who, in the mind of the Black poet, scrubs the floors of a nation in order to create Black diplomats and university professors. It is she who, while seeming to cling to traditional restraints, drives the young on into the fire hoses and one day simply refuses to move to the back of the bus in Montgomery."

The original production script also included a scene in Act II, Scene 2, that clarified this image of Mama. However, the entire scene, along with the character of Mrs. Johnson, was eliminated in order to trim the show's playing time. It has now been published for the first time in the addendum of the 1984 Samuel French edition and has been included in several recent productions. The original producers may have sacrificed too much, underestimating the persistence of the Mammy stereotype in the American psyche. The perception of Lena Younger as a conservative, retarding force has been a difficult one to shed. Although the dialogue in this scene is carried by Mrs. Johnson, a nosy neighbor and somewhat humorous character, Mama's responses clearly place her in the militant forefront. Mrs. Johnson, always the happy bearer of bad news, makes explicit the danger in the family's move and Mama's quiet determination to take the risk.

> JOHNSON: I guess y'all seen the news whats all over the colored paper this week . . .
>
> MAMA: No—didn't get mine yet this week.
>
> JOHNSON: You mean you ain't read 'bout them colored people that was bombed out their place out there? . . . Ain't it something how bad these here white folks is getting here in Chicago! Lord, getting so you think you right down in Mississippi! . . . Course I thinks it's wonderful how our folks keeps on pushing out . . . Lord—I bet this time next month y'all's names will have been in the papers plenty— . . . "NEGROES INVADE CLYBOURNE PARK—BOMBED!"
>
> MAMA: We ain't exactly moving out there to get bombed.
>
> JOHNSON: Oh, honey—you know I'm praying to God every day that don't nothing like that happen! But you have to think of life like it is—and these here Chicago peckerwoods is some baaaad peckerwoods.
>
> MAMA: We done thought about all that, Mis' Johnson.

The conversation continues with Mrs. Johnson carrying most of the dialogue, while Mama speaks briefly, but with quiet authority. Then Lena Younger makes a surprising philosophical connection.

> JOHNSON: Sometimes . . . [Beneatha] act like she ain't got time to pass the time of day with nobody ain't been to college. Oh—I ain't criticizing her none. It's just—you know how some of our young people gets when they get a little education . . . 'Course I can understand how she must be proud and everything—being the only one in the family to make something of herself! I know just being a chauffeur ain't never satisfied Brother none. He shouldn't feel like that, though. Ain't nothing wrong with being a chauffeur.
>
> MAMA: There's plenty wrong with it.
>
> JOHNSON: What?
>
> MAMA: Plenty. My husband always said being any kind of servant wasn't a fit thing for a man to have to be. He always said a man's hands was made to make things, or to turn the earth with—not to drive nobody's car for em—or . . . carry they slop jars. And my boy is just like him—
>
> JOHNSON: Mmmmm mmmm. The Youngers is too much for me! . . . You sure one proud-acting bunch of colored folks. Well—I always thinks like Booker T. Washington said that time—"Education has spoiled many a good plow hand"—
>
> MAMA: Is that what old Booker T. said?
>
> JOHNSON: He sure did.
>
> MAMA: Well, it sounds just like him. The fool.
>
> JOHNSON: Well—he was one of our great men.
>
> MAMA: Who said so?

The physical image of Mama (large, dark, dominant) suggests the Mammy stereotype of countless American plays and films, but her criticism of Booker T. Washington's ideas in this passage aligns her with Washington's intellectual opponent, W. E. B. DuBois. DuBois and other militant advocates for civil rights founded the National Association for the Advancement for Colored People (NAACP), the organization that provided much of the legal bases for protesting segregation. The Washington/DuBois debate framed the philosophical and political issues facing Black-Americans and the fight for human and civil rights early in this century. The stereotype of the Black Mammy suggests complicity with Washington's emphasis on accommodation and economic self-sufficiency. However, in an ironic twist, Hansberry equates Mama's determination with the militant spirit of DuBois's position and Walter's entrepreneurial interests with the materialism associated with Washington's philosophy. Lena Younger is not the accommodating Mammy who chooses the passive, safe path, but rather the folk figure, the courageous spirit that lends credence and power to the militant struggle. In her own determined way, she gives birth to revolutionaries and is herself a progressive force. The explicit reference to Washington in this scene illuminates the "revolutionary" aspect of Lena and sharp-

ly delineates the philosophical difference between Mama and Walter.

Hansberry's final and most definitive framing of the philosophical issues occurs at the beginning of Act III in the dialogue between Asagai and Beneatha. Abridged in early publications of the script, most of this exchange was cut from the film. As in the earlier Walter/Travis scene, the placement of this scene is important. It occurs just after the highly emotional moment when Walter and Mama discover that the money is gone. The audience, affected by the sheer magnitude of the loss, is now invited to reflect on the family's future. At a time when Mama's faith is being sorely tested and the materialistic underpinnings of Walter's faith have been destroyed, what values will shape the family's response? Here Hansberry places a key dialogue—the debate between Asagai and Beneatha. Some critics [for example Max Lerner in "A Dream Deferred," *New York Post*, 8 April 1959] dismiss this section as a distracting, verbose passage, out of place in this realistic piece of theatre. Yet a closer examination of the unabridged scene reveals its crucial role in the philosophical progression of the theme.

The question here is not whether the family should move or stay, but rather what they will learn from this tragedy. Will they act out of an affirmation of life or be paralyzed by despair? Asagai focuses on Beneatha, but Hansberry focuses her critique on Walter and all those who would base their future on the acquisition of things. As the money goes, so goes Beneatha's and Walter's faith in humankind. "Man is foul!" Beneatha says, "And the human race deserves its misery! . . . From now on, I worship truth—and the truth is that people are puny, small and selfish." The logical extension of this "truth" is to ignore human values and to act, if one does at all, out of selfishness and the needs of the existential moment. This idea enables Walter later in Act III to consider any means to recover the lost money. But Asagai counters:

> Truth? Why is it that you despairing ones always think that only you have the truth? I never thought to see *you* like that. You! Your brother made a stupid, childish mistake—and you are grateful to him. So that now you can give up the ailing human race on account of it. You talk about what good is struggle; what good is anything? Where are we all going? And why are we bothering?

Beneatha responds:

> And you cannot answer it! All your talk and dreams about Africa and Independence. Independence and then what? What about all the crooks and petty thieves and just plain idiots who will come into power to steal and plunder the same as before—only now they will be black and do it in the name of the new Independence— You cannot answer that.

Asagai shouts over her: "I live the answer!" Asagai proposes his being, his life, his very existence—and the meaning that commitment creates—as the embodiment of his answer. Asagai acts out of a belief in the transcendent power of man and woman, a belief that cannot be shaken by the loss of money, material things, or even the devastation of human betrayal. This faith will be his armor when he returns to his troubled homeland to fight against terrible odds—poverty and ignorance, not to mention the British and the French—to achieve the full liberation of his people.

Asagai expresses in philosophical and political terms the affirmation that Lena Younger has lived. At this moment, he is her symbolic son—the long-desired reuniting of Africans and Afro-Americans through shared beliefs, not color alone. The debate anticipates the ambivalence of Walter's emotions as he is torn, up to the very end of the play, between an act of despair and an act of affirmation. Ironically, affirmation carries no assurances. For just as Asagai does not know whether he will be revered or murdered for his efforts on behalf of his people, so Walter and the Younger family will face an uncertain future in their new neighborhood. Although Asagai prevails in the debate, Walter must peer into the abyss of despair and lost pride before he can finally acknowledge the progressive, enlightened values of his forebears—the spirit of life which has allowed humankind to transcend its condition.

The play repudiates the kind of materialism that values money and acquisition over human dignity and life. The spirit of humankind, Hansberry insists, must affirm freedom, justice, integrity, caring—at the expense of comfort or even life itself. It is a courageous statement made in the face of the desperate economic needs of the Youngers of the nation. It is offered as a framework for the liberation struggles of the world, in defiance of traditional American notions of success. The uncut scene in Act III gives full expression to the debate and heightens the philosophical questions implicit in the Youngers' struggle. When this scene is cut, as in the film, or abridged, as in the early publications and the original production, the import of Hansberry's philosophical position is diminished and the intellectual dimensions of Beneatha and Asagai are trivialized. The Yale production used the full version of this scene with great success. [Markland Taylor in "*Raisin, Jerusalem* a Case of Good vs. Poor Playwriting," *New Haven Register,* 13 November 1983] even claimed that this scene could well be the climax of the play.

Hansberry's sensing of future trends was most evident in another casualty of the original production script: Beneatha adopts a natural hairstyle (long before the "Afro" became popular) and a bourgeois George Murchison is surprisingly appreciative of the look. But the most dramatic change in the play occurred long before the show went into rehearsal. In an earlier version of the script, Hansberry wrote a more somber ending in which the family is shown sitting in the darkened living room of their new house, armed and awaiting an attack by their white neighbors. The accepted and ever popular upbeat ending, which shows a jubilant family moving to their new home, was no less true than the other ending. This more positive view did, however, emphasize the Younger's evolution and progress rather than the violent, retrogressive attitudes of the racists who awaited them.

Despite the loss of much of the play's philosophical dimension, *A Raisin in the Sun* was a smashing success in 1959 and has continued to attract audiences for a quarter of a century. The productions that recent audiences have applauded are for the most part based on an expanded text that includes portions of the scenes discussed in this essay and that provides greater definition of major characters and theme. The heavy financial risks associated with professional productions resulted in a necessarily conservative handling of the original production and robbed early audiences of the full import of Hansberry's achievement. It may have been asking too much of 1959 audiences to cope with the full vision of the play. Only the very naive would have expected them to accept the intellectual dimension emanating from the experiences of a working-class Black family and the pen of a Black woman writer during the heat and turmoil of those days. The timeliness of the play has not diminished. Its criticism of materialistic values is more poignant amidst the affluence and poverty of American society in the 1980s. At the same time, its depiction of the Black struggle against pernicious, persistent racism remains current as racial intolerance continues to pervade the country's institutions, albeit in more subtle forms. Perhaps because the idea of Black stage characters is not as exotic as it once was, the 1980s audience can perceive the full meaning of the play. Perhaps they are more capable of comprehending the theatre of Black experience, not only as literal portrayal, but as a metaphor for the American experience. Hansberry, however, did not wait for such enlightenment on the part of her audience; she insisted on restoring many of the deleted scenes as soon as possible. It is to her credit that she did so. Her literary executor, Robert Nemiroff, has continued in the same spirit, making other scenes available since the playwright's death. The expanded text has revitalized the play for this generation and has added a new dimension to the exploration of Black experience in the American theatre. (pp. 441-52)

> *Margaret B. Wilkerson, " 'A Raisin in the Sun': Anniversary of an American Classic," in* Theatre Journal, *Vol. 38, No. 4, December, 1986, pp. 441-52.*

Amiri Baraka   (essay date 1987)

[*A leading dramatist in the Black Arts and Theater Movement of the 1960s, Baraka (who wrote until 1967 under the name LeRoi Jones) received world-wide acclaim for his first professional production,* Dutchman *(1964) and is considered a seminal figure in the development of African-American literature. Reputed to be the "Malcolm X of literature," he once dismissed* A Raisin in the Sun *as "middle class." In the following excerpt, Baraka reappraises Hansberry's drama, now lauding the work as "aesthetically powerful and politically advanced" in depicting the tensions and frustrations building up in the African-American community just prior to the beginning of the Civil Rights Movement.*]

In the wake of its twenty-fifth anniversary, Lorraine Hansberry's great play *A Raisin in the Sun* is enjoying a revival of a most encouraging kind. Complete with restorations of the text of scenes and passages removed from the first production, the work is currently being given a new direction and interpretation that reveal even more clearly the play's profoundly imposing stature, continuing relevance, and pointed social analysis. At major regional theaters in city after city *Raisin* has played to packed houses and, as on the night I saw it, standing ovations. It has broken or approached long-standing box office records and has been properly hailed as "a classic," while the *Washington Post* has called it succinctly: "one of the handful of great American dramas . . . in the inner circle, along with *Death of a Salesman, Long Day's Journey into Night,* and *The Glass Menagerie.*"

For a playwright who knows, too well, the vagaries and realities of American theater, this assessment is gratifying. But of even greater significance is the fact that *A Raisin in the Sun* is being viewed by masses of people, black and white, in the light of a new day.

For *Raisin* typifies American society in a way that reflects more accurately the real lives of the black U.S. majority than any work that ever received commercial exposure before it, and few if any since. It has the life that only classics can maintain. Any useful re-appreciation of it cannot be limited, therefore, to the passages restored or the new values discovered, important though these are: it is the play itself, as a dramatic (and sociopolitical) whole, that demands our confirmation of its grandeur.

When *Raisin* first appeared in 1959, the Civil Rights Movement was in its earlier stages. And as a document reflecting the *essence* of those struggles, the play is unexcelled. For many of us it was—and remains—the quintessential civil rights drama. But any attempt to confine the play to an era, mind-set, an issue ("Housing") or set of topical concerns was, as we now see, a mistake. The truth is that Hansberry's dramatic skills have yet to be properly appreciated—and not just by those guardians of the status quo who pass themselves off as dramatic critics. For black theater artists and would-be theorists especially, this is ironic because the play is probably the most widely appreciated—particularly by African Americans—black drama that we have.

Raisin lives in large measure because black people have kept it alive. And because Hansberry has done *more* than document, which is the most limited form of realism. She is a *critical realist,* in a way that Langston Hughes, Richard Wright, and Margaret Walker are. That is, she *analyzes* and *assesses* reality and shapes her statement as an aesthetically powerful and politically advanced work of art. Her statement cannot be separated from the characters she creates to embody, in their totality, the life she observes: it becomes, in short, the living material of the work, part of its breathing body, integral and alive.

George Thompson in *Poetry and Marxism* points out that drama is the most expressive artistic form to emerge out of great social transformation. Shakespeare is the artist of the destruction of feudalism—and the emergence of capitalism. The mad Macbeths, bestial Richard III's, and other feudal worthies are actually shown, like the whole class, as degenerate—and degenerating. (pp. 9-10)

Hansberry's play, too, was political agitation. It dealt with the very same issues of democratic rights and quality that were being aired in the streets. It dealt with them with an unabating dramatic force, vision, political concreteness and clarity that, in retrospect, are awesome. But it dealt with them not as abstractions, fit only for infantile-left pamphlets, but as they are *lived.* In reality.

All of *Raisin's* characters speak *to* the text and are critical to its dramatic tensions and understanding. They are necessarily larger than life—in impact—but crafted meticulously from living social material.

When the play opened on Broadway, Lena Younger, the emotional adhesive of the family, was given a broad, aggressive reading by Claudia McNeil. Indeed, her reading has been taken as the model and somewhat institutionalized in various productions I've seen.

The role itself—of family head, folksy counsel, upholder of tradition—has caused many people to see her as the stereotyped "black matriarch" of establishment and commercial sociological fame. Carrying with them (or rebelling against) the preconceived baggage of that stereotype, and recalling the play through the haze of memory (or from the compromised movie version), they have not bothered to look more closely at the actual woman Hansberry created—and at *what* tradition she in fact upholds. (p. 11)

[In the recent New York revival of the play, Olivia Cole's reading of Lena] was revelation and renewal.

Ms. Cole came at the role from the inside out. Her Lena is a woman, black, poor, struggle-worn but proud and loving. She was in the world *before* the rest of the family, before many of us viewing the play. She has seen and felt what we have not, or what we cannot yet identify. She is no quaint, folksy artifact; she is truth, history, love—and struggle—as they can be manifest only in real life. (p. 12)

Similarly, the new interpreters of Walter Lee . . . are something "fresh," like our kids say. They bring a contemporary flavoring to the work that consists of knowing—with more certainty than, say, Sidney Poitier could have in the original—the frustration and rage animating the healthy black male, *post*-civil rights era. They play Walter Lee more aggressively, more self-consciously, so that when he does fall we can actually hate him—hate the frivolous, selfish male-chauvinist part of ourselves. And when he stands up at the finale and will not be beaten, we can cry with joy.

Part of the renewed impact of the play comes with the fresh interpretation of both director and actors. But we cannot stop there! The social materials that Hansberry so brilliantly shaped into drama are not lightweight. For me this is the test of the writer: no matter the skill of the execution—*what* has been executed? What is it he or she is talking about? Form can never be dismissed, to say the least, particularly by an artist. But in the contradiction between form and content, content must be the bottom line—though unless the form be an extension of (and correctly serve) that content, obviously even understanding of the content will be flawed.

Formalist artists must resort to all kinds of superficial aberrations of form because usually they have nothing to say.

Brecht said how much safer the red is in a "non-objective" painting than the red of blood rushing out of the slain worker's chest. . . . And it is one reason why some critics will always have a problem with the realism of a Hansberry—and ignore the multilayered richness of her form.

A Raisin in the Sun is about *dreams,* ironically enough. And how those psychological projections of human life can come into conflict like any other product of that life. For Lena, a new house, the stability and happiness of her children, are her principal dream. And as such this is the completion of a dream she and her late husband—who has literally, like the slaves, been *worked* to death—conceived together.

Ruth's dream, as mother and wife, is somewhat similar. A room for her son, an inside toilet. She dreams as one of those triply oppressed by society—as worker, as African American, and as woman. But her dream, and her mother-in-law's, conflicts with Walter Lee's. He is the chauffeur to a rich white man and dreams of owning all and doing all the things he sees "Mr. Arnold" do and own. On one level Walter Lee is merely aspiring to full and acknowledged humanity; on another level he yearns to strut his "manhood," a predictable mix of *machismo* and fantasy. But Hansberry takes it even further to show us that on still another level Walter Lee, worker though he be, has the "realizable" dream of the black petty bourgeoisie. "There he is! *Monsieur le petit bourgeois noir*—himself!," cries Beneatha, the other of Lena Younger's children. "There he is—Symbol of a Rising Class! Entrepreneur! Titan of the system!" The deepness of this is that Hansberry can see that the conflict of dreams is not just that of individuals but, more importantly, of classes. Not since Theodore Ward's *Big White Fog* (1938) has there been a play so thoroughly and expertly reflective of class struggle within a black family.

Beneatha dreams of medical school. She is already socially mobile, finding a place, as her family cannot, among other petty bourgeois aspirants on the rungs of "education," where their hard work has put her. Her aspiration is less caustic, more attainable than Walter's. But she yearns for something more. Her name Beneatha (as who ain't?) should instruct us. She is, on the one hand, secure in the collegiate world of "ideas" and elitism, above the mass; on the other, undeceived by the myths and symbols of class and status. Part militant, part dilletante, "liberated" woman, little girl, she questions everything and dreams of service to humanity, an identity beyond self and family in the liberation struggles of her people. Ah, but will she have the strength to stay the course?

Hansberry has Beneatha grappling with key controversies of the period, but also some that had yet to clearly surface. And she grapples with some that will remain with us until society itself is changed: The relationship of the intellectual to the masses. The relationship of African Americans to Africans. The liberation movement itself and the gnawing necessity of black self-respect in its many guises (e.g., "straightened" hair vs. "the natural"). Written in 1956 and first seen by audiences in the new revivals, the part of the text in which Beneatha unveils her hair—the "perm" cut off and she glowing with her original woolly crown—

precedes the "Afro" by a decade. Dialogue between Beneatha and her mother, brother, Asagai and George Murchison digs into all these still-burning concerns.

Similarly, Walter Lee and Ruth's dialogues lay out his male chauvinism and even self- and group-hate born of the frustration of too many dreams too long deferred: the powerlessness of black people to control their own fate or that of their families in capitalist America where race is place, white is right, and money makes and defines the man. Walter dreams of using his father's insurance money to buy a liquor store. This dream is in conflict not only with the dreams of the Younger women, but with reality. But Walter appreciates only his differences with—and blames—the women. Throughout the work, Hansberry addresses herself to issues that the very young might feel only *The Color Purple* has raised. Walter's relationship to his wife and sister, and Beneatha's with George and Asagai, gives us a variety of male chauvinism—working class, petty bourgeois, African.

Asagai, the Nigerian student who courts Beneatha, dreams of the liberation of Africa and even of taking Beneatha there: "We will pretend that . . . you have only been away for a day." But that's not reality either, though his discussion of the dynamics and dialectics of revolution—and of the continuity of human struggle, the only means of progress—still rings with truth!

Hansberry's warnings about neo-colonialism and the growth (and corruption) of a post-colonial African bourgeoisie—"the servants of empire," as Asagai calls them—are dazzling because of their subsequent replication by reality. As is, above all, her sense of the pressures mounting inexorably in this one typical household, and in Walter Lee especially, and of where they must surely lead. It was the "explosion" Langston Hughes talked about in his great poem "Harlem"—centerpiece of his incomparable *Montage of a Dream Deferred,* from which the play's title was taken—and it informs the play as its twinned projection: dream or coming reality.

These are the categories Langston proposes for the dream:

> Does it dry up
> Like a raisin in the sun?

Dried up is what Walter Lee and Ruth's marriage had become, because their respective dreams have been deferred. When Mama Lena and Beneatha are felled by news of Walter Lee's weakness and dishonesty, their life's will—the desired greening of their humanity—is defoliated.

> Or fester like a sore—
> And then run?

Walter Lee's dream has festered, and in his dealings with the slack-jawed con man Willie (merchant of the stuff of dreams), his dream is "running."

We speak of the American Dream. Malcolm X said that for the Afro-American it was the American Nightmare. The little ferret man . . . is the dream's messenger, and the only white person in the play. His name is Lindner (as in "neither a borrower nor a Lindner be"), and the thirty or so "pieces of silver" he proffers are meant to help the niggers understand the dichotomous dream.

"But you've got to admit that a man, right or wrong, has the right to want to have the neighborhood he lives in a certain kind of way," says Lindner. Except black folks. Yes, these "not rich and fancy" representatives of white lower-middle America have a dream, too. A class dream, though it does not even serve them. But they are kept ignorant enough not to understand that the real dimensions of that dream—white supremacy, black "inferiority," and with them ultimately, though they know it not, fascism and war—are revealed every day throughout the world as deadly to human life and development—even their own.

In the post-civil rights era, in "polite" society, theirs is a dream too gross even to speak of *directly* anymore. And this is another legacy of the play: It was one of the shots fired (and still being fired) at the aberrant white-supremacy dream that is American reality. And the play is also a summation of those shots, that battle, its heightened statement. Yet the man, Lindner, explains him/themself, and there is even a hint of compassion for Lindner the man as he bumbles on in outrageous innocence of all he is actually saying—that "innocence" for which Americans are famous, which begs you to love and understand me for hating you, the innocence that kills. Through him we see this other dream:

> Does it stink like rotten meat?
> Or crust and sugar over—
> Like a syrupy sweet?

Almost everyone else in the play would sound like Martin Luther King at the march on Washington were we to read their speeches closely and project them broadly. An exception is George Murchison (merchant's son), the "assimilated" good bourgeois whose boldest dream, if one can call it that, is to "get the grades . . . to pass the course . . . to get a degree" en route to making it the American way. George wants only to "pop" Beneatha after she, looking good, can be seen with him in the "proper" places. He is opposed to a woman's "thinking" at all, and black heritage to him "is nothing but a bunch of raggedy-ass spirituals and some grass huts." The truth of this portrait is one reason the black bourgeoisie has not created the black national theaters, publishing houses, journals, galleries, film corporations, and newspapers the African American people desperately need. So lacking in self-respect are members of this class of George's, they even let the Kentucky Colonel sell us fried chicken and giblets.

The clash between Walter Lee and George, one of the high points of class struggle in the play and a dramatic tour de force, gives us the dialogue between the *sons* of the house and of the field slaves. (pp. 12-18)

When *Raisin* appeared the movement itself was in transition, which is why Hansberry could sum up its throbbing profile with such clarity. The baton was ready to pass from "George's father" as leader of the "Freedom Movement" (when its real muscle was always the Lena Youngers and their husbands) to the Walter Lees and Beneathas and Asagais and even the Georges.

In February 1960, black students at North Carolina A & T began to "sit in" at Woolworth's in a more forceful attack on segregated public facilities. By the end of 1960, some 96,000 students across the country had gotten involved in these sit-ins. In 1961, Patrice Lumumba was assassinated, and black intellectuals and activists in New York stormed the United Nations gallery. While Ralph Bunche (George's spiritual father) shrank back "embarrassed"—probably more so than by slavery and colonialism! But the Pan African thrust had definitely returned.

And by this time, too, Malcolm X, "the fire prophet," had emerged as the truest reflector of black mass feelings. It was of someone like Malcolm that Walter Lee spoke as in a trance in prophecy while he mounts the table to deliver his liquor-fired call to arms. (Nation of Islam headquarters was Chicago where the play is set!) Walter Lee embodies the explosion to be—what happens when the dream is deferred past even the patience of the Lena Youngers.

Young militants like myself were taken with Malcolm's coming, with the immanence of explosion. (pp. 18-19)

We thought Hansberry's play was part of the "passive resistance" phase of the movement, which was over the minute Malcolm's penetrating eyes and words began to charge through the media with deadly force. We thought her play "middle class" in that its focus seemed to be on "moving into white folks' neighborhoods," when most blacks were just trying to pay their rent in ghetto shacks.

We missed the essence of the work—that Hansberry had created a family on the cutting edge of the same class and ideological struggles as existed in the movement itself and among the people. What is most telling about our ignorance is that Hansberry's play still remains overwhelmingly popular and evocative of black and white reality, and the masses of black people dug it true.

The next two explosions in black drama, Baldwin's *Blues for Mr. Charlie* and my own *Dutchman* (both 1964) raise up the militance and self-defense clamor of the movement as it came fully into the Malcolm era. . . . But neither of these plays is as much a statement from the African American majority as is *Raisin.* For one thing, they are both (regardless of their "power") too concerned with white people.

It is Lorraine Hansberry's play which, though it seems "conservative" in form and content to the radical petty bourgeoisie (as opposed to revolutionaries), is the accurate telling and stunning vision of the real struggle. . . . The Younger family is part of the black majority, and the concerns I once dismissed as "middle class"—buying a house and moving into "white folks' neighborhoods"—are actually reflective of the essence of black people's striving and the will to defeat segregation, discrimination, and national oppression. There is no such thing as a "white folks' neighborhood" except to racists *and to those submitting to racism.*

The Younger family is the incarnation—*before* they burst from the bloody Southern backroads and the burning streets of Watts and Newark onto TV screens and the *world* stage—of our common ghetto-variety Fanny Lou Hamers, Malcolm X's, and Angela Davises. And their burden surely will be lifted, or one day it certainly will "explode." (pp. 19-20)

Amiri Baraka, "'A Raisin in the Sun's' Enduring Passion," in "A Raisin in the Sun"; and "The Sign in Sidney Brustein's Window" by Lorraine Hansberry, edited by Robert Nemiroff, New American Library, 1987, pp. 9-20.

FURTHER READING

OVERVIEWS AND GENERAL STUDIES

Baldwin, James. "Sweet Lorraine." *Esquire* LXXII, No. 5 (November 1969): 139-40.

Reminisces about his personal relationship with Hansberry, praising her skill and relating her artistic aims: "Lorraine made no bones about asserting that art has a purpose, and that its purpose was action: that it contained the 'energy which could change things'."

Carter, Steven R. *Hansberry's Drama: Commitment amid Complexity.* Urbana: The University of Illinois Press, 1991, 199 p.

Provides an overview of Hansberry's cultural views and their relation to her artistic goals; interprets her completed and nearly-completed dramas and screenplays; and assesses her dramatic achievements.

Cheney, Anne. *Lorraine Hansberry.* Boston: Twayne, 1984, 174 p.

Full-length study of Hansberry that chronicles her life and analyzes her works.

Davis, Arthur P. "Lorraine Hansberry." In his *From the Dark Tower: Afro-American Writers 1900 to 1960,* pp. 203-07. Washington, D.C.: Howard University Press, 1974.

Discusses the themes in Hansberry's *A Raisin in the Sun* and *The Sign in Sidney Brustein's Window.*

Freedomways 19, No. 4 (Fourth Quarter 1979).

Special issue devoted to Hansberry that includes essays by James Baldwin, Nikki Giovanni, Alex Haley, Ossie Davis, and Lonne Elder and a comprehensive bibliography of writings by and about Hansberry.

Killens, John Oliver. "Broadway in Black and White." *African Forum* 1, No. 3 (Winter 1966): 66-76.

Cites *A Raisin in the Sun* and *The Sign in Sidney Brustein's Window* as examples of outstanding achievements by an African American in the media of theater, film, and television, while arguing that "the great hope of the country is to unleash the tremendous store of black creative energy upon this North American nation and give it a new lease on life."

Whitlow, Roger. "1940-1960: Urban Realism and Beyond." In his *Black American Literature: A Critical History,* pp. 107-46. Chicago: Nelson Hall, 1973.

Contends that *A Raisin in the Sun* is about the "dreams" of the Younger family, while *The Sign in Sidney Brustein's Window* represents the "dreams" of the dramatist: her dream involves the "integrity of art" and the "integrity and moral courage of other people."

A RAISIN IN THE SUN

Adams, George R. "Black Militant Drama." *American Imago* 28, No. 2 (Summer 1971): 107-28.

Provides a psychological analysis of *A Raisin in the Sun,* declaring the drama an "ego-play" because it describes "how a Black family comes to the right relationship with 'reality'." Adams defines "reality" as the white value system.

Atkinson, Brooks. "The Theater: 'A Raisin in the Sun'." *The New York Times* (16 March 1959): 345.

Asserts that "*A Raisin in the Sun* has vigor as well as veracity and is likely to destroy the complacency of any one who sees it. . . . If there are occasional crudities in the craftsmanship, they are redeemed by the honesty of the writing."

Review of *A Raisin in the Sun. The Catholic World* 189, No. 1,130 (May 1959): 159.

Considers *A Raisin in the Sun* "an honest play of contemporary life, splendidly acted."

Cruse, Harold. "Lorraine Hansberry." In his *Crisis of the Negro Intellectual,* pp. 267-84. New York: Quill, 1984.

Maintains that "*A Raisin in the Sun* expressed through a medium of theatrical art that current, forced symbiosis in American interracial affairs wherein the Negro working class has been roped in and tied to the chariot of racial integration by the Negro middle class."

Mitchell, Loften. "The Nineteen-Fifties and the Millenium." In his *Black Drama: The Story of the American Negro in the Theatre,* pp. 142-82. New York: Hawthorne Books, 1967.

Asserts that *A Raisin in the Sun* sparked a resurgence in African-American theater.

Robertson, Nan. "Dramatist Against Odds." *The New York Times* (8 March 1959): II, 3.

Discusses the singular achievement of *A Raisin in the Sun* and relates Hansberry's artistic goals and her reflections about the play.

Tallmer, Jerry. "Broadway, New York." In *International Theatre Annual No. 4,* pp. 62-85. New York: Grove Press, 1959.

Praises the original cast of *A Raisin in the Sun* and describes the drama as "the single most revolutionary American play—quietly revolutionary—to come along in any of the years of my maturity."

Review of *A Raisin in the Sun. Theatre Arts* XLIII, No. 5 (May 1959): 22-4.

Asserts that Hansberry has written "very simply, very honestly and very rewardingly of a Negro family and its trials and aspirations in present day Chicago." The work is declared "a solidly dramatic play that is wide in emotional range and long on conviction."

THE SIGN IN SIDNEY BRUSTEIN'S WINDOW

Bain, Myrna. "Everybody's Protest Play." *National Review* (23 March 1965): 249-50.

Claims that *The Sign in Sidney Brustein's Window* has "no plot" and that it "should have closed on opening night" because in the play "protesting . . . is ritual first and drama second, if at all."

Gassner, John. "Lorraine Hansberry: *The Sign in Sidney Brustein's Window.*" In his *Dramatic Soundings: Evaluations and Retractions Culled from 30 Years of Dramatic Criticism*, pp. 579-80, edited by Glenn Loney. New York: Crown, 1968.

> Claims that *The Sign in Sidney Brustein's Window* "fails to cohere": "the overall action failed to define itself except as portions of an unwritten novel about the life history and harassments of the fictive hero Sidney Brustein."

Hansberry, Lorraine. "Village Intellect Revealed." *The New York Times* (11 October 1964): II, 1, 3.

> Discusses the germination of *The Sign in Sidney Brustein's Window.* Hansberry states that she does not write about "the Negro question" but about "various matters which have both Negro and white characters in them."

Holtan, Orley I. "Sidney Brustein and the Plight of the American Intellectual." *Players: The Magazine of American Theatre* 46, No. 5 (June / July 1971): 222-25.

> Analysis of *The Sign in Sidney Brustein's Window.* Holtan commends the dramatist's call for commitment and lauds the breadth and complexity of the work, but acknowledges that the play may perhaps lack cohesion.

Lewis, Theophilus. Review of *The Sign in Sidney Brustein's Window. American National Catholic Weekly Review* (5 December 1964): 758-59.

> Observes that "the characters are recognizable Village residents, and their separate stories range from the appealing to the ludicrous. The stories, however, do not jell in a cohesive drama."

McCarten, John. "Hansberry's Potpourri." *The New Yorker* (24 October 1964): 93.

> Negative review of *The Sign in Sidney Brustein's Window.* McCarten considers the work an overwrought, unfaithful depiction of Greenwich Village.

Miller, Jordan Y. "Lorraine Hansberry." In *The Black American Writer*, pp. 157-70, edited by C. W. E. Bigsby. Deland, Fla.: Everett / Edwards, 1969.

> Praises Hansberry's skills as a dramatist, citing *The Sign in Sidney Brustein's Window* as proof that Hansberry was not an "accidental" success.

Neal, Lawrence P. "*The Sign in Sidney Brustein's Window.*" *Liberator* IV, No. 12 (December 1964): 25.

> Maintains that *The Sign in Sidney Brustein's Window* demonstrates that "where there is corruption nothing survives" and states that the play "shows much more scope than *Raisin in the Sun,* although it lacks the sharpness of focus that *Raisin* has."

"Borrowed Bitchery." *Newsweek* (26 October 1964): 101-02.

> Disparages *The Sign in Sidney Brustein's Window,* declaring that "in shifting her suffering to the backs of others, in using every easy trick to destroy what threatens her, [Hansberry] has betrayed not only the function of art, but social responsibility, political possibility, her own cause and, most radically, herself."

Redding, Saunders. "In Search of Reality." *The Crisis: A Record of the Darker Races* 73, No. 3 (March 1966): 175-76.

> Review of *The Sign in Sidney Brustein's Window.* Saunders states that "it just misses being great. Miss Hansberry tried to sum up in . . . a single character all the

social anxieties, the cultural confusion and the emotional debris that litter and torment our days. The remarkable thing is that Miss Hansberry nearly succeeded."

"Guilt Collectors." *Time* (23 October 1964): 67.

> Review of *The Sign in Sidney Brustein's Window* that finds it "overloaded, overwritten, and overwrought." The critic adds that Hansberry needs to "recover the dramatic directness and drive of her prizewinning first play, *A Raisin in the Sun.*"

OTHER MAJOR WORKS

Clurman, Harold. "Theatre: 'Les Blancs'." *The Nation* (30 November 1970): 573.

> Objects to the generally negative critical reception of *Les Blancs* and finds that the play is "a forceful and intelligent statement of the tragic impasse of white and black relations all over the world."

Farrison, W. Edward. "Lorraine Hansberry's Last Dramas." *CLA Journal* XVI, No. 2 (December 1972): 188-97.

> Notes the success of the "original and vivid dialogue" in *The Drinking Gourd* and declares the drama "a compact yet comprehensive, authentic, and vivid portrayal" of American plantation slavery. Farrison adds that *What Use Are Flowers?* is "a brave venture into philosophical drama" that nevertheless does nothing to augment Hansberry's reputation.

Gottfried, Martin. "Theater: 'Les Blancs'." *NY Theater Critics' Reviews* XXXI, No. 22 (16 November 1972): 155-56.

> Declares that *Les Blancs* is "a didactic play, existing for its ideas rather than its theater. Its characters are stereotypes, created as points of view rather than as people, and its language heavy with information."

Hentoff, Nat. "'They Fought—They Fought!'" *The New York Times* (25 May 1969): II, 1, 18.

> Praises Hansberry's *To Be Young, Gifted and Black* as "a whirl of probing, celebrating, and moving on" that accurately portrays Hansberry's racial pride and lively spirit.

Kerr, Walter. Review of "Les Blancs." *The New York Times* (29 November 1970): II, 3.

> Acknowledges some flaws in *Les Blancs*—such as various underdeveloped characters—but claims that faults in the work are compensated for by "the candor and drive of the play's speech."

Powell, Bertie J. "The Black Experience in Margaret Walker's 'Jubilee' and Lorraine Hansberry's 'The Drinking Gourd'." *CLA Journal* XXI, No. 2 (December 1977): 304-11.

> Notes that *The Drinking Gourd* not only depicts the Black experience in America during the time of slavery, but also reveals that although some white people were "caught up within the evils of slavery by virtue of their existence," they did not relinquish their humanity.

MEDIA ADAPTATIONS

A Raisin in the Sun. Columbia, 1961.

> The award-winning film adaptation starring Sidney Poitier and Claudia McNeil. Hansberry wrote the screen-

play for this version, which was directed by Daniel Petrie.

A Raisin in the Sun. American Playhouse/NBLA Productions, 1989.

A made-for-television presentation with Danny Glover and Esther Rolle. First aired on PBS, this production was directed by Bill Duke.

For further information on Hansberry's life and career, see *Black Literature Criticism,* Vol. 2; *Black Writers; Contemporary Authors,* Vols. 25-28; *Contemporary Authors New Revision Series,* Vol. 109; *Contemporary Literary Criticism,* Vols. 17, 62; and *Dictionary of Literary Biography,* Vols. 7, 38.

Henrik Ibsen

1828-1906

INTRODUCTION

Full name Henrik Johan Ibsen; also wrote under the pseudonym Brynjolf Bjarme.

Norwegian playwright and poet Henrik Ibsen is regarded as the father of modern drama. He changed the course of Western drama by bringing realism and social concerns to the forefront of European theater, which had been circumscribed by romanticism. His provocative portrayals of contemporary social issues placed his works at the center of cultural debate and made Ibsen at once the most famous, praised, and vilified playwright of the nineteenth century. As the controversies over his choice of subject matter have faded, critics have focused on the universality of the playwright's concerns and the revolutionary aspects of his dramaturgy: striking visual imagery, deft symbolism, and starkly poetic dramatic prose. Ibsen's technical craftsmanship and psychological insight mark his lasting legacy to world literature; in addition, the major themes of his works—self-realization, idealism, guilt, illusion, and the conflict between art and life—poignantly document the frustration and potential of the individual in society.

Born to wealthy parents in Skien in 1828, Ibsen endured a life of poverty after his father went bankrupt in 1836. At the age of fifteen Ibsen left home, apprenticing himself as a pharmacist's assistant in Grimstad, where he remained for the next six years. When he was no more than eighteen, a liaison with a servant woman ten years his senior resulted in an illegitimate child; Ibsen continued to support his son for the next fourteen years, but strove to keep the relationship a secret. Oppressed by poverty and the small-town life of Grimstad, Ibsen pinned his hopes for escape on admission to the university to study medicine. His review of Latin texts for his entrance examinations provided the inspiration for Ibsen's first drama, *Catilina* (*Catiline*), which was published with the aid of a friend in 1850 but failed to arouse interest. Later that year he moved to Christiania (now Oslo), where he studied for eighteen months at a preparatory school but failed the Greek and mathematics sections of his examinations and never became a fully matriculated student. Already the editor of a student newspaper, Ibsen decided to devote all of his attention to writing, and over the next year he published poetry, helped edit a satirical journal, and contributed articles to a radical weekly. He also completed his first play ever produced, the one-act *Kaempehøien* (*The Warrior's Barrow*), which was staged in Christiania on 26 September 1850 and raised Ibsen's hopes for a career as a dramatist.

In November of 1851 Ibsen was offered a job as a playwright in residence for the newly formed Norwegian Theatre in Bergen, the country's first theater to employ Norwegian actors and concentrate on Norwegian, rather than Danish, speech. After a modest grant allowed him to study theater in Copenhagen and Dresden, Ibsen returned

to Bergen in 1852, where he fulfilled his contract by writing one new historical romance every year; in addition, he gained invaluable practical experience by gradually taking on the duties of a producer. Ibsen had a hand in the production of no fewer than 145 plays over the next five years, including his own dramas *Fru Inger til Østraat* (*Lady Inger of Ostraat*) and *Gildet på Solhaug* (*The Feast at Solhaug*)—the latter being his first play to achieve any measure of success. In 1857 Ibsen became the artistic director of the Norwegian Theatre in Christiania. He married Suzannah Thorensen a year later; the couple's only son, Sigurd, was born in 1859. Despite Ibsen's prodigious efforts as a writer and producer, the Norwegian Theatre could not compete with the established, Danish-dominated Christiania Theatre, and it went bankrupt in 1862. A university grant to collect folk tales in western Norway and a temporary job at a meager salary as a literary adviser to the Christiania Theatre followed. *Haermaendene på Helgeland* (*The Vikings at Helgeland*) and *Kjaerlighedens komedie* (*Love's Comedy*) were successfully produced, but mounting debts, overwork, and critical attacks brought Ibsen to the point of a breakdown. His continued petitions to the government for a grant to travel and write were denied, one bringing the response that he "deserved a whipping instead of a stipend." However, an 1864 production of *Kongsemnerne* (*The Pretenders*) earned him a small royalty, and shortly thereafter he was awarded a state grant for foreign travel. With the aid of some friends, Ibsen paid what he could of his debts and left Norway for Rome. He spent the next 27 years living abroad in a self-imposed exile, returning to his homeland for only two short visits; his departure marked the end of his practical association with the theater.

Ibsen's years in Italy brought a breakthrough in his career. His verse dramas *Brand* and *Peer Gynt* were immediate popular and critical successes, establishing Ibsen as Scandinavia's most popular playwright. Several grants and an annual stipend followed, and Ibsen astonished his friends in Rome with his newfound confidence, the elegance of his dress, and the new cut of his beard. In 1868 Ibsen moved to Germany to escape political unrest in Italy. There he abandoned poetry as a dramatic medium and published *De unges forbund* (*The League of Youth*) and the monumental, two-part *Kejser og Galilaeer* (*Emperor and Galilean*)—his last play set in the past. *Samfundets støtter* (*The Pillars of Society*), a realistic work with a contemporary setting and modern colloquial dialogue, was published in 1877; it marked the first of the so-called social problem plays that consolidated Ibsen's worldwide fame. In the ensuing decades he produced at almost exactly two-year intervals twelve works of modern realism which both thrilled and shocked theater patrons and critics alike and provoked heated debates. The frank treatment of the controversial subjects of women's rights, venereal disease, euthanasia, suicide, and frigidity in such plays as *Et dukkehjem* (*A Doll's House*), *Gengangere* (*Ghosts*), *Vilanden* (*The Wild Duck*), and *Hedda Gabler* brought Ibsen scorn for his lack of artistic decorum and praise for his championing of social reform. In 1891 he returned with his wife to Norway, where he published his last four dramas. In works such as *Bygmester Solness* (*The Master Builder*) and *Når vi døde vågner* (*When We Dead Awaken*), Ibsen experimented with what he called the "new weapons" of mystical symbolism. In 1898, on the occasion of his seventieth birthday, Ibsen received international accolades in public celebrations that hailed him as the world's greatest living dramatist. Ibsen suffered a series of apoplectic strokes in the years following 1901 which left him unable to write or walk. He died in Christiania in 1906, and his country honored him with a state funeral.

Critics generally divide Ibsen's massive body of work into three phases. The first consists of his early romantic plays, primarily written in verse, in which Ibsen drew heavily on traditional folk tales and Norse sagas for subject matter. The second phase consists of the realistic prose dramas on social concerns for which the playwright is most famous. In his final period, Ibsen continued to deal with modern, realistic themes, but made increasing use of symbol and metaphor to convey a mystical, visionary insight into human psychology.

These periods were preceded by his academic effort, *Catiline,* an otherwise undistinguished verse melodrama whose themes on the importance of the individual, the quest for self-realization, and the nature of idealism prefig-

ure much of Ibsen's later work. The playwright continued to explore these concerns in his early romantic dramas, which heroically portray his country's past. Melodramas such as *The Feast at Solhaug* and *The Vikings at Helgeland* and the verse satire *Love's Comedy* are notable primarily for their idiosyncratically Norwegian characters and the emerging note of social criticism. Ibsen's masterpieces from his early romantic period are the epic verse dramas *Brand* and *Peer Gynt,* complementary works whose protagonists embody the Scandinavian life and character. The pictures of the unyielding, uncompromising minister Brand and vacillating but lovable opportunist Peer combine to form not only a critique of Norway's spiritual character, but a sweeping allegory of idealism and human limitation.

In the harsh tragedies and satirical comedies of the second phase of Ibsen's career, the dramatist departed from romantic lyricism to capture modern, natural dialogue within a strictly economical form that hinged on retrospective exposition—the gradual revelation of past events leading to the climax. Ibsen also placed increasing emphasis on the set, props, and mise-en-scène, supplementing his text with complex visual imagery to reinforce his key themes. Ibsen first developed these techniques in *The Pillars of Society,* but it was the scandal surrounding his depiction of the collapse of a middle class marriage in *A Doll's House* and his treatment of the tragedy of inherited venereal disease in *Ghosts* that demonstrated the power of Ibsen's dramaturgy. These works engendered controversies about the propriety of depicting such events in literature and on the stage that would persist throughout the 1880s and 1890s. Indeed, critic and playwright Bernard Shaw coined the term "Ibsenism" to refer to a critique of contemporary morality in dramatic form. This term reflected—and perpetuated—the critical emphasis on Ibsen's works as issue-oriented "thesis dramas" which examined specific social ills. However, the enduring power and appeal of these works has led later critics to explore their revolutionary dramaturgy as well as their universal themes.

Commentators have likened Nora's slamming of the door as she leaves her husband and children in *A Doll's House* to a bomb going off in the drawing rooms of the Victorian era. Early criticism of the play, both positive and negative, often concentrated on the work solely as a feminist tract. Many critics viewed Nora's departure as the moral of the drama and either hailed Ibsen as a champion supporting women's rights or excoriated him as a villain advocating divorce and child abandonment. Ibsen himself stated that he sought to portray "the problem of mankind in general" in *A Doll's House,* and modern critics have examined the play in this light, arguing that the complexity and ambiguity of the work transcends a narrow, tendentious commentary on the institution of marriage. The subtle facets of Nora's characterization and her supposed metamorphosis have become focuses for many commentators, as have the ramifications of the drama's sub-plot, in which Kristine and Krogstad's impending marriage contrasts Nora and Torvald's crumbling relationship. Other critics have examined the symbolism of the Christmas tree and Nora's party costume, arguing that they represent a world of deceptively beautiful appearances. Seen from this perspective, the work emerges not only as an attack on the stultifying conventions of society, but as a testament to the need for freedom and self-expression.

Oppressive social demands and buried truths lie at the heart of *Ghosts,* which portrays the tragedy of Mrs. Alving, a woman who would not leave her loveless marriage and later realizes that her son Oswald has inherited his father's syphilis. As the initial scandal about the play's subject matter subsided, critics turned their attention from the literal facts surrounding the transmission of the disease to its symbolic importance; many have maintained that Oswald's grisly inheritance represents the sin, guilt, and corruption of the past, which exerts control in the present. Numerous commentators have likened the play to ancient Greek tragedy, comparing Mrs. Alving to a classical tragic hero and asserting that in *Ghosts* psychology and heredity take the place of fate in governing human action. Ibsen thus depicts a deterministic universe that throws into high relief the hypocrisy of the self-righteous religious and moral authorities who refuse to confront the truth; this refusal to face the truth emerges as a recurring theme in Ibsen's ensuing dramas.

Critics have often interpreted *En folkefiende* (*An Enemy of the People*) and *The Wild Duck* as reflections not only of mankind's search for truth, but as Ibsen's reaction to the hostile response to *Ghosts* and his growing disillusionment with the form of his social dramas. The well-meaning attempts of Dr. Stockmann to expose his town's corruption despite great personal cost in the ironic comedy *Enemy of the People* are contrasted with the misguided philanthropy of Gregers Werle in *The Wild Duck;* Werle's revelation that Hedvig may not be the legitimate daughter of Hjalmer Ekdal shatters the happiness of the Ekdal family, thus reinforcing the necessity of life-sustaining illusions. *The Wild Duck* stands at a period of transition in Ibsen's work, as its elements of naturalistic detail provide the basis for complex and enigmatic symbolism that has been subject to a variety of interpretations. The significance of the wild duck from which the play derives its title has dominated critical commentary on the drama, with some critics following the lead of Ibsen's Gregers Werle in likening the Ekdal's family pet to several of the play's characters; others assert that the domesticated wild creature serves as a metaphor for modern man's existence. Some have found the manifold symbolism of the play ambiguous and confusing, but many assert that Ibsen's symbols are a refreshing and self-renewing expression of the themes of illusion and reality central to the play. Ibsen's emphasis on fantasy and the imagination is also evident in *Rosmersholm, Freun fra havet* (*The Lady from the Sea*), and *Hedda Gabler,* dramas which continued to herald Ibsen's last period with their dynamic symbolism and their shift in focus away from an examination of the individual's relationship to society and toward an exploration of personal psychology.

Nowhere does Ibsen provide a more complex character study than in *Hedda Gabler,* his portrait of a frustrated aristocratic woman trapped in a bourgeois marriage and repelled by her impending motherhood. The drama's particular social and economic milieu has served as the departure point for many critics' examination of the work, as has Hedda's motivations for her marriage to the dull scholar George Tesman and her subsequent destructive behavior. Numerous commentators have analyzed the work as a tragedy, attempting to locate mythic underpinnings in the drama and discussing Hedda as a tragic figure. The symbolic importance of the play's props, mise-en-scène, and verbal imagery is a dominant trend in recent criticism of *Hedda Gabler,* and critics assert that symbols such as Hedda's dueling pistols and the portrait of her father symbolize various aspects of her psychological struggle between creativity and control—the pistols representing her powerful destructive impulses and the portrait representing the domineering aristocratic code of her past. The tragic conclusion of the drama seems to posit no reconciliation between the impulsive and destructive universe of Hedda and the humane yet limited world of Tesman, and her death stands as an ironic comment on the human desire for a beautiful and perfect act.

The irreconcilable tension between art and life permeates the works of profound mystical symbolism that define Ibsen's final period. Critics have found confessional, autobiographical elements in *The Master Builder, Lille Eyolf* (*Little Eyolf*), *John Gabriel Borkman,* and *When We Dead Awaken.* The protagonists in each of these dramas— an architect, a writer, a financier, and a sculptor— experience the conflict between the demands of vocation and personal life. Critics have pointed out a correlation between Solness's architecture in *The Master Builder* and Ibsen's own oeuvre, likening Solness's churches, houses, and towers to Ibsen's romantic dramas, domestic social plays, and visionary and symbolic works; this has led to speculation that Solness's fear of being surpassed by succeeding generations and his guilt over neglecting his family represent Ibsen's own anguish and concern over his life and work. These overarching themes of freedom of expression, guilt, and idealism unite Ibsen's final dramas with the entire body of his work. Each of Ibsen's plays transcends its specific parochial issues to convey yet another facet of the human enigma, and Ibsen's impact on succeeding generations of playwrights undoubtedly assures him a place as one of the world's greatest dramatists.

PRINCIPAL WORKS

PLAYS

Catilina [as Brynjolf Bjarme] 1850 (revised 1875)
  [*Catiline,* published in *Early Plays: Catiline, The Warrior's Barrow, Olaf Liljekrans,* 1921]
Kaempehøien 1850 (revised 1853)
  [*The Warrior's Barrow,* published in *Early Plays: Catiline, The Warrior's Barrow, Olaf Liljekrans,* 1921]
Fru Inger til Østraat 1855
  [*Lady Inger of Østraat,* published in *The Collected Works of Henrik Ibsen,* 1906-12]

Gildet på Solhaug 1856 (revised 1883)
[*The Feast at Solhaug,* 1909]
Olaf Liljekrans 1857
[*Olaf Liljekrans,* published in *Early Plays: Catiline, The Warrior's Barrow, Olaf Liljekrans,* 1921]
Haermaendene på Helgeland 1858
[*The Vikings at Helgeland,* published in *The Collected Works of Henrik Ibsen,* 1906-12]
Kjaerlighedens komedie 1862
[*Love's Comedy,* 1898]
Kongsemnerne 1863
[*The Pretenders,* 1907]
Brand 1866
[*Brand,* 1891]
Peer Gynt 1867
[*Peer Gynt,* 1902]
De unges forbund 1869
[*The League of Youth,* published in *Ibsen's Prose Dramas,* 1890]
Kejser og Galilaeer 1873
[*Emperor and Galilean,* 1876]
Samfundets støtter 1877
[*The Pillars of Society,* published in *The Pillars of Society and Other Plays,* 1888]
Et dukkehjem 1879
[*Nora,* 1882; also published as *A Doll Home,* 1882; also published as *A Doll's House,* 1889]
Gengangere 1881
[*Ghosts,* 1890]
En folkefiende 1882
[*An Enemy of Society,* published in *The Pillars of Society and Other Plays,* 1888; also published as *An Enemy of the People,* 1939]
Vilanden 1884
[*The Wild Duck;* published in *Ibsen's Prose Dramas,* 1890]
Rosmersholm 1886
[*Rosmersholm,* 1889]
Fruen fra havet 1888
[*The Lady from the Sea,* 1890]
Hedda Gabler 1890
[*Hedda Gabler,* 1891]
Bygmester Solness 1892
[*The Master Builder,* 1893]
Lille Eyolf 1894
[*Little Eyolf,* 1894]
John Gabriel Borkman 1896
[*John Gabriel Borkman,* 1897]
Når vi døde vågner 1899
[*When We Dead Awaken,* 1900]

OTHER MAJOR WORKS

Digte af Henrik Ibsen (poetry) 1871
[*Lyrics and Poems from Ibsen,* 1912]
Samlede Vaerker, 10 vols. (dramas, poetry, and scenarios) 1898-1902
Breve udg Henrik Ibsen (letters) 1904
[*Letters of Henrik Ibsen,* 1905]
The Collected Works of Henrik Ibsen, 12 vols. (dramas, poetry, and scenarios) 1906-12

AUTHOR COMMENTARY

Notes on *A Doll's House* (1879)

[*The following are two of Ibsen's early studies for* A Doll's House: *a brief note discussing the major themes of the drama and a detailed scenario outlining the plot, characterization, and dialogue. Ibsen centers his thoughts on the plight of women in a society defined by men. The essay date given, 1879, is that of the first publication of* A Doll's House.]

There are two kinds of spiritual law, two kinds of conscience, one in man and another, altogether different, in woman. They do not understand each other; but in practical life the woman is judged by man's law, as though she were not a woman but a man.

The wife in the play ends by having no idea of what is right or wrong; natural feeling on the one hand and belief in authority on the other have altogether bewildered her.

A woman cannot be herself in the society of the present day, which is an exclusively masculine society, with laws framed by men and with a judicial system that judges feminine conduct from a masculine point of view.

She has committed forgery, and she is proud of it; for she did it out of love for her husband, to save his life. But this husband with his commonplace principles of honor is on the side of the law and looks at the question from the masculine point of view.

Spiritual conflicts. Oppressed and bewildered by the belief in authority, she loses faith in her moral right and ability to bring up her children. Bitterness. A mother in modern society, like certain insects who go away and die when she has done her duty in the propagation of the race. Love of life, of home, of husband and children and family. Now and then a womanly shaking off of her thoughts. Sudden return of anxiety and terror. She must bear it all alone. The catastrophe approaches, inexorably, inevitably. Despair, conflict, and destruction.

(Krogstad has acted dishonorably and thereby become well-to-to-do; now his prosperity does not help him, he cannot recover his honor.)

•

SCENARIO: FIRST ACT

A room comfortably, but not showily, furnished. A door to the right in the back leads to the hall; another door to the left in the back leads to the room or office of the master of the house, which can be seen when the door is opened. A fire in the stove. Winter day.

She enters from the back, humming gaily; she is in outdoor dress and carries several parcels, has been shopping. As she opens the door, a porter is seen in the hall, carrying a Christmas tree. She: Put it down there for the present. (Taking out her purse) How much? Porter: Fifty öre. She: Here is a crown. No, keep the change. The porter thanks her and goes. She continues humming and smiling contentedly as she opens several of the parcels she has brought. Calls off to find out if he is home. Yes! At first, conversation through the closed door; then he opens it and goes on talking to her while continuing to work most of the time, standing at his desk. There is a ring at the hall door; he does not want to be disturbed; shuts himself in. The maid opens the door to her mistress's friend, just arrived in town. Happy surprise. Mutual explanation of the state of affairs. He has received the post of manager in the new joint-stock bank and is to begin at New Year's; all financial worries are at an end. The friend has come to town to look for some small employment in an office or whatever may present itself. Mrs. Stenborg encourages her, is certain that all will turn out well. The maid opens the front door to the debt collector. Mrs. Stenborg terrified; they exchange a few words; he is shown into the office. Mrs. Stenborg and her friend; the circumstances of the collector are touched upon. Stenborg enters in his overcoat; has sent the collector out the other way. Conversation about the friend's affairs; hesitation on his part. He and the friend go out; his wife follows them into the hall; the Nurse enters with the children. Mother and children play. The collector enters. Mrs. Stenborg sends the children out to the left. Big scene between her and him. He goes. Stenborg enters; has met him on the stairs; displeased; wants to know what he came back for? Her support? No intrigues. His wife cautiously tries to pump him. Strict legal answers. Exit to his room. *She:* (repeating her words when the collector went out) But that's impossible. Why, I did it from love!

SECOND ACT

The last day of the year. Midday. Nora and the old Nurse. Nora, driven by anxiety, is putting on her things to go out. Anxious random questions of one kind and another intimate that thoughts of death are in her mind. Tries to banish these thoughts, to make light of it, hopes that something or other may intervene. But what? The Nurse goes off to the left. Stenborg enters from his room. Short dialogue between him and Nora. The Nurse re-enters; looks for Nora; the youngest child is crying. Annoyance and questioning on Stenborg's part; exit the Nurse; Stenborg is going in to the children. Doctor enters. Scene between him and Stenborg. Nora soon re-enters; she has turned back; anxiety has driven her home again. Scene between her, the Doctor, and Stenborg. Stenborg goes into his room. Scene between Nora and the Doctor. The Doctor goes out. Nora alone. Mrs. Linde enters. Scene between her and Nora. Lawyer Krogstad enters. Short scene between him, Mrs. Linde, and Nora. Mrs. Linde in to the children. Scene between Krogstad and Nora. She entreats and implores him for the sake of her little children; in vain. Krogstad goes out. The letter is seen to fall from outside into the letter box. Mrs. Linde re-enters after a short pause. Scene between her and Nora. Half confession. Mrs. Linde goes out. Nora alone. Stenborg enters. Scene between him and Nora. He wants to empty the letter box. Entreaties, jests, half-playful persuasion. He promises to let business wait till after New Year's Day; but at 12 o'clock midnight . . . ! Exit. Nora alone. *Nora:* (looking at the clock) It is five o'clock. Five; seven hours till mid-

night. Twenty-four hours till the next midnight. Twenty-four and seven—thirty-one. Thirty-one hours to live.

THIRD ACT

A muffled sound of dance music is heard from the floor above. A lighted lamp on the table. Mrs. Linde sits in an armchair and absently turns the pages of a book, tries to read, but seems unable to fix her attention; once or twice she looks at her watch. Nora comes down from the party; so disturbed she was compelled to leave; surprise at finding Mrs. Linde, who pretends that she wanted to see Nora in her costume. Helmer, displeased at her going away, comes to fetch her back. The Doctor also enters, to say good-by. Meanwhile Mrs. Linde has gone into the side room on the right. Scene between the Doctor, Helmer, and Nora. He is going to bed, he says, never to get up again; they are not to come and see him; there is ugliness about a deathbed. He goes out. Helmer goes upstairs again with Nora, after the latter has exchanged a few words of farewell with Mrs. Linde. Mrs. Linde alone. Then Krogstad. Scene and explanation between them. Both go out. Nora and the children. Then she alone. Then Helmer. He takes the letters out of the letter box. Short scene; good night; he goes into his room. Nora in despair prepares for the final step, is already at the door when Helmer enters with the open letter in his hand. Big scene. A ring. Letter to Nora from Krogstad. Final scene. Divorce. Nora leaves the house. (pp. 151-54)

> *Henrik Ibsen, notes on "A Doll's House," in* Playwrights on Playwriting: The Meaning and Making of Modern Drama from Ibsen to Ionesco, *edited by Toby Cole, Hill and Wang, 1960, pp. 151-54.*

Notes on *Ghosts* (1881)

[*Below are Ibsen's extant notes for his preliminary studies for* Ghosts. *Culled from several sources, including the jottings on the back of an envelope addressed to "Madame Ibsen," these memoranda encapsulate Ibsen's thoughts on the plight of modern man, the major themes of* Ghosts, *and other issues. According to the playwright, "Marriage for external reasons . . . brings a Nemesis upon the offspring." The essay date given, 1881, is that of the first publication of* Ghosts.]

The play is to be like a picture of life. Belief undermined. But it does not do to say so. "The Orphanage"—for the sake of others. They are to be happy—but this too is only an appearance—everything is ghosts.

A leading point: She has been a believer and romantic—this is not entirely obliterated by the standpoint reached later—"Everything is ghosts."

Marriage for external reasons, even when these are religious or moral, brings a Nemesis upon the offspring.

She, the illegitimate child, can be saved by being married to—the son—but then—?

•   He was dissipated and his health was shattered in his youth; then she appeared, the religious enthusiast; she saved him; she was rich. He was going to marry a girl who was considered unworthy. He had a son by his wife, then he went back to the girl; a daughter.

• These modern women, ill-used as daughters, as sisters, as wives, not educated according to their gifts, prevented from following their calling, deprived of their inheritance, embittered in temper—it is these who furnish the mothers of the new generation. What will be the result?

• The keynote is to be: The prolific growth of our intellectual life, in literature, arts, etc.—and in contrast to this: all of mankind gone astray.

The complete human being is no longer a product of nature, he is an artificial product like grain, and fruit trees, and the Creole race and thoroughbred horses and dogs, the vine, etc.

The fault lies in that all mankind has failed. If a man claims to live and develop in a human way, it is megalomania. All mankind, and especially the Christian part of it, suffers from megalomania.

• Among us, monuments are erected to the *dead,* since we have a duty toward them; we allow lepers to marry; but their offspring . . . ? The unborn . . . ? (pp. 154-55)

> *Henrik Ibsen, notes on "Ghosts," in* Play-wrights on Playwriting: The Meaning and Making of Modern Drama from Ibsen to Io-nesco, *edited by Toby Cole, Hill and Wang, 1960, pp. 154-55.*

Notes on *Hedda Gabler*   (1890)

[*The following excerpts from Ibsen's preliminary notes for* Hedda Gabler *detail the genesis and evolution of the drama. Beginning with an idea for a play based on the prominent novelist Camilla Collett, who believed that she was the real-life model for the heroine in Ibsen's* The Lady from the Sea, *the playwright developed the characterization and plot to mold the complex and enigmatic Hedda, a passionate yet fearful woman who realizes she is not suited for motherhood but cannot discover her mission in life. The numbered sections indicate the various sources for these notes—which include loose sheets, notebooks, and the back of a calling card—and often refer to earlier versions of characters' names. The essay date listed, 1890, is that of the first publication of* Hedda Gabler.]

(1)

• This married woman more and more imagines that she is an important personality, and as a consequence feels compelled to create for herself a sensational past—

• If an interesting female character appears in a new story or in a play, she believes that it is she who is being portrayed.

• The masculine environment helps to confirm her in this belief.

• The two lady friends agree to die together. One of them carries out her end of the bargain. But the other one who realizes what lies in store for her loses her courage. This is the reversal—

• "He has such a disgusting way of walking when one sees him from behind."

• She hates him because he has a goal, a mission in life. The lady friend has one too, but does not dare to devote herself to it. Her personal life treated in fictional form.

• In the second act the manuscript that is left behind—

• "The lost soul" apologizes for the man of culture. The wild horse and the race horse. Drinks—eats paprika. House and clothes. Revolution against the laws of nature—but nothing stupid, not until the position is secure.

(2)

• The pale, apparently cold beauty. Expects great things of life and the joy of life.

The man who has now finally won her, plain and simple in appearance, but an honest and talented, broad-minded scholar.

(3) .

• The manuscript that H. L. leaves behind contends that man's mission is: Upward, toward the bearer of light. Life on the present foundations of society is not worth living. Therefore he escapes from it through his imagination. By drinking, etc.—Tesman stands for correct behavior. Hedda for blasé oversophistication. Mrs. R. is the nervous-hysterical modern individual. Brack represents the personal bourgeois point of view.

• Then H. departs this world. And the two of them are left sitting there with the manuscript they cannot interpret. And the aunt is with them. What an ironic comment on humanity's striving for progress and development.

• But Holger's double nature intervenes. Only by realizing the basely bourgeois can he win a hearing for his great central idea.

• Mrs. Rising is afraid that H., although "a model of propriety," is not normal. She can only guess at his way of thinking but cannot understand it. Quotes some of his remarks—

• One talks about building railways and highways for the cause of progress. But no, no, that is not what is needed. Space must be cleared so that the spirit of man can make its great turnabout. For it has gone astray. The spirit of man has gone astray.

• *Holger:* I have been out. I have behaved obscenely. That doesn't matter. But the police know about it. That's what counts.

• H. L.'s despair lies in that he wants to master the world but cannot master himself.

• Tesman believes that it is he who has in a way seduced H. L. into indulging in excesses again. But that is not so. It is as Hedda has said: that it was *he* she dreamed of when she talked about "the famous man." But she does not dare tell Tesman this.

• To aid in understanding his own character, L. has made notes in "the manuscript." These are the notes the two of them should interpret, want to interpret, but *cannot* possibly.

• Brack is inclined to live as a bachelor, and then gain admittance to a good home, become a friend of the family, indispensable—

• They say it is a law of nature. Very well then, raise an opposition to it. Demand its repeal. Why give way. Why surrender unconditionally—

• In conversations between T. and L. the latter says that he lives for his studies. The former replies that in that case he can compete with him.—(T. lives *on* his studies) that's the point.

• L. (Tesman) says: I couldn't step on a worm! "But now I can tell you that I too am seeking the professorship. We are rivals."

(4)

• She has respect for his knowledge, an eye for his noble character, but is embarrassed by his insignificant, ridiculous appearance, makes fun of his conduct and remarks.

(5)

• The aunt asks all sorts of ambiguous questions to find out about those things that arouse her imagination the most.

• NOTES: One evening as Hedda and Tesman, together with some others, were on their way home from a party, Hedda remarked as they walked by a charming house that was where she would like to live. She meant it, but she said it only to keep the conversation with Tesman going. "He simply cannot carry on a conversation."

The house was actually for rent or sale. Tesman had been pointed out as the coming young man. And later when he proposed, and let slip that he too had dreamed of living there, she accepted.

He too had liked the house very much.

They get married. And they rent the house. [In a footnote, Ibsen states "Both of them, each in his and her own way, have seen in their common love for this house a sign of their mutual understanding. As if they sought and were drawn to a common home. Then he rents the house. They get married and go abroad. He orders the house bought and his aunt furnishes it at his expense. Now it is their home. It is theirs and yet it is not, because it is not paid for. Everything depends on his getting the professorship."]

But when Hedda returns as a young wife, with a vague sense of responsibility, the whole thing seems distasteful to her. She conceives a kind of hatred for the house just because it has become her home. She confides this to Brack. She evades the question with Tesman.

• The play shall deal with "the impossible," that is, to aspire to and strive for something which is against all the conventions, against that which is acceptable to conscious minds—Hedda's included.

• The episode of the hat makes Aunt Rising lose her composure. She leaves—That it could be taken for the maid's hat—no, that's going too far!

That my hat, which I've had for over nine years, could be taken for the maid's—no, that's really too much!

• *Hedda:* Yes, once I thought it must be wonderful to live here and own this house.

Brack: But now you are contradicting yourself.

Hedda: That may be so. But that's how it is anyway.

• *Hedda:* I don't understand these self-sacrificing people. Look at old Miss Rising. She has a paralyzed sister in her house, who has been lying in bed for years. Do you suppose she thinks it is a sacrifice to live for that poor creature, who is a burden even to herself? Far from it! Just the opposite. I don't understand it.

• *Hedda:* And how greedy they are for married men. Do you know what, Judge Brack? You don't do yourself any good by not getting married.

Brack: Then I can practically consider myself married.

Hedda: Yes, you certainly can—in one way—in many ways even—

Brack: In many ways? What do you mean by that?

Hedda: No thanks. I won't tell you.

• When Mrs. Elvsted says that the first part of Lövborg's book deals with the historical development of "Sociology," and that another volume will appear later, Tesman looks at her a little startled.

• Very few true parents are to be found in the world. Most people grow up under the influence of aunts or uncles—either neglected and misunderstood or else spoiled.

• Hedda rejects him because he does not dare expose himself to temptation. He replies that the same is true of her. The wager! . . . He loses . . . ! Mrs. Elvsted is present. Hedda says: No danger—He loses.

• Hedda feels herself demoniacally attracted by the tendencies of the times. But she lacks courage. Her thoughts remain theories, ineffective dreams.

• The feminine imagination is not active and independently creative like the masculine. It needs a bit of reality as a help.

• Lövborg has had inclinations toward "the bohemian life." Hedda is attracted in the same direction, but she does not dare to take the leap.

• Buried deep within Hedda there is a level of poetry. But the environment frightens her. Suppose she were to make herself ridiculous!

• Hedda realizes that she, much more than Thea, has abandoned her husband.

• The newly wedded couple return home in September—as the summer is dying. In the second act they sit in the garden—but with their coats on.

• Being frightened by one's own voice. Something strange, foreign.

- NEWEST PLAN: The festivities in Tesman's garden—and Lövborg's defeat—already prepared for in the 1st act. Second act: the party—

- Hedda energetically refuses to serve as hostess. She will not celebrate their marriage because (in her opinion, it isn't a marriage)

- *Holger:* Don't you see? I am the cause of your marriage—

- Hedda is the type of woman in her position and with her character. She marries Tesman but she devotes her imagination to Eilert Lövborg. She leans back in her chair, closes her eyes, and dreams of his adventures. . . . This is the enormous difference: Mrs. Elvsted "works for his moral improvement." But for Hedda he is the object of cowardly, tempting daydreams. In reality she does not have the courage to be a part of anything like that. Then she realizes her condition. Caught! Can't comprehend it. Ridiculous! Ridiculous!

- The traditional delusion that one man and one woman are made for each other. Hedda has her roots in the conventional. She marries Tesman but she dreams of Eilert Lövborg. . . . She is disgusted by the latter's flight from life. He believes that this has raised him in her estimation. . . . Thea Elvsted is the conventional, sentimental, hysterical Philistine.

- Those Philistines, Mrs. E. and Tesman, explain my behavior by saying first I drink myself drunk and that the rest is done in insanity. It's a flight from reality which is an absolute necessity to me.

- *E. L.:* Give me something—a flower—at our parting. Hedda hands him the revolver.

Then Tesman arrives: Has he gone? "Yes." Do you think he will still compete against me? No, I don't think so. You can set your mind at rest.

- Tesman relates that when they were in Gratz she did not want to visit her relatives—

He misunderstands her real motives.

- In the last act as Tesman, Mrs. Elvsted, and Miss Rysing are consulting, Hedda plays in the small room at the back. She stops. The conversation continues. She appears in the doorway—Good night—I'm going now. Do you need me for anything? Tesman: No, nothing at all. Good night, my dear! . . . The shot is fired—

- CONCLUSION: All rush into the back room. Brack sinks as if paralyzed into a chair near the stove: But God have mercy—people don't *do* such things!

- When Hedda hints at her ideas to Brack, he says: Yes, yes, that's extraordinarily amusing—Ha ha ha! He does not understand that she is quite serious.

- Hedda is right in this: There is no love on Tesman's part. Nor on the aunt's part. However full of love she may be.

Eilert Lövborg has a double nature. It is a fiction that one loves only *one* person. He loves two—or many—alternately (to put it frivolously). But how can he explain his position? Mrs. Elvsted, who forces him to behave correctly, runs away from her husband. Hedda, who drives him beyond all limits, draws back at the thought of a scandal.

- Neither he nor Mrs. Elvsted understands the point. Tesman reads in the manuscript that was left behind about "the two ideals." Mrs. Elvsted can't explain to him what E. L. meant. Then comes the burlesque note: both T. and Mrs. E. are going to devote their future lives to interpreting the mystery.

- Tesman thinks that Hedda hates E. L.

Mrs. Elvsted thinks so too.

Hedda sees their delusion but dares not disabuse them of it. There is something beautiful about having an aim in life. Even if it is a delusion—

She cannot do it. Take part in someone else's.

That is when she shoots herself.

The destroyed manuscript is entitled "The Philosophy Ethics of Future Society."

- Tesman is on the verge of losing his head. All this work meaningless. New thoughts! New visions! A whole new world! Then the two of them sit there, trying to find the meaning in it. Can't make any sense of it. . . .

- The greatest misery in this world is that so many have nothing to do but pursue happiness without being able to find it.

- "From Jochum Tesman there developed a Jørgen Tesman—but it will be a long, long time before this Jørgen gives rise to a George."

- The simile: The journey of life = the journey on a train.

H.: One doesn't usually jump out of the compartment.

No, not when the train is moving.

Nor stand still when it is stationary. There's always someone on the platform, staring in.

- *Hedda:* Dream of a scandal—yes, I understand that well enough. But commit one—no, no, no.

- *Lövborg:* Now I understand. My ideal was an illusion. You aren't a bit better than I. Now I have nothing left to live for. Except pleasure—dissipation—as you call it . . . Wait, here's a present (The pistol)

- Tesman is nearsighted. Wears glasses. My, what a beautiful rose! Then he stuck his nose in the cactus. Ever since then—!

- NB: The mutual hatred of women. Women have no influence on external matters of government. Therefore they want to have an influence on souls. And then so many of them have no aim in life (the lack thereof is inherited)—

- Lövborg and Hedda bent over the photographs at the table.

He: How is it possible? *She:* Why not? *L.:* Tesman! You couldn't find words enough to make fun of him. . . .

Then comes the story about the general's "disgrace," dismissal, etc. The worst thing for a lady at a ball is not to be admired for her own sake . . . *L.:* And Tesman? He took you for the sake of your person. That's just as unbearable to think about.

• Just by marrying Tesman it seems to me I have gotten so unspeakably far away from him.

• *He:* Look at her. Just look at her! . . . *Hedda:* (stroking her hair) Yes, isn't she beautiful!

• Men and women don't belong to the same century. . . . What a great prejudice that one should love only *one!*

• Hedda and Brack talk about traveling to the small university towns. *Hedda:* Now I'm not counting that little trip through the Tyrol—

Brack: (to Tesman) Are you blind and deaf? Can't you see? Can't you hear—

Tesman: Ah. Take the manuscript. Read to me!

• The demoniacal element in Hedda is this: She wants to exert her influence on someone—But once she has done so, she despises him. . . . The manuscript?

• In the third act Hedda questions Mrs. Elvsted. But if he's like that, why is he worth holding on to. . . . Yes, yes, I know—

• Hedda's discovery that her relations with the maid cannot possibly be proper.

• In his conversation with Hedda, Lövborg says: Miss H—Miss—You know, I don't believe that you are married.

• *Hedda:* And now I sit here and talk with these Philistines—And the way we once could talk to each other— No, I won't say any more . . . Talk? How do you mean? Obscenely? Ish. Let us say indecently.

• NB!! The reversal in the play occurs during the big scene between Hedda and E. L. *He:* What a wretched business it is to conform to the existing morals. It would be ideal if a man of the present could live the life of the future. What a miserable business it is to fight over a professorship!

Hedda—that lovely girl! *H.:* No! *E. L.:* Yes, I'm going to say it. That lovely, cold girl—cold as marble.

I'm not dissipated fundamentally. But the life of reality isn't livable—

• In the fifth act: *Hedda:* How hugely comic it is that those two harmless people, Tesman and Mrs. E., should try to put the pieces together for a monument to E. L. The man who so deeply despised the whole business—

• Life becomes for Hedda a ridiculous affair that isn't "worth seeing through to the end."

• The happiest mission in life is to place the people of today in the conditions of the future.

L.: Never put a child in this world, H.!

• When Brack speaks of a "triangular affair," Hedda thinks about what is going to happen and refers ambiguously to it. Brack doesn't understand.

• Brack cannot bear to be in a house where there are small children. "Children shouldn't be allowed to exist until they are fourteen or fifteen. That is, girls. What about boys? Shouldn't be allowed to exist at all—or else they should be raised outside the house."

• H. admits that children have always been a horror to her too.

• Hedda is strongly but imprecisely opposed to the idea that one should love "the family." The aunts mean nothing to her.

• It liberated Hedda's spirit to serve as a confessor to E. L. Her sympathy has secretly been on his side—But it became ugly when the public found out everything. Then she backed out.

• MAIN POINTS:

1. They are not all made to be mothers.

2. They are passionate but they are afraid of scandal.

3. They perceive that the times are full of missions worth devoting one's life to, but they cannot discover them.

• And besides Tesman is not exactly a professional, but he is a specialist. The Middle Ages are dead—

• *T.:* Now there you see also the great advantages to my studies. I can lose manuscripts and rewrite them—no inspiration needed—

• Hedda is completely taken up by the child that is to come, but when it is born she dreads what is to follow—

• Hedda must say somewhere in the play that she did not like to get out of her compartment while on the trip. Why not? I don't like to show my legs. . . . Ah, Mrs. H., but they do indeed show themselves. Nevertheless, I don't.

• Shot herself! Shot herself!

Brack (collapsing in the easy chair): But great God— people don't *do* such things!

• NB!! Eilert Lövborg believes that a comradeship must be formed between man and woman out of which the truly spiritual human being can arise. Whatever else the two of them do is of no concern. This is what the people around him do not understand. To them he is dissolute. Inwardly he is not.

• If a man can have several male friends, why can't he have several lady friends?

• It is precisely the sensual feelings that are aroused while in the company of his female "friends" or "comrades" that seek release in his excesses.

• Now I'm going. Don't you have some little remembrance to give me—? You have flowers—and so many other things—(The story of the pistol from before)—But you won't use it anyhow—

• In the fourth act when Hedda finds out that he has shot himself, she is jubilant. . . . He had courage.

Here is the rest of the manuscript.

• CONCLUSION: Life isn't tragic. . . . Life is ridiculous. . . . And that's what I can't bear.

• Do you know what happens in novels? All those who kill themselves—through the head—not in the stomach. . . . How ridiculous—how baroque—

• In her conversation with Thea in the first act, Hedda remarks that she cannot understand how one can fall in love with an unmarried man—or an unengaged man—or an unloved man—on the other hand—

• Brack understands well enough that it is Hedda's repression, her hysteria that motivates everything she does.

• On her part, Hedda suspects that Brack sees through her without believing that she understands.

• *H.:* It must be wonderful to take something from someone.

• When H. talks to B. in the fifth act about those two sitting there trying to piece together the manuscript without the spirit being present, she breaks out in laughter. . . . Then she plays the piano—then—d—

• Men—in the most indescribable situations how ridiculous they are.

• NB! She really wants to live a *man's* life wholly. But then she has misgivings. Her inheritance, what is implanted in her.

• Loving and being loved by aunts . . . Most people who are born of old maids, male and female.

• This deals with the "underground forces and powers." Woman as a minor. Nihilism. Father and mother belonging to different eras. The female underground revolution in thought. The slave's fear of the outside world.

• NB!! Why should I conform to social morals that I know won't last more than half a generation. When I run wild, as they call it, it's my escape from the present. Not that I find any joy in my excesses. I'm up to my neck in the established order. . . .

• What is Tesman working on?

• *Hedda:* It's a book on the domestic industries of Brabant during the Middle Ages.

• I have to play the part of an idiot in order to be understood. Pretend that I want to rehabilitate myself in the eyes of the mob—today's mob.

• When I had finished with my latest book, I conceived the idea for a brilliant new work. You must help me with it. I need women, Hedda—! In the Middle Ages the female conscience was so constituted that if she discovered she had married her nephew, she was filled with rancor—

• Shouldn't the future strive for the great, the good, and the beautiful as Tesman says it should? Yes! But the great, the good, the beautiful of the future won't be the same as it is for us—

• *H.:* I remember especially a red-headed girl whom I have seen on the street. *Br.:* I know whom you mean—*H.:* You called her—it was such a pretty name—*Br.:* I know her name too. But how do you know it was pretty? *H.:* Oh, Judge Brack, you are an idiot.

• The passenger and his trunk at the railway station. P. decides where he is going, buys his ticket. The trunk is attended to—

• Hedda: Slender figure of average height. Nobly shaped, aristocratic face with fine, wax-colored skin. The eyes have a veiled expression. Hair medium brown. Not especially abundant hair. Dressed in a loose-fitting dressing gown, white with blue trimmings. Composed and relaxed in her manners. The eyes steel-gray, almost lusterless.

• Mrs. Elvsted: weak build. The eyes round, rather prominent, almost as blue as water. Weak face with soft features. Nervous gestures, frightened expression—

• See above. E. L.'s idea of comradeship between man and woman. . . . The idea is a life-saver!

• If society won't let us live morally with them (women), then we'll have to live with them immorally—

• *Tesman:* The new idea in E. L.'s book is that of progress resulting from the comradeship between man and woman.

• Hedda's basic demand is: I want to know everything, but keep myself clean.

• I want to know everything—everything—everything—

H.: ——

H.: If only I could have lived like him!

• Is there something about Brabant? *B.:* What on earth is that? . . .

• The wager about the use of both pistols.

• *Miss T.:* Yes, this is the house of life and health. Now I shall go home to a house of sickness and death. God bless both of you. From now on I'll come out here every day to ask Bertha how things are—

• In the third act H. tells E. L. that she is not interested in the great questions—nor the great ideas—but in the great freedom of man. . . . But she hasn't the courage.

• The two ideals! *Tesman:* What in the name of God does he mean by that? What? What do we have to do with ideals?

• The new book treats of "the two ideals." Thea can give no information.

(6)

• NB! Brack had always thought that Hedda's short engagement to Tesman would come to nothing.

Hedda speaks of how she felt herself set aside, step by step, when her father was no longer in favor, when he retired and died without leaving anything. Then she realized, bitterly, that it was for his sake she had been made much of. And then she was already between twenty-five and twenty-six. In danger of becoming an old maid.

She thinks that in reality Tesman only feels a vain pride in having won her. His solicitude for her is the same as is shown for a thoroughbred horse or a valuable sporting dog. This, however, does not offend her. She merely regards it as a fact.

Hedda says to Brack that she does not think Tesman can be called ridiculous. But in reality she finds him so. Later on she finds him pitiable as well.

Tesman: Could you not call me by my Christian name?

Hedda: No, indeed I couldn't—unless they have given you some other name than the one you have.

Tesman puts Lövborg's manuscript in his pocket so that it may not be lost. Afterward it is Hedda who, by a casual remark, with tentative intention, gives him the idea of keeping it.

Then he reads it. A new line of thought is revealed to him. But the strain of the situation increases. Hedda awakens his jealousy.

• In the third act one thing after another comes to light about Lövborg's adventures in the course of the night. At last he comes himself, in quiet despair. "Where is the manuscript?" "Did I not leave it behind me here?" He does not know that he has done so. But after all, of what use is the manuscript to him now! He is writing of the "moral doctrine of the future"! When he has just been released by the police!

• Hedda's despair is that there are doubtless so many chances of happiness in the world, but that she cannot discover them. It is the want of an object in life that torments her.

When Hedda beguiles T. into leading E. L. into ruin, it is done to test T.'s character.

• It is in Hedda's presence that the irresistible craving for excess always comes over E. L.

Tesman cannot understand that E. L. could wish to base his future on injury to another.

• *Hedda:* Do I hate T.? No, not at all. I only find him boring.

• *Brack:* But nobody else thinks so.

Hedda: Neither is there any one but myself who is married to him.

Brack: . . . not at all boring.

Hedda: Heavens, you always want me to express myself so correctly. Very well then, T. is not boring, but I am bored by living with him.

Hedda: . . . had no prospects. Well, perhaps you would have liked to see me in a convent (home for unmarried ladies).

Hedda: . . . then isn't it an honorable thing to profit by one's person? Don't actresses and others turn their advan-

tages into profit. I had no other capital. Marriage—I thought it was like buying an annuity.

Hedda: Remember that I am the child of an old man—and a worn-out man too—or past his prime at any rate—perhaps that has left its mark.

Brack: Upon my word, I believe you have begun to brood over problems.

Hedda: Well, what cannot one take to doing when one has gone and got married.

(7)

• *E. L.:* It's impossible for me to call you Mrs. T. You will always be H. G. to me.

• Both Miss T. and B. have seen what lies in store for Hedda. . . . T. on the other hand cries out: My God, I had no idea.

• When E. L. tells H. that he cannot possibly confess to Thea that her and his book has been lost, H. says: I don't believe a word of that. *E.L.:* No, but I know how terribly dismayed she will be. (pp. 156-70)

> *Henrik Ibsen, notes on "Hedda Gabler," in* Playwrights on Playwriting: The Meaning and Making of Modern Drama from Ibsen to Ionesco, *edited by Toby Cole, Hill and Wang, 1960, pp. 156-70.*

OVERVIEWS AND GENERAL STUDIES

Kenneth Muir   (essay date 1959)

[*A British critic, educator, editor, and translator, Muir has published numerous volumes of Shakespearean criticism as well as other theatrical studies. In the essay below, originally given as a lecture at Wayne State University in 1959, Muir examines the last period of Ibsen's work, including* The Master Builder, Little Eyolf, John Gabriel Borkman, *and* When We Dead Awaken. *The critic asserts that the protagonist in each of these dramas is a genius who faces "the conflicting claims of vocation and of the personal life." The conflict between art and life is a theme that links together not only this last sequence of plays, argues Muir, but all of Ibsen's writing.*]

The last period of Ibsen's work includes four plays, beginning with *The Master Builder* in 1892 and ending with *When We Dead Awaken* (1899), a year before his breakdown. Between these two plays appeared two others, *Little Eyolf* and *John Gabriel Borkman.* All four plays are linked together in theme, and the last of them, sub-titled a dramatic epilog, was intended primarily as an epilog to the sequence which began with *The Master Builder,* and secondarily to the whole of Ibsen's previous work. The hero of each of the four plays is a genius—builder, writer, financier, sculptor—and each play is concerned, to some degree, with the conflicting claims of vocation and of the personal life. The successful career of Solness, the Master

Builder, has been at the expense of his wife's happiness. The work on "Human Responsibility" to which Allmers devotes his life is made an excuse for irresponsibility in his personal relationships. John Gabriel Borkman marries a woman he does not love and breaks with a woman he does love for the sake of his career. And the sculptor, Rubeck, in *When We Dead Awaken* sacrifices life to art and thereby ruins his art and destroys the life of the woman who loves him.

Many modern writers have been concerned with this conflict between life and art. It is expressed most forcibly, perhaps in Yeats' lines:

> The intellect of man is forced to choose
> Perfection of the life, or of the work,
> And if it take the second must refuse
> A heavenly mansion, raging in the dark.

But the same conflict is implied by many other writers—in Keats's exclamation, for example, that the poet was the most unpoetical creature in existence, or in the anecdote which provided Henry James with the germ of *The Ambassadors,* an anecdote he was able to turn to such superb use because he was conscious of the way he himself had been forced to sacrifice life to art. W. D. Howells, meeting Jonathan Sturges in Paris, laid his hand on his shoulder and said to him:

> Oh, you are young, you are young—be glad of it: be glad of it and *live.* Live all you can; it's a mistake not to. It doesn't so much matter what you do—but live. This place makes it all come over me. I see it now. I haven't done so—and now I'm old. It's too late. It has gone past me— I've lost it. You have time. You are young. Live!

This, then, or something like it, may have been one of the germs of Ibsen's last plays. But the conflict between the desire to be a great poet and the desire to live had been expressed in one of his early poems more than thirty years before he wrote *The Master Builder.* It describes the building of a castle in the clouds, with two wings, the large one sheltering a deathless poet, the small one serving as a young girl's bower. As time passes, something goes wrong with the plan. The large wing is too small for the poet, and the little wing falls into ruin. The poem expresses (I presume) Ibsen's early realisation that his poetic vocation might crowd out of his life ordinary human relationships and pleasures; and some of the symbolism in *The Master Builder* seems to recall this poem.

The four heroes of his last plays are all compelled to recognize their guilt. Solness, in the opinion of some critics, has failed to achieve his potentialities; and he is at least ruthless and unscrupulous in the way he makes use of others— Kaja, Brovik and Ragnar. Allmers not merely wastes his time on what will clearly be an unreadable treatise on "Human Responsibility"; he marries his wife for her money and treats Little Eyolf, the crippled child, as a means of ministering to his egotism. Borkman suffers no remorse for the ruin he has caused to thousands of innocent people by his criminal speculations, and it is only at the end of the play that he recognizes his sin in casting off Ella Rentheim. Rubeck realises too late that he has sacrificed Irene, and his love for Irene, to his ambitions as a

sculptor. The sin of all four men is egotism, and in particular the masculine egotism of the artist.

Another of Ibsen's poems seems to have links with *The Master Builder:*

> Snug in their cosy home they both enjoyed
> The days of autumn and the dark Decembers.
> There was a fire—the house was all destroyed,
> And they must grope among the ash and embers.
>
> For somewhere in the midst of them may be
> One jewel that can never be consumed;
> And if they go on searching patiently
> One may well find it where it lies entombed.
>
> But though those homeless two may find again
> That precious gem the fire could not destroy
> Never will she her burnt-out faith obtain,
> Nor he retrieve his charred and vanished joy.

In *The Master Builder* we hear of a mysterious fire which enabled Solness to make his fortune, but which estranged him from his wife; and his wife speaks of the lost jewels.

But the immediate experience which inspired the play was Ibsen's meeting, in the Tyrol, with a young Viennese girl, Emilie Bardach. Some time later, while he was planning the play, he said:

> Do you know, my next play is already hovering before me? of course in vague outline. But of one thing I have got firm hold. An experience: a woman's figure. Very interesting, very interesting indeed. Again a spice of devilry in it.

He went on to describe Emilie Bardach, a remarkable woman for the time, who had told Ibsen that she had no wish to marry, preferring to lure husbands away from their wives. "She did not get hold of me," Ibsen declared, "but I got hold of her—for my play. Then I fancy she consoled herself with someone else." But Ibsen, who was over sixty, was not quite so detached as he pretended. Emilie Bardach was not the bird of prey he afterwards described. He admitted that she had warmth of heart and womanly understanding; he wrote on a photograph, "To the May-Sun of a September life"; and he told her in a letter:

> I cannot repress my summer memories, nor do I want to. I live through my experiences again and again. . . . To transmute it all into a poem I find, in the meantime, impossible.

Once *The Master Builder* was written, and Emilie Bardach had provided the inspiration he needed, Ibsen, quite ruthlessly and unscrupulously, broke off his correspondence with her. When the play was published he was furious when she sent him a photograph signed "Princess of Orangia"—Solness' name for Hilde. Ibsen's use of Emilie for his own artistic purposes is a slight indication that Rubeck's treatment of Irene, Borkman's treatment of Ella, and Solness's treatment of Kaja, Hilde and Aline are based on Ibsen's knowledge of his own egotism and ruthlessness where his art was concerned.

It would be wrong to exaggerate the extent to which Ibsen expressed his own personal conflicts in his plays. Although he admitted that to write poetry was to hold a doomsday over oneself, and although he frequently introduced into his work his private obsessions, he invariably universalised them. Some interpretations of *The Master Builder* probably stress too much the personal elements in the play and stress too little the universal elements. It is true that Ibsen himself had an excessive fear of being superseded by the younger generation of dramatists; but the fear of the younger generation in *The Master Builder* has much wider implications than the personal one. Solness confesses to Dr. Herdal:

> SOLNESS: Sooner or later the luck must turn, you see.
>
> HERDAL: Nonsense! What should make the luck turn?
>
> SOLNESS: The younger generation.
>
> HERDAL: Pooh! The younger generation! You are not laid on the shelf yet. I should hope. Oh no—your position is probably firmer now than it has ever been.
>
> SOLNESS: The luck will turn. I know it—I feel the day approaching. Some one or other will take it into his head to say: Give me a chance! And then all the rest will come clamoring after him, and shake their fists at me and shout: Make room—make room! Yes, you wait and see, doctor—presently the younger generation will come knocking at my door—
>
> HERDAL: Well, and what if they do?
>
> SOLNESS: What if they do? Then there's an end of Halvard Solness.

At this moment there is a knock at the door which announces the arrival of Hilde Wangel, who symbolizes the younger generation. Solness welcomes Hilde as an ally, though she turns out to be his destroyer. This dramatises what is perhaps a universal ambivalence in the attitude of the older generation to the younger, in the attitude of parents to children. Parents regard their children with a mixture of love and fear, as the protectors of their old age and the projection of their own desires, but also as their rivals and usurpers. In some plays the conflicting attitudes are dramatised as separate children. In *King Lear,* for example, the good child, Edgar, who lovingly cares for his father, is contrasted with the ruthless Edmund, who supplants him; and the loving Cordelia is contrasted with her ruthless sisters. Hilde, in *The Master Builder,* is partly the bird of prey, and partly the ally and inspirer of Solness, who feels that she gives him a new lease of life.

Ten years before, when Hilde was still a child, Solness had built a church-tower at Lysanger and had climbed the tower with the customary wreath. Afterwards (according to Hilde's story) he had told her she looked like a little princess, and he had promised to return in ten years' time to buy a kingdom for her. As he has not returned to Lysanger she has come to demand the promised kingdom.

Later in the play we hear more about the incident at Lysanger. Solness, as he hung the wreath over the weather vane told the Almighty that he would never build churches again—"Only homes for human beings." But he came to realise that "building homes for human beings is not worth talking of. . . . Human beings haven't any use for these homes of theirs. Not for being happy in." He therefore builds a house with a tower; and he promises Hilde that he will build for her a castle in the air, "with a foundation under it."

The meaning of this is disputed. On the one hand, there are some critics who assume that Ibsen was thinking of himself as the Master Builder—the churches with towers symbolizing his early poetic plays, the homes for human beings symbolizing his prose dramas dealing with social problems, and the houses with towers symbolizing his later, more symbolic plays. On the other hand it has been suggested that whatever the autobiographical strain in *The Master Builder,* the three periods of Solness' work have a much wider significance. Some of Ibsen's early plays, *Brand, Peer Gynt,* and *Emperor and Galilean,* were essentially religious. In the prose plays of the middle period he was mainly concerned with the problems of society and of the relationship of the individual to society. In the plays of the final period Ibsen had come to realise that programs of reform were not enough. He had turned from conventional religion to advocate the creation of a new society based on reason—a society without cramping conventions, without hypocrisy, and without the faults of nineteenth century capitalism. He came to realise that man does not live by bread alone. He needs spiritual food also. As we should put it today—the welfare state is not enough. This interpretation has a much wider reference than to Ibsen's development as a dramatist.

A third interpretation stresses the fact that Solness fears the younger generation because he fears retribution for his refusal to build churches. The house with a tower—symbolizing a sort of humanistic religion, is, like the Tower of Babel, a challenge to God. Miss Bradbrook thinks that Solness' refusal to build for the greater glory of God is a refusal "to be the kind of artist he might have been—and become a lesser kind of artist"; and Professor Una Ellis-Fermor in the preface to her recent translation stresses the element of self-deception in Solness' character, his ruthless imposition of his will on others which he justifies by a myth about himself "that he is at once the director and victim of strange daemonic powers." Ibsen "leads him to destruction by the agency of the only one of his victims who had strength enough to challenge him to make good his pretensions."

We should not expect too precise a symbolism in the play, nor assume that one interpretation necessarily rules out the other. Indeed, those I have mentioned by no means take all the evidence into consideration. One of the things stressed by Ibsen in the second act is the sickly conscience of Solness and the robust conscience of Hilde. He makes clear that by robust conscience he does not mean unscrupulousness: for Hilde, though she is compared to a bird of prey, is unable to steal Solness from his wife once she has got to know her. The implication seems to be that Solness is still riddled with superstition and with a sense of guilt; and he is not strong enough to live according to the new morality in which he professedly believes. Another symbol which is not really explained by the interpretations

I have mentioned is Solness' determination to build a castle in the air—"One with a foundation under it." It is linked with his decision to climb the tower himself. We should not assume, I think, that Ibsen had gone back on his criticism of living by illusions; or that he was repeating the theme of *The Wild Duck* that hardly anyone can live except by illusions. Although Solness himself was doubtless suffering from illusions, one does not get the impression that the castles in the air were themselves illusions. I suspect that these castles represent both the life of the imagination and the communion of souls. Ibsen, we are told, strongly approved of a French performance of the play in which the love of Solness and Hilde was stressed and in which the tower in the last act was a symbol of that love.

The burning of Solness' old home (and the sacrifice of his children) can also be interpreted in different ways. It can symbolize the ruthlessness of the Master Builder in pursuit of success; it can symbolize the price which has to be paid by the artist by reason of his dedication; and it can symbolize the price which has to be paid for creating a new society—this, you will recall, was the theme of Keats's *Hyperion*—the scrapping of old customs, old conventions, old traditions, old ways of thought, with all the suffering which that involves. Mrs. Solness is one who clings futilely to the past. She does not really mind about the loss of her sons, but she minds desperately about the loss of trivial things. She tells Hilde:

> No, it's the small losses in life that cut one to the heart. To lose all the things that other people think next to nothing of. . . . All the old portraits on the walls were burnt. And so were all the old silk dresses. They'd been in the family for generations. And all Mother's and Grandmother's lace—that was burnt too. . . . And then all the dolls. . . . I had nine beautiful dolls . . . they were all burnt up, poor dears. There was no one who thought of saving *them*. Oh, it's so miserable to think about.

It is no wonder that Hilde, after this conversation, tells Solness: "I have just come up out of a vault."

It is significant, no doubt, that Mrs. Solness does everything in a spirit of loveless duty. She is contrasted with Hilde, who is guided entirely by her heart. Whereas in the last act Mrs. Solness wears a white shawl like a shroud, Hilde wears a nosegay of flowers. The spontaneous morality of Hilde is contrasted with the dead morality of Mrs. Solness. Solness is destroyed because he is tied by his past, and because his sickly conscience does not allow him to achieve in reality what he has imagined.

Alfred Allmers, the hero of *Little Eyolf,* is another egotistical self-deceiver. He has married the wealthy Rita partly to provide for his supposed sister Asta, the woman he really loves, and partly to secure the leisure to write his treatise on "Human Responsibility." When he subconsciously realises that the book is no good he devotes himself to the education of their crippled child, Little Eyolf. Rita, not unnaturally, is jealous first of the book (in which he is more interested than in her) and then of Little Eyolf. Almost in answer to her unspoken wishes, Little Eyolf is

drowned; and the rest of the play consists of the mutual recriminations of Allmers and Rita and the exposure of their guilt—that Allmers loves Asta, that he married Rita for her money, that he will never finish his book, that his love for Eyolf was essentially selfish, that Eyolf was crippled when Rita and Allmers were engaged in passionate love, that Allmers no longer loves Rita and would like to live again with Asta when he finds she is not really his sister. Rita is also exposed, though not so devastatingly, because of her possessiveness and jealousy, because she did not love her own child, because she had half wished the child were dead, and because she had no purpose in life except her love for her husband.

This long exposure of the shams and self-deceptions of the Allmers family is the real substance of the play, and the process is started before the death of Little Eyolf on Allmers' return from his walking tour in the mountains, when he recognized that he must give up his book on "Human Responsibility" and that he is no longer in love with Rita. When Rita hears that Allmers is coming home, she puts on a white dress, covers the lamps with rose-pink shades, and sets champagne on the table. Allmers ignores the sexual invitation and refuses to drink the champagne, though Rita is still young and attractive. The sympathies of the audience are largely on her side when she warns Allmers that if he ceases to love her physically she will find consolation elsewhere, when she confesses her jealousy of his work, for which he neglected her, and when she declares she will not be regarded merely as Eyolf's mother:

> I'm not interested in your quiet affection. I want the whole of you, entirely. . . . I'm not going to be put off with scraps and leavings, Alfred—never in this world!

We even sympathise when she says that she wishes she had never borne Little Eyolf, though this death wish is fulfilled at the end of the first act. The mysterious Rat Wife, a sort of female Pied Piper, who offers to rid them of anything that worries them, is a symbol of Rita's evil wish.

The death of Little Eyolf reveals to Allmers and Rita that their son was really a stranger to them and that they are now bound together not by love but by guilt. One by one the veils of illusion are stripped away from their marriage, so that they are compelled to recognize that Allmers had married for the sake of his book, that his love for Rita was almost entirely physical and therefore subject to change, that he had betrayed both her and Asta, whom he really loved, that the book, which was an excuse for his selfishness, would never be written, and that even his love for little Eyolf was largely selfish, and partly a substitute for his love for Asta. He is, moreover, revealed as a self-righteous prig, savage and bitter in his criticisms of Rita, and quite prepared to desert her for Asta. Rita, for her part, is made to recognize her partial responsibility for Eyolf's crippling and his subsequent death, both things being caused by her lack of maternal feeling. She is made to admit her possessiveness in love which leads her to be jealous of Asta, of Eyolf, and even of Allmers's book. But in the end it is Rita who begins the process which leads to their reconciliation. She pleads with Allmers to take up his work again and says she is now willing to share him with the book: this leads to Allmers telling of his experience on the mountains when he thought he would die "and enjoyed the peace and well-being of the presence of death." All-mers hates the slum children who did nothing to save Lit-tle Eyolf from drowning. But Rita tells him that when he leaves her she will try and look after these children:

> RITA: As soon as you've left me, I shall go down to the shore and bring all those poor, outcast children up here with me to our place. . . .
>
> ALLMERS: In our little Eyolf's place!
>
> RITA: Yes, in our little Eyolf's place. They shall have Eyolf's rooms to live in. They shall have his books to read. His toys to play with. They shall take turns at sitting in his chair at table.
>
> ALLMERS: If this is in real earnest—everything you're saying—then there must have been a change in you.
>
> RITA: Yes. There has, Alfred. You've seen to that. You have made an empty place in me. And I must try to fill it up with something. Something that could seem like love.

Allmers admits that they have done nothing for the out-cast children, and it is therefore not surprising that the children did not risk their lives to save Eyolf. Rita explains her determination by her wish to put into practice the the-ories of the book on "Human Responsibility" and by her wish to make her peace with Little Eyolf's wide open eyes; and Allmers agrees to stay with her to help in her work. He has been converted from theory to practice, from ego-tism to unselfishness, from pride to humility. The ending of the play is not the less moving for the second-rate and unpromising character Allmers seems to be in the first two acts of the play. He succeeds against all likelihood in doing what Blake called "annihilating the selfhood" so that the play does not end tragically as *The Master Builder* which preceded it and *John Gabriel Borkman* which followed it.

John Gabriel Borkman is another play dealing with self-deception, with the betrayals practised by a man who has the excuse of genius. Borkman is a former bank director who had served a prison sentence for embezzlement; and right to the end of the play he breathes no word of remorse for the ruin he has caused to innocent people. He still re-fuses to admit his guilt. But he is not a common criminal. He is a man gifted with great imaginative power and vast ambitions. Although he thirsts for power, he wishes to use that power for beneficent purposes, to set free the buried metal for the service of man. When Ella speaks of the freezing breath coming from his kingdom, he replies rhap-sodically:

> That breath is like the breath of life to me. That breath comes to me like a greeting from impris-oned spirits. I can see them, the millions in bondage; I feel the veins of metal that stretch out their curved, branching, luring arms to me. I saw them before me like shadows brought to life—that night when I stood in the cellar of the bank with the light in my hand. You wanted your freedom then. And I tried to do it. But I hadn't the strength. The treasure sank into the abyss again. But I will whisper it to you here in the stillness of the night. I love you, where you lie as though dead in the depth and in the dark! I love you, you treasures that crave for life—with all the shining gifts of power and glory that you bring. I love, love, love you!

Soon after this speech, Borkman feels a metal hand clutch-ing his heart, and he falls dead. But the retribution which overtakes him is not through his financial dishonesty or his overweening ambition. He is condemned by Ella Rent-heim—and by the audience—because he jilted Ella and married her sister Gunhild for the sake of his career. He was thereby guilty of a betrayal of both women through his egotism, as Allmers had betrayed both Rita and Asta. Ella accuses him of "a terrible crime."

> BORKMAN: Which? What do you mean?
>
> ELLA: I mean the crime for which there's no for-giveness.
>
> BORKMAN: You must be out of your mind.
>
> ELLA: You are a murderer! You have committed the deadly sin! You have killed the power to love in me. Do you understand what that means? It speaks in the Bible of a mysterious sin for which there is no forgiveness. I've never been able to see till now what it could be. Now I do see. The great unpardonable sin—it's the sin of killing love in a human creature. . . . You deserted the woman you loved! Me, me, me! The dearest thing you had in the world—you were ready to hand it over for gain. *That's* the double murder you made yourself guilty of. The murder of your own soul and mine.

Borkman refuses to admit his guilt, and just before he dies—and perhaps this is the real cause of his death—Ella again accuses him of murdering her power of loving, of selling her heart "for the kingdom, and the power and the glory."

The main theme is reinforced by the character of Foldal, a clerk who had written a poetic drama which has never been produced but which he regards as the justification for his life, excusing his comparative failure in his career. Ibsen had originally intended to introduce this character into *The Lady from the Sea* sixteen years before. The scene between Foldal and Borkman provides the only comic relief in the play. Borkman pretends for years that he believes that Foldal has written a masterpiece; and Fol-dal pretends to believe that Borkman will be rehabilitated. When Borkman reveals accidentally that he does not really admire the play, Foldal retorts by telling him that he does not believe that Borkman will ever recover his lost power.

> BORKMAN: Haven't you sat here, putting hope and faith and trust into me with your lies?
>
> FOLDAL: They weren't lies, as long as *you* be-lieved in my vocation. As long as you believed in me, so long I believed in you.
>
> BORKMAN: Then we've been deluding each other mutually. And perhaps deluding our-selves—both of us.

FOLDAL: But isn't that at bottom what friendship is, John Gabriel?

This exchange between the two failures not only brings out their self-deception but also serves to link the play with the tragedy of the three artists who are the heroes of the other plays of Ibsen's last period.

The last play of all, **When We Dead Awaken,** is, as we have seen, an epilog to the whole series. All the heroes of the last plays are living a kind of posthumous existence. Solness is waiting to be superseded by the younger generation; Allmers had confronted death on the mountain, though both he and Rita undergo a kind of resurrection at the end of the play. Borkman's life, after his release from jail, is a life of illusion, a posthumous life; and both Rubeck, the sculptor, and his former model, Irene, had died spiritually long before.

This point is made explicit in the last scene when Irene explains why she had not stabbed Rubeck, as she had intended:

> RUBECK: And why did you hold your hand?
>
> IRENE: Because it flashed upon me with a sudden horror that you were dead already—long ago.
>
> RUBECK: Dead?
>
> IRENE: Dead. Dead, you as well as I. We sat there by the Lake of Taunitz, we two clay-cold bodies—and played with each other.

Years before Irene had been the model for the central figure in Rubeck's masterpiece, "Resurrection Day": "figured in the likeness of a young woman, awakening from the sleep of death. . . . It was to be the awakening of the noblest, purest, most ideal woman the world ever saw." Rubeck was afraid that if he touched Irene, if he desired her, he would be unable to complete his masterpiece. As Irene complained, he put the work of art before the human being. And when the work of art was finished, Rubeck said to Irene: "I thank you from my heart. This has been a priceless episode for me." Whereupon she left him: and when they meet again after many years she accuses him of the sins of a poet:

> Because you are nerveless and sluggish and full of forgiveness for all the sins of your life in thought and act. You have killed my soul—so you model yourself in remorse, and self-accusation, and penance.

Rubeck's sin was to subordinate life to art; and when Irene left him he lost most of his inspiration. He altered his masterpiece. The figure modelled on Irene, with its ideal beauty, was no longer in the foreground. On the plinth he carved "men and women with dimly-suggested animal faces." He had learnt worldly wisdom. After his marriage with the young Philistine, Maia, he finds his inspiration has deserted him. He makes portrait busts for wealthy patrons which on the surface appear to be excellent likenesses but into which he contrives to put his own hatred of his fellowmen.

At bottom they are all respectable, pompous

horse faces, and self-opinionated donkey muzzles, and lop-eared, low-browed dog skulls, and fatted swine snouts, and sometimes dull, brutal, bull fronts as well.

It is clear that Rubeck has betrayed himself as an artist by sacrificing love to art. When we meet him at the beginning of the play he is famous and successful but bored with his marriage, despising the public, despising the critics, and believing in nothing. He reminds one of the bitter lines in *Little Gidding*—lines added as an afterthought—in which Mr. Eliot describes the dreadful state of the successful literary man who is without grace:

> Let me disclose the gifts reserved for age
>   To set a crown upon your lifetime's effort.
>   First, the cold friction of expiring sense
> Without enchantment, offering no promise
>   But bitter tastelessness of shadow fruit
>   As body and soul begin to fall asunder.
> Second, the conscious impotence of rage
>   At human folly, and the laceration
>   Of laughter at what ceases to amuse.
>
> And last, the rending pain of re-enactment
>   Of all that you have done, and been; the
>   shame
>   Of motives late revealed, and the awareness
> Of things ill done and done to others' harm
>   Which once you took for exercise of virtue.
>   Then fools' approval stings, and honor stains.

The meeting with Irene underlines Rubeck's guilt. She has been mad—perhaps is still mad—and she is followed by a Sister of Mercy who acts as her keeper. She looks like a corpse newly risen from the grave. She speaks of herself as dead; and she says she has killed her two husbands and all her children. She herself, she tells Rubeck,

> was dead for many years. They came and bound me—laced my arms together behind by back.— Then they lowered me into a vault, with iron bars before the loophole. And with padded walls—so that no one on the earth above could hear the grave-shrieks.—But now I am beginning, in a way, to rise from the dead.

At the end of the play Rubeck and Irene climb a mountain; they hear the blasts of wind which "sound like the prelude to the Resurrection Day"; and in spite of warnings they continue to climb, partly because Irene is afraid of being caught by her keeper and partly because Rubeck confesses his sin of putting "the dead clay image above the happiness of life—of love" and wishes to pass through the mists with Irene "to the summit of the tower that shines in the sunrise." Although they are killed by the avalanche, they have, before the end, risen from the dead.

The flight from the Sister of Mercy, whose "Pax vobiscum" is the curtain line of the play, is intended, I suspect, to have a symbolic meaning. The attempt to reach the summit is an heroic refusal (in Ibsen's view) to return to the strait jacket of conventional religion. It is also contrasted with the behaviour of the other two characters of the play—Rubeck's wife, Maia, and the eccentric hunter, Ulfheim, with whom she has spent the night on the mountain, and with whom she intends to live. As Maia and Ulfheim descend from the mountain into the valley below, the song of Maia is heard:

> I am free! I am free! I am free!
> No more life in the prison for me!
> I am free as a bird! I am free.

The prison from which she is escaping is her married life with Rubeck. She is escaping into the freedom of the purely sensual life, the only kind of life for which she is fitted. Although Rubeck has sinned against Irene, against Maia, and even against his art, he is redeemed at the end.

He and Irene, even though they are destroyed, aim higher than the other pair, who do not rise above the level of the cave man. The climbing of the mountain means something different for the two couples. Rubeck had promised both Irene and Maia that he would take them up to a high mountain and show them all the glory of the world. And he promised Maia, in the words of the Tempter, that all that glory should be hers. But he found that Maia was not born to be a mountain climber; and when she does climb the mountain it is with the primitive Ulfheim who can only offer her hunting and sexual love. When Irene and Rubeck climb the mountain, they do so as a symbol of their resurrection, the resurrection of the love Rubeck had formerly spurned, "an ascent to the Peak of Promise, where all the powers of light may freely look on them—and all the powers of darkness too."

When We Dead Awaken has been condemned by many critics. Archer thought its interest was largely pathological, that it was "a piece of self-caricature" and that Ibsen sacrificed the surface reality to the underlying meaning. Certainly the play is entirely unrealistic in its method; but I can see no signs in it of mental decay. It rounds off brilliantly the last period of Ibsen's work, and it throws light on the significance of the three plays which preceded it.

This last work of Ibsen's was the subject of the first published work of another great writer. James Joyce contributed a long article on the play to the *Fortnightly Review* in 1900; and he concluded that the play may rank with the greatest of the author's work—"if, indeed, it be not the greatest."

It is significant that at the end of a long life devoted exclusively to his art, Ibsen should express in all these last plays his belief in the primacy of life, in the supreme importance of personal relationships. Rubeck tells his wife:

> All the talk about the artist's vocation, and the
> artist's mission, and so forth, began to strike me
> as being very empty and hollow and meaningless
> at bottom.

Maia asks: "Then what would you put in its place?" Rubeck replies, "Life, Maia." It should be remembered that these words were written at the end of the Nineties, when the idea of art for art's sake was often discussed. Ibsen shows in all four plays that if life is subordinated to art, art itself suffers. The same point is made, without words, when Irene appears, striding, like a marble statue. The children at play catch sight of her and run to meet her. We are made to realise the life of which she has been deprived because Rubeck denied the love in his heart. (pp. 91-113)

Kenneth Muir, "Ibsen," in his Last Periods of Shakespeare, Racine, Ibsen, *Wayne State University Press, 1961, pp. 89-116.*

Daniel Haakonsen   (essay date 1966)

[*In the following essay, Haakonsen explores the ambiguous conclusions of Ibsen's realistic plays by focusing on the recurring theme of sacrifice in* Ghosts, Rosmersholm, The Master Builder, The Wild Duck, Hedda Gabler, *and* John Gabriel Borkman. *In each case, the critic asserts, the main character is an idealist whose blind actions cause innocent victims to suffer; as the protagonist realizes this and comes to identify himself with his victim, the simultaneous insight and guilt mark both man's greatness and his limitation. Haakonsen maintains that the endings of these plays encompass this duality in "a poetic and dramaturgically relevant expression of ambiguity."*]

Ibsen's realistic plays belong to a type of drama of revelation. That is to say, the action takes the form of revealing what has been kept secret in the past. The theatre audience watches this process of revelation with increasing understanding and may be excused for thinking that in the end everything will be clear. And yet we know that the ending on the contrary often leaves the audience in a disturbed and bewildered state.

Among all the dramatists of the world Ibsen is in fact the unrivalled master of the sort of endings which may be called ambiguous—if the critic is kind. If not, it may just as well be called confusing.

Let me remind you of one or two of these endings.

One play closes with a woman standing in anguish on the stage. She does not know what to do with her son who has fallen seriously ill, and this problem: what is she to do? is imposed upon us without any answer being given. The *conclusion* of the play, if that word may be used in a context like this, seems to be the character's suffering combined with her uncertainty of mind.

Another play ends up with a man and a woman leaving the stage in order to throw themselves into the water, confessing they that they don't really know why they behave as they do. Is she following him into death, or is he following her? The question is an important one in this play. But they don't know how to answer it. You are following me, they say, and I am following you! Are we expected to have a deeper insight into their suffering and into their total behaviour? Are we perhaps expected to know a better answer than the dramatist himself?

Instead of bowing respectfully to our impressive sphinx, we ought perhaps to ask ourselves whether the endings of Ibsen's plays are due to a dramatic shortcoming, or whether the effect of these endings may be dissipated by a clear-cut explanation, or finally whether the confusion they sometimes produce in our mind may be transformed into a poetically and dramatically relevant expression of ambiguity.

I should like to make a modest attempt in this paper to throw a little more light on these questions. For this purpose I will try a new approach, and in doing so, I am not thinking particularly of the plays in which Ibsen seems to solve the conflicts by means of a clearly stated conclusion, of the kind to be found in *Pillars of Society, A Doll's House, An Enemy of the People, The Lady from the Sea,* or *Little Eyolf.* On the contrary we will try a study of the plays in which the conflict leads to a catastrophe. And in these plays I should like to call your attention to an almost forgotten theme, perhaps the only one that might possibly make the sense of suffering and catastrophe deeper and clearer. I am thinking of the act of sacrifice. But first let me say a word or two to explain what I mean by sacrifice.

In using this word I mean any form of suffering associated with the human will, whether we have the same person suffering and willing this suffering, or whether we have one person suffering and another person willing his suffering. A car accident would not qualify as a sacrifice. But with voluntary renunciation of one of the blessings of life—in extreme cases of life itself—an act of sacrifice occurs; and the same is true in another way when a person's life is vitally affected for the worse by the will of another. In the world of drama a character has a choice of three kinds of sacrifice: he can sacrifice himself or someone or something dear to him; another person may sacrifice him or *his;* he may sacrifice another person or his property. Just why this should happen is in this context of subordinate importance. It may be done to appease the gods, it may be done in the interests of justice, liberty, or one's native land, or it may be done for purely personal reasons.

Now, looking for sacrifice in Ibsen's plays, we first find it as an ingredient in two different themes. We might call these 'the passionate idealist' and 'the doomed hero'.

Let us briefly consider 'the passionate idealist'. In the drama we frequently encounter characters who are prepared to sacrifice other people's lives and happiness in order to promote their own desires and plans. King Creon sacrifices Antigone, and Macbeth is ready to 'wade through slaughter to a throne'. In such cases the ultimate goal may well be dictated by the highest morals and ideals, as when Brutus sacrifices Julius Caesar, or when Hamlet seeks the life of his uncle.

Akin to such characters, and yet very different from them, are the idealists in Ibsen's plays. In this context the likeness is more important than the difference, and may easily be pointed out: in nearby all Ibsen's plays we find that the main character has been unable to make his way through life without sacrificing the lives and the happiness of others to his idealism. (Why we call him 'passionate' will soon be explained.)

May we for a moment leave this theme, and turn to Number 2.

The *doomed hero* is a dramatic theme usually associated with tragedy. Sometimes the hero represents a revolt against the will of the gods, or a challenge to the moral order. With his hubris the hero has set aside all considerations of law and justice, and in the closing stages of the drama he is struck down by retribution and suffers a crushing defeat. His suffering—his death or destruction—comes in the guise of a judgment: the will of the gods or the inherent justice of the social order sacrifices him in order to restore moral balance. King Oedipus and his fate may serve as an example.

'The doomed hero' is a type with which Ibsen was highly familiar. Rebekka West [in *Rosmersholm*] personally describes her death as an act of expiation for the sins of the past. The main character in *The Master Builder* [Halvard Solness] foresees retribution long before he falls from his tower. Death comes to John Gabriel Borkman just as Ella Rentheim pronounces moral judgment on his life—to mention a few examples.

It is an easy matter to envisage one very simple combination of these themes in Ibsen's dramas: The hero has sacrificed the life and happiness of others to his idealism. The retribution therefore overtakes the hero. The moral to be deduced would then be that no one has the right to develop his own personality or interests, or even promote his own ideals, at the expense of other people; and the dramatic pattern is the same as that constantly made use of in the history of drama. Macbeth pays the penalty of his many murders. In Nordic literature, a generation before Ibsen, Adam Oehlenschläger, using the same pattern, had produced what at the time was regarded as a model tragedy, his *Hakon Jarl.* In this play the hero, a champion of the old Norse gods, sacrifices his son to ensure fortune in battle, but fate turns against him and destroys him.

But this simple method of linking the themes together does not provide a suitable pattern in Ibsen's case. This will be seen if we take a closer look at the idealism of his plays.

This idealism seems to be destructive simply because idealism is a cover for deep and blinding passions.

Mrs. Alving's demand for purity in her husband [in *Ghosts*]—which has proved too much for him—is in fact combined with an intense loathing of her husband and with a dangerous attraction for Pastor Manders. Rebekka West personally states that when—with her kind of idealism—she released Rosmer from his unnatural marriage, and removed Beate, she was acting under the influence of an irresistible passion for Rosmer. Hedda Gabler wears a mask of indifference; but once she has sent Ejlert Løvborg to his death, and is sitting in front of the fire burning his manuscript, flames of passion consume her which she cannot conceal. In his great monologue in the last act John Gabriel Borkman reveals that, though he was inspired by an ideal, ambition and an enormous lust for power have driven him relentlessly on. In these plays human lives are sacrificed not to *any* form of idealism, but to one which feeds on deep-rooted passions.

The idealist, then, is shown as 'blinded' during the first phase of his action, that is to say at the time when his behaviour is a menace to others. He acts under the influence of violent emotional pressure, or as a result of some outside influence, or at any rate without being in possession of a full and free consciousness.

Here, however, a strange fact has to be taken into consideration: when the hero recovers his sight, and detects the blind spot in his former idealism, he nevertheless chooses to continue his former line.

Before the conclusion is reached he has plenty of opportunity of revising the aims that have had such dire consequences. But he still continues to be guided by the same form of idealism as before. Even Rebekka West, who has so obviously seen the error of her ways and been compelled to make a complete change in her philosophy of life, continues to work with the same object in mind as when she first came to Rosmersholm; and in the last scene of the play, where her 'conversion' is clearly and openly revealed, she completes her task, in spite of everything, of replacing Beate.

A closer investigation will also reveal that Mrs. Alving, too, in her new spiritual state, ends by completing the sacrifice of her son, or at least by realising the possibility of doing so. She actually does so involuntarily, under duress. But Solness and Borkman still continue in the last scene, in full freedom, to reflect the essential characteristics of their former life. And the same can be said of Gregers Werle [in *The Wild Duck*] and of Hedda Gabler.

This means that if the inner renewal that takes place in the main character has a bearing on the innate ethics of the play, we cannot apply the simple crime-and-punishment pattern to the action in Ibsen's drama. We must not, in fact, condemn his heroes out of hand on the basis of what may be called their crime. And we must not look at the catastrophe as a judgment of justice which restores the moral balance on the stage by the sacrifice of the hero. For in that case the development of the hero himself would be separated from the deepest meaning of the dramatic action.

In order to arrive at an interpretation of the sacrifice themes which will prove more suitable to Ibsen's plays, it might be useful to look at the characters who are not sacrificing anybody, but who are themselves being sacrificed by the passionate hero.

When there is a sacrifice, there must be a victim too. And sometimes in a drama the victim's fate becomes an independent force and has its own impact on the action. This will often be the case when the victim is an innocent man or woman. In fact, the person who suffers most on the stage is not always guilty. He may equally well be what we should call innocent. This is true, for instance, of the main character in [August] Strindberg's *Dream Play*. Among secondary characters who are made to suffer, Ophelia in *Hamlet* springs to mind. And if the innocent suffering occupies an independent and important place in the drama, we might speak about 'the innocent victim' as a separate sacrifice theme.

Ibsen's realistic plays make diligent use of this theme, without, however, applying it to the main character. We find no daughter of Indra in Ibsen's last period. For a parallel we should turn rather to Shakespeare's Ophelia. And yet, although the main characters in Ibsen's dramas are not usually presented as innocent victims, this theme nevertheless occupies a prominent place in his work. Osvald in *Ghosts,* Hedvig in *The Wild Duck,* Beate in *Rosmersholm,* Ella Rentheim in *John Gabriel Borkman,* these all

serve to illustrate the theme, and there would be no difficulty in adding to this list.

In certain cases the action culminates in the sacrifice of this victim, as in *The Wild Duck,* where Hedvig's fate proves the decisive turning-point. In other cases, as in *Ghosts* and *Rosmersholm,* the entire retrospective revelation is concentrated, so to speak, in the fate of the victim, Osvald or Beate. The further the veil is drawn aside to reveal the secrets of the past, the clearer the light that is shed on his—or her—bitter fate. And in actual fact, as we have already pointed out, the fact of sacrifice is in several cases completed in the present, even though its origins may have to be sought far back in the past. On the whole, therefore, it would be right to say that Ibsen has placed a great deal of emphasis on what we have called 'the innocent victim', and this sacrifice theme deserves a closer study.

At first sight one might be struck with the ample possibilities this theme offers to the dramatist who aims to give his plays a marked social perspective. The *guilty* will tend to focus the interest of the audience on *his* problems; the *innocent,* who has no moral accounts to settle, often focusses interest on the milieu. His mind is, as it were, a potential meeting point for the forces in conflict. His suffering may be indicative of dangerous upheavals in a particular milieu, in society, or even in a civilisation.

Now there are among the dramatists some with a more markedly metaphysical approach who assign a still more extensive social function to the innocent victim. They make it clear that the victim suffers, not only on account of moral chaos in society, but also for the benefit of the divided community. It is not the guilty who suffers; it is the innocent, but his suffering is to be regarded as vicarious. As we know, vicarious suffering is a central concept in the great religions of the world. The community or the whole nation is purged when one chosen person suffers the consequences of the moral shortcomings of the others, thereby expiating their guilt and restoring the moral balance.

Instinctively one would of course assume that a metaphysical projection of the innocent victim of this nature would be alien to Ibsen. We may readily accept his use of the sacrifice theme to illustrate the *social* aspect; but surely it would be unreasonable to expect him to go further than this?

The answer is that the idea of a vicarious victim on the stage has certainly not always been foreign to Ibsen. Some time before *Love's Comedy* (1862), he had started on a prose play, *Svanhild,* which may be considered a preparation for *Love's Comedy.* In this prose work, which took shape while the decisive process of maturing was going on in the mind of the playwright, there is a passage which is well worth nothing. Here we find the chief male character, Falk, musing on the name of the chief female character, Svanhild. This has been taken from the Wolsung Saga, which describes how Svanhild was torn to pieces by four horses, according to Falk because there was something 'rotten in the social conditions in this country', and Nemesis was called on to 'restore the balance'. The most important part of Falk's speech is as follows:

You see, when the human order has been violated in this way for long periods, when conditions are such that marriages are contracted without love, and love cannot flourish except by crime, then from time to time a victim must suffer in order to appease the wrath of the gods. And the victim must be the best that the family can offer. This is what happened to Svanhild: terrible things had been going on in her family, and those who committed them got away with it. She was innocent, and was torn to pieces by four horses. That is just about what might be called *Fatum.*

It will thus be seen that at this period Ibsen fully accepted the idea of vicarious suffering; and an analysis of the chief works he wrote between 1862 and 1873 would reveal that this concept was one that remained with him for a long time. Nevertheless it is difficult to believe that he could have made any use of it during his realistic period, where all his ideas were presented in such a way that they can be understood and accepted by the ordinary down-to-earth human intelligence. The idea of vicarious suffering seems to have little in common with the world of ideas in which modern man exists.

It might of course be possible, nevertheless, to assume the existence of an intermediate stage between the innocent victim considered as a battle-ground of conflicting forces and the same victim considered as a healing force.

The innocent victims of the conflict portrayed on the stage might, for example, in their limited human existence, reflect an attitude lacking in the main character. In a world of moral chaos and disorder they present a picture of mankind undivided and largely free from guilt. If the hero, with his greater degree of involvement and his heightened consciousness, could share this attitude, this would prove of momentous importance to the world depicted in the play.

This is precisely what happens in a number of Ibsen's plays; and it is perhaps the most characteristic feature of the use he makes of the sacrifice themes. It is obvious that the process of revelation allows the innocent victims to emerge with greater clarity, but at the same time, as revelation proceeds, another development occurs: the hero becomes increasingly identified with his victim, and step by step assumes more and more of his nature.

Let us consider a little more closely how this is carried out. For the purpose of demonstrating it, I have chosen *Ghosts,* and I take it that there is no need to remind you of the action of this play. All I need do, to illustrate my point, is to show that the action may be said to proceed from the interplay of two different plots.

The main plot springs from Mrs. Alving's attempts to cleanse the house of all traces of the past, so that her son may live a life of freedom and purity.

Side by side with this plot we have another, namely Osvald's struggle to overcome his fears. His purpose is to win the affection of the maid Regine, as she represents in his eyes a source of happiness which could help him to overcome his disease, and also because, in the last resort, this robust young woman might be persuaded to take his life,

if necessary, so that he need not be haunted by the fear of outliving himself.

These aims—the mother's and the son's—clash, because Mrs. Alving knows what no one else does: that Osvald and Regine are half-brother and half-sister. Half-way through the play, however, Mrs. Alving makes a bold attempt to reconcile Osvald's aims with her own. She reveals the truth about Osvald's father; she does so in order to give the two—half-brother and half-sister—an opportunity to make their choice in a spirit of enlightened freedom. Her confession is interrupted by a blaze of light from the Children's Home, which goes up in flames during the night; and when she returns to the subject again some hours later, we suddenly realise that Mrs. Alving has in fact succeeded in uniting the two plots, though in an unforeseen manner, charged with tragic irony. Mrs. Alving now has to occupy the place of Regine in Osvald's plot: *she* is now the person who has to promise him that she will liberate him from his fear. And if she is to remain the loving mother, running her home in such a way as to serve her son's best interests, she can apparently only do so by shielding him from life.

So much, then, for the actual structure of the play. It shows us in a simple schematic way that Mrs. Alving is forced to accept full responsibility for her son. His fate is now in her hands. And with this in mind it may be natural to ask: How does this fill and enrich her world? What is Osvald actually bringing into the life of Mrs. Alving?

He obviously brings his own sufferings. In fact, on the deeper plane, one of the most significant features of his tragedy is that Osvald's material existence and all the suffering it entails fill Mrs. Alving's heart to an increasing extent.

Ibsen's method of showing that this is going on is very, very simple. He makes the process comprehensible, and to a certain extent even visible on the stage, with the help of a familiar pattern from everyday life. Mrs. Alving opens her heart to the helpless Osvald, as though he were an ill-treated child. In Act 2 we have a scene in which Osvald unburdens himself to her, in the same way as any unhappy child would go for consolation to its mother. But because the pattern of this conversation is on the mother-and-child level, the effect is extra poignant when the grown-up man says:

> Mother, may I sit beside you on the sofa?
> Yes, do, my dear.
> There is something I must tell you, Mother.
> Well?
> Because I can't bear it any longer.

It is a sad story indeed to which the mother has to listen. The young painter's mind is permanently affected; he will never be able to work again. He is like a living corpse.

The same basic pattern is used, with certain modifications, when Mrs. Alving towards the close of the play is told the whole truth about Osvald's illness.

> Mother, we are going to have a talk . . . And
> then I'll no longer have this feeling of dread . . .
> Mother, I know you are quite strongminded,

You must sit quite calmly when you hear what
it is . . .

Next comes the scene when Osvald *refuses* to carry his
burden:

I never asked you for life. And what sort of life
is this you've given me? I don't want it! Take it
back!

This causes Mrs. Alving to flee in panic, but Osvald stops
her with words which cannot fail in their effect:

Have you a mother's heart for me, and yet can
see me suffer from this unutterable dread?

Once again she assumes full responsibility for the need of
her child, and gives him her heroic promise. Immediately
afterwards, for the fourth and last time, she hears her son
turn to her like a helpless child coming to its mother. This
is when, with his brain faculties impaired, he asks her to
give him the sun.

When the famous closing scene is reached, one of the main
strands of the tragedy is brought to its conclusion, the one
which transfers the son's sufferings to his mother. 'I cannot bear it any longer', was Osvald's remark on the first
occasion when he asked his mother to share his burden.
And the words Mrs. Alving finally utters sound like an
echo: 'This cannot be borne'.

As a final indication of her identification with her son we
have the last scene, where Mrs. Alving is staring at Osvald
in speechless horror, and clutching her hair. This has the
same visual effect on the stage as Osvald created the first
time his pain was openly expressed, when he had pressed
his hand in despair to his head.

The main character—the idealist who caused others to
suffer—adopts, as it were, the fate of her victim, and
makes it her own.

This highly interesting pattern is also present in other
Ibsen plays, for instance in **Rosmersholm.**

In the spring of 1963 Dr. John Northam delivered a series
of lectures in Kristiansand. One of the lectures was an extensive analysis of *Rosmersholm* [*Dividing Worlds: Shakespeare's* The Tempest *and Ibsen's* Rosmersholm, 1965]. In
this play the victim is named Beate and the two heroes are
named Rosmer and Rebekka. It is fairly evident that the
revelation process in the play brings to Rosmer an increasing insight into the victim's fate. Rosmer has been completely ignorant of the reasons for her suicide. But of equal
importance is the relation between Rebekka and her victim, Beate, who is so strongly associated with the spirit of
Rosmersholm. In his lecture Dr. Northam examined Rebekka's development and pointed out that even before she
went the same way as Beate and went into the mill race,
she had come to understand the strength and the value of
the Rosmersholm tradition, and was subsequently prepared to go beyond mere understanding to the point of
total acceptance of them. In the end she dies in this
Rosmersholm tradition of her own choice.

Personally I would put it as follows: she suffers the same
death for the sake of Rosmer as she had previously forced
her victim to suffer, and in this way she takes upon herself

the fate of her victim. It is no coincidence that in the last
scene she stands on the stage enveloped in the white shawl
which is associated with the dead Beate, and that the last
remark in the play, after Rosmer and Rebekka have been
swept to their death in the mill race, runs as follows: 'The
lady (i.e. Beate) took them.'

The development here mentioned, a development which
results in the hero's identifying himself with his victims,
could be traced in other plays. But to illustrate this it
would be necessary to undertake a series of analyses for
which there is no time in the space of a lecture. Suffice it
to mention one clue that indicates that a similar development may have taken place in other dramas apart from
Ghosts and **Rosmersholm,** namely the manner in which
the hero dies frequently links him very closely to his victim. In **John Gabriel Borkman** Ella Rentheim's heart is
broken as a result of John Gabriel's betrayal, yet it is John
Gabriel himself who dies of a heart attack. Hedda Gabler
has sacrificed Ejlert Løvborg by handing him her pistol,
and she dies by her own hand from a bullet fired from a
pistol that is the companion to the one she gives Ejlert.
Solness falls from his tower because Hilde waves to him,
thus evoking the applause of the crowd; and the fatal signal is made with a white shawl, the shawl used to drape
the neck of the victim of the play, Alline Solness. After
Hedvig has taken her life, in **The Wild Duck,** and Gregers
has realised his share of the responsibility for her death,
his final resolve is to follow in her footsteps.

What conclusions are we to draw from the development
I have endeavoured to trace in **Ghosts,** and which may
perhaps be parallelled in other plays of Ibsen?

First and foremost that the innocent victim's *sole* function
is not to place the guilt of the hero in relief. That he has
this function is of course undeniable. In **Ghosts** the action
which Mrs. Alving seems forced to undertake in the last
scene clearly indicates her guilt, and entails its own punishment. Identifying herself with her victim, the heroine
is herself struck down by the fate her victim suffered. In
this way she is doomed, and there is no further need for
moralising.

But the close companionship that has developed between
herself and Osvald has also brought a new sense of purity
into her life, and this gives her action a new aspect. She
is no longer led astray by her Victorian upbringing or
blinded by secret passion. Like her son, she now sees the
value of 'joy in living' and she would dearly have liked to
have given Osvald this precious gift. Since this cannot be,
she is prepared—still in the spirit of Osvald—to obey her
conscience, despite all conventions. Whether it would be
right to allow the use of morphia, and whether in practice
she would bear it, may be considered irrelevant in this context. One thing is certain: the blind idealist has recovered
her sight, and is now endeavouring to act independently.
And the mere endeavour to do so is a sign of heroism, because one of the alternatives she has to face is terrible almost beyond human understanding.

My purpose in this lecture was not to give an exhaustive
interpretation of **Ghosts.** It was, as you will remember, to
discuss whether confusion or ambiguity is the right word

for the endings of Ibsen's plays, and to do so by considering the use Ibsen makes of the sacrifice themes. Some kind of sacrifice is in fact involved in the final struggle and suffering of the hero, and his experience of catastrophe.

Considering the sacrifice themes, especially in **Ghosts,** I found that the third of them, 'the innocent victim', reflects an attitude which has been lacking in the main character in the period when her idealism was most destructive. But at the end of the tragedy we clearly see that the heroine shares this attitude. Because of this change the ending of **Ghosts** must be described, not as confusing, but as ambiguous in a dramatically acceptable manner. The uncertainty I mentioned in the beginning: what is Mrs. Alving going to do? has as its main function to depict her anguish and leave the audience in a state of mind where ambiguity may be experienced. This ambiguity itself may be defined as follows:

The ending constitutes at one and the same time a judgment on Mrs. Alving's life and a demonstration of her new form of idealism. Considered in the context of the past, the final scene on the stage is a testimony to the heroine's guilt towards her son. She is a doomed hero. But thanks to her identification with her victim and all the consequences this entails the scene may also be considered in quite a different context, in that of the present. In that case it is a testimony to her heroic devotion to her son. Her attitude is thus illuminated from two different angles.

The act of sacrificing another person to oneself, and the act of sacrificing oneself to another, are both portrayed on the stage, and the final anguish experienced by Mrs. Alving exposes at one and the same time her guilt and her innocence, her greatness and her limitation. (pp. 21-34)

> Daniel Haakonsen, *"The Function of Sacrifice in Ibsen's Realistic Drama,"* in Contemporary Approaches to Ibsen *by Alex Bolckmans and others, Universitetsforlaget, 1966, pp. 21-34.*

Martin Esslin   (essay date 1980)

[*Esslin is a prominent and sometimes controversial critic of contemporary theater who is perhaps best known for coining the term "theater of the absurd." His* The Theatre of the Absurd *(1961) is a major study of the avant-garde drama of the 1950s and early 1960s that focuses on the works of Samuel Beckett, Eugene Ionesco, and Jean Genet. In the essay below, Esslin details Ibsen's influence on the modern theater. The critic affirms the social and political impact of Ibsen's portrayal of the moral issues of his day, and posits that the lasting power of his dramas lies in his revolutionary dramatic methods and techniques. The plays of Ibsen heralded the modern era with their complex characterization, psychological tension, and poetic symbolism, argues Esslin, who points to an underlying theme in all of Ibsen's works: "the problem of* Being, *the nature of the self."*]

In the English-speaking world today Henrik Ibsen has become one of the three major classics of the theatre: Shakespeare, Chekhov and Ibsen are at the very centre of the standard repertoire, and no actor can aspire to the very first rank unless he has played some of the leading roles

in the works of these three giants. Among this triad, Ibsen occupies a central position which marks the transition from the traditional to the modern theatre. While Ibsen, like all great dramatists who came after him, owed an immense debt to Shakespeare, Chekhov (who regarded Ibsen as his 'favourite writer' [*The Life and Letters of Anton Tchekhov,* Koteliansky and Tomlinson, eds., 1925]) was already writing under Ibsen's influence. Ibsen can thus be seen as one of the principal creators and well-springs of the whole modern movement in drama, having contributed to the development of all its diverse and often seemingly opposed and contradictory manifestations: the ideological and political theatre, as well as the introspective, introverted trends which tend towards the representation of inner realities and dreams.

Ibsen's first and most obvious impact was social and political. His efforts to make drama and the theatre a means to bring into the open the main social and political issues of the age shocked and scandalised a society who regarded the theatre as a place of shallow amusement. And Ibsen's position seems unique in the history of drama in that he seems to have been the only playwright who, in his lifetime, became the centre of what almost amounted to a political party—the *Ibsenites* who in Germany, England, and elsewhere appear in the contemporary literature as a faction of weirdly dressed social and political reformers, advocates of socialism, women's rights, and a new sexual morality (as in the Ibsen Club, in Shaw's *The Philanderer*). Again and again one can find, in the contemporary literature, the anxious father who inquires of his daughter about to introduce him to her fiancé-to-be whether by chance the young man reads Ibsen and Nietzsche, thus *revealing* himself to be a dangerous subversive element. And the fact that Ibsen had become the symbol and figurehead of what amounted to a counter-culture has had a very considerable influence on the subsequent fluctuations of his posthumous fame and the appreciation of his plays by both the critics and the public.

It was not Ibsen himself, who greatly disliked this development, but a number of his early critics, admirers, and followers—[Bernard] Shaw, [William] Archer, [Georg] Brandes, [Edmund] Gosse, and others—who formulated the doctrines of Ibsenism which persisted for a long time and indeed still persist, inasmuch as Shaw's *The Quintessence of Ibsenism* is still (and deservedly) read as a masterpiece of Shavian polemical writing. The effect of this phenomenon was that Ibsen could, for a long time, be regarded as a principally political playwright commenting on topical social and moral issues. As a result, when some of the main objectives of what had been regarded as his closest concerns had been attained (for example: women's suffrage, a more tolerant attitude to sexual conduct, and the rejection of religious intolerance) the view spread that Ibsen had outlived his fame and become thoroughly out of date. Brecht expressed this view in 1928 when he declared that Ibsen's **Ghosts** had become obsolete through the discovery of Salvarsan as a remedy against syphilis. Yet the very fact that a playwright's work could be seen as having played a vital part in bringing about a change in public opinion and social attitudes had an immense effect on the status of drama as a medium of expression, and its status as an experimental laboratory for social thought and social change. As Brecht put it in 1939: 'The drama of Ibsen, Tolstoy, Strindberg, Gorki, Chekhov, Hauptmann, Shaw, Kaiser and O'Neill is an experimental drama. These are magnificent attempts to give dramatic form to the problems of the time' [Bertolt Brecht, *Gessamelte Werke*, Vol. VII]. It will be noticed that Ibsen's name comes first in Brecht's list of the masters of the new kind of serious, experimental drama. And deservedly so: it was Ibsen who established that tradition, and proved that the theatre could be a forum for the serious consideration of the problems of the age. He is thus the founder and source of the whole strand of modern political and ideological theatre. Brecht himself, who developed a style of playwriting which radically rejected the convention of drama that Ibsen used, can thus be seen to have followed a trail blazed by Ibsen. And indeed, Brecht did acknowledge a direct indebtedness to Shaw who in turn was a professed follower of Ibsen.

This is one of the lines of descent of the contemporary drama we can clearly derive from Ibsen. It was Ibsen whose revolutionary impact and ultimate success showed that drama could be more than the trivial stimulant to maudlin sentimentality or shallow laughter which it had become—at least in the English-speaking world—throughout the nineteenth century.

It is usually assumed that the shock caused by Ibsen, and the furiously hostile reaction his early plays provoked, were due to this political and social subversiveness. But that is only one part of the truth. Another important cause of this virulent reaction by audiences and critics alike lay in the revolutionary nature of Ibsen's dramatic method and technique. This is an aspect which is far more difficult for use to comprehend today as we have become completely conditioned to precisely this then 'revolutionary' convention. Much of the fury directed at the time against Ibsen had nothing to do with his supposed obscenity, blasphemous views, or social destructiveness. What was criticised above all was his *obscurity* and *incomprehensibility.* Ibsen, it was said again and again, was a *mystificateur* who was obscure on purpose in order to maskthe shallowness of his thinking, and whose dark hints and mysterious allusions were never cleared up in his plays. This view is perfectly expressed in a notice of **Rosmersholm** by Clement Scott in the London *Daily Telegraph* (19 February 1891):

> The old theory of playwrighting was to make your story or study as simple and direct as possible. The hitherto accepted plan of a writer for the stage was to leave no possible shadow of a doubt concerning his characterisation. But Ibsen loves to mystify. He is as enigmatical as the Sphinx. Those who earnestly desire to do him justice and to understand him keep saying to themselves: granted all these people are egotists or atheists, or agnostics, or emancipated, or what not, still I can't understand why he does this or she does that.

The matter could not be put more clearly: in the then traditional convention of playwriting (a convention which, indeed, had existed from the very beginnings of dramatic writing) not only was every character labelled as either a villain or a hero, but was also—through soliloquies, asides, or confessions to a confidant—constantly informing the audience of his most secret motivations. The audience therefore did not have to deduce the motivations of the characters from their actions; they *knew* what their motivations were *before* they acted. Playgoers had been used to this convention for centuries. It was only when the demand for realism, of which the later Ibsen was the principal exponent, closed these windows into the inner world of the characters that the audience was faced with the problem of having to decide for themselves what the motivations of many of the characters' otherwise unexplained actions might be. No wonder that audiences unprepared for a manner of presentation that confined itself to the simulation of ordinary, everyday conversation, which hardly ever includes the full disclosure of hidden desires or deep motivations, could not make head or tail of what was supposed to be happening. Moreover, this development coincided in time with the discovery of the unconscious portion of the human psyche—the recognition that in most cases people do not even *know* their own motivations and could thus not express them even if the dramatic convention allowed them to do so. The modern convention of dramatic dialogue is, accordingly, diametrically opposed to the classical one. Now the art consists precisely in opening insights into the characters' unconscious motivations and feelings through the interstices between the most trivial everyday exchanges of small talk.

While Ibsen was by no means the only, or even the first, naturalistic playwright to apply this technique, he was certainly regarded as the most representative and also the most extreme in its application—quite apart from obviously being the greatest master practitioner of it in his own time. The introduction of this *principle of uncertainty* into drama certainly represents a fundamental revolution in dramatic technique, a revolution which is still with us and continues to dominate dramatic writing of all kinds, including the dialogue techniques of avant-garde cinema (as in the work of Robert Altman or John Cassavetes, where the dialogue is out of focus and overlaps so that no more than a general sense emerges). So far has this technique been developed that Ibsen now tends to appear to us overmeticulous and obvious in motivating his characters, however daring in breaking entirely new ground he might have appeared to his contemporaries. What is beyond doubt is that the line of development extends directly from Ibsen to Chekhov, who refined the technique of oblique or indirect dialogue and evolved the concept of the sub-text hidden beneath the explicit language of the dialogue, as well as to Wedekind who was the first to employ deliberately non-communicating dialogue so that the characters—too involved in themselves to listen to what their partners say—deliver what amounts to two monologues in parallel. And it is from Chekhov and Wedekind that the masters of contemporary non-communicating dialogue, such as Harold Pinter and Eugène Ionesco, can trace their ultimate descent.

To illuminate how direct this line of descent is, one has only to point out that James Joyce was not only an enthusiastic admirer of Ibsen in his youth but that he also wrote a very Ibsenite play—the much undervalued and neglected *Exiles*—which, in fact, makes this principle of uncertainty of motives its main theme. It is the subject raised in the final dialogue between Rosmer and Rebecca West in *Rosmersholm:* that one can, in fact, never know another human being's true motivation. Rosmer and Rebecca, because of the impossibility of any full and final awareness that the other's love is pure, can confirm their devotion to each other only in their willingness to die for love—whereas Richard Rowan, the highly autobiographical hero of Joyce's play, admits: 'I can never know, never in this world. I do not wish to know or to believe. I do not care. It is not in the darkness of belief that I desire you. But in restless, wounding doubt . . . ' Here this modern *principle of uncertainty* in human motivation is not only offered to the spectators, left in doubt about the characters' true feelings, but to the characters themselves whose love in fact is seen to spring directly from that very uncertainty; for full knowledge and total security would be an endpoint, the beginning of stagnation and complacency and thus the death of love, which must constantly renew itself out of risk and uncertainty. It is no coincidence that Harold Pinter adapted this play and twice directed performances of it. His deliberate abandonment of supplying motivations of any kind to his characters in plays like *The Homecoming, Old Times* or *No Man's Land* might be regarded as continuing the practice of Joyce and thus, ultimately, of Ibsen.

Affinities and organic evolutionary links in technique between writers like Ibsen, Joyce, and Pinter also highlight the close connection between the technique and form of their work and its subject matter. The method of writing dialogue itself opens up the problem of human communication, motivation, and the nature of the personality—the self. Here too Ibsen stands at the very well-spring of modern literature. And even writers whose technique has very little in common with that of Ibsen are organically linked with him in this respect. James Joyce, the dedicated Ibsenite, links Ibsen with another great writer of our time, Samuel Beckett—in spite of the fact that Beckett's anti-illusionist and non-realist techniques are diametrically opposed to those of Ibsen's plays. For, I venture to suggest, both Beckett and Ibsen are ultimately deeply concerned with a subject matter of fundamental modernity: the problem of *Being,* the nature of the self, with the question of what an individual means when he uses the pronoun *I.* How can the self be defined? Can one even speak of a consistent entity corresponding to an individual's self? This, it seems to me, is the fundamental and underlying subject matter of Ibsen's *oeuvre* which was masked, for his contemporaries, by its surface preoccupation with social and political questions. Moreover, it is this problem which links Ibsen's earlier poetic drama with his later prose plays.

Here again Ibsen's uncanny ability to reflect the main currents of thought of his time emerges; for the problem of human identity, the nature of the self, seems to derive directly from the decline of religious belief which was the mainspring of the intellectual upheavals and revolutions of the nineteenth century to which Ibsen's entire *oeuvre* responded. As long as man was deemed to have an eternal essence, a soul which had been especially created for him

by God and destined to persist—in Heaven or Hell—for all subsequent eternity, there was no problem about the nature of human identity. Each individual was believed to have his own special character and potential, which he might or might not fully develop to its utmost realisation, but which eventually would emerge into eternity. [Emanuel] Swedenborg saw each individual in *Heaven and Hell* as bearing the outward form and features of his or her deepest nature. It was with the loss of transcendental beliefs of this nature that human identity became a problem. Was man the chance product of his genetic inheritance or of his environment? And if so, what was the true inner core of his self, its permanent component, as against the multitude of contradictory impulses which at any moment pull him in this or that direction?

Ibsen, although he insisted that he read few books and confined himself to reading the newspapers right down to the advertisements, was a brilliant sounding-board for all the philosophical cross-currents of his time, whatever the means by which he might have become aware of them. Already the protagonists of *The Pretenders,* or Julian in *Emperor and Galilean,* reflect the problem of the self, the need to search for the self's real core, and the awareness that the realisation of one's true self is the highest human objective. Brand, who is torn between the abstract dictates of his faith on the one hand (a faith he experiences as an implacable imperative existing outside himself), and his impulsive human instincts towards his child and his wife on the other, brings this problem of identity into particularly sharp focus. So also does Peer Gynt, who realises that being sufficient to oneself (that is, merely living by one's contradictory, momentary, instinctive, sensual impulses) actually leads to failure in developing a self. The image of the onion with its core of nothingness is indeed very Beckettian, which is another way of saying 'existentialist'.

For the nothingness at the centre of our own perception of ourselves is, with [Søren] Kierkegaard (whom Ibsen, even if he had never read him, must have understood intuitively from the climate of discussion around him) and with [Jean-Paul] Sartre, precisely the realisation of human *freedom.* The scene, at the end of *The Lady from the Sea* where Ellida has to be given her total freedom by her husband before she can freely decide to commit herself to him, seems to me the perfect expression of the existentialist position in drama (rivalled only by another great and even earlier proto-existentialist play, Kleist's *Prince of Homburg*). Here a character, Ellida, finds her true self by an act of her own will. Self-realisation as the creation of an integrated self out of nothing—the mere welter of instinctive drives—is the way out of the despair engendered by the disappearance of the notion of a God-centred and pre-ordained selfhood. In the case of Ellida, her encounter with the Stranger had conjured up before her a *false self-image* dictated by her animal attraction to him. And here again we are in a very modern field of ideas, the idea of *false consciousness*—a self-image which could easily have become destructive by preventing the potential integration of the personality in a harmonious balance between conflicting drives and needs, just as Brand's and Julian's false self-images ultimately lead to their downfall, or as Peer

Gynt's failure to transcend the mere indulgence of his sensuality probably does (for, surely, the final vision of Peer's return to Solveig is no more than a fantasy, a dream image). Ellida's decision to commit herself—in full freedom—to Wangel seems to provide her with a valid, workable and harmoniously integrated self which, however, still remains precarious and problematic.

It is curious that the part of the Stranger, that giver of a false and destructive self-image to Ellida is, in another play, *The Master Builder,* played by Ellida's own step-daughter—Hilda Wangel. There Solness has transmitted his own false (because self-deceptive) self-image to Hilda who, years later, returns to confront him with it and to demand its realisation in action. Here the problematic nature of the human self is posed in a particularly brilliant dramatic form: Solness is faced with the reflection of his own now certainly obsolete idea of himself (which was a falsehood even at the time when he implanted it in Hilda's mind) in a manner which is reminiscent of the way Krapp is brought to confront his former and falsely romantic self in Beckett's play *Krapp's Last Tape.* The dramatic techniques could not be more different, but in substance the two plays resemble each other very closely. In Ibsen's play it is Hilda's memory which plays the part of the tape-recorder in Beckett's bleakly economical recreation of the same situation.

False consciousness, deceptive self-images, the *I* experiencing itself as the *Not-I* (to quote a Beckettian expression which has become the title of one of his play)—these are expressions of a twentieth century cluster of problems for which Ibsen had his own terminology: he called this syndrome the *Life-lie* or, in a different perspective, the *lure of the ideal.* Peer Gynt's self-indulgence is, in this context, akin to Hjalmar Ekdal's complacency and self-deception—and the destructiveness of commitment to an abstract ideal on the part of Gregers Werle, to Brand's rigidity in blindly following the dictates of an abstract, revealed faith. John Gabriel Borkman, who has sacrificed his capacity for love, his human sensuality, to a Napoleonic self-image to which he still clings long after it has lost all reality, puts the problem of the self to discussion as much as the figure of Rubek, who betrayed both his capacity for love and for real greatness as an artist by opting for the compromise of worldly success and wealth—Peer Gynt's sufficiency to one's baser impulses. Always there is a conflict between irreconcilable aspects of the self, which the individuals concerned have failed to integrate into an harmonious, well-balanced whole.

If one looks at the underlying theme of Ibsen's *oeuvre* in this way, his preoccupation with the problem of women's rights, which so scandalised his contemporaries, also appears in a different perspective: Ibsen himself repeatedly insisted that in writing *A Doll's House* he had not, basically, been concerned with feminism, but merely with the problem of Nora's self-realisation as a human being. If Hilda Wangel destroys Solness by imposing upon him the self-image of a conquering hero unafraid to ascend the highest tower, so Helmer has imposed upon Nora the degrading role and self-image of a child-wife; and in walking ˙ of the marriage she merely—that seems to have been

the point Ibsen was concerned with—asserts her human rights to fashion her own self-image and to create her own integrated self.

Conversely, in what I feel is Ibsen's most 'modern' play, *Hedda Gabler,* we are presented with a character whose self-realisation is made tragically impossible by a number of external factors beyond her control. Hedda is basically a creative personality who cannot realise her potential in a society which does not allow women to live as independent human beings, while her sexual drive towards Løvborg cannot come to fruition because her rigid conditioning by having been brought up as an upper-class lady makes it impossible for her to defy convention by becoming Løvborg's mistress (as Thea, who has not been so conditioned, does). Thus Hedda is trapped in a truly tragic dilemma. Her seeming wickedness results from the confusion and contradictions within her own self-image between, on the one hand, her need to reject the role into which her upbringing and society have forced her (the dutiful and middle-class housewife and mother-to-be) and, on the other, her inability to do so because of the strength of her conditioning and the pressure of public opinion. Her destructiveness is thus merely her creativeness gone wrong, her tragic failure to achieve true selfhood.

Sexuality, and especially female sensuality, which did not officially exist at all for the Victorians, was seen by Ibsen as one of the dangerous instincts insofar as its suppression by the demands of society forced the individual into false or inadequate integrations of his self. Mrs Alving's failure to break out of her marriage in *Ghosts* foreshadows Hedda Gabler's inability to give herself to Løvborg, and is shown by Ibsen to elicit similarly tragic results. In *Little Eyolf* the conflict is between motherhood and uninhibited female sensuality. Rita Allmers is the most openly sexually voracious character in Ibsen's plays: here the rejection of motherhood derives from an undue concentration on the sensual aspect of sex. The child is maimed because the mother neglected him while engaged in the sexual act; and Eyolf ultimately dies because his mother wishes him dead as an obstacle to her uninhibited indulgence of sexual activity. But Rita's exaggerated sexual drive may well spring from her husband's equally disproportionate commitment to his ideal, his work as a philosopher, which has led him to neglect both her sexual needs and their child's emotional and educational demands.

Ultimately this problem of the self is that of the missing core of the onion, the ultimate nothingness at the heart of the personality, the absence of a pre-ordained integrating principle which would automatically harmonise the conflicting drives and instincts that propel the individual in a multitude of centrifugal, disintegrating directions. That is why self-realisation, the creation of such an integrating principle by an act of will has become the task which confronts all of Ibsen's heroes. Seen from this angle, the problem of guilt in a play like *Rosmersholm* also appears in a new and more contemporary light. Here the false solutions arrived at in the past, the false self-images they have created, come between the individual and the ultimate realisation of his or her true self-image. The tradition of the Rosmers is as stifling as the upper-class rigidities of General Gabler's family; and false concepts of duty, on the one hand, and Rebecca's admittedly selfish instinctive sexuality, on the other, create what to these characters must appear as a situation without a way out. Whether, as Freud suggested, Rebecca West felt guilty under the curse of Oedipus (just having learned that she had committed incest with her father) or whether she felt that she had attained to a love of such purity that she could not, under the pressure of Victorian ideas, contemplate its sexual consummation—these characters are trapped in veritable labyrinths of false consciousness.

These are the thematic elements in Ibsen's *oeuvre* which, in my opinion, not only link him to the main preoccupations of contemporary drama but also constitute his continued relevance to the concerns of our time.

There is, however, another aspect of his work which makes Ibsen peculiarly relevant to the dramatic literature of our time. Contemporary drama—whether it is the *epic theatre* created by Brecht; the *absurdist* strain represented by playwrights like Beckett, Genet, Ionesco, and Pinter; or the *documentary* strain of contemporary political theatre—is essentially anti-illusionist, anti-realistic (if realism is understood as the quasi-photographic reproduction of the external appearance of the phenomenal world). Ibsen is generally regarded as the antithesis of this position, as a realist, even a naturalist, who in the most influential phase of his activity strove for complete photographic verisimilitude: a world of rooms without a fourth wall.

This view of Ibsen is correct, up to a point. But Ibsen's essentially poetic genius also propelled him away from photographic realism. That there are dream-like elements, highly reminiscent of the introspective fantasy world of the Absurdists, in Ibsen's earlier plays, in **Brand** and **Peer Gynt,** that there is a vast epic sweep that transcends all realism in **The Pretenders** and **Emperor and Galilean,** is only too obvious. Again and again in these plays the action shifts from the external world into the protagonists' dreams or fantasies: the voice from the avalanche in **Brand,** the Troll scenes in **Peer Gynt,** Peer Gynt's shipwreck, the whole Button Moulder sequence and, indeed, the final vision of Solveig, are dreamlike projections of the characters' inner visions. When Ibsen made the decision to devote himself to realistic prose drama these dream and fantasy elements were—on the surface—suppressed. Yet they are continuously present, nevertheless. They emerge above all in what has come to be regarded as Ibsen's increasing resort to symbolism. Having renounced the use of *poetry in the theatre* (in the form of verse or grandly poetic subject matter) Ibsen made more and more use of *poetry of the theatre* which emerges from the sudden transformation of a real object into a symbol, from the metaphoric power of an entrance or an exit, a door opening or closing, a glance, a raised eyebrow or a flickering candle.

It is my contention—and conviction—that the continuing power and impact of Ibsen's plays spring from precisely this poetic quality. If we accept that all fiction, however realistic its form, is ultimately the product of the imagination, the fantasy-life, the daydreaming of its author, then even the most realistic drama can be seen, ultimately, as a fantasy, a daydream. The more creative, the more complex, the more original, the more poetic the imagination of the writer, the greater will be this element in his work. It is one of the hallmarks of the best work of some of our foremost contemporary playwrights that they are conscious of this position and make use of it. The plays of Edward Bond and Harold Pinter, to name but those who most readily come to mind, are examples of this tendency: they are conceived as working both on the level of extreme realism and at the same time on that of fantasy and dream. In this they have surely been anticipated by Ibsen. The continued and undiminished impact of even Ibsen's most seemingly political plays owes, in my opinion, a great deal to that immense hidden and mysterious power which springs from the co-existence of the realistic surface with the deep subconscious fantasy and dream elements behind it: the simulated forest wilderness in the attic of **The Wild Duck,** the white horses of **Rosmersholm,** the ghosts that haunt Mrs Alving, the mysterious Stranger of **The Lady from the Sea,** the spectral Rat Wife of **Little Eyolf,** Borkman's self-created prison, Løvborg's manuscript as Hedda's aborted dream-child, the haunting appearance of the destructive and seductive Hilda Wangel in **The Master Builder,** Aline's dolls in the same play—they all are powerful poetic metaphors, fantasy-images as well as real objects and forces which can be perceived in a sober, factual light.

For, ultimately, the power of all drama springs from its innermost poetic nature as a metaphor of reality, a representation of the whole of reality which of necessity must include the internal world, the world of the mind (both conscious and subconscious), as well as the external reality of rooms, furniture, and cups of coffee. As soon as that external reality is put on the stage it becomes, by the very nature of the theatrical phenomenon, an image, a metaphor of itself: *imaged,* imagined, and by that very fact a mental, a fantasy phenomenon. 'Alles Vergaengliche ist nur ein Gleichnis', as Goethe puts it in the final scene of *Faust:* all our ephemeral, evanescent reality is itself, ultimately merely metaphor, symbol.

It is this quality of the metaphorical power, the poetic vision behind the realistic surface of Ibsen's later plays—their impact as images, and the complex allusive representations of those aspects of human existence, those problems that lie beyond the expressive resources of merely discursive language—in which their real greatness and enduring impact lies. And these, precisely, are the elements in Ibsen which are both highly traditional as well as continuously contemporary, continuously modern. (pp. 71-82)

Martin Esslin, "Ibsen and Modern Drama," in Ibsen and the Theatre: The Dramatist in Production, *edited by Errol Durbach, New York University Press, 1980, pp. 71-82.*

A DOLL'S HOUSE

Elizabeth Hardwick   (essay date 1972)

[*The following excerpt is from an examination of the portrayal of women in Ibsen's dramas which was first presented at a conference in 1972. Hardwick explores the character of Nora, finding her "the most sympathetic of his heroines." Attempting to account for Nora's change in the course of* A Doll's House *"from the girlish, charming wife to the radical, courageous heroine setting out alone," the critic argues that the character has displayed throughout the play "a gift for life and a fundamental common sense" which has been "made falsely to appear giddy and foolish by the empty, dead conventionality of Helmer." Thus, Hardwick claims, Nora is a consistent character and "the woman who has decided to leave her husband [is] the very same woman we have known before."*]

There has been recently an accretion of interest in the women characters in Ibsen: in the plight of Mrs. Alving [in **Ghosts**], the chaos of Hedda Gabler, the ambition of Rebecca West [in **Rosmersholm**]. These are all dramatically interesting portraits, but world literature offers more complex and richly imagined women. What newly strikes us about Ibsen may be just what we had a decade or so ago thought was stodgy about him—he sees women not only as individual characters and destinies caught up in dramatic conflicts but also as a "problem." He seems alone, so far as I can remember, in suggesting that he has given thought to the bare fact of being born a woman. To be female: What does it mean?

He worried about the raw canvas upon which the details of character were painted. First you are a woman and then you are restless, destructive, self-sacrificing, whatever you happen to be. No doubt there is some Scandinavian texture in all this, some socialistic brooding, something to do with the masterful Thoresen women in his wife's family, with his wife herself. Women seemed very strong to him, unpredictable; they set his literary imagination on fire and so he needed them, but he didn't want to be engulfed, drowned by new passions. He was not domestic and liked living in hotels and hired places in Italy or Germany, summering in cottages by a lake, writing, not necessarily needing the whole sweep of the feminine plan of house, permanence for possessions, roots.

What can **A Doll's House** be for us? Nora's leaving her husband can scarcely rivet our attention. The only thing more common and unremarkable would be her husband's

The tarantella scene from the world premiere of A Doll's House. *Danish Royal Theatre, Copenhagen, 1879.*

leaving her. The last line, the historic "speech," is in the famous stage direction that ends the play. "From below is heard the reverberations of a heavy door closing." The door is the door of self-determination. We have some idea why it is at last opened, but why had it, before, been closed?

A Doll's House is about money, about the way it turns locks. Here is the plot once more. Nora Helmer is the charming young mother of three children. She has been married for eight years. When we first meet her she is full of claims to happiness, but it is rather swiftly revealed that strenuous days and nights lie in the past. Still the marriage has life in it and Nora thinks she is happy. Indeed she is on the brink of being happier—things have taken a good turn. Nora's husband, Helmer, has been a struggling lawyer, but it is typical of his character that the courage and aggressiveness needed to survive as a solitary professional are not quite suitable to his temperament. He requires the corporate frame. Helmer has just been named manager of the Joint Stock Bank. It is a promotion in self-esteem, in social position, best of all in money.

It is Christmas Eve, the tree is brought in by a porter and almost the first line of the play is, "How much?" Nora gives the man a crown and in her first exclamation of liberation says, "Keep the change!" This gratuity, this enlargement of possibility and personal expansiveness are the very sweetness of life to Nora. Her money worries have been overwhelming; natural generosity, pleasant extravagance have had to be sacrificed. True, the new money is still maddeningly not quite there. Helmer's increased salary will not begin for three months. No matter, Nora has bought presents for the family instead of, as in previous years, sitting up all night making the trimmings and the gifts herself. In a mood of hope and indulgence she nibbles some sweets her husband, true to our own dental beliefs, has "forbidden" her in the interest of sound teeth.

In his first exchanges with Nora, Helmer calls her "his twittering lark," and his "squirrel," his little "spendthrift," his "featherbrain." These are not insults—far from it. The words represent the coins of affection they have been living on in the lean days. But still we see right off that Helmer is prudent and Nora is eager for room in life, for spontaneity. "No debts! No borrowing!" the husband announces. But he loosens up a bit with the prodigal demands of the holiday season and counts out some bills for Nora. "Money!" she says, sounding the thundering chord. When she is asked what she wants for Christmas, she declares that she would like cash. Helmer finds the occasion to frown over her likeness to her father when it comes to spending; the husband believes in the inheritance of acquired characteristics, and while he adores his little wife, he can see she is not entirely free of genetic imperfection.

At this point a visitor is announced. The social world of Ibsen's plays is greatly restricted, enclosed in a narrow frame, cut off by the very geography of Norway; the long, dark winters make for social repetition, and there is a kind of solitude at the center of everything. When the bell rings and the eyebrows lift at the unexpected caller, it is, unless it be that odd member of the triangular mystery, almost sure to be an old school friend of either the wife or the husband. Everyone else you know is right there, so to speak. This small-town life has moral consequences always; the players live with the threat of trouble over the most petty matters. When Rosmer changes some of his theological ideas [in *Rosmersholm*] it is a scandal. Error or past dissipation casts a long, long shadow. Small towns always remember you when you were young; they seldom believe all the good things they hear you have done later, since you went off someplace else.

The visitor in *A Doll's House* is Mrs. Linde. She has arrived on Christmas Eve. Those who call upon school friends they haven't seen for years are in a state of emergency. Something awful has happened out there. But in Ibsen's plays they receive a rather guarded welcome. No one has much to give; money, love, friendship come at a high price. This is a bourgeois world just hanging on, even petty bourgeois in the amount of money on hand. Most of the characters can claim only education and profession, not riches. Nora's husband has been made manager of the bank in the nick of time; Hedda Gabler's husband, Tesman, is a professor with very little money; her father was a military man who left nothing; Eilert Lövborg is poor; his mistress, Thea, is poor; Rebecca West in *Rosmersholm* is poor. Mrs. Alving in *Ghosts* has enough money, but disasters such as she has known are worse than poverty.

Mrs. Linde is a confidante, a device, rather thinly sketched, but in her outlines of practicality and heavy duties she is an interesting contrast to Nora. Mrs. Linde has come to town to get a job. Money has had its way with her since birth. Her father died and she gradually had to look after her mother and her younger brothers. She married at last, seeking minimal security, forgoing love. But ill luck dogged her still. Her husband died but not before his business fell into trouble. He left her without money and even without "a sorrow or a longing to remember." It had been a complete blank—and no pension at the end of it. She survived. Mrs. Linde is steadfast if somewhat depressed. She has always worked.

At this point Nora starts to reveal the real plot of the play. Hearing of Mrs. Linde's troubles, of her lifelong sacrifices, Nora cannot resist admitting the troubles she, the happy, lucky young wife, has known. She has got herself into a mess on behalf of those she loves and she is proud of her steady, if unconventional, efforts to extricate herself. Nora too has made decisions, borne burdensome consequences. Yes, she has a husband and "three of the loveliest children," but she has had to find ways, she has had to work— "light fancy work . . . crochet and embroidery and things of that sort"—and copying late at night. Her secret is that she took on nothing less than the responsibility of saving her husband's life.

Helmer, when they were first married, had lost his health in the struggle to survive in the harsh commercial climate of Norway. We have no reason to doubt that he might have died without a trip south, to the sun. The bitter Norwegian winters, the coughs, the lung disease, the bronchial threats are perfectly convincing. "How lucky you had the money to spend," the penny-worn Mrs. Linde says about their year in Italy.

Of course they hadn't the money to spend. Nora, without telling her husband, who would have certainly refused or vetoed the idea, had borrowed the money from the disgraced moneylender, Krogstad. This man had been a schoolmate of Helmer's, an admirer of Mrs. Linde's, a small-town embarrassment to himself and his family because he had at some time been guilty of forgery, had not actually been sentenced, but had lived on—forced into usury—with a small post in Helmer's bank and no position in society. Nora turned to Krogstad for her secret negotiations on the money for the year in Italy; she also forged her dying father's name to the note because she didn't know what else to do. But they had their year in the sun, her husband is well, and she has been scrupulously paying back the loan with interest all these years, doing "fancy work," and saving pennies from her household money.

Lies had to be told, but Nora never doubted that she had done something both necessary and honorable. Also, the trip to Italy was one of those necessities that happily coincided with the heart's desire. When she gets out her pretty costume and dances the tarantella in a Mediterranean celebration of joy, we see that in saving her husband's life she has had the best year of her own. "I seem the fool I am not," said Cleopatra [in Shakespeare's *Antony and Cleopatra*].

Mrs. Linde speaks of being alone and childless and Nora cries out, "So utterly alone. How dreadful that must be!" And yet when Mrs. Linde faces her present situation, her mother dead, the boys raised and on their own, Nora suddenly says, "How free you must feel!" Mrs. Linde finds only "an inexpressible emptiness." She has no one to live for and yet "you have to be always on the strain." This woman has had a hard life of lonely work. She is thoroughly capable, even shows a talent for business, and Helmer is easily able to offer her a job in his bank.

Still, Mrs. Linde is a paradox, the sort of puzzle at the very heart of this play. She is capable and hard-working, but *she is not independent*. Nora is impractical and inexperienced, loves "beautiful gloves," and wants the house to be nice—she is also *intrinsically independent* and free-spirited. In the end she leaves her husband and her children in order to find herself, but it is not the final gesture that makes her free. Anna Karenina left her husband and her son [in Leo Tolstoy's *Anna Karenina*], but she was tragically dependent, driven finally by the torments of love to a devastating jealousy and to suicide.

Mrs. Linde, with her business experience, is prudent and conventional like Helmer. She tells Nora, "A wife can't borrow without her husband's consent." Nora thinks that is nonsense, a technicality. (In this conclusion she shows herself prophetic of modern American practice.) She is not, like Krogstad, dishonest and self-pitying. Instead she seems to enjoy the triumph of the borrowing and the struggle to repay. She has nothing but the most honorable intentions toward the money and the interest. Krogstad is a true forger, always wanting to make a leap without taking the consequences. He whines about his reputation. "All paths barred." It is strongly suggested that he would have been more respected if he had gone to jail. Instead

he has somehow edged out of that but has not been able to push away the cloud over his name.

No one understands vice better than Ibsen. He knows what a Krogstad is like. The outcast does not care about reality, but only about fancy. Krogstad holds Nora's fate in his hands; the fact that she has almost repaid the money does not impress him. He knows about the forging of her father's name. Well enough. She must make Helmer keep him on at the bank, give him that little bit of respectability. And then suddenly the minor post is not sufficient. Krogstad begins to dream, a true forger's dreaming. He will not be a mere clerk; no, he must be Helmer's right-hand man and soon become the manager himself! This flamboyant soaring, done in only a few lines, is masterly. (Old Father Ibsen dreaming over his schnapps, no doubt.) In the end, Mrs. Linde and Krogstad decide to share the future. It is a case of supply and demand.

Helmer finds out about the borrowing and the forgery. He flies into a rage and nowhere shows the "miracle" of understanding or of male chivalry Nora had pretended to expect. He thinks she's a treacherous little idiot who can tear down in a moment of folly all a man has built up by his most painful efforts. When he sees that it may not all be revealed, that they can get by with it, his fury abates. But Nora has suffered a moral disappointment. Helmer is not only a donkey, but a coward as well. She makes her decision to leave him and her children because she feels she has been deceiving herself about marriage and happiness and must now learn what life is really about.

The change from the girlish, charming wife to the radical, courageous heroine setting out alone has always been a perturbation. Part of the trouble is that we do not think, and actresses and directors do not think, the Nora of the first acts, the bright woman—with her children, her presents, her nicknames, her extravagance, her pleasure in the thought of "heaps of money"—can be a suitable candidate for liberation. No, that role should by rights belong to the depressed, childless, loveless Mrs. Linde and her lonely drudgery. The truth is that Nora has always been free; it is all there in her gaiety, her lack of self-pity, her impulsiveness, her expansive, generous nature. And Nora never for a moment trusted Helmer. If she had done so she would long ago have told him about her troubles.

Nora kept her secret because she took pride in having assumed responsibility for her husband's life. She also kept quiet out of a lack of faith in her husband's spirit, a thorough knowledge of his conventionality and fear. Even as he is opening the letter that tells of the borrowing and forgery, *before he knows*, she thinks, Goodbye, my little ones. Of course her worst fears are true. Helmer behaves very badly, saying I told you so, and babbling on about her being her father's daughter. Had Nora stayed with him, we can imagine a rather full store of grievance would be in the closet. At the least Helmer would be eternally joking about her foolishness and looking into his wallet at night.

It is difficult to play Nora on the stage. Not that the role is demanding in the usual ways, but rather because of the intellectual and emotional distance this spirited young wife must travel. It is common to link the early Nora and the late Nora by an undercurrent of hysteria in the beginning of the play—a preparation of the ground by a sprinkling of overly bright notes, a little breathlessness and hurry. Hysterical worry will not connect the two Noras. Her panic is a fleeting thing, based upon reality. It has to do with the pressing practical problem of the odious Krogstad's determination to use Nora for his own dishonest purposes.

The hysteria, the worry will not open the door. The only way the two can be reconciled is for the players and the audience to give up their idea that an independent, courageous woman cannot be domestic, pleasure-loving, and charming. If the play were written today, Nora would have left Helmer long ago. They are ill-matched. She has a gift for life and a fundamental common sense made falsely to appear giddy and girlish by the empty, dead conventionality of Helmer.

An exchange about debt: Helmer says, Suppose a catastrophe happened to a man and his family was left with a coffin of unpaid bills; Nora answers, "If anything so dreadful happened, it would be all the same to me whether I was in debt or not." She shows this sort of undercutting intelligence and genuineness throughout the play. Her mind has always been free and original; she is liberated by her intelligence and high spirits.

Strange that Helmer should want a doll's house and yet be so hostile to details of domestic creation. Over and over he leaves the stage with an air of insufferable self-love when there is anything to do with sewing or household affairs. In one scene he mocks the arm movements of a woman knitting. He flees from the presence of the children when they come in from the cold outside, saying, "Only mothers can endure such a temperature."

Nora's children—this is a hedge of thorns. Abandon Helmer, all right, but bundle up the children and take them with you, arranging for his weekend and vacation visits. Even in Ibsen's day one actress refused the part saying, "I could never abandon my children." Nora's love for the children seems real. The nurse points out that they are used to being with their mother more than is usual. Helmer, again lecturing about heredity, says lying mothers produce criminal children. Nora shudders, remembering her interest payments. The nurse she will finally leave the children with is the one who has raised her, but still the step is a grave one. In one of the most striking bits of dialogue between husband and wife, Helmer says, " . . . no man sacrifices his honor, not even for one he loves." "Millions of women have done so," Nora replies.

When Helmer says that she cannot leave her children, she might have said, "Millions of men have done so," and in that been perfectly consistent with current behavior. Nora seems to be saying that she cannot raise her own children in the old way and that she needs time to discover a new one.

Nevertheless the severance is rather casual and it drops a stain on our admiration of Nora. Ibsen has put the leaving of her children on the same moral and emotional level as the leaving of her husband and we cannot, in our hearts,

assent to that. It is not only the leaving but the way the play does not have time for suffering, changes of heart. Ibsen has been too much a man in the end. He has taken the man's practice, if not his stated belief, that where self-realization is concerned children shall not be an impediment.

In William Archer's Preface to *A Doll's House* he had the idea that the woman who served as the model for Nora had actually, in real life, borrowed the money to redecorate her house! There is something beguiling in this thought, something of Nora Helmer in it. The real case was a dismal and more complicated one. The borrowing woman was an intellectual, a sort of writer, who had some literary correspondence with Ibsen. A meeting was arranged and the biographer, Halvdan Koht, says that "she was hardly what he [Ibsen] expected, but young, pretty and vivacious." She was invited to Dresden, and Ibsen called her "the lark." Some years later the lark married and borrowed money secretly to take her husband south for his health. She had trouble paying the money back and the Ibsens urged her to confess to her husband. She confessed and he, in fury, demanded a divorce. The poor wife suffered a nervous breakdown, was sent to an asylum. "In this catastrophe the marriage was dissolved."

The play and the true happening are a wonderfully rich psychological comment on each other. When we learn that the model for Nora was intelligent and ambitious everything falls into place. There is no need to wonder about motivation or changes of character, sudden revelations. Ibsen has not made Nora a writer, but he has, if we look carefully, made her extremely intelligent. She is the most sympathetic of all his heroines. There is nothing bitter, ruthless, or self-destructive in her. She has the amiability and endurance that are the clues to moral courage. Nora is gracious and fair-minded. Even when she if leaving Helmer, she thanks him for being kind to her. With Dr. Rank, the family friend, who is in love with her, she is honest and her flirtation has none of the heavy cynicism of Hedda Gabler's relation with *her* family friend, Judge Brack, and none of the bitter ambitiousness of Rebecca's relationship with Rosmer. Nora is not after anything and we cannot imagine her in nihilistic pursuit of an architect (*The Master Builder*) or the sculptor (*When We Dead Awaken*). Nora's freedom rests upon her affectionate nature.

The habit is to play Nora too lightly in the beginning and too heavily in the end. The person who has been charming in Acts 1 and 2 puts on a dowdy traveling suit in Act 3 and is suddenly standing before you as a spinster governess. If the play is to make sense, the woman who has decided to leave her husband must be the very same woman we have known before. We may well predict that she will soon be laughing and chattering again and eating her macaroons in peace, telling her friends—she is going back to her hometown—what a stick Helmer turned out to be. Otherwise her freedom is worth nothing. Nora's liberation is not a transformation, but an acknowledgment of error, of having married the wrong man. Her real problem is money—at the beginning and at the end. What will she live on? What kind of work will she do? Will she get her children back? Who will be her next husband? When the curtain goes down it is only the end of Volume One.

Because Nora is free and whole she does not present the puzzling tangle of deceit and subterfuge, suppressed rage and dishonesty, that are so peculiar a tendency in the women in Ibsen's other realistic plays. *A Doll's House* is a comedy, a happy ending—except for the matter of the children. The play was published more than ninety years ago and we have found out very little we could add. In the case of grating marriages the children are still there, a matter of improvisation, resistant to fixed principles. Fortunately some of Ibsen's more far-out heroines—Hedda Gabler, Rebecca West, and Irene—are childless and this makes their suicides and falling off a mountain easier on the moral sensibilities of the audience. (pp. 37-48)

> Elizabeth Hardwick, *"Ibsen's Women," in her* Seduction and Betrayal: Women and Literature, *Random House, 1974, pp. 31-84.*

M. C. Bradbrook   (essay date 1982)

[*In the essay below, Bradbrook asserts that the plot of* A Doll's House *hinges on the complex network of interrelated characters, with foils such as Kristine, Krogstad, and Dr. Rank commenting on the relationship between Nora and Torvald. The play's tension results not only from the contrast between its characters, asserts the critic, but from its manipulation of the techniques of the "well-made plays" typical of Ibsen's day. The self-conscious theatricality of the work is evident in the representation of the characters themselves, maintains Bradbrook, who notes that the "characters think they are living in the theatre, they make up plays for themselves but find they are in a different drama."*]

At Christmas 1879—though not quite immediately—the appearance of *A Doll's House* brought the fame of Henrik Ibsen to England. The social emancipation of women, especially through literary women, had been established a generation earlier; in 1845 Elizabeth Barrett Browning had eloped to Italy, and George Eliot, who had gone abroad in 1854 to live with G. H. Lewes, was, by the end of the 1870s, a venerated figure. In this year, 1879, Sarah Bernhardt came to London, having walked out of the Comédie Francaise and slammed the door.

But in the preliminary notes for his play Ibsen had set forward a position so radical that it might well be used today as a feminist manifesto:

> There are two kinds of moral law, two kinds of conscience, one in man, and a completely different one in woman. They do not understand each other; but in matters of practical living the woman is judged by a man's law, as if she were not a woman but a man . . . A woman cannot be herself in contemporary society, it is an exclusively male society, with laws drafted by men, and with counsel and judges who judge feminine conduct from the masculine point of view . . . She has committed a crime and is proud of it because she did it for love of her husband and to save his life . . . Now and then like a woman, she shrugs off her thoughts. Sudden return of

dread and terror. Everything must be borne alone.

However, at the end of the 'Ibsen decade' (the 1880s) when the play had appeared in London, Milan, Paris and Budapest Ibsen told the Society for Extended Female Education in Vienna, in 1891, that it was not about women's rights but the rights of humanity in general; in 1898 he repeated this to the Norwegian Women's Rights League ('What courage!' observed Nigel Dennis), adding 'I am not even quite sure what women's rights are' [Michael Meyer, *Henrik Ibsen,* 1971].

In the terms of a later generation his interests were psychological rather than sociological; he said he did not believe in 'external revolutions'; the revolution 'must come from within'.

Ibsen's work made its effect in translation into languages he did not always understand; it was read much more than performed. Today it survives because of its power in performance. Modern rediscovery of Ibsen followed the stage and broadcast revivals of the 1950s. The full impact of this play survives across language barriers because Ibsen has employed all the arts of the theatre. Perhaps because the theatre in which he was trained had relied on translations for most of its performances and had little of its own, Ibsen succeeded in developing (at the age of fifty-one and in his fifteenth play) a reticulation or meshing of human relationships which elastically adapts itself in live action; the space between the characters, the links that divide and unite them, the space between actors and audience, and the flow of empathy that sustains performance, each derives from Ibsen's employment of all the kinds of communication possible in drama. Words and sub-text, the setting and the invisible, eliminated or superseded drafts upon which Ibsen worked forward to his final form supply a 'complex variable' capable of all the modulations recently chronicled in Daniel Haakonsen's *Henrik Ibsen, mennesket og kunstneren* [1981].

The original Nora, Betty Hennings, had begun her career as a ballerina; one of Ibsen's final inspirations, Nora's tarantella, embodies the heroine's terror and despair, while concentrating her power as Eve, the prime delight and temptress of men. Like the dance of Anitra in *Peer Gynt,* the dance of the Capri fishergirl belongs to an untamed Southern scene, but it has now been transported from Egypt to the cosy little home with its stove, draped table and upright piano, from which the dancer will depart into a Norwegian night.

The delicious life-giving power radiating from Nora must be controlled and kept jealously for her male circle: 'You and papa have done me a grave wrong', she finally tells her husband. Nora's forging of her dying father's signature has outraged her husband equally as a lawyer and as President of the Bank; but to her the gold of his wedding ring has become a bigger fraud, since the President is found to be spiritually bankrupt, totally self-deceived.

Livsglaeden, that untranslateable word, the fountain of life, dances in the faded images of the little skylark, the little squirrel; an actress can still embody it. Nowhere else in Ibsen do the lineaments of animal desire show as plainly as in Torvald Helmer's 'Don't want to? don't want to? aren't I your husband?' Payment on the nail is the protector's right; it is no 'demand of the ideal'.

Whatever harsh privation his new urban environment inflicted on man's primal energies, the child-wife and father-husband relation, that popular model for happy marriages in the mid-nineteenth century, immensely fortified the home as enclosure, cradle and prison. The skylark, the pet squirrel plays in a cage. At the end, Torvald's magnanimous act of forgiving his wife leaves her in exactly the position that he had seen as being his own under the blackmailer's power:

> Here I am, in the grip of a man without a conscience; he can do whatever he likes with me, demand anything he wants, order me about just as he chooses . . . and I daren't breathe a word.

The happy state of affairs to which Torvald later looks forward was a sort of spiritual cannibalism: 'Open your whole heart to me, and I shall become both your will-power and your conscience.' At the beginning, he had been forbidding his baby doll to eat macaroons or do mending in the drawing-room; he kept the key of the letter-box in his pocket, and when Nora inadvertently let slip a word of criticism, he straightway asserted his authority over her by dispatching Krogstad's letter of dismissal. For once he and Krogstad agree as lawyers in thinking that Nora's disappearance or suicide would not absolve him from possible accusations of having instigated her forgery. Nora's rejection of his sexual approach is dismissed with 'What's this? You've played the fool with me long enough, little Nora.' Finally, he opens her last letter from Krogstad, refusing to give it her. Her childish pet name (she was christened Eleanora, as Ibsen explained to his family, who gave that name to his grand-daughter) means that to translate 'Nora', something like 'Nolly-dolly' is needed.

The eternal child-wife must remain unconscious of the sexual implications of her own pretty games whilst she daydreams about legacies from elderly admirers. She is expert at undressing herself in imagination for Dr Rank. She dresses up and plays parts for Torvald almost like Harold Pinter's girls. In Ibsen's first draft she reveals that her father liked her to write poetry and learn French, but Torvald preferred dramatic recitations, and disapproved of French literature; his own fantasies of secret mistresses and bridal nights, revealed in his cups, come out of cheap novelettes. Dr Rank slips into calling her 'Nora' but the truly familiar 'du' is reserved for the men between each other, the two women together, and the husband and wife; three different linkings of the threads. Inside 'Nolly-dolly' another self is growing up. She may enjoy playing at secrets, the secrets of the Christmas tree; but her copying work (in the first draft *not* a secret from Torvald) makes her feel 'almost like a man'; and at the news of Torvald's power to dismiss such bank employees as Krogstad, she feels an impulse to swear.

The audience is never told of the emergent adult growing in the chrysalis of the doll's house; they are left to fill her in, or fill her out. Her unconscious growth towards maturity is accompanied by self-delusive dreams of Torvald, the chivalrous knight-errant; and by blank disregard for the concerns of others. When her instinct to love and cherish is in collision with brute facts, she cannot bear to hurt, and would rather lie. She is not alone in this.

> There wasn't the slightest chance that they could go to the lighthouse tomorrow, Mr Ramsay snapped out irascibly.
> How did he know? she asked. The wind often changed. The extraordinary irrationality of her remark, the folly of women's minds enraged him. She flew in the face of facts, made his children hope what was utterly out of the question, in effect, told lies. He stamped his foot on the stone 'Damn you' he said . . . To pursue truth with such astonishing lack of consideration for other people's feelings, to rend the thin veils of civilisation so wantonly, so brutally, was to her so horrible an outrage of human decency that, without replying, dazed and blinded, she bent her head as if to let the pelt of jagged hail, the drench of dirty water, batter her unrebuked. There was nothing left to be said. [Virginia Woolf, *To The Lighthouse*, 1927]

Nora begs Krogstad to think of her children, and his reply 'Did you or your husband think of mine?' is quite as devastating as Torvald's 'I am saved, Nora, I am saved', when he finds the fatal IOU has been returned. (In the first draft he says 'We are saved'.)

In a letter to Brandes, written as early as 1871, Ibsen had described the scientists and artists of every age as showing a family likeness—the artist possessing as instinct or intuition what the scientist learnt as knowledge. In the psychology of everyday life Ibsen and Strindberg anticipated Freud, who was himself later to comment on the 'case' of Rebekka West [in ***Rosmersholm***].

Since *A Doll's House* is not psychiatry but drama, the whole plot is woven in a network of relationships. The characters are symbiotically linked so that the minor figures supply a 'feed' to the main figures at a much deeper level than that of the narrative.

Rank and Krogstad are both old school friends of Torvald, Kristine of Nora; each presents a shadow side of the twin. The cross-relationships become a closed system. We do not know what Torvald's chief clerk is like, the details of Rank's practice were suppressed; we do not know whether Nora's childbirths were hard or easy, or what was the character of Krogstad's first wife. But we know that Kristine has been forced by necessity to develop her masculine qualities, to become a breadwinner (also, earlier, to sell herself in the marriage-market). The hard, cold insight which makes her tell Krogstad she won't resign the job at the bank in which she has displaced him 'for that wouldn't help you at all' created what is eventually Nora's equally hard, cold insight into her own situation. Kristine deliberately stops Krogstad from claiming back his letter of disclosure; replacing Dr Rank as ruthless experimenter, she detonates the explosion. Yet Kristine herself is hungry for a home, hungry to be needed, as Nora is hungry for freedom. She had long ago broken Krogstad as Nora breaks Torvald ('I felt as though the ground were cut from under my feet') but now the family for whom she sacrificed herself are no longer in need of her, she feels desolate and empty. In the first draft she was still supporting her brothers; this detracts from her egoistic energy, as she greets the future in words that anticipate Nora's. Tidying up a little, and putting ready her outdoor clothes, to meet Krogstad who is waiting below:

> What a change! O what a change! [literally a turning in the road]. People to work for—people to live for. A home that needs to *feel* like home! Well, now I'll set to, straight away. [In the first draft, 'We'll set to'] . . . I wish they'd hurry! Ah, there they are! Get my things.

But the competent Kristine radiates from no fountain of life; 'she's a bore, that woman', says Torvald. Malice would recall the epigram 'She lives for others. You can tell the others by the hunted look in their eyes.' When Nora comes in after putting off her fancy dress, Torvald cries 'What's this? Not going to bed? You've changed?', and she replies 'Yes, Torvald, I've changed.' There is no verbal echo in the Norwegian, as there is in English, but to dress for a journey links the two scenes dramatically and in action. As Kristine finds a city home, Nora sets out for her birthplace, in search of herself.

In her last speech Nora brings together her whole life, the dead father and her eight years marriage 'with a stranger' so that the past looms into the present at several levels, not only at the one of her dangerous secret. Torvald reproaches her for her ingratitude, and blames himself for having turned advocate for the defence when sent by his ministry to investigate her father's affairs. Ibsen suppressed the passage from the first draft, where he says that he could find no trace of the 1200 dollars her father was supposed to have given her just before his death, for it would be tactless to enquire why Torvald, the lawyer, did not check fully the details of a transaction from which so unexpectedly he had benefited. An audience should not have its notice drawn to the inconsistency. It has rightly been allowed to feel, earlier, that Nora has some basis for her dreams of Torvald's chivalry in the kindness he had shown her 'poor papa'.

As we never hear about anyone outside the charmed circle of home, so the close detail and meshing of the foreground distinguish *A Doll's House* from its immediate predecessor, *Pillars of the Community* (1877). Here women's rights are shown in a feminine group ranging from the emancipated Lona to the patient Martha, who, like Solveig in *Peer Gynt,* sits at home spinning and waiting for her lover to return. Though Ibsen had begun the art of elimination and of carving in high relief, Bernick's relations with his whole community dominate. (The women do not supply the action of the play.) A large cast of nineteen are found flowing in and out of the garden-room at Bernick's. The irony is far more direct ('Just repaired! and in your own yard, Mr Bernick! . . . now if she's been one of those floating coffins you hear about in the bigger countries!'), and is not so fully integrated with the language of stage movement.

By contrast, Torvald's address to Nora through the half-open door as, unknown to him, she is 'changing', allows him in half-soliloquy to cast himself as a hero, till in his inflation he triumphantly reaches the cheap image of a dove rescued from a hawk—almost becoming something birdlike. The script must be his alone—to her earlier cry 'You mustn't take it on yourself!' he had snapped 'Stop play-acting!' Her language from this moment is naked, plain (in contrast to her horror when Dr Rank spoke out to her of his love). But at the end, when Torvald in a mixture of threat and appeal says 'Then only one explanation is possible . . . you don't love me any more', her simple 'No; that's it. Exactly' brings back the angry cross-examining lawyer: 'Then perhaps you can also explain to me?' In the first draft she had attacked Torvald; in the final version she defines and describes, gives orders to her husband, to which he responds with bewildered questions. The last difficult definition of the 'miracle' that their 'common life' (*samliv*) 'might become a marriage' (*ekteskap*) annihilates Torvald as lawyer and as man.

The word's power is extended in its context. The silences of Dr Rank, his 'Thanks for the light', and the black cross above his name on the visiting card that, according to social ritual, has been dropped, anticipate the depth of Nora's own speech. Her inner death does not leave enough relationship to merit reproaches.

These depths belong with Shakespeare's *Macbeth* and [Jean] Racine's *Andromaque*. When Lady Macbeth says 'He that's coming / Must be provided for', or Pyrrhus 'Rien ne vous engage à m'aimer en effet', breaking by his obtuseness the barrier of Hermione's control, then a long-built tension explodes; but Ibsen contrives this in the speech of everyday life. (Lady Macbeth is indeed matter of fact, but the context is high poetry.)

In Ibsen's prose the tensions come partly from the relation between the characters, partly from that between his play and what was expected of such dramas (the model of [Augustin Eugène] Scribe). On stage the first audience, while enjoying the charm of Nora, actually took Torvald's point of view and thought him a decent husband. In the theatre they followed the familiar code which Ibsen was breaking. It was reading that convinced them of his intention. By the time he had finished drafting and redrafting *A Doll's House* the original notes did not apply, and he was justified in saying it was not a question of women's rights. The tensions come from the marriage between the word and its context, and this works as rhythm works in poetry. But the verse rhythms of Ibsen were very simple; it was only in prose that he gained the classic freedom of his great predecessors.

As he said again and again, his resources were within; he created out of himself, yet he did not subsequently impose an interpretation. He would not tell actors how to play their roles, nor tell the audience how Mrs Alving acted with the morphine: 'That everyone must decide for himself.' The plays grew into contexts he did not know. One translation was called 'Breaking a Butterfly'. [Gerhart] Hauptmann wrote 'Before Sunrise', and [Eugène] Brieux 'Damaged Goods' out of *Ghosts;* [Bernard] Shaw put back a lot of theory, and wrote *Candida*.

It is still difficult to accept Ibsen's assertion that he was not depicting Laura Keiler, his disciple, who to take her sick husband to Italy in 1876 had borrowed without his knowledge; and afterwards, when her guarantor fell ill, wrote a poor piece of work which Ibsen refused to recommend to his publisher. It was after this that she desperately forged a cheque; her husband turned on her, tried to take the children and obtain a divorce, for she had collapsed, and put her in a mental hospital with violent patients. Later she went back to him.

On a second occasion Ibsen refused even to make a public denial of any connection between Laura Keiler and his play, when [Georg] Brandes had launched an attack on her. Since Laura Keiler's story was widely known the general public could not fail to make the connection, although for Ibsen the originating story bore no relation to the work he had made. Ibsen was later to say that he did not depict himself in his plays, disclaiming identification with his 'enemy of the people', Dr Stockmann. He risked even more in the later plays, but these were built on enigmas and paradoxes. In *When We Dead Awake* the sculptor describes how he changed his own work.

Something much nearer Laura Keiler's story (and her feminism) appears in the preliminary notes for what was then termed *A Modern Tragedy;* the germinative process produced something very different. In Mrs Keiler's story there was no Dr Rank, no Krogstad, no Mrs Linde, no dramatic context for the events which made the narrative 'line' into a dramatic web.

The play is not a dramatic monologue for Nora with supporting assistance. The great final scene impresses with its truth, but not as a transcript of anything that could actually happen; it is itself the 'miracle' it postulated. Passions are disentangled from the criss-cross tangles of ordinary life; all the characters being at once so closely enmeshed with each other, yet so isolated from any other crowd or chorus figures, the detail is not realistic.

Ibsen said that as well as character, his people must have a fate. Nora's fate is to embrace an unknown future—to carry the bright flame of her vitality into the dark. 'Out into the storm of life' is one of Borkman's most ironic fantasies [in *John Gabriel Borkman*]; Nora seeks a deep solitude. 'It is necessary that I stand alone.'

'I look into myself; there is my battleground', said Ibsen; his characters say the same:

> Within, within! that is my call
> That is the way I must venture. That is my path.
> One's own innermost heart—*that* is the world.
>
> [Innad! innad! Det er ordet!
> Dit gaar veien. Der er sporet!
> Eget hjerte—*det* er kloden.]
>
> [*Brand*]

The characters of Ibsen's plays stem most clearly from his own innermost heart when he has sometimes to drive out minor, gesticulatory, symbolic figures who come irrelevantly. In the first draft of *A Doll's House,* Dr Rank talks of a patient, a miner who blew his own right hand off when in drink. Rank may have his special reasons to be hard on this sort of case. (He thinks social care for social failures is turning Norway into a clinic!) The self-mutilated, the murderer in *Brand,* the conscript in *Peer Gynt,* are almost

as innocent as the victims in *The Wild Duck* and old Foldal in *John Gabriel Borkman.* Brendel challenges Rebekka to chop off her finger or her ear, Hedda's demands on Løvborg have a squalid sequel. Consul Bernick puts the case of the engineer's need to send a workman to almost certain death. Ibsen killed part of himself. Here, more subtly, Torvald's cruelty is closely linked with squeamishness. The ruthless visionary, the expansive self-intoxicated orator, the down-and-out with visions of grandeur, the doomed child, the woman of narrow aims and iron will, the doctor who judges, are all part of Ibsen's inner society. ([William Butler] Yeats termed his own 'the circus animals'.) Some ghosts found local homes in people Ibsen met, others represent only facets of himself; none is simply repeated. The black comedy or satire from *Pillars of the Community* is concentrated in aspects of Torvald.

Ibsen had freed himself, at the cost of exile, from years of humiliating subservience in theatres at Oslo and Bergen. He had learnt the craft as a junior stage-manager, who also wrote to order: cheap reproductions of Romanticism gave models for his ideals of Norwegian nationalism. His history plays developed a very limited originality, and it was only after eleven years and five plays that he broke free in *Love's Comedy* (1862). Two years later he left for Rome where he wrote *Brand,* declaring the truest form of love is hate.

A Doll's House returns to Norway's urban scene, but also transforms the elements of the well-made plays on which he had toiled so long. It retains old melodramatic tricks, object the sensitive critics of the twentieth century. Rather, it is [Victorien] Sardou *plus,* Scribe *plus,* Ibsen's stagiest work. The characters think they are living in the theatre, they make up cheap plays for themselves but find they are in a different drama. Stage satire does not prevent the use of basic theatrical experience. Ibsen had lived thirteen years in the Norwegian doll's house and written seven plays before he slammed the door.

A Doll's House was composed in Italy where he had gone on his first emancipation—it remained for him the land where feelings were released. The final draft was completed by the sea, always for him a source of primal energies. (For ten years, living in Germany, he had denied himself the sea.) The tarantella of the Capri fishergirl must have come out of his surroundings; he was living in the beautiful little city whence [John] Webster's Duchess of Malfi took her title, but this earlier feminist rebel could not have been known to him.

The successive drafts are Ibsen's substitute for stage rehearsals (which in his day were perfunctory). Today, a director may try out something in rehearsal, only to discard it. Even when a play begins its run considerable modifications to the text, as well as to blocking and presentation, evolve from the effects of full performance. It is not unknown for a whole set to be changed.

If Norway and Scribe had played Torvald to Ibsen's Nora, his exorcism gave him a figure which he grew to know ever more distinctly as an individual. One day he told Susannah, his wife, that he had seen Nora; she came to him and put her hand on his shoulder. Her hands were important (he even broke through his usual amenability to object of one actress that her hands were not right for the part). In an early draft she suddenly sees them as criminal, and shrinks with horror as she decks the Christmas tree ('Not with these hands!'). Her hysteria takes the form of stroking a muff and crying 'Pretty, pretty gloves!'

Ibsen told Susannah that she was wearing a blue woollen dress; blue was his favorite colour. As an old man, he guiltily conspired with his beautiful daughter-in-law, Bergliot, to buy an expensive set of blue velvet curtains for his dreary apartment. (Susannah was conspicuously lacking in the gift of home-making, shared by many of Ibsen's fascinating women.)

Laura Keiler in 1871 had received from Ibsen that telling observation 'Intellectually, man is a long-sighted animal . . . we see most clearly at a distance; details distract; one must remove oneself from what one wants to describe; one describes the summer best on a winter day'. He continued, 'It is not a matter of willing to go in this direction, but of willing what one absolutely must because one is oneself and cannot do otherwise.'

One sees society best in solitude perhaps. Ibsen's final version, after a long gestation, usually came quickly. After 1877 the regular rhythm evolved of one play every two years, with about two months in late summer and early autumn for the final shaping. It was a natural rhythm, like breathing or sleeping, that came at maturity, at first in a controlled way. Other rhythms, like swimming or riding, often become instinctive with practice.

In his verses **'The Portrait of the Artist at Home'**, Ibsen described 'his children', his creations dancing round him, living a life of their own, rosy and fresh as if from a bath; if he betrays his presence, the play stops. All theatre—in *A Doll's House* metatheatre also—for him takes the form of a children's game (hide-and-seek). The play had taken hold of him, he accepts its autonomy 'living to live in a world of time beyond me . . . lips parted, the hope, the new ships'. T. S. Eliot's poem about the integration of his own art with that of the past drew from Shakespeare the vision of a girl, a daughter:

> What is this face, less clear, and clearer,
> The pulse in the arm, less strong and stronger—
> Given or lent? More distant than stars and
>   nearer than the eye . . . this form, this face,
>   this life
> Living to live in a world of time beyond me.
>   [*Marina*]

At the price of deep solitude, total insulation, the liberation of imaginative forms results in an orchestration of their actions which comes from the depths. Ibsen had said **'Brand** began to grow within me like an embryo', but it was at first as a poem, not a drama. The dramatic form suddenly asserted itself. Ibsen was a dramatist as Chopin was a pianist; he could use no other form. But Ibsen wrote concertos and symphonies, not sonatas; he remained free from the actual presence of the theatre, yet clearly bound to it. In the title of *A Doll's House* both his separation from and his ingestion of the theatre where he had learnt his trade is faintly adumbrated; for to look into the peep-

show of the nineteenth century's picture-stage is indeed to look into a doll's house (with furniture painted on the backcloth). Not as the result of planning, but of steady, patient work on experience that has been 'lived through'— as he phrased it—the final form emerged; imperative, autonomous, a mimesis that generates new forms of mimesis, with their own life, within the audience and through the years.

Creative opportunities for this third mimesis by the audience are still open. (For example, in this age when racial inequalities have largely replaced sexual inequalities as ground for public concern, the effect of having a white Torvald and a black Nora might be worth some director's experiment.)

The integration of conscious and unconscious functions in the verbal and non-verbal languages of the play generates valid new performance in the live theatre. In a book much studied by Ibsen, it is said of wisdom that 'remaining in herself, she maketh all things new'. (pp. 81-91)

> *M. C. Bradbrook, " 'A Doll's House' and the Unweaving of the Web," in her* Women and Literature, 1779-1982: The Collected Papers of Muriel Bradbrook, Vol. 2, *Barnes and Noble, 1982, pp. 81-92.*

Carol Strongin Tufts   (essay date 1986)

[*Tufts argues that examining* A Doll's House *in terms of the "narcissistic personality" as defined by modern psychologists can help highlight Nora's complexity, explain the actions of the secondary characters, and elucidate the drama's theme of isolation. The critic maintains that, beyond mere self-absorption or preoccupation with their problems, the characters in* A Doll's House *demonstrate delusions of self-importance that drive every element of the plot.*]

I am not a member of the Women's Rights League. Whatever I have written has been without any conscious thought of making propaganda. I have been more the poet and less the social philosopher than people generally seem inclined to believe. . . . To me it has seemed a problem of mankind in general. And if you read my books carefully you will understand this. . . . My task has been the *description of humanity*. To be sure, whenever such a description is felt to be reasonably true, the reader will read his own feelings and sentiments into the work of the poet. These are then attributed to the poet; but incorrectly so. Every reader remolds the work beautifully and neatly, each according to his own personality. Not only those who write but also those who read are poets. They are collaborators. [Henrik Ibsen, *Ibsen: Letters and Speeches,* Evert Sprinchorn, ed., 1964]

To look again at Ibsen's famous and often-quoted words— his assertion that *A Doll's House* was not intended as propaganda to promote the cause of women's rights—is to realize the sarcasm aimed by the playwright at those nineteenth-century "collaborators" who insisted on viewing his play as a treatise and Nora, his heroine, as the romantic standard-bearer for the feminist cause. Yet there is also a certain irony implicit in such a realization, for directors, actors, audiences, and critics turning to this play a little over one hundred years after its first performance bring with them the historical, cultural, and psychological experience which itself places them in the role of Ibsen's collaborators. Because it is a theatrical inevitability that each dramatic work which survives its time and place of first performance does so to be recast in productions mounted in succeeding times and different places, *A Doll House* can never so much be simply reproduced as it must always be re-envisioned. And if the spectacle of a woman walking out on her husband and children in order to fulfill her "duties to [her]self " is no longer the shock for us today that it was for audiences at the end of the nineteenth century, a production of *A Doll House* which resonates with as much immediacy and power for us as it did for its first audiences may do so through the discovery within Ibsen's text of something of our own time and place. For in *A Doll House,* as Rolf Fjelde has written [in his introduction to Ibsen's *The Complete Major Prose Plays,* 1978], "[i]t is the entire house . . . which is on trial, the total complex of relationships, including husband, wife, children, servants, upstairs and downstairs, that is tested by the visitors that come and go, embodying aspects of the inescapable reality outside." And a production which approaches that reality through the experience of Western culture in the last quarter of the twentieth century may not only discover how uneasy was Ibsen's relationship to certain aspects of the forces of Romanticism at work in his own society, but, in so doing, may also come to fashion a *Doll House* which shifts emphasis away from the celebration of the Romantic belief in the sovereignty of the individual to the revelation of an isolating narcissism—a narcissism that has become all too familiar to us today.

The characters of *A Doll House* are, to be sure, not alone in dramatic literature in being self-preoccupied, for self-preoccupation is a quality shared by characters from Oedipus to Hamlet and on into modern drama. Yet if a contemporary production is to suggest the narcissistic self-absorption of Ibsen's characters, it must do so in such a way as to imply motivations for their actions and delineate their relationships with one another. Thus it is important to establish a conceptual framework which will provide a degree of precision for the use of the term 'narcissism' in this discussion so as to distinguish it from the kind of self-absorption which is an inherent quality necessarily shared by all dramatic characters. For that purpose, it is useful to turn to the criteria established by the Task Force on Nomenclature and Statistics of the American Psychiatric Association [*DSM-III: Diagnostic Criteria Draft,* 1978] for diagnosing the narcissistic personality:

  A. Grandiose sense of self-importance and uniqueness, e.g., exaggerates achievements and talents, focuses on how special one's problems are.
  B. Preoccupation with fantasies of unlimited success, power, brilliance, beauty, or ideal love.
  C. Exhibitionistic: requires constant attention and admiration.
  D. Responds to criticism, indifference of oth-
  ers, or defeat with either cool indifference, or with marked feelings of rage, inferiority, shame, humiliation, or emptiness.
  E. At least two of the following are characteristics of disturbances in interpersonal relationships:
    (1) Lack of empathy: inability to recognize how others feel, e.g., unable to appreciate the distress of someone who is seriously ill.
    (2) Entitlement: expectation of special favors without assuming reciprocal responsibilities, e.g., surprise and anger that people won't do what he wants.
    (3) Interpersonal exploitiveness: takes advantage of others to indulge own desires for self-aggrandizement, with disregard for the personal integrity and rights of others.
    (4) Relationships characteristically vacillate between the extremes of over-idealization and devaluation.

These criteria, as they provide a background against which to consider Nora's relationship with both Kristine Linde and Dr. Rank, will serve to illuminate not only those relationships themselves, but also the relationship of Nora and her husband which is at the center of the play. Moreover, if these criteria are viewed as outlines for characterization—but not as reductive psychoanalytic constructs leading to "case studies"—it becomes possible to discover a Nora of greater complexity than the totally sympathetic victim turned romantic heroine who has inhabited most productions of the play. And, most important of all, as Nora and her relationships within the walls of her "doll house" come to imply a paradigm of the dilemma of all human relationships in the greater society outside, the famous sound of the slamming door may come to resonate even more loudly for us than it did for the audiences of the nineteenth century with a profound and immediate sense of irony and ambiguity, an irony and ambiguity which could not have escaped Ibsen himself.

Thus to take up first the relationship of Nora and Kristine Linde, a reading of the initial conversation between the two women reveals a certain narcissistic motivation behind Nora's response to her old friend. A director staging the scene might here discover a woman who becomes progressively exhibitionistic as she displays her own happiness and good fortune in the face of Kristine's misery, a woman who, filled with a sense of her own importance in managing the loan which saved Torvald's life, makes Kristine into the audience so long denied her, a kind of mirror to reflect her own self-admiration back to her. Although she makes use of Kristine as a confidante, she appears to have little sense of her as a person separate from herself and no real empathy for her suffering. In fact, her initial treatment of her suggests a self-absorption which borders on callousness as she chatters away about her own happiness and good fortune to this childhood friend who, left with nothing, has come to ask a job of her husband.

Although it may be argued that her initial conversation with Kristine is little more than a part of the machinery of the well-made play, providing the necessary "occasion" that enables the playwright to set out his exposition, Ibsen could have created a Nora who displays genuine empathy and compassion for her childhood friend. Instead, it is possible to find a character whose self-preoccupation leads her, at best, to trivialize and, at worst, to dismiss the situation and suffering of her friend, as in this first conversation between the two women:

> MRS. LINDE: (*in a dispirited and somewhat hesitant voice*). Hello, Nora.
>
> NORA: (*uncertain*). Hello—
>
> MRS. LINDE: You don't recognize me.
>
> NORA: No, I don't know—but wait, I think— (*Exclaiming.*) What! Kristine! Is it really you?
>
> MRS. LINDE: Yes, it's me.
>
> NORA: Kristine! To think I didn't recognize you. But then, how could I? (*More quietly.*) How you've changed, Kristine!
>
> MRS. LINDE: Yes, no doubt I have. In nine—ten long years.
>
> NORA: Is it so long since we met! Yes, it's all of that. Oh, these last eight years have been a happy time, believe me. And so now you've come in to town, too. Made the long trip in the winter. That took courage. . . . To enjoy yourself over Christmas, of course. Oh, how lovely! Yes, enjoy ourselves, we'll do that. . . .
>
> (Act I)

And although she goes on to remark that Kristine has grown paler and thinner since the last time they met, Nora essentially glosses over the implications of the great change in her friend to bubble over with her own happiness and to assume that because she will be enjoying herself this Christmas, Kristine must be in town to do the same.

While there is, on one level, a certain degree of nervousness here in Nora's initial reaction to Kristine—a desire to hide her shock at Kristine's changed appearance through a kind of good-natured obtuseness—there may also be, on a deeper level for an actress playing the part, a wish to avoid the need to acknowledge the reasons for the change she sees in the other woman. And what such a wish comes to imply as the conversation continues is her failure to see Kristine as a separate person, a person whose pain is as real, as legitimate, as her own joy. Here is Nora, who has made her entrance this Christmas Eve "*humming happily to herself,*" carrying "*an armload of packages,*" possessing money enough to tell the delivery boy to "keep the change" for the crown which she gives him. In her own home and about to become financially well-off as Kristine is not, Nora finds her attractiveness and vitality daily verified by the attentions of her husband and Dr. Rank. In contrast, Kristine, homeless and dressed in traveling clothes, is a woman worn out and devoid of all but the most modest of expectations, her complete exhaustion exemplified by the fact that she has been passed coming up the stairs by Dr. Rank, himself dying of congenital degeneration of the spine and so not the fastest person on his feet.

Kristine, of course, is used by Ibsen as a foil to Nora, who will become homeless precisely as her old friend acquires a home. She will find herself alone in the world just as Kristine ends her own loneliness in marriage to Krogstad. Yet as the play begins, Nora, caught up in her satisfaction in the prospect of being able to pay off the loan and in her joy and pride in her home and family and in Torvald's promotion at the bank, only acknowledges that Kristine has become a widow *after* she has remarked on how happy the last eight years have been for herself. "Oh, I knew it, of course," Nora admits; "I read it in the papers. Oh, Kristine, you must believe me; I often thought of writing you then, but I kept postponing it, and something always interfered." But Nora's stress here remains on herself. As Kristine goes on to say that she now has nothing, neither children nor money, she can respond, "So completely alone. How terribly hard that must be for you," only immediately to add, "I have three lovely children. You can't see them now; they're out with the maid." Consistent with her behavior up to this point, she plays lip service to Kristine's hardships one minute only to flaunt her own blessings the next, for Nora, who adores seeing her children, assumes that her impoverished and childless friend must adore seeing them too and never supposes that the sight of those children might instead intensify Kristine's childlessness and desolation. Although she does go on to insist that Kristine "tell" her "everything," for, Nora says, "I don't want to be selfish. I want to think only of you today," she cannot help adding, "But there *is* something I must tell you. Did you hear the wonderful luck we had recently?" And with this question, Nora has managed again to turn the subject of the conversation back to herself.

Now Nora can go on to report that Torvald has been made manager of the bank. Ironically, this is probably the only news in which Kristine has any real interest, since it is possible that she has endured Nora's self-congratulatory chatter only because it is she who is Kristine's entrée to Torvald, the successful man who might be prevailed upon to help her to find a job. What is most important here, however, is that Nora seems unable, for all her stated desire to do so, to focus on Kristine herself. It is only after Nora has told how "light and happy" she feels, for it will be "lovely to have stacks of money and not a care in the world"—this to someone who has been left with nothing, "[n]ot even a sense of loss to feed on"—and has talked about the difficult period of Torvald's illness, that she pulls herself up short to say, "But how disgusting of me—I'm talking of nothing but my own affairs." Yet so far, Nora has done little else.

For a while after this the conversation turns to Kristine, who describes her last three years as "one endless workday without rest." Yet now with her mother dead and her brothers able to provide for themselves, Kristine can only reply to Nora's "How free you must feel" with "No—only unspeakably empty. Nothing to live for now." To try to fill up that emptiness, as well as out of financial necessity, she has come to town to find a "steady job, some office work." But it is as if Nora has managed not to hear the desperation in her words and, identifying only with the work that she too has had to take on, says, "Oh, but Kristine, that's so dreadfully tiring, and you already look so

tired. It would be much better for you if you would go off
to a bathing resort." Again, Nora's response, as it suggests
her inability to recognize how Kristine feels, also suggests
her narcissism, for although Nora can understand having
had to work hard—after all, she has had to do that herself—she seems unable to comprehend the utter desolation
which exhausts Kristine now that her "burdens" have
been removed. And it is the callousness implicit in that response which provokes Kristine's bitter reply: "I have no
father to give me travel money, Nora."

As Kristine finally makes her realize that she has come to
ask Torvald's assistance in finding a job, Nora jumps at the
chance to be her intermediary, not only because she is "so
eager to help," but also, for a director and an actress responding to Ibsen's suggestion of her narcissism, because
she can use the opportunity to demonstrate the power she
has over Torvald. "Just leave it to me," she tells Kristine,
"I'll bring it up so delicately—find something attractive
to humor him with. Oh, I'm so eager to help you." To this
Kristine replies, in a line heavy with sarcasm, "How very
kind of you, Nora, to be so concerned over me—doubly
kind, considering you really know so little of life's burdens
yourself."

Kristine's reply, however, is not just an understandable response to the recital she has had to endure of Nora's happiness and good fortune, nor is it simply an indication of
her self-admitted bitterness, for there may also be an implicit sense of pride here which points to her own narcissism. Beneath the barely disguised sarcasm of her words
is the suggestion of Kristine's sense of her own importance, her belief that her problems and her sacrifices have
not only been greater than those of Nora, but that they
are, by implication, unique in the world, that they make
her somehow special, superior. If Kristine's line is read
with such a suggestion in mind—and if she herself is considered from what, for an actress playing the part, could
very well be her own view of Nora's treatment of her
throughout the play as little more than a prop, or convenience, in a relationship without mutual concern or reciprocity—the motivation Ibsen has provided for her actions at the end of the play takes on a new complexity as
she deters Krogstad from asking for the return of the letter
that has been the source of Nora's agony.

On the surface of it, Torvald must, of course, read that letter, since that is what brings about the play's denouement,
and Kristine is speaking for Ibsen when she says, "I've
seen such incredible things in this house. Helmer's got to
learn everything; this dreadful secret [Nora's forging of
her father's signature in order to procure the loan] has to
be aired; those two have to come to a full understanding;
all these lies and evasions can't go on" (Act III). Also, in
terms of the play's structure, it is obvious that Nora treats
Kristine as little more than a prop because that is the way
Ibsen treats her: it is Kristine's presence which provides
the opportunity for Nora to express those feelings which
she must keep hidden from Torvald. Yet beneath the matter of the play's mechanics, it is possible to see Kristine's
own narcissism as a subconscious force which compels her
not only to desire some revenge against the friend who has
always been luckier and more privileged than she—who

has, in fact, ironically turned out to have problems that
surpass her own in their uniqueness—but which also
causes her to feel firm in her conviction that her hardships
and suffering have conferred moral superiority upon her:
in her own eyes, she believes herself absolutely justified in
knowing what will be best for the Helmers' marriage.

To see narcissism as a subconscious motive for Kristine's
action here is also to see a certain irony in her desire to
marry Krogstad. Another of the gears in the machinery
of Ibsen's well-made play, that marriage, founded as it
seems to be on truth and equality between the partners,
is meant to function as the foil to the marriage of the Helmers, the realistically attainable possibility which they
have failed to achieve. Yet as she proposes that "we two
shipwrecked people . . . reach across to each other,"
Kristine tells Krogstad,

> I have to go on living. All my born days, as long
> as I can remember, I've worked, and it's been my
> best and my only joy. But now I'm completely
> alone in the world; it frightens me to be so empty
> and lost. To work for yourself—there's no joy in
> that. Nils, give me something—someone to work
> for.
>
> (Act III)

By placing the emphasis here on the urgency of Kristine's
own needs, an actress may find that what she is really asking is that Krogstad return to her the sense of self that she
lost when her mother died and her brothers became self-
sufficient. When Krogstad, all too aware of his status as
social outcast, can only reply, "And do you really have the
courage then?" Kristine's answer again places her own
longing first as she says, "I need to have someone to care
for," adding only after this, "and your children need a
mother. We both need each other."

With the hint of narcissistic motivation for Kristine's proposal to Krogstad comes the irony that what she is attempting to reproduce is the one situation that made her
feel unique and important, for she will care and work and
sacrifice for the morally crippled Krogstad and his children as she had cared and worked and sacrificed for her
invalid mother and younger brothers. Such a relationship
is the only one that she desires, the only one she can envision, not because she is inherently selfless, but because it
allows her to maintain an idealized image of herself. Krogstad may say, "I don't believe all this. It's just some hysterical feminine urge to go out and make a noble sacrifice,"
and Kristine may answer, "Have you ever found me to be
hysterical?" (Act III), but earlier she has also told him,
"you've never understood me." The irony here is that such
understanding might allow him to know that her "urge to
go out and make a noble sacrifice" is not motivated by hysteria so much as it may be motivated by the narcissistic
need to recreate the one situation that has made her feel
important and unique and without which she feels empty,
a situation in which he and his children will serve as props
for her own idealized sense of self.

It is that air of self-important uniqueness that lies behind
Kristine's condescending tone in remarking Nora's kindness toward her—considering, as Kristine sees it, how little of "life's burdens" the other woman really knows—and

it is her attitude that prompts Nora to confess the "big thing": that it was she who raised the money necessary for the trip to Italy that saved Torvald's life (Act I). When the astonished Kristine asks her how she could have obtained the money, Nora replies, "I could have gotten it from some admirer or other. After all, a girl with my ravishing appeal—" and later goes on to speak of her fantasy of a "rich old gentleman who had fallen in love with me . . . [a]nd . . . died, and when his will was opened, there in big letters it said, 'All my fortune shall be paid over in cash, immediately, to that enchanting Mrs. Nora Helmer'." Told only half in jest, this fantasy not only foreshadows the scene Nora will play out with Dr. Rank in Act II, but it also reveals Nora's keen awareness of the power of her "ravishing appeal."

It is that "appeal" which she knows to be, but will not acknowledge as the basis of her relationship with Dr. Rank: the sexually charged subtext of this "friendship" in which Nora can be seductive and Rank seduced, but only so long as neither admits that this is what is really happening. Even more important, however, it is also that "ravishing appeal" which Nora knows to be at the center of her relationship with Torvald, for as she goes on to tell Kristine about the loan, she speaks of it as a secret to be held in reserve for "sometime, years from now, when I'm no longer so attractive . . . when Torvald loves me less than now, when he stops enjoying my dancing and dressing up and reciting for him." And although Nora immediately dismisses this possibility as "ridiculous! That'll never happen," it is her knowledge that her "beautiful, happy home" is built on that "appeal," the perfect complement to Torvald's "masculine pride," that suggests the mutually narcissistic terms of their marriage. Moreover, Nora's seemingly sudden transformation from the "little lark" of the first two acts to the determined woman of the third act who is able to slam the door on her "doll house" and walk out into the world becomes much less sudden if it is seen that the narcissistic terms of that marriage cease to be mutual from the moment Torvald reacts to Krogstad's letter.

As Nora talks to Kristine, admirable as her resourcefulness in obtaining and repaying the loan may be, her confession implies a kind of competition over who has endured the most and worked the hardest and ends as a device to elicit the other person's astonishment and awe. If Kristine takes pride in her sacrifices for her mother and brothers, Nora not only proves that she too has been capable of sacrifice, but that the terms of that sacrifice have been much more daring. Like Kristine, Nora views her problems and her deeds as unique; and although it is true that her obtaining of the loan has indeed been unique insofar as she is a woman in a society in which women, to look ahead to the resonant line from *Hedda Gabler,* "don't do such things," her act of forgery has been committed by others before her: Krogstad, after all, is at the bottom of the social ladder because, as he says, "it was nothing more and nothing worse that I once did—and it wrecked my whole reputation" (Act I). As for Nora's hardships—her husband's illness, her scrimping and saving and working at copying at night to repay the loan—they, too, are not unique, for the mere presence of Kristine, as well as of Dr. Rank, attests to human suffering as a commonplace occur-

rence. And it is Nora's failure to respond to Kristine's pain with any real degree of empathy that hints at a narcissism which will also carry over into her relationship with Dr. Rank. It becomes, therefore, quite in keeping with Nora's character that she can say as Kristine leaves to see about finding a room, "What a shame we're so cramped here, but it's quite impossible for us to—" (Act I)— sentiments echoed by Torvald in Act III as he returns late at night from the masquerade party upstairs and tells Kristine, "I hope you get home all right. I'd be happy to— but you don't have far to go." Although Kristine may be useful as an audience and a mirror to reflect Nora back to herself, the presence of such a house guest would be an inconvenience which she prefers not to have intrude on her holiday. Having listened to, but not really having taken in Kristine's account of her emotional and financial impoverishment, she will not put herself out to make room for her in her "beautiful, happy home."

A director and an actress developing the suggestion of narcissism in Nora's first conversation with Kristine can carry that suggestion further in Act II in the scene which takes place between Nora and Dr. Rank. Here Rank becomes for Nora the "rich old gentleman" of her fantasy, the way out of Krogstad's blackmail. The crux of this scene involves Nora's sexual teasing of Rank, her hitting him *lightly on the ear* with the flesh-colored silk stockings she has been dangling before him under the pretext of displaying part of the costume she will wear to dance the tarantella on the following night. The effect of all this is that Rank responds to her request for "an exceptionally big favor," a "great proof" of his "friendship," with the confession of his love for her, a confession which first causes her to call for a lamp to be brought in and then to say, "Ah, dear Dr. Rank, that was really mean of you."

In order to see how this scene works in terms of the narcissism that has already been implied by Nora's conversation with Kristine, it is first necessary to acknowledge Rank's most important functions in the mechanism of Ibsen's well-made play. As is obvious, Ibsen has created Rank, this friend of both husband and wife, as a means of clarifying the play's main issue and building the case which must culminate in Nora's departure from her husband and children. Thus Rank serves to emphasize Torvald's limitations, his shallowness, and his lack of courage and compassion, for Rank, who knows that he is dying and that the process will not be a pretty one, knows too that Torvald "with his sensitivity" has "a sharp distaste for anything ugly," and so tells Nora, "I don't want him near my sickroom. . . . I won't have him there. Under no condition. I'll lock my door to him" (Act II). Also, as the walking emblem of the sins of the parents being visited upon their children, Rank's dying of congenital syphilis helps to provide motivation for Nora's decision to leave her children, since she believes that "The way I am now, I'm no use to them" (Act III), an idea reinforced in her mind by Torvald's earlier pronouncement, made in reference to Krogstad, that "It's usually the mother's influence that's dominant" on children who "go bad" (Act I). Moreover, Nora's friendship with Rank also reveals how much of herself her relationship with her husband has cost her, for as she tells Kristine,

Torvald loves me beyond words, and, as he puts it, he'd like to keep me all to himself. For a long time he'd almost be jealous if I even mentioned any of my old friends back home. So of course I dropped that. But with Dr. Rank I talk a lot about such things, because he likes hearing about them.

(Act II)

It is, therefore, no wonder that Nora can so ironically say in describing to Rank the difference in her feelings for Torvald and for him, "you see, there are some people that one loves most and other people that one would almost prefer being with" (Act II).

Yet the underlying narcissism which has caused Nora to be so tactlessly obtuse in her conversation with Kristine can now be seen as leading her into unconscious cruelty in her manipulation of Rank whom she tantalizes with her silk stockings in a desperate attempt to make fantasy into reality and to transform him into the dreamed-of "rich old gentleman" so taken with her "ravishing appeal" that he becomes her financial savior. In so doing, not only does she exploit his feelings with no regard for his personal integrity—the cost to him of confessing his love and the importance he places on that confession as he tells her, "I swore to myself you should know this before I'm gone"—but she also fails to appreciate the literal reality which has prompted him to speak at all: his knowledge that "Within a month I'll probably be laid out and rotting in the churchyard. . . . But the worst of it is all the other horror before it's over." What angers and appalls Nora is not that Rank loves her, but that in telling her of that love he has done exactly the one thing which she has not wanted him to do, for, as she says, "you came out and told me. That was quite unnecessary. . . . Why did you have to be so clumsy, Dr. Rank! Everything was so good." For the actress playing Nora, the "everything" that was "so good" may be felt as a narcissistic sense of entitlement with its freedom to allow her to bask in Rank's attention and admiration, even to ask "an exceptionally big favor" of him, without ever having to acknowledge her responsibility in eliciting the feelings which she knows, even before he says it, place his "body and soul" at her "command." And thus the final cruelty here becomes her failure to consider how that "everything" must have felt to Rank himself, how what was "so good" for her was, ironically, so bittersweet for him.

To see Nora's behavior in this scene with Rank as being consistent with the narcissism that has already been implied as motivation for many of her words and actions up to this point is to go beyond the need for the usual kind of justification for that behavior such as that offered, for example, by a critic like F. L. Lucas [in his *The Drama of Ibsen and Strindberg,* 1962] who begins with the assumption that "grief is egotistic" so that he may go on to insist:

Nora, under the shadow of her own disaster, cannot really believe in his. Here, indeed, she may seem a little *too* obtuse. She is not callously selfish . . .; she is simply, in her worried distraction, insensitive and blind. And so, self-centred like a child on her own perplexities, but

hoping for help from her old friend, she now slips into innocent coquetries, which kindle this lonely man on the edge of the grave to a guarded declaration of passion.

Yet even Lucas must admit that "it is Nora" who, "in this instant, grows 'ugly'." And though he may rationalize that ugliness by seeing Nora as the victim of a "father-fixation" which causes her to view Rank as a father substitute, "a kind of sugar-daddy" whom she can play with and tease but to whom "she cannot give . . . the sympathetic compassion of a mature woman, only the petulance of a priggish child," this incident of the silk stockings is indeed so jarring to the totally sympathetic romantic view of Nora that its distastefulness may have led Eva Le Gallienne to cut it from her translation of the play.

Complete sympathy for Nora, however, may require cutting all those "ugly" words and actions which Ibsen himself gave her and accepting without criticism the romanticism which she at once embraces and embodies. While it may indeed be true, as Elaine Hoffman Baruch has stated [in "Ibsen's *Doll House:* A Myth for Our Time," *Yale Review* 69, 1980], that Nora "ultimately rejects a romanticism that rests on illusion and fantasy [as] she accepts a more profound romantic value in her assertion of the primacy of the individual over all other claims," it is precisely this "assertion of the primacy of the individual over all other claims" which, as Ibsen has drawn it here, may be seen as causing this character to become as much a victimizer as she is a victim, as much the exploiter of others as she has been exploited by them. What is important, as Patricia Meyer Spacks has pointed out [in "Confrontation and Escape in Two Social Dramas," *Modern Drama* 11, 1968], is to recognize that while "Nora is self-dramatizing too, . . . Ibsen never allows us to accept her at her own valuation. Much of the tension, the vitality, the complexity of Ibsen's play derives from this fact." Moreover, Nora is not the only character engaged in self-dramatization, driven by a need to see an idealized image of herself reflected back to her in the eyes of others. This, after all, is what Kristine has also attempted and, though in one aspect she has failed as the tremendous energy of Nora's need has come to dominate her own, she does finally succeed when Krogstad allows her, in essence, to make her "noble sacrifice" for him and his children. It is this same kind of self-dramatization which also provides much of the motivation for Rank's behavior, not only in his speeches to Nora about his imminent death, but in the staging of his final farewell to the Helmers, complete with the condemned man's request for a last cigar as he leaves to deposit in their mailbox the calling card marked with "a black cross over the name . . . announcing his own death" (Act III).

Thus, as Inga-Stina Ewbank has noted [in "Ibsen's Dramatic Language as a Link between His 'Realism' and His 'Symbolism'," in *Contemporary Approaches to Ibsen,* 1966], "For most of this play, the dialogue brings out what the action implies: that the central characters are all playing parts before each other," so that "the fancy dress ball on the floor above, for which there is no plot-necessity, . . . functions as a telling image of human relationships." And the irony of Rank's final farewell here is that his carefully staged exit has no more than a momentary effect on the Helmers who, as Ewbank has also noted, are themselves involved in the play's "central game, or part, playing [which] is, of course," their "whole marital relationship." Caught up in the scenario of her planned self-sacrifice as she waits for Torvald to read Krogstad's letter and so bring about the "miracle" of which she has been dreaming, Nora can only react to the announcement of Rank's imminent death by transforming it into her own as she tells Torvald, "If it has to happen, then it's best it happens in silence" (Act III). And Rank ceases to exist for her except as the excuse to put Torvald off sexually so that he may at last read his mail. It is Torvald's own narcissistic reaction to Rank's black-marked calling cards which foreshadows his equally narcissistic reaction to Krogstad's letter. Sounding very much like the histrionic Hjalmar Ekdal of Ibsen's later play *The Wild Duck,* Torvald's initial response implies more about the dramatizing self-consciousness of the speaker than it does about any real feeling he might have for the plight of the individual who has occasioned the speech: "Ah, my poor friend!" says Torvald, "Of course I knew he wouldn't be here much longer. But so soon—And then to hide himself away like a wounded animal." For Torvald soon reveals his true feelings as he continues:

> He'd grown right into our lives. I simply can't imagine him gone. He with his suffering and loneliness—like a dark cloud setting off our sunlit happiness. Well, maybe it's best this way. For him, at least. . . . And maybe for us too, Nora. Now we're thrown back on each other, completely. (*Embracing her.*) Oh you, my darling wife, how can I hold you close enough?
>
> (Act III)

Torvald, in effect, immediately proceeds to answer his own question by revealing his cherished romantic fantasy of himself as gallant knight and his wife as damsel in distress: "You know what, Nora—time and again I've wished you were in some terrible danger, just so I could stake my life and soul and everything for your sake." But Torvald's fantasy has also been Nora's own, the "miracle" for which she waits. This shared fantasy, which comes to fail them both, can be seen as the central game of their marriage, the very foundation of the mutual narcissism which has bound them together. And as he reads Krogstad's letter, it is that foundation itself which begins to crumble.

For Torvald, it was Nora's "ravishing appeal"—her "scamper[ing] about and do[ing] tricks" (Act II), but most of all her "innocence" and "helplessness"—which fed his grandiose sense of self-importance, providing him with the constant attention and admiration his narcissism required. Yet because Torvald over-idealized Nora as he over-idealized their marriage itself, the news that his "little lark" has not only not been innocent, but that she has in fact also been capable of action in the world outside the "doll house," can, for an actor playing the part, provide motivation for the instant shift Torvald makes from over-idealization to utter devaluation:

> Oh, what an awful awakening! In all these eight years—she who was my pride and joy—a hypo-

crite, a liar—worse, worse—a criminal! How infinitely disgusting it all is! The shame! . . . Oh, to have to say this to someone I've loved so much! Well, that's done with.

> (Act III)

And it is in that "awful awakening" too that the actor playing Torvald in a contemporary production of the play can come to realize an even deadlier threat that this character feels to his vision of himself, a threat which, like Nora's own action, resides in the world outside the "doll house," for in dealing with Krogstad, she has placed her husband in the power of the one person who refuses to validate his sense of self-importance. Looking at him, Krogstad does not see the powerful man of affairs, the soon-to-be manager of the bank, but his old teenage "crony" still to be addressed on a "first-name basis . . . in front of" all those "others" who possess the ultimate power to confirm or destroy Torvald's image of himself in the greater world outside the "doll house." Thus it is no wonder that all that now concerns the panic-stricken Torvald is "saving the bits and pieces, the appearance," since it is "the appearance" which has always been for him "all that matters."

Yet as Krogstad's second letter arrives and that "appearance" is no longer under threat, though Torvald may shout, "I'm saved. Nora, I'm saved!" the irony is that he has already destroyed the mutual terms of the narcissism which has bound him together with his wife. It is important, therefore, to reconsider the reason for Nora's act in finally leaving Torvald, since that reason may not be nearly so transparent as the assertion of selfhood which most productions of the play have made it—nor as relatively straightforward as a critic such as Baruch, for example, has described it: that is, because he has failed "to live up to her image of him." In fact, that reason finally becomes even more subtle than Torvald's simply laying bare a narcissistic self-concern in which there has been no care for his wife. For Ibsen has provided a much more ironic complexity of motivation for Nora's final action if Torvald, in his own self-concern, is viewed as having essentially denied her the ultimate act that could have completed and made perfect her own idealized vision of herself. Nora may indeed have been awaiting the "miracle" in which her husband was supposed to "step forward, take the blame on" himself "and say: I am the guilty one"; but the real essence of that "miracle" would have been her own response, since as she tells her husband:

> You're thinking I'd never accept such a sacrifice from you? No, of course not. But what good would my protests be against you? That was the miracle I was waiting for, in terror and hope. And to stave that off, I would have taken my life.
>
> (Act III)

As Arthur Ganz has pointed out [in "Miracle and Vine Leaves: An Ibsen Play Rewrought," *PMLA* 94, 1979], "Torvald has been, in one of Ibsen's ultimate ironies, almost as much Nora's 'doll' (the puppet-hero of her dreams) as she has been his. . . ." And the greatest irony of all may be that what that "puppet-hero" has denied her has not been his own sacrifice for her sake, but rather the opportunity to prevent his sacrifice with a more daring one of her own. What was to be accomplished by such a sacrifice is not necessarily, as Ganz has seen it, "the abnegation of the self that she had assented to in her doll's house," but rather the narcissistic affirmation of an idealized self which will never have to face the time when, as Nora has feared from the beginning, "Torvald loves me less than now, when he stops enjoying my dancing and dressing up and reciting for him" (Act I). In sacrificing herself to save her husband, Nora could have remained forever the perfect object of his love.

Thus to follow Ibsen's suggestion of Nora's narcissism throughout the play also makes it possible to see a more subtle irony in Torvald's failure to perform the "miracle" in which she has placed all her hope. For she has been enthralled by a dream of self-sacrifice from the moment Kristine tells her tale of suffering in the service of others, and it is that dream which her husband betrays. Robbed of it and of the idealized self-image that has been at its center, she can only respond to him with the rage which, despite its muted quality, is the mirror image of his own response to Krogstad's letter. Because she has over-idealized Torvald as he has over-idealized her, Nora, as her husband has done before her, utterly devaluates the eight years of their marriage. But though she tells him, "You don't understand me. And I've never understood you either—until tonight" (Act III), the irony is that they have understood each other all too well until tonight when narcissistic need of each to maintain an idealized self-image has come to exclude the identical need of the other.

Stripped of the narcissistic dream of self-sacrifice, Nora now speaks of fulfilling her "Duties to herself"; as she tells Torvald, "I believe that, before all else, I'm a human being, no less than you—or anyway, I ought to try to become one." Yet although our sympathies as an audience are with her as she appears to recognize the hollowness of her former ideal and as she courageously prepares to leave her home so that she may try to "stand completely alone . . . to discover myself and the world out there"—which is to say, to discover an authentic self—Ibsen has imbued Nora's exit from her "doll house" with irony and a certain ambiguity. And that irony and ambiguity are rooted in Nora's own lack of any real substance on which to base her quest as well as in the possibility that the world outside the "doll house" is much the same as the world within its walls.

The fact is, as Spacks has pointed out, that although Nora "now testifies to the need for facing reality . . . she is still supported by an image of herself as heroine, a dream of romantic defiance of society in all its power," as she determines to discover "who's right, the world or I." And it is because Nora has replaced one idealized self-image with another that she may find herself with nothing on which to build an authentic self in a world that, as Ibsen portrays it, is filled with individuals engaged in a masquerade in which there may be nothing beneath the mask. If Nora is seen as remaining as much the narcissist as she has always been, the troublesome issue of the relative ease with which she appears to leave her children can at last be resolved, for her first concern has always been herself. The real irony here, then, is that the woman who only moments ago

was so completely prepared to sacrifice her own life for the sake of her husband ends by calling upon her "duties to herself" and leaves her children, as Marvin Rosenberg has stated [in "Ibsen vs. Ibsen or: Two Versions of *A Doll's House*," *Modern Drama* 12, 1969], "in the hands" of that same husband whom she "knows to be so corrupt [that] she will not even trust herself with him."

Equipped now with the baggage of a new narcissistic self-image, Nora closes the door on the "doll house" which has been her home with Torvald to find herself facing another door which opens into the larger "doll house," the world in which she and all the characters live and move. Taking Ibsen at his "insistence that his individual works should be regarded as parts of a thematic whole, modern Ibsen commentators," as Roslyn Belkin has written ["Prisoners of Convention: Ibsen's 'Other' Women," *Journal of Women's Studies in Literature* 1, No. 2, 1979], "have discerned that, in varying ways, Ibsen's entire canon continues the nineteenth century Romantic tradition which argues for the supremacy of the individual over any kind of repressive social convention." Yet looking at the influences exercised by that Romantic tradition, we at the end of the twentieth century, even more than Ibsen's contemporaries, have come to know its excesses which, as in the case of the cult of the "supremacy of the individual," too often become, like Nora's tarantella, a wild dance to be performed before enraptured spectators who will reflect the performance back to the dancer. And so it is in recasting *A Doll House* for a contemporary production that we may discover that Ibsen, the social critic, saw two sides to the Romantic celebration of the supremacy of the individual. Also Ibsen, the poet whose task was the "description of humanity," wrote more prophetically than even he may have known, for his Nora finally did not so much slam the door on the past as the playwright himself, going far beyond the issue of women's rights, opened the door connecting that past with the future. (pp. 140-58)

> *Carol Strongin Tufts, "Recasting 'A Doll House': Narcissism as Character Motivation in Ibsen's Play," in* Comparative Drama, *Vol. 20, No. 2, Summer, 1986, pp. 140-59.*

GHOSTS

Francis Fergusson   (essay date 1949)

[Fergusson is one of the most influential drama critics of the twentieth century. In his study The Idea of a Theater, *he claims that the fundamental truths present in all drama are defined exclusively by myth and ritual, and that the purpose of dramatic representation is, in essence, to confirm the "ritual expectancy" of the society in which the artist works. Fergusson's method has been described as a combination of the principles of Aristotle's* Poetics *and the principles of modern myth criticism. In his discussion of* Ghosts *in* The Idea of a Theater, *excerpted here, Fergusson detects elements of three conflicting types of drama in the work: a formulaic "well-*

*made" thriller, a realist "thesis play" about a specific so-
cial question, and a traditional tragedy. Although Ibsen
constructed* Ghosts *as a straightforward thesis play, the
critic suggests, Mrs. Alving's seeking, striving spirit is
characteristic of a tragic hero. Fergusson argues further
that whereas the drama's ending satisfies the requirements of both the well-made and thesis play, Mrs. Alving's tragedy is "truncated," for she achieves no tragic
insight or awareness.]*

THE PLOT OF GHOSTS: THESIS, THRILLER, AND TRAGEDY

Ghosts is not Ibsen's best play, but it serves my purpose,
which is to study the foundations of modern realism, just
because of its imperfections. Its power, and the poetry of
some of its effects, are evident; yet a contemporary audience may be bored with its old-fashioned iconoclasm and
offended by the clatter of its too-obviously well-made plot.
On the surface it is a *drame à thèse* [thesis play], of the
kind [Eugène] Brieux was to develop to its logical conclusion twenty years later: it proves the hollowness of the
conventional bourgeois marriage. At the same time it is a
thriller with all the tricks of the Boulevard entertainment:
Ibsen was a student of Scribe in his middle period [Augus-
tin Eugène Scribe was the originator of the "well-made

play"]. But underneath this superficial form of thesis-
thriller—the play which Ibsen started to write, the angry
diatribe as he first conceived it—there is another form, the
shape of the underlying action, which Ibsen gradually
made out in the course of his two-years' labor upon the
play, in obedience to his scruple of truthfulness, his profound attention to the reality of his fictive characters' lives.
The form of the play is understood according to two conceptions of plot, which Ibsen himself did not at this point
clearly distinguish: the rationalized concatenation of
events with a univocal moral, and the plot as the "soul"
or first actualization of the directly perceived action.

Halvdahn Khot, in his excellent study *Henrik Ibsen,* has
explained the circumstances under which **Ghosts** was
written. It was first planned as an attack upon marriage,
in answer to the critics of **A Doll's House.** The story of the
play is perfectly coherent as the demonstration and illustration of this thesis. When the play opens, Captain Alving
has just died, his son Oswald is back from Paris where he
had been studying painting, and his wife is straightening
out the estate. The Captain had been accepted locally as
a pillar of society but was in secret a drunkard and debauchee. He had seduced his wife's maid, and had a child
by her; and this child, Regina, is now in her turn Mrs. Alving's maid. Mrs. Alving had concealed all this for some-

Maurice Wilkinson as Pastor Manders, Frederick Lewis as Oswald, and Mary Shaw as Mrs. Alving in Ghosts. *New York, 1903.*

thing like twenty years. She was following the advice of the conventional Pastor Manders and endeavoring to save Oswald from the horrors of the household: it was for this reason she had sent him away to school. But now, with her husband's death, she proposes to get rid of the Alving heritage in all its forms, in order to free herself and Oswald for the innocent, unconventional "joy of life." She wants to endow an orphanage with the Captain's money, both to quiet any rumors there may be of his sinful life and to get rid of the remains of his power over her. She encounters this power, however, in many forms, through the Pastor's timidity and through the attempt by Engstrand (a local carpenter who was bribed to pretend to be Regina's father) to blackmail her. Oswald wants to marry Regina and has to be told the whole story. At last he reveals that he has inherited syphilis from his father—the dead hand of the past in its most sensationally ugly form—and when his brain softens at the end, Mrs. Alving's whole plan collapses in unrelieved horror. It is "proved" that she should have left home twenty years before, like Nora in *A Doll's House;* and that conventional marriage is therefore an evil tyranny.

In accordance with the principles of the thesis play, *Ghosts* is plotted as a series of debates on conventional morality, between Mrs. Alving and the Pastor, the Pastor and Oswald, and Oswald and his mother. It may also be read as a perfect well-made thriller. The story is presented with immediate clarity, with mounting and controlled suspense; each act ends with an exciting curtain which reaffirms the issues and promises important new developments. In this play, as in so many others, one may observe that the conception of dramatic form underlying the thesis play and the machine-made Boulevard entertainment is the same: the logically concatenated series of events (intriguing thesis or logical intrigue) which the characters and their relationships merely illustrate. And it was this view of *Ghosts* which made it an immediate scandal and success.

But Ibsen himself protested that he was not a reformer but a poet. He was often led to write by anger and he compared the process of composition to his pet scorpion's emptying of poison; Ibsen kept a piece of soft fruit in his cage for the scorpion to sting when the spirit moved him. But Ibsen's own spirit was not satisfied by the mere discharge of venom; and one may see, in *Ghosts,* behind the surfaces of the savage story, a partially realized tragic form of really poetic scope, the result of Ibsen's more serious and disinterested brooding upon the human condition in general, where it underlies the myopic rebellions and empty clichés of the time.

In order to see the tragedy behind the thesis, it is necessary to [turn] to the distinction between plot and action, and to the distinction between the plot as the rationalized series of events, and the plot as "the soul of the tragedy." The action of the play is "to control the Alving heritage for my own life." Most of the characters want some material or social advantage from it—Engstrand money, for instance, and the Pastor the security of conventional respectability. But Mrs. Alving is seeking a true and free human life itself—for her son, and through him, for herself. Mrs. Alving sometimes puts this quest in terms of the iconoclasms of the time, but her spiritual life, as Ibsen gradually discovered it, is at a deeper level; she tests everything—Oswald, the Pastor, Regina, her own moves—in the light of her extremely strict if unsophisticated moral sensibility: by direct perception and not by ideas at all. She is tragically seeking; she suffers a series of pathoses and new insights in the course of the play; and this rhythm of will, feeling, and insight underneath the machinery of the plot is the form of the life of the play, the soul of the tragedy.

The similarity between *Ghosts* and Greek tragedy, with its single fated action moving to an unmistakable catastrophe, has been felt by many critics of Ibsen. Mrs. Alving, like Oedipus, is engaged in a quest for her true human condition; and Ibsen, like Sophocles, shows on-stage only the end of this quest, when the past is being brought up again in the light of the present action and its fated outcome. From this point of view Ibsen is a plot-maker in the first sense: by means of his selection and arrangement of incidents he defines an action underlying many particular events and realized in various modes of intelligible purpose, of suffering, and of new insight. What Mrs. Alving sees changes in the course of the play, just as what Oedipus sees changes as one veil after another is removed from the past and the present. The underlying form of *Ghosts* is that of the tragic rhythm as one finds it in [Sophocles's] *Oedipus Rex.*

But this judgment needs to be qualified in several respects: because of the theater for which Ibsen wrote, the tragic form which Sophocles could develop to the full, and with every theatrical resource, is hidden beneath the clichés of plot and the surfaces "evident to the most commonplace mind." At the end of the play the tragic rhythm of Mrs. Alving's quest is not so much completed as brutally truncated, in obedience to the requirements of the thesis and the thriller. Oswald's collapse, before our eyes, with his mother's screaming, makes the intrigue end with a bang, and hammers home the thesis. But from the point of view of Mrs. Alving's tragic quest as we have seen it develop through the rest of the play, this conclusion concludes nothing: it is merely sensational.

The exciting intrigue and the brilliantly, the violently clear surfaces of *Ghosts* are likely to obscure completely its real life and underlying form. The tragic rhythm, which Ibsen rediscovered by his long and loving attention to the reality of his fictive lives, is evident only to the histrionic sensibility. As Henry James put it, Ibsen's characters "have the extraordinary, the brilliant property of becoming when represented at once more abstract and more living": i.e., both their lives and the life of the play, the spiritual content and the form of the whole, are revealed in this medium. A Nazimova, a Duse, could show it to us on the stage. Lacking such a performance, the reader must endeavor to respond imaginatively and directly himself if he is to see the hidden poetry of *Ghosts.*

MRS. ALVING AND OSWALD: THE TRAGIC RHYTHM IN A SMALL FIGURE

As Ibsen was fighting to present his poetic vision within

the narrow theater admitted by modern realism, so his protagonist Mrs. Alving is fighting to realize her sense of human life in the blank photograph of her own stuffy parlor. She discovers there no means, no terms, and no nourishment; that is the truncated tragedy which underlies the savage thesis of the play. But she does find her son Oswald, and she makes of him the symbol of all she is seeking: freedom, innocence, joy, and truth. At the level of the life of the play, where Ibsen warms his characters into extraordinary human reality, they all have moral and emotional meanings for each other; and the pattern of their related actions, their partially blind struggle for the Alving heritage, is consistent and very complex. In this structure, Mrs. Alving's changing relation to Oswald is only one strand, though an important one. I wish to consider it as a sample of Ibsen's rediscovery, through modern realism, of the tragic rhythm.

Oswald is of course not only a symbol for his mother, but a person in his own right, with his own quest for freedom and release, and his own anomalous stake in the Alving heritage. He is also a symbol for Pastor Manders of what he wants from Captain Alving's estate: the stability and continuity of the bourgeois conventions. In the economy of the play as a whole, Oswald is the hidden reality of the whole situation, like Oedipus' actual status as son-husband: the hidden fatality which, revealed in a series of tragic and ironic steps, brings the final peripety [reversal] of the action. To see how this works, the reader is asked to consider Oswald's role in Act I and the beginning of Act II.

The main part of Act I (after a prologue between Regina and Engstrand) is a debate, or rather agon [conflict], between Mrs. Alving and the Pastor. The Pastor has come to settle the details of Mrs. Alving's bequest of her husband's money to the orphanage. They at once disagree about the purpose and handling of the bequest; and this disagreement soon broadens into the whole issue of Mrs. Alving's emancipation versus the Pastor's conventionality. The question of Oswald is at the center. The Pastor wants to think of him, and to make of him, a pillar of society such as the Captain was supposed to have been, while Mrs. Alving wants him to be her masterpiece of liberation. At this point Oswald himself wanders in, the actual but still mysterious truth underlying the dispute between his mother and the Pastor. His appearance produces what the Greeks would have called a complex recognition scene, with an implied peripety for both Mrs. Alving and the Pastor, which will not be realized by them until the end of the act. But this tragic development is written to be acted; it is to be found, not so much in the actual words of the characters, as in their moral-emotional responses and changing relationships to one another.

The Pastor has not seen Oswald since he grew up; and seeing him now he is startled as though by a real ghost; he recognizes him as the very reincarnation of his father: the same physique, the same mannerisms, even the same kind of pipe. Mrs. Alving with equal confidence recognizes him as her own son, and she notes that his mouth-mannerism is like the Pastor's. (She had been in love with the Pastor during the early years of her marriage, when she wanted

to leave the Captain.) As for Oswald himself, the mention of the pipe gives him a Proustian intermittence of the heart: he suddenly recalls a childhood scene when his father had given him his own pipe to smoke. He feels again the nausea and the cold sweat, and hears the Captain's hearty laughter. Thus in effect he recognizes himself as his father's, in the sense of his father's *victim;* a premonition of the ugly scene at the end of the play. But at this point no one is prepared to accept the full import of these insights. The whole scene is, on the surface, light and conventional, an accurate report of a passage of provincial politeness. Oswald wanders off for a walk before dinner, and the Pastor and his mother are left to bring their struggle more into the open.

Oswald's brief scene marks the end of the first round of the fight, and serves as prologue for the second round, much as the intervention of the chorus in the agon between Oedipus and Tiresias punctuates their struggle, and hints at an unexpected outcome on a new level of awareness. As soon as Oswald has gone, the Pastor launches an attack in form upon Mrs. Alving's entire emancipated way of life, with the question of Oswald, his role in the community, his upbringing and his future, always at the center of the attack. Mrs. Alving replies with her whole rebellious philosophy, illustrated by a detailed account of her tormented life with the Captain, none of which the Pastor had known (or been willing to recognize) before. Mrs. Alving proves on the basis of this evidence that her new freedom is right; that her long secret rebellion was justified; and that she is now about to complete Oswald's emancipation, and thereby her own, from the swarming ghosts of the past. If the issue were merely on this rationalistic level, and between her and the Pastor, she would triumph at this point. But the real truth of her situation (as Oswald's appearance led us to suppose) does not fit either her rationalization or the Pastor's.

Oswald passes through the parlor again on his way to the dining room to get a drink before dinner, and his mother watches him in pride and pleasure. But from behind the door we hear the affected squealing of Regina. It is now Mrs. Alving's turn for an intermittence of the heart: it is as though she heard again her husband with Regina's mother. The insight which she had rejected before now reaches her in full strength, bringing the promised pathos and peripety; she sees Oswald, not as her masterpiece of liberation, but as the sinister, tyrannical, and continuing life of the past itself. The basis of her rationalization is gone; she suffers the breakdown of the moral being which she had built upon her now exploded view of Oswald.

At this point Ibsen brings down the curtain in obedience to the principles of the well-made play. The effect is to raise the suspense by stimulating our curiosity about the facts of the rest of the story. What will Mrs. Alving do now? What will the Pastor do—for Oswald and Regina are half-brother and sister; can we prevent the scandal from coming out? So the suspense is raised, but the attention of the audience is diverted from Mrs. Alving's tragic quest to the most literal, newspaper version of the facts.

The second act (which occurs immediately after dinner) is ostensibly concerned only with these gossipy facts. The

Pastor and Mrs. Alving debate ways of handling the threatened scandal. But this is only the literal surface: Ibsen has his eye upon Mrs. Alving's shaken psyche, and the actual dramatic form of this scene, under the discussion which Mrs. Alving keeps up, is her pathos which the Act I curtain broke off. Mrs. Alving is suffering the blow in courage and faith; and she is rewarded with her deepest insight: "I am half inclined to think we are all ghosts, Mr. Manders. It is not only what we have inherited from our fathers and mothers that exists again in us, but all sorts of dead ideas and all kinds of old dead beliefs and things of that kind. They are not actually alive in us; but they are dormant all the same, and we can never be rid of them. Whenever I take up a newspaper and read it, I fancy I see ghosts creeping between the lines. There must be ghosts all over the world. They must be as countless as the grains of sand, it seems to me. And we are so miserably afraid of the light, all of us." This passage, in the fumbling phrases of Ibsen's provincial lady, and in William Archer's translation, is not by itself the poetry of the great dramatic poets. It does not have the verbal music of [Jean] Racine, nor the freedom and sophistication of Hamlet, nor the scope of the Sophoclean chorus, with its use of the full complement of poetic and musical and theatrical resources. But in the total situation in the Alving parlor which Ibsen has so carefully established, and in terms of Mrs. Alving's uninstructed but profoundly developing awareness, it has its own hidden poetry: a poetry not of words but of the theater, a poetry of the histrionic sensibility. From the point of view of the underlying form of the play—the form as "the soul" of the tragedy—this scene completes the sequence which began with the debate in Act I: it is the pathos-and-epiphany following that agon.

It is evident, I think, that insofar as Ibsen was able to obey his realistic scruple, his need for the disinterested perception of human life beneath the clichés of custom and rationalization, he rediscovered the perennial basis of tragedy. The poetry of *Ghosts* is under the words, in the detail of action, where Ibsen accurately sensed the tragic rhythm of human life in a thousand small figures. And these little "movements of the psyche" are composed in a complex rhythm like music, a formal development sustained (beneath the sensational story and the angry thesis) until the very end. But the action is not completed: Mrs. Alving is left screaming with the raw impact of the calamity. The music is broken off, the dissonance unresolved—or, in more properly dramatic terms, the acceptance of the catastrophe, leading to the final vision or epiphany which should correspond to the insight Mrs. Alving gains in Act II, is lacking. The action of the play is neither completed nor placed in the wider context of meanings which the disinterested or contemplative purposes of poetry demand.

The unsatisfactory end of *Ghosts* may be understood in several ways. Thinking of the relation between Mrs. Alving and Oswald, one might say that she had romantically loaded more symbolic values upon her son than a human being can carry; hence his collapse proves too much—more than Mrs. Alving or the audience can digest. One may say that, at the end, Ibsen himself could not quite dissociate himself from his rebellious protagonist and see her action in the round, and so broke off in anger, losing his

tragic vision in the satisfaction of reducing the bourgeois parlor to a nightmare, and proving the hollowness of a society which sees human life in such myopic and dishonest terms. As a thesis play, *Ghosts* is an ancestor of many related genres: Brieux's arguments for social reform, propaganda plays like those of the Marxists, or parables *à la* [Leonid Nikolaivich] Andreev, or even [Bernard] Shaw's more generalized plays of the play-of-thought about social questions. But this use of the theater of modern realism for promoting or discussing political and social ideas never appealed to Ibsen. It did not solve his real problem, which was to use the publicly accepted theater of his time for poetic purposes. The most general way to understand the unsatisfactory end of *Ghosts* is to say that Ibsen could not find a way to represent the action of his protagonist, with all its moral and intellectual depth, within the terms of modern realism. In the attempt he truncated this action, and revealed as in a brilliant light the limitations of the bourgeois parlor as the scene of human life.

THE END OF GHOSTS: THE TASTELESS PARLOR AND THE STAGE OF EUROPE

Oswald is the chief symbol of what Mrs. Alving is seeking, and his collapse ends her quest in a horrifying catastrophe. But in the complex life of the play, all of the persons and things acquire emotional and moral significance for Mrs. Alving; and at the end, to throw as much light as possible upon the catastrophe, Ibsen brings all of the elements of his composition together in their highest symbolic valency. The orphanage has burned to the ground; the Pastor has promised Engstrand money for his "Sailor's Home" which he plans as a brothel; Regina departs, to follow her mother in the search for pleasure and money. In these eventualities the conventional morality of the Alving heritage is revealed as lewdness and dishonesty, quickly consumed in the fires of lust and greed, as Oswald himself (the central symbol) was consumed even before his birth. But what does this wreckage mean? Where are we to place it in human experience? Ibsen can only place it in the literal parlor, with lamplight giving place to daylight, and sunrise on the empty, stimulating, virginal snow-peaks out the window. The emotional force of this complicated effect is very great; it has the searching intimacy of nightmare. But it is also as disquieting as a nightmare from which we are suddenly awakened; it is incomplete, and the contradiction between the inner power of dream and the literal appearances of the daylight world is unresolved. The spirit that moved Ibsen to write the play, and which moved his protagonist through her tragic progress, is lost to sight, disembodied, imperceptible in any form unless the dreary exaltation of the inhuman mountain scene conveys it in feeling.

Henry James felt very acutely the contradiction between the deep and strict spirit of Ibsen and his superb craftsmanship on one side, and the little scene he tried to use—the parlor in its surrounding void—on the other. "If the spirit is a lamp within us, glowing through what the world and the flesh make of us as through a ground-glass shade, then such pictures as Little Eyolf and John Gabriel are each a chassez-croisez of lamps burning, as in tasteless parlors, with the flame practically exposed," he wrote in

London Notes. "There is a positive odor of spiritual paraffin. The author nevertheless arrives at the dramatist's great goal—he arrives for all his meagerness at intensity. The meagerness, which is after all but an unconscious, an admirable economy, never interferes with that: it plays straight into the hands of his rare mastery of form. The contrast between this form—so difficult to have reached, so 'evolved,' so civilized—and the bareness and bleakness of his little northern democracy is the source of half the hard frugal charm he puts forth."

James had rejected very early in his career his own little northern democracy, that of General Grant's America, with its ugly parlor, its dead conventions, its enthusiastic materialism, and its "non-conducting atmosphere." At the same time he shared Ibsen's ethical preoccupation, and his strict sense of form. His comments on Ibsen are at once the most sympathetic and the most objective that have been written. But James's own solution was to try to find a better parlor for the theater of human life; to present the quest of his American pilgrim of culture on the wider "stage of Europe" as this might still be felt and suggested in the manners of the leisured classes in England and France. James would have nothing to do with the prophetic and revolutionary spirit which was driving the great continental authors, Ibsen among them. In his artistry and his moral exactitude Ibsen is akin to James; but this is not his whole story, and if one is to understand the spirit he tried to realize in Mrs. Alving, one must think of [Søren] Kierkegaard, who had a great influence on Ibsen in the beginning of his career.

Kierkegaard (in *For Self-Examination*) has this to say of the disembodied and insatiable spirit of the times: " . . . thou wilt scarcely find anyone who does not believe in—let us say, for example, the spirit of the age, the *Zeitgeist.* Even he who has taken leave of higher things and is rendered blissful by mediocrity, yea, even he who toils slavishly for paltry ends or in the contemptible servitude of ill-gotten gains, even he believes, firmly and fully too, in the spirit of the age. Well, that is natural enough, it is by no means anything very lofty he believes in, for the spirit of the age is after all no higher than the age, it keeps close to the ground, so that it is the sort of spirit which is most like will-o'-the-wisp; but yet he believes in spirit. Or he believes in the world-spirit (*Weltgeist*) that strong spirit (for allurements, yes), that ingenious spirit (for deceits, yes); that spirit which Christianity calls an evil spirit—so that, in consideration of this, it is by no means anything very lofty he believes in when he believes in the world-spirit; but yet he believes in spirit. Or he believes in 'the spirit of humanity,' not spirit in the individual, but in the race, that spirit which, when it is god-forsaken for having forsaken God, is again, according to Christianity's teaching, an evil spirit—so that in view of this it is by no means anything very lofty he believes in when he believes in this spirit; but yet he believes in spirit.

"On the other hand, as soon as the talk is about a holy spirit—how many, dost thou think, believe in it? Or when the talk is about an evil spirit which is to be renounced—how many, dost thou think, believe in such a thing?"

This description seems to me to throw some light upon Mrs. Alving's quest, upon Ibsen's modern-realistic scene, and upon the theater which his audience would accept. The other face of nineteenth century positivism is romantic aspiration. And Ibsen's realistic scene presents both of these aspects of the human condition: the photographically accurate parlor, in the foreground, satisfies the requirements of positivism, while the empty but stimulating scene out the window—Europe as a moral void, an uninhabited wilderness—offers as it were a blank check to the insatiate spirit. Ibsen always felt this exhilarating wilderness behind his cramped interiors. In *A Doll's House* we glimpse it as winter weather and black water. In *The Lady from the Sea* it is the cold ocean, with its whales and its gulls. In *The Wild Duck* it is the northern marshes, with wildfowl but no people. In the last scene of *Ghosts* it is, of course, the bright snow-peaks, which may mean Mrs. Alving's quest in its most disembodied and ambivalent form; very much the same sensuous moral void in which Wagner, having totally rejected the little human foreground where Ibsen fights his battles, unrolls the solitary action of passion. It is the "stage of Europe" before human exploration, as it might have appeared to the first hunters.

There is a kinship between the fearless and demanding spirit of Kierkegaard, and the spirit which Ibsen tried to realize in Mrs. Alving. But Mrs. Alving, like her contemporaries whom Kierkegaard describes, will not or cannot accept any interpretation of the spirit that drives her. It may look like the *Weltgeist* when she demands the joy of living, it may look like the Holy Ghost itself when one considers her appetite for truth. And it may look like the spirit of evil, a "goblin damned," when we see the desolation it produces. If one thinks of the symbols which Ibsen brings together in the last scene: the blank parlor, the wide unexplored world outside, the flames that consumed the Alving heritage and the sunrise flaming on the peaks, one may be reminded of the condition of Dante's great rebel Ulysses. He too is wrapped in the flame of his own consciousness, yet still dwells in the pride of the mind and the exhilaration of the world free of people, *il mondo senza gente.* But this analogy also may not be pressed too far. Ulysses is in hell; and when we explore the Mountain on which he was wrecked, we can place his condition with finality, and in relation to many other human modes of action and awareness. But Mrs. Alving's mountains do not place her anywhere: the realism of modern realism ends with the literal. Beyond that is not the ordered world of the tradition, but *Unendlichkeit,* and the anomalous "freedom" of undefined and uninformed aspiration.

Perhaps Mrs. Alving and Ibsen himself are closer to the role of Dante than to the role of Ulysses, seeing a hellish mode of being, but free to move on. Certainly Ibsen's development continued beyond *Ghosts,* and toward the end of his career he came much closer to achieving a consistent theatrical poetry within the confines of the theater of modern realism. He himself remarked that his poetry was to be found only in the series of his plays, no one of which was complete by itself. (pp. 148-61)

Francis Fergusson, " 'Ghosts' and 'The Cherry Orchard': The Theater of Modern Realism," in his The Idea of a Theater: A Study of Ten Plays, the Art of Drama in Changing Perspec-

tive, Princeton University Press, 1949, pp. 146-77.

Robert W. Corrigan   (essay date 1959)

[*Corrigan views Mrs. Alving in* Ghosts *as divided between her intellectual ideals and an "emotional inheritance" over which she has no control. The sense of guilt she experiences, he claims, results from her attempt to intellectually break free of "those values which she emotionally still accepts." The critic then goes on to argue that Ibsen's presentation in* Ghosts *of a person who is destroyed attempting to live rationally in an irrational world overthrows traditional definitions of tragedy, which "celebrated man's ability to achieve wisdom through suffering."*]

> What profit has man of all his labour wherein he laboureth under the sun? One generation passeth away, and another generation cometh; but the earth abideth forever. . . . The sun also ariseth, and the sun goeth down, and hasteth to the place where he arose.
>
> *Ecclesiastes*

Ghosts created the biggest stir in Europe of all of Ibsen's plays. It was the hallmark of the Free Theatre movement. Antoine at the Théâtre Libre, Brahm at the Freie Buehne, and Grein at the Independent Theatre in London all produced this play as a symbol and a harbinger of their freedom. But the play was violently received. It shocked respectable middle-class audiences everywhere; it was condemned and banned; for the young turks of liberalism it was a banner to be waved on high. From the beginning the play had a notoriety that Ibsen only partially intended.

Fortunately, *Ghosts* is now seen in clearer perspective and we tend to be amused by the critical reaction of the Nineties. But *Ghosts* is still a controversial play. The number of respectable interpretations currently making the rounds is large and when you get on the subject of *Ghosts* as tragedy—well, it is one of those plays, like [Arthur Miller's] *Death of a Salesman,* it just won't stay settled and is always good for an argument. The four major interpretations of the play usually advanced are: First, Ibsen wrote *Ghosts* as an answer to the objections raised by Nora's flight from her husband and children in *A Doll's House.* Tied to a worse husband than Helmar, Mrs. Alving, instead of leaving him, had decided to stay, and to cover up the "corpse" of her married life with respectable trappings. Second: Mrs. Alving and Oswald are the victims of a two-fisted fate which takes the form of the laws of heredity in a mechanistic world and the stultifying and debilitating conventions of respectability. Third: Hereditary disease was for Ibsen the symbol of all the determinist forces that crush humanity, and, therefore, he sought to put in opposition to these forces the strongest of all instincts—maternal passion. And, finally, there is a fourth group of critics who dismiss the play as irrelevant except as an historical landmark. They argue that although the play may have been revolutionary in its day, today any dramatic conflict which presents suffering and a shot of penicillin as its alternatives is not very convincing. All of these interpretations—and they have been persuasively argued by responsible critics—seem to me to be either misreadings of the play or beside the point. They are comments about the play, but they are ancillary and fail to recognize the underlying conflict of the play. For this reason most modern commentaries on *Ghosts* fail to describe and interpret the central action which Ibsen is imitating, and this has resulted in many limited or erroneous discussions of the play as a tragedy. It is this central action and its tragic implications which I wish to discuss, and this can best be done by first turning to Ibsen the man and the artist.

I

Ibsen's biography is a study in conflict and contradiction. The gadfly of bourgeoisie morality was helplessly bourgeois; the enemy of pietism was a guilt-ridden possessor of the worst kind of "Lutheran" conscience; the champion of the "love-life of the soul" was incapable of loving; the militant spokesman against hypocrisy and respectability was pompous and outraged at any breach of decorum. Ibsen's life is the contradiction of those values affirmed in his plays. This should not confuse us, however, if we will look even briefly at some of the significant events in a life that was really quite dull.

Ibsen was born into an atmosphere of fairly prosperous parochial respectability. His father was a small-time shipping tycoon in the little town of Skien. In 1836, when Ibsen was eight years old, his father went bankrupt and was accused of embezzlement and forgery. The charges were never proved, but the family was ostracized and reduced to a grubbing kind of poverty. When Ibsen was sixteen he left his family, amidst bitter renunciations on both sides, never to see or correspond with them again. Even when his parents died he failed to return or write. He wrote to a friend on the occasion of his father's death that he was "unable to offer assistance of any kind." So at sixteen Ibsen went to the dismal town of Grimstead as an apprentice in pharmacy. Here he had an illegitimate son, Hans Jakob, and once again was "run out of town." He left Grimstead, leaving mother and child stranded, and never took the slightest interest in them. He went to Christiana (now Oslo) to begin his career as a writer and failed. In 1851 he was hired as director and dramaturg of the new Bergen National Theatre. Again, Ibsen was a failure. Letters and memoirs of actors in his company show him to have been incompetent as both a director and as a manager; and the plays written expressly for the theatre in his role as dramaturg were all miserable flops. Furthermore, he must have felt failure in his personal life. He fell in love three times in Bergen, and in each instance the girl's father broke off the affair because Ibsen was not suitable as a son-in-law. By 1857 he was on the verge of being fired; friends stepped in and got him a job as director of the newly organized Norwegian Theatre in Christiana. But failure followed him and by 1862 the National Theatre was bankrupt both artistically and financially and Ibsen was bitterly denounced by the press. Once again, friends came to his aid and he was given a small dole in the form of a literary scholarship to study abroad.

The story of Ibsen's success as an international playwright is well-known and in 1891 he returned to Norway as a celebrity. In Christiana, where he settled for good, he became something of a national institution and was far from disliking such a status. All the frustration, humiliation, and rejection he had endured in youth and early manhood were now amply compensated for. He was wealthy and internationally famous. As if anxious to do full justice to his literary and social position, Ibsen increased his air of excessively dignified respectability. So much so that in all his external habits he was even more strict and methodical than those philistines whom he had ridiculed so aggressively in his plays. Immaculately dressed in his frock-coat and silk tophat, he took his daily walks along the same streets, sat at the same table in the same cafe (where the customers all respectfully rose whenever he entered), and went home at the same time—with the regularity of clockwork. He was also fond of displaying his numerous decorations and medals, which he used to collect and covet with the relish of a *nouveau riche* enjoying all the external insignia of his own importance.

In short, Ibsen became a "pillar of society" in his last days; he was a regular speaker at the Norwegian equivalents of the Rotary Club, the AAUW, Labor Unions, and the Better Business Bureau. In his speeches he praised all of these groups and gratefully accepted their adulation and honors. His study walls were covered with plaques and certificates from civic organizations and only a bust of [August] Strindberg—a bust that captured the penetrating and demonic quality of Strindberg's gaze—acted as an antidote to this display of middle-class self-righteousness. On March 15th, 1900 Ibsen had a stroke, and another in the following year. These paralytic strokes were followed by amnesia and for six years he lay helplessly senile. He died on May 23rd, 1906, at the age of seventy-eight.

The clue to the meaning of all Ibsen's plays lies in this strange biography. Ibsen's plays are a continuous act of expiation. Certainly, it is significant that bankruptcy and the resultant rejection by society appears in four of his plays; the desire to restore the family honor is central to two more; and there are illegitimate children in eight plays. Thematically, the plays are, almost without exception, patterned in a similar way: a hidden moral guilt and the fear of impending retribution. Structurally, the plays are epilogues of retribution. All of the plays after *Peer Gynt,* begin on a happy note late in the action. In each case the central figure has a secret guilt which is soon discovered. As the play progresses, by series of expository scenes (scenes which delve into the past and are then related to the present condition of the characters), a sense of the foreboding doom of impending retribution envelops the action and each of the plays ends with justice, in the form of moral fate having its way. And finally, beginning with *Ghosts,* Ibsen introduces the theme of expiation. In every play following *Ghosts,* at least one of the central characters feels the need to exorcise his guilt, doubt, or fear by some form of renunciation.

Perhaps more important is the fact, that as Ibsen's art developed these themes and attitudes changed in tone and form. The guilt, which had been specific in the early days—Bernick's lie [in *The Pillars of Society*], Nora's forgery [in *A Doll's House*], Mrs. Alving's return—becomes more and more abstract, nebulous, and ominous as best

evidenced in the nameless guilt of Solness [in *The Master Builder*] and Rosmer [in *Rosmersholm*]. The fear, which in the early plays had been the fear of discovery, becomes a gnawing anxiety. Self-realization, which in *Brand* is presented in terms of the Kierkegaardian imperative of either/or is realized in the later plays in an ambiguous kind of self-destruction. And finally, significant action on the part of the characters has tendencies towards becoming a frozen stasis of meaningless activity and contemplation.

Ibsen's life and his work are closely interwoven. Ibsen, rejected from society as a young man, had good reason to see the blindness of bourgeois respectability in his exile. And yet his sharp criticism of society is always balanced by his desire to be a part of that very society he saw and knew to be false. Over and over again in his plays and letters he condemns the hypocrisy, the intellectual shallowness, and the grim bleakness of his Scandinavian homeland. But he returned to it in pomp and circumstance. Herein lies the crux to an understanding of Ibsen's art in general and *Ghosts* in particular. More and more we see that both in Ibsen the man and in the characters of his plays the basic struggle is within.

Ibsen lived in a time of revolution; he was a maker of part of that revolution; and he knew full well that all the things he said about bourgeois society were true. But despite his rational understanding, his intellectual comprehension of this fact, he was driven by deeper forces within him not only to justify himself to that false society, but to become a part of it. It is this struggle within himself between his rational powers and the Trolls of the Boyg that best explains his life and work. Ibsen's plays are his attempts to quell the guilt he felt for desiring values which he knew to be false. In support of this point, I call attention to two important bits of evidence: the first is a letter written by Ibsen to Peter Hanson in 1870:

> While writing *Brand,* I had on my desk a glass with a scorpion in it. From time to time the little animal was ill. Then I used to give it a piece of soft fruit, upon which it fell furiously and emptied its poison into it—after which it was well again. Does not something similar happen to us poets? The laws of nature regulate the spiritual world also. . . .

The second is a short poem entitled **"Fear of Light"** (presently, I shall relate the significance of that title to *Ghosts*):

> What is life? a fighting
> In heart and brain with Trolls.
> Poetry? that means writing
> Doomsday-accounts of our souls.

I contend that Ibsen's plays were attempts—attempts that were bound to fail, just as Mrs. Alving's attempts were bound to fail—to relieve Ibsen of his guilt and at the same time were judgments of his failure to overcome the Trolls (which first appear as Gerd in *Brand*), those irrational forces and powers within man over which he has no control.

Keeping these facts in mind, let us now turn to *Ghosts.* One does not have to be a very perceptive student of the theatre to realize that the "ghosts" Ibsen is talking about are those ghosts of the past that haunt us in the present. In fact, Ibsen has often been criticized for using his ghost symbolism with such obviousness, such lack of subtlety, and so repetitiously. Certainly, when reading the play we feel this criticism is justified. Oswald's looking like Captain Alving; his interest in sex and liquor; his feelings toward Regina; his syphilitic inheritance; Pastor Mander's influence over Mrs. Alving, the orphanage, and the fire are only a few of the "ghosts" that Ibsen uses as analogues to his theme. Alrik Gustafson puts it this way [in "Some Notes on Themes, Character, and Symbol in *Rosmersholm,*"*Carleton Drama Review* I, No. 2]:

> Symbols are, of course, a commonplace in Ibsen's dramas, but in his early plays before *The Wild Duck* he uses symbolistic devices somewhat too obviously, almost exclusively to clarify his themes. Any college sophomore can tell you after a single reading of *Pillars of Society, A Doll's House,* or *Ghosts* what the symbols expressed in these titles mean. The symbols convey *ideas*—and little else. They have few emotional overtones, are invested with little of the impressive mystery of life, the tragic poetry of existence. They tend to leave us in consequence cold, uncommitted, like after a debate whose heavy-handed dialectic has ignored the very pulse-beat of a life form which it is supposed to have championed.

But *Ghosts* is concerned with more than the external manifestations of an evil heritage. In those oft-quoted lines that serve as a rationale for the play, Mrs. Alving says:

> I am half inclined to think we are all ghosts, Mr. Manders. It is not only what we have inherited from our fathers and mothers that exists again in us, but all sorts of old dead ideas and all kinds of old dead beliefs and things of that kind. They are not actually alive in us; but there they are dormant, all the same, and we can never be rid of them. . . . There must be ghosts all over the world. . . . And we are so miserably afraid of the light, all of us . . . and I am here, fighting with ghosts both without and within me.

The ghosts of plot and symbol are the manifestations of Mrs. Alving's struggle with the ghosts within. It is this internal conflict, a conflict similar to Ibsen's personal struggle, that is the play's central action.

To define this action more explicitly, I would say that Ibsen is imitating an action in which a woman of ability and stature finds her ideals and her intellectual attitudes and beliefs in conflict with an inherited emotional life determined by the habitual responses of respectability and convention. As the play's form evolves it becomes apparent that the values Mrs. Alving affirms in intellectual terms are doomed to defeat because she has no control over her emotional inheritance—an inheritance of ghosts which exists, but which cannot be confined to or controlled by any schematization of the intelligence.

Every significant choice that Mrs. Alving has ever made and the resultant action of such a decision is determined by these ghosts of the past rather than by intellectual deliberation. To mention but a few instances: Her marriage to Captain Alving in conformity to the wishes of her mother and aunts; her return to her husband; her reaction to the Oswald-Regina relationship; her acceptance of Manders after she has seen and commented upon the hypocrisy of the scene with Engstrand; her failure to tell Oswald the "straight" truth about his father; the horror of her reaction when Oswald is indifferent to his father's life; and finally, the question mark with which the play ends. All of these scenes are evidence that Mrs. Alving's ideals of freedom and her rhetorical flights into intellectual honesty are of no use to her when it comes to action. Perhaps, I can make my point more clear by briefly developing two of the above mentioned episodes.

As the second act opens, Mrs. Alving comes to a quick decision about Oswald's relationship with Regina: "Out of the house she shall go—and at once. That part of it is clear as daylight." I will return to the relationship of light to enlightenment, but for the moment we see that Mrs. Alving's decision is based upon an emotional response determined by her inheritance of respectability. Then, Mrs. Alving and the pastor begin to talk; and Mrs. Alving always talks a good game. After better than four pages of dialogue, Mrs. Alving is finally able to exclaim: "If I were not such a miserable coward, I would say to him: 'Marry her, or make any arrangement you like with her—only let there be no deceit in the matter.'" The pastor is properly shocked when Mrs. Alving gives him the "face the facts of life" routine; but her liberation, which is only verbal, is short lived! Manders asks how "you, a mother, can be willing to allow your . . ." This is Mrs. Alving's reply: "But I am not willing to allow it. I would not allow it for anything in the world; that is just what I was saying."

Or to take another situation. In Act I, Mrs. Alving tells Manders what her husband was really like: "The truth is this, that my husband died just as great a profligate as he had been all his life." In Act II, she is telling Manders of all the things she *ought* to have done and she says: "If I had been the woman I ought, I would have taken Oswald into my confidence and said to him: 'Listen, my son, your father was a dissolute man.'" In the third act circumstances have forced Mrs. Alving to tell Oswald the truth about his father: "Your poor father never found any outlet for the overmastering joy of life that was in him. And I brought no holiday spirit into his house, either; I am afraid I made your poor father's home unbearable to him, Oswald."

When we come to see the big scenes in this way, we then recall the numerous small events that create the network of the action and give the play its texture. Such things come to mind as Mrs. Alving's need of books to make her feel secure in her stand, and the neat little bit in the first act where Mrs. Alving reprimands Oswald for smoking in the parlor, which Ibsen then underscores by making it an issue in the second act.

Ibsen's plays are filled with such incidents; those little events that tell so much. I am of the persuasion that Ibsen is not very good at making big events happen; as appealing as they may be to a director, they tend to be theatrically inflated; they are melodramatic in the sense that the action of the plot is in itself larger than the characters or the situation in the play which create such events. Ibsen is the master of creating the small shocking event, or as Mary McCarthy puts it: "the psychopathology of everyday life." Nora's pushing off the sewing on the widow Christine [in *A Doll's House*]; Hjalmer letting Hedwig do the retouching with her half-blind eyes as he goes off hunting in the attic; his cutting of his father at Werle's party [in *The Wild Duck*]; and the moment when Hedda intentionally mistakes Aunt Julia's new hat for the servant's [in *Hedda Gabler*], are all examples of this talent. These are the things we know we are capable of! This is the success (and the limitation) of the naturalistic convention "which implies a norm of behavior on the part of its guilty citizens within their box-like living rooms."

But to return to the main business at hand: the conflict for Mrs. Alving, then, is not how to act. She just acts; there is no decision, nor can there be, for she has no rational control over her actions. Herein lies the conflict. Just because Mrs. Alving has no control over her actions, does not mean she escapes the feelings of guilt for what she does and her inability to do otherwise. Her continual rhetoricizing about emancipation and her many acts of renunciation are attempts to satisfy these feelings of guilt. For example, and I am indebted to Wiegand here [Hermann Weigand, *The Modern Ibsen*, 1925], the explicit reasons she gives for building the orphanage do not account sufficiently for her use of the expression, "the power of an uneasy conscience." There is a big difference between fear that an ugly secret will become known and an evil conscience. Mrs. Alving's sense of guilt is the result of an intellectual emancipation from the habits of a lifetime; it is an emancipation from those values which she emotionally still accepts. It is precisely for this reason that her attempts at expiation are never satisfactory—they are not central to and part of her guilt.

To put it another way, Mrs. Alving's image of herself as liberated from outworn ideas is at odds with what in fact she is, a middle-aged woman bound by the chains of respectability and convention. It is for this reason, in a way similar to [Jean-Paul] Sartre's characters in the hell of *No Exit*, that she suffers. She is aware of the disparity between image and fact: "I ought" is a choric refrain that runs through her conversation; and she constantly looks for ways to affirm her image and assuage her guilt. And yet, the very fact that she accepts the image of herself as free, when experience has proven otherwise time and time again, explains why she is defeated in every attempt at atonement.

The sun finally rises. Ibsen has been preparing for this from the beginning. As the past is gradually revealed in the play and as the issues of the action come into sharper focus, "light" becomes more and more important in Ibsen's design. The play opens in the gloom of evening and rain; Mrs. Alving, at least according to Ibsen's stage directions, plays most of her important revelation scenes at the window, the source of light; as Mrs. Alving decides to quell Oswald's "gnawing doubts," she calls for a light; Oswald's big speech about the "joy and openness of life" uses the sun as its central metaphor; the light that reveals—tells the truth—how impossible it is for Mrs. Alv-

ing to atone for her guilt has its source in the flames of the burning orphanage; and, finally, it is the sun, the source of all light, that reveals the meaning of the play's completed action. Mr. Alving is still trapped within the net of her own inheritance. She, as she has already told us and as Ibsen tells us in his poem, **"Fear of Light,"** is afraid to face the real truth about herself. This fear is something over which she has no control.

If we can empathize with Mrs. Alving, and I think we can, we have been lead to feel, as she believes, that as the light comes out of darkness, as the pressures of reality impinge upon her with unrelenting force, she will be capable of an act of freedom. We want to believe that she will affirm the image that she has of herself as a liberated human being by an action that is expressive of that freedom, even if that action is the murder of her own son. We want to feel that the light and heat of the sun will have the power to cauterize the ghosts of her soul. But if we have been attentive to the developing action, if we but recall what events followed the "lesser lights;" then we realize that there can be no resolution. Mrs. Alving can give only one answer, "No!"

Mrs. Alving, like Oswald, who is the most important visible symbol of the ghosts, is a victim of something over which she has no control. We are reminded of Oswald's famous speech in the second act: "My whole life incurably ruined—just because of my own imprudence. . . . Oh! if only I could live my life over again—if only I could undo what I have done! If only it had been something I had inherited—something I could not help." We have known all along that Oswald is a victim, so Ibsen is telling us for a purpose. The reason, as a study of his other plays will attest, is that for Ibsen the external is always the mirrored reflection of what's within. Mrs. Alving is also a victim! Like Oswald, she is doomed just by being born. And since she never comes to understand herself; since she never realizes and accepts the disparity of her image of herself and the truth about herself, she can never—in a way that Oedipus, a similar kind of victim, can—resolve the conflict.

For Mrs. Alving the sun has risen and just as she cannot give Oswald the sun, so the light of the sun has not been able to enlighten her. This, I believe is the conflict in the play and the developed meanings of this conflict form the play's central action.

But is this action tragic? How, if at all, is *Ghosts* a tragedy? It seems to me that there are two possible answers to these questions and the answer will depend largely on which interpretation of the play one accepts. The prevelant interpretation is the one which claims that this is a play of social protest and reform. The adherents of such a view can gather together a great deal of evidence in support of their case: all of Ibsen's plays from **League of Youth** to **The Wild Duck;** passages from the play themselves, like Oswald's speech on the freedom of Europe; numerous of Ibsen's public speeches, and several of his letters. With this interpretation the play is saying that if man would only see how hypocritical and outmoded his values were then the disasters that occur in the play need never have taken place. This view has as its fundamental premise that social evils can be cured and that when they are man is capable of living with a "joy of life." But if this is true, if all you have to do is be honest with yourself—and such a view assumes this is possible—and if men would see the falseness of social conventions and change them, then it seems to me the eternal elements of tragedy are dissolved in the possibility of social reform. Tragedy is concerned with showing those destructive conflicts within man that exist because man is a man no matter what age he may happen to be a part of, and no matter what kind of a society he may live in. John Gassner puts it this way [in *The Theatre in Our Times,* 1954]:

> Tragedy requires an awareness of "life's impossibilities," of limitations imposed upon man by the nature of things and by the nature of man, which cannot be poetically dissolved by sentiment or "reformed" out of existence.

In some ways, I think Ibsen did intend *Ghosts* to be a play of social reform, but if this is the case, he created more than he planned. In all of his early plays, the plays we think of as the social reform plays, Ibsen is much like Mrs. Alving; he believed intellectually in freedom and wrote and talked a good deal about it, but is this the whole story? The disassociation of the ideals men live by and the facts of their living is a central theme in Ibsen's work, but it is interesting to note that even in *Ghosts* the possibility of the "happy illusion" is presented. It is a hint that Ibsen is coming to feel that the conflict between truth and ideals can never be reconciled. By the time of *Rosmersholm,* even the free souls are tainted, the reformers are corrupt, and the man trying to redeem himself is shown to be capable only of realizing that he cannot be redeemed. Rosmer's death is an act of expiation, but suicide is decided upon only after Rosmer discovers the impossibility of redemption within society by means of freer and more honest views and relations.

Thus, while it is true that Ibsen, both in his public pronouncements and in his plays prior to *Ghosts,* gives us evidence that he believes optimistically in the possibility of social reform; that he believes that finally the sun will rise and continue to shine if man works long and diligently at facing the truth, I wonder if Ibsen is in fact whistling as he walks in the night through a graveyard. I wonder if Ibsen, even as early as *Ghosts,* isn't being a Mrs. Alving. Certainly this passage from a letter written during the composition of *Ghosts* permits us to wonder:

> The work of writing this play has been to me like a bath which I have felt to leave cleaner, healthier, and freer. Who is the man among us who has not now and then felt and acknowledged within himself a contradiction between word and action, between will and task, between life and teaching on the whole? Or who is there among us who has not selfishly been sufficient unto himself, and half unconsciously, half in good faith, has extenuated this conduct both to others and to himself?

The alternative interpretation of *Ghosts* is the one which I have outlined in this essay. Mrs. Alving is a victim in a conflict over which she has no control. What are the implications of such a view to tragedy?

In 1869 Ibsen wrote a significant letter to the critic George Brandes. In this letter he says:

> There is without doubt a great chasm opened between yesterday and today. We must continually fight a war to the knife between these epochs.

What Ibsen meant in this letter was that to live in the modern world is to be, in many important ways, different from anyone who ever lived before. Now this doesn't mean that man has changed; human nature is still the same, but Ibsen felt that the modern way of looking at man had changed in a way that was significantly new.

Joseph Wood Krutch pursues this problem in his recent book, *"Modernism" in the Modern Drama.* Krutch develops his argument by pointing out that since Greek times the Aristotelian dictum that "man is a reasoning animal" had been pretty universally accepted. This view did not deny man's irrationality, but it did assert that reason is the most significant human characteristic. Man is not viewed as pre-eminently a creature of instincts, passions, habits, or conditioned reflexes; rather, man is a creature who differs from the other animals precisely in the fact that rationality is his dominant mode.

The modern view assumes the opposite premise. In this view men are not sane or insane. Psychology has dissolved such sharp distinctions; we know that normal people aren't as rational as they seem and that abnormal people don't act in a random and unintelligible way. In short, the dramatist of our age has had to face the assumption that the rational is relatively unimportant; that the irrational is the dominant mode of life; and that the artist must realize, therefore, that the richest and most significant aspects of human experience are to be found in the hidden depths of the irrational. "Man tends to become less a creature of reason than the victim of obsessions, fixations, delusions, and perversions." [Krutch].

It is this premise that all of the great dramatists at the end of the 19th century, beginning with Ibsen, had to face. How is one to live in an irrational world? How is one to give meaning to life in a world where you don't know the rules? How are human relationships to be meaningfully maintained when you can't be sure of your feelings and when your feelings can change without your knowing it? Ibsen's plays, beginning with *Ghosts,* dramatize man destroyed by trying to live rationally in such a world. But to accept irreconcilable conflict as the central fact of all life; to make dissonance rather than the harmony of reconciliation the condition of the universe is to accept as a premise a view of life which leads in drama, as in life, to a world in which men and women, heroes and heroines, become victims in a disordered world which they have not created and which they have no moral obligation to correct.

It is this process, which began in the drama when Ibsen came to see man as a victim of irrational powers, of the Trolls, over which he has no control, that leads to the sense of futility that so completely dominates a great deal of modern drama. This is the kind of futility that is expressed in our text from Ecclesiastes (as it is in Hemingway's novel); but is this sense of futility generative of what we traditionally associate with tragedy?

The traditional forms of tragedy have been affirming in the sense that they celebrated man's ability to achieve wisdom through suffering. Such tragedy saw man as a victim, to be sure, but it also saw man as having those heroic qualities and potentialities which permitted him to endure his suffering and be significantly enlightened by them in such a way that victory was realized even in defeat.

The central conflict of *Ghosts* is not peculiar to the modern world. The disassociation of fact and value is a common theme in all tragedy. But there is a significant difference when this theme is used before Ibsen. Traditional tragedy celebrates the fact that, although most of us are incapable of it, the values men wish to live by can, if only for a moment, be realized through the actions of the tragic hero. It celebrates the fact that man's capacity for greatness is often expressed in the committing of an action which is horrifying and ought not to happen and yet which must happen. In this way the possibility that man's actions and his values can be in harmony is realized. This is the affirmation of tragedy; this is the meaning of the sun that resolves so many traditional tragedies. In this kind of tragedy the hero goes through the "dark night of the soul" with all its pain, suffering, doubt, and despair; but man is viewed as one responsible for and capable of action, even if that action is a grasping for the sun. Because of this fundamental difference in view, in traditional tragedy the dark night passes away and the sun also rises on the rebirth and affirmation of a new day.

This sunrise of traditional tragedy, which celebrates the "joy and meaning of life," is not the sunrise of futility. It is not the sunrise which sheds its rays as an ironic and bitter joke on a demented boy asking his equally helpless mother: "Mother, give me the sun, The sun—the sun!"

Perhaps Mrs. Alving is more tragic than Oedipus, Hamlet, or Lear; but if she is, her tragedy must be evaluated by new canons of judgment; for she differs from her predecessors in kind and not degree. (pp. 171-80)

> Robert W. Corrigan, "The Sun Always Rises: Ibsen's 'Ghosts' as Tragedy?" in Educational Theatre Journal, *Vol. XI, No. 3, October, 1959, pp. 171-80.*

John Northam   (essay date 1973)

[*In the following excerpt from his* Ibsen: A Critical Study, *a book-length examination of the playwright and his major works, Northam focuses on Mrs. Alving in* Ghosts, *placing her in the context of the society depicted in the play. According to the critic, Mrs. Alving "has always been at war" with her society, which subtly coerces women to sacrifice their "personal integrity to social demands." Her continuing struggle to break free of her condition and discover truth makes Mrs. Alving "a great fighter against a terrible opponent" in Northam's estimation.*]

The ironies compressed into [the final scene of *Ghosts*] are likely to be almost as unendurable for the audience as for

Mrs Alving. She worked so hard to create for her son a corner of health and sanity in a corrupt world; that son is mentally diseased. She planned to clear the house of all other but herself and her beloved child; she has succeeded, but only in this appalling travesty. She thought that she could bring the long, hateful comedy to a neat end, scaling off all consequences, but she has unwittingly written a final act which is tragic. She worked to preserve a life and must now decide whether to destroy it.

The sum of these reversals to her expectations amounts to a condemnation of Mrs Alving; not for her trying, but for the mode of her trying. The essential quality in her is ambiguity, that strangely constant mingling within the one woman of radical and conformist; she is strong enough to try to think for herself, but too cowardly to act in any other way than that required by the society she has, in part, seen through. Her radicalism itself is never complete; it may, under Oswald's influence, expand, but at no point can she fully liberate herself from the influence upon her, acknowledged or unacknowledged, of dead social habits. All that can be said of her at the end of the play is that at least at that moment she is being forced to face facts as they really are; what she will make of the experience we cannot know.

Thus the play could be taken as the trial and condemnation of a misguided, inadequate woman. If Mrs Alving had been true to her own feelings she would not have married Alving, or remained with him once married; had she been true to her own sense of the genuine, she would not have decided to rectify the disaster of her life by preserving appearances, whose falsity she recognised, in order to appease society. It is a strong indictment and the play undoubtedly levels it at her; and yet an account that stopped there would seem to me not to acknowledge much else that is offered.

For all her misguidedness, Mrs Alving remains in the imagination as a splendid woman. This impression comes partly from her personality and character taken by and for themselves. She has been so strong, to have coped with a life like that without weakness and to have coped alone. She must have had nerves and a will of steel to have conceived and carried out a plan of such complexity and long duration without losing heart. She always fights to control and shape events, never allowing herself to be passively overwhelmed. She is indeed a strong woman. And we can only admire the direction in which her strength is constantly directed. Misguided or not, blinkered though she may be in ways unsuspected by herself, she is always trying to see through pretence and hypocrisy to the truth behind it. She often fails to get through, and she initially fails to act on the truth that she has discovered, but that is the direction her bent of mind leads her in. And out of her private understanding she hopes for one single thing: to create the possibility of a decent life.

There is an element of selfishness in all this, yet even that is forgiveable in a mother. She wants her boy to herself. But she is no child-devourer; Oswald has always been free to come and go; but for his illness he could return to Paris; Mrs Alving relishes the thought of his staying but she has never suggested it, still less demanded or engineered it.

The element of maternal selfishness is minor compared with the selflessness that has made her sacrifice her own happiness to her son's well-being. Everything that she has done has been directed towards that.

Thus even on a narrow view of Mrs Alving as a character in isolation she seems to merit deep respect and not mere blame. For the full assessment we need to see her in her context.

In simple terms, Mrs Alving has always been at war with society. Her stature, and her achievements, must be gauged in relation to her antagonist. And here the play creates a force of peculiar horror. Society is presented as an openly coercive force, but that is not its chief characteristic. We see it in action upon Manders and through him upon Mrs Alving. The coercion is strong, certainly not negligible, but it is not remarkable.

Society's real power lies in its unobtrusiveness. The trap it lays for Mrs Alving is one into which she and millions of other women have slipped without recognising that it was a trap. There is nothing openly coercive about the advice of relations when it comes to choosing a husband. Mrs Alving was not aware of facing a great crisis in her life when she decided that Alving was the best catch in social terms; and yet in that choice she subdued her own feelings to the criteria created by society. The essential falsification occurred then, yet who could have identified such a crisis in so commonplace a decision? Part of the power of society in *Ghosts* is that it works through small-scale events which do not proclaim their real significance at the moment of occurrence. Brand could identify his crises; Mrs Alving could not.

Yet once in, the consequences are fatal and inescapable. From the initial falsification all others flow; and these too hide their significance in unobtrusiveness. When Mrs Alving sent Oswald away from home and made arrangements for Regine and so on, she was being false to her knowledge of the truth, but she was conditioned by society to accept without question that this was the reasonable way to act. Her plans were reasonable submissions to society that followed from her first reasonable submission. And she has gone on living for years without having much reason to recognise that such submission of personal integrity to social demands could be critical and fatal.

And yet in the end the magnitude of crisis must become clear. To submit, to the extent that Mrs Alving has, to society is to cause terrible corruption to set in. Oswald's disease is the outward and spectacular sign of the corruption, of its secretiveness and of its fatal inevitability, but it is not the only form of corruption. There is corruption of will, corruption of courage, corruption of integrity, of relationships—indeed a creeping invasion through many different veins and arteries of the play simultaneously. In *Brand* the sequence of events was linear; Brand moved on from one crisis and its consequences to the next. In *Ghosts* the various streams of corruption move apparently independently and in unsuspected ways towards the one moment of dissolution.

Perhaps Ibsen's greatest discovery in *Ghosts* was the way in which his protagonist must necessarily be involved in modern society. Falk, in *Love's Comedy,* by virtue of his favoured status as student, was allowed to stand outside the social structure he condemned. Though affected by his antagonism to his surroundings, he was not contaminated by them. Nor was Brand; even though he was woven into his community far more intimately than Falk, his small parish can serve only as an emblem of real modern social existence; and he too, Ibsen seemed to imagine, could preserve his spiritual integrity.

Mrs Alving cannot preserve hers entirely from the corruption she later comes to identify. However clearly she may, by the time the play begins, recognise that she married for the wrong reason, may have acted wrongly since, may need to revise and enlarge her sense of truth and honesty, she constantly reveals that society continues to influence her ways of thought and action. Ibsen can see now that no individual, not even one with the basic integrity of a Mrs Alving, can escape permeation by the very corruption by society that their integrity makes them identify and oppose. Significantly one of the images of that permeation is the gloom which envelops, as an all-pervasive natural force, the action of so much of the play.

This is Mrs Alving's antagonist, and it is in its peculiar fashion powerful enough to explain and justify total submissiveness in all the individuals who compose it. Mrs Alving is conditioned; she is partly submissive, deliberately and unconsciously; but she is never totally subdued. And this refusal to give up trying to discover what is the truth and the right way to respond to it is again significantly defined through the image of a great natural force, the sun. Notwithstanding her wounds and blemishes, indeed because of them, Mrs Alving emerges as a great fighter against a terrible opponent.

In *Ghosts,* then, Ibsen has entered more deeply into the nature of modern society and its relationship to the heroic individual; he has also created a dramatic form for embodying his vision. Whatever else it may be, *Ghosts* cannot reasonably be assessed as a mere surrender on Ibsen's part to theatrical expediency or as a betrayal of the poetic copiousness of *Love's Comedy, Brand* and *Peer Gynt* to the seductions of naturalism. Its form is essential to the vision.

The language, for instance, is limited in range because this is one of the effects society has on its members. It educates them to think decorously and to express themselves with conventional neatness. Anyone who tries to break these limitations must create his own language and in Oswald's shapeless rhetoric the impression of overemphasis, of straining after effects not to hand in the common use of language, is indicative not of Ibsen's verbal impoverishment but of the spiritual impoverishment of the society that cannot accommodate Oswald; and, as we have seen, Mrs Alving's reduction of his vision to the careful patterning that she has been educated in illuminates the same point from a different angle. Ibsen can no longer imagine for his modern hero that degree of mental and spiritual autonomy that allowed Falk and Brand to be fully articulate poets. Their significance lies in their being poets of living, men with a vision of a finer life than society offers, but their ability to be poets in words, to speak out with full-blooded rhetoric to expound, explore, define their visions, is one way of asserting that they are spiritually free men. But they were so only because Ibsen had not, at that time, really sensed the power of modern society: Falk can stand outside it, Brand encounters a simplified version, an emblem. Nobody, not even Mrs Alving, can preserve his autonomy in the face of the complexity of power that society now represents for Ibsen, and the language is one means of expressing this fact.

The same is true of the setting. Mrs Alving's handsome room may be less spectacular than Brand's mountains and ice-church but it is not to be despised for its ordinariness. The set mirrors Ibsen's conviction that it is by its unobtrusiveness, by its very reasonableness and seemliness, that society is able to exercise its power; the very decency of appearances helps him emphasise the horror of discovering that the attractive setting is a monstrous snare, and the limiting of the action to one room takes away the illusion, still preserved in *Love's Comedy* and *Brand*, that there is somewhere else to go. In modern society, as Ibsen sees it, there is nowhere else; the great battles must be fought out amongst comfortable furniture in a handsome house; the mountains offer no escape to Mrs Alving: they are remote images of ultimate truth, not to be trodden as they were by Falk and Brand. The setting is an essential part of Ibsen's harsher vision.

The setting is created partly by verbal, partly by visual imagery. Both kinds indicate further advances beyond the artistry and vision of his earlier works. The extremity of imagery in *Brand*, those blatant and massive symbols of opposition—storm, mountains, ice-church, narrow dale, sunshine and so forth—help create what amounts to an almost comforting sense of clarity. The opposed values are identified for us; the crises that arise out of the opposition are made manifest not merely to us but to the protagonist. In *Ghosts* everything is made less precise. Instead of storm, steady drizzle and mist, not a challenge so much as an enervating atmosphere; instead of miserable dale, Mrs Alving's country house, outwardly a haven. There are no sharp indices of crisis; we have to discover them as Ibsen now sees them, as latent and lurking. Out of this lack of clarity comes a further virtue. Instead of establishing his imagery *ab initio* [from the beginning], as he does in *Love's Comedy* and in *Brand*, and then working by repetition, Ibsen allows his imagery to grow organically, establishing itself and its significance progressively. He works not by massive and blatant groupings but by small affinities gradually discovered. Yet he holds all this together, more successfully than in *Brand*, by creating a feeling of tempo, of inevitable movement towards a climax. All of the imagery is ultimately controlled by the image of Oswald's disease and by the image of day dispersing night. Thus Ibsen can represent deviousness and cryptic consequence without losing his sense of the essential unity of the action or of the pace in which the action moves. There is little feeling of development or progression in *Love's Comedy;* in *Brand* there is progression of a relatively simple linear kind, with little feeling of tempo; *Ghosts* moves much more impressively.

In *Ghosts* the vision is enriched and the form for its expression brought almost to perfection. Not quite to perfection because there are signs, here and there, that the effort to elucidate for himself the pattern that underlies the seemingly petty detail of modern living led him into oversimplification, both of vision and form, in the interests of clarity. Some of the cross-weaving of images into patterns is of this kind—the equation of the drizzle with the spiritual climate, or of Oswald with the Orphanage, does not need the kind of emphasis it is given. Manders need not be as inadequate as he is to give a reasonable representation of society's inadequacies.

Ghosts has its imperfections but it is a great play for all that. Though different in kind it is arguably a finer dramatic poem than *Brand,* if by poem we mean an imaginatively organised structure of imagery constituting a profound and unified vision. Less debatably, Mrs Alving is a more convincing kind of hero than Brand, by virtue of her fuller involvement in a society more fully understood and represented. From *Love's Comedy* and *Brand* we gain insight into the issues that govern the quality of living; in *Ghosts* the issues are played out upon our nerves and feelings as we experience, with Mrs Alving, what it feels like to be a woman like that condemned to live in such a world. *Ghosts* is, above all, an experience, immediate and immensely painful. And yet, for all its greatness, it marks only Ibsen's entry into artistic maturity; the greatest works are amongst those that follow. (pp. 106-12)

> *John Northam, in his* Ibsen: A Critical Study, *Cambridge at the University Press, 1973, 237 p.*

THE WILD DUCK

Lionel Trilling   (essay date 1967)

[*A respected American critic and literary historian, Trilling was also an essayist, editor, novelist, and short story writer. His exploration of liberal arts theory and its implications for the conduct of life led Trilling to function not only as a literary critic, but as a social commentator as well. A liberal and a humanist, Trilling judged the value of a text by its contribution to culture and, in turn, regarded culture as indispensable for human survival. In the following essay, originally published in* The Experience of Literature (1967), *Trilling suggests that* The Wild Duck *reflects Ibsen's awareness that "people cannot bear much reality, [and] some can bear even less than others." Hjalmar Ekdal, the critic notes, "knows that in order to get through life he needs all the help that illusion can give him." Significantly, Trilling adds, illusion and "make-believe" are "the very essence of one of man's most characteristic and important activities, that of art."*]

In T. S. Eliot's *Murder in the Cathedral,* the Archbishop Becket utters a sentence which has become famous—"Human kind," he says, "cannot bear very much reality." The sad dictum may serve to summarize the purport of

The attic set for Ingmar Bergman's 1972 production of The Wild Duck. *Royal Dramatic Theatre, Stockholm.*

The Wild Duck. And the play goes on to suggest that it is wicked for one person to seek to impose upon another a greater amount of reality than can comfortably be borne. That this should be the "message" of a play by Henrik Ibsen came as a great surprise—indeed, a shock—when **The Wild Duck** was first presented in 1884.

And even now it is likely to startle any reader or playgoer acquainted with the author's characteristic early work. For Ibsen was an outstanding figure in the movement of modern art and intellect that subjected all existing institutions, and the conventions of thought and feeling, to relentless scrutiny in the interests of truth; it was the stern judgment of this movement that society is a contrivance to mask or evade or distort reality. The effort to discriminate between what is real and what is illusory is of course not a new endeavor for literature. But in the modern epoch it has been undertaken with a new particularity and aggressiveness, and by none more than by Ibsen. He had made his reputation with four plays—**Pillars of Society, A Doll's House, Ghosts,** and **An Enemy of the People**—and in each of them he had pressed home the view that falsehood, whether in the form of social lies and hypocrisy or of self-deception, weakens the fabric of life and deprives human kind of its dignity. Expectably enough, his work had met with resistance by the larger part of his audience, that is to say, the more conventional part. But by the same token, the "advanced" minority, a growing force in European culture, received him as a master of truth. In his lifetime and for many years after his death, people spoke of "Ibsenism," by which they meant the radical questioning of all established and respectable modes of life and the un-

yielding opposition to sham and pretense. It can therefore be imagined with what bewilderment and dismay the Ibsenites received a play which said that truth may be dangerous to life, and not every man is worthy to tell it or receive it, and that the avoidance and concealment of the truth, or even a lie, may have a vital beneficence.

In speaking of the fate of Oedipus, I remarked that although we feel apprehension as Oedipus approaches closer and closer to the knowledge that will destroy him, and although we may wish to warn him against continuing his investigation, we do not really want the dreadful truth to stay hidden from him. As I put it, "we do not want Oedipus to remain oblivious of the truth about himself. An Oedipus who prudently gave up his search would be an object of condescension, even of contempt. . . . " This is of course pretty much the feeling on which Gregers Werle proceeds when he resolves to bestow on Hjalmar Ekdal the terrible gift of reality. Hjalmar does not know that his wife had once been secretly the mistress of the elder Werle and that he is not in point of biological fact the father of his daughter. Gregers discloses the true state of affairs because he wants Hjalmar to "face reality" in order to gain the dignity which is presumed to follow upon that disagreeable confrontation. Why, then, do we blame Gregers for making the revelation?

The answer is that Hjalmar is not Oedipus, as poor Hjalmar himself well knows until he is tempted to believe otherwise. Perhaps no moment in the play is more bitterly affecting than that in which, after the disclosure has been made, Hjalmar says, "Do you think a man can recover so easily from the bitter cup I've just emptied?" Gregers replies, "Not an ordinary man, no. But a man like you—!" And Hjalmar desperately and feebly tries to accept the moral heroism that has been ruthlessly thrust upon him: "Good Lord, yes, I know that. But you mustn't be driving me, Gregers. You see, these things take time."

It may indeed be true that people cannot bear very much reality, but some can bear even less than others. Hjalmar is one of those who can bear scarcely any at all. Yet it might be said that in his weakness there is a kind of strength. Whatever his announced claims for himself may be, in his heart of hearts he estimates himself fairly accurately. Until Gregers comes into his life with high talk of what the "summons to the ideal" ought to mean to "a man like you," Hjalmar knows that in order to get through life he needs all the help that illusion can give him, and he takes all the help he can get. It is plain enough that Hjalmar does not really believe he will vindicate the family honor and rehabilitate his old father by making a fortune as an inventor, but the double pose of righter of wrongs and of lonely man of genius sustains and comforts him. We can scarcely suppose that the truth about his wife and daughter had all these years lain very far from his consciousness; if he had wanted to grasp it, he could have reached out for it long ago. He had no such desire, and in consequence he is established in a small but cozy way of life, provided with an affectionate wife who cheerfully performs not only her own tasks but his, and an adoring daughter; he lives in such self-esteem as may arise for the uncontradicted assertion of his natural superiority. In the light of his wife's goodness of heart, it is not of the least importance that this simple woman was once another man's mistress; in the light of his daughter's boundless affection and trust, it is of no consequence that he had not actually engendered her; and Hjalmar had seen to it that what did not matter was never allowed to come into his consciousness. But once the explicit truth is forced upon him, it does its destructive work. We may feel that it should not have had the effect upon the poor man that it does have; we comment on the pettiness of his pride, on how accomplished he is in nursing his grievance. Yet if we consider the sexual ethos of his time, we recognize that only a saint or a philosopher could have received the revelation with magnanimous good sense. The fact that Hjalmar is neither saint nor philosopher does not decisively distinguish him from most men.

The device by which Ibsen suggests the possible beneficence of illusion is a charming one, and also deeply moving, even more in actual presentation on the stage than on the printed page—it is always an electrifying moment for the audience when the forest in the garret is first revealed to view. There is something strangely affecting in a fiction, a mere fancy, that stands before us as a palpable actuality, to be seen and entered into; and the actuality of the forest is made more than palpable by its being inhabited by the beautiful and tragic wild duck. When first the sliding door is pushed back to reveal the moonlit scene, we have the sense that we have been permitted to look out through Keats's "magic casements, opening on the foam / Of perilous seas, in faery lands forlorn."

For the Ekdals, this fictive forest is a source not only of pleasure but of life itself. It calls forth their best emotions. Toward it, especially toward its most notable denizen, the wounded wild duck, Hedvig directs the natural grace of her spirit, and it is the means by which old Lieutenant Ekdal reconciles himself to his ruined old age. Even Hjalmar rises above his uneasy self-regard and surrenders to a childlike innocence when he comes under the spell of this avowed illusion, which so touchingly binds the family together. The little wilderness is a mere game which the Ekdals play, but into all the activities of human kind, even the most serious and practical, some element of the game is introduced; "make believe" and "as if " do not come to an end with childhood. And the "let's pretend" of play is the very essence of one of man's most characteristic and important activities, that of art.

Hjalmar's father, Lieutenant Ekdal, the simple-minded old hunter, who in his best days had been the mighty killer of actual bears, plays the forest game with the perfectly clear consciousness that it is a game, even though it is also, for him, life itself; and Hedvig plays it as a child, with an absolute commitment to it but with no real confusion of the fancy with reality. And when Hjalmar plays it, he too knows it for what it is. But there are illusions from which some people in *The Wild Duck* cannot detach themselves. Hjalmar must have some rôle which will conceal from his own perception and that of the world the fact that he is a man of no talent or distinction. In school he had been known as a great declaimer of poetry and therefore as a person of notable sensibility and high ideals, and it is partly the illusioned memory of Hjalmar as he was in the past that leads Gregers to intervene on behalf of his friend's moral dignity; Gregers accepts without question Hjalmar's claim to being a wronged man and an unfulfilled genius. Molvik, the former theological student, is a feckless drunkard but he takes heart from the rôle that Dr. Relling invents for him, that of a "demonic" character, a personality which manifests its power in the "wildness" of a supernal intoxication. As for Gregers himself, we can scarcely fail to see that his behavior as the uncompromising idealist is dictated not only by his grievance against his robust father but also by his desire to acquire a moral status that will mask the emptiness of his unloving heart.

People like these, living by illusions of personal distinction, did not always exist. Like the bereaved doctor of Chekhov's "Enemies" and Gabriel Conroy of Joyce's "The Dead," they are the creatures of modernity, especially of that aspect of modernity which Hegel, in his *Philosophy of History,* called the "secularization of spirituality." What Hegel meant by that phrase is suggested by the authority that Ibsen himself achieved and the means by which he achieved it. Where once the moral life of human kind had been chiefly in the keeping of the Church, it was now, by Ibsen's time, increasingly in the charge of playwrights, novelists, poets, and philosophers. Where once life had been relatively simple under the Church's guidance or direction, it was now complex in response to the questioning of writers. Where once it had been concerned with the fulfilment of the duties that were appropriate to one's station in life, it was now concerned with the fulness of a person's life as an individual, with its integrity and dignity, with the proud, vexed commitment to the ideal, that new moral and spiritual sanction which would have been quite incomprehensible a century or two earlier. Ibsen had done much to forward the "secularization of spirituality" and to advance the new self-consciousness, demanding that people be heroes of the spirit. *The Wild Duck* was written in a moment of brilliant self-doubt. This was perhaps induced by the disaffection from his disciples that any master may feel when he perceives how his own hardwon ideas are distorted by those who make easy use of them. But this turning of Ibsen upon himself cannot be attributed merely to his desire to discomfit his Ibsenite followers and to detach himself from the doctrinaire conception of what he had done. It came also, we feel sure, from a magnanimous mind's awareness of the difficulty of life and the impossibility of forcing upon it any single rule, even that of reality. (pp. 22-7)

> *Lionel Trilling, "Henrik Ibsen: 'The Wild Duck',"* in his *Prefaces to The Experience of Literature, Harcourt Brace Jovanovich, 1979, pp. 22-7.*

Ruth Harmer   (essay date 1970)

[*Harmer contends that Gina Ekdal is "the truly heroic figure in* The Wild Duck.*" The numerous conflicting critical interpretations of the drama, she claims, result from regarding Hjalmar, Old Ekdal, or Gregers as the hero. After disqualifying each of these characters in turn, Harmer asserts that Gina, "with her loving-kindness, her life-truth," is the play's protagonist. Furthermore, the critic argues, far from being the play's hero, Gregers, "with his 'claim of the ideal,' his death-truth," is Gina's antagonist.*]

When a play is widely acclaimed as a masterpiece by critics who disagree radically about its nature and meaning, it may be that the work possesses such richness of content, such poetic density, that critics are unable to comprehend its totality; it may be that it contains an element so alien to conventional notions that they are unwilling to follow where the playwright's vision has led. The critical confusion generated by Henrik Ibsen's *The Wild Duck* since it was first published in 1884 suggests that sometimes both elements are involved.

Although many of its earliest readers and audiences found it "obscure and morbid," as Professor Otto Reinert of the University of Oslo noted several years ago [in his *Modern Drama,* 1962], "today it is generally considered one of Ibsen's greatest plays in prose." Yet there is currently very little more agreement about the kind of play it is than there was during Ibsen's lifetime. George Brandes, an admiring contemporary, said in 1898 that it was "perhaps the most pessimistic play that Ibsen had yet written" [*Henrik Ibsen, A Critical Study*]. Nine years later, Edmund Gosse categorized it [in his *Ibsen*] as a "brilliant, but saturnine and sardonic tragi-comedy," whose theme was of such a "topsy-turvy nature" that it had "made Ibsen as nearly 'rollicking' as he ever became in his life." Ibsen, who also regarded it as a tragi-comedy, complained of a Copenhagen production in 1898 because "it exaggerated the play's farcical side" [quoted in F. L. Lucas, *The*

Drama of Ibsen and Strindberg, 1962]. Recently, British critic F. L. Lucas, who considers it a "bitter tragedy," marveled that an American critic ("a Professor Weigand") had said: "*The Wild Duck* does not begin as a comedy and end as a tragedy. It is a comedy from start to finish." Robert Raphael, another American critic, has labeled it an analysis and satire of transcendentalism, "only potentially frightening and often even quite farcical" ["Illusion and the Self in *The Wild Duck, Rosmersholm,* and *The Lady from the Sea,"* *Ibsen: A Collection of Critical Essays,* ed. Rolf Fjelde, 1965].

The mode of representation partly accounts for the play's being held, like the players in *Hamlet,* best for "tragical-comical-historical-pastoral"—what the critic will. Highly realistic in its rendering of "ordinary" people in an "ordinary" world of social events and institutions, of domestic occupations and preoccupations, it records the details of existence with a photographic literalness. *The Wild Duck* is also naturalistic in its emphasis on the importance of heredity and environment as dominant forces in shaping men's destinies and in its emphasis on the mean and trivial facts of daily life. But above all, it is an intensely poetic, highly "romantic" play dominated by the symbolism of the wild bird and the "heavenly" attic, where it dwells with the poor and the meek and the "wounded" in the blessedness of love.

Although the action itself is relatively unified and simple, following the pattern of homecoming and holocaust set in *Ghosts* and other plays, the complexity of the antecedent action, revealed with tantalizing skill during the five acts, is also partly responsible for the varied responses to the play.

The sequence of tragic events was set in motion many years earlier by Håkon Werle, a wealthy Norwegian merchant and manufacturer, during his ruthless rise to fortune and his only somewhat less ruthless career as a sexual adventurer. The "battlefield" of his past is strewn with victims. His wife, a puritanical, impoverished gentlewoman, was driven to madness and death by his treatment. His son, Gregers, passionately attached to his mother while loathing and fearing his father, had fled the house to a fifteen-year exile at one of Werle's enterprises in the mountains. Some outsiders fared no better by their association with him. Lieutenant Ekdal, Werle's business partner and the father of Gregers' best friend, Hjalmar, had been imprisoned and ruined for a theft of government timber—a crime that brought profit, not punishment to the man chiefly responsible, Werle. To cloak the consequences of his seduction of Gina, his wife's maid, Werle arranged to marry her off to the unsuspecting Hjalmar.

Now old and lonely and nearly blind, Håkon Werle is ready to settle gracefully into dying. He wishes to give the management of his businesses to his son, to exchange his town house for Gregers' mountain retreat. He summons Gregers home.

The curtain rises on a party to which all the "best people" in town have been invited to celebrate the Werles' reconciliation. But even before the after-dinner coffee and liqueurs have been tasted, it becomes apparent that the fatted calf had been slaughtered and served prematurely. Gregers has no intention of playing the part of the prodigal son—of becoming his father's business partner or of being a guest at the wedding feast of his father and Mrs. Sörby, Werle's housekeeper and current mistress. He has returned in the role of avenging angel, bent on retribution for the wrongs done his adored mother and Old Ekdal.

During his conversation with Hjalmar, while the others are joking broadly and eating hugely, Gregers acquires another mission. He realizes that his father's setting up Gina and Hjalmar in the photography business, thus making possible their marriage, was simply an inexpensive means of shielding himself from scandal. Hjalmar's child, Hedvig, is undoubtedly Werle's. Gregers leaves his father's house, announcing that he will reveal to his friend that "what he calls his home is built upon a lie!"

To accomplish that, Gregers moves into the house that Hjalmar occupies with his wife, daughter, father, and two lodgers: Molvik, a student of theology and a dedicated drunkard; and Relling, a disillusioned doctor who ministers to the spiritually sick patients he encounters in "the great hospital" that is the world by concocting for them life-sustaining illusions, sometimes—as in the case of Molvik—of a high-proof, alcoholic content.

In spite of the poverty and eccentricity of its inhabitants, the house is a strange and wonderful place—a home in which people are protected by love, ennobled by happiness. Out of the scraps thrown to them by Werle and his servants and the miserable sums realized from the photographic business and Old Ekdal's copying work, out of their imaginings and generous feelings, they have created a kind of paradise in the great attic that is stocked with rabbits, pigeons, tame fowl of various kinds, and the wild duck given to them by one of Werle's employees after his master had wounded it and his dog had retrieved it from the bottom of the marsh, where it had gone to die. There, Old Ekdal, wearing the Army uniform that had been stripped from him by his imprisonment, can fancy himself again a mighty hunter. There Hjalmar can love his father, whom he denies in "polite company," and can indulge with dignity his desire to perpetuate his childhood in play. There, Hedvig, who is becoming blind, finds joy in tending the creatures of the forest, in reading the books left behind by a former tenant, and in the companionship of her grandfather and her father, whom she idolizes.

Gregers, with his mad preoccupation with absolute truth, refuses to recognize the miracle that love has wrought. The attic is not heaven to him, but "the depths of the sea." He will be like his father's dog: "one that goes to the bottom after wild ducks when they dive and bite themselves fast in tangle and sea-weed, down among the ooze." Hjalmar, he convinces himself, has "sunk down to die in the dark" and must be rescued from his contentment since that is only "an effect of the marsh poison."

He will not be dissuaded from that by his father, by Gina, or by Dr. Relling, who warns him bluntly that if he comes dunning the "insolvent" household with his claim of the ideal while Relling is on the premises he will go "head-foremost down the stairs." Gregers tells his friend—

although Hjalmar has protested that "in my house nobody ever speaks to me about unpleasant things. . . . It's not good for me"—that Gina had been his father's mistress. Far from feeling the "new consecration" that Gregers had expected him to feel, Hjalmar is still reeling from that blow when Mrs. Sörby arrives with a document from Werle awarding Old Ekdal a hundred crowns a month for life, a gift that will be passed on to Hedvig when her grandfather dies. Hjalmar, for the first time, associates Hedvig's incipient blindness with that of Werle. He thrusts the child from him and leaves.

However, not even that wound is mortal. Dr. Relling takes him out with Molvik to get terribly drunk; and by mid-hangover the next morning, fed and soothed by Gina, Hjalmar is beginning to recover. But Gregers' mission is not yet finished. In order to induce in his three unwitting victims the "true frame of mind for selfsacrifice and forgiveness," he persuades Hedvig that she must kill the wild duck: "to make a free-will offering, for his sake, of the dearest treasure you have in the world!"

The loving little girl agrees, although by the next (the final) act she changes her attitude about the sacrifice:

> Yesterday evening, at the moment, I thought there was something so delightful about it; but since I have slept and thought of it again, it somehow doesn't seem worth the while.

Gregers persuades her that she must exhibit the "true, joyous, fearless spirit of sacrifice," and after Hjalmar again rejects her, she creeps into the attic with the pistol—the weapon which both Hjalmar and Old Ekdal had contemplated using against themselves. Unable to bring herself to kill the wild duck, she kills herself. And the play ends.

With action so direct and straightforward, what does give rise to perplexities and confusion? The answer, I believe, lies in the characters, in Ibsen's marvelously intricate characterizations.

The writer himself anticipated some problems. In a letter to his publisher, Frederik Hegel, on September 2, 1884, accompanying the manuscript, Ibsen noted:

> In some ways this new play occupies a position by itself among my dramatic works, its plan and method differing in several respects from my former ones. . . . I hope that my critics will discover the points alluded to. At any rate, they will find several things to squabble about and several things to interpret.
> [*Letters and Speeches*, ed. Evert Sprinchorn]

Since much of the letter emphasized his attitude toward the characters, it is reasonable to assume that they constitute at least one of the "points alluded to"—although not specified by him:

> Long, daily association with the characters in this play has endeared them to me, in spite of their manifold failings. And I hope that they may find good and kind friends among the great reading public, and more particularly among the actor tribe—for all of them, without exception, are rewarding roles. But the study and represen-

tation of these characters will not be an easy task.

August Lindberg, who directed the first production of **The Wild Duck** on January 30, 1885 at the Royal Dramatic Theater in Stockholm and who played the role of Hjalmar, expressed himself "dizzy" with the theatrical richness of the play:

> Such great opportunities for us actors! Never before have we been faced with such possibilities. . . . The people in the play are completely new, and where would we get by relying on old theaterical clichés?

The characters were so "completely new," Ibsen's characterizations of heroic and villainous figures were so compassionate, and his refusal to deny tragic stature to common men and women was so remarkably daring that it is small wonder that critics were and have continued to be in disagreement about the principal participants in the struggle and their significance.

Unwilling to risk approaching that "limit of knowledge" that Ibsen dared in creating his people, following their predilictions, insisting that theme comes before character rather than follows from it, critics have hurled labels with wildest abandon. Perhaps the best indication of how confused matters are may be gained from the summing up by Professor Theodore Jorgenson in his recent study [*Henrik Ibsen: A Study in Art and Personality*, 1945]. He says that if the need of illusions is taken as the main theme, the leading tragic character is Hjalmar Ekdal; if it is absolute idealism, Gregers Werle; if it is the belief that the finest are destroyed by the prophets of absolute idealism and the illusion-ridden masses, it is Hedvig. "Thus **The Wild Duck** may be regarded as three plays in one." On the other hand, Professor Jorgensen earlier in his analysis had asserted that in **The Wild Duck** Ibsen was seeking a new method— to substitute for a leading character a symbol that could "tie all the heterogeneous elements of the drama together and give it the necessary unity." In addition to all those "major" possibilities for the heroic role, Dr. Relling has also been offered as candidate.

Relling's candidacy as protagonist, I think, is easiest to dismiss, for the reasons that Professor Reinert and others have pointed out: his structurally unprepared late arrival; his place among the chorus as commentator; his flawed character—as Mrs. Sorby says, he has "frittered away all that was good in him"; his questionable remedies for his patients' ills. To be sure, he has helped to protect the ego of Molvik by diagnosing him as a "demonic personality" rather than an alcoholic and that of Hjalmar by leading him to believe that his laziness is but the incubation period of a great inventor, but his nostrums are those of a quacksalver rather than a doctor.

Nor is it posible to accept seriously the notion that Hedvig is the protagonist. The delicate, shy, loving little girl is essentially where Relling insists that she must be: "outside of all this." We weep over her willingness to turn the pistol against herself rather than the wild duck; we are not participants in the anguished struggle.

Although Gregers Werle has been suggested as the leading tragic character as well as "a kind of bitter self-parody by Ibsen of his own reforming fervour" [F. L. Lucas], he is neither a heroic nor a farcical character. Indeed, two of the characters he calls to mind are Iago [in Shakespeare's *Othello*] in his wanton destruction of another man's happiness and (here the resemblance is closer, I think) Roger Chillingworth [in Nathaniel Hawthorne's *The Scarlet Letter*] in the systematic manner in which he violates the sanctity of a human heart.

Gregers makes himself believe that his intentions are good, that all he desires is to free his friend from false illusions so that he can rebuild his life and marriage on the solid foundations of truth and justice. But Ibsen calls attention to what he is up to through the pointed comments of Relling. When Gregers talks about the "marsh vapors" in the house, Relling retorts sharply: "Excuse me—may it not be you yourself that have brought the taint from those mines up here?" When Gregers speaks about ideals, Relling brings him up coldly: "While I think of it, Mr. Werle, junior—don't use that foreign word: ideals. We have the excellent native word: lies."

Gregers fancies that his goodness is apparent, but Gina sees him clearly. When Hjalmar returns from the party with the news that he has seen Gregers, she asks simply: "Is Gregers as ugly as ever?" The exterior ugliness matches what is within. his love for his joyless mother has poisoned his heart and mind. Gregers acts not from love, but from hatred. His one moment of insight comes when he tells his father that: "If I am to go on living, I must try to find some cure for my sick conscience." His father is correct when he replies that it will never be sound. Gregers is powerless to destroy his father, but he is succesful in his assault on the Ekdals. And in his spiritual pride, he indicates his readiness to go right on playing God. Unchastened by the ruin of his friend's marriage, by the suicide of the child, he tells Relling grandly as the curtain falls that he is *glad* his destiny is what it is: "to be the thirteenth at the table"—that is, to play Christ. It is not surprising, as Lucas has noted, that when the play was performed in Italy, "realistic" Italians called to Gregers "in a storm of fury and disgust"—'*Basta! Basta! Imbecille!*'

Far more likely a candidate for the role, as August Lindberg seems to have recognized quickly, is Hjalmar—a character shaped by Ibsen with exquisite skill. Hjalmar is a catalog of frailties. He is greedy, consuming vast quantities of butter and beer so that Gina and Hedvig have to starve themselves in order that the food bills may be paid; he is lazy, napping all afternoon, playing in the attic, dreaming about the inventions that will happen without his exertions; he is proud of his appearance, his curly locks, his still young figure; he is thoughtless, forgetting to bring home from the Werle party the gift he had promised Hedvig (he returns with a menu instead!). Hjalmar is a coward, denying his father at the party because Old Ekdal is not socially acceptable, rejecting Hedvig because of conventions; he is pretentious, posing as an authority to his simple family and trying to maintain his reputation for sophistication by discouraging Hedvig from reading. He is full of self pity and sentimentality, and he is almost utterly shallow. Briefly ennobled by the death of Hedvig, his sorrow, we feel with Dr. Relling, will quickly pass, and "before a year is over, little Hedvig will be nothing to him but a pretty theme for declamation."

But he is not totally to blame. "Ekdal's misfortune," as Dr. Relling points out, "is that in his own circle he has always been looked upon as a shining light." Brought up by two "high-flown, hysterical maiden aunts" and an overly fond father:

> When our dear, sweet Hjalmar went to college, he at once passed for the great light of the future amongst his comrades too.
>
> He was handsome, the rascal—red and white—a shop-girl's dream of manly beauty; and with his superficially emotional temperament, and his sympathetic voice, and his talent for declaiming other people's verses and other people's thoughts. . . .

Moreover, his failings are human failings, and they are free from malice. He is gentle; he is not suspicious—it would never have occurred to him to think ill of Old Werle or Gina or anyone else. Within the framework of his limited capacity, he is affectionate—genuinely fond of his father, his child, his wife. And his romantic dreams are directed to doing something for Hedvig, making it possible for his father to go publicly in uniform. He is the victim rather than the protagonist, the soul for possession of which Gregers is struggling against . . . Gina. For here is the truly heroic figure in *The Wild Duck.* Striving, suffering, enduring, she has been casually dismissed by critics as simple or even "weak." Admittedly, she appears an unlikely figure to assume the tragic mantle, "shuffling quietly in and out in her felt slippers, with that see-saw walk of hers." But once she had been beautiful. Old Werle's unremitting pursuit of her indicates that she had been lovely to look at; Hedvig reflects her. Even the unperceptive Gregers notices that "she promises to be very like you, Mrs. Ekdal."

What was once an external has become an inner glow. With nothing to begin with—no education, as her speech larded with malapropisms points out; with no one to protect her (she had fled the Werle house only to be forced into a sexual relationship with Old Werle by her mother); with only a weak and dissolute young fop for a husband—her love for Hjalmar had enabled her to create a world of happiness and contentment. As hard-working as Hjalmar is lazy, she cleans and cooks for Relling and Molvik as well as her husband, Hedvig, and Hjalmar's father. She drudges as if she were receiving a favor instead of conferring one. She manages the photography business so that Hjalmar may occupy himself peacefully with his no-invention, telling clients to come during the afternoon so that they will not interfere with his nap. She is gentle with Old Ekdal, allowing him to make her house into the wild duck's domain, not reproaching him for closeting himself with the bottle that Werle's servant had given him, gently humoring the poor old man. She endures the presence of Molvik and Relling with grace, is tender with Hedvig, and transforms Hjalmar from a young man with "bad ways" into "a moral of a husband." She asks nothing for herself, although she is not wantless—dreaming of the time when

she and Hedvig would "be able to let ourselves go a bit, in the way of both food and clothes."

For all her apparent simplicity, she is perceptive about essentials: Gregers' evil, Hjalmar's weaknesses, Hedvig's adolescent problems, the late Mrs. Werle's cruelty and coldness. Her reactions are not lethargic, but marvelously controlled, as we know from the way she waits with barely concealed anguish for the blow to fall when Hjalmar returns from his disastrous walk with Gregers:

> HJALMAR: It seems to me your voice is trembling.
>
> GINA: (*putting the lamp-shade on*). Is it?
>
> HJALMAR: And your hands are shaking, are they not?

Critics are not to be blamed unduly for failing to recognize Gina's stature. Such love is not easy to comprehend. When Hjalmar rushes out of the house leaving havoc behind, her one concern is to get the child quieted; her silence about the affair with Werle was imposed by love for Hjalmar: "I'd come to care for you so much. . . ." Neither is the dignity that she exhibits easy to comprehend. After Gregers has put her as well as Hjalmar through one of the bitterest moments of both their lives, she says simply: "God forgive you, Mr. Werle." She allows herself one anguished cry when Relling announces that Hedvig is dead: "Oh, my child, my child." Then she picks up again her burden as guardian of what is left of the devastated house. Directing Hjalmar to help her carry the child's body to her own room, "it musn't lie here for a show," she comforts him: "We must help each other to bear it. For now at least she belongs to both of us."

It is not surprising, I think, that Ibsen was so concerned about who played the role. In a letter to Lindberg, thanking him for his performance as Hjalmar and for the "exemplary" rehearsing and staging of the play, Ibsen strongly protested that the part of Gina had not been "entrusted" to Mrs. Hwasser, one of the leading players, as he had been "absolutely certain" it would have been. "I do feel absolutely convinced that the part of Gina will not be handled properly until it is given to Mrs. Hwasser."

If Gina is accepted as the protagonist, problems of theme are resolved, and the play does not—as Professor Reinert has charged—"insist on its own meaninglessness." Two main forces are in conflict: Gregers, with his "claim of the ideal," his death-truth; Gina, with her loving kindness, her life-truth. Also involved is the compromise, equivocating force: Dr. Relling, with his escape and illusion, his life-lie. The play is designed to show us that only hers is worth struggling for, only that saves life as well as art from meaninglessness. (pp. 419-27)

> *Ruth Harmer, "Character, Conflict, and Meaning in 'The Wild Duck',"* in Modern Drama, *Vol. XII, No. 4, February, 1970, pp. 419-27.*

Ronald Gray (essay date 1977)

[*Gray judges* The Wild Duck *a confused and poorly*

*written play. Hjalmar is, he claims, naive to the point of
"simple-mindedness," and Gregers is "a man slightly
crazed," whose motives in revealing the truth to Hjalmar
remain obscure. Gray particularly attacks Ibsen's use of
symbolism, especially that of the wild duck, which, he
insists, has so many possible meanings that its use leads
to confusion and ambiguity.*]

An initial weakness [in *The Wild Duck*] shows as early
as the exposition. Ibsen starts traditionally enough with
the device of a conversation between two servants, one
permanent, the other hired only for the evening, and
therefore needing to be told who everyone is. Tennant
calls this clumsy [in his *Ibsen's Dramatic Technique*,
1948], but it is acceptable, however well-worn, as a swift
means of sketching in the background. It is in the scene
between Gregers Werle and Hjalmar Ekdal, later in Act
One, that more serious difficulties become noticeable.

There is a complex situation to be divulged: first, that fourteen years ago Werle senior has had a child, Hedvig, by
his former housekeeper, Gina, and has arranged for the
mother to marry Hjalmar, whom he has set up in business
as a professional photographer. Then it needs to be explained that old Werle has also—perhaps for confidential
reasons of his own connected with a business deal—looked
after Hjalmar's aging father, that Hjalmar has no suspicion of the reason for this, or for his own specially favoured treatment. It also has to be brought out that the son,
Gregers, is beginning to believe that his father is motivated
by a certain self-interest.

These events may pass well enough as credible at a performance, when there is no time to consider them. As on
other occasions, Ibsen gains by not presenting them as
staged action. Reflection shows that the story depends on
some considerable degree of naivety in Hjalmar, and a
willingness in old Werle to gamble on very long odds. We
are asked to believe that after Werle discovered Gina's
pregnancy he first dismissed her from her job as his housekeeper, then arranged matters so that Hjalmar took up
lodgings in her mother's house, and finally waited until
Hjalmar not only fell in love with Gina but married her
before her pregnancy became obvious to him—and then
failed to notice that she gave birth rather soon after their
marriage. Given that Hjalmar is extraordinarily naive, or
very willing to be deceived, this is not impossible. But with
only four or five months for all this to happen—Hjalmar
could hardly have failed to notice if Gina had given birth
within three or four months of marriage—the time-
scheme is rather tight.

A greater awkwardness arises from the needs of the exposition. Gregers, who describes Hjalmar as his 'best and
only friend', must be brought into conversation with him
in such a way that Hjalmar reveals all the facts about his
engagement and marriage, and, while suspecting nothing
himself, causes Gregers to see the hidden hand of his self-
interested father in all the ostensibly generous benefactions intended to hush up the past. This is dramatically
useful: the audience hears just what Gregers hears, and
puts two and two together just as he does: its interest is
actively engaged. The question arises, though, how
Gregers can be so completely uninformed about the affairs

of so close a friend. He has been away, it appears, for sixteen or seventeen years, working 'up at Håidal', 'slaving
away like any ordinary clerk', and in the whole of that
time he has never been back to town or heard any news
except what his father chose to tell him in postscripts to
business letters. He did learn that Hjalmar Ekdal's father
had been in prison on account of a dishonest business deal,
which almost involved Werle senior also (hence the elder
man's only apparently charitable care for old Ekdal), but
this did not induce him to write to Hjalmar, despite his
own father's involvement. And Hjalmar did not write to
Gregers because Werle senior told him that Gregers was
offended with him, old Ekdal having nearly brought his
own father into disgrace:

> GREGERS: And you think I was against you on
> that account? Whoever gave you that idea?
>
> HJALMAR: I know you were, Gregers. It was
> your father himself who told me.
>
> GREGERS: (*amazed*) My father! Indeed. Hm!
> Was that the reason you never let me hear from
> you . . . not a single word?
>
> HJALMAR: Yes.
>
> GREGERS: Not even at the time when you went
> and became a photographer?
>
> HJALMAR: Your father said there was no point
> in writing to you about anything.
>
>   (Act I)

Ibsen has covered every conceivable objection that a critic
of the Scribe school [of the "well-made play"] could make.
As an exposition this cannot be faulted: there is an explanation for everything. But the demands of the exposition
have required the characters to seem naive or unintelligent
to a degree that makes them in themselves less interesting.
The exposition has taken precedence over the character-
drawing.

It is, again, not impossible for such a man as Gregers to
leave his parents' home—even when his mother, to whom
Gregers was devoted, was still alive—and to seclude himself in some remote part of the country for years on end,
never inquiring about his best friend, learning nothing of
events from his mother, not returning for her funeral, not
getting in touch with his best friend when the friend's father is failed (a fact which Gregers knew), and maintaining himself on a pittance. But such a hermit seems eccentric to a degree that can damage the play. One wants to
know why he acts so queerly, and Ibsen gives no sign of
interest in that question.

It is not impossible for a man, marrying a woman in the
circumstances in which Hjalmar married Gina, to remain
unsuspicious, and not to tell his close friend either that the
marriage had taken place or that a daughter had been
born, simply because he had been given a rather unlikely
reason why the friend should be offended. (What offence
could Hjalmar have given Gregers by virtue of old Ekdal's
business deal having come near to incriminating Werle senior?) But such simple-mindedness and gullibility are too
frequent a feature of Ibsen's characters for one not to feel
that the sheer technical difficulties have prevented the por-

trayal of characters possessing more subtle qualities, or else that Ibsen was little interested in the real complexities of behaviour.

There is here not merely a technical question of an unlikely exposition. It is not the creaking revelation of the dramatist's labour caused by Hjalmar's repeated questions— 'Surely you know that?', 'Gregers, didn't you kow?', 'Maybe you didn't know anything about that either?', 'Don't you remeber she was called Gina?', and so on— that matters most. Hjalmar himself is one of those many characters in Ibsen for whom it is hard to find a more charitable name than 'booby'. Ibsen seems to parade him for the audience's scorn. He is made to ask at Mrs Sörby's party whether the vintage makes any difference to wine, and having learned that it does, to show off his knowledge at home to his wife and daughter. He is mockingly asked by the Fat Guest to recite some poetry, which he 'used to do so prettily', and has at the time no retort to this insult, but again boasts at home as though he had put everyone in their places. There is in all this a psychological interest, in seeing Hjalmar turn his defeats into satisfactions. He is a sort of prim and unbending Micawber [in Charles Dickens's *David Copperfield*]. When his daughter Hedvig asks if he has remembered to bring her home a titbit from the dinner-party, he has not—which might happen to anyone—but offers to show her the menu and tell her what the courses tasted like. Only after she has shown her unquestioning devotion, offering to bring him first his flute, then some beer, does he show any sign of being aware of her, but then he goes straight into his rôle as hagridden but loving father of the family, plays his flute 'with much "feeling" ', and declares there is no place like home. Hedvig kills herself, in the end, to please him, and the play means to show how his falsity drove her to it. As with Helmer Torvald, the demonstration is laid on with a trowel.

Gregers is equally near to a caricature, though again not altogether incredible. His absence of curiosity about his old friend need not be taken as a mark of his character, rather as a distortion caused by technical considerations. The difficulty about being moved by the play comes from his unreasoning and fanatical insistence on opening Hjalmar's eyes to the truth. The need for this is never discussed. Gregers merely speaks of freeing Hjalmar from 'all the lies and deceit that are causing his ruination,' and is never challenged to say what that ruination is. So far as the play shows us, Hjalmar is comfortably off in his marriage, and it might be more to the point to ask him to show consideration for Hedvig and his wife, rather than to insist on his knowing his daughter is illegitimate. Gregers never reflects on the likely consequences of telling Hjalmar the truth about the past, but assumes the results can only be good, and this blindness in both of them is not offered so that we may understand it: it is the mainstay of the play.

As Relling says, Gregers is 'an acute case of inflamed scruples'. But he is precisely that, a 'case', not a man with whom one feels any degree of affinity, such as Relling implies when he goes on to say Gregers' disease is 'a national illness'. If the issue could be presented in those terms it might well have that extension of meaning from the individual to the more general which a play needs for real suc-

cess. A Norwegian 'national illness' is likely to be shared by other nations too: there can be few people with no desire at all to remove splinters from other people's eyes. But the objection is not that in *Ghosts,* by contrast, the Norwegian disease is rather hushing things up than revealing them. It is rather that the deep need most people feel to get at the truth is not adequately represented by Gregers' bald-headed rush at it. We suppress the truth about ourselves for reasons of which Gregers is ignorant; we have more inhibitions than his puritan zeal comprehends, and Ibsen, in showing the results of zeal of that order, is plugging away at the obvious. The place for such a grotesque is farce.

Gregers' proposal to Hedvig that she should show her love for her father by sacrificing the wild duck, her dearest possession, is a crux of the play: without it there could be no catastrophe. But this is based on no better grounds than Gregers' revelation to Hjalmar about Hedvig's parentage. In his first wild reaction to that news, Hjalmar turned on Hedvig in a fit of bad temper and said he would like to wring the duck's neck. There was no reason to take this any more seriously than other unthinking things he says throughout the play. But as though grateful to the dramatist for giving him a cue, Gregers reminds Hedvig in Act Four that her father used such language, and turns it into a pretext for sacrificing the bird for Hjalmar. At this point, when Gregers says, 'Supposing you offered to sacrifice the wild duck for *his* sake . . .Suppose you were ready to sacrifice for him the most precious thing you had in the world,' the play ceases to be about any desire for truth and becomes at best—but it is not really this—a study of a man slightly crazed. (The number of characters whose sanity one begins to doubt increases from here on.)

Gregers is surely not meant to be crazed, despite the remarks to this effect which his father makes about him. One indication of that is his similarity, on this particular point, with other Ibsen characters, so many of whom expect their relatives or friends to behave as Gregers suggests Hedvig should. Nora supposes her husband will quite certainly destroy his own reputation to preserve hers, and is astonished when he does not. Rosmer accepts willingly Rebecca West's idea that she should drown herself to restore his faith in mankind [in *Rosmersholm*]. Hedda suggests suicide to Løvborg [in *Hedda Gabler*]. Oswald takes it for granted that Regine will end his life if he asks her to [in *Ghosts*]. The sacrifice Gregers proposes is nothing like so great as some of these, which are not presented as acts of madness, and in some cases seem to be seen as great, tragic necessities. (A parodistic version of the Ten Commandments was current among some radical thinkers in late nineteenth-century Norway, including a Commandment to take one's own life. But Ibsen does not have such modern Albigensians in mind.) Besides, Gregers' case is not studied by the dramatist; it is simply the means by which the plot is furthered, and this puts an end to any serious pretensions. Gregers, again, gives no account of how he thinks his proposed course of action will help anybody. With the zeal of a leech he fastens onto the idea of self-sacrifice, as he does to the idea of truth, and is astounded by the results of his inspirations.

With two such men as Gregers and Hjalmar at the centre the play is bound to remain at a crude level; humanly speaking it does, however, also introduce a new kind of play, in which symbolism is more important than in any previous work of Ibsen's. Hitherto, symbolism had generally been only apparent here and there. Bernick's leaky ships [in *The Pillars of Society*], Nora's forgery [in *A Doll's House*], Oswald's disease [in *Ghosts*], Stockmann's sewers [in *An Enemy of the People*] all had at least a metaphoric value. But so far no play had made the symbol so predominant, or so interrelated with all the characters' lives, as the wild duck is, and on this account it is possible to discuss here the question of Ibsen's achieving a *poésie de théâtre*.

The bird is certainly an image with many potential meanings. It can expand with something like the iridescence of poetry, by virtue of its ambiguity, for it never stands for any one thing. In some places it seems to be associated with despair: it is compared implicitly with 'some people in this world that dive straight to the bottom the moment they get a couple of bullets in them, and never come up again,' and is thus linked, sometimes explicitly, with the despair of old Ekdal and Hedvig. They are the people who have, like the duck, dived to the bottom of the river or sea, and clung fast there, or so the explicit parallels suggest, though it is not clear how this can be said of Hedvig: the symbol is forced upon her, yet she is not remotely like her shattered grandfather. Gregers' self-imposed task, as he sees it, is to dive down like a well-trained dog, and save both Hjalmar and Hedvig, who to his way of thinking have gone down to die in the dark. (It really is not true: Hjalmar is too self-centred for despair, and Hedvig is spirited in her difficult situation.) Yet the bird also stands for the opposite of despair. In one sense it is the creature that tried to commit suicide when it was only slightly hurt, in another, it is, as Hedvig says, the most important thing in the room, 'because she's a *real* wild bird'. The place where it lives is also the place where the clock does not work, which leads Gregers to say, with the disclosure of symbolism characteristic of him, that 'time stands still in there . . . beside the wild duck'. We may be chary of accepting this offer of a symbol at face value—the metaphor is so pressed into service—but the suggestion is surely that there is something of eternity about the duck. Is it that total freedom Skule dreamed of [in *The Pretenders*], and Brand, and Julian [in *Emperor and Galilean*], perhaps? But if we choose to think that, the attribution is tacked on. There is nothing more timeless or eternal about the duck than the fact that the clock in the same room has stopped; the duck has no function in the play that could be described in this particular symbolical way.

Other ambiguities include the fact that, though the bird symbolises the depths, it lives in the highest part of the building, and that, though 'wild', it lives cooped up in the attic, even though it is often said to have been saved. (This relationship between imprisonment and freedom will seem more notable still in Hedda Gabler's desire to liberate Løvborg.)

The rôle of the dog which rescues the duck is equally ambiguous. The purpose of the dog which belonged to Gregers' father was not to save the duck's life by refusing to let it bite fast to the weeds on the sea-bed, but to bring it back to the hunter, who for some reason kept it alive where he would normally have killed it. (What was old Werle doing, sending a duck with two slugs in its body and a damaged neck as a pet for Hedvig? Presumably he shot it in order to eat it.) Gregers, however, when he says that he would like to be a dog, speaks as though his purpose would be to rescue the duck, or people in a similar situation. His lack of success, indeed the bungled job he makes of the whole operation, is related to this confusion in the symbols themselves. Gregers does not know what he intends by 'liberating' Hjalmar and Hedvig; he plunges in and brings Hedvig, at least, straight to her death.

These are not poetic images: the ambiguity is not enlivening but confusing, both to audience and to characters. Yet it almost seems at times as though Ibsen were aware of this, as though he were presenting in Gregers a parody of himself. That he is to a degree such a parody, so far as Ibsen was a man continually concerned with 'the claims of the ideal', is self-evident. That he is a parody of Ibsen's 'poetic' character needs more showing, and cannot be said so definitely in every case. Yet the hint is often proffered.

In *The Wild Duck,* more than in any other play, Ibsen seems to ridicule the habit of talking in a double sense, in inappropriate metaphors, as when Gregers is asked by Hjalmar what he would most like to be, if not himself.

> HJALMAR: (*laughs*) Ha! ha! And if you weren't Gregers Werle, what is it you would want to be?
>
> GREGERS: If I could choose, I should most of all like to be a clever dog.
>
> GINA: A dog!
>
> HEDVIG: (*involuntarily*) Oh, no!
>
> GREGERS: Yes, a really absurdly clever dog, the sort that goes down to the bottom after wild ducks, when they dive down and bite fast on to the seaweed and the tangle down there in the mud.
>
> HJALMAR: You know, Gregers . . . I don't understand a word of what you are saying.
>
> (Act 2)

Yet the possibility of a certain self-ridicule by Ibsen looks more remote when he at once follows this dialogue with another in which Gina's hard-headedness turns to a kind of awe, only increased by the comments of the innocent child Hedvig:

> GINA: (*staring into space, her sewing on her lap*) Wasn't that funny, him saying he wanted to be a dog?
>
> HEDVIG: I'll tell you what, Mother . . . I think he meant something else.
>
> GINA: And what else might that be?
>
> HEDVIG: Well, I don't know. But it was just as though he meant something different from what he was saying—all the time.
>
> (Act 2)

This heavy underlining, of a symbolical sense which must already be thoroughly clear to the audience, might well be a mark of Ibsen's involvement with his symbols to the point of not realising how obvious they are. Yet he also provides a contrast in the character of Gina, one of whose chief rôles is making a down-to-earth, crudely common-sensical interpretation of every metaphor used. If Gregers speaks of a poisoned atmosphere she at once protests that she aired the place this morning, and when Relling speaks of 'inflamed scruples' she almost thinks they are physiological. Uncertainty about the irony comes from the fact that Gina's misunderstanding is so gross: a 'poisoned' atmosphere is not so very unusual an expression, and we half sense that the joke is on her, for what it is worth.

Yet there must surely be irony in the scene in which Hedvig's dead body is discovered, however movingly it may be staged. For Gina this is an instant when she is desolated; her response is pure motherly grief. For Hjalmar his daughter's death is something to be denied, for Relling it is an occasion to reprove Hjalmar for his sentimentality. For Gregers, it is a symbol:

> HJALMAR: Well, Relling . . . why don't you say something?
>
> RELLING: The bullet hit her in the breast.
>
> HJALMAR: Yes, but she'll be coming round.
>
> GINA: (*bursts into tears*) Oh my little one!
>
> GREGERS: (*huskily*) In the briny deep . . .
>
> (Act 5)

Gregers' line is grotesque, not only because of the fact that he speaks symbolically, but because of the particular words he uses, which could hardly make the symbolism more obvious. I have quoted here James McFarlane's translation, which may slightly overdo the exaggeration: it is difficult to say, but perhaps 'the vasty deep,' being a Shakespearean quotation, has something to be said for it. What is certain is that in Act Three Ibsen has deliberately drawn attention to the oddity of these words. When Gregers uses them for the first time, Hedvig at once asks why he uses that particular phrase. It is true that the alternatives she proposes are closer to one another in sound than 'the briny deep' is to 'the seabed': where Gregers says *på havsens bund,* which uses a slightly archaic and 'poetic' form of the genitive, she suggests as more natural *havets bund* or *havbunden,* and clearly his phrase, though only slightly different in Norwegian, sounds out of place to her. When it is repeated after Hedvig's death, the oddity must strike us, and the incongruousness of Gregers' response must be brought home to us. (On the other hand, Hedvig admits that she herself uses the archaism for the room of the wild duck, so that the repetition of it reflects on her also.)

Ibsen, then, wanted the moment of Hedvig's death to be tinged with criticism of the man whose blundering way of speaking has helped to bring it about. Gregers has implanted in Hedvig's mind the idea that she herself is the wild duck who must be sacrificed, and now he is refusing to face the consequences. But it is the symbolical mode, rather than the idealism, which is criticised through the

'poetic' words, and that same mode is the chief feature of the play Ibsen is presenting.

He had no real need of a symbol at all, in order to cope dramatically with the shattering of illusions. Gregers could simply have humiliated Hjalmar to the point where Hedvig would do anything, even kill herself to demonstrate to him that he was still loved. The device of the duck seems to give a greater scope to the play, to hint at Freedom in a more than local sense, but only serves to produce a less moving, more confusing work. The duck is a mere *fait divers* [trivial fact], and the play would be more telling without it.

Any resistance we may still feel to the idea that Ibsen is ironically detached from such symbolising probably comes from the awareness that for his own part, as a dramatist, he continues to use symbolism, both now and in later plays, in exactly the same way. There is comedy in the moment when Gregers asks Hedvig whether she is so certain the loft is really only a loft, as there is in his prim retort to Relling's accusation that he carries the 'claim of the ideal' around in his back-pocket: 'It is in my breast that I carry it.' Yet it is Ibsen who makes Gina say that Gregers has lit a stove and then damped it too much, and finally thrown water all over it and the floor too. Gina cannot herself mean that symbolically, but Ibsen means us to understand it so, and to see in it an epitome of all the mess that Gregers causes throughout the play. Ibsen is by now incapable of writing without some degree of symbolism, and that is precisely what prevents *The Wild Duck* from being deeply moving. Take, for instance, the actual moment of Hedvig's death, which is as artificial as anything Ibsen wrote:

> HJALMAR: . . . Suppose the others [Mrs Sörby and old Werle] came along, their hands loaded with good things, and they called to the child: 'Come away from him. With us, life is awaiting you . . .'
>
> GREGERS: (*quickly*) Well, what then, d'you think?
>
> HJALMAR: If I then asked her: 'Hedvig, are you willing to give up life for my sake'? (*Laughs scornfully*) Oh yes! I must say. You would soon hear the sort of answer I would get!
>
> (*A pistol shot is heard within the loft.*)
>
> (Act 5)

Such appropriate coincidences are not uncommon in Ibsen's plays. Whether Hedvig has heard what Hjalmar has said and misinterpreted it is uncertain. She may have understood 'life' to mean not life with Mrs Sörby but life of any kind, and the pistol shot may be an answer saying that she does love Hjalmar, enough to sacrifice herself, or that she is in despair at his (only recently and unexpectedly expressed) doubt about her love. The indisputable point is that the pistol-shot is, metaphorically, an answer, and that same fact is what makes the moment stagey. It is also a quality not of any particular character but of the play.

The final touch is given in the conversation between Gregers and Relling, just before the curtain falls. They have been discussing whether Hedvig's death will have any notable effect on Hjalmar, or whether he will be ennobled by it or return to wallowing deeper and deeper in self-pity. Gregers is convinced that some good will come of the sacrifice he has unwittingly caused:

> GREGERS: If *you* are right and *I* am wrong, life will no longer be worth living.
>
> RELLING: Oh, life wouldn't be so bad if we could only be left in peace by these blessed people who come running round to us poor folk with their claims of the ideal all the time.
>
> GREGERS: (*staring into space*) In that case I am glad my destiny is what it is.
>
> RELLING: If I may ask—what is your destiny?
>
> GREGERS: (*turning to leave*) To be thirteenth at table.
>
> RELLING: The devil it is! [Literally 'Devil believe that'.]
>
> (Act 5)

Gregers' portentousness still leaves some doubt about the significance of this exchange. He is still talking in a symbol, and rather an obscure one. Whether he means merely that it is unlucky to be thirteenth, or that he is the Christ-figure among the twelve others, or the Judas-figure, is disputable, and no doubt Ibsen intended ambiguity here as he did in the case of the wild duck itself: to himself Gregers is a Christ, to others a Judas. It is both good and bad that the claim of the ideal should be presented—that might well be Gregers' view. But Ibsen himself has carefully made that remark possible, and given the symbol a basis in the reality of the play's action. Gregers actually was thirteenth, or at any rate one of thirteen, at table in Act One, as was carefully brought out at the time, and this seems to lend a kind of weight to what would otherwise be a remark out of the blue. On the other hand, Relling's scepticism and his colloquial reference to the Devil (echoing the same unintentional use of the word by Regine at the beginning of *Ghosts,* and several other similar uses scattered through the plays) suggest a final negative, or at least a doubt.

There is an intriguing quality here, tempting us to unravel the puzzle. In reality, though, there is no unravelling it: it is an indeterminate ending as well as a portentous one, and that is the most serious criticism that the play has to meet, at this point. In the final moment Ibsen is not really concerned about the death of Hedvig, any more than Gregers was. He is concerned to maintain the ambiguity of his position, both maintaining his symbolism and decrying the impulse which draws him towards it. In that comprehensiveness, he may have felt, lay the only full realisation of himself as an artist. (pp. 99-111)

> *Ronald Gray, in his* Ibsen—A Dissenting View: A Study of the Last Twelve Plays, *Cambridge University Press, 1977, 231 p.*

Rolf Fjelde   (essay date 1986)

[*Fjelde examines* The Wild Duck *as an artistic expression of Ibsen's dissatisfaction with the social realism of his own early plays. The Ekdals's loft provides a place for "life-enhancing free play of the imagination," an activity, Fjelde suggests, Ibsen had come to recognize as essential in human life. With this drama, the critic concludes, "fantasy and myth are once again openly admitted to the Ibsenian stage."*]

The Wild Duck is the most elusive of the entire group of Ibsen's so-called realistic dramas, and designedly so. It is as evasive as Hjalmar Ekdal is to being pinned down; it refuses accommodation to a clearly dominant set or direction of values; it is the work of the final cycle closest to fulfilling Wallace Stevens' line that "A poem must resist the intelligence / Almost successfully." From appearing to be a relatively simple, even cynical retraction of didactic and messianic tendencies in the preceding four plays—Ibsen's corrective self-criticism—it becomes, under continued examination, more and more mysterious, as versions of the truth erode other versions, and key facts—Hedvig's paternity, the disability of Gregers's mother, the benign or malign character of Haakon Werle, the circumstances of and responsibility for the original, actionable transgression of boundaries in the forests—are displaced from knowledgeability. Indeed, if the play asserts anything, it would seem to insist that, given the degree of opacity of human being to human being in this world, let the benefit of the doubt be on the side of caring about what we cannot take for granted—the feelings of a rejected child, the multiple significations of the wild duck.

Of the many perspectives **The Wild Duck** affords on its arrangement of material, the one I would like briefly to emphasize here is both integral to the peculiar power that the play exerts, and yet too often neglected in its larger implications: namely, its symbolic reflection of Ibsen's own self-liberating progress as an artist. Although Ibsen's dramatic actions and thematic interests in the first four plays of the cycle are in fact allusive and far-ranging, it was their issue-oriented content that gave them immediate impact among audiences and readers and ensured their author's controversial international fame. That property of the initial quartet of dramas was undoubtedly focused and reinforced by Georg Brandes's "Inaugural Lecture" of 1871, which was then incorporated the following year in the first volume of *Main Currents in Nineteenth-Century Literature,* a book which Ibsen described in a letter to its author as "one of those works which place a yawning gap between yesterday and today." In the text of the "Inaugural Lecture" one finds the pronouncement that Ibsen, then in the throes of completing the immense ideological summation of *Emperor and Galilean,* appears to have seized upon as a strategy of advance to his next stage of development: "What keeps a literature alive in our days is that it submits problems to debate." If this was to be the path to a living, contemporaneous drama that would have the stature of serious literature, then the evidentiary submission of problems—whatever else the play might contain—would have to be as clear, defined and detailed as possible. Logically, inevitably, photographic naturalism became the ostensible style of *Pillars of Society* in treating the "problem" of business ethics; of *A Doll House* in dealing with inequities in marriage; *Ghosts* in confronting parental resonsibilities to truth and to children, even to the brink of euthanasia;

and *An Enemy of the People* in challenging environmental pollution with Dr. Stockmann's evolutionary argument against the democratic dogma of majority rule.

After nearly a decade of inciting thought on such questions via a technique that meticulously reproduced the surfaces of modern life—of trying his luck as a "photographer," as he had bitterly phrased it to Bjørnson after the disappointing critical response to *Peer Gynt*—Ibsen found he could no longer suppress his inherently poetic vision. The fifth play in the series, in effect, cracked the photographic plate and imprinted the realistic action with patterns that were not easily reconciled with strict verisimilitude. *The Wild Duck* is thus a pivotal work that represents simultaneously the thinking through of a crucial artistic reassessment and the universalizing disguise of that reassessment and the universalizing disguise of that reassessment within a work of complex, humanistic art. It is one of the earliest examples of that twentieth-century phenomenon throughout the arts, not least in drama—e.g. Pirandello's *Six Characters*—that finds its characteristic expression by taking the medium itself as its subject matter.

The setting that dominates the play, spanning four of its five acts, is the Ekdal studio apartment with its huge skylight, symptomatically a room originally designed for an artist, but currently occupied by a photographer. It is thus a precise replica of the predicament, described above, of the playwright's own career. Moreover, in its twofold division, it simulates a kind of scenic model of the artist's mind. Downstage is a practical, utilitarian foreground for eating, entertaining, discussing the success or failure of incursions into the world, and doing one's professional work, i.e. taking photographs—in short, a spacialized persona comprehending various kinds of interactions with what's "out there." Upstage lies a mysterious, evocative background that the inhabitants of the studio, all save the chief negotiator with prosaic actuality, Gina, instinctively gravitate toward, full of flotsam and jetsam of past human culture and saving remnants of a diminished natural wilderness. The pragmatic foreground is composed around an old-fashioned portrait camera, with its attractive, warmly shellacked wood, black bellows and tripod, as well as its outlying vials of chemicals and retouching tools—the mechanism by which objective reality is reproduced with minimal modification; the numinous background is attuned to the hidden (it should always be concealed or obscured from the audience), charismatic source of meaning identified with the wild duck.

From this angle of approach, the two principal *external* settings apart from the Ekdal home can be aggregated together as the essential reality outside the artist's mind, the chief categories of being-in-the-world with which that mind must cope. That outer dimension is comprised of two planes of experience: the salon and home office in the Werle mansion, and the disorderly apartment occupied by Relling and Molvik—high society and the lower depths. Again, symptomatically, when the artiste manqué Hjalmar ventures into each of them, in Act One and between Acts Four and Five, he returns humiliated, prompt to reassert his uncontested status of command among his own in the studio and the loft. His chagrin stems not merely

from the fiasco of his attempts at outward adjustment, of his very presence, in the two exterior settings, but as well, on the psychodramatic level, from the low esteem accorded art in the social, "real" world. In the salon, a piano interlude—Schumann or Grieg, one supposes—is regarded as synonymous with tedium or torture by the competitive worldlings; and an album of photographs on display proves of absorbing interest to the artist alone—otherwise it functions as the nineteenth century equivalent of a coffee table ornament, a mere morsel of entertainment, an item of consumption that is "so good for the digestion" to page through [Ibsen, in *The Complete Plays*, trans. Rolf Fjelde]. In the lower depths, on the other hand, art effectively ceases to exist. The failed doctor and the spoiled priest have enough to do just keeping body and soul, their two professional concerns, together.

That the play incorporates a sense of frustration with the inability of art to penetrate the external world and be recognized as such when constricted within Brandes's issue-oriented, social engineering formula is borne out by the fact that no play after *The Wild Duck* adopts a problem play format, even as a vehicle for larger world-historical and/or mythic content. A second impetus toward a reconstituting of method may well derive from Ibsen's suspicion that, by yielding to a reductive, utilitarian role, he was merely being used for others' ends, since what characterizes both levels of the world of actuality beyond the studio/loft is manipulation. From the bastion of worldly power, Haakon Werle has provided Hjalmar with his occupation, much of his income, his wife and possibly even his child with a stealth that deludes Hjalmar into believing that he has attained each through the exercise of his own productive, or reproductive powers. Relling, in a complementary and far more ironic role, has supplied the *geistliche* counterpart to these basic familial props by manipulating Hjalmar—or, comparably, the photographic naturalist?—into the impossible dream of achieving a great invention in photography, elevating it into both a true art and a science, which then becomes the buoying life-lie that keeps him afloat.

As a result Hjalmar has lapsed into a hollow, inflated, albeit deludedly content shell of a human being, alienated from his true self and knowledge of his factual circumstances in nearly every department of his life. And just as Ibsen at this time was turning away from *théâtre utile*, the writing of plays aimed instrumentally at the reformation of society, the Ekdal family group, Hjalmar included, like emblems of contemporary urbanized sensibility, living boxed up in cities while starved for deeper, richer veins of consciousness, turn instinctively toward the loft, that setting identified so strongly with Hedvig, who finds it not a materially diminished realm at all, but a source of endless fantasy and enchantment which she has secretly named "the depths of the sea."

What Hedvig, her father and Old Ekdal have done with the loft is best described by a phrase J. R. R. Tolkien uses [in *The Tolkien Reader*] in discussing the role of fantasy in literature: they have sub-created a Secondary World, apart from and independent of the Primary World ruled by considerations of acquisitive opportunism and practical utility, i.e. Werle and Gina, respectively. The Primary World exists in historical time; the world within the loft is a domain where time has had a stop. The Primary World is a place where poaching timber from state land has long, life-determining consequences; the Secondary World of the Ekdals' sub-creation is one where such consequences can be, or persuasively appear to be, abolished, through a compensatory, life-enhancing free play of the imagination. The objects and creatures gathered inside, moreover, in their odd juxtaposition, exhibit the quality Tolkien deemed imperative for successful fantasy: arresting strangeness.

That quality extends as well to the origin of the loft's objects. They were left there, we are told, by an old sea captain known only as "the Flying Dutchman." The name evokes the fifteenth-century legend made familiar via Heine's poetry and Wagner's opera, wherein a timeless curse, everlasting till Judgment Day, associated with the sea, is counterposed to a land realm bound to time, and wherein the legendary action, also situated in Norway, portrays another daughter, likewise misunderstood, who goes down precipitously of her own will, like the ship, the Flying Dutchman, and its cargo in the depths of the sea. It is as if the salvaged contents of the loft, like the maimed, mysterious Wild Duck that rules it, have been recovered out of that same sea—just as Ibsen had once written in an early article of criticism ["Professor Welhaven on Paludan-Müller's Mythological Poems," *The Drama Review* XII, No. 2], that mythic ideas must be drawn up intact from the sea-depths of the collective consciousness of the race, to be examined and speculated upon as an acceptable, even essential, phase of their consistent development. The Secondary World of fantasy, Ibsen is proclaiming through the vernacular symbolism of his art, must be identified with and derived from the legendary and the mythic; and the claims of the latter, for which the modern psyche is starved in the positivistic contemporary foreground of science, technology and utilitarian realism, are no less rightfully compelling than the claims of society reflected one-sidedly in Brandes's program for serious literature.

With this restoration of balance, this declaration of artistic independence, fantasy and myth are once again openly admitted to the Ibsenian stage, instead of being intricately and ingeniously disguised in the realistic actions, characters and settings, as in the immediately preceding plays of the cycle. Ibsen's outworn luck as a photographer reunites him with his true vocation as a dramatic poet, and the lyric Pegasus shot out from under him, in Bjørnson's dismissive phrase, is reborn in *The Wild Duck* with hooves that strike an authentic, if more subdued fire. We find it again, appropriately, in the primordial, ghostly white horses of Rosmersholm, a place that bears resemblance to a fairytale castle in some enchanted kingdom where children never cry and grownups never laugh; in the mesmerizing Stranger who rises up like a merman out of a watery grave to claim a lady obsessed with the sea as his bride; in a soignée belle's erotic fantasies of a gifted writer as a vine-crowned Dionysus whose death will emblazon a rebirth of tragedy in a trivialized society; in a master builder who has constituted himself as an omnipotent god capable of direct contact, mind to mind, with a spirit choir of help-

ers and servers swarming in attendance. These and other such fantastic elements in the later plays are neither psychologized away nor credulously affirmed; rather, they are phenomenologically bracketed, presented "as if," to be tested, interpreted and incorporated within each individual's cognition of the humanly possible. For in between *An Enemy of the People* and *The Wild Duck,* Ibsen sets forth a new goal to replace Brandes's dictum: that "In these times every piece of creative thinking should attempt to move the frontier markers" [Ibsen, *Letters and Speeches,* ed. Evert Sprinchorn].

Eric Bentley has reminded us that Ibsen was a realist on the outside, a fantasist inside, while Wagner, his early contemporary in innovation, was a fantasist outside, a realist within; and he notes, in *The Playwright As Thinker,* that on the whole the former combination worked better, in giving us "supple strength, fine irony and rich polyphony" in plays like *The Wild Duck.* But Ibsen, by these means, accomplished at least two additional things. He gives us, first, the full and true measure of the world we inhabit more accurately than the pure realists, a world where fantasy, or its equivalent, sits as the interior steersman setting a course incalculable by realistically calibrated estimations of motive and behavior. He was wise enough to recognize that whereas reason and science had their considerable areas of authority—witness those irrefutable analyses of the town's polluted waters—a dangerous fantasy or, more profoundly, a destructive myth could be countered only by a more adequate, humane and compelling fantasy or myth. In that holistic sense, his works remain a collective survival manual and basic training course in the efforts of the race to read and anticipate itself.

But Ibsen's legacy is not restricted to those works alone. The fertile equation factored out in *The Wild Duck,* its unique blend of romanticism, realism, naturalism and symbolism, constitutes the far from exhausted potential of an artistic method he has bequeathed to his successors. Those who study the Ibsen canon in the conventional magpie manner, gleaning techniques for how to develop a character, build a scene or render a social problem stageworthy are guilty, as Dr. Stockmann might say, of setting the intakes of the life-giving waters too low. The greater part of the major plays, that appear so canny, so intricately and ingeniously wrought—and indeed are, in product and result—could only have been achieved in process, shaped by the deep, ulterior currents of the active unconscious, bearing the formal, interpersonal structures on inspired confluences of metaphor and symbol, fantasy and myth. There is, in fact, no more finely honed poetic drama concealed as prose than Henrik Ibsen's—*drama,* one must emphasize, where the medium of the poetry is words always propulsively bent toward defining human lives and destinies. The sooner that truth is generally recognized in exegesis and production, the more fruitfully his pioneering example will enable others to add his full repertory of expression to their own, empowering enrichments of style that proceed, not from mere prowess in technique, but from a changed and amplified vision of the range of human potential—just such a vision as animates the self-reflexive form of *The Wild Duck.* (pp. 35-44)

Rolf Fjelde, " 'The Wild Duck' as a Portrait of the Artist in Transition," in The Play and Its Critic: Essays for Eric Bentley, *edited by Michael Bertin, University Press of America, 1986, pp. 35-44.*

HEDDA GABLER

Bernard Shaw   (essay date 1890)

[*Shaw is one of the best-known dramatists to write in the English language since Shakespeare. He is closely identified with the intellectual revival of the British theater, and in his dramatic theory he advocated eliminating romantic conventions in favor of a theater of ideas, grounded in realism. During the late nineteenth century, Shaw was a prominent literary, art, music, and drama critic, and his reviews were known for their biting wit and brilliance. In the excerpt below from an essay written in 1890, Shaw provides a detailed analysis of Hedda's character, asserting that the central conflict of the drama pits Hedda's instinctive desires against the conventional ideals of her society. Beginning with a description of Hedda's life and marriage before the play begins, he provides a chronological account of her actions and motivations to characterize her as a coward and bully with "no conscience, no convictions."*]

Hedda Gabler has no ethical ideals at all, only romantic ones. She is a typical nineteenth-century figure, falling into the abyss between the ideals which do not impose on her and the realities she has not yet discovered. The result is that though she has imagination, and an intense appetite for beauty, she has no conscience, no conviction: with plenty of cleverness, energy, and personal fascination she remains mean, envious, insolent, cruel in protest against others' happiness, fiendish in her dislike of inartistic people and things, a bully in reaction from her own cowardice. Hedda's father, a general, is a widower. She has the traditions of the military caste about her; and these narrow her activities to the customary hunt for a socially and pecuniarily eligible husband. She makes the acquaintance of a young man of genius who, prohibited by an ideal-ridden society from taking his pleasures except where there is nothing to restrain him from excess, is going to the bad in search of his good, with the usual consequences. Hedda is intensely curious about the side of life which is forbidden to her, and in which powerful instincts, absolutely ignored and condemned in her circle, steal their satisfaction. An odd intimacy springs up between the inquisitive girl and the rake. Whilst the general reads the paper in the afternoon, Lövborg and Hedda have long conversations in which he describes to her all his disreputable adventures. Although she is the questioner, she never dares to trust him: all the questions are indirect; and the responsibility for his interpretations rests on him alone. Hedda has no conviction whatever that these conversations are disgraceful; but she will not risk a fight with society on the point: it is easier to practise hypocrisy, the homage that

truth pays to falsehood, than to endure ostracism. When he proceeds to make advances to her, Hedda has again no conviction that it would be wrong for her to gratify his instinct and her own; so that she is confronted with the alternative of sinning against herself and him, or sinning against social ideals in which she has no faith. Making the coward's choice, she carries it out with the utmost bravado, threatening Lövborg with one of her father's pistols, and driving him out of the house with all that ostentation of outraged purity which is the instinctive defence of women to whom chastity is not natural, much as libel actions are mostly brought by persons concerning whom libels are virtually, if not technically, justifiable.

Hedda, deprived of her lover, now finds that a life of conformity without faith involves something more terrible than the utmost ostracism: to wit, boredom. This scourge, unknown among revolutionists, is the curse which makes the security of respectability as dust in the balance against the unflagging interest of rebellion, and which forces society to eke out its harmless resources for killing time by licensing gambling, gluttony, hunting, shooting, coursing, and other vicious distractions for which even idealism has no disguise. These licenses, being expensive, are available only for people who have more than enough money to keep up appearances; and as Hedda's father, being in the army instead of in commerce, is too poor to leave her much more than the pistols, her boredom is only mitigated by dancing, at which she gains much admiration, but no substantial offers of marriage.

At last she has to find somebody to support her. A good-natured mediocrity of a professor is the best that is to be had; and though she regards him as a member of an inferior class, and despises almost to loathing his family circle of two affectionate old aunts and the inevitable general servant who has helped to bring him up, she marries him *faute de mieux* [for lack of something better], and immediately proceeds to wreck this prudent provision for her livelihood by accommodating his income to her expenditure instead of accommodating her expenditure to his income. Her nature so rebels against the whole sordid transaction that the prospect of bearing a child to her husband drives her almost frantic, since it will not only expose her to the intimate solicitude of his aunts in the course of a derangement of her health in which she can see nothing that is not repulsive and humiliating, but will make her one of his family in earnest.

To amuse herself in these galling circumstances, she forms an underhand alliance with a visitor who belongs to her old set, an elderly gallant who quite understands how little she cares for her husband, and proposes a *ménage à trois* to her. She consents to his coming there and talking to her as he pleases behind her husband's back; but she keeps her pistols in reserve in case he becomes seriously importunate. He, on the other hand, tries to get some hold over her by placing her husband under pecuniary obligations, as far as he can do it without being out of pocket.

Meanwhile Lövborg is drifting to disgrace by the nearest way: drink. In due time he descends from lecturing at the university on the history of civilization to taking a job in an out-of-the-way place as tutor to the little children of

Minnie Maddern Fiske as Hedda and George Arliss as Brack, in Fiske's 1903 revival of Hedda Gabler *at the Manhattan Theatre.*

Sheriff Elvsted. This functionary, on being left a widower with a number of children, marries their governess, finding that she will cost him less and be bound to do more for him as his wife. As for her, she is too poor to dream of refusing such a settlement in life. When Löborg comes, his society is heaven to her. He does not dare to tell her about his dissipations; but he tells her about his unwritten books, which he never discussed with Hedda. She does not dare to remonstrate with him for drinking; but he gives it up as soon as he sees that it shocks her. Just as Mr. Fearing, in Bunyan's story [*The Pilgrim's Progress*], was in a way the bravest of the pilgrims, so this timid and unfortunate Mrs. Elvsted trembles her way to a point at which Lövborg, quite reformed, publishes one book which makes him celebrated for the moment, and completes another, fair-copied in her handwriting, to which he looks for a solid position as an original thinker. But he cannot now stay tutoring Elvsted's children; so off he goes to town with his pockets full of the money the published book has brought him. Left once more in her old lonely plight, knowing that without her Lövborg will probably relapse into dissipation, and that without him her life will not be worth living, Mrs. Elvsted must either sin against herself and him or against the institution of marriage under which

Elvsted purchased his housekeeper. It never occurs to her that she has any choice. She knows that her action will count as "a dreadful thing"; but she sees that she must go; and accordingly Elvsted finds himself without a wife and his children without a governess, and so disappears unpitied from the story.

Now it happens that Hedda's husband, Jörgen Tesman, is an old friend and competitor (for academic honors) of Lövborg, and also that Hedda was a schoolfellow of Mrs. Elvsted, or Thea, as she had better now be called. Thea's first business is to find out where Lövborg is; for hers is no preconcerted elopement: she has hurried to town to keep Lövborg away from the bottle, a design she dare not hint at to himself. Accordingly, the first thing she does in town is to call on the Tesmans, who have just returned from their honeymoon, to beg them to invite Lövborg to their house so as to keep him in good company. They consent, with the result that the two pairs are brought together under the same roof, and the tragedy begins to work itself out.

Hedda's attitude now demands a careful analysis. Lövborg's experience with Thea has enlightened his judgment of Hedda; and as he is, in his gifted way, an arrant *poseur* and male coquet, he immediately tries to get on romantic terms with her (for have they not "a past"?) by impressing her with the penetrating criticism that she is and always was a coward. She admits that the virtuous heroics with the pistol were pure cowardice; but she is still so void of any other standard of conduct than conformity to the conventional ideals, that she thinks her cowardice consisted in not daring to be wicked. That is, she thinks that what she actually did was the right thing; and since she despises herself for doing it, and feels that he also rightly despises her for doing it, she gets a passionate feeling that what is wanted is the courage to do wrong. This unlooked-for reaction of idealism, this monstrous but very common setting-up of wrong-doing as an ideal, and of the wrongdoer as hero or heroine *qua* wrongdoer, leads Hedda to conceive that when Lövborg tried to seduce her he was a hero, and that in allowing Thea to reform him he has played the recreant. In acting on this misconception she is restrained by no consideration for any of the rest. Like all people whose lives are valueless, she has no more sense of the value of Lövborg's or Tesman's or Thea's lives than a railway shareholder has of the value of a shunter's. She gratifies her intense jealousy of Thea by deliberately taunting Lövborg into breaking loose from her influence by joining a carouse at which he not only loses his manuscript, but finally gets into the hands of the police through behaving outrageously in the house of a disreputable woman whom he accuses of stealing it, not knowing that it has been picked up by Tesman and handed to Hedda for safe keeping. Now Hedda's jealousy of Thea is not jealousy of her bodily fascination: at that Hedda can beat her. It is jealousy of her power of making a man of Lövborg, of her part in his life as a man of genius. The manuscript which Tesman gives to Hedda to lock up safely is in Thea's handwriting. It is the fruit of Lövborg's union with Thea: he himself speaks of it as "their child." So when he turns his despair to romantic account by coming to the two women and making a tragic scene, telling Thea that he has cast the manuscript, torn into a thousand pieces, out upon the fiord; and then, when she is gone, telling Hedda that he has brought "the child" to a house of ill-fame and lost it there, she, deceived by his posing, and thirsting to gain faith in the beauty of her own influence over him from a heroic deed of some sort, makes him a present of one of her pistols, only begging him to "do it beautifully," by which she means that he is to kill himself in some manner that will make his suicide a romantic memory and an imaginative luxury to her for ever. He takes it unblushingly, and leaves her with the air of a man who is looking his last on earth. But the moment he is out of sight of his audience, he goes back to the house where he still supposes the manuscript to lie stolen, and there renews the wrangle of the night before, using the pistol to threaten the woman, with the result that he gets shot in the abdomen, leaving the weapon to fall into the hands of the police. Meanwhile Hedda deliberately burns "the child." Then comes her elderly gallant to disgust her with the unromantically ugly details of the deed which Lövborg promised her to do so beautifully, and to make her understand that he himself has now got her into his power by his ability to identify the pistol. She must either be the slave of this man, or else face the scandal of the connection of her name at the in-

quest with a squalid debauch ending in a murder. Thea, too, is not crushed by Lövborg's death. Ten minutes after she has received the news with a cry of heartfelt loss, she sits down with Tesman to reconstruct "the child" from the old notes she has piously preserved. Over the congenial task of collecting and arranging another man's ideas Tesman is perfectly happy, and forgets his beautiful Hedda for the first time. Thea the trembler is still mistress of the situation, holding the dead Lövborg, gaining Tesman, and leaving Hedda to her elderly admirer, who smoothly remarks that he will answer for Mrs. Tesman not being bored whilst her husband is occupied with Thea in putting the pieces of the book together. However, he has again reckoned without General Gabler's second pistol. She shoots herself then and there; and so the story ends. (pp. 110-18)

> *Bernard Shaw, in his* The Quintessence of Ibsenism, *revised edition, Constable and Company, 1913, 210 p.*

Erling E. Kildahl   (essay date 1961)

[*Below, Kildahl stresses the importance of the play's particular setting in shaping the characterization and action of* Hedda Gabler. *Outlining the changing political, economic, and social climate in Norway in 1890, the critic asserts that Hedda's tragedy results from her adherence to an outmoded aristocratic caste system that did not acknowledge recent economic and political developments.*]

Hedda Gabler by Henrik Ibsen is a drama of psychological drives conditioned by a specific socio-economic environment. The particular social system against which the play is etched is its strongest determinant of character and character development. The woman Hedda Gabler is the product of a singular social heritage and *milieu*. She cannot but lose her unique magnetism if she is removed from her setting.

In a letter to his French translator, Count Prozor, Ibsen states his goal in writing ***Hedda Gabler:***

> It was not my purpose to deal with what people call problems in this play. What I principally wanted to do was to depict human beings, human emotions and human destinies upon a groundwork of certain of the social conditions and principles of the present day. [Henrik Ibsen, *Letters,* trans. and ed. J. N. Laurvik and M. Morison, 1905]

The purpose of this paper is to clarify the "social conditions and principles" which existed in Norway in 1890, how they affect the behavior of the persons in the play, and their over-all significance to the play.

Myriad political changes occurred in Norway between 1814, when the Eidsvold constitution was established, and 1885, when the last aristocratic remnants of power were relinquished by King Oscar II. Farmers organized and became a political power in the nation; labor groups banded together and joined forces with the farmers; full religious freedom was won and established; humane criminal laws and punishments were adopted, to name only a few.

Economic upheaval accompanied the political shifts. Crown lands became available to everyone by public sale; laws governing the borrowing of money were liberalized; lumbering and manufacturing industries were broadened and intensified; commerce with other nations and within Norway quickened the pulse of life.

By 1890, the year the play was published, these political and economic innovations were in the process of destroying the traditional foundations of society, and had brought about the "social conditions and principles" against which Henrik Ibsen set *Hedda Gabler.* Although the social foundations of old Norway were in a transitional period, the long-established social strata were still discernible when Ibsen wrote the play; they had not yet conformed to political and economic realities.

The Norwegian social structure was similar to the German model in form and rigidity. Aristocrats, officials of the state, officers of the army, and large landowners constituted the leisure class. Next in importance were the professional classes: doctors, professors, lawyers, and important merchants who operated the large and growing merchant marine. Below them in prestige were the middle-classes, including burghers, small business men, artisans, ships' captains and officers, small landowners, and minor district officials who had privileges dating from the middle ages. At the bottom of the social scale came the laborers and landless farmers, both in bloodless revolt, upon whom fell the basic maintenance of the state.

In the play Hedda is a representative of the highest class whose style of living is told us at the outset. The maid and Miss Tesman, George's aunt, are conversing:

> BERTA: Most like she'll be terrible grand in her ways.
>
> AUNT JULIA: Well, you can't wonder at that—General Gabler's daughter! Think of the sort of life she was accustomed to in her father's time. Don't you remember how we used to see her riding down the road along with the General? In that long black habit—and with feathers in her hat?

Ibsen wanted no doubts to exist about this matter. To eliminate any misunderstanding in the mind of his French translator, he stresses the importance of caste in a letter to Count Prozor: "Hedda as a personality is to be considered rather as her father's daughter than as her husband's wife."

After her father's death Hedda found herself in her late twenties, a spinster. But no eligible suitor who was her social equal was available for the aloof Hedda. She was forced to make a concession to circumstances, a decision most unlike her: she married the best of the lot, a plodding would-be professor, George Tesman.

His capture of Hedda Gabler was a victory for him and for his social-climbing Aunt Julia, who rejoices: "Ah, dear, dear—if my poor brother could only look up from his grave now, and see what his little boy has grown into!" And later, talking to George, "And that you should be the one to carry off Hedda Gabler—the beautiful Hedda Ga-

bler! Only think of it!" The phrase runs through the play like an unbelieving, awe-struck whisper.

Tesman has accomplished the improbable—married Hedda Gabler—a feat that would have been impossible in his father's early manhood. And Aunt Julia hopes to capitalize on it. She buys a new hat " . . . so that Hedda needn't be ashamed of me if we happened to go out together." (This is a liberty we are quite sure Hedda will never permit.)

Aunt Julia has eagerly and quite recklessly mortgaged her annuity to furnish the newlyweds' home, an act of daring that astounds George. Only one event is lacking to make Aunt Julia's happiness complete: the birth of a child who will fuse the blood of the Tesmans and the Gablers.

When Hedda appears, she wastes no time putting Aunt Julia in her place. She rebuffs the offered embrace by holding out her hand, snubs her attempt at humor, insults her pride in the new hat (at which Aunt Julia's resentment flares, a reaction hastily stilled) and finally Hedda discourages her hopes for a child.

After Aunt Julia departs, George asks Hedda: "If you could only prevail on yourself to say *du* to her. For my sake, Hedda? Eh?" to which she replies, "No no, Tesman—you really mustn't ask that of me. I have told you so already. I shall try to call her 'aunt,' and you must be satisfied with that." No common familiarity for Hedda! (Note, in this regard, her avoidance of addressing her husband by his given name except in scorn. Always, otherwise, it is *Tesman*—a distant, patronizing *Tesman*).

The sympathetic understanding that binds together Rebecca West and Johannes Rosmer and takes them to their deaths at the conclusion of *Rosmersholm* is totally foreign to Hedda Gabler's nature. Her breeding, her tradition, and her roots in an ancient system of mores preclude it, and we realize that the gaping void which separates her from Tesman and his aunt will never be bridged—least of all with a child.

Thea Elvsted enters the scene. A daughter of the lower middle-class, she will end, we feel at the play's conclusion, as the second wife and true help-mate of George Tesman, Professor—a not in considerable rise for a girl who began her career as a servant-housekeeper. She is the embodiment of the new Norway, the New Woman, in this play. Ibsen has, portrayed the type more fully as Nora in *A Doll's House,* a strain of her is in Rebecca West, and he will present a youthful version of her in *The Master Builder.* Thea, like Nora, has asserted her individuality, renounced a distasteful marriage, and gained freedom. She has obeyed her impulses and followed her yearning to Christiania. We meet her when she comes to Hedda, who was a childhood school acquaintance, seeking Eilert Lövborg:

> THEA: . . . My husband did not know that I was coming.
>
> HEDDA: What! Your husband didn't know it!
>
> THEA: No, of course not . . . Oh, I could bear it no longer, Hedda! I couldn't indeed—so utterly alone as I should have been in future.

HEDDA: Well? And then?

THEA: So I put together some of my things—
and then I left the house.

HEDDA: Why, my dear, good Thea—to think of
you daring to do it!

to which Thea firmly rejoins:

> I shall never go back to him again.

The marriages of Thea Elvsted and Hedda have an obvious parallel—both are odious, but the contrast in the methods the two women take to dissolve them does not appear until the end of the play. However, the social attitudes dictating the courses of action become clear very shortly:

HEDDA: Then you have left your home—for
good and all?

THEA: Yes. There was nothing else to be done.

HEDDA: But then—to take flight so openly . . .
what do you think people will say of you, Thea?

THEA: *They must say what they like, for aught
I care. I have done nothing but what I had to do.*

The italics are mine. Hedda is totally incapable of such words.

Any struggle between these two women, one simple but action-minded, the other intelligent but incapable of action, must result in defeat for Hedda. Mrs. Elvsted is unpretentious (at one point Eilert Lövborg labels her "stupid") but she recognizes her individual rights and acts accordingly. She saves herself regardless of possible social ostracism. Hedda, often mistakenly identified with the free, modern woman, would never do so. Thea realizes the nature of the changes which have revolutionized Norway and adapts her life to them. Hedda, on the other hand, is incapable of compromise or change. The social matrix by which she was formed prohibits such alternatives—she will break before she bends—that is her tragedy.

Eilert Lövborg's precise place in the social fabric which encompasses *Hedda Gabler* is less easily determined than that of any other character in the play. His social position is never definitely stated by Ibsen and clues in the dialogue as to his background are mere hints, shadowy and indistinct.

We are given a glimpse of his past in Act I. Tesman and Judge Brack discuss him:

TESMAN: Well—no doubt he has run through all
his property long ago; and he can scarcely write
a new book every year—eh?

BRACK: You must remember that his relations
have a good deal of influence.

TESMAN: Oh, his relations, unfortunately, have
entirely washed their hands of him.

BRACK: At one time they called him the hope of
the family.

TESMAN: At one time, yes! But he has put an end
to all that.

From this exchange we know he comes from a propertied, influential family (probably of the second layer, the professional class); that he is an intellectual; that he has failed to fulfill his promise; and that his family has dissociated itself from him. In Act II in a short scene between Hedda and Lövborg, that information is elaborated:

LOVBORG: —When I used to come to your father's in the afternoon—and the General sat over at the window reading his papers—with his back towards us—

HEDDA: And we two on the corner sofa—

LOVBORG: Always with the same illustrated paper before us—

HEDDA: For want of an album, yes.

LOVBORG: Yes, Hedda, and when I made my confessions to you—told you about myself, things that at that time no one else knew! There I would sit and tell you of my escapades—my days and nights of devilment.

In those earlier days then, he had been socially acceptable by both Hedda and her father, the General. His social position allowed him to call upon them, and those visits led to a confidential friendship. With that development, it is reasonable to presume that romance and marriage became future possibilities. Such eventualities could become realities, however, only if Lövborg renounced his "escapades and devilment," fulfilled his promise, and succeeded in some conventional manner.

But quite suddenly their friendship was irrevocably breached when he made sexual advances which she rejected. We learn about it later on in the same scene partially quoted above:

LOVBORG: It was you that broke with me.

HEDDA: Yes, when our friendship threatened to develop into something more serious. Shame upon you, Eilert Lövborg! How could you think of wronging your—your frank comrade?

When this reunion scene between Hedda and Lövborg is read in its entirety, we learn that Hedda was an avid and provocative listener and questioner in those bygone conversations. A study of the dialogue allows little doubt that from his viewpoint she led him on, aroused his passions, and tempted him into assuming that she would welcome more serious and overt advances on his part—that she would be willing to participate in similar escapades.

Hedda was fully capable of thinking of and hinting at illicit delights of love (and still is, in the play, with Judge Brack). But in her circle (and, we assume, in Lövborg's at that time) flirtation was acceptable only as long as it remained mere coquetry. There was a point in flirtation beyond which neither partner was to venture. Supposedly both participants in the delightful game knew the rules. They knew the point at which this activity, which was exciting and acceptable, became serious, unacceptable, and a violation of an understood taboo. In their youthful affair, Hedda obeyed the social law and Lövborg transgressed it.

Lövborg's violation of this social law during his youth is puzzling, granted we are correct in our placement of him in the social spectrum of the time. There are two possible explanations for his behavior: one, he did not know that his attempt to win Hedda's favors, carried beyond the acceptable limits, was violating a taboo, and two, he knew but didn't care. In either case, it gives us an interesting view of his background which is at variance with the information we have garnered about him thus far in this paper. If he came from the professional class (and that conclusion seems reasonable from the internal evidence in the play), the questions arise: why did he not know how far he could go in this love game? And, if he did know, why did he not care? His training, the aspirations of his family, the stiff mores of his time and place all conspired to make him aware of socially unacceptable behavior and to make him heedful of his actions.

Lövborg's passionate response to Hedda's provocations may seem a natural reaction to us today. But such a belief ignores entirely the strength of the caste system of the time and place, with its network of restrictions and inhibitions, which was a powerful brake on headstrong impulses and passions.

Here is an example of the conflicting elements that Ibsen utilized to suggest a shadowy, vague, and shifting social frame for Eilert Lövborg, a man who somehow does not fit any class. In his youth a rebel against his "good" family, later a bohemian consorting with the red-haired, gun-carrying Mlle. Diana, gifted, undisciplined, undefined, and always disturbing, Eilert Lövborg was created and employed by Ibsen as a symbol of the equally undefined and disturbing changes which were taking place in the social structure of Norway.

Lövborg's social transgression, even though it occurred long before the action of the play begins, and fascinating as it is in itself for the insight it affords us into his background, has an even greater significance. It is a pivotal event because it is Hedda's motivational mainspring throughout the play. We learn that this improper advance triggered a set of socially conditioned reactions from Hedda which was sharp, verging on the outraged. Her aristocratic lineage, birth, training, and pride flared into near violence. Her sense of caste and caste proprieties demanded instant satisfaction. She threatened to shoot him. We first hear of it in that same scene in Act II:

> LOVBORG: Oh, why did you not carry out your threat? Why did you not shoot me down?
>
> HEDDA: Because I have such a dreadful fear of scandal.

Although she did not carry out her threat because of her fear of scandal which would besmirch her proud name, she had no choice but to react the way she did, and Eilert Lövborg's name was removed from the list of eligible young men. As a result, when she was ready to marry, she had to settle upon Tesman (whom she basically detested), who was the best of the young men available. Utter boredom was her only offspring from that incongruous union and, in the play, that boredom prompts her to set in train the events which lead ultimately to her destruction.

When Lövborg makes his appearance in Act II we know that he is attempting, with Thea Elvsted's help, to re-establish himself in society. He has given up his "repulsive habits" for her sake and has written a new book which will win him fame. All comes to naught. An alcoholic, he is tricked by Hedda into taking a drink, gets drunk, loses his manuscript, contemplates suicide, and dies a repulsive death.

Judge Brack is Hedda's social equal, one of her caste. Ibsen is at some pains to establish this fact. First, the position he gives him, that of a state functionary, is conclusive in itself; second, Ibsen plants the closeness of Brack's friendship with Hedda when Tesman says to him, near the end of Act I: "Think of Hedda, my dear fellow! You, who know her so well—."; third, the dramatist endowed him with an unmistakable aristocratic style in his speech. Judge Brack talks Hedda's language, the language of images, nuances, murmurs, sighs, and lifted eyebrows which is so masterfully demonstrated during their conversation in the early part of Act II:

> BRACK: Fortunately your wedding journey is over now.
>
> HEDDA: (Shaking her head). Not by a long—long way. I have only arrived at a station on the line.
>
> BRACK: Well, then the passengers jump out and move about a little, Mrs. Hedda.
>
> HEDDA: I never jump out . . . because there is always someone standing by to—
>
> BRACK: (laughing). To look at your ankles, do you mean?
>
> HEDDA: Precisely.
>
> BRACK: Well but, dear me—
>
> HEDDA: (with a gesture of repulsion). I won't have it. I would rather keep my seat where I happen to be—and continue the tête-a-tête.
>
> BRACK: But suppose a third person were to jump in and join the couple.
>
> HEDDA: Ah—that is quite another matter!
>
> BRACK: A trusted, sympathetic friend—
>
> HEDDA: —with a fund of conversation on all sorts of lively topics—
>
> BRACK: —and not the least bit of a specialist!
>
> HEDDA: (with an audible sigh). Yes, that would be a relief indeed.
>
> BRACK: (hears the front door open, and glances in that direction). The triangle is completed.
>
> HEDDA: (half aloud). And on goes the train.

Although by birth and vocation Judge Brack is an aristocrat-professional, and by temperament a dandy and *bon-vivant*, he is by taste and choice a discreet *roué* who shuns marriage and seeks quiet triangular arrangements with married women. And here, precisely, is where he has compromised his caste and his honor. He is willing to exercise his considerable talents and go to great lengths, including blackmail, to achieve that goal with Hedda.

Judge Brack is a master of the techniques and methods by which he satisfies his illicit desires, but his sensibilities have become blunted by years of self-indulgence and that weakness leads him to make a fatal error in his strategy to conquer Hedda. Brack refuses to believe that she will not compromise herself, her caste, or her pride. Just as, at an earlier time, Eilert Lövborg, for an unknown reason, misinterpreted her coquetry as willingness to engage in a sexual affair, so now Judge Brack, because his sensitivity is dulled, makes the same mistake:

> BRACK: Well, fortunately, there is no danger, so long as I say nothing.
>
> HEDDA: (looks up at him). So I am in your power, Judge Brack. You have me at your beck and call, from this time forward.
>
> BRACK: (whispers softly). Dearest Hedda—believe me, I shall not abuse my advantage.
>
> HEDDA: I am in your power none the less. Subject to your will and your demands. A slave, a slave then! (Rises impetuously.) No, I cannot endure the thought of that! Never!
>
> BRACK: (looks half-mockingly at her). People generally get used to the inevitable.

At play's end he stands revealed in his caste betrayal. He has subverted a code of behavior to his own degrading designs and has turned his back to everything which he should uphold. The extent of his personal social disintegration is expressed in the final speech of the play, his fatuous "Good God!—people don't do such things." Judge Brack has been away from his own kind for such a long time that he has lost touch completely. If anyone should have recognized that people—people of Hedda Gabler's type, people proudly bound to a rigid social code—*do* do such things, it should have been Judge Brack.

The "social conditions and principles" that Ibsen had in mind when he wrote *Hedda Gabler* are of crucial importance in the play. They constitute the molding and tempering forces which dictate the behavior of all the play's characters. Because each character is a part of a tightly woven social fabric, he becomes an exceptionally real, three-dimensional person, and the atmosphere of the play is vibrant and alive. Unfolding in that atmosphere and against the backdrop of those "social conditions and principles" the play has meaning, unity, and dimension.

In conception and execution, *Hedda Gabler* is a brilliantly subtle and complex masterpiece of human relationships dictated and largely controlled by the intricacies of the social *milieu* of the time and place. Because Henrik Ibsen created those human relationships and set them amidst an unobtrusive yet omnipresent social fabric, *Hedda Gabler* is one of the most striking dramaturgical achievements of all time.

The purpose of this paper has been to clarify the "social conditions and principles" which existed in Norway in 1890, how they affect the behavior of the persons in *Hedda Gabler,* and their over-all significance to the play. It is hoped that an understanding of those conditions and principles, while not offering a solution to all the problems of the play, will help to eliminate some of them.

Perhaps we can never fully understand the drives of the persons in this play, and it may be just as well that it is so. If all its hidden facets of character could be exposed and its deep mines of behavior motivation could be exhausted, no enigma would remain. But, like *Hamlet, Hedda Gabler* retains its secret and its mystery and, with them, its lasting fascination. (pp. 207-13)

> Erling E. Kildahl, "The 'Social Conditions and Principles' of Hedda Gabler," in Educational Theatre Journal, *Vol. XIII, No. 3, October, 1961, pp. 207-13.*

Patricia Meyer Spacks   (essay date 1962)

[*In the essay below, Spacks asserts that the enduring power of* Hedda Gabler *lies not only in the complex characterization of Hedda, but in its overall structure and its underlying themes about the role of women and the nature of society. The principal characters in the drama duplicate Hedda's desire to control the destinies of others, argues the critic, depicting in microcosm a restrictive society that denies freedom to all of its members—especially women. Seen from this larger perspective, concludes Spacks, "what seems to be a study of an abnormal woman turns into a study of an abnormal society," and Hedda emerges as a character demanding sympathy as well as condemnation.*]

Although Ibsen's *Hedda Gabler* has recently enjoyed considerable off-Broadway success, critical confusion about the play has not appreciably abated. Reviews of the recent production merely emphasized the conflicting views which have been advanced since *Hedda Gabler* first appeared in 1890. It seems to be a play about an extraordinary woman—but extraordinary in precisely what way? Is she naturally cruel and malicious, or is she made so by the events one sees on stage? In a review entitled "A Beautiful Snake," Whitney Balliett in the *New Yorker,* after admitting that various social problems are dealt with in the play, insists that Ibsen "was primarily interested in exploring ironically the cold depths of that changeless and most fascinating of all women—the bitch." Alan Pryce-Jones, on the other hand, in *Theatre Arts,* complained that the New York production made Hedda's bitchiness too immediately apparent. "To give the play its full impact, we ought to discover only slowly the full awfulness of which she is capable. . . . It is the shock of coming home to a humdrum existence, to unexpected poverty, that releases the devil in her." But a minority opinion in *The Commonweal,* by Richard Gilman, suggests that "Hedda is not a *femme fatale* or a study in neurotic behavior as much as she is a locus for energy turned in upon itself, an arena for the struggle of being with non-being."

These representative opinions suggest the nature of the critical controversy, and hint at the difficulty of finding a coherent reading of the play. Ever since Ibsen himself insisted that *Hedda* was about a character, not ideas, commentary has tended to center on the complex and mysterious title figure. But no interpretation based solely on the enigmatic Hedda quite accounts for the play's power, a power available even in the mid-twentieth century, despite the implausibilities of motivation (Hedda's marriage to Tesman, for example), of speech (Miss Tesman on the subject of invalids), and of action (Mrs. Elvsted's convenient production of the working notes of Lövborg's book). This power seems to derive both from the total structure of the play and, Ibsen's insistence notwithstanding, from a subterranean structure of ideas. That ideas about the nature of womanhood and of society are at work here is immediately suggested by Ibsen's own working notes on *Hedda.* A section headed "Main Points" contains these comments:

1. They are not all made to be mothers.

2. They are passionate but they are afraid of scandal.

3. They perceive that the times are full of missions worth devoting one's life to, but they cannot discover them.

These statements certainly outline Hedda's problems, but the phraseology, the "they" which obviously applies to women in general, hints that Ibsen had a broader application in mind. And there is even a sense in which Hedda's problems are duplicated, not only by the other women in the play, but by the men as well. The desire to control someone's destiny, announced explicitly by Hedda ("For once in my life I want the power to shape a human destiny") is shared, in more or less devious forms, by all the other important characters; this theme dictates the action of the drama, in the Aristotelian sense, and accounts for its most profound overtones.

A yearning to shape a destiny is quite clearly the center of Hedda's motivation, and its demonstration in her case involves all the major symbols of the play. The destinies at Hedda's disposal are somewhat limited. Her own destiny does not seem to be under her control: her marriage to Tesman is proof of that. She married, without love (she hates the very word), because she had danced herself tired and wasn't "getting any younger"; even General Gabler's daughter was forced to accept marriage as the only recourse, and not even General Gabler's daughter, in a loveless marriage to a virtual non-entity ("a thoroughly worthy man" who "may still go far," but about whose capacities Hedda obviously has serious doubts)—not even she can retain control over her own future under these circumstances. There are financial restrictions, for one thing, so that she cannot entertain as she had wished; and, of greatest symbolic importance, there is the unwanted pregnancy, the visible emblem of Hedda's subjection.

But if she cannot control her own life, perhaps she can dominate others. Her human contacts consist almost entirely of efforts, sometimes quite random and meaningless, to assert her dominance. Her husband seems a defenseless victim for Hedda to exercise her power on, but he is hardly worth bothering with, as Hedda herself suggests. Aunt Rina and the maid are easy prey; Hedda merely practices on them. Mrs. Elvsted seems almost as vulnerable, although she turns out to have hidden resources, as, of course, do Lövborg and Judge Brack. Even Tesman eludes Hedda at last. There remains the most obvious object of control: the unborn child. In motherhood, one would think, Hedda could gratify her need to form the lives of others: she would not be a good mother, but perhaps she would be a more satisfied woman. But this avenue, of course, she totally rejects; and the reason for her rejection points to the most essential quality of her character.

For Hedda Gabler wants power—not responsibility. The antithesis between the two concepts is at the heart of the play; Hedda's unwillingness to accept responsibility is the central aspect of her perversity. She rejects normal, two-way marriage, rejects the very idea of love, rejects the normal functions of motherhood. And, unwilling even to accept full responsibility for the actions she really commits ("I suddenly get impulses like that and I simply can't control them"), she cannot go to bed with Eilert or in any other way brave social disapproval.

The burning of the manuscript, the "child" of Eilert and Thea, underlines the ambivalence of Hedda's nature. It is, of course, most obviously an assertion of her power, a dramatic attempt to form the destinies of others. But it is also, equally apparently, an expression of her perversity: a willful destruction of the fruit of a male-female union, a demonstration of her jealousy of those who, freer than she can ever be, can defy society and find a genuine "vocation." The only vocation she finds open for herself is the manipulating of others—perhaps she can get Jörgen to go into politics, to combat her boredom. But she herself painfully recognizes the inadequacy of such plotting, and the superiority of the way which Eilert and Thea have found. And her strength—her ability to act ruthlessly and powerfully—is intimately involved with her weakness, her inability to accept responsibility or defy society directly.

In the past, it has seemed possible to her that she can turn the weakness to her advantage, make it into a strength. Her pre-marital relationship with Eilert, as it is revealed in the play, seems to have been an extended effort in this direction. She had power over Lövborg—he says so himself—and exercised it, "in a devious way, if you please," for the sake of a *vicarious* sense of freedom, unable then or ever to brave social restrictions herself. The vine leaves that she wishes to see in his hair are the symbol of beauty achieved by defiance of society; his dissipated life in the past, the dissipation she urges him toward in the present, represent to her the possibility of escaping rather than submitting to narrow social limits. It is entirely for her own sake that she manipulates him: not merely for the joy of controlling a destiny, but for the immediate joy of knowing that she has, with perfect safety, with no apparent responsibility, caused a violation of conventional restrictions. Even her attempt to drive Eilert to suicide has a similar direct motivation: it is for the sake of preserving her illusions as well as for the sake of asserting power. Her dialogue with Judge Brack, after his report of the suicide, makes the point perfectly explicit:

> HEDDA: Oh, what a sense of freedom there is in this act of Eilert Lövborg's.
>
> BRACK: Freedom, Mrs. Hedda? Of course, it is freedom for him.

HEDDA: I mean for me. It gives me a sense of freedom to know that an act of deliberate courage is still possible in this world—an act of spontaneous beauty.

Judge Brack then goes on to demonstrate that this view of the situation is a "beautiful illusion." It is, in this respect, identical with all Hedda's views of the essential nature of reality: there is a sense in which, almost consciously, she insists on remaining in the world of illusion. She rejects the basic functions of women—marriage, motherhood; she rejects the real world of responsibility; her preservation of the sense of power and control depends on her withdrawal from reality for the sake of illusion. When Lövborg tries to find out why their intimacy had ended, Hedda cries out, "I realized the danger; you wanted to spoil our intimacy—to *drag it down to reality*" (italics mine). What she means, apparently, is that Lövborg wanted to turn their relationship into a sexual one, in which Hedda would have been forced to participate directly, instead of gaining vicarious fulfillment through his freedom. Her unwillingness to be dragged down to reality remains paramount: Hedda can't stand to talk about money, can't stand any mention of her pregnancy.

Her desperate suicide is, of course, Hedda's dramatic attempt to reconcile the opposed sides of her character. Now, for the first time, she decides to assert her dominance by controlling her *own* destiny, to reconcile beauty and reality. The beauty is to come from the willed act; death itself is ugly, in Hedda's view: she will have nothing to do with Aunt Rina's death. But her suicide is to be an act of defiance, of assertion, of profound meaning—and Hedda, at the last, would rather mean than be. It is, of course, a totally appropriate final irony that this heavily weighted act should be reacted to merely as a violation of social convention ("people don't *do* such things"), with no recognition of the deep significance inherent in such a violation on Hedda's part.

The other characters in the play, motivated to a greater or lesser extent by the same need to control a destiny, are not all so unsuccessful as Hedda. Mrs. Elvsted, indeed, who seems to be set up, thematically and descriptively, in contrast to Hedda (abundant, curly golden hair versus sparse brown hair; willingness to ignore conventional standards for the man she loves versus Hedda's inability either to love or to ignore convention), is conspicuously successful in the areas where Hedda fails. But it is a mistake to sentimentalize her, as some readers of the play have done, to see her as the "good woman" opposed to Hedda's evil. Matters are by no means so clear-cut. Like Hedda, for example, whose perversity is emphasized by this fact, Thea Elvsted seems strangely removed from normal maternal and connubial impulses. Like Hedda, she has made a loveless marriage, a marriage of convenience. She has no children of her own. Her stepchildren she has apparently abandoned without a qualm. Her "child" is the manuscript: it is she who suggests the identification. This substratum of coldness is obscured, in Thea's case, by the fact that she so brilliantly fits the stereotype of the gentle, clinging, defenseless little woman. But Ibsen is at some pains to point out that the gentleness, the clinging quality, are merely her modes of achieving ends rather similar to

Hedda's. She is as conscious as Hedda herself of the power-motif:

HEDDA: Tell me, Thea—how did this friendship start between you and Eilert Lövborg?

MRS. ELVSTED: It grew gradually. I began to have a sort of power over him.

HEDDA: Really?

MRS. ELVSTED: Yes. After a while he gave up his old habits. Oh, not because I asked him to—I never would have dared do that. But I suppose he realized how unhappy they made me, and so he dropped them.

It is almost a parody of ladies'-magazine manipulation: the poor, misguided man gives up his bad habits and never realizes he is being "handled." Hedda's outbursts of jealousy ("I think I shall have to burn your hair off, after all!") are in a sense justified: the best testimony to this fact is Eilert's "she's somehow broken my courage—my defiant spirit." Eilert, to be sure, has a tendency to romanticize himself, and this remark is in a sense a self-justification for weakness. Yet it underlines Thea's success in exercising power: her power is felt by Eilert as much as Hedda's has been in the past.

Like Hedda—like all women, Ibsen seems to suggest, because women's possibilities are limited by their social role—Mrs. Elvsted looks outside herself for a destiny to control, and it is for this reason that she is so resilient at the end of the play. Unlike Hedda, she has not run out of available victims. She ends with a vision of twofold control: she can be to Tesman what she has been to Lövborg ("If I could only inspire your husband in the same way!" she says to Hedda), and she can even continue to form Eilert's destiny posthumously. One wonders, of course, about the reality of the love she professes for Lövborg. Love and the lust for power, the polar extremes of all great visions of human emotional capacity from Christianity to Freudianism, seem to be absolutely antithetical for Hedda; as one sees with increasing clarity the extent to which the desire for control is central also in Thea, it is difficult to believe that it is not, in her also, finally a substitute for love.

The ways in which the need for control can be disguised through gentleness, "femininity," are sketched also in the more shadowy character of Miss Tesman, Aunt Julianne. The only unmarried woman in the play, she has an obsessive interest in Hedda's prospective children. The normal interest of the maiden aunt, one might feel, except that the other two female characters have been importantly defined by their *lack* of interest in real children. In this context, the spinster's deep concern seems yet another instance of the perversity which envelops the world of the play. Her mode of control is sacrifice. "I simply must have someone to live for," she says; and again, "One can always find some poor invalid who needs to be taken care of." She is certainly a "good" woman; her desire to help is unexceptionable. Yet it is not hard to sympathize with Hedda, however much one condemns her brutality toward the old lady: the audience or reader, too, can easily feel that Aunt Julianne is eager to worm her way into the lives of others, that she has a strong *potentiality* of subtle dominance, in a peculiarly feminine way.

On the masculine side, the need to dominate is also apparent, and also subtly handled. It is most clear in Judge Brack, who is in some ways Hedda's male counterpart. He, too, avoids responsibility ("generally speaking, I have a great respect for the state of matrimony, but I confess, that as an individual—"); he, too, clearly wants power; to be "cock-of-the-walk" by "back ways," to assert masculine sexual dominance. "I'm exceedingly glad that you have no sort of hold over me," remarks Hedda in the third act, and Judge Brack replies with an ambiguous laugh and an equally ambiguous remark, taken by Hedda as a veiled threat. The resolution of their relationship is explicitly and emphatically in terms of the power-motif.

> HEDDA: That means you have me in your power, Judge! You have me at your beck and call from now on.
>
> BRACK: Dearest Hedda—believe me—I shall not abuse my advantage.
>
> HEDDA: I am in your power, all the same. Subject to your commands and wishes. No longer free—not free! . . . No. I won't endure that thought. Never!
>
> BRACK: *looks at her half mockingly.* People manage to get used to the inevitable.

This interchange is, of course, one of the precipitating causes of Hedda's suicide.

The other two men, like the two women besides Hedda, conceal their desire for control in devious ways. Tesman seems an obvious weakling, with no opportunity for domination. He doesn't assert himself in his marriage; he loves to wait on Hedda: in this respect he resembles his aunt. But when he is given his first opportunity to control a destiny, when the manuscript of Eilert's book falls into his hands, he demonstrates a singular ambiguity of response. He doesn't give the manuscript back to Eilert or tell any of the others that he's found it ("I didn't want them to know—for Eilert's sake, you see"); when, the next day, he calls on Eilert "to tell him the manuscript was safe," he leaves no message; he does not mention the manuscript to Mrs. Elvsted, although he meets her immediately after his failure to find Eilert. Of course he lacks the sort of courage which Hedda has so abundantly; it is she who, for her own reasons, actually destroys the manuscript. And when she has done so, Tesman is free to adopt once more the strong moral tone he is most comfortable with. Finally, he shares with Mrs. Elvsted the opportunity, so satisfying to them both, of controlling Eilert's destiny after his death. For this goal, he willingly abandons control of his own future. ("I'll devote my life to it! . . . My own work will simply have to wait.") "You know," he says, "sorting out and arranging other people's papers—that's something I'm particularly good at—." And our ultimate scorn for Tesman is based partly on the fact that this statement seems so profoundly true: this is the only sort of control, the only variety of power, that is readily available to him.

Eilert is a more complicated case. He, too, tempts one to sentimentalize about him, and certainly he is the pleasan-test person in the play—but he, too, has his faults. In the past he has made an abortive effort to exercise some control over Hedda, to make her become his mistress. Not only did he fail in that effort, but he was subjugated, instead, to *her* ideas of freedom and beauty. Lövborg is the one person in the play who, during the time of the action, is primarily concerned to control his *own* destiny: Hedda skillfully perverts that concern into a desire to demonstrate to others how efficiently he can manage himself. (There are, of course, already elements of this desire in Lövborg: he does not propose to compete with Tesman for the professorship, but he wants everyone to know that he could have done so.) But paradoxically, this man who wishes only to control his own life has as little power to do so as Hedda. And this is because he is the focus of other people's efforts at control. His dissipation in the past was largely Hedda's responsibility; his success in the present has been under Mrs. Elvsted's supervision and inspiration. He is as concerned as Hedda herself about the opinions of others, once she has suggested that others may be thinking badly of him: the suggestion that Mrs. Elvsted has lost faith in him starts him on his course of dissipation once more. After the loss of the manuscript, he confesses that he has no force of his own. In his final appearance on stage, he apparently goes off to commit suicide under the influence of Hedda; and the final irony is that even his mysterious death seems not to have been, after all, the result of his own will and control. ("Did he threaten to shoot [Mademoiselle Diana], and did the pistol go off then—or did she grab the pistol, shoot him, afterwards putting it back into his pocket.") As far as direct control is concerned, then, he is totally unsuccessful. Yet in another sense—this is the ultimate, vital twist of the play—he controls the destinies of the very people who have controlled his: Hedda, Tesman, Mrs. Elvsted. For this business of control is not, as it turns out, a one-way matter: the victim, the object of control, forms the life of his manipulators as inevitably as they form his. Hedda is driven to suicide by Eilert's final denial, in action, of her principles. Mrs. Elvsted and Tesman are driven together by Eilert's death; their future course of action is dictated by his memory and his manuscript. And one has little hope that their relationship will prove, ultimately, any more fruitful than the other relationships will prove, ultimately, any more fruitful than the other relationships that the drama presents: in this world of power-need, fruitfulness is an unlikely resolution.

For it is, after all, a *world* that we glimpse in the play. Unlike many of Ibsen's other works, ***Hedda Gabler*** presents no characters who seem to stand primarily as representatives of society and social pressure. Yet "society" looms in the background: "what people will think" is a constant issue. And the group we see on the stage seems ultimately a social microcosm, suggests exactly why and how society exercises so much restrictive and destructive force. These are people all turned on one another, all obsessed with control of one another: the freedom that Hedda so yearns for becomes in this context clearly impossible. There is no room for freedom; Eilert's apparent freedom in the past was illusory. Even if one wishes only to control his own life, he finds himself cut off from this possibility because there are so many other people who also want to control his life, who *insist* on controlling it. The psychological fact becomes, for Ibsen, ultimately a social fact: what seems to be a study of an abnormal woman turns into a study of an abnormal society. The futile condition of women ("They perceive that the times are full of missions worth devoting one's life to, but they cannot discover them") is both partial cause and effect of a profound social chaos, a modern Hobbesian world in which people are forced to band together for fear of one another—and if they do not fear one another, they should.

Here is the ultimate source of the pessimism one feels in this play: there is no escape from this world and its pressures, and disaster, of one sort or another, is always implicit in it. One can imagine the story of Mrs. Elvsted, or Tesman—any character in the play. It would lack the interest of Hedda's story, for it would deal with a far more commonplace individual, but it would be the story of an equally frustrated life. And the sense one has that Hedda is not, ultimately, completely a villainess, that she deserves and demands sympathy as well as condemnation, comes partly from the recognition, which the play forces on its readers and viewers, that Hedda's difference from the rest lies mainly in the fact that she is more straightforward in the expression of the drives that dominate them all. She attempts, as much as she can, "masculine" solutions for her problems; and in a society where men demonstrate such "feminine" deviousness and participate in "feminine" values, where women have little scope for straightforward action, she is tragically doomed to failure. The play's disturbing quality, its ability to leave the viewer strangely uneasy, comes partly from the fact that it condemns not only Hedda, but the world which surrounds her—a world not in the least dated, a society with troublesome affinities to our own. (pp. 155-64)

> Patricia Meyer Spacks, "The World of Hedda Gabler," in The Tulane Drama Review, *Vol. 7, No. 1, Fall, 1962, pp. 155-64.*

Sandra E. Saari   (essay date 1977)

[*Below, Saari examines the plot of* Hedda Gabler *to establish a unifying pattern in the action of the drama: the attempt to "re-create the past in a perfected form." Recurring images of hair, fire, pistols, and vine leaves underscore Hedda's attempts to re-enact events from her past, argues the critic, who points to a similar desire on behalf of all of the principal characters. Hedda's suicide results from her recognition that re-creating her past life is impossible, concludes Spacks, yet the act itself ironically fulfills her desire for a perfect and beautiful deed.*]

Most scholarly criticism of Henrik Ibsen's *Hedda Gabler* inevitably focuses on an analysis of Hedda's character and motives. But a dramatic consideration prior to the *why* of character and motive is: *what* is Hedda doing? Plot, the most important element of tragedy according to Aristotle, is an imitation of an action. Yet the character of Hedda is so compelling that the action of *Hedda Gabler* has been denied even by Henry James: "his drama is essentially that supposedly undramatic thing, the picture not of an action but of a condition" [in *Ibsen: The Critical Heritage*, Michael Egan, ed., 1972]; and has been severely deemphasized by a critic of such stature as M. C. Bradbrook:

Eva Le Gallienne as Hedda Gabler. 1928.

"As, however, the centre of the play is not a problem but a personality there is less emphasis on the story—on the links of cause and effect" [*Ibsen the Norwegian: A Revaluation,* 2nd ed., 1946]. Obviously it is not readily apparent what Hedda is doing. However, an analysis of the structure of the play, and in particular the structure of the four dominant image patterns, reveals the nature of Hedda's actions and that, together with an analysis of the secondary characters' actions, establishes the unity of the play's action.

In broadest terms, the structure of *Hedda Gabler* is identical to that of all Ibsen's mature plays—the movement from delusion or illusion, with respect to the past, to recognition. Specifically this structure in *Hedda Gabler* consists in a series of attempts by Hedda to reinstate the past in her present life, a series that culminates in her suicide, her final recognition of the delusory nature of that project. Using retrospective exposition, Ibsen counterpoints each revelation of an incident from Hedda's past life with a re-enactment of that incident in the play's forward action. For example, the retrospective exposition in Act II reveals that Hedda and Lövborg used to sit together on a sofa in her father's house, ostensibly looking at a book but actually engaged in clandestine conversation; the forward action in Act II has Lövborg and Hedda in an identical posture using the same pretext for a similar purpose. Ibsen has counterpointed that past incident by having Hedda, fully aware of its past import, re-create it in the present. During this conversation, Hedda is able to treat Tesman as no more of a threat than her father had been on similar occasions. Furthermore, until reminded by Tesman, Hedda completely forgets about the imminent arrival of her present rival, Thea, so successfully has she disengaged herself from the present and immersed herself in re-creating the past. This pattern, as will be shown below, is the dominant pattern of Hedda's actions. Thus the major action of the play—the action the plot imitates; that which, as Francis Fergusson states, "is to be used to indicate the direction which an analysis of a play should take" [*The Idea of a Theater: A Study of Ten Plays,* 1949]—is to re-create the past in a perfected form.

I

Since unity of action demands that all characters be engaged in that action, a preliminary step in this analysis is to demonstrate that the secondary characters participate in the action of re-creating the past in a perfected form. Two of the three major secondary characters are historians—by their stipulated vocation they are re-creators of the past—and the third is an historian's amanuensis.

Jörgen Tesman spent his six-month honeymoon rummaging through European archives to gather notes on medieval domestic industries. Ibsen's conception of this pursuit is indicated by an early note for the play: "And then Tesman isn't really a scholar, but a specialist. The Middle Ages are dead" [*The Oxford Ibsen,* Vol. VII, ed. James Walter McFarlane, 1966]. Tesman's lifework is to recreate the dead past; for him the present is empty of significance until it has been completed, until it has become the past. Ibsen reinforces this characterization of Tesman repeatedly. To Aunt Julle's covert inquiries about Hedda's pregnancy, Tesman responds with total lack of comprehension; his focus on the history of mankind has rendered unrecognizable the shape of the present and the prospects for the future. Lövborg's manuscript about the future of civilization elicits Tesman's astonished remark, "Amazing! It just wouldn't enter my head to write about anything like that." The ultimate demonstration of Tesman's chronic retrospection and absence of foresight occurs in the last act. Tesman is able to comprehend Lövborg's vision of the future only when he is able to deal with it as a problem of re-creating the past. Tesman and Thea begin to reconstruct Lövborg's manuscript from her fragmentary notes. The suggestion of ridicule that lingers about Tesman during the play precipitates here as Tesman first puts aside his own work in order to re-create Lövborg's, and then, to have more time for this reconstruction, hands over his own wife to Brack in the classical comic manner of the husband blindly arranging his own cuckoldry. He eagerly immerses himself in a re-creation of the past: he makes arrangements to go to his childhood home with his former sweetheart to reconstruct the manuscript of a dead friend. Tesman instinctively seeks the comfort and security of the completed and therefore predictable past. His is the benighted comic extreme of a pattern that Hedda pursues seriously and knowingly.

Lövborg also began as an historian, but he is more than that by the time the play begins. His first volume was on the history of civilization. He repudiates its worth, "I wrote a book that nobody could disagree with," and

claims that his next volume, on the future of civilization, "is the real thing. I put some of myself into this one." Lövborg's relation to the past is the antithesis of Tesman's. Whereas Tesman can see his life only in terms of the safely distanced, completed past and finds present events such as Lövborg's competition for his appointment a near catastrophe, Lövborg, to the contrary, has come to terms with the past—with the historical past in his first volume and with his personal disreputable past by the publication of that first, highly praised volume, which redeems his reputation. Having fully recognized and articulated the past, Lövborg is freed from it and freed for "the real thing," which involves risk, involves exercising one's freedom by acting in a manner that has *not* already been publicly sanctioned or approved because it is merely a reiteration of the past. Thus Lövborg provides a pattern for Hedda to emulate. But Hedda represents for him an aspect of the past that still has power; she pulls Lövborg back into that past. Becoming intoxicated, he loses his manuscript, which represents the future, and re-creates his drunken past, complete with the orgy at Mlle. Diana's; he lapses into his former state of disgrace. This re-creation is brought to completion by his death, which assures that he will not emerge again from that past.

Thea is the third character who is identified with the historian's re-creation of the past. A kind of auxiliary historian, she is amanuensis first to Lövborg and then to Tesman. When Lövborg tells her that they will cease working together, Thea responds, "What am I to do with my life, then?" Though this seems to be evoked by her intense passion for Lövborg, such an interpretation is thoroughly discredited by her later actions. Minutes after learning of Lövborg's death, Thea is immersed with Tesman in an "eager examination" of the notes for Lövborg's manuscript. Hedda explicitly defines this action as a reversion to past habit: "Isn't this strange for you, Thea? Now you're sitting here together with Tesman . . . as you used to sit with Ejlert Lövborg." Thea, unaware of Hedda's mockery or of the inherent irony of her own posture, earnestly answers, "Oh yes, oh God . . . if only I could inspire your husband in the same way." Thea has found what she is to do with her life: with Tesman substituted for Lövborg, she can continue her previous habit of taking and organizing someone else's notes. The pocketful of notes she produces in Act IV is the complement of Tesman's suitcase of notes in Act I. The two figures merge over Lövborg's literary remains. Like Tesman, Thea feels very uncomfortable and inept in dealing with the dynamic, changeable present and, like Tesman, she retreats into the psychically safe posture of recreating the already actualized and therefore uneventful past. She too becomes an historian, a re-creator rather than a creator—in the terminology of the play, "an academic."

"You're something of an academic too, in your own line," Hedda accuses Brack. Like Tesman, Brack seeks to perpetuate his habitual pattern. His is the *ménage à trois.* Since his previous triangular arrangement has evidently disappeared—in the Earlier Draft this point is very specific: "In the last six months I've lost no less than three"— his action in the play is to re-create such a pattern with Hedda and Tesman. His polite interest in Tesman's well-being, and his ostensible concern for and ultimate discrediting of Lövborg have as an end the securing of this triangle. His gaining control over Hedda in the last act assures his full participation in such a triangle. Brack thereby completes the re-creation of his past pattern.

The other two secondary characters also reflect the major action of re-creating the past. Aunt Julle, but a short time after Aunt Rina's death, contemplates filling the empty spot: "Poor Rina's little room won't be left empty, you may be sure of that! [. . .] Oh, there's always some poor invalid or other who needs a bit of care and attention, unfortunately." Like Thea, Aunt Julle finds the habit of a relationship stronger than her response to the individual and so seeks to perpetuate the habit. Her disposition of Berte to Tesman's house has the same motive behind it. She tells Berte, "Jörgen must have you in the house with him, you see. He simply must. You've always looked after him, ever since he was a little boy." Berte becomes a living image of the transferral of past habit from Aunt Julle's household to Tesman's. She is an incarnation, in the Tesman's household, of the imposition of the past upon the present in the same manner that the portrait of General Gabler represents Hedda's own past. That the General is merely a portrait while Berte is an ubiquitous presence stresses the domination of the Tesman influence that threatens Hedda—her attempts to reassert her past are everywhere hedged by the inveterate habits of the Tesmans. Of these opposing poles of power, Ibsen says: "Jörgen Tesman, his old aunts, and the faithful servant Berte together form a picture of complete unity. They think alike, they share the same memories and have the same outlook on life. To Hedda they appear like a strange and hostile power, aimed at her very being" [Letters and Speeches, Evert Sprinchorn, ed., 1964].

II

Around Hedda, the central character, the plot and structure of the play coalesce, as she attempts to re-create her past both materially and mimetically. As opposed to a character like Mrs. Alving in **Ghosts,** for whom the past is re-enacted in the present against her intentions and despite her attempts to avoid it, Hedda intends and attempts to re-enact the past. In this she is distinct among Ibsen protagonists. And in this respect she is a direct outgrowth of one aspect of Ellida Wangel in **The Lady from the Sea.** Ibsen once wrote, "After Nora, Mrs. Alving had to come" [Letters and Speeches], indicating that the latter was the manifestation of Nora's rejected alternative; one can say of this play, "After Ellida, Hedda Gabler had to come." Ellida is powerfully drawn to her past, represented in the character of A Stranger, but she ultimately chooses not to return to it. Hedda has made the opposite choice.

Act I reveals Hedda's prior arrangements for establishing a physical, material replica of her past life. The Falk villa, formerly owned by a *statsraadinde,* is of proper class and magnitude for Hedda, and it formed the basis of her marriage: "It brought on engagement and marriage and honeymoon and the whole lot." But her assessment of this replication of the past is negative.

HEDDA: Ugh . . . I think it smells of lavender

and pot-pourri in all the rooms. . . . But perhaps Aunt Julle brought that smell in with her.

BRACK: [laughs] No, I think it's more probably a relic of the late lamented Lady Falk.

HEDDA: Yes, it has a sort of odour of death.

Rather than revivifying her past, the house entombs her in its own history. Hedda's replication of her material past further deteriorates at the end of Act I, when the appurtenances of her caste—the social life, the footman, and the saddle-horse, all of which Tesman has promised—are denied. By the end of Act I, Ibsen has clearly indicated that the material past with which Hedda has been trying to surround herself will not materialize perfectly. Act I closes with Hedda taking refuge from this material insufficiency in her pistols, those objects from her past that will ultimately destroy her.

The structure and plot of the remaining three acts revolve around Hedda trying to re-create the past mimetically. Perhaps an appropriate way to describe Hedda's transition is in theatrical terms. Hedda has tried to re-create the set in Act I; in Acts II-IV she will try to re-enact various scenes from her past: that is, she will attempt to re-create and participate in past events by imitating those events in the present.

Hedda's attempts to re-create the past mimetically begin with the opening scenes of Act II. In quick succession there are three scenes of increasingly elaborate replication of the past. Hedda, shooting her pistol down into the garden, sees Brack, pretends he is her target, and fires. Brack's response to this pistol play includes the somewhat cryptic remark, "Do you still play at that game?" Two things are noteworthy in this response. This is one of several references to Hedda's game playing; other characters in the play do not see her actions as having serious purpose. And, more important for the immediate discussion, Hedda's action is identical to a series of past actions: "Do you *still* play at that game?" The second scene is more protracted.

BRACK: [leans forward slightly] Well, my lady, what do you say to a comfortable little gossip.

HEDDA: [leans further back in the sofa] Doesn't it seem to you that it's an eternity since we talked together? Oh . . . I don't count those few words last night and this morning.

BRACK: But . . . between ourselves? Just the two of us, you mean?

HEDDA: Well, yes. More or less.

This preamble to their conversation points to this tête-à-tête being an enjoyable repetition of many such past events. Hedda and Brack are re-establishing their mutual participation in a former pattern. The third reduplicated scene in Act II is the Hedda-Lövborg tête-à-tête on the sofa, discussed earlier. Here, because the passions involved are stronger, Hedda immerses herself even more completely in the past than she has in the previous two scenes. Thus, in these three scenes that begin Act II, Ibsen establishes the mode of Hedda's action: the reanimation of the past through mimetic re-creation of that past.

III

The larger movement of the play involves this type of re-creation on an extended scale. In the three scenes just discussed, the re-creation is concurrent with the narration of the past event. However, in the broader perspective of the play as a whole, simultaneity is not the pattern. Rather, the compelling tension of the plot derives precisely from the disjunction of the retrospective narration and the mimetic recreation. The deliberate construction of this non-synchronous presentation is apparent if one compares the Earlier Draft and the final copy. The images associated with the larger re-enactment of the past—the hair, the fire, the pistol, the vine leaves in the hair—are so explicitly elaborated by Ibsen between the Earlier Draft and the completed play that their structural importance becomes preeminent. As a result of this structure, the play acquires a kind of teleology: events reported from the past, particularly those involving threats or desires, take on a looming potential for becoming manifest in the present action of the play, and the present becomes focused on a re-creating, a perfecting, and a consummation of that past.

Three of the four images associated with this larger re-enactment are introduced in Act I: the hair, the fire, and the pistol. At the first mention of Thea's name, Hedda responds: "That woman with the provoking hair that everyone made such a fuss of. An old flame of yours, too, I'm told." By using the Norwegian idiom *gamle flamme,* "old flame," to express the relationship between Tesman and Thea, Ibsen, from the outset, connects the fire image with that of Thea's hair. The first private conversation between Hedda and Thea explicitly delineates this relationship and details the past desire that presses for fulfillment:

> MRS. ELVSTED: Yes, but you were in the class above me. Oh, I was dreadfully frightened of you in those days!
>
> HEDDA: Frightened? Of me?
>
> MRS. ELVSTED: Oh, dreadfully frightened. When we met on the steps you always used to pull my hair.
>
> HEDDA: No, did I really?
>
> MRS. ELVSTED: Yes, and you once said you were going to burn it off.
>
> HEDDA: Oh, that was just something I said, you know.
>
> MRS. ELVSTED: Yes, but I was such a fool in those days.

Here are five elements described from the past that are to be recreated. The first four are: 1) Hedda's being *en klasse over,* "in the class above," Thea; 2) Thea being dreadfully frightened of Hedda; 3) Hedda bullying Thea by pulling her hair; and 4) Thea having been "such a fool." In addition there is the not yet actualized and therefore most important element: 5) Hedda's threat to burn Thea's hair. By the end of Act II, Hedda has reconstituted these elements in their essential significance: 1) she has demonstrated her superiority over Thea in maneuvering Lövborg to drink the cold punch; 2) she has so frightened Thea that Thea

cries, "Let me go! Let me go! I'm frightened of you, Hedda"; 3) she has bullied Thea by pinching her arm, making her cry "Ow!"; and 4) she concludes the scene by calling Thea "you little goose," having made her the fool again. However, the most important of the re-created elements is Hedda's repetition of her threat at the end of Act II: "I think I'll burn your hair off after all." This threat, disclaimed by Hedda in Act I ("Oh, yes, but that was just something I said, you know."), is now delivered with a passionate intensity that simultaneously affirms and discounts as mock repetition the intent of the words. Thus the content of one sequence of the retrospective exposition of Act I has become manifest in the forward action of the play by the end of Act II through Hedda's deliberate recreation of that action. And the threat involving the hair and the fire images has been potently re-activated.

The third of the images introduced in Act I is the pistol, which is also associated with a threat. Thea, reporting Lövborg's conversation about "someone or other from . . . from his past. Someone he can't really forget," makes this statement: "He said that when they parted, she threatened to shoot him with a pistol." Though positive identification of this menacer is delayed until Act II, Hedda's immediate discounting of the story provides a clue to her own implication. Her retort, "Oh, rubbish! People don't have such things here," is similar to the response she gave when Thea mentioned the threat to burn her hair. Social convention provides a disclaimer: people may say extreme things but they will act within narrowly defined limits of social propriety. The menacing image of the pistol also closes Act I. Hedda contemptuously tosses out the threat that, stripped of other pastimes, she will while away her bored hours playing with her pistols. Tesman responds with alarm, running and shouting after her, "No, for the love of God, my darling Hedda . . . don't touch those dangerous contraptions!" And, as if in response to Tesman's agitated shock at the very thought of such outlandish behavior, a pistol shot startles the audience at the beginning of Act II. Hedda is making good her threat to amuse herself with pistols. Farther into the act, during her tête-à-tête with Lövborg, Hedda is identified as the past menacer with the pistol:

> LOVBORG: It was you who broke it off.
>
> HEDDA: Yes, because there was an imminent danger that the game would become a reality. Shame on you, Ejlert Lövborg, how could you offer such violence to . . . to your confidential companion!
>
> LOVBORG: [*presses his fists together*] Oh, why didn't you play it out! Why didn't you shoot me down, as you threatened!
>
> HEDDA: I'm too much afraid of a scandal.

Again, through retrospective exposition, an event from Hedda's past is revealed that still remains to be fulfilled, to be brought to conclusion, and so, because of the suspended action, has psychological duration into the present. Lövborg is emotionally wrought up by the remembered threat and invokes its memory in a perfected form: "Why didn't you shoot me down, as you threatened!" Like the hair and fire threat, the pistol threat too, having been introduced merely as a reported event, now gains a new potency because of the emotional atmosphere associated with it. Both threats have been summoned into the present in Act II and await fulfillment.

The fourth major image of the play is that of *vinlöv i haaret,* "vine leaves in the hair." Unlike the other three images, this is not immediately associated with a looming threat made in the past by Hedda, nor is its past significance for Hedda even identifiable upon its introduction into the play. The final lines of Act II contain Hedda's triumphant vision: "And then . . . at ten o'clock . . . then Ejlert Lövborg will come . . . with vine leaves in his hair." Since vine leaves in the hair are a familiar public symbol of the victor's wreath, the poet's laurel, and the Dionysian crown, this statement does not seem to require any reference to Hedda's past to obtain meaning. The subsequent references to this image during Act III likewise seem obvious in their import. Hedda, speaking to Thea at the beginning of the act, still envisions: "Ejlert Lövborg, he's sitting there [at Judge Brack's party] reading aloud . . . with vine leaves in his hair." The customary connotations of the victorious poet-prophet are emphasized. This vision is somewhat blurred when Tesman comes home from Judge Brack's party and reports Lövborg's actions:

> TESMAN: And then to know that . . . with all his talents . . . unfortunately he's quite beyond hope of reform, all the same.
>
> HEDDA: I suppose you mean he's got more courage than the rest?
>
> TESMAN: No, good Lord . . . he just can't keep himself under control at all, you know.
>
> HEDDA: Well, and what happened then . . . in the end?
>
> TESMAN: Yes, well, I'd almost have described it as an orgy, Hedda.
>
> HEDDA: Did he have vine leaves in his hair?
>
> TESMAN: Vine leaves? No, I didn't see anything like that. But he made a long and incoherent speech about the woman who had inspired him in his work. Yes, that's how he expressed it.

Hedda, attempting to fashion a desirable image of Lövborg, tries to cast Tesman's statements in a light that will correspond to her vision—first by adding courage beyond conventional morality to the picture of the person and then by adding to the description of the orgy the vine leaves in the hair to transform it into a celebration of the Dionysian rite. The contrast between her exalted, highly figurative vision and Tesman's prosaic, literalist responses further underlines the disparity between them and demonstrates the poetic heights Hedda ascends to create her vision. There follows the progressive deterioration of that vision. First Tesman tells her he has found Lövborg's carelessly lost manuscript: the poet-prophet has let slip through his fingers his prophecy. Then Judge Brack gives a more complete account of the actions of the previous night, concluding with a description of Lövborg's engaging in a brawl and being taken to the police station. Far

from being the victor, Lövborg is the captive. Hedda finally responds, reluctantly relinquishing her vision: "So that was how it was. He didn't have vine leaves in his hair." Brack is baffled: "Vine leaves, my lady?" Though Brack, Tesman, and Thea have been unaware of any significance in Hedda's phrase, the audience is aware. The exoteric meaning of this image has been reinforced in various contexts. However, not until the end of Act III is the esoteric significance of vine leaves in the hair revealed. Lövborg, having lost the manuscript sees no future for himself:

> HEDDA: And what are you going to do, then?
>
> LOVBORG: Nothing. Just put an end to it all. The sooner the better.
>
> HEDDA: [*takes a step towards him*] Ejlert Lövborg . . . listen to me . . . Couldn't you let it happen . . . beautifully?
>
> LOVBORG: Beautifully? [*Smiles.*] Crowned with vine leaves, as you used to imagine?

Though a universal symbol, vine leaves in the hair are also a private symbol for Hedda that represents her past projection of an idealized Lövborg. Her many references to vine leaves in the hair in Acts II and III are seen here, at the end of Act III, to be referring to this ideal from the past that she is trying to re-create and actualize in the present. In her private world from the past, Lövborg is the antithesis of everything Tesman represents in the play. Lövborg represents beauty, courage, concern for reputation rather than for income—in short, the vine leaves in the hair symbolize for Hedda the freedom of the superior individual from the normal constraints of society. Hedda's response to Lövborg at this juncture is, "Oh, no, I don't believe in those vine leaves any more." Nevertheless, she attempts to re-create the past despite her avowed disbelief, for she goes on to say, "But beautifully all the same! Just for this once!" Though she has relinquished the hope of an enduring, actualized state of beauty, she still holds fast to the possibility of a singular manifestation of that ideal, a unique bodying forth *for én gangs skyld,* literally, "for one time's sake," in time and in behalf of time, of her perfected vision from the past.

IV

The final scenes of Act III bring together all four images—hair, fire, pistol, and vine leaves in the hair—into the climax of the play. Here Hedda attempts to re-create the past in a perfected form by acting to accomplish the threats she had formulated in the past: she gives Lövborg her pistol and she burns the manuscript. During Acts II and III she had tried, as we have seen, to re-create her vision of Lövborg with vine leaves in his hair. When her aspirations are thwarted, she proceeds to enact the threats she had delivered in the past. She gives Lövborg the pistol, insisting that he recognize it as the one that "was aimed at you, once." Lövborg responds, "You should have used it then." And Hedda, bringing the "then" into the present, retorts, "Well . . . ! You use it now." She endeavors to recapture her vision of Lövborg as a representative of the new man who is not bound by social dictates: "And beautifully, Ejlert Lövborg. Promise me that!" Significantly, whereas Lövborg had previously bid goodbye to Hedda as

Tesman's wife, *"Farvel, frue,"* he now, after receiving her pistol, salutes her with her maiden name, *"Farvel, Hedda Gabler."* Hedda, momentarily, is the person that she was: she has succeeded briefly in recapturing the past.

The scene concluding Act III is the culmination of the threat to burn Thea's hair. The manuscript has been clearly identified by Lövborg and Thea as their child, earlier in the act. Hedda repeats that identification as she burns the manuscript; thus her action on one level is a *Kindermord,* a child-killing. But there is another significant identity to notice. Hedda identifies the child first as Thea's, and then, most importantly, singles out Thea's specific attribute, her curly hair. Considered structurally, in the light of Hedda's prior threat to burn off Thea's hair, this scene is a fulfillment of that unfulfilled past, with the "child" being the representative of an attribute of the parent. Ibsen's additions to the Earlier Draft of the play (entitled "Hedda" in the *Samlede Verker* and "Hedda Gabler: Earlier Draft" in *The Oxford Ibsen*) verify the importance of this correspondence. In the Earlier Draft, Thea's hair is mentioned only twice, in the stage directions: Hedda touches Thea's hair in Acts II and IV. There is no *description* of Thea's hair in the stage directions, no identification of her as a woman with "provoking" hair, no reference to the hair-pulling episodes of schooldays nor to the threat of burning; nor does Act II, consequently, end with the re-invoking of that threat. And finally, there is no reference in the burning scene of Act III to Thea "with the curly hair." It seems obvious that these references to Thea's hair, by their absence in the Earlier Draft and their presence in the final copy, are of a piece, and that the *"Du med krushaaret!"* "You with the curly hair!" is meant to be the culmination of the series, the fulfilling of the threat. In other words, Ibsen has added in the final copy an image that functions structurally to alter the action of the play significantly at this point from a simple *Kindermord* event to a more complex event that entails the fulfilling of a threat from the past.

This addition certainly cannot be a fortuitous occurrence: there are similar additions with respect to the structural images that function between Hedda and Lövborg—the images of the pistol and the vine leaves in the hair. Though the pistols appear prominently in the Earlier Draft, there are noteworthy alterations and additions in the final copy. Most outstanding is the threat. Hedda's threat to shoot Lövborg with her pistol, just as her threat to burn Thea's hair, is absent in the Earlier Draft and present in the final copy. In the Earlier Draft, the following references to the pistols are absent: the report by Thea in Act I of a woman who threatened to shoot Lövborg when they parted; the comment by Brack at the beginning of Act II about Hedda still playing "that game" with the pistols; Lövborg's impassioned remark in Act II that Hedda should have shot him as she threatened; and finally the culmination of the threat, Hedda's giving Lövborg the pistol at the end of Act III and saying, "It was aimed at you, once." In the Earlier Draft, Lövborg had not been threatened by Hedda; in fact, he had asked for the pistol with which to kill himself. The addition of this structure of the pistol imagery in the final copy changes Hedda's motive in giving Lövborg the pistol. In the Earlier Draft, she explicitly states that the reason

for her maneuvering Lövborg to attend Judge Brack's party is "to see whether [she] could lure him to his downfall," and the reason for her wanting Tesman to burn Lövborg's manuscript is "to see whether [she] has any power over [Tesman]." In the final copy, this motive, her testing of her power, is made considerably less egregious by the absence of these lines and the presence of the longstanding threat that is finally brought to its culmination. The overall effect of the addition of the structures connected with the pistol imagery and the hair-burning imagery is to change Hedda's action from that of obtaining power over people to that of seeking to re-create her past.

The vine leaves in the hair imagery is totally absent from the Earlier Draft. Without this imagery at the end of Act II, the idea of Lövborg *living* a glorious life beyond the confines of society is muted to the point of obscurity. Because of the insubstantiality of that aspect, Hedda's dominant motive in the Earlier Draft seems to be an attempt to maneuver Lövborg so that he will *die* beautifully, and Hedda becomes much more the necrophile. As they stand in the final copy, these two ideas balance each other: Hedda's original desire is that Lövborg *live* beautifully, and only after that possibility has been denied, first by Tesman and then by Brack, only after she has had demonstrated to her the impossibility of her aspirations for Lövborg's beautiful life, does she turn to the possibility of his beautiful death. Her visions of his life and of his death have in common the qualitative distinction indicated by the vine leaves in the hair imagery, Hedda's symbol from her past of beauty. And once again, the addition in the final copy of a coherent structure of imagery establishes that ultimately Hedda is attempting to re-create the past.

In her attempt to re-create her past in a perfected form, Hedda has moved through four stages: 1) the re-creation of the material past; 2) the re-creation of actual scenes from her past, such as the tête-à-têtes with Brack and Lövborg; 3) the re-creation of her dominion over Thea and of her image of Lövborg as totally free and superior to society, at the end of Act II; 4) and, when this latter re-creation malfunctions, the re-creation in a perfected form of the threats to Thea and Lövborg at the end of Act III.

Act IV begins with Hedda "dressed in black . . . walking aimlessly around the darkened room." The funereal appearances of Hedda, then Berte, and finally Aunt Julle seem an appropriate consequence of the destruction at the end of Act III. Aunt Julle's conversation reveals that Aunt Rina has died; and Hedda, after hearing how Tesman's aunt "passed over so quietly . . . and so gently," goes through the formal motions of condolence, all the while awaiting news of a death which is, in contradistinction, bold and proud. In a situation similar to the one in which she was seeking news of Lövborg's triumph at Brack's party in Act III, Hedda now is confronted with a series of three messengers with increasingly complete reports. In Act III, she heard first from Tesman, who knew very little; then from Brack, who knew a great deal more; and finally from Lövborg himself, who presented an altered version fit for Thea's ears and then the total truth meant only for Hedda. In Act IV the pattern repeats. The first messenger is Tesman, who knows nothing but fears that something is amiss; the second messenger is Thea, who had heard "incredible rumors" and something about a hospital, and fears "that he [Lövborg] may have met with an accident." The third messenger is Brack, who, as always, has made it his business to be thoroughly informed. His first story is modified for Thea's benefit, and his final story is the complete truth, meant only for Hedda. As in Act III, Hedda is now loath to give up her vision of what she is seeking to re-create. When Thea speaks of the hospital, Hedda rejects the suggestion: "Oh, no . . . that can't be possible!" Brack substantiates that Lövborg is in fact in the hospital and "is not expected to live." Hedda must accept the news about the hospital as a warp in her perfect design. Rather than allowing Brack to continue delivering, without intervention, the version designed for Thea, Hedda herself begins to furnish the details of Lövborg's death, details that correspond to her vision. She insists that Lövborg has killed himself: "Yes, I'm certain he did"; and after the emotive reactions of the others, she asserts confidently, "Shot himself!" With each of Brack's affirmations, she becomes more exultant, her vision becoming confirmed at last. But then Brack states that Lövborg was shot in the breast.

> HEDDA: [*to Brack*] He was shot in the breast?
>
> BRACK: Yes . . . as I said.
>
> HEDDA: Not in the temple?
>
> BRACK: In the breast, Mrs. Tesman.
>
> HEDDA: Well . . . the breast is good, too.
>
> BRACK: I beg your pardon, Mrs. Tesman?
>
> HEDDA: [*evasively*] Oh no . . . nothing.

Hedda has been so positive about what she thought was the necessary pattern of events, so certain that her re-creation was perfect this time, that she simply cannot comprehend at first what Brack says, and she demands instead to hear that Lövborg was "shot in the temple" so that the beauty of his death will be equivalent to that most beautiful of deaths—Werther's. Only grudgingly will she allow that Lövborg has been shot in the breast. Having accepted that obstacle, she declares triumphantly, "At last . . . a really courageous act." "I say that there is beauty in this deed." With Lövborg, Hedda is translated out of the Tesman world into that perfected world of her past.

When Brack and Hedda are alone, Hedda exults in the completion of her vision: "It's a liberation to know that an act of spontaneous courage is yet possible in this world. An act that has something of unconditional beauty." This is the diction of a person raised to the heights of inspiration. In the Earlier Draft, Ibsen had a line in Hedda's next speech that explicitly stated what the nature of her inspiration was: her attempt to re-create the past in a perfected form—the theme that has been developed throughout this essay. There she said, "But now I can see him as I used to see him."

Brack, however, then delivers the line that provides the denouement for the play and that, in general terms, is the denouement of every mature play of Ibsen. Brack says, interrupting Hedda's ethereal bemusings, "It pains me, my

lady . . . but I am compelled to disabuse you of a beautiful illusion." Hedda: "Illusion?" And Brack delivers a series of short, sharp blows: Lövborg was at Mlle. Diana's boudoir, where he was talking wildly; he was found there with a discharged pistol in his breast pocket; and the bullet, far from being deliberately and calmly placed in the breast, was accidentally discharged into his groin. Hedda becomes progressively more distressed and revolted with each detail that so debases her original vision. Finally, looking up "with an expression of revulsion," she acquiesces: "That as well! Oh . . . everything I touch seems destined to turn into something mean and farcical." Finally Hedda has been brought to the recognition that it is impossible to re-create the past, that one cannot live in it, that the attempt to live in the past is based on illusion. Since she finds the present intolerable, with Thea claiming Tesman and reclaiming the dead Lövborg, and with Brack asserting his design, Hedda summons up the courage to act. The recognition of the impossibility of re-creating and thus living in the past gives her the strength openly to defy her society for the first time. She breaks the expected funereal mood by playing "a wild dance tune" and then performs, herself, a beautiful action: she shoots herself in the temple. This, of course, fulfills her vision from the past, the vision of the beautiful deed. And the plot of the play has reached completion: the perfected form has been attained, the form which never changes and for which there is no future—death. Hedda has in fact, though not in the manner she originally anticipated, succeeded in recreating the past in a perfected form. (pp. 299-313)

> *Sandra E. Saari, " 'Hedda Gabler': The Past Recaptured," in* Modern Drama, *Vol. XX, No. 3, September, 1977, pp. 299-316.*

Lisa Elaine Low   (essay date 1982)

[*In the following essay, Low defends Hedda against the critical contention that she is simply perverse and destructive. The critic asserts that the society depicted in* Hedda Gabler *is so restrictive and stultifying that it must be annihilated, and therefore Hedda's suicide marks her as a hero. "If life is criminal," she concludes, "destruction is heroic."*]

> JOAN: What! Must I burn again? Are none of you ready to receive me?
>
> CAUCHON: The heretic is always better dead. And mortal eyes cannot distinguish the saint from the heretic.
>
> [Bernard Shaw, *Saint Joan*]

Especially because she commits unforgivable crimes against the apparently defenseless, Hedda Gabler is difficult to defend. It is madness to stand by her, for this would require, apparently, either re-examination of our first instinct, to survive; or to party openly with the devil. For there can be no question, Hedda Gabler is a destroyer. She is not just, like a profferer of lotus, a detainer. She is a destroyer. Like Clytemnestra, she is a man slayer. Like Medea, she is an infant slayer. She kills at the end of Act III, one child; and at the end of Act IV, another: Lovborg's manuscript; Tesman's embryo. As if to eliminate all possible futures, she kills past and present, parent and child. And then, she kills herself.

It is this, her killing of herself, which gives us pause. Because it is that act, and that act alone, which wins our sympathy; or, if not that, at least that conviction that there is something substantial in Hedda, though not visible, which goes beyond our conventional ideas of the way things are. The final line of the play, Brack's baffled

> But good God! People don't *do* such things!

articulates our numb confusion at her suicide. People don't do such things; not at least, in any well-made world.

And yet, just as we are astonished by Hedda's death, we also believe in it, for in participating in Hedda Gabler's universe we have stood with electric wires to our temples. We leave the play breathless, having seen, for a close and shocking instant, a cross of lightning flash against the dark chaos of the way things are. We have not language, like Judge Brack, even to articulate an appropriate response. And yet it is just this, that gap between heroic articulation and ineffability, between what is to be borne and what must be ignored, that insures the impact of the play. Between the climax of the shot, and the anti-climax of Tesman's

> Shot herself! Shot herself in the temple! Can you imagine!

there is a split second. It is just enough time to see what it is we can stand and what we can not. In spite of order, there is chaos; in spite of art, there is death; in spite of painted teacups and well-placed flowers, there is the hideous truth of our mortality. Then we shrink back, like Brack, into our chairs and the rest is silence.

We are, I think, meant to be above Tesman. Like all comic figures, he is to be laughed at. But it is only because we recognize in him that so unloved portion of ourselves that we withdraw laughing. We are all of us best at arranging other people's papers; and in such a world there is no room for Heddas or for Ejlerts, for people who do do such things; people who refuse, not only because they will not, but because they can not—to arrange other people's papers. This is a world unprepared to recognize, and if to recognize, unprepared to accept, its saints—except, that is, in the repose of death.

Hedda Gabler is a play about two characters who, for all their exquisite sensibility and passion, are impotent. Ibsen, like Shaw, anatomized the world, but only to be ignored. And like Shaw, he was bitterly disappointed Brack's final

> But good God! People don't *do* such things!

reflects not only Brack's but the audience's limitations. It prophesies critical response to the play, for not even yet are we willing to read the real implications of *Hedda Gabler*. *Hedda Gabler* condemns a society infatuated with regulation; one that has not a speculative mind, and one that turns its face from truth. And, as it condemns that society, it condemns us. Tesman, Thea, and Brack are as we are—slow-footed to the stable, perversely insensitive to the tragic. But the final point of this play goes just beyond the devastation of a frankly indifferent human communi-

ty. It looks, too, out over, or down into, the twentieth century abyss. Hedda's vital spirit is trapped in the space between the human and the metaphysical void. As an aristocrat tied to a dying religion caught in a bourgeois world; as a nineteenth century woman of extreme sensibility locked inside the cramped cell of her husband's petty ideas, Hedda Gabler is an emphatic metaphor for what it is like to be passionately human in the void.

In *Hedda Gabler* Ibsen marks as his hero not a resuscitator, but a destroyer of life. And Hedda is a hero, for life itself, the ridiculous folly of human mediocrity, juxtaposed against the great futility of all human enterprise—even Lovborg's sterile triumphs, which represent not only the maximum that has been, but that can be said and done for mankind—is a crime. If life itself is criminal, destruction is heroic. That is the point, anyway, of the flood. It is also the peculiar paradox which shadows our confused recognition of Hedda's death. And yet to give this much credit, this much applause, this much love to Hedda must be to discredit ourselves; that, and to grant her the robes of a God; for only God can call for the flood, can tamper against us with his Biblical mathematics, and still be called holy.

It has not been the custom to call Hedda holy. It has not been the custom, in fact, to see in her redemptive impulses. On the contrary, critics have found Hedda gravely unpleasant. Boyeson refers, for example, to Hedda's "complete perversion of womanhood" [*A Commentary on the Writings of Henrik Ibsen,* 1894]. Le Gallienne calls her repugnance at pregnancy "twisted" [Introduction to *Six Plays by Henrik Ibsen,* 1957]. For his part, Shaw says of Hedda that she has "no ideals"; that she has "no heart, no courage, no conviction . . . she remains mean, envious, insolent, cruel" [*The Quintessence of Ibsenism,* 3rd ed., 1926]. Elizabeth Hardwick, too, disapproves of Hedda, calling her "mean-spirited and petty in both large and small matters" [*Seduction and Betrayal: Women and Literature,* 1974]. Caroline Mayerson is less generous. To her Hedda is a "confused and irresponsible egotist" whose "colossal egotism" finds its "final self-dramatization" in a suicide negated by Brack and Tesman who "have the curtain lines" ["Thematic Symbols in *Hedda Gabler*" in *Ibsen: A Collection of Critical Essays,* 1965]. Harold Clurman calls Hedda not only a "moral coward" but a "corrupting and malefic force" [*Ibsen,* 1977]. Even in Grant Allen's preposterously cavalier comment that Hedda is "nothing more nor less than the girl we take down to dinner in London nineteen times out of twenty" we sense that Hedda is not altogether well-liked [cited by Le Galliene].

That this has been her lamentable history can not be surprising. Hedda is selfish by all accounts; she is narcissistic, mean, and cruel. Her deeds are extravagantly unkind: she insults, mocks, snubs, and destroys. She marries a man as spiritually shallow as he is physically repulsive in order, one thinks, to avoid the hazards of sexual relations. She is by her own admission a coward, and by her own admission everything she touches turns ludicrous and mean. She does nothing to help, but only to destroy; she is committed to no cause but destruction; she is, in fact, a woman of no earthly attachments. She despises the very idea of motherhood, of caring for the sick, of acting as midwife to a great mind's manuscript; she finds love, sexuality, and life, for that matter, offensive; and she has, by her own confession, but one thing she is really good at: boring herself to death! No, there is no possibility whatever of defending Hedda; not, anyway, if we consider her in the light of convention.

But it is not, of course, in this light that Ibsen wishes us to scrutinize Hedda. To condemn her, as she has been condemned, is to subject her to the same conventional mores which the play seeks to subvert. True, we have come some way from Boyeson's comment in 1894, that Hedda "laughs at the ridiculous idea of loving her husband, without perceiving how she dishonours herself by the admission." And Hedda's sins, though still myriad, have been given the honor of metaphysical breathing space. As a result of Freud and Nietzsche, Sartre and de Beauvoir, Hedda Gabler is beginning, if not to be well-liked, then at least to be fathomed. The apparently socially deplorable has been given psychological depth, and tragic stature. Conventional interpretation has been subverted until it is not Hedda, but the social and metaphysical atmosphere in which she stands that is intolerable. And this is all to the good. It is what Ibsen must intend: for *Hedda Gabler* describes a world of human as well as cosmic complacency. Here, because the community is like the void, a blank table of curvilinear space, the only possible response to the tragic is a dull, flattened, and diminishing echo. In such a universe both Hedda Gabler and Ejlert Lovbort can not survive. In such a universe, death is the only possible solution, not just for Hedda and Ejlert, Hedda's unborn child and Ejlert's manuscript, but for the race.

In a note jotted for the play Ibsen writes, "Life is not tragic. Life is ridiculous. And that can not be borne" [*The Oxford Ibsen,* Vol. VII, James Walter McFarlane, ed., 1966]. Hedda is emblematic of Ibsen's vision of the potential of the race. In her raised clenched fists, in her passion for pistols, we see not just cynicism but nihilism. Against Hedda, the artist's *elan vital,* Ibsen sets the Tesmans. Their well-furnished drawing room represents a microcosm of a world committed to booties and book cutting. It is a world bent upon stagnation, upon studying the already ossified Middle Ages. It is a passive, silent world where indifference is a juggernaut to passion. Past this mask of quotidian activity, just past the window pane, is the autumn foliage, the dying out of the year, the gradual falling off of souls into death. The Tesmans, inversions of the life force, spawn mediocrity and castrate true fecundity. Against them Hedda, who can not quite literally explode with frustrated instinct, does the next best thing: she blows her brains out. All the intellectual pressure explodes, and in the aftermath the equilibrium long sought for mercy's sake is complete.

Hedda's death is, like a cross of lightning, momentary. It is almost absurd; it expresses an unutterable darkness which pulls Ibsen, like Hardy, feet first into the twentieth century. In *Hedda Gabler,* life is ridiculous because it is futile, and because people, moving as they do in a fog of indifference and imbecility, of conventions as static as the Middle Ages, are ludicrous and mean. It is not, then, as Hardwick claims, that Hedda is "mean-spirited and petty" but that her community is; and it is not that Hedda represents "a complete perversion of womanhood" but that mankind itself has gone astray. It is not that Hedda is without ideals or courage. By her own, and by Ibsen's definition, it is courage which allows her finally to settle not only Ejlert's, but her own account with life.

Death, then, is the final measure of Tesmanic mediocrity, for even death can not break into, or move the dark stream of obscure consciousness. Brack is too cunning and Tesman, Thea, and Miss Tesman are too oblivious of human complexity to recognize in death tragedy. Rina's grave illness, and her passing, are comic. And what tragedy inheres in Ejlert's death is undercut at once by Brack's perversion of the facts to buffer a Thea who, when she discovers the truth, sets out immediately to reestablish her relationship with Ejlert in Tesman. Hedda's death, too, is futile. But it is not, as Mayerson would have us believe, because Hedda is foiled and Brack and Tesman have the curtain lines. Nor is it a reassertion of the good, a foiling of a "nihilistic villainess" who kills herself as if backing away from the mirror and crucifix of Lovborg's recovered manuscript. In fact, Ibsen calls Tesman's attempt to recover the manuscript "the burlesque touch."

It is this darkness, then, that justifies Hedda's suicide and Ejlert's death. In these final acts Hedda—bent upon determining a destiny, upon changing, somehow, a world of no consequence—moves out of contained into actual violence, out of obscurity into heroism. She steps out of a Leyden jar not to join but to reject mediocrity; for Hedda recognizes, in Ejlert's behalf, not only that his design for the future will be tampered with by the Christmas trade, but that the impotence of the Tesmans always circumscribes the potence of the Lovborgs.

Hedda and Ejlert stand as two principles warring in Ibsen's own intelligence: destructive against procreative, nihilistic against optimistic. Hedda's victory, her huge will, summons the play's dying fall. With Lovborg's death the world descends into an everlasting hell. All hope is abandoned. And so, because tragedy requires hope, and human self-esteem, there can be little tragedy here. On the contrary, Hedda and Ejlert stand in a world universally dark. Pressed up against a windowpane that looks out of nothingness into nothingness, they merely exchange the consequence of one nothingness for another.

It is in her cage, then, as a nineteenth century woman of passion prohibited from self-assertion, that Hedda becomes an emphatic metaphor for the human condition. Her "tragedy" is both socially realistic, as in [Arthur Miller's] *Death of a Salesman,* and metaphysical, as in [Samuel Beckett's] *Waiting for Godot,* for Hedda's watch is not so very different from Didi and Gogo's. As activity in *Godot* is a mere substitute for death, for Hedda, who commits suicide, it is death's equivalent.

Through Hedda, Ibsen describes a chaos tied up into a corset, an ill-made universe compressed into a well-made play. Hedda's suicide, Ejlert's death, the burning of the manuscript, the annihilation of Tesman's child are the last acts of mercy, the last creative gestures, the last making, rather than the masking of the fact of death in a world of passive violence. Only a corset here prevents the encroachment of the void, and a corset is, as far as the community is concerned, all that is necessary.

Ibsen's world, in **Hedda Gabler,** is beyond dejection. Here he calls for Biblical mathematics, the flood, universal extinction. With what materials the world has at hand, things can not be restored. What Hedda destroys—Ejlert, herself, the manuscript, the infant—is the possibility of an improved world. Considering the extant conditions, the unlikelihood of the flood

> Shot herself! Shot herself in the temple!
> Can you imagine?

Considering Ibsen's grimmest insight

> Life is not tragic. Life is ridiculous

Hedda does the best she can. As in Harry Hope's "I wish that death or Hickey would come" here the grotesque mock-Christ-cum-Madonna is come. And, as in [Eugene O'Neill's] *The Iceman Cometh,* what Christ leaves behind is not a rejuvenated society; not a society which recognizes in this burst of passion potential after all, but dumb obscurity. When the smoke clears, the good are gone.

As in *Hamlet,* there is a bloody stage when the curtain falls. But in **Hedda Gabler** there is no Fortinbras, no principle to bring in a new order. Nor is there here an Horatio who, for love, would sacrifice his life for the dead hero. Nor here an Horatio who shall tell a tale of woe. Here there is only the burlesque attempt to reconstruct what was, if not literally, then at least figuratively torn into shreds and thrown out upon the windy, silent fjords: a reinvented, humane future. (pp. 43-9)

> *Lisa Elaine Low, "In Defense of Hedda," in* Massachusetts Studies in English, *Vol. VIII, No. 3, 1982, pp. 43-9.*

FURTHER READING

AUTHOR COMMENTARY

Sprinchorn, Evert, ed. *Ibsen: Letters and Speeches.* New York: Hill and Wang, 1964, 360 p.
  Compilation of Ibsen's correspondence, lectures, and prefaces, including an 1874 speech given to Norwegian students in which he discusses his ambivalent feelings toward his homeland and his view that "to be a poet means essentially to see . . . in such a way that whatever is seen is perceived by his audience just as the poet saw it."

OVERVIEWS AND GENERAL STUDIES

Bradbrook, M. C. *Ibsen the Norwegian: A Revaluation.* New Edition. Hamden, Conn.: Archon Books, 1966, 173 p.
  Influential study of the dramatist by a noted theatrical scholar. Bradbrook examines Ibsen's work in the context of his own life and the spirit of the times in which he lived.

Brandes, George. *Henrik Ibsen, A Critical Study. With a 42 page essay on Björnstjerne Björnson.* 1899. Reprint. New York: Benjamin Blom, 1964, 171 p.
  Analysis by the prominent scholar and contemporary of the playwright. Brandes's study comprises three "impressions," written at various points in Ibsen's career and documenting the critic's evolving appreciation of the dramatist's work.

Brustein, Robert. "The Fate of Ibsenism." In his *Critical Moments: Reflection on Theatre & Society 1973-1979,* pp. 124-38. New York: Random House, 1980.
  Contends that, despite the fact that "Ibsen is now beginning to suffer the deadly fate of the classic author—to be included in the anthologies and excluded from the imaginative life of the people, to be universally accepted without being much liked or understood," the dramatist's works continue to have relevance in the modern world.

Chesterton, G. K. "Ibsen." In his *Handful of Authors: Essays on Books & Writers,* edited by Dorothy Collins, pp. 134-42. New York: Sheed and Ward, 1953.
  Regards Ibsen's technique of realism both liberating and confining. "Ibsen was a very great man who made art as realistic as it can well be; it cannot be entirely realistic. But if it were entirely realistic, it would be almost entirely romantic," Chesterton claims.

Clurman, Harold. *Ibsen.* New York: Macmillan Publishing Co., 1977, 223 p.
  Examines Ibsen's dramas as a unified body of work. Clurman observes contradictions and inconsistencies in Ibsen's work, but interprets these as evidence of the playwright's struggles with, and ultimate rejection of, both the "old faith" of religion and the "new truth" of science.

Deer, Irving. "Ibsen's Self-Reflexivity in *A Doll's House* and *The Masterbuilder.*" In *Within the Dramatic Spectrum: The University of Florida Department of Classics Comparative Drama Conference Papers,* Volume VI, edited by Karelisa V. Hartigan, pp. 35-44. Lanham, Md.: University Press of America, 1986.
  Argues that *A Doll's House* and *The Master Builder* are "dramas about dramas," reflecting both Ibsen's "struggle to create a new kind of drama and their own struggle to create a new way of acting in the world." Deer observes that "each play shows protagonists who are conceived as expressing themselves through theatrical means—performing, plotting, playing in old dramatic forms, searching for new ones."

Dowden, Edward. "Henrik Ibsen." In his *Essays Modern and Elizabethan,* pp. 26-60. New York: E. P. Dutton, 1910.
  Examines Ibsen's works, centering on the philosophical themes of self-realization and the search for truth.

Durbach, Errol, ed. *Ibsen and the Theatre: The Dramatist in Production.* New York: New York University Press, 1980, 144 p.
  Collection of studies that focus on the performance aspects of Ibsen's work.

Esslin, Martin. "Ibsen: *An Enemy of the People, Hedda Gabler, The Master Builder.*" In his *Reflections: Essays on Modern Theatre,* pp. 29-48. Garden City, N. Y.: Doubleday, 1969.
  Outlines structure and characterization in *An Enemy of*

the People, Hedda Gabler, and The Master Builder. Esslin focuses on the dramatic symbolism in each play and examines Ibsen's protagonists as tragic figures.

Forster, E. M. "Ibsen the Romantic." In his Abinger Harvest, pp. 83-8. New York: Harcourt, Brace, 1936.
Reprints Forster's 28 March 1928 article for the New Republic in which he examines romantic elements in Ibsen's later plays. Forster argues that Ibsen's poetic language, symbolism, and settings lend a romantic undercurrent to many of his domestic dramas.

Gassner, John. "Ibsen in the Contemporary Theatre." In his The Theatre in Our Times: A Survey of the Men, Materials and Movements in the Modern Theatre, pp. 105-13. New York: Crown Publishers, 1954.
Records the impact of Ibsen's dramas on succeeding generations of playwrights.

Gray, Ronald. Ibsen—A Dissenting View: A Study of the Last Twelve Plays. Cambridge: Cambridge University Press, 1977, 231 p.
Negative appraisal of Ibsen as a literary craftsman. Gray's discussion of The Wild Duck is excerpted above.

Hurt, James. Catiline's Dream: An Essay on Ibsen's Plays. Urbana: University of Illinois Press, 1972, 206 p.
Traces recurring themes and structures in Ibsen's body of work. Hurt argues that Ibsen's dramatic power "results in large part from the connections Ibsen was able to make between his personal stresses and those in his society."

Lavrin, Janko. Ibsen: An Approach. London: Methuen & Co., 1950, 139 p.
Biographical and critical study of the author that follows "the development of Ibsen the dramatist parallel with that of Ibsen the man."

Northam, John. Ibsen: A Critical Study. Cambridge: Cambridge University Press, 1973, 237 p.
Close analysis of six of Ibsen's plays as essentially poetic works. The dramas Northam considers include Brand, The Wild Duck, and Hedda Gabler; his comments on Ghosts are excerpted above.

Norwegian Research Council for Science and the Humanities. Contemporary Approaches to Ibsen. Oslo: Universitetsforlaget, 1966, 134 p.
Collection of essays on various aspects of Ibsen's work by such noted critics as Inga-Stina Ewbank, Francis Fergusson, and John Northam.

Shaw, Bernard. The Quintessence of Ibsenism: Now Completed to the Death of Ibsen. London: Constable and Company, 1926, 210 p.
General appraisal of Ibsen's work by the renowned playwright and early supporter of Ibsen's dramatic techniques. Shaw's discussion of Hedda Gabler is excerpted above.

Styan, J. L. "Ibsen's contribution to realism." In his Modern drama in theory and practice, Volume 1: Realism and naturalism, pp. 17-30. Cambridge: Cambridge University Press, 1981.
Traces Ibsen's increasing use of realism in his drama and the challenges such a shift presents to actors and directors attempting to stage the plays. Styan particularly examines early productions of A Doll's House and Ghosts.

Weigand, Hermann J. The Modern Ibsen: A Reconsideration. New York: Henry Holt and Company, 1925, 416 p.
Detailed examination of twelve of Ibsen's dramas, from Pillars of Society through the final plays.

Winter, William. "Ibsenites and Ibsenism." In The American Theatre as Seen by Its Critics 1752-1934, edited by Montrose J. Moses and John Mason Brown, pp. 94-101. New York: Cooper Square Publishers, 1967.
Reprint of a 1913 discussion of Ibsen and his influence on theatrical practices by a prominent commentator. Winter, a fierce opponent of Ibsen's dramatic techniques, charges that "Ibsen is not a dramatist, in the true sense of that word, and Ibsenism, which is rank, deadly pessimism, is a disease, injurious alike to the Stage and to the Public."

Zucker, A. E. Ibsen: The Master Builder. New York: Henry Holt and Company, 1929, 312 p.
Biographical and critical study of Ibsen that attempts to "present a portrait of the man, painted largely from materials furnished by men and women who actually knew him."

A DOLL'S HOUSE

Archer, William. "Ibsen and English Criticism." The Fortnightly Review XLVI, No. CCLXXI (1 July 1889): 30-7.
Surveys English critical reaction to Ibsen's drama, focusing on A Doll's House. Archer objects to the truisms that Ibsen is "overly didactic" and lacks "artistic propriety."

Baruch, Elaine Hoffman. "Ibsen's Doll House: A Myth for Our Time." The Yale Review: A National Quarterly LXIX, No. 3 (March 1980): 374-87.
Considers A Doll's House a prophetic work that anticipates modern feminism. According to Baruch, the drama is a "feminist play par excellence" in which Ibsen "explores the nature of freedom for both sexes and considers the relationship of the individual to past and present as well as to the family and the state."

Britain, Ian. "A Transplanted Doll's House: Ibsenism, Feminism and Socialism in Late-Victorian and Edwardian England." In Transformations in Modern European Drama, edited by Ian Donaldson, pp. 14-54. Atlantic Highlands, N. J.: Humanities Press, 1983.
Examines the critical reaction to A Doll's House in late nineteenth- and early twentieth-century England. Britain examines letters, reviews, and press accounts to determine the play's appeal to English socialists as a feminist text.

Davies, H. Neville. "Not just a bang and a whimper: the inconclusiveness of Ibsen's A Doll's House." Critical Quarterly 24, No. 3 (Autumn 1982): 33-43.
Examination of the Christine Linde-Nils Krogstad and the Dr. Rank sub-plots and their bearing on the central action of A Doll's House. Davies remarks that the main plot is "unresolvably inconclusive": it "ends with a question mark, and the two sub-plots, which do not end inconclusively, point in opposite directions."

Kindelan, Nancy. "Ibsen's A Doll House and the Theatre of the Grotesque." In All the World: Drama Past and Present,

Volume II, edited by Karelisa V. Hartigan, pp. 41-52. Washington, D. C.: University Press of America, 1982.

> Argues that Ibsen's use of physical symbols—the Christmas tree, the tarantella, Nora's costume, and the wedding ring—manifests the tradition of the Theatre of the Grotesque. Kindelan also draws on Jungian psychology to detail Nora's struggle for growth against the restrictive morals of her society.

Quigley, Austin E. "*A Doll's House* Revisited." *Modern Drama* XXVII, No. 4 (December 1984): 584-603.

> Maintains that the overriding theme of *A Doll's House* concerns the complex ways in which inherited roles and values constrain individual freedom. The structure of the drama itself embodies this theme, argues Quigley, by synthesizing the inherited plot of the traditional "well-made play" with novel verbal and visual imagery.

Rosenberg, Marvin. "Ibsen vs. Ibsen or: Two Versions of *A Doll's House.*" *Modern Drama* XII, No. 2 (September 1969): 187-96.

> Compares the first and final drafts of *A Doll's House* to determine that Ibsen the "artist and craftsman" was in conflict with Ibsen "the social thinker" in this play.

Shafer, Yvonne. "Complexity and Ambiguity in Ibsen's *A Doll House.*" *Literature in Performance* 5, No. 2 (April 1985): 27-35.

> Focuses on the relationship between Nora and Torvald to dispute the contention that *A Doll's House* is a one-dimensional thesis drama. Shafer cites a 1979 University of Texas production directed by Michael Kahn to show how rich, human portrayals of the Helmers reveal "subtle ironies, paradoxes, and unanswered questions" inherent in Ibsen's drama.

Simonds, W. E. "Henrik Ibsen." *The Dial* X, No. 119 (March 1890): 301-03.

> A favorable assessment of *A Doll's House,* occasioned by the publication of Henrietta Frances Lord's English translation of Ibsen's text. Simonds offers a biographical sketch of the playwright and a synopsis of *A Doll's House,* asserting that the relationship between Nora and Torvald Helmer is not a marriage but "a partnership in sensuality in which one of the parties is an innocent victim."

Templeton, Joan. "The *Doll House* Backlash: Criticism, Feminism, and Ibsen." *Publications of the Modern Language Association* 104, No. 2 (January 1989): 28-40.

> Surveys the critical controversy concerning feminist ideology in *A Doll's House.* Templeton contrasts commentary extolling Nora as "the principal international symbol for women's issues" with the contention that the play is "completely indifferent" to the question of women's rights.

GHOSTS

Konrad, Linn B. "Father's sins and mother's guilt: dramatic responses to Darwin." In *Drama, Sex and Politics.* Themes in Drama 7, edited by James Redmond, pp. 137-49. Cambridge: Cambridge University Press, 1985.

> Examines the metaphor of disease in *Ghosts* as part of a discussion on the impact of Darwin's theory of evolution on the drama of the late nineteenth century.

Moore, George. "Note on *Ghosts.*" In *Impressions and Opinions,* pp. 215-26. 1891. Reprint. New York: Benjamin Blom, 1972.

> Review of an early French production of *Ghosts.* In this work, Moore observes, "we learn that though there be no gods to govern us, . . . nature, vast and unknown, forever dumb to our appeal, holds us in thrall."

Scott, Clement. Review of *Ghosts.* In *Specimens of English Dramatic Criticism: XVII-XX Centuries,* edited by A. C. Ward, pp. 182-89. London: Oxford University Press, 1945.

> Harshly negative appraisal of the London premiere of *Ghosts* by a prominent theater critic. Scott attacks nearly every aspect of the drama, including its characterization, structure, and themes, and concludes that *Ghosts* is "a dull, undramatic, verbose, tedious, and utterly uninteresting play."

Stein, Walter. "*Ghosts* and the Death of God." *The Critical Quarterly* 9, No. 2 (Summer 1967): 109-19.

> Argues that in *Ghosts* Ibsen experiments with a new form of tragedy, one that takes place in a deterministic universe without a God or religion—the underpinnings of traditional definitions of tragedy.

THE WILD DUCK

Crompton, Lois. "The 'Demonic' in Ibsen's *The Wild Duck. The Tulane Drama Review* 4, No. 1 (September 1959): 96-103.

> Traces Ibsen's use of the concept of the "demonic"—referring to someone who has been frustrated or betrayed—which Relling first employs to describe the conduct of the drunkard Molvik. According to Crompton, Ibsen employs the idea ironically, applying it to the "comfort-loving" Hjalmar, adding, however, that by the play's end Hjalmar's "external calm has been shattered, and a new note has been sounded: that of demonic protest."

MacCarthy, Desmond. Review of *The Wild Duck.* In *Specimens of English Dramatic Criticism: XVII-XX Centuries,* edited by A. C. Ward, pp. 237-41. London: Oxford University Press, 1945.

> Assessment of an early London production of *The Wild Duck,* which the critic finds missed the note of "hard pity" in the play. MacCarthy judges this one of Ibsen's finest works and admires its presentation of "the fundamental weakness of human nature."

Mueller, Janel M. "Ibsen's Wild Duck." *Modern Drama* XI, No. 3 (1969): 347-55.

> Examines Ibsen's symbolic use of the wild duck in the play. Although Gregers successively associates the bird with Old Ekdal and Hjalmar, Mueller claims, Ibsen subtly indicates that these interpretations are incorrect while linking Hedvig with the wounded creature.

Simon, John. "*The Wild Duck.*" In his *Singularities: Essays on the Theater, 1964-1973,* pp. 35-51. New York: Random House, 1975.

> Defends Ibsen against critics who charge that "he is preoccupied with the dreariest bourgeois realities to the point of becoming a bore." Simon counters that *The Wild Duck* and Ibsen's other plays contain "meanings so manifold and self-renewing that there is no danger of their ever being exhausted."

HEDDA GABLER

Braunmuller, A. R. "*Hedda Gabler* and the sources of symbolism." In *Drama and Symbolism,* edited by James Redmond, pp. 57-70. Cambridge: Cambridge University Press, 1982.

> Explores symbolism in *Hedda Gabler.* Braunmuller examines the significance of Hedda's pregnancy, Lövborg's manuscript, Mademoiselle Diana, and General Gabler's pistols in an extended discussion of the nature and function of symbols in the drama.

Clancy, James H. "*Hedda Gabler:* Poetry in Action and in Object." In *Studies in Theatre and Drama: Essays in Honor of Hubert C. Hefner,* edited by Oscar G. Brockett, pp. 64-72. The Hague, Netherlands: Mouton, 1972.

> Discusses visual metaphors in Ibsen's *Hedda Gabler.* Clancy asserts that the set design and symbols such as Hedda's pistols and Lövborg's manuscript constitute a "non-verbal poetry" that underscores the play's key themes.

Dorcy, Michael M. "Ibsen's *Hedda Gabler:* Tragedy as Denouement." *College English* 29, No. 3 (December 1967): 223-27.

> Argues that Ibsen's treatment of the time element in *Hedda Gabler* denies the heroine tragic stature. Dorcy asserts that Hedda does not act out of free will and that her death is a "catastrophic re-action" to her pressing circumstances.

Durbach, Errol. "The Apotheosis of Hedda Gabler." *Scandinavian Studies* 43, No. 1 (1971): 143-59.

> Explores Hedda's death against a background of Classical Greek tragedy. Durbach maintains that Hedda's death elevates her to divine status, thereby reconciling the struggle between Dionysian passion and Apollonian control.

Fuchs, Elinor. "Mythic Structure in *Hedda Gabler:* The Mask behind the Face." *Comparative Drama* 19, No. 3 (Fall 1985): 209-21.

> Stresses the mythological underpinnings of *Hedda Gabler.* Fuchs likens Hedda to Hecate, Lövborg to Dionysus, and the plot to ancient fertility cult traditions, asserting that Ibsen sought to satirize the diminished vitality of modern man.

Gates, Joanne E. "Elizabeth Robins and the 1891 Production of *Hedda Gabler.*" *Modern Drama* XXVIII, No. 4 (December 1985): 611-19.

> Chronicles the 1891 London staging of *Hedda Gabler,* jointly produced by American actresses Elizabeth Robins and Marion Lea. Gates asserts that the translation's fidelity to Ibsen's text and the daring production style changed the course of English drama by securing "new and important enthusiasts to the Ibsen movement."

Gosse, Edmund. "Ibsen's New Drama." *The Fortnightly Review* (1 January 1891): 4-13.

> A favorable assessment of Ibsen's newly published *Hedda Gabler.* Gosse centers his remarks on the "complex and morbid" characterization of the heroine.

James, Henry. "Henrik Ibsen." In his *Essays in London and Elsewhere,* pp. 230-47. New York: Harper, 1893.

> Includes James's essay "On the Occasion of *Hedda Gabler,*" which focuses on the protagonist's character and motivation to depict Hedda as "the study of an exasperated woman."

Le Gallienne, Eva. *Preface to Ibsen's 'Hedda Gabler': With a New Translation of the Play.* London: Faber and Faber, n.d., 202 p.

> Explores Hedda's character and the motivation for her actions. Le Gallienne, who performed the role in 1948, renders a step-by-step analysis from Hedda's perspective of the events in the play.

Olsen, Stein Haugom. "Why Does Hedda Gabler Marry Jœrgen Tesman?" *Modern Drama* XXVII, No. 4 (December 1985): 591-610.

> Contrasts the creative, impulsive tendencies of Hedda and Lövborg with the conventional morality of Tesman and his family. Denying any heroism to the destructive acts of Hedda and Lövborg, Olsen upholds the humane yet limited moral order defined by the Tesmans.

For further information on Ibsen's life and career, see *Twentieth-Century Literary Criticism,* Vols. 2, 8, 16, 37; and *Contemporary Authors,* Vol. 104.

Wole Soyinka

1934-

INTRODUCTION

Full name Akinwande Oluwole Soyinka.

Recipient of the 1986 Nobel Prize in literature, Soyinka has been called Africa's finest writer. The Nigerian playwright's unique style blends traditional Yoruba folk-drama with European dramatic forms to provide both spectacle and penetrating satire. His works reflect his philosophy that an artist should function as "the record of the mores and experience of his society" and document twentieth-century Africa's political turmoil and its struggle to reconcile tradition with modernization. However, as Eldred Durosimi Jones has stated, the author's work touches on universal themes as well as addressing specifically African issues: "His concern is with man on earth. Man is dressed for the nonce in African dress and lives in the sun and tropical forest, but he represents the whole race."

Soyinka was born in Aké, a Nigerian village populated by members of the Yoruba tribe. As a young child, he was exposed to the pull between African tradition and Western modernization. Soyinka's grandfather introduced him to the pantheon of Yoruba gods and to other tribal folklore, while his parents were greatly influenced by the British colonial experience: his mother was a devout Christian convert and his father the headmaster of the village school established by the British. As Soyinka matured, the conflict between the two divergent cultures became apparent to him. His father began urging Wole to leave Aké to attend the government school in Ibadan and, during a visit, his grandfather administered a scarification rite of manhood against the boy's parents' wishes. The induction involved ritual incisions around Soyinka's ankles intended to protect him from being poisoned and to strengthen him for conflicts with larger opponents. Soyinka was also consecrated to the god Ogun, an explorer, artisan, and hunter in Yoruba folklore. Ogun is a recurring figure in Soyinka's work and has been named by the author as his muse.

After gaining admission to University College in Ibadan in 1952, Soyinka published some poems and short stories in *Black Orpheus,* a Nigerian literary magazine. Two years later, he left Africa to attend the University of Leeds in England where he received an honors degree in English in 1957. After receiving his degree, he worked for two years as a script-reader for the Royal Court Theatre in London. This position allowed Soyinka to watch the direction and stage-management of the theater during a period of English dramatic revival. His one-act play *The Invention* was presented with readings of Soyinka's poetry as *The Invention and Other Tales* at the Royal Court in 1959. In the play Soyinka attacked racism through comic satire by portraying an incident that causes South Africa's black population to lose their skin color, only to be subjected to discrimination in new ways. Though critics admired the play's ideas, many claimed Soyinka did not properly de-

velop them. In the same year the Arts Theatre of Ibadan presented a double-bill of Soyinka's *The Swamp Dwellers* and *The Lion and the Jewel,* two dramas he had begun following the completion of his degree. The productions were highly successful and led to a Rockefeller Foundation research fellowship in African traditional drama.

In 1960, shortly after independence from colonial rule had been declared, Soyinka returned to Nigeria to begin research on Yoruba folklore and drama. He incorporated elements of both into his next play, *A Dance of the Forests,* which many critics consider Soyinka's first important drama. The play warns the newly independent Nigerians that the end of colonial rule does not mean an end to their country's problems, and it depicts the inhabitants of a small town coming to terms with their past. It was first performed on 10 October 1960 as a part of the Nigerian independence celebration in a production by the 1960 Masks, an acting company Soyinka had recently formed; the author himself played the part of Forest Father. *A Dance of the Forests,* given special notice by the Swedish Academy Nobel Prize committee, addresses many of the themes central to his later dramas, including physical sacrifice and the depravity of human nature. Also in 1960 an

Ibadan student group first produced Soyinka's *The Trials of Brother Jero,* a humorous play about human frailty and temptation. The work centers on Brother Jeroboam, a false prophet who manipulates his followers. Critics have admired the play's ironic conclusion, in which Jero is allowed to continue deceiving his followers, noting its wider applications to the sinister political machinations of African dictatorships.

From 1960 to 1963, Soyinka made his creative base in Ibadan, where he produced plays by fellow African dramatists and wrote a one-act tragedy, *The Strong Breed.* This drama concerns Eman, an educated young Nigerian who, unwilling to follow his father as symbolic carrier of his village's sins but unable to completely reject his ties to the community, offers his life in sacrifice to the villagers. In 1962 Soyinka became a lecturer at the University of Ife but, increasingly committed to social protest, resigned for political reasons a year later. In 1963 he turned to the revue format with *The Republican,* which gave him an outlet for pointed political satire. The work, comprising a series of sketches, introduced his new company, the Orisun Players, an acting troupe dedicated to presenting new Nigerian dramas in English. Another revue followed in 1965 with *Before the Blackout,* as did the first performance of *Kongi's Harvest* in Lagos. In this work, Soyinka attacks Africa's tyrannical dictators by representing the clash between their governmental systems and the traditional African social structures they replaced.

The Road, Soyinka's next work, was presented in London for the Commonwealth Arts Festival in 1965. For this piece, the playwright shifted from a conventional narrative form to a metaphorical parable about humankind's search for truth in a chaotic universe. In the play, a character called the Professor searches for the "Word" which will allow him to unite the worlds of the spirit and the flesh; by moving road signs, he creates accidents he hopes will reveal the truth he seeks. Critics have praised the innovation of this highly symbolic work, but have also remarked on its heavy use of metaphor and overall ineffectiveness. Also in 1965 Soyinka was arrested by the Nigerian police, accused of forcing a radio announcer at gunpoint to broadcast incorrect election results. No evidence was ever produced, however, and Soyinka was released after three months. Two years later he was appointed chairman of the department of theater arts at the University of Ibadan and published his first collection of poetry *Idanre and Other Poems* as well as his first novel *The Interpreters.* He was arrested again that same year during Nigeria's civil war, in which the Ibo people were attempting to form their own country, Biafra. Soyinka was strongly opposed to the conflict, especially to the Nigerian government's brutal policies toward the Ibo. He traveled to Biafra to establish a peace commission composed of leading intellectuals from both sides; when he returned, the Nigerian police accused him of helping the Biafrans buy jet fighters. Although he was never formally charged with any crime, Soyinka was held for more than two years, mostly in solitary confinement. He was released in 1969 and his prison diary was published in 1972 as *The Man Died: Prison Notes of Wole Soyinka.*

Soyinka directed his drama *Madmen and Specialists* in 1970. In this work, set in an unspecified time and place, a doctor—who is trained as a specialist in torture—returns home after a war and uses his new skills on his father. The play's major themes concern the loss of faith and rituals and the disintegration of the traditional family unit. Still discontented with the Nigerian political climate, Soyinka left the country in 1971, accepting a fellowship at Churchill College, Cambridge in 1972. A year later London's National Theatre commissioned and produced *The Bacchae of Euripides,* Soyinka's adaptation of the classical drama. In the same year Soyinka published his second novel, *Season of Anomy,* and returned to his character of Brother Jeroboam in the play *Jero's Metamorphosis.* Satirically examining the relationship of church and state, the play depicts Jero scheming for the right to perform the last rights for those condemned to public execution. Soyinka then moved to Ghana to edit *Transition,* a magazine on African culture, not returning to Nigeria until 1975, when he was appointed professor of comparative literature at the University of Ife and published an additional poetry collection, *Poems of Black Africa.*

In 1976 he produced the essay collection *Myth, Literature and the African World* and *Ogun Abibiman,* a volume of poetry. His next play, *Death and the King's Horseman,* received its first staging in 1976. This work concerns the failure of Elesin, horseman of a recently deceased king, to follow his master to the next life. Although the drama is based on actual incidents in 1946 Nigeria toward the end of British colonial rule, Soyinka has stated that he considers the political aspects of the play to be minor. "The action, the tragedy of *Death and the King's Horseman* could have been triggered off by circumstances which have nothing to do with the colonial factor," he has claimed. "But the tragedy of a man who fails to fulfill an undertaking is a universal tragedy." The work, like *A Dance of the Forests,* received special notice by the Swedish Academy on the occasion of Soyinka's Nobel Prize in literature.

In 1977 Soyinka adapted Bertolt Brecht's *The Threepenny Opera* as *Opera Wonyosi* and published his autobiography, *Aké: The Years of Childhood,* in 1981. His 1983 drama *Requiem for a Futurologist* portrays the misdeeds of Eleazar Hosannah, an evangelist's protegé who attempts to destroy his master Godspeak Igbehodan by predicting his death and taking out an obituary. Ironically, as the play progresses, the more Dr. Godspeak protests that he is still alive, the more people accuse him of actually being dead. The play, though not well-received initially, gave "full rein to Soyinka's comic genius as well as his gift for barbed social satire," Jones has commented. Soyinka next completed *A Play of Giants,* a harsh attack on modern African political leaders, in 1984. This satire concerns African heads of state who meet in New York at the United Nations and, while having their images sculpted, casually discuss the brutality of their regimes.

International recognition of Soyinka's work came when he won the Nobel Prize in 1986. At that time he remarked "I think the prize is a recognition of the whole African literary tradition on which my work is based, by the outside world and by the African world itself." Currently Soyinka is the chairman of the editorial board of *Transition,* which was revived in 1991 for the purpose of "exchanging opinions and ideas, with Africa at its center." Along with Henry Louis Gates, Jr., and Kuame Anthony Appiah, Soyinka published the first new issue in May 1991.

Many of Soyinka's plays focus upon dichotomies of good versus evil and progress versus tradition. *The Swamp Dwellers* condemns African superstition and glorification of the past, whereas *The Lion and the Jewel* cautions against the opposite extreme and affirms positive African values while rejecting incongruous European elements. In *The Swamp Dwellers,* Igwezu turns his back on the past as he resists the domination of his community by the Kadiye, the Chief Priest to the Serpent of the Swamps. Ultimately, Igwezu forsakes his village for the city. In contrast, *The Lion and the Jewel,* which Jones calls "a harmonious blend of words, song, dance, and mime," embraces the past as it lampoons the indiscriminate acceptance of Western modernization. The plot revolves around Sidi, the village beauty, and the rivalry between her two suitors: the Baroka, the old village chief with many wives, and Lakunle the enthusiastically Westernized schoolteacher who dreams of molding Sidi into a "civilized" woman. In the end, Sidi rejects Lakunle for the Baroka.

A Dance of the Forests presents a complex view of the interrelatedness of the past, present, and future. In this drama three mortals—Rola the prostitute, Adenebi the Council Orator, and Demoke the carver—invite the spirits of their ancestors to visit earth to share in "The Gathering of the Tribes" (representing Nigeria's independence celebrations in October 1960). Although each of the three human characters has a link in a former life to these ancestors, the two spirits who appear for the festivities are not the noble figures the mortals expected. Commentators have noted that *A Dance of the Forests* appears to criticize Africans for deemphasizing the present and glorifying the past while warning the young Nigerian nation to avoid this pitfall. Soyinka's skill in incorporating dancing, drumming, and singing to reinforce his theme has often been praised. Critics also note the work's resemblance to William Shakespeare's *A Midsummer Night's Dream,* pointing out that both plays contain forest- and spirit-world settings, disguises, prologues, and a play-within-a-play.

In the bitterly satirical *Kongi's Harvest* Soyinka attacks the repressive political regimes of contemporary Africa. The action involves Daodu and Segi and their failed attempt to overthrow the government of Kongi, the president of Isma. Kongi himself has recently deposed the country's king. He wishes to bring his nation into the modern world, but the people cling to traditional ways and, as a result, his government becomes dictatorial. Since the revolt fails, the play offers no optimistic ending "in which evil is put down and a brand-new regime of good succeeds," Jones claims; nevertheless, Daodu and Segi have "led an assertion of life against the death principle that Kongi represents." In 1970 the American dramatist and actor Ossie Davis adapted and directed a film version of *Kongi's Harvest,* with Soyinka in the role of Kongi.

Many critics acknowledge Soyinka's *Death and the King's Horseman* as one of his most powerful works, full of "the stateliness and mystery of Greek tragedy" as Holly Hill noted in her London *Times* review of the 1987 Lincoln Center production. The play opens just after the king of a Nigerian village has died. Tradition states that the king's horseman must accompany his master to the next world by committing a sacrificial suicide in which he brings about his death through his own willpower. On the night his death is to occur, the horseman Elesin Oba takes a new bride as is the custom, but against advice he chooses a young virgin. When the British District Officer Simon Pilkings learns that the ritual suicide is about to take place, he immediately intervenes. Wishing to avoid controversy prior to a Royal visit, he has Elesin jailed. Pilkings and his wife Jane are then surprised by the arrival of Olunde, Elesin's son, who has returned from his studies in England upon hearing of his father's fate. When Elesin is ultimately unable to find the will to leave his young bride, Olunde takes his own life, thus completing his father's communal duty. *Death and the King's Horseman* received mixed reviews from critics in its revival at New York's Lincoln Center. Some reviewers commended its tragic form, rich language, and effective dramatization of metaphysical issues, while others disliked the crude, satirical portrayal of the British characters, a slow pace due to lengthy poetic speech, and difficult mystical passages.

Commentators have divided Soyinka's work into pre- and post-prison phases. Although social and political satire have always been a staple of Soyinka's work, even in such lighthearted examples as *The Lion and the Jewel* and *The Trials of Brother Jero,* critics have discerned an increased anger and pessimism in his work after 1967. Some, for instance, have noted a change in tone between the two Jero plays, with *Trials* cited for its light comic touch and *Jero's Metamorphosis* for its dark satirical portrayal of the main character. In his plays Soyinka increasingly denounces the succession of military-run governments that have appeared in Nigeria and other African nations. *Kongi's Harvest,* as already noted, is a general indictment of authoritarianism, while *Opera Wonyosi* and *A Play of Giants* feature readily identifiable caricatures of Jean-Bédel Bokassa, Idi Amin, and other notorious political figures.

Soyinka's work is frequently described as demanding but rewarding reading. Although his plays are widely praised, they are infrequently performed, especially outside Africa. The dancing and choric speech often found in them are unfamiliar and difficult for non-African actors to master, a problem Hill noted in her review of *Death and the King's Horseman.* However, as Thomas Hayes stresses, Soyinka provokes change and greater understanding in his audiences. "His drama and fiction have challenged the West to broaden its aesthetic and accept African standards of art and literature. His personal and political life have challenged Africa to embrace the truly democratic values of the African tribe and reject the tyranny of power practiced on the continent by its colonizers and by many of its modern rulers."

PRINCIPAL WORKS

PLAYS

The Swamp Dwellers   1958
The Invention and Other Tales   1959
The Lion and the Jewel   1959
†*The Trials of Brother Jero*   1960
A Dance of the Forests   1960
The Republican   1963 [revised with new sketches as *The New Republican,* 1963]
The Strong Breed   1963
Three Plays   1963
Before the Blackout   1965
Camwood on the Leaves   1965   (radio play)
The Detainee   1965   (radio play)
Kongi's Harvest   1965
The Road   1965
Madmen and Specialists   1970
The Bacchae of Euripides: A Communion Rite   1973
†*Jero's Metamorphosis*   1973
Death and the King's Horseman   1975
Opera Wonyosi   1977
Requiem for a Futurologist   1983
A Play of Giants   1984

OTHER MAJOR WORKS

The Interpreters   (novel)   1965 [first published 1970]
Idanre and Other Poems   (poetry)   1967
The Fourth Stage: Through the Mysteries of Ogun to the Origin of Yoruba Tragedy   (essay)   1969 [published in *The Morality of Art: Essays Presented to G. Wilson Knight*]
Poems from Prison   (poetry)   1969 [enlarged edition published as *A Shuttle in the Crypt, 1971*]published as *A Shuttle in the Crypt,* 1971]
Plays from the Third World: An Anthology [editor]   (dramas)   1971
The Man Died: Prison Notes of Wole Soyinka   (prose)   1972
Season of Anomy   (novel)   1973
Poems of Black Africa [editor]   (poetry)   1975
Myth, Literature and the African World   (essays)   1976
Ogun Abibiman   (poetry)   1976
Aké: The Years of Childhood   (autobiography)   1981
Mandela's Earth and Other Poems   (poetry)   1988
Isarà: Voyage around Essay   (prose)   1989

*These works were published as *Three Plays* in 1963.

†These works were published as *The Jero Plays* in 1973.

AUTHOR COMMENTARY

An Evening with Wole Soyinka   (1986)

[*The following interview was conducted in late 1986, soon after Soyinka had won the Nobel Prize in literature. Soyinka talks with Anthony Appiah about receiving the Nobel Prize and discusses his play* Death and the King's Horseman. *A variant form of this interview appeared in 1987 in* The New Theater Review *under the title "Easing the Transition."*]

[Appiah]: *Now that you've had three months or so to think about it, can you tell us what you think the significance is of the award of the Nobel Prize, first of all to you and then to you as an African?*

[Soyinka]: To me, it's been hell. (Laughter.) On one level, yes. I understand what Bernard Shaw meant when he was given the Prize and he said he could forgive the man who invented dynamite, but it took the mind of a devil to invent the Nobel Prize for literature. I share some of this feeling, but only to a certain extent. The other side of the coin, of course, is that it increases one's literary family, increases one's awareness of the need of many activities, many paths, many concerns of the common Earth we inhabit. It increases an awareness of the need of people to fasten onto a voice, a representative, and that refers to your question about Africa in particular. So, it's of great importance, I think, not so much to me as to the literary craftsmen of my continent, to those who share my political concerns for the continent, to those who share the longing for a brotherhood/sisterhood which transcends the African continent and reaches out into the diaspora. The way in which the Prize has been received by people all over the world, particularly the African diaspora—in the West Indies, in the United States, and across the various language boundaries—has reinforced my insistent conviction that the African world is not limited by the African continent.

I noticed that when you gave your Nobel lecture, you chose to discuss apartheid and southern Africa. Did you feel that that was a particularly important thing to do at that moment?

A lot of my writing has been concerned with injustice, with inhumanity, with racism, inside and outside of my immediate environment, which is Nigeria. This is a world platform, and I could not think of any more appropriate moment for voicing this particular level of my literary concerns. I thought it was most appropriate, yes. (pp. 777-78)

How does it enhance or change your position when you're speaking within Nigeria?

I've always insisted that I do not accept any kind of double standards. I do not accept a distinction, excuses on behalf of either our own black oppressors or the white oppressors of our race. In other words, the more one emphasizes the oppression which we receive from outside, the more we obtain the moral strength and the moral authority to criticize our own black oppressors. So this is equally important. Many African heads of state sent messages, personal telegrams, telexes, etc., and for me this means they have already accepted the imperative of the moralities which guide my work. So now it becomes a little bit more difficult for many of them to say, "Oh, you are criticizing us to the outside world!" when they understand that a kind of moral authority attaches to events of this kind and they have identified themselves with it. Otherwise, I'll tell them, "Take back your congratulatory telegrams." (Laughter.)

I wonder if this wouldn't be a good moment to go back a bit in time and ask you to comment on **Aké,** *your book about your early childhood. Could you say something about the process of writing about your early life?*

You know, one recaptures certain aspects of some elements of smells and sounds, either by actually smelling and hearing them or by suddenly missing them, because something triggers off the memory. You suddenly realize that a certain slice of your life is disappearing, and you get a feeling that you want to set it down in one form or another. This period of my childhood belongs to that sudden realization of a lost period, a lost ambience, a lost environment. I don't like autobiographies, because they're mostly lies, but there's a period of innocence in which one can write down things quite frankly. Even *Aké* is not totally truthful. (Laughs.) You have to expunge some things. You are embarrassed by some things, so you leave them out. But this is obviously more truthful because of the lack of inhibition than many other things I write about my life. It's not lying—you don't tell untruths, you just do not tell all the truth. It's part and parcel of the protection of human dignity. I've always been repelled by the general Euro-American habit of telling all, revealing all the dirty secrets of human relationships, even without asking permission of those who share this personal relationship with you. (Laughter, applause.)

So the childhood is one period in which there is really nothing much to hide, and I'd always wanted to set it down. I spoke to my publisher, he gave me a small advance, and I spent it. It took three years after that before I could enter the frame of mind to recapture this particular life in the way I wanted to set it down.

Aké *was very successful in this country—it's a widely read book—, and that success makes plain how intelligible you have made the world of your childhood to those of us who in different ways didn't share it, because we lived either in other parts of Africa or in other parts of the world. There presumably are, however, problems in presenting your work, especially as a dramatist, because of the different traditions of interpretation of theater and performance in Nigeria, in West Africa, in Africa, and in the rest of the world. Could you reflect a little while on some of the ways in which these problems affect the production that you're now engaged in,* **Death and the King's Horseman?**

It's interesting that you ask that question apropos of *Aké,* because in one of the sessions with the company, some of the cast expressed their difficulty in finding a sort of corresponding experience in their own lives with the content, theme, and characters in **Death and the King's Horseman.** I have to confess that I was very impatient about this kind

of difficulty. But, remarkably, one of the actresses—and a white one at that—said to the others, "Well, why don't you read *Aké?*" At least one portion is, in fact, very significant in terms of the position of the women in **Death and the King's Horseman.**

But, as I said and admit freely, I have a very impatient attitude towards this. I grew up, as many of us did, on the fare of European literature. Even in school we didn't have too much problem understanding the worlds of William Shakespeare, Bernard Shaw, Galsworthy, Moliere, and Ibsen, and, frankly, I'm irritated when people from outside my world say they find it difficult to enter my world. It's laziness, it's intellectual laziness . . . especially today when communication is a matter of course. There are economic relations between all the nations of the world. I see in Nigeria millionaires, multi-corporations, a constant exchange of films, video tapes, radio, music; Fela comes here with his music. I find no difficulty at all in entering into Chinese literature, Japanese literature, Russian literature, and this has always been so. I think the barrier is self-induced. "This is a world of the exotic, we can not enter it." The barrier is self-created. By now it has to be a two-way traffic. There can be no concessions at all; the effort simply has to be made.

But at the same time the work of a director principally involves responsibility towards the audience. He must always find idioms, whether in the field of music, poetry, or scenography, to interpret what might be abstruse elements. The director must bring out images in concrete terms which are merely in verbal terms within the book. When he moves a play from one area to another, the director seeks certain symbols, certain representational images in order to facilitate—because you're encapsulating a history of a people within a couple of hours. If you take

Christine Clinton as Alu and Adisa Ajetunmodi as Makuri perform a scene from Soyinka's The Swamp Dwellers *in the 1959 Ibadan Arts Theatre production.*

[Shakespeare's] *Coriolanus* to Africa, it's the responsibility of the director to try to transmit the metaphors within that particular language, the visual images, in terms which cannot be too remote. But then again I believe that the audience must not be overindulged, and once as a director I feel I have satisfied myself, that I've eased the transition, the rest is up to the audience. They can take it or leave it. (Applause.)

I take it that part of the passion of your remarks is in response to some of the ways in which your work has been received in the United States and in Europe, perhaps more in the United States.

I have to say Europeans are a little bit—if one can make comparisons—more receptive. Americans are very insular. I suppose that's because you have so many cultures in America, and Americans don't feel they have to go outside what is already here. But there's a great deal of insularity in America, and that applies not merely to culture, but to politics. Americans don't even make an attempt to understand the politics of outside nations. They think they do, but they do not. And I mean this on all levels. I speak not merely of the taxi driver who asked me, "Yea, what's happening, man. You're from Neegeria. Is that in *Eeran?*" (Laughter.) I find the same attitude even among university lecturers. Not so long ago there was a professional, very intelligent, highly trained, and I happened to remark that one of my ways of relaxing is just to go into the bush and do some hunting. And he said, "Oh, what do you use for hunting?" What he was asking was, "Is it clubs? Or bows and arrows?" I mean we've been fighting wars with cannons and guns in Africa for I don't know how long. I said, "No, it's catapult." (Laughter.) So, it's the same thing with culture. Americans are far more insular.

I'd like to talk a little more about **Death and the King's Horseman.** *Is this a political play, or would you rather read it as relatively apolitical, by contrast, for example, to* **A Play of Giants?**

Of course there's politics in *Death and the King's Horseman.* There's the politics of colonization, but for me it's very peripheral. The action, the tragedy of *Death and the King's Horseman* could have been triggered off by circumstances which have nothing to do with the colonial factor—that's very important to emphasize. So it's political in a very peripheral sense. The colonial factor, as I insist, is merely a catalytic event. But the tragedy of a man who fails to fulfill an undertaking is a universal tragedy. I regard it as being far, far, far less political than *A Play of Giants,* yes.

You've said that **Horseman** *is fundamentally a metaphysical play. That might invite the speculation that it is a difficult play, since* metaphysical *is a word—I know this as a philosopher—which invites difficulties. Is there something you want to say, in advance of people's seeing it, about the metaphysical issues, the issues of death and transition, which the play addresses?*

All his life, the principal character, the Elesin Oba—the Horseman of the King—, has enjoyed certain unique privileges for a certain function. At the critical moment he fails to fulfill that function, so he's doomed. That's

straightforward. But then, one asks, how is it that, in the first place, such a function was the norm for a community of people? We can ask that from this distance. And that's not so long ago. In fact, societies like this still exist.

I've given my company current examples from India, for instance, of human sacrifice and so on to the goddess Kali, which were in the newspapers quite recently. So one must begin by understanding what is the spiritual context of a people for whom this is not an aberration, not an abnormality, and one finds it in the world view, the metaphysical beliefs of the Yoruba people.

We believe that there are various areas of existence, all of which interact, interlock in a pattern of continuity: the world of the ancestor, the world of the living, and the world of the unborn. The process of transition among these various worlds is a continuing one and one which is totally ameliorated. For instance, the function of ritual, of sacrifice—whether it's a ram or a chicken—, the function of seasonal ceremonies, is in fact allied to the ease of transition among these various worlds.

So, in effect, death does not mean for such a society what it means for other societies. And it's only if one establishes this kind of context, through whatever symbolic means, that one can begin—distanced as you and I are from this particular kind of society, even if we are part of the world. It's only by exposing this world as a hermetic, self-regulating universe of its own that a tragedy of a character like Elesin can have absolute validity. So within that context, this is what enables him. For him it's not death.

At the same time, even journeying from New York to Boston is an activity of loss. You leave something behind. It involves a pain. How much you want to live in this world which you know very well, which is concrete, which one can only relate to in symbolic terms. And so for Elesin the difficulty does exist as a human being within this world. But he's been brought up to believe, and his whole community believes, in the existence of these various worlds which are secure and even concrete in their own terms. And his failure to make that transfer from one to the other, *that* really is the tragedy of Elesin.

You spoke just now of **Horseman** *as a tragedy, which of course it is. I think the concept of tragedy tends to get used in our culture very much and in a debased form and with very little sense of classical tragedy. You chose, very deliberately I think, to frame* **Horseman** *as a classical tragedy. Is that not a difficulty, turning once again to the problems of production? Is it not difficult to produce a tragedy for a contemporary American audience? Not because it's alien or exotic or African, but because the concept of tragedy required to enter this world is a distant one to many people?*

Yes. But that's only if one begins by accepting the European definition of tragedy. I remember my shock as a student of literature and drama when I read that drama originated in Greece. What is this? I couldn't quite deal with it. What are they talking about? I never heard my grandfather talk about Greeks invading Yorubaland. I couldn't understand. I've lived from childhood with drama. I read at the time that tragedy evolved as a result of the rites of Dionysus. Now we all went through this damn thing, so I think the presence of eradication had better begin. It doesn't matter what form it takes. (Applause.)

Nevertheless, whatever their origins, tragedy does have a specific, formal . . .

But I've never made a claim that I'm presenting tragedy in European terms. *Tragedy*—quite apart from the misuse of the word which we know about—whether we translate it in Yoruba or Tre or Ewe, I think we'll find a correlative somewhere in which we're all talking about the same thing. Just as the equivalent of the word *tragedy* in Yoruba can be debased in Africa, so it can be debased in Europe. But ultimately there is a certain passage of the human being, a certain development or undevelopment of the human character, a certain result in the processes of certain events which affects the human being which has that common definition of tragedy in no matter what culture. And it is to that kind of linguistic bag, that symbolic bag, which audiences in theater must attune themselves, whether it is Japanese tragedy or Chinese tragedy.

There may be difficulties, but I think they're very superficial. As I explained to some of my company, "You say you have difficulty looking for some parallel experience in America. But what do you call what happened to Richard Nixon? If ever there was a tragic character, that is it. Begin from there." (Laughter.) Just begin from there. We all have these experiences; it's universal. It's only in the details we differ. What happens to a man psychologically in terms of his valuation within the community in which he resides, the fall from—to use a cliché—grace to grass, that's the element of tragedy. (pp. 777-83)

Wole Soyinka and Anthony Appiah, in an interview, in Black American Literature Forum, *Vol. 22, No. 4, Winter, 1988, pp. 777-85.*

OVERVIEWS AND GENERAL STUDIES

Eldred Durosimi Jones   (essay date 1988)

[*In the following excerpt, Jones provides background in Yoruba culture for a better understanding of Soyinka and his works. Jones states that Soyinka "has taken a deep and scholarly interest in the culture of his people," which provides him with "a base of ideas from which his works flow."*]

Wole Soyinka has his roots in Yoruba culture, as even a cursory reading of his works soon shows, but his experience extends far wider; his formal education and his working experience have brought him into contact with ideas from the whole modern world. This other half of his experience is also represented in his work. His imagery ranges from tropical yam roots to the falling acorns of Tegel. But he starts as a Yoruba.

Apart from having been born a Yoruba and thus being naturally a part of the culture, Soyinka has taken a deep and scholarly interest in the culture of his people. His in-

Soyinka performs the role of Forest Father (right) in the 1960 Masks staging of A Dance of the Forests.

terest in the language is strikingly illustrated by his thoughtful translation of one of the most popular works of Yoruba literature, D. O. Fagunwa's *Ogboju ode ninu Irunmale* under the title *The Forest of a Thousand Daemons*. In a very significant Translator's Note prefixed to the work, Soyinka demonstrates the linguistic discretion he had to exercise. His explanation of his choice of the word 'daemon' is illustrative of the point. He writes: 'The spelling is important. These beings who inhabit Fagunwa's world demand at all costs and by every conceivable translator's trick to be preserved from the common or misleading associations which substitutes such as *demons, devils* or *gods* evoke in the reader's mind. At the same time, it is necessary that they transmit the reality of their existence by the same unquestioning impact and vitality which is conveyed by Fagunwa in the original.' Some of the results of the translator's ingenuity are new words like Ghommids, dewild, Gnom (without an e) and kobold, It is worth noting that these beings from Yoruba tradition found in Fagunwa's world (and in the forests of Tutuola) are also found in Soyinka's own forests in his play *A Dance of the Forests.* The Crier's summons in that play is:

> To all such as dwell in these Forests; Rock devils,
> Earth imps, Tree demons, ghommids, dewilds, genies
> Incubi, succubi, windhorls, bits and halves and such
> Sons and subjects of Forest Father, and all
> That dwell in his domain . . .

Soyinka shares in this respect the same mythological world as Fagunwa and Tutuola.

His scholarly interest in this world is further demonstrated in his essay 'The Fourth Stage' in which he develops a theory of Yoruba tragedy by examining the ideas underlying the Yoruba concepts of being, and in particular, the ideas underlying Yoruba theology. The effect of this deep scholarly interest in Yoruba culture endows Soyinka with a base of ideas from which his works flow. Indeed some knowledge of Yoruba culture is necessary for any serious study of this author's work.

YORUBA CULTURE

The Yoruba are one of Africa's most remarkable peoples. Their culture is not only rich, but shows a remarkable capacity for survival in areas far removed from its original home. Yoruba culture survives robustly for example in Brazil and other parts of South America, the Caribbean, and in Sierra Leone, areas which centuries ago, largely through the slave trade, came into contact with Yoruba of the diaspora.

The original home of the Yoruba is of course Western Nigeria. G. J. Afolabi Ojo, himself a distinguished Yoruba scholar defines their cultural area thus [in his *Yoruba Culture*, 1966]: '. . . the area where Yoruba culture is typical coincides with the six western provinces of Western Nigeria [Oyo, Ibadan, Abeokuta, Ijebu, Ondo, Lagos]; Ilorin Division of Ilorin Province; and Kabba Division of Kabba Province'.

Soyinka was born in Abeokuta, an area which still retains the highest density of Yoruba speakers—over 90 per cent of the population, according to Ojo.

GODS, SPIRITS, ANCESTORS

Traditional Yoruba life is dominated by religion. The Yoruba are surrounded by gods and spirits with whom the lives of mortals interact. In what is more an idiomatic expression for the idea of multiplicity than an actual count, the Yoruba ascribe to themselves four hundred and one gods. (Soyinka prefers to translate a similar expression *Irunmale,* not literally as four hundred deities but as 'a thousand and one'.) The total count of deities probably can never be given since local areas have some deities peculiar to them. There are of course major deities who are recognized and worshipped all over Yorubaland. Olodumare (Olorun) is the supreme god—'Creator, king, Omnipotent, All-wise, All-knowing, Judge, Immortal, Invisible and Holy'. He is worshipped through minor deities, and although constantly invoked in oaths, the Yoruba do not represent him physically or build shrines to him. In deference to Yoruba tradition (and because he would not know what he looked like anyway) Kola, the artist in Soyinka's novel *The Interpreters,* does not represent Olodumare in his painting of the Yoruba Pantheon. (He appears as Forest Head in *A Dance of the Forests.*) The gods represented in Kola's canvas are Orisa Nla, the principal deity under Olodumare, Esu, the spirit of disorder, evil and change, Sango, god of lightning and electricity, Sopona (Obaluwaiye) of smallpox, Erinle, Esumare, and

Soyinka's favourite god, Ogun. The duality of this last god, the seeming contradiction in his nature—he is both the creative and the destructive essence—makes him an enigmatic symbol both in Soyinka's own creative work and in his criticism. Man in his capacity both for creation and destruction is a reincarnation of this contradictory god of the forge. In 'The Fourth Stage' for example Soyinka writes thus about Ogun:

> As for Ogun, he is best understood in Hellenic values as a totality of the Dionysian, Apollonian and Promethean values. Nor is this all. Transcending even today, the distorted myths of his terrorist reputation, traditional poetry records him as 'protector of orphans', 'roof over the homeless', 'terrible guardian of the sacred oath'; Ogun stands in fact for a transcendental humane but rigidly restorative justice.

Below the deities, in Yoruba belief, are numerous spirits of the ancestors and of things. Some of the gods in fact are ancestors who have been elevated into deities. Thus Sango was once the third Alafin (king) of Oyo. Gods and the spirits of the ancestors are thus very close to each other. Trees, peculiar land formations, rivers etc., all could become imbued with spirits which make them sacred. Human life itself is regarded as part of a continuum of life stretching from the spirits of unborn children through bodily existence to the spirits of departed ancestors. The abiku child who appears as a symbol at the end of *A Dance of the Forests* and is also the subject of a poem is a manifestation of a restless child spirit who is constantly shuttling back and forth between the land of the unborn spirits and this life, causing itself to be born over and over again by the same mother only to plague her by its death. These are the gods and spirits which make up the teeming population of Soyinka's forests in *A Dance of the Forests.*

The ancestors are worshipped through the *egungun,* masked figures who, if the ceremonies are duly observed, become possessed by the spirits they represent, and are able to speak with unearthly wisdom. Soyinka makes use of this idea of possession in both *A Dance of the Forests* and *The Road,* two of his most important plays. In contrast to this proper use of masks, he offers the travesty of the District Commissioner and his wife in *Death and the King's Horseman,* prancing about in the 'fancy dress' of captured *egungun* regalia, ironic symbols of a tragic alienation. The carving of masks and other objects for the worship of these numerous ancestors and deities has made the Yoruba probably the most prolific as well as the most artistic wood carvers in the world. A good impression of both their skill and sheer output (it must be remembered that the light wood used is highly perishable necessitating constant replacement) can be gained from Ulli Beier's illustrated booklet, *The Story of Sacred Wood Carvings From One Small Yoruba Town.* The carver is central to Yoruba life and worship; this central position is reflected in the symbolic role of Demoke the carver in *A Dance of the Forests* who becomes a representative of humanity.

YORUBA OCCUPATIONS AND FESTIVALS

Farming is the most important occupation of the Yoruba although quite interestingly they are also an urban people, their farms being situated a long way from their homes. Hunting, fishing, weaving, dyeing and trading are other occupations, but it is the regular rhythm of farming—clearing the farm, hoeing it, sowing it, and reaping the harvest—which dictates the larger patterns of life. A failure of crops is a disaster of the greatest magnitude. In Soyinka's symbolism such a failure becomes a symbol for destruction and the very negation of life, while the image of a successful and plenteous harvest represents the positive forces of life. The big Yoruba festivals predominantly come at the time of harvest when there is plenty to eat and drink. Harvest thus has associations of both piety and joy, as is reflected in Soyinka's poem **'Idanre'**.

Some trees and crops have come to be prominent in the culture and assume symbolic stature. Dr Ojo lists among these, yam, kola, oil palm, and maleguetta pepper. These appear in this symbolic role in Soyinka's works; indeed all of them appear in a single poem **'Dedication'**. Palm wine, one of the products of the oil palm, is the universal drink; thirst quencher as well as drink of ceremony and celebration. Tutuola's most famous character, the Drinkard, undertakes his perilous pilgrimage to the land of the dead in pursuit of his dead palm wine tapster without whose services life was insupportable. Palm wine assumes almost a mystical role in Soyinka's work. It is the wine of Professor's special version of the rite of communion in **The Road.** Egbo has to have a gourd of the best on his visit with the unnamed girl to his shrine in **The Interpreters.** Soyinka's special interest in palm wine (artistic and gastronomic) is exemplified by a celebration of the rites of the Harmattan solstice which he organized at the University of Lagos and for which he composed poems both in Yoruba and English, all around the theme of palm wine.

Yoruba culture is rich in ceremonies ranging from the simple ceremonies of regular worship (the principal deities are worshipped every four days) through family ceremonies associated with birth, marriage, death, to the big annual festivals of particular gods, and special ceremonies relating to the crowning and the rule of Obas (kings). Ulli Beier in his booklet *A Year of Sacred Festivals in One Yoruba Town* describes with pictures eleven of the major festivals celebrated in this town of six thousand inhabitants. His list is limited to the big town festivals and does not include the more numerous smaller family and personal celebrations.

The principal external features of these festivals are drumming, singing, dancing, feasting and sacrifice. Poetic praise songs (oriki) and prayers are recited, mimetic dances re-enact events whose originals are lost in mythological gloom, sacrifices, often of freshly killed animals, are offered, and pent-up spirits are released in general dancing. Oyin Ogumba [in 'The Traditional Content of the Plays of Wole Soyinka,' *African Literature Today* 4 (1970)] has pointed out how the Yoruba festival has influenced Soyinka's plays:

> But by far the most significant traditional element in these plays is the overall design of a festival. This is particularly true of the plays, namely **Kongi's Harvest, The Strong Breed** and **A Dance of the Forests.** In each of these plays, the prevailing mood is that of the preparation for or celebration of a great event which produces so much excitement or tension in the whole populace that everybody thinks of nothing but the great event. This is, in fact, the atmosphere that prevails when important ceremonies are performed in traditional Africa, and Soyinka in these plays very often catches the essence of the festival mood with the drumming, bustle and other manifestations of a holiday.

The head of Yoruba government is the Oba. He is a king who rules surrounded by ceremony, and combines both political and priestly functions. The Oba's spiritual authority is exemplified in **Kongi's Harvest** in which, even when the Oba's political authority has been eroded by the new regime of Kongi, he still has reserves of moral and spiritual authority with which to compel deference from the functionaries of the new regime. Baroka, the wily Bale of Ilujinle, is another of Soyinka's evocations of the Yoruba traditional ruler.

All Yoruba culture is enshrined in the language, a highly tonal and musical language which gives the impression of being chanted rather than spoken. These rhythmic and tonal qualities do not come over into English, which is a language of a very different type. What does flow over into Soyinka's English is the wealth of imagery and proverbial formulas which he uses with remarkable effect. Soyinka thinks in images, and his poems in particular are elaborate formulations of imagery which only reveal their full meaning when the image code is broken. His fondness for puns, which sometimes seems over-indulged in English, is also probably an overflow from the word puzzles, tongue-twisters and other verbal tricks of his original language.

CHRISTIAN INFLUENCES

His Yoruba traditional background provides the key to one part of Soyinka, but it is well to remember that there are other influences as well, so universal that they cannot be so easily identified. Although Soyinka received his basic formal education up to university level in Nigeria, the content of this education was essentially Christian-European. He has declared that he is no longer a practising Christian, but the influence of Christianity on his work is quite apparent. He has a facility of Biblical reference which could only come of years of early Bible study. A complete list of Biblical references in Soyinka's work would be impressive, but only a few illustrations are given here.

In **The Interpreters,** Dehinwa who deliberately slams the door to aggravate Sagoe's already splitting headache becomes Jael (*Judges* 4, 21) who drove a tent pin through Sisera's temples. In the same novel, Joe Golder, dissatisfied with his complexion (too light for a Negro) felt 'like Esau cheated of my birthright', a reference to the well-known story of Esau and Jacob (*Genesis* 27, 36). The Life of Christ must have made a deep impression, for there are Christ figures all over Soyinka's work, often with verbal links with the Bible. **'The Dreamer'** is an obvious example. He hangs

> Higher than trees a cryptic crown
> Lord of the rebel three
> Thorns lay on a sleep of down

And myrrh; a mesh
Of nails, of flesh
And words that flowered free

This picture obviously derives from Christ on the Cross. There are parallels too between Eman in *The Strong Breed* and Christ. Both men are victims of people for whom they worked, and each died high on a sacred tree leaving the people stunned by their deaths. Willing sacrifice is one of Soyinka's recurrent themes.

The miracle of the feeding of the five thousand (*Mark,* 6), is ironically recalled in the last section of the poem '**Ikeja, Friday, Four O'clock**' in the words: 'Let nought be wasted, gather up for the recurrent session / Loaves of lead, lusting in the sun's recession.' There are undertones of Christ's entry into Jerusalem in '**Easter**'. Some of the references are so natural that they could have been unconscious. Quite obviously, like Dehinwa, Sagoe, and Egbo in *The Interpreters,* Soyinka had large doses of Sunday School.

OTHER INFLUENCES

His higher education, started at Ibadan, was continued at Leeds where he read English. The Leeds syllabus is very wide in scope, and must have brought Soyinka into contact with the whole range of modern European and American literature. He was one of G. Wilson Knight's memorable pupils. The great literary critic in his preface to *The Golden Labyrinth,* acknowledges his debt to Soyinka's interpretation of the character of King Lear, which in turn influenced his conception of the work. The English poet Thomas Blackburn, after whom Soyinka wrote his poem '**By Little Loving**', was another Leeds contact. Describing his other experiences in Britain and continental Europe Soyinka himself said: 'I worked in a nightclub partly as a barman and partly as a bouncer. During one of the long vacations, I worked as a bricklayer in Holland. Then I taught in a variety of schools in Britain. From very good grammar schools to those which qualify to be called borstals.' An interest in and facility of reference to other mythologies, but particularly Greek mythology, is obvious in his later work. *Shuttle in the Crypt,* his essay '**The Fourth Stage**' and, of course, his adaptation of *The Bacchae* of Euripides copiously illustrate this.

Perhaps even more significant was Soyinka's attachment to the Royal Court Theatre, the home of the English Stage Society, where he was a play reader. Some of his early pieces were tried out there. '**The Invention**' and excerpts from other works formed the programme at the Sunday night productions of that theatre on November 1, 1959. The attachment to the Royal Court put him in contact with the work of the *avant-garde* European playwrights as well as the work of traditional dramatists. (English reviewers of his plays have seen influences on his work ranging from Ben Jonson, through Wycherley, Ibsen and Chekov to Wesker and Pinter.) Soyinka has travelled widely since over a vast area of the world, and no doubt being a sensitive man has been influenced. His work is, however, a truly original manifestation of his whole vast range of experiences. Certainly this range of experiences has given him a world-wide view of mankind, even though he naturally chooses to treat man mainly through the African environment.

He is primarily an African writer and whatever influence his work has on the rest of the world—he is now performed in Britain, continental Europe and America—his primary audience is in Africa where his works should be read and performed a great deal more there than they are. Among the plays, the shorter works, particularly the comedies, are performed fairly often, but the major plays far too seldom. The main reason for this is that the major plays do make considerable demands on the skill of actors and the ingenuity of directors, and tropical Africa does not have professional companies which can put on the plays with the degree of professional skill that they require.

SOYINKA AND THE STAGE

Soyinka himself is conscious of the need for companies which would keep a body of players together under expert direction long enough for them to develop the necessary skills for the production of the new African drama which draws on African traditional methods of presentation as well as the techniques of European and other traditions of theatre. On his return from England he formed 'The 1960 Masks', the company which put on *A Dance of the Forests* in Nigeria's independence year. Later he formed Orisun Theatre. His hope for permanent theatre groups is still far from fulfilment, but he has used university theatre groups as the nuclei of acting companies which have performed his plays both within and outside Nigeria.

Soyinka is himself a skilled actor and director whose productions of his own plays demonstrate the fact that a professional production is not necessarily an elaborate production. He directed the première of *Kongi's Harvest* on the floor of the conference hall of the Federal Palace Hotel in Lagos without benefit of a proper stage, but by expert lighting, and the sensitive use of music and movement he pulled off an excellent production. Not every director is a Soyinka, and it must be admitted that plays like *A Dance of the Forests* present formidable problems of staging. Conversely, elaborate facilities may not in themselves effect a successful production. At least one critic suggests that the direction of *The Bacchae* failed to respond adequately to the demands of the text: 'Faced with a text that calls for precise and meaningful gesture, for narrative clarity, and for a theatre language based on ritual, the director has opted for imitation orgies, fake horror, and whooped-up excitement' [Albert Hunt, 'Amateurs in Horror', reprinted in James Gibbs (ed.), *Critical Perspectives on Wole Soyinka,* 1980].

Soyinka's other work, particularly the poetry, has the reputation of being difficult. What this really means is that it demands close and sensitive reading—as does his novel *The Interpreters.* Very few writers, however, repay this attention more copiously than Soyinka does. However complex he may be, though, it seems ludicrous that in Africa reading lists which include T. S. Eliot's poetry with its background of classical European mythology and mysticism, should exclude Soyinka on grounds of difficulty.

BASIC CONCERNS

Soyinka's life is inseparable from his work, much of which arises from a passionate, almost desperate, concern for his society. This concern is apparent in his poetry, drama and essays, but is not merely literary. It shows itself in his letters to the Nigerian papers which can always be relied upon to rouse enthusiastic support or bitter opposition. Indeed it is this very concern, and the speed with which he translates ideas into action that puts him so often at odds with institutions and governments. His dramatic resignation from the University of Ife, the celebrated Radio Station episode, and his detention during most of the Nigerian Civil War are all examples of Soyinka in uncomfortably exposed positions as a result of deeply held convictions. And yet, Soyinka constantly insists that he is not a 'committed' writer. All that this really means, as he explains in the *Spear* interview [*Spear,* May 1966], is that he is 'not committed to any ideology'. There can be few writers who believe more deeply in freedom and are prepared to sacrifice as much for it. In his own words:

> I believe there is no reason why human beings should not enjoy maximum freedom. In living together in society, we agree to lose some of our freedom. To detract from the maximum freedom socially possible, to me, is treacherous. I do not believe in dictatorship benevolent or malevolent.

It is from deeply held convictions like these that the 'works' both literary and social flow. Soyinka is a unified personality; the artist and the man are one.

The essential ideas which emerge from a reading of Soyinka's work are not specially African ideas although his characters and their mannerisms are African. His concern is with man on earth. Man is dressed for the nonce in African dress and lives in the sun and the tropical forest, but he represents the whole race. The duality of man's personality, his simultaneous capacity for creation and destruction which makes him almost at every moment a potential victim of his own ingenuity, is a universal trait of *homo sapiens* who has been given by his creator the gift of free will. In *A Dance of the Forests,* the Yoruba style deity, Forest Father, represents the creator, and Demoke the Yoruba carver represents man. Any universal god or any abstraction for the source of life could take Forest Father's place just as any man of sensibility could take the place of the Yoruba artist.

SALVATION AND THE INDIVIDUAL WILL

Soyinka sees society as being in continual need of salvation from itself. This act of salvation is not a mass act; it comes about through the vision and dedication of individuals who doggedly pursue their vision in spite of the opposition of the very society they seek to save. They frequently end up as the victims of the society which benefits from their vision. The salvation of the society then depends on the exercise of the individual will. Thus the act of Atunda, the Yoruba slave who fragmented the unified essence and produced many individual essences or gods, is celebrated in 'Idanre' as are other individual deities or inspired men (prophets) who by the exercise of their individual will

transformed the lives of men. The Yoruba figure then is paralleled by figures from all universal religions. Atunda is a symbol for a universal idea which Yoruba mythology and religion conveniently supplies.

If the individual will is so important, society must enable it to be exercised freely. For Soyinka any form of political repression is a suppression of this individual will, which is the force through which new ideas and new life proceed. The suppression of the individual will is thus a suppression of the very forces of life. This is the point of the play *Kongi's Harvest,* to give just one prominent example of the theme. This is not a Yoruba or an African idea. If it has validity, this is a general validity. The clash between the individual and the society which Soyinka so often portrays in African terms is a universal phenomenon; the martyr who is the positive product of the clash is also fortunately (I reproduce Soyinka's irony) universal.

The individual with a vision for society has to communicate this vision and to disseminate it if society is to be improved by it. The tragic irony which appeared in a number of Soyinka's works was that the visionary remained misunderstood and isolated, and often died before his message was understood. Soyinka's own experience, as he saw men whose views and attitudes he thought held promise for Nigeria—Victor Banjo and Major Fajuyi, for example—die without seeing their ideas reach any fulfilment, would have confirmed how often this circumstance attended human affairs. It was still the duty of the visionary to pursue his course, lonely or not, since as in the case of his dreamer in the poem of that name, the ideas once sown may sprout even after the death of the sower. False prophets, by contrast, seem to produce more instant growths, like seeds on stony ground. In works like *Kongi's Harvest* the focus is turned a little on *groups* of faithful followers of reformist leaders. Segi and Daodu had their groups of women and young farmers in opposition to the tyranny of Kongi's rule in *Kongi's Harvest.* In *The Man Died* Soyinka is impressed by the strength conveyed by the song of the group of Ibo prisoners, and his post-prison novel, *Season of Anomy,* portrays a community with a philosophy and a corporate vision as a catalyst for reform. This is a shift of emphasis. The leaders are still there, still dreaming and daring often alone—Ofeyi, like Orpheus, has to take the decision to make his journey through Hell alone—but attention is also given to the supporting group of ordinary men and women who are the society.

CONCERN FOR LIFE

Soyinka's work celebrates life, and deprecates its opposite. This opposite includes minor internal repressions, but it also embraces the general wastefulness of war. This is an aspect of Soyinka's work that is more obviously relevant to the whole modern world. Again he finds Yoruba mythology handy with the enveloping images. Ogun, temporarily maddened by drink, and indiscriminately killing friend and foe, is a personalization of the idea of the senseless waste that war brings. The message of 'Idanre' is a universal one, equally applicable (only more so) to those who are armed with nuclear weapons as to those who have only swords. The Nigerian Civil War, a national catastrophe gloomily foreshadowed in *A Dance of the Forests,* was thus to Soyinka an awful and unnecessary waste, a negation of the principle of life. Since to him literature was only one manifestation of life, he involved himself totally in efforts to frustrate the pursuit of the war, with results in terms of personal suffering which are only too well-known.

A minor variation on the destruction of human potential, is man's destruction of the environment. This is a theme—pollution—which has become popular in recent years in the industrialized world. In many parts of Africa it still seems remote. Indeed Africa is at the stage when it is actually clamouring for the factors of pollution as fast as it can obtain them. In one of his earliest plays (and funniest, so that the point is often missed) Soyinka gives the 'backward' Oba of Ilujinle a plea for the environment:

> And the wish of one old man is
> That here and there,
> Among the bridges and the murderous roads,
> Below the humming birds which
> Smoke the face of Sango, dispenser of
> The snake-tongued lightning; between this mo-
>   ment
> And the reckless broom that will be wielded
> In these years to come, we must leave
> Virgin plots of lives, rich decay
> And the tang of vapour rising from
> Forgotten heaps of compost, lying
> Undisturbed . . .

Human life presents constant challenges and constant choices, and man has to thread his way through all the contradictory alternatives. Soyinka himself seems to prefer the personality of Ogun who has always lived a life amidst the challenges and the risks of wrong choices. Ogun (unlike the eternal penitent Obatala who forbids wine to his worshippers), 'in proud acceptance of the need to create a challenge for the constant exercise of will and control, enjoins the liberal joy of wine'. A similar characteristic of Dionysos is no doubt one of the reasons why Soyinka found Euripides' play *The Bacchae* an interesting one to adapt. It is in response to the challenges that man moves towards true wisdom, battered and bruised by his experiences. This is the kind of pilgrimage through all life's opportunities and hazards that Soyinka gives the young interpreters in his novel.

These are the kinds of huge concerns which remain in the mind when the particular mannerisms through which they are expressed in individual works have been forgotten. These are the sorts of ideas which give Wole Soyinka his universal appeal. (pp. 3-14)

> *Eldred Durosimi Jones, in his* The Writing of Wole Soyinka, *third edition, Heinemann Educational Books Ltd., 1988, 242 p.*

DEATH AND THE KING'S HORSEMAN

PRODUCTION REVIEWS

Clive Barnes   (review date 2 March 1987)

[*Barnes is an English critic who has worked as the associate editor and chief drama and dance critic for the* New York Post *since 1978. He also served as dance critic (1965-78) and daily drama critic (1967-78) for the* New York Times. *The following review comments on the 1987 Lincoln Center production of* Death and the King's Horseman. *Barnes applauds Soyinka's play, calling it "poetically fascinating in its grasp of souls and their journeys." Though he criticizes Soyinka for portraying the British through "crude, cartoon-like" political satire and for the "far-fetched parallel" he draws between Yoruban ritual suicide and a fancy masquerade attended by the British colonialists, Barnes appreciates the work for lyrically presenting "eternal matters of the soul" with "a stern note of tragedy."*]

Most plays if they were to be seen in terms of music drama take on the aspect of operas, operettas, or Broadway musicals.

Once in a while one gets a play whose texture, sense of static contemplation, and general thematic complexity suggests more a cantata or oratorio.

Such a work is **Death and the King's Horseman,** by the 1986 Nobel-laureate Nigerian playwright Wole Soyinka, which was opened by the Lincoln Center Theater at the Vivian Beaumont last night. It is thoughtful, static, and epic.

It is concerned with the transcendent power of religious duty. Its dramatic strands are rich, varied, and at times twisted, arrestingly, to what at first seem to be cross purposes, until those purposes stand unravelled and revealed.

The play, which dates from 1975, is based on a real incident that happened in Nigeria in 1946, at the end of the British Colonial rule. Soyinka, for various dramatic reasons, small but pertinent, has pushed the incident back two years.

Its story is embedded in the myth and ritual of the Yoruba people, the dominant race of Southern Nigeria, where the play is set.

It opens in a town marketplace. A great king has died and is to be given a ceremonial burial. The climax of the ceremony must be the death of Elesin, the traditional "Horseman" of the King—in life, the King's closest friend and adviser.

According to ritual and custom, Elesin will die and follow his master; his death will be willed by himself. He will commit ritual suicide simply by ceasing to live, an act of human destiny.

Yoruba religion sees the world as one of transition between that which is to come, that which is, and that which was. Such natural transitions are the heart of Yoruban culture. Elesin's death symbolizes such transitions.

The preparations are in hand. On the night of his death, Elesin, as is the custom, will take a new bride, and he chooses, against advice, a young virgin.

The ritual comes to the ears of the local British District Officer, Simon Pilkings, who with his wife is about to a attend a fancy-dress ball to be held at the British Residency in honor of some visiting Royal personage.

Horrified at the idea of ritual suicide, Pilkings issues orders that such a pagan procedure be stopped.

At the ball, where with strange insensitivity the Pilkings have gone dressed in ceremonial Yoruba burial garments, Pilkings is worried by news of a disturbance in town.

He and his wife are also surprised by the arrival of Elesin's son Olunde, whom they had helped, against parental wishes, to go to England to study medicine. Olunde has, it seems, come back to play his part in his father's dance of death.

From the play's slow start—it is like a windy version of a Yeats poetic drama, with the principal characters attempting a Shakespearean stature—it moves, with the arrival of the British, into crude, cartoon-like political satire.

Here the tone changes; the high-flown poetry evaporates, and with the authenticity of the broadly comic English, we are reminded that Soyinka once spent six years on the staff of London's Royal Court Theater.

At this point the play seems to be precisely about that very "facile tag of 'clash of cultures,' " which Soyinka specifically warns against in his smuggish "Author's Note" in the program. It is almost Kiplingesque.

But then the play shows its final hand. The blowhard, uncertain, ecstatic, yet oddly worldly character Earle Hyman has been portraying as Elesin becomes clear: the man is a moral renegade.

He has not the strength to will the transition of death. The powers of present flesh, indicated by his choice of the beautiful virgin, are too much for him. It is left to his son to make the final statement.

This play in three movements—and again the musical comparision is not unintentional—is difficult to empathize with.

The concept of ritual suicide accompanying a King's death is repellent to our present European sensibility; and Soyinka's sly comparision between Yoruba ritual and the make-believe finery of a fancy-dress ball is far-fetched, for the latter is scarcely a matter of life and death.

But the play does force one to consider the inflexible morality of belief (the Spanish Inquisition, and perhaps even Adolf Hitler, subscribed to such moralities) and the threnodic theme and structure of the play eventually becomes overwhelmingly impressive.

Whatever else the play is, from the broad canvas of its opening to its final processional ceremony, it is dealing lyrically with eternal matters of the soul and human belief. And, in the end, it is that universal concern that colors the play purple, and gives it the stern note of tragedy.

Soyinka has directed the play himself—a little self-indulgently perhaps with regards to the comedy, but his sense of the ritual and passion is unerring.

David Gropman's settings handle the supposedly intransigent Beaumont stage with great skill, Pat Collins's lighting suggests the African night as well as the African sun, while Judy Dearing's costumes make all the right Nigerian and Colonial noises.

Of the performances Hyman's complex rendering of the deviously heroic Elesin, the King's reluctant horseman, is superb in its sense of nervous confidence and final moral collapse.

The rest seem authentically Nigerian. From Trazana Beverley the female conscience of the Market to Eriq La Salle in the Sidney Poitier-like role (Soyinka should watch out for Hollywood stereotypes while he is so busy giving America lessons) of the noble eldest son.

Alan Coates and Jill Larson are admirably straightforward as the British couple trapped in an alien web.

This is both a play of wonder, and a play worth wondering

about; imperfect, difficult to Western ears, but poetically fascinating in its grasp of souls and their journeys.

> Clive Barnes, "In the Heart of Africa: A Clash of Cultures," in New York Post, March 2, 1987.

Frank Rich   (review date 2 March 1987)

[*Since 1977, Rich has been the chief cinema and television critic for* Time *magazine. He is also a contributor to* Ms., *the* New York Times, *and* Esquire. *Below, Rich calls Soyinka's* Death and the King's Horseman *"baffling" and "stupefying." The critic contends that the production's poor acting overshadowed the play's interesting discussion of metaphysical issues and rich language, adding that, despite the author's claims to the contrary, the drama was easily reduced to a "clash of cultures."*]

There's a lot of reading material available to those unsuspecting theatergoers who stumble into Wole Soyinka's **Death and the King's Horseman** at the Vivian Beaumont. The Lincoln Center Theater management has seen fit to provide not only a plot synopsis in the Playbill but also a handbill containing a second synopsis (longer but still unilluminating), descriptions of the leading characters and historical background and, finally, an author's note in which the playwright gives his own work a rave review. Is somebody trying to tell us something? I'm afraid so. Even with the elaborate documentation, **Death and the King's Horseman** is frequently baffling in this production, and even when it's coherent, it's stupefying. During the first half, one hears the constant sound of Playbills rustling, as the audience tries to figure out what's going on. After intermission comes a kind of resigned hush, most of the survivors having given up.

As anyone who has read Mr. Soyinka's childhood memoir, **Aké**, knows, he is one of the world's outstanding writers—that rare recent Nobel laureate (1986) whose prize did not prompt widespread critical dispute. What Mr. Soyinka does not seem to be is a stage director, at least when working with largely American casts. In 1984 at Yale, he mounted his brilliant, savage satire about African dictators, **A Play of Giants,** with all the comic verve of a window dresser arranging a department-store display of mannequins. Mr. Soyinka's staging of **Death and the King's Horseman**—nearly as static and more incompetently performed—eviscerates a work that could well offer some of the "threnodic essence" the author's note describes.

Written in the mid-1970's, the play was inspired by an actual incident in the Nigeria of 1946. The King's Horseman, a chief in the ancient city of Oyo, prepares to commit suicide so he may join his recently deceased King in the next world. Before this Yoruban ritual is carried out, however, a Colonial District Officer intervenes in the name of British notions of "civilization." The inexorably tragic results of this interference, like Mr. Soyinka's use of a five-act structure, lend **Death and the King's Horseman** a classical shape.

In his program note, the playwright argues that it would

be "facile," "prejudicial" and "reductionist" to say this work is about a "clash of cultures." Yet that's the way the drama comes across here. Much of the evening is lavished on detailed illustration and explanation of Yoruban cultural traditions—which stand in stark contrast to the behavior of the English twits, who are seen preparing for a decadent costume ball even as they decry the Africans' "barbaric," "savage" and "feudalistic" ways. In a similar vein, the chief's honorable ritual suicide is set in didactic opposition to the white man's "mass suicide" of World War II—this, in spite of Mr. Soyinka's claim that he changed the story's timeframe from postwar 1946 to 1944 only "for minor reasons of dramaturgy."

Because of the poor acting, the virtues of the play's political arguments, metaphysical ambitions and rich language alike are rendered moot. The lead actors—Earle Hyman (the King's Horseman), Ben Halley Jr. (the village "Praise Singer" or "griot") and Trazana Beverley (leader of the women's chorus)—do Yoruban culture no favor by mangling their poetic speeches with odd phrasings, absurdly clipped final consonants and unintentional lapses into broad American accents. The bright Judy Dearing costumes aside, the singing, dancing and chanting inhabitants of the Oyo marketplace seem equally unconvincing. Whether laughing in studied unison or engaging in mock flirtations during scene transitions, these are patronizingly presented "natives" reminiscent of the unspontaneous extras in Dino De Laurentiis film epics like "Hurricane" and the remake of "King Kong."

The English fare even worse. (Mr. Soyinka wrote the play while at Cambridge University.) Their dialogue is standard B-movie colonialese—"You're just a savage like all the rest!" shrieks the District Officer's wife to an educated, outspoken African—and they spend too much time cocking their ears toward the ominous beat of distant village drums. In the roles of the colony's most burdened white couple, Alan Coates and Jill Larson are so caricatured that even Rudyard Kipling might find their upper lips a bit stiff.

Whatever the other faults of the production, the much-maligned Beaumont auditorium itself is not to blame: David Gropman's parched white set, lighted with typical finesse by Pat Collins, effectively thrusts the action forward into the audience. Still, one can't so easily absolve the Beaumont's artistic director, Gregory Mosher, who previously produced **Death and the King's Horseman**—also under its author's direction—in Chicago in 1979. Is this what's meant by beating a dead horse?

> Frank Rich, "Soyinka's 'Death and the King's Horseman'," in The New York Times, March 2, 1987, p. C13.

Allan Wallach   (review date 2 March 1987)

[*In the following assessment of the New York production of* Death and the King's Horseman, *Wallach judges the play ineffective as a tragedy. The critic claims that Earle Hyman failed to convey Elesin Oba's "infectious enjoyment of life" and eventual despair and that this character's metaphysical journey through ritual suicide was "more a subject for debater's points than an event that grips the imagination."*]

Elesin Oba is a life-embracing Yoruba chief whose principal role is to die. As the king's horseman, he must go to his death in a ritual sacrifice on the day of his master's ceremonial burial, so that he may accompany him into the next world.

This ultimate service—and a British officer's inability to comprehend it—is the subject of **Death and the King's Horseman,** by Wole Soyinka, winner of the 1986 Nobel Prize for Literature. Only now, a decade after its first performance in Soyinka's native Nigeria, has the play arrived on a New York stage, Lincoln Center's Vivian Beaumont.

The author has directed the production himself (as he did earlier ones in Chicago and Washington), giving it a bright wash of color. At the beginning, vendors troop down the Beaumont's aisles before hawking their wares in a bustling market. Elesin embraces both a new marriage and his ritual death to the accompaniment of throbbing drums and costumed dancers. These occasions contrast sharply with the politely correct costume ball held by pallid British colonials.

The drama in **Death and the King's Horseman** is more subdued than the colorful set pieces. Lengthy poetic speeches make emotions remote and give the play a slow, almost stately pace. The climactic scene has the inevitability of Greek tragedy, but its impact is curiously muted.

Soyinka wrote that the play is based on events that took place in Oyo, an ancient Yoruba city of Nigeria, in 1946, although he set the action back to the time of World War II for reasons of dramaturgy.

In his telling, Elesin (Earle Hyman) is a man whose robust vigor is manifested by his attentions to the women vendors in the market. As he banters with the "Praise Singer" (Ben Halley Jr.), he seems more attached to this world and its pleasures than prepared for the next. He even plans to take a young wife, choosing the future daughter-in-law of Iyaloja, "Mother" of the Market (Trazana Beverley).

When the district officer, Simon Pilkings (Alan Coates), receives word of the proposed death ceremony, he dispatches police to seize and incarcerate Elesin. Pilkings and his wife, Jane (Jill Larson), head off to the ball—blithely unconcerned that their costumes, the attire of a Yoruba death cult, are deeply offensive to Nigerians. In that inappropriate costume, Pilkings sets in motion a disastrous chain of events.

Much of the play's force depends on the central performance. Hyman plays Elesin with the requisite good humor in the early scenes, yet he doesn't convey what the author calls "that infectious enjoyment of life which accompanies all his actions." Later, his despair falls short of tragic dimension.

Other performances are capable, although Coates and Larson are hampered by the thinly drawn roles of well-meaning whites. As the Mother of the Market, Beverley is a commanding figure, and Eriq La Salle is effective as

Elesin's son, a medical student who has returned from England to bury him.

The son also has the burden of lecturing Mrs. Pilkings on colonialism and the folly of meddling in affairs beyond outsiders' understanding. He makes a telling point when he compares the interference in one man's ritual suicide with the acceptance of "mass suicide" in World War II.

Soyinka has warned against giving the play the facile label of "clash of cultures." The confrontation, he wrote, "is largely metaphysical, contained in the human vehicle which is Elesin and the universe of the Yoruba mind . . . " On the Beaumont's vast stage, the human dimension is diminished. The desired journey of the king's horseman is more a subject for debaters' points than an event that grips the imagination.

> *Allan Wallach, "Soyinka on Sacrifice and Understanding," in* Newsday, *March 2, 1987.*

John Beaufort   (review date 4 March 1987)

[*In the following review, Beaufort praises the 1987 Lincoln Center production of* Death and the King's Horseman, *calling it a "fascinatingly rich tapestry in dramatic form." He notes especially Earle Hyman's "exceptional strength, authority, and eloquence" in portraying the king's horseman Elesin Oba.*]

Toting their wares, the market people converge from the aisles onto the blazingly lit stage of the Vivian Beaumont Theater. Their convergence, with drums and singing, establishes the extraordinary pulse and teeming human presence of **Death and the King's Horseman,** Wole Soyinka's poetic drama set in 1944 Nigeria. The play is having its New York premiere at Lincoln Center. This prelude of color and motion transports the spectator to the scene of the events that follow.

The marketplace hubbub climaxes with the arrival of Elesin, Horseman of the King (Earle Hyman). Elesin is about to meet the ritual, self-imposed death which will, according to tribal superstition, join him with the king, whose demise occurred a month previously. ("No one will kill him. He will simply die.") The scene includes the first of the flights of eloquence in which Mr. Soyinka establishes the flamboyantly noble character of the king's horseman. It is left to Olohun-iyo, the Praise Singer (Ben Halley Jr.) to express the crowd's fervent admiration of this legendary warrior, the late king's closest friend.

Elesin (pronounced El-ee-shin) responds in a variety of ways to the general adulation. After briefly teasing his admirers, he delivers an ironic commentary on the "Not I" behind which the frightened hide when death approaches. Finally he selects a beautiful young girl, already betrothed, to be his "bride" before he ends his life.

Soyinka quickly shifts the scene to the bungalow veranda where British District Officer Simon Pilkings (Alan Coates) and his wife, Jane (Jill Larson), are tangoing in anticipation of the evening's fancy-dress ball at the British residency. They are interrupted by Sergeant Amusa (Ernest Perry Jr.), who is appalled and terrified to discover them wearing "death" costumes confiscated from some recently arrested cultists. When Pilkings is apprised of Elesin's intention, he begins trying to avert the fatal ritual.

Death and the King's Horseman chronicles the tragic effects of his blundering efforts. (The play is based on an actual incident.) The situation is complicated by the arrival of Elesin's eldest son, Olunde (Eriq La Salle), who has been studying medicine in England. To the dismay of the naively well-meaning Jane, Olunde accepts his father's forthcoming self-sacrifice.

Nobel laureate Soyinka dramatizes the complex of countercurrents in a variety of ways. Such intense confrontations as those between the Pilkings and Olunde contrast with the hilarious free-for-all in which some obstreperous schoolgirls make fools of three black policemen. Underneath it all lie the irreconcilables of a situation in which obtuse occupiers run roughshod over a native population. Apart, however, from his contempt for the contemptuous British, the author gives no indication of whether he condemns or condones Elesin's death-willing act.

Notwithstanding four pages of background notes, some of the play's more extended poetic and mystical passages may create difficulties of understanding for the uninitiated spectator. But *Death and the King's Horseman* is nevertheless a fascinatingly rich tapestry in dramatic form. As his own director, Soyinka has staged a performance that blends individual elements with the populous pageant that embraces the plot's unfoldment.

Mr. Hyman brings exceptional strength, authority, and eloquence to the central role of Elesin. This magnificent actor is equal to every demand of the role, whether Elesin is glorying in his warriorship or physically diminishing into an almost wraithlike figure. Besides those already mentioned, the fine cast includes Trazana Beverley as the "Mother" of the Market, Sylvia Best as the silent Bride, Abdoulaye N'Gom as the Pilkings's Christian houseboy, and Dillon Evans as the British Resident.

The large ensemble contributes to the sense of ritual, rhythmic movement, and atmosphere, as do the accompanying drummers (Kimati Dinizulu, Yomi Obileye, Tunji Oyelana, Edwina Lee Tyler).

Judy Dearing's resplendent costumes set the visual tone. The production . . . is equally well served by David Gropman's scenery and Pat Collins's lighting.

> John Beaufort, "Nigerian Drama Blends Plot, Pageantry," in The Christian Science Monitor, *March 4, 1987, p. 23.*

CRITICAL COMMENTARY

Mark Ralph-Bowman   (essay date 1983)

[*In the following essay, Ralph-Bowman explains Soyinka's* Death and the King's Horseman *as the converging of two movements. The first, in acts one and three, focuses on Elesin Oba, who represents "the embodiment of the mythology and the history of his people," while the* second, in acts two and four, centers on the "sterile, existential wasteland" of the white colonialists. In act five, the two movements meet in the sacrifice of Elesin's European-educated son Olunde whose death, the critic contends, represents "a significant and uncompromising affirmation of traditional cosmology." Ralph-Bowman claims blasphemy is the main reason for Elesin's failure: by refusing sacrificial suicide, Elesin denies his community and ignores his sacred duty. He then compares Elesin to African leaders who have forsaken their own culture and embrace alien, Western values.]

> But most of you may face up to the reality, the hard brutal facts of our social and economic reality. You may face up to these honestly, and up to the consequences, as to where your duty and responsibility lies. You may refuse and follow the parade and march-past of all parasitical and retrograde forces into the dung-heap of history.
> [Y. B. Usman, *For the Liberation of Nigeria*]

As the war of Biafran secession receded into the past, Nigerians faced once more the issues they had confronted before the hostilities began in July 1967. In certain senses the scars of the civil war may never be healed, but in others the war changed nothing and the issues facing the nation remained the same. There was the question of federal unity, coupled with the vexed question of religious divisions; the quest for a national language; the return to civilian rule, but perhaps the most important and fundamental to all was the matter of oil revenues and how most productively to use them. This problem of how to distribute wealth was neither unique nor new to Nigeria but, after more than a decade of independence, a reassessment of the situation was in order. At about the time of independence Wole Soyinka had written three plays each of which contributed to the birth of a nation. With the reassertion of one nation implied by the federal victory in the civil war the time was ripe for a review of the ideals and admonitions that had informed *A Dance of the Forests, The Lion and the Jewel,* and *The Swamp Dwellers.* Some fourteen years after independence Soyinka goes back to events that occurred fourteen years before it. While too much ought not to be made of this fact it is probably not accidental in the work of a man with as strong a sense of history as Soyinka's. It is difficult to resist the sense of déjà vu in the selection of events in *Death and the King's Horseman,* difficult to resist the conclusion that the forces at work in colonial 1946 are seen by Soyinka to be at work in postcolonial 1974.

A synopsis of the plot of *Death and the King's Horseman* makes the play seem pretty uncomplicated. The king of Oyo has died and the tradition requires his chief horseman, Elesin Oba, to die in order to accompany him on his journey to the world of the ancestors. It is the eve of Elesin Oba's death and there is an atmosphere charged with excitement and expectation, such as is appropriate for any significant religious event. On his last day in this life the Horseman can be denied nothing, not even a new bride whose

> wrapper was no disguise
> For thighs whose ripples shamed the river's
> Coils around the hills of Ilesi.

Ben Halley, Jr. as the Praise Singer and Earle Hyman as Elesin in the 1987 production of Death and the King's Horseman *directed by Soyinka.*

Meanwhile, the English Prince of Wales is visiting the town and the District Officer, Simon Pilkings, is anxious that all goes smoothly. He feels that a ritual suicide by a major figure in the local hierarchy during the Prince's visit would not enhance his career prospects in the colonial service. He decides to intervene. He arrests the Horseman. Olunde, Elesin Oba's son, away in England against his father's wishes, having heard that his father is to die, returns to pay his last respects. The failure of his father to die in the appropriate manner is spiritually and socially disruptive as well as shameful, so Olunde takes his father's place.

It is in the nature of synopses to fail to do justice to the work in question and nowhere is this more true than in this instance. *Death and the King's Horseman* is complex and tightly woven and, as one has come to expect from Soyinka, enigmatic. The enigma of this play is not of Soyinka's making, though it is of his choosing. At the heart of this play is a religious mystery. Not that *Death and the King's Horseman* is a religious treatise but, if one is to appreciate the full significance of the consternation caused by Elesin Oba's failure to "commit death" one has to appreciate something of the cosmology fundamental to the play.

In **"The Fourth Stage"** and later in *Myth, Literature and the African World,* Soyinka explores what he understands to be the relation in Yoruba cosmology between man, the gods, and the ancestors. The essence of this cosmology, as he expounds it, is in direct contradiction to the Christian and European emphasis on the individual and individual salvation. For the Yoruba the emphasis is on community,

and community in this context makes no distinction between the dead, the living, and the unborn. The emphasis is on continuity, on maintaining the continuous and contiguous relationship of these three stages of being. All-important in this relationship is the Fourth Stage, which is the vital link between the three stages. Soyinka sees the Fourth Stage in contradistinction with the Christian concept of Death in which man is essentially changed. The Fourth Stage is to Soyinka the world neither of the dead nor of the living; its ineffable nature is explored in *Death and the King's Horseman* through the image of the Passage.

The play itself opens with the stage direction "A passage through a market. . . . " Elesin Oba himself first appears along another passage and after his taunting, satirical Not-I Bird dance he calls on all present to

> Watch me dance along the narrowing path
> Glazed by the soles of my great precursors.

His sighting of the young girl and his wish to marry her as his last act in this world precipitates a heated discussion in the course of which the image of the Passage develops from a passage to passage itself, from a route to a process. Elesin Oba commands thus:

> All you who stand before the spirit that dares
> The opening of the last door of passage,
> Dare to rid my going of regrets!

Elesin Oba is "the voyager at his passage." He is about to undergo a transition, but it is more subtle than that. He is not only to undergo a transition, to go along the Passage, he is Transition itself, he is the Passage. In accepting that the young girl and Elesin Oba be married, Iyaloja expresses the hope that any child of the union should be

> neither of this world nor of the next. Nor of the one behind us. As if the timelessness of the ancestor world and the unborn have joined spirits to wring an issue of the elusive being of passage . . . Elesin!

When Elesin Oba brings the stained cloth of the marriage bed to Iyaloja as proof of the consummation of the marriage he declares

> It is no mere virgin stain, but the union of life and the seeds of passage . . . When earth and passage wed, the consummation is complete only when there are grains of earth on the eyelids of passage.

Thus the Passage is conceived as both the passing through a stage of existence and that stage of existence itself, it is both passing and to pass, both gerund and infinitive. Thus Elesin Oba is both the mediator between the dead and the living as well as mediation itself. He is both act and actor, which brings him paradoxically close to the Christian theology of the relationship between the Father and the Son. Such is the significance of Elesin Oba and his role in the play and this significance explains one reason why the drama should not be trivialized into a matter of "culture conflict."

Elesin Oba, however, fails. This failure does not mean that Soyinka is portraying the collapse of a cosmology or the failure of traditional wisdom or values. As with most tragedy—and several critics of this play gratuitously point out a five-act structure analogous to that of classic western tragedy—one major critical problem posed by the play is to find the affirmation concealed by the disaster. From this play one of the most forceful impressions carried away is that of Elesin Oba's failure. How can failure such as his be understood to be affirmation?

The answer is that the play is not about failure, a fact that becomes clear if the "five-act structure" is ignored and the whole western tradition of individual tragedy forgotten. Soyinka has charged [in *The Man Died*] that we should

> suspect all conscious search for the self's authentic being; this is favourite fodder for the enervating tragic Muse. *I do not seek; I find.* Let actions alone be the manifestations of the authentic being in defence of its authentic visions. History is too full of failed prometheans bathing their wounded spirits in the tragic stream.

The structure of *Death and the King's Horseman* is that of two converging movements, one of which begins with Elesin Oba in Act One and follows him through Act Three to Act Five where it fuses with the other which begins in Act Two, proceeds through Act Four and fuses with the first when Olunde replaces Elesin Oba as the being of passage.

The first movement is dominated by Elesin Oba, a dramatic creation unrivalled in African drama beside whom even such a character as Oduwale in Rotimi's *The Gods Are Not To Blame* seems paltry. The ability to bring the character

of Elesin Oba off the page and onto the stage will for long be the yardstick of an actor's skill. Elesin dances, boasts, teases, jokes, lusts, and finally despairs his way to dramatic immortality, and great will be the performance that carries each stage of this process to a successful conclusion. But it is not merely an individual that Soyinka has created, for, through this character come reverberations not only of earlier Soyinkan creations but also the great figures of Yoruba mythology. D. S. Izevbaye [in "Mediation in Soyinka: The Case of the King's Horseman" in *Critical Perspectives on Wole Soyinka*, edited by James Gibbs, 1981] has pointed out the significance of Esu Elegba in this context: Esu Elegba whom he describes as "the principle of uncertainty, fertility and change, the one god who makes possible the reconciliation of opposites." Izevbaye has also pointed out the "Ogun-like courage of Elesin in the climactic Third Act." Besides these there is another suggestive resonance in this character, Oranyan. Oranyan, son of the great progenitor of the Yoruba who had as one responsibility the defence of his people. This defence Oranyan undertook single-handed while the people stood by, like a Greek chorus, forbidden to intervene. Elesin Oba, on behalf of his people, also single-handed, had to join the dead king to prevent the destruction of his people. The other characters do not intervene, even at the iconoclastic intervention of Pilkings.

Thus Elesin Oba is an embodiment of the mythology and the history of his people and a performance of the play is, as [Femi] Osofisan suggests [in *Theatre in Africa*, 1978] "the ritual itself." The play is a celebration of Yoruba culture and is to be enacted through an "evocation of music from the abyss of transition" (Soyinka's note on the play). In this respect it accords with the distinction Soyinka makes between western drama and African drama in *Myth, Literature and the African World*.

> The serious divergences between a traditional African approach to drama and the European will not be found in lines of opposition between creative individualism and communal creativity, nor in the level of noise from the auditorium— this being the supposed gauge of audience participation—at any given performance. They will be found more accurately in what is a recognisable Western cast of mind, a compartmentalising habit of thought which periodically selects aspects of human emotion, phenomenal observations, metaphysical intuitions and even scientific deductions and turns them into separatist myths (or 'truths') sustained by a proliferating superstructure of presentation idioms, analogies and analytical modes . . . the difference which we are seeking to define between European and African drama as one of man's formal representation of experience is not simply a difference of style or form, nor is it confined to drama alone. It is representative of the essential difference between two world views, a difference between one culture whose very artifacts are evidence of a cohesive understanding of irreducible truths and another, whose creative impulses are directed by period dialectics.

Death and the King's Horseman is not a literary enactment of some significant but past moment, of some unique historical event or personality, but, in the words of the Christian church, a sacramental activity. Yet, Elesin Oba fails. Is the play therefore a sacrament of failure, a celebration of the impotence of tradition, a Yoruba version of Frederich Nietzsche's "God is Dead"?

Were one to study the play as a classic five-act construction, such a conclusion as that suggested might be reached since Elesin Oba is the "protagonist" and he fails. If, however, one observes the structure to be that of two converging movements, such a reading is impossible. The main thrust of the first movement has been pointed out above. The second movement begins in Act Two in the house of the District Officer, Simon Pilkings. This house and the Residency in Act Four represent a sterile, existential wasteland. Pilkings and his wife have no religious awe themselves and deride such awe whenever they are confronted by it, dismissing it as "mumbo-jumbo" and "nonsense." Jane Pilkings observes, with a tellingly condescending contradiction, "I think you've shocked his big pagan heart *bless him*" (my emphasis). Who or what is to confer blessings from their cosmological vacuum? Neither she nor her husband respect Egungun, Islam, Christianity, or traditional wisdom, yet Jane can pronounce to Olunde later in the play that "life should never be thrown deliberately away." If there is no respect for death there can be no respect for life. It is in this essentially pagan environment that the second movement of the play begins.

In Act Two, besides the Pilkings, Soyinka introduces three characters although one of them, Olunde, is only announced and does not appear until Act Four. The other two, Sergeant Amusa and Joseph, demonstrate differing, yet related, responses to the colonial experience, which is depicted in this play more in terms of its spiritual than its physical or political significance. Both Amusa and Joseph have been spiritually colonized. Both have taken alien religions and both have, by virtue of those religions, been cut off from their cultural roots. Sergeant Amusa is an emasculated figure of mockery who is routed by the market women while pursuing his confused idea of duty, although he does, ultimately, resist the crude bullying of Pilkings. Joseph manages to retain a chilling dignity in his confrontation with Pilkings, but his victory over the D.O. is ultimately hollow since it is clear he has no place outside the enervated missionary circles of the Very Reverend Macfarlane, as is evidenced by his ignorance of what is taking place in the market. Ignorance of events in the market is ignorance of the real world since "Oja L'aiye, Orun n'ile" [The world is a market, heaven is home]. Thus it would appear from the examples of Joseph and Amusa that entanglement with "the ghostly ones" and their ways, more importantly, a separation from the traditional values and beliefs of the culture, leads to an alienated deracination. Act Two also leads us to believe that Elesin Oba's son has deserted his home, its responsibilities, and its values. Olunde is described as a sensitive young man who "should be munching rose petals in Bloomsbury" but whose mind is set on being a doctor and who is actively trying to maintain contact with his father's great enemy, Pilkings. Olunde, with the assistance of Pilkings, "escaped" from the "close confinement" imposed by his father and ran away to England. Given the picture of Amusa and Joseph,

one's expectation is for a newer model of Soyinka's earlier Frankenstein monstrosity, Lakunle.

In Act Four Olunde appears, having heard of the death of the King and wishing to pay his respects to his father whom he expects to find dead. Rather than a man whose roots have been pulled up and despite his "sober western suit," Olunde turns out to be a man whose experience of the world outside has brought a deeper understanding of his heritage and his relation to it. Soyinka is careful not to press the implications of that understanding too early in the play:

> JANE: . . . and to tell the truth, only this evening, Simon and I agreed that we never really knew what you left with.
>
> OLUNDE: Neither did I. But I found out over there. I am grateful to your country for that. And I will never give it up.

In good time Soyinka will reveal the depth of Olunde's conviction. In Olunde's cosmology it is crucial that Elesin Oba dies to join the dead king so the world should not, in the words of Praise Singer, "be wrenched from its true course" or smashed "on the boulders of the great void." When Elesin Oba fails, Olunde undertakes the task of trying to avoid the catastrophe. When, in Act Five, Olunde's body is carried onto the stage the two converging movements of the play meet and through this meeting the affirmation of the play occurs. One movement began in the market place, the world, and led to Elesin Oba's realization of the cause of his failure:

> My will was squelched in the spittle of an alien race, and all because I had committed this blasphemy of thought—that there might be the hand of the gods in a stranger's intervention.

The other movement began in the cultural rag-and-bone shop of the colonial bungalow and developed through to Olunde's death. That death is a significant and uncompromising affirmation of traditional cosmology and a significant and uncompromising indictment of a generation of leaders who have betrayed both it and their trust.

I have suggested that **Death and the King's Horseman** was Soyinka's judgement on the decade or so of Nigerian history up to the time of its composition, more especially of that period in the aftermath of the civil war. In **The Man Died** (a richly suggestive title in the context of **Death and the King's Horseman**) Soyinka writes:

> A war of solidity; for solidity is a far more accurate word than unity to employ in describing a war which can only consolidate the very values that gave rise to the war in the first place, for nowhere and at no time have those values been examined. Nowhere has there appeared a programme designed to ensure the eradication of the fundamental iniquities which gave rise to the initial conflicts.
>
> There will be victors of course, but not the sacrificing masses of Biafra or the rest of the nation. Being glutted and satiated with the expected bonus of war, the élitist pyramid will elide in the natural mechanism of satiation, the fart, will

suck in new élitist sectors, creating a self-consolidating regurgitive, lumpen Mafiadom of the military, the old politicians and business enterprise. After all, a people's combative will is not limitless. The war will have put it to such an intolerable strain that little of it will be left over to challenge the war (power) profiteers when they begin to ride the nation to death. As they will, puffed with the wind of victory, incontestable rulers, the only beneficiaries of the stench of death.

It is one of the triumphs of **Death and the King's Horseman** that it avoids the pitfalls inherent in the tone of Soyinka's bitter prognostication in **The Man Died.** In the play he has avoided splenetic rage, rather transforming it into a compassionate masterpiece. His mood in **The Man Died** is almost uniformly destructive while **Death and the King's Horseman** is effectively constructive. Using Elesin Oba Soyinka has cast in human and humane form the "élitist pyramid [that] will elide in the natural mechanism of satiation." Elesin Oba is victim of his own strengths that are, as is so often the case with the great Prometheans whose cause European tragedy espouses, the cause of his weakness. Soyinka has made Elesin's failure both individual and representative since, as well as being a finely delineated individual character, Elesin Oba is also, as was suggested earlier, the embodiment of the culture of his people and as such he has an awful responsibility. It is quite simply that on him depends the future, on him depends existence itself. Within the cosmology of this play there is no distinction between the future in this incarnation and that of the ancestors. In this context it is worth noting the significance of placing a play of immediate, contemporary relevance in 1946. The implication of the contiguity of past, present, and future is that in any ultimate, essential sense, there is not past, present, or future, only a now, so that failure is external, irrevocable, total destruction in which the ancestors are destroyed along with everything else. The world of the ancestors cannot exist independently of this world nor this world independently of them. A failure now is as final as in 1946, 1846, or 2046. It is for this reason that Iyaloja, mother of the market, mother of the world, allows Elesin Oba no pity when she confronts him in prison:

> You have betrayed us. We fed you sweetmeats such as we hoped awaited you on the other side. But you said No, I must eat the world's left-overs. We said you were the hunter who brought the quarry down; to you belonged the vital portions of the game. No, you said, I am the hunter's dog and I shall eat the entrails of the game and the faeces of the hunter. We said you were the hunter returning home in triumph, a slain buffalo pressing down on his neck; you said wait, I first must turn up this cricket hole with my toes. We said yours was the doorway at which we first spy the tapper when he comes down from the tree, yours was the blessing of the twilight wine, the purl that brings night spirits out of doors to steal their portion before the light of day. We said yours was the body of wine whose burden shakes the tapper like a sudden gust on his perch. You said, No, I am content to lick the dregs from each calabash when the drinkers are

done. We said, the dew on the earth's surface was for you to wash your feet along the slopes of honour. You said No, I shall step in the vomit of cats and the droppings of mice; I shall fight them for the left-overs of the world.

This is a sprawling, searching, evocative speech, as potent in powerful allusions as a brimful keg of palm wine. Through its immediate and direct condemnation of Elesin Oba comes a more far-reaching condemnation of a leadership addicted to leftovers. As with all finely wrought images this one allows the mind ample space to travel from the particular to the general. As the speech proceeds, before the mind's eye passes a sordid picture of devastation and waste: the history of a continent of proud people and magnificent creatures, but the creatures have been destroyed to make feather fans for the chorus girls of Las Vegas, handbags for Mayfair, coats for Paris, aphrodisiacs for Tokyo, while the proud people are reduced to porters or to dependence on Red Cross handouts, erased like the Amerindian or the Aborigine at the instigation of a stranger's intervening economy. Where palm wine and millet beer were suitable refreshment in the past, now only champagne and scotch whisky will do for a man and Babycham for a lady. "Junk food" is ubiquitous. From Coca-Cola to corn flakes the picture is the same as people are

> pressured into dietary tastes and habits whose high cost is related less to nutritive value than to the promotion, packaging and profits of foreign brand owners.
>
> [Susan George, *How the Other Half Dies,* 1977]

It is not accidental that such dietary changes occur as the result of marketing policy. Susan George quotes the board chairman of International Flavours and Fragrances advising others on how to market their products successfully (emphasis added):

> How often we see in developing countries that the poorer the economic outlook, the more important the small luxury of a flavoured soft drink or smoke . . . to the dismay of many would-be benefactors, the poorer the malnourished are, the more likely they are to spend a disproportionate amount of whatever they have on some luxury rather than on what they need. . . . Observe, study, learn [how to sell in rapidly changing rural societies]. *We try to do it at IFF. It seems to pay off for us. Perhaps it will for you too.*

And vultures worry at the piles of imported tin cans that result from this callous indifference. Businessmen from Europe compete with each other for franchises to import food banned in Europe or America. International drug consortia peddle dangerous drugs with criminal irresponsibility knowing they will be distributed by unqualified pharmacists unable to read the instructions written in the minutest of print. Y. B. Usman had this to say on the subject in 1977:

> The peasant in Funtua, Gboko, and Umuahia does not only fail to benefit in any way from this purchase of shares [in transnational companies] by his "countrymen" but actually loses in three

major ways. In the first place, these companies and their agencies are more effectively exploiting him through lower prices (and wages paid to his son in the factory), hoarding, shoddier goods, since they have richer and more powerful "indigenes" working directly for them. Secondly, these companies are more effectively manipulating and milking the peasant by looting the public wealth through tax evasion, foreign exchange rackets, contracts and purchases, because the public institutions are run by people who are their shareholders. Thirdly, the peasant is ultimately divested of his farm because the indigenous shareholder has made so much profit through dividends and hoarding and inflation that he puts him into debt, buys off his farm, creates a large estate (actually a private holiday resort) and makes him both landless and unemployed. That is why when they were squabbling over these shares we asked who made up this "North" likely to benefit from these shares of the "West"; and who made up "the nation" that is supposed to benefit from this "indigenisation". That is why we asked why these companies which were productive were not taken over by public institutions at federal, state, local government levels and by trade union, co-operatives and other collective institutions. Those companies which were not producing anything useful like those importing cosmetics, trinkets and drinks should just be closed down. You can see why the question of whose nation is quite fundamental.

It is not unreasonable to claim that the imaginative scope of Iyaloja's speech of condemnation encompasses all of these visions and more.

At the end of the speech that raises such a ghastly spectre Iyaloja says, "We called you leader and oh, how you led us on." Soon after this assault by Iyaloja comes Elesin Oba's admission of the cause of his failure. From the time of his incarceration he began to probe for the reasons of his failure:

> in the house of *osugbo,* those who keep watch through the spirit recognised the moment, they sent word to me through the voice of our sacred drums to prepare myself. I heard them and I shed all thoughts of earth. I began to follow the moon to the abode of gods . . . servant of the white king, that was when you entered my chosen place of departure on feet of desecration.

This is the initial excuse of a broken man who is trying to find a scapegoat. It is, at bottom, the culture-conflict excuse, a rationalization employed to excuse a setting loose of the responsibilities implied by his culture and his place in it, just another in the train of feeble rationalizations in the process of the accumulation of leftovers. At the nadir of his spiritual fortunes Elesin Oba uses the culture-conflict excuse, but Olunde demonstrates that those who whine of culture conflict employ Eurocentric formulae with no substance. It is no accident that Soyinka wants to avoid the simplistic interpretation of *Death and the King's Horseman* being "about" culture conflict.

Somewhat later in Act Five, alone with his weeping, faith-ful young bride, Elesin Oba is compelled to a more truthful analysis:

> First I blamed the white man, then I blamed my gods for deserting me. Now I feel I want to blame you for the mystery of the sapping of my will. But blame is a strange peace offering for a man to bring a world he has deeply wronged, and to its innocent dwellers. Oh little mother, I have taken countless women in my life but you were more than a desire of the flesh. I needed you as the abyss across which my body must be drawn, I filled it with earth and dropped my seed in it at the moment of preparedness for my crossing. You were the final gift of the living to their emissary to the land of the ancestors, and perhaps your warmth and youth brought new insights of this world to me and turned my feet leaden on this side of the abyss. For I confess to you, daughter, my weakness came not merely from the abomination of the white man who came violently into my fading presence, there was also a weight of longing on my earth-held limbs. I would have shaken it off, already my foot had begun to lift but then, the white ghost entered and all was defiled.

But it is the mother of the world, Iyaloja, who forces from him the awful truth. It is her catalog, discussed above, of his failure as a leader that compels him to acknowledge how he came to fail in his duty. He realizes that

> it is when the alien hand pollutes the source of will, when a stranger force of violence shatters the mind's calm resolution, this is when a man is made to commit the awful treachery of relief, commit in his thought the unspeakable blasphemy of seeing the hand of the gods in this alien rupture of his world. I know it was this thought that killed me, sapped my powers and turned me into an infant in the hands of unnamable strangers.

In the production of the play at Bayero University in Kano in 1979, Nelson Okonkwo playing Elesin Oba spat the words "unnamable strangers" into the ear of one of the policeman detailed by Pilkings to guard him. It was a gesture of defiance but it was also a gesture of self-repudiation since he had become as much a lackey of the colonial presence as that representative of the "native administration." This gesture is followed by his dreadful confession:

> My will was squelched in the spittle of an alien race, and all because I had committed this blasphemy of thought—that there might be the hand of the gods in a stranger's intervention.

Thus the cause of Elesin Oba's failure is, ultimately, blasphemy, which is to say, betrayal. Unable to withstand the attraction of a life of addiction to leftovers he tried to convince himself that the leftovers were wholesome, that the neglect of his historically enshrined, sacred duty to the dead and the living was legitimate. If this neglect of duty could be explained as the will of the gods, then infraction of that duty could be seen as fulfilment and his inability to "commit death" would be meritorious. The greatest and deepest betrayal, the archetypal betrayal, is that that claims to be an honoring of the contract with those being betrayed. It is an act that precludes respect for its proponent. As a leader of his people at a particular time in their history Elesin Oba had a particular responsibility to them: to withstand the adulteration of the life-sustaining essence of the society. Instead he rationalized and was fatally compromised.

When Elesin Oba asks that the world forgive him, we come to the crux of the play. Elesin who has brought laughter and tears, who has earned respect and for whom nothing but good has been desired, this man has now to be cast off and rejected. The pathos of the situation asks that he be forgiven but sentimentality has to be renounced. The integrity of the play demands it, but, more significantly, the integrity of the society requires it. Elesin Oba is a dramatic creation with the mythic proportions of the great figures of literature. He has the grandeur, dignity, and pathos of Oedipus; the questing anguish of Hamlet; the restless and aspiring soul of Peer Gynt; the arrogance of Nietzsche's superman; the sense of comedy, love of life, and sensual proclivities of Dionysus; and the pathetic, rationalizing weakness of Richard II. Though a creation of such stature he has to be totally and unequivocally renounced: "I have no father, eater of left-overs."

In the final analysis, however, the renunciation of Elesin Oba is not undertaken in a spirit of disdain or contempt, rather as a kind of scorification. Elesin Oba may have failed as a leader but he is still a man and his body deserves the respect accorded to the bodies of men, "However sunk he was in debt he is no pauper's carrion abandoned on the road." He is dramatically central to this play and in a performance cannot but dominate the proceedings. Yet, as with those leaders on the actual "world stage" whom he represents and who also dominate the proceedings and often wrench the world from its true course and plunge it into chaos, if the integrity of the people is to be maintained both Elesin Oba and the leaders have to be finally, but humanely, renounced. "Forget the dead," Iyaloja commands, "forget even the living. Turn your mind only to the unborn" who are, in Ayi Kwei Armah's words, "The Beautyful Ones."

It might appear from the foregoing that Soyinka could be accused of espousing a form of romantic primitivism. The opposite is the case. Olunde is the character who embodies the play's contemporary and significant affirmation and he is neither primitive nor romantic. He is the character we might expect to embrace the "sophisticated" leftovers of an alien culture much as do Dr. Faseyi in *The Interpreters* or Brempong in [Awi Kwei] Armah's *Fragments*. Olunde shows that once the essence of the culture is fully embraced then exposure to glittering eye-catching dross has no effect. There will be snapping of fingers around the head but no abandoning of hard-won harvests or rapid dialog with the legs. With the death of Olunde and the joining of the two movements of the play, not only have the roles of father and son been reversed, but also Elesin Oba has changed roles with Joseph and Amusa. They both salvage some dignity from their plight; he salvages nothing. Elesin

> is gone at last into the passage but oh, how late it is. His son will feast on the meat and throw

him bones. The passage is clogged with droppings from the King's stallion; he will arrive all stained in dung.

The wallowers in the detritus of an alien culture in this world wallow in the dung for eternity. Olunde who went to Europe with an ambivalent mind learned what is fundamental to his integrity and to the integrity of his people: the contiguity of past, present, and future. Those who betray the present destroy not just themselves but the entire community—forever.

The difficulty confronting anybody attempting to follow Olunde's "model" of procedure is that it is vague and prescribes no formula for the potential acolyte. No doubt Yakubu Nasidi [in "Literature and Politics: 'Kongi's Harvest' as Political Drama," *Work in Progress* [Zaria], No. 3, 1980] would see this vagueness as "indicative of the incoherence of the playwright's political intuition." It is, perhaps, more useful to regard Soyinka as giving instructions similar to those of another intellectual giant of contemporary Nigeria, Yusufu Bala Usman who in 1975 instructed graduates thus:

> A direct, honest and frank question defines a problem, and if there is the will to tackle it, that is half-way to its solution. One might even say that the most fundamental problem of contemporary Nigeria is the way we ask questions.

It is significant that both Usman and Soyinka direct their followers towards questioning. In ideological terms they are poles apart, as indeed were Marx and Shakespeare—that did not prevent Marx from using Shakespeare to shed light on his ideas. Soyinka's prescription is for individuals to undertake a vigorous journey of self-discovery with no route indicating how obstacles may be negotiated, guaranteeing only that it will demand great, perhaps the ultimate, self-sacrifice. It is a route familiar to Soyinka himself so it is propounded with some authority. Few people, however, have the moral and spiritual stature for such a challenge while for the majority even the idea of it is a luxury. How shall a truck pusher, a lorry-park tout or a market woman find time for such an activity? Since the play does not speak directly to the common man it might be rejected by those with that particular ideological prescription for art. It is, after all, the Marxian critic might justifiably object, merely bourgeois entertainment whose silent ideology is to reduce the masses to political irrelevance. "In this play," Izevbaye writes in an article already referred to, "Soyinka stresses the importance of honor for the well-being of man by pointing out the need for the transcendence of material goals." As this comment assumes, the play centers on the upper echelons of a hierarchical society; Olunde's example is for the leaders in that society and the play is about such leaders. Soyinka has renounced "inert historical scarecrows" and "ideological dragons" and writes of the world as he understands it, not as others do. The play is unashamedly hierarchical, as is the society that is depicted. Soyinka is a leader in that society. In his own right he stands on the pinnacle of his achievement thundering his condemnation of those leaders who betray their calling and their trust, dragging the people into "dung and vomit . . . lips reeking of the left-overs of lesser men." From another pinnacle, sometimes cynically dubbed an ivory tower, that other giant—Usman—also thunders (emphasis added)

> transnationals . . . are owned, controlled and geared to operate in order to suck wealth from the Third World to Western Europe, America and Japan. This is made possible not because of any technological superiority, but because the classes in the Third World countries like Nigeria are essentially intermediaries, or, if you like, trading-post agents and *lack the will, capacity and political base with which to break their strangleholds.*

Soyinka's Praise Singer—guardian of culture, custodian of history and chider of misdemeanor—laments of the failure of his erstwhile leader:

> Elesin, we placed the reins of the world in your hands yet you watched it plunge over the edge of the bitter precipice. You sat with folded arms while evil strangers tilted the world from its course and crashed it beyond the edge of emptiness—you muttered, there is little that one man can do, you left us floundering in a blind future. Your heir has taken the burden on himself.
>
> (pp. 81-97)

> *Mark Ralph-Bowman, " 'Leaders and Left-Overs': A Reading of Soyinka's 'Death and the King's Horseman'," in* Research in African Literatures, *Vol. 14, No. 1, Spring, 1983, pp. 81-97.*

James Booth   (essay date 1988)

[*In the following excerpt, Booth disagrees with Soyinka's insistence that the District Officer Simon Pilkings and his wife Jane, white colonists in his play* Death and the King's Horseman, *are incidental to the drama. Booth contends, rather, that the colonists' inability to comprehend Yoruban values—specifically those relating to ritual suicide—gives the audience "the impression of a wider confrontation of cultures" and thus provides a major point of interest in the drama.*]

Two complementary techniques are used in [*Death and the King's Horseman*] to convey its sacrificial theme: one direct and highly poetic, the other indirect and realistic. In the virtuoso first and third acts, the richly textured rhetoric of the Yoruba characters translates the audience into a world of apparently timeless natural rhythms. The community expresses itself in terms of praise song and threnody, enthralling in their metaphysical intensity, but affording only an impressionistic insight into customs and social structure.

> ELESIN. The world I know is good.
>
> WOMEN. We know you'll leave it so.
>
> ELESIN. The world I know is the bounty
> Of hives after bees have swarmed.
> No goodness teems with such open hands
> Even in the dreams of deities.
>
> WOMEN. And we know you'll leave it so.
>
> ELESIN. I was born to keep it so. A hive

> Is never known to wander. An anthill
> Does not desert its roots. We cannot see
> The still great womb of the world—
> No man beholds his mother's womb—
> Yet who denies it's there? Coiled
> To the navel of the world is that
> Endless cord that links us all
> To the great origin. If I lose my way
> The trailing cord will bring me to the roots
>
> WOMEN. The world is in your hands.

It is only through the contrasting prose of acts 2 and 4 that the actual specifics of the sacrificial custom are explored, by means of dialogues between African and white characters. Despite Soyinka's insistence on the incidental quality of the Europeans, it cannot be denied that one of the main ways in which the play's Yoruba values are dramatically defined is by contrast with the attitudes of the uncomprehending whites. Theatrically, this is a most effective device, since the overwhelming majority of any audience (black or white) will be ideologically more attuned to individualistic ideology than to the communalist values represented in the central religious sacrifice of the play. They will need an imaginative bridge to take them into its world, and this is supplied by their anticolonialism, which Soyinka skillfully evokes. As David Richards has demonstrated [in "Òwe l'esin òrò: Proverbs Like Horses: Wole Soyinka's *Death and the King's Horseman,*" *Journal of Commonwealth Literature* 19. 1 (1984)], one key strategy is to contrast the rich communal wisdom of the Yoruba proverbial idiom with the tinny vocabulary of skepticism and secularity employed by Pilkings and Jane. The problem with this indirect method is the (deliberate) thinness of treatment of the Europeans. On occasion the spectator may feel that the white characters are being perfunctorily manipulated by the playwright, and when this occurs, doubt may arise about the authenticity of the other, African side of the antithesis.

One of the central passages where a white character is thus used to define specific Yoruba values is the long conversation between Olunde and Jane in act 4, which constitutes Olunde's only appearance (alive) in the play. The scene is the crux of the action, since it is this apparently Westernized medical student's surprising decision to kill himself that constitutes the play's central act of faith in the efficacy of sacrifice. Elesin's failure to sacrifice himself is more easily understandable. Even a spectator quite out of sympathy with the play's religious theme can empathize with his guilt and remorse for surrendering to the temptations of the world and the flesh. Olunde's decision to take the opposite direction is far more problematic, both psychologically and dramatically. It is significant then that our view of Olunde should be determined so exclusively by what occurs during this single dialogue with Jane.

Soyinka appears in much of the scene to be drawing a deliberate contrast between the attitudes of the African character and the European toward self-sacrifice:

> JANE. Mind you there is the occasional bit of excitement like that ship that was blown up in the harbour.

OLUNDE. Here? Do you mean through enemy action?

JANE. Oh no, the war hasn't come that close. The captain did it himself. I don't quite understand it really. Simon tried to explain. The ship had to be blown up because it had become dangerous to the other ships, even to the city itself. Hundreds of the coastal population would have died.

OLUNDE. Maybe it was loaded with ammunition and had caught fire. Or some of those lethal gases they've been experimenting on.

JANE. Something like that. The captain blew himself up with it. Deliberately. Simon said someone had to remain on board to light the fuse.

OLUNDE. It must have been a very short fuse.

JANE. (shrugs) I don't know much about it. Only that there was no other way to save lives. No time to devise anything else. The captain took the decision and carried it out.

OLUNDE. Yes . . . I quite believe it. I met men like that in England.

JANE. Oh just look at me! Fancy welcoming you back with such morbid news. Stale too. It was at least six months ago.

OLUNDE. I don't find it morbid at all. I find it rather inspiring. It is an affirmative commentary on life.

JANE. What is?

OLUNDE. That captain's self-sacrifice.

JANE. Nonsense. Life should never be thrown deliberately away.

OLUNDE. And the innocent people round the harbour?

JANE. Oh, how does one know? The whole thing was probably exaggerated anyway.

The theatrical effect of this interchange is clear. The audience sympathizes with Olunde's sensitive approval of heroic self-sacrifice and condemns the white woman's obtuse failure to recognize its spiritual nobility. But although this scene works well enough theatrically, it is, on closer examination, oddly imprecise in effect. Olunde's skeptical question about the short fuse is left hanging unsatisfactorily, and the audience is in danger of becoming preoccupied with the thematically extrinsic mechanics of the blurred story rather than with its clear spiritual lesson. Jane, moreover, fails strangely to see the point of her own account, and this despite Olunde's assurance that she is "somewhat more understanding" than her husband. In this respect she seems thematically unhelpful. Indeed the audience may feel puzzled by her blundering struggle to understand (with her husband's help) an incident the implications of which are so patently obvious. She is in danger of appearing not as an imperceptive European, but as a simple half-wit—or worse, a perfunctory puppet of the playwright. And her frivolous reduction of the tragedy to

the level of social diversion ("the occasional bit of excitement," "such morbid news. Stale too") seems odd, even from an empty-headed socialite, since from the evidence we are given it seems reasonable to infer that the captain's action has saved the lives of some of her white compatriots on the coast.

Clearly, the chief point this episode is intended to raise, with typical Soyinkan complexity, is that self-sacrifice is as characteristic of Europe as of Africa. The essential similarity between the sacrifices of Olunde and the captain carries a significant message of "common humanity" for the audience. Indeed the desire to include this sacrificial parallel seems to be one of the "minor reasons of dramaturgy" behind Soyinka's moving of the play's action from 1946 to the period of the war. In the European tradition of Carton in *A Tale of Two Cities* and Captain Oates of the Antarctic, this captain has "played the white man," as it were, dying when required, that others may live. Significantly for the effect of the scene as a whole however, the sacrifice of the captain is entirely secular and practical. He dies to preserve the physical rather than the metaphysical safety of his community, and his action can be appreciated with no act of faith. The sacrifice of Olunde which it foreshadows is, in contrast, essentially religious.

This contrast between the sacrifices reinforces a consistent pattern in the play. The range of concepts and feelings exhibited by the whites is confined consistently within practical, secular, often reductive limits, while the African characters retain a monopoly of the spiritual and metaphysical, both in language and action. Olunde's language in describing his experience in Britain shows this clearly: "I found your people quite admirable in many ways, their conduct and courage in this war for instance." The whites may have "conduct and courage," but these solid and useful qualities only make them insensitive to the different, more elusive values of others. Significantly it is Olunde's experience of this white obtuseness which has been instrumental in bringing him to a full appreciation of his own roots:

> OLUNDE. Don't make it so simple, Mrs. Pilkings. You make it sound as if when I left, I took nothing at all with me.
>
> JANE. Yes . . . and to tell the truth, only this evening, Simon and I agreed that we never really knew what you left with.
>
> OLUNDE. Neither did I. But I found out over there. I am grateful to your country for that. And I will never give it up.
>
> JANE. Olunde, please, . . . promise me something. Whatever you do, don't throw away what you have started to do. You want to be a doctor. My husband and I believe you will make an excellent one, sympathetic and competent. Don't let anything make you throw away your training.

Jane cannot see the health of Olunde's community in any terms but the medical: he must not "throw away" his training as a doctor. Similarly she speaks of "protecting" Elesin from the consequences of "a barbaric custom." Olunde, however, understands that his father's assent to sacrifice gives him "the deepest protection the mind can conceive."

It may be objected that this kind of analysis is in danger of forcing a typicality on the characters that Soyinka does not intend. He is not opposing "Europe" against "Africa," it may be argued, and the feeble Jane in particular is simply a "catalyst" here, not a representative of European culture. No larger thematic significance should be read into the fact that the playwright has chosen to make her a shallow chatterer, flustered by the first hint of deeper values, rather than (say) a thoughtful Christian familiar with the Western tradition of martyrdom and self-sacrifice. The choice of characterization is simply a theatrical expedient to throw Olunde's spiritual firmness into better relief. Nor should any significance be read into the absence from the play of any spiritually aware white character. Soyinka has explained in his prefatory note that the whites are not the center of his focus, and their treatment is only incidental to his essentially Yoruba theme.

Such a reading is naive and quite disregards the inevitable theatrical effect on any audience, white, black, or mixed, of a prolonged stage confrontation between a white, who happens to be materialistic and spiritually shallow, and a black, who is depicted as profoundly and organically religious. Without the intervention of some kind of positive theatrical check (a thoroughly Westernized black character or a religious white perhaps) no amount of prefatory protestation can stop the characters becoming, in effect, representatives for the versions of their cultures that are presented. Moreover the impact of this scene on stage is indeed one of gladiatorial combat between cultural antitheses. Its rhetoric consistently generates a sense that the characters do stand for wider cultural principles. Olunde continually uses such phrases as "your people," "you white races," of "the white races." "You white races know how to survive; I've seen proof of that," he exclaims bleakly to Jane. Against Jane and her people he opposes "our people." "We," unlike "you," he asserts, have not "mastered the art of calling things by names which don't remotely describe them." In "your" newsreels, he says to Jane, murderous defeats are described as victories. He bitterly concludes that by their war "the white races" are "wiping out their so-called civilisation for all time and reverting to a state of primitivism the like of which has so far only existed in your imagination when you thought of us." The "you" here is clearly not simply Jane. The white woman responds with an insistence that her husband is genuinely concerned "for you. For your people" and protests that Olunde has not seen "us at our best." She admits that there are "many things we don't really grasp about your people." The very pronouns "you" and "we" have by this time become heavily charged with generalized significance and seem to encompass whole cultures. If the scene is not intended to impress the audience as a confrontation between "Europe" and "Africa," such repeated antithetical and generalizing vocabulary is extremely unfortunate. In fact, of course, it is precisely the impression of a wider confrontation of cultures that compels the audience's involvement and makes this scene such vivid and gripping theater. Its brilliant effect on stage certainly does

not derive from any subtle discussion of Yoruba metaphysics.

It is difficult not to feel, on reflection, that this crucial scene is more in the nature of a series of propaganda points than anything more dramatically respectable, though these points are scored with great skill and satiric accuracy. The frivolous "fancy dress" use to which Jane is putting the spirit mask, for instance, is a potent visual focus in performance, and Olunde's dry and telling reproach is guaranteed to stir any audience:

> OLUNDE. (mildly) And that is the good cause for which you desecrate an ancestral mask?
>
> JANE. Oh, so you are shocked after all. How disappointing.
>
> OLUNDE. No I am not shocked Mrs. Pilkings. You forget that I have now spent four years among your people. I discovered that you have no respect for what you do not understand.

Jane of course has no adequate answer, not having been given the necessary philosophical depth or eloquence by her creator. This is very plausible and allows for a sharp and dramatically satisfying effect. Throughout the scene the audience is cajoled by a series of such pointed contrasts into a belief in the desirability, and the plausibility, of Olunde's self-sacrifice. He is called a "savage" by Jane and an "impudent nigger" by the aide-de-camp. Jane, as we have seen, fails to respond to the nobility of a parallel secular self-sacrifice performed by a fellow white, and Pilkings assaults Olunde's father with his "albino's hand." The effect of these negative contrasts with the "Europe" that appears embodied on the stage is to lure the audience into an unexamined imaginative assent to the proposition that there is something peculiarly African about Olunde's sacrifice and also that it is spiritually and psychologically necessary. Olunde claims never to have doubted the necessity of the sacrificial custom. But, in dramatic terms, instead of the Europeans being "incidental" to his sacrifice, as this should imply, there is too much of an appearance that his decision has been precipitated *by* his interaction with Europeans. It becomes his way of "making a point," as it were.

But at this crucial thematic moment, when an articulate, Western-educated medical student is about to submit himself to ritual immolation, one might feel justified in expecting a more complex exploration of the question of understanding and respect between African and European cultures. This is particularly important here, since whatever cultural humility these confrontations elicit in the play's spectators will almost certainly have been imbibed from the traditions of Jane's Europe, going back to Montaigne's celebrated remark [in his *Essays*] on the Brazilian cannibals he met in Rouen: "I do not believe, from what I have been told about this people, that there is anything barbarous or savage about them, except that we all call barbarous anything that is contrary to our own habits." The same Europe that produced the barbarism of the *conquistadores* and the slave trade also produced the tradition of cultural relativism to which Olunde appeals here. Without the intellectual tradition of Thomas More, Montaigne,

Swift, Frobenius, Conrad, E. M. Forster, and Margaret Mead behind it, Olunde's remark would possess little force. But neither Olunde nor the playwright chooses to explore this complexity. Are we intended to infer that cultural relativism and humility are strikingly more characteristic of Olunde's Yoruba people than of Jane's Europeans? What are Olunde's deeper feelings and mental processes as he reproaches Jane for lacking the cultural eclecticism that he himself is about to discard? Is there no conflict in his mind between the scientific perspectives of his English medical education and the metaphysical perspectives of his Yoruba religion?

It will be objected here that this whole approach is too literal and takes insufficient account of the metaphorical impact of what is, after all, a poetic drama, not a historical documentary. The demand for a more detailed exploration of Olunde's psychology and a greater thematic explicitness reduces what is essentially a symbolic assertion of spiritual transcendence to a question of mere plausibility and realistic coherence. Soyinka is not writing a polemic aimed at securing the practical reintroduction of ritual suicide; he is merely using the historical incident as a particularly vivid imaginative symbol of sacrifice in general and of traditional Yoruba communalism in particular. It is this metaphorical level of the play which is stressed by most of the critics and on which Soyinka insists in his prefatory note. This argument carries a great deal of force. The religious motive of Olunde's sacrifice is not intended to command the audience's approval on a literal level. Very few will be inclined to accept that the gods or "cosmic totality" really require self-immolation of the kind prescribed by Yoruba tradition. Olunde's sacrifice is to be seen as the metaphorical vehicle for a more universal tenor. It symbolizes the determination to be true to one's roots and to assert the value of higher duty against both the internal threat of materialistic self-interest (Elesin's tragic flaw) and the external threat of an imposed alien culture. Viewed as the freely willed sacrifice of individual self on behalf of a religious principle, Olunde's decision achieves metaphorical universality and can command the respect of spectators with widely different views on religion and philosophy.

One major problem with this version remains the very specific and historically concrete context in which Olunde (in contrast to his father) is presented. The action at this point is firmly situated in a particular place and a recent time: colonial Oyo during World War II. And, as we have seen, this colonial context largely determines the dramatic presentation of Olunde's mind. Jane and Olunde argue, in the prose of common debate, about the nature of colonialism, the difference between white and black cultures, and about the horrors of war, their tone ranging from politeness to passionate offense. This is no stylized, poetic setting of metaphorical suggestiveness, such as was evoked in acts 1 and 3. It is more reminiscent of the realistic British drama of class antagonisms produced by John Osborne and Arnold Wesker in the 1950s and 1960s. In this context it is difficult for the audience to refrain from asking literal, unmetaphorical questions about the motivations and beliefs of the characters—and of the playwright.

There is moreover a second problem, generated by the dual nature of Olunde's sacrifice. As it is dramatically presented, in the context of the interference of the Pilkingses, it appears as an assertion of spiritual and cultural freedom. But in its Yoruba context it has a quite different meaning, as the inevitable sacrifice of human life required by cosmological necessity. In this aspect it is philosophically quite distinct from the more familiar sacrifice of self and is founded on a principle opposite to personal moral conviction—communal or "cosmic" totality. Though both sacrifices involve the death of an individual for the sake of the larger good, they are otherwise so ideologically different that it is difficult to see how the one can stand as a metaphor for the other with any coherence. But in Olunde's case the two modes of sacrifice are thoroughly blended and confused in a most unusual way. He *chooses* to die because he rejects his European education and the colonial restraint of the Pilkingses, thus gaining the audience's anti-imperialist sympathy. But more fundamentally, he *must* die, irrespective of his own choice. He has inherited his unworthy father's role, and the unalterable cosmic law ordains that his blood must be spilled. The conflict between the levels of the metaphor seems unresolvable. (pp. 532-39)

> *James Booth, "Self-Sacrifice and Human Sacrifice in Soyinka's 'Death and the King's Horseman',"* in Research in African Literatures, *Vol. 19, No. 4, Winter, 1988, pp. 529-50.*

FURTHER READING

AUTHOR COMMENTARY

Brown, Wesley. "Nobel Laureate Wole Soyinka." *Essence* 18, No. 4 (August 1987): 35.

> Interview in which Soyinka comments on what he sees as the cultural snobbery of Americans, the Black American search for a cultural identity, and the difficulty for individuals and nations to accept foreign cultures. "The greatest threat to freedom," he claims, "is the absence of criticism."

Gates, Henry Louis, Jr. "Wole Soyinka: Writing, Africa and Politics." *The New York Times Book Review* (23 June 1985): 1, 28-9.

> Interview conducted by American critic and scholar Henry Louis Gates, Jr., in which Soyinka discusses his career as a politically active Nigerian writer.

OVERVIEWS AND GENERAL STUDIES

Banham, Martin. "African Literature II: Nigerian Dramatists in English and the Traditional Nigerian Theatre." *The Journal of Commonwealth Literature* No. 3 (July 1967): 97-102.

> Examines what Banham perceives as a trend in the Nigerian theater: the fusion of the international language of English with the traditional African art form of Yoru-

ban Folk Opera, especially seen in Soyinka's *Kongi's Harvest* and *The Road.*

Black American Literature Forum (Wole Soyinka Issue, Part 1) 22, No. 3 (Fall 1988).

Issue focusing on Soyinka's receipt of the Nobel Prize in literature in 1986. Contains his Nobel Prize speech denouncing racism and human inequality, calling instead for "its complement: universal suffrage—and peace."

Black American Literature Forum (Wole Soyinka Issue, Part 2) 22, No. 4 (Winter 1988).

Issue devoted to the study of Soyinka's drama, novels, and other works. Includes essays devoted to *Requiem for a Futurologist, Death and the King's Horseman,* as well as interviews with Soyinka in which he discusses his drama and poetry.

Gibbs, James, ed. *Critical Perspectives on Wole Soyinka.* Washington, D. C.: Three Continents Press, Inc., 1980, 274 p.

Includes critical essays on Soyinka's plays, poetry, and prose.

Jones, Eldred Durosimi. *The Writing of Wole Soyinka.* London: James Currey, 1988, 242 p.

Offers background on the influences in Soyinka's life which affect his work, as well as commentary on the playwright's dramas from *The Swamp Dwellers* to *Requiem for a Futurologist.*

Katrak, Ketu H. *Wole Soyinka and Modern Tragedy: A Study of Dramatic Theory and Practice.* New York: Greenwood Press, 1986, 192 p.

Study of Soyinka which attempts to understand his reliance on the Yoruba world-view in his drama. "Despite a predilection for the metaphysical in his plays," Katrak contends, Soyinka "never loses his overriding concern with society, with the value of the protagonist's self-knowledge for his people."

Maclean, Una. "Soyinka's International Drama." *Black Orpheus: A Journal of African and Afro-American Literature* No. 15 (August 1964): 46-51.

Discussion of the international appeal of Soyinka's drama. Maclean claims that, although an understanding of Nigerian mythology and customs aids in the appreciation of Soyinka's plays, it is not essential since the playwright explains any African references in the course of his dialogue.

Maduakor, Obi. *Wole Soyinka: An Introduction to His Writing.* New York: Garland Publishing, 1986, 339 p.

Study of Soyinka attempting to clarify the "difficulties" in his works, including his subject matter and technical innovations. Chapter three concentrates on Soyinka's five metaphysical plays: *A Dance of the Forests, The Road, Madmen and Specialists, The Bacchae of Euripides,* and *Death and the King's Horseman.* Maduakor categorizes these plays as metaphysical because of their themes of death, their abstract content, and their African world view.

Moore, Gerald. *Wole Soyinka.* New York: African Publishing Corporation, 1971, 114 p.

Traces Soyinka's career in the theater from his early work through the production of *Kongi's Harvest* in 1965. Moore attempts to relate each work "to the author's

total activity in the theatre and in society at the time of its conception."

Ogumba, Oyin. "The Traditional Content of the Plays of Wole Soyinka." In *African Literature Today: A Journal of Explanatory Criticism,* edited by Eldred D. Jones, pp. 2-18. London: Heinemann, 1972.

Attempts to determine the nature of Soyinka's borrowing from traditional African forms and ideas in his dramas. Ogumba notes the presence of African expressions, songs, and, more importantly, the design of festival in Soyinka's drama.

Peters, Jonathan. "*A Dance of the Forests:* The Universal Dome of Continuity" and "*The Road, Kongi's Harvest, Madmen and Specialists:* Masks of Deification and Defecation." In his *A Dance of Masks: Senghor, Achebe, Soyinka,* pp. 161-221. Washington, D. C.: Three Continents Press, 1978.

Considers chronologically four of Soyinka's dramas to show the major themes the dramatist entertains and his development as an artist. Peters claims that "man seems to be a doomed animal in Soyinka's work, a prey or victim of his fellows or of some of his dubious inventions dubbed progress and civilization."

Sekoni, 'Ropo. "Metaphor as Basis of Form in Soyinka's Drama." *Research in African Literature* 14, No. 1 (Spring 1983): 45-57.

Compares the repeated images and episodes in the Yoruba ritual "Obatala Festival" to Soyinka's dramatic technique in *A Dance of the Forests* and *Kongi's Harvest.* Sekoni determines that the repetition of metaphor is an important structural feature of both the ritual and Soyinka's plays.

Wright, Derek. "The Ritual Context of Two Plays by Soyinka." *Theatre Research International* 12, No. 1 (Spring 1987): 51-61.

Considers the use of the annual "rite of the carrier" in Soyinka's *The Strong Breed* and *The Bacchae of Euripides.* In this ritual, the evils of the previous year are projected into a material object and removed from the village by a person who is then allowed to return to the community.

Yankowitz, Susan. "The Plays of Wole Soyinka." *African Forum: A Quarterly Journal of Contemporary Affairs* 1, No. 4 (Spring 1966): 129-33.

Examines six of Soyinka's dramas, including *A Dance of the Forests, The Lion and the Jewel, The Swamp Dwellers, The Road, The Trials of Brother Jero,* and *The Strong Breed.* Yankowitz notes that each of these plays, in styles ranging from prose to poetry to song, examines the modern themes of alienation, hypocrisy, sin, and expiation "within the framework of a civilization seeking new values without destroying its heritage."

INDIVIDUAL WORKS

Hill, Holly. "Vicious Circle: Holly Hill Reports from New York on Public Resistance to Theatrical Quality." *The Times* (London) (6 April 1987): 17.

Commends the Lincoln Center for its production of *Death and the King's Horseman.* Hill believes the play "has the stateliness and mystery of Greek tragedy."

Lindfors, Bernth. "Begging Questions in Wole Soyinka's *Opera Wonyosi*." *Ariel* 12, No. 3 (July 1981): 21-33.

> Reveals the degree to which Soyinka transformed the original texts of the plays from which he adapted *Opera Wonyosi:* John Gay's *The Beggar's Opera* and Bertolt Brecht's *The Threepenny Opera.* Lindfors calls *Opera Wonyosi* Soyinka's attempt to "contribute to the reform of contemporary Nigeria through song, dance, and satirical laughter."

Sotto, Wiveca. *The Rounded Rite: A Study of Wole Soyinka's Play* The Bacchae of Euripides. Lund Studies in English 72, edited by Claes Schaar and Jan Svartvik. Lund: Liber Fölag Lund, CWK Gleerup, 1985, 187 p.

> In-depth study of Soyinka's *The Bacchae of Euripides* which offers background on the influences on the playwright and the dramatic form of the play.

MEDIA ADAPTATIONS

Kongi's Harvest. Calpenny Nigerian Films-Herald Productions, 1971.

> Film version of Soyinka's play directed by American actor Ossie Davis and starring Soyinka as the African dictator Kongi. 85 minutes.

For further information of Soyinka's life and career, see *Black Literature Criticism,* Vol. 3; *Contemporary Authors,* Vols. 13-16, rev. ed.; *Contemporary Literary Criticism,* Vols. 3, 5, 14, 36, 44; and *Dictionary of Literary Biography Yearbook 1986.*

John Millington Synge

1871-1909

INTRODUCTION

Full name Edmund John Millington Synge.

The author of *The Playboy of the Western World* and *Riders to the Sea,* Synge is considered the greatest dramatist of the Irish Literary Renaissance, a movement that sought to create a new literature out of the heritage, language, and folklore of the Irish people. In his unsentimental but compassionate portrayal of Irish peasants and his highly imaginative and poetic dialogue patterned after the vernacular spoken by the rural population in the West of Ireland, Synge attempted to capture the essence of the Irish spirit, which he described in his preface to *Playboy* as "fiery and magnificent, and tender."

Born in Rathfarnham, a town near Dublin, into a middle-class Protestant family, Synge was raised by his devoutly religious mother after his father's death in 1872. Due to his poor health, he was educated at home by private tutors. Influenced by his reading of the works of Charles Darwin, Synge broke from his religious upbringing at the age of fourteen, and his ill feelings towards Christianity often arise in his plays. He studied Hebrew and Irish at Trinity College in Dublin, and, after earning his Bachelor's degree, he traveled extensively in Germany, France, and Italy, intent on a career in music. Eventually judging himself better suited to literary endeavors, he moved in 1895 to Paris, where he studied at the Sorbonne. The following year, he encountered two fellow expatriates, the political activist Maud Gonne and the poet and dramatist William Butler Yeats. Synge briefly joined Gonne's Irish League, an organization dedicated to liberating Ireland from English rule, but quickly became disillusioned with the militant tactics she advocated. Yeats, the most prominent figure of the Irish Literary Renaissance, had a more lasting influence on Synge: he urged him to return to Ireland and to write about the peasants of the three small islands off the country's western coast, known collectively as the Aran Islands or, simply, Aran. The advice appealed to Synge, and he subsequently spent many summers on the islands observing the customs and dialect of the peasants. In their Anglo-Irish dialect, in their stories and legends, and in their spiritual beliefs—which he viewed as a hybrid of Christian teachings and the stronger, more exciting element of ancient paganism—Synge discovered the inspiration for most of his dramatic works.

In 1903 Synge settled in Dublin, where the Irish National Theatre Society staged his first play, *In the Shadow of the Glen.* Presenting the story of a suspicious husband who fakes his own death in order to determine whether his young wife is faithful, and who has his worst fears confirmed, the play shocked Irish audiences with its ironic depiction of marriage. However, it found popularity in the more liberal atmosphere of England. In 1905 Yeats and the dramatist Lady Gregory produced Synge's *The Well of the Saints* at the new Abbey Theatre. Containing

Synge's most acerbic characterizations of Irish peasants in the sarcastic, feuding blind couple Martin and Mary Doul, and in a Saint of questionable virtue, the play greatly impressed Yeats with its colorful dialogue; yet it, too, offended Dubliners. The first production of *The Playboy of the Western World* incited a public outrage in 1907 when audiences took exception to its coarse language and what they considered an unflattering portrayal of the Irish peasantry. Attempts to disrupt performances of the drama were so hostile that police were called to the Abbey Theatre to protect the players. News of the so-called *Playboy* riots earned an international reputation for Synge, who defended the play against charges that no Irish citizen would behave as his characters did by insisting that the characterizations and the plot of the play were taken from actual events. Two years later, Synge died of Hodgkin's disease, leaving *Deirdre of the Sorrows* complete but only partially revised.

Synge is remembered primarily for his innovations as a linguistic stylist. While his dialogue, as he professed, was taken directly from the speech of Irish peasants, he used his aesthetic sensibilities to bring out the inherent poetic qualities of the Anglo-Irish dialect. As Yeats suggested, in response to objections that Synge's dialogue was not entirely "natural," "Perhaps no Irish countryman had ever that exact rhythm in his voice, but certainly if Mr. Synge had been born a countryman, he would have spoken like that." Synge's achievement, critics maintain, was the use of this style to compliment the themes pervading his works: the possibilities and limitations of speech, the disparity between reality and illusion, and the painfulness of everyday existence. Exhibiting all of these themes in a highly compressed format, *Riders to the Sea* is a one-act tragedy set inside an Aran cottage. The play presents vivid descriptions of the daily actions of the islanders and focuses on the danger of their custom of fishing in small boats, called curraghs. Synge renders the fatalism native to a region in which the people depend on the sea for their livelihoods and exist in constant fear of sudden and violent storms. In the course of the play, Maurya, who has already lost four of her six sons to drowning, discovers that her son Michael has also drowned. She protests in vain as her last remaining son, Bartley, subsequently sets forth on what will be another fatal expedition. She expresses her grief by keening, the ritual shrieking over a corpse, but ultimately assesses her situation in a characteristically simple and fatalistic pronouncement: "I've had a husband, and a husband's father, and six sons in this house—six fine men, though it was a hard birth I had with every one of them and they coming to the world—and some of them were found and some of them were not found, but they're gone now the lot of them." Critics have compared *Riders to the Sea* to Greek tragedy due to its compactness of narrative and its symbolic structure, which mirrors the cyclical nature of human existence in the intertwined stories of the two deaths. Commentators also observe that the play contains numerous allusions to Greek and Irish myth, as well as the Book of Revelations. It is esteemed as Synge's most artful and poetic work, but the bleakness of its subject matter has prevented it from being widely produced.

The Playboy of the Western World, on the other hand, is Synge's most frequently produced play. Set in rural County Mayo, the play opens in a country shebeen, an unlicensed drinking establishment, run by Michael James Flaherty and his daughter, Pegeen Mike. Shawn Keogh, Pegeen's timid suitor, and several local peasants are gathered in the pub when newcomer Christy Mahon arrives, in flight from the civil authorities of County Kerry. Christy tells the group how he recently killed his father, and then progressively embellishes the account while the villagers respond to him as a hero and poet. A rivalry consequently develops among the local women, most notably Pegeen and Widow Quin, for Christy's attentions, and Pegeen pledges her love to the fugitive. When his father appears, injured but alive, the villagers, including Pegeen, turn against Christy because he no longer represents the romantic hero they had envisioned him to be; when he makes another attempt on his father's life, the group prepares to lynch him. Christy and his father are reconciled when Old Mahon saves his son from the lynching mob, and they leave the village together. The drama ends with Pegeen mourning the loss of Christy, "the only playboy of the western world."

Criticism on *The Playboy of the Western World* typically

stresses the thematic opposition between reality and imagination in the drama, tracing Christy's development toward self-realization as an individual and as a poetic persona. The play's portrayal of his transformation is praised for suggesting a variety of mythological and biblical archetypes. For example, *Playboy* is often discussed in terms of the central themes and plot structures of the legends surrounding the hero Cuchulain from Irish mythology, and the drama's treatment of patricide is compared to that in Sophocles's tragedy *Oedipus Rex.* Some commentators, emphasizing the rejection of Christy by his former admirers in the play's third act, have argued that Synge presents him as a Christ figure. However, comic and ironic elements in *Playboy* have caused critics to debate the degree of parody involved in Synge's approach to such prototypes. Christy, for example, is also considered a mock or secularized Christ in light of the drama's pagan themes and ironic use of religious allusions and expressions. *Playboy* has garnered much critical attention for eluding traditional classifications of comedy and tragedy, and is cited as an early example of the modern tragicomedy.

Synge was an important catalyst in the development of Irish drama, for in bringing Anglo-Irish dialect to the stage he greatly influenced his successors, among whom Sean O'Casey and Brendan Behan are notable examples. He remains one of the most revered figures in modern drama, and *Playboy of the Western World* is considered by some the finest play written in English during the twentieth century.

PRINCIPAL WORKS

PLAYS

In the Shadow of the Glen   1903
Riders to the Sea   1904
The Well of the Saints   1905
The Playboy of the Western World   1907
The Tinker's Wedding   1909
Deirdre of the Sorrows   1910

OTHER MAJOR WORKS

The Aran Islands   (essays)   1907
Poems and Translations   (poetry)   1909
Collected Works. 4 vols.   (dramas, essays, and poetry)   1962-68

AUTHOR COMMENTARY

Preface to *The Playboy of the Western World*   (1907)

[*In this preface, which received its first publication in*

1907, Synge emphasizes the folk origins of the language in his plays and envisions a drama that will contain both joy and reality.]

In writing **The Playboy of the Western World,** as in my other plays, I have used one or two words only that I have not heard among the country people of Ireland, or spoken in my own nursery before I could read the newspapers. A certain number of the phrases I employ I have heard also from herds and fishermen along the coast from Kerry to Mayo or from beggar-women and ballad-singers nearer Dublin; and I am glad to acknowledge how much I owe to the folk-imagination of these fine people. Any one who has lived in real intimacy with the Irish peasantry will know that the wildest sayings and ideas in this play are tame indeed, compared with the fancies one may hear in any little hillside cabin in Geesala, or Carraroe, or Dingle Bay. All art is a collaboration; and there is little doubt that in the happy ages of literature, striking and beautiful phrases were as ready to the story-teller's or the playwright's hand, as the rich cloaks and dresses of his time. It is probable that when the Elizabethan dramatist took his ink-horn and sat down to his work he used many phrases that he had just heard, as he sat at dinner, from his mother or his children. In Ireland, those of us who know the people have the same privilege. When I was writing **In The Shadow of the Glen,** some years ago, I got more aid than any learning could have given me from a chink in the floor of the old Wicklow house where I was staying, that let me hear what was being said by the servant girls in the kitchen. This matter, I think, is of importance, for in countries where the imagination of the people, and the language they use, is rich and living, it is possible for a writer to be rich and copious in his words, and at the same time to give the reality, which is the root of all poetry, in a comprehensive and natural form. In the modern literature of towns, however, richness is found only in sonnets, or prose poems, or in one or two elaborate books that are far away from the profound and common interests of life. One has, on one side, Mallarmé and Huysmans producing this literature; and on the other, Ibsen and Zola dealing with the reality of life in joyless and pallid words. On the stage one must have reality, and one must have joy; and that is why the intellectual modern drama has failed, and people have grown sick of the false joy of the musical comedy, that has been given them in place of the rich joy found only in what is superb and wild in reality. In a good play every speech should be as fully flavoured as a nut or apple, and such speeches cannot be written by any one who works among people who have shut their lips on poetry. In Ireland, for a few years more, we have a popular imagination that is fiery and magnificent, and tender; so that those of us who wish to write start with a chance that is not given to writers in places where the springtime of the local life has been forgotten, and the harvest is a memory only, and the straw has been turned into bricks. (pp. 174-75)

> *J. M. Synge, in a preface to* The Complete Plays, *edited by T. R. Henn, Methuen, 1981, pp. 174-75.*

OVERVIEWS AND GENERAL STUDIES

W. B. Yeats   (essay date 1905)

[*The leading figure of the Irish Literary Renaissance and a major poet in twentieth-century literature, Yeats was also an active critic of his contemporaries' works. As a critic he judged the writings of others according to his own poetic values of sincerity, passion, and vital imagination. Yeats was one of the founders of the Irish National Theatre Society at the Abbey Theatre and in this capacity worked closely with Synge during the composition and production stages of his plays. In the following excerpt from his preface to* The Well of the Saints, *first published in 1905, Yeats recollects a pivotal encounter with Synge in Paris and extols his powers as a dramatist.*]

Six years ago I was staying in a students' hotel in the Latin Quarter, and somebody, whose name I cannot recollect, introduced me to an Irishman, who, even poorer than myself, had taken a room at the top of the house. It was J. M. Synge, and I, who thought I knew the name of every Irishman who was working at literature, had never heard of him. He was a graduate of Trinity College, Dublin, too, and Trinity College does not, as a rule, produce artistic minds. He told me that he had been living in France and Germany, reading French and German literature, and that he wished to become a writer. He had, however, nothing to show but one or two poems and impressionistic essays, full of that kind of morbidity that has its root in too much brooding over methods of expression, and ways of looking upon life, which come, not out of life, but out of literature, images reflected from mirror to mirror. He had wandered among people whose life is as picturesque as the Middle Ages, playing his fiddle to Italian sailors, and listening to stories in Bavarian woods, but life had cast no light into his writings. He had learned Irish years ago, but had begun to forget it, for the only language that interested him was that conventional language of modern poetry which has begun to make us all weary. I was very weary of it, for I had finished *The Secret Rose,* and felt how it had separated my imagination from life, sending my Red Hanrahan, who should have trodden the same roads with myself, into some undiscoverable country. I said: 'Give up Paris. You will never create anything by reading Racine, and Arthur Symons will always be a better critic of French literature. Go to the Aran Islands. Live there as if you were one of the people themselves; express a life that has never found expression.' I had just come from Aran, and my imagination was full of those grey islands where men must reap with knives because of the stones.

He went to Aran and became a part of its life, living upon salt fish and eggs, talking Irish for the most part, but listening also to the beautiful English which has grown up in Irish-speaking districts, and takes its vocabulary from the time of Malory and of the translators of the Bible, but its idiom and its vivid metaphor from Irish. When Mr. Synge began to write in this language, Lady Gregory had already used it finely in her translations of Dr. Hyde's lyrics and plays, or of old Irish literature, but she had listened with different ears. He made his own selection of word and phrase, choosing what would express his own personality. Above all, he made word and phrase dance to a very strange rhythm, which will always, till his plays have created their own tradition, be difficult to actors who have not learned it from his lips. It is essential, for it perfectly fits the drifting emotion, the dreaminess, the vague yet measureless desire, for which he would create a dramatic form. It blurs definition, clear edges, everything that comes from the will, it turns imagination from all that is of the present, like a gold background in a religious picture, and it strengthens in every emotion whatever comes to it from far off, from brooding memory and dangerous hope. When he brought *The Shadow of the Glen,* his first play, to the Irish National Theatre Society, the players were puzzled by the rhythm, but gradually they became certain that his Woman of the Glen, as melancholy as a curlew, driven to distraction by her own sensitiveness, her own fineness, could not speak with any other tongue, that all his people would change their life if the rhythm changed. Perhaps no Irish countryman had ever that exact rhythm in his voice, but certainly if Mr. Synge had been born a countryman, he would have spoken like that. It makes the people of his imagination a little disembodied; it gives them a kind of innocence even in their anger and their cursing. It is part of its maker's attitude towards the world, for while it makes the clash of wills among his persons indirect and dreamy, it helps him to see the subject-matter of his art with wise, clear-seeing, unreflecting eyes; to preserve the integrity of art in an age of reasons and purposes. Whether he write of old beggars by the roadside, lamenting over the misery and ugliness of life, or of an old Aran woman mourning her drowned sons, or of a young wife married to an old husband, he has no wish to change anything, to reform anything; all these people pass by as before an open window, murmuring strange, exciting words. (pp. 298-300)

Mr. Synge has in common with the great theatre of the world, with that of Greece and that of India, with the creator of Falstaff, with Racine, a delight in language, a preoccupation with individual life. He resembles them also by a preoccupation with what is lasting and noble, that came to him, not, as I think, from books, but while he listened to old stories in the cottages, and contrasted what they remembered with reality. The only literature of the Irish countrypeople is their songs, full often of extravagant love, and their stories of kings and of kings' children. 'I will cry my fill, but not for God, but because Finn and the Fianna are not living,' says Oisin in the story. Every writer, even every small writer, who has belonged to the great tradition, has had his dream of an impossibly noble life, and the greater he is, the more does it seem to plunge him into some beautiful or bitter reverie. Some, and of these are all the earliest poets of the world, gave it direct expression; others mingle it so subtly with reality that it is a day's work to disentangle it; others bring it near by showing us whatever is most its contrary. Mr. Synge, indeed, sets before us ugly, deformed or sinful people, but his people, moved by no practical ambition, are driven by a dream of that impossible life. (pp. 303-04)

W. B. Yeats, "Preface to the First Edition of 'The Well of the Saints'," in his Essays and Introductions, The Macmillan Company, 1961, pp. 298-305.

Patrick A. McCarthy (essay date 1988)

[*McCarthy is an American educator and critic specializing in modern English and Irish literature. In the following essay, he examines Synge's relationship to the Irish Literary Renaissance.*]

At the end of James Joyce's *A Portrait of the Artist as a Young Man,* Stephen Dedalus, budding Irish poet, proclaims his intention "to forge in the smithy of my soul the uncreated conscience of my race." By "conscience" Stephen means, among other things, "consciousness," and it is typical of the writers of his generation that Stephen regards the Irish racial or national consciousness as something that must be developed through literature; most writers, however, imagined that their poems, novels, and plays were a means of resuscitating Ireland's national cultural identity rather than creating it *ab ovo.* Supposedly written in Stephen's diary on April 26, 1902, the passage also implies that the ongoing Irish Literary Renaissance or Revival—an identifiable phenomenon at least since 1894, when William Patrick Ryan wrote a book on the subject—had not succeeded in creating or even resurrecting the "conscience" of the Irish race. That task would remain for Stephen and his own creator, both of whom believed that forging the Irish national consciousness was a

Sketch of Synge by John Yeats.

task best performed somewhere on the continent, out of reach of Irish lawsuits, censorship, and other threats to artistic integrity.

The flights from Ireland of Joyce and Stephen, and their rejection of the Irish Renaissance, reverse the pattern of John Millington Synge's career. In his early and mid-twenties Synge had traveled and studied extensively on the continent, first studying music and then immersing himself in the works of Goethe, Lessing, Ibsen, Huysmans, and other European writers, but by 1902 he had turned his attention to his native land, making several trips to the Aran Islands in search of authentic Irish cultural roots and determining that he would make his own contributions to the Irish conscience within (if not always in full agreement with) the established national literary and dramatic movement. It seems ironic that Synge, a product of the Anglo-Irish Ascendancy class, would play a major role in the revival of interest in native Irish culture while the Catholic-educated Joyce felt so alienated from the literary movement that he had Stephen write in his diary about his fear of the Gaelic-speaking Irish peasantry. The fact is, however, that the Irish Literary Renaissance was dominated by Anglo-Irish writers like William Butler Yeats, Lady Augusta Gregory, and Synge. Joyce was less an Irishman than a Dubliner, and his disdain for rural life may have led him to feel a greater affinity with nineteenth-century Continental writers than with the primitive and archaic Celtic literature that drew its power from an identification with natural forces; conversely, Synge, an accomplished amateur naturalist, was attracted to the concept of an Irish cultural identity defined in terms of imagination and natural spontaneity rather than religion and social class. This somewhat romantic version of Irish nationality served as a foundation for many of the productions of the Literary Revival.

Frank O'Connor has noted [in his *Short History of Irish Literature,* 1968] that "the [literary] tradition that Yeats, Synge and Lady Gregory had picked up from Petrie, Ferguson and Standish O'Grady, was largely a Protestant one"; yet he has also observed that the major writers of the literary movement were "people who had spent a considerable part of their youth in the country, whereas its opponents were mainly . . . townsmen." In the Preface to *The Playboy of the Western World,* Synge wrote of his fascination with the Irish peasantry's "popular imagination that is fiery and magnificent, and tender," citing qualities that Joyce rarely found in Ireland. Years later, in "The Municipal Gallery Revisited," Yeats was to write movingly of the faith in the common life of the countryside that underlay his own writings as well as those of Synge and Lady Gregory:

> John Synge, I and Augusta Gregory, thought
> All that we did, all that we said or sang
> Must come from contact with the soil, from that
> Contact everything Antaeus-like grew strong.

Like Tolstoy and other Slavophile writers of nineteenth-century Russia, the advocates of the Irish Renaissance stressed the importance of basing a modern cultural identity upon contact with the soil. There are, however, two crucial differences between the literary situations in Ireland and in Russia: Russia was not ruled by another country, nor was the Russian language in serious danger of disappearing. In Ireland, on the other hand, the nation's political subservience to England and the consequent loss of the Irish language as a major factor in Irish life meant, for many people, that a national literary renaissance could take place only in the medium of a foreign tongue.

The Irish Literary Renaissance, which attempted this compromise between the native tradition and the imported language, was one of three distinct, although in some ways parallel, movements that challenged the English political and cultural domination of late nineteenth- and early twentieth-century Ireland. The other movements were those of Irish political nationalism, which took as its goal land reform, "home rule," or even complete independence from Great Britain; and the revival and promotion of Irish Gaelic culture, especially through the Gaelic League's attempt to return the Irish language to a position of prominence and influence within Irish life. Synge had contact, at various times, both with Irish nationalism and with the Gaelic League, but the relationship was rarely a happy one. In Paris he was for several months a member of Maud Gonne's nationalistic organization L'Association Irlandaise, but in April 1897 he resigned, citing as his reason the "revolutionary and semi-military" nature of the organization. Later, he supported the goal of Irish economic self-sufficiency but objected to the idea that the Abbey Theatre should produce didactic, nationalistic dramas. As to the Gaelic League, Synge was enthusiastic about preserving the Gaeltacht (Gaelic-speaking) areas of the West, but he "declared himself opposed to the reimposition of the language on the rest of the country" [Declan Kiberd, *Literature and the Changing Ireland,* 1982]. Synge's ambivalent attitudes toward political and linguistic forms of nationalism are similar to those of Yeats and other writers closely associated with the Irish Literary Renaissance, for whom Irish political independence and the promotion of the Irish language were less important for their own sakes than as part of the attempt to forge a distinctly Irish cultural identity that incorporated both the Celtic and the Anglo-Irish populations.

Opinions vary as to when the Irish Literary Revival began, but most literary historians would agree that the phase of Irish literature during which writers were most conscious of the Literary Renaissance as a significant factor in Irish cultural life started around 1890 and came to a conclusion shortly after the establishment of the Irish Free State in 1922. As the terms revival and renaissance imply, the writers believed they were resurrecting a national literature that had once been extensive and important. Critics often call attention to the 1878 publication of Standish O'Grady's *History of Ireland: Heroic Period,* with its redactions and adaptations of Irish myths, as a seminal event in the years leading up to the Literary Renaissance, for O'Grady's book reminded the Irish that they were the inheritors of a significant body of literature whose forms and values owed nothing to those of the English literary tradition. George Russell (AE), who articulated a central belief of the Irish Renaissance when he said that "A nation exists primarily because of its own imagination of itself," described his response to O'Grady's stories as that of a man "who suddenly feels ancient memories rushing at him, and knows he was born in a royal house." The patriotic pride engendered in many Irishmen by O'Grady's books was reinforced over the next few decades by other English versions of Gaelic stories and poems. One of the most popular and influential of those versions was Lady Gregory's *Cuchulain of Muirthemne,* whose Preface, written by W. B. Yeats, includes the claim that "If we will but tell these stories to our children the Land will begin again to be a Holy Land, as it was before men gave their hearts to Greece and Rome and Judea." Rarely was the Literary Revival's claim for the merits of pagan Ireland made more explicitly, but similar assumptions about the revitalizing power of myth underlay much of the literature of the time.

Cuchulain of Muirthemne (1902) and its companion volume, *Gods and Fighting Men* (1904), were important not only because they presented readers with English versions of Irish myths, but because Lady Gregory's prose style, which she called the "Kiltartan dialect," showed that an Irish dialect of English could be a sensitive and flexible medium for literary expression. Even earlier uses of Irish dialect may be found in Douglas Hyde's *Beside the Fire* (1890) and *Love Songs of Connacht* (1893). As Richard Fallis observes [in his *Irish Renaissance,* 1977], Hyde's demonstration of the literary possibilities of Irish English constituted "a process of preservation and innovation," both a reminder of the richness of the Gaelic literary tradition and a means of helping some aspects of that tradition survive in the English-speaking world. This combination of traditional and individual elements helped to make the Literary Renaissance a particularly vital phase of Irish literature, but it also led to conflicts with traditionalists who objected to the more experimental productions of the movement or to language and themes that they regarded as inaccurate portrayals of Irish life.

Since he was one of the authors most often attacked for these reasons, it is interesting to note that in **"An Epic of Ulster,"** his review of *Cuchulain of Muirthemne,* Synge dealt with the issue of linguistic authenticity in literary works. After noting Hyde's pioneering use of an authentic Irish dialect and crediting Hyde with influencing Yeats's style and that of other recent Irish writers, Synge observed that some of Lady Gregory's passages contain echoes of Old Testament or Oriental style. Far from objecting to the book on the grounds that its speech is not always legitimate peasant dialect, however, he argued that "This union of notes, fugitive as it is, forms perhaps the most interesting feature of the language of the book", and that "in her intercourse with the peasants of the west Lady Gregory has learned to use [an Elizabethan] vocabulary in a new way, while she carries with her plaintive Gaelic constructions that make her language, in a true sense, a language of Ireland." As the subject of Synge's language is dealt with elsewhere in this book, I will not go into it in detail here, but it is worth noting that Hyde's style, and Lady Gregory's, appealed to Synge in part because they seemed to capture the ancient spirit of the country while allowing the individual writer the freedom to develop an individual mode of expression and that Synge's own dramatic dialogues involve a similar combination of genuine peasant speech and some other effects that, if not always linguisti-

cally accurate, are faithful to the very intense and concrete nature of rural Irish speech.

Aside from the use of dialect by Hyde and Lady Gregory, the most significant influence of Synge's style was probably the Irish language itself, which he first studied at Trinity College, beginning in 1888. The Professor of Irish was a Protestant clergyman, James Goodman, whom Synge later accused of ignorance, or at least indifference, toward "the old literature of Ireland [and] the fine folktales and folk-poetry of Munster and Connacht." At Trinity, a bastion of pro-British sentiment, the course in Irish was taught in the Divinity School, and the motivation for offering the course was religious rather than literary: training in Irish was deemed useful to Protestant clergymen who might be assigned to Gaelic-speaking areas of the country. The reading material for the course, an Irish version of the Gospel of St. John, was uninspiring, but Synge took a prize in Irish and went on to read, in the original Irish, both *The Children of Lir* and *Diarmuid and Grainne.* In 1898, Synge studied Old Irish at the College de France under the direction of the distinguished scholar Henri d'Arbois de Jubainville and met Richard Irvine Best, whose translation of de Jubainville's *Le Cycle mythologique irlandais et la mythologie celtique* Synge later reviewed. Shortly after completing his course of study with de Jubainville, Synge set out on his first trip to the Aran Islands.

The trip to Aran has become part of the folklore of histories of the Irish Literary Renaissance. William Butler Yeats several times told the story of how he had met Synge in Paris in 1896 (originally Yeats's arithmetic would have made it 1899) and had told him to "go to the Aran Islands and find a life that had never been expressed in literature, instead of a life where all had been expressed." Declan Kiberd has argued persuasively that the influence of Best and de Jubainville was a more significant factor than Yeats's advice in Synge's decision to make his historic journey, but Yeats nonetheless came to regard Synge as in some sense his creation and defended his plays against hostile critics. After Synge's death, Yeats idealized him as "that enquiring man John Synge. . . . That dying chose the living world for text" ("In Memory of Major Robert Gregory"), and in his Nobel Prize acceptance speech, Yeats said that Synge and Lady Gregory should have been standing on either side of him as he accepted the award from the King of Sweden. Yeats's proprietary interest in Synge was of considerable value in promoting Synge's career and preserving his place within the pantheon of the Literary Revival, so that the literal truth of Yeats's story is in one sense less important than the crucial combination of Yeats's influence and the Aran trip in bringing Synge to a prominent position within the literary movement.

A consideration of Synge's relationship to Yeats is inseparable from an understanding of his place in the Irish Renaissance, for Yeats was far more than an important poet within the literary movement: he was also its chief organizer and propagandist and the first internationally known writer to place his reputation squarely behind the movement. In many ways, the Irish Literary Renaissance was an extension of Yeats, an organ for the achievement of his goal of creating a national (but not nationalistic) literature for Ireland. Synge, however, was far from being a mere follower or imitator of Yeats, as we might gather from a 1904 letter to Stephen MacKenna in which Synge declares,

> I do not believe in the possibility of "a purely fantastic, unmodern, ideal, spring-dayish, Cuchulainoid National Theatre," because no drama—that is to hold its public—can grow out of anything but the fundamental realities of life which are neither modern or unmodern, and, as I see them, are rarely fantastic or spring-dayish.

Synge's emphasis on "the fundamental realities of life" sets him apart from Yeats, who was usually more concerned with rising above those realities. The difference may be seen in their treatments of the Deirdre legend: Yeats's *Deirdre* (1907) is concentrated, ritualistic, highly symbolic, whereas Synge's **Deirdre of the Sorrows** (1910) is almost a domestic tragedy by comparison. Likewise, the blank verse of *Deirdre,* with its elevated diction, contrasts with the prose style of **Deirdre of the Sorrows,** which closely resembles that of Synge's peasant dramas. The same rejection of what Synge regarded as "fantastic or spring-dayish" tendencies in the literary movement's uses of Irish mythology may be seen in his poem **"The Passing of the Shee,"** whose subtitle—*"After looking at one of A. E.'s pictures"*—singles out the most otherworldly Irish Revival figure as the inspiration for its more profane vision of saying adieu to the fairies while

> We'll search in Red Dan Sally's ditch,
> And drink in Tubber fair,
> Or poach with Red Dan Philly's bitch
> The badger and the hare.
>
> (I.38)

Similarly, the description of Kate Cassidy's wake in **The Playboy of the Western World** includes Michael James Flaherty's boast that "you'd never seen the match of it for flows of drink, the way when we sunk her bones at noonday in her narrow grave, there were five men, aye, and six men, stretched out retching speechless on the holy stones" (IV, 151). This scene is a long way removed from the delicate lyricism of "The Wanderings of Oisin" or the sentimental idealism of *Cathleen Ni Houlihan,* whose author was to invoke the name of this popular play when he rebuked the crowd that protested Synge's far greater play.

The **Playboy,** in fact, contains several elements that distinguish it from more conventional Abbey Theatre fare and from the "Cuchulainoid" aspect of the literary movement generally. Chief among these elements is the parody of Irish mythic heroism embodied in the portrayal of Christy Mahon, a timid young man who becomes a champion athlete, successful ladies' man, and great braggart "by the power of a lie." Several critics, of whom M. J. Sidnell was the earliest and Declan Kiberd the most thorough and persuasive, have called attention to Synge's use of mythic elements in this play, although Kiberd wisely warns against seeking extensive one-to-one correspondences between the play and mythic narratives such as those included in Lady Gregory's *Cuchulain of Muirthemne.* More subversive of the professed aims of the Literary Renais-

sance, perhaps, is the play's constant insistence that greatness is always found elsewhere—in another county, perhaps, or in a heroic past like the one that Pegeen invokes in the first act, asking:

> Where now will you meet the like of Daneen Sullivan knocked the eye from a peeler, or Marcus Quin, God rest him, got six months for maiming ewes, and he a great warrant to tell stories of holy Ireland till he'd have the old women shedding down tears about their feet. Where will you find the like of them, I'm saying?

The irony here cuts both ways, satirizing both the present, in which we constantly imagine that there are no more great men (although we might create one, if he tells the right story), and the supposedly heroic past itself, a time when a prison term for molesting animals gives a man the status of a hero.

Ironically, Synge's parodic versions of Irish mythic tales are often close in spirit to the original stories, since medieval Irish literature contains more than its share of ludicrous and grotesque elements. In *The Irish Comic Tradition,* Vivian Mercier has written [in his *Irish Comic Tradition,* 1962] of the pervasiveness in Irish and Anglo-Irish literature of the very elements—satire, parody, the macabre and the grotesque, and the like—that characterize Synge's plays and some of his poems; and in *Synge: The Medieval and the Grotesque,* Toni O'Brien Johnson has demonstrated that Synge frequently used medieval sources in a manner consistent with the spirit of the originals. Synge was, in fact, capable of adopting the persona of a medieval Irish satirist, for example in his poem **"The Curse,"** which plays on the belief in the magical power of the satirist to cause his victims severe physical pain.

Although he recognizes the satiric element in Synge's work, Mercier argues that Synge "stands almost entirely outside the Gaelic literary tradition" because, "unlike the class-conscious Gaelic poets and satirists, Synge sympathizes with the underdog and the outcast, be he tramp or tinker, parricide or blind beggar." Indeed, one of the sharpest distinctions between Synge and Yeats might be seen in their different satiric perspectives: both satirize the money-grubbing tendencies of the Irish bourgeoisie—Synge in the persons of Dan Burke and Michael Dara, Yeats in the person of William Murphy and others who, in "September 1913," believe that "men were born to pray and save"—but Synge's critique of the middle class comes from the perspective of the outcast, whereas Yeats imagined that he was defending the ideals of a vanishing aristocracy.

The distinction here may be related to the difference between Synge's and Yeats's attitude toward the Irish past. For Yeats, the past represented a coherent, organic state like the one Ruskin associated with the Middle Ages. Alex Zwerdling says, accurately, that Yeats found Irish heroic literature appealing, in part, because it "presented a picture of a hierarchical society ruled by kings, a world whose simplicity of organization emphasized both the sharp distinction between noble, freeman, and slave and the unity created by their mutual interdependence" [*Yeats and the Heroic Ideal,* 1965]. The association of the Irish myths with a vision of organic unity is implied also in Yeats's re-current concern with the heroic figure of Cuchulain, for Cuchulain "combined the roles of warrior, aristocrat, po-litical leader, and visionary" in a manner that is impossi-ble in the modern world.

To the extent that the recovery of a coherent community is associated with the desire to resurrect the sense of na-tional cultural identity, this emphasis on the stability and coherence of the past, and on the importance of a model of community based on the heroic tales, is one of the most salient features of the Irish Renaissance. It is not, howev-er, an important aspect of Synge's work: the only model of a coherent community to be found in the plays is the one in **Riders to the Sea,** a contemporary (although highly archaic) society in which people are bound together through their common struggle against the destructive forces of Nature. Elsewhere—for example, in **The Well of the Saints** and **The Playboy of the Western World**— Synge satirized communities as places dominated by petti-ness, conformity, and hypocrisy. To Hugh Kenner's per-ceptive comment that in Synge's plays "those who set forth have chosen better than those who choose to stay" [*A Colder Eye,* 1983], we might add G. J. Watson's obser-vation that "the tramp-figure or social reject is [Synge's] version of the isolated artist type, the more so as Synge al-ways endows him (the Tramp and Nora, Martin Doul, Christy) with the artist's imagination and heightened elo-quence" [*Irish Identity and the Literary Revival,* 1979]. This sympathy for the outcast and alienation from all communities, so characteristic of Synge, would later be-come an important factor in Yeats's poems (the Crazy Jane poems are particularly good examples), as Yeats's disillusionment with the course of events in Ireland led him to a position not far removed from the one Synge had occupied years before.

Synge's preference for outcasts and dissenters, which is ev-ident from the beginning of his career, is related not only to his alienation from some aspects of the literary move-ment but also to the movement's increasing alienation from the public. The twin attacks on **The Playboy of the Western World**—by nationalists and by religious zeal-ots—were undoubtedly spurred, in part, by suspicions about the "Irishness" of an Irish Literary Revival domi-nated by Anglo-Irish Ascendancy writers, and the split deepened when Yeats called in the Royal Irish Constabu-lary, an arm of the British government, to quell the distur-bances. Synge believed that he was making a good argu-ment for the legitimacy of his art when he wrote, in the Preface to the **Playboy,** that the play included "one or two words only, that [he had] not heard among the country people of Ireland" and that much of his material for **The Shadow of the Glen** had come from listening to servant girls through "a chink in the floor of the old Wicklow house where [he] was staying"; the first comment was dis-missed as obviously untrue and the second as an admission that he was an Ascendancy interloper whose works could be nothing more than a caricature of the real Ireland. Nor did the controversy end with Synge's death, for more than two decades later, in 1931, Daniel Corkery's *Synge and Anglo-Irish Literature* praised Synge for his attempt to

portray the Irish peasantry but often faulted the works for what Corkery believed were inaccuracies of portrayal.

Corkery's book is often regarded as the production of an ethnic chauvinist; yet it must be admitted that conflict be-tween the Irish Literary Revivalists and the community whose cultural identity they set out to resurrect and re-shape was inevitable. The example of Charles Stewart Par-nell, another Ascendancy class champion of the Catholic peasantry who had been rejected by many of his country-men, became for Joyce and Yeats the prototype of the martyred culture hero, and Robin Skelton has argued per-suasively that the nationalists who objected to the **Playboy** did so in part because Christy's career—adulation fol-lowed by betrayal and scapegoating—"bore sufficiently close a resemblance to that of Parnell to make them un-comfortable" ["The Politics of J. M. Synge," *Massachu-setts Review* 18, No. 1 (1977)]. It might well be added that the public was more likely to see itself portrayed by the small-minded communities of the **Playboy** or **The Well of the Saints** than by the drifters and beggars who are sup-posed to gain our sympathy.

The conflict between individual and community that is central to Synge seems at times almost a paradigm of the tension between the literary movement and its public. Christy Mahon, it might be argued, resembles Synge him-self as much as he does Parnell, so that the action of the play accurately predicts the public hostility that it engen-dered. Later, in his poem "On Those that Hated 'The Playboy of the Western World', 1907," Yeats depicted Synge as "great Juan" stared at and reviled by the "eu-nuchs" of Dublin, and elsewhere Yeats campaigned to in-stall Synge within the ranks of the great Irish heroes. Synge's view of heroism was considerably more ironic than Yeats's, and the plays often constitute a critique of the cult of the hero: the **Playboy** and, in a different way, **The Well of the Saints** examine the extent to which illu-sions are necessary to produce a semblance of heroism. Nonetheless, as Seamus Deane has argued [in his *Celtic Revivals,* 1985], "Synge is not writing out the failure of heroism. He is registering its failure in regard to society or, conversely, society's failure in regard to it."

Finally, it may be remarked that the plays continually re-flect the dominant concerns of the movement for Irish cul-tural revival. The fact that the only people who actually die in the plays are members of two endangered species— Aran Islanders, in **Riders to the Sea,** and Irish mythic he-roes, in **Deirdre of the Sorrows**—is typical of the concern that traditional Irish life, in many ways so superior to the urban life surrounding the Abbey Theatre, is slipping away, never to be recovered; the revolt against authority figures—a significant factor in every play except **Riders to the Sea,** and a minor factor even there, through Maurya's recognition of the limitations of priestly knowledge—has a good deal to do with the demand for Irish cultural self determination; and the struggle of the lonely artist-figure against his or her imaginative inferiors suggests the paro-chialism against which Synge and the other Literary Re-vivalists believed they were doomed to struggle. If Synge objected to the "Cuchulainoid" aspects of the literary movement, he never doubted the importance and validity of its main goal: to develop in the English language an Irish literature whose range and subtlety are comparable to those of the best English writers of the time and to do so by relying on subjects that are grounded in Irish life and legend but are universal in their handling of the fundamental problems of life. As the first authentic genius of the Irish theater, Synge was one of the few writers who were most responsible for the success of the Irish Literary Renaissance and the development of a modern Irish literature that is both rooted in Celtic tradition and relevant to the cultural needs of twentieth-century Ireland. (pp. 161-70)

> Patrick A. McCarthy, "Synge and the Irish Literary Renaissance," in A J. M. Synge Literary Companion, *edited by Edward A. Kopper, Jr., Greenwood Press, 1988, pp. 161-71.*

RIDERS TO THE SEA

CRITICAL COMMENTARY

R. L. Collins   (essay date 1947)

[*In the following essay, Collins describes the qualities that make* Riders to the Sea *unique among Synge's dramas and claims that the play captures the essence of the Aran Islands.*]

A peculiarly persistent contradiction has developed in the critical treatment of John Millington Synge. Despite the variety of opinion, both in time and kind, there have emerged certain uniformities: Synge's work is of a piece; he discovered late what he could do; creatively, he did much the same thing from his first to his last play—although here there is always recognition that **Deirdre of the Sorrows** differs in content, if not in manner, from the other plays.

Alongside this uniformity—and usually unaware of the contradiction involved—there has been a steady, if unequal, division of opinion as to Synge's greatest work. Most critics have chosen to think **Riders to the Sea** the apex, although there is a smaller group who place that play in a distinctly inferior rank to that of **The Playboy of the Western World,** or even **The Well of the Saints** or **The Shadow of the Glen.** This is not a mere matter of enthusiasm for a particular work—it is tantamount to a complete act of exclusion. To the admirers of **Riders to the Sea,** the other plays are good journeyman work, only here and there having the seal of greatness. To those who praise most highly one of the other plays, **Riders to the Sea** is mechanically good, but at its best a mere school exercise.

The contradiction arises out of the same people maintaining the two things—that Synge's work is unified, yet that one part is clearly set aside from the remainder. All the critics are aware of a distinction. But they do not try to analyze this distinction and they do not seem to recognize

further that the distinction so marked between **Riders to the Sea** and the other plays is present because there was a dichotomy in the man. Creatively, Synge was pulled towards two contrary objectives; in his memoirs there is evidence everywhere of this strain, but the struggle is not immediately apparent in the creative works. It is not present, that is, within the corpus of a single play. The struggle is there nevertheless: one side of Synge's nature finds expression in **Riders to the Sea;** the other side, in all the other plays.

In all the plays save **Riders to the Sea** the reader or spectator detects easily the thread that holds them together—that unifies them, that marks them as products of a single pen and a single attitude. Despite the obvious technical differences of **The Shadow of the Glen, The Well of the Saints, The Playboy of the Western World,** and **Deirdre of the Sorrows,** the view of life by the author is the same in all. The fear of all the characters is that life will be unfulfilled—beauty dies—the paralysis of old age creeps in. Martin Doul, Christy Mahon, and Naisi have a family likeness: they are all poets, all "fine, fiery fellows with great rages when their temper's roused"; and Pegeen, Nora Burke, and Deirdre have within them the same desire for a full and vigorous life. They are all hard women to please; the cry of each is essentially the same: Nora, "a long while sitting here in the winter . . . with the young growing behind me and the old passing"; Deirdre, looking forward to almost certain death and recalling with anguish the seven perfect years with Naisi just concluding, "Woods of Cuan, woods of Cuan, dear country of the east!"; and Pegeen, standing proud and wretched with the life that had beckoned so ironically now closing around her, saying, "Oh my grief, I've lost him surely. I've lost the only Playboy of the Western World."

In all these plays the identification of reader and spectator is with the characters: in their fortunes, in their hopes and fear, he participates, and the plays stand or fall on the interest aroused by the characters.

In **Riders to the Sea,** however, the thread is broken and the play stands apart from the other work of Synge. Many critics have tacitly recognized this fact and some, indeed, have briefly suggested the measure of difference separating **Riders to the Sea** from the other work. Darrell Figgis says that "we know, and are vitally interested in, Macbeth, and his tragedy is poignant to us with a sense of personal loss. But we do not know Maurya thus. She is not a person to us. She is the soul of a mother set before a cliff of terror. We shudder for all mothers of Aran in her, whereas 'Out, out, brief candle!' comes to us from a man whose magnificence won us." And L. A. G. Strong comments on the play's "steady, eternal rhythm, to which the actors move like puppets, or creatures in a dream. They are fated, but it is the eternal pulse of Nature that governs them."

But no one, I believe, has studied the problem closely, no one has distinctly marked wherein **Riders to the Sea** is set apart from the other plays, and no one has assigned the reasons for the isolated nature of the play. These reasons Synge himself recorded, if unconsciously, in the notebooks of his visits to the Aran Islands.

Brigit O'Dempsey, Sara Allgood, and Maire O'Neill in the 1906 production of Riders to the Sea.

In the record of Synge's first journey to Aran there occurs this passage:

> On the low sheets of rock to the east I can see a number of red and grey figures hurrying about their work. The continual passing in this island between the misery of last night [when the islands were shrouded in one of their recurrent mists] and the splendour of today, seems to create an affinity between the moods of these people and the moods of varying rapture and dismay that are frequent in artists, and in certain forms of alienation. Yet it is only in the intonation of a few sentences or some old fragment of melody that I catch the real spirit of the island, for in general the men sit together and talk with endless iteration of the tides and fish and of the price of help in Connemara.

Homely touches of character—men sitting together and talking endlessly of tides and fish and the price of kelp in Connemara—is this not the basis of drama? And especially in Synge's peasant drama is not this steady humdrum of life basically felt and undeniably necessary no matter what bizarre events, what "variations from the ordinary types of manhood," what wild sayings and ideas come into

the plays? That is, is it not necessary if the artist has for an intention the desire to depict Life in terms of lives?

No one will deny that such a desire was Synge's in all of his plays save **Riders to the Sea.** But in that play Synge sought, I believe, to achieve a synthesis of the effect Aran had had upon him; in other words, he attempted to put that "intonation of a few sentences," that "old fragment of melody," which seemed to him the real spirit of the islands, into creative form. A few characters were necessary, for he chose the vehicle of drama, but they were, it seems to me, deliberately de-humanized—and this fact accounts for the great gulf separating **Riders to the Sea** from Synge's other plays.

There are, it is true, many realistic details offered in **Riders to the Sea,** the clean white boards for the coffin, the bit of new rope being eaten by the pig with the black feet, the stick Michael brought from Connemara—in a sense, too many, for as George Moore said they occasionally make the play seem little more than the contents of Synge's notebook. Yet these details of life as it is lived in one poor cottage Synge offers not for their everyday human values (as he does, for example, with Pegeen's enumeration of things to be sent against her wedding day in Jimmy Farrell's creel cart by Mr. Sheamus Mulroy, Wine and Spirit Dealer, Castlebar), but for the brilliant light they help to shed in the author's presentation of the spirit of the place. And, if it is objected that humanity is surely present in Nora's cry—"isn't it a pitiful thing when there is nothing left of a man who was a great rower and fisher, but a bit of an old shirt and a plain stocking?"—or in Maurya's terrifying "I've seen the fearfulest thing any person has seen since the day Bride Dara seen the dead man with the child in his arms," even these are unearthly wails that can be identified with the music that is implicit in Synge's conception of the spirit of the place. Their burden, though expressed by human beings here, is the same as that note Synge kept hearing in the cormorants over the islands: "There is one plaintive note which they take up in the middle of their usual babble, and pass on from one to another along the cliff with a sort of inarticulate wail, as if they remembered for an instant the horror of the mist."

Synge's character delineation in *Riders to the Sea,* like that in all his plays, is that of the notebook writer. He observed life closely, jotted down his impressions, and then he refined these impressions—omitting all that seemed irrelevant, converting the individual to the universal, and making all speech both articulate and memorable. But the characters in *Riders to the Sea* end—I think deliberately—by being bloodless creations.

Following the description of the dangerous exertions that are required of the Aran men merely to launch and land one of their curraghs safely, Synge says, "This continual danger, which can only be escaped by extraordinary dexterity, has had considerable influence on the local character, as the waves have made it impossible for clumsy, foolhardy, or timid men to live on these islands."

In the re-created play Synge's deft use of his observation and conclusion may be seen. For, despite the fact that all the men in Maurya's family, up to and at last including Bartley, have lost their battle to the sea, neither the reader nor the spectator ever thinks of any of them as having been "clumsy, foolhardy, or timid." Certainly not "timid," because they live out their lives in the face of repeated warnings. Not "clumsy," despite the awkwardness of a riderless pony knocking man and horse into the sea, for Bartley is here combatting a supernatural force. The hand of Fate is on him doubly: he leaves without his mother's blessing and her vision has foretold the event. And not "foolhardy," despite the attempts of Maurya to prevent Bartley from going on the sea, for the young priest has not forbade the trip, and the economic motive driving Bartley is strong: "This is the one boat going for two weeks, and the fair will be a good fair for horses I heard them saying below."

But after this is said and after we are aware how successful Synge has been in transferring from notebook to play this sense of extraordinary stoical character in the figure of Bartley, we must yet notice the significant hiatuses in the drama in this connection. Bartley answers no questions put by his mother, he offers only the explanation of the fair for the necessity of his journey, he does not defend himself against her pleas, he does not try to soften his departure. It is true that to Maurya's question, "Isn't it a hard and cruel man won't hear a word from an old woman, and she holding him from the sea?" Cathleen offers the argument of necessity and inevitability that "It's the life of a young man to be going on the sea, and who would listen to an old woman with one thing, and she saying it over?" It is true, also, that after Bartley's abrupt departure Cathleen indicates that he turned back for a moment at the door dumbly seeking Maurya's blessing.

But this is all that Synge attempts or allows in the matter of human relationships when there was room for so much. And the omission is due, I believe, not so much to the desired economy, certainly not to hasty writing—but to the fact that Synge is dealing here not with people but with abstractions. It is the spirit of loneliness, of continual struggle ending only in death, of stoical acceptance of defeat that *Riders to the Sea* is to embody. The theme, the picture, the language are everything; the people are nothing. They hardly achieve even the abstraction of being the Mother, the Son, the Daughter. In *The Shadow of the Glen,* as in *Lear,* pity naturally accompanies the other emotions; in *Riders to the Sea,* in a situation potentially more pathetic, there is only dry-eyed despair and this arises out of our witnessing a crystallized moment in time and space and not out of sympathy with the characters.

At the close of the first of the Aran notebooks, written just after Synge had left the islands when, standing on the Galway shore, he could look across the bay to the islands and attempt an evaluation of his recent experiences, this insight appears:

> I have come out of an hotel full of tourists and commercial travellers, to stroll along the edge of Galway bay, and look out in the direction of the islands. The sort of yearning I feel towards those lonely rocks is indescribably acute. This town, that is usually so full of wild human interest, seems in my present mood a tawdry medley of all that is crudest in modern life.

One may surmise that in such a mood as this *Riders to the Sea* was written. It is instructive to note that the "wild human interest," so much a part of *The Shadow of the Glen, The Well of the Saints, Deirdre of the Sorrows,* and *The Playboy of the Western World*—being specifically mentioned in the Preface to the last named play as a necessity for imaginative drama—at times is definitely antipathetic to Synge. His yearning at this moment is not to the people of Aran but "to those lonely rocks," as it was, I believe, throughout the composition of *Riders to the Sea.*

The characters of *Riders to the Sea* are made a race apart. Although Synge succeeds in making them symbolic of an everlasting struggle between man and natural forces, of man's fortitude and capacity for endurance, of man's dignity in the face of suffering, he does not attempt to individualize, to humanize, to provide them with the little touches that make created characters lifelike.

In most of the plays Synge's method of incorporating vivid details from the notebooks was to associate them with character—usually successfully, occasionally so that they protruded. There is the Tramp in *The Shadow of the Glen,* for example—a man who has lived his life in the back hills, with the mists and the storms, "walking round in the long nights . . . the time a little stick would seem as big as your arm, and a rabbit as big as a bay horse, and a stack of turf as big as a towering church in the city of Dublin." A man of courage, yes, but also a man who knows of things that cannot be explained rationally. He is willing enough to sit with Nora's "dead" husband at her request, but he is wise enough to take precautions against evil: "Maybe if you'd a piece of grey thread and a sharp needle—there's great safety in a needle, lady of the house—I'd be putting a little stitch here and there in my old coat, the time I'll be praying for his soul, and it going up naked to the saints of God." In Inishmaan the old story-teller, Pat Dirane, had told Synge of the efficacy of having a sharp needle on his person to ward off harm from the fairies, and Synge had noted that "Iron is a common talisman with barbarians, but in this case the idea of exquisite sharpness was probably present also, and, perhaps, some feeling for the sanctity of the instrument of toil, a folk-belief that is common in Brittany."

In contrast, there is Martin Doul, with his eyesight restored, grumbling at the amount of work being put upon him by his present master, Timmy the smith, and accusing him of all kinds of cruelty: "Oh, God help me! I've heard tell you stripped the sheet from your wife and you putting her down into the grave, and that there isn't the like of you for plucking your living ducks, the short days, and leaving them running around in their skins, in the great rains and the cold." Now, this recollection of Synge's having seen in a cottage in Inishmaan "all the women down on their knees plucking the feathers from live ducks and geese" is vivid, even more so than the original incident, perhaps justifies itself because of that fact, is appropriate enough for the sharp-tongued Martin, but is woefully inappropriate when applied to the brawny Timmy who would never be doing woman's work.

But the fact to be noted in both these examples is that Synge makes a conscious effort—here and again and again in the plays—to relate incident to character, to focus sharply the characteristic trait. In *Riders to the Sea,* however, the normal, expected human traits are not present. And in great part they are not present because Synge, having been impressed by the isolation of Aran and the resultant other-worldliness of its inhabitants, attempted in this play to record their distinction from ordinary folk. But Synge's method was not to display differences in personality between the islanders and other people; instead he almost completely denied all personality and individuality in favor of depicting the forces that governed the lives of these people.

When Synge was on his way back to Aran for his second visit, he met the boy Michael, his guide around Inishmaan on the first visit. Michael was now living and working on the mainland; and Synge "was singularly struck with the refinement of his nature, which has hardly been influenced by his new life, and the townsmen and sailors he has met with." Later in the day, Synge, Michael, and a friend of Michael's sat outside near the sea. "The day was unbearably sultry, and the sand and sea near us were crowded with half-naked women, but neither of the young men seemed to be aware of their presence. Before we went back

to the town a man came out to ring a young horse on the sand close to where we were lying, and then the interest of my companions was intense." Imagine Christy, Martin Doul, even Naisi and the Tramp being indifferent to the women. But only by an act of will can Bartley, or for that matter Nora and Cathleen, be thought of in terms of romantic love. Passion there is in the young men—but it is expressed in terms of the fairly primitive struggle between man and horse. So also in *Riders to the Sea.* The emphasis lies here because Synge had been thus impressed time after time by the lives of the islanders. Human relationships on the islands, when described at all, are always portrayed in terms of violence—the fierce mother love, the wild scorn of the girls for Synge when they learn he is a bachelor, the violent games of the young men and girls. And violence, while never an actuality before the spectator in *Riders to the Sea,* is omnipresent: it is the unseen force that governs the lives of the characters and accounts for the unceasing tension of the play. Certainly there are wild, free actions in all the plays, but in all except *Riders to the Sea* the violence arises out of character, or the action of character upon character. In *Riders to the Sea* it is the thing itself—crystallized and separated from its source of origin as from the people it affects. The characters serve only to identify and to concentrate attention upon the abstract force.

Perhaps it goes without saying that in the subordinate characters of the children and the neighbors who bring in the body of Bartley and fall into a deliberate frieze of grief around the apron of the stage, it is easy to see and to say that lifelikeness is sacrificed in favor of the abstraction. But what of the central character of Maurya? Is she too in a sense unhuman?

When Synge returned to Inishmaan for the second time, he lived again with the family he had visited on his first trip. He found changes in the household; Michael was working on the mainland, another son had gone to America. Synge was shown a letter from the latter saying that he was leaving New York to take up his life a few hundred miles inland—a letter that gave great grief to the mother, for "when she hears them talking of railroads and inland cities where there is no sea, things she cannot understand, it comes home to her that her son is gone forever. . . . The maternal feeling is so powerful in these islands that it gives a life of torment to the women. Their sons grow up to be banished as soon as they are of age, or live here in continual danger on the sea; their daughters go away also, or are worn out in their youth with bearing children that grow up to harass them in their own turn a little later."

No one will deny that this maternal feeling is strong in Maurya—no one fails to grasp the torment her life has been in the loss one after the other of her husband and sons. But, as Synge directs the course of the play, the torment is in retrospect—Nora, indeed, being amazed at her mother's calm acceptance of new disaster. The magnificent speeches of Maurya at the close of the play do not plumb emotional depths—nor were they intended to. They are not the direct lament of "Absalom! Oh, my son Absalom!" or the five-fold "never" of Lear; they are the circumscribed grief of one in sackcloth and ashes—

mourning in a prescribed, ritualistic manner. Cathleen offers a natural reason for her mother's passivity—"An old woman will be soon tired with anything she will do, and isn't it nine days herself is after crying and keening, and making great sorrow in the house?"—but the true explanation lies elsewhere. It is to be found in the rigid control Synge exercised over the play, constantly forcing consideration away from Maurya and her troubles, and on to the spirit of strength, fortitude, and resignation that comes from constant conflict with the overpowering forces of wind and wave.

And as Maurya is the distinct center of the play, so the core of Maurya and hence of the play is this composite of qualities—violence, grief, endurance, strength, resignation—that for Synge spelled Aran. In all his other plays Synge sought to express his requisites of drama, *reality* and *joy*, in terms of people; in *Riders to the Sea* he attempted and achieved an essence. He put into creative terms what he had seen and, as an artist, been deeply affected by: "The whole sight of wild islands and sea was as clear and cold and brilliant as what one sees in a dream, and alive with singularly severe glory that is in the character of the place." (pp. 278-84)

> *R. L. Collins, "The Distinction of 'Riders to the Sea'," in* The University of Kansas City Review, *Vol. XIII, No. 4, Summer, 1947, pp. 278-84.*

Paul M. Levitt   (essay date 1969)

[*In the essay below, Levitt explores the narrative structure of* Riders to the Sea, *suggesting that it contributes significantly to the symbolic meaning of the play.*]

Riders to the Sea is of considerable technical interest because of the methods by which Synge obtained intensity and compression within a single act. So clearly did Synge insinuate early in the play a subsequent course of action, that there can be no doubt how the play will end. Indeed, Synge's successful communication of the inevitability of an early death for the fishermen of the Aran Islands has frequently been commented on. Charles Tennyson observes [in "Irish Plays and Playwrights," *The Quarterly Review* CCXV (July 1911)] that "in *Riders to the Sea* . . . the interest is not that of doubt. . . . The certainty [of Bartley's death] is so great that there is hardly even the interest of suspense." This verdict is echoed by Ernest Boyd, Percival Wilde, Alan Price, and others. However, in none of these discussions is there any attempt to see how the imagery and the structure of the action extend the borders, and hence the meaning, of the play to create a sense of fate and timeless repetition.

The major thematic strain of recurring death is initiated in the title of the play and is maintained through allusions to the books of Exodus and Revelation. The biblical allusions combine not only literary levels, but also temporal levels: they bring together past, present, and future in a continuum of NOW. The title *Riders to the Sea* alludes to the fatal ride in Exodus by Pharaoh's horsemen who pursued the Israelites to the midst of the sea and, in consequence, suffered the Lord's wrath for their disobedience.

("Then sang Moses and the children of Israel this song unto the Lord, and spake, saying, I will sing unto the Lord, for he hath triumphed gloriously: the horse and his rider hath he thrown into the sea" [Ex. 15:1]. In particular, the title applies to Michael and Bartley, the two sons of Maurya's who figure in the play, and upon whom Maurya's vision centers. Synge gives to all the drowned fishermen of the Aran Islands, including all the men in Maurya's family, the fate associated with Pharaoh's horsemen. He thus expands the dimensions of the tragedy and gives the play universality.

However, Synge is even more indebted to the Revelation of Saint John the Divine than to Exodus for the imagery and allusions in *Riders*. The revelation purports to be the revelation of Jesus Christ to His servant John in Patmos "to shew . . . things which must shortly come to pass" (Rev. 1:1). It sums up the theme of earthly mortality present in both testaments, while developing, among other things, the Alpha and Omega metaphor—the end of life on earth and the beginning of the life to come. *Riders*, too, concerns the Alpha and Omega of life. And as well, *Riders* has a vision of the future (and also memories of death in the past), and an overall plan which shows "things which must shortly come to pass."

The impression of an unbroken cycle of death inevitably working itself out is a direct result of the organization in the play. By interweaving the elements of the action in such a way as to suggest the presence of a fatal nexus binding each male member of the family to the next, Synge captures the timeless rhythm of recurring death. Through the figures of the two horsemen—Michael and Bartley—are symbolically represented the death of the first rider in the past and the death of the last rider in the present. The riders to the sea are the beginning and the ending, the first and the last riders, victims of the relentless repetition of the eternal pattern.

The play begins as the tragedy, begun many years before, nears completion. Four sons, a husband, and a husband's father have already drowned. There is fear that a fifth son (Michael) has drowned, and that the sixth son (Bartley), the last, is readying himself to go down to the sea. The exposition establishes the relationship between those who have died in the past and those who will die shortly. The present action portrays Nora and Cathleen's concern to identify "a shirt and a plain stocking [that] were got off a drowned man in Donegal" in order to determine if they are Michael's, and the concern of all three women—Maurya and her daughters, Nora and Cathleen—as to whether or not Bartley will leave.

Thus, the lines along which this tragedy of fate will proceed are clear. While we anxiously wait for the completion of an event (Michael's journey) which began before the play opened, we are witness to the start of a new event (Bartley's forthcoming trip). The first event is sustained long enough to permit the second event to begin. This organization contributes to the sense of an inexorable fate, because the overlapping actions proclaim the relatedness of both events. Even as Bartley is preparing to journey to the sea, we suspect that his passage is a renewal of Michael's passage, as Michael's was a renewal of the journeys of the men who preceded him. The very nature of the pattern seems to demand that Bartley must die too.

Bartley's fate, which we have guessed at all along, is first realized, symbolically, in his exit speech:

> BARTLEY (taking the halter.) I must go now quickly. I'll ride down on the red mare, and the gray pony'll run behind me. . . . The blessing of God on you. (He goes out.)

Those familiar with the Apocalypse will have a presentiment of tragedy, knowing that the red mare and the gray pony invoke the memory of the Four Horsemen (Rev. 6:1-8). The apocalyptic symbolism here at once reinforces the biblical imagery of the title and focuses attention on Bartley's exit, emphasizing the likelihood of his dying. Moreover, not only does the apocalyptic symbolism foreshadow the death of Bartley at the end of the play, but it also prepares us for the continuation and development of that symbolism in Maurya's dream.

Shortly after Bartley has gone, Maurya leaves to overtake him in order to give him the bread which the girls have baked for his trip. At this point, Synge returns the action to the question of Michael's fate, that is, to the identification of the clothing. By doing so, he emphasizes through the very organization of the play the theme of a beginning-to-end cycle relentlessly and fatally working itself out in the deaths of Maurya's sons and husband and husband's father. To begin the second action, Bartley's departure, before the first action, the identification of Michael's clothes, is concluded, gives the impression of the separate actions being related. [Levitt adds in a footnote: "Synge was also obliged for dramatic reasons to begin a second action before he could resolve the first. Not to have overlapped the actions would have created a 'dead spot' following the resolution of the Michael question, which in turn would have compelled Synge to find 'something' to occupy the stage from the time that Michael's death is discovered until the time Bartley's subsequent death is known. (Not many plays can stand such 'dead spots,' and especially not a one-act play.) Synge does not permit any relaxation of tension or interest; the Michael question sustains the suspense until the Bartley question is reintroduced."]

As Maurya returns from looking for Bartley, she enters slowly, in silence. She is still holding the bread. We sense that Maurya's weary and reticent entrance is the result of her having missed Bartley. We would little suspect that it is because she *has seen* Bartley. Consequently, almost half the scene is played ironically, because it is played under the assumption that Maurya's depression is the result of her unsuccessful attempt to intercept Bartley. Her eventual revelation, therefore, is doubly effective, revealing at once the irony of her having in fact seen Bartley and the vision which is at the heart of the play's meaning.

Cathleen breaks the silence, asking, "You didn't give him his bit of bread?" But Maurya does not answer. Instead, there is a stage direction which tells us that "Maurya begins to keen softly, without turning round." The bread has gone undelivered; Maurya has not made contact with Bartley. In all times, bread has been equated with life and the living. The important allusion here is that of coming forward, making contact, receiving the bread. To fail to make contact is, symbolically, to die.

Maurya reveals that she has seen "Michael himself." To which Cathleen answers: "You did not, mother; it wasn't Michael you seen, for his body is after being found in the far north, and he's got a clean burial by the grace of God." But Maurya is not to be put off, and Cathleen's contradiction only urges her to a complete revelation of what it is she has seen:

> MAURYA [a little defiantly]. I'm after seeing him this day, and he riding and galloping. Bartley came first on the red mare; and I tried to say "God speed you," but something choked the words in my throat. He went by quickly; and "the blessing of God on you," says he, and I could say nothing. I looked up then, and I crying, at the gray pony, and there was Michael upon it—with fine clothes on him, and new shoes on his feet.

What Maurya has seen is, apocalyptically, the end of Michael and Bartley's life on earth. (And certainly nowhere is the imagery of Revelation more evident than in Maurya's vision.) The allusion underlying her vision reinforces the idea of a terrible destiny being visited upon the men in her family. We are uneasy upon hearing what it is that Maurya has seen, remembering the red horse and the gray (pale) horse Bartley and Michael ride and the fine clothes and new shoes that Michael's phantasm wears. For the red and gray ponies remind us of the Four Horsemen—and death. Michael's fine clothes remind us of the new linen in Revelation: "And to [the righteous] was granted that [they] should be arrayed in fine linen, clean and white: for the fine linen is the righteousness of saints" (Rev. 19:8). "And the armies *which were* in heaven followed [the Word of God] upon white horses, clothed in fine linen, white and clean" (Rev. 19:14). What Maurya has seen is a vision of death and the promise of the life to come. The horses Michael and Bartley ride symbolize the brothers' deaths, and Michael's new clothes his life to come. In terms of the dramatic action, Michael and Bartley represent the Alpha and Omega of male life in their family. (The "first" of Maurya's last two remaining sons, Michael, has already concluded his fatal ride as the last son, Bartley, is beginning his.) By dramatizing only the final steps in the fatal pattern, Synge is letting the part stand for the whole. The Michael and Bartley action represents in small the larger cycle of mortality which has taken the lives of eight men. Moreover, Synge emphasizes the chronology of this cycle by having the "first" son (Michael) dressed in fine clothes and the last son (Bartley) not. This is to indicate in time that Michael is already dead, but Bartley has not died yet, although fated to die.

Hence, Maurya's vision is completely functional; it serves to secure the imagery and meaning in the play and to implement the theme. The figure of the red and gray horses reinforces the timelessness of Michael's and Bartley's ride and the meaning of the play's title; it introduces the richness of the death imagery in Revelation, while the mention of "fine clothes" suggests the salvation of the righteous.

Expanding and extending the significance of Maurya's vision and the theme of an inexorable fate, Synge, in what is perhaps the finest touch in the play, dramatizes the idea of recurrent death by repeating in the background (of the stage) in pantomime the dreadful homecoming pageant which Maurya is describing in the foreground. At the same time that Maurya is recounting the men who have passed from her to death and the scenes of their dying and their homecoming, a similar scene (a "ghost scene") is re-enacted in silence, as the townspeople, bearing the dead Bartley, enter noiselessly in the background.

> MAURYA. . . . There were Stephen, and Shawn, were lost in the great wind, and found after in the Bay of Gregory of the Golden Mouth, and carried up the two of them on the one plank, and in by that door.
>
> [She pauses for a moment, the girls start as if they heard something through the door that is half open behind them.]
>
> NORA (in a whisper). Did you hear that, Cathleen? Did you hear a noise in the north-east?
>
> CATHLEEN (in a whisper). There's some one after crying out by the seashore.
>
> MAURYA (continues without hearing anything). There was Sheamus and his father, and his own father again, were lost in a dark night, and not a stick or sign was seen of them when the sun went up. There was Patch after was drowned out of a curragh that turned over. I was sitting here with Bartley, and he a baby, lying on my two knees, and I seen two women, and three women, and four women coming in, and they crossing themselves, and not saying a word. I looked out then, and there were men coming after them, and they holding a thing in the half of a red sail, and water dripping out of it—it was a dry day, Nora—and leaving a track to the door.
>
> [She pauses again with her hand stretched out toward the door. It opens softly and old women begin to come in, crossing themselves on the threshold, and kneeling down in front of the stage with red petticoats over their heads.]

Maurya's speech by itself is a testament to a life of suffering, recalled at a prophetic moment of sheer hopelessness. Furthermore, by means of the pantomime, Synge captures the ritualistic significance of death and creates a fugal quality in the whole play. It is here that Synge finally harvests the labor of constructing a pattern of repetitive action in which background, theme, and language are repeatedly interwoven.

Throughout the play Synge has been emphasizing the inevitability of premature and violent death suffered by the Aran islanders. The background of a relentless and formidable sea has been particularly influential in persuading us to this idea. In addition, Synge's language reinforces the theme and mood. Almost chant-like, the redundant cadences of Synge's prose seem to duplicate the awful regularity of the sea and the keening of the women.

In the final speeches of the play, Synge again returns to the idea of an unalterable fate which links Maurya's dead.

He gains the effect of concatenated deaths by repeating the news of Michael's death and, at the same time, revealing Bartley's death. While handing Maurya the few recovered pieces of Michael's clothing, Cathleen explains to her that they were found in the far north. Then in the next speech, Nora, in a most dehumanizing description tells how the dead Bartley is come home: a speech which echoes Maurya's description of a moment before in the pantomime scene, of how Patch's drowned body was carried into the house. "They're carrying a thing among them and there's water dripping out of it and leaving a track by the big stones." Maurya's, Cathleen's, and Nora's speeches, following one after another, as they do, give the effect of being related. Bartley's death is confirmed when Cathleen, almost too afraid to ask what she already knows, whispers, "Is it Bartley it is?" Without even hearing the reply of "one of the women"—"It is surely, God rest his soul"—we know that the dread cycle is completed.

As Bartley is brought in, Cathleen asks how he was drowned. This is important because the reply to her question by one of the women—"The gray pony knocked him into the sea, and he was washed out where there is a great surf on the white rocks"—brings us back to the symbolism of the horses in Revelation. But it is to be remembered that Bartley was riding the red mare, which means that the gray pony caused Bartley to be thrown from his own horse into the sea below. It is fitting that when Bartley dies, his death is caused by the gray pony, the horse specifically associated with death. ("And I looked, and behold a pale horse: and his name that sat on him was Death" [Rev. 6:8].) Also, it is meaningful that Bartley's death resulted from his having been thrown into the sea, because if we remember from Exodus that "the horse and his rider hath [the Lord] thrown into the sea," and the analogue to be found in the meaning of the title, **Riders to the Sea,** we are reminded by both that being thrown into the sea is equated with death.

Furthermore, "the white rocks" to which Bartley's body was carried by the surf are the same ones that Cathleen has mentioned earlier in the play in conjunction with a stormy sea. Cathleen asks: "Is the sea bad by the white rocks, Nora?" By alerting us to the rocks early in the play (rocks associated with a bad sea), Synge foreshadows the place of Bartley's death. By mentioning the rocks a second time, Synge emphasizes the point that death is always close at hand and that it occurs in familiar places. Also, the double reference to the white rocks serves, in the overall design of the play, to introduce the threat of the sea and to summarize its symbolism. By significant repetition Synge links the beginning and ending of **Riders,** reinforcing our sense of the cyclical action operating in the play.

Briefly, then, in **Riders,** Synge captures the pattern of death by focusing on a point shortly before the end of the cycle, dramatizing only the last two deaths in the family—those of Michael and Bartley. In this way, and by careful exposition, he compresses past and present action into the closing moments of a tragedy long unfolding. It is this organization, combined with the biblical imagery in the play, which gives **Riders** its extraordinary compactness and intensity, making of the prior drowning and the present tragedy one unbroken action. (pp. 53-61)

Paul M. Levitt, "The Structural Craftmanship of J. M. Synge's 'Riders to the Sea'," in Éire-Ireland: A Journal of Irish Studies, Vol. IV, No. I, 1969, pp. 53-61.

Daniel J. Casey (essay date 1972)

[*Casey is an American scholar, editor, and fiction writer whose works are inspired by his Irish heritage. In the following excerpt, he examines the mood and "pagan fatalism" of the Aran setting of* Riders to the Sea.]

Yeats's well-publicized counsel to the young Synge, as they stood outside the Hotel Corneille in Paris in 1896, may have spurred his intent to visit Aran, but Synge's early concern for the Wicklow peasants, his non-apostolic motive for studying Irish at Trinity, his literary involvement with Le Braz, Loti, and Renan, and his interest in Jubainville's Celtic mythology lectures at the Sorbonne also anticipated the journeys to the Islands. And it is true that Synge probably would have failed in the concert halls and that Arthur Symons was the better critic of French literature. In May, 1898, some seventeen months after Yeats's historic Paris dictum, Synge's enthusiasm lured him from the Wicklow Pale onto the western rocks to begin his literary novitiate. He turned west to experience a world he had long wondered at, a world of myth and reality that he would later express as it had never before been expressed.

In the Aran notebooks, Synge recognized the stark cultural disparity that stood between the islanders and himself: on his second visit, he entered: "In some ways these men and women seem strangely far away from me. They have the same emotions that I have, and the animals have, yet I cannot talk to them when there is much to say, more than to the dog that whines beside me in a mountain fog." But with each succeeding visit to Aran the distance was narrowing, while the allurement for the Fir Bolg and their posterity increased. By October, 1902, when the text of [*Riders to the Sea*] was complete, Synge's imagination was alive with myth, epic, and fairy and folk tales, for he had, since his first Aran visit, continued his Celtic studies at the Sorbonne, reviewed for *The Speaker* four Irish titles—*Danta Amhrain is Caointe Sheathruin Ceitinn, Cuchulain of Muirthemne, Donegal Fairy Stories,* and *Foras Feasa Ar Eirinn*—written the essay, "**La Vieille Littérature Irlandaise,**" participated in the Breton folk revival, and compiled and edited nearly a score of notebooks in *The Aran Islands.*

The Aran sketches furnished plots for his dramas, and his reflections added an aesthetic perspective. Pat Dirane, the sgéalái of Inishmaan, provided **"He That's Dead Can Do No Hurt",** and the oldest man on the island gave him the details of the infamous Lynchehaun murder story. Synge transferred Dirane's tale to the Harney cottage in the Wicklow Hills and made *In the Shadow of the Glen* of it. He removed the ancient's tale of the patricide from Achill and the Arans to a shebeen in Mayo, and there created *The Playboy of the Western World.* Though he adapted the plot of *The Well of the Saints* from a medieval French farce, he also remembered Martin Coneely's miraculous Aran well at *Teampall an Ceatrair Alainn* (The Church of the Four Comely Persons), where blindness and epilepsy were cured. Four of Synge's six plays might have been set in Aran, but only in *Riders to the Sea* is there the urgency of capturing the pristine qualities of the Aran requiem. *Riders to the Sea* is folk drama as no other Synge play is folk drama; it harkens back to antiquity and draws its strength from the mood of pagan fatalism that pervades the place.

I. IMPLICATIONS OF SETTING

Riders to the Sea is an Aran requiem that opens sometime before the Celtic dawn and ends abruptly in the midst of a curious funeral in the Celtic twilight. It is a dramatic episode that depends in the end on mythical, symbolic, and allegorical interpretation, and in the beginning on John Millington Synge's Aran experience.

Understanding the implications of setting in *Riders to the Sea* contributes to an appreciation of the tragedy. Critics have indeed examined the playwright's conscious art, his use of form, ironic technique, and dialect; few have responded intuitively to *an domhain shair* (the western world) or inquired into Synge's dependence on the cottage on Inishmaan to set his dramatic elegy. A cursory reading of the prose sketches, *The Aran Islands,* is unlikely to resolve the problem of response to setting in *Riders,* though it will assuredly be a step in that direction. The resolution begins on a quay in Galway or aboard a turf-stacked hooker out of Carraroe. It comes of peering through a mist-laden bay for a glimpse of "a wet rock in the Atlantic". Essentially the tragedy derives its force from the interacting preternatural powers emanating from the omnipotent sea, the subterranean recesses of the defiant islands, and the mysterious psyche of the Aranmen themselves. The fuller sense of tragedy comes, of course, in the final cathartic realization of man's tenuous existence in the cosmos.

Riders to the Sea is, we are told, set on "An Island off the West of Ireland"; it is set on Inishmaan, the middle island in the Aran group. Conjecture as to Synge's reasons for an Inishmaan cottage setting may seem pointless. Hadn't he witnessed the aftermath of a drowning there and heard islanders' whispered versions of the tragedy? But for Synge the fisher cottage suggests more than a tragic tale; it suggests a barren windswept landscape, megalithic monuments, and the dark descendants of the Fir Bolg, a folk whose race memory is crowded with mythic allusions. Inishmaan, where more Irish is spoken, and where "the life is perhaps the most primitive that is left in Europe", provided more than an atmosphere, it provided the reason for the drama itself. The aged thatcher on Inisheer confided:

> Long ago we used all to be pagans, and the saints used to be coming to teach us about God and the creation of the world. The people on the middle island were the last to keep a hold on the fire-worshipping, or whatever it was they had in those days, but in the long run a saint got in among them and they began listening to him though they would often say in the evening they

believed, and then say the morning after that, they did not believe.

Synge sought to be witness to the most extraordinary endemic instincts and to participate, however vicariously, in the Gaelic experience. In *The Aran Islands* we have something of his observations and his reflections; in *Riders to the Sea* an aesthetic representation of those instincts and that experience.

II. THE ARAN SKETCHES AS A SOURCE

George Moore's remark that the details in *Riders to the Sea* "occasionally make the play seem little more than the contents of Synge's notebooks" has more than a hint of truth in it. Among the playwright's impressions scattered through the Aran sketches are recollections of the tragic and near-tragic incidents that contribute to the dramatic episode. During his first visit to Inishmaan in May and June, 1898, Synge was intrigued by the ceremony that attended the death of an old woman in the neighboring cottage. The mournful keen at the wake and the repetitious thud of the hammer on the coffin he overheard from a distance. The following morning he recorded details of the burial—the manner in which the coffin was loosely sewn in sailcloth and borne by three cross-poles lashed to the lid; the procession of men followed by old women with red petticoats drawn over their heads; the ritual in which each old woman led an ancient recitative, bending her forehead to a stone, while the rest swayed rhythmically and intoned an incomprehensible chant; the interment, accompanied by a rumbling of thunder and a rain of hailstones; and finally the primordial recessional keen that concluded the burial. Synge was completely absorbed in the ancient lament and noted:

> The grief of the keen . . . seems to contain the whole passionate rage that lurks somewhere in every native of the island. In this cry of pain the inner consciousness of the people seems to lay itself bare for an instant and to reveal the mood of the beings who feel their isolation in the face of a universe that wars on them with wind and seas. They are usually silent, but in the presence of death all outward show of indifference or patience is forgotten, and they shriek with pitiable despair before the horror of the fate to which they are all doomed.

The emphasis on aboriginal pagan ritual to the near exclusion of Catholic ritual—only the mass and an old man's simple prayer are mentioned—is evidence of what struck Synge as the most primitive of human instincts.

During his second visit to Inishmaan in September and October, 1899, he experienced what he called "the darker side of life in the islands". Gone was the vernal vitality of May and June, and in its stead came the somber grays and blacks of autumn, the unwelcome chill of the southwest wind, and the thundering waves that broke on the rock shelves to inundate the landscape. Synge's curragh passage to Aranmore was a memorable confrontation between four skilled Inishmaan rowers and an angry sea, and in his providential escape from drowning, he realized that life on the middle island held more than an aura of pagan fatalism, that the malevolent sea had a destructive

force that Aranmen knew they could not reckon with. *Riders to the Sea,* Synge's nature-elegy, springs, then, from the same roots as does early Irish nature poetry, and his understanding of primitive man's communion with nature and the elements is the understanding that lies beneath the "nature mystique" Ellis-Fermor [in *The Irish Dramatic Movement,* 1964] has attributed to his work.

During the autumns of 1900 and 1901, Synge witnessed a sequence of events that bore even more directly on his composition of *Riders.* In 1900 he noted, "Now a man has been washed ashore in Donegal with one pampooty on him, and a striped shirt with a purse in one of the pockets, and a box of tobacco." The islanders trying to identify the drowned man as a fisherman from Inishere or Inishmaan, received confirmation from the man's sister, who was able to remember details about his clothes, his stockings, and his purse and tobacco.

> "Ah!" she said, "it's Mike sure enough, and please God they'll give him a decent burial".
>
> Then, she began to keen slowly to herself. She had loose yellow hair plastered round her head with the rain, and as she sat by the door suckling her infant, she seemed like a type of woman's life upon the islands.

The visions of the dead man's disconsolate mother searching the sea, his keening sister identifying the corpse, and the suckling infant were faithfully recorded; the archetypal image of grief-stricken woman and the death-rebirth pattern were suggested to the writer. On this third Aran journey Synge again committed every vivid impression to the notebooks, including his doleful memory of the drove of pigs being transported to an English slaughterhouse by a local jobber.

During the final visit to the island in September and October, 1901, he added to his mournful impressions. One night as a hurricane was howling, Norah, a young married woman, was dying of typhus; as she was not expected to live beyond morning, coffin boards had to be borrowed from a man who had put the boards aside two years before for his aged mother. The headless body of a young man had been washed ashore after floating for several weeks in the sea, and once again keening and hammering could be heard in the vicinity of the wake cottage. The young man had taken a curragh to tow horses from a hooker to the shore of the south island. The curragh was swamped by waves and the young man was lost, but according to the lad relating the story, there were signs and prophesies preceding the drowning. Not only had the young man's dog sat beside him crying a warning, his mother had a vision of him riding a horse to the slip; she saw him catch his horse, then a second horse . . . and afterward he went out and was drowned.

Synge described the burial and funeral of the young man as "one of the strangest scenes I have met with". The mourners beat on the closed coffin; both men and women raised the keen; an old man splashed holy water on the bereaved. The gravediggers accidentally turned up the skull of the young man's maternal grandmother, and his mother seized the skull and took it aside keening and shrieking over it in wild despair. At last Synge wandered down to the shore and joined fishermen who were dragging with nets, and as he broke bread with them he reflected:

> . . . I could not help feeling that I was talking with men who were under a judgment of death. I knew that every one of them would be drowned in the sea in a few years and battered naked on the rocks, or would die in his own cottage and be buried with another fearful scene in the grave-yard I had just come from.

Shortly afterward, the old man in the cottage where Synge lodged told a revenant tale of a mother who had been abducted by fairies but returned at night to nurse her infant. The captive spirit directed her own escape on Oidche Shamhna. She would be riding, she said, among the fairy host behind a young man on a gray horse, and her rescuers were to throw something over the two riders to release them from the fairy spell.

This sequence of connected impressions provides the episode and explains the origin of many of the playwright's "allusions". Details have been accounted for: Michael's stocking and shirt, the white boards for the coffin, the pig destined for the slaughterhouse, the vision of the rider and the two horses, the gray pony of Shamhna, and others. The wake and burial have been twice described. If Synge's tragedy succeeds, one is tempted to attribute its success to his realism, his talent for accurately representing character and situation. But, in truth, *Riders to the Sea* succeeds largely because it realized an Aran-consciousness and has a subtle awareness that character and situation are somehow subordinated to setting. Synge begins with a composite of impressions, but he manages to translate those impressions to a moving dramatic elegy.

III. THE AESTHETIC SENSE

In the aesthetic representation, Synge consciously ladens each descriptive detail, dialogue, and action with far-reaching significance, creating, as it were, continuous symbolic multiplication. The new rope that hangs by the white boards suggests deadly uses: to lash the coffin shut, to drag the pig with the black feet to slaughter, to halter the red mare that will destroy Bartley. At the same time the brevity—the playwright's restricted development of character, confinement of movement within the cottage kitchen, resistance to extended dialogue—serves to emphasize what does occur on stage. Maurya has already lost her husband and five sons; only one son remains to be buried, and his fate is symbolically sealed with his every action. His death is, in fact, anticlimactic. The focus is clear and the dramatic action is brief. The opening dialogue between Cathleen and Nora, for example, focuses immediate attention on Maurya's condition and the cause of it, and introduces the ensuing conflict between Bartley and Maurya. It is audience awareness of symbolic multiplication and response to the implications of setting that contributes to the sense of dramatic progression. In effect, the playwright has in several minutes implied that an island family will be annihilated by the sea and that supernatural forces are impotent as intercessors.

The symbols, echoes, and allusions are archetypal; they are drawn directly from a primitive folk engaged in the most elemental struggle—the struggle for survival in nature. The activity is activity of hearth—kneading bread, spinning yarn, and raking fire—and the characters are more types than *personae;* they are mother, son, and daughters before they are Maurya, Bartley, Cathleen, and Nora. Only Maurya, in her miraculous transfiguration from petulant old woman to pagan priestess of antiquity, moves beyond type. As the tragic figures in the elegy, Maurya must elicit sympathy. Her plight, the plight of island women and women everywhere, is that she be tormented by sons who live in the face of death and by daughters who are to be subject to the same torments as she. Maurya's final capitulation shows a sense of relief from death, lamentation, and uncertainty. "No man at all can be living for ever, and we must be satisfied" is natural and spontaneous, rather than profound and reflective, for it is, like most of Synge's memorable speeches, drawn from actual dialogue or correspondence. *Riders to the Sea* reaches Greek-perfection, not because it is Aristotelian, but because it translates a primitive Gaelic experience which is also universal.

The playwright is obviously less concerned with character development and dramatic action than he is with effecting a pervasive fatalistic mood. Bartley's death blends with Michael's death, and the deaths of Stephen and Shawn, and Sheamus and Patch, and with the deaths of their father and grandfather before them. And Synge's color scheme—the black, white, gray, and red—suggest always death and destruction. The somber mood of the island requiem is, of course, dominated by blackness—the blackness of night, of cliffs of the north, of the knot on Michael's clothing, of "hags that do be flying on the sea". There are white rocks in the sea by which man is devoured and white boards by which he is swallowed into the earth. The spectral gray pony of Maurya's vision that carried the apparition of Michael and that knocked Bartley into the sea exists in a half-light and serves to meld the world of the dead and the world of those soon to die. In the end, though, it is the crimson of martyrdom and sacrifice that spills over the stage as old women, red petticoats drawn over their heads, file into the foreground and raise a frightful keen.

Synge's rendering of the Gaelic idiom also contributes to the ominous and mournful effect. The sea is, we are told, "middling bad" by the white rocks, but there is "a great roaring in the west" that threatens to worsen it and there is "a power of young men floating round in the sea". References to gusting winds, turning tide, and the star against the moon forebode evil. And Nora, referring to Bartley's hunger, says, "And it's destroyed he'll be . . . "; Cathleen emphasizes the ambiguous intent with "It's destroyed he'll be, surely." Dialogue is aesthetically appropriate to mood, and the episode culminates in a forceful elegiac impression rather than a dramatic resolution.

The playwright moves toward a solemn requiem for a mortal man, but mortality, the common denominator that makes all men riders to the sea, marks the ceremony a requiem for humanity. Maurya, now prophetess-priestess in an order older than that of Melchizedek, presides instinctively in the liturgy. The victim, shrouded in a bit of sailcloth, lies before her on the sacrificial table ringed in red, while the swaying, chanting mourners lend the scene an atmosphere of pagan desperation. The rubrics are curious, suggestive of a ceremony that has evolved from pagan-Christian syncretism over a millennium and a half. The celebrant kneels at the head, the two servers at the feet, the community close at hand. The ritual is deceptively complicated. Maurya rises, drops Michael's clothing across Bartley's feet, then sprinkles the body with holy water. She kneels, crosses herself, and prays silently. When she rises again, it is to spread the clothes and sprinkle them with what remains of the water. She turns the cup mouth downward on the table symbolically, and lays her hands on Bartley's feet. She kneels again. The women continue to keen inarticulately in the background as Maurya half prays half chants the *threnos,* a lament for Bartley, for Michael, for herself, and for suffering human-kind. Maurice Bourgeois explains [in his *John Millington Synge and the Irish Theatre,* 1965], "To Synge the Irish peasant is a latter-day Pagan on whose old-time heathen-dom the Christian faith has been artificially and superficially grafted".

There is no young priest at this requiem; there is only the traditional priestess of the pre-Celt. Christianity cannot commune with nature, and its antecedent, a religion that lives on in dim mythology, *can* commune, even if it is powerless to contradict what has been preordained. Synge found that the islanders did not distinguish between the natural and the supernatural, that in time of crisis they reverted to ancient belief and ancient ritual, and to the race tendency to credit signs and visions and prophecies. Human opposition to the cosmic design is futile; resignation is all that is left to man. What becomes important, then, is that Michael have a clean burial, that Bartley have a fine coffin and a deep grave, and that Maurya have a great sleep after Samhain. [In a footnote, Casey defines Samhain as "the ancient Feast of the Dead, when spirits were abroad in the land".]

Riders to the Sea is not an accurate representation of life and death on Inishmaan, nor is it meant to be. The playwright has selected from the incidents aspects of Aran life, and he has extended those aspects imaginatively. The various criticisms—that the play is too brief, that dialogue is inappropriate, that character and situation are undeveloped—are unfounded. Synge accomplished what he had set out to accomplish, a dramatic elegy that was rooted in the primitive response to death in Aran.

If art can be accepted as collaboration, Synge's reasons for coming as an outsider and immersing himself in Gaeltacht traditions are apparent. His experiences, sitting huddled by a turf fire in an Inishmaan cottage listening to a wizened Gaelic storyteller, or inquiring into the vanishing vestiges of an ancient mythology, began that collaboration. Confronted with a rich trove of primary materials, he found that his imagination was overwhelmed. P. A. O'Síocháin accurately summarized Synge's aesthetic mission:

> He did pick up much of the Celtic imagery which he wrote into an exquisite word texture in English. He undoubtedly inherited some of it,

but his approach to Gaelic and to the Gaelic way of life was that of a semi-foreigner with a poetic mind, a keen intelligence, and a capacity for dedication. He was attracted by the grand vision of his dreams for his own personal ambition, and in the Gaelic and in the Aran Islands he knew that he had found something profoundly unique could he but absorb it and translate it into words of drama and literature.

> [*Aran: Islands of Legend,* 1962]

Synge did absorb it and translate it into the words of drama.

To return to the perhaps too obvious premise, that Synge's art begins in his fascination for the exotic world of the Gael and in his awareness of his cultural distances from that world, is to affirm the playwright's aesthetic. "If an Irishman of modern culture dwells for a while in Inishmaan or Inisheer, or, perhaps, anywhere among the mountains of Connacht, he will not find there any trace of an external at-homeness but will rather yield himself up to the entrancing newness of the old". Out of Synge's representation of the Gaelic traditions that lived on Aran in his time were born the finest dramas of the Celtic Revival. (pp. 89-99)

> *Daniel J. Casey, "An Aran Requiem: Setting in 'Riders to the Sea'," in* The Antigonish Review, *No. 9, Spring, 1972, pp. 88-100.*

THE PLAYBOY OF THE WESTERN WORLD

PRODUCTION REVIEWS

The Irish Times   (review date 28 January 1907)

[*In the following review originally published in* The Irish Times *in 1907, the critic disapproves of the frank language in* The Playboy of the Western World.]

Mr. J. M. Synge's new comedy, **The Playboy of the Western World,** was produced in the Abbey Theatre on Saturday night by the National Theatre Society. The theatre was crowded with an audience the majority of whom were prepared to give a friendly reception to the latest work of a playwright who had already proved himself possessed of ability to present an effective stage representation of Irish people. On those who visited the Abbey Theatre on Saturday night for the first time, however, the performance must have produced a strange impression. The majority of theatre-goers are not accustomed to 'remorseless truth' in characterisation, and after witnessing **The Playboy** they will be rather strengthened than otherwise in their preference for the conventional form of stage representation. Mr. Synge set himself the task of introducing his audience to a realistic picture of peasant life in the far West of Ireland, and he succeeded in accomplishing his purpose with a remarkable degree of success. The roadside publichouse, in which the action of the play takes place, and the peas-

Sara Allgood, Barry Fitzgerald, and Arthur Shields in The Playboy of the Western World.

ants who come upon the scene, are true to life; the atmosphere of 'the West' is all around, and the dialogue full and free. There is much to commend in Mr. Synge's work, but it is open to serious question whether he has been well advised in regard to some of the dialogue. While there is not a word or a turn of expression in the play that is not in common use amongst peasants, it is quite another matter to reproduce some of the expressions on a public stage in a large city. People here will not publicly approve of the indiscriminate use of the Holy Name on every possible occasion, nor will they quietly submit to the reproduction of expressions which, to say the least, are offensive to good taste, however true they may be to actual life. A large section of Saturday night's audience very properly resented these indiscretions on the part of the author, and brought what, in other respects, was a brilliant success to an inglorious conclusion. Mr. Synge, we are afraid, must to some extent sacrifice the 'remorseless truth' if his play is to be made acceptable to healthy public opinion. As to the acting of the piece, it was worthy of the highest commendation. Mr. W. G. Fay took the principal part of Christopher Mahon, and gave an admirable representation of the part, and Miss Maire O'Neill was also excellent as Margaret

Flaherty. Mr. F. J. Fay was very good as Shawn Keogh, the rival of Christy Mahon, and the other parts were well filled by Mr. A. Power, Mr. Arthur Sinclair, Mr. J. A. O'Rourke, Mr. J. M. Kerrigan, Mr. U. Wright, Mr. Harry Young, Miss Sara Allgood, Miss Bright O'Dempsey, Miss Alice O'Sullivan, and Miss Mary Craig. *The Playboy* will be repeated each evening during this week. (pp. 248-50)

> *A review of "The Playboy of the Western World," in* Specimens of English Dramatic Criticism: XVII-XX Centuries, *edited by A. C. Ward, Oxford University Press, 1945, pp. 248-50.*

The Irish Times   (editorial date 30 January 1907)

[The following editorial, originally published in 1907 on page one of an edition of The Irish Times, *calls for an end to the "crude and violent" demonstrations against* The Playboy of the Western World.]

The National Theatre Company cannot complain that Dublin's reception of Mr. Synge's play, **The Playboy of the Western World,** at the Abbey Theatre has been lacking in warmth. The play, Mr. Synge tells us, was 'made to amuse'. Perhaps a section of our countrymen can only achieve amusement by working themselves into a violent passion. At any rate they have amused themselves during the last two nights by making such a pandemonium at the Abbey Theatre that the actors have been obliged to go through their parts in dumb show. The charges made against the play in defence of this rowdy conduct are that its plot and characters are an outrageous insult to the West of Ireland and its people, and that some of its language is vulgar, and even indelicate. The hero of the play is a disreputable tramp, who only ceases to be courted by the women of a Western village when they discover that he is not really a parricide. Such an incident would be uncommon in any civilised country. The 'Irish Ireland' critics of Mr. Synge's play have decided that it would be absolutely impossible in Ireland—just as they decided previously, in the case of *Countess Cathleen,* that it would be impossible for any Irish-woman to sell her soul to the devil, and, in the case of *The Spell,* that it would be impossible for any Irish-woman to believe in the potency of a love-philtre. 'Calumny gone raving mad' is how the *Freeman's Journal* describes **The Playboy of the Western World,** and during the last two nights considerable bodies of apparently intelligent young men have endorsed that verdict by appearing to go raving mad at the Abbey Theatre.

It need hardly be said that no well-balanced mind can defend for a single moment the *Sinn Fein* party's crude and violent methods of dramatic criticism. Let us admit at once that Mr. Synge's play has serious faults. It seems to be granted by his most enthusiastic admirers that some of his language has the material fault of being indelicate and the artistic fault of obscuring the essential realities of the play. An error in taste, however, is not a crime, and the shriekings of an infuriated mob are not the proper method of rebuking it. As to the main incident of the play being impossible, Mr. Synge had produced *prima facie* evidence in favour of its possibility. The idea, he says, was suggested to him by the fact that a few years ago a man who committed a murder was kept hidden by the people on one of the Arran Islands until he could get off to America. Mr. Synge refers us also to the case of Lynchehaun, who was a most brutal murderer of a woman, and yet, by the aid of Irish peasant women, managed to conceal himself from the police for months. The fact is that while, in our opinion, there are aspects of Mr. Synge's play which may be justly and severely criticised, the *Sinn Fein* shouters have ignored these altogether, and have founded their objections on a theory of Celtic impeccability which is absurd in principle, and intolerable when it is sought to be rigidly imposed as a canon of art. Our own criticism of the play is based solely on artistic considerations. We blame Mr. Synge, for instance, for not having made his motive clear to his audience. Hardly any member of the gathering which witnessed the first production on Saturday night seems to have been able to guess what the author was 'driving at'. In another column that clever writer, 'Pat', evolves an interesting and plausible theory of what was in Mr. Synge's mind. Even, however, if it were a true theory Mr. Synge appears to have failed to give his audience a definite appreciation of it. But, if Mr. Synge is correctly represented in an 'interview' which he gave yesterday to an evening newspaper, 'Pat's' motive was not really his motive—in fact, he had no serious motive at all. He is said to have stated that the play is an extravaganza, that he wrote it to please himself, and that its Irish setting was a mere accident. If this can be a true explanation we confess that we find it hard to defend *The Playboy of the Western World.* The idle aim of a mere extravaganza does not justify the grimly realistic treatment of a distinctly unpleasant theme. A serious purpose, clearly brought home, would have vindicated the play. If, however, Mr. Synge was simply a humourist, then he has played with edged tools, and he can hardly lay claim to that feeling of self-approval which was the consolation of the Roman actress when she, too, was hissed from the stage.

Yet even if the faults of Mr. Synge's play were much greater than we take them to be, the treatment which it has received from a section of the public is utterly indefensible. Mr. Synge is an artist, and, as such, not immune from criticism; but it ought to be intelligent criticism. The claim—not now advocated for the first time—that people should be allowed to howl down a play or a book merely because it offends their crude notions of patriotism cannot be tolerated for a moment, if there is ever to be such a thing as independent thought in Ireland. We heartily endorse everything that Mr. W. B. Yeats said yesterday on this subject.

When I was a lad (said Mr. Yeats) Irishmen obeyed a few leaders; but during the last ten years a change has taken place. For leaders we now have societies, clubs, and leagues. Organised opinion of sections and coteries has been put in place of these leaders, one or two of whom were men of genius. . . . There are some exceptions, as heretofore, but the mass only understand conversion by terror, threats, and abuse.

It is high time for thoughtful Irishmen of all parties to make a stand for freedom of thought and speech against

bodies which seek to introduce into the world of the mind the methods which the Western branches of the United Irish League have introduced into politics. For this reason we sympathise with the plucky stand which the National Theatre Company is making against the organised tyranny of the clap-trap patriots. We hope, however, that the next battle will be over a play to which, as a work of art, we shall be able to give a more wholehearted approval than we find it possible to offer to *The Playboy of the Western World.* (pp. 250-53)

> *A review of "Playboy of the Western World," in* Specimens of English Dramatic Criticism: XVII-XX Centuries, *edited by A. C. Ward, Oxford University Press, 1945, pp. 250-53.*

Pat (pseudonym of P. D. Kenney)   (essay date 30 January 1907)

[*In the following essay originally published in* The Irish Times *in 1907, Kenney defends* The Playboy of the Western World *as a "highly moral play," contending that the audience must penetrate its vulgar exterior to find the valuable message about the Irish people.*]

Dublin audiences are said to be very critical, and those at the Abbey Theatre are said to be the most critical of them, but they have not yet permitted themselves to see *The Playboy of the Western World,* and I hope the plucky players will play on until there is a chance to understand, when the screaming has exhausted itself. The screamers do not know what they are missing.

In a way there are two plays, one within another, and unless the inner one is seen, I am not surprised at the screaming about the outer one, which in itself is repellent, and must so remain until seen in the light of the conception out of which it arises, as when we welcome a profane quotation in a sermon, recognising a higher purpose that it is employed to emphasise. *The Playboy of the Western World,* is a highly moral play, deriving its motive from sources as pure and lofty as the externals of its setting are necessarily wild and vulgar; and I cannot but admire the moral courage of the man who has shot his dreadful searchlight into the cherished accumulation of social skeletons. He has led our vision through the Abbey-street stage into the heart of Connacht, and revealed to us there truly terrible truths, of our own making, which we dare not face for the present. The merciless accuracy of his revelation is more than we can bear. Our eyes tremble at it. The words chosen are, like the things they express, direct and dreadful, by themselves intolerable to conventional taste, yet full of vital beauty in their truth to the conditions of life, to the character they depict, and to the sympathies they suggest. It is as if we looked into a mirror for the first time, and found ourselves hideous. We fear to face the thing. We shrink at the word for it. We scream.

True, a play ought to explain itself; but then, the audience has not yet permitted it to explain itself. Perhaps the externals are unworkably true to the inherent facts of life behind them; but that is a superficial matter, and though it is hard for an artist to select language less strong than the truth impelling him, I think a working modification may be arrived at without sacrificing anything essential. Mr. Synge must remember the shock was sincere.

'Pegeen' is a lively peasant girl in her father's publichouse on the wild wayside by the Western sea, and it is arranged for her to marry 'Shaneen Keogh', the half idiot, who has a farm, but not enough intelligence to cut his yellow hair. There is no love. Who could think of loving 'Shaneen'? Love could not occur to her through him. He has not enough intelligence to love. He has not enough character to have a single vice in him, and his only apparent virtue is a trembling terror of 'Father Reilly'. Yet there is nothing unusual in the marriage of such a girl to such a person, and it does not occur to her that love ought to have anything to do with the matter.

Why is 'Pegeen' prepared to marry him? 'God made him; therefore let him pass for a man', and in all his unfitness, he is the fittest available! Why? Because the fit ones have fled. He remains because of his cowardice and his idiocy in a region where fear is the first of the virtues, and where the survival of the unfittest is the established law of life. Had he been capable, he would have fled. His lack of character enables him to accept the conditions of his existence, where more character could but make him less acceptable, and, therefore, less happy. Character wants freedom, and so escapes, but the 'Shaneens' remain to reproduce themselves in the social scheme. We see in him how the Irish race die out in Ireland, filling the lunatic asylums more full from a declining population, and selecting for continuance in the future the human specimens most calculated to bring the race lower and lower. 'Shaneen' shows us why Ireland dies while the races around us prosper faster and faster. A woman is interested in the nearest thing to a man that she can find within her reach, and that is why 'Pegeen' is prepared to marry her half idiot with the yellow hair. 'Shaneen' accepts terror as the regular condition of his existence, and there is no need for him to emigrate with the strong and clever ones who insist on freedom for their lives.

Such is the situation into which the 'Playboy' drifts, confessing in callous calmness that he has killed his father, and claiming sanctuary as potboy in the publichouse—not, by the way, a convincing position in which to disguise a murderer. Women do not choose murderers for their husbands, but the 'Playboy' is a real, live man, and the only other choice is the trembling idiot, who would be incapable even to kill his father. Instinctively and immediately, 'Pegeen' prefers the murderer. Besides, there is the story of why he 'stretched his father with the loy'. The father had wanted to force him into a marriage with a woman he hated. The son had protested. The father had raised the scythe, but the son's blow with the spade had fallen first. Murder is not pleasant, but what of the other crime—that of a father forcing his son to marry a woman he hated? Were it not for this crime, the other could not have followed. A real, live man was new and fascinating to 'Pegeen', even a parricide, and the man who had killed his father, rather than marry a woman he hated, might at least be capable of loving sincerely. Then, he was a man who had achieved something, if only murder, and he had achieved the murder obviously because his better charac-

ter had not been permitted to govern him. When trembling idiocy tends to be the standard of life, intelligence and courage can easily become criminal, and women do not like trembling men. In their hearts, they prefer murderers. What is a woman to do in conditions of existence that leave her a choice only between the cowardly fool and the courageous criminal?

The choice itself is full of drama, the more tragic because it is the lot of a community. The woman's only alternatives are to be derelict or to be degraded; poor 'Pegeen' personifies a nation in which the 'Shaneens' prevail, and in which strong, healthy men can stay only to be at war with their surroundings. It is the revolt of Human Nature against the terrors ever inflicted on it in Connacht, and in some subtle way of his own the dramatist has succeeded in realising the distinction; so that when even the guilt is confessed, we cannot accept the 'Playboy' quite as a murderer, and we are driven back to the influences of his environment for the origin of his responsibility, feeling that if we do not permit men to grow morally, we are ourselves to blame for the acts by which they shock us. Such are Synge's insights into life and character in Connacht. Can the Western peasantry have a truer friend than the one who exhibits to criticism and to condemnation the forces afflicting their lives?

The peasant women of Connacht are no more partial to murderers than other women in other countries, but we must take the conduct of women anywhere in the light of their environment, and we must take the conduct of men in the same way. The difference between a hero and a murderer is sometimes, in the comparative numbers they have killed, morally in the favour of the murderer; and we all know how the 'pale young curate' loses his drawing-room popularity when the unmarried subaltern returns from his professional blood-spilling. It is not that women love murder; it is that they hate cowardice, and in 'Pegeen's' world it is hard for a man to be much better than a coward. Hence the half-idiot with the yellow hair, who, controlling his share of the nation's land, can inflict his kind on the community generation after generation.

The fierce truth and intensity of the dramatist's insight make strength of expression inevitable, but, confining myself strictly to the artistic interest, I feel that the language is overdone, and that the realism is overdone. They irritate, and, worse still, they are piled up to such excess in the subsidiaries of expression as to make us lose sight in some measure of the dramatic essentials. As to the discussions on feminine underclothing, I have often heard discussions more familiar among the peasantry themselves, without the remotest suggestion of immorality, and if Dublin is shocked in this connection, it is because its mind is less clean than that of the Connacht peasant woman.

In itself, the plot is singularly undramatic by construction, suggesting drama rather than exploiting 'cheap' effect. We have to think down along the shafts of light into Connacht in order to realise the picture at the end of the vista, but when we see it we find it inevitable and fascinating. The play is more a psychological revelation than a dramatic process, but it is both.

I have not said much to suggest 'comedy', which is the official adjective for this play. I have tried to bring out the unseen interests that await criticism and appreciation while the Abbey Street audiences scream. It is a play on which many articles could be written.

There was a large audience last night, mainly there to 'boo', but they must pay to come in, so that the management stands to make money, and to be heard in the end. (pp. 254-59)

> *Pat [P. D. Kenny], "That Dreadful Play," in* Specimens of English Dramatic Criticism: XVII-XX Centuries, *edited by A. C. Ward, Oxford University Press, 1945, pp. 254-59.*

CRITICAL COMMENTARY

Louis Untermeyer   (essay date 1908)

[*A poet during his early career, Untermeyer is better known as an anthologist of poetry and short fiction, an editor, and a master parodist. Notable among his anthologies are* Modern American Poetry *(1919),* The Book of Living Verse *(1931),* New Modern American and British Poetry *(1950), and* A Treasury of Laughter *(1946). Untermeyer was a contributing editor to the* Liberator *and the* Seven Arts, *and served as poetry editor of the* American Mercury *from 1934 to 1937. In the following essay, Untermeyer focuses on the poetic language of* The Playboy of the Western World.]

Costume design for a 1920 production of The Playboy of the Western World, *drawn by the Russian-born French artist Marc Chagall.*

Under the fanfare of the wrangling schools, a new voice is making itself heard, and strange, peasant-like harmonies announce the advent of another figure. It is to simple but exotic strains—to the melodies of rustic flute and weather-beaten strings that the spirit of J. M. Synge is disclosed—the spirit of bogs and peatmarshes, the spirit of unfettered poetry. Wild poetry itself is in his utterance, for although Mr. Synge writes entirely in prose, his sentences are so steeped in similes of the skies that his very commonplaces are filled and colored with all the *nuances* of rhythm. The sunlight filters through his lines and the spell of scenic splendor is over all his work. This very poetic quality is at one time the most obvious and most indefinable characteristic of the four prose plays with which Mr. Synge has declared himself. Nor is dramatic power lacking; as the following passage between the two disillusioned beggar-folk (the man and wife in *The Well of the Saints*) testifies:

> MARY DOUL.—I wouldn't rear a crumpled whelp the like of you. It's many a woman is married with finer than yourself should be praising God if she's no child, and isn't loading the earth with things would make the heavens lonesome above, and they scaring the larks and the crows and the angels passing in the sky.

> MARTIN DOUL.—Go on now to be seeking a lonesome place where the earth can hide you away; go on now, I'm saying, or you'll be having men and women with their knees bled, and they screaming to God for a holy water would darken their sight, for there's no man but would liefer be blind a hundred years, or a thousand itself, than to be looking on your like.

Even in this scrap, torn from its context, there is the natural burst of speech that is almost lyric. William Butler Yeats has pointed out [in his preface to *The Well of the Saints*] that 'it blurs definition, clear edges, everything that comes from the will; it turns imagination from all that is of the present, like a gold background in a religious picture. . . . Perhaps no Irishman had ever that exact rhythm in his voice, but certainly if Mr. Synge had been born a countryman, he would have spoken like that. It makes the people of his imagination a trifle disembodied; it gives them a kind of innocence even in their anger and their cursing.'

In *The Playboy of the Western World* . . . , he himself explains this absence of prosiness in a remarkably spirited preface (the Shavian worshippers notwithstanding). In this he acknowledges his debt to the fishermen and ballad-singers, the beggar women and peat gatherers; from Kerry to Mayo or near Dublin he borrows the phrases from the folk imagination of these people. 'Any one who has lived in real intimacy with the Irish peasantry will know that the wildest sayings and ideas in this play are tame, indeed, compared with the fancies one may hear in any little hill-side cabin in Geesala or Carraroe or Dingle Bay. All art is a collaboration; and there is little doubt that in the happy ages of literature, striking and beautiful phrases were as ready to the storyteller's hand as the rich cloaks and dresses of his time [or the playwright's].' And so Mr. Synge goes on to tell how, when he was writing *The Shadow of the Glen* (a tremendous little one-act play), he got more aid than any learning could have given him from 'a chink in the floor of the old Wicklow house where I was staying, that let me hear what was being said by the servant girls in the kitchen.' The keynote of the preface, however, may be found in the next to last sentence where he maintains—'In a good play every speech should be as fully flavored as a nut or apple, and such speeches cannot be written by any one who works among people who have shut their lips on poetry.' 'Give up Paris; you will never create anything by reading Racine,' Yeats told him. 'Go to the Aran Islands. Live there as if you were one of the people themselves; express a life that has never found expression.'

All of which has borne fruit in this play itself, which, though it may lack the delicate suggestion and the haunting minor cadences of his *Riders to the Sea,* contains fresher and more virile writing than anything the prophets of the 'Celtic revival' have produced. The characters move naturally and seemingly of their own warm will,—they are peasants of to-day who live with hot words on their lips and hot blood in their hearts—peasants who believe in the beauty of the actual and who concern themselves little with esoteric sysmbolism, or the fates of Deirdre and Naois.

Christy Mahon, a young Irish Peer Gynt, but with more dreams and less fire than the Norwegian ne'er do well, confesses to the murder of his father and thereby gains the respect of the community in general, and the girl Pegeen in particular. This, and the subsequent chorus of admiration from the countryfolk, furnishes the first shock to the unprepared reader—a shock from which the theatergoers in Dublin did not recover, until provoked by further outrages against what they considered the sanctity of the drama, they had vented their disapproval in rather medieval manners at the Abbey Theater early last year. Later, when the Widow Quin and Pegeen bid openly for Christy's favor and vie with each other before the bashful braggart the shock is aggravated, and finally in the second act, when the village girls and the widow hotly woo him, the climax is reached. These passages are boldly written and forceful dialogues, and though the writer of this cannot vouch for their genuineness, they have the almost unmistakable ring of truth. Intensely modern it is yet highly poetic. It is Shaw, without his sophistries and smart speeches—it is the 'Life force' revealing itself with neither paradox, decoration, nor apology. And in a country where the sex relation is a topic unfit for public mention—a topic for the fashionable clubman on one hand and the psychopath on the other—all of this was, naturally, unpardonable.

But it will succeed in spite of the 'prurient prudes' (as Charles Reade was wont to call that estimable class). Mr.

Synge is not writing for to-day, but for the years to come in such passages as these:

> It's that you'd say surely if you seen him and he after drinking for weeks, rising up in the red dawn, or before, it may be, and going out into the yard as naked as an ash-tree in the moon of May, and shying clods against the visages of the stars till he had put the fear of death into the banbhs and screeching sows.

> I've told my story no place till this night, Pegeen. . . . I've said it nowhere till this night, for I've seen none the like of you the eleven long days I am walking the world, looking over a low ditch or a high ditch, on my north or south, into stony scattered fields, or scribes of bog, where you'd see young limber girls, and fine prancing women making laughter with the men.

The imagery of the first quotation and the delicate naturalism of the second can only be matched with prose like this:

> It's little you'll think if my love's a poacher's love or an earl's itself, when you'll feel my two hands stretched around you, and I squeezing kisses on your puckered lips, till I'd feel a kind of pity for the Lord God (who) is all ages sitting lonesome in his golden chair.

But it is futile to quote; the play is full of such lines, and illuminated with the most skilful character-delineation. Mr. Synge calls it a 'comedy in three acts,' but in reality it is at one time history, pastoral, pastoral-comical, historical-pastoral, tragical-historical, etc. There are moments of truly glorious farce (such as the return of Old Mahon, supposedly 'destroyed' by Christy), and there are times (notably in the last act) when the play verges perilously on rather bitter tragedy. But it is a comedy for all that, even though the ending may not be the conventional happy one, for this unflinching dramatist has no intention of flinging a sop to Cerberus.

Taking it all in all the play (in conjunction with Mr. Synge's other dramas) points with promise to the reincarnation of poetry in prose, the beautiful growing up through the common.

It is to the chronicler of the peasant of to-day that we must look for the fulfilment of this promise, and should Mr. Synge continue to carry out this wonder, he shall have put the whole world in his debt. (pp. 364-67)

> *Louis Untermeyer, "J. M. Synge and The Playboy of the Western World," in* Poet Lore, *Vol. XIX, No. III, Autumn, 1908, pp. 364-67.*

Eric Salmon (essay date 1970)

[*In this excerpt, Salmon discusses the function of language and the disparity between reality and illusion in* The Playboy of the Western World.]

The question of the relationship of reality to illusion, and the expression of this question as a major theme, lies, of course, at the very heart of [*The Playboy of the Western World*] (perhaps at the heart of all theater). The central structure of the plot of *Playboy* depends upon it, and its ramifications extend from this central structure not only into subsidiary elements of the plot but also into the portrayal of the characters themselves and into the language which they all use. There is an apt illustration of this in Pegeen's speech in Act III when she says, "and myself, a girl was tempted often to go sailing the seas till I'd marry a Jew-man with ten kegs of gold, and I not knowing at all there was the like of you drawing nearer, like the stars of God." What she is, in fact, saying here is that the conventional romantic idea of mating and marriage and a young girl's imagining of their purposes, is very different indeed from the reality when it comes. The chief illustration, however, and the most direct, of the reality-illusion theme, is Christy's story of the murder and the differing attitudes to this story of Christy himself, of Pegeen, of the gullible and credulous villagers, of Old Mahon when he eventually turns up and, interestingly, of the suspicious Philly. To all of them, the story is what they want it to be and its shape and texture is conditioned not by any factual reality, but by the need of a particular personality to be sustained by a particular illusion. Pegeen, who is much the most clear-sighted and honest person in the play in the long run, comes finally to realize this when she says, "I'll say, a strange man is a marvel, with his mighty talk; but what's a squabble in your back yard, and the blow of a loy, have taught me that there's a great gap between a gallous story and a dirty deed." When Christy first enters, and before we have heard the first telling by him of the story of how he killed his father, all the indications are that Christy is expecting the response of his story to be one of fright, horror and the threat of retribution. He finds, however, even from the very first vague and cautious hint that he gives them of what he has done, that their reaction is quite otherwise and it is their respect, which quickly modulates through admiration to extravagant praise, which encourages him to tell the story at all. When he first tells it, it has all the aspects of a plain, unvarnished tale, which Christy himself in all probability believes (though even at this point, the play seems to provoke the interesting doubt as to whether Christy really *does* think that his father is dead or, on the other hand, that he ran away not because he was afraid of being accused of murder, but because he was afraid of the anger of his father when his father recovered sufficiently from the blow to pursue him: it seems to me that this case can be argued with equal force in either direction and that the resultant ambiguity is deliberate and serves only to add richness to the play's central theme). The fact remains that when the story is first told, it is told in plain straightforward terms and mentions only the actual fact, namely, that "I just riz the loy and let fall the edge of it on the ridge of his skull, and he went down at my feet like an empty sack, and never let a grunt or groan from him at all." Under the influence of the obvious and increasing admiration which his story and his situation produces, when next he tells the story (in his first tête-à-tête with Pegeen, later in Act I) there is a significant detail added: he says, "the way it was a bitter life he led me till I did up a Tuesday and halve his skull." In other words, the blow which he gave his father has now developed into a much more flamboyant and heroic-sounding one. Early in the next act, he tells the story again, this time to a group of village girls, to whom he says, "and I hit a blow on the ridge of his skull, laid him stretched out, and he split to the knob of his gullet." Evidently a heavier, more powerful, more heroic and devastating a blow than the one mentioned before! Note that with a single stroke he now manages to cleave his way significantly further through his father's anatomy than when last he mentioned the matter. It is also significant—and a piece of gorgeous comic irony—that the story now, as told to the village girls, has the full trappings of romantic detail, including a report of the alleged conversation that passed between Christy and his father, leading up to the dramatic killing and culminating in an atavistic statement that raises the whole thing to the level of ritual murder: Christy says—"impressively" according to the stage direction—"with that, the sun came out between the cloud and the hill, and it shining green in my face. 'God have mercy on your soul' says he, lifting a scythe; 'or on your own' says I, raising the loy." Susan and Honor, two of the girls who are listening to him with rapt attention, at this point say, "that's a grand story" and "he tells it lovely." There is one further version of the story worth noting: talking to the Widow Quin, later in Act II, Christy says, "from this out, I'll have no want of company when all sorts is bringing me their food and clothing, the way they'd set their eyes upon a gallant orphan cleft his father with one blow to the breeches belt." Short of hacking his poor father clean in two in one go, the story can go no further and it is immediately after this final version of cleaving to the breeches belt that the father himself arrives (with head swathed in bandages, it is true, but with gullet and belt-line still intact) and Christy's fine story and the fantasies which have clung gloriously and cloud-like around it, begins at this point to disintegrate. The question of how *much* of the story is factual is held constantly before us by the play and by its superb comic method. Obviously, the way in which Christy tells the story, altering it as he goes along, getting more and more patently into the realms of fantasy, moves us, in the audience, to doubt his word: but how *much* of his word are we to doubt? Before Old Mahon appears, we have even begun to doubt whether the father ever really existed at all. But we are not sure: perhaps, after all, he *does* exist. It is our admission of this possibility and our simultaneous doubt about it that helps to move the comic situation forward through the play. And the theme of illusion-reality is reflected not only in Christy and his telling of the story and not only in the central position which this story obviously occupies in the structure and plot of the play, but also in the responses and reactions of the other characters to the situation and the story. How much of this gorgeously romantic stuff do they *really* believe, we ask ourselves? Perhaps they are simply allowing Christy his necessary illusion and providing themselves with a share in it by giving him an audience. And yet this may not be the case at all: certainly, it is perfectly evident from the play itself that it is not equally the case with all the characters concerned. The central question remains, the question of the relationship in true experience of reality to illusion, and this question is also raised, of course, by the *quality* of the responses of the other characters to Christy's story. I have had the rather curious experience of discussing this play fairly extensively and on a number of different occasions with different groups of university students in Canada and the

United States: in all these discussions there has always been one—and sometimes more than one—student who has been genuinely horrified by what he or she regarded as the callousness and immorality of the characters who listen to Christy's story and accord it a place of honour and renown, rather than rushing out and summoning the nearest policeman. The people who adopt this argument tend also to extend it to include the play itself and its author, as well as the characters; they suggest that it is an immoral work and that Synge's purpose in writing it was the immoral purpose of glorifying, or at the very least defending, patricide. To judge the play and Christy's story in this way is to make the prime mistake of treating the theater not as a poetic medium but an informational one, as though the play were there to *tell* us something rather than to reflect obliquely a sense of the world. It is the very fact that the explicit, observable, surface responses of the characters are *not* the same as might be anticipated in a parallel situation in "real life" that should signal to us that the inhibitions and inarticulations of real life are not what we are here concerned with, that the mirror is seeking to catch a reflection of the life beneath the surface—and not only the life of the individual or even the practical manifestations of the spirit of life in humanity and human communities, but the very nature of that spirit itself, as if the author had been impelled to seek to persuade us to share his vision of those subterranean channels that course under all life and his sense of wonder at the sudden, unaccountable, illogical irruptions of that stream forced violently to the surface of "ordinary" living. The qualities, then, of the different responses of the characters are not to be judged as if this were a social worker's casebook, but as parts of an entity the nature of which is not simply being examined or reported upon but is being actively recreated in the hearts of the audience, one of the elements of that entity being the sense of reality and illusion as twin pulses in the veins of the universe. This is not to say that the characters have no reality as people: they have, but the reality is a quintessential one, not a mundane or literal one and to try to judge their attitudes by reference to a particular moral code is to ignore the fact that they are, so to say, "permanent people," whereas a moral code is a temporary structure erected for the convenience of a particular society and erected, moreover, on the basis of co-operate *behaviour,* not individual reality. The one character whose stance with regard to Christy is, right from the start, a conventionally "moral" one is Shawn Keogh. When he hears Christy's story for the first time he immediately says—though with great timidity—"that'd be a queer kind to bring into a decent quiet household with the like of Pegeen Mike—A bloody-handed murderer the like of him." The play, however, has already set up Shawn as a figure of fun worthy only to be dismissed with laughter: this point is well established even before Christy arrives. And immediately after his mundane moral utterance quoted above, he is summarily dismissed from the cottage by Pegeen, and it is Christy, the fantasy-merchant, the reality-and-illusion boy, who is left in triumph and sole possession. By first making fun of and then dismissing Shawn and his "ordinary" point of view, the play is, in fact, directing our attention away from surface responses and literal interpretations and re-directing us towards the reali-

ty-and-illusion metaphor which Christy and his story are rapidly becoming in the play.

This same metaphor is contained also, throughout the length of the play, in the form and frame and imagery of the language, quite apart from the use of that language for the representation of characters. It shows most often and most clearly, as one would expect, in the conversation of Pegeen and Christy, but all the others have touches of it, too—Philly's story of playing in the graveyard when he was a little boy: "for when I was a young lad there was a graveyard beyond the house with the remnants of a man who had thighs as long as your arm. He was a horrid man, I'm telling you, and there was many a fine Sunday I'd put him together for fun, and he with shiny bones, you wouldn't meet the like of these days in the cities of the world"—the Widow Quin's account of her own lurid past—Michael James's account of Kate Cassidy's funeral: " . . . for you'd never see the match of it for flows of drink, the way when we sunk her bones at noonday in her narrow grave, there were five men, aye, and six men, stretched out retching speechless on the holy stones." One has, throughout, from all of them, the vivid impression of a life full of riot and revelry in an austere place, the sustaining illusions of fantasy intertwined with the stony facts of physical experience: it is worth noting, for example, that in Philly's story of the graveyard and Michael James's story of the funeral, the grim appurtenances of death are taken quite simply and easily as being the natural accompaniment of fun and enjoyment. This, in a play with a different aesthetic orientation, would be callous and brutal, a sign of decadence and depravity: in *Playboy,* it is not callous and brutal, since the play itself has already established quite clearly for us the organization of its own metaphors towards an imaginative consideration of the reality-illusion theme. There is another image which threads through the language of this play and which carries this same general implication: this is the image of the poet as a great talker, as a weaver of romance, as a purveyor of a life that contains a greater truth. Pegeen says to Christy, at various points in the play, " . . . and you walking the world telling out your story to young girls or old," "you said the like of that, may be, in every cot and cabin where you've met a young girl on your way," "if you weren't destroyed travelling, you'd have as much talk and streeleen, I'm thinking, as Owen Roe O'Sullivan or the poets of the Dingle Bay and I've heard all times it's the poets are your like, fine fiery fellows with great rages when their temper's roused." And when she is depressed and thinks that she might lose him she says " . . . but we're only talking, maybe, for this would be a poor thatched place to hold a fine lad as the like of you." At one point, in ecstasy, she exclaims " . . . and any girl would walk her heart out before she'd meet a young man with your like for eloquence, or talk, at all." Throughout this kind of speech there is the strong suggestion that one can make a world, create a reality, out of great talk. And the images are so vivid and connect at so many points with the audience's own sense of the core of reality in the natural world, that it is simply inadequate to dismiss this talk, as some people have done, as merely being infected with Irish blarney. Nor can one account for it purely in terms of the psychology, realistically considered and represented, of the characters. By constantly provoking our minds to the awareness of gorgeous dreams, it challenges us to confess to ourselves, if we can, what we believe the nature of reality to be. (pp. 114-19)

[The language in the play] been commented on many times before but what has not, perhaps, been sufficiently emphasized in these comments is the self-parody in which Synge's language indulges. Alan Price has glanced at this idea [in his *Synge and the Anglo-Irish Drama*, 1961], but only in passing and then only as a vague possibility: "In presenting this immense deal of talk to one poor ha' p'orth of action Synge may have intended, among other things, to have a sly grin at blather and blarney. . . . " This makes it sound peripheral—something consciously added by the author after the really solid business of the play was complete. The self-satirising quality of the language seems to me much more integral to the play's whole purpose, and essential to its structure, than this would imply. It is not an addition or bonus; it is both a vehicle for conveying one of the central meanings of the play and a part of that meaning in itself.

Synge's language in **Playboy of the Western World** is far more extravagant than in any of the rest of his plays: it sounds more like great oratorical, declamatory speech and it indulges in gratuitously extravagant metaphor far more than any other Synge play. It does this without in any way distorting the characters which it is portraying: rather, it elevates them to its own level, interprets them in its own medium, so that, though each is distinctive and talks in his own way, yet in a certain sense it is true that they all use the same kind of language. And this kind of language is a powerful, moving and evocative one, glorifying both by precept and example the "gift of the gab." It is most significant that over and over again there are references to the power of good talk. "There's praying," says the Widow Quin after one of Christy's more extravagant utterances: "Aid me for to win her and I'll be asking God to stretch a hand to you in the hour of death and lead you short cuts through the Meadows of Ease and up the floor of Heaven to the Footstool of the Virgin's Son." Pegeen's comments on Christy's fine talk have already been quoted. The bravery and the fine language go together, but even allowing for this, the language of this play is unduly extravagant and seems curiously to be aware of this itself. It is well to remember that Christy, replying to Pegeen's praise of his eloquence, says: "Let you wait to hear me talking until we're astray in Erris when Good Friday's by. . . . " His talk up to now, he says, has been lenten stuff only, labouring under a self-denying ordinance; but with a return to its natural fulness and in a holiday mood, how much more persuasive will it be! He is admitting that intuitively he recognizes that language which is big enough, fine enough and sensitive enough to convey the exact *nuances* of the subtle and hard-to-apprehend truth, contains by the same token the power to deceive. And so throughout the play the language, with an almost insolent ease, weaves a fantasy of heroic romanticism (which is yet a reality and more than a fantasy) and at the same time mocks itself and parodies itself for its own skill and the effect that it knows it can obtain. This is why some of Christy's images and metaphors are so extravagant—the one about the loneliness of God, for example, or the one that likens the bishops to holy prophets straining to look through the windows of heaven to see Helen of Troy walking in beauty and glory on the earth. It is noteworthy that in both of these images, and in several others in the play, the rectitude of the humble Christian is contrasted with the wild vigor and sheer animal enjoyment of a Pan-like paganism, always with the Christian imprisoned in some way, regretfully refusing (or being prevented from accepting) the vitality of Pan but envying this vitality all the same. (Ibsen often reflects the same sense, though with a flatness of language of which Synge thoroughly disapproved.) The direct points which the dialogue is making in these instances do not require, for the purposes of the plot, such overstatement and bravura: but nevertheless the overstatement and bravura is not an excrescence, but is a way of adding depth to the ironic point concerning language and the power of language. This cord binds the main senses of the play together in a marvellous unity. It carries with it a reflection of all the other meanings, simultaneously realized—the reality-and-illusion theme is echoed in the overstatement of the language—(How *real* are these metaphors? How seriously are we to take them? A delicious ambiguity is preserved by the play on this point: they seem right, they feel right, the play lends them its authority, and yet deliberately and quite consciously draws attention to their extravagance. Where are we to believe that reality lies?)—the business of violence and gentleness, one could argue, is also reflected in the structure and flavour of this heady language—the incandescence of the creative moment, in which people are changed and destinies born, is reflected in the way that the language tugs forward to its climatic points, urged on alike by rhetoric and metaphor—the isolating loneliness of the individual soul is hinted at both by the desperate eloquence itself (Why is it so necessary to talk bravely and to reflect the exactitude of a burning truth if not to establish some kind of contact with someone else?) and by the self-mockery of the language which admits that nine times out of ten the attempt to establish contact is bound to be a failure—the uneasy co-existence of nobility and banality in all human experience is doubly reflected in the language of the play: first, by the presence of this great talk in the middle of mundane and grubby circumstances, and, secondly, by the juxtaposition of strikingly contrasted images within the language itself. The one theme which by its nature could not be contained within the actual framework and nature of the language is the one concerned with the apparent necessity for conventional morality. The language here is used to explain and enunciate this theme but can hardly be said to contain it within its own form. This theme is a discursive and polemical one and not therefore one that would be capable of being obliquely reflected by the form and frame of language: some degree of direct explication is needed. Not that the nature of the language changes in these moments, nor does it betray or desert or damage them, but this particular theme is rather outside the language than contained within its blood-stream.

This language has often been praised for its marvellously decorative effect and the praise is, indeed, just; it would be the greatest mistake, however, to regard its *function* as being a decorative one. The decoration is, so to say, an aesthetic bonus, but the true function of the language is to provide the play with a spine or, if one may change one's metaphor, a motive power for all its parts. The language in **Playboy of the Western World** is in fact the play's organizing principle. It is poetic in the strict and commonsense meaning of that word and its poetry works in this play, as all great art works, obliquely. Art is, by definition, an oblique statement: if it states its purpose directly, it is no longer art; if its purpose could be stated directly there would be no need for art at all. It is no derogation, therefore, to remark that the language does not say what on the surface it appears to say: it says more, it talks of things taller, deeper and higher than what appears on the surface. Robin Skelton has noted an interesting thing in this connection. In his Introduction to **Four Plays and The Aran Islands** (1962), he says: "The speech of Synge's plays is not merely a faithful recording of the speech he heard in Aran, Wicklow and Kerry, however; it is also a dramatic construction. In fusing together Gaelic and English locutions, Synge has provided a speech which clearly implies the situation of his characters, all of whom can be regarded as partaking of two worlds. On the one hand they are jostled by their pasts, and aware of legends and superstitions; they are aware of being a race beyond the polite confines of society. On the other they are aware of social pressures and their gaiety or their sadness, and their imaginative fervour, are closely connected to their sense of social unease. They are displaced people in their own country." The form of the language has become the meaning of the play, or at least one of its meanings.

The fact . . . that this play's stature has not always been readily recognized, is due, I think, to the play's own profundity and density of texture and to the—at first glance—forbidding austerity of its theatrical and dramatic means: it appears somehow too simple to be capable of saying more than at first glance appears, and since this glance reveals to the unwary only things which are silly or offensive or both, misunderstanding and a dislike are from that point on almost inevitable. And the lack of simplicity in the language, until one realizes its central place in the structure of the piece, serves only to increase the impression that an attempt is being made to inflate something small and ordinary into something impressive. Only the cultivation of a sensitivity of the same order as that of the play itself can release the explosive and magnificent energies of the **Playboy**'s comic vision and vitality. (pp. 125-28)

> *Eric Salmon, "J. M. Synge's 'Playboy': A Necessary Reassessment," in* Modern Drama, *Vol. XIII, No. 2, September, 1970, pp. 111-28.*

Robin Skelton   (essay date 1971)

[*Skelton is an English-born Canadian poet, essayist, and editor, whose poetry reflects the duality of his cultural background and his wide-ranging interests in art and music. A renowned scholar of the Irish Literary Renaissance, Skelton has edited volumes of Synge's dramas and poetry, and has written extensive studies on Synge's life and works. In the following excerpt, he examines* The Playboy of the Western World *in relation to Miguel de Cervantes's* Don Quixote (1605-15); The New

Testament; and Shanachie, or folklore of the Irish countryside. Skelton also discusses the characterizations of Pegeen Mike, The Widow Quin, and Christy Mahon.]

After the first-night riot [incited by a performance of **The Playboy of the Western World** at the Abbey Theatre] Synge was reported as telling the *Evening Mail* that he had not attempted 'to represent Irish life as it is lived', and as saying:

> I wrote the play because it pleased me, and it just happens that I know Irish life best, so I made my methods Irish.

He was reported as calling his play 'a comedy, an extravaganza, made to amuse', and saying, 'I never bother whether my plots are typically Irish or not; but my methods are typical.'

Synge's own account of what he said in that interview is included in a letter to Stephen MacKenna:

> He—the interviewer—got in my way—may the devil bung a cesspool with his skull—and said, 'Do you really think, Mr Synge, that if a man did this in Mayo, girls would bring him a pullet?' The next time it was, 'Do you think, Mr Synge, they'd bring him eggs?' I lost my poor temper (God forgive me that I didn't wring his neck) and I said, 'Oh well, if you like, it's impossible, it's extravagance (how's it spelt?). So is *Don Quixote!*' He hashed up what I said a great [deal] worse than I expected, but I wrote next day politely backing out of all that was in the interview. That's the whole myth. It isn't quite accurate to say, I think, that the thing is a generalization from a simple case. If the idea had occurred to me I could and would just as readily have written the thing as it stands without the Lynchehaun case or the Aran case. The story—in its *essence*—is probable, given the psychic state of the locality. I used the cases afterwards to controvert critics who said it was *impossible*.

The Lynchehaun case and the Aran case are both instances of men being wanted by the police for murder being given sanctuary by the peasants. The letter to MacKenna makes it clear that Synge's claim to naturalistic reporting was, in this case as in others, a defensive response to criticism. The reference to *Don Quixote* is intriguing and worth bearing in mind.

The letter which Synge wrote to the press as a consequence of the interview is also significant. Synge explained:

> **The Playboy of the Western World** is not a play with 'a purpose' in the modern sense of the word, but although parts of it are, or are meant to be, extravagant comedy, still a great deal more that is behind it, is perfectly serious when looked at in a certain light. That is often the case, I think, with comedy, and no one is quite sure to-day whether 'Shylock' and 'Alceste' should be played seriously or not. There are, it may be hinted, several sides to **The Playboy**. 'Pat', I am glad to notice, has seen some of them in his own way. There may be still others if anyone cares to look for them.

'Pat' was Patrick Kenny, who had seen the play largely as a prophecy of the downfall of an Ireland that was exporting its strongest inhabitants and being emotionally and spiritually debilitated by the institution of arranged and loveless marriages. Another interpretation was offered by the *Evening Mail* reviewer, who thought the play might be an allegory, though he found it too obscure for him. He suggested that 'the parricide represents some kind of nation-killer, whom Irish men and Irish women hasten to lionize'. Most reviewers, however, took a more naïve line. The *Freeman's Journal* saw the play as an 'unmitigated, protracted libel upon Irish peasant men and, worse still upon Irish girlhood', and referred to it as a 'squalid, offensive production, incongruously styled a comedy . . . '. D. J. O'Donoghue, in a letter to the same paper, said:

> The continuous ferocity of the language, the consistent shamelessness of all the characters (without exception), and the persistent allusions to sacred things make the play even more inexcusable as an extravaganza than as a serious play. . . .

In a letter to M. J. Nolan of 19 February Synge wrote:

> With a great deal of what you say I am most heartily in agreement—as where you see that I wrote the *P.B.* directly, as a piece of life, without thinking or caring to think, whether it was a comedy tragedy or extravaganza, or whether it would be held to have, or not to have, a purpose—also where you speak very accurately and rightly about Shakespeare's 'mirror'. In the same way you see . . . that the wildness and, if you will, vices of the Irish peasantry are due, like their extraordinary good points of all kinds, to the *richness* of their nature—a thing that is priceless beyond words. . . . Whether or not I agree with your final interpretation of the whole play is my secret. I follow Goethe's rule to tell no one what one means in one's writings.

If we add together all these public and private comments of Synge we get a fairly clear notion, not of the precise 'meaning' he himself attached to his play, but of his attitudes towards the play's message element. Firstly, he insists that the play is credible in terms of actuality, but should not be labelled comedy, tragedy or extravaganza. He suggests that there are 'several sides' to the play, and, while calling it 'a piece of life', indicates that it does have a meaning or meanings and is more than a simple piece of entertainment. He clearly indicates the central ambiguity of mood by his reference to Shylock and Alceste, and also, more significantly, by his reference, when being questioned by a reporter, to *Don Quixote*. Don Quixote is, like Christy Mahon, a fantasist and an 'outsider'. He was used by Cervantes to comment upon the vices and absurdities of the society of his time. He is himself a fool, but ultimately much less of a fool than the acceptably conventional realists he encounters, for his folly and his fantasy are supported and dignified by a view of the world which is obsessively idealistic and chivalrous, whereas the other people lack any real conviction or vision. Moreover, in several instances, Quixote persuades others to share for a while his fantasy and to see themselves as fair ladies, nobles and knights, in a world of dragons and heroism. Sometimes self-consciously, sometimes humorously or even derisively, they gain through him a sense of the glories that are gone and of the dignity they no longer feel they possess. Finally, however, Quixote is most usually rejected, and rides away, accompanied by his faithful, awed, yet sceptical Sancho Panza, to find new wonders and irradiate other commonplaces with the ideal illumination of his fantasy.

It is not difficult to see Christy Mahon as a Don Quixote figure, at once saviour and fool, hero and clown, visionary and madman. The difference is that it is, at least in part, the peasants who create the vision for him. Initially he is only a scared boy, convinced in his simplicity that he has killed his father. Praised and admired for his derring-do, he becomes both a braggart and a visionary, his words elevating the commonplace into such poetry that Pegeen Mike and even the Widow Quin are dazzled by his eloquence. Inspired thus he becomes, in fact, the hero, winning all the prizes at the races, and though finally he falls from grace when his father returns from the dead, he retains at the close of the action that heroic self-confidence which he has been given.

It is at the end of the play, however, that the Quixote element gives way to another, for Christy again 'kills' his father and is immediately viewed with horror and both beaten and betrayed.

It is here that Synge's Shylock parallelism applies. As long as Shylock's 'bargain' remained a distant threat and a fantasy Bassanio regarded him amiably. When, however, he attempted to perform in reality what had been disregarded when merely imagined, he was not only regarded with horror but condemned for a crime of conspiracy which had previously been tolerated and even jested over. The parallelism is obviously inexact, but points to Synge's understanding the essential part played by that element of the grotesque and brutal which some of his audience condemned. In one of his sketches for the play Synge, as in *The Tinker's Wedding* plan, attached descriptive epithets to each movement and each small episode. The first act he saw as moving from 'comedy and locality' through 'Molièrian climax of farce', 'savoury dialogue', 'Poetical', 'Rabelaisian' to the final 'diminuendo ironical'. The second act uses the words 'character', 'comedy' and 'Poetical' to describe its shape. In the third act alone, after Old Mahon and Christy meet face to face, is the word 'drama' used (IV. 296-7). At that point, indeed, the whole play alters its perspective and characters once found endearing are found to be ignorant, vicious and treacherous.

George Moore recognized this shift in the play when he wanted Synge to alter the ending, saying, 'Your end is not comedy, it ends on a disagreeable note.' Moore found the physical violence at the end most unacceptable.

> The burning of Christy's legs with the coal is quite intolerable and wouldn't be acceptable to any audience—French, German or Russian. The audience doesn't mind what is said, but what is done—the father coming in with his head bandaged with a dangerous make-up.

Moore later recanted, but his letter must have entertained Synge, for surely one of the points made about the Mayo folk is that they don't 'mind what is said, but what is done', a point which could only be driven home by the emphasis upon physical actuality provided by the coal incident and the bloody head of Old Mahon actually 'killed' in front of them.

It is at this point that the relationship between language and actuality comes into the picture. Throughout the play there has been, to quote D. J. O'Donoghue, 'continuous ferocity of language'. The action itself, however, only erupts into violence the once, and, as Pegeen Mike says, 'there's a great gap between a gallous story and a dirty deed' (IV. 169). It is not only the ferocity of the language that is important; it is what O'Donoghue calls 'the persistent allusions to sacred things'.

That the play constantly uses religious words is obvious enough. The first impression one receives is that the almost indiscriminate appeals to divinity are intended to point to the use of Christian terminology as a medium for imprecation and a vehicle for superstition. The dignity of the references contrasts with the pettiness of their occasion. It is one way to create comic incongruity and show the spiritual decadence of the west, a decadence which has gone so far that, for all the religious verbiage, the only acceptable Redeemer turns out to be a young man who has killed his Da in a scuffle, not Christ Messiah but Christy Mahon.

Once the notion of Christy as in some way related to Christ enters the picture, however, it is likely to dominate it. Stanley Sultan, in a well argued essay ["A Joycean Look at *The Playboy of the Western World,*" in Maurice Harmon, ed., *The Celtic Master,* 1969], presents a view of Christy as a Promethean figure whose rebellion against his father symbolizes for the Mayo peasants their wish to revolt against the oppressive forces of the Church as represented by 'the Holy Father' in Rome and 'Father Reilly' nearer at hand. 'Stop tormenting me with Father Reilly,' cries Pegeen to Shawn, she being the girl most attracted to the heroic view of parricide. Dr Sultan, however, goes on from this to suggest that 'the ***Playboy*** presents a carefully developed analogue to the ministry and crucifixion of Jesus'.

At first blush this may seem an extreme view, but once the analogy has been hypothesized a number of details appear to support it. The village girls bring the newly arrived Christy 'presents' and announce 'Well, you're a marvel! Oh, God bless you! You're the lad surely!", thus parodying the Epiphany. The triumphant entry of Christy into the house after his ride to victory in the sports, applauded by all the crowds, is followed, after a while, by a judgment scene in which the crowd's mood changes. The episode begins when the betrothal of Pegeen and Christy is blessed by Michael:

> . . . so may God and Mary and St Patrick bless you, and increase you from this mortal day.
>
> CHRISTY *and* PEGEEN. Amen, O Lord! (IV. 157)

Old Mahon then rushes in and identifies himself. Pegeen is convinced and turns on Christy:

CHRISTY. You've seen my doings this day, and let you save me from the old man; for why would you be in such a scorch of haste to spur me to destruction now?

PEGEEN. It's there your treachery is spurring me, till I'm hard set to think you're the one I'm after lacing in my heart strings half-an-hour gone by. *To* MAHON. Take him on from this, for I think bad the world should see me raging for a Munster liar and the fool of men.

MAHON. Rise up now to retribution, and come on with me.

CROWD *jeeringly.* There's the playboy! There's the lad thought he'd rule the roost in Mayo. Slate him now, Mister.

CHRISTY *getting up in shy terror.* What is it drives you to torment me here, when I'd ask the thunders of the might of God to blast me if I ever did hurt to any saving only that one single blow.

MAHON *loudly.* If you didn't, you're a poor good-for-nothing, and isn't it by the like of you the sins of the whole world are committed?

CHRISTY *raising his hands.* In the name of the Almighty God. . . .

(IV. 161-2)

The echoes of the New Testament here are indisputable. In other parts of the play we are reminded of the parable of the Good Samaritan, when the moaning stranger is left to himself 'in the gripe of the ditch' by Shawn and Michael. The binding and wounding of Christy echoes the binding and wounding of Christ and his projected hanging recalls the crucifixion. Pegeen's betrayal of him is Judas-like; after offering intense affection she brings him total betrayal. If we see Christy Mahon as a distorted reflection of Christ Messiah, then we can see Father Reilly and the Holy Father and Shawn Keogh as representatives of the Old Testament religion and those Sadducees and Pharisees whom Christ opposed. That the hypothesis we posited has some basis is clear enough. Dr Sultan, however, is more emphatic than we might wish. He says:

> . . . what Synge has concretely presented is a mirror-image of the story of Jesus' mission of exhortation to obedience to His Father. And it is this fact which makes the sudden and shocking reversal in the last minutes of the play comprehensible. Like Jesus, when Christy confronts with the true significance of his message those who have followed and praised him, they prepare to have him executed by the standard method used for common criminals. The crucifixion is no less complete and sudden a reversal in a triumphant short earthly career; and it came about precisely because the people would not risk secular and spiritual trouble when the issue arose.

Later in his essay he says:

> It is through his exploitation in ***Playboy*** of the ministry and crucifixion of Jesus that Synge crystallized the elements of the play into a coherent masterpiece. The analogue both helps to motivate, and articulates precisely the nature of the reciprocal effects of Christy on the people of

Mayo and the people on him. Further more, the comic action of Christy's glorification and re-union with his father, and the bitter denouement of rejection and betrayal, are not disparate but integral: the Christ analogue simply and elo-quently establishes that they are complementary to each other in a single pattern.

The trouble with this view of the *Playboy* is that the Christ analogue is intermittent. We cannot easily avoid be-lieving in the Christy-Christ parallelism at the judgment scene; apart from anything else Old Mahon's rhetorical question, 'Isn't it by the like of you the sins of the whole world are committed?', reminds one instantaneously of that Christ who took upon him all the sins of the world. The parallelism with the Good Samaritan story is also ex-tremely obvious. Nevertheless, we would have to be ludi-crously ingenious to find similarly exact counterparts to the love-talk between Christy and Pegeen (should we see her as the Church, the bride of Christ?), to Widow Quin (the temptation in the wilderness?) and the double 'death' of Old Mahon (the Nativity and the Resurrection?). It would be better, perhaps, to consider one or two more fun-damental attributes of the play before allowing ingenuity to outdistance reason.

The Playboy of the Western World is, in my definition, a shanachie play. It originated, at least partly, in a story told Synge by Pat Dirane, the shanachie of Inishmaan. If we look at the other stories told Synge by shanachies, espe-cially in the Aran islands, we may be able to get another perspective upon the play.

The first thing that strikes one about the stories, as op-posed to the anecdotes, that Synge heard, is their extraor-dinary richness of echo. . . . A story of Diarmuid paral-lels that of the Shirt of Nessus. Another long story, that of the widow's son who, having killed a great many flies, thinks himself a hero and goes out into the world, has ech-oes of several of Grimm's stories, Greek myths, and medi-eval romances. Indeed, all the stories told Synge on Aran and elsewhere could be analysed as conflations of several older stories, and most of them contain archetypal ele-ments.

If we look at the structure of the *Playboy* in these terms it becomes apparent that it has several characteristics in common both with the shanachie story and the shanachie anecdote. Firstly the material of the play has been created from many disparate sources. Dr Saddlemyer lists three passages from *The Aran Islands,* twelve from *In Wicklow, West Kerry and Connemara,* and five from various note-books, and all these, either in language or theme, relate di-rectly to different parts of the play. Moreover, the 'Good Samaritan' episode in the *Playboy* relates to the death of Patch Darcy in *The Shadow of the Glen;* Christy telling us he is 'handy with ewes' is reminiscent of the use of that image in the same play, and the 'poet's talking' of Christy recalls the 'poetry' of the Douls in *The Well of the Saints.* Christy says to Pegeen:

> Let you wait to hear me talking till we're astray in Erris when Good Friday's by, drinking a sup from a well, and making mighty kisses with our wetted mouths, or gaming in a gap of sunshine

with yourself stretched back unto your necklace in the flowers of the earth.

> (IV. 149)

Martin Doul says to Molly Byrne:

> Let you come on now, I'm saying, to the lands of Ivereagh and the Reeks of Cork, where you won't set down the width of your two feet and not be crushing fine flowers, and making sweet smells in the air.

> (IV. 117)

Some of these echoes of earlier writings may have been un-conscious, but Synge's own defensive emphasis upon his play's actuality makes it clear that he was aware of the conglomerate character of his work. Moreover, as one looks through the worksheets for the *Playboy* there are numerous indications of a highly conscious process of gathering, reconstructing, and paring.

If, then, the *Playboy* is as conglomerate as many of the shanachie tales in its fusing together of separate events and ascribing them all to one occasion, does it have other attri-butes of those tales also?

It is here that the mythic element in the *Playboy* falls into place. Just as the O'Connor story can be related, at differ-ent places, to several older and archetypal stories and leg-ends, so *The Playboy of the Western World* can, at differ-ent times, be related with differing degrees of precision to the New Testament, to *Don Quixote,* and to stories current among the folk of the west of Ireland. Synge has, indeed, not only created a play from shanachie material; he has created a play which has precisely the same kind of rich-ness as the shanachie material, a play fitfully illuminated by archetypal echoes and allusions, which, nevertheless, retains coherence, not upon the mythic, but upon the nar-rative level. The 'psychic state of the locality' is expressed in a language of such strength that it dominates and uni-fies the play. *The Playboy of the Western World* is not al-legory or parable or myth or anti-myth. If it must be given a label, the label must be invented, for the method of con-struction and the manipulation of echo and theme are en-tirely original, and very few other playwrights have prof-ited by Synge's discoveries. Among these, however, and obviously, is Sean O'Casey whose mature drama uses the same shifting levels of meaning, the same intermittent symbolist power, and the same ferocity and lyricism of speech. (pp. 115-23)

That Synge, in working out his play, thought in terms of character as much as theme is clearly observable from the worksheets. There are continual changes in speeches, but almost all appear to be made in order to clarify the rela-tionships of the characters and make the development of the plot more credible. There are no crudely symbolist speeches, as there are in the drafts of *The Tinker's Wed-ding.* Queries and hesitations relate to human encounters rather than to archetypal references, though it is notice-able that in the discarded drafts there are many uses of re-ligious terminology and these increase as the play pro-ceeds. It was, it appears, from a rigorous exploration of 'the psychic state of the locality' and of the inter-relationship of characters, each a vehicle for attitudes and principles endemic in that locality, that Synge developed the mythic richness which Stanley Sultan sees as a Christian analogue that coheres and dignifies the drama. (p. 125)

It is with Pegeen Mike, the Widow Quin and Christy Mahon that we should be most concerned. Pegeen Mike differs from the other girls in the energy of her passions, the liveliness of her tongue, and the decisiveness of her temper. Rejecting Shawn Keogh, she also rejects the paternal authoritarianism of the Church, as she, too, pays little heed to the authority of her own father. Attracted by Christy, she uses him to further her search for identity, freedom, and romance, finding his words and his deeds heroic and poetic. When Old Mahon returns to life she is angered by having been fooled. When Old Mahon is killed the second time and Christy set upon and tied, it is she who leads in the tying and it is she who ruthlessly burns him with the lighted turf. Pegeen's intensity of feeling leads her towards both total acceptance and total rejection. Her spirit is akin to the Playboy's in its extreme vitality, and it is this that attracts her to him and also causes her to reject him.

Pegeen contrasts with Widow Quin who, like the village girls, finds Christy attractive, but, unlike Pegeen, does not expect integrity in her hero. She is not too perturbed by the arrival of Old Mahon, and delightedly connives at the suppression of the true facts. She herself wants Christy as her man, but her morality is dubious. She offers him other girls as if she were to be his procuress rather than his bride, and her view of life appears to be totally unprincipled. She is a strong character in the play and dominates most of the action when she is on stage. By her candid self-seeking she reveals the moral confusion of her friends and neighbours. They swear by their God, and take His name in vain. The Widow rarely uses the name of God. Indeed, in the whole play she uses the word only twice. The first occasion is when she tells Christy:

> When you see me contriving in my little gardens, Christy Mahon, you'll swear the Lord God formed me to be living lone and that there isn't my match in Mayo for thatching or mowing or shearing a sheep.
>
> (IV. 89)

The second is when she says of Pegeen to Christy:

> God help her to be taking you for a wonder, and you a little schemer making up a story you destroyed your da.
>
> (IV. 125)

Her attitude to the hectic religious language of the others is well shown when Christy asks her to help him win Pegeen.

> CHRISTY. . . . Aid me for to win her, and I'll be asking God to stretch a hand to you in the hour of death, and lead you short cuts through the Meadows of Ease, and up the floor of Heaven to the Footstool of the Virgin's Son.
>
> WIDOW QUIN. There's praying!
>
> (IV. 129-31)

The Widow Quin observes the goings-on with a mixture of detached amusement, sympathy, and mischievous opportunism. She sees Christy and Pegeen for what they are.

This, however, is her limitation. For Christy's world is not the real one. It is a world of high words and great claims, and he is so intoxicated and elevated by his dream that he actually makes it come true. He does show himself a leader of men, in that he wins the contests on the sands, as if he were a hero at the Greek games. He is admired by the girls and, even after his downfall, he retains some of their affection. Moreover, while he does not become a father-killer, he does become his father's master. Words have created the reality they pictured. Moreover, he now understands the importance of having a proper conceit of himself, and knowing his dignity as a unique human creature. This has been given him as much by the times of glory as by the hours of defeat. For all his blusterings, his elaborate appeals to the heavenly powers, and his confusions of Christian values, he has discovered something which is more important than Pegeen's belief in the need for integrity, and than Widow Quin's materialist realism, and than Shawn Keogh's submission to his Church. He embodies the wildness, the richness, the idealism and the romanticism of the west in his own person, and he has found that it is possible to transfigure existence with the poetry of energy and passion.

Rejecting Christy, Pegeen realizes that she has rejected the only one who had the secret of transforming the dullness of life into radiance. She herself made him; she, with her passion for idealism and rebellion, convinced him of his own glory, but then the creation outdistanced the creator who became afraid of the creature she had invented. Pegeen is, after all, no more than a village girl and, at least according to the Widow Quin, not particularly exceptional. Christy, however, is exceptional. He becomes much more than a village hero. He becomes an orphic figure whose music survives his destruction. He becomes, indeed, an immortal, for he sees himself living out a 'romping lifetime from this hour to the dawning of the judgment day' (IV. 173).

Pegeen is another of Synge's passionate, disturbed women hungry for freedom and romance, and she comes closer to success than her predecessors. Nevertheless, her pride and the fundamental puritanism of her temperament make it impossible for her to accept the consequences of her own dream. She cannot accept the Romancer that is Christy, nor can she face his loss without grief. She represents an Ireland that dreaming of independence cannot accept the consequences of the dream becoming reality any more than that faith in spiritual power to which she gives lip service. For Christy is a representative of faith and spiritual power. He will be 'master of all fights from now' (IV. 173), because of that faith. Poverty of spirit is the disease Pegeen and all Ireland must recognize.

It is now that the utility of the Christ-Christy analogue can be seen. Christy is a poor man who achieves spiritual authority by pursuing, through times of weakness and despair, a vision of freedom that transfigures his own life and that of the people about him. His betrayal and crucifixion cannot break his spirit. He faces death and hell with courage and gaiety. Betrayed by those who crowned him king, he nevertheless triumphs. A parody of Christ rather than a reflection of Him, he gives the society he enters the exact leader they wish for—one of those whom Pegeen describes when she laments the passing of the great ones of the past such as 'Daneen Sullivan knocked the eye from a peeler' and Marcus Quin who told 'stories of holy Ireland till he'd have the old women shedding down tears about their feet' (IV. 59). Societies get the leaders they deserve and Christy Mahon is more fitted for Mayo than Christ Messiah, but even Christy is betrayed. There is no wonder perhaps that this play aroused many of its more perceptive but over-sensitive spectators to fury. (pp. 128-31)

> *Robin Skelton, in his* The Writings of J. M. Synge, *The Bobbs-Merrill Company, Inc., 1971, 190 p.*

FURTHER READING

AUTHOR COMMENTARY

Synge, John Millington. *The Autobiography of J. M. Synge.* Dublin: The Dolmen Press, 1965, 46 p.
> Assembles extracts from Synge's notebooks. The volume includes fourteen photographs taken by Synge on the Aran Islands.

OVERVIEWS AND GENERAL STUDIES

Benson, Eugene. "Demythologising Cathleen Ni Houlihan: Synge and His Sources." In *Irish Writers and the Theatre*, pp. 1-16. Irish Literary Studies, edited by Masaru Sekine, Vol. 23. Totowa, N.J.: Barnes and Noble, 1986.
> Asserts that in reworking the source material for his dramas, Synge accented themes of sexuality and death.

Bourgeois, Maurice. *John Millington Synge and the Irish Theatre.* London: Constable & Co., 1913, 338 p.
> Early study of Synge's works. Bourgeois provides the reader with information on every aspect of the publication and performance of Synge's works, primary and secondary bibliographies, a genealogy, notes on first performances, and a list of portraits of Synge.

Corkery, Daniel. *Synge and Anglo-Irish Literature: A Study.* Dublin: Cork University Press, 1931, 247 p.
> Important critical survey which devotes a chapter to each of the plays.

Figgis, Darrell. "The Art of J. M. Synge." *The Fortnightly Review* n.s. XC, No. DXXXX (1 December 1911): 1056-68.
> Praises Synge's dramas for their characterization, language, and overall philosophy.

Gaskell, Ronald. "The Realism of J. M. Synge." *The Critical Quarterly* 5, No. 3 (Autumn 1963): 242-48.
> Concedes that Synge's plays convey an expansive sense of reality, but argues that he never matched the dramatic intensity of Bertolt Brecht or Federico Garcia Lorca because his characters are too passive.

Gassner, John. "John Millington Synge and the Irish Muse." In his *Masters of the Drama*. Rev. ed., 542-74. n.p., Dover Publications, 1954.
> Overview of Synge's career.

Gerstenberger, Donna. *John Millington Synge.* New York: Twayne Publishers, 1964, 157 p.
> Concise introduction to Synge's works.

Greene, David H., and Stephens, Edward M. *J. M. Synge: 1871-1909.* New York: The Macmillan Company, 1959, 321 p.
> Seminal critical biography.

Grene, Nicholas. *Synge: A Critical Study of the Plays.* Totowa, N.J.: Rowman and Littlefield, 1975, 202 p.
> Detailed discussion of each of Synge's plays, considering his "development as a dramatist and the origins of that development."

Harmon, Maurice, ed. *J. M. Synge Centenary Papers, 1971.* Dublin: The Dolmen Press, 1972, 202 p.
> Collection including essays by Seamus Deane, Ann Saddlemyer, and David H. Greene.

Howarth, Herbert. "John Millington Synge." In his *Irish Writers, 1880-1940: Literature under Parnell's Star,* pp. 212-44. London: Rockliff, 1958.
> Sketch of Synge highlighting his relationship to his contemporaries.

Howe, P. P. *J. M. Synge: A Critical Study.* London: Martin Secker, 1912, 215 p.
> Early examination of Synge's works. Howe notes: "This book is an essay in dramatic criticism . . . , seeking to make clear the beauty and the value of the plays, and their place in English drama."

Johnston, Denis. *John Millington Synge.* New York: Columbia University Press, 1965, 48 p.
> Brief overview of the writer and his works.

Kiberd, Declan. *Synge and the Irish Language.* Totowa, N.J.: Rowman and Littlefield, 1979, 294 p.
> Investigates Synge's grasp of the Gaelic language and his experimentation with the Gaelic literary tradition.

Kronenberger, Louis. "Synge." In his *Thread of Laughter,* pp. 279-88. New York: Alfred A. Knopf, 1952.
> Hails Synge as "one of the most clearly and musically dissenting voices to the whole theater of Ibsen and Shaw, to the whole tradition of the realistic or satiric problem play, to the whole theory of art as having an immediate purpose or ulterior motive."

McMahon, Seán. " 'Leave Troubling the Lord God': A Note on Synge and Religion." *Éire-Ireland* XI, No. 1 (1976): 132-41.
> Challenges the opinion that Synge was irreligious and anti-clerical.

Mikhail, E. H., ed. *J. M. Synge: Interviews and Recollections.* New York: Barnes & Noble, 1977, 138 p.
> Collects assorted comments, interviews, and obituary tributes by Synge's contemporaries.

Price, Alan. *Synge and the Anglo-Irish Drama.* London: Methuen & Co., 1961, 236 p.
> Discusses Synge's works and chronicles the progress of the Abbey Theatre.

Pritchett, V. S. "The End of the Gael." In his *In My Good Books,* pp. 155-60. 1942. Reprint. Port Washington, N.Y.: Kennikat Press, 1970.

> Compares the literary missions of James Joyce and Synge.

Saddlemyer, Ann. " 'A Share in the Dignity of the World': J. M. Synge's Aesthetic Theory." In *The World of W. B. Yeats: Essays in Perspective,* edited by Robin Skelton and Ann Saddlemyer, pp. 241-53. Seattle: University of Washington Press, 1965.

> Examines Synge's notebooks in order to chart the development of his aesthetic beliefs.

———. "In Search of the Unknown Synge." In *Irish Writers and Society at Large,* pp. 181-98. Irish Literary Studies, edited by Masaru Sekine, Vol. 22. Totowa, N.J.: Barnes and Noble, 1985.

> Psychological study based on biographical data and the writer's notebooks.

Skelton, Robin. "The Politics of J. M. Synge." *The Massachusetts Review* XVIII, No. 1 (Spring 1977): 7-22.

> Characterizes Synge's politics as basically Socialist, but adds that, unlike many of his contemporaries who slipped into dogmatism, he maintained a sense of irony and skepticism in his views.

Whelan, F. A. E., and Hull, Keith N. " 'There's Talking for a Cute Woman!': Synge's Heroines." *Éire-Ireland* XV, No. 3 (Fall 1980): 36-46.

> Study of women in Synge's plays that states, "With the exception of Maurya in *Riders to the Sea,* each woman initiates movement away from [physical or social isolation] toward a life of greater vitality through passion, wildness, or beauty."

Williams, Raymond. "J. M. Synge." In his *Drama: From Ibsen to Eliot,* pp. 154-74. London: Chatto & Windus, 1965.

> Argues that Synge's works surpass the boundaries of both satirical and regional drama.

Yeats, John Butler. "Synge and the Irish." In his *Essays Irish and American,* pp. 51-61. Dublin: The Talbot Press, 1918.

> Encomium of Synge, celebrating the poetry of his dramas and the greatness of his character.

Yeats, W. B. *The Cutting of an Agate.* London: Macmillan and Co., 1919, 223 p.

> Contains Yeats's "Preface to the First Edition of *The Well of the Saints,*" "Preface to the First Edition of John M. Synge's *Poems and Translations,*" and "J. M. Synge and the Ireland of His Time."

RIDERS TO THE SEA

Beerbohm, Max. "Some Irish Plays and Players." In his *Around Theatres,* pp. 314-19. New York: Simon and Schuster, 1954.

> Positive review of a triple bill at the Irish Theatre featuring *Riders to the Sea, In the Shadow of the Glen,* and Yeats's *The King's Threshold.*

Currie, Ryder Hector, and Bryan, Martin. "*Riders to the Sea:* Reappraised." *The Texas Quarterly* XI, No. 4 (Winter 1968): 139-46.

> Emphasizes the psychological dimension of *Riders to the Sea.*

Van Laan, Thomas F. "Form as Agent in Synge's *Riders to the Sea.*" *Drama Survey* 3, No. 3 (February 1964): 352-66.

> Argues that in *Riders* Synge discovered the method for creating a modern tragedy.

PLAYBOY OF THE WESTERN WORLD

Bessai, Diane E. "Little Hound in Mayo: Synge's Playboy and the Comic Tradition in Irish Literature." *Dalhousie Review* 48, No. 3 (Autumn 1968): 372-83.

> Cites a number of stories from Irish folklore as sources for the action of *Playboy.*

Bigley, Bruce M. "*The Playboy of the Western World* as Antidrama." *Modern Drama* XX, No. 2 (June 1977): 157-67.

> Interprets *Playboy* as a drama that opposes the conventions of both comedy and tragedy.

Ditsky, John. "Synge's Savage Sermon." In his *Onstage Christ: Studies in the Persistence of a Theme,* pp. 46-58. Totowa, N.J.: Barnes & Noble, 1980.

> Detects parallels to the New Testament in *Playboy.* "Synge can be seen to have created Christy, Christ and Christ-bearer," Ditsky writes, "as a bringer of good news—a carrier of the ideas of love as the key to human development back to a community of principles supposedly Christian, presumably the religion of love."

Gutierrez, Donald. "Coming of Age in Mayo: Synge's *The Playboy of the Western World* As a Rite of Passage." *Hartford Studies in Literature* VI, No. 2 (1974): 159-66.

> Interprets *Playboy* as a "puberty rite of passage."

Hart, William. "Synge's Ideas on Life and Art: Design and Theory in *Playboy of the Western World.*" *Yeats Studies,* No. 2 (1972): 35-51.

> Discusses *Playboy* as the most complete expression of Synge's overall philosophy.

Kauffman, Stanley. Review of *Playboy of the Western World.* In his *Persons of the Drama: Theater Criticism and Comment,* pp. 117-20. New York: Harper & Row, 1976.

> Review of a 1971 performance of *Playboy* emphasizing how perceptions of the play have altered over time.

Kilroy, James F. "The Playboy as Poet." *PMLA* 83, No. 2 (March 1968): 439-42.

> Proposes that Christy Mahon's verbal ability improves over the course of the play. Kilroy writes: "Synge . . . is portraying the gradual growth of a poet."

———. *The "Playboy" Riots.* Dublin: The Dolmen Press, 1971, 101 p.

> Reprints newspaper articles concerning the protests that arose over *Playboy.*

MacLean, Hugh H. "The Hero as Playboy." *The University of Kansas City Review* XXI, No. 1 (Autumn 1954): 9-19.

> Discusses Christy Mahon "as scapegoat, as false Messiah, and as the Hero at length re-united with his Father."

Parker, Randolph. "Gaming in the Gap: Language and Liminality in *Playboy of the Western World.*" *Theatre Journal* 37, No. 1 (March 1985): 65-85.

> Argues that the basis of *Playboy's* "thematic matrix" is the gap between language and reality.

Waters, Maureen. "The Comic Hero." In her *Comic Irish-*

man, pp. 58-81. Albany: State University of New York Press, 1984.

> Compares Christy Mahon to the tradition of comic characters in Irish literature. The traditional figure "uses language to dazzle and evade, to create a mask which conceals his true nature," writes Waters. "Christy is the exception, the man who finally becomes the antithetical self, the hero he is reputed to be."

Whitaker, Thomas R., ed. *Twentieth Century Interpretations of "The Playboy of the Western World": A Collection of Critical Essays.* Englewood Cliffs, N.J.: Prentice-Hall, 1969, 122 p.

> Includes essays by W. B. Yeats, Cyril Cusack, and David H. Greene.

For further information on Synge's life and career, see *Contemporary Authors,* Vol. 104; *Dictionary of Literary Biography,* Vols. 10, 19; and *Twentieth-Century Literary Criticism,* Vols. 6, 37.

John Webster

1580?-1634?

INTRODUCTION

Critics often rank the English dramatist John Webster second only to William Shakespeare among Jacobean tragedians, and his two major works, *The White Devil* and *The Duchess of Malfi,* are more frequently revived on stage than any plays of the period other than Shakespeare's. Webster's tragedies, while highly regarded as poetic drama by some commentators, have also been attacked by others as being excessively grim and horrifying: his plays present a world in chaos, seemingly devoid of morality or any human feeling other than passionate sensuality. However, in performance Webster's highly charged verse often imbues his characters with a unique dignity and power.

No portraits of Webster are known to exist, and for over three hundred years little was known about his life. It was only recently that investigators uncovered information that provides some details. He was born in London, the eldest son of John Webster, a prosperous coachmaker and member of the prestigious guild, the Merchant Taylors' Company. (Coachmaking was a relatively new trade and did not yet have its own professional association.) Given his father's status, Webster was probably educated at the highly respected Merchant Taylors' School. Noting the prominence of legal concerns in Webster's dramas, scholars speculate that he may have also had some legal training. A John Webster was enrolled at the Middle Temple—the equivalent of a law school—but it is not certain that this was the playwright. Records indicate that, like his father, Webster was a respected member of the community. It is also known that he married Sara Peniall around 1605 and that they raised a large family. On his father's death Webster assumed the elder Webster's membership in the Merchant Taylors' Company. Scholars usually date Webster's death to around 1634, the year that Thomas Heywood referred to him in the past tense in his *Hierarchie of the Blessed Angels.*

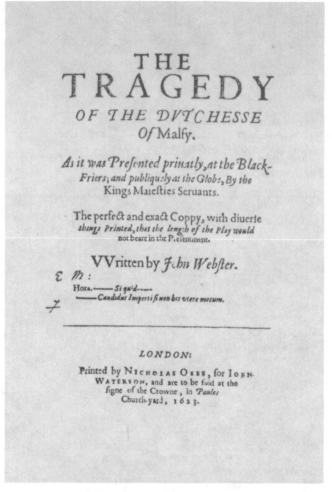

Title page of the 1623 edition of The Duchess of Malfi.

Webster's career in the theater began with collaborative work for Philip Henslowe, a man perhaps best known as the proprietor of London's Rose Theatre. Henslowe's *Diary,* which provides an invaluable view of English drama of the time, records in May 1602 that he paid Webster, Anthony Munday, Michael Drayton, Thomas Middleton, and Thomas Dekker for the now lost *Caesar's Fall or The Two Shapes.* In October 1602 Henslowe paid Webster, Dekker, Heywood, Henry Chettle, and Wentworth Smith for a play called *Lady Jane.* This work no longer survives and is considered by scholars to be an early version of *Sir Thomas Wyat,* a history play by various hands. Also in October, Webster and Heywood were advanced money for a play called *Christmas Comes But Once a Year.* Although he appears to have had no further connection with Henslowe, Webster continued to collaborate on dramatic works, and towards the end of 1604 he and Dekker wrote *Westward Ho,* a scandalous city comedy of middle-class London life. This satire spurred John Marston, George Chapman, and Ben Jonson to respond with the even more scandalous *Eastward Ho.* Dekker and Webster returned with *Northward Ho* in 1605, which many critics consider to be the better of the two Dekker-Webster comedies.

Webster's greatest accomplishments as a dramatist, *The White Devil* and *The Duchess of Malfi,* both reflect a sense of darkness encompassing human existence and a profound consciousness of evil and suffering in the world. Webster wrote during the Jacobean period, an age that questioned the preceding Elizabethan era's worldview, which was founded on the belief that all social, political, and even spiritual relations were defined in an unchanging hierarchy. The suggestion that chaos lies beyond such order—glimpsed in Elizabethan dramas such as Shakespeare's *King Lear*—became increasingly explicit in Jacobean drama. In particular, English society grew steadily more concerned over Machiavellianism, the political theory derived from the writing of Niccolo Machiavelli, an Italian statesman who, in his 1513 work *The Prince,* described politics as an amoral and ruthless striving to acquire and maintain power. The spread of such ideas contributed to the deterioration of belief in traditional values and fostered a general fear of societal disarray, in which people would be left to drift aimlessly through an amoral world.

The influence of this pessimistic worldview is evident in Webster's first independent work, *The White Devil.* Based on Italian historical events, the tragedy relates a complex tale of love, murder, and revenge. It centers on the adulterous passion between the Duke of Brachiano and Vittoria Corombona, who together plot and direct the murders of their spouses. Brachiano's brothers-in-law, to avenge their sister's death, instigate successful murder plots against the Duke and his mistress. At the center of this corrupt world is Flamineo, Vittoria's brother and secretary to Brachiano. Completely amoral and unscrupulous, he willingly performs any service necessary to satisfy his employer's passions, including murder and procuring his sister for Brachiano. Flamineo also functions as a chorus figure in the play, cynically commenting on the action. Vittoria is a unique Jacobean heroine: although thoroughly corrupt, she is nonetheless sympathetic. Strong-willed and independent, she chooses to live in accordance with her own desires and eloquently acquits herself during the course of the play. As D. C. Gunby has observed, "Vittoria is a white devil, but she is also a brilliant and resourceful woman, beautiful, courageous and highly intelligent, and we cannot help responding to her with some sympathy and warmth." While acknowledging the poignancy of Webster's presentation of Vittoria, who struggles—albeit unsuccessfully—to control her own life, some critics maintain that the absence of any positive, truly moral figure makes the world presented in the play one of unrelieved bleakness.

Webster's next drama, *The Duchess of Malfi,* is widely acclaimed as his masterpiece. Algernon Charles Swinburne maintained that "This tragedy stands out among its compeers as one of the imperishable and ineradicable landmarks of literature," and many subsequent critics have echoed this opinion. Like *The White Devil, The Duchess of Malfi* is based on Italian history. The widowed Duchess, against the wishes of her brothers, secretly marries her servant Antonio. The brothers—the fanatical Ferdinand and the scheming Cardinal—plant a spy, Bosola, in their sister's household. A character similar to Flamineo in *The White Devil,* Bosola is even more complex, vacillating between delight in his sinister role and a sense of degradation. When Bosola uncovers the truth about the Duchess's marriage, her brothers ruthlessly harass her, drive her from her home, and eventually imprison her. In a famous scene, she is tormented by madmen performing a stylized dance around her, and she is ultimately murdered. Critics have argued that Ferdinand's obsession with his sister is in part incestuous and that his descent into the madness of lycanthropy—the belief that he is a wolf—indicates that

theatrically and spiritually he turns into a beast. Scholars agree that the Duchess herself is one of the greatest tragic heroines of the period. Her attitude of Christian resignation in the face of her brothers' vicious cruelty imbues her with a profound dignity, and the depiction of her murder is commonly judged one of the most moving scenes in all Jacobean drama.

Scholars note a significant decline in Webster's dramaturgy following the composition of *The Duchess of Malfi.* Most agree that his next play, the tragicomic *Devil's Law-Case,* is the most difficult of Webster's works to assess. Its nearly incoherent plot involves a large number of shocking and absurd schemes, which preclude dramatic unity. It has only been performed once—in 1980—since Webster's time. Webster also contributed thirty-two character sketches to the sixth edition of Thomas Overbury's *New and Choice Characters, of Several Authors* (1615), and continued to collaborate on plays. *Appius and Virginia,* perhaps written with Heywood around 1634, is a Roman tragedy about the corrupt judge Appius who seeks to possess Virginia, the daughter of a famous general. Although admired by nineteenth-century critics for its classical simplicity of construction, this drama is not now highly regarded. Other plays attributed either wholly or partially to Webster include the lost works *Guise* and *The Late Murder of the Son upon the Mother.* He is also believed to have contributed to *Anything for a Quiet Life* and *A Cure for a Cuckold,* both of which survive only in carelessly printed editions.

Over the centuries Webster's critical reputation has fluctuated. From his own time to the present, some critics have praised the poetic brilliance of Webster's tragic vision, while others have scorned his plays as confused and excessively violent. To his peers, Webster was a slow, careful writer who "borrowed" lines from his fellow playwrights and used them to create powerful scenes. Although such borrowing was not uncommon during the Jacobean era, Webster utilized others' material to such a degree that he was satirized in Henry Fitzjeffrey's 1617 poem, "Notes from Blackfriars." Calling the playwright "Crabbed Websterio," Fitzjeffrey jeered:

> Heer's not one word *cursively* I have *Writ,*
> But hee'l *Industriously* examine it.
> And it some 12. monthes hence (or there *about*)
> Set in a shamefull sheete, my errors *out.*
> But what care I it *will* be so obscure,
> That none shall understand him (I am sure).

The great number of printings and revivals of Webster's plays during the seventeenth century attests to their continued popularity. In the eighteenth century, however, his reputation was eclipsed by a growing interest in Shakespeare. Webster was known mainly to bibliographers and scholars, who considered his plays scarcely more than period pieces, fine examples of the drama of the past but with little to offer contemporary audiences. In fact, his tragedies were performed only five times during the eighteenth century. In 1808 Charles Lamb renewed interest in Webster's plays with an enthusiastic appreciation of them in his *Specimens of English Dramatic Poets Who Lived about the Time of Shakespeare.* The noted critic William Hazlitt subsequently found that *The White Devil* and *The Duchess of Malfi* "come the nearest to Shakespeare of any thing we have upon record." The first collected edition of Webster's works appeared in 1830, and the first nineteenth-century production of *The Duchess of Malfi* took place twenty years later. With this staging began a new phase of criticism: response to the play as acted. Critics of the period were sharply divided on the merit of Webster's works, with one group agreeing with Hazlitt and celebrating the poetic power of Webster's tragic vision, while the other attacked what they saw as absurd improbabilities, gross excesses, and episodic structures in the tragedies. William Archer, a member of the second group, argued that "Webster was not, in the special sense of the word, a great dramatist, but was a great poet who wrote haphazard dramatic or melodramatic romances for an eagerly receptive but semi-barbarous public."

In the twentieth century, debate continues as to Webster's moral outlook, with the critics who see it as fundamentally negative outnumbering those who assert that the plays reveal a profound belief that personal integrity can be maintained in a chaotic universe. Evaluations of Webster's artistry have revealed an intricate relationship between dramatic structure, characterization, and imagery in his plays. Examining Webster's use of language, Clifford Leech observed that "Webster excels in the sudden flash, in the intuitive but often unsustained perception. At times he startles us by what may be called the 'Shakespearian' use of the common word."

Both lauded and maligned for centuries, the dramatic art of John Webster remains difficult to assess. While undeniably horrifying, his depictions of people struggling to make sense of their lives in an apparently meaningless world possess a curiously modern sensibility. *The White Devil* and *The Duchess of Malfi* retain a vitality that continues to appeal to actors, audiences, and critics. That Webster's best works are still performed, read, and debated is perhaps the finest testament to his standing as a dramatist.

PRINCIPAL WORKS

PLAYS

Caesar's Fall or The Two Shapes 1602 [with Anthony Munday, Michael Drayton, Thomas Middleton, and Thomas Dekker; no longer extant]

The Famovs History of Sir Thomas Wyat. With the Coronation of Queen Mary, and the coming in of King Philip. 1602 [with Dekker, Henry Chettle, Thomas Heywood, and Wentworth Smith; published 1607]

Christmas Comes But Once a Year 1602 [with Heywood, Chettle, and Dekker; no longer extant]

West-ward Hoe 1604 [with Dekker; published 1607]

North-ward Hoe 1605 [with Dekker; published 1607]

The White Divel, or, The Tragedy of Paulo Giordano Ursini, Duke of Brachiano, With The Life and Death of

Vittoria Corombona the famous Venetian Curtizan 1612 [published 1612]

The Tragedy Of The Dvtchesse Of Malfy 1614 [published 1623]

The Guise unknown date [no longer extant]

The Deuil's Law-Case. Or, When Women goe to Law, the Deuill is full of Businesse. A new Tragecomedy c. 1619-22 [published 1623]

Anything for a Quiet Life c. 1621 [by Middleton and perhaps Webster; published 1662]

The Late Murder of the Son upon the Mother, or Keep the Widow Waking 1624 [with Dekker, John Ford, and William Rowley; no longer extant]

A Cure for a Cuckold c. 1624-25 [with Rowley; published 1661]

Appius and Virginia: A Tragedy 1634 [published 1654]

OTHER MAJOR WORKS

Induction to John Marston's *The Malcontent* 1604

* *A Monumental Columne, Erected to the Memory of Henry, Late Prince of Wales* (poetry) 1613

* *Monuments of Honor. Derived from Remarkable Antiquity, and Celebrated in London. At the Confirmation of John Gore* (poetry) 1624

*Webster contributed poems to these collections of elegiac and panegyric verse.

OVERVIEWS AND GENERAL STUDIES

Ian Jack (essay date 1949)

[*In the excerpt below, Jack maintains that there is no correspondence between the moral axioms of "degree"—the hierarchical ordering of nature and society—and the Machiavellian life presented in Webster's drama. Machiavellianism, a philosophy derived from Niccolo Machiavelli's political manifesto* The Prince *(1513), stresses the single-minded, ruthless, and amoral cunning of the individual as a means of obtaining and maintaining power. This disassociation, Jack continues, is the dramatist's fundamental flaw.*]

Disintegration characterizes the view of life which inspired Webster's best-known plays. It is perfectly true, as Dr. Tillyard remarks [in *The Elizabethan World Picture*], that Webster, like the rest of his age, inherited 'the Elizabethan world-picture'; but in his work we see that world-picture falling in ruins. When Dr. Tillyard goes on to say that Webster's characters belong 'to a world of violent crime and violent change, of sin, blood and repentance, yet to a world loyal to a theological scheme', and adds: 'indeed all the violence of Elizabethan drama has nothing to do with a dissolution of moral standards: on the contrary, it can afford to indulge itself just because those standards were so powerful', he is overlooking the highly significant differences between Elizabethan drama and Jacobean drama, and uttering a dangerous half-truth. No doubt there is a definite 'theological scheme' behind Webster, in the sense that it was familiar to his audience and himself, and could therefore be drawn on for imagery; but *The White Divel* and *The Dutchesse of Malfy* are our best evidence that the Elizabethan theological scheme could no longer hold together.

Henry James [in *The Art of Fiction*] pointed out that the ultimate source of a novel's value is the quality of the mind which produced it; and the same is true of drama. Great tragedy can be written only by a man who has achieved—at least for the period of composition—a profound *and balanced* insight into life. Webster—his plays are our evidence—did not achieve such an insight. The imagery, verse-texture, themes and 'philosophy' of his plays all point to a fundamental flaw, which is ultimately a moral flaw.

If one reads through *The White Divel* and *The Dutchesse of Malfy,* noting down the *sententiæ* [concise statements of principles] and moralizing asides of the various characters, one finds oneself in possession of a definite attempt at a 'philosophy', a moral to the tale:

> *Integrity of life, is fames best friend,*
> *Which nobly (beyond Death) shall crowne the*
> * end.*
> > *[The Dutchesse of Malfy,* V.v.146]

This philosophy is Stoical and Senecan, with a Roman emphasis on the responsibilities of Princes:

> The lives of Princes should like dyals move,
> Whose regular example is so strong,
> They make the times by them go right or wrong.
> > *[The White Divel* I.ii.81]

But this background of moral doctrine has nothing to do with the action of the plays: so far from growing out of the action, it bears all the marks of having been superimposed by the poet in a cooler, less creative mood, than that in which the Duchess and Flamineo had their birth. There is no correspondence between the axioms and the life represented in the drama. This dissociation is the fundamental flaw in Webster.

What was wrong, apparently, was that there was available no philosophy of life which kindled Webster's imagination as certain aspects of Hell, or Chaos, kindled it. No moral order represented itself to his imagination as real. Consequently his plays contain brilliant passages of poetry—they appear whenever he touches on the small area which acted as his inspiration—but lack imaginative coherence. They have indeed a unity, the unity for which the 'mist' is a symbol; but one mood, isolated and out of focus, cannot be the basis of a profound tragic vision. Webster himself seems to have understood this better than some of his more enthusiastic critics; but his attempt to shore up chaos with a sententious philosophy is a flagrant artistic insincerity. Webster fails to realize his Senecan philosophy as he realizes his glimpses of Hell.

We might say that Webster suffered from the poverty—the philosophical poverty—of the tradition in which he worked; but the fact that he chose to write in the Revenge tradition at all is itself evidence of a lack of harmony in his own mind. For other traditions were available, notably the tradition of Morality, to which Shakespeare's great tragedies owe more than has even yet been understood. Webster's choice of the Revenge tradition, his failure to give life to his Senecan moralizings, and (we may add) the fact that his work contains no convincing statement of the *positive* aspect of the doctrine of Degree, are all related: Degree and Order—as we come to see—were not real enough to Webster to stir his imagination. A lower concept of the Universe, and of Man's place in it, was all that he could compass.

This explains the fascination which the 'Machiavellian' had for Webster. To the conservative Elizabethan the Machiavellian doctrine seemed merely the denial of that Order and Degree which held the Universe together: Machiavellianism was anarchism. It is not surprising that a mind as unbalanced as Webster's should have allowed the Machiavellian ideal to usurp the place in his thought which a more conservative poet would have reserved for Degree. As a consequence, there is a remarkable number of 'politicians' in his two plays.

Flamineo in *The White Divel* is a good example. He acts as pander to his sister Vittoria, contrives her husband's death, and treats his mother with a cold, sub-human ferocity:

> I pray will you go to bed then,
> Least you be blasted.
> > [I.ii.264]

He treacherously murders his brother in his mother's presence, and proclaims that nothing but a limitation of his natural ability prevents him from double-crossing his master, Brachiano: 'I had as good a will to cosen him, as e'er an Officer of them all; but I had not cunning enough to doe it' [V.iii.56-8]. He tries to corrupt even Giovanni with cynical advice. It is only when he is listening to the 'superstitious howling' [V.iv.59] of his mother over the brother whom he has killed that Flamineo's Machiavellianism proves imperfect:

> I have a strange thing in mee, to th' which
> I cannot give a name, without it bee
> Compassion.
> > [V.iv.109]

Flamineo's philosophy is simply that

> *Knaves do grow great by being great mens apes.*
> > [IV.ii.246]

He explains his own villainy by saying:

> . . . I made *a kind of path*
> To her [Vittoria's] & mine owne preferment.
> > [III.i.36-7]

Flamineo's attitude to women proves him a 'Courtier' of a very different cast from Castiglione's ideal:

> I visited the Court, whence I return'd
> More courteous, more letcherous by farre.
> > [I.ii.319]

His attitude to women is that of 'the cynic'. He regards a woman's modesty as 'but the superficies of lust' [I.ii.18], and makes love to Zanche 'just as a man holds a wolfe by the eares' [V.i.150]—to prevent her from turning on him. He looks on women—and on all humanity—as mere animals: 'women are like curst dogges'; human love-making he regards as the coupling of mare and stallion. There is something peculiarly fiendish about his ironical comment, as he eavesdrops at the love-making of Vittoria and Brachiano:

> BRAC: [enamoured] Nay lower, you shall weare my Jewell lower.
>
> FLAM: [aside] *That's better, she must weare his Jewell lower.*
>
> [I.ii.218]

There is an infinite weariness in Flamineo's voice when he says:

> O, no othes for gods sake!
>
> [IV.ii.150]

The strident courage which Flamineo shows in dying—

> Strike thunder, and strike lowde to my farewell
> [V.vi.276]

—is a quality which he shares with all Webster's Machiavellians; and this, the one admirable quality in so many of his characters, manifests Webster's peculiarly limited and deformed notion of ethics. We find in Webster only the virtue of Hell: the courage of despair. The stridency of this pagan courage is very evident when Brachiano cries:

> . . . *Monticelso,*
> *Nemo me Impune laces* [s] *it,*
>
> [III.ii.186]

or when Francisco proclaims:

> *Flectere si nequeo superos, Acheronta movebo.*
> [IV.i.143]

Denied insight into any virtue other than Stoical courage, Webster tries to erect unflinchingly perseverance in evil into the sum of moral goodness. In the process he is disingenuous. As [Charles] Lamb remarked [in *Specimens of English Dramatic Poets*], 'This White Devil of Italy sets off a bad cause so speciously, and pleads *with such an innocence-resembling boldness,* that we . . . are ready to expect, when she has done her pleadings, that . . . all the court will rise and make proffer to defend her in spite of the utmost conviction of her guilt'. Vittoria is dishonourable: Webster simply makes her behave as if she were honourable. This is an artistic insincerity—a lie in the poet's heart—of which Shakespeare would not have been guilty; but Webster, having no profound hold on any system of moral values, found it easy to write for Vittoria dissembling verse which in its righteous simplicity seems to proclaim her honesty in the face of her accusers.

It is consonant with Webster's unbalanced outlook that the distinguishing mark of his Machiavellian 'heroes' is their individualism. In Shakespeare individualism is an infallible mark of villainy:

> Richard loves Richard; that is, I am I.
> [*Richard III,* V.iii.236]

Like Richard III, Iago and Edmund in Shakespeare, Lo-

dovico, the Cardinal, Bosola and Flamineo are all individualists, and all villains.

The atmosphere in which Webster's characters live is the atmosphere of a corrupt Court. The description of 'France' at the beginning of *The Dutchesse of Malfy* sets off the scene of Webster's play by contrast:

> In seeking to reduce both State and People
> To a fix'd Order, the[ir] juditious King
> Begins at home . . .
>
> [I.i.8]

To point the contrast, Bosola—who is one of the 'dissolute, and infamous persons' [I.i.10] who are banished from any healthy Court—enters just as this speech is finished. If Webster were an orthodox Elizabethan, the rest of the play would be an illustration of what happens in a state of which the Prince himself is evil:

> Death, and diseases through the whole land
> spread.
>
> [I.i.16]

But while the atmosphere of the play is precisely the atmosphere described in these opening lines, there is in Webster, as we have already mentioned, no convincing statement of the positive aspect of Degree; we do not for a moment believe that when the Duke and Cardinal are dead the state of Amalfi will return to a condition of health and normality. While the atmosphere of Webster's plays is as unhealthy as that of 'Vienna' in *Measure for Measure,* there is in Webster no Messianic Duke to return and save the state from chaos. The 'mist' of the two plays is all-embracing: we can form no notion of another world which will be revealed when the rottenness of Amalfi has come to a head and been purged away. Comfortable words spoken at the end of *The White Divel* and *The Dutchesse of Malfy* carry no conviction; if we take evil away from Webster's world, nothing is left.

This explains the curious futility of all Webster's characters. When Bosola is asked how Antonio was killed, he answers:

> In a mist: I know not how,
> Such a mistake, as I have often seene
> In a play.
>
> [V.v.120]

Very similar in tone is the reply of the Duke in *The Dutchesse of Malfy,* when he is asked why he brought about the death of the Duchess; he replies that he had hoped to gain

> An infinite masse of Treasure by her death.
> [IV.ii.304]

This explanation is so off-hand and perfunctory that it can only be termed an *excuse:* the Duke is in fact at a loss to find any plausible reason for his actions.

All Webster's characters, indeed, and particularly his most consummate 'politicians', have only the most tenuous hold on reality; they are characterized by the same motiveless malignity that Coleridge noticed in Iago. But whereas Iago is a subordinate character in *Othello,* so that we are prepared to accept the convention by which he is simply 'The Villain', a man who desires evil because it is his nature to do so, Webster's plays are almost entirely peopled by such characters.

Without adopting the attitude of the 'naturalistic' critic, we must maintain that there are too many inconsistencies in Webster's plays; and whereas inconsistencies are readily passed over when—as in Shakespeare—they are subservient to some important dramatic purpose, in Webster there is no deeper purpose than to make our flesh creep, and we feel an inevitable resentment.

There is in fact something a trifle ridiculous about Webster. When we have seen his two plays we have indeed 'supp'd full of horrors', and overheard 'talk fit for a charnel'. An irruption of real humour—humour of the Shakespearean sort—would knock Webster's waxworks into a cocked hat. He is too evidently bent on exploiting the emotions of his audience.

Webster, that is to say, is a decadent. He is decadent in the sense that he is incapable of realizing the whole of life in the form in which it revealed itself to the Elizabethans. By concentrating exclusively on the narrow aspect of life revealed in one mood, he threw the relations of the whole out of harmony. In his work the proper relations between the individual and society, between God and Man, are overthrown. The sensationalism of his plays is the stigma of an outlook on life as narrow as it is intense. Webster sees the human situation as a chaotic struggle, lit indeed by flashes of 'bitter lightning', but fated to sink again into a mist of confusion and sub-human activity. (pp. 38-43)

> Ian Jack, "The Case of John Webster," in Scrutiny, *Vol. XVI, No. 1, March, 1949, pp. 38-43.*

Adair Mill   (essay date 1956)

[*In the excerpt below, Mill charges that critics who claim Webster perceives the world as hopelessly corrupt make the mistake of attributing to the author the views expressed by his characters. Mill argues that Webster in* The White Devil *and* The Duchess of Malfi *depicts fascinating sinners set against the background of a world that is implicitly moral.*]

A reader who approached either **The White Devil** or **The Duchess of Malfi** with the expectation that Webster is to paint a world of evil, sin, despondency and despair from which there is no escape imaginable or redemption possible, save for momentary flashes of mystical illumination, could not fail to be bewildered, perplexed and disappointed by the plays themselves. Far from portraying an utterly evil and sinful world, Webster, in my opinion, directs his attention away from general conceptions of the world as a whole to a keen and penetrating psychological study of a group of sinful and evil people, an analysis of their characters, and a sympathetic recreation of their passions and sentiments. Far from symbolising or shadowing forth the world as Webster conceived it, these characters are obvious exceptions to the general rule, figures that fascinate because of their strangeness, their pervisity. Vittoria, Flamineo, Brachiano and Lodovico; Ferdinand, the Car-

dinal and Bosola, and even, to a certain extent, the Duchess and Antonio, are all exceptional characters set off against a background of the most orthodox and conventional morality. If we are to use the phrase 'Webster's world' we should, I think, apply it to this world of orthodox religion, conventional morality and common-place platitudes which forms the firm and indispensable foundation for the gloom and terror of these plays. Unless one accepts this fact the plays become vague and wavering in intention, and obscure and self-contradictory in meaning. Nonexistent problems, such as the supposed contradiction between the implicit and explicit meaning of the plays, perplex and irritate the reader; critics complain of the lack of any moral teaching in plays that are filled with moral platitudes and common-places, of the failure to portray education through suffering on the part of a playwright whose intention was to show that suffering is a result of sin and that virtue is its own reward, of the lack of a mystical redemption from despair in a world that despair has never touched, however lost and despairing single, individual members of that world may be.

When the basic attitudes of life, religion and morality are traditional and conventional, when the playwright accepts without question the moral and spiritual values of his time, he may be forgiven if he fails to define these values clearly and fully, and it may be regarded as a venial fault if he fails to make the moral principles underlying his play unmistakably apparent to a critic belonging to a different age with totally different moral and religious assumptions. Webster does not, however, provide his modern critics with this excuse for misunderstanding and misinterpretation. Although he may leave general concepts such as virtue and justice undefined, yet he makes his moral and religious position sufficiently clear, and points in a broad and effective background of general principles against which his brilliant studies of moral perversity or weakness are portrayed. The first scene of a Jacobean play is almost always of immense importance in so far as it sets the tone, atmosphere and general attitude of the play. **The White Devil** is no exception to this rule. In this case, however, the first scene is devoted not only to setting forth the general moral principles that form a basis for the play as a whole but also to giving a brief but brilliantly effective sketch of Lodovico's character—with the unfortunate result that some modern critics have allowed themselves to be misled into regarding Lodovico's outlook as being identical with the author's own. The word 'banished' with which the play opens has been taken as the key-word to the play and the author's whole attitude to life. Nothing could be more absurdly far from the truth. It is the key-word to Lodovico's character, but that character only becames clear when seen against the general principles of morality enunciated by Antonelli and Gasparo. The sane, orthodox outlook of the two gentleman serves as a foil to the dark, insane perversity of Lodovico's attitude. The two friends pour out the story of his heinous crimes in order to try to convince him that he has been justly punished, that to harbour any grudge or grievance against his judges is absurd and unjustifiable, and that his personal disaster is not only just but might well prove beneficial in so far it has given him an opportunity of seeing the results of his conduct and so of reforming his way of life. They accuse him of having ruined the noblest earldom by his prodigality, of having sold his estates to purchase luxuries and dainties, of having allowed himself and his fortune to become the prey of flatterers and sycophants, of having indulged in all kinds of excesses and extravagances, drunkenness and debauchery, and of having committed horrible and bloody murders. From the list of these crimes it is not very difficult to uncover the principles that form the foundation of the moral principles accepted by Antonelli and Gasparo; duty to society (consisting, in the case of great men, in performing their duties towards their inferiors and their dependants), duty to one's family (in preserving one's estates, wealth and honour intact), and one's duties towards oneself (in controlling one's passions and appetites, in refusing to allow oneself to become the tool of evil men or evil desires, and in remaining true to certain rational and accepted principles of moral conduct). It is, of course, by no means logically inevitable that that the theory of morality that we have attributed to Antonelli and Gasparo should also be attributed to Webster. Nevertheless, the fact that it is allowed to set the moral of the first scene of the play allows us to assume, at least tentatively, that it may approximate to the basic moral principles upon which the author has built the ethical fabric of his play. There are a number of other alternatives. Antonelli and Gasparo might be meant to represent an orthodox and traditional philosophy which the author wishes to prove untenable; they might represent a purely conventional outlook serving as a contrast to the pessimistic but realistic attitude of Lodovico; they might serve as puppets to put forward conventional and accepted opinions that the author might shelter behind if he were attacked for the daring, 'atheist' opinions put forward in the play; or they might stand for the view of life that the author accepted in his conscious mind but which he subconsciously rejected in favour of a despairing and outrageous nihilism. The first three, all of which presuppose that Webster was more or less in conscious agreement with the world-view held by a Lodovico, could only be accepted if supported by external evidence, or if it were proved that there was no other means of removing the obscurities or of solving the contradictions of the play; yet far from solving our problems such a supposition only raises more. The whole purport and teaching of the play, which is that sin brings its own punishment, only falls into place if we assume that Webster accepts the orthodox morality and the conventional outlook of his time, and that he regards Lodovico, Flamineo, Vittoria and Brachiano as examples of perversity and evil. A Jacobean audience would immediately accept the moral principles taken for granted by Antonelli and Gasparo as the norm, and the grotesque outrageousness of Lodovico's sentiments make it quite clear that he is intended to represent the exceptional and the pathological:

> GASPARO: You have acted certain murders here in Rome Bloody and full of horror.
>
> LODOVICO: 'Las, they were flea-bitings.
>   (I. i. 31-32)

The manner in which he spurns Antonelli's conventional but nevertheless apt description of the uses of adversity serves to give the audience a striking insight into the depths of his insane sense of grievance:

> ANTONELLI: and so affliction Expresseth virtue fully, whether true Or else adulterate.
>
> LODOVICO: Leave your painted comforts: I'll make Italian cut-works in their cuts If ever I return.
>   (I. i. 48-52)

It is quite obvious that Webster meant the audience to be shocked and horrified by Lodovico's statements, and equally obvious that the attitude to life, religion and morality revealed in the sentiments of a Lodovico, a Vittoria, or any other of the 'atheistical' characters in Webster's plays were meant to reveal the terror of that hell that an evil person carries around with him. Moreover the word 'Italian' in the above quotation is of considerable significance here as we shall find that the evil characters in Webster are conceived not only as horrifying exceptions in a more or less sane and stable, though imperfect, world, but as strange, fascinating, unfamiliar figures to be found in the Italy of the Renaissance but utterly foreign to English soil. Thus Webster's principal characters, far from representing the author's general attitude to man and the world that he inhabits, are at two removes from such a straightforward universality—first because they are obvious exceptions to the normal run of human beings, and secondly because they are represented as being typical of Renaissance Italy, a country which, in the eyes of an English Protestant of the Elizabethan and Stuart periods, was immoral, irreligious and evil.

As for the point of view that would make Webster subconsciously in agreement with the pessimists, nihilists and atheists of his dramas, I find it difficult to accept such excursions into the domain of psycho-analysis, expecially when carried out by amateurs, as one of the legitimate activities of a literary critic. If the play as it stands is obscure, unsatisfying, and vague in meaning and intention then I suppose that there is a certain amount of justification for such desperate expedients as the psycho-analysis of a dead man's mind. But where the play is, as in this case, perfectly clear and straight-forward if one accepts the author's explicit commentary on his own play, and obscure and unsatisfying only if one assumes that the author's real meaning differs from that commentary, then it is clear that the reader and critic should keep to the straight-forward, obvious interpretation of the play's outlook. The desire to represent Webster as being in substantial agreement with the sentiments and attitude of the evil characters in his plays probably springs from the inability of certain critics to accept the rather naive and unsophisticated ethical code to be found side by side with the most penetrating psychological analysis, just as the inability of some Romantic critics to accept the dogmatic religious and moral outlook of [John] Milton tempted them into attributing to the poet a sympathy with the outlook of the Devil.

In *The White Devil* Webster makes his ethical position perfectly clear by means of the sentiments placed in the mouth of Cornelia. The scene in which she makes her first appearance on the stage is an unforgettable example of the imaginative brilliance of Webster's theatrical invention, which employs as its medium not only the speech, sentiments and actions of the characters but also the stage setting, and the movement and disposition of the characters on the stage. The adulterous lovers occupy the centre of the stage, with Flamineo and Zanche, the pander and the negress, on one side, and Cornelia, Vittoria's mother, listening behind. There is thus a sort of double chorus— Flamineo commenting cynically on the progress made by Brachiano and Vittoria in their criminal lust, Cornelia bewailing the sinfulness of her daughter and the viciousness of her son. It is in this scene that the moral setting of the play is most vividly revealed and most effectively impressed on the spectator's mind, and the fact that the rest of the action of the play represents a substantial proof of the truth of the *sententiae* contained in Cornelia's first speech should permit us to regard this play as being not only just as much of a morality play as any of Shakespeare's, but but as a morality play with perhaps an even more explicit and straightforward moral attitude than any of Shakespeare's.

> Many fears are fall'n upon me: O, my heart!
> My son the pander! Now I find our house
> Sinking to ruin. Earthquakes leave behind,
> Where they have tyrannized, iron, or lead, or
>   stone;
> But, woe to ruin, violent lust leaves none.
>   (I.ii.206-10)

This speech, and it worthy of remark that Webster does not disdain the help of the conventional rhymed couplet in order to point a common-place, would seem to imply that virtue is capable of preserving a house and family from ruin, and that prosperity is more commonly to be found consorting with virtue than with vice—a platitude upon which, indeed, the rest of the play is a commentary. There is nothing to suggest that virtue is impossible in Webster's world. On the contrary, it is usually spoken of as something far less surprising and far more easily acceptable than vice or sin. The extraordinarily effective introduction of the young Giovanni in Act II scene i brings before our eyes a living example of that virtue which is generally, in Webster, confined to abstract formulation in the sentences. The moral attitude revealed is one typical of the Humanist Renaissance, and differs in no way from the Elizabethan ideals manifested in the works of [Philip] Sidney and [Edmund] Spenser. This brief but memorable scene contains in brief the true character and education of a prince. He should be trained by example rather than by precept, and in this no teacher can be superior to his own father—one of the arguments for the superior virtue of an aristocracy of birth. His virtue should be of power to withstand temptation and adversity, and should be formed on the Roman model of courage, discretion, self-control and justice, together with a real sense of his responsibilities as a ruler and prince. The classical humanistic basis of Webster's morality is revealed in Francesco's remark,

> See, a good habit makes a child a man,
> Whereas a bad one makes a man a beast.
>   (II.i.140-41)

For Webster, as for Shakespeare and other thinkers of a typically Renaissance cast of mind, the highest compliment that can be paid to any human being is to describe him as a 'man'. Although certain aspects of humanity may be 'beastly', there is a world of difference between a true man and a beast, and a man who lives a virtuous life is worthy of the greatest admiration and respect. That this is no unattainable ideal in Webster is shown by the demonstration of Giovanni's sense of justice with which the play ends. This surely proves that Webster's world is not incorrigibly evil and that his hope lies rather in the actions of good men like Giovanni rather than in a mystical faith in something indefinable and far. Webster's attitude to princes and great men is, as a matter of fact, sufficient to defeat any attempt to make Webster a pessimist. There are many bitter and cynical attacks on great men throughout the play but it must be borne in mind that these are placed in the mouths of the two most notorious villains, Lodovico and Flamineo. Lodovico is a boldly and effectively drawn character, an admirable example of what the nineteenth century called a nihilist and the seventeenth century an atheist. His whole outlook is based on a sense of grievance, and thus on a sense of denial and revolt. He is a typical specimen of that type of man who believes himself to be essentially worthy and good, but who has been treated, in his own opinion, with harsh injustice by the world and particularly by the great. This sense of grievance and despised virtue drives him into a diabolical obsession with crime and destruction (but it is significant that his mania for destruction is always directed against sinful people) and ultimately with self-destruction.

>   I do glory yet
>
> That I can call this act mine own. For my part,
> The rack, the gallows, and the torturing wheel,
> Shall be but sound sleeps to me: here's my rest:
> I limn'd this night-piece, and it was my best.
>   (V.vi.295-99)

This diabolical obsession draws a sharp contrast between himself and Flamineo, whose sins are committed out of no passionate obsession with sin itself or out of any sense of grievance, but purely and deliberately to advance himself in the world and, by making himself a pander and a tool to the vicious desires of the great, better his financial position. The mean and abject nature of his crimes stands in vivid contrast to the Satanic darkness of Lodovico's. Moreover whilst Lodovico's crimes are committed against the wicked, so that his sin consists mostly in appropriating to himself the task of punishing sin, which rightly belongs to God and the prince, Flamineo's crimes are directed against the pure and the innocent and the virtuous. It would seem rather surprising to accept any statements made by these characters on life or morality as worthy of credence, and more surprising still to attribute them to the author. Yet if we are to accept Webster as a pessimist it must be on the strength of sentiments expressed by characters such as these, since it is in their speeches that typical 'Websterian' attitudes are to be found, and rarely outside. Taking their remarks on great men (since few things reveal optimism or pessimism so clearly as one's attitude to the great) we shall find that they give us valuable insight into the characters of the two men, but only in the case of Flamineo any hint as to the position taken up by Webster himself. One of the outstanding features of Lodovico's character is his lack of insight into other's characters and motives, and his rather remarkable lack of practical intelligence and imagination. This is clearly revealed in the first scene of the play, indeed in the first word. He never attempts to refute the accusations that Antonelli and Gasparo bring against him—yet he finds it impossible to understand how he could have been sentenced to banishment, he sees nothing but the most bewildering injustice in the way he has been treated. In this scene he attacks great men for their cruelty and injustice, to be mildly reprehended by his two friends for doing so. But the most telling incident, so far as his attitude to great men is concerned is his falling so easy a victim to Francesco's simple stratagem, and in being so easily persuaded that the Cardinal, by a present of gold, wishes to assure him of his secret sympathy and encouragement in the crime he is about to commit. The attack on great men which immediately follows is thus almost comically ironic.

> O the art,
> The modest form of greatness! that do sit,
> Like brides at wedding-dinners, with their looks turned
> From the least wanton jest, their puling stomach
> Sick of the modesty, when their thoughts are loose,
> Even acting of those hot and lustful sports
> Are to ensue about midnight: such his cunning:
> He sounds my depth thus with a golden plummet.
> I am doubly arm'd now. Now to the act of blood.
> There's but three Furies found in spacious hell,
> But in a great man's breast three thousand dwell.
>
> (IV.iii.145-55)

Here we have the ridiculous situation of a man so cynical and intent on seeing evil everywhere that he is easily tricked into believing the Cardinal a hypocrite. If we are to interpret correctly Lodovico's judgments on great men or indeed on any aspect of morality or society, it must be as indices to Lodovico's character and certainly not as sententiae revealing anything of Webster's own attitudes and beliefs. Flamineo's observations must, on the other hand, be given much more serious consideration as they contain more than a little universal validity. Flamineo differs from Lodovico in nothing so much as in the power of his intelligence and the keenness of his insight into other's characters and motives for action. Lodovico's sense of grievance dulls his intelligence and insight; Flamineo's mean ambition serves to sharpen his. His understanding of character is keen and shrewd, his judgments are based on clearsighted observation and an only too lucid insight into the seamier side of human nature.

> Fie, fie, my lord,
> Women are caught as you take tortoises,
> She must be turned on her back.
>
> (IV.ii.153-55)

This statement is absolutely typical of Flamineo's 'sententiae', and of those of all the 'melancholy' character's of Jacobean drama. It is a statement almost universally true, a statement that shocks one into perceiving a valuable even though only a partial truth, but one to which there are, of course, notable exceptions—exceptions which are far more important than the norm. Flamineo's remarks concerning great men are, however, more worthy of credence and more likely to reflect the opinions of the author since, whereas the remark on women is intended not so much as a reasoned judgment as a piece of advice to Brachiano on how to behave towards Vittoria, his remarks concerning great men are made on the death of Brachiano, on the collapse of all his hopes and the failure of all his schemes and intrigues, a moment when Jacobean villains are permitted to have a glimpse of the truths that they have ignored.

> To see what solitariness is about dying princes! as heretofore they have unpeopled towns, divorced friends, and made great houses unhospitable, so now, O justice! where are their flatterers now? Flatterers are but the shadows of princes' bodies; the least thick cloud makes them invisible. . . . He was a kind of statesman that would sooner have reckoned how many cannon bullets he had discharged against a town, to count his expense that way, than how many of his valiant and deserving subjects he lost before it.
>
> FRANCISCO: Oh, speak well of the duke.
>
> FLAMINEO: I have done. Wilt hear some of my court-wisdom? To reprehend princes is dangerous and to over-commend some of them is palpable lying.
>
> (V.iii.42-67)

There is no suggestion that all princes are bad. In fact it is all but explicitly stated that some are good and virtuous. This opinion is also more than implied in the closing aphorism of the conjurer:

> Both flowers and weeds spring when the sun is warm,
> And great men do great good or else great harm.
>
> (II.ii.55-6)

That power for good as well as for evil lies in the hands of great men acquits Webster of any possible charge of unalleviated pessimism as far as the body politic is concerned, and his continually emphasising, both in the sententiae and in the action of the play, that vice and sin and selfish irresponsibility on the part of a ruler brings ruin and destruction in its wake lends his whole outlook an undeniably optimistic colouring. That great men can put their virtue into action and so bring order and justice to the countries under them frees Webster not only from the charge of pessimism but also from that of fatalism and determinism. It would indeed be strange for a fatalist to lay so much emphasis on the virtue of the young Giovanni and to depart from the historical truth in order to make him the instrument of justice at the end of the play, thus making quite clear his belief in the efficacy of individual character and effort.

It would seem, therefore, that there is little reason or justification for suggesting that Webster's outlook, concious or unconscious, can be identified with the outlook of a Flamineo, a Lodovico or a Brachiano. I should suggest, on the contrary, that *The White Devil* is at once a psychological drama and a morality play, in which the psychological studies are set against a background of the most orthodox and conventional morality, and an attitude to life which differs little if at all from that which had been held by a typical Elizabethan such as Sir Philip Sidney, and in which the sentences are designed to inculcate the moral truth, exemplified by the play itself, that uninhibited lust brings murder and ruin and remorse in its train, that vice brings its own punishment and virtue its own reward. In this play the author sets out to demonstrate the terrible effects of lust and unbridled passion as well as to analyse psychologically various forms of perversion and despair. There is nothing to suggest that the characters are ever considered as anything but horrifying exceptions to the general rule—exceptions even in the immoral and irreligious Italy of their birth. If one's own outlook on life happens to find adequate expression in the sentiments of a Vittoria or a Lodovico, a Brachiano or a Flamineo, one should at least refrain from crediting Webster with the same attitudes. If these outrageous sentiments are taken as being the truth as Webster saw it then we transform a beautifully constructed, clearly conceived drama into a bewildering skein of contradictions, ambiguities, 'tensions' and unconscious meanings. A Jacobean audience must certainly have seen Vittoria's 'noble and resolute' end as the shocking and horrifying end in store for the unrepentant sinner and atheist, and I can see no reason for supposing that that was not also the view of the author.

Critics are almost unanimous in perceiving a falling-off in the author's powers as we pass from *The White Devil* to *The Duchess of Malfi.* The poetry is less beautiful, the imagery less striking and original, the characters less clearly and boldly drawn, the construction of the play less sure. Yet in many ways it is the more interesting and even the more fascinating play, and one which, I think, gives one more food for thought and to which one turns more readily than *The White Devil.* Although the characters may seem less firmly drawn a further acquaintance with the play reveals this as the sign of a psychological curiosity and insight far in advance of that displayed in *The White Devil.* The characters of Bosola and the Duchess are far more complex and life-like than any of the characters in the preceding play. As for the moral attitude, the values accepted by the author as the bases of his thought and the ethical foundation of his morality play (for this play is just as much a morality as *The White Devil*) remain constant. The point of interest has, however, shifted. In *The White Devil* the author was concerned with the effects of lust and unbridled appetite. In *The Duchess of Malfi* he is concerned with the more complex and subtle theme of integrity.

> Integrity of life is fame's best friend,
> Which nobly beyond death, shall crown the end.
>   (V.v.145-46)

In *The Duchess of Malfi* all the principal characters, the Duchess herself, Antonio, Bosola, Ferdinand, the Cardinal, even the waiting-maid Cariola, are all examples of a lack of true integrity, an inability to see themselves truly and clearly, an inability to perceive the difference between what they are, what they pretend to be, and what they imagine themselves to be. They all lack one of the essential characteristics of integrity—the courage to face up to their own character and their own position in society, thus

achieving true self-knowledge and a sense of responsibility and duty. In Ferdinand this flaw takes the form of the extraordinary contradiction between his insane jealousy of his sister's honour and his own vicious, vulgar, debauched and brutal character. The cold Machiavellianism of the Cardinal is a more obvious manifestation of a lack of integrity consisting as it does in maze of lies and hypocrisy—a maze in which he finally finds his own ruin. Antonio is clear-sighted, reasonable and honest, both as regards himself and his own position, and as regards the people around him. His lack of integrity takes the form of a certain weakness of character which prevents him from acting with the same truth and frankness that we find in his thought and observation, and leads him into the devious paths of deceit and shame. This weakness of character in Antonio is all the more striking when seen against the background of his true and manly virtues and ideals. We feel that there is no trace of vain-glory but only an honest appraisement of his own worth in his declaration to the Duchess:

> Were there nor heaven
> Nor hell, I should be honest: I have long serv'd
>   virtue,
> And ne'er ta'en wages of her.
>   (I.i.503-05)

The degradation into which Antonio is dragged by the split between his ideals and his actions is strikingly symbolised by his appealing to truth at the very moment that he is entering upon a course of secrecy and hypocrisy.

> Truth speak for me;
> I will remain the constant sanctuary
> Of your good name.
>   (I.i.526-28)

This lack of integrity brings about a tragic decline in Antonio's character. Nothing could point the pernicious nature of the disease that is eating at his soul more clearly than the contrast between the Antonio of the above quotations and the Antonio of Act III, who seems quite cheerfully prepared to accept the fact that the Duchess is popularly regarded as a strumpet and himself as a dishonest and corrupt parasite provided that their lives are safe. From a noble and honest courtier he dwindles into an ineffective and insignificant hanger-on at court.

None of these characters, however, have the absorbing psychological interest of Bosola, another study in lack of integrity and one of the most fascinating characters in Jacobean drama. In him Webster has incorporated features of both Flamineo and Lodovico and has thus produced a man who may lack the bold and effective outlines of these characters but who has infinitely more complexity and, I think it may be argued, even more truth to life. Almost incomprehensible in his extraordinary contradictions and vacillations he is a brilliant example of Webster's ability to trace the terrible results of a despair that takes the form of self-pity and self-contempt: a weak man with no very strong or stable moral principles he has nevertheless a sincere respect for virtue and a sincere pity for the innocent and the weak in their sufferings, yet he is driven by the sense of defiance and revolt that springs from his self-contempt to indulge in cruelties of the most diabolical and unspeakable and calculated sadism against that Duchess that he admires and pities. Yet even his self-contempt is not courageously faced but is rather a secret and malignant tumour hidden under a bitter sense of grievance.

But the real tragedy of a lack of integrity rests in the portrait of the Duchess herself. If Antonio fails through weakness, the Duchess fails through an almost deliberate blindness. She refuses to face either the true nature of her actions or their inevitable consequences. In marrying Antonio she flouts the desires of her brothers, contravenes the conventions of her society, rejects the responsibilities of a Duchess and defies the Church of God. Yet she clings to her brothers' friendship, has an exaggerated regard for her own reputation and good name, demands the respect due to a Duchess, and appeals to God and to heaven. All these contradictions spring essentially from a lack of integrity, an inability, or rather a refusal, to look courageously and honestly at herself, her character and her actions, a wishful blindness to the incompatibility of her duties and her desires. "I am blind", she declares to Antonio, and Cariola asks her if she sleeps "Like a madman, with your eyes open." Webster's Duchess degenerates from the noble and virtuous aristocratic lady portrayed by Antonio in the opening scene into the fallen woman, whom the common rabble call a strumpet, of the later sections of the play, still clinging pathetically to the illusion that her reputation is safe, her good name unspotted, her position as a Duchess still worthy of respect. Webster traces the course of this degeneration in a bold and effective manner. Her greedy gorging of the apricots in Act II reveals in the most striking fashion how the 'spirit of greatness and of woman in her' has degenerated into tetchiness and mere sensual indulgence. The light-hearted badinage in Act III scene ii, which would be charming set against a background of frank and passionate love, is almost disgusting when played against a background of mean hypocrisy and deceit. In the same scene she saves her husband's life by destroying his reputation and good name and proclaiming him a thief and a scoundrel. And so, as the play progresses, the miserable couple have recourse to more and more shameful ways of avoiding shame. The Duchess descends deeper and deeper into the pit of despair and dishonour without ever succeeding, without, indeed, even attempting, to come to terms with herself or with life. Perhaps the most bitter irony in a play built upon irony is the Duchess' declaration to Bosola, 'I am Duchess of Malfi still'. She has forfeited all right to respect as a ruler, and as a woman, yet she peevishly and vainly attempts to demand respect from the villainous Bosola. But her flaw rests in a lack of integrity and not in actual sin, so that in spite of her degeneration she retains much of the essential virtue and nobility of her character to the end, however tormented, petulant and hysterical she may become. Her last commands respecting her children show that she has not forfeited all right to be respected as a mother, and she meets death with fortitude far truer and more dignified than the defiance of a Vittoria. Nothing reveals the characters of the personages in Webster's plays so significantly as their deaths, and it is most revealing that of all his principal characters only Isabella in *The White Devil* and the Duchess in *The Duchess of Malfi* have faith in heaven. Antonio's mind remains in this world, he has no faith in anything beyond the present life and all he can hope to acquire is a kind of Stoic fortitude. As for the other characters their minds are far from heaven, and they die in a defiant or resigned despair. Only the Duchess turns to heaven in quiet confidence. And yet, even here, I feel, it is not so much a passionate and redeeming faith as mere orthodox piety. Her belief is sincere but it is not strong enough to transform her. Heaven is no more than her last refuge when her world falls in ruins about her. Death is to 'serve as mandragora to make her sleep.' On her reviving for a few moments she calls first on her lover and then for mercy, a pathetic rather than an inspiring end.

With the pathetic horror of this death we reach the end of Act IV. Webster has often been criticised for having dragged the play on through another act. It cannot be denied that this does constitute a superficial weakness in the play, although one not nearly so striking on the stage as in the study since the final scenes are theatrically most effective. Moreover the fifth act appears an unnecessary appendix only if we concentrate all our interest on the story of the Duchess and forget that the play is partly a psychological analysis of various forms of despair and lack of integrity, partly a morality play demonstrating the terrible results of these weaknesses in various individuals. Up to the end of the fourth act the Duchess has been the centre of interest, but after her death the various other forces at work in the other characters are shown working their authors' ruin. The means by which each is brought to destruction are both psychologically true and morally edifying. The vicious, turbulent Ferdinand through bestial madness, the cold, Machiavellian Cardinal through overcunning, Bosola by the man whose vices he had served and in an attempt to redeem, too late, his past crimes, Antonio in facing up to the danger that he ought to have faced years before. The fifth act is thus, devoted to showing the effects on the mind of a lack of integrity, and also to proving Webster's thesis that sin is its own punishment and brings in its train the inevitable consequences of perplexity, despair and death.

It has been pointed out that there is no sense of redemption in a Websterian tragedy, and this has been taken as an indication of the depth of his despair and pessimism. But redemption is a mystical state to which only those may attain who have passed through utter despondency and despair, who have lost faith irrecoverably in all the intellectual and rational categories that give a meaning and a purpose to life. Such a man must have recourse to something beyond mere reason and the intellect, and finds salvation in the absurdity of faith. That there is no redemption in Webster does not testify to a lack of faith and hope, but merely to an absence of despair and despondency. A writer with so unquestioning an acceptance of the conventional social, moral and religious standards has no need whatsoever of a mystical faith. In a note to [his edition of] *The Duchess of Malfi* Lucas quotes a passage from the *Countess of Pembroke's Arcadia* in which the original of two of Webster's most pessimistic statements are to be found.

"In such a shadowe, or rather pit of darkness, the *wormish* mankinde lives, that neither they knowe how to foresee, nor what to feare: and are like tenisbals, tossed by the racket of the hyer powers." No one would dream of suggesting that Sidney conceived a world of utter corruption in which goodness and virtue is simply unimaginable, and there seems to me to be as little reason for suggesting that Webster did so. The pessimistic statements generally quoted to demonstrate the darkness of Webster's outlook are usually to be found in the mouths of evil or sinning characters. They are psychologically true in so far as they represent the outlook of such a character, and they are morally edifying in so far as they present to the audience a shocking and terrifying picture of the world in which sinners and atheists live, but they rarely put forward what Webster or any normal Jacobean could possibly have regarded as an acceptable picture of life and the world. Sometimes such statements are placed in the mouths of 'melancholy' characters such as Bosola or Flamineo, and these may truly represent the authors sentiments, and act as a kind of chorus to the drama. Such are the remarks on women, on sex, on the court, on bodily corruption and the omnipotence of the passions. Such remarks are quite capable of bringing down in ruins the conventional and facile optimism of the nineteenth and twentieth centuries, but the tougher and firmer faith of the Renaissance, based on the double foundations of humanism and religion, thus combining the classical respect for man and the created world with the religious concepts of the Fall, original sin and grace, was able to withstand much stronger blows. The Elizabethan could attack a woman for painting, and at the same time accept as normal that she should look for 'the face she had before the world was made'. He could turn with revulsion from the act of sex and all the functions of the body, yet respect the sacred bond of marriage and the equally holy ties between parents and children. The terms optimist and pessimist are not really applicable to men of that period, since either word implies a limiting of experience, a tendency to look at the world from a certain point of view and a tendency to close one eyes to certain aspects of life. Whether idealist or realist, and the Elizabethans and Jacobeans were usually both idealist and realist at one and the same time, they looked at life much more objectively and fearlessly than has been customary since the eighteenth century. A certain number of the Jacobeans were attracted by the gloomier aspects of life, but because writers such as Webster displayed brilliant psychological insight into the various forms of despair and an unforgettable power of imagination in bringing these to life through the medium of dialogue, sentiments, imagery, action and stage-setting, there is nothing in this to prove that Webster shared these sentiments with his characters. Nor is there any reason for accepting Ellis-Fermor's attractive and poetic conceit that Webster, from his pit of darkness, could perceive, now and again, the 'stars' that 'shine still'. This is justified neither by Webster's general outlook nor by the quotation so rudely dragged from its context and so anachronistically interpreted. The allusion is to a remark made by Bosola in answer to the Duchess' wild curses.

DUCHESS: I'll go pray;—
No, I'll go curse.

BOSOLA: Oh, fie!

DUCHESS: I could curse the stars—

BOSOLA: Oh, fearful!

DUCHESS: And those three smiling seasons of the year
Into a Russian winter: nay, the world
To its first chaos.

BOSOLA: Look you, the stars shine still.

DUCHESS: Oh, but you must
Remember, my curse hath a great way to go.
(IV.i.121-23)

Bosola's 'The stars shine still', far from revealing mystical faith and serenity only emphasises the utter vanity of the Duchess' defiance and despair. As a matter of fact 'the stars shine still' could suggest mystical serenity only to generations brought up on romantic emotional nature symbolism. To a Jacobean they would be the ornaments spangling the black weed of night, or influences guiding the destinies of men. It is surely obvious that Bosola's remark is meant to emphasise the impotence of the Duchess' rage, and the senselessness of all revolt against ineluctable fate.

[Christopher] Marlowe has been indicated as the dramatic predecessor of the Jacobean playwrights in general and of Webster in particular because of the influence of [Niccolo] Machiavelli on his conception of life and morality. Even a desultory comparison of Marlowe and Webster, however, should serve to underline what we have been attempting to prove—that there is nothing unconventional or revolutionary in Webster's outlook. Whereas Marlowe's whole attitude towards the world is strongly affected by the teaching of Machiavelli and by Machiavellianism, Machiavelli's influence on Webster seems to me to be confined to the portrayal of certain characters, and does not affect his general outlook. If we compare [Marlowe's] *Edward II* with **The White Devil** and **The Duchess of Malfi**, one cannot but be struck by the very great contrast between the two playwrights. In Webster there is no doubt as to what is good and what is bad, the distinction between good and evil is clear-cut. In **The White Devil** we have some obviously vicious characters, and others as obviously virtuous. In **The Duchess of Malfi,** since the author is concerned not so much with the simple conceptions of vice and virtue as with the more ambiguous quality of lack of integrity, and the characters of Antonio, the Duchess and even Bosola are a complex of virtues and vices, virtues and failings, there is not the same obvious distinction between good and evil characters, but there is an equally clear distinction between good and evil, a distinction no less clear because left largely implicit. In *Edward II,* however, there is no such definite moral background. One may set aside the Queen as an adulterous vixen, Mortimer as a ruthless usurper, the nobles as a set of brutes and only Kent and the young prince as virtuous characters, but what is one to make of the King, of Gaveston, of Spencer and Baldock? Edward is portrayed as a despicably weak and contemptible effeminate and hedonist, Gaveston as a vindictive and scheming pervert, Spencer and Baldock as ambitious, cynical and unscrupulous Machiavellians. And yet it is in these degenerate and vicious characters that one finds a real capacity for loyalty and love. That he should depict love as proliferating in such a dunghill is of the greatest significance for a true understanding of Marlowe's thought. For the moment, however, I shall rest content in indicating the vast difference between Marlowe's outlook and Webster's—the latter's resting firmly on rational categories such as virtue, justice, integrity, the latter's resting rather vaguely on emotional concepts such as love, loyalty and innocency. In portraying a Machiavellian character such as Mortimer Marlowe was indeed the predecessor of Webster (and of almost all the Elizabethan and Jacobean dramatists), but in his pessimism and cynicism coupled with faith in love and loyalty as redeeming characteristics Marlowe is obviously much closer to Shakespeare than to Webster, and has progressed far beyond Webster's comparatively naive and unquestioning outlook.

Some poets, such as Shakespeare, approach the world directly and imaginatively, and convey their conception of life in the form of characters and symbols that shadow forth reality as they themselves perceive it. Others accept a conventional world-view, and against this accepted pattern weave their own particular embroideries. In the case of the play-wright this may mean accepting a world-view which has already been crystallised into intellectual dogmas and rational principles, and portraying against this the characters, sentiments and actions of men. The first takes man as a glass through which to portray the world and reality; the second takes the analysis and creation of character, and the pointing of the accepted codes of morality as an end in itself. Webster belongs to the second category, and any attempt to force him into the first merely serves to obscure the moral purport of the play and dull the brilliance of the psychological analysis. (pp. 17-34)

> *Adair Mill, "John Webster as a Moralist," in* Litera, *Vol. 3, 1956, pp. 15-34.*

Ian Scott-Kilvert   (essay date 1964)

[*In the excerpt below, Scott-Kilvert provides background on Webster's place in the Jacobean theater and investigates his stagecraft and use of language. He also provides a brief survey of Webster's minor works and collaborations.*]

The years of Webster's apprenticeship in the theatre coincided with a period of intense disillusion in the national life. The decline of landed wealth and the pursuit of money-making in its place, the downfall of the brilliant but erratic Earl of Essex, the death of Queen Elizabeth and the conspicuous absence of the magic of sovereignty in her successor, the disgrace and imprisonment of Raleigh, the series of conspiracies aimed at the throne and culminating in the Gunpowder Plot—these and many parallel events combined to produce a sense of the breakdown of established standards and beliefs, which was quickly reflected in the drama. Shakespeare and [George] Chapman, survivors of the Elizabethan age, approach tragedy by way of the historical play, and we find them at all times keenly aware of the sanctity of kingship and the hierarchy of degree. Their protagonists are men and women of unques-

tioned authority, whose public life is brought to ruin by private weaknesses. The tragedy of Othello or of Antony lies not only in the hero's betrayal—real or imaginary—by his beloved, but in the collapse of his soldiership.

But with the younger generation of tragedians, [John] Marston, Webster, [Cyril] Tourneur and [Thomas] Middleton, we feel at once the absence of this ideal order. The new playwrights are oppressed by an apparently irreconcilable conflict between the world of earthly experience and the world of the spirit:

> While we look up to heaven, we confound
> Knowledge with knowledge. O, I am in a mist!
> (*The White Devil*, V.vi.)

Humanity, they are compelled to recognize, is no better for its new-found knowledge, but rather more inhuman: indeed what marks out the tragedy of this period is the ingenuity and elaboration of the dramatists' conception of evil. The bond of nature is cracked, and the pragmatic creed of [Niccolo] Machiavelli, with its assumption of the natural weakness and wickedness of men and its insistence upon *la verità effetuale della cosa,* has become the reality which forces itself upon the playwright's vision. Beyond this code of self-seeking, all is uncertainty, 'a mist' as Webster repeatedly describes it; the divine powers are indifferent, and the heavens high, far off and unsearchable.

By comparison with the Elizabethan approach, the new dramatic poetry is noticeably more sceptical, more sophisticated, more aware of inner contradictions. The very title, *The White Devil,* contains a multiplicity of meanings, which begin with the Elizabethan proverb, 'the white devil is worse than the black', and may be applied not only to Vittoria but to the hero, Bracchiano, and indeed to the society in which the play is set. The new poetry is also more condemnatory and satirical in tone, and in the case of Webster (though not of Marston and Tourneur, who caricature and distort to intensify the effect of their satire) it is more naturalistic in its handling of character and event. For Webster's audience *The White Devil* was a strikingly topical play: the actions which it depicts had taken place barely a quarter of a century before. And just as a subject which is remote in legend or history seems to emphasize the influence of fate upon the outcome, so the choice of a modern theme creates the opposite illusion: the more contemporary the characters, the greater their apparent freedom of action. Certainly by comparison with plays such as *Romeo and Juliet* or *Othello* the plots of Webster's tragedies owe very little to chance: at first glance his characters strike us as wilful to the last degree in courting their own downfall. Of course freedom and compulsion are necessarily the coordinates upon which all tragedy is plotted, and every dramatist of consequence discovers as it were a new equation for the act of choice, which is the starting point for a tragic situation. But a closer study suggests that Webster differs from most of his contemporaries in choosing *not* to make this issue explicit. When Bosola exclaims

> We are merely the stars' tennis-balls, struck and
>   bandied
> Which way please them
>   (*The Duchess of Malfi,* V.iv.)

we know that this is only a half-truth in the design of the tragedy, and in fact the continuous uncertainty as to whether fate or chance rules the world contributes powerfully to the horror which the play inspires in us.

What perhaps most astonishes the modern reader of Jacobean tragedy is the divergence between the avowed purpose of the dramatist and the actual effect of the drama, between the impression intended and the impression conveyed. Both the poets and the critics of the time were convinced that Renaissance tragedy was more improving than Greek. They found fault with the latter for its rebellious protest against divine providence, and praised the former for demonstrating, in [George] Puttenham's phrase, 'the just punishment of God in revenge of a vicious and evil life'. Similarly the playwrights constantly defend the theatre against the attacks of the Puritans by stressing its reformative value. Yet in *The White Devil* it is perfectly clear that Webster's sympathies are strongly drawn towards the guilty lovers, while in *The Duchess of Malfi* the sufferings inflicted upon the heroine are out of all proportion to her offence. It was this discrepancy between the precept and the practice of Elizabethan and Jacobean tragedy which prompted [Thomas] Rymer's indignant question—which he might as well have applied to Webster's tragedies as to Othello—'If this be our end, what boots it to be virtuous?' Webster's sympathy, not only in his tragedies but also in his later plays, consistently goes out to what he calls 'integrity of life', that is the determination to remain what you are, in the face of suffering, misfortune and death: admiration for this quality can scarcely be reconciled with conventional notions of good and evil. (pp. 13-16)

. . . . .

In the history of literature tragedy is generally regarded as an exceptionally stable form, which has somehow preserved throughout the centuries a recognizable resemblance to its Greek originals. But these resemblances are deceptive. Greek drama is essentially religious. Its primary concern is not to study the personality of the hero but to interpret the regulation of human affairs by the actions of the gods: its plots are drawn from a single body of mythology and its form is rigidly stylized. Elizabethan tragedy is essentially secular. The playwrights abandoned the scriptural or allegorical material which had supplied the themes of the mediaeval drama, and turned their attention instead to English and Roman histories or French and Italian *novelle*. The mysteries which they explore are those

> Of fate and chance and change in human life

and this change of direction has never been reversed. But if Elizabethan and modern tragedies share some resemblances in theme, they share very few in form or technique, and the reader will be led far astray if he expects the Elizabethan play to conform to the dramatic methods of [Henrik] Ibsen and his successors, themselves strongly influenced by the techniques of modern fiction.

The vital point to be grasped here—admirably developed by Miss M. C. Bradbrook in her *Themes and Conventions of Elizabethan Tragedy* [1934]—is that the Elizabethan playwright did not set out to devise a plot in the form of a logical or internally consistent narrative. The essential ingredients for his drama were striking episodes and memorable language. He could not, as his modern counterpart can, conceal his lack of poetic inspiration by attention to the details of construction. [William Butler] Yeats's criticism of the speech of modern dramatic characters is well-known: 'When they are deeply moved, they look silently into the fire-place', and he was referring to the modern playwright's assumption that he can achieve his emotional effect through the placing and sequence of events, rather than through the eloquence of his dialogue. To Elizabethan audiences eloquence was the very breath of drama, and they were interested above all in how a character spoke and acted in a moment of crisis rather than in how he arrived there. In this respect an Elizabethan tragedy is more like the score of an opera than the text of a novel. The elements of place and time, for example, are treated as freely and flexibly as possible. If they lend themselves to dramatic exploitation, well and good, but they possess few rights of their own. Much of the sustained effect of terror and anguish which is built up in the fourth act of *The Duchess of Malfi* depends on the vagueness of the location and the suspension of time during the Duchess's imprisonment.

This is not to say that the Elizabethans were incapable of the kind of mechanical dexterity which was so much admired by William Archer. Shakespeare achieves something of this cog-wheel effect in *Othello,* and [Ben] Jonson in *Volpone,* while [Francis] Beaumont and [John] Fletcher were still more adroit in the plotting of their material. But most of the playwrights of the period were not thinking along the lines of the Aristotelian whole, and it would be difficult to select any play as a typical specimen of Elizabethan or Jacobean dramatic structure. Since the source material varied so widely, and since plays tended to be conceived as a series of striking situations, every major playwright developed a dramatic form of his own, the mould of which was shaped by the nature of his poetic gifts. At its best the imaginative pressure and concentration of the language of Jacobean tragedy sweeps away the problems of dramatic illusion. The poets created a speech which could be simple or ceremonious by turns, and was at once direct in its elementary sense and rich in secondary meanings. In *The White Devil,* for example, Webster achieves one of the most powerful openings in the whole range of Jacobean drama. Lodovico's cry of 'Banish'd!' not only sums up the initial situation of the play and casts the shadow of the revenger over all that follows, but in a deeper sense it suggests the self-excommunication of this blood-crazed figure from the normal instincts of humanity. It is at once followed by other metaphors central to the play's meaning, such as those which hint at Vittoria's career— 'Fortune's a right whore' and 'an idle meteor soon lost i'th'air'. The best of Webster's poetry, like that of Shakespeare, Tourneur, Middleton and other contemporaries, possesses this power of prefiguring the action by means of dramatic images which leap from the particular to the general and reveal the moral universe that surrounds the characters and the setting.

Webster is one of those rare dramatists who in his first independent play achieves at a single bound the height of his poetic powers. *The White Devil* offers us Jacobean verse in its full maturity: here Webster is exploiting after his own fashion many of the developments in style and versification which Shakespeare had first introduced into his great tragedies. The end-stopped blank verse pentameter has been completely remoulded, passages of any length are frequently enjambed, the rhythms of colloquial speech are counterpointed against the regular beat of the line, and the style and tone of the dialogue clearly reflects the demand for a greater naturalism in expression and performance. Like the best of his rivals in the theatre Webster quickly establishes a dramatic idiom which is unmistakably his own. Unlike his fellow satirists Marston and Tourneur, he shows himself sympathetic even to the most villainous of his characters and keenly aware of their individual and unpredictable qualities, and he shares something of Shakespeare's gift for coining images which can project a character within a single line of verse or prose.

The tone of his verse is at once witty, sardonic, allusive, full of nervous energy. His handling of metre is often as harsh and irregular as [John] Donne's, and his frequent habit of introducing resolved feet reflects the complexity or deliberate outlandishness of his figures of speech:

> Mark her, I prithee: she simpers like the suds
> A collier hath been washed in . . .
> > (*The White Devil,* V.iii.)

Elsewhere when he aims at a sententious effect he produces a *rallentando* through a sequence of heavily stressed monosyllables:

> This busy trade of life appears most vain
> Since rest breeds rest, where all seek pain by
> > pain.
> > (*The White Devil,* V.vi.)

If he lacks the architectonic sense, he comes nearest of all his contemporaries to Shakespeare in his power to produce striking yet subtle variations of mood, of strength and of pace within a scene. Some of his finest effects are achieved by sudden transformations of this kind, as in *The White Devil* with the entry of the boy Giovanni in mourning for his mother immediately after the passion and tumult of the court scene, or with Ferdinand's eavesdropping upon the careless jesting of the lovers in *The Duchess of Malfi.* While other dramatists employ song to great effect, Webster in *The White Devil* and *The Duchess of Malfi* without invoking the aid of music uses the dramatic lyric in a completely original fashion to introduce a different emotional dimension. Of Cornelia's lines:

> Call for the Robin-red-breast and the wren,
> Since o'er shady groves they hover,
> And with leaves and flowers do cover
> The friendless bodies of unburied men
> > (*The White Devil,* V.iv.)

[Charles] Lamb wrote:

> I never saw anything like this dirge, except the ditty which reminds Ferdinand of his drowned father in *The Tempest.* As that is of the water, watery, so this is of the earth, earthy. Both have that intenseness of feeling which seems to re-

solve itself into the elements which it contemplates.

These achievements represent the peaks of Webster's art. On the other hand he is curiously unenterprising in his use of the soliloquy, which he normally employs merely to give notice of his characters' intentions rather than to explore their inmost qualities. And besides his didactic habit of rounding off an episode with a conventional platitude, he is apt to interrupt the progress of a scene with a tedious moral fable, thus destroying much of the tension which he has carefully built up.

This habit brings us to his borrowings from other authors. Commentators long ago remarked that his plays, especially *The White Devil* and *The Duchess of Malfi,* contain many sentiments, images and even whole sentences which have been lifted from contemporary writers, in particular from [Michel de] Montaigne, [Philip] Sidney, and the Scottish dramatist William Alexander. Of course originality was less highly prized in Webster's age than it is today. Quotation or adaptation from classical or foreign authors was regarded as a mark of erudition, and plagiarism was even to some extent encouraged by the educational system of the time which required students to keep a commonplace book. Mr. F. L. Lucas defends Webster's imitation and contends that he almost always transmuted what he borrowed into something different and better. This is often the case, but it does not tell us the whole story. Certainly Webster excels in the final stroke, the expansion of some hitherto unremarked detail, which transforms a second hand perception into a touch of perfect aptness. He was not the kind of author who plagiarized in order to save himself mental effort. On the contrary he was an exceptionally laborious artist who took great pains to weave his borrowings into the texture and atmosphere of his plays. Nevertheless his borrowings so far exceeded the normal that they came to affect his methods of composition. If we analyse the sequence of his dialogue in passages where the borrowing can be traced, it becomes clear that his imagination was often prompted by what he had read rather than by his own invention. This habit of working from a commonplace book explains the peculiarly conceit-laden and disjointed style which Webster employs in a passage such as the following, which contains images drawn from three different authors:

> Thou shalt lie in a bed stuffed with turtle-feathers, swoon in perfum'd linen like the fellow was smothered in roses. So perfect shall be thy happiness that as men at sea think land and trees and ships go that way they go, so both heaven and earth shall seem to go thy voyage. Shalt meet him, 'tis fixed with nails of diamonds to inevitable necessity.
> > (*The White Devil,* I.ii.)

In the same way his longer verse passages do not flow as Shakespeare's do with an opulent succession of metaphors, in which each image springs naturally from its predecessor. Instead they often consist of a series of undeveloped metaphors or similes so loosely strung together that any one might be removed without damage to the rest, and the borrowing habit also seems to be responsible for the abrupt transitions of thought and feeling which so often occur in his verse. But when all this has been said, the fact that Webster's finest flights are often launched with the help of a borrowed idea does not diminish their effect. The study of his sources is valuable not in a derogatory sense, but because the identification of the original often helps to penetrate a meaning, clarify a dramatic effect, or define the qualities of a character which the commentators have missed.

Webster's use of figures of speech is closely related to his conception of tragedy, and his imagery throws much light upon the inner meaning of his plays. Both *The White Devil* and *The Duchess of Malfi,* for example, are pervaded by images of the fair show that masks inward corruption or poison, and the calm weather that hides an impending storm, and each of these sequences of metaphor is skilfully woven into the play so as to suggest the deceitfulness of fortune. The Elizabethan delight in the familiar objects and traditional beauties of the created world lies far behind him, and in his choice of metaphor and simile he deliberately singles out the curious, the grotesque and the sinister. His universe is a place of fear—it is noticeable that he is one of the few Elizabethans who does not celebrate the sublime and healing qualities of music. The birds which figure in his poetry are visualized in captivity or awaiting death, and when he describes the characteristics of plants or minerals it is the deformed and the deadly which fascinate him—witness his references to hemlock, mildew, poison, snakes and the mysterious properties of the mandrake. Often his visual symbols suggest a fearful immediacy, an icy touch, a suffocating embrace, a physical contact with the horrible. He strives to express and reconcile incongruity, above all that of the mortality of the graveyard and the sensuality of the living body. The symbolic act to which his imagination continually returns is that of tearing away the mask and uncovering the dreadful shape in the effort to resist the horror of death.

His poetry and prose follow two distinct styles of expression. The first is sophisticated, intellectually agile, staccato and restless in rhythm. In the second we find his imagination working at white heat, for he is a poet of brief and blinding insight rather than of steady illumination. This is the style which is reserved for the climaxes of his plays and which pervades his most highly wrought passages:

> Your beauty! O, ten thousand curses on't
> How long have I beheld the devil in crystal!
> Thou hast led me, like an heathen sacrifice,
> With music and with fatal yokes of flowers
> To my eternal ruin. Woman to man
> Is either a god or a wolf.
>
> (*The White Devil,* IV.i.)

> I am not mad yet, to my cause of sorrow:
> The Heaven o'er my head seems made of molten
>   brass,
> The earth of flaming sulphur, yet I am not mad.
> I am acquainted with sad misery
> As the tanned galley-slave is with his oar;
> Necessity makes me suffer constantly
> And custom makes it easy.
>
> (*The Duchess of Malfi,* IV.ii.)

At these moments Webster's language is unadorned. His vocabulary becomes predominantly Anglo-Saxon, en-

riched by the rare Latin word, his rhythm steady, his tone prophetic: his words seem to wield an absolute power, with which they suddenly gather together the thought and emotions of the whole play, state the tragic issue and create the moment of vision.

Webster's contribution to the Overbury collection of *Characters* is of interest because the Character as a literary genre noticeably influenced the dramatic writing of the time. Theories of psychological classification such as the doctrine of the humours were in the air, and Theophrastus's treatise aroused an interest in a similar analysis of manners and sociology. Bishop Hall was the pioneer of the form and in his *Characterismes of Vertues and Vice* he handles the subject in broader and more concrete terms than his Greek model. Thus while Theophrastus remarks that 'The Flatterer is a person who will say as he walks with another, "Do you observe how people are looking at you?" ' Hall individualizes his portrait as follows: 'The Flatterer is blear-eyed to ill and cannot see vices . . . Like that subtle fish, he turns himself into the colour of every stone . . . He is the moth of liberal men's coates, the earewig of the mightie, the bane of courts, a friend and slave to the trencher, and good for nothing but to be factor for the Divell.'

Webster develops his character-writing along similar lines. Clearly the form was congenial to him: it demanded a mannered, compressed, carefully cadenced prose, gave scope for ingenious and extravagant imagery and lent itself equally to satirical commentary and moral exhortation. It is noticeable that in his two major tragedies Webster puts almost all this type of prose into the mouths of his two satirical commentators, Flamineo and Bosola. Among the Overbury *Characters* connoisseurs of Webster's powers of invective will appreciate his sketch of 'A Jesuit', and of 'A Rimer' ('A Dung-Hille not well laid together'), but in general he succeeds better in praise than in blame. The best pieces written in his happier vein are the characters of 'An Excellent Actor', 'A Franklin', and—a surprising contribution for Webster—'A Fayre and Happy Milke-Mayd'. This last may be seen as the complete antithesis of his tragic heroines, and in fact Bosola, when he finally urges the Duchess to lay aside her youth, her beauty and her desire to live, tells her (IV.iii):

> Thou art some great woman sure, for riot begins
> to sit on thy forehead (clad in grey hairs) twenty
> years sooner than on a merry milk-maid's.

. . . . .

Webster's drama is often criticized as episodic and lacking in architectonic power. Certainly the plots of *The White Devil* and *The Duchess of Malfi* are overloaded with detail, and there are moments when the playwright wilfully abandons dramatic truth for the sake of an immediately striking effect. Nevertheless each of these tragedies embodies a dramatic idea which is sufficiently powerful to hold it together. It is impossible to say the same of his later plays. At least five years separate *The Duchess of Malfi* from Webster's next play, and in that interval the changing mood of the theatre has been at work. Both Jacobean tragedy and comedy at their best had been bent on the pursuit of reality. The characteristics of the 'new wave' of tragi-comedy, of which the most skilful practitioners were Beaumont and Fletcher, had been sketched as early as 1609 in the latter's preface to *The Faithful Shepherdess:*

> A tragie-comedie is not so called in respect of mirth and killing, but in respect it wants deaths, which is inough to make it no tragedie, yet brings some near it, which is inough to make it no comedie.

This was a formula with insidious possibilities. Shakespeare, it is true, turns it to sublime use in his final romances. There he contrives to raise the action to a higher plane, on which at the end of each play the confused purposes of sinful humanity are transcended by a divine forgiveness. But in other hands the new mode suggests little more than a weary longing to lay aside the ultimate questions and seek relief from the painful integrity of great art, whether tragic or comic. Suspense or surprise in an exotic setting, sudden reversals of situation or transformations of sentiment—in short entertainment of an agreeably romantic kind—now become the dramatist's principal aim, and to achieve the unforeseen he must be prepared to distort character, confuse motive and ignore the normal consequences of human actions. These tendencies become increasingly apparent in Webster's later plays, the more regrettably so, because his genius was obviously so unsuited to satisfy the new taste. John Fletcher, the originator of the tragi-comic mode, was a sufficiently ingenious and versatile playwright to make this irresponsible treatment of the drama plausible. When Webster attempts such effects the result seems as unnatural as it is clumsy: in fact, as one might expect, the scenes which redeem his post-tragic plays are those in which his instinct prompts him to work against the prevailing fashion.

This division of purpose is most apparent in his last independent play, *The Devil's Law-Case.* Here he abandons courtly for bourgeois life and makes no attempt to draw a coherent moral. Nevertheless, a number of recognizable characteristics survive from his earlier work. Once again it is a woman's passion which dominates the plot and asserts an even more astonishing defiance of conventional standards. The play opens with Leonora, a sixty year old widow, cynically arranging with her son Romelio a marriage of convenience for her daughter Jolenta. Mother and son are well aware that Jolenta is in love with another aristocratic wooer, Contarino, but have no compunction in allowing a duel to take place between the suitors. But when Romelio tries to make certain of the wounded Contarino's death by disguising himself as a Jewish physician and stabbing his supposed patient, it transpires that Leonora has fallen in love with Contarino, and in revenge hires an unscrupulous lawyer to prove her own son illegitimate and thus disinherit him. The climax is reached in the trial scene—Webster excels throughout his career in the drama of the court-room—in which the corrupt eloquence of the prosecuting lawyer is matched by the resource of Romelio and the perspicacity of the upright advocate Crispiano. Leonora's case collapses, but this does not prevent a grotesque *dénouement* whereby she is matched 'happily ever after' with the young Contarino, Jolenta with her prescribed husband Ercole, and Romelio with a nun whom he had seduced years before.

The figure who dominates the play and links it with the world of the tragedies is the Neapolitan merchant Romelio. This character represents yet another of Webster's Machiavellian studies, shrewder and more experienced than Flamineo, as quick-witted and resolute as the Cardinal. When he disguises himself as a Jewish physician, Webster is clearly evoking the memory of Marlowe's Barabas, the Jew of Malta, and appears to be depicting Romelio as a thorough-paced villain. But later when he is visited in prison by a Capuchin friar to prepare him for death—an episode strongly reminiscent of the death-cell scene in *Measure for Measure*—the humour and steadiness of temper which underlie Romelio's courage make a powerful appeal to our sympathy:

> FRIAR: Pray tell me, do you not meditate of death?
>
> ROME: Phew, I tooke out that lesson When once I lay sicke of an Ague: I do now Labour for life, for life! Sir, can you tell me Whether your Toledo or your Millain blade Be best temper'd?
> *(The Devil's Law-Case,* V.iv.)

Romelio is by far the most vital of Webster's tragi-comic creations and it is certainly the role into which he poured the best of his later dramatic poetry.

Anything For a Quiet Life, a comedy written mainly in prose in collaboration with Middleton, is the least interesting play of any in which Webster took a hand. It makes fun of the marriage of an elderly knight to a young, capricious and self-willed girl. Lady Cressingham bullies her husband into parting with his estate, disinheriting his eldest son and sending away his younger children, but at the end of the play she is suddenly presented in a completely different light as a sensible wife, who has rid her husband of his ruinous obsessions with alchemy and gambling. *A Cure for A Cuckold,* attributed to Webster and Rowley and probably written some four years later, at least provides more dramatic tension. The hero, Lessingham, is told by his mistress that he will succeed in his wooing only if he kills his best friend for her sake. Although he is prepared to comply, both parties contrive to evade this harsh condition, and the unscrupulousness of Lessingham's action is forgotten in a conventionally happy ending. The play is chiefly memorable for its duelling scene on Calais sands, for its sequel when Lessingham pretends that he has fulfilled his mistress' command, and last but not least for Rowley's comic creation of the returned mariner, Compass. In the following year appeared *The Fair Maid of the Inn,* which is generally regarded as the joint work of Webster, Massinger and Ford. In this play Webster returns to a theme which resembles that of *The Devil's Law-Case,* the disowning of a son (Cesario) by his mother (Mariana), though on this occasion the object is to save him from danger. But once again we find a hero whose shifts of affection and equivocations in his dealings with the heroine are finally rewarded by marriage. Webster's contribution to this play is mainly limited to the second act and the last three scenes, and his sardonic style shows itself most plainly in a satirical creation, the fantastic charlatan Forobosco.

With ***Appius and Virginia*** Webster returns finally to tragedy—that is if we follow those scholars who place the play
at the end rather than the beginning of his career. There
is evidence for either conclusion, but Mr. Lucas makes a
strong case when he argues that the portrait of the Roman
lawyer in this play is such an accomplished creation that
it is far more likely to have followed the equally sophisticated Cantilupo of ***The Devil's Law-Case*** than to have
preceded the crude caricature of an advocate that we find
in ***The White Devil***. There is also the argument from topical allusion, which suggests that the starving of the
Roman army, which plays an important part in the plot,
refers to the scandalous neglect and hardships suffered by
an English contingent despatched to the Low Countries
in the year 1624-5. Those critics who prefer the later date
attribute only a minor share of collaboration to Heywood.
The play reflects something of the blunt, unsophisticated
quality of early Roman history. The action is straightforward, the sequence of emotions easily predictable, the
characters drawn with rigid, somewhat elementary
strokes: in particular the character of the martyred Virginia possesses far too little freedom of choice to stand comparison with Webster's earlier heroines. But amidst the artificiality of Caroline tragedy the rough simplicity of Vir-
ginius's farewell to his daughter stands out powerfully.
And in Appius's speech before execution, Webster expresses for the last time the tribute he can never withhold
from courage—especially in a villain:

> Think not, lords
> But he that had the spirit to oppose the gods
> Dares likewise suffer what their powers
>   inflict . . .
> Now with as much resolvéd constancy
> As I offended will I pay the mulct . . .
>   Learn of me, Clodius,
> I'll teach thee what thou never studiedst yet
> That's bravely how to dy . . .
>   (***Appius and Virginia***, V.ii.)

•

> Webster was much possessed by death
> And saw the skull beneath the skin

writes T. S. Eliot. Certainly in his tragedies the menace
and the mystery of death become the preoccupation which
in the end overpowers all others, so that the dramatist
seems deliberately to hold his characters on the brink of
eternity as he questions them in their dying moments.
Time and again his imagination returns to study the different responses of humanity to this ordeal that none can escape: now it is the sudden, uncontrollable dread voiced by
Bracchiano:

> O thou soft natural death, that art joint-twin
> To sweetest slumber: no rough-bearded comet
> Stares on thy mild departure: the dull owl
> Beats not against thy casement: the hoarse wolf
> Scents not thy carrion. Pity winds thy corse
> Whilst horror waits on princes

and

> On pain of death, let no man name death to me,
> It is a word infinitely terrible.
>   (***The White Devil***, V.iii.)

or Flamineo's wry mockery, which masks a total and desperate uncertainty in all things spiritual:

> LOD: What dost think on?
> FLA: Nothing; of nothing: leave thy idle ques-
>   tions
> I am i'th' way to study a long silence.
> To prate were idle, I remember nothing.
> There's nothing of so infinite vexation
> As man's own thoughts . . .
> We cease to grieve, cease to be fortune's slaves
> Nay cease to die by dying . . .
>
>   I do not look
> Who went before, nor who shall follow me;
> No, at myself I will begin and end
>   (***The White Devil***, V.vi.)

or the Duchess of Malfi's resolution and assurance:

> What would it pleasure me to have my throat
>   cut
> With diamonds, or to be smothered
> With cassia, or to be shot to death with pearls?
> I know death hath ten thousand several doors
> For men to take their exits: and 'tis found
> They go on such strange geometrical hinges
> You may open them both ways: any way, for
>   heaven's sake
> So I were out of your whispering: tell my broth-
>   ers
> That I perceive death, now I am well awake,
> Best gift is they can give, or I can take.
> I would fain put off my last woman's fault,
> I'll not be tedious to you
>   (***The Duchess of Malfi***, IV.ii.)

or, as a final comment, the stoical fatalism of Bosola:

> Yes, I hold my weary soul in my teeth,
> 'Tis ready to part from me . . .
>   O, I am gone.
> We are only like dead walls or vaulted graves
> That, ruined, yield no echo. Fare you well—
> It may be pain, but no harm to me to die
> In so good a quarrel: O this gloomy world,
> In what a shadow, or deep pit of darkness
> Doth womanish and fearful mankind live.
> Let worthy minds ne'er stagger in distrust
> To suffer death, or shame, for what is just
> Mine is another voyage.
>   (***The Duchess of Malfi***, V.v.)

Webster was also 'possessed' by the contrast between the
wilful pretensions and desires of men and women and the
reality which lies in wait for them. He does not follow
Shakespeare's conception of tragedy as a fateful and exceptional conjunction of character and circumstance,
whereby a man

> Carrying, I say, the stamp of one defect . . .
> His virtues else, be they as pure as grace . . .
> Shall in the general censure take corruption
> From that particular fault
>   (*Hamlet*, I.iv.30-5)

for to Webster corruption is a matter of the general doom,
not the particular fault. The world, as he sees it, is a pit
of darkness through which men grope their way with a
haunting sense of disaster, and the ordeal to which he sub-

mits his characters is not merely the end of life but a struggle against spiritual annihilation by the power of evil: it is noticeable that none of them, however intolerable the blows of fate, seeks refuge in suicide. The nature of this struggle is beset by a terror which is Webster's most original contribution to tragic art. At the end of a Shakespearean tragedy the forces of evil have spent themselves, the hero has in some measure learned wisdom. At the end of *The White Devil* death merely interrupts the worldly concerns of the protagonists, leaving them face to face with damnation. Only in *The Duchess of Malfi* do we receive a suggestion of a further vision, a hint that the spiritual chaos of the early seventeenth century is not eternity.

Webster is not an easy dramatist to appreciate, nor does he yield up his best at a first reading. His plots lack the unity and the impetus which are the reward of devotion to a single dominant theme. But judged by his individual scenes he remains, after Shakespeare, the most profound and theatrically accomplished tragedian of his age, who excels equally in the sudden *coup de théâtre* or in the gradual heightening of tension and the capacity to play upon the nerves of his audience. He surpasses Middleton and [John] Ford in the imaginative depth and concentration of his poetry, and Chapman and Tourneur as a creator of living men and women and of roles which can still hold the stage. He succeeds better than any of his contemporaries in re-creating the colour and the spiritual climate of Renaissance Italy—in *The White Devil,* as Mr. Lucas says, we know at once that we have crossed the Alps. On the strength of his two great plays he stands in the history of English tragedy as second only to Shakespeare. (pp. 29-45)

> *Ian Scott-Kilvert, in his* John Webster, *Longmans, Green & Co., 1964, 51 p.*

Ralph Berry   (essay date 1972)

[*Berry is a Canadian scholar and critic who has written numerous studies on the works of William Shakespeare and his contemporaries. In the excerpt below, he focuses upon the themes of evil and the law in Webster's dramatic works, and defends the plays against the criticism that they are too complex and "literary" to be effective on stage. Berry concludes: "the intellectual concerns of Webster seem to me perfectly compatible with the needs of the theatre."*]

The ends-means equation must dominate a discussion of Webster's art. The first necessity of baroque is that the audience should be gripped, excited, moved. But major art rests on foundations that remain valid after the turbulence of the immediate emotions has died. And these foundations must include the content—I do not mean, the subject matter—of the drama. That can afford an answer to the question: what are the positive concerns of the playwright? What, even more simply, are his plays about?

The obvious answer is that the *sententiae* [concise statements of principles] constitute the moral concerns of the plays. These are the points where the action halts, the text leaps into inverted commas, and a moral generalization is enunciated on the situation of the characters. Naturally,

most of the action is completely opposed to the drift of the *sententiae,* and Ian Jack [in 'The Case of John Webster', *Scrutiny* XVI, 1949] sees in this the fundamental flaw of Webster:

> . . . this background of moral doctrine has nothing to do with the action of the plays: so far from growing out of the action, it has all the marks of having been superimposed by the poet in a cooler, less creative mood than that in which the Duchess and Flamineo had their birth. There is no correspondence between the axioms and the life represented in the drama. This dissociation is the fundamental flaw in Webster.

The dissociation is certainly a fundamental fact of Webster; but it prefers no charge against the playwright. It is obviously true that 'There is no correspondence between the axioms and the life represented in the drama'. This is on a par with writing: 'There is no correspondence between Clytemnestra's action in killing Agamemnon and the views expressed by the chorus.' For this is what the *sententiae* amount to. They fulfil, in diffused form, the function of the chorus; and the practice of Euripides (especially) and Sophocles had demonstrated that the choric viewpoint, though an important one, is not final and definitive. And the drama consists essentially of the gap between the choric morality and the actions of the principal characters. Webster himself, *in propria persona* [in his own person], had lamented that he could not include in his play 'the sententious Chorus . . . the passionate and weighty Nuntius', but found the true correlative of the chorus. His *sententiae* outline a body of conventional moral wisdom, to which his characters refer, but to which they cannot adhere. Such a situation is not much unlike life itself. It is curious that Webster should be censured for a most original dramatic procedure: that is, the development of the old chorus not into a self-contained unit of expression (Enobarbus, Thersites [in Shakespeare's *Antony and Cleopatra* and *Troilus and Cressida, respectively*]) but as a part of the character's mind. As a depiction of a disintegrating world order, this procedure deserves some recognition in the twentieth century.

The *sententiae* do not, in themselves, tell us what the plays are about. A broad indication, of a sort, is supplied by the plots. The plots of Webster's three plays, taken alone, afford inadequate but not misleading statements of his intentions. *The White Devil* is essentially a pattern of evil-doers and of retribution; *The Duchess of Malfi* reveals humanity, rather than evil-doers, gripped by a malevolent or indifferent fate; *The Devil's Law-Case* is a story of wrong unpunished. Such are the stories, and such the essences of his three plays. But to demonstrate fully the playwright's design one must look elsewhere.

The concerns of Webster are located in the imagery of his plays. The imagery is the basic content of his work; it reveals the primary symbols through which Webster's imagination expresses itself. It is not solely a matter of verbal imagery; . . . the interconnections of action, character, and words make all partial analyses highly provisional. But a study must be based on the words of the text. These texts are massive growths of imagery; it would be misleading to speak of a 'pattern of imagery' as a sort of necklace of verbal brilliants that rest on the otherwise unadorned body of the play. On the contrary, *The White Devil* and *The Duchess of Malfi* would have virtually no text left were one to remove the imagery. The motifs that can be discerned here offer the best indications of Webster's concerns.

The method for establishing image themes, as developed by Caroline Spurgeon, Wilson Knight, and Wolfgang Clemen, lends itself to varying emphases but in essence remains constant. Two stages are necessary: first, a descriptive analysis, by subject matter, of the play's images; second, a reclassification of the images that brings together images from various groups into one thematic category. The second stage of the analysis concentrates on the images that seem to play a special and functional part in the movement of the play. Usually the analyst can obtain certain clues, apart from his own judgement, in locating these special images. One is likely to find, on a comparison with other plays by contemporary dramatists, or with other plays by the same dramatist, that certain motifs leap into prominence. Thus Caroline Spurgeon [in *Shakespeare's Imagery*, 1935] found a major significance in some ten images of clothing in *Macbeth*. Webster, however, usually makes his thematic points through a considerable weight of iterative imagery. They give the impression (which is supported by his own admission of being a slow worker) of being deployed in accordance with a conscious intellectual design.

A primary classification of Webster's images reveals his fascination with certain areas of subject matter. Images of animals and disease figure very largely in all three of his plays. *The White Devil* and *The Duchess of Malfi* draw heavily, in addition, on images that embody the opposition of appearance and reality. Passing from images, defined strictly, to words significantly repeated in the two tragedies, one finds many references to devils and to witches; and in the Machiavellian group, to 'great men', 'princes', 'politic', and 'policy'. These are the data which a secondary classification must interpret. All of these images and words are subsumed in a single theme, that of evil. Evidently, this theme is embodied in the actions of the leading characters. His plays are saturated with a consciousness of human evil.

There is a further area of subject matter, treated in all three plays, which points towards the other grand theme that dominates the imagination of Webster. It is the Law. Numerically far fewer than those embodying the theme of evil, images of the Law occur at critical points in *The White Devil* and *The Duchess of Malfi*. (The Law is, of course, the substance of the plot itself in *The Devil's Law-Case*, and the dialogue there contains a multitude of literal references in addition to certain metaphors.) The idea of the Law is supported by a number of verbal counters that present aspects of the same concept: justice, revenge, service, payment, reward. Moreover, an important aspect of the Law—retribution—is present in the many images of storm in the two tragedies. Finally, we can note that the trial scene is the theatrical centre of *The White Devil* and *The Devil's Law-Case,* and a miniature trial (the dialogue of Ferdinand and Bosola) is correspondingly placed (IV.

ii) in *The Duchess of Malfi*. The images of the Law, together with its associated terms, stand for the mechanisms whereby man governs himself—and by which the universe governs him. They constitute one of the two major themes that dominate Webster's imagination. While other themes of importance exist in his plays—most notably, the theme of knowledge in *The Duchess of Malfi*—only these themes figure largely in all three plays.

The relationship between evil and the Law is the intellectual tension that grips *The White Devil, The Duchess of Malfi,* and *The Devil's Law-Case.* The resolution of that tension is the main concern of each play; for while human evil may be a constant, the Law is not. It is presented in turn as a simple retributive mechanism that punishes wrongdoers, as the ineluctable fate that awaits a sinful humanity, and as a moral and ethical code of human conduct—a central, albeit unfulfilled, ideal.

The thematic concerns of this playwright do, however, raise criticisms of a quite different order from those I have considered earlier. The mass of imagery of which each tragedy is composed invites, to my mind, two objections that have not been urged against Webster in the past. They can conveniently be considered at this point. First, it may be said that the sheer bulk of the imagery is altogether too much strain upon the audience. The ornamentation of a baroque facade is one thing; the spectator has no fixed time in which to absorb the implications of the manifold detail. The dense imagery of a Webster play is a different matter, since the audience must be supposed to be capable of assimilating it without preparation and within a given time-limit. It is true that *The Duchess of Malfi* is slightly lighter in texture than *The White Devil,* and *The Devil's Law-Case* contains a much smaller quantity of imagery than the tragedies. Perhaps Webster had listened to the complaint that his audience needed much more non-metaphoric dialogue on which to 'rest' their minds. Even if one allows for heavy cuts in performance, one is still left with a residual play of high metaphorical content. This 'overloading' of the audience's mind is undoubtedly a deliberate objective of Webster's art; it complements his other varieties of sensationalism. But in practice the two tragedies must always pose formidable problems of assimilation. I think it a telling charge to level against Webster's stagecraft.

The second objection lying in wait for the expounder of themes is that the plays are too literary and schematic. The patterns of imagery may be so obtrusive as to impair the effectiveness of the plays in performance, since a play is in the first instance a record of human activity, not an aggregation of symbols conveniently broken down into lines of dialogue. Either the playwright, or the critic, is too schematic; on one of these horns the critic can be gored. The critic must take his chance, but can plead that his *schema* is an abstraction, an aid to interpretation, not a model that represents formally the play experience. The critic's *schema* does not correspond to the play in the same way that a map does to the terrain. Webster's *schema* requires careful identification. I believe that Webster worked, very slowly and deliberately, towards a definite intellectual objective; and that he excluded from his work ideas and material that might conflict with that design. The ideas that constitute his intellectual objective are constantly re-embodied in the words and actions of his characters. And the implications and associations of those words are . . . highly restrictive in value. It sounds like a formula for dead theatre. How, then, can we account for the continuing life of Webster on stage? The answer, I suggest, is that the play structure contains much more than the ideas that may be abstracted. The characters of a Webster play obstinately maintain a life of their own; they assert it against the very text.

That this is possible, the themes of their nature admit. For evil and the Law have quite different implications for the theatre. The Law is readily embodied in action; and since the tragedies are much concerned with reward (Flamineo and Bosola) and punishment (almost all the leading characters) the concept can readily be elaborated in a fairly programmatic way, one that leaves untouched the separate questions of character and psychology. But Webster's emphasis on the evil of his stage society does not exclude counter-suggestions. Flamineo and Bosola are not invulnerable to the occasional impulse of decency; Brachiano dies trying to shield 'that good woman', Vittoria, from poison; Lodovico urges his master not to expose himself to danger; Ferdinand is the wreck of a prince, a part invariably allotted to an actor of distinction; the marble facade of the Cardinal cracks at the last. As with character, so with the body. . . . [The] body is invariably alluded to as the symbol of corruption and mortality. It is one of the most consistent correspondences that Webster employs. But the stage actors are, to appearances, very far from corrupt. The Duchess and Vittoria are beautiful women; Brachiano has none of the physical grossness of his historical source (a pointer, this, to Webster's intentions); Antonio must be a pretty enough fellow, and Julia finds plenty to admire in Bosola. Certainly, all this may be held to embody the appearance-reality opposition in a rather schematic form. But its effect on the audience must be an impression of complexity, of opposed tendencies and suggestions. And that impression, naturally, is heightened by the blurring and inconsistency of character that I have already considered. In brief, the intellectual concerns of Webster seem to me perfectly compatible with the needs of the theatre. (pp. 77-82)

> *Ralph Berry, in his* The Art of John Webster, *Oxford at the Clarendon Press, 1972, 174 p.*

Robert Freeman Whitman   (essay date 1973)

[*Whitman is an American scholar whose works include* The Play Reader's Handbook *(1966),* Beyond Melancholy: John Webster and the Tragedy of Darkness *(1973), and* Shaw and the Play of Ideas *(1977). In the following excerpt from* Beyond Melancholy, *Whitman examines the structural unity of Webster's tragedies, finding that the "technique of setting up tension by confronting us with persons or principles that we intellectually and ethically must condemn and at the same time impulsively approve of is basic to Webster's dramatic method."*]

Finding the underlying order behind apparent chaos is a pleasure common to artists and critics. While art is too complex a human activity to be reduced to any simple formula, surely not the least among its functions is as a stay against confusion. The pattern revealed may be only partial and tentative; as [Michel de] Montaigne warned, "Thou seest but the order and policie of this little little Cell wherein thou art placed: . . . This law thou aleagest is but a municipall law, and thou knowest not what the universall is." But however circumscribed his vision may be, the artist somehow appeals to man's perennial need for reassurance that his experience, as an individual and as a species, is part of a coherent and meaningful economy.

So it is that the structural unity, and the ethical consistency lying behind it, . . . so often denied to Webster's plays, may be the source of both aesthetic and critical satisfaction. For the viewer there may be the renewed hope for a moral universe, a gratification of which he is at best only half aware. And for the critic there is the much more self-conscious pleasure of contemplating an artistic whole. But this is not enough. The appeal of order has its limits; and the fact is that we demand something more. That "consistency is the hobgoblin of little minds" is true in a human if not a logical sense. There is that in us—call it what you will—that resents too much order, rebels against a mechanistic universe which pays only lip service to the individual.

Nor is artistic control and ethical consistency sufficient to explain the dramatic impact or define the tragic vision of Webster's tragedies. It does not account, for instance, for the tremendous imaginative appeal which the ostensibly "bad" characters, Vittoria and Flamineo and Bosola, have for us and, apparently, for Webster. It is certainly no accident that he gives Flamineo and Bosola a significantly higher percentage of the lines than any other characters. And it is all very well to say that the world is evil, earthly pleasure mere vanity, and Vittoria a wicked creature putting up a bold front; this is simply not adequate to our response to her. At her trial, for example, we know intellectually that she is evil, as Webster makes perfectly clear in the preceding and subsequent action, that appearances are deceptive, and that we are only seeing her as she would be seen. We are aware of the speciousness of her noble self-justification, and of the vitality being wasted in a bad cause. But the fact remains that, in spite of the essential justice of Monticelso's charges, when Vittoria hurls the names of Whoore and Murdresse back in his face, we can hardly help reacting as Flamineo does later: "Th'art a noble sister, / I love thee now." This does not mean that we are fooled and think she is "good." Indeed, we admire her proud defiance not in spite of her being a brazen strumpet, but because of it. Were she innocent she would be pitiable, but far less exciting. As it is, she appeals to the amoral, refractory impulse in all of us that rebels at the self-righteous morality of the Cardinal; she is, in a sense, the vicarious assertion of our freedom from law.

By letting, nay, encouraging us to respond to Vittoria in this fashion Webster has neither lost control of his character nor renounced conventional morality. . . . [He] never permits us to forget what Vittoria really is, and it is not conventional standards that are being undercut so much as hers. We know her, and yet, in spite of our better judgments, we are pleased when her pointed jabs at Monticelso strike home.

Webster, not very successful in his few soliloquies, is certainly at his best in dramatic dialogues, scenes of verbal fencing where the tension is sustained by pulling our sympathies first one way and then another by the justness or wit or even the striking metaphors of the participants. Most of the memorable scenes in either play would fit into this category: the by-play between Vittoria and Brachiano early in *The White Devil,* the confrontation of Brachiano and Francisco, the scene in the House of Convertites, the wooing of Antonio by the Duchess, or the conversation between the Duchess and Bosola in prison. Vittoria's trial is one of the best of these, and it is a masterpiece of juggling, of double-dealing, of forcing us into a kind of moral and imaginative schizophrenia.

The trial scene opens with the expulsion of the too-eloquent court lawyer, an incident which perhaps serves the very practical purpose of explaining why an ecclesiastical trial should be conducted in the vernacular, but which also has the much more important function of eliminating the middleman and bringing the two principals face to face. The brief episode ends in a draw, for while we admire the accused's boldness, and the tone of her defense is established at once ("I will not have my accusation clouded, / In a strange tongue: All this assembly / Shall heare what you can charge mee with"), Francisco's open contempt for the pompous latinizer is equally engaging. But behind the apparent ingenuousness there has been politic maneuvering by both sides; Monticelso has furthered his plan to ruin Vittoria by publishing her adultery as widely as possible, and the ground has been laid for her very just complaint later: "If you bee my accuser / Pray cease to be my Judge."

As the duel between the two antagonists begins, the advantage, as far as our sympathies lie, is probably with Monticelso. We know Vittoria for an adulteress and at least an accomplice in murder, and the Cardinal's promise to the court, "You see my Lords what goodly fruict she seemes, / . . . I will but touch her and you straight shall see / Sheele fall to soote and ashes," and his characterization of her behavior, " . . . In musicke banquets and most ryotous surfets / This whore, forsooth, was holy?" are both striking in language and, from what we have already seen of her, all too just. The high point of his charge is his lengthy "character" of a whore, rich in the pungent, somewhat grotesque metaphors that so delighted Webster: "Sweete meates which rot the eater, . . . Shipwrackes in Calmest weather, . . . They are those flattering bels have all one tune / At weddings, and at funerals, . . . Worse then dead bodies, which are beg'd at gallowes / And wrought upon by surgeons, to teach man / Wherin hee is imperfect." Everything that Vittoria represents, viewed morally, socially, rationally, is set forth in this speech; and intellectually, we must assent. But at the same time we are viewing Vittoria in a dramatic context, and this is not evidence, but slander. Monticelso has given us a series of colorful but somewhat irrelevant abstractions, not the living, passionate woman we see before us. As Vittoria says,

"This carracter scapes me," and we are inclined to agree with the English Ambassador, " . . . the Cardinals too bitter,"—even while we know better!

With this burst of vicious generalizations Monticelso seems to have shot his bolt, and while the overt tide of the trial turns against Vittoria, we are inexorably caught up in the vitality and resoluteness of her defense. Just after his long speech the Cardinal accuses her of "impudence" for not wearing mourning for her husband, and when she replies, "Had I forknowne his death as you suggest, / I would have bespoke my mourning," we want to cry, "Touché!"—although we know perfectly well that not only did she foreknow the murder, she had at once provoked and urged it. Monticelso is reduced almost to snarling impotence, and Vittoria, "so intangled in a cursed accusation" that she "must personate masculine virtue," seems to take control of the situation, and hurls defiance in his face: "To the point! / Find mee but guilty, sever head from body: / Weele part good frindes: I scorne to hould my life / At yours or any mans intreaty, Sir." His commonplaces seem powerless now: "Well, well, such counterfet Jewels / Make trew ones oft suspected"; and she picks them up brilliantly: "You are deceaved. / For know that all your strickt-combined heads, / Which strike against this mine of diamondes, / Shall prove but glassen hammers, they shall breake— / These are but faigned shadowes of my evels. Terrify babes, my lord, with painted devils, / I am past such needlesse palsy."

Monticelso's reply is interrupted by his brief but dramatic altercation with her lover, an incident that breaks the main line of action, but in no way weakens Vittoria's cause in our eyes. Brachiano's patent hypocrisy, like hers, is overshadowed by a glorious gesture, and his proud defiance of the common enemy is sympathetically identified with hers. After her lover leaves, Vittoria is even more on the defensive, but she parries well. If we sum up all her faults, we know that "beauty and gay clothes, a merry heart, / And a good stomacke to a feast," are *not* all the poor crimes we could charge her with; but Monticelso has little more than vague, circumstantial evidence, rumor, "what is ordinary and Ryalto talke," to bring against her. And when the accuser-judge passes sentence, we feel that it is *he* who has made a "corrupted triall," that he has indeed "ravisht justice," and our better judgments are submerged in the poetry of Vittoria's last great burst of defiance:

> I will not weepe,
> No I do scorne to call up one poore teare
> To fawne on your injustice—beare me hence,
> Unto this house of—what's your mittigating
>   Title?
>
> MONTICELSO: Of convertites.
>
> VITTORIA: It shal not be a house of convertites—
> My minde shall make it honester to mee
> Then the Popes Pallace, and more peaceable
> Then thy soule, though thou art a Cardinall—
> Know this, and let it somewhat raise your
>   spight,
> Through darkenesse Diamonds spred their ritchest light.

By the time she has left the stage the balance of our sympathies has gone over completely to her side; but if we have been carried away by her passionate self-justification, it has been at the expense of all rational and moral considerations. And Webster gives us ample opportunity *not* to be taken in, to see his heroine coldly and dispassionately, for he not only frames the episode with others which show Vittoria in a far less favorable light, but reminds us of her true nature throughout, in the accusations of Monticelso, in her sometimes blatant evasions and hypocrisy, and in permitting her to descend to something close to billingsgate. But the fact is that we simply don't care.

Webster is obviously playing with us, skillfully and with a purpose. One thing that he accomplishes, probably the most important, is the involvement of the audience, forcing them at least momentarily into a position that rationally they should reject. He has set up two antagonists as clearly opposed—although neither is simon-pure—as "right" and "wrong," and we acquiesce, perhaps half consciously, to Vittoria's code, we become committed to her "side"; and insofar as her tragedy lies in what she is rather than in what happens to her, it is our tragedy as well.

This technique of setting up tension by confronting us with persons or principles that we intellectually and ethically must condemn and at the same time impulsively approve of is basic to Webster's dramatic method. He creates situations in which conventional codes of conduct are flagrantly violated and then persuades us, by exploiting our latent admiration for high spirits and audacity, our instinctive rebelliousness against convention and authority, and the appeal of sheer poetry, to sympathetic identification with the violators. Thus he presents us at once with a conflict that is theatrically dramatic and a dilemma that is morally involving.

Our attitude towards Vittoria is subject to the same disjunctive treatment in the final act. Again we are caught up in admiration for this proud, bold girl who defies death with the same resolution as she defied society. But Webster makes sure that the tribute is paid only at the price of conscience. As she is dying, her brother delivers her epitaph: "Fare thee well. / Know many glorious woemen that are fam'd / For masculine vertue, have bin vitious, / Onely a happier silence did betyde them. / Shee hath no faults, who hath the art to hide them." What Flamineo means as high praise we should see as a fairly accurate characterization of the standards by which they both lived. By such brazen flaunting of all morality Webster makes sure that the approbation we accord Vittoria cannot be justified on any grounds but her own.

This is, of course, a somewhat risky maneuver. We may be such stern moralists that whatever aura of glamour Webster has managed to throw around the figure of Vittoria is completely dispelled by Flamineo's cynical comment. And if this is the case, much of the effectiveness of the play, or at least of her role, is lost, for she is then nothing more than a bad woman who has her just deserts. But for most of us, I think, this does not happen. The image of Vittoria as a glorious rebel holds, and we are forced to keep our moral judgments at least partially in abeyance,

to make that compromise between reason and instinct that is, perhaps, central to all tragedy.

A similar dichotomy exists in many other episodes, and in connection with other characters. Our attitude towards Brachiano, especially in the scene in which he confronts Francisco and Monticelso, is torn by our recognition that the man is an amoral and unfeeling libertine and imminent murderer and our pleasure in his assertion of independence before those self-righteous representatives of moral and social conformity. We are dazzled by the magnificent defiance of his cry: "Were she whore of mine, / All thy loud Cannons, and thy borrowed Switzers / Thy Gallies, nor thy sworne confederates, / Durst not supplant her;" and it takes more than Francisco's reply, "Let's not talke on thunder— / Thou hast a wife, our sister . . . ," to restore our vision. Only the following scene, between Brachiano and Isabella, can do that.

Even before our moral sense has been stunned by these gestures of defiance our attitude towards this adulterous pair is ambiguous. In the earlier scene where they profess their mutual passion we know perfectly well that they are moved by lust and plotting murder, and yet their frank contempt for convention and the joy and vitality of their self-indulgence, especially when set against the sour impotence of old Camillo, give them a kind of justification that is barely shaken by Flamineo's counterpoint of cynical commentary, and that makes Cornelia's outraged morality an unwelcome intrusion.

Many of the episodes in *The Duchess of Malfi* seem designed to produce much the same ambivalent response, although here the situation is made dramatically and psychologically more complex because most of the central characters, unlike those in *The White Devil,* seem aware from the beginning of the conflict between the demands of society and morality on the one hand and the need for love and security on the other. A good deal has been said elsewhere about whether or not the Duchess should be viewed as "wrong" in her union with Antonio. Certainly she sees the danger of leaving "the path of simple virtue," and considers herself "going into a wildernesse, / Where I shall find nor path, nor friendly clewe / To be my guide." Antonio fears that he is being tempted by "a sawcy and ambitious divell," and warns himself that "he's a foole / That (being a-cold) would thrust his hands i'th' fire / To warme them." And there is considerable pathos in their mutual reassurances that "We are now man, and wife, and 'tis the Church / That must but eccho this." There is of course no question but that our sympathies lie even more with this couple than with Vittoria and Brachiano in their comparable scene. They are not murderers, and they make some attempt to conform to propriety in their private "wedding." They have given themselves to love, and by no criterion but the strictest morality could we possibly condemn them. Yet they have bound themselves to the world, and the world betrays them. They are in the wrong, and they know it. And the wooing episode derives much of its power from the fact that these lovers are defying religion, society and family to fulfill their passion.

Other scenes in the play, already effective in terms of the plot alone, gain dramatic impact from the tension created by the fact that we cannot help but see the illicit, or at least improper, alliance as basically "good," while those who claim vengeance in the name of family and morality are just as obviously "bad." Indeed, almost the only important episode where this feeling is not in some degree present, where the conflict seems to be at least temporarily resolved, is that in which Bosola prepares the Duchess for death. It is significant that by this point Bosola has announced that his "business shalbe comfort," and has morally disassociated himself from Ferdinand's revenge, and the Duchess has turned her back on worldly love and pride and happiness. Nevertheless, even here the mood of quiet acceptance may be undermined by a conflicting feeling that the price demanded for reconciling virtue and happiness is too high.

It is probably in connection with Bosola and Flamineo that the ambiguity of our attitudes is most pronounced. Both are malcontents, and through most of the action completely cynical, materialistic, and amoral. One is a pandar for his sister, the other a spy and informer, and both are murderers. There is seemingly little to recommend them, and yet with their withering contempt for all pretension and self-conceit, their vitality and quick wit, and their fondness for extravagant and colorful language that is almost always startlingly apt, they are thoroughly engaging. I suspect that it is in large part their very cynicism and amorality that intrigues us, appealing to our basic urge to be free of morality and all the limitations it implies. In a sense we envy their freedom, for they are what we, unless we are psychopaths, can never be. This is particularly true of Flamineo. Bosola, characteristically, is more complex, and throughout the play is aware of the ambivalence of his own feelings, resenting the fact that worldly necessity forces him to submerge his own good nature. As he says to Ferdinand: "I would have you curse your selfe now, that your bounty / (Which makes men truly noble) ere should make / Me a villaine: . . . Thus the Divell / Candies all sinnes o'er."

These two characters are paradoxical in another sense, too, for they are at once ministers of Heaven and of Hell. Bosola's comment on the speech just quoted is, "Sometimes the Divell doth preach," and the remark is an appropriate one. He and Flamineo are the most outspoken in their defiance of conventional morality, and yet it is often their scurrilous sneers or hypocritical piety that remind us where morality in a given situation lies. . . . [It] is Flamineo's running commentary that keeps the lovers' "grand passion" in its proper perspective in *The White Devil,* and Bosola's sharp tongue deflates not only the pretensions of Ferdinand and the Cardinal but the self-delusion of Antonio and the Duchess.

This kind of "double vision," as has already been suggested, is characteristic of many aspects of Webster's two tragedies. Each play represents a complex of antitheses: the surface appearance and the hidden reality, honesty and sincerity which violate convention and immorality wearing the guise of piety, attractive vice and unattractive virtue, the appeal of freedom and the need for law. The characters, and our attitudes towards them, are ambivalent, and the structure of the plays intensifies this quality. Both

Bosola and Flamineo seem obsessed with tearing the painted face from things to reveal the corruption and hypocrisy beneath: "Theres nothing so holie but money will corrupt and putrifie it" (*WD.,* III. ii. 23); or "Though we are eaten up of lice, and wormes, / And though continually we beare about us / A Rotten and dead body, we delight / To hide it in rich tissew" (*DM.,* II. i. 57-60). The happiest scenes, of love and marriage and birth, are constantly undercut by intimations of mortality, and elsewhere the metaphors of hidden evil, disease, poison, death, run like a litany, almost always conjoined with the notion of the fair and promising exterior. "The devill in christall!" The White Devil. Webster seems to be presenting us with a series of ambiguities: the ambiguity of appearances, the ambiguity of good and evil, the ambiguity of life itself.

And it is in this quality that the heart of Webster's tragic vision lies. But the ambiguity lies not so much in the thing itself, in the external world, as in the duality and frailty of human nature. If man were purely a thinking creature, and if the thinking instrument were flawless, there would be no ambivalence, and no tragedy. But even within that "little, little cell" where man is qualified to see, he is in a mist, his vision hopelessly distorted by passion and prejudice and ignorance, by hopes of happiness and fears of death. Within the plays what is evil is generally painfully clear, but what virtue is, or how it is to be followed by blind, double-natured man, is tragically obscure. "While we looke up to heaven wee confound / Knowledge with knowledge." Montaigne had said: "Of all vanities, man is the greatest; that man, who presumeth of his knowledge, doth not yet know what knowledge is"; and: "Wee are farre enough from being honest according to God: For, wee cannot be such according to our selves. Human wisedome could never reach the duties, or attaine the devoires it had prescribed unto it selfe. . . . Is he unjust in not dooing that, which he cannot possibly atchieve? The lawes which condemne us, not to be able; condemne us for that we cannot performe." Perhaps the most succinct statement of this dilemma comes from another Pyrrhonist, Fulke Greville, in a chorus in *Mustapha,* published at about the same time that Webster was writing *The White Devil* (1609):

> Oh, wearisome condition of humanity,
> Born under one law, to another bound;
> Vainly begot, and yet forbidden vanity,
> Created sick, commanded to be sound.
> What meaneth nature by these divers laws?
> Passion and reason self-division cause.

The problem of reconciling the inherent limitations of human nature to the demands of a stable, Divinely ordered, and therefore absolute moral universe is hardly a new one, and the answers man has put forward are several. The *contemptus mundi* tradition offered one: that this world was, through God's will and man's Fall, a dark pit of vanity and temptation, that we must scorn all things tainted by flesh and the Devil and wait with faith for the next world, where the order in all its glory would be revealed. When faith faltered, as it did before the tradition died out, and contempt for the world was divorced from its theological context, nothing was left but the bleakest despair in an irrational, meaningless, worthless world where man was thrust willy-nilly to suffer, with neither guide nor hope. This *might* be Webster's world—if it were not for the haunting sense, in the dying cries of Flamineo and Bosola, in the constant reminders of a moral framework, and, most explicitly, in the quiet faith of the Duchess's renunciation, that there *is* something more.

Montaigne's answer to the dilemma . . . was not far from that of *contemptus mundi,* and his despair in wretched, self-deluded mankind was balanced by a belief in another world beyond his comprehension. But instead of *rejecting* this transient and deceptive world, he embraces it as all we have, as God's gift to make the best of we can. Perhaps in another life we may see the one true light—but sufficient unto the day is the revelation thereof.

The most important difference between the viewpoints of Montaigne and Webster is that while Montaigne saw man and the world as hopelessly imperfect, and the way to Heaven too far beyond our capacities to be even attempted, he could accept these limitations with equanimity, do his best, "play the man well and duly," and take the promise of a better world on something like faith. Webster, on the other hand, was not satisfied to accept the injustice of the paradox that man is "created sick, commanded to be sound." Montaigne could see life as a comedy; for Webster it was a tragedy.

Of Webster's characters only the Duchess finds her way out of the dilemma, but it is significant that the last part of the play belongs to Bosola, who, more humanly frail, tries to find the Heaven he glimpsed in the Duchess' eyes, and fails. And while we must admire the Duchess, it is to Bosola that we feel the closest. And this is the genius of Webster. By forcing us to compromise our moral instincts in favor of human weakness, he draws us into the same dilemma as his characters. Reason yearns for an ordered, stable, moral world—and eternity, too. But instinct demands something more. We want pleasure, too, and love, comfort now as well as later, and the security of power as well as law; above all, we would be ourselves, self-reliant individuals free to follow the requirements, not of some impersonal Will, but of our own natures.

We too would look up to Heaven, but the Devil and the mist stand in its light. We would follow the law, but in the bewildering confusion of demands, of God and society and human nature, of reason and instinct, of the need for order and the need for freedom, where *is* the law? This is, perhaps, the essence of man's tragedy. Not that he wants that which he cannot have, but that he needs things which are mutually exclusive. Much of the power of Webster's tragedies derives from the skill with which he capitalizes on these two basic and contradictory impulses of human nature. The only dignity which his central characters possess lies in their assertion of their individuality, the resolute defiance of morality and society with which they claim their right to be themselves and follow the world. And, for Webster's purposes and our sympathy, it is all they need. But it is only half the story. The other half, the order which they must violate to gain their "freedom," is equally compelling, for them and for us; and if it sometimes does not seem so dramatically, it is only because Webster could take something for granted in the way of a moral sense in

his audience. Besides, he did not want to weight the issue, for he could not afford to pre-judge. He isn't *telling* us where "right" lies; this is no moral tract, but tragedy.

The structure of the two plays, both as entities and in individual scenes, intensifies the antithetical "pull" of these two impulses, and the tension thus set up is the substance of Webster's drama. But it is not only dramatic, it is tragic,—because the conflict is irreconcilable, and because it is ours as well as theirs. And at the heart of tragedy lies our unanswered question: why?

The total effect of Webster's plays presents a similar paradox. He provides us, as I think most great drama does, with a sense of satisfaction in the reaffirmation of an ordered and moral world where the forces of rebellion and chaos are put down—but also with a feeling of awe and even terror at the price that a revolt with which we can so easily identify ourselves must pay. And this, perhaps, is what Aristotle meant by pity and fear. (pp. 192-205)

> *Robert Freeman Whitman, in his* Beyond Melancholy: John Webster and the Tragedy of Darkness, *Institut für Englische Sprache und Literatur, Universität Salzburg, 1973, 226 p.*

THE WHITE DEVIL

PRODUCTION REVIEWS

F. L. Lucas　(review date 17 October 1925)

[*Lucas was an English man of letters who is best known as the editor of John Webster's works and as a literary critic. In addition to his position as poetry critic of the* New Statesman, *he wrote several noteworthy works, including* Authors, Dead and Living *(1926) and* The Decline and Fall of the Romantic Ideal *(1936). In 1925, Lucas was preparing* The Complete Works of John Webster *when* The New Statesman *asked him to review the Renaissance Theatre revival of* The White Devil. *In his assessment, Lucas laments the "fatal lack of dignity throughout" the performance as well as the truncated adaptation of the script.*]

I do not know whether Mr. Bernard Shaw witnessed the Renaissance Theatre's production of Webster's *White Devil.* If so, it must have cost him some effort not to rise up in the auditorium, as the curtain fell, and say: "You see (as so often) I was right. How many more revivals of Elizabethan plays will it take to make you understand why I labelled Webster 'a Tussaud laureate,' or why I urged that a statue should be put up in Deptford to the benefactor of mankind who stabbed Marlowe, and Mr. Swinburne be sentenced for life to sell picture-postcards of it to American tourists?" Certainly the ghost of the late Mr. William Archer could be heard murmuring in the pit his refrain of "poor Webster." Only Webster himself was absent; for the play we saw was assuredly not his.

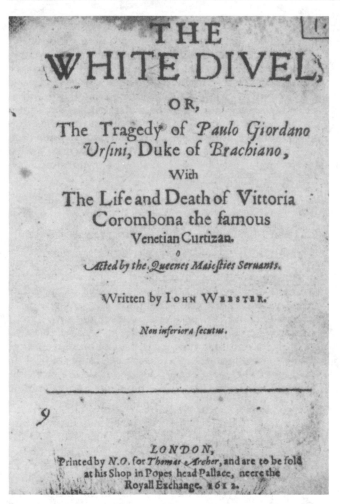

Title page of the 1612 edition of The White Devil.

Webster wrote a play of this title about a woman and a great lord in Renaissance Italy who fell in love with one another. Her brother became their pander; from their adultery followed the murders of the wife of one, of the husband and younger brother of the other; and, last of all, from those three murders death came to the three murderers in their turn. Now, if a dramatist chooses such characters for a play, it becomes one of his first and most difficult problems how to secure for them the sympathy of his audience. They may be bad; but when they come to their bad end, we must feel that it is tragic, not a good riddance. It is the problem Shakespeare faced and solved in *Macbeth*. And so Webster had solved it here, could plays be foolproof. How were we to be made to care what became of these beings who felt no shame and knew no pity and kept no faith? How was [John] Milton in like case to make us care for the Devil himself [in *Paradise Lost*]? By making these characters magnificent amid, and in spite of, the guilt that brings their ruin, Vittoria wins us because with all the clay of her cunning and her heartlessness Webster has mixed such a fire of beauty and intellect, of pride and passion and indomitable courage, that we forget the blood on her hands and the wrongs of the kindly Isabella; and when in the trial-scene she stands at bay, with the bril-

liance of another Mary Stuart, against both worlds, the power of State and church, of Florence and of Rome, we cry: "Not guilty," despite ourselves and truth. But Webster did not rely, to gain this sympathy, on his heroine's qualities alone. Instead of showing us her lover as he was in history, so fat that he had a dispensation about kneeling in the Papal presence, he gilded with the brightest gold of his poetry the splendid figure of Paolo Giordano Ursini, Duke of Brachiano; that her sin might be palliated by the greatness of the temptation, as Vittoria's splendour palliated his. We have to picture some prince of the Italian Renaissance, a ruthless but successful soldier and statesman, riding through life as proudly as Bartolommeo Colleoni rides through Venice still. Yet not even this was enough. As further excuse, Webster made Vittoria's husband, not the good-hearted youth he seems really to have been, but a cold, hairless, witless pedant, almost a Renaissance Dr. Casaubon, prating of alchemy and adages. Here, then, were two great figures and a great temptation; it only remained to find a devil; Webster took the Machiavelli of popular imagination and made him Flamineo. And yet, lest even he and his black familiar Zanche should lack our pity at the last, to Flamineo he gave a devil's wit, and to both that unwincing courage, that gift of dying game, which in his eyes covered so many sins. For always Webster had meant that we should shudder with pity, though we felt the justice, when amid a storm of poetry his characters fall before us, like the star of the Son of the Morning from heaven, bright and bitter and baleful to the end.

But he had not reckoned with the modern producer. It was essential that the personal appearance of the characters turn our sympathies in the right direction from the first; and accordingly the worst was to be feared when the Duke of Brachiano appeared as a rather insignificant-looking young Lothario, shorter than most of the characters on the stage, particularly his own Duchess; and the bald wittol Camillo as a handsome young fool provided with one of Clarkson's bushiest golden wigs. I do not wish to split hairs, but on their evidence alone it might be doubted whether the producer had properly read the play. For it is clear from the text that Brachiano had curly hair, Francesco white hair, and Camillo not much of any sort. None of these details was observed: the first mattered not a pin, the second made the Duke of Florence look, instead of a grey intriguer, fifteen years too young, but the third showed a complete misunderstanding of Camillo's part. And it soon became apparent that more than wigs was wrong. The actors gave the impression of having been left by the producer to conceive their own characters without any particular regard for the play. Thus, the Duke of Florence seemed to have vowed with all the determination of the youthful Queen Victoria, "I *will* be good"; for the naturally pleasant character of Mr. Charles Carson had so overlaid the treacherous Medici he was meant to be, that when in Act V., disguised in a dressing-gown as a Moor, he had to take his share in poisonings and stranglings, it was impossible to believe that it was the same person. Similarly his ally the Cardinal adopted such a stage-Anglican air of sweetness and light, and rebuked Vittoria in the trial-scene so much more with sorrow than anger, that it seemed most unfair when the English Ambassador suddenly observed, "The Cardinal's too bitter." But it was not in this charitable light that Elizabethan audiences were accustomed to seeing scarlet Cardinals; and the sympathy which should have gone out to Vittoria's courage in the teeth of the tempest vanished when the tempest never broke. If anyone in the whole play should rant, it is the Cardinal.

And yet even these things mattered less than the fatal lack of dignity throughout; it was for the main characters to give some impression of the princeliness of that proud society which set the standard of culture for all Europe. There were moments when the actors managed to keep still and allow Webster's poetry to give for an instant that illusion; but most of the time there was such a flapping and flopping (who can hope to speak passionate verse lying on one elbow on the floor?) that the memory reverted longingly to Mr. [William Butler] Yeats' project for rehearsing a company in barrels on wheels, to be moved, *when* necessary, by the producer with a pole. Miss Cowie as the heroine, attractive as she looked, seemed in needless uncertainty how far she was a great lady, how far a designing minx. But if she had little dignity, Mr. Esmé Percy's Brachiano had none. To cower crossing himself in abject agonies of terror on his deathbed was not a thing, whatever his faults, that the "strong heart" of Paolo Giordano would have stooped to do; it destroyed our pity; and to turn the character of the Orsini into a pert young lover out of a French comedy, mouthing that his heart was "looth to break," was almost enough in itself to wreck the play. And why, to continue the dreary tale, estrange us from Cornelia by dressing her like the matron of an orphanage? Or make up Zanche so like a comic negress that it was inconceivable how Flamineo could ever have become entangled with her? True, she is a Moor and gibed at as such; but so was Othello. It was indeed ironic enough that we complex moderns, who find Elizabethan characters so elementary, "mere violences" as a recent critic has put it, should yet ourselves show such *naïveté* in rendering Webster's subtleties, such a complete misdirection of his appeals to the sympathies of his audience. The one character who seemed to have some sense of the gifts Webster meant him to possess was Mr. Hardwicke's Flamineo. He was a little too genial, too little the cold, deep, cynical toad, whose sudden spurts of venom can never warm his blood into more than a moment's passion. But he was a great relief.

The plot itself fared no better than the characters. Vittoria's husband and Brachiano's wife had to be murdered; to represent this Webster adopts the crude but at least lucid method of a pair of conjurer's dumb-shows, in which the execution of both crimes is magically made visible to Brachiano. These were entirely cut, and the curtain rose on the trial of Vittoria without the audience knowing for what she was to be tried. One could mentally see the fog of mystification rising from the stalls. And the omission was the more unfortunate that the dumb-shows, little as one would expect it, proved, when the play was acted at Cambridge, eerily effective. Similarly at the end where Giovanni and his followers burst in and Lodovico, after murdering Vittoria, is himself led off to execution, exclaiming:

> For my part
> The racks, the gallows, and the torturing wheel

> Shall be sound sleeps to me.

the speech was left as a curtain, though the appearance of the ministers of justice was cut altogether and it became impossible to see why the words were uttered. And there was little consolation for this shearing away of vital parts in the retention of a great deal of obscure bawdry that needed a glossary in order to be understood. After things like this one watched with resignation how smaller dramatic points were missed—how Brachiano exclaimed on the awfulness of dying "'mongst women howling," when not a woman on the stage had uttered a murmur; how, when in his madness he cries:

> I'll do a miracle, I'll free the court
> From all foul vermin. Where's Flamineo?

a long pause before the last three words was allowed to destroy all the sinister irony of the juxtaposition. Indeed, most of the speakers continued the good old English tradition of always breaking up blank verse, and even couplets, into as many unrecognisable fragments as possible: "Those are the killing griefs that dare not . . . speak." In consequence not even Webster's poetry could save him or do its part in creating his atmosphere, his sense of the vastness of death and the brave, brief light of human courage in its gloom. At moments the play showed signs of life—in the scene of Giovanni's questions about the dead, in the last scene of all—but they were moments and no more.

The Renaissance Theatre is such an admirable institution in theory that it is all the greater pity when it has such failures as this. But it is clear that in simple justice to the Elizabethans, if they cannot be done better, they had better not be done at all. The actors at least knew their parts—which is more than can be said of some Phœnix productions in the past; properly produced, the play might have been a different thing. It is there I suspect that the difficulty largely lies. The similar failure of the ***Duchess of Malfi,*** as acted by the Phœnix Society in 1919, seems to have been partly due to a similar lack of control; so that Mr. James Strachey could write bitterly of it at the time: "Finally there was Ferdinand, who in a happier world would have been an actor-manager, as was shown by his conviction, not shared in this case by the other actors, that he was the central figure of the play." The consequence of such disasters is that Webster's reputation is written down as an overrated superstition, while choruses of critics chant: "The play's a jest and all things show it . . ." It is indeed more than a jest, and Webster's fame would die, if that were possible, of a few more such revivals. (pp. 11-13)

> *F. L. Lucas, "Playing the Devil," in* New Statesman, *Vol. XXVI, No. 651, October 17, 1925, pp. 11-13.*

CRITICAL COMMENTARY

Hereward T. Price (essay date 1955)

[*Price finds that Webster uses imagery in* The White Devil *to "convey the basic conflict of his drama, the conflict between outward appearance and inner substance or reality." This imagery, Price maintains, is linked in*

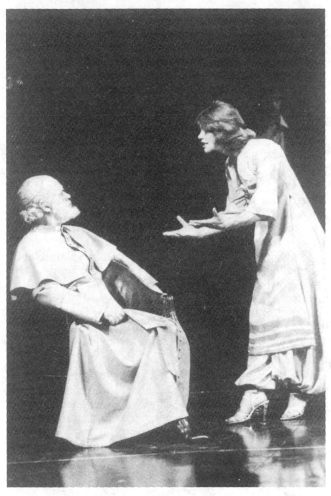

The trial scene (III.ii) in a 1976 production of The White Devil
with Patrick Magee as Monticelso and Glenda Jackson as Vittoria.

*the action and the language. The repeated references to
poison, for example, are accompanied by a number of
actual poisonings in the play.*]

For many generations symbolism has dominated the poetry of America and Europe. In time, of course, the critics found out what was happening and they began to investigate the movement. They have carried their investigations further and further afield over the literature of the last four centuries and in the process they have enormously widened our knowledge of poetry. Through their labors we read with clearer eyes and a deeper enjoyment than before.

Shakespeare has, naturally, received a great deal of attention. He is indeed the center of a lively controversy about the exact function which he intended imagery to perform. One body of critics sees the Shakespearian play as a symbol at large made up of many smaller symbols. Such integration into a coherent form does not, of course, constitute for this school the whole truth about a play. They do not ignore the other structure of plot or of characterization. But they assert that a study of the elaborate interdependence of Shakespeare's images will afford us a valuable key to his meaning. Other critics refuse to recognize in Shake-

speare any planned and complex correlation of imagery. Some even treat the idea with scorn.

We ought to approach this problem not as if it were something peculiar to just one writer but from the viewpoint of general Elizabethan practice. Not enough work has been done on other Elizabethans. We may perhaps obtain some light on Shakespeare by studying the technique of his contemporaries. Possibly, by establishing likeness or difference, by comparison or contrast, we shall come to see Shakespeare's characteristic tendencies more clearly. I have chosen Webster to investigate because in the depth, the subtlety, and the complexity of his imagery he comes nearer than any other Elizabethan dramatist to the power of Shakespeare. Moreover his sombre rendering of life's terrors provides something that our generation can respond to immediately and with perfect comprehension.

While Webster approaches Shakespeare in many aspects of his imagery, there can be no comparison between them in range. Shakespeare wrote a large number of plays over a long period of time. Webster, on the other hand, is known chiefly for the **White Devil** and the **Duchess of Malfi,** which were written fairly close together. They resemble one another in the nature of the symbols used. In fact the **Duchess of Malfi** even takes over symbols from the **White Devil.** The resolute consistency with which Webster elaborates an extended sequence of diverse but interrelated images distinguishes the **White Devil** and the **Duchess of Malfi** not only from Webster's other work but also from the rest of the Elizabethan drama. (pp. 717-18)

Before we begin, we must first point out that there was a stock of images common to all Elizabethan drama. We must, for instance, train ourselves to recognize proverbs. Elizabethan critics regarded them as an ornament of style, readers delighted in them, and poets would try to give pleasure by interweaving proverbs or reminiscences of proverbs into their work. Many figures that appear to be brilliant inventions turn out on inspection to be old proverbs. When Bosola says: "Thou sleep'st worse, then if a mouse should be forc'd to take up her lodging in a cats eare" (**Duchess of Malfi** IV. ii. 135-36), he appears to have hit upon a striking figure. In reality he is only employing a proverb well known to the Elizabethans. They would approve of the passage because Webster gave to an old saw a novel application.

I pass over shortly the question of Webster's debts to contemporary authors. He notoriously lifted his images from a large number of writers, especially from [Philip] Sidney and from [Michel de] Montaigne. But it is also true that he rarely borrows without improving on his source. His mind was a sieve through which only the essential elements passed. He trims his borrowings so closely as to achieve the utmost economy and sharpness of phrase. At other times Webster uses what in his source is flat or merely logical in order to show his characters turning to passion or violence, and in Webster it sounds like the grinding of teeth in a curse. Or elsewhere by a slight change in rhythm or wording he transforms the prosaic into haunting poetry. When he conveyed other people's bright ideas, Webster was following the conventional Renaissance practice of imitation, and he could plead the conventional justification that he put his imitation to very good use. Whatever he took he worked into the essential substance of the play.

If we then ask what really distinguishes Webster from other Elizabethans, we find it in his consistent use of a double construction, an outer and an inner. He gives us figure in action and figure in language. These he fuses so intimately as to make the play one entire figure. Now it is possible to say that this would be true of all drama. But, if we except Shakespeare, no other dramatist works so resolutely as Webster at making figure in action and figure in word conform to one another all the way through. Most Elizabethan dramatists tend to use figure for its power of enhancing a speech, a scene, or a particular moment in a play. But in the *White Devil* and the *Duchess of Malfi* a figure is usually one of a series of figures, all of which are focussed on the same control point. The verbal images dovetail into one another exactly as they closely parallel the figure in action, rising and falling with it, inseparable from it. Webster is important in the history of English dramatic art just because of this exact and sustained correlation. The severe self-discipline necessary to achieve Webster's superb uniformity of effect is most unusual among writers in England. It might almost be called un-English; it is certainly un-Elizabethan.

For Webster the figure-in-words appears at first sight to be the more important. The action gives the impression of being loose, and while it leads up to violent explosions, as for instance, murders, Webster does not primarily exploit such happenings for their value as sensation. Like every dramatist he keeps us hanging in fear and hope about the thing that is to happen, but he interests us far more in what moves the minds of his characters. He works up to a sudden speech or perhaps only to a sudden line to reveal as by lightning the essential quality of a life or even the meaning of the whole play. That is his *grand coup*. In his two great plays a cruel villain plans to destroy a group of people. The event interests us, of course, but we are much more deeply occupied in watching Webster turn inside out the minds of good and bad characters in a successive, deep, and rich revelation. It is only after inspecting the play very carefully that we discover how much our interest in character has been kept up and repeatedly stimulated by Webster's skillful manipulation of action, his use of contrast, and especially by his superb timing.

The general function of imagery in Webster is of course the same as in all other drama. It is the most pregnant expression of truth. It reveals character, it does the work of argument, it emphasizes mood, and it prefigures the events to come. In Webster the foreshadowing is typically ironical. The good that is promised turns out to be evil. Webster especially uses imagery to convey the basic conflict of his drama, the conflict between outward appearance and inner substance or reality. He gives us a universe so convulsed and uncertain that no appearance can represent reality. Evil shines like true gold and good tries to protect itself by putting on disguise or a false show. What is hidden rusts, soils, festers, corrupts under its fair exterior. The devil is called the "invisible devil."

Most powerfully of all Webster uses poison to express the

relation between fair show and foul truth. Poison kills all the more certainly because it is not seen or even suspected. In the *White Devil* Webster weaves into his lines about thirty references to poison. Parallel to this the action itself contains a number of notable poisonings. In addition Webster uses *devil* as a key-word. In the *White Devil* it occurs twenty-six times. The relentless repetition of the same kind of figure, the heaping up of the same words, time and again, cannot be accidental. Such frequency of occurrence shows that there must be method, conscious and deliberate.

I begin with the *White Devil.* Lucas [in his edition of the play] explains the meaning of the title, "a devil disguised under a fair outside" and he backs up his definition by many quotations. The *N.E.D.* gives the following meanings for *white:* morally pure, stainless, innocent; free from malignity, beneficent; propitious, auspicious, happy; highly prized, pet, darling; fair-seeming, specious, plausible. In the conflict between these meanings lies the irony of the title. Probably Webster also had in mind two Elizabethan proverbs, *The White devil is worse than the black* and *The devil can transform himself into an angel of light.* The very title of the play, then, is a figure of the sort we have been discussing. Vittoria is the white devil: white to outside view, inside the black devil.

Lodovico opens the play with a series of figures that express the relation between deceptive appearance and the bitter reality. (He is to end the play by sacrilegiously putting on the disguise of a friar in order to commit a series of murders.)

> LODO: . . . Fortun's a right whore.
> If she give ought, she deales it in small percels,
> That she may take away all at one swope.
> This tis to have great enemies, God quite them:
> Your woolfe no longer seemes to be a woolfe
> Then when shees hungry.
>
> GAS: You terme those enemies
> Are men of Princely ranke.
>
> (I.i.4-10)

Here we have two themes at which Webster labors persistently, both pertaining to the difference between seeming and being. First we have Fortune that makes a show of favor in order to deceive. Secondly, the rich and powerful are not regarded as wolves, however wolfish they may be. Only the penniless and hungry adventurer is looked upon as a beast of prey. The magnificence of rank covers a multitude of sins. The unrelenting repetition of this kind of figure binds all the scenes of the play into a whole of the highest possible unity. Webster varies the figure to include hidden disease or indeed any kind of rottenness that develops unseen.

Webster then introduces that particular theme of hidden corruption, of magnificent rank covering sin, that is the overt subject of the play. Brachiano now lives in Rome, "And by close pandarisme seekes to prostitute / The honour of Vittoria Corombona" (I. i. 41-2). Close pandarism is, of course, hidden pandarism, pandarism that is kept close. Act I.ii is concerned most of all with the *close pandarisme.* Here is corruption of the vilest sort. Vittoria's brother, Flamineo, undertakes to corrupt his sister's honor. He asks Brachiano to conceal himself, using an ominous word that foretells the end: "Shrowd you within this closet, good my Lord" (I. ii. 33). He then goes on to seduce Vittoria from her husband Camillo and win her over for Brachiano. At the same time Camillo is tricked into believing that Flamineo is persuading Vittoria to come back to him. The scene that follows may appear to be the ordinary stuff of Elizabethan drama. Flamineo tricks Camillo, and the trick is everywhere in Elizabethan comedy and tragedy. Camillo stands apart, watching Flamineo and Vittoria talking, and commenting on what he sees. That also is common form in Elizabethan drama. Camillo's most important comment is: "A vertuous brother, a my credit" (145). The difference between Webster and other Elizabethans lies in the exact correspondence between his figures-in-word and figures-in-action. Camillo is entirely deceived by appearances, the seeming good cloaks horrible evil. Webster uses the old tricks of the stage but he fills them with his own meaning.

And now Webster follows up with figures that promise happiness, only to deceive. Flamineo foretells for Vittoria the delights which the affair with Brachiano will bring to her: "Thou shalt lye in a bed stuft with turtles feathers, swoone in perfumed lynnen like the fellow was smothered in roses—so perfect shall be thy happinesse, that as men at Sea thinke land and trees and shippes go that way they go, so both heaven and earth shall seeme to go your voyage. Shalt meete him, tis fixt with nayles of dyamonds to inevitable necessitie" (148-153).

These lines contain one of the main ironies of the play. Webster grants Brachiano and Vittoria no happiness. While for a brief moment "heaven and earth *seem* to go their voyage," only Flamineo's last prophecy comes true. Necessity binds them all together in a way Flamineo did not foresee. And what horror and revulsion Webster conveys in the one word *happy,* coming from the mouth of the brother and pander and used of the sister he is seeking to prostitute.

For the rest of the scene Webster pursues the difference between appearance and reality in a long series of figures. He piles up these figures especially to describe the fair outside of Camillo that covers only a "lousy slave" (45-48, 100-102, 125 f).

Then Webster makes Vittoria narrate a dream in which she suggests to Brachiano how he may murder her husband and his own wife. She invents the figure of a yew tree to represent the marriages of Vittoria to Camillo and of Brachiano to Isabella. Vittoria speaks of the *eu* to Brachiano and of course she means *you*. As we shall see Webster repeats the figure of the *yew* later on (IV. iii. 123-26). The marriages represented by the yew were rooted in decay and could not prosper.

In connection with the dream Webster identifies Vittoria for the first time as the devil. Flamineo says: "The divell was in your dreame" (240) and follows almost at once: "Excellent Divell. / Shee hath taught him in a dreame/To make away his Dutchesse and her husband" (246-248).

A little later Cornelia introduces the first mention of poison:

> O that this faire garden,
> Had [with] all poysoned hearbes of Thessaly,
> At first bene planted . . . rather [then] a buriall
>　　plot,
> For both your Honours.
>
>　　　　　　　　　　　(264-268)

Flamineo sums up the scene by speaking of the ways of policy as winding and indirect, flowing like rivers with "crooke bendings" and imitating "the suttle fouldings of a Winters snake." (346) "Subtle" implies deceit, and a snake, "anguis in herba," strikes from concealment and kills by poison.

The happiness they are all so confident of turns out to be Dead Sea fruit. In the case of Vittoria and Brachiano Webster defers the ironic event, but in the next scene (II.i) with Isabella he makes it follow upon the too confident forecast at once. Isabella is certain she can win back Brachiano:

> 　　　　I do not doubt
> As men to try the precious Unicornes horne
> Make of the powder a preservative Circle
> And in it put a spider, so these armes
> Shall charme his poyson, force it to obeying
> And keepe him chast from an infected straying.
> 　　　　　　　　　　(II. i. 13-18)

Notice the themes of *poison* and *infection*. Poison kills without being seen, infection corrupts long before its effects are visible—here are the two most frequent themes of the play. Of course, Isabella's attempt to recover Brachiano is a complete failure.

> Isa: You are as welcome to these longing armes,
> As I to you a Virgine.
>
> Brac: O your breath!
> Out upon sweete meates, and continued Phys-
> 　　icke!
> The plague is in them.
>
> Isa: You have oft for these two lippes
> Neglected Cassia or the naturall sweetes
> Of the Spring-violet. . . .
>
> 　　　　　　　　　　(165-170)

She fails, and notice that Brachiano in this speech can no longer see her as she is. Not only does Webster show evil disguised, he shows us also that Brachiano's foulness prevents him from seeing the good.

Brachiano curses his marriage and cruelly casts Isabella off. But she, in her love for her husband, pretends that it is she who has broken up the marriage. She "puts on an act" of spiteful jealousy and rage and convinces her brother the Duke that she is but a "foolish, mad, and jealous woman." Here again Webster gives us the appearance that deceives. But this time it is purest goodness that cloaks itself in evil. Webster's world is so corrupt that goodness itself works to deceive. No appearance is true.

The next scene is full of figure-in-action. In two dumb-shows a conjurer reveals how the Duchess and Camillo are murdered. In the one show villains lay poison on the picture of Brachiano—and depart laughing. The Duchess kneels before the picture, does three reverences to it, kisses it thrice, and the poison on it kills her. Brachiano, watching the dumb show, exclaims, "Excellent." Such pitiless confrontation of opposites is the strongest of irony. In the second dumb-show Flamineo, Camillo, and others drink healths. Flamineo and Camillo "compliment" one another as to who shall first use the vaulting-horse, and then Flamineo breaks Camillo's neck.

And now that Brachiano has lost his wife and Vittoria her husband, the way seems clear for the promised happiness. But Flamineo and Vittoria are arrested immediately. Here is Webster's method. Vittoria is promised happiness if she submits to Brachiano, Isabella thinks she can "charm the Duke's poison," "keep him from an infected straying." Both are deceived by the event. Isabella dies of Brachiano's poison, Vittoria is arrested even before she sees Brachiano. Webster builds his figures into the construction of the play, the whole of the play is in them, and that gives them their power.

But there is more in this scene. Here we see the characteristic polarity of Webster's method in the extreme. The murderers "depart laughing," Isabella is all humility, devotion, and love, and even in her dying agony manages to prevent anyone else from being poisoned by the picture. Brachiano sees his wife's supreme love and the tortures of her death, and remarks, "Excellent, then shee's dead." The principle of polarity is clear.

This polarity is seen in the figures of appearance and reality all through the play.

In the famous trial-scene (III.ii) Vittoria faces her accuser with superb intellectual resource. Judge and defendant fight one another with figure, and for every figure the Cardinal hurls at Vittoria, she immediately retorts with another. The Cardinal proceeds to strip her of her fairseeming in order to show the foul heart inside. He will point out her follies in more "natural red and white" than that upon her cheek. She seems to be goodly fruit but is like the apples of Sodom and Gomorrah, so that when he touches her, she will fall to soot and ashes. Night by night she counterfeited a prince's court. Again and again he comes back to that word *counterfeit.* "This whore, forsooth, was holy," "Ha," exclaims Vittoria, "whore, what's that?" It is her only blunder. In twenty lines the Cardinal informs her with abundant detail:

> They are first,
> Sweete meates which rot the eater: In mans
>   nostrill
> Poison'd perfumes. They are coosning Alcumy,
> Shipwrackes in Calmest weather . . .
>   . . . conterfetted coine . . .
> You, gentlewoman!
> Take from all beasts, and from all mineralls
> Their deadly poison.
>
> (83-106)

Again Webster's figures show the polarity—or the irony—he loves. Sweetmeats which rot, shipwrecks in calmest weather, the stretch between these opposites is the source of Webster's strength.

The Cardinal also fixes on Vittoria the name of devil.

> I am resolved
> Were there a second Paradice to loose
> This Devell would betray it.

VIT: O poore charity!
Thou art seldome found in scarlet.

> (71-4)

CARD: You know what Whore is; next the devell, Adultry,
Enters the devell, Murder.

> (112-13)

If the devill
Did ever take good shape behold his picture.

> (224-25)

That is, she is the White Devil.

She retorts with spirit and throws back at him the reproach of falseness: "These are but faigned shadowes of my evels. / Terrify babes, my Lord, with *painted* devils" (150-51). But this only strengthens Webster's theme of appearance and reality. She displays a splendid spirit, she is magnificent in intellect and courage, and she is—a whore and a murderess.

The Cardinal in passing sentence again insists on her rottenness: "Such a corrupted triall have you made / Both of your life and beauty . . ." (269-270). Vittoria raves at him and leaves the court with a figure that reverses the ideas of appearance and reality in Vittoria's favor: "Through darkenesse Diamonds spred their richest light" (306). Again we see the polarity of Webster's figure, the stark contrast of darkness and rich light. This line also shows Webster's habit of summing up a movement in its closing words. The light will become rich through the darkness, in adversity Vittoria's character will show its richest light.

In the next scene (III.iii) Webster continues to harp on the theme of corruption. Flamineo is the chief speaker: "A Cardinall . . . theres nothing so holie but mony will corrupt and putrifie it" (23-4). "Religion; oh how it is commeddled with policie. The first bloudshed in the world happened about religion" (36-7).

In the next scene (IV.i) the Cardinal and the Duke play at fence, trying to deceive one another. The Cardinal preaches dissimulation, the false front, the concealed intrigue: "We see that undermining more prevailes / Then doth the Canon" (15-16). He lends the Duke a black book in which he has collected the names of notorious offenders in the city. The list is so large that it demonstrates the immense rottenness of Society. And again Webster rams into us his idea of corruption concealed by outward show: "See the corrupted use some make of bookes: / Divinity, wrested by some factious bloud, / Draws swords, swels battels, and orethrowes all good" (99-101).

In the next scene the Duke sends a love-letter to Vittoria, suggesting that she should elope with him. He hopes it will be played into Brachiano's hands. This is exactly what happens. Brachiano believes Vittoria has been unfaithful and his rage with her brings insight.

> Your beautie! ô, ten thousand curses on't.
> How long have I beheld the devill in christall!
> Thou hast lead mee, like an heathen sacrifice,
> With musicke, and with fatall yokes of flowers
> To my eternall ruine.
>
> (IV. ii. 88-92)

The *devill in christall* is the White Devil. Music and flowers lead to ruin. Here again the principle of polarity is clear. Vittoria answers Brachiano:

> What have I gain'd by thee but infamie?
> Thou hast stain'd the spotlesse honour of my
>   house . . .
> I had a limbe corrupted to an ulcer,
> But I have cut it off; and now Ile go
> Weeping to heaven on crutches.
>
> (IV. ii. 109-23)

A stain on honor, corruption, the ulcer: here Webster pursues relentlessly the same themes.

But the letter has a second effect. Brachiano and Vittoria make up their quarrel and then resolve to adopt the suggestion in the letter and run away to Florence. Again the trick succeeds, appearances deceive, they deceive most dangerously when they flatter. The suggestion to elope to Florence seemed wonderful. It promised to Vittoria and Brachiano liberty and the enjoyment of their love. But when the Duke hears that they have fled, he exclaims that is exactly what he has been aiming at. "Thy fame, fond Duke, / I first have poison'd; directed thee the way / To marrie a whore; what can be worse?" (IV. iii. 57-9).

The word *poison'd* links this piece of treachery with the other poisonings in the play. The Duke has destroyed by means of something whose apparent sweetness concealed its deadliness. He has really taken the Cardinal's hint and "undermined" the lovers.

Meanwhile the Cardinal has been elected Pope. He sees Lodovico talking with the Duke and warns him to conjure from his breast that cruel devil. He especially warns him against his plan to kill Brachiano: "Like the blacke, and melancholicke Eugh-tree, / Do'st thinke to root thy selfe in dead mens graves, / And yet to prosper?" (IV. iii. 123-25). Here, as we have already mentioned, Webster recalls Vittoria's fable of the ewe-tree in I.ii and this links the beginning with the end of the play, one murder with the other. But after the Pope has left, the Duke sends a servant to Lodovico with a thousand crowns. Lodovico can only think that they come from the Pope. He soliloquizes on the art of great ones in concealing their designs. Here again Webster gives us the figure of false show in action. Such a trick may be common enough in Elizabethan drama, but the sharp irony of it has an intricacy that is peculiar to Webster. Lodovico believes that the holy churchman is dissembling with him. In reality it is the Duke who is fooling him. This world is so full of false shows that we deceive ourselves even when we recognize that trickery is afoot.

The deceitfulness of appearances dominates the close of the play. Villainy is cloaked under a show of holiness, and again events that seem to promise happiness turn to disaster. In IV. iii Lodovico takes the sacrament to prosecute the murder of Brachiano and Vittoria in their palace, i.e., he uses the false show of holiness for murder. Webster opens V. i. by a magnificent wedding procession of Brachiano, Vittoria, and their household. Flamineo remains on the stage. He speaks: "In all the weary minutes of my life, / Day nere broke up till now. This mariage / Confirmes me happy." *Hortensio.* "'Tis a good assurance. / Saw you not yet the Moore that's come to Court?" (V. i. 1-4). Even at the first moment of Flamineo's happiness, Webster shows him about to be destroyed. The Moor is the Duke in disguise and he has brought with him the murderers Lodovico and Antonelli disguised as holy men, as Capuchins. Disguise is not, as it may be elsewhere, merely a convention, something to be expected in a play of blood. It is the meaning of the play that these murderers use the mask of holiness to kill.

Again we see the polarity of Webster's method. The brilliant marriage-procession and Flamineo's assurance of happiness are immediately followed by a dialogue between the three disguised murderers. Flamineo, with unconscious irony, sums up this passage with a commonplace about the deceitfulness of appearances: "Glories, like glow-wormes, afarre off shine bright / But lookt to neare, have neither heat nor light" (38-9). The couplet has many facets. The glow-worm may point at the marriage, at the happiness so soon to be blasted. It may also refer, as Mr. Lucas's note shows, to "persons of paltry eminence." But it all illustrates Webster's method. The situation is figure-in-action reinforced by figure-in-words.

Act V. ii opens with a typical mixture of figure-in-action and figure-in-word. Cornelia enters with her son Marcello. She is wearing a crucifix. Marcello says: "I have heard you say, giving my brother sucke, / Hee tooke the Crucifix betweene his hands, / And broke a limb off." *Cor.* "Yes: but 'tis mended" (V. ii. 11-13). At this point Flamineo enters and runs his brother Marcello through. This incident, again, shows Webster's characteristic polarity. The mother is giving suck to her child: he breaks the crucifix. Since the crucifix has been mended, she is entirely without fear: at that very moment: Enter Flamineo. *Flamineo runnes Marcello through.* The thought is mirrored twice, in the language, and in the action.

Cornelia is at first deceived by appearances. She cannot believe that Marcello is dead, "he is not dead, hee's in a trance" (V. ii. 29). There is a tragic chasm here between appearance and reality. Brachiano enters and Cornelia, in a moment of superb greatness, lies to him in order to save Flamineo's life. She is torn between two emotions, love for the murdered son and love for the son that murdered him. The only thing that could come out of these twisted emotions was the lie. And now to illustrate the sharpness of Webster's irony, we are compelled to reproduce the text as it stands.

> FLA: [to the Duke]. At your pleasure.
> *Lodovico sprinkles Brachiano's bever with a poison.*
> Your will is law now—Ile not meddle with it.
>
> (75-6)

Webster mingles many figures in this short passage, all focussed on the falseness of appearances. Brachiano's will is law *now,* in a few seconds he will be dead. At the same time Lodovico secretly sprinkles poison into the strong helmet that Brachiano will put on his head in order to protect his life. And of course there is the treachery of Lodovico, disguised as a monk, and therefore honored as a guest, evil concealed under a robe of religion.

At the moment of death Brachiano repeats the actions of his wife as she was dying. She had prevented those about her from touching the poisoned picture. Brachiano says to Vittoria: "Do not kisse me, for I shall poyson thee" (V. iii. 27). In this repetition there is terror. The moral law has not been mocked, it has vindicated itself with a resolute exactness. "An eye for an eye . . ." But further, Brachiano speaks the horrible truth about his love. It was posion for Vittoria.

At the end of Brachiano's life he sees the false show dissolve and he is confronted with the terrible reality. He is made to see the full horror of his life and of death. In death, "horrour waights on Princes" (35). His agonized ravings seem to be nonsense but they make grim sense. He speaks of quails (i.e., loose women) who feed on poison. He sees the Devil come to visit him. And when Vittoria says "heer's nothing," he answers: "Nothing? rare! nothing! when I want monie, / Our treasurie is emptie; there is nothing, / Ile not bee us'd thus" (V. iii. 107-09). So far as he is concerned, this answer sums up the play. His adventure with Vittoria promised happiness and he has had nothing.

And then comes the last false show. The two assassins enter, disguised as friars. They hold up the crucifix to him. Then they throw off their disguise and reveal themselves to him. They add to his torments by piling reproaches on him, they call him devil, they say his art was poison. They glory in detailing to him the poisons that are melting his brains. But on the very threshold of death Brachiano's love finds its final great expression. He shouts "Vittoria! Vittoria!" His love is still undefeated and in his extremity he calls to her for help. It reminds one of "Pompilia, will you let them murder me."

Here Webster achieves a level of greatness in understanding the depth of a man's soul which he sustains throughout the play. Brachiano has murdered his wife and the husband of his mistress, but he is yet capable of a deep and selfless love for the woman he dishonors. Appearances deceive in two ways; they disguise the good as well as the evil. It would appear that two people so debased and ruthless as Vittoria and Brachiano must be incapable of a great love. But in Webster no one is thoroughly evil. After Vittoria and Brachiano have committed all their crimes and their expectations have turned against them, this love, a source of so much evil and suffering, remains a thing of strength and beauty. Probably in his final cry "Vittoria! Vittoria!" Brachiano transcends his crimes and brings salvation upon himself. Webster shows the same transfiguration in Vittoria, who, on learning of Brachiano's death, exclaims, "O well! this place is hell!"

Vittoria comes running in but the pretended friars push her out of the room. "What! will you call him again / To live in treble torments? *for charitie, / For Christian charitie,* avoid the chamber." (172-74). Once more the grim irony, the fairest of appearances is used to conceal the foulest of crimes. As quickly as possible, to prevent any

more interruptions, Lodovico strangles Brachiano with "a true love-knot" sent from the Duke of Florence.

In the concluding scenes Webster rings the changes on the figures he has been employing throughout the play. Lodovico and Gasparo enter, still disguised as churchmen, and confront Vittoria and Flamineo with the horrible truth that they are to die. Vittoria pleads:

> O your gentle pitty:
> I have seene a black-bird that would sooner fly
> To a mans bosome, then to stay the gripe
> Of the feirce Sparrow-hawke.
>
> GAS: Your hope deceives you.
>
> (V. vi. 184-87)

This is a terrible speech, fundamental to the play. Man, made in the image of his Creator, is false to this image. He is viler in his cruelty than the beasts. And hope in this play always deceives.

Webster repeats the idea of false show when he makes Vittoria appeal to Lodovico: "You, my Deathsman! / Me thinkes thou doest not looke horrid enough, / Thou hast to[o] good a face to be a hang-man" (210-12). But Lodovico is as pitiless as Gasparo. In his turn he calls her "thou glorious strumpet," that is, she is still the white devil, her glorious beauty covering only foulness. But the truth is, she is now really glorious. Both she and Flamineo are great in death. Webster plays on the word *glorious.* Flamineo says:

> Th'art a noble sister,
> I love thee now . . .
> Know many glorious woemen that are fam'd
> For masculine vertue, have bin vitious,
> Onely a happier silence did betyde them.
> Shee hath no faults, who hath the art to hide them.
>
> (241-47)

Part of this problem of appearance and reality arises from the greatness of soul which is revealed or uncovered in the "devils" of the play. Strip some veils of appearance from them and they are foul, strip those other veils from them and their hearts are seen to harbor an inviolable greatness.

Webster does not leave us without reverting to another principal figure—the deceitfulness of fortune.

> VIT: My soule, like to a ship in a blacke storme,
> Is driven I know not whither.
>
> FLA: Then cast ancor.
> Prosperity doth bewitch men seeming cleere,
> But seas doe laugh, shew white, when Rocks are neere.
>
> (248-51)

Finally the end of the play curiously echoes the beginning. Giovanni has the last word: "Let guilty men remember their blacke deedes, / Do leane on crut[c]hes, made of slender reedes." To the last bitter word of the play men's trust is deceived. In *The White Devil* Webster was something of a pioneer. Rich as Elizabethan drama is in imagery, nobody before Webster had elaborated a system of figure so intricately linked and so profound. (pp. 718-30)

Hereward T. Price, "The Function of Imagery in Webster," in PMLA, *Vol. LXX, No. 4, September, 1955, pp. 717-39.*

D. C. Gunby   (essay date 1971)

[*In the following excerpt, Gunby surveys the various literary influences on Webster's composition of* The White Devil *and argues that the author carefully wove his source material into a play that is "rich in character and incident" and "subtly planned and executed."*]

Few plays in English have generated greater critical disagreement than **The White Devil**. A recent editor [John Russell Brown], picking his way through a tangle of conflicting opinions, summarised the situation thus:

> Critical opinion cannot speak with certain or united voice about Webster's purposes; it has proved possible to talk of him as an old-fashioned moralist, as a sensationalist, as a social dramatist, as an imagist or dramatic symphonist, as a man fascinated by death, or a man halting between his inherited and his individual values.

This diversity of critical approaches, although confusing, represents a challenge, testifying as it does to the depth and complexity of the play. In making our own way to the heart of **The White Devil,** we need constantly to remind ourselves of this complexity and to test the approach adopted here against those suggested by other critics.

THE DRAMATIST AND HIS AIMS

The slowness and difficulty with which John Webster wrote were, it seems, common knowledge in the literary circles of Jacobean London. When, in 1617, one Henry Fitzjeffrey of Lincoln's Inn wished to attack Webster, he found the most telling satiric thrust to be a portrait of 'Crabbed *(Websterio)* / The Play-wright, Cart-wright' in the throes of composition:

> Was ever man so mangl'd with a *Poem*?
> See how he draws his mouth awry of late,
> How he scrubs: wrings his wrests: scratches his
>   *Pate.*
> A *Midwife*! helpe! By his *Braines coitus,*
> Some *Centaure* strange: some huge *Bucephalus,*
> Or *Pallas* (sure) ingendred in his *Braine,*
> Strike, *Vulcan,* with thy hammer once againe.

It may be that **The White Devil** was written with even greater deliberation than usual or simply that in this, his first major unaided venture, Webster felt more vulnerable than in later years to criticism of his artistic method. Whatever the reason, in the address to the reader with which he prefaced the 1612 Quarto of the play, the dramatist devotes some time to replying to 'those who report I was a long time in finishing this tragedy'. 'I confess', he says,

> I do not write with a goose-quill, winged with two feathers, and if they will needs make it my fault, I must answer them with that of Euripides to Alcestides, a tragic writer: Alcestides objecting that Euripides had only in three days composed three verses, whereas himself had written

three hundred: 'Thou tell'st truth,' (quoth he) 'but here's the difference,—thine shall be read for three days, whereas mine shall continue three ages.'

Webster provides further evidence of the scale against which he wished to be measured when, at the end of the preface, he names those fellow dramatists in whose company he would be read:

> Detraction is the sworn friend to ignorance: for mine own part I have ever truly cherish'd my good opinion of other men's worthy labours, especially of that full and height'ned style of Master Chapman, the labour'd and understanding works of Master Jonson: the no less worthy composures of the both worthily excellent Master Beaumont, and Master Fletcher: and lastly (without wrong last to be named) the right happy and copious industry of Master Shakespeare, Master Dekker, and Master Heywood, wishing what I write may be read by their light:

Though the list is catholic, setting essentially lightweight writers like [Thomas] Dekker and [Thomas] Heywood cheek by jowl with [Ben] Jonson and Shakespeare, it makes Webster's critical preferences very plain. For though he praises the ease and fluency of Shakespeare, Dekker and Heywood, and offers a generalised tribute to Beaumont and Fletcher, he reserves pride of place for the 'full and height'ned style of Master Chapman' and 'the labour'd and understanding works of Master Jonson'.

In seeking to emulate these two writers in the creation of tragedy learned and weighty enough to stand comparison with those of the ancients, Webster recognised, as Jonson and [George] Chapman did, the impossibility of adhering in every particular to the forms of Greek and Roman tragedy. Borrowing at length, significantly enough, from Jonson's preface to his first learned tragedy, *Sejanus* (1605), Webster explains this fact to his reader:

> If it be objected this is no true dramatic poem, I shall easily confess it,—*non potes in nugas dicere plura meas: ipso ego quam dixi,*—willingly, and not ignorantly, in this kind have I faulted: for should a man present to such an auditory, the most sententious tragedy that ever was written, observing all the critical laws, as height of style, and gravity of person, enrich it with the sententious *Chorus,* and as it were lifen death, in the passionate and weighty *Nuntius:* yet after all this divine rapture, *O dura messorum ilia,* the breath that comes from the uncapable multitude is able to poison it.

We may wonder, perhaps, to what extent a disclaimer of this kind demonstrated more the writer's competence in and familiarity with the formal austerities of classical drama than his desire to write according to this convention. But at the same time we must recognise that he is setting up the critical laws of the ancients as standards to be aspired to. The chorus and nuntius might have to be dispensed with, Jonson admitted in his preface to *Sejanus,* and also the 'strict Lawes of *Time*', but 'the other offices of a *Tragick* writer'—'truth of argument, dignity of persons, grauity and height of Elocution, fulnesse and frequencie of Sentence'—could—and should—be discharged.

These 'offices', his preface implies, Webster too upheld. With them, therefore, an examination of *The White Devil* should begin.

TRUTH OF ARGUMENT

Although the copious marginal documentation of his two learned tragedies, *Sejanus* and *Catiline,* shows his respect for a detailed knowledge of the historical events he was dramatising, Jonson did not believe that 'truth of argument' meant simply 'historicity of argument'. Like Chapman, he believed that

> hee is call'd a *Poet,* not hee which writeth in measure only; but that fayneth and formeth a fable, and writes things like the Truth. For, the Fable and Fiction is (as it were) the forme and Soule of any Poeticall work, or *Poeme.*

As a historian Jonson sought to remain true to his sources. As a poet and dramatist, he knew that he was entitled to shape a historical argument, providing it with a form and unity which, merely re-told, it would not possess.

The historical facts which lie behind *The White Devil* are these. Vittoria Accoramboni was born at Gubbio, a small town in the Apennines, on 15 February 1557. The family was poor, though of good standing, and Vittoria, as one of eleven children, came to realise that her future prosperity depended upon her beauty, which was considerable. Her mother, who was of the same opinion, took her to Rome, where she met, fell in love with, and (in June 1573) was married to Francesco Peretti, a nephew of Cardinal Montalto. At first all went well, but Vittoria was gay and given to extravagance, while Francesco was very much under the thumb of his stern and parsimonious uncle, and trouble developed to a point at which Vittoria began looking for a wealthier protector. In 1580 she found one (perhaps through the agency of her brother, Marcello, then the Duke's chamberlain) in Paolo Giordano Orsini, Duke of Bracciano.

Bracciano had been married in 1558 to Isabella de Medici, by whom he had had three children, including, in 1572, a son and heir, Virginio. In 1576, however, he had discovered that Isabella had a lover, a distant relative of his named Troilo Orsini, and she had died in suspicious circumstances, probably strangled by Bracciano himself. In 1581 he took steps to provide as conveniently for the freedom of Vittoria, by having Peretti murdered in the street. Within a fortnight Bracciano and Vittoria were married in secret.

The next four years the couple spent trying to reverse or evade an order from the Pope, Gregory XIII, that they should separate. Vittoria herself spent a period in Castel St. Angelo, during which, temporarily abandoned by Bracciano, she tried unsuccessfully to commit suicide. Upon her release, however, the liaison was resumed, and in October 1583 the couple were married a second time, in public at Bracciano. Just as a further enforced separation seemed inevitable Pope Gregory died. During the interregnum Bracciano, having secured the opinion of pliant theologians that the prohibitions imposed by the previous Pope had died with him, married Vittoria a third time. Within hours their arch-enemy, Cardinal Montalto, was proclaimed Pope, taking the title of Sixtus V.

Curiously enough the new Pope did not exact the vengeance that might have been expected, though they continued to suffer his severe disfavour. Accordingly the Duke and his wife left Rome, travelling first to Venice, then Padua, and finally, on account of his deteriorating health, to Salo on Lake Garda. There, on 13 November 1585, he died. Vittoria, after an outburst of despair in which she tried to shoot herself, settled down to enjoy her very comfortable widowhood, having been lavishly provided for in Bracciano's will. This very lavishness was, however, her undoing, for the Medici relatives of Bracciano's first wife became alarmed at the inroads being made upon the inheritance of the Duke's heir, Virginio. After seeking to reach a compromise, which Vittoria refused, they decided to have her murdered. The task was undertaken by a kinsman and former confidant of Bracciano, Lodovico Orsini, who invaded her palace at the head of a band of followers, and killed both Vittoria and her young brother Flamineo. Four days later (on 27 December 1585) Lodovico, having been found guilty by the authorities in Padua, was executed. Within the next few days many of his followers suffered the same fate.

That the facts of history and Webster's dramatisation of them differ in many respects is at once apparent. There are, firstly, numerous changes of name: Francesco Peretti, for example, becomes Camillo, while his uncle, Cardinal Montalto, is renamed Monticelso. Secondly, there are changes of role. Historically, both Isabella de Medici and Vittoria's mother were less than admirable: Webster makes them both virtuous. Lastly, there are alterations to the pattern of events. Historically, Isabella's death had nothing to do with Bracciano's love for Vittoria, but took place four years prior to their first meeting. The manner of Bracciano's death too is altered. In the play he is poisoned: in fact he died a natural death; a victim of his obesity. Nor is there historical warrant for Flamineo's cowardly murder of Marcello, or Cornelia's madness, while Lodovico's capture was actually accomplished only after a regular siege of the palace in which he had taken refuge.

For these departures from history two explanations are possible. The first is that the sources of Webster's information were themselves inaccurate. The second is that he deliberately altered the facts to meet his artistic requirements.

What we know of the sources suggests that they were, to some extent, responsible for Webster's divergences from historical fact. If Dr. Gunnar Boklund [in *The Sources of The White Devil,* 1957] is right, then Webster's primary source was one of a regular series of newsletters sent to the Fugger banking family in Augsburg by one of its many Italian agents. From this letter he would have gathered not only the broad outlines of the whole affair, but also several major departures from fact: that Isabella was still alive when Bracciano met Vittoria; that the Duke's son was named Giovanni; that Lodovico himself stabbed Vittoria; and that the Pope took no further part in the pursuit of Vittoria after Bracciano's death. He would also have learned that 'foul play was suspected' over the death of Bracciano. The Fugger newsletter was certainly not Webster's only source, however. The manner in which Brachiano is poisoned is probably taken from Boaistuau's *Theatrum Mundi,* where we learn of a certain Florentine knight who 'died suddenly' after his helmet was poisoned during a tournament, while the behaviour of the two 'friars' at the bedside of the dying man is borrowed from [Desiderius] Erasmus' colloquy, *Funus.* For the details of the conclave scene two sources are possible. The less likely is John Florio's *A Letter Lately Written from Rome* (1585), which recounts the death of Gregory XIII and the election of Sixtus V. The other is Hierome Bignon's *A Brief, but an Effectuall Treatise of the Election of Popes* (1605), which, though dealing with the election of Leo II in 1605, relates more closely to the scene in *The White Devil.*

Even taking into account all the proven inaccuracies of source, however, we are left with a considerable number of changes which must, unless a hitherto undiscovered source comes to light, be taken as Webster's own. Some of these we may put down to his desire to tighten the structure of his digressive and episodic tale. The capture of Lodovico and his accomplices immediately after the murders achieves this end. So, too, does the conflation, in the career of Webster's Flamineo, of aspects of the lives of two of Vittoria's brothers; the villainous Marcello, and Flamineo, the innocent sufferer in the final calamity. Other changes are dictated by Webster's dramatic sense. Vittoria married to the young Peretti would have to be unequivocally condemned for her behaviour towards her husband: Vittoria married to Camillo may be felt to have some cause for dissatisfaction, if not for inciting her lover to murder him. Similarly, the great trial scene (III, ii), though without warrant in history, is essential to the play: the lingering incarceration which Vittoria in fact suffered formed no workable basis for dramatic action of the kind Webster sought.

Finally, the didactic purpose in some of Webster's alterations, sometimes secondary to his dramatic or aesthetic motives and sometimes paramount, cannot be ignored. The creation of Marcello and the unhistorical virtues of Cornelia and Isabella are examples of this didactic purpose: like Marcello, the two women are needed as examples of virtue by which others may be measured. There are didactic implications, too, in the manner of Brachiano's death, in the creation of Zanche, in Francisco's choice of disguise, and in the grotesque mock-death which Flamineo stages at the beginning of the final scene. All of these changes reinforce the meaning which Webster perceived in the chronicle-like formlessness of the original narrative, a meaning which seemed to him to justify his reshaping of the facts of history in pursuit of 'truth of argument'.

DIGNITY OF PERSONS

The 'dignity of persons' which Jonson lists among the 'offices of a *Tragick* writer', and whose value Webster also recognised, is an expression of the important Renaissance critical concept of decorum. The principles of universality and verisimilitude upon which this concept chiefly relied had their origin in Aristotle's four basic requirements for characterisation: that characters should be good; that they should be drawn with propriety (that is, true to type); that they should be true to life; and that they should be self-consistent. The *reductio ad absurdum* of these general and undogmatic observations was the elaborate critical structure developed chiefly by Italian theorists whose concern was the detailed prescription of the proper traits for every character-type in the dramatist's range.

Both as dramatist and as critic, Jonson rejected such prescriptions. 'I am not of that opinion', he remarks in *Discoveries,* 'to conclude a *Poets* liberty within the narrowe limits of lawes, which either the *Grammarians,* or *Philosophers* prescribe. For, before they found out those Lawes, there were many excellent Poets, that fulfill'd them. He did not abandon the concept of decorum, but, holding that 'rules are ever of lesse force, and valew, then experiments' he chose to rely on his own experience and judgement rather than theoretical prescriptions.

Webster, as *The White Devil* proves, also combines adherence to critical precepts with a pragmatic approach to their application. In striving for what he calls 'gravity of person' he creates characters sufficiently typical to satisfy the requirements of decorum, yet at the same time distinctively individual. Brachiano and Francisco, for example, are both Dukes, and both portrayed as such. Yet while sharing that dignity of mien and awareness of rank which decorum demanded of an aristocrat, they differ quite radically in other respects. Brachiano is brave, as a Duke should be (cowardice being allowed only among the lower orders of society), but his courage is of the noisy, obvious kind, and accompanied by a tendency to bully and bluster. Francisco, on the other hand, is devious, and chooses to undermine his opponent rather than attack him openly. In part such differences too can be attributed to decorum, which demands that men should be shown as old or young, and not as inhabitants of the no-man's-land of middle age, so that Webster varies history to make Brachiano a young man, subject to the fiery impetuosity of the typical youth, and his brother-in-law and contemporary, Francisco, old and experienced. Other influences can be traced, however, in the individualisation of Webster's characters. One is humour psychology, with its definition of four basic personality types reinforcing the concept of the typical inherent in the idea of decorum. Another is the native tradition in English drama, the morality play, which while dealing basically in types of vice and virtue, added individual and highly realistic detail in the interests of immediacy. In Brachiano, therefore, the attributes of the choleric man are added to those of the young Duke, while Francisco is not merely an old Duke, but also phlegmatic in temperament and a descendant of the morality vice.

The other major characters exhibit the same combination of the typical and the individual. Monticelso is a Cardinal, sharing characteristics with the princes of the Church found in *The Duchess of Malfi,* Middleton's *Women Beware Women,* and Shirley's *The Cardinal.* Yet he holds our interest as a individual, a man who, by contrast with Francisco, begins by seeking revenge but ends by abjuring it. Isabella, for her part, is type-cast as the noble and faithful wife, but individualised as more than this, while in Giovanni sufficient is added to the stock portrait of the child prince to make him one of the more attractive of the children in Jacobean drama. Lodovico, like Bosola after him, is in some respects a reluctant villain, recognising the claims of morality even as he flouts them.

Decorum demanded a strict division between the characters of one social class and another. In Marcello and Cornelia, types of the honest soldier and virtuous mother, we find this class distinction clearly observed. With Flamineo, the university-educated secretary, it is less clearcut, though we are kept aware of the differences in social standing between him and his employer as well as, in a more subtle way, between him and his counterpart in the malcontent tradition, Lodovico. In Vittoria, however, social distinctions are thoroughly blurred. One minute vulgarly vituperative, she can in the next display courage, wit and eloquence equalling (and in some ways surpassing) the aristocratic magnificence of Brachiano, Francisco and Monticelso. In so doing, of course, she also violates another of decorum's basic tenets. Aristotle observed that 'There is a type of manly valour; but valour in a woman, or unscrupulous cleverness, is inappropriate.' Vittoria, who admits that in self-defence she is forced to 'personate masculine virtue', combines masculine traits and feminine in a way which blatantly violates the distinctions demanded between the sexes. This blurring of accepted canons might support Ian Jack's complaint [in 'The Case of John Webster', *Scrutiny*, XVI, 1949] that Webster commits an 'artistic insincerity' in making the guilty Vittoria seem innocent. In fact it not only makes Vittoria one of the most complex and intriguing of Jacobean heroines, but also serves to warn us against the combination of attractiveness and criminality which the epithet 'white devil' comprehends.

GRAVITY AND HEIGHT OF ELOCUTION

Renaissance man inherited a tradition which placed a high value on the art of rhetoric and ascribed a deep significance to language. 'No glasse', says Jonson in *Discoveries*,

> renders a mans forme, or likenesse, so true as his speech. Nay, it is likened to a man; and as we consider feature, and composition in a man; so words in Language: in the greatnesse, aptnesse, sound, structure, and harmony of it.

It is not surprising, therefore, to find the doctrine of decorum extended to cover what a man says as well as how he acts, or to find theorists like Minturno prescribing in detail what is appropriate, both in manner and in matter, in the speech of the different character-types. In determining this, however, critics were guided not only by the character and status of the speaker, but also by the genre to which the work in which he appeared belongs. Confusing what in Aristotle is an ethical distinction between men 'above our own level of goodness, or beneath it, or just as we are', the Italian theorists determined that tragedy, as the highest of the forms of scenic (or dramatic) poetry, demanded the depiction of persons of noble birth. To do justice to this combination of noble themes and aristocratic characters, decorum and the theory of genres alike demanded an 'elevated' style, *sublime* or *altisonum.*

While generally cavalier in their attitude to other rules governing the 'correct' writing of tragedy, English dramatists agreed that, for the tragic protagonists at least, it was necessary to achieve what Jonson calls 'gravity and height of elocution' and Webster 'height of style'. In search of this goal, Webster pursued—to a degree unequalled, so far as is known, by any other dramatist of the time—a policy of literary borrowing.

The knowledge that more than three-quarters of all that Webster wrote was borrowed from the works of others comes as a shock in an age critical of plagiarism. To the Jacobean, however, reared in a rhetorical tradition which commended 'imitation', borrowing was to be censured only when, as with Thomas Lodge, it took the form of large-scale theft. For the rest,

> this is one kinde of fruit gotten by readinge, that a man may imitate that which he lyketh and alloweth in others, and such speciall poyntes and sayinges as hee is especially delighted & in loue withall, by apt and fitte deriuation maye wrest to serue his owne turne and purpose [Franciscus Patricius, *A Moral Methode of ciuile Policie*, 1576].

The style which Webster forges by making his borrowings 'serue his owne turne and purpose' reflects to some extent the method of composition. Tense and tightly-knit, the speeches present themselves not as sustained poetic utterances (there are only a handful of these, all formalised in some way, in the entire play), but as a series of phrases or fragments of sense. The effect, which constant variations in the pace and tone of the verse reinforce, is of a nervous and at times disjunctive movement, with almost epigrammatic intensity of significance. Often elliptical in grammar and syntax, intricate in its shifts of thought and feeling, and full of puns and quibbles, Webster's language demands close and constant attention. This it repays by its richness and diversity, its subtle ironies and moments of utter simplicity, and its ability to convey nuances of character. It repays us, above all, in its imagery, which, as in Flamineo's warning to Marcello, 'When age shall turn thee / White as a blooming hawthorn', reveals that quality of unexpectedness, that capacity to relate the apparently unrelated or invert accepted metaphoric associations, which is characteristically metaphysical. It is paradoxical that, admiring Jonson and Chapman, and striving to emulate their achievements in the tragic mode, Webster developed an 'elevated' style which has little in common with theirs, but much with the poetry of John Donne.

FULLNESS AND FREQUENCY OF SENTENCE

To sixteenth-century men, the chief function of literature was didactic. Among Italian critics, only [Lodovico] Castelvetro disagreed, claiming that 'poetry was invented exclusively to delight and give recreation'. Prudently, in opposing a generally held critical 'truth', he went to Aristotle for his defence:

> Those who insist that poetry was invented mainly to profit, or to profit and delight together, let them beware lest they oppose the authority of Aristotle, who . . . seems to assign nothing but pleasure to it; and if, indeed, he concedes some

utility to it, he concedes it accidentally, as is the case with the purgation of fear and of pity by means of tragedy.

Not unexpectedly, orthodox theorists also cited Aristotle, linking his concept of *catharsis* and the demand for 'goodness' among the requisites for character with Horace's *prodesse* and *utile* and the Platonic notion of utility, to produce a case for the primacy of instruction over delight. To the modern mind, this argument seems highly suspect, involving a distortion of Aristotle's meaning, as well as a highly selective reading of Horace's description of the role of the poet as 'aut prodesse . . . aut delectare . . . aut simul et iucunda et idonea dicere vitae' (*either* to profit *or* to delight *or* to utter words at once both pleasing and helpful to life). To the sixteenth-century writer or critic, however, steeped in a medieval Christian tradition as well as a classical pagan one, it seemed both right and natural that poetry should assume the function of moral philosophy, just as it seemed logical to derive from Aristotle's theories a view of tragedy as moralistic as this of Minturno's:

> the tragic poet . . . sets before us the characters . . . of men who seem in the eyes of other men to be outstanding for their dignity, power, and indeed every favour of fortune, and nevertheless sink to extreme unhappiness because of some human error. This he does so that we may see that no trust is to be put in the smooth course of events, that there is nothing on earth so lasting and stable that it cannot fall and die, nothing so firm and strong that it cannot be overthrown, nothing so happy and exalted that it cannot be made unhappy and brought low; and so that when we contemplate so great a change of fortune in others, we may take heed lest misfortunes come to us against our hope and against our expectation, and so that when they do happen—since things of this sort are wont to happen to men—we may bear them with an un-ruffled soul.

In emphasising these lessons, *sententiae* or generalised moral comments were assigned a major role. All the English dramatists used them: some, like Fletcher, in a perfunctory and extraneous fashion; others, like [John] Marston, Chapman and Jonson, as an integral part of the moral structure of their plays. No one, however, makes more frequent use of the 'sentence', or assigns it a more important role, than Webster. Unable, as he tells us in his prefatory address, to 'enrich' *The White Devil* with a 'sententious *Chorus*' because of 'the uncapable multitude', he follows the next best course, and distributes his choric commentary amongst the leading characters.

In the Quarto of 1612 these choric statements are often distinguished typographically, as at IV. ii. 246-47 or V. vi. 250-54. Just as often, however, a maxim will appear (because, it seems, of the differing habits of the two compositors employed in setting the play) without typographical indication. In I, i, for example, at least seven passages warrant consideration as *sententiae,* including the final couplet:

> Great men sell sheep, thus to be cut in pieces,
> When first they have shorn them bare and sold
>   their fleeces.
>
>   (I. i. 62-3)

Marked or unmarked, however, the maxims scattered so liberally throughout *The White Devil* play an important part in forming and controlling our response to the action.

A similar effect is achieved through the use of the tale, examples of which occur in *The White Devil* at II, i, 335-56 and IV, ii, 222-35. Until recently, critics generally deplored Webster's use of these set-pieces, joining Rupert Brooke [in *John Webster and the Elizabethan Drama,* 1916] in labelling them 'long-winded, irrelevant, and fantastically unrealistic'. Recognition that the tales are not irrelevant, but bear strongly upon the events they interrupt, has brought with it a better understanding of Webster's aims, and an awareness that only through extensive stylisation can he create the extra-dramatic interludes necessary for chorically directed reflection.

What is the audience to reflect upon? What are the lessons which *The White Devil* seeks to convey? In answering we must, I think, distinguish between (without separating) two levels of didactic intention: the immediate and the ultimate. On the immediate level, the play has much to say about the perils of court life, and the illusory nature of greatness. The reader is to learn, in Webster's own words, of 'courtly reward and punishment', and having discovered that 'Glories, like glow-worms, afar off shine bright / But look'd to near, have neither heat nor light', to conclude, with Vittoria: 'O happy they that never saw the court, / Nor ever knew great man but by report'. More importantly, he is to recognise the futility of the parasite's frenzied search for advancement, and acknowledge, as Flamineo belatedly does, that 'rest breeds rest, where all seek pain by pain'.

Underlying these lessons are others more universal in significance. 'While we look up to heaven we confound / Knowledge with knowledge', says the dying Flamineo. Webster is at pains to prevent his reader making a similar mistake by stressing the indivisibility of the material and the spiritual, and placing the everyday in an eternal perspective. Life and death, heaven and hell, salvation and damnation; these form the frame of reference within which Webster demonstrates the workings of a pattern of retribution as apt as it is inexorable, and proves that, despite the sufferings of the virtuous, good must eventually triumph over evil.

Described thus, *The White Devil* might be taken for a medieval morality play, austere in form, simplistic in its underlying assumptions, and single-minded in its presentation of a thesis. . . . [It] is, in fact, none of these things; . . . despite the Augustinian rigour of the beliefs upon which it is founded, the play is rich in character and incident, subtly planned and executed, and, as the critical conflicts over its meaning prove, far from obvious. Nor does this imply a conflict between the play's meaning and its form. On the contrary, the very richness of *The White Devil* reinforces its message. Vittoria is a white devil, but she is also a brilliant and resourceful woman, beautiful, courageous and highly intelligent, and we cannot help responding to her with some sympathy and warmth. In doing so we are not only paying tribute to Webster's ability to create a living character, but also demonstrating the force of his argument by following, to some extent, in the footsteps of Brachiano. Adapting Marshall McLuhan's famous phrase, we might say that in *The White Devil* the medium is part of the message. (pp. 7-20)

D. C. Gunby, in his Webster: The White Devil, *Edward Arnold, 1971, 64 p.*

THE DUCHESS OF MALFI

PRODUCTION REVIEWS

The Times, London   (review date 25 November 1919)

[*In the following review of the 1919 Phoenix Society production of* The Duchess of Malfi, *the critic maintains that the play is "no longer a live classic, but a museum-classic, a curio for connoisseurs"; nevertheless, he praises Cathleen Nesbitt's Duchess and William Rea's Bosola.*]

The difficulty of reviving a Jacobean "tragedy of blood" in this sceptical age of ours is that just when the author, like the Fat Boy, "wants to make your flesh creep" he is more likely to provoke you to laughter. There was certainly some tittering yesterday afternoon towards the close of *The Duchess of Malfi,* when Bosola killed first Antonio and then the Cardinal and then Duke Ferdinand, but not till after Ferdinand had run him through the body, so that there were four corpses on the floor in a heap.

Why does the multiplication table have this disturbing effect? Why is one violent death tragic, while four at once become comic? But Webster has other means of making your flesh creep, which have by no means lost their efficacy. No one, we think, was tempted even to smile at the ghastly incidents by which the poor Duchess was mentally tortured, before being strangled—the severed hand thrust into hers, the silent entry of the masked and hooded executioners bearing her coffin, and, "creepiest" of all, her encirclement by a crowd of gibbering, wailing madmen. After these horrors, her death by the cord—a quiet, almost peaceful martyrdom—came as a relief. This, at any rate, was on the true tragic level, and there is a good deal of poetry (though more of ratiocination) in the play, with a phrase here and there that thrills you—Ferdinand's "laughing hyena" and Delio's "these wretched eminent things." But to get yourself back into the frame of mind of the original public for whom Burbage played Ferdinand, or even of the later public for whom Betterton played Bosola, is, we fear, out of the question. In other words, *The Duchess of Malfi* is no longer a live classic, but a museum-classic, a curio for connoisseurs.

But if the play as a whole, as an organic work of art, can now only be taken historically, some of its personages are still live enough and still interesting. Duke Ferdinand appeals to us as a good specimen of a Renaissance monster of deadly hate and fiendish cruelty. (He was played by Mr.

Robert Farquharson, an old hand at these monsters, whose style and whose very affectations are in keeping with the monstrous.) The Cardinal (Mr. Ion Swinley) is by comparison a tame villain, but a good *cinquecento* type, too, toying with his mistress in his scarlet robes, and poisoning her when she becomes a nuisance. Antonio, the honest husband (Mr. Nicholas Hannen), cuts rather a poor, passive figure, consulting his own safety and deserting his wife.

But the martyred Duchess is a creation of pure beauty, the one ennobling element in the tragedy, and beautifully, nobly, she was played by Miss Cathleen Nesbitt. And Bosola, the villain, introspective, moralizing, philosophic, is of fascinating interest—as curious a study in criminal pathology as Iago himself. Mr. William Rea played him with an air of melancholy reverie and aloofness which gave him immense distinction. Nor did a certain Irish accent do any harm, for English spoken by an Irishman has always the blest merit of clear enunciation.

A review of "The Duchess of Malfi," in The Times, *London, November 25, 1919, p. 10.*

The Times, London   (review date 19 April 1945)

[*In 1945 George Rylands produced* The Duchess of Malfi *at London's Haymarket Theatre with a cast that included the noted Shakespearean actors John Gielgud, Peggy Ashcroft, Cecil Trouncer, and Leon Quartermaine. In the following review, the critic lauds the entire production, particularly Trouncer's Bosola.*]

Of the several revivals in recent years of Webster's "tragedy of blood"—each an unavailing attempt to reanimate a classic which time has tamed—this is the most resolute.

Mr. John Gielgud and his producer, Mr. George Rylands, indeed the whole of their company, have meant business. Not much more in the way of staging and acting could well be done to put us into the frame of mind of the original public for whom Burbage played Ferdinand. And the reward of all this care and accomplishment last night was that the audience, though naturally it could not discard its thwarting modernity, followed all that happened on the stage with a respectful curiosity which rose at times to emotional sympathy and never once descended to misplaced tittering.

Those who know the play and the almost insuperable problems which it sets the present-day producer will not regard such praise as faint. That we do not smile at the heap of corpses on which the final curtain falls implies that the actors have fixed attention with Ferdinand's soul-stricken ravings, with the Cardinal's unequal struggle against implacable fate, and with Bosola's strangely intense remorse—thus flouting Johnson's opinion that the genius of the play comes in and goes out with the Duchess.

It is true, however, that while the Duchess lives in the person of Miss Peggy Ashcroft, the players' adventure seems less perilous than it afterwards becomes. Her wooing of the steward is delightful in its ease and certainty of touch, and her indiscreet gossipings with her husband, her maid, and the open-eared Bosola have the authentic sparkle that

A scene from a 1946 New York production of The Duchess of Malfi, *with Whitfield Connor as Antonio, Donald Eccles as Ferdinand, and Elisabeth Bergner as the Duchess.*

happiness assumed as a matter of right may confer. Nor does she fail when she is called upon to communicate the horror of the tortures and to reveal the resistant spirit of the doomed woman. The tortures, "the mortification by degrees," are perhaps more decorative than horrible. To be anything else would require an apparatus of grisliness which no modern producer can effectively employ, resolute though he may be.

Mr. Gielgud plays Duke Ferdinand less as a Renaissance monster of deadly hate and fiendish cruelty coveting his sister's wealth than as a petulant pervert, a reading to which the text apparently lends itself. But the supreme attraction of the revival is Mr. Cecil Trouncer's superbly vital study of Bosola as a murderer of fortune prematurely aged in the galleys who appears to look deeply into wickedness with the paradoxical desire of seeing good blossom there. Beside this completely observed character the Cardinal of Mr. Leon Quartermaine and the hero of Mr. Leslie Banks are but sketches, though these sketches do not lack accomplishment.

A review of "The Duchess of Malfi," in The Times, *London, April 19, 1945, p. 6.*

James Redfern   (review date 27 April 1945)

[*In the review below, Redfern praises nearly every aspect of George Rylands's 1945 production of* The Duchess of Malfi. *He notes that Peggy Ashcroft's portrayal of the Duchess is done with "an unselfconscious art and a purity of style," that John Gielgud's performance as Ferdinand is "masterly and one of the subtlest, most finished pieces of acting he has ever given us," and that Cecil Trouncer's Bosola is "beyond criticism."*]

It is very rare to find that a long-established reputation is not justified, and this superb production of **The Duchess of Malfi** makes no exception, but is sufficient to prove the greatness of Webster's tragedy as acclaimed by Lamb and the best English critics for centuries. It is indeed a magnificent play, which rivets our attention unfailingly from the brilliant opening scene—which plunges us into the heart of the story—to the death of the noble Duchess; after which a contemporary audience may find itself lacking the staying-power of the Elizabethans and think the scenes in which the guilty murderers meet their just fate superfluous. I was astonished to see that one of the London dailies called the play "out-moded," which statement shows a woeful lack of imagination and seriousness in any writer of these times, when the bloodthirsty, sadistic horrors practised for years in German concentration camps put the crimes of Webster's and other Elizabethan "tragedies of blood" quite in the pale—but also show how much deeper into human nature the dramatists of our classic period were used to dig.

Great drama requires great acting, and I am glad to say that in this fine and deeply satisfying production it gets it. Peggy Ashcroft portrays the noble simplicity of the unhappy Duchess with an unselfconscious art and a purity of style few actresses can command, and only wants a trifle more grandeur to be perfection. John Gielgud's representation of her twin-brother Ferdinand is masterly and one of the subtlest, most finished pieces of acting he has ever given us. If Leon Quartermaine's charm were less natural, and more devilishly calculated his performance as the Cardinal would also have been beyond criticism, as is Cecil Trouncer's magnificent performance as Daniel de Bosola. All good critics have agreed that Webster's invention of this character is an outstanding example of dramatic creation, and those who wonder how it is that honest, loyal men can become the tools of unscrupulous, treacherous and blood-thirsty villains can find in Webster's Bosola a convincing exposition of how and why it can happen. The character of Bosola, indeed, is one of those illuminating revelations by means of which great art helps to explain the actualities of life. As for the character of Ferdinand, it alone is sufficient to prove that long before psycho-analysis and other semi-scientific jargon of the psychologists a gifted writer could delve quite as far into human character as a Freud or any other quasi-medical specialist.

> James Redfern, in a review of "The Duchess of Malfi," in The Spectator, Vol. 174, No. 6096, April 27, 1945, p. 383.

Punch   (review date 2 May 1945)

[*The reviewer here finds Rylands's production of* The Duchess of Malfi *"an uncomfortable form of enchantment" due to the combination of horror and powerful characterization.*]

Round about the cauldron go. There is a strong magic in this midnight. JOHN WEBSTER, thickening the hell-broth with most of the terrors of the Jacobean stage, enchants all that he puts in. It is, to be sure, an uncomfortable form of enchantment. There is no hey-nonny-nonny about it. The Websterian night is feverish: now it stifles, now freezes. ("Methinks 'tis very cold," says *Bosola* to *Antonio,* "and yet you sweat: you look wildly.") With this dramatist we fear to glance behind; the fiend is at our elbow. *The Duchess of Malfi* may be a lesser work than *The White Devil.* We may lament its fifth-act cluster of corpses and the grinding apparatus of horror. Yet who—Mr. Bernard Shaw excepted—can listen in mockery to *Bosola's* dirge (like the rustle of a winding-sheet) or remain quite unaffected by the dews and damps, the fever-chills, the sudden hectic flushes, the charnel-splendours of Webster's verse and prose?

We know next to nothing of this dramatist's life. Even the dates of his birth and death are uncertain. Playgoers admired him as a First Gravedigger, a man about the tomb; none could make more of the worm, the canker, and the grief, or penetrate so shrewdly what *Bosola* in *The Duchess* calls the "shadow, or deep pit of darkness" in which "womanish and fearful" mankind lives. WEBSTER was the Jacobean Theatre Royal: to-day, when he is revived at the Theatre Royal, Haymarket, he can still hold the stage superbly—though not with his once-potent tricks of waxen figures, severed hands, and routs of madmen. (The last *danse macabre* just fails to chill.)

We need not linger over the plot. It is enough to say that the young widowed *Duchess* weds in secret *Antonio,* steward of her household; that her brothers, *Ferdinand Duke of Calabria* and a corrupt Cardinal, respectively wolf and fox, seek her doom; and that *Daniel de Bosola,* a scoundrel with both a downright relish and a curious intricacy of mind, becomes her torturer in a procession of protracted death. The fifth act is the usual mopping-up operation.

Bosola is the play's overmastering part. This mercenary, ripe for any enterprise, has a lurking conscience and an out-and-out way of expressing himself that must have endeared him mightily to his first audiences. Mr. CECIL TROUNCER, skilled in black vesper's pageants, now presents the fellow with a dark pleasure and raises the hair with his utterance of the dirge: " 'Tis now full tide 'tween night and day; End your groan and come away." Few could bring more grace to the *Duchess* than Miss PEGGY ASHCROFT. She commands the part from the rapture of the wooing to the moment when, her face "folded in sorrow," she can say yet: "I am Duchess of Malfi still." *Ferdinand of Calabria,* frenzied and wolfish, is a part to stun the modern actor, but Mr. JOHN GIELGUD sustains its passion. "A very salamander lives in's eye To mock the eager violence of fire." His brother the Cardinal fades before *Ferdinand:* Mr. LEON QUARTERMAINE, rich speaker though he is, lacks the ominous sunset quality of this scarlet sin. Mr. LESLIE BANKS'S *Antonio,* on the other hand, is a good match for the *Duchess.* The actor's charm masks the poorness of the part, which (we are here persuaded) acts better than it reads. Altogether the tragedy has returned to the stage under an auspicious star: it is happy in Mr. GEORGE RYLANDS'S production, and in the sombre magnificence of the sets by Mr. ROGER FURSE.

> J. C. T., in a review of "The Duchess of Malfi," in Punch, Vol. CCVIII, No. 5441, May 2, 1945, p. 382.

CRITICAL COMMENTARY

William Archer   (essay date 1920)

[*A Scottish dramatist and critic, Archer is best known as one of the earliest and most important translators of Henrik Ibsen's plays and as a drama critic of the London stage during the late nineteenth and early twentieth centuries. Archer valued drama as an intellectual product and not as simple entertainment. For that reason he did a great deal to promote the "new drama" of the 1890s, which dealt largely with pressing social and*

"The Masque of the Madmen": lunatics torment the Duchess (Judy Parfitt) in a 1961 Royal Court Theatre production of The Duchess of Malfi.

moral concerns. Throughout his career he protested critical overvaluation of Elizabethan and Restoration drama, claiming that modern works were in many respects equal to or better than their centuries-old predecessors. In the essay below, Archer finds The Duchess of Malfi *a "fundamentally bad" play and charges that Webster's admirers such as Charles Lamb and Algernon Charles Swinburne failed to differentiate between poetic and dramatic merit.*]

The long-delayed reaction against the cult of the lesser Elizabethans, initiated by Charles Lamb and caricatured by Swinburne, is being powerfully promoted by the activities of the Phoenix Society, which has recently been founded for the production of Elizabethan and Restoration plays. John Webster's **Duchess of Malfi,** revived last November at Hammersmith, had a very 'bad Press.' The privilege of listening to its occasional beauties of diction was felt to be dearly bought at the price of enduring three hours of coarse and sanguinary melodrama. But dramatic criticism in these days is so restricted in space that no one, so far as I have seen, has studied the structure of this famous 'masterpiece,' and shown that, even apart from its embroidery of horrors, the play is a fundamentally bad one. It is true that technical standards are not absolute,

but vary in relation to the material conditions of the stage for which a play is designed. But even under Elizabethan conditions, there was nothing, except his singular inexpertness, to prevent Webster from telling his story well. Massinger, or even Middleton, would have made a very different thing of it.

There can be no doubt that the orthodox criticism of the past century placed **The Duchess of Malfi** only a little lower than Shakespeare's greatest tragedies. Lamb's eulogy I shall cite in its due place. For the present let us listen to Swinburne (*Age of Shakespeare*):

> The crowning gift of imagination, the power to make us realise that thus and not otherwise it was, that thus and not otherwise it must have been, was given—except by exceptional fits and starts—to none of the poets of their time but only to Shakespeare and Webster . . . Except in Aeschylus, in Dante and in Shakespeare, I, at least, know not where to seek for passages which in sheer force of tragic and noble horror . . . may be set against the subtlest, the deepest, the sublimest passages of Webster.

Swinburne, it will be noted, ignores structure and development, and centres his attention on 'passages.' Passage-worship is the vice of this whole school of criticism.

Let us now recall to memory the main features of *The Duchess of Malfi.* Lest I be suspected of misrepresenting the plot, I quote the summary of it given by a twentieth-century admirer, the lamented Rupert Brooke (*John Webster and the Elizabethan Drama*):

> The Duchess of Malfi is a young widow forbidden by her brothers Ferdinand and the Cardinal to marry again. They put a creature of theirs, Bosola, into her service as a spy. The Duchess loves and secretly marries her steward, Antonio, and has three children. Bosola ultimately discovers and reports this. Antonio and the Duchess have to fly. The Duchess is captured, imprisoned and mentally tortured, and put to death. Ferdinand goes mad. In the last act he, the Cardinal, Antonio and Bosola are all killed with various confusions and in various horror.

To this concisely accurate argument of the play I will only subjoin that the butcher's bill is by no means complete. Brooke tells only of five corpses: to these we must add the Cardinal's mistress Julia, two of the Duchess's children, her maid Cariola, and a servant—ten in all. The murders in *Hamlet* run to only half that number.

The First Act ushers us slowly into the theme, with a series of character-sketches of the Duchess and her two brothers, delivered by Antonio to his confidant, Delio. Then the 'Arragonian brethren,' as they are called, coarsely and brutally warn their sister against marrying again. It need scarcely be said that they are taking the best possible means to make her defy their tyranny; but Webster might reply that if all men were experts in feminine psychology, drama would disappear both from life and from the stage. A more serious objection to their conduct is that it has no assignable motive. There is not the smallest reason why they should object to their sister's making an open and honourable marriage. Towards the end of the play, this thought seems to strike Ferdinand, and he tells us that

> He had a hope,
> Had she continued widow, to have gained
> An infinite mass of treasure.

But it is hard to guess how this can be, seeing that the Duchess has a surviving son by her first marriage. This son, the reigning Duke of Malfi, is only once alluded to: the Duchess herself seems quite to have forgotten his existence: but it is at one point quite explicitly mentioned, and deprives the conduct of the Duke and Cardinal of the last vestige of reason.

Be this as it may, the brethren instal Bosola, a disreputable soldier of fortune, as their spy or 'intelligencer,' and take themselves off. No sooner are their backs turned than the Duchess sends for Antonio, and, in a scene of some charm, proposes to him a secret union.

In the Second Act, we start a cumbersome underplot, concerned with the Cardinal's mistress, Julia, which serves no purpose except to provide us with a scene of lust and murder in the last Act. We presently find that the Duchess is

about to give birth to a child, and that the lynx-eyed Bosola, though he suspects her condition, has no idea who is the father. We see him ferreting around the Duchess's apartments at the time of her lying-in; and his suspicions are confirmed when he picks up a calculation of the child's nativity which Antonio has casually dropped. What should we say of a modern dramatist who should bring about the revelation of a deadly secret through the inconceivable folly of a leading character, who first composes a compromising document, and then drops it in the actual presence of a man whom he knows to be a spy!

Bosola now takes Antonio to be accessory to the Duchess's amour (he expresses the idea more briefly); but he is apparently incapable of putting two and two together, and so does not suspect him of being the father of the child. He of course informs the Duke and the Cardinal of his discovery, and Ferdinand goes into an epilepsy of fury at the idea of 'the royal blood of Arragon and Castile' being 'thus attainted.' He proposes to 'lay her general territory waste,' to 'hew her to pieces,' to 'make a sponge of her bleeding heart,' and to boil down her child into a broth and administer it to the unknown father. He is an agreeable gentleman, is Ferdinand, Duke of Calabria.

And now comes a curious and characteristic point. In spite of the foaming fury of the Arragonians, they do nothing at all to avenge their precious 'honour,' or to save it from further stains. They stand idly by for at least a couple of years, while the Duchess, at her leisure, bears two more children to Antonio! If there exists a common-sense principle so clear and compulsive that it may fairly be called a law, it is surely that a violent passion, once aroused, must 'ne'er feel retiring ebb, but keep due on' till it has vented itself in destructive action. What should we say if a modern dramatist presented to us such a broken-backed play? It may be urged that Webster was only following his narrative source in giving the Duchess and Antonio three children. But he was under no obligation to follow it. His business was to compress the very prolix narrative, as it appears in [William] Paynter's *Palace of Pleasure,* into a good play. And in Paynter there is no detective set to watch the Duchess. Bosola does not appear until the very end of the story, when he is hired to murder Antonio. What is so ridiculous in Webster is the position of this paid spy, who is a member of the Duchess's household for three years, and watches her producing a surreptitious family, without ever discovering who the father is. Can there be the least doubt that Webster ought to have made the brothers leave their sister unwatched until scandalous rumours reached them, that they should then have sent an agent to find out what was going on, and that, on his discovering the secret, the catastrophe should have followed like a thunder-clap? The part Webster assigns to Bosola is a glaring example of constructive inefficiency.

At last Ferdinand determines to look into matters for himself, and, by an infantile artifice, is made to discover clearly the Duchess's amour, but still without identifying her lover. As there was never any doubt of the fact of her amour, this elaborate scene leaves matters precisely where they stood two years before, except that the Duchess knows she is discovered. This being so, she determines to send Antonio out of danger, by pretending to dismiss him on a charge of peculation. Then Bosola, who has at last begun to suspect Antonio, by feigning to defend his character, lures the Duchess into a confession that he is the father of her children. These two scenes—the Duchess's dismissal of Antonio, and Bosola's discovery of her secret—are really dramatic, showing an adroit application of means to ends. And now, when at last all is out, one naturally expects the action to hurry up a little. But no such matter. Bosola, instead of trying to prevent Antonio's flight, aids and abets the Duchess in her design of following him to Ancona. It is not his fault that she does not entirely elude her brothers' vengeance. The flight to Ancona, it may be said, is part of the original story. But, once more, Webster was in no way bound to follow Paynter; and in the story there is at this point no Bosola to behave with inept inconsistency.

Presently, when he might with advantage have followed Paynter, Webster renounces his guidance. The Duchess having rejoined Antonio, Paynter provides a good reason for their parting again. They see a troop of horse approaching with the evident intention of capturing them; and, as they cannot both escape, the Duchess urges Antonio, who is well mounted, to ride off with their eldest son, she herself, as she fondly believes, having nothing to fear from her brothers. This plausible ground for their separation is ignored by Webster.

We now come to the act—the Fourth—which has earned for Webster the reputation of a superb tragic poet. Antonio has escaped to Milan, and the Duchess is back in Amalfi, where Ferdinand favours her with a visit. Alleging that he has 'rashly made a solemn vow never to see her again,' he begs her to receive him in the dark. Then, affecting to 'seal his peace with her,' he thrusts upon her a dead man's hand. She at first receives it as his, remarking

> You are very cold:
> I fear you are not well after your travel

—and then cries 'Ha! lights!—O, horrible!' Is the invention of this ghastly practical joke—for it is Webster's: he did not find it in his original—is it a thing to be admired, and to earn its inventor a place only a little below Aeschylus and Shakespeare? I submit that any morbid-minded schoolboy could have conceived it, and that the humblest melodramatist of to-day would not dare to affront his transpontine audiences by asking them to applaud such a grisly absurdity.

Next the ingenious Ferdinand draws a curtain, and shows the Duchess wax figures of Antonio and their son, apparently lying dead. It is manifestly impossible that Ferdinand can have secured portraits in wax of the man and child; yet the Duchess takes the figures for reality, and is duly horrified. It would have been infinitely easier, safer and more dramatic to have lied to her in words. This waxen lie is the device of a dramatist whose imagination works on the level of a Tussaud Chamber of Horrors.

Then comes the famous and much-admired Dance of Madmen which Ferdinand provides to enliven his sister's last moments. It is preluded by the Duchess's beautiful speech to Cariola:

> I'll tell thee a miracle:
> I am not mad yet, to my cause of sorrow:
> The heaven o'er my head seems made of molten
>   brass,
> The earth of flaming sulphur, yet I am not mad.
> I am acquainted with sad misery
> As the tann'd galley-slave is with his oar.

That Webster was a poet no one denies; yet this same poet, on the next page, treats us to a song by a madman, sung 'to a dismal kind of music' says the stage-direction, of which this is the first verse:

> O, let us howl some heavy note,
> Some deadly, dogged howl,
> Sounding as from the threatening throat
> Of beasts and fatal fowl!

When the eight madmen have gone through their frigid antics and talked their dismal nonsense, Bosola enters disguised as an Old Man, announces himself as a tomb-maker, and talks a great deal of fantastic stuff 'fit for a charnel,' as the Duchess aptly observes. Then enter 'Executioners, with a coffin, cords, and a bell,' who proceed to strangle, on the open stage, first the Duchess, and then the struggling, shrieking, biting and scratching Cariola. From the modern editions it would seem that they also strangle in sight of the audience the Duchess's two young children. But when we read the original quarto, in the light of our better knowledge of the structure of the Elizabethan stage, we see that the children were strangled behind the scenes, and their bodies revealed by the drawing of a curtain.

Now it was of this scene in especial that Charles Lamb wrote:

> What are 'Luke's iron crown,' the brazen bull of Perillus, Procrustes' bed, to the waxen images which counterfeit death, the wild masque of madmen, the tomb-maker, the bellman, the living person's dirge, the mortification by degrees! To move a horror skilfully, to touch a soul to the quick, to lay upon fear as much as it can bear, to wean and weary a life till it is ready to drop, and then step in with mortal instruments to take its last forfeit; this only a Webster can do. Writers of an inferior genius may 'upon horror's head horrors accumulate'; but they cannot do this. They mistake quantity for quality, they 'terrify babes with painted devils,' but they know not how a soul is capable of being moved; their terrors want dignity, their affrightments are without decorum.

I yield to no one in my love and reverence for Charles Lamb; but I cannot conceal my conviction that a more topsy-turvy criticism than this was never penned. Others, forsooth, 'mistake quantity for quality'! If ever any man did so it was surely Webster. We may be wrong in thinking his quality very poor, but there can be no mistake as to his quantity being excessive. Other people's terrors 'want dignity'—is Ferdinand's trick with the dead man's hand a dignified terror? Other people's 'affrightments are without decorum'—is the masque of lunatics a decorous affrightment? Is all this calculated 'to touch a soul to the quick'? If ever there was a crude and unblushing appeal to the physical nerves, this is surely it.

With the death of the Duchess, the interest of the play is over; for Antonio is admittedly a shadowy character as to whose fate we are very indifferent; and though we are willing enough to see Ferdinand, the Cardinal and Bosola punished, we could quite well dispense with that gratification. Webster, however, is not the man to leave any of his *dramatis personae* alive if he can help it; so, as Rupert Brooke says, he kills off his criminals 'with various confusions and in various horror.' The Cardinal's irrelevant mistress, Julia, dies of kissing a poisoned book—a favourite incident with the Elizabethans. The Cardinal himself is killed by Bosola, his attendants disregarding his cries for help, because he has told them that he will very likely imitate the ravings of his mad brother, and no one must pay any attention—a piece of imbecile ingenuity such as tyros in playwriting are apt to plume themselves upon. Bosola kills Antonio by mistake, and Ferdinand and Bosola kill each other. There is scarcely room on the stage for all the corpses; which is perhaps the reason why, in the Phoenix revival, Ferdinand stands on his head to die, and waves his legs in the air.

All the editors of *The Duchess of Malfi* make a bald statement that Lope de Vega treated the same theme; but I have seen no comparison between Lope's play and Webster's. It is not one of his well-known works; but after some trouble I discovered it at the British Museum and read it. The Spanish and the English conventions are so very different that minute comparison is hardly possible. *El Mayordomo de la Duquesa de Amalfi* is not so much a play as an opera, full of brilliant bravura passages. But Lope's play is a much less barbarous product than Webster's; and I have no hesitation in saying that his catastrophe is immeasurably superior. It is highly concentrated, and, though rather too horrible for modern tastes, intensely dramatic. The Duchess and Antonio have parted, as in the original story. Then Ferdinand (here called Julio) succeeds in persuading them that he is reconciled to their union, and that Antonio has only to return to Amalfi for all to end happily. We see Antonio pass from one room into another in which he expects to find the Duchess; and then we see the Duchess hurrying to meet Antonio; but when the curtains are opened behind which she expects to find him, what she does find is a table set forth with three salvers on which are the heads of Antonio and their two children. This plunge from the height of joyful expectancy to the abyss of anguish and despair is incalculably more dramatic than Webster's laborious piling up of artificial horrors. After a pathetic outburst of lamentation, the Duchess, who has been poisoned, falls dead.

Lope's conclusion, too, is humanised by the fact that the Duke of Amalfi, the Duchess's legitimate son, whom Webster only mentions in passing, warmly espouses his mother's cause. I should be glad to know what the admirers of Webster's Duchess make of the fact that she never gives a word or a thought to the offspring of her first marriage.

This attempt to apply rational canons of dramatic construction to an Elizabethan 'masterpiece' will doubtless be regarded in many quarters as little less than sacrilegious. The time is surely approaching, however, when the criticism of the Elizabethans will no longer be left to scholars

who know nothing of the theatre (Lamb's own plays show clearly how little he understood it), and who have not the elementary power of distinguishing between poetic and specifically dramatic merit. (pp. 126-32)

> William Archer, "The Duchess of Malfi," in The Nineteenth Century and After, *Vol. LXXXVIII, No. DXV, January, 1920, pp. 126-32.*

Kenneth Rexroth (essay date 1967)

[*Rexroth was a prominent American critic and translator. As a critic, his acute intelligence and wide sympathy allowed him to examine such varied subjects as jazz, Greek mythology, the works of D. H. Lawrence, and the cabala. As a translator, Rexroth was largely responsible for introducing the West to both Chinese and Japanese classics. In the excerpt below, Rexroth praises* The Duchess of Malfi *as a work that transcends traditional definitions of tragedy and melodrama, and adds "an entirely new dimension to drama."*]

The drama of Shakespeare is distinguished, even in the plays where he is still learning his craft, by an extraordinary coherence of all the artistic processes, of creation, of structure of the work itself, of response in audience or reader. Subjective-objective, classical-romantic, expressionistic-architectural, realism-symbolism—such antitheses are subsumed in a synthesis of completely integrated communication. It is this massive integrity which has led innumerable critics to postulate a man, Shakespeare, who is far better organized than most humans, let alone most writers or people of the theater. Even the plays that seem to reflect a period of personal tragedy and disillusion, such as *Hamlet* or *Troilus and Cressida*, show few signs of any fragmentation of personality in their author—whatever may be the case with their heroes and heroines.

Few contemporary artists in any medium could be found to show forth better the schism in the most fundamental nature—the very sources—of creativity, which has become so characteristic of all the arts since the early years of the nineteenth century, than Ben Jonson and John Webster, writing three centuries ago. The difference is so great that we seem to be dealing with two distinct operations of the mind. The plays of Jonson are classic in structure and objective in their delineation of motives and behavior, but also they are conceived of as taking place "out there." The esthetic process, from creator to spectator, occurs in material which is independent of either of them once it has been formed.

Webster is not the least interested in what happens "out there." He uses poetry, drama, acting, stage effects solely to work inside the spectator. The material of Webster is the collective nervous system of his audience. This is beyond romanticism and its subjectivity. Nothing would appear quite like it until, following [Edgar Allan] Poe, [Stephane] Mallarmé 300 years later would make the method explicit. Yet how explicit? We have no name for it, and that in a field ever fertile with jargon—criticism and esthetics. And few critics watching *The Duchess of Malfi* or reading *L'Après-midi d'un Faune* are aware of what is happening to them.

The Duchess of Malfi is a fashionable play, a revival of the tragedy of blood so popular at the beginning of Elizabethan drama. So are *Macbeth* and *Hamlet.* Webster is a conscious, deliberate disciple of Shakespeare. So are Beaumont and Fletcher. It is one of the first tragedies that can be called decadent, both in its verse structure and in its somewhat phosphorescent dramaturgy—the greatest of a class that includes Tourneur, Ford, and Shirley and would be imitated, carefully but with only limited success, by Shelley in *The Cenci.* Yet it really isn't like any of these plays.

In the very first scene of *Duchess,* Webster, wasting no time, starts out to do something quite different from Shakespeare in *Macbeth* or Shelley in *The Cenci.* Shakespeare is building a character, setting a scene, creating a psychological environment that will define the character and the tragedy of Macbeth himself—out there. Shelley does that, too, but he is more interested in himself, in expressing himself, perhaps in scaring himself a little. We call it romantic subjectivism.

In the opening scene of *Duchess,* Antonio and Delio carry on a dialogue which seems objective enough. They describe, as they appear, all the important characters, their interrelations, and hint at the potentialities for tragedy these relationships embody. But in what an extraordinary fashion! Webster uses a standard device, the opening dialogue, "Hello, old friend, what's been going on while I've been gone?" to string together a series of carefully concealed assaults on the nerves of his audience:

> If it chance
> Some cursed example poison it near the head,
> Death and diseases through the whole land
> 　spread. . . .
>
> I do haunt you still. . . .
>
> They are like plum trees that grow crooked over standing pools. They are rich and over laden with fruit but none but crows, pies and caterpillars feed on them. . . .
>
> Places in court are like beds in hospital, where this man's head lies at that man's foot, and so lower and lower.

Corruption—the idea echoes with the word throughout the first act in what purports to be the ordinary conversation of a court. It is a court where the head sickens and the members rot, but over and above the careful setting of a situation, Webster is striving to affect the audience directly. This play is going to take place inside the heads—in each individual brain—of the audience.

Is this melodrama? The play is certainly a melodrama by conventional definition, but this is more like hypnotism. As the play goes on, horror seeps into the most commonplace statements until language loses its informative role and becomes a kind of argot whose aim always is not communication between the characters but manipulation of the minds of the audience. Meanwhile, the action goes on,

bodies move in space with uncanny haste and glow with foxfire. The stage is lit with decay.

Melodrama is supposed to be bad art. Is *The Duchess of Malfi* great art? It certainly is great melodrama, probably the greatest ever written, and in addition—and more importantly—it adds an entirely new dimension to drama, or even to art as a whole. If great art makes us confront the profoundest meanings of life, *Duchess* is hardly art at all, because it literally doesn't mean much. When we leave the play our nerves have been rubbed raw and tortured. Does this make them more acute receptors? It may just as well dull our sensitivity as sharpen it. We are left nervously exhausted by a novel such as [Choderlos de Laclos's] *Les Liaisons Dangereuses,* but we are also left prostrate by a long look into the abysm of deliberate evil, and our valuations of human conduct and our responses to those valuations have been subtly reorganized. The good and evil that struggle in *The Duchess of Malfi,* once the play is over, vanish. The Duchess changes her costume and is just an actress, impatient to be gone to a late supper.

In recent years the estheticians and critics who try to establish a moral ground of justification for the arts have shifted their position to a kind of physiological esthetic: "The arts work upon us through abstract, purely artistic qualities. They do not teach or even communicate. The experience of the subtle architectonics of a great work of art makes us more refined, more efficient organisms, and the cumulative effects of such experiences through life make us better men." There is not an iota of empirical evidence for this notion. On the contrary, society has always been suspicious of "esthetes" as secret rascals given to shocking depravities. This is not true, either; Oscar Wilde's Dorian Grey and the heroes of [Charles Marie Georges] Huysmanns's novels are excessively rare types. Although it follows the conventions of tragedy and deals, with great psychological penetration, with the slow corruption of consciously chosen evil, *The Duchess of Malfi* is not a nerve tonic or a moral stimulant. It is simply very great entertainment and its own excuse for being.

Kenneth Rexroth, "The Duchess of Malfi," in Saturday Review, *Vol. L, No. 9, March 4, 1967, p. 21.*

FURTHER READING

OVERVIEWS AND GENERAL STUDIES

Berry, Ralph. *The Art of John Webster.* Oxford: At the Clarendon Press, 1972, 174 p.

> Focuses on the general theme in Webster's works that the law must oppose evil. Berry also finds analogies to the baroque visual arts in *The White Devil, The Duchess of Malfi,* and *The Devil's Law Case.*

———. "Masques and Dumb Shows in Webster's Plays." In *The Elizabethan Theatre VII,* edited by G. R. Hibbard, pp.

124-46. Port Credit, Ontario: P. D. Meany Company in collaboration with the University of Waterloo, 1980.

Argues that Webster parodied the masque genre to challenge the traditional concepts of order, hierarchy, and ceremony.

Bogard, Travis. *The Tragic Satire of John Webster*. Berkeley: University of California Press, 1955, 158 p.

Maintains that Webster used the techniques of satire and tragedy to skillfully create powerful drama.

Bradbrook, M. C. *John Webster: Citizen and Dramatist*. New York: Columbia University Press, 1980, 218 p.

A useful study in two parts: the first provides a historical context for Webster, and the second offers a survey of his career as a dramatist.

Courtade, Anthony E. *The Structure of John Webster's Plays*. Salzburg: Institut für Anglistik und Amerikanistik, 1980, 172 p.

Maintains that rather than violating Jacobean dramatic conventions, Webster "manipulated the episodes, character, concepts, language and physical action of his major works to create a very clear statement on mankind."

Dent, R. W. *John Webster's Borrowing*. Berkeley: University of California Press, 1960, 323 p.

Line-by-line examination of Webster's major works which reveals their sources. The critic describes Webster's borrowing as very careful and extensive.

Hunter, G. K. and S. K. Hunter, eds. *John Webster: A Critical Anthology*. Harmondsworth: Penguin, 1969, 328 p.

Reprints previously published criticism under three headings: Contemporaneous Criticism, the Developing Debate, and Modern Views. Each section contains an introductory overview.

Leech, Clifford. *John Webster: A Critical Study*. London: The Hogarth Press, 1951, 122 p.

Seminal study of Webster's life and dramatic writings. Leech finds that the shorter speeches in Webster's works impress more than the longer passages, and that his plays excel in their flashes of brilliant verse.

Moore, Don D. *John Webster and His Critics: 1617-1964*. Baton Rouge: Louisiana State University Press, 1966, 199 p.

Surveys the wealth of critical investigations of Webster and traces twentieth-century productions of his works.

——, ed. *Webster: The Critical Heritage*. London: Routledge & Kegan Paul, 1981, 161 p.

Reprints important commentary on Webster to trace his critical reputation from his time to the end of the nineteenth century. Includes remarks by Henry Fitzjeffrey, William Hazlitt, and William Archer.

Morris, Brian, ed. *John Webster*. London: Ernest Benn Limited, 1970, 237 p.

This volume, part of the Mermaid Critical Commentaries series, includes essays by prominent Webster critics.

Murray, Peter B. *A Study of John Webster*. The Hague: Mouton, 1969, 274 p.

Overview of Webster's collaborative efforts and independent dramas which addresses what the critic contends is Webster's overall theme: How is humanity to behave in an evil world?

Ridley, M. R. "Webster." In his *Second Thoughts: More Studies in Literature*, pp. 74-132. London: J. M. Dent & Sons, 1965.

Close examination of *The White Devil* and *The Duchess of Malfi* that finds that Webster's characterization goes beyond stereotypes into genuine human portraits.

Schuman, Samuel. *John Webster: A Reference Guide*. Boston: G. K. Hall, 1985, 280 p.

Annotated bibliography of writings on the dramatist, covering the period from 1602 to the 1980s.

Stodder, Joseph Henry. *Moral Perspectives in Webster's Major Tragedies*. Salzburg: Institut für Englische Sprache und Literatur, 1974, 164 p.

Study of the actions and speeches of the major characters of *The White Devil* and *The Duchess of Malfi*. Stodder attempts to demonstrate Webster's technique of balancing good and evil between characters and within each character.

Swinburne, Charles Algernon. Entry in *The Encyclopædia Britannica*, eleventh edition, Vol. 28, pp. 462-63. Cambridge: At the University Press, 1911.

Laudatory evaluation of Webster and his place in English stage history.

West, Muriel. *The Devil and John Webster*. Salzburg: Institut für Englische Sprache und Literatur, 1974, 319 p.

Traces Webster's use of devil and witchcraft imagery in *The White Devil* and *The Duchess of Malfi*.

Whiteside, George. "John Webster: A Freudian Interpretation of His Two Great Tragedies." In *The Analysis of Literary Texts: Current Trends in Methodology*, edited by Randolph D. Pope, pp. 201-11. Ypsilanti, Mich.: Bilingual Press/Editorial Bilingüe, 1980.

Brief examination of Vittoria from *The White Devil* and the Duchess from *The Duchess of Malfi* that finds in the earlier play a good woman and a passionate woman are depicted as two separate entities, representing the dramatist's "despairing view of the way things actually are." Whiteside notes that the Duchess is an ideal maternal figure, reflecting Webster's idea of how things should be.

THE WHITE DEVIL

Boklund, Gunnar. *The Sources of The White Devil*. Cambridge, Mass.: Harvard University Press, 1957, 226 p.

Discusses the historical background of the drama and traces the possible sources for Webster's version, which, the critic maintains, presents "various degrees of evil at war."

Dallby, Anders. *The Anatomy of Evil: A Study of John Webster's "The White Devil."* Lund: Gleerup, 1974, 236 p.

Structural analysis which finds a tightly woven pattern of images, language, mood, and morality in the play.

Holland, George. "The Function of the Minor Characters in *The White Devil*." *Philological Quarterly* 52 (1973): 43-54.

Argues that the secondary characters provide a social context for judging the major figures of the play.

Kistner, A. L. and M. K. Kistner. "Traditional Structures in *The White Devil.*" *Essays in Literature* 12, No. 2 (Fall 1985): 171-88.

Maintains that the drama has three complex interwoven "structuring patterns"—tragedy of state, revenge tragedy, and morality play—which play off one another to create dramatic coherence and organization.

Layman, B. J. "The Equilibrium of Opposites in *The White Devil:* A Reinterpretation." *PMLA* 74, No. 4 (September 1959): 336-47.

Suggests that the emphasis of Webster's works on deceptive appearance is in reaction to the Machiavellianism he saw around him.

McLeod, Susan H. "Duality in *The White Devil.*" *Studies in English Literature 1500-1900* XX, No. 2 (Spring 1980): 271-85.

Finds the organization of the drama based on the duality suggested by its title.

THE DUCHESS OF MALFI

Baker, Susan C. "The Static Protagonist in *The Duchess of Malfi.*" *Texas Studies in Literature and Language* 22, No. 3 (Fall 1980): 343-57.

Maintains that the audience undergoes moral growth in reacting to the unchanging nature of the Duchess in the face of the horrors she suffers.

Boklund, Gunnar. *The Duchess of Malfi: Sources, Themes, Characters.* Cambridge, Mass.: Harvard University Press, 1962, 189 p.

Discusses the historical background of the drama and traces the possible sources for Webster's version.

Brennan, Elizabeth M. Introduction to *The Duchess of Malfi* by John Webster, pp. vii-xxvii. New York: Hill and Wang, 1965.

Provides a general overview of the drama as well as a biographical sketch of Webster and discussions of the play's sources and early performances.

Driscoll, James P. "The Integrity of Life in *The Duchess of Malfi.*" *Drama Survey* 6, No. 1 (Spring-Summer 1967): 42-53.

Maintains that the theme of the drama is the integrity of life in the face of adversity. Driscoll relates this theme to "the ancient motifs of vengeance, justice, morality, and honor," which, he claims, Webster invests with a "new vitality and intensity."

Giannetti, Louis D. "A Contemporary View of *The Duchess of Malfi.*" *Comparative Drama* 3, No. 4 (1969): 297-307.

Examination of *The Duchess of Malfi* as "an 'action' intended to be physically embodied on a stage." Giannetti finds that studying the visual aspects of the play highlights its complexity.

Jankowski, Theodora A. "Defining/Confining the Duchess: Negotiating the Female Body in John Webster's *The Duchess of Malfi.*" *Studies in Philology* LXXXVII, No. 2 (Spring 1990): 221-45.

Argues that the character of the Duchess challenges Jacobean views regarding the "representation of the female body and woman's sexuality."

Kiefer, Frederick. "The Dance of the Madmen in *The Duchess of Malfi.*" *The Journal of Medieval and Renaissance Studies* 17, No. 2 (Fall 1987): 211-33.

Examines a sixteenth-century engraving in an attempt to explain the appearance of the madmen before the Duchess.

Knight, G. Wilson. "*The Duchess of Malfi.*" *The Malahat Review* No. 4 (October 1967): 88-113.

Examination of the imagery of *The Duchess of Malfi.* Knight finds the tragedy "perhaps the most beautiful and profound creation of a mood in our literature."

Leech, Clifford. *Webster: The Duchess of Malfi.* London: Edward Arnold, 1963, 64 p.

General introduction to the play which assesses its relation to Jacobean tragic conventions, as well as its construction, themes, and characterizations.

Luckyj, Christina. " 'Great Women of Pleasure': Main Plot and Subplot in *The Duchess of Malfi.*" *Studies in English Literature 1500-1900* 27, No. 2 (Spring 1987): 267-83.

Refutes the commonly held perception that the subplot of the Cardinal's mistress is unnecessary by demonstrating that it acts as a mirror of the primary plot.

Luecke, Jane Marie. "*The Duchess of Malfi:* Comic and Satiric Confusion in a Tragedy." *Studies in English Literature 1500-1900* IV, No. 2 (Spring 1964): 275-90.

Maintains that the critical confusion concerning the drama is due to its mix of satiric and comic elements. Luecke concludes that while the drama succeeds as satire and comedy, it fails as tragedy.

Mitchell, Giles and Eugene Wright. "Duke Ferdinand's Lycanthropy as a Disguise Motive in Webster's *The Duchess of Malfi.*" *Literature and Psychology* XXV, No. 3 (1975): 117-23.

Offers a psychoanalytic interpretation of Ferdinand which reveals the psychological relationships between incest, lycanthropy, and necrophilia in Webster's tragedy.

Rabkin, Norman, ed. *Twentieth Century Interpretations of the Duchess of Malfi: A Collection of Critical Essays.* Englewood Cliffs, N. J.: Prentice-Hall, 1968, 120 p.

Collection of previously published material by prominent scholars.

Randall, Dale B. J. "The Rank and Earthy Background of Certain Physical Symbols in *The Duchess of Malfi.*" *Renaissance Drama* n.s. XVIII (1987): 171-203.

Examines the symbolic significance of two stage properties: the severed hand and the apricots, finding that "both are charged with a range of allusion that is capable of casting light on some of the play's major ideas."

Spivack, Charlotte. "*The Duchess of Malfi:* A Fearful Madness." *Journal of Women's Studies in Literature* 1, No. 2 (Spring 1979): 122-32.

Finds the Duchess a feminine archetype in her roles as wife and mother as well as political ruler. She is a complete woman, the critic maintains, whose integrity and power to change others transforms her male tormentors.

Thayer, C. G. "The Ambiguity of Bosola." *Studies in Philology* LIV, No. 2 (April 1957): 162-71.
   Depicts Bosola as a "complex and elusive" character who is also a major tragic protagonist.

For further information on Webster's life and career, see *Dictionary of Literary Biography,* Vol. 58.

August Wilson

1945-

INTRODUCTION

Wilson emerged in the 1980s as a major figure in American theater. His dramas, for which he has received such prizes as the Tony Award, the New York Drama Critics' Circle Award, and the Pulitzer Prize, are part of a play-cycle in progress devoted to the African-American experience throughout the twentieth century. "I'm taking each decade and looking at one of the most important questions that blacks confronted in that decade and writing a play about it," Wilson has explained. "Put them all together and you have a history." Praised for their vivid characterizations and richly poetic dialogue, Wilson's dramas often center upon conflicts between African Americans who have found a way to come to terms with the harsh realities of their lives and those who have not. He commented: "I've tried to fuse my artistic consciousness and my political consciousness. I may be saying there's an illness here, but I don't know what the prescription is." Wilson's perceptive, somber explorations of African-American history prompted Samuel G. Freedman to describe the dramatist as "one part Dylan Thomas and one part Malcolm X, a lyric poet fired in the kiln of black nationalism."

Wilson grew up in a Pittsburgh ghetto called the Hill, the son of a white father and a black mother; his mother worked as a janitor to support her six children after their father abandoned them. Wilson experienced rampant racism in many of the schools he attended; finally, frustrated by a teacher's false accusation of plagiarism, he dropped out of school in the ninth grade, thereafter educating himself by reading extensively at the local library. "I didn't think this at the time, but in retrospect it was one of the best things that could have happened," Wilson has noted. "Suddenly I had the freedom to explore and develop my mind. I went to the library to read things I didn't know anything about. I read anything I wanted to." He discovered the works of such African-American writers as Ralph Ellison, Langston Hughes, and Arna Bontemps; and, inspired by their powerful, skilled use of elements drawn from their heritage, he began to write poetry and short stories. In 1968, while involved in the civil rights movement, Wilson cofounded Black Horizon on the Hill, a community theater aimed at increasing the political awareness and activism of the residents of the area. The playhouse became a forum for his first dramas.

Wilson's professional breakthrough occurred in 1978 when he was invited to write plays for a black theater founded, in St. Paul, Minnesota by Claude Purdy, a former Pittsburgh director. In this new milieu, Wilson began to recognize poetic qualities in the language of his native city. While his first two dramas, *Black Bart and the Sacred Hills* and *Jitney,* garnered little notice, his third, *Ma Rainey's Black Bottom,* was accepted by the National Playwright's Conference at the Eugene O'Neill Theater

Center in Connecticut, where it drew the attention of Lloyd Richards, the artistic director of the Yale Repertory Theater. Richards later recalled: "I sensed in August Wilson's writing an extraordinary pulse, a powerful range of voices in tune with those I remember from my own youth." Richards directed *Ma Rainey* at Yale and later took the play to Broadway. Since then, often with Richards in the role of mentor and director, all of Wilson's plays have had their first staged readings at the Playwright's Conference, followed by runs at the Yale Repertory Theater and regional theaters before opening on Broadway.

Ma Rainey's Black Bottom, set in the 1920s, is an exploration of racism. The play depicts an imaginary episode in the life of legendary black singer Gertrude "Ma" Rainey, regarded by many as the mother of the blues. The action takes place in a recording studio and involves four musicians who are waiting for Ma's arrival. As the details of the musicians' lives unfold through their conversation, the audience becomes aware of the racism that these black performers have had to face. Eventually, Ma Rainey arrives, and the attitudes of the group's white manager and the owner of the studio reveal continuing exploitation of

Ma and her band. The play climaxes when one of the musicians, Levee, who has been irreparably scarred by the violent oppression he has suffered, vents his frustrations on the others. While some critics found the plot insubstantial and viewed the ending as contrived, Wilson was praised for the vitality of the characterizations of *Ma Rainey*. The thorough development of the characters, each of whom is a realistic, non-stereotypical personality, was enhanced by Wilson's use of authentic, lively dialogue.

Wilson's second play to appear on Broadway, the Pulitzer Prize-winning *Fences,* received unanimous praise from reviewers. An examination of the destructive and far-reaching consequences of racial injustice, the drama is set in the late 1950s, on the eve of the Civil Rights Movement. *Fences* revolves around Troy Maxson, an outstanding high school athlete who was ignored by major league baseball because of his color. Struggling through middle-age as a garbage man, Troy's bitterness results in family conflicts. His son Cory, who also aspires to an athletic career, must battle his father's envy of him, and Troy's wife Rose is humiliated by his adultery. Many critics see in Wilson's treatment of family divisions the influence of such playwrights as Arthur Miller, Tennessee Williams, and Eugene O'Neill. Wilson has commented: "My concern was the idea of missed possibilities. Music and sports were the traditional inroads for blacks, and in both *Ma Rainey* and *Fences,* with both Levee and Troy, even those inroads fail."

Joe Turner's Come and Gone, the third installment in Wilson's play-cycle, debuted while *Fences* was still running on Broadway, an unprecedented accomplishment in the New York theater for an African-American playwright. Generally regarded as more mystical than Wilson's other works, *Joe Turner* is about the struggles of blacks who migrated north in the decades following the Civil War. The play takes place in 1911 in the Pittsburgh boardinghouse owned by Seth and Bertha Holly. Following seven years of forced labor at the hands of Joe Turner, an infamous Southerner who frequently abducted blacks and held them as indentured servants, Herald Loomis travels to Pennsylvania in search of his wife. Loomis's journey ends at the Holly boardinghouse, where the other black residents are also searching for some kind of connection and wholeness in their lives. Partially assimilated into white America, they nevertheless embrace the African traditions of their past. At the end of Act I, the boarders sing and dance a *juba,* an African celebration of the spirit. Their shared joy represents an achievement of unity—evidence that they have found a way to cope with the trauma of slavery and the harsh reality of white persecution. Loomis, however, is unable to join in the *juba.* Instead, he abruptly puts an end to the celebration with a terrifying vision of the bones of slaves who perished on the voyage from Africa to America. At the end of the play, Loomis achieves a measure of acceptance of his situation through a symbolic blood-letting. *Joe Turner* was an immensely popular and critical success—Wilson himself has cited it as his personal favorite—and reviewers have lauded Wilson's skillful use of African myth and legend to create a richly poetic drama.

The Piano Lesson, which examines the confrontation of African-American tradition with possibilities for the future, won a Pulitzer Prize before appearing on Broadway. A piano serves as a major element in this play, which is set in 1936 in Doaker Charles's Pittsburgh home. Decades earlier, the white slave-owner of the Charles family traded Doaker's father and grandmother for the piano, and the grief-stricken grandfather carved African totems of his wife and son in the piano's legs. Later, Doaker's elder brother was killed in a successful conspiracy to steal the piano, which now sits, untouched and revered, in Doaker's living room. Conflict arises when Boy Willie, Doaker's nephew, wants to sell it to purchase land, sacrificing a symbol of the past to the pragmatic concerns of the present. However, he is opposed by his sister, who wishes to keep the piano because of the family history it represents. *The Piano Lesson* was praised by most critics, including Frank Rich, who asserted: "Whatever happens to the piano, . . . the playwright makes it clear that the music in *The Piano Lesson* is not up for sale. That haunting music belongs to the people who have lived it, and it has once again found miraculous voice in a play that August Wilson has given to the American stage." Some reviewers, however, did not feel that *The Piano Lesson* met the high dramatic standards set by Wilson's earlier works, viewing the play as static and judging the playwright's use of a ghost onstage glaringly ineffective. While David Patrick Stearns admitted that "some scenes are among the most compelling, eloquent drama Wilson has ever written," he also felt that certain aspects of the play were "obnoxious" and "numbingly repetitious." His ultimate verdict was that *The Piano Lesson* needed "all the endorsement power the Pulitzer offers. Though easy to respect, it isn't always easy to enjoy."

Despite such criticism, Wilson continues to command widespread respect and has added another work to his play-cycle: *Two Trains Running.* This drama, set in 1969 in Pittsburgh's Hill District, received its first performance at the Yale Rep on 27 March 1990. In an interview, Nick Flournoy, a companion of Wilson's for over twenty-five years, summed up his friend's career: "August Wilson is on a trek. He's saying who you are and what you are are all right. It's all right to be an angry nigger. It's all right to be whatever you are."

PRINCIPAL WORKS

PLAYS

Black Bart and the Sacred Hills   1981
Jitney   1982
Ma Rainey's Black Bottom   1984
Fences   1985
Joe Turner's Come and Gone   1986
The Piano Lesson   1987
Two Trains Running   1990

AUTHOR COMMENTARY

Preface to *Three Plays* (1991)

[*In the following preface to the volume that collects* Ma Rainey's Black Bottom, Fences, *and* Joe Turner's Come and Gone, *Wilson discusses his formative influences, including blues music, the art of Romare Bearden, and black writers such as Amiri Baraka and Ed Bullins.*]

"Where to begin?" is among the first questions an artist asks himself. I have always told anyone who asks for my advice to begin anywhere, and that beginning will lead them, whether backward or forward, to the place they want to go. That the place where they arrive may be a place they have wanted to go to unknowingly or perhaps even unwillingly is the crucible in which many a work of art is fired. Romare Bearden has said art is born out of, among other things, necessity. One always knows his wants better than his needs. Each of these plays was a journey. At the end of each, out of necessity, emerged an artifact that is representative, the way a travel photo is representative, of the journey itself. It is the only record.

I have said elsewhere and will repeat here that writing a play is for me like walking down the landscape of the self, unattended, unadorned, exploring what D. H. Lawrence called "the dark forest of the soul." It is a place rife with shadows, a place of suspect quality and occasional dazzling brightness. What you encounter there are your demons which you have occasionally fed, trying, as Hansel, to make your way back home. You find false trails, roads closed for repairs, impregnable fortresses, scouts, armies of memory, and impossible cartography. It is a place where the cartographers labor night and day remaking the maps. The road is sometimes welcoming and its wide passages offer endearment with each step only to narrow to a footpath that has led you, boatless, to the edge of a vast and encompassing ocean. Occasionally, if you are willing to negotiate the perils, you arrive strong, brighter of spirit, to a place that sprouts yams and bolls of cotton at your footfall.

So I will begin this preface where these plays began, in 1965, with a twenty-year-old poet wrestling with the world and his place in it, having discovered the joy and terror of remaking the world in his own image through the act of writing.

To write is to fix language, to get it down and fix it to a spot and have it have meaning and be fat with substance. It is in many ways a remaking of the self in which all of the parts have been realigned, redistributed, and reassembled into a new being of sense and harmony. You have wrought something into being, and what you have wrought is what you have learned about life, and what you have learned is always pointed toward moving the harborless parts of your being closer to home. To write is to forever circle the maps, marking it all down, the latitude and longitude of each specific bearing, giving new meaning to something very old and very sacred—life itself.

As a twenty-year-old poet faced with how little you know about life, you profess to know everything. What you know most assuredly is that you are going to live until you die. What you have, almost without knowing you have it, is a sense of immortality that allows you to approach the mine fields with the blind faith of innocence and the assurance of an indefatigable spirit that rivals St. George in his willingness to slay the dragon. *If only you could get those damn words down on paper!*

I lived in a rooming house in Pittsburgh in those early days, and as I bedded down each night with my immortal self the guns of social history and responsibility that went boom in the night and called the warriors to their stations were largely ignored. If I heard them at all they had no relation to my bearing as a poet determined to answer the question of how many angels could sit on the head of a pin, despite the fact that I was having trouble identifying the angels and the size of the pin.

Most of the truly important moments in our lives go by unnoticed. We recognize them only in retrospect after we have chosen one road or another and have seen where it has taken us. Only after we have kissed the woman for the last time unknowingly, or have left her final nakedness and been marked by the unsurety and the bruise, do these moments have any resonance.

Sometimes you are privileged to recognize these moments when they occur, and from one day to the next, life, in a single stroke of gluttony, has knocked over the lamps and rearranged the maps. One night in the fall of 1965 I put a typewritten yellow-labeled record titled "Nobody in Town Can Bake a Sweet Jellyroll Like Mine," by someone named Bessie Smith, on the turntable of my 78 rpm phonograph, and the universe stuttered and everything fell to a new place.

Although the business of poetry is to enlarge the sayable, I cannot describe or even relate what I felt. Suffice it to say it was a birth, a baptism, a resurrection, and a redemption all rolled up in one. It was the beginning of my consciousness that I was a representative of a culture and the carrier of some very valuable antecedents. With my discovery of Bessie Smith and the blues I had been given a world that contained my image, a world at once rich and varied, marked and marking, brutal and beautiful, and at crucial odds with the larger world that contained it and preyed and pressed it from every conceivable angle.

"Youth is sweet before flight, and a mighty furnace is its kiln," I have written my daughter as she approaches her twenty-first birthday and wrestles, in her becoming womanhood, with the social welter of America in the nineties. My own youth is fired in the kiln of black cultural nationalism as exemplified by Amiri Baraka in the sixties. It posited black Americans as coming from a long line of honorable people with a cultural and political history, a people of manners with a strong moral personality that had to be reclaimed by strengthening the elements of the culture that made it unique and by developing institutions for preserving and promoting it. The ideas of self-determination, self-respect, and self-defense which it espoused are still very much a part of my life as I sit down to write. I have stood them up in the world of Bessie Smith on the ground captured by the blues. Having started my beginning consciousness there it is no surprise that I would mature and my efforts at writing would come to fruition on the same ground. I saw the blues as a cultural response of a nonliterate people whose history and culture were rooted in the oral tradition. The response was to a world that was not of their making, in which the idea of themselves as a people of imminent worth that belied their recent history was continually assaulted. It was a world that did not recognize their gods, their manners, their mores. It despised their ethos and refused to even recognize humanity. In such an environment the blues was a flag bearer of self-definition, and within the scope of the larger world which lay beyond its doorstep, it carved out a life, set down rules, and urged a manner of being that corresponded to the temperament and sensibilities of its creators. It was a spiritual conduit that gave spontaneous expression to the spirit that was locked in combat and devising new strategies for engaging life and enlarging itself. It was a true and articulate literature that was in the forefront of the development of both character and consciousness.

I turned my ear, my heart, and whatever analytical tools I possessed to embrace this world. I elevated it, rightly or wrongly, to biblical status. I rooted out the ideas and attitudes expressed in the music, charted them and bent and twisted and stretched them. I tested them on the common ground of experience and evidence and gave my whole being, muscle and bone and sinew and flesh and spirit, over to the emotional reference provided by the music. I learned to read between the lines and tried to fill in the blank spaces. This was life being lived in all its timbre and horrifics, with zest and purpose and the affirmation of the self as worthy of the highest possibilities and the highest celebration. What more fertile ground could any artist want?

Though my discovery of Bessie Smith and the blues provided me with an aesthetic with which to frame my growing ideas of myself as part of something larger, it was not until I discovered the art of Romare Bearden that I was able to turn it into a narrative that would encompass all of the elements of culture and tradition, what [James] Baldwin had so eloquently called "the field of manners and ritual of intercourse" that sustains black American life. Bearden had accomplished in painting an expression as full and varied as the blues. My discovery of his work was akin to my discovery of Bessie Smith, a moment of privilege and exaltation that comes from recognizing yourself as a vital part of a much larger world than you had imagined. "I try to explore, in terms of the life I know best, those things which are common to all cultures," Bearden had said. I took it as my credo and sought to answer Baldwin's call for a profound articulation of the black tradition that could sustain a man once he left his father's house. Armed with Bearden and the blues I began to look at myself in ways I hadn't thought of before and in which I have never ceased to think of since. I began to work with the idea that I would try to put in my work all the things I saw in his, the spirit and texture and substance and grace and elegance. But how?

Many writers anxious to see results often ignore the very thing that can produce them—craft with all its tentacles, its many facets and applications. As I was a poet and writer of short fiction, the crafting of a play was new to me. I didn't know the rules, the elements, or the tools. But, since I had been writing for fifteen years, I was not without discipline. I knew that to write and to write well one must be uncompromising and make choices based on one's heart and mind and execute them with craft. But what craft? The craft I knew was the craft of poetry and fiction. To my mind, they had to connect and intercept with the craft of playwrighting at some point and all I had to do was find that point. Fiction was a story told through character and dialogue, and a poem was a distillation of language and images designed to reveal an emotive response to phenomena that brought it into harmony with one's knowledge and experience. Why couldn't a play be both?

I thought that in order to accomplish that I had to look at black life with an anthropological eye, use language, character, and image to reveal its cultural flashpoints and in the process tell a story that further illuminated them. This is what the blues did. Why couldn't I? I was, after all, a bluesman. Never mind I couldn't play a guitar or carry a tune in a bucket. I was cut out of the same cloth and I was on the same field of manners and endeavor—to articulate the cultural response of black Americans to the world in which they found themselves. And so I began, not tentatively, but straight ahead, unswerving, unmitigating. I had, after all, nothing to lose.

An artist who stands before a blank canvas is Picasso (or Matisse, since Picasso himself said "There is no one but Matisse"), until proven otherwise. Artists have the same tools: color, line, mass, form, and their own hearts beating, their own demons, and their own necessity. When I sat down to write I realized I was sitting in the same chair as Eugene O'Neill, Tennessee Williams, Arthur Miller, Henrik Ibsen, Amiri Baraka, and Ed Bullins. I felt empowered by the chair. I was confronted by the same blank piece of paper, the same problems of art and craft—how to invest the characters with a life and history, how to invent situations that challenged the characters' beliefs, forced them into action, and prompted them to stand beside the consequences ready to reengage life on the new field of memory and observable phenomena. Feeling that sense of power, there were no rules. I was on a new adventure, with the blues and what I call the blood's memory as my only guide and companion. These plays are the result.

I could not have accomplished any of this if the black playwrights working in the sixties had not laid the groundwork. Amiri Baraka, Ed Bullins, Philip Hayes Dean, Richard Wesley, and Ron Milner are but a few of those who were particularly vocal. I have an enormous respect for their talents and work and I place myself in that long line of the tradition of African-American letters that has nurtured us all. Also none of these plays would exist in the form they are in if it were not for Lloyd Richards and the Eugene O'Neill Theater Center. Started by George White with characteristic vision, the Eugene O'Neill Theatre Center is the home of the National Playwrights' Conference where each summer fifteen playwrights are invited, from among the approximate fifteen hundred who submit their work, to participate. My relationship with the O'Neill began in 1980 when my good friend Rob Penny sent me the O'Neill brochure inviting submissions, on which he wrote, in his increasingly cryptic style, "Do This!" I did, and they promptly rejected five of my scripts until the summer of 1982 when I submitted *Ma Rainey's Black Bottom* and was invited by Lloyd Richards and his staff to participate in the conference. That was the first of many enjoyable summers I spent at the O'Neill working on my plays. The O'Neill's contribution to the development of my plays and my work as a playwright should not be overlooked. In each instance the O'Neill conference has been the catalyst for major rewriting and rethinking. As I am not the kind of writer who sets everything in concrete with a chisel from beginning to end, from the O'Neill to Broadway each play has enjoyed the unselfish energies of many talented theater professionals who, by their insights and provocations, have contributed to important changes in the texts. I worked with Bill Partlan as the director on both *Ma Rainey* and *Fences* and benefited from his stagings. Edith Oliver provided wise and insightful comments as my dramaturge on *Fences* and *Joe Turner.* Michael Feingold, as usual witty and brilliant, was my dramaturge on *Ma Rainey.* Amy Saltz was the director on *Joe Turner* and her staging proved to be illuminating and resulted in more rewriting. Among the many happy events in my career was my meeting of Charles Dutton at the O'Neill in 1982. He is a rare actor of enormous talent whose intuitive sensibilities closely match my own. His inventive portrayal of Levee in *Ma Rainey* inspired me to write the roles of Harold Loomis in *Joe Turner* and Boy Willie in *The Piano Lesson* for him. I am still challenged to write a role to match his talent.

I met Lloyd Richards in the Exxon Building in New York City in 1982. The occasion was the annual luncheon given for the O'Neill playwrights. I don't think either one of us placed any undue importance on the meeting. I don't think either one of us knew what lay in store for us. When the house lights went down on the opening night performance of *Ma Rainey's Black Bottom* at the Yale Repertory Theatre on April 6, 1984, I marked it more as an accomplishment than as a point of departure for a journey through the landscape of the American theater. As it turns out it was both, and I count myself fortunate to have had Lloyd Richards as my guide, my mentor, and my provocateur. More than anyone, he can stand in loud witness to the birth and growth of these plays. From the O'Neill to Yale to Broadway, each step, in each guise, his hand has been firmly on the tiller as we charted the waters from draft to draft and brought the plays safely to shore without compromise. We were guided by the text, our own visions, and occasionally by the seat of our pants, to a port that has been worthy of the cruise. I count him as a true friend and invaluable colleague.

There is a moment in *Joe Turner's Come and Gone* at the end of the first act when the residents of the household, in an act of tribal solidarity and recognition of communal history, dance a Juba. Herald Loomis interrupts it to relate a terrifying vision of bones walking on the water. From the outset he has been a man who has suffered a spir-itual dislocation and is searching for a world that contains his image. The years of bondage to Joe Turner have disrupted his life and severed his connection with his past. His vision is of bones walking on water that sink and wash up on the shore as fully fleshed humans. It is not the bones walking on the water that is the terrifying part of the vision—it is when they take on flesh and reveal themselves to be like him. "They black. Just like you and me. Ain't no difference." It is the shock of recognition that his birth has origins in the manifest act of the creator, that he is in fact akin to the gods. Somewhere in the Atlantic Ocean lie the bones of millions of Africans who died before reaching the New World. The flesh of their flesh populates the Americas from Mississippi to Montevideo. Loomis is made witness to the resurrection and restoration of these bones. He has only to reconcile this vision with his learned experiences and recognize he is one of the "bones people." At the end of the play he repudiates the idea that salvation comes from outside of himself and claims his moral personality by slashing his chest in a bloodletting rite that severs his bonds and demonstrates his willingness to bleed as an act of redemption.

I am reminded of a twenty-year-old poet in a rooming house in Pittsburgh in 1965 who came face to face with himself and did not find it wanting. (pp. vii-xiv)

> *August Wilson, in his* "Three Plays," *University of Pittsburgh Press, 1991, 318 p.*

OVERVIEWS AND GENERAL STUDIES

Hilary DeVries   (essay date 1987)

[*In the following essay, DeVries examines the recurring themes in Wilson's cycle of plays regarding the black experience. She identifies the most pervasive theme as* "the need for black Americans to forge anew their identity, an identity that is at once African and American."]

In August Wilson's most recent play, *The Piano Lesson,* the young protagonist Boy Willie declares: "That's all I wanted. To sit down and be at ease with everything. But I wasn't born to that. When I go by on the road and something ain't right, then I got to try and fix it." The speaker is the son of a slave determined to transform his family's racial legacy into a self-determining future; but the words also bear witness to their author's aspirations as one of this country's leading black playwrights.

In the black American theatrical tradition, often distinguished as much by political circumstance as individual accomplishment, August Wilson has emerged as a compelling new voice. Chronicling the history of black Americans through the 20th century, Wilson draws on his background as a poet to enrich his more recently honed talents as a dramatist. His three best-known plays, *Ma Rainey's Black Bottom, Fences* and *Joe Turner's Come and Gone,* evince both their author's fecund use of language and a storyteller's narrative touch.

The plays' cumulative intent, however, is as pedagogic as it is expository. Wilson describes his artistic agenda as an attempt to "concretize" the black American tradition, to demonstrate how that tradition "can sustain a man once he has left his father's house." Indeed, the theme that surges through Wilson's work is the need for black Americans to forge anew their identity, an identity that is at once African and American.

In the seven years he has been writing plays—his first efforts resulted in a handful of seldom if ever produced one-acts—Wilson has undertaken an ambitious, systematic project: each work is to be set in a different decade from 1900 to the present. "I'm taking each decade and looking back at one of the most important questions that blacks confronted in that decade and writing a play about it," says Wilson. "Put them all together and you have a history."

The dramatic chronicle that has resulted thusfar is peopled by striking protagonists earmarked by the eras in which they lived: Levee, the impetuous young trumpeter of *Ma Rainey,* struggles to survive in a white entertainment world during the '20s; Loomis, the forbiddingly Dickensian protagonist of *Joe Turner,* fights to regain his identity after seven years of forced labor in the early 1900s; Troy, the tyrannical patriarch of *Fences,* rages at social injustice prefiguring that of the explosive '60s. Collectively they constitute Wilson's overt literary intent: "You should be able to see a progression through the decades from Loomis to Levee to Boy Willie [in *The Piano Lesson*] to Troy. Says drama critic Ernie Schier, "August is a better chronicler of the black experience in this country than Alex Haley. In 40 years, he will be the playwright we will still be hearing about."

Ironically, Wilson is emerging at a time when few black American playwrights are finding and keeping a national audience, when politically and artistically the country is more attuned to the racial injustices of South Africa than to the dilemmas of its own black population. Nonetheless, after nearly two decades of writing both poetry and drama and four years of almost exclusive collaboration with director Lloyd Richards at the O'Neill Theater Center and Yale Repertory Theatre, Wilson is entering a new and broader arena.

The Piano Lesson received its first staged reading at the O'Neill this past summer. A trio of Wilson's other plays are currently crisscrossing the country. *Fences,* starring James Earl Jones, is set to open in New York in March after runs last season at the Goodman Theatre in Chicago and (with a different cast) at Seattle Repertory Theatre. The Yale production of *Joe Turner* has just completed the first of its regional theatre stopovers at Boston's Huntington Theatre Company. And—although *Ma Rainey* never recouped its investment during its commercial New York run two years ago, despite its critical heralding and a 1984 Tony nomination—Wilson is tilting anew at Broadway. In addition to the upcoming New York run of *Fences,* Wilson has just completed the book for a new musical about black jazz musician Jelly Roll Morton, which is to star Gregory Hines and open on Broadway in the spring under Jerry Zaks's direction. "I consider this a jazz-blues folk

opera," says Wilson, "an encapsulation of the history of black music until 1928."

The undertaking is further evidence of Wilson's commitment to his delineated literary turf—history, that individual and collective process of discovery that, as the author says, "becomes doubly important if someone else has been writing yours for you." His plays maintain a contemporary involvement with the past, and punctuate each era with its own particular totems. By mining black American music, which Wilson sees as one of the few traditionally acceptable venues for black American culture, Wilson is able to reveal the cumulative history informing his protagonists: nearly all his characters are in search of their individual songs of identity. Wilson describes Loomis's metaphysical journey in *Joe Turner,* for example, as a "song in search of itself."

Its musical allusions aside, Wilson's writing is a poetic melding of African and Western imagery. His use of ethnographically specific folklore borders on the mystical and reinforces the distinctively non-linear narrative style which the playwright ascribes to an "African storytelling mode." While some have been slow to warm to this non-traditional dramatic structure, others have praised it as indigenous to the black oral tradition, a heritage that embraces African as well as Bible Belt oral patterns and serves as Wilson's own palimpsest. "It is writing based on centuries of 'hearing'," says director Claude Purdy, who staged Wilson's *Fences* at GeVa Theatre in Rochester, N.Y.

Wilson describes his work as an attempt to confront "the glancing manner in which white America looks at blacks and the way blacks look at themselves." By probing the sociological archetype with sufficient metaphor but without conspicuous didactism, Wilson has set himself apart from many of the so-called angry young black playwrights, including Ed Bullins and Amiri Baraka, whose work proliferated during the late '60s. "I can only do what I do because the '60s existed," Wilson reasons. "I am building off that original conflict."

Although he maintains that "the one thing that has best served me as a playwright is my background in poetry," Wilson first came to the theatre out of a search for a broader forum in which to voice his social concerns; initially he thought about a legal career. But after a boyhood spent on the streets of Pittsburgh—Wilson dropped out of school at age 15—the playwright says "my sense of justice [became] very different from what the law says. It just happened that my talent lies with words." Claude Purdy, now director-in-residence at St. Paul's Penumbra Theatre, confirms Wilson's motives: "August came out of the '60s with a responsible attitude, eager to explore his community's culture and do something for his people."

As a co-founder of Pittsburgh's Black Horizons Theatre, Wilson wrote his early one-acts during the height of the black power movement as a way, he says, "to politicize the community and raise consciousness." Today Wilson prefers the label of "cultural nationalist."

"An interviewer once asked me if having written these plays I hadn't exhausted the black experience. I said,

'Wait a minute. You've got 40,000 movies and plays about the white experience, and we don't ask if you've exhausted your experience.' I'll never run out of material. If I finish this cycle, I'll just start over again. You can write forever about the clash between the urban North and the rural South, what happened when [blacks] came to the cities, how their lives changed and how it affected generations to come."

It is an outspoken assertion from this usually reserved 41-year-old Pittsburgh native now residing in St. Paul. Wilson's conversational style only hints at his transplanted Midwest roots. With his soft-spoken affability and almost old-fashioned politeness, he hardly appears the source for the chorus of vibrant voices—by turns soft and genial, angry and defiant—one hears in his plays.

"After I turned 20, I spent the next 10 to 15 years hanging out on streetcorners, following old men around, working odd jobs. There was this place called Pat's Cigar Store in Pittsburgh. It was the same place that Claude McKay mentioned in his book *Home to Harlem.* When I found out about that, I said, 'This is a part of history,' and I ran down there to where all the old men in the community would congregate."

Although Wilson originally channeled his literary efforts into poetry, his move to Minnesota in the early 1970s served as a catalyst, permitting those colloquial voices and his own skills as a dramatist to come into their own. Initially working as a script writer for the local science museum's children's theatre while firing off "five plays in three years" to the O'Neill, Wilson did not conceive of himself as a playwright until he received the first of several writing grants. After submitting *Jitney* to Minneapolis's Playwrights' Center, Wilson was awarded a Jerome Foundation fellowship in the late 1970s. (He has subsequently received Bush, Rockefeller, McKnight and Guggenheim fellowships.) "I walked in and there were 16 playwrights," Wilson remembers about that encounter with the Playwrights' Center. "It was the first time I had dinner with other playwrights. It was the first time I began to think of myself as one."

It was this "two hundred bucks a month for a year" that afforded Wilson the opportunity to rework a one-act about a blues recording session into what became the full-length *Ma Rainey,* his first play accepted by the O'Neill and the most naturalistic of his dramas. Set in a Chicago recording studio in 1927, the play is a garrulous and colloquially accurate look at the exploitation of black musicians. Through Wilson's carefully orchestrated verbal riffs, the characters' struggle for identity slowly escalates to a violent conclusion.

In *Ma Rainey,* the struggle is predicated not only upon friction between the white recording executives and the black musicians but also upon subtle conflicts within the black community itself. Ma, the recording star, knows the limits of her commercial success, admitting, "It's just like I been a whore"; the elderly pianist, Toledo, is an African nationalist who argues, "We done sold ourselves to the white man in order to be like him"; Levee, the headstrong trumpeter, is intent on making it in the white world, on

seeing his name in lights. Unable to confront his white oppressors, Levee fatally lashes out at his own. Wilson describes Levee's condition in a rhetorical question: "How can I live this life in society that refuses to recognize my worth, that refuses to allow me to contribute to its welfare?"

It is a question that Wilson probes again in *Fences,* written partly as a response to criticism of *Ma Rainey*'s bifurcated focus. "*Fences* was me sitting down saying, 'Okay, here is a play with a large central character.' " It was also the writer's attempt to create a protagonist who, unlike the impatient and intransigent Levee, had achieved a grudging parity with his times, albeit a smoldering suppression of desire suitable to the political realities of the 1950s. "Unlike Levee, Troy didn't sell his soul to the devil," says Wilson.

A former Negro League ballplayer past his prime by the time Jackie Robinson broke the color barrier, Troy Maxson can be considered Wilson's most overtly didactic character. "I had to write a character who is responsible and likes the idea of family," says the playwright. This sense of responsibility—for one's own destiny as well as one's own family—is pivotal for Wilson, not only in its metaphysical ramifications but in its more pragmatic applications as well. "We have been told so many times how irresponsible we are as black males that I try and present positive images of responsibility," says the writer. "I started *Fences* with the image of a man standing in his yard with a baby in his arms."

It is this sense of individual accountability that Wilson's other protagonists—Loomis in *Joe Turner* and Boy Willie in the yet-to-be-produced *Piano Lesson*—confront in more mystical terms. "In *Ma Rainey* and *Fences,*" Wilson explains, "the two roads into white American society traditionally open to blacks, entertainment and sports, fail the characters." As a result, the leading figures in the subsequent plays do not establish their identities relative to the white world; they rediscover themselves as Africans. "If black folks would recognize themselves as Africans and not be afraid to respond to the world as Africans, then they could make their contribution to the world as Africans," says Wilson.

Set in 1911 in order to get closer to this "African retentiveness," *Joe Turner* is infused with so much non-Western mysticism and folklore—ghosts, myths, chants and spells—that the narrative can be seen as a spiritual allegory. Based partly on a painting by black artist Romare Bearden, "Mill Hand's Lunch Bucket," as well as the legend of the actual slave hunter Joe Turner, the play is rife with historical detail as well as religious feeling. Loomis's search for his own past after seven years of bondage symbolizes the quest of an entire race. "As a whole, our generation knows very little about our past," explains Wilson. "My generation of parents tried to shield their children from the indignities they'd suffered."

For Loomis, the journey towards self-knowledge includes two apocalyptic moments—baptismal exorcisms that bracket the play's two acts and reverberate with violence. In the first of these cathartic steps, Loomis confronts his vision of "bones walking on top of water," a mythic image of ancestral suffering. In the final scene, Loomis faces both Christianity and African myth, and with a single symbolic act, finds himself purged from his past and a free man. As Loomis states, "I don't need anyone to bleed for me, I can bleed for myself."

It is a moment of individual transmogrification that Wilson examines again, and to even stronger effect, in **The Piano Lesson.** Although Wilson intends to rewrite this latest entry in his historical cycle next summer, the play's inherent dramatic conflict—a brother and sister argue over their shared legacy, the family piano—and its crisp scenic construction bode well for its arrival on stage. The piano itself is Wilson's clearest, most fully realized symbol, one that resounds with African and Western significance while forming the fulcrum of the play's metaphysical debate. "The real issue is the piano, the legacy. How are you going to use it?" says Wilson.

There are two choices, one taken up by Berneice, who wants to preserve the blood-stained piano as a totem to the family's violence-wracked past. Her brother, Boy Willie, however, is intent on literally capitalizing on the family's history to create a new future; he wants to sell the piano and buy the land which their father originally farmed as a slave. "I ain't gonna be no fool about no sentimental value," Boy Willie says. "With that piano I get the land and I can go down and cash in the crop." As Wilson describes his character's position, "I often wonder what the fabric of American society would be like if blacks had stayed in the South and somehow found a way to [economically] develop and lock into that particular area. That's what Boy Willie is articulating. He wants to put his hands to better use."

Willie's desire encapsulates the playwright's overall intent. "I think it's largely a question of identity. Without knowing your past, you don't know your present—and you certainly can't plot your future," Wilson says. "You go out and discover it for yourself. It's being responsible for your own presence in the world and for your own salvation." (pp. 22-5)

Hilary Devries, "A Song in Search of Itself," in American Theatre, *Vol. 3, No. 10, January, 1987, pp. 22-5.*

MA RAINEY'S BLACK BOTTOM

PRODUCTION REVIEWS

Clive Barnes (review date 12 October 1984)

[*A British-born American drama and dance critic, Barnes has been called "the first, second and third most powerful critic in New York." He has refrained from exploiting his influence, however, and has adopted an informal, conversational writing style in his reviews. Barnes insists that criticism of the arts is a public service; therefore, the function of a reviewer is to advise and inform audiences rather than determine a production's success or failure. As a result, Barnes has also earned the reputation of being "the major newspaper critic easiest to please." His commentary has appeared regularly in the* New York Times *and the* New York Post. *In the following review, Barnes praises the characterizations and technical aspects of* Ma Rainey's Black Bottom *but finds that "nothing much happens" in terms of the plot.*]

It is a strange kind of play, **Ma Rainey's Black Bottom,** that arrived on Broadway at the Cort last night, coming via the Yale Repertory Company.

Perhaps it is not so much a play as a slice of life, or an exposition of the black experience—the black experience between the wars, around the end of the 1920s.

August Wilson, the playwright, has set his drama in Chicago in 1927, in a recording studio, during a session in which the famed Ma Rainey (correctly called "the Mother of the Blues") recorded *Ma Rainey's Black Bottom* and the even more famous *Moonshine Blues.*

This event is a historical happening—but Wilson very reasonably takes it from there. The play does have something to do with the legendary Rainey, and, rather more, the relationship between the black artist and the white, exploitative world of his or her time.

For this is essentially a political play, and although Ma Rainey—and perhaps her singing of the blues and the very blues spirit—inspired Wilson's work, Ma is not even the principal character at her own session.

The focus is on the four musicians that the singer had as her accompaniment. In real life her players were often excellent, and included the likes of Louis Armstrong, Tommy Ladnier, Tampa Red. Here, in fiction, the four of them are not the likes of Armstrong, but they are black men and they are talking, and joking, but most of all talking, about the black experience.

Much is explained, but—and this is the crucial fault of the play—nothing much happens. Until right at the end, when, as if Wilson who had scarcely started his play suddenly found he had run out of time and had to finish it, there is an eruption of sorts, feasible in life but scarcely credible in the tidier domain of drama.

The dialogue is racy, salty, pertinent—but it hangs in the air, its social content being so much more evident than its dramatic context.

The characters—both black and, to a lesser extent, white—are fine. For the most part the writing avoids cliche and stereotype, although the white cop on the take, and the white studio owner on the make, veer close to the danger zone.

Yet the imperious Ma, high-handed, shrewd, proud, and even jealous of her rival Bessie Smith, and Ma's motley crew—sharply representative of their race, time, and profession—are drawn with the observation of life.

Director Lloyd Richards, who has been associated with this play both at Yale and, earlier, at the O'Neill Play-

Charles S. Dutton as Levee, Leonard Jackson as Slow Drag, and Theresa Merritt as Ma Rainey in the original production of Ma Rainey's Black Bottom.

wrights' Center, has done a tremendous job in preparing *Ma Rainey's Black Bottom* for the stage.

The seedy but attractive setting by Charles Henry Mc-Clennahan and the crisply period costumes by Daphne Pascucci help all along the line, but Richards' major assist comes from a cast, most of whom seemingly live the play rather than act it.

Theresa Merritt as Ma Rainey has a presence even off-stage, which she is for most of the play, while her quartet, squabbling in the dusty foreground and dramatic spotlight, is nothing less than magnificent.

Joe Seneca as the phlegmatic leader, Robert Judd as a hazily philosophic pianist, Leonard Jackson as the cheerful, hedonistic bass player, and—best of all—Charles S. Dutton as an embittered, complex, new-wave trumpeter, become their roles with grace.

They are playing in a play that is never really there, but thanks to their skills, as well those of Wilson and Richards, to many audiences this may not be overwhelmingly evident.

In such lucky, but happy, circumstances *Ma Rainey's Black Bottom* might yet wriggle its way to glory. But watch out for that ending, friends!

Clive Barnes, " 'Ma Rainey'—The Black Experience," in New York Post, *October 12, 1984.*

Frank Rich   (review date 12 October 1984)

[*Rich provided drama reviews for* Time *and the* New York Post *prior to becoming the* New York Times *drama critic in 1980. In the following favorable review, he describes* Ma Rainey's Black Bottom *as "a searing inside account of what white racism does to its victims."*]

Late in Act I of *Ma Rainey's Black Bottom,* a somber, aging band trombonist (Joe Seneca) tilts his head heavenward to sing the blues. The setting is a dilapidated Chicago recording studio of 1927, and the song sounds as old as time. "If I had my way," goes the lyric, "I would tear this old building down."

Once the play has ended, that lyric has almost become a prophecy. In *Ma Rainey's Black Bottom,* the writer August Wilson sends the entire history of black America crashing down upon our heads. This play is a searing inside account of what white racism does to its victims—and it floats on the same authentic artistry as the blues music it celebrates. Harrowing as *Ma Rainey's* can be, it is also funny, salty, carnal and lyrical. Like his real-life heroine, the legendary singer Gertrude (Ma) Rainey, Mr. Wilson articulates a legacy of unspeakable agony and rage in a spellbinding voice.

The play is Mr. Wilson's first to arrive in New York, and it reached here, via the Yale Repertory Theater, under the sensitive hand of the man who was born to direct it, Lloyd Richards. On Broadway, Mr. Richards has honed *Ma Rainey's* to its finest form. What's more, the director brings us an exciting young actor—Charles S. Dutton— along with his extraordinary dramatist. One wonders if the electricity at the Cort is the same that audiences felt when Mr. Richards, Lorraine Hansberry and Sidney Poitier stormed into Broadway with *A Raisin in the Sun* a quarter-century ago.

As *Ma Rainey's* shares its director and Chicago setting with *Raisin,* so it builds on Hansberry's themes: Mr. Wilson's characters want to make it in white America. And, to a degree, they have. Ma Rainey (1886-1939) was among the first black singers to get a recording contract—albeit with a white company's "race" division. Mr. Wilson gives us Ma (Theresa Merritt) at the height of her fame. A mountain of glitter and feathers, she has become a despotic, temperamental star, complete with a retinue of flunkies, a fancy car and a kept young lesbian lover.

The evening's framework is a Paramount-label recording session that actually happened, but whose details and supporting players have been invented by the author. As the action swings between the studio and the band's warm-up room—designed by Charles Henry McClennahan as if they might be the festering last-chance saloon of *The Iceman Cometh*—Ma and her four accompanying musicians overcome various mishaps to record "Ma Rainey's Black Bottom" and other songs. During the delays, the band members smoke reefers, joke around and reminisce about past gigs on a well-traveled road stretching through whorehouses and church socials from New Orleans to Fat Back, Ark.

The musicians' speeches are like improvised band solos— variously fizzy, haunting and mournful. We hear how the bassist Slow Drag (Leonard Jackson) got his nickname at a dance contest, but also about how a black preacher was tortured by being forced to "dance" by a white vigilante's gun. Gradually, we come to know these men, from their elusive pipe dreams to their hidden scars, but so deftly are the verbal riffs orchestrated that we don't immediately notice the incendiary drama boiling underneath.

That drama is ignited by a conflict between Ma and her young trumpeter Levee, played by Mr. Dutton. An ambitious sport eager to form his own jazz band, Levee mocks his employer's old "jugband music" and champions the new dance music that has just begun to usurp the blues among black audiences in the urban North. Already Levee has challenged Ma by writing a swinging version of "Ma Rainey's Black Bottom" that he expects the record company to use in place of the singer's traditional arrangement.

Yet even as the battle is joined between emblematic representatives of two generations of black music, we're thrust into a more profound war about identity. The African nationalist among the musicians, the pianist Toledo (Robert Judd), argues that, "We done sold ourselves to the white man in order to be like him." We soon realize that, while Ma's music is from the heart, her life has become a sad, ludicrous "imitation" of white stardom. Levee's music is soulful, too, but his ideal of success is having his "name in lights"; his pride is invested in the new shoes on which he's blown a week's pay.

Ma, at least, senses the limits of her success. Though she acts as if she owns the studio, she can't hail a cab in the white city beyond. She knows that her clout with the record company begins and ends with her viability as a commercial product: "When I've finished recording," she says, "it's just like I'd been some whore, and they roll over and put their pants on." Levee, by contrast, has yet to learn that a black man can't name his own terms if he's going to sell his music to a white world. As he plots his future career, he deceives himself into believing that a shoeshine and Uncle Tom smile will win white backers for his schemes.

Inevitably, the promised door of opportunity slams, quite literally, in Levee's face, and the sound has a violent ring that reverberates through the decades. Levee must confront not just the collapse of his hopes but the destruction of his dignity. Having played the white man's game and lost to its rigged rules, he is left with less than nothing: Even as he fails to sell himself to whites, Levee has sold out his own sense of self-worth.

Mr. Dutton's delineation of this tragic downfall is red-hot. A burly actor a year out of Yale, he is at first as jazzy as his music. With his boisterous wisecracks and jumpy sprinter's stance, he seems ready to leap into the stratosphere envisioned in his fantasies of glory. But once he crash lands, the poison of self-hatred ravages his massive body and distorts his thundering voice. No longer able to channel his anger into his music, he directs it to God, crying out that a black man's prayers are doomed to be tossed "into the garbage." As Mr. Dutton careens about with unchecked, ever escalating turbulence he transforms an anonymous Chicago bandroom into a burial ground for a race's aspirations.

Mr. Dutton's fellow band members are a miraculous double-threat ensemble: They play their instruments nearly as convincingly as they spin their juicy monologues. Aleta Mitchell and Lou Criscuolo, as Ma's gum-chewing lover and harried white manager, are just right, and so is Scott Davenport-Richards, as Ma's erstwhile Little Lord Faunteroy of a young nephew. It's one of the evening's more grotesquely amusing gags that Ma imperiously insists on having the boy, a chronic stutterer, recite a spoken introduction on her record.

Miss Merritt is Ma Rainey incarnate. A singing actress of both wit and power, she finds bitter humor in the character's distorted sense of self: When she barks her outrageous demands to her lackeys, we see a show business monster who's come a long way from her roots. Yet the roots can still be unearthed. In a rare reflective moment, she explains why she sings the blues. "You don't sing to feel better," Miss Merritt says tenderly. "You sing because that's a way of understanding life."

The lines might also apply to the play's author. Mr. Wilson can't mend the broken lives he unravels in *Ma Rainey's Black Bottom.* But, like his heroine, he makes their suffering into art that forces us to understand and won't allow us to forget. (pp. C1, C3)

Frank Rich, "Wilson's 'Ma Rainey's' Opens," in The New York Times, *October 12, 1984, pp. C1, C3.*

Edwin Wilson   (review date 16 October 1984)

[*In the review below, Wilson commends the acting and direction of the Broadway production of* Ma Rainey's Black Bottom *but declares that while "there is an abundance of atmosphere and banter, and a strong racial statement," there is "not much of a play."*]

"Vamp until ready" was a phrase that often appeared on sheet music in the 1920s and 1930s. It meant that the piano player was to improvise until the soloist sang the song. In *Ma Rainey's Black Bottom,* the new play at the Cort Theatre, playwright August Wilson does plenty of vamping, but has trouble getting to the tune. There is an abundance of atmosphere and banter, and a strong racial statement, but not much of a play.

The scene is a Chicago recording studio in the 1920s. A group of black musicians, the backup band for singer Ma Rainey, the "mother of the blues," is waiting for Ma to come for a recording session. Cutler (Joe Seneca), the trombonist, is straw boss of the group. Toledo (Robert Judd), the pianist, is an inveterate leader whose pseudoscholarly lectures are a constant irritant to Levee (Charles S. Dutton), a flashy trumpet player in a wide-striped suit and shiny new shoes. Waiting for Ma along with the musicians are her manager (Lou Criscuolo) and the owner of the recording company (John Carpenter), both white men.

Also waiting is the audience. For almost an hour there is no sign of Ma, and therefore no drama. While waiting, the musicians rehearse occasionally, but mostly they bicker among themselves. Levee, for instance, younger than the others, is a songwriter who aspires to lead his own band. He continually taunts the others for playing in what he calls a "jug band."

When Ma does appear, she makes a grand entrance. Accompanied by a simpering nephew (Scott Davenport-Richards) and a high-style lady friend (Aleta Mitchell), she enters the studio like an ocean liner coming into port. Dressed in shimmering fuchsia and pink sequins, Theresa Merritt as Ma is an amply endowed woman for whom the waves part. Once in the studio, she takes charge, ordering her manager and the record producer to do her bidding. She refuses to sing until someone goes out in the cold to get her a Coca Cola, and insists that she will not record the title song unless her nephew provides a spoken introduction. The fact that he badly stutters leaves her undeterred.

The theme of the play is racial injustice. Ma and her trombonist compare notes on their mistreatment as black entertainers; Levee tells how he was forced to witness white men rape his mother when he was eight years old. And Ma takes obvious relish in turning the tables on her white manager and producer. The evening ends in a melodramatic murder that results from black frustration.

Unfortunately, polemics do not make a play. The band's infighting amounts only to extended byplay, and Ma herself does little more than issue ultimatums to her underlings. We are even shortchanged on the actual music. Only two songs are performed in full.

Offsetting Mr. Wilson's shortcomings as a playwright are the performances and the direction. The cast is first-rate, especially Charles S. Dutton and Theresa Merritt, who gives a flawless performance. Also, director Lloyd Richards has created a vivid sense of stage life. Their work, however, remains a prelude waiting for a drama.

Edwin Wilson, "Ma Rainey," in The Wall Street Journal, *October 16, 1984.*

CRITICAL COMMENTARY

Philip E. Smith, II   (essay date 1986)

[*In the essay below, Smith discusses the historical background of* Ma Rainey's Black Bottom *and the major themes of the play. He concludes that* Ma Rainey's *"is a blues-as-drama about the consequences of not understanding the relationship of self to history and culture."*]

August Wilson's new play, [*Ma Rainey's Black Bottom*], about a 1927 Ma Rainey recording session in Chicago dramatizes the production of blues race-records as a critique of commercial and racial exploitation of blacks by whites. But this critique underlies the play as a kind of "given," a basic slice of American life upon which another kind of drama is enacted. Wilson's characters present American blacks' strategies for survival and their dissemination of attitudes toward exploitation by means of playing the blues, singing the blues, telling the blues, and living the blues. So Wilson's play itself constitutes a dramatic "playing" of the blues wherein language, representation, and action on stage encompass several kinds of blues performances.

Kenneth Burke's ideas about "Literature as Equipment for Living" [in his *The Philosophy of Literary Form,* 1973] offer an approach to understanding the play, the blues, and the play-as-blues. Burke suggests that a work of literature "is the strategic naming of a situation. It singles out a pattern of experience that is sufficiently representative of our social structure . . . for people to 'need a word for it' and to adopt an attitude towards it." The word for it, August Wilson's strategic naming as dramatized in *Ma Rainey's Black Bottom,* is "blues." A brief recollection of some background about the blues will be useful before proceeding to the play.

The experience that blues names is rooted in the history

of black people emerging from slavery into a dislocated role as the exploited and racially separate bottom class in our society. Imamu Amiri Baraka, in his book renaming American blacks *The Blues People,* has observed that:

> some kind of graph could be set up using samplings of Negro music proper to whatever moment of the Negro's social history was selected, and that in each grouping of songs a certain frequency of reference could pretty well determine his social, economic, and psychological states at that particular period. From the Neo-African slave chants through the primitive and classical blues to the scat-singing of the be-boppers: all would show definite insistences of reference that would isolate each group from the others as a social entity.

August Wilson sets his play in a significant moment of the "Blues People's" history when the "classic blues" as sung by Ma Rainey was emerging from its origins in "country" or "primitive" blues, which in turn grew out of diverse traditions such as African music, the spiritual, and the Anglo-American folk ballad. The blues came north early in the twentieth century with blacks who migrated to find jobs in cities and industry. In the 1920's and 30's blues were increasingly shunned by middle-class blacks who tried to assimilate into the mainstream of white culture, but lower-class blacks, especially recently arrived migrants, often kept in touch with their southern cultural heritage of blues music. By the mid-1940's, Baraka claims, some middle-class blacks "had wandered completely from the blues tradition, becoming trapped in the sinister vapidity of main-line American culture."

Even by 1927, black music and culture had undergone a major transformation which was manifested in blues performances and the associated production of entertainment and commodities for profit. As Baraka points out:

> Blues, until the time of the classic blues singers, was largely a *functional* music; and it emerged from a music, the work song, that did not exist except as a strictly empirical communication of some part of the black slave's life. But the idea of the blues as a form of music that could be used to entertain people on a professional basis, *i.e.,* that people would actually pay to see and hear blues performed, was a revelation. And it was a revelation that gave a large impetus to the concept of the 'race' record.

Ma Rainey based her career as musical performer and celebrity on the new market for blues. She had begun as a vaudeville artist and started singing the blues in 1902 after hearing a young girl who came to her tent in a small town in Missouri and performed a blues lament. Rainey recognized the power and appeal of blues songs and found them to be very popular with her rural, southern, tent-show audiences. Blues songs were a mainstay of her live and recorded performances until she retired in 1935.

The blues became a mass-produced commodity through the promotion and sale of race records in the 1920's. The first blues race record, Mamie Smith's version of "Crazy Blues," appeared on the OKeh label in 1920; after its commercial success, production increased rapidly, as did ad-

vertising and distribution. By 1927, the year of the play's setting, over 500 titles were released, and sales to blacks were estimated to be ten million records. However, the classic blues, like the country blues, had only a limited period of popularity before more "advanced" forms of jazz appropriated and replaced the older music.

August Wilson began work on his play while listening to a Ma Rainey record he bought in 1976:

> I listened and I began to write. My first idea was to explore the economic exploitation of black musicians. The play took place entirely in the recording studio. I wrestled with that a while and abandoned it. I came back to the play in 1978 and I began to hear the voices of the band members. So I decided to open the door to the band room and see who was inside. The whole time I was writing, I was listening to records in my room. I was listening to the male blues singers—Charlie Patton, Son House—because I was writing the men in the band. And I was trying to write honestly, to aquire [sic] the force of the blues.

If Wilson's major black characters have their origins in country and classic blues performers and their songs, then it is not far-fetched to think of several of the stories told by the band members as prose blues, or equipment for living in white America. The play portrays a single day's recording session, almost with the rigor of the neo-classical unities of time, place, and action, and with a unity of purpose that brings together the separate stories and perspectives of the ensemble of characters, but principally Ma Rainey and her accompaniment band: Cutler, the trombonist and leader; Toledo, the pianist; Slow Drag, the bassist; and Levee, the trumpeter. The central focus of the many blues performances in the play is suggested in dialogue between Ma Rainey and Cutler.

> MA RAINEY: White folks don't understand about the blues. They hear it come out but they don't know how it got there. They don't understand that's life's way of talking. You don't sing to feel better. You sing 'cause that's a way of understanding life.

> CUTLER: That's right. You get that understanding and you done got a grip on life to where you can hold your head up and go on to see what else life got to offer.

The description of blues as a way of understanding life recalls Burke's strategies and Baraka's theory of blues as a graph of black social history. This moment of significant dialogue offers a way of approaching the central dramatic conflict between Levee, the young trumpet player, and the other major black characters. While Cutler and Ma Rainey see the blues as a way of understanding life, Levee disdains their kind of blues as old-fashioned, rural entertainment unsuited to a new breed of urban blacks. Levee has rural roots (he comes from a farm in the Mississippi delta), but he wants to become a bandleader and recording artist, so he writes music in a new style which Sturdyvant, the white manager of the recording studio, encourages. In the opening moments of the play, Sturdyvant rejects Ma Rainey's previous records as "garbage"; he wants to hear more of Levee's new sound, which will jazz up Ma's blues. Sturdyvant and Irvin, Ma's white manager, have also chosen a list of songs for the day's recording session.

Which songs and how they will be played become a focus of the play, with Sturdyvant, Irvin, and Levee against Ma and the rest of the band. Wilson dramatizes the whites' assumptions about power and domination of blacks through this issue. The conflict is strongest in relation to the title song, "Ma Rainey's Black Bottom," which Sturdyvant and Irvin want to have recorded in Levee's jazzed-up version. Levee argues with the rest of the band in the rehearsal room until Irvin commands them to play Levee's version; when Ma arrives at the studio and hears it being rehearsed, she countermands the order, and insists on *her* version. Wilson shows that Ma must constantly assert herself against the manipulations and arguments of the whites. Her authority is partially economic: she says, "They don't care nothing about me. All they want is my voice. Well, I done learned that and they gonna treat me like I want to be treated no matter how much it hurt them. . . . As soon as they get my voice down on them recording machines, then it's just like if I'd be some whore and they roll over and put their pants on. Ain't got no use for me then." But she also has spiritual authority: her version of the blues comes from her felt sense of black experience, as she tells Irvin: "What you all say don't count with me. You understand? Ma listens to her heart. Ma listens to the voice inside her. That's what counts with Ma."

That spiritual authority underlies Ma's economic power; it might be called her "blues understanding" of life, the accumulated wisdom of her own experience and of a more general black consciousness. To supplement Ma's consciousness and authority, Wilson gives the members of the band their own moments in the play to express a blues understanding or strategy toward life. They tell stories, sometimes boasting, sometimes ironically self-critical, sometimes satiric, which embody strategies for survival or happiness. They serve as parables, reprimands, and lessons for one another, and especially for Levee, whose arrogance and Faustian willingness to sell his soul to the white man the others find repugnant.

The story-telling begins with humor; Levee arrives in the studio proudly sporting new shoes, and bragging that the music he's written for Sturdyvant is "art," not that "old jug band music" the band usually plays for Ma. Toledo wins his bet that Levee can't even spell "music," and tells a story to illustrate why Levee, with his pretensions about music, is a fool. Toledo then establishes his position as a kind of self-taught intellectual aware of the African heritage, and as a spokesman for the need to resist looking to the white man for approval. Levee responds by making fun of Toledo's shoes as "clod-hoppers" and "old brogans" suited to an "old sharecropper." Levee's solution for the problems of black people is to forget them, as Irvin and Sturdyvant have urged; he sings and dances a few lines of "Doctor Jazz": "when the world goes wrong and I have got the blues / He's the man who makes me put on my dancing shoes."

This performance provides for more exposition of the central conflict. Toledo condemns blacks who only want to

have a good time, and again shows up Levee as a "fool" who doesn't understand that "the colored man ought to be doing more than just trying to have a good time all the time," that "every living colored man in the world got to do his part." When Levee resists being called a "fool," Toledo calls him a "devil," and Slow Drag tells a story of an Alabama man who sold his soul to the devil. Levee angrily wishes that he could sell his soul; Toledo warns him about blasphemy, but Levee dares God to strike him down. By using the language of "fool" and "devil" and the issues of intelligence and religion, Wilson heightens the emotional strains between Levee and the band and establishes a framework of topics and issues on which, in the second act, he builds a parallel explosion of tensions when the band again argues with Levee about "fools" and "devils."

Act I proceeds with alternating scenes of Ma in the studio and the band's rehearsal. Ma's strategies for survival are demonstrated in the way she makes Irvin fix an altercation with the police and in her later insistence on recording her own version of her song. The band hears the story of how Slow Drag got his name, and Toledo's story, addressed to Levee, about how blacks are the leftovers from the great "stew" of history. Toledo's point is that Levee's "black ass" has already been eaten for supper by the white man, but that Levee is too much of a toady and fool to know it. Levee refuses Toledo's advice, and not until the end of the act, when his version of the song has been rejected by Ma, and the other band members accuse him of being "spooked up" by the white man, does Levee tell his own story.

Wilson gives Levee the concluding minutes of the act to reveal how his personal history has produced those attitudes which the other blacks condemn. Levee relates how, as a boy of eight, he took his daddy's knife to fight a gang of eight or nine white men who assaulted and raped his mother. In the fight he was severely stabbed and slashed; he raises his shirt to show the band "a long ugly scar." The scar and story emphasize how Levee has been scarred emotionally, too; he goes on to relate and endorse his father's revenge: how he smiled, sold his farm and moved, then returned to stalk and kill four whites before he was caught and lynched. So, Levee says, "that taught me how to handle them. So you all just back up and leave Levee alone about the white man. I can smile and say yessir to whoever I please. I got time coming to me." To underline this moment, Wilson calls for a long pause, and then has Slow Drag sing the apocalyptic chorus of a blues-spiritual, "If I Had My Way," which ends "I would tear this old building down."

Levee may have earned some respect or understanding by showing the other band members that he has paid his dues to resisting the white man. Slow Drag's quotation of the song suggests the empathy and fantasy in the blues tradition, that blacks wish for the power of Samson to bring down the whole oppressive building of white society. But, as Toledo knows, it would take all the blacks, everywhere, to do it, not one Samson. Levee's strategy for survival, to smile and say yessir, but to advance only himself, to write and sell music to white men, to be inspired by Doctor Jazz and the white man's advice to forget his troubles, to buy new Florsheim shoes and clothes and scorn those who wear country clod-hoppers, to reject his rural heritage and the solidarity and wisdom of the older band members, in short, to sell his soul to the devil and leave behind his roots and the crimes against his family, all make him into a black man alienated from the blues people, into a foolish Faustian individualist searching for money, fashion, fame, sexual pleasure, dancing, and all the urban "good times" he feels he is owed to make up for the scars he bears on his body and his soul.

At the end of the first act, Wilson has established that Levee wants the power and success Ma Rainey has earned, but without the solidarity with an older blues tradition that gives her a feeling of spiritual authority, and that offers strategies for living to the other members of the band. In the second act these tendencies are further developed. Ma reaffirms her control over the white record producers and over the band. Levee chases Ma's sexually provocative protegé, Dussie Mae, and promises to show her a "good time" in Memphis. After several false starts, Ma sings her version of the song, which also promises good times, dancing, and sexual pleasure. But the recording is botched and Levee is blamed for disconnecting the microphone cord.

In the rehearsal room again, the members of the band provoke Levee by calling him a fool; Toledo tells a self-critical story about having been a fool in marriage, which leads Toledo and Levee to make conflicting statements about life and death which reflect their attitudes about the racial conflicts in the play. Toledo has an accepting view: "Oh, life is fair. It's just in the taking what it gives you." Levee rejects this view: "Life ain't nothing," he says, "now death . . . death got some style! Death will kick your ass and make you wish you never been born!"

Wilson follows the life and death exchange with a reprise of the topic of selling souls to the devil. Toledo expands the idea to include the condition of American blacks who try to assimilate white culture: "We done sold ourselves to the white man in order to be like him. Look at the way you dressed . . . that ain't African. That's the white man. We trying to be just like him. We done sold who we are in order to become someone else. We's imitation white men." But Levee continues to reject historical and cultural analyses; he prefers to see himself as an autonomous individual: "I'm Levee. Just me. I ain't no imitation nothing." He affirms that he wants to be like Ma Rainey and command white men to obey. The others argue that Levee doesn't understand how little the whites value her, and Cutler tells an illustrative story of a Reverend Gates who was humiliated and made to dance by a gang of whites, then accused of heresy for dancing with a cross and a Bible. So, Cutler concludes, "the white folks don't care nothing about Ma Rainey. She's just another nigger who they can use to make some money." The story provokes Levee into a violent anti-religious diatribe which reveals another side to his wish for alliance with the devil: his hatred of the white man's God who won't strike down the "crackers," and who hates blacks. As they fight, Levee pulls a knife, menacing Cutler, then challenges God, screaming his rage that God didn't save his mother from

rape, and as Wilson says in the stage directions, "begins to stab upwards in the air, jumping, trying to reach God."

The dramatization of Levee's alienation from man and God is complete, and all that remains is the catastrophe. Ma fires Levee for improvising too much; Sturdyvant betrays Levee's hopes of being a bandleader and recording star then compounds the ignominy by buying his songs for a paltry five dollars each; and, finally, Toledo accidentally steps on Levee's new shoe with his country clod-hoppers. Levee loses control; Wilson's stage direction says "All the weight in the world suddenly falls on Levee and he rushes at Toledo with his knife in his hand." He kills Toledo before anyone can stop him, and Wilson ends the play with a blackout and a thematic atmospheric device: "The sound of a trumpet is heard, LEVEE's trumpet, a muted trumpet struggling for the highest of possibilities and blowing back pain and warning."

The concluding blues note suggests Levee's "version" of the play: his Faustian, individualist strategy toward life is a failure; further, he has dealt a crippling blow against his fellow blacks because he kills the most critical and knowledgeable character in the play. Toledo has pointed out the essential truths of American blacks' existence in 1927; but Levee wants to reject his relation to history, his African roots, and the need for solidarity among members of his race. Toledo has also shown the crucial flaw of blacks since before slavery: selling themselves to the white man, trying to assimilate, to be like him. Levee refuses to believe or understand Toledo's critique. Levee penetrates to one truth, however—it gives him a kind of power to know that God isn't on the black man's side, and it turns him away from the blues tradition and other black people who, like Toledo, believe that life is fair.

Levee foreshadows the next generation of blacks after those who sang and played the classic blues: he is a modern, urban, alienated man, refusing to recognize that his individualism cripples him by refusing to understand how he is scarred in spirit, not just body. Behind the mask of Doctor Jazz, Levee's master is death, or perhaps the devil in whiteface; Levee has nowhere to turn but to himself when he rejects the traditions and strategies of the blues people. He cannot bear the tremendous weight of his own rage, and with his strategy of selling himself to the white man exploded and betrayed, Levee is left without Ma's strength of heart and her spiritual authority; he can only bring down a more valuable man as he caves in upon his own inauthentic self.

August Wilson's play, then, is a blues-as-drama about the consequences of not understanding the relationship of self to history and culture. The lesson of Levee's Faustian break with his own blues tradition is sung, played, and told by the characters of a drama which fuses the naturalistic, representational, ensemble play with black American culture and music: with the blues as equipment for living. (pp. 177-85)

Philip E. Smith, II, " 'Ma Rainey's Black Bottom': Playing the Blues as Equipment for Living," in Within the Dramatic Spectrum, *edited by Karelisa V. Hartigan, University Press of America, 1986, pp. 177-86.*

FENCES

PRODUCTION REVIEWS

Allan Wallach   **(review date 27 March 1987)**

[*In the following review, Wallach regards* Fences *not as a "rage at racial injustice," but as a drama that depicts "a black man forced to come to terms with an unfeeling white world."*]

In the old days of the Negro Leagues, he had a big home run swing, hitting the ball far beyond the fences of now-forgotten stadiums. Now a 53-year-old sanitation worker, his body gone to paunch, Troy Maxson finds fences hemming him in instead of challenging him. But he's still gutsy and expansive, a man who can brag about wrestling with death and make you see it as a struggle between equals.

Troy is a yarn-spinner, a teller of raunchy jokes, a womanizer, a demanding husband, a harsh, inflexible father. James Earl Jones gives this role at the heart of August Wilson's *Fences* its full measure of earthiness and complexity. His superlative acting matches his memorable Jack Jefferson in *The Great White Hope*.

When Jones' Troy Maxson is laughing with his pal while they share a pint of gin, the play swells to match his over-sized dimensions. At other times, however, when he is fighting with his athlete son or scrapping with his put-upon wife, *Fences* shrinks to the conventional confines of a family play.

Wilson, whose ***Ma Rainey's Black Bottom*** was such a remarkable playwriting debut, hasn't given *Fences* the same flashes of poetry and flashpoint of rage at racial injustice, even though both elements are present. The family conflicts are curiously schematic, giving the impression that Wilson was less interested in such routine fare than in depicting a black man forced to come to terms with an unfeeling white world.

The central struggle pits Troy against his son, Cory (Courtney B. Vance), a high-school football star who's good enough, in the thawing racial environment of 1957, to have a college recruiter after him. Evoking his own crushed sports career, Troy insists that Cory keep his after-hours job at the A&P and give up football. "The white man," he growls, "ain't gonna let you get nowhere with that football no way."

The original cast of Fences.

Cory's feelings about his domineering father emerge in a flat question, "How come you ain't never liked me?"—evaded by Troy in a speech about fulfilling his family responsibility (a word that resounds throughout *Fences*). And the boy's loaded accusation—Troy is afraid his son will surpass him athletically—is left unexplored.

There is more passion in the fight between Troy and his wife, Rose (Mary Alice), when he tells her that another woman is carrying his child. Rose's anger and humiliation have her pounding on his massive chest. Troy's description of the life that led him to stray is like Churchill strained through a garbage man's bone-weariness: "I give you my sweat and my blood. I ain't got no tears. I done spent them."

The fence Troy is building to enclose their tiny yard serves as a metaphor both for Rose's desire to fence in her rambling husband and for the barriers erected between family members.

Wilson's sharply attuned ear for the rhythms of his characters is displayed by the men who show up in the yard (a beautifully detailed set by James D. Sandefur), where a ball suspended on a rope serves as a sad memento of Troy's career. Troy's brother (Frankie R. Faison), his mind destroyed by a wartime injury, stumbles in trailing his pathetic delusions, and his son from a previous marriage (Charles Brown) keeps showing up to borrow money and nurse his illusion that he is a jazzman.

Lloyd Richards (who also directed *Ma Rainey*) has given the play an understanding production, although it grows languid on occasion. In the good supporting cast, Mary Alice's intensely felt Rose and Ray Aranha's drinking crony are most notable.

Jones' performance is at its heartiest in the bouts of drinking and bantering. He mingles indignation and humor when Troy describes the racial barriers he is battering at his job, and he warms with the linked memories of an early sexual encounter and a showdown with his own hard father.

The actor makes us see the fragility beneath Troy's harshness and the pride in his talk of providing for his family, however meanly. At those times, *Fences* becomes a rich portrait of a man who scaled down his dreams to fit inside his run-down yard.

> Allan Wallach, "Fenced in by a Lifetime of
> Resentments," in Newsday, March 27, 1987.

Clive Barnes   (review date 27 March 1987)

[*In the following highly favorable review, Barnes contends that "what makes 'Fences' so engrossing, so embracing, so simply powerful, is [Wilson's] startling ability to tell a story, reveal feeling, paint emotion."*]

Once in a rare while, you come across a play—or a movie or a novel—that seems to break away from the confines of art into a dense, complex realization of reality. A veil has been torn aside, the artist has disappeared into a transparency. We look with our own eyes, feel with our own hearts.

That was my reaction to August Wilson's pulsing play *Fences*, which opened last night at the 46th Street Theater, with James Earl Jones in full magnificent cry heading a cast of actors as good as you could find anywhere.

I wasn't just moved. I was transfixed—by intimations of a life, impressions of a man, images of a society.

Wilson, who a couple of seasons back gave us the arresting but fascinatingly flawed *Ma Rainey's Black Bottom,* always insists in interviews that he is writing from the wellspring of black experience in America.

This is undoubtedly true. Had Wilson been white, his plays would have been different—they would have had a different fire in a different belly.

But calling Wilson a "black" playwright is irrelevant. What makes *Fences* so engrossing, so embracing, so simply powerful, is his startling ability to tell a story, reveal feeling, paint emotion.

In many respects, *Fences* falls into the classic pattern of the American realistic drama—a family play, with a tragically doomed American father locked in conflict with his son. Greek tragedy with a Yankee accent.

The timing of the play—the late '50s—is carefully pinpointed in the history of black America as that turning point in the Civil Rights movement when a dream unfulfilled became a promise deferred.

The hero is Troy Maxson—and I suggest that he will be remembered as one of the great characters in American drama, and Jones always recalled as the first actor to play him.

Troy is as complex and as tormented as black America itself. He started life as a refugee from the South, and as a thief and, eventually, a killer.

Life in a penitentiary gave him the iron determination to reshape his life—as did, later, a feverish brush with death.

Prison also taught him baseball; when he came out, he became a temperamental star of the Negro Leagues. And now—in 1957—he can look at the likes of Jackie Robinson and Hank Aaron, making it in the Major Leagues of big-time whiteball, with a mixture of anger, envy and contempt.

A garbage collector, Troy has typically had to fight through his union to become the first black driver of a garbage truck. Equally typically, he hasn't even got a driver's license.

He sees himself as a man fenced in with responsibilities, but he has created some of those fences himself—some intended to keep people out, some to keep people in.

He is a family man—with a second wife, Rose, and their son Cory, as well as Gabriel, his brother, half-crazed by a war injury, and Lyons, Troy's older son by a previous marriage.

His life is secure—but limited. His son wants to go to college on a football scholarship, but Troy, wary of professional sports, refuses to let him try his luck.

Troy—although fully aware of his wife's qualities and warned by his best friend, Jim—falls in love with a younger woman, who becomes pregnant.

What is particularly pungent about Wilson's play is how the story and the characters are plugged into their particular historic relevance, ranging from the lessons of prison to the metaphors of baseball. It is this that makes the play resonate with all its subtle vibrations of truth and actuality.

This is in no sense a political play—but quite dispassionately it says: This is what it was like to be a black man of pride and ambition from the South, trying to live and work in the industrial North in the years just before and just after World War II.

The writing is perfectly geared to its people and its place. It jumps from the author's mind onto the stage, its language catching fire in the rarefied atmosphere of drama.

However fine the play is—and it is the strongest, most passionate American dramatic writing since Tennessee Williams—no praise can be too high for the staging by Lloyd Richards.

Helped by the cinematic accuracy of James D. Sandefur's setting, Richards has made the play into a microcosm in which we can see the tiny reflections of parts of ourselves, parts of America and parts of history.

He gives every actor a sense of purpose and belonging—and makes the play their nightly story. Wonderful acting, but also marvelous direction.

James Earl Jones remakes himself in Troy's image. It is a performance of such astonishing credibility that it offers the audience a guilty sense of actually spying on the character, unobserved and unwanted.

But this is only one performance of note; in her way, Mary Alice, as Troy's wife, is just as powerful, her pain and reality just as painfully real. And then there is Courtney B. Vance as Troy's alienated son, another performance of bewildering truth and honesty.

Add to these Ray Aranha, Charles Brown, Frankie F. Faison, and Karima Miller, and you have an ensemble cast as good as you will ever find.

Fences gave me one of the richest experiences I have ever had in the theater.

> Clive Barnes, "Fiery 'Fences'," *in* New York Post, *March 27, 1987.*

Edwin Wilson   (review date 31 March 1987)

[*In the following review, the critic discusses the characterization of Troy in* Fences *and praises Wilson's ability to "strike at the heart, not just of the black experience, but of the human condition."*]

In the second act of **Fences,** the new play at the 46th Street Theater, the main character, Troy, has just told Rose, his wife of 18 years, that he is about to be a father. Rose had not even known that Troy was seeing another woman, let alone that the woman was pregnant by him. The audience

James Earl Jones as Troy Maxson in Fences.

watches anxiously for a scream or a torrent of outrage from Rose, but before she can utter a word, Troy's brother Gabriel comes around the corner of their house carrying a red rose he wishes to present to Rose. Because Gabriel is a half-wit, as a result of a World War II head injury, the audience knows that the fury between Rose and Troy must be suspended until they deal with Gabriel. Later, when Rose's pent-up anger bursts out, it is all the more devastating because of the delay.

The tableau of the scene—Rose facing Troy as Gabriel enters with his flower—signals a crosscurrent of emotions at once infinitely complex but immediately recognizable. It's the kind of scene only a real dramatist could conceive, a playwright like August Wilson. More than in his previous play, **Ma Rainey's Black Bottom,** Mr. Wilson in **Fences** demonstrates that he can strike at the heart, not just of the black experience, but of the human condition.

The scene of **Fences** is the back yard of the Maxson house in a Northern industrial city, and the time is 1957. Despite the modest surroundings, the hero, Troy Maxson, is larger than life, especially as played by the expansive James Earl Jones. A garbage worker by trade, he had been a ballplayer who might have had a chance at the big leagues if he had not played in the days before racial discrimination had ended. In addition to his wife, Rose (Mary Alice), and their son, Cory (Courtney B. Vance), Troy has his best friend, Jim Bono (Ray Aranha), and a son from a former marriage, Lyons (Charles Brown), who comes around every payday to borrow money.

The fence in the title refers specifically to a picket fence

Troy is building around the back yard at Rose's request. But symbolically it refers to the many fences in the lives of the characters: Those that people want to escape from as well as those they build around others. Troy, for instance, prevents Cory, a high-school senior, from having an interview that might lead to a football scholarship to college. Troy claims it is for the boy's own good, but both Rose and Cory know it is out of jealousy: Troy doesn't want Cory to succeed in sports when he was unable to. On the other hand, Troy himself wants to escape from the confines of this station in life: to be a driver on the garbage truck instead of a collector. Even more, he wants to escape from the monotony of his life by continuing to be married to Rose while also having an affair with the woman he has made pregnant.

A man of great humor with an enormous appetite for life, Troy takes on everyone, including God and death (he holds lengthy, personal conversations with both). Along with his zest for living and his appeal, however, Troy is exceedingly selfish toward those around him, not only Rose and Cory, but his brother, Gabriel, whom he has taken advantage of financially. In short, Troy is a complex character, and part of Mr. Wilson's strength as a dramatist is that he shows the man whole, with the full measure of his shortcomings as well as his strengths.

Another impressive quality of Mr. Wilson's play is that it is not a polemical piece. Because the play is set in the late '50s, just before the civil-rights movement exploded, racial discrimination is very much a part of the fabric of the play, affecting the situation of every character. As important as it is, however, that is not the main focus. Rather, it is the universal quality of the people.

The play begins slowly. Much of the first half consists of conversations between Troy and the others, and though these exchanges are thoroughly amusing and true-to-life, they are short on action. At the start of the second act, however, the fireworks begin and continue detonating until the end. In scene after scene, raw nerve ends are exposed and we sense the full depth of the ambition, the frustration, the pain, as well as the love these characters feel.

The effect is all the more forceful thanks to a strong production. James D. Sandefur has designed an authentic back yard to the Maxsons' brick house, complete with tree, back porch, an alleyway lined with telephone poles, and in the distance, the vista of industrial plants. It captures the confined world that is a haven for Rose, but a closed stockade Troy and Cory want to escape from.

Lloyd Richards has provided taut, effective direction, bringing out the best in each performer but also achieving a beautifully balanced ensemble. Individual actors are at their best, including Mr. Jones, who, in his towering performance as Troy, is much less mannered than in other recent outings.

Toward the end of the play, Troy is a lonely man: Rose, Cory and Bono have all ostracized him. As his life becomes increasingly empty, however, the play grows richer and richer, and reminds us once again of the way in which good drama, well acted, can touch us. It's an experience that's been in short supply on Broadway lately. So **Fences**

is an especially welcome and important addition to the season.

Edwin Wilson, "Wilson's 'Fences' on Broadway . . . " in The Wall Street Journal, *March 31, 1987.*

JOE TURNER'S COME AND GONE

PRODUCTION REVIEWS

Clive Barnes (review date 28 March 1988)

[*In the following favorable review, Barnes compares* Joe Turner's Come and Gone *to a Eugene O'Neill family drama. Barnes affirms that the play* "is about the results of slavery; it is about separation. Separation from roots, separation from kith and kin, separation within one's own psychic self."]

A man searching for wholeness, a man digging for the roots of his existence, a man reaching into his past to move into his future—this man, disturbed, battered, embittered, is the hero of August Wilson's play **Joe Turner's Come and Gone,** which opened last night at the Ethel Barrymore Theater.

With it, Wilson moves another step into his grand dramatic design of providing a panoramic view of the American black experience since the days of Lincoln.

This is the third play in the series to reach Broadway, and, like its predecessors, **Ma Rainey's Black Bottom** and the still-running Tony Award-winning **Fences,** it stands completely on its own, while still opening yet another window on Wilson's overall theme, and revealing yet another aspect of his compelling theatrical genius.

Joe Turner is set in a Pittsburgh boarding house in 1911. The scene is peaceful, domestic. A sunny morning. A woman getting breakfast. A man, her husband and master of the house, just home from work.

Into this scene—which seems fugitively like a genre painting, an interior with figures—people, life, and themes gradually intrude. Black people, black life, black themes. This is an America that, in this time slot, few artists have explored. Few have even noticed.

Wilson starts his play with the leisureliness of a Eugene O'Neill slowly pinpointing this family—a boarding house in industrial America, filled with transients. These are Wilson's dispossessed—refugees both from the Africa they were wrested from, and the American South from which they have emigrated.

The mood, however, is funny, odd, eccentric . . . very cozy, very O'Neill himself in blackface, but this is certainly not an amused rendition of *Ah, Wilderness* played on the black notes of nostalgia's piano.

Joe Turner is a blues lament on a cold street—the memory of a loss. Yet also—for Wilson is an irrepressible, even if often depressed, optimist—the prescription for a future, a hope for a mending.

Into this respectable Pittsburgh boarding house there erupts a huge, straggling man, with staring eyes, a shabby coat, a big battered hat, holding onto a daughter as if his life depended on it. The name is Herald Loomis, and his pain is as formidable as his person.

He is looking for his wife, whom he has not seen in nine years. Where he comes from, what he is doing, why he is searching, these are questions that at first hang unanswered in the play like mist in the air.

Other people walk in and out of the play, in and out of the boarding house—there is a Sunday chicken dinner which ends in the joy of a singing-dancing-chanting "Juba," an impromptu celebration of the spirit.

Into this joy Loomis suddenly rushes in. He tells of visions, of a sea of skeletons. He has a kind of fit—epileptic perhaps, or some terrible seizure of the soul.

He is both encouraged and quieted down by Bynum Walker, the house's senior resident and an old man with wisdom and the gift of "mending." African society might have called him a conjur-man or a witch-doctor.

In Pennsylvania 1911, Bynum is simply an eccentric who has seen strange things, knows about herbs and blood, and may have occult power. Bynum believes that every man has a song to sing—the soulsong of his inner journey—and must find it, keep it, sing it.

And Loomis? What is the mystery of his search? Why must he find his wife?

And, for that matter, who was Joe Turner, whom Bynum sings the blues about?

That last much I'll tell you, and leave the rest to Wilson. Joe Turner—now still oddly memorialized in a famous blues by the pappy of New Orleans, W. C. Handy—was at the turn of the century the brother of a Tennessee governor.

His little trick was to lure blacks into an illegal crap game, arrest them, shove them into a chain gang, and sell them off as indentured workers for seven years. It was the last wicked flick of the slave traders' whip.

But Wilson's play is not about slavery. It is about the results of slavery; it is about separation. Separation from roots, separation from kith and kin, separation within one's own psychic self.

He is writing about blacks in 1911, but his apocalyptic vision is so clear—okay, it's a clear look at a muddy vessel—that what he has to say about the atavistic demands of everyone's tribal pasts (we are all tribes of the same monkeygod) and the need to mend ourselves into communal wholeness, must strike a universal note.

But the play is black. The idiom is the black theater, as is the language and the form. In many ways its verbal riffs and emotional cadenzas resemble jazz, so don't go expecting the Grieg-like music and manicured form of Ibsen.

That music and that form has, in fact, been beautifully caught—in all, its confusing mixture of fact and metaphor, naturalism and symbolism—by Lloyd Richards's staging, which starts with the painterly setting by Scott Bradley and the somber costumes of Pamela Peterson, and ends with the play's fulfilment.

Richards—long Wilson's director and collaborator—understands the pulse of the play, the slow start, the emotional build, the final catharsis. The aftertaste. So important, this—the play after the play, the play that dissolves in your mind as you start to walk down the street.

The ensemble performances are very much subservient to the concept, and some, like moments of the play itself, are deliberately conventional. All are good, but two have the responsibility of shaping of the play, and these are magnificent.

Delroy Lindo as the shambling, dispossessed Loomis is tremendous, casting his bulky shadow over the whole play. Just as important is the subtle, diffident performance of Ed Hall as the medicine man, Bynum Walker.

Here is a lovely, moving play that carries you with it like a matchbox on a flood.

> Clive Barnes, *"O'Neill in Blackface,"* in New York Post, *March 28, 1988.*

Frank Rich   (review date 28 March 1988)

[*In the review below, Rich judges the major theme of* Joe Turner's Come and Gone *to be the black man's "search for identity into a dark and distant past."*]

August Wilson continues to rewrite the history of the American theater by bringing the history of black America—and with it the history of white America—to the stage. In *Joe Turner's Come and Gone,* Mr. Wilson's third play to reach New York, that history unfolds with the same panoramic sweep that marked *Ma Rainey's Black Bottom* and *Fences.* As the new play's characters hang out in the kitchen and parlor of a black boardinghouse in the Pittsburgh of 1911, they retrace their long hard roads of migration from the sharecropping South to the industrialized North, and those tales again hum with the spellbinding verbal poetry of the blues. Whether a lost young woman is remembering how her mother died laboring in the peach orchards or a bitter man named Herald Loomis (Delroy Lindo) is recounting his seven years of illegal bondage to the Mississippi bounty hunter Joe Turner, Mr. Wilson gives haunting voice to the souls of the American dispossessed.

But to understand just why the play at the Barrymore may be Mr. Wilson's most profound and theatrically adventurous telling of his story to date, it is essential to grasp what the characters do not say—to decipher the history that is dramatized in images and actions beyond the reach of logical narrative. In *Joe Turner,* there are moments when otherwise voluble men reach a complete impasse with language, finding themselves struck dumb by traumatizing thoughts, and memories that they simply "ain't got the words to tell." And there are times when the play's events also leap wildly off the track of identifiable reality. Late in Act I, Herald Loomis becomes so possessed by a fantastic vision—of bones walking across an ocean—that he collapses to the ground in a cyclonic paroxysm of spiritual torment and, to the horror of his fellow boarders, scuttles epileptically across the floor on his back, unable to recover his footing and stand up.

These are occasions of true mystery and high drama, and they take Mr. Wilson's characters and writing to a dizzying place they haven't been before. That place is both literally and figuratively Africa. Though on its surface a familiar American tale about new arrivals in the big city searching for jobs, lost relatives, adventure and love, *Joe Turner's Come and Gone* is most of all about a search for identity into a dark and distant past. That search leads the black characters back across the ocean where so many of their ancestors died in passage to slavery—and it sends Mr. Wilson's own writing in search of its cultural roots. As the occupants of the Pittsburgh boardinghouse are partly assimilated into white America and partly in thrall to a collective African unconscious, so Mr. Wilson's play is a mixture of the well-made naturalistic boardinghouse drama and the mystical, non-Western theater of ritual and metaphor. In *Joe Turner,* the clash between the American and the African shakes white and black theatergoers as violently as it has shaken the history we've all shared.

To achieve his sophisticated end, Mr. Wilson has constructed an irresistible premise. *Joe Turner* begins when the bizarre Loomis, imposing and intense in Mr. Lindo's riveting performance, comes knocking fiercely at the boardinghouse door with his delicate 11-year-old daughter (Jamila Perry) incongruously in tow. With his years of servitude to Joe Turner at last behind him, Loomis is searching for the wife who deserted him at the start of his captivity a decade earlier. But Loomis is a "wild-eyed, mean-looking" man who looks as if he "killed somebody gambling over a quarter"; he's so pitch-black in mood and dress that there must be more to his story. Bynum Walker (Ed Hall), an eccentric fellow boarder with a penchant for clairvoyance and other forms of old-country voodoo, becomes obsessed with the strange intruder, intent on linking Loomis somehow to the supernatural "shining man" who haunts his own search for the "secret of life."

Yet the metaphysical cat-and-mouse game played by Bynum and Loomis is only the spine of *Joe Turner.* Everyone in the boardinghouse is looking, each according to his own experience, for either a lost relative or a secret of life, or both. The proprietor (Mel Winkler), the son of a free man, seeks salvation by becoming a typical American entrepreneur; he has no sympathy for a new young tenant (Bo Rucker) who arrives in Pittsburgh with rustic cotton-picking manners and crazy dreams of escaping menial labor with his guitar music. The women of the house also range across a wide spectrum—from a worldly cynic (Kimberly Scott) to a naïve romantic searching for a man (Kimberleigh Aarn) to the good-hearted proprietress (L. Scott Caldwell) who believes that laughter is the best way "to know you're alive."

By throwing such varied individuals together, Mr. Wilson creates a kaleidoscopic pattern of emotional relationships,

including some tender, funny and sexy courtships sparked by the endearingly boisterous Mr. Rucker. But each character also has a distinct relationship to the black past, just as each has a different perspective on the white urban present. It's only when all the boardinghouse residents spontaneously break into an African "juba," singing and dancing at a Sunday fried-chicken dinner, that the extended family of *Joe Turner* finds a degree of unity and peace. As Bynum says to anyone who will listen, each man must find his own song if he is to be free. Loomis, the sole character who fails to join in the juba, must find his song if he is to reconnect to life and overthrow the psychic burden of his years of slavery. Only then will Joe Turner—the play's symbol of white oppression as well as the subject of the W. C. Handy blues song that gave it its title—be truly gone.

As usual with Mr. Wilson, the play overstates its thematic exposition in an overlong first act. There are some other infelicities, too, most notably the thin characterization of a pair of children. While one wishes that the director, Lloyd Richards, had addressed these flaws with more toughmindedness during the two years of refinement that followed the play's premiere at the Yale Repertory Theater, the production is in every other way a tribute to its extended development process in resident theaters around the country. The first-rate cast, which also includes Raynor Scheine as a benign white river rat and Angela Bassett as a fervent convert to the white god that failed her ancestors, forms a supple, harmonic ensemble. Mr. Richard's staging is equally conversant with scenes of romantic flirtation, rending tableaux of divided families and galvanic climaxes in which the past erupts in a frenzy of exorcism.

The oblique, symbiotic relationship between Mr. Hall's otherworldly Bynum and Mr. Lindo's Loomis is particularly impressive. The two men's subliminal, often unspoken connection emerges like a magnetic force whenever they are onstage together. Loomis, we're told, was in happier days the deacon of the "Abundant Light" church. Under Mr. Hall's subtle psychological prodding and healing, Mr. Lindo gradually metamorphoses from a man whose opaque, defeated blackness signals the extinction of that light into a truly luminous "shining man," bathing the entire theater in the abundant ecstasy of his liberation. The sight is indescribably moving. An American writer in the deepest sense, August Wilson has once again shown us how in another man's freedom we find our own.

> Frank Rich, *"Panoramic History of Blacks in America in Wilson's 'Joe Turner',"* in The New York Times, *March 28, 1988, p. C15.*

John Beaufort   (review date 30 March 1988)

[*In the following review, Beaufort hails the Broadway production of* Joe Turner's Come and Gone *as "the most searching of the growing cycle of August Wilson dramas about the black American experience."*]

Joe Turner's Come and Gone is the most searching of the growing cycle of August Wilson dramas about the black American experience. It was preceded on Broadway by *Ma Rainey's Black Bottom* (the 1920s) and the current *Fences* (the 1950s), winner of the Pulitzer Prize and other awards. The transcendent new work further explores the personal sufferings and struggles born of a diaspora that began with slavery and continued with the post-emancipation migration of blacks to the industrial North.

In the present work, the struggle is as much for self-identity and self-realization as for lost kinfolk. *Joe Turner* is set in Pittsburgh in 1911. Swinging in mood from the richly comic to the poignantly tragic, the play constitutes what Mr. Wilson has described as "a boardinghouse play." Its inspiration comes from a painting by the late Romare Bearden and its title from a W. C. Handy blues ballad about the actual Joe Turner.

The action occurs in the simple but hospitable boarding house operated by Seth Holly (Mel Winkler), a hardworking factory hand and part-time tinsmith, and his good-hearted wife, Bertha (L. Scott Caldwell). The $2-a-week rate covers room and two meals a day. The boarders include Bynum Walker (Ed Hall), an amateur "voodoo" man with claims to mystic healing and "binding" powers; Jeremy Furlow (Bo Rucker), a newcomer from the South with a guitar under his arm and an eye for the girls; Mattie Campbell (Kimberleigh Aarn), a pretty woman in search of the husband who deserted her after the death of their two children; and humorous, worldly-wise Molly Cunningham (Kimberly Scott).

The cheerful, occasionally explosive course of events takes a darker turn with the arrival of Herald Loomis (Delroy Lindo) and his 11-year-old daughter Zonia (Jamila Perry). Loomis, a one-time church deacon, has been a victim of the notorious Joe Turner, a bounty hunter who kidnapped blacks and sold them into plantation servitude. After completing his term, Loomis has taken to the road in search of the wife from whom circumstances separated him.

Seth's suspicions of the black-clad, seemingly sinister Loomis explode into hostility when a "juba" celebration leaves the stranger writhing and out of control. Although the benign Bynum proves his healing gift, it requires an even more violent eruption to bring the complex, multifaceted play to its affirmingly mystical resolution.

While Wilson's dialogue abounds in folk-flavored vernacular, his lyric flights (especially as spoken by Mr. Hall's Bynum) give *Joe Turner* its extra dimension of poetic drama. The author also proves once more that he has moved far beyond the conventional "race play." The crimes of Joe Turner are presented as merely part of the pattern of subjugation that black Americans have historically endured. No great stir is caused among the boarders when Rutherford Selig (Raynor Scheine), a white traveling tin salesman who earns a little on the side for tracking down lost loved ones, tells how his father used to apprehend runaway slaves for their masters.

The performance staged by Lloyd Richards, Wilson's longtime collaborator, at the Ethel Barrymore Theatre is sensitively attuned to the resonances of *Joe Turner's Come and Gone.* Hall and Mr. Lindo create the central dynamic for a human drama of heroic proportions. Besides those already mentioned, the good cast includes Angela Bassett as Loomis's finally appearing wife and Richard Parnell Habersham as a little boy next door. A murky

background of smokestacks and bridges looms above the cozy boardinghouse premises of Scott Bradley's setting. The Yale Repertory Theatre production, lighted by Michael Gionnitti and costumed by Pamela Peterson, expands the scope and range of what is becoming a magnificent project.

> John Beaufort, "New Chapter in Wilson Saga
> of Black Life," in The Christian Science Mon-
> itor, *March 30, 1988, p. 21.*

FURTHER READING

AUTHOR COMMENTARY

DeVries, Hilary. "August Wilson—A New Voice for Black American Theater." *The Christian Science Monitor* (16 October 1984): 29-30.
> Interview in which DeVries explores the origins of Wilson's plays and his strong involvement with black history.

Wilson, August. "How to Write a Play Like August Wilson." *The New York Times* (10 March 1991): 5, 17.
> Adaptation of a talk given by Wilson in 1991 at Manhattan's Poetry Center in which he discusses his personal writing techniques.

OVERVIEWS AND GENERAL STUDIES

Brown, Chip. "The Light in August." *Esquire* III, No. 4 (April 1989): 116, 118, 120, 122-27.
> Detailed article tracing Wilson's literary career and events in his personal life.

Christiansen, Richard. "August Wilson: A Powerful Playwright Probes the Meaning of Black Life." *Chicago Tribune* (9 February 1986): 12, 13.
> Chronicles Wilson's literary career and examines several of the themes of his plays.

DeVries, Hilary. "A Street-Corner Scribe of Life in Black America." *The Christian Science Monitor* (27 March 1987): 1, 8.
> Discusses the themes, imagery, and language of Wilson's play-cycle on the black American experience.

Freedman, Samuel G. "Wilson's New *Fences* Nurtures a Partnership." *The New York Times* (5 May 1985): 80.
> Centers on the collaborative efforts of Wilson and Lloyd Richards, the artistic director of the Yale Repertory Theater.

———. "A Voice from the Streets." *The New York Times Magazine* (10 June 1987): 36, 40, 49, 70.
> Traces Wilson's life from early childhood to the present, illuminating aspects that helped determine the form and content of his plays.

Harrison, Paul Carter. "August Wilson's Blues Poetics." In *Three Plays,* by August Wilson, pp. 291-317. Pittsburgh: University of Pittsburgh Press, 1991.

Examines the influence of the oral and blues music traditions on Wilson's dramas, suggesting that the plays "arguably represent the culmination of political, social, and aesthetic objectives presaged by the Harlem Renaissance in the twenties and the Black Arts Movement of the sixties."

Mitgang, Herbert. "Wilson: From Poetry to Broadway Success: *Ma Rainey's* is First Hit for Author." *The New York Times* (22 October 1984): C15.

Traces Wilson's career development through the first production of *Ma Rainey's Black Bottom* at the Yale Repertory Theater.

Poinsett, Alex. "August Wilson: Hottest New Playwright." *Ebony* XLIII, No. 1 (November 1987): 68, 70, 72, 74.

Biographical article focusing on Wilson's career and the impact of cultural heritage on his writing.

Staples, Brent. "August Wilson." *Essence* 18, No. 4 (August 1987): 51, 111, 113.

Examines blues music and oral tradition as utilized by Wilson in his dramas.

MA RAINEY'S BLACK BOTTOM

Kauffmann, Stanley. "Bottoms Up." *Saturday Review* 11, No. 1 (January-February 1985): 83, 90.

Examines the characters in *Ma Rainey's Black Bottom*, finding Ma "an absolute monarch." Although admitting a somewhat contrived plot, Kauffmann praises Wilson's use of "dramatic metaphor and dialogue that frequently flies."

Richards, David. "Look! Ma!: *Rainey* Brings Life to Tired Broadway." *The Washington Post Book World* (18 November 1984): H1, H4.

Admits some structural flaws in *Ma Rainey's Black Bottom*, but generally praises Wilson for his characterizations and dialogue.

FENCES

Rich, Frank. "Family Ties in Wilson's *Fences*." *The New York Times* (27 March 1987): C3.

Review that describes *Fences* as an often formulaic but nevertheless masterful dramatic tour de force.

Simon, John. "Wall in the Family." *New York* (6 April 1987): 92.

Finds that despite a loss of spontaneity in the second act, *Fences* brings "life, in all its bittersweetness" to the stage.

Staples, Brent. "*Fences:* No Barrier to Emotion." *The New York Times* (5 April 1987): II; 1, 39.

Personal reflection on the social and emotional realism of *Fences*, stating that "this play with virtually no concessions to the middle class has enfolded the universal in the particular, in a way that results in total accessibility" for the audience.

JOE TURNER'S COME AND GONE

Kleiman, Dena. "*Joe Turner*, the Spirit of Synergy." *The New York Times* (19 May 1986): C11.

Examines the collaboration between Wilson and Lloyd Richards on the production of *Joe Turner's Come and Gone*, especially their efforts to dramatize the lead character's "desperate search for himself" and how his "quest for identity is eventually realized."

Richards, Lloyd. "Preface to *Joe Turner's Come and Gone*." *Theater* XVII, No. 3 (Summer/Fall 1986): 64.

Discusses the importance of oral tradition in Wilson's plays. Calling Wilson "a fantastic storyteller, who captures the drama of storytelling in plays," Richards explains that "the storytelling, like the ritual of purification by blood in the play, allows the characters to face their day to day problems, and confront their own sense of mortality."

THE PIANO LESSON

Brustein, Robert. "The Lesson of *The Piano Lesson*." *The New Republic* (21 May 1990): 28-30.

Negative review in which Brustein claims that Wilson's artistic vision is limited to the black experience and that he should "develop the radical poetic strain that now lies dormant in his art."

Rich, Frank. "A Family Confronts Its History in August Wilson's *Piano Lesson*." *The New York Times* (17 April 1990).

Favorable review that examines the themes and symbolism of *The Piano Lesson*, claiming that the play "rattles history and shakes the audience on both sides of the racial divide."

Stearns, David Patrick. "*The Piano Lesson:* Heavy on Drills." *USA Today* (17 April 1990).

Mixed review in which Stearns states that Wilson's play is at times "compelling" and "eloquent" but generally "as tedious as a piano lesson."

For further information on Wilson's life and career, see *Black Literature Criticism*, Vol. 3; *Contemporary Authors*, Vols. 115, 122; and *Contemporary Literary Criticism*, Vols. 39, 50, 63.

CUMULATIVE INDEXES

This Index Includes References to Entries in These Gale Series

Contemporary Literary Criticism presents excerpts of criticism on the works of novelists, poets, dramatists, short story writers, scriptwriters, and other creative writers who are now living or who have died since 1960.

Twentieth-Century Literary Criticism contains critical excerpts by the most significant commentators on poets, novelists, short story writers, dramatists, and philosophers who died between 1900 and 1960.

Nineteenth-Century Literature Criticism offers significant passages from criticism on authors who died between 1800 and 1899.

Literature Criticism from 1400 to 1800 compiles significant passages from the most noteworthy criticism on authors of the fifteenth through eighteenth centuries.

Classical and Medieval Literature Criticism offers excerpts of criticism on the works of world authors from classical antiquity through the fourteenth century.

Short Story Criticism compiles excerpts of criticism on short fiction by writers of all eras and nationalities.

Poetry Criticism presents excerpts of criticism on the works of poets from all eras, movements, and nationalities.

Drama Criticism presents criticism of the works of dramatists of all eras, movements, and nationalities.

Children's Literature Review includes excerpts from reviews, criticism, and commentary on works of authors and illustrators who create books for children.

Contemporary Authors Series encompasses five related series. *Contemporary Authors* provides biographical and bibliographical information on more than 97,000 writers of fiction and nonfiction. *Contemporary Authors New Revision Series* provides completely updated information on authors covered in *CA*. *Contemporary Authors Permanent Series* consists of listings for deceased and inactive authors. *Contemporary Authors Autobiography Series* presents specially commissioned autobiographies by leading contemporary writers. *Contemporary Authors Bibliographical Series* contains primary and secondary bibliographies as well as analytical bibliographical essays by authorities on major modern authors.

Dictionary of Literary Biography encompasses four related series. *Dictionary of Literary Biography* furnishes illustrated overviews of authors' lives and works. *Dictionary of Literary Biography Documentary Series* illuminates the careers of major figures through a selection of literary documents, including letters, interviews, and photographs. *Dictionary of Literary Biography Yearbook* summarizes the past year's literary activity and includes updated entries on individual authors. *Concise Dictionary of American Literary Biography* comprises six volumes of revised and updated sketches on major American authors that were originally presented in *Dictionary of Literary Biography*.

Something about the Author Series encompasses three related series. *Something about the Author* contains well-illustrated biographical sketches on juvenile and young adult authors and illustrators from all eras. *Something about the Author Autobiography Series* presents specially commissioned autobiographies by prominent authors and illustrators of books for children and young adults. *Authors & Artists for Young Adults* provides high school and junior high school students with profiles of their favorite creative artists.

Yesterday's Authors of Books for Children contains heavily illustrated entries on children's writers who died before 1961. Complete in two volumes.

Literary Criticism Series
Cumulative Author Index

This index lists all author entries in the Gale Literary Criticism Series and includes cross-references to other Gale sources. References in the index are identified as follows:

AAYA: *Authors & Artists for Young Adults*, Volumes 1-7
CA: *Contemporary Authors* (original series), Volumes 1-135
CAAS: *Contemporary Authors Autobiography Series*, Volumes 1-14
CABS: *Contemporary Authors Bibliographical Series*, Volumes 1-3
CANR: *Contemporary Authors New Revision Series*, Volumes 1-35
CAP: *Contemporary Authors Permanent Series*, Volumes 1-2
CA-R: *Contemporary Authors* (first revision), Volumes 1-44
CDALB: *Concise Dictionary of American Literary Biography*, Volumes 1-6
CLC: *Contemporary Literary Criticism*, Volumes 1-69
CLR: *Children's Literature Review*, Volumes 1-25
CMLC: *Classical and Medieval Literature Criticism*, Volumes 1-8
DC: *Drama Criticism*, Volume 1-2
DLB: *Dictionary of Literary Biography*, Volumes 1-112
DLB-DS: *Dictionary of Literary Biography Documentary Series*, Volumes 1-9
DLB-Y: *Dictionary of Literary Biography Yearbook*, Volumes 1980-1990
LC: *Literature Criticism from 1400 to 1800*, Volumes 1-18
NCLC: *Nineteenth-Century Literature Criticism*, Volumes 1-34
PC: *Poetry Criticism*, Volumes 1-3
SAAS: *Something about the Author Autobiography Series*, Volumes 1-13
SATA: *Something about the Author*, Volumes 1-66
SSC: *Short Story Criticism*, Volumes 1-9
TCLC: *Twentieth-Century Literary Criticism*, Volumes 1-43
YABC: *Yesterday's Authors of Books for Children*, Volumes 1-2

Bach, Richard (David) 1936-....... CLC 14
See also CANR 18; CA 9-12R; SATA 13

Bachman, Richard 1947-
See King, Stephen (Edwin)

Bachmann, Ingeborg 1926-1973..... CLC 69
See also CA 93-96; obituary CA 45-48

Bacon, Sir Francis 1561-1626 ...... LC 18

Bacovia, George 1881-1957 .... TCLC 24

Bagehot, Walter 1826-1877 ...... NCLC 10
See also DLB 55

Bagnold, Enid 1889-1981 .... CLC 25
See also CANR 5; CA 5-8R;
obituary CA 103; SATA 1, 25; DLB 13

Bagryana, Elisaveta 1893-......... CLC 10

Bailey, Paul 1937-............... CLC 45
See also CANR 16; CA 21-24R; DLB 14

Baillie, Joanna 1762-1851 .... NCLC 2

Bainbridge, Beryl
1933-.... CLC 4, 5, 8, 10, 14, 18, 22, 62
See also CANR 24; CA 21-24R; DLB 14

Baker, Elliott 1922-............ CLC 8, 61
See also CANR 2; CA 45-48

Baker, Nicholson 1957-........... CLC 61

Baker, Russell (Wayne) 1925-...... CLC 31
See also CANR 11; CA 57-60

Bakshi, Ralph 1938-.............. CLC 26
See also CA 112

Bakunin, Mikhail (Alexandrovich)
1814-1876 .... NCLC 25

Baldwin, James (Arthur)
1924-1987 ..... CLC 1, 2, 3, 4, 5, 8, 13,
15, 17, 42, 50, 67; DC 1
See also BLC 1; CANR 3,24; CA 1-4R;
obituary CA 124; CABS 1; SATA 9, 54;
DLB 2, 7, 33; DLB-Y 87;
CDALB 1941-1968; AAYA 4

Ballard, J(ames) G(raham)
1930-......... CLC 3, 6, 14, 36; SSC 1
See also CANR 15; CA 5-8R; DLB 14

Balmont, Konstantin Dmitriyevich
1867-1943 .... TCLC 11
See also CA 109

Balzac, Honore de
1799-1850 .... NCLC 5; SSC 5

Bambara, Toni Cade 1939- .... CLC 19
See also BLC 1; CANR 24; CA 29-32R;
DLB 38; AAYA 5

Bandanes, Jerome 1937- .... CLC 59

Banim, John 1798-1842 .... NCLC 13

Banim, Michael 1796-1874 ...... NCLC 13

Banks, Iain 1954-................ CLC 34
See also CA 123

Banks, Lynne Reid 1929-.......... CLC 23
See also Reid Banks, Lynne

Banks, Russell 1940- .... CLC 37
See also CANR 19; CA 65-68

Banville, John 1945-.............. CLC 46
See also CA 117, 128; DLB 14

Banville, Theodore (Faullain) de
1832-1891 .... NCLC 9

Baraka, Imamu Amiri
1934- .... CLC 1, 2, 3, 5, 10, 14, 33
See also Jones, (Everett) LeRoi
See also BLC 1; CANR 27; CA 21-22R;
CABS 3; DLB 5, 7, 16, 38; DLB-DS 8;
CDALB 1941-1968

Barbellion, W. N. P. 1889-1919 ... TCLC 24

Barbera, Jack 1945-.............. CLC 44
See also CA 110

Barbey d'Aurevilly, Jules Amedee
1808-1889 .... NCLC 1

Barbusse, Henri 1873-1935 .... TCLC 5
See also CA 105; DLB 65

Barea, Arturo 1897-1957 .... TCLC 14
See also CA 111

Barfoot, Joan 1946-.............. CLC 18
See also CA 105

Baring, Maurice 1874-1945 .... TCLC 8
See also CA 105; DLB 34

Barker, Clive 1952- .... CLC 52
See also CA 121

Barker, George (Granville)
1913-..................... CLC 8, 48
See also CANR 7; CA 9-12R; DLB 20

Barker, Howard 1946-............ CLC 37
See also CA 102; DLB 13

Barker, Pat 1943-................ CLC 32
See also CA 117, 122

Barlow, Joel 1754-1812 .... NCLC 23
See also DLB 37

Barnard, Mary (Ethel) 1909-....... CLC 48
See also CAP 2; CA 21-22

Barnes, Djuna (Chappell)
1892-1982 ... CLC 3, 4, 8, 11, 29; SSC 3
See also CANR 16; CA 9-12R;
obituary CA 107; DLB 4, 9, 45

Barnes, Julian 1946-.............. CLC 42
See also CANR 19; CA 102

Barnes, Peter 1931- .... CLC 5, 56
See also CA 65-68; DLB 13

Baroja (y Nessi), Pio 1872-1956.... TCLC 8
See also CA 104

Barondess, Sue K(aufman) 1926-1977
See Kaufman, Sue
See also CANR 1; CA 1-4R;
obituary CA 69-72

Barrett, (Roger) Syd 1946-
See Pink Floyd

Barrett, William (Christopher)
1913-..................... CLC 27
See also CANR 11; CA 13-16R

Barrie, (Sir) J(ames) M(atthew)
1860-1937 .... TCLC 2
See also CLR 16; YABC 1; CA 104;
DLB 10

Barrol, Grady 1953-
See Bograd, Larry

Barry, Philip (James Quinn)
1896-1949 .... TCLC 11
See also CA 109; DLB 7

Barth, John (Simmons)
1930- ...... CLC 1, 2, 3, 5, 7, 9, 10, 14,
27, 51
See also CANR 5, 23; CA 1-4R; CABS 1;
DLB 2

Barthelme, Donald
1931-1989 ..... CLC 1, 2, 3, 5, 6, 8, 13,
23, 46, 59; SSC 2
See also CANR 20; CA 21-24R, 129;
SATA 7; DLB 2; DLB-Y 80

Barthelme, Frederick 1943-........ CLC 36
See also CA 114, 122; DLB-Y 85

Barthes, Roland 1915-1980 .... CLC 24
See also obituary CA 97-100

Barzun, Jacques (Martin) 1907- .... CLC 51
See also CANR 22; CA 61-64

Bashevis, Isaac 1904-1991
See Singer, Isaac Bashevis

Bashkirtseff, Marie 1859-1884 ... NCLC 27

Basho, Matsuo 1644-1694 .... PC 3

Bass, Kingsley B. 1935-

Bassani, Giorgio 1916-............. CLC 9
See also CA 65-68

Bataille, Georges 1897-1962 .... CLC 29
See also CA 101; obituary CA 89-92

Bates, H(erbert) E(rnest)
1905-1974 .... CLC 46
See also CA 93-96; obituary CA 45-48

Baudelaire, Charles
1821-1867 .... NCLC 6, 29; PC 1

Baudrillard, Jean 1929-........... CLC 60

Baum, L(yman) Frank 1856-1919 ... TCLC 7
See also CLR 15; CA 108; SATA 18;
DLB 22

Baumbach, Jonathan 1933- ...... CLC 6, 23
See also CAAS 5; CANR 12; CA 13-16R;
DLB-Y 80

Bausch, Richard (Carl) 1945- ...... CLC 51
See also CA 101

Baxter, Charles 1947-............. CLC 45
See also CA 57-60

Baxter, James K(eir) 1926-1972 .... CLC 14
See also CA 77-80

Bayer, Sylvia 1909-1981
See Glassco, John

Beagle, Peter S(oyer) 1939-......... CLC 7
See also CANR 4; CA 9-12R; DLB-Y 80

Beard, Charles A(ustin)
1874-1948 .... TCLC 15
See also CA 115; SATA 18; DLB 17

Beardsley, Aubrey 1872-1898 ..... NCLC 6

Beattie, Ann 1947-... CLC 8, 13, 18, 40, 63
See also CA 81-84; DLB-Y 82

Beattie, James 1735-1803 .... NCLC 25

Beauvoir, Simone (Lucie Ernestine Marie
Bertrand) de
1908-1986 ... CLC 1, 2, 4, 8, 14, 31, 44,
50
See also CANR 28; CA 9-12R;
obituary CA 118; DLB 72; DLB-Y 86

Becker, Jurek 1937-............. CLC 7, 19
See also CA 85-88; DLB 75

Becker, Walter 1950-............. CLC 26

Caballero, Fernan 1796-1877..... NCLC 10

Cabell, James Branch 1879-1958 ... TCLC 6
See also CA 105; DLB 9, 78

Cable, George Washington
1844-1925 .... TCLC 4; SSC 4
See also CA 104; DLB 12, 74

Cabrera Infante, G(uillermo)
1929-.................CLC 5, 25, 45
See also CANR 29; CA 85-88

Cade, Toni 1939-
See Bambara, Toni Cade

CAEdmon fl. 658-680........... CMLC 7

Cage, John (Milton, Jr.) 1912-..... CLC 41
See also CANR 9; CA 13-16R

Cain, G. 1929-
See Cabrera Infante, G(uillermo)

Cain, James M(allahan)
1892-1977 .... CLC 3, 11, 28
See also CANR 8; CA 17-20R;
obituary CA 73-76

Caldwell, Erskine (Preston)
1903-1987 .... CLC 1, 8, 14, 50, 60
See also CAAS 1; CANR 2; CA 1-4R;
obituary CA 121; DLB 9, 86

Caldwell, (Janet Miriam) Taylor (Holland)
1900-1985 .... CLC 2, 28, 39
See also CANR 5; CA 5-8R;
obituary CA 116

Calhoun, John Caldwell
1782-1850 .... NCLC 15
See also DLB 3

Calisher, Hortense 1911-.... CLC 2, 4, 8, 38
See also CANR 1, 22; CA 1-4R; DLB 2

Callaghan, Morley (Edward)
1903-1990 .... CLC 3, 14, 41, 65
See also CANR 33; CA 9-12R;
obituary CA 132; DLB 68

Calvino, Italo
1923-1985 .... CLC 5, 8, 11, 22, 33, 39;
                                    SSC 3
See also CANR 23; CA 85-88;
obituary CA 116

Cameron, Carey 1952-........... CLC 59

Cameron, Peter 1959-............ CLC 44
See also CA 125

Campana, Dino 1885-1932....... TCLC 20
See also CA 117

Campbell, John W(ood), Jr.
1910-1971 .... CLC 32
See also CAP 2; CA 21-22;
obituary CA 29-32R; DLB 8

Campbell, Joseph 1904-1987 .... CLC 69
See also CANR 3, 28; CA 4R;
obituary CA 124; AAYA 3

Campbell, (John) Ramsey 1946- .... CLC 42
See also CANR 7; CA 57-60

Campbell, (Ignatius) Roy (Dunnachie)
1901-1957 .... TCLC 5
See also CA 104; DLB 20

Campbell, Thomas 1777-1844 .... NCLC 19

Campbell, (William) Wilfred
1861-1918 .... TCLC 9
See also CA 106

Camus, Albert
1913-1960 ... CLC 1, 2, 4, 9, 11, 14, 32,
                        63, 69; DC 2; SSC 9
See also CA 89-92; DLB 72

Canby, Vincent 1924-............. CLC 13
See also CA 81-84

Canetti, Elias 1905-......... CLC 3, 14, 25
See also CANR 23; CA 21-24R; DLB 85

Canin, Ethan 1960-.............. CLC 55

Cape, Judith 1916-
See Page, P(atricia) K(athleen)

Capek, Karel
1890-1938 .... TCLC 6, 37; DC 1
See also CA 104

Capote, Truman
1924-1984 ..... CLC 1, 3, 8, 13, 19, 34,
                        38, 58; SSC 2
See also CANR 18; CA 5-8R;
obituary CA 113; DLB 2; DLB-Y 80, 84;
CDALB 1941-1968

Capra, Frank 1897-.............. CLC 16
See also CA 61-64

Caputo, Philip 1941-............. CLC 32
See also CA 73-76

Card, Orson Scott 1951-.... CLC 44, 47, 50
See also CA 102

Cardenal, Ernesto 1925-.......... CLC 31
See also CANR 2; CA 49-52

Carducci, Giosue 1835-1907...... TCLC 32

Carew, Thomas 1595?-1640 .... LC 13

Carey, Ernestine Gilbreth 1908-.... CLC 17
See also CA 5-8R; SATA 2

Carey, Peter 1943-.......... CLC 40, 55
See also CA 123, 127

Carleton, William 1794-1869...... NCLC 3

Carlisle, Henry (Coffin) 1926-...... CLC 33
See also CANR 15; CA 13-16R

Carlson, Ron(ald F.) 1947-........ CLC 54
See also CA 105

Carlyle, Thomas 1795-1881 ...... NCLC 22
See also DLB 55

Carman, (William) Bliss
1861-1929 .... TCLC 7
See also CA 104

Carpenter, Don(ald Richard)
1931-....................... CLC 41
See also CANR 1; CA 45-48

Carpentier (y Valmont), Alejo
1904-1980 .... CLC 8, 11, 38
See also CANR 11; CA 65-68;
obituary CA 97-100

Carr, Emily 1871-1945.......... TCLC 32
See also DLB 68

Carr, John Dickson 1906-1977 ...... CLC 3
See also CANR 3; CA 49-52;
obituary CA 69-72

Carr, Virginia Spencer 1929-....... CLC 34
See also CA 61-64

Carrier, Roch 1937-............. CLC 13
See also DLB 53

Carroll, James (P.) 1943-......... CLC 38
See also CA 81-84

Carroll, Jim 1951- .... CLC 35
See also CA 45-48

Carroll, Lewis 1832-1898........ NCLC 2
See also Dodgson, Charles Lutwidge
See also CLR 2; DLB 18

Carroll, Paul Vincent 1900-1968.... CLC 10
See also CA 9-12R; obituary CA 25-28R;
DLB 10

Carruth, Hayden 1921- .... CLC 4, 7, 10, 18
See also CANR 4; CA 9-12R; SATA 47;
DLB 5

Carter, Angela (Olive) 1940-..... CLC 5, 41
See also CANR 12; CA 53-56; DLB 14

Carver, Raymond
1938-1988 ... CLC 22, 36, 53, 55; SSC 8
See also CANR 17; CA 33-36R;
obituary CA 126; DLB-Y 84, 88

Cary, (Arthur) Joyce (Lunel)
1888-1957 .... TCLC 1, 29
See also CA 104; DLB 15

Casanova de Seingalt, Giovanni Jacopo
1725-1798 .... LC 13

Casares, Adolfo Bioy 1914-
See Bioy Casares, Adolfo

Casely-Hayford, J(oseph) E(phraim)
1866-1930 .... TCLC 24
See also BLC 1; CA 123

Casey, John 1880-1964
See O'Casey, Sean

Casey, John 1939- .... CLC 59
See also CANR 23; CA 69-72

Casey, Michael 1947-............. CLC 2
See also CA 65-68; DLB 5

Casey, Patrick 1902-1934
See Thurman, Wallace

Casey, Warren 1935- .... CLC 12
See also Jacobs, Jim and Casey, Warren
See also CA 101

Casona, Alejandro 1903-1965 ...... CLC 49
See also Alvarez, Alejandro Rodriguez

Cassavetes, John 1929-1991....... CLC 20
See also CA 85-88, 127

Cassill, R(onald) V(erlin) 1919-... CLC 4, 23
See also CAAS 1; CANR 7; CA 9-12R;
DLB 6

Cassity, (Allen) Turner 1929- .... CLC 6, 42
See also CANR 11; CA 17-20R

Castaneda, Carlos 1935?-.......... CLC 12
See also CA 25-28R

Castedo, Elena 1937- .... CLC 65
See also CA 132

Castellanos, Rosario 1925-1974..... CLC 66
See also CA 131; obituary CA 53-56

Castelvetro, Lodovico 1505-1571..... LC 12

Castiglione, Baldassare 1478-1529 ... LC 12

Castro, Rosalia de 1837-1885 ..... NCLC 3

Cather, Willa (Sibert)
1873-1947 ...... TCLC 1, 11, 31; SSC 2
See also CA 104; SATA 30; DLB 9, 54;
DLB-DS 1; CDALB 1865-1917

Catton, (Charles) Bruce
1899-1978 .... CLC 35
See also CANR 7; CA 5-8R;
obituary CA 81-84; SATA 2;
obituary SATA 24; DLB 17

Cauldwell, Frank 1923-
See King, Francis (Henry)

Caunitz, William 1935- .... CLC 34

Causley, Charles (Stanley) 1917-..... CLC 7
See also CANR 5; CA 9-12R; SATA 3;
DLB 27

Caute, (John) David 1936-......... CLC 29
See also CAAS 4; CANR 1; CA 1-4R;
DLB 14

Cavafy, C(onstantine) P(eter)
1863-1933 .... TCLC 2, 7
See also CA 104

Cavanna, Betty 1909-............. CLC 12
See also CANR 6; CA 9-12R; SATA 1, 30

Caxton, William 1421?-1491? .... LC 17

Cayrol, Jean 1911-............... CLC 11
See also CA 89-92; DLB 83

Cela, Camilo Jose 1916-...... CLC 4, 13, 59
See also CAAS 10; CANR 21; CA 21-24R

Celan, Paul 1920-1970 ...... CLC 10, 19, 53
See also Antschel, Paul
See also DLB 69

Celine, Louis-Ferdinand
1894-1961 ..... CLC 1, 3, 4, 7, 9, 15, 47
See also Destouches,
Louis-Ferdinand-Auguste
See also DLB 72

Cellini, Benvenuto 1500-1571 .... LC 7

Cendrars, Blaise 1887-1961........ CLC 18
See also Sauser-Hall, Frederic

Cernuda, Luis (y Bidon)
1902-1963 .... CLC 54
See also CA 89-92

Cervantes (Saavedra), Miguel de
1547-1616 .... LC 6

Cesaire, Aime (Fernand) 1913- .. CLC 19, 32
See also BLC 1; CANR 24; CA 65-68

Chabon, Michael 1965?-........... CLC 55

Chabrol, Claude 1930- .... CLC 16
See also CA 110

Challans, Mary 1905-1983
See Renault, Mary
See also CA 81-84; obituary CA 111;
SATA 23; obituary SATA 36

Chambers, Aidan 1934- .... CLC 35
See also CANR 12; CA 25-28R; SATA 1

Chambers, James 1948-
See Cliff, Jimmy

Chambers, Robert W. 1865-1933... TCLC 41

Chandler, Raymond 1888-1959 ... TCLC 1, 7
See also CA 104

Channing, William Ellery
1780-1842 .... NCLC 17
See also DLB 1, 59

Chaplin, Charles (Spencer)
1889-1977 .... CLC 16
See also CA 81-84; obituary CA 73-76;
DLB 44

Chapman, Graham 1941?- .... CLC 21
See also Monty Python
See also CA 116; obituary CA 169

Chapman, John Jay 1862-1933 ..... TCLC 7
See also CA 104

Chappell, Fred 1936- .... CLC 40
See also CAAS 4; CANR 8; CA 5-8R;
DLB 6

Char, Rene (Emile)
1907-1988 .... CLC 9, 11, 14, 55
See also CA 13-16R; obituary CA 124

Charles I 1600-1649 .... LC 13

Chartier, Emile-Auguste 1868-1951
See Alain

Charyn, Jerome 1937- ...... CLC 5, 8, 18
See also CAAS 1; CANR 7; CA 5-8R;
DLB-Y 83

Chase, Mary (Coyle) 1907-1981 ...... DC 1
See also CA 77-80, 105; SATA 17, 29

Chase, Mary Ellen 1887-1973 .... CLC 2
See also CAP 1; CA 15-16;
obituary CA 41-44R; SATA 10

Chateaubriand, Francois Rene de
1768-1848 .... NCLC 3

Chatier, Emile-Auguste 1868-1951
See Alain

Chatterji, Bankim Chandra
1838-1894 .... NCLC 19

Chatterji, Saratchandra
1876-1938 .... TCLC 13
See also CA 109

Chatterton, Thomas 1752-1770 .... LC 3

Chatwin, (Charles) Bruce
1940-1989 .... CLC 28, 57, 59
See also CA 85-88,; obituary CA 127

Chaucer, Geoffrey c. 1340-1400 ..... LC 17

Chayefsky, Paddy 1923-1981....... CLC 23
See also CA 9-12R; obituary CA 104;
DLB 7, 44; DLB-Y 81

Chayefsky, Sidney 1923-1981
See Chayefsky, Paddy
See also CANR 18

Chedid, Andree 1920-........... CLC 47

Cheever, John
1912-1982 ..... CLC 3, 7, 8, 11, 15, 25,
64; SSC 1
See also CANR 5, 27; CA 5-8R;
obituary CA 106; CABS 1; DLB 2;
DLB-Y 80, 82; CDALB 1941-1968

Cheever, Susan 1943-.......... CLC 18, 48
See also CA 103; DLB-Y 82

Chekhov, Anton (Pavlovich)
1860-1904 ...... TCLC 3, 10, 31; SSC 2
See also CA 104, 124

Chernyshevsky, Nikolay Gavrilovich
1828-1889 .... NCLC 1

Cherry, Caroline Janice 1942-
See Cherryh, C. J.

Cherryh, C. J. 1942-............. CLC 35
See also CANR 10; CA 65-68; DLB-Y 80

Chesnutt, Charles Waddell
1858-1932 .... TCLC 5, 39; SSC 7
See also BLC 1; CA 106, 125; DLB 12, 50,
78

Chester, Alfred 1929?-1971 .... CLC 49
See also obituary CA 33-36R

Chesterton, G(ilbert) K(eith)
1874-1936 .... TCLC 1, 6; SSC 1
See also CA 104; SATA 27; DLB 10, 19,
34, 70

Chiang Pin-Chin 1904-1986
See Ding Ling
See also obituary CA 118

Ch'ien Chung-shu 1910-........... CLC 22

Child, Lydia Maria 1802-1880 .... NCLC 6
See also DLB 1, 74

Child, Philip 1898-1978 .... CLC 19
See also CAP 1; CA 13-14; SATA 47

Childress, Alice 1920-........... CLC 12, 15
See also BLC 1; CLR 14; CANR 3, 27;
CA 45-48; SATA 7, 48; DLB 7, 38

Chislett, (Margaret) Anne 1943?-.... CLC 34

Chitty, (Sir) Thomas Willes 1926- .. CLC 11
See also Hinde, Thomas
See also CA 5-8R

Chomette, Rene 1898-1981
See Clair, Rene
See also obituary CA 103

Chopin, Kate (O'Flaherty)
1851-1904 .... TCLC 5, 14; SSC 8
See also CA 122; brief entry CA 104;
DLB 12, 78; CDALB 1865-1917

Christie, (Dame) Agatha (Mary Clarissa)
1890-1976 ...... CLC 1, 6, 8, 12, 39, 48
See also CANR 10; CA 17-20R;
obituary CA 61-64; SATA 36; DLB 13

Christie, (Ann) Philippa 1920-
See Pearce, (Ann) Philippa
See also CANR 4; CA 7-8

Christine de Pizan 1365?-1431?....... LC 9

Chulkov, Mikhail Dmitrievich
1743-1792 .... LC 2

Churchill, Caryl 1938- .... CLC 31, 55
See also CANR 22; CA 102; DLB 13

Churchill, Charles 1731?-1764....... LC 3

Chute, Carolyn 1947-............. CLC 39
See also CA 123

Ciardi, John (Anthony)
1916-1986 .... CLC 10, 40, 44
See also CAAS 2; CANR 5; CA 5-8R;
obituary CA 118; SATA 1, 46; DLB 5;
DLB-Y 86

Cicero, Marcus Tullius
106 B.C.-43 B.C.............. CMLC 3

Cimino, Michael 1943?-........... CLC 16
See also CA 105

Cioran, E. M. 1911-............. CLC 64
See also CA 25-28R

Cisneros, Sandra 1954-........... CLC 69
See also CA 131

Clair, Rene 1898-1981 .... CLC 20
See also Chomette, Rene

Clampitt, Amy 19??-............. CLC 32
See also CA 110

Clancy, Tom 1947-............. CLC 45
See also CA 125

Clare, John 1793-1864 .... NCLC 9
See also DLB 55

Ghiselin, Brewster 1903- . . . . CLC 23
See also CANR 13; CA 13-16R

Ghose, Zulfikar 1935-. . . . . CLC 42
See also CA 65-68

Ghosh, Amitav 1943- . . . . CLC 44

Giacosa, Giuseppe 1847-1906 . . . . . . TCLC 7
See also CA 104

Gibbon, Lewis Grassic 1901-1935. . . TCLC 4
See also Mitchell, James Leslie

Gibbons, Kaye 1960- . . . . CLC 50

Gibran, (Gibran) Kahlil
1883-1931 . . . . TCLC 1, 9
See also CA 104

Gibson, William 1914- . . . . CLC 23
See also CANR 9; CA 9-12R; DLB 7

Gibson, William 1948- . . . . CLC 39, 63
See also CA 126

Gide, Andre (Paul Guillaume)
1869-1951 . . . . TCLC 5, 12, 36
See also CA 104, 124; DLB 65

Gifford, Barry (Colby) 1946- . . . . CLC 34
See also CANR 9; CA 65-68

Gilbert, (Sir) W(illiam) S(chwenck)
1836-1911 . . . . TCLC 3
See also CA 104; SATA 36

Gilbreth, Ernestine 1908-
See Carey, Ernestine Gilbreth

Gilbreth, Frank B(unker), Jr.
1911- . . . . CLC 17
See also CA 9-12R; SATA 2

Gilchrist, Ellen 1935- . . . . CLC 34, 48
See also CA 113, 116

Giles, Molly 1942- . . . . CLC 39
See also CA 126

Gilliam, Terry (Vance) 1940-
See Monty Python
See also CA 108, 113

Gilliatt, Penelope (Ann Douglass)
1932- . . . . CLC 2, 10, 13, 53
See also CA 13-16R; DLB 14

Gilman, Charlotte (Anna) Perkins (Stetson)
1860-1935 . . . . TCLC 9, 37
See also CA 106

Gilmour, David 1944-
See Pink Floyd

Gilpin, William 1724-1804 . . . . . . NCLC 30

Gilroy, Frank D(aniel) 1925- . . . . CLC 2
See also CA 81-84; DLB 7

Ginsberg, Allen
1926- . . . CLC 1, 2, 3, 4, 6, 13, 36, 69
See also CANR 2; CA 1-4R; DLB 5, 16;
CDALB 1941-1968

Ginzburg, Natalia 1916- . . . . . . CLC 5, 11, 54
See also CA 85-88

Giono, Jean 1895-1970. . . . . CLC 4, 11
See also CANR 2; CA 45-48;
obituary CA 29-32R; DLB 72

Giovanni, Nikki 1943- . . . . . CLC 2, 4, 19, 64
See also BLC 2; CLR 6; CAAS 6;
CANR 18; CA 29-32R; SATA 24;
DLB 5, 41

Giovene, Andrea 1904-. . . . . CLC 7
See also CA 85-88

Gippius, Zinaida (Nikolayevna) 1869-1945
See Hippius, Zinaida
See also CA 106

Giraudoux, (Hippolyte) Jean
1882-1944 . . . . TCLC 2, 7
See also CA 104; DLB 65

Gironella, Jose Maria 1917- . . . . CLC 11
See also CA 101

Gissing, George (Robert)
1857-1903 . . . . TCLC 3, 24
See also CA 105; DLB 18

Gladkov, Fyodor (Vasilyevich)
1883-1958 . . . . TCLC 27

Glanville, Brian (Lester) 1931- . . . . . . CLC 6
See also CANR 3; CA 5-8R; SATA 42;
DLB 15

Glasgow, Ellen (Anderson Gholson)
1873?-1945. . . . . TCLC 2, 7
See also CA 104; DLB 9, 12

Glassco, John 1909-1981 . . . . CLC 9
See also CANR 15; CA 13-16R;
obituary CA 102; DLB 68

Glasser, Ronald J. 1940?- . . . . CLC 37

Glendinning, Victoria 1937-. . . . . CLC 50
See also CA 120

Glissant, Edouard 1928-. . . . . CLC 10, 68

Gloag, Julian 1930- . . . . CLC 40
See also CANR 10; CA 65-68

Gluck, Louise (Elisabeth)
1943- . . . . CLC 7, 22, 44
See also CA 33-36R; DLB 5

Gobineau, Joseph Arthur (Comte) de
1816-1882 . . . . NCLC 17

Godard, Jean-Luc 1930-. . . . . CLC 20
See also CA 93-96

Godden, (Margaret) Rumer 1907-. . . CLC 53
See also CLR 20; CANR 4, 27; CA 7-8R;
SATA 3, 36

Godwin, Gail 1937-. . . . CLC 5, 8, 22, 31, 69
See also CANR 15; CA 29-32R; DLB 6

Godwin, William 1756-1836. . . . . . NCLC 14
See also DLB 39

Goethe, Johann Wolfgang von
1749-1832 . . . . NCLC 4, 22, 34
See also DLB 94

Gogarty, Oliver St. John
1878-1957 . . . . TCLC 15
See also CA 109; DLB 15, 19

Gogol, Nikolai (Vasilyevich)
1809-1852 . . . . . NCLC 5, 15, 31; DC 1;
                                                      SSC 4
See also CAAS 1, 4

Goines, Donald 1937?-1974
See also BLC 2; CA 124; obituary CA 114;
DLB 33

Gokceli, Yasar Kemal 1923-
See Kemal, Yashar

Gold, Herbert 1924-. . . . . . . CLC 4, 7, 14, 42
See also CANR 17; CA 9-12R; DLB 2;
DLB-Y 81

Goldbarth, Albert 1948-. . . . . CLC 5, 38
See also CANR 6; CA 53-56

Goldberg, Anatol 1910-1982 . . . . . . CLC 34
See also obituary CA 117

Goldemberg, Isaac 1945- . . . . CLC 52
See also CANR 11; CA 69-72

Golding, William (Gerald)
1911- . . . . . CLC 1, 2, 3, 8, 10, 17, 27, 58
See also CANR 13; CA 5-8R; DLB 15

Goldman, Emma 1869-1940. . . . . . . TCLC 13
See also CA 110

Goldman, William (W.) 1931- . . . . CLC 1, 48
See also CA 9-12R; DLB 44

Goldmann, Lucien 1913-1970 . . . . . . CLC 24
See also CAP 2; CA 25-28

Goldoni, Carlo 1707-1793 . . . . LC 4

Goldsberry, Steven 1949-. . . . . CLC 34

Goldsmith, Oliver 1728?-1774. . . . . . . LC 2
See also SATA 26; DLB 39

Gombrowicz, Witold
1904-1969 . . . . CLC 4, 7, 11, 49
See also CAP 2; CA 19-20;
obituary CA 25-28R

Gomez de la Serna, Ramon
1888-1963 . . . . CLC 9
See also obituary CA 116

Goncharov, Ivan Alexandrovich
1812-1891 . . . . NCLC 1

Goncourt, Edmond (Louis Antoine Huot) de
1822-1896 . . . . NCLC 7

Goncourt, Jules (Alfred Huot) de
1830-1870 . . . . NCLC 7

Gontier, Fernande 19??-. . . . . CLC 50

Goodman, Paul 1911-1972. . . . CLC 1, 2, 4, 7
See also CAP 2; CA 19-20;
obituary CA 37-40R

Gordimer, Nadine
1923- . . . . . CLC 3, 5, 7, 10, 18, 33, 51
See also CANR 3; CA 5-8R

Gordon, Adam Lindsay
1833-1870 . . . . NCLC 21

Gordon, Caroline
1895-1981 . . . . CLC 6, 13, 29
See also CAP 1; CA 11-12;
obituary CA 103; DLB 4, 9; DLB-Y 81

Gordon, Charles William 1860-1937
See Conner, Ralph
See also CA 109

Gordon, Mary (Catherine)
1949- . . . . CLC 13, 22
See also CA 102; DLB 6; DLB-Y 81

Gordon, Sol 1923-. . . . . CLC 26
See also CANR 4; CA 53-56; SATA 11

Gordone, Charles 1925- . . . . CLC 1, 4
See also CA 93-96; DLB 7

Gorenko, Anna Andreyevna 1889?-1966
See Akhmatova, Anna

Gorky, Maxim 1868-1936 . . . . TCLC 8
See also Peshkov, Alexei Maximovich

Goryan, Sirak 1908-1981
See Saroyan, William

Gosse, Edmund (William)
1849-1928 . . . . TCLC 28
See also CA 117; DLB 57

Gotlieb, Phyllis (Fay Bloom)
1926- . . . . CLC 18
See also CANR 7; CA 13-16R; DLB 88

Author Index

Hauptmann, Gerhart (Johann Robert)
1862-1946 .... **TCLC 4**
See also CA 104; DLB 66

Havel, Vaclav 1936- .... **CLC 25, 58, 65**
See also CA 104

Haviaras, Stratis 1935- .... **CLC 33**
See also CA 105

Hawes, Stephen 1475?-1523? .... **LC 17**

Hawkes, John (Clendennin Burne, Jr.)
1925- ...... **CLC 1, 2, 3, 4, 7, 9, 14, 15,
27, 49**
See also CANR 2; CA 1-4R; DLB 2, 7;
DLB-Y 80

Hawking, Stephen (William)
1948- .... **CLC 63**
See also CA 126, 129

Hawthorne, Julian 1846-1934 ..... **TCLC 25**

Hawthorne, Nathaniel
1804-1864 ... NCLC 2, 10, 17, 23; SSC 3
See also YABC 2; DLB 1, 74;
CDALB 1640-1865

Hayashi Fumiko 1904-1951 .... **TCLC 27**

Haycraft, Anna 19??-
See Ellis, Alice Thomas
See also CA 122

Hayden, Robert (Earl)
1913-1980 .... **CLC 5, 9, 14, 37**
See also BLC 2; CANR 24; CA 69-72;
obituary CA 97-100; CABS 2; SATA 19;
obituary SATA 26; DLB 5, 76;
CDALB 1941-1968

Hayman, Ronald 1932- .... **CLC 44**
See also CANR 18; CA 25-28R

Haywood, Eliza (Fowler) 1693?-1756 .. **LC 1**
See also DLB 39

Hazlitt, William 1778-1830 ...... **NCLC 29**

Hazzard, Shirley 1931- .... **CLC 18**
See also CANR 4; CA 9-12R; DLB-Y 82

H(ilda) D(oolittle)
1886-1961 .... **CLC 3, 8, 14, 31, 34**
See also Doolittle, Hilda

Head, Bessie 1937-1986 .... **CLC 25, 67**
See also BLC 2; CANR 25; CA 29-32R;
obituary CA 119

Headon, (Nicky) Topper 1956?- .... **CLC 30**
See also The Clash

Heaney, Seamus (Justin)
1939- .... **CLC 5, 7, 14, 25, 37**
See also CANR 25; CA 85-88; DLB 40

Hearn, (Patricio) Lafcadio (Tessima Carlos)
1850-1904 .... **TCLC 9**
See also CA 105; DLB 12, 78

Hearne, Vicki 1946- .... **CLC 56**

Hearon, Shelby 1931- .... **CLC 63**
See also CANR 18; CA 25-28

Heat Moon, William Least 1939- ... **CLC 29**

Hebert, Anne 1916- .... **CLC 4, 13, 29**
See also CA 85-88; DLB 68

Hecht, Anthony (Evan)
1923- .... **CLC 8, 13, 19**
See also CANR 6; CA 9-12R; DLB 5

Hecht, Ben 1894-1964 .... **CLC 8**
See also CA 85-88; DLB 7, 9, 25, 26, 28, 86

Hedayat, Sadeq 1903-1951 .... **TCLC 21**
See also CA 120

Heidegger, Martin 1889-1976 ...... **CLC 24**
See also CA 81-84; obituary CA 65-68

Heidenstam, (Karl Gustaf) Verner von
1859-1940 .... **TCLC 5**
See also CA 104

Heifner, Jack 1946- .... **CLC 11**
See also CA 105

Heijermans, Herman 1864-1924 ... **TCLC 24**
See also CA 123

Heilbrun, Carolyn G(old) 1926- ..... **CLC 25**
See also CANR 1, 28; CA 45-48

Heine, Harry 1797-1856
See Heine, Heinrich

Heine, Heinrich 1797-1856 .... **NCLC 4**
See also DLB 90

Heinemann, Larry C(urtiss) 1944- .. **CLC 50**
See also CA 110

Heiney, Donald (William) 1921- ..... **CLC 9**
See also Harris, MacDonald
See also CANR 3; CA 1-4R

Heinlein, Robert A(nson)
1907-1988 ...... **CLC 1, 3, 8, 14, 26, 55**
See also CANR 1, 20; CA 1-4R;
obituary CA 125; SATA 9, 56; DLB 8

Heller, Joseph
1923- .... **CLC 1, 3, 5, 8, 11, 36, 63**
See also CANR 8; CA 5-8R; CABS 1;
DLB 2, 28; DLB-Y 80

Hellman, Lillian (Florence)
1905?-1984 ..... **CLC 2, 4, 8, 14, 18, 34,
44, 52; DC 1**
See also CA 13-16R; obituary CA 112;
DLB 7; DLB-Y 84

Helprin, Mark 1947- ..... **CLC 7, 10, 22, 32**
See also CA 81-84; DLB-Y 85

Hemans, Felicia 1793-1835 ...... **NCLC 29**

Hemingway, Ernest (Miller)
1899-1961 ... **CLC 1, 3, 6, 8, 10, 13, 19,
30, 34, 39, 41, 44, 50, 61; SSC 1**
See also CA 77-80; DLB 4, 9; DLB-Y 81,
87; DLB-DS 1; CDALB 1917-1929

Hempel, Amy 1951- .... **CLC 39**
See also CA 118

Henley, Beth 1952- .... **CLC 23**
See also Henley, Elizabeth Becker
See also CABS 3; DLB-Y 86

Henley, Elizabeth Becker 1952-
See Henley, Beth
See also CA 107

Henley, William Ernest
1849-1903 .... **TCLC 8**
See also CA 105; DLB 19

Hennissart, Martha
See Lathen, Emma
See also CA 85-88

Henry, O. 1862-1910 ... **TCLC 1, 19; SSC 5**
See also Porter, William Sydney
See also YABC 2; CA 104; DLB 12, 78, 79;
CDALB 1865-1917

Henry VIII 1491-1547 .... **LC 10**

Hentoff, Nat(han Irving) 1925- ..... **CLC 26**
See also CLR 1; CAAS 6; CANR 5, 25;
CA 1-4R; SATA 27, 42; AAYA 4

Heppenstall, (John) Rayner
1911-1981 .... **CLC 10**
See also CANR 29; CA 1-4R;
obituary CA 103

Herbert, Frank (Patrick)
1920-1986 .... **CLC 12, 23, 35, 44**
See also CANR 5; CA 53-56;
obituary CA 118; SATA 9, 37, 47; DLB 8

Herbert, Zbigniew 1924- .... **CLC 9, 43**
See also CA 89-92

Herbst, Josephine 1897-1969 ...... **CLC 34**
See also CA 5-8R; obituary CA 25-28R;
DLB 9

Herder, Johann Gottfried von
1744-1803 .... **NCLC 8**

Hergesheimer, Joseph
1880-1954 .... **TCLC 11**
See also CA 109; DLB 9

Herlagnez, Pablo de 1844-1896
See Verlaine, Paul (Marie)

Herlihy, James Leo 1927- .... **CLC 6**
See also CANR 2; CA 1-4R

Hermogenes fl.c. 175- .... **CMLC 6**

Hernandez, Jose 1834-1886 ...... **NCLC 17**

Herrick, Robert 1591-1674 .... **LC 13**

Herriot, James 1916- .... **CLC 12**
See also Wight, James Alfred
See also AAYA 1

Herrmann, Dorothy 1941- .... **CLC 44**
See also CA 107

Hersey, John (Richard)
1914- .... **CLC 1, 2, 7, 9, 40**
See also CA 17-20R; SATA 25; DLB 6

Herzen, Aleksandr Ivanovich
1812-1870 .... **NCLC 10**

Herzl, Theodor 1860-1904 .... **TCLC 36**

Herzog, Werner 1942- .... **CLC 16**
See also CA 89-92

Hesiod c. 8th Century B.C.- ...... **CMLC 5**

Hesse, Hermann
1877-1962 ... **CLC 1, 2, 3, 6, 11, 17, 25,
69; SSC 9**
See also CAP 2; CA 17-18; SATA 50;
DLB 66

Heyen, William 1940- .... **CLC 13, 18**
See also CAAS 9; CA 33-36R; DLB 5

Heyerdahl, Thor 1914- .... **CLC 26**
See also CANR 5, 22; CA 5-8R; SATA 2,
52

Heym, Georg (Theodor Franz Arthur)
1887-1912 .... **TCLC 9**
See also CA 106

Heym, Stefan 1913- .... **CLC 41**
See also CANR 4; CA 9-12R; DLB 69

Heyse, Paul (Johann Ludwig von)
1830-1914 .... **TCLC 8**
See also CA 104

Hibbert, Eleanor (Burford) 1906- .... **CLC 7**
See also CANR 9, 28; CA 17-20R; SATA 2

Higgins, George V(incent)
1939- .... **CLC 4, 7, 10, 18**
See also CAAS 5; CANR 17; CA 77-80;
DLB 2; DLB-Y 81

Higginson, Thomas Wentworth
        1823-1911 .... **TCLC 36**
        See also DLB 1, 64

Highsmith, (Mary) Patricia
        1921- .... **CLC 2, 4, 14, 42**
        See also CANR 1, 20; CA 1-4R

Highwater, Jamake 1942- .... **CLC 12**
        See also CLR 17; CAAS 7; CANR 10;
        CA 65-68; SATA 30, 32; DLB 52;
        DLB-Y 85

Hijuelos, Oscar 1951- .... **CLC 65**
        See also CA 123

Hikmet (Ran), Nazim 1902-1963.... **CLC 40**
        See also obituary CA 93-96

Hildesheimer, Wolfgang 1916- ..... **CLC 49**
        See also CA 101; DLB 69

Hill, Geoffrey (William)
        1932- .... **CLC 5, 8, 18, 45**
        See also CANR 21; CA 81-84; DLB 40

Hill, George Roy 1922- .... **CLC 26**
        See also CA 110, 122

Hill, Susan B. 1942- .... **CLC 4**
        See also CANR 29; CA 33-36R; DLB 14

Hillerman, Tony 1925- .... **CLC 62**
        See also CANR 21; CA 29-32R; SATA 6

Hilliard, Noel (Harvey) 1929- ...... **CLC 15**
        See also CANR 7; CA 9-12R

Hillis, Richard Lyle 1956-
        See Hillis, Rick

Hillis, Rick 1956- .... **CLC 66**
        See also Hillis, Richard Lyle

Hilton, James 1900-1954 .... **TCLC 21**
        See also CA 108; SATA 34; DLB 34, 77

Himes, Chester (Bomar)
        1909-1984 .... **CLC 2, 4, 7, 18, 58**
        See also BLC 2; CANR 22; CA 25-28R;
        obituary CA 114; DLB 2, 76

Hinde, Thomas 1926- .... **CLC 6, 11**
        See also Chitty, (Sir) Thomas Willes

Hine, (William) Daryl 1936- .... **CLC 15**
        See also CANR 1, 20; CA 1-4R; DLB 60

Hinton, S(usan) E(loise) 1950- ..... **CLC 30**
        See also CLR 3, 23; CA 81-84; SATA 19,
        58; AAYA 2

Hippius (Merezhkovsky), Zinaida
        (Nikolayevna) 1869-1945...... **TCLC 9**
        See also Gippius, Zinaida (Nikolayevna)

Hiraoka, Kimitake 1925-1970
        See Mishima, Yukio
        See also CA 97-100; obituary CA 29-32R

Hirsch, Edward (Mark) 1950-... **CLC 31, 50**
        See also CANR 20; CA 104

Hitchcock, (Sir) Alfred (Joseph)
        1899-1980 .... **CLC 16**
        See also obituary CA 97-100; SATA 27;
        obituary SATA 24

Hoagland, Edward 1932- .... **CLC 28**
        See also CANR 2; CA 1-4R; SATA 51;
        DLB 6

Hoban, Russell C(onwell) 1925- .. **CLC 7, 25**
        See also CLR 3; CANR 23; CA 5-8R;
        SATA 1, 40; DLB 52

Hobson, Laura Z(ametkin)
        1900-1986 .... **CLC 7, 25**
        See also CA 17-20R; obituary CA 118;
        SATA 52; DLB 28

Hochhuth, Rolf 1931-........ **CLC 4, 11, 18**
        See also CA 5-8R

Hochman, Sandra 1936-.......... **CLC 3, 8**
        See also CA 5-8R; DLB 5

Hochwalder, Fritz 1911-1986 ...... **CLC 36**
        See also CA 29-32R; obituary CA 120

Hocking, Mary (Eunice) 1921-..... **CLC 13**
        See also CANR 18; CA 101

Hodgins, Jack 1938-.............. **CLC 23**
        See also CA 93-96; DLB 60

Hodgson, William Hope
        1877-1918 .... **TCLC 13**
        See also CA 111; DLB 70

Hoffman, Alice 1952-............. **CLC 51**
        See also CA 77-80

Hoffman, Daniel (Gerard)
        1923-.................. **CLC 6, 13, 23**
        See also CANR 4; CA 1-4R; DLB 5

Hoffman, Stanley 1944-............ **CLC 5**
        See also CA 77-80

Hoffman, William M(oses) 1939- ... **CLC 40**
        See also CANR 11; CA 57-60

Hoffmann, E(rnst) T(heodor) A(madeus)
        1776-1822 .... **NCLC 2**
        See also SATA 27; DLB 90

Hoffmann, Gert 1932- .... **CLC 54**

Hofmannsthal, Hugo (Laurenz August
        Hofmann Edler) von
        1874-1929 .... **TCLC 11**
        See also CA 106; DLB 81

Hogg, James 1770-1835 .... **NCLC 4**

Holbach, Paul Henri Thiry, Baron d'
        1723-1789 .... **LC 14**

Holberg, Ludvig 1684-1754 .... **LC 6**

Holden, Ursula 1921-............. **CLC 18**
        See also CAAS 8; CANR 22; CA 101

Holderlin, (Johann Christian) Friedrich
        1770-1843 .... **NCLC 16**

Holdstock, Robert (P.) 1948-....... **CLC 39**

Holland, Isabelle 1920- .... **CLC 21**
        See also CANR 10, 25; CA 21-24R;
        SATA 8

Holland, Marcus 1900-1985
        See Caldwell, (Janet Miriam) Taylor
        (Holland)

Hollander, John 1929-...... **CLC 2, 5, 8, 14**
        See also CANR 1; CA 1-4R; SATA 13;
        DLB 5

Holleran, Andrew 1943?-.......... **CLC 38**

Hollinghurst, Alan 1954-.......... **CLC 55**
        See also CA 114

Hollis, Jim 1916-
        See Summers, Hollis (Spurgeon, Jr.)

Holmes, John Clellon 1926-1988.... **CLC 56**
        See also CANR 4; CA 9-10R;
        obituary CA 125; DLB 16

Holmes, Oliver Wendell
        1809-1894 .... **NCLC 14**
        See also SATA 34; DLB 1;
        CDALB 1640-1865

Holt, Victoria 1906-
        See Hibbert, Eleanor (Burford)

Holub, Miroslav 1923-............. **CLC 4**
        See also CANR 10; CA 21-24R

Homer   c. 8th century B.C.-....... **CMLC 1**

Honig, Edwin 1919-.............. **CLC 33**
        See also CAAS 8; CANR 4; CA 5-8R;
        DLB 5

Hood, Hugh (John Blagdon)
        1928- .... **CLC 15, 28**
        See also CANR 1; CA 49-52; DLB 53

Hood, Thomas 1799-1845........ **NCLC 16**

Hooker, (Peter) Jeremy 1941-...... **CLC 43**
        See also CANR 22; CA 77-80; DLB 40

Hope, A(lec) D(erwent) 1907-.... **CLC 3, 51**
        See also CA 21-24R

Hope, Christopher (David Tully)
        1944-..................... **CLC 52**
        See also CA 106

Hopkins, Gerard Manley
        1844-1889 .... **NCLC 17**
        See also DLB 35, 57

Hopkins, John (Richard) 1931-...... **CLC 4**
        See also CA 85-88

Hopkins, Pauline Elizabeth
        1859-1930 .... **TCLC 28**
        See also BLC 2; DLB 50

Horgan, Paul 1903- .... **CLC 9, 53**
        See also CANR 9; CA 13-16R; SATA 13;
        DLB-Y 85

Horovitz, Israel 1939- .... **CLC 56**
        See also CA 33-36R; DLB 7

Horwitz, Julius 1920-1986........ **CLC 14**
        See also CANR 12; CA 9-12R;
        obituary CA 119

Hospital, Janette Turner 1942-..... **CLC 42**
        See also CA 108

Hostos (y Bonilla), Eugenio Maria de
        1893-1903 .... **TCLC 24**
        See also CA 123

Hougan, Carolyn 19??-.......... **CLC 34**

Household, Geoffrey (Edward West)
        1900-1988 .... **CLC 11**
        See also CA 77-80; obituary CA 126;
        SATA 14, 59; DLB 87

Housman, A(lfred) E(dward)
        1859-1936 .... **TCLC 1, 10; PC 2**
        See also CA 104, 125; DLB 19

Housman, Laurence 1865-1959 ..... **TCLC 7**
        See also CA 106; SATA 25; DLB 10

Howard, Elizabeth Jane 1923-... **CLC 7, 29**
        See also CANR 8; CA 5-8R

Howard, Maureen 1930-.... **CLC 5, 14, 46**
        See also CA 53-56; DLB-Y 83

Howard, Richard 1929- ...... **CLC 7, 10, 47**
        See also CANR 25; CA 85-88; DLB 5

Howard, Robert E(rvin)
        1906-1936 .... **TCLC 8**
        See also CA 105

Jacobs, Jim 1942-
See Jacobs, Jim and Casey, Warren
See also CA 97-100

Jacobs, W(illiam) W(ymark)
1863-1943 . . . . **TCLC 22**
See also CA 121

Jacobsen, Jens Peter 1847-1885 . . **NCLC 34**

Jacobsen, Josephine 1908- . . . . **CLC 48**
See also CANR 23; CA 33-36R

Jacobson, Dan 1929- . . . . **CLC 4, 14**
See also CANR 2, 25; CA 1-4R; DLB 14

Jagger, Mick 1944- . . . . **CLC 17**

Jakes, John (William) 1932- . . . . **CLC 29**
See also CANR 10; CA 57-60; DLB-Y 83

James, C(yril) L(ionel) R(obert)
1901-1989 . . . . **CLC 33**
See also CA 117, 125; obituary CA 128

James, Daniel 1911-1988
See Santiago, Danny
See also obituary CA 125

James, Henry (Jr.)
1843-1916 . . . **TCLC 2, 11, 24, 40; SSC 8**
See also CA 132; brief entry CA 104;
DLB 12, 71, 74; CDALB 1865-1917

James, M(ontague) R(hodes)
1862-1936 . . . . **TCLC 6**
See also CA 104

James, P(hyllis) D(orothy)
1920- . . . . **CLC 18, 46**
See also CANR 17; CA 21-24R

James, William 1842-1910 . . . . . **TCLC 15, 32**
See also CA 109

Jami, Nur al-Din 'Abd al-Rahman
1414-1492 . . . . **LC 9**

Jandl, Ernst 1925- . . . . **CLC 34**

Janowitz, Tama 1957- . . . . **CLC 43**
See also CA 106

Jarrell, Randall
1914-1965 . . . . **CLC 1, 2, 6, 9, 13, 49**
See also CLR 6; CANR 6; CA 5-8R;
obituary CA 25-28R; CABS 2; SATA 7;
DLB 48, 52; CDALB 1941-1968

Jarry, Alfred 1873-1907 . . . . **TCLC 2, 14**
See also CA 104

Jeake, Samuel, Jr. 1889-1973
See Aiken, Conrad

Jean Paul 1763-1825 . . . . **NCLC 7**

Jeffers, (John) Robinson
1887-1962 . . . . **CLC 2, 3, 11, 15, 54**
See also CA 85-88; DLB 45;
CDALB 1917-1929

Jefferson, Thomas 1743-1826 . . . . **NCLC 11**
See also DLB 31; CDALB 1640-1865

Jeffrey, Francis 1773-1850 . . . . **NCLC 33**

Jellicoe, (Patricia) Ann 1927- . . . . . . **CLC 27**
See also CA 85-88; DLB 13

Jenkins, (John) Robin 1912- . . . . **CLC 52**
See also CANR 1; CA 4R; DLB 14

Jennings, Elizabeth (Joan)
1926- . . . . **CLC 5, 14**
See also CAAS 5; CANR 8; CA 61-64;
DLB 27

Jennings, Waylon 1937- . . . . **CLC 21**

Jensen, Johannes V. 1873-1950 . . . . **TCLC 41**

Jensen, Laura (Linnea) 1948- . . . . . . **CLC 37**
See also CA 103

Jerome, Jerome K. 1859-1927 . . . . **TCLC 23**
See also CA 119; DLB 10, 34

Jerrold, Douglas William
1803-1857 . . . . **NCLC 2**

Jewett, (Theodora) Sarah Orne
1849-1909 . . . . **TCLC 1, 22; SSC 6**
See also CA 108, 127; SATA 15; DLB 12, 74

Jewsbury, Geraldine (Endsor)
1812-1880 . . . . **NCLC 22**
See also DLB 21

Jhabvala, Ruth Prawer
1927- . . . . **CLC 4, 8, 29**
See also CANR 2, 29; CA 1-4R

Jiles, Paulette 1943- . . . . **CLC 13, 58**
See also CA 101

Jimenez (Mantecon), Juan Ramon
1881-1958 . . . . **TCLC 4**
See also CA 104

Joel, Billy 1949- . . . . **CLC 26**
See also Joel, William Martin

Joel, William Martin 1949-
See Joel, Billy
See also CA 108

John of the Cross, St. 1542-1591 . . . . **LC 18**

Johnson, B(ryan) S(tanley William)
1933-1973 . . . . **CLC 6, 9**
See also CANR 9; CA 9-12R;
obituary CA 53-56; DLB 14, 40

Johnson, Charles (Richard)
1948- . . . . **CLC 7, 51, 65**
See also BLC 2; CA 116; DLB 33

Johnson, Denis 1949- . . . . **CLC 52**
See also CA 117, 121

Johnson, Diane 1934- . . . . **CLC 5, 13, 48**
See also CANR 17; CA 41-44R; DLB-Y 80

Johnson, Eyvind (Olof Verner)
1900-1976 . . . . **CLC 14**
See also CA 73-76; obituary CA 69-72

Johnson, Fenton 1888-1958
See also BLC 2; CA 124;
brief entry CA 118; DLB 45, 50

Johnson, James Weldon
1871-1938 . . . . **TCLC 3, 19**
See also Johnson, James William
See also BLC 2; CA 125;
brief entry CA 104; SATA 31; DLB 51;
CDALB 1917-1929

Johnson, James William 1871-1938
See Johnson, James Weldon
See also SATA 31

Johnson, Joyce 1935- . . . . **CLC 58**
See also CA 125, 129

Johnson, Lionel (Pigot)
1867-1902 . . . . **TCLC 19**
See also CA 117; DLB 19

Johnson, Marguerite 1928-
See Angelou, Maya

Johnson, Pamela Hansford
1912-1981 . . . . **CLC 1, 7, 27**
See also CANR 2, 28; CA 1-4R;
obituary CA 104, DLB 15

Johnson, Samuel 1709-1784 . . . . **LC 15**
See also DLB 39, 95

Johnson, Uwe
1934-1984 . . . . **CLC 5, 10, 15, 40**
See also CANR 1; CA 1-4R;
obituary CA 112; DLB 75

Johnston, George (Benson) 1913- . . . **CLC 51**
See also CANR 5, 20; CA 1-4R; DLB 88

Johnston, Jennifer 1930- . . . . **CLC 7**
See also CA 85-88; DLB 14

Jolley, Elizabeth 1923- . . . . **CLC 46**
See also CA 127

Jones, D(ouglas) G(ordon) 1929- . . . . **CLC 10**
See also CANR 13; CA 29-32R, 113;
DLB 53

Jones, David
1895-1974 . . . . **CLC 2, 4, 7, 13, 42**
See also CANR 28; CA 9-12R;
obituary CA 53-56; DLB 20

Jones, David Robert 1947-
See Bowie, David
See also CA 103

Jones, Diana Wynne 1934- . . . . **CLC 26**
See also CLR 23; CANR 4, 26; CA 49-52;
SAAS 7; SATA 9

Jones, Gayl 1949- . . . . **CLC 6, 9**
See also BLC 2; CANR 27; CA 77-80;
DLB 33

Jones, James 1921-1977 . . . . **CLC 1, 3, 10, 39**
See also CANR 6; CA 1-4R;
obituary CA 69-72; DLB 2

Jones, (Everett) LeRoi
1934- . . . . **CLC 1, 2, 3, 5, 10, 14, 33**
See also Baraka, Amiri; Baraka, Imamu
Amiri
See also CA 21-24R

Jones, Louis B. 19??- . . . . **CLC 65**

Jones, Madison (Percy, Jr.) 1925- . . . **CLC 4**
See also CAAS 11; CANR 7; CA 13-16R

Jones, Mervyn 1922- . . . . **CLC 10, 52**
See also CAAS 5; CANR 1; CA 45-48

Jones, Mick 1956?- . . . . **CLC 30**
See also The Clash

Jones, Nettie 19??- . . . . **CLC 34**

Jones, Preston 1936-1979 . . . . **CLC 10**
See also CA 73-76; obituary CA 89-92;
DLB 7

Jones, Robert F(rancis) 1934- . . . . **CLC 7**
See also CANR 2; CA 49-52

Jones, Rod 1953- . . . . **CLC 50**
See also CA 128

Jones, Terry 1942?- . . . . **CLC 21**
See also Monty Python
See also CA 112, 116; SATA 51

Jong, Erica 1942- . . . . **CLC 4, 6, 8, 18**
See also CANR 26; CA 73-76; DLB 2, 5, 28

Jonson, Ben(jamin) 1572(?)-1637 . . . . . **LC 6**
See also DLB 62

Jordan, June 1936- . . . . **CLC 5, 11, 23**
See also CLR 10; CANR 25; CA 33-36R;
SATA 4; DLB 38; AAYA 2

Jordan, Pat(rick M.) 1941- . . . . **CLC 37**
See also CANR 25; CA 33-36R

Kessler, Jascha (Frederick) 1929-.... **CLC 4**
See also CANR 8; CA 17-20R

Kettelkamp, Larry 1933-.......... **CLC 12**
See also CANR 16; CA 29-32R; SAAS 3;
SATA 2

Kherdian, David 1931-........... **CLC 6, 9**
See also CLR 24; CAAS 2; CA 21-24R;
SATA 16

Khlebnikov, Velimir (Vladimirovich)
1885-1922 .... **TCLC 20**
See also CA 117

Khodasevich, Vladislav (Felitsianovich)
1886-1939 .... **TCLC 15**
See also CA 115

Kielland, Alexander (Lange)
1849-1906 .... **TCLC 5**
See also CA 104

Kiely, Benedict 1919-.......... **CLC 23, 43**
See also CANR 2; CA 1-4R; DLB 15

Kienzle, William X(avier) 1928- .... **CLC 25**
See also CAAS 1; CANR 9; CA 93-96

Kierkegaard, SOren 1813-1855... **NCLC 34**

Killens, John Oliver 1916-........ **CLC 10**
See also CAAS 2; CANR 26; CA 77-80,
123; DLB 33

Killigrew, Anne 1660-1685.......... **LC 4**

Kincaid, Jamaica 1949- .... **CLC 43, 68**
See also BLC 2; CA 125

King, Francis (Henry) 1923-..... **CLC 8, 53**
See also CANR 1; CA 1-4R; DLB 15

King, Martin Luther, Jr. 1929-1968
See also BLC 2; CANR 27; CAP 2;
CA 25-28; SATA 14

King, Stephen (Edwin)
1947-.........**CLC 12, 26, 37, 61**
See also CANR 1, 30; CA 61-64; SATA 9,
55; DLB-Y 80; AAYA 1

Kingman, (Mary) Lee 1919-....... **CLC 17**
See also Natti, (Mary) Lee
See also CA 5-8R; SAAS 3; SATA 1

Kingsley, Sidney 1906-............ **CLC 44**
See also CA 85-88; DLB 7

Kingsolver, Barbara 1955-........ **CLC 55**
See also CA 129

Kingston, Maxine Hong
1940-................**CLC 12, 19, 58**
See also CANR 13; CA 69-72; SATA 53;
DLB-Y 80

Kinnell, Galway
1927-..........**CLC 1, 2, 3, 5, 13, 29**
See also CANR 10; CA 9-12R; DLB 5;
DLB-Y 87

Kinsella, Thomas 1928- ...... **CLC 4, 19, 43**
See also CANR 15; CA 17-20R; DLB 27

Kinsella, W(illiam) P(atrick)
1935-.....................**CLC 27, 43**
See also CAAS 7; CANR 21; CA 97-100

Kipling, (Joseph) Rudyard
1865-1936 .... **TCLC 8, 17; PC 3; SSC 5**
See also YABC 2; CANR 33; CA 120;
brief entry CA 105; DLB 19, 34

Kirkup, James 1918- .... **CLC 1**
See also CAAS 4; CANR 2; CA 1-4R;
SATA 12; DLB 27

Kirkwood, James 1930-1989 .... **CLC 9**
See also CANR 6; CA 1-4R;
obituary CA 128

Kis, Danilo 1935-1989 .... **CLC 57**
See also CA 118, 129; brief entry CA 109

Kivi, Aleksis 1834-1872 .... **NCLC 30**

Kizer, Carolyn (Ashley) 1925-... **CLC 15, 39**
See also CAAS 5; CANR 24; CA 65-68;
DLB 5

Klappert, Peter 1942-............. **CLC 57**
See also CA 33-36R; DLB 5

Klausner, Amos 1939-
See Oz, Amos

Klein, A(braham) M(oses)
1909-1972 .... **CLC 19**
See also CA 101; obituary CA 37-40R;
DLB 68

Klein, Norma 1938-1989 .... **CLC 30**
See also CLR 2, 19; CANR 15; CA 41-44R;
obituary CA 128; SAAS 1; SATA 7, 57;
AAYA 2

Klein, T.E.D. 19??-................ **CLC 34**
See also CA 119

Kleist, Heinrich von 1777-1811.... **NCLC 2**
See also DLB 90

Klima, Ivan 1931-................ **CLC 56**
See also CANR 17; CA 25-28R

Klimentev, Andrei Platonovich 1899-1951
See Platonov, Andrei (Platonovich)
See also CA 108

Klinger, Friedrich Maximilian von
1752-1831 .... **NCLC 1**

Klopstock, Friedrich Gottlieb
1724-1803 .... **NCLC 11**

Knebel, Fletcher 1911-........... **CLC 14**
See also CAAS 3; CANR 1; CA 1-4R;
SATA 36

Knight, Etheridge 1931-1991...... **CLC 40**
See also BLC 2; CANR 23; CA 21-24R;
DLB 41

Knight, Sarah Kemble 1666-1727 ..... **LC 7**
See also DLB 24

Knowles, John 1926- ......**CLC 1, 4, 10, 26**
See also CA 17-20R; SATA 8; DLB 6;
CDALB 1968-1987

Koch, C(hristopher) J(ohn) 1932-... **CLC 42**
See also CA 127

Koch, Kenneth 1925- .... **CLC 5, 8, 44**
See also CANR 6; CA 1-4R; DLB 5

Kochanowski, Jan 1530-1584....... **LC 10**

Kock, Charles Paul de
1794-1871 .... **NCLC 16**

Koestler, Arthur
1905-1983 .... **CLC 1, 3, 6, 8, 15, 33**
See also CANR 1; CA 1-4R;
obituary CA 109; DLB-Y 83

Kohout, Pavel 1928-............. **CLC 13**
See also CANR 3; CA 45-48

Kolmar, Gertrud 1894-1943....... **TCLC 40**

Konigsberg, Allen Stewart 1935-
See Allen, Woody

Konrad, Gyorgy 1933-.......... **CLC 4, 10**
See also CA 85-88

Konwicki, Tadeusz 1926-..... **CLC 8, 28, 54**
See also CAAS 9; CA 101

Kopit, Arthur (Lee) 1937- .... **CLC 1, 18, 33**
See also CA 81-84; CABS 3; DLB 7

Kops, Bernard 1926-.............. **CLC 4**
See also CA 5-8R; DLB 13

Kornbluth, C(yril) M. 1923-1958.... **TCLC 8**
See also CA 105; DLB 8

Korolenko, Vladimir (Galaktionovich)
1853-1921 .... **TCLC 22**
See also CA 121

Kosinski, Jerzy (Nikodem)
1933- .... **CLC 1, 2, 3, 6, 10, 15, 53**
See also CANR 9; CA 17-20R; DLB 2;
DLB-Y 82

Kostelanetz, Richard (Cory) 1940- .. **CLC 28**
See also CAAS 8; CA 13-16R

Kostrowitzki, Wilhelm Apollinaris de
1880-1918
See Apollinaire, Guillaume
See also CA 104

Kotlowitz, Robert 1924-............ **CLC 4**
See also CA 33-36R

Kotzebue, August (Friedrich Ferdinand) von
1761-1819 .... **NCLC 25**

Kotzwinkle, William 1938- ... **CLC 5, 14, 35**
See also CLR 6; CANR 3; CA 45-48;
SATA 24

Kozol, Jonathan 1936-............ **CLC 17**
See also CANR 16; CA 61-64

Kozoll, Michael 1940?-............ **CLC 35**

Kramer, Kathryn 19??-............ **CLC 34**

Kramer, Larry 1935- .... **CLC 42**
See also CA 124, 126

Krasicki, Ignacy 1735-1801....... **NCLC 8**

Krasinski, Zygmunt 1812-1859 .... **NCLC 4**

Kraus, Karl 1874-1936............ **TCLC 5**
See also CA 104

Kreve, Vincas 1882-1954 .... **TCLC 27**

Kristofferson, Kris 1936-.......... **CLC 26**
See also CA 104

Krizanc, John 1956-............. **CLC 57**

Krleza, Miroslav 1893-1981......... **CLC 8**
See also CA 97-100; obituary CA 105

Kroetsch, Robert (Paul)
1927-.................**CLC 5, 23, 57**
See also CANR 8; CA 17-20R; DLB 53

Kroetz, Franz Xaver 1946- .... **CLC 41**
See also CA 130

Kropotkin, Peter 1842-1921....... **TCLC 36**
See also CA 119

Krotkov, Yuri 1917-............. **CLC 19**
See also CA 102

Krumgold, Joseph (Quincy)
1908-1980 .... **CLC 12**
See also CANR 7; CA 9-12R;
obituary CA 101; SATA 1, 48;
obituary SATA 23

Krutch, Joseph Wood 1893-1970.... **CLC 24**
See also CANR 4; CA 1-4R;
obituary CA 25-28R; DLB 63

Krylov, Ivan Andreevich
1768?-1844................. **NCLC 1**

Lee, Don L. 1942-................. CLC 2
    See also Madhubuti, Haki R.
    See also CA 73-76

Lee, George Washington
    1894-1976 .... CLC 52
    See also BLC 2; CA 125; DLB 51

Lee, (Nelle) Harper 1926-...... CLC 12, 60
    See also CA 13-16R; SATA 11; DLB 6;
    CDALB 1941-1968

Lee, Lawrence 1903- .... CLC 34
    See also CA 25-28R

Lee, Manfred B(ennington)
    1905-1971 .... CLC 11
    See also Queen, Ellery
    See also CANR 2; CA 1-4R;
    obituary CA 29-32R

Lee, Stan 1922-.................. CLC 17
    See also CA 108, 111

Lee, Tanith 1947-................ CLC 46
    See also CA 37-40R; SATA 8

Lee, Vernon 1856-1935 .... TCLC 5
    See also Paget, Violet
    See also DLB 57

Lee-Hamilton, Eugene (Jacob)
    1845-1907 .... TCLC 22
    See also CA 117

Leet, Judith 1935- .... CLC 11

Le Fanu, Joseph Sheridan
    1814-1873 .... NCLC 9
    See also DLB 21, 70

Leffland, Ella 1931- .... CLC 19
    See also CA 29-32R; DLB-Y 84

Leger, (Marie-Rene) Alexis Saint-Leger
    1887-1975 .... CLC 11
    See also Perse, St.-John
    See also CA 13-16R; obituary CA 61-64

Le Guin, Ursula K(roeber)
    1929- .... CLC 8, 13, 22, 45
    See also CLR 3; CANR 9; CA 21-24R;
    SATA 4, 52; DLB 8, 52;
    CDALB 1968-1987

Lehmann, Rosamond (Nina) 1901- ... CLC 5
    See also CANR 8; CA 77-80; DLB 15

Leiber, Fritz (Reuter, Jr.) 1910-.... CLC 25
    See also CANR 2; CA 45-48; SATA 45;
    DLB 8

Leimbach, Marti 1963-............ CLC 65

Leino, Eino 1878-1926 .... TCLC 24

Leiris, Michel 1901-............. CLC 61
    See also CA 119, 128

Leithauser, Brad 1953-........... CLC 27
    See also CANR 27; CA 107

Lelchuk, Alan 1938-.............. CLC 5
    See also CANR 1; CA 45-48

Lem, Stanislaw 1921-........ CLC 8, 15, 40
    See also CAAS 1; CA 105

Lemann, Nancy 1956-............. CLC 39
    See also CA 118

Lemonnier, (Antoine Louis) Camille
    1844-1913 .... TCLC 22
    See also CA 121

Lenau, Nikolaus 1802-1850 ...... NCLC 16

L'Engle, Madeleine 1918- .... CLC 12
    See also CLR 1, 14; CANR 3, 21; CA 1-4R;
    SATA 1, 27; DLB 52; AAYA 1

Lengyel, Jozsef 1896-1975......... CLC 7
    See also CA 85-88; obituary CA 57-60

Lennon, John (Ono)
    1940-1980 .... CLC 12, 35
    See also CA 102

Lennon, John Winston 1940-1980
    See Lennon, John (Ono)

Lennox, Charlotte Ramsay
    1729?-1804................. NCLC 23
    See also DLB 39

Lentricchia, Frank (Jr.) 1940-...... CLC 34
    See also CANR 19; CA 25-28R

Lenz, Siegfried 1926-............ CLC 27
    See also CA 89-92; DLB 75

Leonard, Elmore 1925-......... CLC 28, 34
    See also CANR 12, 28; CA 81-84

Leonard, Hugh 1926-............. CLC 19
    See also Byrne, John Keyes
    See also DLB 13

Leopardi, (Conte) Giacomo (Talegardo
    Francesco di Sales Saverio Pietro)
    1798-1837 .... NCLC 22

Lerman, Eleanor 1952-............ CLC 9
    See also CA 85-88

Lerman, Rhoda 1936-............. CLC 56
    See also CA 49-52

Lermontov, Mikhail Yuryevich
    1814-1841 .... NCLC 5

Leroux, Gaston 1868-1927....... TCLC 25
    See also CA 108

Lesage, Alain-Rene 1668-1747....... LC 2

Leskov, Nikolai (Semyonovich)
    1831-1895 .... NCLC 25

Lessing, Doris (May)
    1919- .... CLC 1, 2, 3, 6, 10, 15, 22, 40;
    SSC 6
    See also CA 9-12R; DLB 15; DLB-Y 85

Lessing, Gotthold Ephraim
    1729-1781 .... LC 8

Lester, Richard 1932-............ CLC 20

Lever, Charles (James)
    1806-1872 .... NCLC 23
    See also DLB 21

Leverson, Ada 1865-1936........ TCLC 18
    See also CA 117

Levertov, Denise
    1923- ...... CLC 1, 2, 3, 5, 8, 15, 28, 66
    See also CANR 3, 29; CA 1-4R; DLB 5

Levi, Peter (Chad Tiger) 1931- ..... CLC 41
    See also CA 5-8R; DLB 40

Levi, Primo 1919-1987........ CLC 37, 50
    See also CANR 12; CA 13-16R;
    obituary CA 122

Levin, Ira 1929- .... CLC 3, 6
    See also CANR 17; CA 21-24R

Levin, Meyer 1905-1981 .... CLC 7
    See also CANR 15; CA 9-12R;
    obituary CA 104; SATA 21;
    obituary SATA 27; DLB 9, 28; DLB-Y 81

Levine, Norman 1924- .... CLC 54
    See also CANR 14; CA 73-76; DLB 88

Levine, Philip 1928-... CLC 2, 4, 5, 9, 14, 33
    See also CANR 9; CA 9-12R; DLB 5

Levinson, Deirdre 1931-.......... CLC 49
    See also CA 73-76

Levi-Strauss, Claude 1908- .... CLC 38
    See also CANR 6; CA 1-4R

Levitin, Sonia 1934-............. CLC 17
    See also CANR 14; CA 29-32R; SAAS 2;
    SATA 4

Lewes, George Henry
    1817-1878 .... NCLC 25
    See also DLB 55

Lewis, Alun 1915-1944............ TCLC 3
    See also CA 104; DLB 20

Lewis, C(ecil) Day 1904-1972
    See Day Lewis, C(ecil)

Lewis, C(live) S(taples)
    1898-1963 .... CLC 1, 3, 6, 14, 27
    See also CLR 3; CA 81-84; SATA 13;
    DLB 15

Lewis (Winters), Janet 1899-....... CLC 41
    See also Winters, Janet Lewis
    See also CANR 29; CAP 1; CA 9-10R;
    DLB-Y 87

Lewis, Matthew Gregory
    1775-1818 .... NCLC 11
    See also DLB 39

Lewis, (Harry) Sinclair
    1885-1951 .... TCLC 4, 13, 23, 39
    See also CA 104; DLB 9; DLB-DS 1;
    CDALB 1917-1929

Lewis, (Percy) Wyndham
    1882?-1957................. TCLC 2, 9
    See also CA 104; DLB 15

Lewisohn, Ludwig 1883-1955...... TCLC 19
    See also CA 73-76, 107;
    obituary CA 29-32R; DLB 4, 9, 28

L'Heureux, John (Clarke) 1934-.... CLC 52
    See also CANR 23; CA 15-16R

Lieber, Stanley Martin 1922-
    See Lee, Stan

Lieberman, Laurence (James)
    1935-..................... CLC 4, 36
    See also CANR 8; CA 17-20R

Li Fei-kan 1904-................. CLC 18
    See also Pa Chin
    See also CA 105

Lifton, Robert Jay 1926-.......... CLC 67
    See also CANR 27; CA 17-18R

Lightfoot, Gordon (Meredith)
    1938-..................... CLC 26
    See also CA 109

Ligotti, Thomas 1953- .... CLC 44
    See also CA 123

Liliencron, Detlev von
    1844-1909 .... TCLC 18
    See also CA 117

Lima, Jose Lezama 1910-1976
    See Lezama Lima, Jose

Lima Barreto, (Alfonso Henriques de)
    1881-1922 .... TCLC 23
    See also CA 117

Limonov, Eduard 1943-........... CLC 67

Lincoln, Abraham 1809-1865 ..... NCLC 18

McGinley, Phyllis 1905-1978 ...... **CLC 14**
See also CANR 19; CA 9-12R;
obituary CA 77-80; SATA 2, 44;
obituary SATA 24; DLB 11, 48

McGinniss, Joe 1942-............. **CLC 32**
See also CANR 26; CA 25-28R

McGivern, Maureen Daly 1921-
See Daly, Maureen
See also CA 9-12R

McGrath, Patrick 1950-........... **CLC 55**

McGrath, Thomas 1916- .... **CLC 28, 59**
See also CANR 6; CA 9-12R, 130;
SATA 41

McGuane, Thomas (Francis III)
1939- .... **CLC 3, 7, 18, 45**
See also CANR 5, 24; CA 49-52; DLB 2;
DLB-Y 80

McGuckian, Medbh 1950-........ **CLC 48**
See also DLB 40

McHale, Tom 1941-1982........ **CLC 3, 5**
See also CA 77-80; obituary CA 106

McIlvanney, William 1936-........ **CLC 42**
See also CA 25-28R; DLB 14

McIlwraith, Maureen Mollie Hunter 1922-
See Hunter, Mollie
See also CA 29-32R; SATA 2

McInerney, Jay 1955- .... **CLC 34**
See also CA 116, 123

McIntyre, Vonda N(eel) 1948- ..... **CLC 18**
See also CANR 17; CA 81-84

McKay, Claude
1889-1948 .... **TCLC 7, 41; PC 2**
See also BLC 3; CA 104, 124; DLB 4, 45,
51

McKay, Claude 1889-1948
See McKay, Festus Claudius

McKay, Festus Claudius 1889-1948
See also BLC 2; CA 124; brief entry CA 104

McKuen, Rod 1933-............. **CLC 1, 3**
See also CA 41-44R

McLuhan, (Herbert) Marshall
1911-1980 .... **CLC 37**
See also CANR 12; CA 9-12R;
obituary CA 102; DLB 88

McManus, Declan Patrick 1955-
See Costello, Elvis

McMillan, Terry 1951- .... **CLC 50, 61**

McMurtry, Larry (Jeff)
1936- .... **CLC 2, 3, 7, 11, 27, 44**
See also CANR 19; CA 5-8R; DLB 2;
DLB-Y 80, 87; CDALB 1968-1987

McNally, Terrence 1939-...... **CLC 4, 7, 41**
See also CANR 2; CA 45-48; DLB 7

McPhee, John 1931-.............. **CLC 36**
See also CANR 20; CA 65-68

McPherson, James Alan 1943-..... **CLC 19**
See also CANR 24; CA 25-28R; DLB 38

McPherson, William 1939- .... **CLC 34**
See also CA 57-60

McSweeney, Kerry 19??-.......... **CLC 34**

Mead, Margaret 1901-1978........ **CLC 37**
See also CANR 4; CA 1-4R;
obituary CA 81-84; SATA 20

Meaker, M. J. 1927-
See Kerr, M. E.; Meaker, Marijane

Meaker, Marijane 1927-
See Kerr, M. E.
See also CA 107; SATA 20

Medoff, Mark (Howard) 1940-... **CLC 6, 23**
See also CANR 5; CA 53-56; DLB 7

Megged, Aharon 1920-............. **CLC 9**
See also CANR 1; CA 49-52

Mehta, Ved (Parkash) 1934-....... **CLC 37**
See also CANR 2, 23; CA 1-4R

Mellor, John 1953?-
See The Clash

Meltzer, Milton 1915- .... **CLC 26**
See also CLR 13; CA 13-16R; SAAS 1;
SATA 1, 50; DLB 61

Melville, Herman
1819-1891 ...... **NCLC 3, 12, 29; SSC 1**
See also SATA 59; DLB 3, 74;
CDALB 1640-1865

Membreno, Alejandro 1972- .... **CLC 59**

Mencken, H(enry) L(ouis)
1880-1956 .... **TCLC 13**
See also CA 105, 125; DLB 11, 29, 63;
CDALB 1917-1929

Mercer, David 1928-1980.......... **CLC 5**
See also CANR 23; CA 9-12R;
obituary CA 102; DLB 13

Meredith, George 1828-1909...... **TCLC 17**
See also CA 117; DLB 18, 35, 57

Meredith, George 1858-1924..... **TCLC 43**

Meredith, William (Morris)
1919- .... **CLC 4, 13, 22, 55**
See also CANR 6; CA 9-12R; DLB 5

Merezhkovsky, Dmitri
1865-1941 .... **TCLC 29**

Merimee, Prosper
1803-1870 .... **NCLC 6; SSC 7**

Merkin, Daphne 1954-........... **CLC 44**
See also CANR 123

Merrill, James (Ingram)
1926-........ **CLC 2, 3, 6, 8, 13, 18, 34**
See also CANR 10; CA 13-16R; DLB 5;
DLB-Y 85

Merton, Thomas (James)
1915-1968 .... **CLC 1, 3, 11, 34**
See also CANR 22; CA 5-8R;
obituary CA 25-28R; DLB 48; DLB-Y 81

Merwin, W(illiam) S(tanley)
1927- ...... **CLC 1, 2, 3, 5, 8, 13, 18, 45**
See also CANR 15; CA 13-16R; DLB 5

Metcalf, John 1938-.............. **CLC 37**
See also CA 113; DLB 60

Mew, Charlotte (Mary)
1870-1928 .... **TCLC 8**
See also CA 105; DLB 19

Mewshaw, Michael 1943-........... **CLC 9**
See also CANR 7; CA 53-56; DLB-Y 80

Meyer-Meyrink, Gustav 1868-1932
See Meyrink, Gustav
See also CA 117

Meyers, Jeffrey 1939- .... **CLC 39**
See also CA 73-76

Meynell, Alice (Christiana Gertrude
Thompson) 1847-1922 .... **TCLC 6**
See also CA 104; DLB 19

Meyrink, Gustav 1868-1932...... **TCLC 21**
See also Meyer-Meyrink, Gustav

Michaels, Leonard 1933-........ **CLC 6, 25**
See also CANR 21; CA 61-64

Michaux, Henri 1899-1984 ...... **CLC 8, 19**
See also CA 85-88; obituary CA 114

Michelangelo 1475-1564............ **LC 12**

Michelet, Jules 1798-1874....... **NCLC 31**

Michener, James A(lbert)
1907- .... **CLC 1, 5, 11, 29, 60**
See also CANR 21; CA 5-8R; DLB 6

Mickiewicz, Adam 1798-1855 ..... **NCLC 3**

Middleton, Christopher 1926-...... **CLC 13**
See also CANR 29; CA 13-16R; DLB 40

Middleton, Stanley 1919-........ **CLC 7, 38**
See also CANR 21; CA 25-28R; DLB 14

Migueis, Jose Rodrigues 1901-..... **CLC 10**

Mikszath, Kalman 1847-1910 ..... **TCLC 31**

Miles, Josephine (Louise)
1911-1985 .... **CLC 1, 2, 14, 34, 39**
See also CANR 2; CA 1-4R;
obituary CA 116; DLB 48

Mill, John Stuart 1806-1873..... **NCLC 11**
See also DLB 55

Millar, Kenneth 1915-1983 .... **CLC 14**
See also Macdonald, Ross
See also CANR 16; CA 9-12R;
obituary CA 110; DLB 2; DLB-Y 83;
DLB-DS 6

Millay, Edna St. Vincent
1892-1950 .... **TCLC 4**
See also CA 103; DLB 45;
CDALB 1917-1929

Miller, Arthur
1915- ...... **CLC 1, 2, 6, 10, 15, 26, 47;**
DC 1
See also CANR 2, 30; CA 1-4R; CABS 3;
DLB 7; CDALB 1941-1968

Miller, Henry (Valentine)
1891-1980 .... **CLC 1, 2, 4, 9, 14, 43**
See also CA 9-12R; obituary CA 97-100;
DLB 4, 9; DLB-Y 80; CDALB 1929-1941

Miller, Jason 1939?-.............. **CLC 2**
See also CA 73-76; DLB 7

Miller, Sue 19??-................. **CLC 44**

Miller, Walter M(ichael), Jr.
1923- .... **CLC 4, 30**
See also CA 85-88; DLB 8

Millett, Kate 1934-............... **CLC 67**
See also CANR 32; CA 73-76

Millhauser, Steven 1943-........ **CLC 21, 54**
See also CA 108, 110, 111; DLB 2

Millin, Sarah Gertrude 1889-1968 .. **CLC 49**
See also CA 102; obituary CA 93-96

Milne, A(lan) A(lexander)
1882-1956 .... **TCLC 6**
See also CLR 1, 26; YABC 1; CA 104, 133;
DLB 10, 77, 100

Milner, Ron(ald) 1938-............ **CLC 56**
See also BLC 3; CANR 24; CA 73-76;
DLB 38

Osceola 1885-1962
See Dinesen, Isak; Blixen, Karen
(Christentze Dinesen)

Oshima, Nagisa 1932- .... **CLC 20**
See also CA 116

Oskison, John M. 1874-1947..... **TCLC 35**

Ossoli, Sarah Margaret (Fuller marchesa d')
1810-1850
See Fuller, (Sarah) Margaret
See also SATA 25

Ostrovsky, Alexander
1823-1886 .... **NCLC 30**

Otero, Blas de 1916- .... **CLC 11**
See also CA 89-92

Ouida 1839-1908................ **TCLC 43**
See also de la Ramee, Marie Louise
See also DLB 18

Ousmane, Sembene 1923-
See also BLC 3; CA 125; brief entry CA 117

Ousmane, Sembene 1923- .... **CLC 66**
See also Sembene, Ousmane
See also CA 125; brief entry CA 117

Ovid 43 B.C.-c. 18 A.D. .... **CMLC 7; PC 2**

Owen, Wilfred (Edward Salter)
1893-1918 .... **TCLC 5, 27**
See also CA 104; DLB 20

Owens, Rochelle 1936-............. **CLC 8**
See also CAAS 2; CA 17-20R

Owl, Sebastian 1939-
See Thompson, Hunter S(tockton)

Oz, Amos 1939- ... **CLC 5, 8, 11, 27, 33, 54**
See also CANR 27; CA 53-56

Ozick, Cynthia 1928-...... **CLC 3, 7, 28, 62**
See also CANR 23; CA 17-20R; DLB 28;
DLB-Y 82

Ozu, Yasujiro 1903-1963.......... **CLC 16**
See also CA 112

P. V. M. 1912-1990
See White, Patrick (Victor Martindale)

Pa Chin 1904-................... **CLC 18**
See also Li Fei-kan

Pack, Robert 1929-.............. **CLC 13**
See also CANR 3; CA 1-4R; DLB 5

Padgett, Lewis 1915-1958
See Kuttner, Henry

Padilla, Heberto 1932-........... **CLC 38**
See also CA 123

Page, Jimmy 1944-.............. **CLC 12**

Page, Louise 1955-.............. **CLC 40**

Page, P(atricia) K(athleen)
1916- .... **CLC 7, 18**
See also CANR 4, 22; CA 53-56; DLB 68

Paget, Violet 1856-1935
See Lee, Vernon
See also CA 104

Paglia, Camille 1947-............. **CLC 68**

Palamas, Kostes 1859-1943 .... **TCLC 5**
See also CA 105

Palazzeschi, Aldo 1885-1974....... **CLC 11**
See also CA 89-92; obituary CA 53-56

Paley, Grace 1922-.... **CLC 4, 6, 37; SSC 8**
See also CANR 13; CA 25-28R; DLB 28

Palin, Michael 1943- .... **CLC 21**
See also Monty Python
See also CA 107

Palliser, Charles 1948?-........... **CLC 65**

Palma, Ricardo 1833-1919....... **TCLC 29**
See also CANR 123

Pancake, Breece Dexter 1952-1979
See Pancake, Breece D'J

Pancake, Breece D'J 1952-1979 .... **CLC 29**
See also obituary CA 109

Papadiamantis, Alexandros
1851-1911 .... **TCLC 29**

Papini, Giovanni 1881-1956...... **TCLC 22**
See also CA 121

Paracelsus 1493-1541............. **LC 14**

Parini, Jay (Lee) 1948- .... **CLC 54**
See also CA 97-100

Parker, Dorothy (Rothschild)
1893-1967 .... **CLC 15, 68; SSC 2**
See also CAP 2; CA 19-20;
obituary CA 25-28R; DLB 11, 45. 86

Parker, Robert B(rown) 1932-...... **CLC 27**
See also CANR 1, 26; CA 49-52

Parkin, Frank 1940-.............. **CLC 43**

Parkman, Francis 1823-1893..... **NCLC 12**
See also DLB 1, 30

Parks, Gordon (Alexander Buchanan)
1912- .... **CLC 1, 16**
See also BLC 3; CANR 26; CA 41-44R;
SATA 8; DLB 33

Parnell, Thomas 1679-1718 .... **LC 3**

Parra, Nicanor 1914-.............. **CLC 2**
See also CA 85-88

Pasolini, Pier Paolo
1922-1975 .... **CLC 20, 37**
See also CA 93-96; obituary CA 61-64

Pastan, Linda (Olenik) 1932- ...... **CLC 27**
See also CANR 18; CA 61-64; DLB 5

Pasternak, Boris
1890-1960 .... **CLC 7, 10, 18, 63**
See also CA 127; obituary CA 116

Patchen, Kenneth 1911-1972... **CLC 1, 2, 18**
See also CANR 3; CA 1-4R;
obituary CA 33-36R; DLB 16, 48

Pater, Walter (Horatio)
1839-1894 .... **NCLC 7**
See also DLB 57

Paterson, Andrew Barton
1864-1941 .... **TCLC 32**

Paterson, Katherine (Womeldorf)
1932- .... **CLC 12, 30**
See also CLR 7; CANR 28; CA 21-24R;
SATA 13, 53; DLB 52; AAYA 1

Patmore, Coventry Kersey Dighton
1823-1896 .... **NCLC 9**
See also DLB 35

Paton, Alan (Stewart)
1903-1988 .... **CLC 4, 10, 25, 55**
See also CANR 22; CAP 1; CA 15-16;
obituary CA 125; SATA 11

Paulding, James Kirke 1778-1860.. **NCLC 2**
See also DLB 3, 59, 74

Paulin, Tom 1949-............... **CLC 37**
See also CA 123; DLB 40

Paustovsky, Konstantin (Georgievich)
1892-1968 .... **CLC 40**
See also CA 93-96; obituary CA 25-28R

Paustowsky, Konstantin (Georgievich)
1892-1968
See Paustovsky, Konstantin (Georgievich)

Pavese, Cesare 1908-1950 .... **TCLC 3**
See also CA 104

Pavic, Milorad 1929-............. **CLC 60**

Payne, Alan 1932-
See Jakes, John (William)

Paz, Octavio
1914- ...... **CLC 3, 4, 6, 10, 19, 51, 65;
PC 1**
See also CANR 32; CA 73-76

p'Bitek, Okot 1931-1982
See also BLC 3; CA 124; obituary CA 107

Peacock, Molly 1947-............. **CLC 60**
See also CA 103

Peacock, Thomas Love
1785-1886 .... **NCLC 22**

Peake, Mervyn 1911-1968....... **CLC 7, 54**
See also CANR 3; CA 5-8R;
obituary CA 25-28R; SATA 23; DLB 15

Pearce, (Ann) Philippa 1920-..... **CLC 21**
See also Christie, (Ann) Philippa
See also CLR 9; CA 5-8R; SATA 1

Pearl, Eric 1934-
See Elman, Richard

Pearson, T(homas) R(eid) 1956- .... **CLC 39**
See also CA 120, 130

Peck, John 1941-................. **CLC 3**
See also CANR 3; CA 49-52

Peck, Richard 1934-.............. **CLC 21**
See also CLR 15; CANR 19; CA 85-88;
SAAS 2; SATA 18; AAYA 1

Peck, Robert Newton 1928-........ **CLC 17**
See also CA 81-84; SAAS 1; SATA 21;
AAYA 3

Peckinpah, (David) Sam(uel)
1925-1984 .... **CLC 20**
See also CA 109; obituary CA 114

Pedersen, Knut 1859-1952
See Hamsun, Knut
See also CA 104, 109, 119

Peguy, Charles (Pierre)
1873-1914 .... **TCLC 10**
See also CA 107

Pepys, Samuel 1633-1703........... **LC 11**

Percy, Walker
1916-1990 ... **CLC 2, 3, 6, 8, 14, 18, 47,
65**
See also CANR 1, 23; CA 1-4R;
obituary CA 131; DLB 2; DLB-Y 80

Perec, Georges 1936-1982 .... **CLC 56**
See also DLB 83

Pereda, Jose Maria de
1833-1906 .... **TCLC 16**

Perelman, S(idney) J(oseph)
1904-1979 ... **CLC 3, 5, 9, 15, 23, 44, 49**
See also CANR 18; CA 73-76;
obituary CA 89-92; DLB 11, 44

Peret, Benjamin 1899-1959 .... **TCLC 20**
See also CA 117

Powers, John R. 1945-............ **CLC 66**
See also Powers, John J(ames)
See also CA 69-72

Pownall, David 1938-............ **CLC 10**
See also CA 89-92; DLB 14

Powys, John Cowper
1872-1963 .... **CLC 7, 9, 15, 46**
See also CA 85-88; DLB 15

Powys, T(heodore) F(rancis)
1875-1953 .... **TCLC 9**
See also CA 106; DLB 36

Prager, Emily 1952-.............. **CLC 56**

Pratt, E(dwin) J(ohn) 1883-1964.... **CLC 19**
See also obituary CA 93-96; DLB 92

Premchand 1880-1936 .... **TCLC 21**

Preussler, Otfried 1923-......... **CLC 17**
See also CA 77-80; SATA 24

Prevert, Jacques (Henri Marie)
1900-1977 .... **CLC 15**
See also CANR 29; CA 77-80;
obituary CA 69-72; obituary SATA 30

Prevost, Abbe (Antoine Francois)
1697-1763 .... **LC 1**

Price, (Edward) Reynolds
1933-......... **CLC 3, 6, 13, 43, 50, 63**
See also CANR 1; CA 1-4R; DLB 2

Price, Richard 1949- .... **CLC 6, 12**
See also CANR 3; CA 49-52; DLB-Y 81

Prichard, Katharine Susannah
1883-1969 .... **CLC 46**
See also CAP 1; CA 11-12

Priestley, J(ohn) B(oynton)
1894-1984 .... **CLC 2, 5, 9, 34**
See also CA 9-12R; obituary CA 113;
DLB 10, 34, 77; DLB-Y 84

Prince (Rogers Nelson) 1958?- ..... **CLC 35**

Prince, F(rank) T(empleton) 1912- .. **CLC 22**
See also CA 101; DLB 20

Prior, Matthew 1664-1721.......... **LC 4**

Pritchard, William H(arrison)
1932-...................... **CLC 34**
See also CANR 23; CA 65-68

Pritchett, V(ictor) S(awdon)
1900- .... **CLC 5, 13, 15, 41**
See also CA 61-64; DLB 15

Probst, Mark 1925-............. **CLC 59**
See also CA 130

Procaccino, Michael 1946-
See Cristofer, Michael

Prokosch, Frederic 1908-1989.... **CLC 4, 48**
See also CA 73-76; obituary CA 128;
DLB 48

Prose, Francine 1947-............. **CLC 45**
See also CA 109, 112

Proust, Marcel 1871-1922 .. **TCLC 7, 13, 33**
See also CA 104, 120; DLB 65

Pryor, Richard 1940-............. **CLC 26**
See also CA 122

Przybyszewski, Stanislaw
1868-1927 .... **TCLC 36**
See also DLB 66

Puig, Manuel
1932-1990 .... **CLC 3, 5, 10, 28, 65**
See also CANR 2, 32; CA 45-48

Purdy, A(lfred) W(ellington)
1918- .... **CLC 3, 6, 14, 50**
See also CA 81-84

Purdy, James (Amos)
1923-............ **CLC 2, 4, 10, 28, 52**
See also CAAS 1; CANR 19; CA 33-36R;
DLB 2

Pushkin, Alexander (Sergeyevich)
1799-1837 .... **NCLC 3, 27**

P'u Sung-ling 1640-1715 .... **LC 3**

Puzo, Mario 1920-......... **CLC 1, 2, 6, 36**
See also CANR 4; CA 65-68; DLB 6

Pym, Barbara (Mary Crampton)
1913-1980 .... **CLC 13, 19, 37**
See also CANR 13; CAP 1; CA 13-14;
obituary CA 97-100; DLB 14; DLB-Y 87

Pynchon, Thomas (Ruggles, Jr.)
1937- ..... **CLC 2, 3, 6, 9, 11, 18, 33, 62**
See also CANR 22; CA 17-20R; DLB 2

Quarrington, Paul 1954?-.......... **CLC 65**
See also CA 129

Quasimodo, Salvatore 1901-1968 ... **CLC 10**
See also CAP 1; CA 15-16;
obituary CA 25-28R

Queen, Ellery 1905-1982 .... **CLC 3, 11**
See also Dannay, Frederic; Lee, Manfred
B(ennington)

Queneau, Raymond
1903-1976 .... **CLC 2, 5, 10, 42**
See also CA 77-80; obituary CA 69-72;
DLB 72

Quin, Ann (Marie) 1936-1973 .... **CLC 6**
See also CA 9-12R; obituary CA 45-48;
DLB 14

Quinn, Simon 1942-
See Smith, Martin Cruz
See also CANR 6, 23; CA 85-88

Quiroga, Horacio (Sylvestre)
1878-1937 .... **TCLC 20**
See also CA 117

Quoirez, Francoise 1935-
See Sagan, Francoise
See also CANR 6; CA 49-52

Rabe, David (William) 1940-... **CLC 4, 8, 33**
See also CA 85-88; CABS 3; DLB 7

Rabelais, Francois 1494?-1553........ **LC 5**

Rabinovitch, Sholem 1859-1916
See Aleichem, Sholom
See also CA 104

Rachen, Kurt von 1911-1986
See Hubbard, L(afayette) Ron(ald)

Radcliffe, Ann (Ward) 1764-1823 .. **NCLC 6**
See also DLB 39

Radiguet, Raymond 1903-1923 .... **TCLC 29**
See also DLB 65

Radnoti, Miklos 1909-1944 .... **TCLC 16**
See also CA 118

Rado, James 1939-.............. **CLC 17**
See also CA 105

Radomski, James 1932-
See Rado, James

Radvanyi, Netty Reiling 1900-1983
See Seghers, Anna
See also CA 85-88; obituary CA 110

Rae, Ben 1935-
See Griffiths, Trevor

Raeburn, John 1941- .... **CLC 34**
See also CA 57-60

Ragni, Gerome 1942-............. **CLC 17**
See also CA 105

Rahv, Philip 1908-1973 .... **CLC 24**
See also Greenberg, Ivan

Raine, Craig 1944-.............. **CLC 32**
See also CANR 29; CA 108; DLB 40

Raine, Kathleen (Jessie) 1908- ... **CLC 7, 45**
See also CA 85-88; DLB 20

Rainis, Janis 1865-1929 .... **TCLC 29**

Rakosi, Carl 1903-............... **CLC 47**
See also Rawley, Callman
See also CAAS 5

Ramos, Graciliano 1892-1953 ..... **TCLC 32**

Rampersad, Arnold 19??-.......... **CLC 44**

Ramuz, Charles-Ferdinand
1878-1947 .... **TCLC 33**

Rand, Ayn 1905-1982........ **CLC 3, 30, 44**
See also CANR 27; CA 13-16R;
obituary CA 105

Randall, Dudley (Felker) 1914-...... **CLC 1**
See also BLC 3; CANR 23; CA 25-28R;
DLB 41

Ransom, John Crowe
1888-1974 .... **CLC 2, 4, 5, 11, 24**
See also CANR 6; CA 5-8R;
obituary CA 49-52; DLB 45, 63

Rao, Raja 1909-.............. **CLC 25, 56**
See also CA 73-76

Raphael, Frederic (Michael)
1931-..................... **CLC 2, 14**
See also CANR 1; CA 1-4R; DLB 14

Rathbone, Julian 1935- .... **CLC 41**
See also CA 101

Rattigan, Terence (Mervyn)
1911-1977 .... **CLC 7**
See also CA 85-88; obituary CA 73-76;
DLB 13

Ratushinskaya, Irina 1954- .... **CLC 54**
See also CA 129

Raven, Simon (Arthur Noel)
1927-...................... **CLC 14**
See also CA 81-84

Rawley, Callman 1903-
See Rakosi, Carl
See also CANR 12; CA 21-24R

Rawlings, Marjorie Kinnan
1896-1953 .... **TCLC 4**
See also YABC 1; CA 104; DLB 9, 22

Ray, Satyajit 1921-................ **CLC 16**
See also CA 114

Read, Herbert (Edward) 1893-1968 .. **CLC 4**
See also CA 85-88; obituary CA 25-28R;
DLB 20

Read, Piers Paul 1941- ...... **CLC 4, 10, 25**
See also CA 21-24R; SATA 21; DLB 14

Reade, Charles 1814-1884 .... **NCLC 2**
See also DLB 21

Reade, Hamish 1936-
See Gray, Simon (James Holliday)

Ryder, Jonathan 1927-
See Ludlum, Robert

Ryga, George 1932- .... CLC 14
See also CA 101; obituary CA 124; DLB 60

Séviné, Marquise de Marie de
Rabutin-Chantal 1626-1696..... LC 11

Saba, Umberto 1883-1957 .... TCLC 33

Sabato, Ernesto 1911- .... CLC 10, 23
See also CA 97-100

Sacher-Masoch, Leopold von
1836?-1895............... NCLC 31

Sachs, Marilyn (Stickle) 1927- ..... CLC 35
See also CLR 2; CANR 13; CA 17-20R;
SAAS 2; SATA 3, 52

Sachs, Nelly 1891-1970 .... CLC 14
See also CAP 2; CA 17-18;
obituary CA 25-28R

Sackler, Howard (Oliver)
1929-1982 .... CLC 14
See also CA 61-64; obituary CA 108; DLB 7

Sacks, Oliver 1933- .... CLC 67
See also CANR 28; CA 53-56

Sade, Donatien Alphonse Francois, Comte de
1740-1814 .... NCLC 3

Sadoff, Ira 1945-................. CLC 9
See also CANR 5, 21; CA 53-56

Safire, William 1929-............ CLC 10
See also CA 17-20R

Sagan, Carl (Edward) 1934-........ CLC 30
See also CANR 11; CA 25-28R; SATA 58

Sagan, Francoise
1935- .... CLC 3, 6, 9, 17, 36
See also Quoirez, Francoise
See also CANR 6; DLB 83

Sahgal, Nayantara (Pandit) 1927-... CLC 41
See also CANR 11; CA 9-12R

Saint, H(arry) F. 1941- .... CLC 50

Sainte-Beuve, Charles Augustin
1804-1869 .... NCLC 5

Sainte-Marie, Beverly 1941-1972?
See Sainte-Marie, Buffy
See also CA 107

Sainte-Marie, Buffy 1941-........ CLC 17
See also Sainte-Marie, Beverly

Saint-Exupery, Antoine (Jean Baptiste Marie
Roger) de 1900-1944 .... TCLC 2
See also CLR 10; CA 108; SATA 20;
DLB 72

Saintsbury, George 1845-1933..... TCLC 31
See also DLB 57

Sait Faik (Abasiyanik)
1906-1954 .... TCLC 23

Saki 1870-1916............... TCLC 3
See also Munro, H(ector) H(ugh)
See also CA 104

Salama, Hannu 1936-............ CLC 18

Salamanca, J(ack) R(ichard)
1922- .... CLC 4, 15
See also CA 25-28R

Sale, Kirkpatrick 1937-........... CLC 68
See also CANR 10; CA 13-14R

Salinas, Pedro 1891-1951......... TCLC 17
See also CA 117

Salinger, J(erome) D(avid)
1919- ...... CLC 1, 3, 8, 12, 56; SSC 2
See also CA 5-8R; DLB 2;
CDALB 1941-1968

Salter, James 1925-......... CLC 7, 52, 59
See also CA 73-76

Saltus, Edgar (Evertson)
1855-1921 .... TCLC 8
See also CA 105

Saltykov, Mikhail Evgrafovich
1826-1889 .... NCLC 16

Samarakis, Antonis 1919- .... CLC 5
See also CA 25-28R

Sanchez, Florencio 1875-1910..... TCLC 37

Sanchez, Luis Rafael 1936-........ CLC 23

Sanchez, Sonia 1934-............. CLC 5
See also BLC 3; CLR 18; CANR 24;
CA 33-36R; SATA 22; DLB 41;
DLB-DS 8

Sand, George 1804-1876......... NCLC 2

Sandburg, Carl (August)
1878-1967 ... CLC 1, 4, 10, 15, 35; PC 2
See also CA 5-8R; obituary CA 25-28R;
SATA 8; DLB 17, 54; CDALB 1865-1917

Sandburg, Charles August 1878-1967
See Sandburg, Carl (August)

Sanders, (James) Ed(ward) 1939- ... CLC 53
See also CANR 13; CA 15-16R, 103;
DLB 16

Sanders, Lawrence 1920-.......... CLC 41
See also CA 81-84

Sandoz, Mari (Susette) 1896-1966 .. CLC 28
See also CANR 17; CA 1-4R;
obituary CA 25-28R; SATA 5; DLB 9

Saner, Reg(inald Anthony) 1931- .... CLC 9
See also CA 65-68

Sannazaro, Jacopo 1456?-1530 ..... LC 8

Sansom, William 1912-1976...... CLC 2, 6
See also CA 5-8R; obituary CA 65-68

Santayana, George 1863-1952..... TCLC 40
See also CA 115; DLB 54, 71

Santiago, Danny 1911-............ CLC 33
See also CA 125

Santmyer, Helen Hooven
1895-1986 .... CLC 33
See also CANR 15; CA 1-4R;
obituary CA 118; DLB-Y 84

Santos, Bienvenido N(uqui) 1911-... CLC 22
See also CANR 19; CA 101

Sappho c. 6th-century B.C.-....... CMLC 3

Sarduy, Severo 1937-............. CLC 6
See also CA 89-92

Sargeson, Frank 1903-1982 .... CLC 31
See also CA 106, 25-28R; obituary CA 106

Sarmiento, Felix Ruben Garcia 1867-1916
See Dario, Ruben
See also CA 104

Saroyan, William
1908-1981 ..... CLC 1, 8, 10, 29, 34, 56
See also CA 5-8R; obituary CA 103;
SATA 23; obituary SATA 24; DLB 7, 9;
DLB-Y 81

Sarraute, Nathalie
1902- .... CLC 1, 2, 4, 8, 10, 31
See also CANR 23; CA 9-12R; DLB 83

Sarton, Eleanore Marie 1912-
See Sarton, (Eleanor) May

Sarton, (Eleanor) May
1912-................. CLC 4, 14, 49
See also CANR 1; CA 1-4R; SATA 36;
DLB 48; DLB-Y 81

Sartre, Jean-Paul (Charles Aymard)
1905-1980 ... CLC 1, 4, 7, 9, 13, 18, 24,
44, 50, 52
See also CANR 21; CA 9-12R;
obituary CA 97-100; DLB 72

Sassoon, Siegfried (Lorraine)
1886-1967 .... CLC 36
See also CA 104; obituary CA 25-28R;
DLB 20

Saul, John (W. III) 1942- .... CLC 46
See also CANR 16; CA 81-84

Saura, Carlos 1932-............. CLC 20
See also CA 114

Sauser-Hall, Frederic-Louis
1887-1961 .... CLC 18
See also Cendrars, Blaise
See also CA 102; obituary CA 93-96

Savage, Thomas 1915-............ CLC 40
See also CA 126

Savan, Glenn 19??-............. CLC 50

Sayers, Dorothy L(eigh)
1893-1957 ....TCLC 2, 15
See also CA 104, 119; DLB 10, 36, 77

Sayers, Valerie 19??-............. CLC 50

Sayles, John (Thomas)
1950-................. CLC 7, 10, 14
See also CA 57-60; DLB 44

Scammell, Michael 19??-.......... CLC 34

Scannell, Vernon 1922- .... CLC 49
See also CANR 8; CA 5-8R; DLB 27

Schaeffer, Susan Fromberg
1941-................. CLC 6, 11, 22
See also CANR 18; CA 49-52; SATA 22;
DLB 28

Schell, Jonathan 1943-............ CLC 35
See also CANR 12; CA 73-76

Schelling, Friedrich Wilhelm Joseph von
1775-1854 .... NCLC 30
See also DLB 90

Scherer, Jean-Marie Maurice 1920-
See Rohmer, Eric
See also CA 110

Schevill, James (Erwin) 1920-...... CLC 7
See also CA 5-8R

Schisgal, Murray (Joseph) 1926-..... CLC 6
See also CA 21-24R

Schlee, Ann 1934-................ CLC 35
See also CA 101; SATA 36, 44

Schlegel, August Wilhelm von
1767-1845 .... NCLC 15

Schlegel, Johann Elias (von)
1719?-1749................... LC 5

Schmidt, Arno 1914-1979......... CLC 56
See also obituary CA 109; DLB 69

Schmitz, Ettore 1861-1928
See Svevo, Italo
See also CA 104, 122

Schnackenberg, Gjertrud 1953- ..... CLC 40
See also CA 116

Schneider, Leonard Alfred 1925-1966
See Bruce, Lenny
See also CA 89-92

Schnitzler, Arthur 1862-1931 ...... TCLC 4
See also CA 104; DLB 81

Schor, Sandra 1932?-1990 .... CLC 65
See also CA 132

Schorer, Mark 1908-1977 .... CLC 9
See also CANR 7; CA 5-8R;
obituary CA 73-76

Schrader, Paul (Joseph) 1946- ...... CLC 26
See also CA 37-40R; DLB 44

Schreiner (Cronwright), Olive (Emilie
Albertina) 1855-1920 .... TCLC 9
See also CA 105; DLB 18

Schulberg, Budd (Wilson)
1914- .... CLC 7, 48
See also CANR 19; CA 25-28R; DLB 6, 26,
28; DLB-Y 81

Schulz, Bruno 1892-1942 .... TCLC 5
See also CA 115, 123

Schulz, Charles M(onroe) 1922- .... CLC 12
See also CANR 6; CA 9-12R; SATA 10

Schuyler, James (Marcus)
1923- .... CLC 5, 23
See also CA 101; DLB 5

Schwartz, Delmore
1913-1966 .... CLC 2, 4, 10, 45
See also CAP 2; CA 17-18;
obituary CA 25-28R; DLB 28, 48

Schwartz, John Burnham 1925- .... CLC 59

Schwartz, Lynne Sharon 1939- ..... CLC 31
See also CA 103

Schwarz-Bart, Andre 1928- .... CLC 2, 4
See also CA 89-92

Schwarz-Bart, Simone 1938- .... CLC 7
See also CA 97-100

Schwob, (Mayer Andre) Marcel
1867-1905 .... TCLC 20
See also CA 117

Sciascia, Leonardo
1921-1989 .... CLC 8, 9, 41
See also CA 85-88

Scoppettone, Sandra 1936- .... CLC 26
See also CA 5-8R; SATA 9

Scorsese, Martin 1942- .... CLC 20
See also CA 110, 114

Scotland, Jay 1932-
See Jakes, John (William)

Scott, Duncan Campbell
1862-1947 .... TCLC 6
See also CA 104; DLB 92

Scott, Evelyn 1893-1963 .... CLC 43
See also CA 104; obituary CA 112; DLB 9,
48

Scott, F(rancis) R(eginald)
1899-1985 .... CLC 22
See also CA 101; obituary CA 114; DLB 88

Scott, Joanna 19??- .... CLC 50
See also CA 126

Scott, Paul (Mark) 1920-1978 .... CLC 9, 60
See also CA 81-84; obituary CA 77-80;
DLB 14

Scott, Sir Walter 1771-1832 ..... NCLC 15
See also YABC 2

Scribe, (Augustin) Eugene
1791-1861 .... NCLC 16

Scudery, Madeleine de 1607-1701 ..... LC 2

Sealy, I. Allan 1951- .... CLC 55

Seare, Nicholas 1925-
See Trevanian; Whitaker, Rodney

Sebestyen, Igen 1924-
See Sebestyen, Ouida

Sebestyen, Ouida 1924- .... CLC 30
See also CLR 17; CA 107; SATA 39

Sedgwick, Catharine Maria
1789-1867 .... NCLC 19
See also DLB 1, 74

Seelye, John 1931- .... CLC 7
See also CA 97-100

Seferiades, Giorgos Stylianou 1900-1971
See Seferis, George
See also CANR 5; CA 5-8R;
obituary CA 33-36R

Seferis, George 1900-1971 ...... CLC 5, 11
See also Seferiades, Giorgos Stylianou

Segal, Erich (Wolf) 1937- .... CLC 3, 10
See also CANR 20; CA 25-28R; DLB-Y 86

Seger, Bob 1945- .... CLC 35

Seger, Robert Clark 1945-
See Seger, Bob

Seghers, Anna 1900-1983 .... CLC 7, 110
See also Radvanyi, Netty Reiling
See also DLB 69

Seidel, Frederick (Lewis) 1936- ..... CLC 18
See also CANR 8; CA 13-16R; DLB-Y 84

Seifert, Jaroslav 1901-1986 ..... CLC 34, 44
See also CA 127

Sei Shonagon c. 966-1017? .... CMLC 6

Selby, Hubert, Jr. 1928- ..... CLC 1, 2, 4, 8
See also CA 13-16R; DLB 2

Sembene, Ousmane 1923-
See Ousmane, Sembene

Sembene, Ousmane 1923-
See Ousmane, Sembene

Senacour, Etienne Pivert de
1770-1846 .... NCLC 16

Sender, Ramon (Jose) 1902-1982 .... CLC 8
See also CANR 8; CA 5-8R;
obituary CA 105

Seneca, Lucius Annaeus
4 B.C.-65 A.D. .... CMLC 6

Senghor, Leopold Sedar 1906- ...... CLC 54
See also BLC 3; CA 116, 125

Serling, (Edward) Rod(man)
1924-1975 .... CLC 30
See also CA 65-68; obituary CA 57-60;
DLB 26

Serpieres 1907-
See Guillevic, (Eugene)

Service, Robert W(illiam)
1874-1958 .... TCLC 15
See also CA 115; SATA 20

Seth, Vikram 1952- .... CLC 43
See also CA 121, 127

Seton, Cynthia Propper
1926-1982 .... CLC 27
See also CANR 7; CA 5-8R;
obituary CA 108

Seton, Ernest (Evan) Thompson
1860-1946 .... TCLC 31
See also CA 109; SATA 18; DLB 92

Settle, Mary Lee 1918- .... CLC 19, 61
See also CAAS 1; CA 89-92; DLB 6

Sevine, Marquise de Marie de
Rabutin-Chantal 1626-1696 ..... LC 11

Sexton, Anne (Harvey)
1928-1974 ... CLC 2, 4, 6, 8, 10, 15, 53;
PC 2
See also CANR 3; CA 1-4R;
obituary CA 53-56; CABS 2; SATA 10;
DLB 5; CDALB 1941-1968

Shaara, Michael (Joseph) 1929- .... CLC 15
See also CA 102; obituary CA 125;
DLB-Y 83

Shackleton, C. C. 1925-
See Aldiss, Brian W(ilson)

Shacochis, Bob 1951- .... CLC 39
See also CA 119, 124

Shaffer, Anthony 1926- .... CLC 19
See also CA 110, 116; DLB 13

Shaffer, Peter (Levin)
1926- .... CLC 5, 14, 18, 37, 60
See also CANR 25; CA 25-28R; DLB 13

Shalamov, Varlam (Tikhonovich)
1907?-1982 .... CLC 18
See also obituary CA 105

Shamlu, Ahmad 1925- .... CLC 10

Shammas, Anton 1951- .... CLC 55

Shange, Ntozake 1948- ...... CLC 8, 25, 38
See also BLC 3; CANR 27; CA 85-88;
CABS 3; DLB 38

Shapcott, Thomas W(illiam) 1935- .. CLC 38
See also CA 69-72

Shapiro, Karl (Jay) 1913- .. CLC 4, 8, 15, 53
See also CAAS 6; CANR 1; CA 1-4R;
DLB 48

Sharp, William 1855-1905 .... TCLC 39

Sharpe, Tom 1928- .... CLC 36
See also CA 114; DLB 14

Shaw, (George) Bernard
1856-1950 .... TCLC 3, 9, 21
See also CA 104, 109, 119; DLB 10, 57

Shaw, Henry Wheeler
1818-1885 .... NCLC 15
See also DLB 11

Shaw, Irwin 1913-1984 .... CLC 7, 23, 34
See also CANR 21; CA 13-16R;
obituary CA 112; DLB 6; DLB-Y 84;
CDALB 1941-1968

Shaw, Robert 1927-1978 .... CLC 5
See also CANR 4; CA 1-4R;
obituary CA 81-84; DLB 13, 14

Skelton, Robin 1925- .... **CLC 13**
See also CAAS 5; CA 5-8R; DLB 27, 53

Skolimowski, Jerzy 1938- .... **CLC 20**

Skolimowski, Yurek 1938-
See Skolimowski, Jerzy

Skram, Amalie (Bertha)
1847-1905 .... **TCLC 25**

Skrine, Mary Nesta 1904-
See Keane, Molly

Skvorecky, Josef (Vaclav)
1924- .... **CLC 15, 39, 69**
See also CAAS 1; CANR 10, 34; CA 61-64

Slade, Bernard 1930- .... **CLC 11, 46**
See also Newbound, Bernard Slade
See also DLB 53

Slaughter, Carolyn 1946- .... **CLC 56**
See also CA 85-88

Slaughter, Frank G(ill) 1908- ...... **CLC 29**
See also CANR 5; CA 5-8R

Slavitt, David (R.) 1935- .... **CLC 5, 14**
See also CAAS 3; CA 21-24R; DLB 5, 6

Slesinger, Tess 1905-1945 .... **TCLC 10**
See also CA 107

Slessor, Kenneth 1901-1971 .... **CLC 14**
See also CA 102; obituary CA 89-92

Slowacki, Juliusz 1809-1849 ..... **NCLC 15**

Smart, Christopher 1722-1771 .... **LC 3**

Smart, Elizabeth 1913-1986 .... **CLC 54**
See also CA 81-84; obituary CA 118;
DLB 88

Smiley, Jane (Graves) 1949- .... **CLC 53**
See also CA 104

Smith, A(rthur) J(ames) M(arshall)
1902-1980 .... **CLC 15**
See also CANR 4; CA 1-4R;
obituary CA 102; DLB 88

Smith, Betty (Wehner) 1896-1972... **CLC 19**
See also CA 5-8R; obituary CA 33-36R;
SATA 6; DLB-Y 82

Smith, Cecil Lewis Troughton 1899-1966
See Forester, C(ecil) S(cott)

Smith, Charlotte (Turner)
1749-1806 .... **NCLC 23**
See also DLB 39

Smith, Clark Ashton 1893-1961 .... **CLC 43**

Smith, Dave 1942- .... **CLC 22, 42**
See also Smith, David (Jeddie)
See also CAAS 7; CANR 1; DLB 5

Smith, David (Jeddie) 1942-
See Smith, Dave
See also CANR 1; CA 49-52

Smith, Florence Margaret 1902-1971
See Smith, Stevie
See also CAP 2; CA 17-18;
obituary CA 29-32R

Smith, Iain Crichton 1928- .... **CLC 64**
See also DLB 40

Smith, John 1580?-1631............. **LC 9**
See also DLB 24, 30

Smith, Lee 1944-................. **CLC 25**
See also CA 114, 119; DLB-Y 83

Smith, Martin Cruz 1942-........ **CLC 25**
See also CANR 6; CA 85-88

Smith, Martin William 1942-
See Smith, Martin Cruz

Smith, Mary-Ann Tirone 1944-..... **CLC 39**
See also CA 118

Smith, Patti 1946- .... **CLC 12**
See also CA 93-96

Smith, Pauline (Urmson)
1882-1959 .... **TCLC 25**
See also CA 29-32R; SATA 27

Smith, Rosamond 1938-
See Oates, Joyce Carol

Smith, Sara Mahala Redway 1900-1972
See Benson, Sally

Smith, Stevie 1902-1971.... **CLC 3, 8, 25, 44**
See also Smith, Florence Margaret
See also DLB 20

Smith, Wilbur (Addison) 1933-..... **CLC 33**
See also CANR 7; CA 13-16R

Smith, William Jay 1918- .... **CLC 6**
See also CA 5-8R; SATA 2; DLB 5

Smolenskin, Peretz 1842-1885.... **NCLC 30**

Smollett, Tobias (George) 1721-1771 .. **LC 2**
See also DLB 39

Snodgrass, W(illiam) D(e Witt)
1926- .... **CLC 2, 6, 10, 18, 68**
See also CANR 6; CA 1-4R; DLB 5

Snow, C(harles) P(ercy)
1905-1980 .... **CLC 1, 4, 6, 9, 13, 19**
See also CA 5-8R; obituary CA 101;
DLB 15, 77

Snyder, Gary (Sherman)
1930- .... **CLC 1, 2, 5, 9, 32**
See also CANR 30; CA 17-20R; DLB 5, 16

Snyder, Zilpha Keatley 1927-...... **CLC 17**
See also CA 9-12R; SAAS 2; SATA 1, 28

Sobol, Joshua 19??- .... **CLC 60**

Soderberg, Hjalmar 1869-1941 .... **TCLC 39**

Sodergran, Edith 1892-1923....... **TCLC 31**

Sokolov, Raymond 1941-........... **CLC 7**
See also CA 85-88

Sologub, Fyodor 1863-1927........ **TCLC 9**
See also Teternikov, Fyodor Kuzmich
See also CA 104

Solomos, Dionysios 1798-1857 ... **NCLC 15**

Solwoska, Mara 1929-
See French, Marilyn
See also CANR 3; CA 69-72

Solzhenitsyn, Aleksandr I(sayevich)
1918-... **CLC 1, 2, 4, 7, 9, 10, 18, 26, 34**
See also CA 69-72

Somers, Jane 1919-
See Lessing, Doris (May)

Sommer, Scott 1951- .... **CLC 25**
See also CA 106

Sondheim, Stephen (Joshua)
1930- .... **CLC 30, 39**
See also CA 103

Sontag, Susan 1933-... **CLC 1, 2, 10, 13, 31**
See also CA 17-20R; DLB 2, 67

Sophocles
c. 496? B.C.-c. 406? B.C...... **CMLC 2;**
DC 1

Sorrentino, Gilbert
1929- .... **CLC 3, 7, 14, 22, 40**
See also CANR 14; CA 77-80; DLB 5;
DLB-Y 80

Soto, Gary 1952-................. **CLC 32**
See also CA 119, 125; DLB 82

Soupault, Philippe 1897-1990 ...... **CLC 68**
See also CA 116; obituary CA 131

Souster, (Holmes) Raymond
1921- .... **CLC 5, 14**
See also CANR 13; CA 13-16R; DLB 88

Southern, Terry 1926- .... **CLC 7**
See also CANR 1; CA 1-4R; DLB 2

Southey, Robert 1774-1843 .... **NCLC 8**
See also SATA 54

Southworth, Emma Dorothy Eliza Nevitte
1819-1899 .... **NCLC 26**

Soyinka, Wole
1934-....... **CLC 3, 5, 14, 36, 44; DC 2**
See also BLC 3; CANR 27; CA 13-16R;
DLB-Y 86

Spackman, W(illiam) M(ode)
1905- .... **CLC 46**
See also CA 81-84

Spacks, Barry 1931-............... **CLC 14**
See also CA 29-32R

Spanidou, Irini 1946-............. **CLC 44**

Spark, Muriel (Sarah)
1918- .... **CLC 2, 3, 5, 8, 13, 18, 40**
See also CANR 12; CA 5-8R; DLB 15

Spencer, Elizabeth 1921-.......... **CLC 22**
See also CA 13-16R; SATA 14; DLB 6

Spencer, Scott 1945-.............. **CLC 30**
See also CA 113; DLB-Y 86

Spender, Stephen (Harold)
1909- .... **CLC 1, 2, 5, 10, 41**
See also CA 9-12R; DLB 20

Spengler, Oswald 1880-1936 ...... **TCLC 25**
See also CA 118

Spenser, Edmund 1552?-1599 .... **LC 5**

Spicer, Jack 1925-1965 .... **CLC 8, 18**
See also CA 85-88; DLB 5, 16

Spielberg, Peter 1929-............. **CLC 6**
See also CANR 4; CA 5-8R; DLB-Y 81

Spielberg, Steven 1947-........... **CLC 20**
See also CA 77-80; SATA 32

Spillane, Frank Morrison 1918-
See Spillane, Mickey
See also CA 25-28R

Spillane, Mickey 1918- .... **CLC 3, 13**
See also Spillane, Frank Morrison

Spinoza, Benedictus de 1632-1677 .... **LC 9**

Spinrad, Norman (Richard) 1940-... **CLC 46**
See also CANR 20; CA 37-40R; DLB 8

Spitteler, Carl (Friedrich Georg)
1845-1924 .... **TCLC 12**
See also CA 109

Spivack, Kathleen (Romola Drucker)
1938- .... **CLC 6**
See also CA 49-52

Spoto, Donald 1941-.............. **CLC 39**
See also CANR 11; CA 65 68

Springsteen, Bruce   1949-.......... CLC 17
  See also CA 111

Spurling, Hilary   1940-............ CLC 34
  See also CANR 25; CA 104

Squires, (James) Radcliffe   1917-.... CLC 51
  See also CANR 6, 21; CA 1-4R

Stael-Holstein, Anne Louise Germaine Necker,
  Baronne de   1766-1817...... NCLC 3

Stafford, Jean   1915-1979... CLC 4, 7, 19, 68
  See also CANR 3; CA 1-4R;
    obituary CA 85-88; obituary SATA 22;
    DLB 2

Stafford, William (Edgar)
  1914-................... CLC 4, 7, 29
  See also CAAS 3; CANR 5, 22; CA 5-8R;
    DLB 5

Stannard, Martin   1947-.......... CLC 44

Stanton, Maura   1946-............. CLC 9
  See also CANR 15; CA 89-92

Stapledon, (William) Olaf
  1886-1950 .... TCLC 22
  See also CA 111; DLB 15

Starbuck, George (Edwin)   1931-.... CLC 53
  See also CANR 23; CA 21-22R

Stark, Richard   1933-
  See Westlake, Donald E(dwin)

Stead, Christina (Ellen)
  1902-1983 .... CLC 2, 5, 8, 32
  See also CA 13-16R; obituary CA 109

Steele, Sir Richard   1672-1729....... LC 18
  See also DLB 84, 101

Steele, Timothy (Reid)   1948-....... CLC 45
  See also CANR 16; CA 93-96

Steffens, (Joseph) Lincoln
  1866-1936 .... TCLC 20
  See also CA 117; SAAS 1

Stegner, Wallace (Earle)   1909-... CLC 9, 49
  See also CANR 1, 21; CA 1-4R; DLB 9

Stein, Gertrude   1874-1946... TCLC 1, 6, 28
  See also CA 104; DLB 4, 54, 86;
    CDALB 1917-1929

Steinbeck, John (Ernst)
  1902-1968 ..... CLC 1, 5, 9, 13, 21, 34,
                                   45, 59
  See also CANR 1; CA 1-4R;
    obituary CA 25-28R; SATA 9; DLB 7, 9;
    DLB-DS 2; CDALB 1929-1941

Steinem, Gloria   1934-............. CLC 63
  See also CANR 28; CA 53-56

Steiner, George   1929-............. CLC 24
  See also CA 73-76; DLB 67

Steiner, Rudolf(us Josephus Laurentius)
  1861-1925 .... TCLC 13
  See also CA 107

Stendhal   1783-1842............. NCLC 23

Stephen, Leslie   1832-1904........ TCLC 23
  See also CANR 9; CA 21-24R, 123;
    DLB 57

Stephens, James   1882?-1950 .... TCLC 4
  See also CA 104; DLB 19

Stephens, Reed
  See Donaldson, Stephen R.

Steptoe, Lydia   1892-1982
  See Barnes, Djuna

Sterchi, Beat   1949-................ CLC 65

Sterling, George   1869-1926....... TCLC 20
  See also CA 117; DLB 54

Stern, Gerald   1925-.............. CLC 40
  See also CA 81-84

Stern, Richard G(ustave)   1928-... CLC 4, 39
  See also CANR 1, 25; CA 1-4R; DLB 87

Sternberg, Jonas   1894-1969
  See Sternberg, Josef von

Sternberg, Josef von   1894-1969..... CLC 20
  See also CA 81-84

Sterne, Laurence   1713-1768......... LC 2
  See also DLB 39

Sternheim, (William Adolf) Carl
  1878-1942 .... TCLC 8
  See also CA 105

Stevens, Mark   19??-.............. CLC 34

Stevens, Wallace   1879-1955..... TCLC 3, 12
  See also CA 104, 124; DLB 54

Stevenson, Anne (Katharine)
  1933-................... CLC 7, 33
  See also Elvin, Anne Katharine Stevenson
  See also CANR 9; CA 17-18R; DLB 40

Stevenson, Robert Louis
  1850-1894 .... NCLC 5, 14
  See also CLR 10, 11; YABC 2; DLB 18, 57

Stewart, J(ohn) I(nnes) M(ackintosh)
  1906-................... CLC 7, 14, 32
  See also CAAS 3; CA 85-88

Stewart, Mary (Florence Elinor)
  1916-................... CLC 7, 35
  See also CANR 1; CA 1-4R; SATA 12

Stewart, Will   1908-
  See Williamson, Jack
  See also CANR 23; CA 17-18R

Still, James   1906-.............. CLC 49
  See also CANR 10, 26; CA 65-68;
    SATA 29; DLB 9

Sting   1951-
  See The Police

Stitt, Milan   1941-................ CLC 29
  See also CA 69-72

Stoker, Abraham
  See Stoker, Bram
  See also CA 105; SATA 29

Stoker, Bram   1847-1912 .... TCLC 8
  See also Stoker, Abraham
  See also SATA 29; DLB 36, 70

Stolz, Mary (Slattery)   1920-....... CLC 12
  See also CANR 13; CA 5-8R; SAAS 3;
    SATA 10

Stone, Irving   1903-1989........... CLC 7
  See also CAAS 3; CANR 1; CA 1-4R, 129;
    SATA 3

Stone, Robert (Anthony)
  1937?- .... CLC 5, 23, 42
  See also CANR 23; CA 85-88

Stoppard, Tom
  1937-... CLC 1, 3, 4, 5, 8, 15, 29, 34, 63
  See also CA 81-84; DLB 13; DLB-Y 85

Storey, David (Malcolm)
  1933-................... CLC 2, 4, 5, 8
  See also CA 81-84; DLB 13, 14

Storm, Hyemeyohsts   1935-......... CLC 3
  See also CA 81-84

Storm, (Hans) Theodor (Woldsen)
  1817-1888 .... NCLC 1

Storni, Alfonsina   1892-1938 .... TCLC 5
  See also CA 104

Stout, Rex (Todhunter)   1886-1975 ... CLC 3
  See also CA 61-64

Stow, (Julian) Randolph   1935- .. CLC 23, 48
  See also CA 13-16R

Stowe, Harriet (Elizabeth) Beecher
  1811-1896 .... NCLC 3
  See also YABC 1; DLB 1, 12, 42, 74;
    CDALB 1865-1917

Strachey, (Giles) Lytton
  1880-1932 .... TCLC 12
  See also CA 110

Strand, Mark   1934-......... CLC 6, 18, 41
  See also CA 21-24R; SATA 41; DLB 5

Straub, Peter (Francis)   1943- ...... CLC 28
  See also CA 85-88; DLB-Y 84

Strauss, Botho   1944-............. CLC 22

Straussler, Tomas   1937-
  See Stoppard, Tom

Streatfeild, (Mary) Noel   1897- ..... CLC 21
  See also CA 81-84; obituary CA 120;
    SATA 20, 48

Stribling, T(homas) S(igismund)
  1881-1965 .... CLC 23
  See also obituary CA 107; DLB 9

Strindberg, (Johan) August
  1849-1912 .... TCLC 1, 8, 21
  See also CA 104

Stringer, Arthur   1874-1950....... TCLC 37
  See also DLB 92

Strugatskii, Arkadii (Natanovich)
  1925-...................... CLC 27
  See also CA 106

Strugatskii, Boris (Natanovich)
  1933-...................... CLC 27
  See also CA 106

Strummer, Joe   1953?-
  See The Clash

Stuart, (Hilton) Jesse
  1906-1984 .... CLC 1, 8, 11, 14, 34
  See also CA 5-8R; obituary CA 112;
    SATA 2; obituary SATA 36; DLB 9, 48;
    DLB-Y 84

Sturgeon, Theodore (Hamilton)
  1918-1985 .... CLC 22, 39
  See also CA 81-84; obituary CA 116;
    DLB 8; DLB-Y 85

Styron, William
  1925-.......... CLC 1, 3, 5, 11, 15, 60
  See also CANR 6; CA 5-8R; DLB 2;
    DLB-Y 80; CDALB 1968-1987

Sudermann, Hermann   1857-1928 .. TCLC 15
  See also CA 107

Sue, Eugene   1804-1857 .... NCLC 1

Sukenick, Ronald   1932-..... CLC 3, 4, 6, 48
  See also CAAS 8; CA 25-28R; DLB-Y 81

Suknaski, Andrew   1942- .... CLC 19
  See also CA 101; DLB 53

Sully Prudhomme   1839-1907...... TCLC 31

Su Man-shu 1884-1918 . . . . TCLC 24
See also CA 123

Summers, Andrew James 1942-
See The Police

Summers, Andy 1942-
See The Police

Summers, Hollis (Spurgeon, Jr.)
1916- . . . . CLC 10
See also CANR 3; CA 5-8R; DLB 6

Summers, (Alphonsus Joseph-Mary Augustus)
Montague 1880-1948 . . . . TCLC 16
See also CA 118

Sumner, Gordon Matthew 1951-
See The Police

Surtees, Robert Smith
1805-1864 . . . . NCLC 14
See also DLB 21

Susann, Jacqueline 1921-1974 . . . . . . CLC 3
See also CA 65-68; obituary CA 53-56

Suskind, Patrick 1949- . . . . CLC 44

Sutcliff, Rosemary 1920- . . . . CLC 26
See also CLR 1; CA 5-8R; SATA 6, 44

Sutro, Alfred 1863-1933 . . . . TCLC 6
See also CA 105; DLB 10

Sutton, Henry 1935-
See Slavitt, David (R.)

Svevo, Italo 1861-1928 . . . . TCLC 2, 35
See also Schmitz, Ettore

Swados, Elizabeth 1951- . . . . CLC 12
See also CA 97-100

Swados, Harvey 1920-1972 . . . . CLC 5
See also CANR 6; CA 5-8R;
obituary CA 37-40R; DLB 2

Swan, Gladys 1934- . . . . CLC 69
See also CANR 17; CA 101

Swarthout, Glendon (Fred) 1918- . . . CLC 35
See also CANR 1; CA 1-4R; SATA 26

Swenson, May 1919-1989 . . . . . CLC 4, 14, 61
See also CA 5-8R; obituary CA 130;
SATA 15; DLB 5

Swift, Graham 1949- . . . . CLC 41
See also CA 117, 122

Swift, Jonathan 1667-1745 . . . . LC 1
See also SATA 19; DLB 39

Swinburne, Algernon Charles
1837-1909 . . . . TCLC 8, 36
See also CA 105; DLB 35, 57

Swinfen, Ann 19??- . . . . CLC 34

Swinnerton, Frank (Arthur)
1884-1982 . . . . CLC 31
See also obituary CA 108; DLB 34

Symonds, John Addington
1840-1893 . . . . NCLC 34
See also DLB 57

Symons, Arthur (William)
1865-1945 . . . . TCLC 11
See also CA 107; DLB 19, 57

Symons, Julian (Gustave)
1912- . . . . CLC 2, 14, 32
See also CAAS 3; CANR 3; CA 49-52;
DLB 87

Synge, (Edmund) John Millington
1871-1909 . . . . TCLC 6, 37; DC 2
See also CA 104; DLB 10, 19

Syruc, J. 1911-
See Milosz, Czeslaw

Szirtes, George 1948- . . . . CLC 46
See also CANR 27; CA 109

Tabori, George 1914- . . . . CLC 19
See also CANR 4; CA 49-52

Tagore, (Sir) Rabindranath
1861-1941 . . . . TCLC 3
See also Thakura, Ravindranatha
See also CA 120

Taine, Hippolyte Adolphe
1828-1893 . . . . NCLC 15

Talese, Gaetano 1932-
See Talese, Gay

Talese, Gay 1932- . . . . CLC 37
See also CANR 9; CA 1-4R

Tallent, Elizabeth (Ann) 1954- . . . . . CLC 45
See also CA 117

Tally, Ted 1952- . . . . CLC 42
See also CA 120, 124

Tamayo y Baus, Manuel
1829-1898 . . . . NCLC 1

Tammsaare, A(nton) H(ansen)
1878-1940 . . . . TCLC 27

Tan, Amy 1952- . . . . CLC 59

Tanizaki, Jun'ichiro
1886-1965 . . . . CLC 8, 14, 28
See also CA 93-96; obituary CA 25-28R

Tarbell, Ida 1857-1944 . . . . TCLC 40
See also CA 122; DLB 47

Tarkington, (Newton) Booth
1869-1946 . . . . TCLC 9
See also CA 110; SATA 17; DLB 9

Tasso, Torquato 1544-1595 . . . . LC 5

Tate, (John Orley) Allen
1899-1979 . . . . CLC 2, 4, 6, 9, 11, 14, 24
See also CA 5-8R; obituary CA 85-88;
DLB 4, 45, 63

Tate, James 1943- . . . . CLC 2, 6, 25
See also CA 21-24R; DLB 5

Tavel, Ronald 1940- . . . . CLC 6
See also CA 21-24R

Taylor, C(ecil) P(hillip) 1929-1981 . . CLC 27
See also CA 25-28R; obituary CA 105

Taylor, Edward 1642?-1729 . . . . LC 11
See also DLB 24

Taylor, Eleanor Ross 1920- . . . . CLC 5
See also CA 81-84

Taylor, Elizabeth 1912-1975 . . . CLC 2, 4, 29
See also CANR 9; CA 13-16R; SATA 13

Taylor, Henry (Splawn) 1917- . . . . . . CLC 44
See also CAAS 7; CA 33-36R; DLB 5

Taylor, Kamala (Purnaiya) 1924-
See Markandaya, Kamala
See also CA 77-80

Taylor, Mildred D(elois) 1943- . . . . . CLC 21
See also CLR 9; CANR 25; CA 85-88;
SAAS 5; SATA 15; DLB 52

Taylor, Peter (Hillsman)
1917- . . . . CLC 1, 4, 18, 37, 44, 50
See also CANR 9; CA 13-16R; DLB-Y 81

Taylor, Robert Lewis 1912- . . . . CLC 14
See also CANR 3; CA 1-4R; SATA 10

Teasdale, Sara 1884-1933 . . . . TCLC 4
See also CA 104; SATA 32; DLB 45

Tegner, Esaias 1782-1846 . . . . NCLC 2

Teilhard de Chardin, (Marie Joseph) Pierre
1881-1955 . . . . TCLC 9
See also CA 105

Tennant, Emma 1937- . . . . CLC 13, 52
See also CAAS 9; CANR 10; CA 65-68;
DLB 14

Tennyson, Alfred 1809-1892 . . . . . NCLC 30
See also DLB 32

Teran, Lisa St. Aubin de 19??- . . . . . CLC 36

Teresa de Jesus, St. 1515-1582 . . . . . . LC 18

Terkel, Louis 1912-
See Terkel, Studs
See also CANR 18; CA 57-60

Terkel, Studs 1912- . . . . CLC 38
See also Terkel, Louis

Terry, Megan 1932- . . . . CLC 19
See also CA 77-80; CABS 3; DLB 7

Tertz, Abram 1925-
See Sinyavsky, Andrei (Donatevich)

Tesich, Steve 1943?- . . . . CLC 40, 69
See also CA 105; DLB-Y 83

Tesich, Stoyan 1943?-
See Tesich, Steve

Teternikov, Fyodor Kuzmich 1863-1927
See Sologub, Fyodor
See also CA 104

Tevis, Walter 1928-1984 . . . . CLC 42
See also CA 113

Tey, Josephine 1897-1952 . . . . TCLC 14
See also Mackintosh, Elizabeth

Thackeray, William Makepeace
1811-1863 . . . . NCLC 5, 14, 22
See also SATA 23; DLB 21, 55

Thakura, Ravindranatha 1861-1941
See Tagore, (Sir) Rabindranath
See also CA 104

Thelwell, Michael (Miles) 1939- . . . . CLC 22
See also CA 101

Theroux, Alexander (Louis)
1939- . . . . CLC 2, 25
See also CANR 20; CA 85-88

Theroux, Paul
1941- . . . . CLC 5, 8, 11, 15, 28, 46
See also CANR 20; CA 33-36R; SATA 44;
DLB 2

Thesen, Sharon 1946- . . . . CLC 56

Thibault, Jacques Anatole Francois
1844-1924
See France, Anatole
See also CA 106

Thiele, Colin (Milton) 1920- . . . . CLC 17
See also CANR 12; CA 29-32R; SAAS 2;
SATA 14

Thomas, Audrey (Grace)
1935- . . . . CLC 7, 13, 37
See also CA 21-24R; DLB 60

Thomas, D(onald) M(ichael)
1935- . . . . CLC 13, 22, 31
See also CANR 17; CA 61-64; DLB 40

Twain, Mark
1835-1910 ... **TCLC 6, 12, 19, 36; SSC 6**
See also Clemens, Samuel Langhorne
See also YABC 2; DLB 11, 12, 23, 64, 74

Tyler, Anne
1941- .... **CLC 7, 11, 18, 28, 44, 59**
See also CANR 11; CA 9-12R; SATA 7;
DLB 6; DLB-Y 82

Tyler, Royall 1757-1826.......... **NCLC 3**
See also DLB 37

Tynan (Hinkson), Katharine
1861-1931 .... **TCLC 3**
See also CA 104

Tytell, John 1939- .... **CLC 50**
See also CA 29-32R

Tyutchev, Fyodor 1803-1873 ..... **NCLC 34**

Tzara, Tristan 1896-1963.......... **CLC 47**
See also Rosenfeld, Samuel

Uhry, Alfred 1947?- .... **CLC 55**
See also CA 127

Unamuno (y Jugo), Miguel de
1864-1936 .... **TCLC 2, 9**
See also CA 104

Underwood, Miles 1909-1981
See Glassco, John

Undset, Sigrid 1882-1949.......... **TCLC 3**
See also CA 104

Ungaretti, Giuseppe
1888-1970 .... **CLC 7, 11, 15**
See also CAP 2; CA 19-20;
obituary CA 25-28R

Unger, Douglas 1952-............. **CLC 34**
See also CA 130

Unger, Eva 1932-
See Figes, Eva

Updike, John (Hoyer)
1932- ...... **CLC 1, 2, 3, 5, 7, 9, 13, 15,**
                    23, 34, 43
See also CANR 4; CA 1-4R; CABS 2;
DLB 2, 5; DLB-Y 80, 82; DLB-DS 3

Urdang, Constance (Henriette)
1922- .... **CLC 47**
See also CANR 9, 24; CA 21-24R

Uris, Leon (Marcus) 1924-....... **CLC 7, 32**
See also CANR 1; CA 1-4R; SATA 49

Ustinov, Peter (Alexander) 1921- .... **CLC 1**
See also CANR 25; CA 13-16R; DLB 13

Vaculik, Ludvik 1926- .... **CLC 7**
See also CA 53-56

Valenzuela, Luisa 1938-........... **CLC 31**
See also CA 101

Valera (y Acala-Galiano), Juan
1824-1905 .... **TCLC 10**
See also CA 106

Valery, Paul (Ambroise Toussaint Jules)
1871-1945 .... **TCLC 4, 15**
See also CA 104, 122

Valle-Inclan (y Montenegro), Ramon (Maria)
del 1866-1936............... **TCLC 5**
See also CA 106

Vallejo, Cesar (Abraham)
1892-1938 .... **TCLC 3**
See also CA 105

Van Ash, Cay 1918-.............. **CLC 34**

Vance, Jack 1916?-.............. **CLC 35**
See also DLB 8

Vance, John Holbrook 1916?-
See Vance, Jack
See also CANR 17; CA 29-32R

Van Den Bogarde, Derek (Jules Gaspard
   Ulric) Niven 1921-
See Bogarde, Dirk
See also CA 77-80

Vandenburgh, Jane 19??-.......... **CLC 59**

Vanderhaeghe, Guy 1951- .... **CLC 41**
See also CA 113

Van der Post, Laurens (Jan) 1906-... **CLC 5**
See also CA 5-8R

Van de Wetering, Janwillem
1931- .... **CLC 47**
See also CANR 4; CA 49-52

Van Dine, S. S. 1888-1939....... **TCLC 23**

Van Doren, Carl (Clinton)
1885-1950 .... **TCLC 18**
See also CA 111

Van Doren, Mark 1894-1972..... **CLC 6, 10**
See also CANR 3; CA 1-4R;
obituary CA 37-40R; DLB 45

Van Druten, John (William)
1901-1957 .... **TCLC 2**
See also CA 104; DLB 10

Van Duyn, Mona 1921-....... **CLC 3, 7, 63**
See also CANR 7; CA 9-12R; DLB 5

Van Itallie, Jean-Claude 1936-...... **CLC 3**
See also CAAS 2; CANR 1; CA 45-48;
DLB 7

Van Ostaijen, Paul 1896-1928..... **TCLC 33**

Van Peebles, Melvin 1932- ..... **CLC 2, 20**
See also CA 85-88

Vansittart, Peter 1920-........... **CLC 42**
See also CANR 3; CA 1-4R

Van Vechten, Carl 1880-1964 ...... **CLC 33**
See also obituary CA 89-92; DLB 4, 9, 51

Van Vogt, A(lfred) E(lton) 1912-..... **CLC 1**
See also CANR 28; CA 21-24R; SATA 14;
DLB 8

Varda, Agnes 1928- .... **CLC 16**
See also CA 116, 122

Vargas Llosa, (Jorge) Mario (Pedro)
1936- ...... **CLC 3, 6, 9, 10, 15, 31, 42**
See also CANR 18; CA 73-76

Vassa, Gustavus 1745?-1797
See Equiano, Olaudah

Vassilikos, Vassilis 1933-........ **CLC 4, 8**
See also CA 81-84

Vaughn, Stephanie 19??- .... **CLC 62**

Vazov, Ivan 1850-1921.......... **TCLC 25**
See also CA 121

Veblen, Thorstein Bunde
1857-1929 .... **TCLC 31**
See also CA 115

Verga, Giovanni 1840-1922 .... **TCLC 3**
See also CA 104, 123

Verhaeren, Emile (Adolphe Gustave)
1855-1916 .... **TCLC 12**
See also CA 109

Verlaine, Paul (Marie)
1844-1896 .... **NCLC 2; PC 2**

Verne, Jules (Gabriel) 1828-1905 ... **TCLC 6**
See also CA 110; SATA 21

Very, Jones 1813-1880........... **NCLC 9**
See also DLB 1

Vesaas, Tarjei 1897-1970.......... **CLC 48**
See also obituary CA 29-32R

Vian, Boris 1920-1959 .... **TCLC 9**
See also CA 106; DLB 72

Viaud, (Louis Marie) Julien 1850-1923
See Loti, Pierre
See also CA 107

Vicker, Angus 1916-
See Felsen, Henry Gregor

Vidal, Eugene Luther, Jr. 1925-
See Vidal, Gore

Vidal, Gore
1925- .... **CLC 2, 4, 6, 8, 10, 22, 33**
See also CANR 13; CA 5-8R; DLB 6

Viereck, Peter (Robert Edwin)
1916- .... **CLC 4**
See also CANR 1; CA 1-4R; DLB 5

Vigny, Alfred (Victor) de
1797-1863 .... **NCLC 7**

Vilakazi, Benedict Wallet
1905-1947 .... **TCLC 37**

Villiers de l'Isle Adam, Jean Marie Mathias
   Philippe Auguste, Comte de
1838-1889 .... **NCLC 3**

Vinci, Leonardo da 1452-1519....... **LC 12**

Vine, Barbara 1930-.............. **CLC 50**
See also Rendell, Ruth

Vinge, Joan (Carol) D(ennison)
1948- .... **CLC 30**
See also CA 93-96; SATA 36

Visconti, Luchino 1906-1976....... **CLC 16**
See also CA 81-84; obituary CA 65-68

Vittorini, Elio 1908-1966...... **CLC 6, 9, 14**
See also obituary CA 25-28R

Vizinczey, Stephen 1933-.......... **CLC 40**

Vliet, R(ussell) G(ordon)
1929-1984 .... **CLC 22**
See also CANR 18; CA 37-40R;
obituary CA 112

Voight, Ellen Bryant 1943- .... **CLC 54**
See also CANR 11; CA 69-72

Voigt, Cynthia 1942- .... **CLC 30**
See also CANR 18; CA 106; SATA 33, 48;
AAYA 3

Voinovich, Vladimir (Nikolaevich)
1932- .... **CLC 10, 49**
See also CA 81-84

Voltaire 1694-1778 .... **LC 14**

Von Daeniken, Erich 1935-
See Von Daniken, Erich
See also CANR 17; CA 37-40R

Von Daniken, Erich 1935-........ **CLC 30**
See also Von Daeniken, Erich

Weiss, Peter (Ulrich)
    1916-1982 .... CLC 3, 15, 51
    See also CANR 3; CA 45-48;
    obituary CA 106; DLB 69

Weiss, Theodore (Russell)
    1916- .... CLC 3, 8, 14
    See also CAAS 2; CA 9-12R; DLB 5

Welch, (Maurice) Denton
    1915-1948 .... TCLC 22
    See also CA 121

Welch, James 1940- .... CLC 6, 14, 52
    See also CA 85-88

Weldon, Fay
    1933- .... CLC 6, 9, 11, 19, 36, 59
    See also CANR 16; CA 21-24R; DLB 14

Wellek, Rene 1903- .... CLC 28
    See also CAAS 7; CANR 8; CA 5-8R;
    DLB 63

Weller, Michael 1942- .... CLC 10, 53
    See also CA 85-88

Weller, Paul 1958- .... CLC 26

Wellershoff, Dieter 1925-........ CLC 46
    See also CANR 16; CA 89-92

Welles, (George) Orson
    1915-1985 .... CLC 20
    See also CA 93-96; obituary CA 117

Wellman, Mac 1945- .... CLC 65

Wellman, Manly Wade 1903-1986 .. CLC 49
    See also CANR 6, 16; CA 1-4R;
    obituary CA 118; SATA 6, 47

Wells, Carolyn 1862-1942 .... TCLC 35
    See also CA 113; DLB 11

Wells, H(erbert) G(eorge)
    1866-1946 ...... TCLC 6, 12, 19; SSC 6
    See also CA 110, 121; SATA 20; DLB 34,
    70

Wells, Rosemary 1943-............ CLC 12
    See also CLR 16; CA 85-88; SAAS 1;
    SATA 18

Welty, Eudora (Alice)
    1909- .... CLC 1, 2, 5, 14, 22, 33; SSC 1
    See also CA 9-12R; CABS 1; DLB 2;
    DLB-Y 87; CDALB 1941-1968

Wen I-to 1899-1946 .... TCLC 28

Werfel, Franz (V.) 1890-1945 ...... TCLC 8
    See also CA 104; DLB 81

Wergeland, Henrik Arnold
    1808-1845 .... NCLC 5

Wersba, Barbara 1932-............ CLC 30
    See also CLR 3; CANR 16; CA 29-32R;
    SAAS 2; SATA 1, 58; DLB 52

Wertmuller, Lina 1928- .... CLC 16
    See also CA 97-100

Wescott, Glenway 1901-1987....... CLC 13
    See also CANR 23; CA 13-16R;
    obituary CA 121; DLB 4, 9

Wesker, Arnold 1932- .... CLC 3, 5, 42
    See also CAAS 7; CANR 1; CA 1-4R;
    DLB 13

Wesley, Richard (Errol) 1945-....... CLC 7
    See also CA 57-60; DLB 38

Wessel, Johan Herman 1742-1785 .... LC 7

West, Anthony (Panther)
    1914-1987 .... CLC 50
    See also CANR 3, 19; CA 45-48; DLB 15

West, Jessamyn 1907-1984 ...... CLC 7, 17
    See also CA 9-12R; obituary CA 112;
    obituary SATA 37; DLB 6; DLB-Y 84

West, Morris L(anglo) 1916-..... CLC 6, 33
    See also CA 5-8R; obituary CA 124

West, Nathanael 1903?-1940 .... TCLC 1, 14
    See also Weinstein, Nathan Wallenstein
    See also CA 125, 140; DLB 4, 9, 28

West, Paul 1930- .... CLC 7, 14
    See also CAAS 7; CANR 22; CA 13-16R;
    DLB 14

West, Rebecca 1892-1983 .. CLC 7, 9, 31, 50
    See also CANR 19; CA 5-8R;
    obituary CA 109; DLB 36; DLB-Y 83

Westall, Robert (Atkinson) 1929-... CLC 17
    See also CLR 13; CANR 18; CA 69-72;
    SAAS 2; SATA 23

Westlake, Donald E(dwin)
    1933- .... CLC 7, 33
    See also CANR 16; CA 17-20R

Westmacott, Mary 1890-1976
    See Christie, (Dame) Agatha (Mary
    Clarissa)

Whalen, Philip 1923- .... CLC 6, 29
    See also CANR 5; CA 9-12R; DLB 16

Wharton, Edith (Newbold Jones)
    1862-1937 ...... TCLC 3, 9, 27; SSC 6
    See also CA 104; DLB 4, 9, 12, 78;
    CDALB 1865-1917

Wharton, William 1925-........ CLC 18, 37
    See also CA 93-96; DLB-Y 80

Wheatley (Peters), Phillis
    1753?-1784................ LC 3; PC 3
    See also BLC 3; DLB 31, 50;
    CDALB 1640-1865

Wheelock, John Hall 1886-1978.... CLC 14
    See also CANR 14; CA 13-16R;
    obituary CA 77-80; DLB 45

Whelan, John 1900-
    See O'Faolain, Sean

Whitaker, Rodney 1925-
    See Trevanian

White, E(lwyn) B(rooks)
    1899-1985 .... CLC 10, 34, 39
    See also CLR 1; CANR 16; CA 13-16R;
    obituary CA 116; SATA 2, 29, 44;
    obituary SATA 44; DLB 11, 22

White, Edmund III 1940-......... CLC 27
    See also CANR 3, 19; CA 45-48

White, Patrick (Victor Martindale)
    1912-1990 .. CLC 3, 4, 5, 7, 9, 18, 65, 69
    See also CA 81-84; obituary CA 132

White, T(erence) H(anbury)
    1906-1964 .... CLC 30
    See also CA 73-76; SATA 12

White, Terence de Vere 1912-...... CLC 49
    See also CANR 3; CA 49-52

White, Walter (Francis)
    1893-1955 .... TCLC 15
    See also BLC 3; CA 115, 124; DLB 51

White, William Hale 1831-1913
    See Rutherford, Mark
    See also CA 121

Whitehead, E(dward) A(nthony)
    1933- .... CLC 5
    See also CA 65-68

Whitemore, Hugh 1936-.......... CLC 37

Whitman, Sarah Helen
    1803-1878 .... NCLC 19
    See also DLB 1

Whitman, Walt
    1819-1892 .... NCLC 4, 31; PC 3
    See also SATA 20; DLB 3, 64;
    CDALB 1640-1865

Whitney, Phyllis A(yame) 1903-.... CLC 42
    See also CANR 3, 25; CA 1-4R; SATA 1,
    30

Whittemore, (Edward) Reed (Jr.)
    1919- .... CLC 4
    See also CAAS 8; CANR 4; CA 9-12R;
    DLB 5

Whittier, John Greenleaf
    1807-1892 .... NCLC 8
    See also DLB 1; CDALB 1640-1865

Wicker, Thomas Grey 1926-
    See Wicker, Tom
    See also CANR 21; CA 65-68

Wicker, Tom 1926-................ CLC 7
    See also Wicker, Thomas Grey

Wideman, John Edgar
    1941- .... CLC 5, 34, 36, 67
    See also BLC 3; CANR 14; CA 85-88;
    DLB 33

Wiebe, Rudy (H.) 1934-..... CLC 6, 11, 14
    See also CA 37-40R; DLB 60

Wieland, Christoph Martin
    1733-1813 .... NCLC 17

Wieners, John 1934-.............. CLC 7
    See also CA 13-16R; DLB 16

Wiesel, Elie(zer) 1928-..... CLC 3, 5, 11, 37
    See also CAAS 4; CANR 8; CA 5-8R;
    SATA 56; DLB 83; DLB-Y 87

Wiggins, Marianne 1948-.......... CLC 57

Wight, James Alfred 1916-
    See Herriot, James
    See also CA 77-80; SATA 44

Wilbur, Richard (Purdy)
    1921- .... CLC 3, 6, 9, 14, 53
    See also CANR 2; CA 1-4R; CABS 2;
    SATA 9; DLB 5

Wild, Peter 1940-................ CLC 14
    See also CA 37-40R; DLB 5

Wilde, Oscar (Fingal O'Flahertie Wills)
    1854-1900 .... TCLC 1, 8, 23, 41
    See also CA 119; brief entry CA 104;
    SATA 24; DLB 10, 19, 34, 57

Wilder, Billy 1906-.............. CLC 20
    See also Wilder, Samuel
    See also DLB 26

Wilder, Samuel 1906-
    See Wilder, Billy
    See also CA 89-92

Wilder, Thornton (Niven)
1897-1975 ..... CLC 1, 5, 6, 10, 15, 35;
DC 1
See also CA 13-16R; obituary CA 61-64;
DLB 4, 7, 9

Wiley, Richard 1944-............. CLC 44
See also CA 121, 129

Wilhelm, Kate 1928-............... CLC 7
See also CAAS 5; CANR 17; CA 37-40R;
DLB 8

Willard, Nancy 1936-........... CLC 7, 37
See also CLR 5; CANR 10; CA 89-92;
SATA 30, 37; DLB 5, 52

Williams, C(harles) K(enneth)
1936-................ CLC 33, 56
See also CA 37-40R; DLB 5

Williams, Charles (Walter Stansby)
1886-1945 ....TCLC 1, 11
See also CA 104

Williams, Ella Gwendolen Rees 1890-1979
See Rhys, Jean

Williams, (George) Emlyn
1905-1987 .... CLC 15
See also CA 104, 123; DLB 10, 77

Williams, Hugo 1942-............. CLC 42
See also CA 17-20R; DLB 40

Williams, John A(lfred) 1925-.... CLC 5, 13
See also BLC 3; CAAS 3; CANR 6, 26;
CA 53-56; DLB 2, 33

Williams, Jonathan (Chamberlain)
1929-...................... CLC 13
See also CANR 8; CA 9-12R; DLB 5

Williams, Joy 1944-.............. CLC 31
See also CANR 22; CA 41-44R

Williams, Norman 1952- .... CLC 39
See also CA 118

Williams, Paulette 1948-
See Shange, Ntozake

Williams, Sherley Anne 1944-
See also BLC 3; CANR 25; CA 73-76;
DLB 41

Williams, Shirley 1944-
See Williams, Sherley Anne

Williams, Tennessee
1911-1983 .... CLC 1, 2, 5, 7, 8, 11, 15,
19, 30, 39, 45
See also CA 5-8R; obituary CA 108; DLB 7;
DLB-Y 83; DLB-DS 4;
CDALB 1941-1968

Williams, Thomas (Alonzo) 1926-... CLC 14
See also CANR 2; CA 1-4R

Williams, Thomas Lanier 1911-1983
See Williams, Tennessee

Williams, William Carlos
1883-1963 ... CLC 1, 2, 5, 9, 13, 22, 42,
67
See also CA 89-92; DLB 4, 16, 54, 86;
CDALB 1917-1929

Williamson, David 1932- .... CLC 56

Williamson, Jack 1908- .... CLC 29
See also Williamson, John Stewart
See also DLB 8

Williamson, John Stewart 1908-
See Williamson, Jack
See also CANR 123; CA 17-20R

Willingham, Calder (Baynard, Jr.)
1922-...................... CLC 5, 51
See also CANR 3; CA 5-8R; DLB 2, 44

Wilson, A(ndrew) N(orman) 1950-... CLC 33
See also CA 112, 122; DLB 14

Wilson, Andrew 1948-
See Wilson, Snoo

Wilson, Angus (Frank Johnstone)
1913-............. CLC 2, 3, 5, 25, 34
See also CANR 21; CA 5-8R; DLB 15

Wilson, August
1945-........... CLC 39, 50, 63; DC 2
See also BLC 3; CA 115, 122

Wilson, Brian 1942-.............. CLC 12

Wilson, Colin 1931-............ CLC 3, 14
See also CAAS 5; CANR 1, 122; CA 1-4R;
DLB 14

Wilson, Edmund
1895-1972 .... CLC 1, 2, 3, 8, 24
See also CANR 1; CA 1-4R;
obituary CA 37-40R; DLB 63

Wilson, Ethel Davis (Bryant)
1888-1980 .... CLC 13
See also CA 102; DLB 68

Wilson, Harriet 1827?-?
See also BLC 3; DLB 50

Wilson, John 1785-1854......... NCLC 5

Wilson, John (Anthony) Burgess 1917-
See Burgess, Anthony
See also CANR 2; CA 1-4R

Wilson, Lanford 1937-....... CLC 7, 14, 36
See also CA 17-20R; DLB 7

Wilson, Robert (M.) 1944-....... CLC 7, 9
See also CANR 2; CA 49-52

Wilson, Sloan 1920-.............. CLC 32
See also CANR 1; CA 1-4R

Wilson, Snoo 1948-............... CLC 33
See also CA 69-72

Wilson, William S(mith) 1932- ..... CLC 49
See also CA 81-84

Winchilsea, Anne (Kingsmill) Finch, Countess
of 1661-1720.................. LC 3

Wingrove, David 1954-............ CLC 68
See also CA 133

Winters, Janet Lewis 1899-
See Lewis (Winters), Janet
See also CAP 1; CA 9-10

Winters, (Arthur) Yvor
1900-1968 .... CLC 4, 8, 32
See also CAP 1; CA 11-12;
obituary CA 25-28R; DLB 48

Winterson, Jeanette 1959-........ CLC 64

Wiseman, Frederick 1930-........ CLC 20

Wister, Owen 1860-1938 .... TCLC 21
See also CA 108; DLB 9, 78

Witkiewicz, Stanislaw Ignacy
1885-1939 .... TCLC 8
See also CA 105; DLB 83

Wittig, Monique 1935?-........... CLC 22
See also CA 116; DLB 83

Wittlin, Joseph 1896-1976........ CLC 25
See also Wittlin, Jozef

Wittlin, Jozef 1896-1976
See Wittlin, Joseph
See also CANR 3; CA 49-52;
obituary CA 65-68

Wodehouse, (Sir) P(elham) G(renville)
1881-1975 ... CLC 1, 2, 5, 10, 22; SSC 2
See also CANR 3; CA 45-48;
obituary CA 57-60; SATA 22; DLB 34

Woiwode, Larry (Alfred) 1941-... CLC 6, 10
See also CANR 16; CA 73-76; DLB 6

Wojciechowska, Maia (Teresa)
1927-...................... CLC 26
See also CLR 1; CANR 4; CA 9-12R;
SAAS 1; SATA 1, 28

Wolf, Christa 1929- .... CLC 14, 29, 58
See also CA 85-88; DLB 75

Wolfe, Gene (Rodman) 1931-...... CLC 25
See also CAAS 9; CANR 6; CA 57-60;
DLB 8

Wolfe, George C. 1954-........... CLC 49

Wolfe, Thomas (Clayton)
1900-1938 .... TCLC 4, 13, 29
See also CA 104; DLB 9; DLB-Y 85;
DLB-DS 2

Wolfe, Thomas Kennerly, Jr. 1931-
See Wolfe, Tom
See also CANR 9; CA 13-16R

Wolfe, Tom 1931-... CLC 1, 2, 9, 15, 35, 51
See also Wolfe, Thomas Kennerly, Jr.

Wolff, Geoffrey (Ansell) 1937- ..... CLC 41
See also CA 29-32R

Wolff, Tobias (Jonathan Ansell)
1945-...................... CLC 39, 64
See also CA 114, 117

Wolfram von Eschenbach
c. 1170-c. 1220 .... CMLC 5

Wolitzer, Hilma 1930-............ CLC 17
See also CANR 18; CA 65-68; SATA 31

Wollstonecraft Godwin, Mary
1759-1797 .... LC 5
See also DLB 39

Wonder, Stevie 1950-............. CLC 12
See also Morris, Steveland Judkins

Wong, Jade Snow 1922-........... CLC 17
See also CA 109

Woodcott, Keith 1934-
See Brunner, John (Kilian Houston)

Woolf, (Adeline) Virginia
1882-1941 .... TCLC 1, 5, 20, 43; SSC 7
See also CA 130; brief entry CA 104;
DLB 36, 100

Woollcott, Alexander (Humphreys)
1887-1943 .... TCLC 5
See also CA 105; DLB 29

Wordsworth, Dorothy
1771-1855 .... NCLC 25

Wordsworth, William 1770-1850.. NCLC 12

Wouk, Herman 1915-........ CLC 1, 9, 38
See also CANR 6; CA 5-8R; DLB-Y 82

Wright, Charles 1935- .... CLC 6, 13, 28
See also BLC 3; CAAS 7; CANR 26;
CA 29-32R; DLB-Y 82

Wright, Charles (Stevenson) 1932-.. CLC 49
See also CA 9-12R; DLB 33

DC Cumulative Nationality Index

DC Cumulative Title Index